S0-DST-806

# SAWYER FAMILIES OF NEW ENGLAND

1636 –1900

ꙮ

# SAWYER FAMILIES OF NEW ENGLAND

## 1636 –1900

by

Eleanor Grace Sawyer

Published by Penobscot Press, Camden, ME 1995

International Standard Book Number 0-89725-240-3
Library of Congress Catalog Card Number 95-70741



First Printing September 1995

This book is available from:

Eleanor G. Sawyer
PO Box 440
Strafford, NH 03884

Manufactured in the United States of America
Printed on 50# acid-free paper

This book is dedicated to my husband,

Colonel Robert Kendal Sawyer.

# ꟸ TABLE OF CONTENTS ꟸ



Please Note: The Sawyer coat of arms illustrated on the title page of this book is one of many such designs that have been seen over the years. It is used here for decorative purposes only, and should by no means be construed as being representative of the Sawyer families decribed herein.

# ➰ PREFACE ➰

This genealogy began in Washington, DC, in the mid-1960's as an effort to trace my husband's direct family line. Initially, I had only a few notes compiled over a lifetime by my father-in-law, which I began to supplement through trips to the National Archives and Library of Congress. I soon found it impossible to connect our earliest known forebear -- my husband's great-great-grandfather -- to his parents, so I decided to start from the other end, to work from the earliest recorded Sawyer in New England and try to make a connection that way.

Published genealogies and family histories promptly led me to William, Thomas, and Edward, the three Sawyer brothers who came to New England in 1636. Thereafter, I had more success, especially after my husband retired and we settled in New England, where I had access to the many libraries, historical societies and archives to be found in that region. Gradually, as my interest grew, I expanded my search far beyond my original purpose, to include as many New England Sawyer family lines as possible during the period 1636-1900. I began supplementing my research by writing to Sawyers listed in telephone books, requesting family information gleaned from bibles, diaries, and similar sources, and was gratified to find so much interest and willingness to help.

Although I cannot list all of the Sawyer "cousins" who so kindly responded with information which I otherwise would not have obtained, I want them to know how much I appreciate their contributions. In addition, I must give special thanks to the following:

Theodora Hoyt Sawyer
Robert L. Taylor
Elizabeth Wescott
Neil Gould Sawyer
Gerald M. Kimball
Clifton R. Sargent
Henry Nathan Sawyer
Frederick W. Sawyer, III
Leonard F. Tibbetts

Also, undying gratitude to Robert D. Ellis and Peter A. Sawyer for technical help.

## HOW THIS BOOK IS ORGANIZED

The great majority of Sawyers living in New England today are descended from three brothers who came to the New World from England in the early 17th century and settled in Massachusetts: Edward at Rowley, William at Newbury, and Thomas at Lancaster. Accordingly, this genealogy is based primarily on each of these individuals' family lines, generation by succeeding generation. Lesser Sawyer lines are covered separately, including lines or families whose origins I could not identify.

As indicated by the book title, this work contains information about Sawyer heads of family from 1636 through 1900. The children of those born in 1900 are listed with their dates of birth, but are not carried forward as future heads of family. In other words, the genealogy of that particular line ends there. There are exceptions, however. Because certain individuals provided information about their family lines beyond the year 1900, that information is included to the extent that it was provided, with no additional research.

Because it is not practicable to carry a woman's genealogy forward after she married and took another surname, the emphasis is on the male members of the family. I have noted only the circumstances of each Sawyer woman's birth, marriage, and death, other minor personal data if available, and her husband's name and origin, if known. Information about the families of married Sawyer women must be sought in the genealogical records of their spouses' families.

The lines of Sawyer males who left New England are not carried beyond their immediate families.

The national census (1790-1900) constitutes the research basis, supplemented by vital records, personal records, obituaries, and the sources listed in Part VII. Original records are used wherever possible, but it has been necessary to rely on many secondary sources because the information is simply not available elsewhere. To have verified all data found in these secondary sources would have been an impossible task, so such information should be viewed as "probable" or "possible" and, at the very least, be used as clues.

Source references are listed below each family entry. First cited is the census, if used, then vital records (VR), family records, and obituaries. Included are additional sources keyed by a capital letter and number to the listings in Part VII, for example N14. This indicates that it refers to the 14th source listed under the letter N. In the interests of space and avoiding repeated detailed references, specific pages within sources are not given, the assumption being that the user is able to find the information in the work cited.

***Family Heads***. The name of each family head appears after the sequence number, in bold upper case lettering, together with his generation number, as for example, 1. **WILLIAM$^1$ SAWYER**. Thereafter he is referred to simply as William$^1$. The date and place of his birth, death, and marriage appear after his name. Other basic information follows, such as his occupation, church membership, military service, and places where he is found, generally in that order. Although this work is a genealogy and not a family history, additional details are included if they seem of sufficient interest.

***Children.*** Married sons with male children are assigned sequence numbers, but only their names, generation numbers, and years of birth and death are shown at this point. All other details appear later, when they reappear as heads of family.

***Double Dating.*** Some dates in the early records are shown as, for example, 1702/03. This reflects a change in the calendar which took place in 1582, and is described in any encyclopedia. Because this is confusing to some people, and is not very important for our purposes, only the "New Style" or modern date is used in this genealogy.

## RESEARCH PROBLEMS

1. The birth date of individuals shown in early records is sometimes the date on which they were actually baptized.

2. Marriage dates in early records sometimes reflect the date on which marriage intentions were filed rather than the actual marriage. Where known, intentions are shown as m.(I).

3. US census records began in 1790. Prior to 1850, they showed only the name of the family head, his marital status, and the number and ages of his sons and daughters. Until 1830, ages were shown within 10 years, in 1830 and 1840 within five years. Beginning in 1850, the names and actual ages of all members of the family were given.

4. Town vital records often disagree with ages shown in the national census. Reconciliation usually shows that the town records are correct.

5. Some town names have been changed over the years. In some cases, towns have been redistricted, with parts becoming separate, incorporated entities with different names.

6. "Junior" after a name does not necessarily mean that a boy was named after his father, for sometimes sons named for an uncle were so called. Or, if a boy died young and a later son of the family received the same name, he might be called "Junior." On the other hand, sons -- especially the first -- were often named for their paternal grandfather, and a middle name was sometimes the maiden name of their mother. There was also a tendency within family lines to use the same Christian names. All this serves as clues.

7. Wills and deeds sometimes refer to persons "related to" another person. This usually meant a brother or sister or, less often, a parent.

8. Gravestones sometimes show the date when the stone was carved or erected rather than the date of death. Data on death certificates, even if provided by a family member, is sometimes erroneous and should be verified elsewhere if possible.

## ABBREVIATIONS

B/ - bought
b. - born/birth
bp. - baptized
bur. - buried
cem. - cemetery
ca. - circa
CH- child/children
d. - died/death
dau. - daughter
div. - divorced
d.y. - died young
edn. - edition
enl. - enlisted
(f) - female
facs.-.facsimile
(m) - male
m. - married/marriage
m.(I) - filed intention to marry
ms. - manuscript
n.d. - no date
n.p.-.no publisher
obit. - obituary
PP. - Privately Printed
PBA - Published by the Author
PBT - Published by the Town
rec. - records
rev. - revised
S/ - sold
SA/ - state archives/(state)
unk. - unknown
unm. - unmarried
VR - vital records
vol. - volume(s)
wid. - widow

AAS - American Antiquarian Society, Worcester MA
ALSOP - Ancient Landmards Society of Parsonsfield ME
DAR - Daughters of the American Revolution
FARC - Federal Archives and Records Center, Waltham MA
LOC - Library of Congress, Washington DC
MASA - Massachusetts State Archives, Boston MA
MHS - Maine Historical Society, Portland ME
MOCA.-.Maine Old Cemetery Association, Augusta ME
MLS - Maine State Library, Augusta ME
MSA - Maine State Archives, Augusta ME
NA - National Archives, Washington DC
NEHGS - NE Historic Genealogical Society, Boston MA
NHHS - NH Historical Society, Concord NH
NHSA - New Hampshire State Archives, Concord NH
NHSL - NH State Library, Concord NH
VSA - Vermont State Archives, Montpelia VT

## SAWYERS OF ENGLAND

Many Sawyer genealogies and family histories say that Edward, William, and Thomas left England on a ship (possibly *Hopewell*) commanded by one "Captain Parker" and arrived in Salem, Massachusetts, sometime in 1636[a] . These same sources say that the three brothers were the sons of John Sawyer of Lincolnshire, England, a farmer who was also said to be a landowner. Although Sawyer is far from an uncommon name in England, I have not been able to find the precise family from which the three boys descended, this despite two research trips to the United Kingdom.

Charles E. Banks' *Topographical Dictionary of English Emigrants To New England* [B20] mentions a William of Leighton Buzzard, son of Francis Sayer[b] and Elizabeth Atkins, both members of old yoeman families which had lived in Hinwick in Poddington, North Bedfordshire, since the early 14th century. Although it has been suggested that this William may have been he who came to America in 1636, such does not seem likely. For one thing, he was christened on 19 September 1602, well before the year 1613 which is generally accepted as the birthdate of William of Newbury. Moreover, he would have been at least 100 years old when he died, somewhat older than our William was at his death. In any case, he had no brother Edward; and although he had a brother Thomas, the latter was born in 1592, 24 years before the birth of Thomas of Lancaster. Thus, lacking better evidence, this candidate may safely be rejected.

---

[a] The only other reference I find to the ship *Hopewell* is in *Hotten's Original Lists* [H74], which indicates that a William and Thomas Sawyer, ages 18 and 23, came to Warwick Squeak, Virginia, on that ship in 1625.

[b] Sayer, Sare, Sawer, Sayard, Seare, Seyer, and Seaire were some of the spelling variations of the name Sawyer, which sometimes appear in more than one form within a single document.

# PART I

## ꟹ EDWARD OF ROWLEY ☙

1. **EDWARD[1] SAWYER**, b. 1608 in England, was the oldest of the three Sawyer brothers who came to New England in 1636, but the least is known about him. A tanner, he lived initially in Ipswich MA, but in 1640 he and Thomas[1] bought lots near each other in nearby Rowley. When Thomas moved on to Nashaway Plantation in 1646, Edward remained in Rowley until his death on 9 Mar 1673.

Various genealogies and family histories state that Edward was married to Mary Peasley and brought her and their three children -- Henry, Mary, and James -- with him to the New World. As a source, these claims usually refer to page 1444 of Thomas Little's *Genealogy and Family History of Maine* [L30], which unfortunately gives no clue as to where he obtained the information.

There seems little doubt that Edward's wife was named Mary, b. ca. 1610 d. 20 Feb 1693, for she was so called in vital records. However, we do not know her maiden name, nor is there any documentary evidence that a "Mary" with three children ever arrived with Edward. The only Mary Peasley I could account for during this period was a daughter of Joseph Peasley of Haverhill MA, born about 1633, who would have been only 12 years old when Edward's first recorded child, Sarah, was born. In any case, this Mary married Henry Sayward of Hampton NH.

As for the three children, Henry appeared in Hampton NH in 1647 and 1662, in York ME in 1675, and was an inhabitant of Portsmouth NH in 1711. It is also worthy of note that the first child of William of Reading (see Part V) was named Henry at a time when first sons were often named for their grandfather, and I have found no earlier Henry Sawyer in New England. This suggests a possibility that Edward's son Henry could have been the father of William of Reading.

We do not know what happened to the daughter, Mary. James Savage's *Genealogical Dictionary of New England*.[S12], page 1638, lists a Mary Sawyer who m.(1) William Mitchell in 1648 and (2) Robert Savoy in 1656, both of Newbury MA; but we do not know who her parents were, and it is perhaps significant that none of her nine children was named Edward, Henry, or James, as we might expect if she were the Mary we seek. I feel that James, the third child attributed to Edward, was probably the weaver who established the Sawyer line in Gloucester MA. See Part IV for more on this question.

According to the vital records of Rowley MA, **Edward[1]** and Mary had the following children:

Sarah, b. 19 Oct 1645, d. 12 Dec 1645.
John, b. 17 Jul 1747, d. in infancy.
2 John[2], 1648-1722.
Ezekiel, b. 165?, d. 18 Sep 1675 at the "Bloody Creek Massacre", Deerfield MA, unm.

Sources: VR Rowley MA. B53, P82b, R29, J13.

### SECOND GENERATION

2. **JOHN[2] SAWYER** [see 1], b. 7 Jun 1648 Rowley MA, d. 2 Apr 1722 Rowley MA, m. Rowley MA Mary Parrat of Rowley MA, b. 15 Jul 1647 d. 28 Sep 1714, dau. Francis and Elizabeth Parrat.

Edward, b. 17 Mar 1674, d. 27 Jun 1675.
Mary, b. 18 Oct 1676, d. 20 Feb 1693.
3 Ezekiel[3], 1678-1727.
Elizabeth, b. 19 Aug 1680, d. 1 Oct 1732, unm.
4 John[3], 1682-1771.

Hannah, b. 4 Jun 1684, d. 27 Sep 1722, m. 10 May 1715 Samuel Woodbury.
Sources: VR Rowley MA, Littleton MA. B53, F15, S60.

## THIRD GENERATION

3. **EZEKIEL$^3$ SAWYER** [see 2], b. 14 Jan 1678 Rowley MA, d. 13 Apr 1727 Rowley MA, m. 27 Dec 1704 Rowley MA Hannah Stickney, b. 23 Jun 1681 d. 13 Dec 1740, dau. John and Hannah (Brocklebank) Stickney.

Mary, b. 25 Sep 1705, d. 22 Feb 1726, unm.
5 Ezekiel$^4$, 1707-1766.
Hannah, b. 17 Apr 1709, d. 14 Apr 1745, m. 3 Jan 1734 Joshua Jackson.
Benjamin, b. 2 Nov 1710, d. 25 Jul 1713.
Jane, b. 16 Oct 1712, d. y.
Marcy, b. 7 Jun 1714, m. 14 Dec 1756 Daniel Goodwin.
Mehitable, b. 9 Mar 1719, d. 3 Apr 1719.
Jane, b. 9 Mar 1719, d. 25 Mar 1724.
Benjamin, b. 29 Jun 1720, d. 8 Jun 1722.
Sources: VR Rowley MA. B53, J1, J16, A25.

4. **JOHN$^3$ SAWYER** [see 2], b. 5 Aug 1682 Rowley MA, d. 25 Mar 1771 Littleton MA, m.(1) 23 May 1710 Rowley MA Elizabeth Tenny, b. 23 Apr 1687 d. 6 Oct 1710, dau. Thomas and Margaret (Hidden) Tenny; m.(2) 19 Nov 1711 Rowley MA Mary Leighton b. 15 Jun 1690 d. 27 Apr 1757, dau. Ezekiel and Rebecca (Woodman) Leighton. Went to Littleton MA 1726.

Moses, b. 23 Jul 1712 Rowley MA, d. 24 Nov 1739 Lancaster MA, m. 16 May 1739 Harvard MA Ruth Robens of Harvard MA, b. ?. He bur. in Old Common Burial Ground, Lancaster MA. Wid. m. Justinian Holden 25 Jun 1741.
Rebecca, b. 10 Oct 1713.
Mary, b. 9 Jul 1715, d. 30 May 1796, m. Apr 1734 Abraham Patch.
Elizabeth, b. 8 Jan 1719, d. 24 Sep 1736.
John, b. 28 Sep 1722 Rowley MA, d. 17 Aug 1739 Harvard MA.
Hannah, b. 28 Apr 1727, m. 19 Jul 1744 Samuel Hoar.
Sarah, b. 8 May 1729, d. 9 Jun 1729.
Sarah, b. 22 Dec 1730, d. 1806, m. 28 Nov 1754 Elias Stone of Harvard MA.
Sources: VR Rowley MA, Harvard MA, Littleton MA. B53, L33, T10, C24, E20, N5, J16, B33.

## FOURTH GENERATION

5. **EZEKIEL$^4$ SAWYER** [see 3], b. 16 Jun 1707 Rowley MA, d. 26 Jun 1766 Rowley MA, m. 10 Dec 1730 Rowley MA Mehitable Jewett, bp. 8 Dec 1706 d. 11 Nov 1774, dau. Aquila and Anne (Tenny) Jewett. Selectman for Rowley MA 1756.

Benjamin, b.28 Dec 1731, d. 8 apr 1736.
John, b. 16 Mar 1734, d. 28 Apr 1736.
Anne, b. 28 Jul 1736, d. 19 Apr 1813, m. 7 Dec 1756 James Todd.
Jane, b. 12 Jul 1738 d. 15 Jan 1813, m. 31 Mar 1767 Nathaniel Barker.
6 Moses$^5$, b. 1740.
7 Ezekiel$^5$, 1742-1817.
8 John$^5$, 1745-1821.
Aquila, b. 17 Apr 1748, d. 30 Nov 1749.
Sources: VR Rowley MA. B53, E20, J14, T10, J16.

## FIFTH GENERATION

6. **MOSES[5] SAWYER** [see 5], b. 24 Aug 1740 Rowley MA, m. 21 May 1771 Rowley MA Elizabeth (Goodhue) Kilbourne, wid. of Daniel, b. ?.

9 Moses[6], b. 1772.

Elizabeth, b. 21 Jun 1778, m. 13 Sep 1798 William Garland of Gilmanton NH.

Eunice, b. 8 Oct 1780.

Sources: Gloucester MA census 1790. VR Rowley MA, N6, B53.

7. **EZEKIEL[5] SAWYER** [see 5], b. 27 Sep 1742 Rowley MA, d. 13 Jan 1817 Bradford VT, m. Mary Payson, b. 11 Mar 1745 d. 6 Jul 1812, dau. Eliot and Mary (Todd) Payson. Revolutionary War: Captain. Farmer. Bradford VT 1795. He bur. in Upper Plain Cem., Bradford VT.

10 Elliot[6], b. 1765. Went to Quebec, Canada.

Ezekiel, b.13 Jan 1768 Rowley MA, d. 17 Jul 1842 Bradford VT, m.(1) 18 Feb 1801 Bradford VT Ruby Taber of Dartmouth MA, b. 7 Sep 1778 d. 24 Mar1813, dau. Stephen and Comfort (Parker) Taber; m.(2) 14 Nov 1813 West Fairlee VT Jane Southworth, b. 1785 d. 25 Dec 1820, dau. Daniel and Anna Moore. (Ezekiel is listed in Bradford VT census 1810, but also in Bath NH census 1810.) CH: Ruby, b. 2 Feb 1802, m. 29 Mar 1827 Bath NH Carleton Johnson; Almira, b. 3 Jun 1804; Moses, b. 1805, d. 16 Apr 1807; MaryAnn, b. 27 Jun 1806, m. 25 Sep 1845 Benjamin Cilley; Hannah, b. 14 May 1808, d. 11 Sep 1887, m. 11 Apr 1843 Daniel Carr; Jane, b. Jun 1810, m. Benjamin Cilley; Harriet, b. 1812, m. 26 Mar 1855 Benjamin Cilley; Ezekiel, b. 1820, d. 12 Oct 1823.

Mary, b. 30 Oct 1770, m.(1) 18 Feb 1794 Jonathan Gage, Hopkinton NH, m.(2) 1803 Joseph Worth.

Mehitable, b. 31 Mar 1773, d. 22 Jan 1862, unm.

Elizabeth, b. 13 Feb 1775, d. 23 May 1855, m. 19 Mar 1807 Jesse Johnson.

11 Joseph[6], 1777-1818.

Hannah, b. 26 Apr 1779, m. Jonathan Johnson.

Jane, b.10 Mar 1782, d. 21 May 1869, m. 8 Apr 1802 Harris Johnson.

Mercy, b. 1 Aug 1784, m. 19 Oct 1803 Isaiah Stone. Went to Ohio.

12 John[6], b. 1786-1847.

Anne, b. 8 Apr 1789, d. 1867, m. 8 Mar 1818 Harvey Smith.

Note: An account of Ezekiel's Revolutionary War experiences is found in [J16].

Sources: Rowley MA census 1790. Bath NH census 1810. Bradford VT census 1800, 1810. VR Rowley MA, SA/VT. B53, W24, N20, M30, C36, B9, J16, D6, R5, C6, N6.

8. **JOHN[5] SAWYER** [see 5], b. 11 Jun 1745 Rowley MA, d. 15 Jun 1821 Scarboro ME, m.(1) 18 May 1769 Rowley MA Elizabeth Smith, b. 7 May 1748 d. 24 Jul 1773; m.(2) 22 Jun 1774 Ipswich MA Abigail Kilbourne of Ipswich MA, b. 12 Oct 1750 d. 2 Dec 1817, dau. Ebenezer and Abigail (Hovey) Kilbourne; m.(3) 4 Dec 1817 Rowley MA Hannah Lancaster, b. 1 Dec 1754 d. 12 May 1851 Rowley MA, dau. Thomas and Priscilla (Mighill) Lancaster. Revolutionary War: In Captain Mighill's Company, Baldwin Regiment. Cordwainer. B/S/land in Scarboro and Cape Elizabeth ME, 1782-1818. John and Abigail both joined Congregational Church, Scarboro ME Sep 1792.

Elizabeth, b. 24 Mar 1770, m. 4 Apr 1790 Daniel Marr.

Benjamin, b. 23 Feb 1772, d. 4 Mar 1772.

John, b. 4 Apr 1773, d. 8 Sep 1773.

Thomas, b. 13 Jul 1775, d. 6 Oct 1798.

John, b. 26 Sep 1777, d. 7 Oct 1799.

Nabby, b. 1780, d. 1799.
13 Ivory$^6$, 1783-1871.
14 Henry$^6$, 1787-1877.
Ezekiel, b. 1790, d. 9 Oct 1799.
Amos Jewett, b. 1793, d. 1799.
Hannah K., b. 1795, d. 30 Oct 1799.
Sources: Scarboro ME census 1790, 1810, 1820. VR Rowley MA, Ipswich MA. F21, B53, R10a, M3, W11.

## SIXTH GENERATION

9. **MOSES$^6$ SAWYER** [see 6], b. 22 Jun 1772 Rowley MA, m.(I) 21 Sep 1794 Rowley MA Hannah Crockett of Barnstead NH, b. ?. According to the 1810 Barnstead census, Moses had one son between 0-10 years old, two dau. between 10-16 years, and one dau. between 16-26 years. I have only been able to identify the son.
15 Moses$^7$, 1800-1871.
Sources: Barnstead NH census 1810. VR Rowley MA, SA/NH.

10. **ELLIOT$^6$ SAWYER** [see 7], b. 9 May 1765 Rowley MA, m. Lucy Young, b. ?. In Stanstead, East Canada, 1804. Carpenter.
Narcissa, b. 1793, m. 10 Feb 1860 Theodore S. Bangs.
Lucy, b. Aug 1796, d. 3 Apr 1865, unm.
16 Elliot P.$^7$, 1798-1874.
Mary P., b. ?, m. 1 Jan 1829 James McDuff.
Betsey, b. ?, m. Albert Woodward.
Maria, b. ?, m. Ogden Fox.
Ruth, b. ?, m. Samuel Webster.
Joseph, b. ?.
Jerusha, b. ?.
John, b. ?.
Sources: Newbury VT census 1800. VR Rowley MA, SA/VT.

11. **JOSEPH$^6$ SAWYER** [see 7], b. 20 Mar 1777 Rowley MA, d. 22 Sep 1818 West Newbury VT, m. 28 Dec 1801 Newbury VT Azubah Chamberlin of Newbury VT, b. 6 Nov 1779 d. 31 Mar 1830, dau. Colonel Remembrance and Elizabeth (Elliot) (Johnson) Chamberlin. Major of militia. He bur. in Upper Plain Cem., West Newbury VT.
17 Remembrance Chamberlin$^7$, 1803-1862.
Elizabeth, b.10 Jan 1805, d. 16 Apr 1879, m. 7 Apr 1828 Hiram Smith.
Amanda, b.1807, d. 13 Nov 1868, m. 30 Jan 1834 Clark Chamberlin.
Mary Payson, b.14 Feb 1809, d. 27 Jun 1850, m. 9 Jul 1833 Joseph Bayley.
18 Ezekiel$^7$, 1811-1863.
19 Jonathan John$^7$, 1813-1865.
Hannah J., b. ?, d. 10 Mar 1865, m. 27 May 1839 Enoch Wiggin.
Joseph, b. 1819 West Newbury VT, d. 13 Sep 1881 Newbury VT, m. Sarah K. Wallace of Newbury VT, b. ?. In California 1849. To Oregon?
Sources: Newbury VT census 1810, 1820 (wid.). VR Rowley MA, SA/VT. B7, W24, B22, C36.

12. **JOHN$^6$ SAWYER** [see 7], b. 27 Oct 1786 Bradford VT, d. 19 Sep 1847 Bradford VT, m. 19 Mar 1816 Lydia W. Dike of Bradford VT, b. 1793 d. 12 Dec 1842.
Mary Dike, b. 27 Feb 1817, m. George Burroughs.

John Hiram, b. 22 Nov 1818 Bradford VT, d. 14 Aug 1896 Bradford VT, m. Sarah Hibbard of Piermont NH, b. 1824 d. 5 Oct 1893. Farmer. Deacon.

Emily Payson, b. Jan 1822, m. 3 Sep 1862 Charles Blanchard.

20 Henry Ezekiel$^7$, 1824-1887.

Lydia Ann, b. 13 Jun 1826, d. 28 Aug 1904.

21 Joseph$^7$, b. 1829.

Elizabeth, b.14 Sep 1831, m. 30 Nov 1852 Ellis McDuffee of Bradford VT.

Edward, b. 20 Feb 1837 Bradford VT.

Jane, b. 20 Feb 1837, m. 6 Feb 1861 Edward Robie of Bradford VT.

Sources: Bradford VT census 1830, 1840, 1850. VR SA/VT. M30, N20.

13. **IVORY$^6$ SAWYER** [see 8], b. 1783 Scarboro ME, d. 17 Jun 1871, m. 29 Jul 1807 Cape Elizabeth ME Abigail Jordan of Cape Elizabeth ME, b. 1783 d. 30 Mar 1860 Gardiner ME. In Scarboro ME, Webster ME, Gardiner ME. She bur. Highland Avenue Cem., Gardiner ME.

Daughter, b. (1800-1810).

Daughter, b. (1810-1820).

Daughter, b. (1810-1820).

22 Alvin$^7$, 1816-1892.

John, b. 31 Oct 1820 Lisbon ME. In Webster ME.

Joan, b. 8 Jun 1823, d. 2 Apr 1902.

Jane, b. 8 Mar 1826.

William, b. 18 Aug 1827 Lisbon ME. In Webster ME.

Sources: Scarboro ME census 1810. Lisbon ME census 1820, 1830. Webster ME census 1840, 1850. Gardiner ME census 1850. VR Gardiner ME, SA/ME. M5.

14. **HENRY$^6$ SAWYER** [see 8], b. 1787 Scarboro ME, d. 11 Jan 1877, m. 13 Feb 1812 Cape Elizabeth ME Lydia Waterhouse, b. 1790 d. 29 Jan 1861. Farmer. B/land in Scarboro ME 1816, 1818. Joined First Church of Scarboro ME 6 Nov 1831.

John H., b. 29 Jun 1814 Scarboro ME, d. 9 Feb 1842 Portland ME, m.(I) 9 Apr 1836 Phebe H. Dyer, b. ?. He bur. in Western Cem., Portland ME. CH: Henrietta E., b. 21 Aug 1839; John H., b. 17 Aug 1842, d. 31 May 1844.

Jane, b. 30 Aug 1815.

23 Francis Osgood$^7$, 1818-1886.

24 Thomas L.$^7$, 1820-1902.

25 Joshua Waterhouse$^7$, b. 1822.

Alexander, b. 27 Mar 1825, d. 16 Oct 1847.

Eliza A., b. 28 Sep 1827, m. 27 Sep 1853 William Q. Turner.

Joseph Scott, b. 11 Mar 1830 Scarboro ME, d. Scarboro ME, m. 25 Jul 1852 Mary J. Libby of Scarboro ME, b. 7 Feb 1831 d. 8 Nov 1913, dau. John and Jane (Milliken) Libby. B/land in Scarboro ME 1855. Promised life care to father for land, 1868. CH: Elizabeth Carolyn, b. ?, died in teens.

Mary E. ,b. 28 May 1833, d. 29 Sep 1911, m. 6 Oct 1855 James Kezer.

Edwin, b. 19 Nov 1835, d. 5 Dec 1838.

Sources: Scarboro ME census 1830, 1840, 1850. Portland ME census 1840. VR Scarboro ME, Cape Elizabeth ME, SA/ME. R10a, M5, S23, K6.

## SEVENTH GENERATION

15. **MOSES[7] SAWYER** [see 9], b. Jun 1800 Barnstead NH, d. 18 Dec 1871 Portsmouth NH, m. 3 Nov 1825 Farmington NH Mary Berry of Strafford NH, b. 12 Feb 1806 d. 14 Aug 1886, dau. John and Susanna (McNeil) Berry. Trashman.

Eliza A. , b. 1827, m. 10 Jul 1851 John C. Wood of Portsmouth NH.
Adeline E., b. 1830, m. 22 Nov 1852 Boston MA Franklin Brewster.
Daniel B., b. ca. 1832 Portsmouth NH. Joiner.
Sylvester J., b. Oct 1837, d. 17 May 1841.
Mary F., b. 1844.
Almira P., b. 1849, m. 26 Mar 1870 Albert A. Ferren.

Sources: Portsmouth NH census 1840, 1850, 1860. VR SA/MA. N6, N14, F15.

16. **ELLIOT P.[7] SAWYER** [see 10], b. 1798 Newbury VT, d. 9 Sep 1874 Bradford VT, m. 18 Jun 1824 Ascot, Canada Lydia Abbott of Ludlow VT, b. Sep 1806 Ludlow VT, d. 31 Mar 1874, dau. Asa and Lydia Abbott. Carpenter. Note: Marriage record says Elliot Eaton. James' death certificate says mother was Lydia A. Holt. Several of their CH were talented singers. More CH listed in [J16].

Samuel, b. ?, drowned in Canada at age 14.
26 Homer E.[8], 1826-1867.
Emily M., b. 1828, m. Ormand Jenny of Methuen MA.
Elzina P., b. 1831, m. George Peters of Bradford VT.
Silas A., b. 1833, m. Abbie E_____, b. ?. Went to New Orleans LA.
Maria L., b. 1835, m. 7 Jan 1857 Lowell MA John Bicknell.
John A., b. ca. 1837 Bradford VT, m. 13 Jul 1864 Boston MA Annie E. Garcelon of Boston MA, b. 1844, dau. Alson and Emily Garcelon. CH: Alson Garcelon, b. 20 May 1867, d. 21 Oct 1886; Silas Gordon, b. 30 Jun 1870 Brighton MA; Maude Lena, b. 10 Jan 1874, d. 1 Jan 1880; Bertha E., b. 8 Oct 1882. Bookkeeper. In livery business. In Allston MA 1869.
27 James Elliot[8], 1841-1898.

Sources: Bradford VT census 1840, 1850. VR Bradford VT, Rowley MA, SA/MA. P12, J16, W61.

17. **REMEMBRANCE CHAMBERLIN[7] SAWYER** [see 11], b. Mar 1803 W. Newbury VT, d. 19 Aug 1862 Newbury VT, m. 29 Aug 1832 Newbury VT Zerniah Brock of Concord NH, b. 6 Nov 1809 d. Jun 1888, dau. Thomas R. and Rebecca (Carr) Brock. Farmer. He bur. in W. Newbury VT.

Azubah, b. 7 May 1833, d. 25 Feb 1842.
28 Joseph[8], b. 5 Aug 1835.

Sources: VR SA/VT. A2, A3, B22.

18. **EZEKIEL[7] SAWYER** [see 11], b. 1811 W. Newbury VT, d. 9 Feb 1863, m. 1838 Lona Howe of Hancock NH, b. 17 Jan 1810 d. 1 Sep 1878, dau. Silas and Phebe Howe. Farmer, stage proprietor. In Wells River VT.

29 George Alfred[8], 1840-1925.
Susan, b. 1842, m. 14 Feb 1865 Joseph Sawyer of Bradford VT.

Sources: Newbury VT Hist, H80, B22.

19. **JONATHAN JOHN[7] SAWYER** [see 11], b. 1813 W. Newbury VT, d. 3 May 1865 Newbury VT, m. 3 Dec 1843 Danvers MA Prudence H. (Brock) Wright of Barnet VT, b. ? d. 1864. Hotel keeper. In Danvers MA, Lawrence MA, Lowell MA.

Sarah E., b. 16 May 1844, d. 21 Aug 1847.

Daughter, b. 12 Apr 1846.
Daughter, b. 18 Dec 1849.
Addie, b. ?. Went to Portland OR.
Frank, b. ?. Went to Portland OR.
Sources: VR Lawrence MA. SA/MA. W24, B22.

20. **HENRY EZEKIEL$^7$ SAWYER** [see 12], b. 2 Feb 1824 Bradford VT, d. 12 Sep 1887, m. 23 May 1849 Bradford VT Amanda Chamberlin, b. 22 May 1826 d. 31 Dec 1902, dau. Moses and Martha (Child) Chamberlin. In Chicago IL.
Harry C., b. 21 Nov 1854, d. 1 Apr 1896.
Sources: VR SA/VT. B22.

21. **JOSEPH$^7$ SAWYER** [see 12], b. 24 Apr 1829, m. 14 Feb 1865 Newbury VT Susan Sawyer of Newbury VT, b. 1842, dau. Ezekiel and Lona (Howe) Sawyer. Hotelkeeper. In Bradford VT 1850, Chicago IL.
Infant, b. ?, d. 11 Aug 1866.
Ruth E., b. Aug 1867, d. 9 Jan 1874 Newbury VT.
Frank E., b. ?. Went to Texas.
Sources: Bradford VT census 1850. VR SA/VT.

22. **ALVIN$^7$ SAWYER** [see 13], b. 4 May 1816 Scarboro ME, d. 8 Dec 1892, m. 2 Sep 1848 Zelamy B. Curtis of Richmond ME, b. Feb 1822 d. 22 Nov 1913, dau. Lowe and Mercy (Bates) Curtis. Carpenter. In Gardiner ME 1850.
Ozro L., b. Oct 1849 Gardiner ME, m. 15 Sep 1892 Mabel Goodnough of Gardiner ME, b. ca. 1873.
Fred W., b. ca. 1852 Gardiner ME.
Sources: Gardiner ME census 1850. VR Gardiner ME, SA/ME. Obit.

23. **FRANCIS OSGOOD$^7$ SAWYER** [see 14], b. 5 Apr 1818 Scarboro ME, d. 17 May 1886 Cape Elizabeth ME, m.(1) 13 Oct 1842 Cape Elizabeth ME Mary J. Jordan, b. 1823 d. 9 Jun 1861 or 7 May 1863; m.(2) 13 Sep 1863 Abby L. Reed, b. Mar 1839 d. 25 Jun 1897, dau. John and Eunice (Tibbets) Reed. S/land in Cape Elizabeth ME 1849. Cooper. Served in militia.
John Edwin, b. 19 Dec 1844 Portland ME, d. 6 Dec 1905, m. 26 Apr 1870 Annie H. Elder, b. 1846. Inspector. CH: Edith A., b. 26 May 1872, d. 14 Jun 1872.
Mary F., b. 9 Sep 1851, d. 22 Jan 1921 Portland ME, unm.
Frank Harwood, b. 14 Jun 1857 Portland ME, m. 13 Jun 1885 Ida H. Whitney, b. Aug 1862. CH: Alberta F., b. 17 May 1886.
William D. Emmons, b. 9 Jun 1871, d. 1925, m. Hattie _____, b. ?.
L. Gertrude., b. 1877, d. 27 Oct 1932, m. Nathaniel Berry.
Sources: Portland ME census 1850. Cape Elizabeth ME census 1880. ME 1880 Census Index. VR Cape Elizabeth ME, SA/ME. R10a.

24. **THOMAS L.$^7$ SAWYER** [see 14], b. 24 Jun 1820 Scarboro ME, d. 27 Oct 1902 Portland ME, m. 7 Jul 1843 Mary J. Turner, b. 1820. Provision dealer. He bur. in Western Cem., Portland ME.
Alexander Scott, b. 18 Jul 1849 Portland ME, d. 8 Apr 1881 Portland ME, m. (1) 5 Dec 1868 Biddeford ME Hannah F. Cole of Biddeford ME, b. ?; m.(2) 31 Dec 1872 Gloucester MA Melvina A. Miller of Rockport MA, b. ?, dau. Charles and Melvina

Miller; m.(3) 29 Jan 1876 Emeline S. Boothby of Limington ME, b. 21 Sep 1840 d. 1881.

Frederick T., b. 1852, d. 17 Jun 1854.

Mary L., b. Oct 1860, d. 21 Jul 1861.

Sources: Portland ME census 1850, 1860, 1880 (w/brother Joshua), ME 1880 Census Index. VR Portland ME, SA/ME, SA/MA. P69, M5.

25. **JOSHUA WATERHOUSE[7] SAWYER** [see 14], b. 16 Dec 1822 Scarboro ME, m.(1)(I) 27 Apr 1844 Sophia A. Dresser, b. 1827 d. 10 May 1858; m.(2) 9 Mar 1859 Ellen M. Winchester of Portland ME, b. 1838.

Sophia D., b. 1845, d. 29 Nov 1846.

30 Robert Henry[8], b. 1847.

Ella Etta, b. 15 Mar 1849.

Abby, b. 30 Mar 1851, m. 14 Nov 1873 Boston MA Charles F. Libby.

Alice W., b. 8 Sep 1859, d. 22 Mar 1862.

Joshua W., b. 16 Jul 1864, d. 29 Jul 1864.

Grace Belle, b. 1865.

Joshua W., b. Dec 1867, d. 21 May 1870.

Adelaide Louise, b. 28 Nov 1868, m. 4 Aug 1890 Portland ME Everett Lewis Plimpton.

Jimmie, b. Aug 1870, d. 8 Nov 1870.

Winchester, b. 8 May 1872.

Ellen Winchester, b. 8 Aug 1875, m. 1 Aug 1895 Hiram A. Sherman.

Marion B., 8 Dec 1879, d. 7 Apr 1894.

Willie, b. 17 Apr 1883.

Sources: Portland ME census 1850, 1860. ME 1880 Census Index. VR SA/ME, SA/MA. R10a, L20, S37, M5.

## EIGHTH GENERATION

26. **HOMER E.[8] SAWYER** [see 16], b. 19 Aug 1826 Stanstead, East Canada, d. 12 Oct 1867 New Orleans LA, m. 28 Oct 1858 Hopkinton MA Sarah Letitia Parker, b. 17 Dec 1839 d. 4 Jan 1888, dau. John and Mary A. (Fales) Parker. Carpenter.

Anna Belle, b. Oct 1863, d. 8 Jan 1865.

31 Homer Eugene[9], 1866-1938.

Sources: Newbury VT census 1850. VR Holliston MA, SA/MA. P12, M30.

27. **JAMES ELLIOT[8] SAWYER** [see 16], b. 23 Apr 1841 Bradford VT, d. 1 Sep 1898 Hanover NH, m.(1) 16 Feb 1867 Ellen Cummings of Bradford VT, b. 12 May 1843 d. 26 Oct 1873 Laconia NH, dau. Isreal and Ruth (Kinney) Cummings; m.(2) 5 Jan 1878 Orford NH Martha J. Underhill of Piermont NH, b. 2 Oct 1851 d. 8 Sep 1919, dau. Samuel H. and Maria (Muchmore) Underhill. Coal dealer. In Bradford VT 1885.

Carrie L., 1 Jan 1868, m. 25 Jan 1893 Elbridge G. Libby.

Homer L., b. 5 Jul 1869, d. 7 Jul 1870.

Lottie, b. 27 Dec 1871, d. 23 Aug 1872.

Son, b. ?, d. 13 Oct 1873.

Leon Elliot, b. Jun 1878 Bradford VT, d. 5 Jun 1901 Bradford VT, m. 21 Jul 1900 Bradford VT Marguerite Dow Bagley, b. ?. CH: Grace E., b. 11 Mar 1901.

Bernard James, b. 17 Jun 1886 Bradford VT, m. 21 Jul 1906 Christa B. Gilbert, b. ?. CH: Helen Agnes, b. 15 Feb 1907; Anne Louise, b. 30 Oct 1908; George Elliot, b. 10 Feb 1911, d. 15 Jan 1927.

Fred Raymond, b. 19 May 1888, m. 30 Jun 1913 Hanover NH Ella L. Morrell, b. ?.
Sources: Bradford VT census 1850. Orford NH census 1880. VR SA/NH, SA/VT. C90.

28. **JOSEPH[8] SAWYER** [see 17], b. 5 Aug 1835 W. Newbury VT, m. 31 Dec 1862 Newbury VT Hannah H. Tyler of Deer Isle ME, b. ?, dau. Daniel Tyler. Farmer, hotelkeeper. In Wentworth NH.

Remembrance Chamberlin, b. 30 Sep 1863 Newbury VT. In Wentworth NH.
32 Frederick W.[9], 1870-1911.
Son, stillborn 7 May 1874.
Sources: VR SA/VT. B22.

29. **GEORGE ALFRED[8] SAWYER** [see 18], b. 7 Mar 1840 Wells River VT, d. 25 Mar 1925 Newbury VT, m. 1 Dec 1864 Newbury VT Sophia B. Shephard of Newbury VT, b. 1843 d. 1920, dau. Jacob and Jane (Johnson) Shephard. Farmer, hotelkeeper.

Ida Belle, b. 13 Oct 1865 d. 1942, m. 1 Jan 1886 Maurice A. Gale.
Lewis A., b. 31 Dec 1869, d. 20 May 1877.
Jennie Lona, b. 15 Dec 1871, d. 8 Feb 1934, m. 25 Nov 1891 Arthur Cheever.
Sue Shephard, b. 18 Feb 1876, m. 28 Nov 1905 Harry M. Hinman.
33 George Alfred[9], 1879-1960.
Sources: VR SA/VT. W24, B22.

30. **ROBERT HENRY[8] SAWYER** [see 25], b. 8 Jun 1847 Portland ME, m. May 1780 Georgia A. Nash of Portland ME, b. ?. In Windham ME.

Annie E., b. 20 Nov 1870, d. 2 May 1872.
34 Robert Henry[9], b. 1873.
Sources: VR SA/ME.

## NINTH GENERATION

31. **HOMER EUGENE[9] SAWYER** [see 26], b. 8 Aug 1866 New Orleans LA, d. 1938, m. 24 Nov 1890 Mary Buckley of Detroit MI, b. ? d. 1928. In Malden MA.

35 Homer Eugene[10], 1892-1968.
Sources: VR SA/MA. P12.

32. **FREDERICK W.[9] SAWYER** [see 28], b. 21 Feb 1870 Newbury VT, d. 13 Jul 1911 Winchester NH, m. 14 Apr 1891 Ida May Black of New Brunswick, Canada, b. ?. Farmer. In Wentworth NH.

John Black, b. 2 Jun 1895.
Hilda M., b. 17 Feb 1901.
Sources: VR SA/NH, SA/VT.

33. **GEORGE ALFRED[9] SAWYER** [see 29], b. 26 Jul 1879 Newbury VT, d. 7 Dec 1960, m. Corinne Blanchard of Sutton MA, b. 11 Dec 1888 d. 21 Jan 1992, dau. Arthur and Celeste Blanchard. In Lebanon NH. He bur. in Oxbow Cem., Newbury VT.

Richard Arthur, b. 11 Oct 1916, m. 25 Apr 1941 Barbara L. Kenny, b. ?. CH: Richard Arthur, b. 29 Jun 1949, d. 18 Dec 1992 Hardwick MA; John Porteous, b. 2 Mar 1952, d. 30 Aug 1985.

Robert Norman, b. 24 Dec 1917 Hartford VT, m. 30 Apr 1944 Pauline Sharp, b. ?. In Woodstock VT. CH: Paula, b. 27 Mar 1948, m. 26 Jun 1984 Richard Reynolds; Peter, b. 27 Nov 1949.

Sources: VR SA/VT. Obit, Richard Arthur Sawyer rec.

34. **ROBERT HENRY⁹ SAWYER** [see 30], b. 4 Mar 1873 Portland ME, m. 12 Nov 1895 Portland ME Edith S. Merry of Portland ME, b. 1874, dau Albert and Alice (Stanley) Merry. Clerk.

Rufus Stanley, b. 22 Aug 1896.

Sources: VR SA/ME.

## TENTH GENERATION

35. **HOMER EUGENE[10] SAWYER** [see 31], b. 8 Apr 1892 Malden MA, d. 12 Nov 1968, m. 7 Feb 1917 Kathryn Motley, b. ? d. 1944. In Dedham MA.

Kathryn, m. Stuart Gillies. Went to Edinburgh, Scotland.

Motley, b. 23 Feb 1920, d. 1982, m. 25 Apr 1942 (div. 1976) Betty Butler.

Sources: P12.

# PART II

## ꩜ WILLIAM OF NEWBURY ꩜

1. Born in England about 1613, **WILLIAM[1] SAYER**[a] was living in Salem MA in 1640, having arrived in America four years earlier with his brothers Edward and Thomas. He moved to Wenham MA in 1643, thence to Newbury MA, where he settled beside the Merrimac River near the West Parish meeting house. There he remained until his death some sixty years later. William was married to Ruth Bitfield (Bidfield? Binford?), b. ?, d. ca. May 1693, daughter of William and Elizabeth and sister of Samuel, a Boston constable. They had the twelve children listed below.[b]

Active in town affairs throughout his life, William was elected to various minor offices: Fence Viewer on April 2, 1668 and April 3, 1671; Surveyor of Highways on March 5, 1677; and Tithing Man on March 24, 1680 and March 22, 1686. He took the oath of allegiance to King Charles II in 1678[c] . Little is known about his personality, but he must have been a compassionate man, judging by two petitions from the town of Newbury to the General Court containing his signature. One was dated May 14, 1654 on behalf of "our loving friend, Lieutenant Robert Pike, of Salisbury," the other written May 21, 1663, protesting a fine imposed upon one Dr. Greenland of Newbury, who had practiced as a physician without a license. Clearly he was religious, for in 1681 he, his wife, his daughter Ruth and her husband, Benjamin Morse, and others, all of Newbury, joined the First Baptist Church of Boston and later helped to establish an early Baptist church in Newbury.

It appears that William had a practical side as well, for by both grant and purchase he acquired a number of acres of land near the main road in the West Parish and there built the home he occupied for the rest of his life. A tax assessor's list of Newbury inhabitants drawn up in August 1688 credits him with "2 houses, 12 acres of plow land, 12 acres of meadow, 1 horse, 4 oxen, 2 two-yr olds, 2 one-yr olds, 9 sheep & 3 hogs" [C91a]. Thus, whatever else he may have been, he was not a poor man.

The precise date of William's death is not recorded, but on March 1st, 1703 his son-in-law, John Emery, was appointed administrator of the estate of "Wm Sawyer of Newberry late deceased ...By right of his Late Wife Mary Sawyer, daughter to the Deceased," with Thomas Treadwell, Jr., and John Knowlton as sureties. On October 4, 1703, however, John Emery "upon Oath makes his return T Tr is no Estate of ye sd Deed to be found," and asked the court to relieve him of his trust. For those of his children who had perhaps not already received some portion of his estate, William had made provisions on 19 May 1693 by a deed of gift to his youngest son, Stephen, stipulating that the latter was to pay to each of his four sisters 20 pounds within five years of his father's death. This deed was acknowledged on 30 May 1693 by William and his wife, Ruth, who "gave up her right of dower," and was recorded on 22 Aug 1694.

Many of William's descendents remained in and around Newbury MA, while others scattered throughout Essex, Suffolk, and Norfolk counties of Massachusetts. A few -- probably William himself -- are buried under ancient grey slabs in the Old Sawyer Hill burial ground in the

---

[a] Originally, William[1] spelled his name Sayer. By 1689, when he signed an inventory of his deceased son's estate, he had added a "w," thereby giving it the modern spelling. There is no indication that either of his brothers spelled their surname Sayer, but on the gravestone of Thomas[1] in Lancaster MA the name is spelled Sawer.

[b] Several secondary works include another child, Bitfield, born after Samuell[2], who allegedly died unm at age 97. The source for this is not given, and no such child appears in the vital records of the period.

[c] On April 27, 1678 the British Government instructed the authorities of the Massachusetts Bay Colony to administer an oath of allegiance to all male subjects who were sixteen years of age or older, and to fine or imprison any who refused to comply.

western part of what is now Newburyport MA, off Ferry Road[d] . Others moved to Maine and New Hampshire and established the roots of Sawyer lines which were to develop elsewhere in New England.

1. William[1] and Ruth had the following children:
2 John[2], 1645-1689.
3 Samuell[2], 1646-1718.
Ruth, b. 16 Sep 1648, d. ca. 1715, m. 27 Aug 1667 Benjamin Morse.
Mary, b. 7 Feb 1650, d. 24 Jun 1659.
Sarah, b. 20 Nov 1651, d. 2 Aug 1732, m. 15 Jan 1669 Joshua Browne.
Hannah, b. 23 Feb 1653, d. 25 Jan 1660.
4 William[2], 1656-1718.
Frances, b. 24 Mar 1658, d. 7 Feb 1660.
Mary, b. 29 Jul 1660, d. 3 Nov 1699, m. 13 Jun 1683 John Emery, Jr.
5 Stephen[2], 1663-1753.
Hannah, b. 11 Jan 1664, d. 28 Aug 1683.
Frances, b. 3 Nov 1670, d. Oct 1744, m. Thomas Treadwell.

Sources: VR Newbury MA. H84, E2, A26, P33, U1, H63, S38, J16, P79.

## SECOND GENERATION

2. **JOHN[2] SAWYER** [see 1], b. 24 Aug 1645 Newbury MA, d. 18 Mar 1689 Newbury MA, m. 18 Feb 1676 Newbury MA Sarah Poore, b. 5 Jun 1655, dau. John and Sarah Poore of Newbury MA. B/land in Haverhill MA 1669. In Newbury MA 1681 and became member of the First Baptist Church. On 25 Feb 1690, letters of administration were granted by the county court at Ipswich MA to Sarah, who brought in a "true inventory to ye best of her knowledge upon oath" and gave bonds in the amount of 400 pounds. Wid. m. 27 Nov 1707 Joseph Bayley of Newbury MA.

Ruth, b. 22 Sep 1677. Had two illegitimate sons, one (Benjamin) b. 6 Jan 1701.
6 William[3], 1679-1759.
Sarah, b. 20 May 1681, m. 29 Jun 1702 Ed Woodman of Newbury MA.
John, b. 25 Apr 1683, d. 19 Mar 1689.
7 Jonathan[3], b. 1685.
8 David[3], 1687-ca. 1747.
9 John[3], 1688-1756.

Sources: VR Newbury MA. U1, H84, L29, B5, E20.

3. **SAMUELL[2] SAWYER** [see 1], b. 22 Nov 1646 Newbury MA, d. 11 Feb 1718 Newbury MA, m. 13 Mar 1671 Newbury MA Mary Emery of Pembroke NH, b. 24 Jun 1652, dau. John andMary (Webster) Emery. Lieutenant in King Philip War. Quaker. Made a Freeman 12 May 1675. Licensed innholder 1693-1716. On 21 Dec 1715, purchased Blue Anchor Tavern with mansion house, barn and stable. S/land 3 Mar 1716. Will dated 10 Feb 1718.

Mary, b. 20 Jan 1672, d. 21 Apr 1745.
10 Samuel[3], 1674-1723.
John, b. 15 Mar 1676 Newbury MA, d. Newbury MA, m.(1) 25 Dec 1700 Newbury MA Mary (Brown) Merrill, wid. of Peter, b. 16 Jan 1671 d. 21 Feb 1707, dau. Isaac and Rebecca (Bailey) Brown; m.(2)(I) 25 Nov 1710 Salem MA Sarah (Wells) Sybley, wid.

---

[d] Many of the oldest stones are sunken or badly eroded by the elements. William1's grave, if there, cannot be identified. Since other members of his immediate family are present, however, and as the cemetery was located near his home, it is reasonable to assume that his remains lie somewhere in the Sawyer Hill burial ground.

of Samuel, b. 27 Aug 1669, dau. John and Sarah (Littlefield) Wells. Mentioned as soldier 26 Aug 1696 in York ME; Sergeant in 1709. CH: Judith, b. 16 Oct 1701, d. 20 Feb 1740, m. 29 Nov 1723 Newbury MA Nathan Chase; John, b. 5 Apr 1704, d. 17 Apr 1723; Lydia, b. 29 Mar 1712, m. 2 Apr 1747 Dr. James Holgate of Haverhill MA; Eunice, b. 21 Jan 1714, d. 1804, m. Mar 1735 Joshua Woodman; Loice, b. 12 Jul 1718, d.1799, m. Nov 1736 Deacon William Calif.

Hannah, b. 12 Jan 1678, d.y.

11 Josiah[3], 1681-1756.

12 Joshua[3], 1682-1768.

Daughter, b. 7 Mar 1684, d. 26 Mar 1684.

13 Benjamin[3], 1686-1725.

Child, b. 15 Nov 1693, d. same day.

Sources: VR Newbury MA. H84, C92, R34, S35, B54, C30, E20, N27, M36.

4. **WILLIAM[2] SAWYER** [see 1], b. 1 Feb 1656 Newbury MA, d. 7 Jun 1718 Wells ME, m. 2 Nov 1677 Sarah (Littlefield) Wells, wid. of John, b. 16 Nov 1650 d. Jan 1735, dau. Francis Littlefield. Narraganset War 1675. Helped organize the First Church of Wells in 1706. Representative in 1707, 1716, 1717. Will was dated three days before his death.

Joseph, b. 14 Aug 1678 Wells ME, d. 10 Aug 1703 Wells ME, m. Mary Fletcher, b. ? d. 10 Aug 1703. Joseph, Mary, and a son were killed by Indians; a second child was taken captive. Brother Francis administered estate 1704.

14 Francis[3], 1681-1756.

15 Daniel[3], 1683-1717.

Hannah, b. 9 Apr 1685, m. 8 Jul 1706 Philip Chesley.

Ruth, b. 26 May 1687, m. 1717 James Sampson.

Sources: VR Newbury MA, Wells ME. Will, T14, F23, N5, H84, B67, H63, S42, P82k, A31.

5. **STEPHEN[2] SAWYER** [see 1], b. 25 Apr 1663 Newbury MA, d. 8 Jun 1753 Newbury MA, m. 10 Mar 1687 Newbury MA Ann Titcomb of Newbury MA, b. 7 Jul 1666 d. 1 Oct 1750, dau. William and Elizabeth (Bitfield, wid. of William Stevens) Titcomb. Corporal in Indian Wars. Quaker in 1690. At time of death, he was the oldest man in Newbury MA.

Ann, b. 1 Aug 1687, m.(1) 15 Oct 1708 Ebenezer Sargent, m.(2) Robert Peasley.

16 Daniel[3], 1688-1781.

Sarah, b. 1691, m. 23 Nov 1711 Nathaniel Weed of Amesbury MA.

17 Stephen[3], 1692-1765.

18 Enoch[3], 1694-1771.

Elizabeth, b. 26 Jan 1703, m. 7 Jan 1723 Zecheus Collins of Lynn MA.

Sources: VR Newbury MA. H84, J16.

## THIRD GENERATION

6. **WILLIAM[3] SAWYER** [see 2], b. 29 Apr 1679 Newbury MA, d. 1759, m. 7 Jan 1702 Newbury MA Lydia Webster of Newbury MA, b. 20 Dec 1681 d. Oct 1773, dau. Isreal and Elizabeth (Lunt) Webster. Wid. in Atkinson NH.

Elizabeth, b. 1 Oct 1702, m. 19 Apr 1739 Thomas Stephens.

Sarah, b. 11 Jan 1705.

Mary, b. 25 Oct 1708, d. 1799, unm.

19 William[4], b. 1710.

Lydia, b. 29 May 1719, d. 6 Mar 1736.

20 Abner[4], 1721-1805.

Sources: VR Newbury MA. H84, L46, N9, C56, C91a.

7. **JONATHAN³ SAWYER** [see 2], b. 4 Mar 1685 Newbury MA, m. 10 Jan 1711 Newbury MA Mary Rawlins of Newbury MA, b. 10 Apr 1683 d. Jun 1768, dau. Nicholas and Rebecca (Long) Rawlins. Mary bur. in Hampstead NH.

Elisha, b. 31 Oct 1714 Newbury MA, m. 2 Nov 1736 Newbury MA Rebecca Pike, b. 16 Feb 1714. CH: Mary, b. 17 Oct 1737, d. 3 Jan 1824 W. Newbury MA; Rebecca, b. 24 Jul 1742; Sarah, b. 13 May 1744, m. 21 Jun 1863 Jesse Page, went to Hampstead NH; Tirzah, b. 15 Mar 1751, m. 9 Nov 1778 Thomas Webber of Hopkinton NH; Bettee, b. 19 May 1757.

21 Abel⁴, 1718-1794.

22 Moses⁴, 1722-1791.

Sources: VR Newbury MA, Hampstead NH. N5, R25.

8. **DAVID³ SAWYER** [see 2], b. 13 Jan 1687 Newbury MA, d. ca. 1747 Scarboro ME, m. 28 Feb 1712 Kittery ME Eleanor Frost of Kittery ME, b. ?, dau. Nicholas and Mary (Small) Frost. In Kittery ME 1711. Church at Sturgeon Creek (now Eliot ME) mentions "Mrs. Sawyer" in 1724. B/land in Scarboro ME 1727. Helped establish First Congregational Church, Scarboro ME, 1728.

John, b. 2 Mar 1713 Kittery ME.

Mary, b. 13 Jul 1714, m. _____ Stevens.

23 David⁴, 1715-1796.

Jonathan, b. 6 Apr 1716, d. 4 Mar 1721.

Sarah, b. 26 Jul 1719, d. 1 Sep 1752, m.(1) 22 Sep 1741 Paul Atkins, m.(2) 1 Apr 1748 John Small.

Stephen, b. 26 Feb 1721 Kittery ME, d. Gorham ME, m. Sarah _____, b. ?. Revolutionary War: Private in Ebenezer Murch's Company, 27 Nov 1779. To Scarboro ME from Kittery, thence to Gorham ME. S/land in Gorham ME 1754. B/land in Gorham ME 1757. S/land in Gorham ME 1775. In Gorham ME 1790, 1799. CH: Rhoda, b. 10 Jul 1743, m. 12 Apr 1765 Stephen Trip; Mary, b. 7 Apr 1745; Sarah, b. 27 Mar 1748, m. 12 May 1767 Abner Trip; Catherine, b. 28 Oct 1750, m. 3 Nov 1768 Joseph Weymouth; Phebe, b. 8 Sep 1754.

Sources: Gorham ME census 1790. VR Newbury MA, Kittery ME, Gorham ME. U1, L30,P82a, Y3, M3, S22, P51, W31.

9. **JOHN³ SAWYER** [see 2], b. 11 Sep 1688 Newbury MA, d. 27 Mar 1756 Newbury MA, m. 25 Nov 1714 Newbury MA Abigail Thurlow, b. 10 Feb 1696 d. 20 Apr 1776 Byfield MA, dau. Jonathan and Mary (Merrill) Thurlow. Fought Indians Nov 1709 at Merrimac River under Captain Thomas Noyes of Newbury MA.

24 Abraham⁴, b. 17 Feb 1716.

Mehitable, b. 8 Apr 1719.

Sarah, b. 10 Nov 1721, m. 17 Jan 1743 Joseph Smith of Rowley MA.

Abigail, b. 9 Mar 1724.

John, b. 31 Jul 1726 Newbury MA, d. 1766 Newbury MA m. 23 Jan 1753 Salisbury MA Mary Buswell of Salisbury MA, b. ?. CH: Anna, b. 29 Jul 1753; Sarah, b. 28 Dec 1755; Abigail, b. ?.

Mary, b. 2 Mar 1729, d. 1819, m.(1) 5 Aug 1756 John Blaisdell of Chelmsford MA, m.(2) 1777 Benjamin Wallingford.

Eliphalet, b. Dec 1735 Newbury MA.

Lydia, b. 29 Jan 1738, m. 10 Nov 1757 Moses Kelly.

Sources: VR Newbury MA, Salisbury MA, Chelmsford MA. H84, E20, M36, C48, K2.

10. **SAMUEL³ SAWYER** [see 3], b. 5 Jun 1674 Newbury MA, d. 21 Apr 1723 Newbury MA, m. 17 Dec 1702 Newbury MA Abigail Goodridge, b. 17 Sep 1675 d. 14 Oct 1722, dau. Joseph and Martha (Moores) Goodridge. Served with Captain Hugh March 1711. Gravestone in Sawyer Hill burial ground, Newburyport MA.

25 Samuel⁴, 1705-1783.
Martha, b. 17 Feb 1707, m. 16 May 1728 Edmund Hale.
Abigail, b. 26 May 1709 d. 26 Sep 1741, m. 11 Dec 1735 Abraham Annis.
Joseph, b. 8 Apr 1711, d. 25 Sep 1723. Mary, b. 3 Oct 1712, d. 24 Jul 1744, m. Oct 1730 Smith Hills.
26 Edmund⁴, 1714-1807.
27 Jacob⁴, 1716-1763.
Sources: VR Newbury MA. N5, K2, C13, A29, H4.

11. **JOSIAH³ SAWYER** [see 3], b. 20 Jan 1681 Newbury MA, d. 4 Apr 1756 Newbury MA, m. 22 Jan 1707 Newbury MA Tirzah Bartlett, b. 20 Jan 1684 d. 2 Sep 1739, dau. Samuel and Elizabeth (Titcomb) Bartlett. Cordwainer 1707. Ship owner. Gravestone in Sawyer Hill burial ground, Newburyport MA.

28 Josiah⁴, 1709-1792.
29 Moses⁴, 1711-1778.
Tirzah, b. 7 Nov 1713, d. 1782, m. Reuben French.
Hannah, b. 1715, d. 6 Sep 1739.
Isreal, b. 9 Oct 1717, d. 2 Aug 1739.
30 Gideon⁴, 1719-1806.
James, b. 12 May 1722, d. 27 Sep 1723.
Sources: VR Newbury MA. H84, E20.

12. **JOSHUA³ SAWYER** [see 3], b. 23 Feb 1682 Newbury MA, d. Jun 1768 Hampstead NH, m. Elizabeth _____, b. ?.

Joseph, b. 19 Nov 1706 Newbury MA, d. 15 Jul 1749 Kingston NH, m. 1 Dec 1729 Newbury MA Dorothy Brown of Newbury MA, b. 10 Aug 1712, dau. Thomas and Elizabeth (Berry) Brown. In Salisbury MA 1732. B/land in Kingston NH 1739, 1742, 1748. Wid. m. 25 May 1749 Kingston NH John Young. CH: son, b. 3 Nov 1733 d. 4 Feb 1734; Miriam, b. 5 Nov 1735, m. 29 Apr 1751 John Young, Jr; Elizabeth, b. 27 Nov 1738, d. 13 Jul 1813, m. 30 Dec 1757 Joseph Brown; Dorothy, b. 14 Dec 1740; Joseph, b. 5 Jun 1743, d. 31 Oct 1745; Judith, b. 6 Oct 1745, m. David Jones; Sarah, b. 13 Oct 1748.
Mary, b. 29 Apr 1709, m. 24 Sep 1729 Titus Wells of Chester NH.
31 Joshua⁴, 1711-1794.
32 Nathan⁴, b. 1714.
Sarah, b. 18 Aug 1716, d. 23 Nov 1781, m. 10 Feb 1735 Benjamin Joy.
Elizabeth, b. ?, m. 19 Jun 1744 William Richardson.
Anne, b. 3 Mar 1721, m. 16 Dec 1742 Moses Morse.
Sources: VR Newbury MA, Salisbury MA. H84, E2, D9.

13. **BENJAMIN³ SAWYER** [see 3], b. 27 Oct 1686 Newbury MA, d. 1725 Amesbury MA, m. 3 Feb 1714 Amesbury MA Elizabeth Jameson of Amesbury MA, b. 28 Dec 1690 d. 22 Dec 1750, dau. John and Esther (Martin) Jameson. In Amesbury MA 1714.

33 Benjamin⁴, 1716-1757.
Elizabeth, b. 2 Sep 1718, d. 7 Feb 1803, m. 30 Aug 1737 Daniel Nichols.

34 John[4], 1721-1801.
Mary, b. 1 Feb 1724, m. 13 Feb 1743 Rowley MA William Stickney.
Sources: VR Newbury MA. R29, H84, S89.

14. **FRANCIS[3] SAWYER** [see 4], b. 6 Mar 1681 Wells ME, d. 31 Aug 1756 Ipswich MA, m.(1) 6 Oct 1705 Elizabeth (Treadwell) Dennis, wid. of Thomas, b.?; m.(2)(I) 15 Jan 1725 Ipswich MA Susannah Low of Ipswich MA, wid. of David, b. 9 Oct 1687 d. 30 May 1748, dau. Robert and Abigail (Ayers) Lord; m.(3) 6 Jan 1749 Ipswich MA Hannah Staniford, b. ? d. Dec 1750; m.(4) 26 Oct 1751 Mary Knowlton, b. 1694 d. Feb 1789. Attended town meeting w/father in Wells ME 1716. B/land in Dover NH 1722, Chichester NH 1744. Owned land in Ipswich MA 1734. S/land Somersworth NH 1755. First seven CH were b. in Wells ME, the last two in Ipswich MA.
35 Joseph[4], 1706-1774.
Elizabeth, b. 5 Sep 1709, d. 29 Apr 1785, m. 25 Apr 1730 Isaac Appleton.
Samuel, b. 11 Jun 1712, d.y.
Abigail, b. 1 Mar 1715, d. 16 Sep 1779, m. 23 Sep 1736 Dan Gilman.
Mary, b. 25 Mar 1717, d. 8 Dec 1786, m. 20 Apr 1751 Abner Harris.
36 Daniel[4], 1719-1813.
Unice, b. 6 Jul 1722, d. 22 Apr 1744, m. 14 May 1743 John Moulton.
Hannah, b. 29 Mar 1729, d. Apr 1731.
37 Samuel[4], 1730-1808.
Sources: VR Ipswich MA. S24, H84, C24, C43, F23, T14, B67.

15. **DANIEL[3] SAWYER** [see 4], b. 26 May 1683 Wells ME, d. 1717 Wells ME, m. Sarah Bolles, b. ?, dau. Joseph and Mary (Call) Bolles of Ipswich MA. Wid. m. 10 Apr 1739 Joseph Hill.
38 William[4], 1706-1768.
Sarah, b. 6 Oct 1708, m. 25 Jan 1726 David Littlefield, Jr.
Lydia, b. 14 Aug 1710, m. 12 Nov 1729 Jeremiah Littlefield.
Daniel, b. 4 Apr 1712, d. 9 Nov 1713.
Hannah, b. 29 Nov 1714, m.(I) 3 Oct 1730 Joseph Hatch.
Sources: H84, N42, A31, B67, T14, G20a.

16. **DANIEL[3] SAWYER** [see 5], b. 28 Jan 1688 Newbury MA, d. 22 Oct 1781 Newbury MA, m. 2 Apr 1714 Newbury MA Sarah Moody, b. 11 Feb 1695 d. 21 Aug 1790, dau. Thomas Moody. Original proprietor of Nottingham NH, 1743. B/S/land in Nottingham NH 1746, 1766, 1767.
39 Humphrey[4], 1716-1797.
Anne, b. 14 Jan 1717, m. 19 Mar 1737 Amesbury MA Samuel Smith.
Elijah, b. Aug 1720, d. 14 Nov 1720.
Judith, b. 5 Sep 1721, d. 1 Jul 1722.
Sources: VR Newbury MA. H84, N16.

17. **STEPHEN[3] SAWYER** [see 5], b. 1692 Newbury MA, d. 5 Jan 1765 Newbury MA, m. (I) 19 Aug 1719 Sarah Rowell, b. 7 Aug 1697, dau. Jacob and Hannah (Barnard) Rowell. Quakers. S/land in Nottingham NH 1733-1742.
40 Jacob[4], 1719-1799.
41 Moses[4], 1721-1816.
Miriam, b. 28 Oct 1723, m. 24 Oct 1744 Joseph Hill of Hampton NH.
Elizabeth, b. 23 Dec 1725, m. 17 Jun 1748 John Brown.
42 Aaron[4], 1729-1805.
Hannah, b. 29 Apr 1731, d. 13 Apr 1781, m. 20 May 1749 Thomas Hanson.
43 Beetfield[4], 1736-1833.

44 Amos[4], 1738-ca. 1824.
45 Micah[4], 1741-1817.
Sources: VR Newbury MA. D47, N16.

18. **ENOCH[3] SAWYER** [see 5], b. 22 Jul 1694 Newbury MA, d. 15 Nov 1771 Newbury MA, m. 29 Sep 1721 Reading MA Sarah Pierpont of Reading MA, b. 3 Oct 1697 d. 3 Sep 1773, dau. Rev. Jonathan Pierpont. Physician.

Child, b. 1722, d. 14 May 1722.
Enoch, Dr., b. 19 Apr 1723 Newbury MA, d. 7 Sep 1805 Newbury MA, m.(1) 30 Mar 1758 Newbury MA Hannah Moody, b. 1 Dec 1730 d. 23 Mar 1790, dau. John Jr. and Hannah (Toppan) Moody; m.(2) 18 Dec 1804 Sarah Parsons, wid., b. ?. Delegate to Federal Constitutional Convention 1788. Physician. CH: Mary, b. 8 Apr 1759, d. 1834, m. 21 Mar 1780 Rev. David Toppan; Judith, b. 12 Jul 1761, d. 1830; Sarah, b. 22 Feb 1763; Hannah, b. 26 Nov 1769, d. Apr 1840 Hallowell ME; son, b. (1784-1790).
Mary, b. 11 Sep 1725, d. 18 Oct 1756.
Anna, b. 15 Sep 1727, d. 16 May 1786.
46 Edmund[4], 1730-1795.
Micajah, b. 23 Sep 1733, d.y.
Sarah, b. Oct 1735, d.y.
47 Micajah[4], 1737-1817.
Sarah, b. 25 Mar 1740, m. 18 Jul 1762 Thomas Parsons.
Sources: Newbury MA census 1790, 1800. VR Newbury MA, Reading MA. Ould Newbury, NEHGReg V34, Abraham Toppan Gen, List of Delegates by County 1788.

## FOURTH GENERATION

19. **WILLIAM[4] SAWYER** [see 6], b. 12 Aug 1710 Newbury MA, d. Plaistow NH, m. 2 Apr 1735 Newbury MA Hannah Follansbee of Amesbury MA, b. 18 Nov 1716, dau. Thomas Follansbee. Hannah B/land in Amesbury MA 1736. William S/land in South Hampton NH 1744. In Plaistow NH 1760. Wid. went to Litchfield ME.

Hannah, b. 11 Mar 1737.
William, b. 27 Mar 1739, d. 1749.
Lydia, b. 1 Feb 1740, d. 1820.
Sarah, b. 19 May 1743.
Mary, b. 28 Jul 1745.
48 David[5], 1748-1835.
William, b. 18 Mar 1753 Newbury MA, d. 4 Mar 1838 Vienna ME, m. Oct 1778 Salisbury MA Abigail Follansbee, b. 1760 d. 20 Dec 1835. Revolutionary War. Physician. Town Treasurer for Goffstown NH 1781. Innholder 1784-1804. CH: Sarah, b. 1787, d. 1829, m. Hallowell ME Jonathan Haines; Abigail, b. ?, m. 10 Jan 1806 Hallowell ME James Gow.
Sources: Newcastle ME census 1790. Hallowell ME census 1800. Readville ME census 1810. Augusta ME census 1820. VR Newbury MA, Salisbury MA. N16, H84, D56, H3, N27, N11, David Young rec.

20. **ABNER[4] SAWYER** [see 6], b. 6 May 1721 Newbury MA, d. 28 May 1805 Hampstead NH, m. 1 Aug 1745 Haverhill MA Mary Foot, b. ?. His m. record says he was from So. Hampton NH. B/land in South Hampton NH 1744. In Hampstead NH 1748.

49 Joshua[5], b. 1746.
Son, b. 1749, d. Nov 1755.

Joseph, b. 25 Jan 1753 Hampstead NH.
Child, b. Aug 1758, d. Dec 1758.
Sarah, b. 19 Dec 1759.
John, b. 26 Mar 1767 Hampstead NH, m.(I) 23 Feb 1790 Susannah Townsend, b. 1769 d. 25 Sep 1846 Haverhill MA. Child b. 1790, d. 26 Sep 1793.

Sources: Hampstead NH census 1790, 1800. VR Newbury MA, Haverhill MA, Hampstead NH.

21. **ABEL[4] SAWYER** [see 7], b. 15 Aug 1718 Newbury MA, d. 15 Apr 1794 Hampstead NH, m.(1) 24 Apr 1744 Newbury MA Abigail Ordway, b. 15 Nov 1719 d. 22 Sep 1778; m.(2) 4 Feb 1779 Newbury MA Mehitable Hale, b. ?.

50 Abel[5], 1744-1821.
Abigail, b. 10 Mar 1748, m. 1772 John Wheeler of Newburyport MA.

Sources: VR Newbury MA.

22. **MOSES[4] SAWYER** [see 7], b. Feb 1722 Newbury MA, d. bef. 19 May 1791 Enfield NH, m.(1) 19 Jun 1759 Kingston NH Sarah Chase of Sandown NH, wid., b. ?; m.(2) Lydia _____, b. ?. B/land in Plaistow NH 1760. S/land in Plaistow NH 1766. B/ land in Hopkinton NH 1766. Elected to town offices in Hopkinton NH: Fence Viewer 1775; Town Moderator 1776; Surveyor of Highways. In 1791 Richard Currier was appointed guardian of Phebe and David. CH listed in will. Lydia and Moses Jr bp. in Amherst NH Congregational Church 1776.

51 Jonathan[5], 1760-1840.
52 Truman[5], b. 1761.
53 Moses[5], b. 1763.
Sarah, b. 6 Mar 1764.
Stephen, b. ca. 1770.
Rhoda, b. ?.
Phebe, b. ?.
David, b. ca. 1775.

Sources: VR Newbury MA, Plaistow NH. N16.

23. **DAVID[4] SAWYER** [see 8], b. 18 Dec 1715 Kittery ME, d. 14 Jul 1796 Saco ME, m.(I) 25 Feb 1737 Biddeford ME Hephzibar Davis of Biddeford ME, b. 4 Jun 1721 d. 8 Oct 1803, dau. John and Elizabeth (Basford) Davis. Hephzibar joined First Congregational Church of Scarborough ME on 21 Aug 1743. In Saco ME 1750. S/land in Scarborough MA 1754. Joined Saco ME church in 1769.

Eleanor, bp. 27 Jan 1740.
54 John[5], 1742-1826.
55 David[5], bp. 1744.
Josiah, bp. 29 Apr 1744 Scarborough ME.
Hephzibar, bp. 2 Mar 1745, m. 9 Dec 1762 Ephraim Bryant.
56 Joel[5], 1746-1825.
Betty, b. 14 Mar 1751, d. 28 Jun 1827, m. 1770 Robert Patterson.
57 William[5], ca. 1753-1841.
58 Abner[5], ca. 1757-1823.
Molly (Mary?), b. 25 Mar 1765 (in Gorham ME?), d. 9 Oct 1815, m. 15 Apr 1786 Jesse Whitney.

Sources: Saco ME census 1790. VR Saco ME, Scarboro ME. S23, Y1, H84, M3, P30.

24. **ABRAHAM$^{4}$ SAWYER** [see 9], b. 17 Feb 1716 Newbury MA, m. 17 Feb 1737 Rowley MA Margaret (Fowler) Hidden of Byfield MA, wid. of Ebenezer, b. ?, dau. Benjamin and Anne (Foster) Fowler. In Byfield MA, Rowley MA.

Benjamin, bp. 14 Oct 1739 Newbury MA, d. 10 Oct 1821, m. 16 Apr 1761 Rowley MA Molly March, b. ?. Revolutionary War. In Byfield MA. He bur. in Kittery ME. CH: Mehitable, bp. 18 Apr 1762; Catherine, bp. 2 Oct 1763; Hannah, bp. 29 Dec 1765; Betty, bp. 10 Dec 1769, m. 25 Jan 1786 Stephen Davis.

Mehitable, b. Jun 1742, d. 27 Oct 1749.

Sarah, bp. 27 Jan 1745, d.y.

Sarah, bp. 16 Oct 1748.

59 Samuel$^{5}$, bp. 1754.

John, bp. 19 Sep 1756, d. 30 Dec 1775 in the Revolutionary War.

Sources: VR Newbury MA, Rowley MA. S90, B53, E20, E17, J16.

25. **SAMUEL$^{4}$ SAWYER** [see 10], b. 4 Jun 1705 Newbury MA, d. 11 Jun 1783 Newbury MA, m. 9 Jul 1728 Newbury MA Mary Kelley, b. 31 Dec 1708, dau. John and Hannah (Somes) Kelley.

Samuel, b. 13 Aug 1729, d. 31 Jul 1737.

Mary, b. 17 Aug 1732, d. 17 Jul 1737.

Judith, b. 17 Jun 1735, d. 26 Jul 1737.

Mary, b. 30 Mar 1739.

60 Samuel$^{5}$, 1741-1786.

61 Joseph$^{5}$, 1744-1818.

John, b. 23 Feb 1746, d. 24 May 1753.

Sources: VR Newbury MA. H84, K2.

26. **EDMUND$^{4}$ SAWYER** [see 10], b. 6 Nov 1714 Newbury MA, d. 18 Feb 1807 Sutton NH, m. 1 Jan 1735 Amesbury MA Sarah Rowell of Amesbury MA, b. 4 Oct 1719, dau. Philip and Sarah (Davis) Rowell. B/land in Amesbury MA 1737. S/land in Amesbury MA 1740. Constable in 1753. Selectman for Hampstead NH 1758. Executor for brother Jacob 1763. S/land in Unity NH 1764. In Hampstead NH 1748, Sutton NH 1758. He bur. in So. Sutton NH.

62 Joseph$^{5}$, 1736-1813.

Jacob, b. 4 Oct 1738 Amesbury MA, d. 8 May 1763 Hampstead NH, m. 25 Nov 1762 Hampstead NH Elizabeth Webster, b. ?. Revolutionary War: In Major Goffe's Company, Hampstead NH, 1 May 1756 - 9 Nov 1756. B/S/land in Merrimac NH 1762, 1763. CH: Son, b. 10 Sep 1763, d. 22 Oct 1763.

63 Enoch $^{5}$, 1741-1817.

Sarah, b. 30 Jan 1744, d. 22 Feb 1822, m. 8 Feb 1769 Caleb Kimball.

Sources: Warner NH census 1790. VR Newbury MA, Amesbury MA, Hampstead NH. H84, N38, L29, M54.

27. **JACOB$^{4}$ SAWYER** [see 10], b. 4 Jun 1716 Newbury MA, d. bef. Mar 1763 Hampstead NH, m. 12 Dec 1744 Newbury MA Elizabeth Savery, b. 1720 d. 8 Mar 1791 Newburyport MA. Will probated 28 Mar 1763.

Jacob, b. 24 Sep 1745 Newbury MA.

Elizabeth, b. 15 May 1748, d. 17 Sep 1804, m. 8 May 1766 Edmund Worth.

Abigail, b. 23 Jul 1750, gave birth to Jeremiah 14 Dec 1773 in Brentwood NH.

Sarah, b. 1 Oct 1752, d. 14 Oct 1830, m. 6 Apr 1772 Enoch Chase.

Lois, bp. 18 May 1755, d. 1755.

Lois, bp. 11 Jul 1756.

Mary, b. 25 Dec 1757, m. 13 Sep 1779 Joshua Follansbee.

Eunice, b. 19 Aug 1761, d. 2 Dec 1838.
Sources: VR Newbury MA. C30.

28. **JOSIAH⁴ SAWYER** [see 11], b. 12 Apr 1709 Newbury MA, d. 10 Jun 1792 South Hampton NH, m. 25 Dec 1735 Newbury MA Mary Ordway, b. 5 Nov 1714 d. 2 Mar 1796, dau. Deacon John and Hannah (Bartlett) Ordway. B/land in So. Hampton NH 1745, in Nottingham NH 1757. B/S/land in Nottingham NH 1769. S/land in Deerfield NH 1769.

64 Josiah$^5$, 1737-1812.
65 Isreal$^5$, 1739-1821.
66 Matthias$^5$, 1741-1818.
67 John$^5$, 1744-1796.
Joshua, b. 1745.
Hannah, b. 25 Apr 1746, d. 23 Sep 1770, unm.
68 Richard$^5$, 1748-1818.
69 Moses$^5$, 1750-1821.
Molly, b. 12 Jan 1754, d. 21 Sep 1779, unm.
Tirzah, b. 15 Jul 1758, d. 2 Sep 1832, unm.

Sources: So. Hampton NH census 1790. VR Newbury MA, So. Hampton NH, Amesbury MA. D28.

29. **MOSES$^4$ SAWYER** [see 10], b. 21 Feb 1711 Newbury MA, d. 30 Aug 1778 Newburyport MA, m. 7 Jan 1752 Newbury MA Hannah Long, b. 1726 d. 19 May 1802. B/land in Kingston NH 1745, 1746. S/land in Kingston NH 1751. S/land in Hawk (Danville) NH 1770.

Moses, b. 11 Nov 1752, d.y.
70 Matthias Plant$^5$, 1754-1777.
71 Moses$^5$, 1756-1799.
Joseph, b. 5 Sep 1758 Newbury MA, d. 22 Apr 1831 Newburyport MA, m. (1) 14 Jun 1790 Newbury MA Sarah (Merrill) Woodman, wid. of Nathan, b. 1753 d. 26 Mar 1791, dau. Enoch and Sarah (Long) Merrill; m.(2) 26 May 1795 Newbury MA Sarah Long of Chester NH, b. 1762 d. 18 Jan 1813; m.(3) 25 Dec 1817 Newbury MA Nancy Roberts b. 12 Feb 1792, dau. Joseph and Anna (Trevett) Roberts. CH: Daughter, b. (1790-1800); Son, b. (1800-1810); Daughter, b. (1800-1810).
Child, b. ?, d. 1760.
Hannah, b. 14 Dec 1761, d. 28 Oct 1763.
Hannah, b. 8 Jul 1764, d. 6 Jan 1850, m. 29 Apr 1786 Jacob Little.
72 Thomas$^5$, 1770-1849.

Sources: Newbury MA census 1800, 1810, 1820, 1830. VR Newbury MA. L29.

30. **GIDEON$^4$ SAWYER** [see 11], b. 15 Dec 1719 Newbury MA, d. 26 Dec 1806 Hawk (Danville) NH, m. 25 Dec 1746 Newbury MA Sarah Bartlett, wid., b. 1724 d. 3 Mar 1797. B/S/land in Kingston NH 1745-1751. B/land in Chester NH 1757. B/land in Hawk (Danville) NH 1770. Will dated 5 Jul 1799.

Sarah, b. 12 Jun 1748 So. Hampton NH, d. 25 May 1765.
73 Gideon$^5$, 1751-1817.
74 James$^5$, 1755-1828.
75 Jotham$^5$, 1757-1824.
Hannah, b. 16 May 1760, d. 4 May 1820, unm.
Tamar, b. 8 Oct 1762, m. 13 Mar 1791 Abner Clough.
Reuben, b. 8 Sep 1765, d. 18 Dec 1789 Northfield NH, unm.

Sources: Hawk NH census 1790. VR Newbury MA, Newburyport MA, Kingston NH. N10, N6, N14, N16.

31. **JOSHUA[4] SAWYER** [see 12], b. 14 Dec 1711 Newbury MA, d. 17 Dec 1794 Hampstead NH, m. 18 Jun 1741 Esther Rogers, b. 8 Oct 1714 d. 18 Jul 1787, dau. John and Esther (Ordway) Rogers. In Hampstead NH 1764.

Elizabeth, b. 20 Jun 1742, d. 17 Oct 1743.

John, b. 25 Mar 1744, d. y.

Joshua, b. 22 Aug 1746 Newbury MA, d. 3 Jun 1827 Henniker NH, m.(1) 4 Feb 1770 Newbury MA Miriam Rogers, b. 20 Jun 1744 d. 17 Jun 1807, dau. Isaac and Anna Rogers; m.(2) 12 Jan 1808 Sarah White, b. 16 Jun 1737 d. 8 Feb 1819. In Hampstead NH 1764, Hopkinton NH 1775. CH: Miriam, b. 14 Feb 1771, d. 16 Aug 1774; Anna, b. 18 Mar 1773, d. 16 Apr 1833, m. 2 Jul 1806 Nathan Blanchard; Joshua, b. 31 May 1780, d. 31 May 1780; Miriam, b. 31 May 1780, d. 1 Jun 1780; Miriam, b. 31 Aug 1784, d. 19 Jul 1787.

76 John[5], 1748-1833.

Joseph, b. 9 Jun 1751 Newbury MA. In Hampstead NH.

77 Stephen[5], 1753-1822.

Esther, b. 24 Aug 1755, d. 11 May 1840, m. 23 Mar 1775 William Richardson.

Edmund, b. 3 Dec 1760 Newbury MA, m. Sarah _____, b. ?. In Franklin NH 1775. Revolutionary War: Private in Captain Osgood's Company at Concord MA 1776; Private in Captain Ebenezer Webster's Company at Battle of Bennington Aug 1777. In Vermont for seven years. Mentioned in Salisbury NH Town Records 1811.

Sources: Hopkinton NH census 1790, 1800. Franklin NH census 1830, 1840. VR Newbury MA, Hampstead NH. N14.

32. **NATHAN[4] SAWYER** [see 12], b. 7 May 1714 Newbury MA, m. Feb 1745 Newbury MA Mary Mors, b. ?. In Boston MA 1759.

Mary, b. 25 Nov 1747 Boston MA.

John, b. 28 Dec 1749 Boston MA, m. 6 Jun 1779 Sarah Jackson, b. ?.

Hannah, b. 14 Feb 1752.

Susannah, b. 29 Oct 1754.

Sarah, b. 27 Aug 1766.

Sources: VR Newbury MA, Boston MA.

33. **BENJAMIN[4] SAWYER** [see 13], b. 2 Mar 1716 Newbury MA, d. 28 Oct 1757 Kingston NH, m. 23 Nov 1737 Kingston NH Mary Bean of Kingston NH, bp. 24 Apr 1718. B/land in Kingston NH 1753.

Benjamin, b. 27 Aug 1738, d. 17 Sep 1738.

Mary, b. 25 Sep 1739, m. 2 Mar 1758 John Darling.

Benjamin, b. 29 Apr 1742 Kingston NH.

John, b. 27 Aug 1751, d. 28 Oct 1757.

Sources: VR Newbury MA, Kingston NH. T20, B40.

34. **JOHN[4] SAWYER** [see 13], b. 5 Sep 1721 Amesbury MA, d. 7 Jul 1801 Amesbury MA, m. 3 Apr 1746 Amesbury MA Elizabeth Kelly, b. 26 Dec 1728 d. 12 May 1794, dau. Richard and Hannah (Bartlett) Kelly. Revolutionary War. B/land in Dunbarton NH 1767.

Esther, b. 13 Mar 1747, m. 15 Oct 1765 Enoch Bayley.

78 Richard[5], 1748-1837.

Moses, b. 10 Apr 1751, d. 17 Apr 1751.

Elizabeth, b. 16 Jun 1752, d. 3 Nov 1753.
Moses, b. 18 Sep 1754, d. 12 Jul 1756.
Elizabeth, b. 1 Dec 1756.
79 John$^5$, 1760-1823.
Hannah, b. 12 Feb 1762, d. 29 Jun 1799.
Lois, b. 28 Jan 1764, d. 12 Apr 1784.
80 Symmes$^5$, 1766-1845.
81 Wyburd$^5$, 1769-1813.
Abigail, b. 22 Dec 1770.
Sources: Amesbury MA census 1790, 1800. H84, B5, K2, E20.

35. **JOSEPH$^4$ SAWYER** [see 14], b. 8 Dec 1706 Wells ME, d. 2 Mar 1774 Berwick ME, m.(1)(I) 6 Jun 1730 Ipswich MA Mary Calef of Ipswich MA, b. 1706 d. 6 Sep 1738, dau. Joseph Hill; m.(2) 7 Feb 1744 Wells ME Mehitable Littlefield, b. 20 Oct 1723 d. 23 Oct 1750, dau. Francis and Hepzibah (Littlefield) Littlefield. Mentioned in Wells ME town records 1735. Judge, physician, merchant. Note: Probate record says he d. 12 Jul 1766.

Joseph, b. 22 Aug 1733, d. 22 Oct 1735.
Susannah, bp. 8 Jun 1735.
Eunice, b. 1 May 1745, d. 25 Apr 1775, m. 25 Apr 1771 Bartholomew Gilman.
Sarah, b. ?, d.y.
Elizabeth, b. 12 Sep 1747, d. 20 Nov 1790, m. May 1771 Tristram Gilman of North Yarmouth ME.
Hepzibah, bp. 10 Sep 1749.
Ebenezer, b. 30 Sep 1750 Wells ME, d. 30 Mar 1778 Wells ME, m. 17 Feb 1774 Boston MA Elizabeth Checkly of Boston MA, b. ?. Delegate from Wells to Provincial Congress Feb 1775. Wid. m. John Lothrop of Boston MA. He bur. in Oceanville Cem., Wells ME. CH: Elizabeth, b. 13 Apr 1777.
Sources: VR Wells ME, Ipswich MA. T14, A31, N5, B67, P82k, M5, N10, L29.

36. **DANIEL$^4$ SAWYER** [see 14], b. 25 Jan 1719 Wells ME, d. 18 Sep 1813 Kennebunk ME, m.(1) (I)22 Nov 1740 Ipswich MA Frances Abbott of Ipswich MA, bp.12 Nov 1721, dau. Arthur and Mercy (Appleton) Abbott; m.(2) Kennebunk ME Joanna (Fidler) Kimball, b. ca. 1743, wid. of Nathaniel, dau. John Fidler. French and Indian Wars.

Sarah, b. ?.
82 Daniel$^5$, b. 1743.
Samuel, b. 21 Sep 1746 Wells ME.
Frances, b. 16 Apr 1749.
Joseph, b. 3 Jun 1750 Wells ME.
Abigail, b. Sep 1752, m. 18 Nov 1773 Aaron Wheelwright.
Susannah, b. 17 Nov 1754.
Mehitable, b. 10 Apr 1757, d. 8 Aug 1813 m.(1) 11 Aug 1778 Solomon Littlefield, m.(2) 15 Nov 1784 Capt Hutson Bishop, m.(3) 15 Apr 1805 Hosea Coombs.
83 Nathaniel$^5$, 1760-1835.
Sources: VR Wells ME, Ipswich MA. B67, N5, H84, A2, A3, P82k, E20, Obit.

37. **SAMUEL$^4$ SAWYER** [see 14], b. 27 Sep 1730 Ipswich MA, d. 7 Nov 1808 Ipswich MA, m. 11 Mar 1753 Elizabeth (Brown) Lakeman, wid., b. ? d. 18 Aug 1808, dau. James Brown. Owned Sawyer's Purchase in Littlefield ME. B/S/land in Lincoln County, 1783-1808. B/S/land in Scarboro ME 1792.

Susan, b. 24 Feb 1754, d. 23 Nov 1825, unm.

Samuel, b. 7 Feb 1755, d.y.
Elizabeth, b. 3 Apr 1757, d. 10 Nov 1842, unm.
Samuel, b. 3 Dec 1758, d.y. James Brown, b. 11 May 1760 Ipswich MA, d. 6 Sep 1840 Ipswich MA, unm.
Samuel, b. 21 Mar 1762 Ipswich MA.
Joseph, b. 15 Jan 1764, d.y.
84 Joseph$^5$, 1765-1851.
85 John$^5$, 1767-1829.
86 George Whitefield$^5$, 1770-1855.
Sources: Ipswich MA census 1790, 1800, 1810, 1820, 1830, 1840. VR Ipswich MA. H84, E20, W13, W14, Annette S. Meany Rec.

38. **WILLIAM$^4$ SAWYER** [see 15], b. 6 Feb 1706 Wells ME, d. 17 Jul 1768 Wells ME, m.(1) Mary Littlefield, b. 1707, m.(2) 25 Apr 1734 Love Bragdon of York ME, b. 19 May 1709, dau. Arthur Bragdon.
Phebe, b. 7 Jul 1728, m. 13 Mar 1743 Spark Perkins of York ME.
Sarah, b. 3 Aug 1729, d.y.
Lydia, b. 14 Feb 1731., d.y.
Daniel, b. 12 Mar 1733 Wells ME, d.y.
87 Samuel$^5$, 1735-1779.
Mary, b. 15 Aug 1736, m. 1764 Daniel Simpson of York ME.
Sarah, b. 25 Jun 1738, m. 21 Jan 1755 Newman Perkins of Wells ME.
88 William$^5$, 1740-1825.
Daniel, b. 1 Apr 1743 Wells ME, m.(1) Abigail Hill, b. ?, m.(2) Elizabeth _____, b. ?. CH: Sarah, b. 1 Jul 1764, d. 10 Jan 1857, m. 20 Oct 1787 John B. Hill; Mary, b. 10 Oct 1780.
Hannah, b. 1 Apr 1744, m. 5 Nov 1767 Abijah Hatch.
Lydia, b. 15 Jul 1750.
Sources: Wells Ch rec, H84, A31, B67, F20, P82k, P32, G20A.

39. **HUMPHREY$^4$ SAWYER** [see 16], b. 12 Feb 1716 Newbury MA, d. 1797 Newbury MA, m. 17 Jun 1742 Lynn MA Hannah Phillips of Lynn MA, b. 1714 d. 1768. Blacksmith. In Weare NH 1788, Newbury MA 1790.
89 Daniel$^5$, 1744-1811.
90 Phillips$^5$, 1746-1821.
Mary, b. 3 Mar 1748.
91 James$^5$, b. 1750.
Anna, b. 28 Mar 1753.
Ezra, b. 13 Jul 1755 Newbury MA, d. Holderness NH. CH: Son, b. (1774-1784); two sons, b. (1784-1790).
Ruth, b. 28 Jun 1757, d. 12 Oct 1760.
Hannah, b. 31 Jan 1760, m. 23 Jan 1782 Pharoah Johnson of Lynn MA.
92 Elijah$^5$, 1762-1839.
93 Humphrey$^5$, 1764-1820.
Sarah, b. 15 Sep 1768, m. 16 Oct 1790 William Weed.
Sources: Newbury MA census 1790. Holderness NH census 1800. VR Newbury MA, Lynn MA. N9.

40. **JACOB$^4$ SAWYER** [see 17], b. 23 Sep 1719 Newbury MA, d. 26 Apr 1799 Dover NH, m.(1) 7 Nov 1743 Susannah Estes of Dover NH, b. 19 Feb 1724 d. 7 Dec 1749, dau. Joseph and Mary (Robinson) Estes; m.(2) 10 Jul 1751 Sarah Hanson, b. 3 Mar 1733 d. 7 May 1802.

Blacksmith. In Dover NH 1743. B/land in Dover NH 1745, 1753, 1761, 1761, 1767. Selectman for Dover NH 1764-1765. Will dated 1794.

Sarah, b. 8 Nov 1744, d. 16 May 1829, m. 22 Oct 1766 Zaccheus Hanson.
94 Stephen[5], 1752-1831.
Patience, b. 26 Sep 1753, d. 30 Jun 1832, m. 4 Oct 1780 Richard Hanson.
Susannah, b. 17 Dec 1758, m. _____ Gerrish.
Micajah, b. 19 May 1760 Dover NH, d. bef. 16 Oct 1813 Dover NH. Nancy Maloney appointed executrix of his estate 16 Oct 1813. Census of 1810 lists no family.
Kezia, b. 12 Jan 1762, m. 30 Apr 1800 Benjamin Kelley.
Lydia, b. 30 Nov 1763, m. _____ Yeaton.
95 Timothy[5], 1766-1820.
96 Jacob[5], 1769-1846.
Mary, b. 13 Nov 1771, d. 25 Feb 1853, m. 1793 Abednego Robinson of Newfields NH.
Content, b. 13 Apr 1774, m. 1 Jul 1812 James Neal of York ME.
97 Enoch[5], 1776-1857.

Sources: Dover NH census 1790, 1810. VR Newbury MA. F20, S69, N5, P82i, E23, H9, B84.

41. **MOSES[4] SAWYER** [see 17], b. 30 Sep 1721 Newbury MA, d. 1816 Dover NH, m.(1) 5 Nov 1744 Huldah Hill of Kittery ME, b. ?, dau. Samuel and Hannah Hill of Kittery ME; m.(2) 28 Aug 1766 Rebecca Swain of Barrington NH, b. 1731 d. 16 Dec 1816, dau. Richard and Margaret Swain. B/land in Dover NH 1754.

Hannah, b. 6 Dec 1748, m. 30 Nov 1768 Moses Canney.
98 Samuel[5], 1751-1827.
Mary, b. 1 Jun 1753, m. 28 Dec 1774 Samuel Brown of Barrington NH.
99 George[5], 1758-1813.
100 Zaccheus[5], 1760-1824.
Loas *(sic)*, b. 24 Jul 1769.
Moses, b. 1771. No family listed in Dover NH census 1820.
Sarah, b. 17 May 1774.
Note: One dau, unidentified, d. 14 May 1787.

Sources: Dover NH census 1790, 1800, wid. 1810. VR Newbury MA, Dover NH. S70, N16.

42. **AARON[4] SAWYER** [see 17], b. 30 Jun 1729 Newbury MA, d. 30 Aug 1805 Amesbury MA, m. 8 Sep 1762 Amesbury MA Rachel Sargent, b. 17 Feb 1732, dau. John and Hannah (Quimby) Sargent. Revolutionary War. Physician. Lived in Sawyer House, Merrimac MA.

101 Stephen[5], 1762-1842.
Hannah, b. 4 Jan 1765, m. 10 Oct 1782 William Pecker.
102 Joshua[5], 1767-1829.
103 Aaron[5], 1773-1862.

Sources: Amesbury MA census 1790, 1800. VR Newbury MA, Amesbury MA. D6, N5, H63, Clifton R. Sargent Jr. rec.

43. **BEETFIELD[4] SAWYER** [see 17], b. 20 Feb 1736 Newbury MA, d. 21 Sep 1833 W. Newbury MA, m.(1) 15 Jun 1769 Phebe Collins of Amesbury MA, b. 6 Mar 1745; m.(2) 1773 Amesbury MA Sarah Colby, b. 16 Feb 1748 d. 1774, dau. Nathaniel and Elizabeth (Clough) Colby; m.(3) 23 Dec 1776 Susannah (Hanson) Varney, b. 15 Jun 1738 d. 25 Feb 1817, wid. of Ezekiel, dau. Robert and Lydia Hanson of Dover NH. In Newton NH, Hill NH.

104 Betfield[5], 1774-1835.
Phebe, b. 29 Jan 1778, d. 1 Sep 1806, m. 24 Feb 1800 Thomas Ordway.
Lydia Hanson, b. 16 Jul 1781, d. 4 Aug 1803.

Sources: Newbury MA census 1790, 1800, 1810. VR Newbury MA. H84, T20.

44. **AMOS⁴ SAWYER** [see 17], 16 Feb 1738 Newbury MA, d. bef. 1824, m. 29 Nov 1764 Newbury MA Mary Peasley of Newton NH, b. ?, dau. John and Lydia Peasley. In Plaistow NH 1771. Will dated Jan 1823.

Sarah, b. 16 Nov 1765, d.y.
105 Stephen⁵, 1767-1844.
106 John⁵, b. 1770.
Lydia, b. 6 Nov 1773, m. 19 Jun 1793 Ebenezar Noyes of Atkinson NH.
Sarah, b. 3 Feb 1777, d. 13 Nov 1837 Plaistow NH. Had an illegitimate son, Moses Copp, Jr., b. 31 Jan 1804.
Amos, b. 28 Jan 1779, d.y.
107 Nathaniel⁵, b. 1780.
Mary, b. 23 May 1783, m.(1) Joseph Smith, m.(2) Samuel Stuart.
Amos, b. 15 May 1788 Plaistow NH.

Sources: Plaistow NH census 1800, 1810, 1820. VR Newbury MA, Plaistow NH. P82g.

45. **MICAH⁴ SAWYER** [see 17], b. 2 Apr 1741 Newbury MA, d. 3 Mar 1817 Newbury MA, m. 7 Dec 1769 Newbury or Amesbury MA Sarah Huntington of Amesbury MA, b. 18 May 1748 d. 10 Apr 1826, dau. John and Abigail (Jones) Huntington. Quaker.

108 Jacob⁵, 1771-1843.
Miriam, b. 31 Dec 1772, d. 3 Feb 1848, m. 26 Nov 1803 Micajah Browne.
Abigail, b. 19 Jan 1775, d. 28 Dec 1851.
Sarah, b. 14 Oct 1777, d. 4 May 1872, m. 17 Jun 1797 Samuel Moody.
109 Stephen⁵, 1780-1874.
John, b. 10 Jul 1784 Newbury MA, d. 1858 Newbury MA, m. 22 Apr 1839 Nancy D. Currin of New Hampshire, b. ?. Farmer.
David, b. 15 Oct 1793 Newbury MA, d. 14 Apr 1866 W. Newbury MA, m.(1) 12 Oct 1820 W. Newbury MA Rebecca Currier, b. 5 Oct 1800 d. 5 Oct 1826; m. (2) 8 Oct 1835 Hannah Folsom, b. 4 Sep 1799 d. 26 May 1883. He bur. in Quaker Cem., W. Newbury MA. CH: Sarah Ann, b. 5 Oct 1821, d. 9 Oct 1837; Edwin, b. 6 Mar 1823, d. 2 Apr 1827; Abigail C., b. 11 Jul 1824, d. 22 Jul 1852; Rebecca J., b. 21 Jan 1826, m. 1 May 1849 W. Newbury MA Daniel E. Moulton; Mary A., b. 25 Dec 1836, d. 15 May 1864; Sarah Ann, b. 12 Dec 1842, d. 31 Aug 1844.

Sources: Newbury MA census 1790, 1800, 1810, 1850. W. Newbury MA census 1830, 1840. VR Newbury MA, Amesbury MA, W. Newbury MA, SA/MA. H92, F23, S65. Nathalie S. Potts rec.

46. **EDMUND⁴ SAWYER** [see 18], b. 28 Apr 1730 Newbury MA, d. 13 Sep 1795 Newbury MA, m. 10 Nov 1763 Newbury MA Hannah Moody, b. 15 Oct 1739 d. 1 Jul 1812, dau. Caleb 3rd and Elizabeth (Emery) Moody. Apothecary, bookseller. B/land Machias Township ME 1791.

Son, stillborn 1 Dec 1764.
110 Enoch⁵, 1767-1808.
Elizabeth, b. 21 Feb 1772, m. 6 Oct 1798 Deacon Nehemiah Haskell.

Sources: Newbury MA census 1790. VR Newbury MA. R10f.

47. **MICAJAH⁴ SAWYER** [see 18], b. 15 Jul 1737 Newbury MA, d. 29 Sep 1817 Newburyport MA, m. 27 Nov 1766 Newburyport MA Sybil Farnham, b. 28 Nov 1746 d. 8 Jul 1842, dau. Daniel and Sybil (Anger) Farnham. Harvard graduate 1756. Physician. He bur. in Old Hill Burying Ground, Newburyport MA.

William, b. 3 Feb 1771 Newburyport MA, d. 1859 Boston MA, unm. Harvard graduate. Physician, merchant. B/S/land in Woodstock VT 1823-1828.
Micajah, b. 24 Jan 1773, d. 2 Jul 1788 Newton MA.
Sibyl, b. 30 Jul 1775, d. Aug 1793.
Joseph, b. 9 Dec 1777, d. Jan 1795 London, England.
Hannah F., b. 12 Nov 1780 d. 28 Dec 1865, m. 20 Jan 1807 George Lee.
Mary Anna, b. 3 Sep 1781, m. 20 Jan 1807 Philip Schyler of New York.
111 Thomas$^5$, b. 1783.
Sources: Newburyport MA census 1790. VR Newbury MA, Newburyport MA. L14. N5.

## FIFTH GENERATION

48. **DAVID$^5$ SAWYER** [see 19], bp.15 May 1748 Newbury MA, d. 13 May 1835 Litchfield ME, m. Abiah Belknap, b. 1748 d. 13 May 1844. Tanner. Selectman for Goffstown NH 1787. In Epping NH, Goffstown NH, Litchfield ME. Both bur. Batchelder Corner Cem., Litchfield ME.
Mary S., b. 1770, m. George R. Freeman.
William, b. ca. 1784.
Son, b. (1784-1790).
Mehitable, b. 19 Feb 1791, m. 19 Apr 1819 Captain John True.
Daughter, b. ?, m. Jonathan Carlton.
Daughter, b. ?, m. _____ Mason.
Sources: Goffstown NH census 1790.Litchfield ME census 1800,1810, 1820, 1830. VR Newbury MA. H1, C46, M5.

49. **JOSHUA$^5$ SAWYER** [see 20], b. 13 Jul 1746 Hampstead NH, m. 22 Mar 1768 Haverhill MA Ruth Peaslee, b. 8 Apr 1749 d. 21 Feb 1827, dau. Nathaniel and Martha (Greeley) (Hutchins, of Haverhill MA?) Peaslee. In Haverhill MA 1768.
Ruth, b. 16 Nov 1768, m. 3 May 1798 George C.Copp.
112 Nathaniel Peaslee$^6$, 1772-1852.
William, b. 15 Feb 1774 Haverhill MA.
Polly, b. 2 Oct 1776.
Sally, b. 19 Apr 1778, d. 10 May 1827.
Patty, b. 25 Dec 1780.
Martha, b. 1782, d. 12 Jul 1848, unm.
113 Joseph$^6$, 1786-1857.
114 Joshua$^6$, 1789-1869.
Sophia, b. ?.
Sources: Haverhill MA census 1790, 1800, 1810, 1820, 1830, 1840, 1850. VR Newbury MA, Haverhill MA, Hampstead NH. K7, G36, C4.

50. **ABEL$^5$ SAWYER** [see 21], b. 9 Jan 1744 Newbury MA, d. 12 Feb 1821 Alfred ME, m. 8 May 1763 Newbury MA Sarah Wheeler, b. 24 May 1741. B/S/land in Maine, 1768-1800.
Sarah, b. 22 Mar 1764, d. 13 Jul 1849, m. 22 Dec 1785 Moses Cheney.
Nathan Wheeler, b. 22 Feb 1767 Newbury MA.
115 Abel$^6$, b. 1771.
116 David$^6$, 1775-1862.
Sources: Newbury MA census 1790. VR Newbury MA. A11, P60.

51. **JONATHAN$^5$ SAWYER** [see 22], b. 22 Dec 1760 Plaistow NH, d. 15 Apr 1840 Rabytown (Enfield) NH, m. Mary _____, b. ?. Revolutionary War: Enl. in Captain Nathaniel Hutchins' Company, Hopkinton NH 1777.

117 Jonathan$^6$, 1783-1860.

Samuel C., b. (1794-1800) Enfield NH, m. 4 Dec 1823 Canaan NH Pamelia Currier of Canaan NH, b. 8 Jan 1798 d. 23 Feb 1856, dau. John and Lois (Morse) Currier. War of 1812. In Enfield NH 1830, Hanover NH 1837. CH: Anne, b. 1826, d. 22 Apr 1849 No. Bridgewater MA, unm; Olivia, b. ca. 1827, m. 25 Nov 1846 Dedham MA Major _____ Kelly; Nancy C., b. ?, m. 22 Nov 1846 Dedham MA Horace M. Haynes; Augusta F., b. ca. 1837, m. Dec 1856 Newton MA John A. Kidd; Mary, b. ?; Burns, b. ?; John, b. ?.

Sources: Enfield NH census 1800, 1810, 1820, 1830. VR Brockton MA, SA/MA. N11, W6, N14.

52. **TRUMAN$^5$ SAWYER** [see 22], b. 21 Dec 1761 Plaistow NH, d. Hyde Park VT, m. 20 Dec 1795 Plainfield NH Lucy Wentworth of Plainfield NH, b. ?. Town Clerk and Town Moderator for Hyde Park VT 1804-1812.

Arannah, b. 11 May 1802, m. 25 Jun 1827 Stowe VT Damaris Wells.

Chester, b. 1 Jul 1804 Hyde Park VT, m. 8 Sep 1833 Johnson VT Hetty Smith, b. ?.

118 Truman$^6$, 1811-1864.

Sources: Enfield NH census 1790. Hyde Park VT census 1800, 1810, 1820, 1830. VR SA/VT. D11, H43.

53. **MOSES$^5$ SAWYER** [see 22], b. 10 Mar 1763 Plaistow NH, d. Canaan NH. Revolutionary War: In Captain Butler's Co., West Point NY 1780. Surveyor of Highways for Canaan NH 1825. In Enfield NH 1790. On Canaan NH tax list 1822. He bur. in Sawyer Hill burial ground, Newburyport MA.

Daughter, b. (1794-1800).

119 Noah$^6$, 1796-1882.

Son, b. (1800-1810).

Daughter, b. (1800-1810).

Daughter, b. (1800-1810).

Sources: Enfield NH census 1790,1800,1810. Canaan NH census 1830, 1840. W6, N14.

54. **JOHN$^5$ SAWYER** [see 23], bp. 13 Jun 1742 Scarborough ME, d. 13 May 1826 Saco ME, m. 25 Oct 1781 Scarborough ME by Rev. Thomas Lecarte Elizabeth Tyler, bp. 22 Apr 1764, dau. Royall and Phebe Tyler.

Elizabeth, b. 20 Jun 1784, d. 18 Jun 1849, m. 27 May 1802 William Trickey.

120 Abraham$^6$, b. 1785.

Mary, b. 12 Jul 1789, d. 23 Jul 1791.

121 John$^6$, 1792-1862.

Martha, b. 10 Oct 1793, d. 21 Jun 1844, m. 18 Oct 1815 Daniel Sawyer.

Abner, b. 31 Mar 1795 Saco ME, m. 1 May 1817 Elizabeth Drew of Scarborough ME, b. ?. CH: Sarah E., b. 24 Aug 1819 Buxton ME, m.(I) 27 Sep 1827 Silas Ladd of Saco ME. In Hollis ME 1820, Buxton ME 1830.

122 Deane$^6$, 1797-1859.

Mary, b. 31 Dec 1799.

William, b. 11 Jun 1802 Saco ME.

Sources: Saco ME census 1790, 1800, 1810. Hollis ME census 1820. Buxton ME 1830, 1840, 1850. VR Saco ME, Buxton ME. Y1, S1, B85.

55. **DAVID[5] SAWYER** [see 23], bp. 29 Apr 1744 Scarborough ME, d. Saco ME, m. 26 Aug 1765 Biddeford ME Hannah Pendexter of Biddeford ME, b. ?. Revolutionary War. In Saco ME 1820.

Hannah, b. 21 Jun 1767, d. 18 Nov 1843, m. 28 Oct 1780 Daniel Patterson.
Betty, b. 2 Apr 1769, d. 24 Aug 1812, m. 22 Jan 1789 Richard Berry Jr.
David, b. 1770, d. at 12 days.
123 David[6], 1771-1805.
Sarah, b. 7 Aug 1774, m.(I) 24 Jun 1798 John Webster.

Sources: Saco ME census 1790, 1800, 1810, 1820. VR Saco ME. S1, Y1, M3, Y3.

56. **JOEL[5] SAWYER** [see 23], b. 9 Feb 1746 Scarborough ME, d. 25 Feb 1825 Saco ME, m. 21 Jan 1768 Biddeford ME Mary Stackpole of Biddeford ME, b. 2 Feb 1750 d. 13 May 1829, dau. Andrew and Mary (Davis) Stackpole. NOTE: [S71] says Mary b. 17 May 1751.

Mary, b. Nov 1769.
124 Joel[6], 1772-1852.
Eleanor, b. 2 Dec 1776, d. 7 Feb 1827, m. 7 Jan 1814 Richard Berry.
Hephzibar, b. 4 Feb 1777, m. 8 Feb 1803 George Dolby of Virginia.
125 Andrew Stackpole[6], 1779-1855.
Nancy, b. 31 Aug 1781, m. 6 Feb 1802 Mark Hutchins of Kittery ME.
Anna, b. ca. 1783.
Elizabeth, b. ca. 1786, m. 14 Sep 1807 Abraham Sawyer. See (120).
Hannah, b. 2 Sep 1788,d.12 Feb 1860, m. 4 Jul 1813 John Billings.
126 Daniel[6], 1792-1876.
127 Tristram[6], 1795-1874.

Sources: Saco ME census 1790, 1800, 1810, 1820. VR Saco ME. S22a, S1, S71.

57. **WILLIAM[5] SAWYER** [see 23], b. ca. 1753 Scarborough ME, d. 2 Oct 1841 Saco ME, m. 30 Nov 1775 Mary Warren, b. 1760 d. 16 Aug 1831, dau. Samuel and Sarah (Gray) Warren. W/son Samuel in 1840. He bur. in Tory Hill Cem., Buxton ME.

128 William[6], 1776-1812.
129 Samuel[6], 1778-1858.
Paulina, b. 17 Nov 1780, m. 13 Mar 1800 David Bryant.
Olive, b. 20 Apr 1782, d. 21 Sep 1861, m. 9 Feb 1805 Stephen Sawyer.
Hannah, b. 6 Aug 1784, d. Dec 1876, m. 8 Sep 1818 Samuel Deering of Paris ME.
David, b. 20 Feb 1786, d. 29 Jan 1803.
Stephen, b. 20 Jun 1788 Saco ME, d. Oct 1810.
Mary, b. 14 Nov 1790, m. 13 Apr 1813 Rishworth Jordan.
Frances, 17 Nov 1792 m. 17 Nov 1812 Daniel Dennet.
James, b. 18 Dec 1794 Saco ME, d. 7 Feb 1872, m. 29 Apr 1820 Bristol ME Mary Waters of Newcastle ME, b. ?. Owned store in Newcastle ME 1825. CH: Daughter, b. (1820-1825); Daughter, b. (1825-1830); Son, b. (1825-1830).

Sources: Saco ME census 1790,1800,1810,1820, 1830. Nobleboro ME census 1830 VR Saco ME, Bristol ME, Nobleboro ME. S1, J9, M5. David Young rec.

58. **ABNER[5] SAWYER** [see 23], b. 1757 Saco ME, d. 15 Nov 1823 Saco ME, m. 18 Feb 1779 Mary Staples of Biddeford ME, b. May 1761 d. 12 Apr 1842, dau. James and Mary (Gray) Staples. Revolutionary War. B/S/land in Brownfield ME 1801-1808. B/land in Lovell ME 1823. Bur. in Boom Road Cem., Saco ME. Wid. in Saco ME 1830.

130 Stephen[6], 1780-1853.

James, b. 8 Feb 1782 Saco ME, d. 25 Feb 1865, m. 18 Feb 1808 Biddeford ME Olive Cole, b. 1790 d. 10 Jan 1857 Saco ME. CH: Son, b. (1810-1815); Daughter, b. (1815-1820).

Abner, b. 20 Sep 1784 Saco ME, d. 27 Sep 1829 Saco ME, m.(I) 25 Oct 1815 Biddeford ME Lucy S. Thatcher of Biddeford ME, b. ? d. 30 Aug 1820, dau. George and Sarah (Savage) Thatcher. CH: Child, b. ?, d. 1816; Daughter, b. ?, d. 22 Jan 1821. (1820 census lists two dau. b. (1810-1820).) NOTE:.[R17] says Abner d. 6 Sep 1829.

William, b. 16 Oct 1788, d. Mar 1789.

Mary, b. 11 May 1789, m. 4 Dec 1816 Daniel Townsend, Jr.

Olive, b. 12 Jul 1791, d. 1857, unm. S/land in Brownfield ME 1826.

David, b. 14 Mar 1793 Saco ME, d. 21 Jan 1834 Saco ME, unm.

Mark, b. 20 Dec 1796, d. 22 Dec 1796.

131 Mark$^6$, 1799-1865.

132 Noah$^6$, 1800-1862.

Sarah, b. 20 Nov 1802.

133 Charles C.$^6$, 1805-1864.

Sources: Saco ME census 1790, 1800, 1810, 1820, wid. 1830, 1840, 1850. VR Saco ME, Biddeford ME. L30, Y3, M5, N5, R10g, P82k, B99,W65, P6. Sawyer family Bible, Robert L. Taylor rec.

59. **SAMUEL$^5$ SAWYER** [see 24], bp. 19 May 1754 Newbury MA, m.(1) 23 Dec 1777 Rowley MA Betty Tenny of Rowley MA; b. 31 Dec 1756 d. Nov 1780, dau. Oliver and Betty (Jewett) Tenny, m.(2) 30 May 1784 Lucy Perley of Boxford MA, b. 22 Jul 1760 d. 30 May 1844, dau. Isaac and Hannah (Lakeman) Perley. Tailor. In Durham NH 1775. Revolutionary War.

Polly, b. 22 May 1782.

Betty, b. 18 Jul 1784, d. 1 Dec 1860.

Margaret, b. 1787, d. 30 Oct 1880, m. 13 Sep 1808 Timothy Dow of Concord NH.

134 Amos B.$^6$, 1795-1882.

135 John$^6$, 1798-1888.

Sources: Hopkinton NH census 1790, 1800, 1810. VR Newbury MA, Rowley MA. B53, T10, P33, T20, S68, E17.

60. **SAMUEL$^5$ SAWYER** [see 25], b. 27 Sep 1741 Newbury MA, d. 24 Dec 1786 Newbury MA, m. 26 Nov 1778 Newbury MA Lydia Morse, b. 25 Feb 1740 d. Nov 1815, dau. John and Lydia (Kelly) Morse. Wid. m. Joseph Chase.

136 Samuel$^6$, 1781-1815.

Sources: VR Newbury MA. K2.

61. **JOSEPH$^5$ SAWYER** [see 25], b. 14 Jul 1744 Newbury MA, d. 15 Dec 1818 Newbury MA, m. 26 Nov 1778 Newbury MA Susannah Bayley of Newbury MA, b. 29 Mar 1758 d. 13 Apr 1805, dau. John and Anna (Chase) Bayley of Newbury MA.

Anna, b. 7 Mar 1779, d. 6 Aug 1807.

Abigail, b. 6 Dec 1781, m. 27 Nov 1813 George Gordon.

Judith, b. 7 Oct 1784, d. 29 Jul 1807.

Mary, b. 24 Apr 1787, m. 1810 Nathan Wiggins.

John, b. 25 Sep 1789 Newbury MA.

Sources: Newbury MA census 1790, 1800, 1810. VR Newbury MA. B5, E20.

62. **JOSEPH$^5$ SAWYER** [see 26], b. 28 Oct 1736 Amesbury MA, d. 29 Nov 1813 Warner NH, m. 9 Sep 1756 Judith Kelly, b. 17 Nov 1738 d. 29 Nov 1821. Justice of the Peace. B/land

Hampstead NH 1756. Admitted to church 1766. S/land Hampstead NH 1769. Went to Warner NH 1771. First seven CH were b. in Hampstead NH, the remainder in Warner NH.

Abigail, b. 1 May 1757, m. Oct 1776 Wells Davis of Warner NH.
137 Edmund$^{6}$, 1759-1827.
Anna, b. 19 Dec 1761, d. 24 Aug 1854, m. 21 Oct 1890 Joseph B. Hoyt.
Son, b. and d. same day, Feb 1764.
Jacob, b. 3 Feb 1765, d. 8 May 1765.
138 Moses$^{6}$, b. 1767.
Sarah, b. 11 Jan 1769, m. 23 Jan 1804 Stephen Badger.
139 Joseph$^{6}$, 1771-1856.
Judith, b. 14 Oct 1772, d. 2 Mar 1865, m. 8 Feb 1795 Salisbury NH John Hoyt.
Hannah, b. 1 Apr 1775, m. Mitchell Gilman.
Lois (Louise?), b. 18 Apr 1777.
140 Richard Kelly$^{6}$, 1779-1838.

Sources: Warner NH census 1790, 1800, 1810. VR Hampstead NH. N38, H83, N6, H84

63. **ENOCH$^{5}$ SAWYER**. [see 26], b. 27 Dec 1741 Amesbury MA, d. 1817 Antrim NH, m. 10 Oct 1765 Hampstead NH Sarah Little of Hampstead NH, b. 20 Aug 1747 d. 5 Dec 1829. Farmer. Revolutionary War. S/land in Unity NH 1764. In Hampstead NH 1764. S/land in Hampstead NH 1769. In Goffstown NH 1774. Delegate to Concord Convention 1779. Representative in 1781. In Antrim NH 1794. Wid. in Antrim NH 1820.

Mary, b. 12 Mar 1766, d. 24 May 1766.
Elizabeth, b. 29 Jun 1767, d. 26 Apr 1855, m. 27 Jun 1785 Jonathan Marsh of Hudson NH.
141 Samuel$^{6}$, 1771-1848.
Abigail P., b. 13 Mar 1774, d. 1861, m. 11 Nov 1813 Josiah Haywood of Alexandria NH.
142 Enoch$^{6}$, 1777-1840.
143 Tristram$^{6}$, 1780-1859.
144 Edmund$^{6}$, 1782-1873.
Sally, b. 22 Jul 1785, d. 12 Oct 1869, unm.
Lucinda, b. 9 Aug 1788, d. 8 Jun 1852, m. 12 Apr 1831 Richard Chase of Hillsboro NH.

Sources: Antrim NH census 1800, 1810, 1820. VR Amesbury MA, Hampstead NH. L29, C30, C54, N38, H1

64. **JOSIAH$^{5}$ SAWYER**. [see 28], b. 28 Jan 1737 Amesbury MA, d. 10 Jun 1812 Deerfield NH, m.(1) 27 Sep 1759 Kensington NH Miriam Eastman, b. 28 Feb 1740, dau. Jeremiah and Elizabeth (Brown) Eastman; m.(2) 24 Aug 1781 Salisbury MA Miriam Morrell, b. 4 Jun 1742, dau. Ebenezer and Abigail (Osgood) Morrell. Farmer, blacksmith. B/land in Nottingham NH 1768, 1769. S/land in Nottingham NH 1769. B/land in Deerfield NH 1769.

145 Josiah$^{6}$, 1760-1833.
146 Jeremiah$^{6}$, 1764-1833.
147 David$^{6}$, 1766-1845.
148 John$^{6}$, 1771-1840.
149 Isreal C.$^{6}$, 1773-184?.
Miriam, b. 8 May 1777, d. 30 May 1817, m. 9 Mar 1798 Elijah Watson.

Sources: Deerfield NH census 1790, 1800, 1810. VR Newbury MA, So. Hampton NH. H84, E2, S50.

65. **ISREAL$^{5}$ SAWYER** [see 28], b. 19 Sep 1739 Newbury MA, d. 19 Jul 1821 So. Hampton NH, m.(1) 24 Nov 1763 Kingston NH Jemima Eastman, b. ? d. 5 Apr 1771; m. (2) 26 Oct 1774

Miriam French of So. Hampton NH, b. 1745 d. 2 Sep 1825. B/land So. Hampton NH 1761. Elected Fence Viewer 1775 and Selectman 1778 for So. Hampton NH.

Jemima, b. 11 Jun 1765, m. 14 Jun 1796 Isiah Palmer.

Molly, b. 2 Mar 1767, m. 22 Nov 1792 Samuel Currier.

Miriam, b. 18 Jul 1775, m. 18 May 1795 Stephen Currier.

Sarah, b. 1 Jul 1777, m. 13 Jan 1804 Thomas Flanders.

Isreal, b. 2 Aug 1779 Newburyport MA, d. 26 Oct 1848 So. Hampton NH, m. Mary Galishan of Newburyport MA, b. 1776 d. 16 Mar 1859. Wid. in So. Hampton NH 1850. CH: Mary, b. 16 Apr 1805, m. 26 Nov 1828 Adam Gale of Amesbury MA; Rebecca A., b. 30 Jan 1807, d. 25 Jul 1896, unm; Jacob Currier. b. 11 Nov 1808, d. 23 Mar 1820; Caroline Williams, b. 26 Dec 1810, d. 8 Sep 1840, unm; Abigail Galishan, b. 26 Sep 1813, d. 2 Jul 1904, unm.

Tirzah, b. 26 Aug 1781, m. Apr 1805 Kingston NH Parker Flanders.

Lydia, b. 17 Apr 1785.

William, b. 20 Jun 1787, d. 29 Jan 1811, unm.

Sources: So. Hampton NH census 1790, 1800, 1810, 1820, 1830, 1840, 1850.VR Newbury MA, Newburyport MA, Amesbury MA, So. Hampton NH, SA/MA, SA/NH. A31, N5, N7, N10, T4, N6.

66. **MATTHIAS$^5$ SAWYER** [see 28], b. 25 Aug 1741 Amesbury MA, d. 22 Jun 1818, m. 25 Jan 1775 Deerfield NH Eunice Sanborn of Deerfield NH, b. ?. B/land in Gilmanton NH 1765.

150 William$^6$, 1776-1824.

151 Isreal$^6$, 1778-1831.

Molly, b. 13 Aug 1780.

Sources: Gilmanton NH census 1790, 1800, 1810. VR Gilmanton NH. N14.

67. **JOHN$^5$ SAWYER** [see 28], b. 7 Apr 1744 Amesbury MA, d. 19 Mar 1796 Salisbury MA, m. 30 Aug 1770 Salisbury MA Abigail Shephard, b. 1742 d. 13 Sep 1823, dau. Jeremiah Shepard. Wid. in Salisbury MA 1800, 1810.

Hannah, b. 25 Oct 1772, d. 11 Nov 1846.

152 John$^6$, 1772-1850.

153 Jeremiah$^6$, 1777-1854.

Sources: Salisbury MA census 1790, 1800, 1810. VR Newbury MA, Salisbury MA. F11a.

68. **RICHARD$^5$ SAWYER** [see 28], b. 20 May 1748 So. Hampton NH, d. 22 Jun 1818 Corinth VT, m. 20 Dec 1773 Elizabeth Clark of Hampton Falls NH, b. ?. B/land in Gilmanton NH 1771. Fence Viewer 1775 and Selectman 1787 for So. Hampton NH. He bur. in Corinth Center VT.

Hannah, b. 31 Oct 1774, m. 2 Jun 1796 Hezikiel Carter.

154 Richard$^6$, 1776-1853.

155 Plant$^6$, 1779-1840.

Betty, b. 1 Sep 1782, d. 4 Feb 1861, m. 17 Mar 1801 David Poore.

Sally, b. 16 Nov 1784, m. John Clifford.

Abigail, b. 15 Aug 1789, d. 7 Jun 1761, m. Stephen Merrill.

Sources: So. Hampton NH census 1790.Corinth VT census 1800, 1810. VR Newbury MA, Newburyport MA, SA/VT. P59.

69. **MOSES$^5$ SAWYER** [see 28], b. 21 Aug 1750 So. Hampton NH, d. 29 Apr 1821 Salisbury NH, m. 16 Jan 1775 So. Hampton NH Ann Fitts, b. 20 Jan 1751 d. 4 Oct 1836, dau. Richard and Sarah Fitts. Revolutionary War. In Concord NH 1773, Salisbury NH 1775. Member of

Congregational Church until 1814 when he joined Carson Hill Church in Boscawen NH. Surveyor of Highways 1786 and Constable 1793 for Salisbury NH. Taught at North Road School 1795. Wid. in Salisbury NH 1830.

156 Moses$^6$, 1776-1847.

157 Isaac Fitts$^6$, 1778-1846.

Polly, b. 30 May 1780 d. 1 Nov 1856, m. 18 Jun 1797 David Pettengill, Jr. [P37] says she d. 1 May 1851.

Nathaniel, b. 13 Mar 1782, d. 22 Mar 1783.

158 Nathaniel$^6$, 1784-1853. Went to Ohio.

Ann, b. 21 Jun 1786, d. 25 Dec 1824, m. 22 Mar 1820 Joseph Walker.

Sarah, b. 5 Jun 1789, m. Sewall Fifield.

Betsey, b. 17 May 1793, d. 20 Oct 1880, m. 1 Nov 1815 Nathaniel Webster.

Sources: Salisbury NH census 1790, 1800, 1810, 1820, 1830. VR Newbury MA, So. Hampton NH. N6.

70. **MATTHIAS PLANT$^5$ SAWYER** [see 29], b. 28 Jan 1754 Newbury MA, d. 29 Jul 1777 Newburyport MA, m. 13 Dec 1775 Newbury MA Mary Little, b. 22 Sep 1759 d. 1849, dau. Colonel Moses and Abigail (Bailey) Little. Wid. m. Joshua Follensbee.

159 George$^6$, 1776-1847.

Sources: VR Newbury MA. L20, B5.

71. **MOSES$^5$ SAWYER** [see 29], b. 23 Nov 1756 Newbury MA, d. 5 Aug 1799 Newbury MA, m. 25 Jul 1781 Newbury MA Hannah Little, b. 21 May 1762 d. 25 Nov 1849, dau. Colonel Moses and Abigail (Bailey) Little. Physician. Wid. m. 3 Jul 1806 James Burnham.

Matthias Plant, b. 11 Jul 1788, d. 31 Mar 1857, unm.

Hannah, b. 14 Feb 1793, d. 30 May 1801.

Joseph, b. 16 Dec 1794 Newbury MA, d. 22 Apr 1831.

Sources: Newbury MA census 1790, 1800, 1810. VR Newbury MA. B5, Roberta Sawyer rec.

72. **THOMAS$^5$ SAWYER** .[see 29], b. 16 Sep 1770 Newbury MA, d. 26 May 1849 Corinth VT, m. 4 Aug 1793 Newbury MA Ann Martin of Amesbury MA, b. ? d. 30 Dec 1848. In So. Hampton NH 1794, Corinth VT 1810.

Sally, b. 12 Feb 1794.

160 Moses$^6$, 1795-1894.

161 Joseph$^6$, 1797-1852.

Charles, b. 30 Oct 1799 So. Hampton NH, d. 18 Feb 1836 Corinth VT, m. 6 Apr 1826 Corinth VT Betsey Rowland, b. 1807 d. 10 Apr 1881. He bur. Corinth Center Cem. CH: Thomas, b. Feb 1828, d. 21 Dec 1832; Caroline L., b. 18 Oct 1829, d. 27 May 1895.

162 Jacob M.$^6$, 1801-1869.

Hannah, b. 3 Oct 1803, d. 2 Jun 1877, m. 7 Mar 1822 Bodwell Ladd.

Jonathan, b. 2 Nov 1805 So. Hampton NH. In Corinth VT.

Sophronia, b. Jan 1809, d. 21 Dec 1809.

Sources: So. Hampton NH census 1800.Corinth VT census 1810, 1820, 1830, 1840. VR Newbury MA, SA/VT. D41.

73. **GIDEON$^5$ SAWYER** [see 30], b. 13 Oct 1751 Kingston NH, d. Oct 1817 Northfield NH, m. Hannah Sherborn, b. 1759 d. 18 Apr 1790. Revolutionary War. Lived in that part of Canterbury NH which later became Northfield NH. On Canterbury tax roll, 1775-1780. Birth recorded in Newbury MA.

Sarah, b. 5 Nov 1777, d. Sep 1822.

163 Gideon[6], 1779-1854.
Hannah, b. 1782, d. 22 Jan 1799.
Lydia, b. 23 Jul 1784, d. 14 May 1826, m. 21 May 1812 Elias Abbott.
Tamar, b. 5 Sep 1787.

Sources:Northfield NH census 1790, 1800, 1810. VR Newbury MA, Newburyport MA. A2, W43, C87, N9.

74. **JAMES[5] SAWYER** [see 30], b. 30 Jan 1755 Kingston NH, d. 8 Nov 1828 Danville NH, m. 19 Feb 1789 Newburyport MA Alla Rand of Sandown NH, b. 1758 d. 21 Jul 1833. Canterbury NH tax list 1780.

Olive, b. 25 Nov 1790, m. 21 Mar 1811 John H. Sanborn.
Sarah, b. 25 Aug 1794, m. 30 Dec 1819 Joseph Boswell.
James, b. 4 Oct 1796 Danville NH, d. 17 Jan 1873 Danville NH, m. 30 Jan 1823 Philena Sanborn, b. 15 Jul 1805 d. 13 Jun 1887 Bristol NH, dau. Moses H. and Susanna (Brown) Sanborn. Both bp. 30 Jan 1832 in Kingston NH. CH: Rose Ann, b. 1845, m. 24 Nov 1864 Kingston NH L. Norris Brown.
Betty, b. 12 Dec 1800, m. 14 Feb 1822 Phinehas Hart.

Sources: Hawke (Danville) NH census 1790. Danville NH census 1800, 1810, 1820, wid. 1830, 1850. 1860, 1870. VR Newbury MA, Newburyport MA, Hampstead NH. L47, M64, N7, T20, N6.

75. **JOTHAM[5] SAWYER** [see 30], b. 15 May 1757 Kingston NH, d. 30 Sep 1824 Stewartstown NH, m. 20 Oct 1779 Newburyport MA Mary Colby, b. 1758 d. 9 Jun 1849. Revolutionary War. In Northfield NH 1790, Stewartstown NH 1818.

Charlotte, b. 15 Aug 1780, m. 3 Nov 1800 Samuel Sargent.
Walker Colby, b. 31 May 1782 Northfield NH.
Timothy Colby, b. 17 May 1785 Northfield NH.
James B., b. 3 Apr 1787 Northfield NH.
Tamar, b. 15 Feb 1788, d. 28 Dec 1870, m.(1) 17 Apr 1791 Canterbury NH Abner Clough, m.(2) 25 Dec 1809 Canterbury NH Jonathan Whitcher. Birthdate from tombstone.
John Colby, b. 9 Apr 1789 Northfield NH.
Reuben, b. 2 Dec 1791 Northfield NH. Town Clerk for Pittsburg NH 1823.

164 Jotham[6] (Jonathan?), b. 1793.
Elijah Colby, b. 12 Sep 1801 Northfield NH, m.(1) Mary E. Currier of Landaff NH, b. 9 Aug 1805 d. 28 Feb 1865; m.(2)2 May 1866 Rebecca _____ of Lisbon NH, b. 1811 d. 21 Sep 1890. In Indian Territory NH 1830, Pittsburg NH 1850. CH: Richard R., b. 1825 in Hatley, Canada, drowned 30 Mar 1850, unm; Mary A., b. ?; Eldula, b. 1829, m. Charles H. Harriman; Timothy G., b. 1835, drowned 30 Mar 1850; Eunice J., b. 1837; Phebia M., b. 1841; Maria, b. 1844, m. 28 Mar 1867 Canaan VT Addison Chase. Jane, b. ?, m. 3 Aug 1881 George William Abbott in Stewartstown NH.

Sources: Northfield NH census 1790, 1800, 1810. VR Newburyport MA. VR SA/NH, SA/VT. C87, H84, N11, N6.

76. **JOHN[5] SAWYER** [see 31], b. 20 Mar 1748 Newbury MA, d. 9 Nov 1833 Lebanon NH, m. 13 Dec 1770 Newbury MA Alice Couch of Salisbury NH, b. 22 Mar 1751, dau. Joseph and Alice (Rowell) Couch. Revolutionary War: Beginning 19 Apr 1775 for two weeks at Cambridge MA; 1 May 1775 for eight months at Winter Hill (in present Somerville MA); Jul 1776 for two months with Captain J. Page in New Hampshire; Nov 1777 for three to four months with Captain P. Moody in Massachusetts. Later built lumber mills in Lebanon NH.

Joseph, b. 20 Apr 1772 Hampstead NH, m. 18 Mar 1798 Canaan NH Elizabeth Richardson of Canaan NH, b. ?. Surveyor of Highways for Dorchester NH 1801. CH: Daughter, b. ca. 1799; Sarah, b. 30 Nov 1773, d. 4 Dec 1863, m. 5 Sep 1893 Jonathan Greeley.

165 Joshua$^6$ b. 1775.

Alice, b. 18 Jan 1778, m. 30 Aug 1798 Enos Collins of Salisbury NH.

Mary, b. 1779, d. 15 Mar 1866, m. 1801 Benjamin Elliott of Henniker NH.

166 John$^6$, 1783-1860.

Enock, b. ca. 1785.

Esther, b. 20 Jun 1786 d. 9 Apr 1853, m. 22 Mar 1810 Joseph Jackman.

Susie, b. ?, m. 12 Nov 1812 Hezikiah White of New York.

Sources: Andover MA census 1790. Salisbury NH census 1800. Dorchester NH census 1810. Canaan NH census 1830. VR Newbury MA, Dorchester NH, Hampstead NH. D45, N6, W6, N14.

77. **STEPHEN$^5$ SAWYER** [see 31], b. Nov 1753 Newbury MA, d. 14 Jun 1822 Salisbury NH, m.(I) 7 Jul 1782 Hampstead NH Elizabeth Johnson, b. 8 Dec 1754 d. 17 Mar 1827, dau. Samuel and Susannah (Davis) Black. Revolutionary War: Private in Colonel Long's Regiment at Ticonderoga NY. He bur. in Franklin NH.

Susannah, b. 10 Jun 1783, d.y.

Joshua, b. 20 Jan 1786, d.y.

167 Samuel$^6$, 1788-1847.

Miriam, b. 5 Feb 1790, m. 11 Oct 1807 Seth C. Collins.

Susanna, b. 11 Jan 1792.

Stephen, b. 31 Dec 1793 Salisbury NH, d. May 1860 Salisbury NH, m. Marinda Hale, b. 1805, dau. Daniel Hale. In Charlestown MA 1830, Franklin NH 1840. Wid. m. 4 Jul 1866 John Shaw of Salisbury NH. CH: Caroline Marinda, b. 1827, d. 26 Nov 1855; Ann Elizabeth, bp. 5 Sep 1830; Frances Matilda, bp. 28 Aug 1831; Ellen C., b. 1835; Laura A., b. 1844, m. 26 Jul 1870 Lindley M. Edwards in Salisbury NH. First two CH b. in Massachusetts.

Joshua, b. 11 Feb 1796 Salisbury NH, d. 18 Aug 1851 Wilmot NH, m. 5 Jun 1823 Jerusha Hale, b. 1799 d. 1 Oct 1882, dau. Daniel and Lydia (Holmes) Hale. Farmer. Wid. m. 1867 Asa Page. CH: Caroline M., adopted, b. 1827 d. 26 Nov 1855, dau. of Joshua's brother Stephen.

Sources: Salisbury NH census 1790, 1800, 1810, 1820, 1860. Franklin NH census 1830, 1840, 1850. Wilmot NH census 1850. VR Newbury MA, Hampstead NH. N38, G36, N9, N10, N11, H90, F11, N6

78. **RICHARD$^5$ SAWYER** .[see 34], b. 2 Dec 1748 Amesbury MA, d. 4 Sep 1837, m.(1) 11 Jan 1770 So. Hampton NH Ann Sargent, b. 13 Jun 1749 d. 8 Sep 1824 So. Hampton NH; m.(2) 26 Oct 1825 Newburyport MA Sarah Frothingham, b. ?.

Martha, b. 13 Jul 1770 d. 27 Nov 1860, m. 1 May 1791 Jonathan Patten.

Carteret, b. 2 Apr 1773, m. 28 Oct 1792 1st cousin Moses Bailey.

168 Moses$^6$, 1775-1843.

169 William$^6$, 1777-1828.

Symes, b. 26 Apr 1783 Amesbury MA, d. 6 Apr 1860, m. 29 May 1805 Sarah Sargent, b. 7 Feb 1789. Farmer. CH: Son, b. (1806-1810); Son, b. (1810-1820); Ann, b. ?, d. 6 Jul 1844.

Sources: Amesbury MA census 1790, 1800, 1810, 1820, 1830, 1850. VR Amesbury MA, Newburyport MA. B5, B17, E20.

79. **JOHN[5] SAWYER** [see 34], b. 16 Feb 1760 Amesbury MA, d. 2 Jul 1823, m. 6 Dec 1780 Amesbury MA Lois Kelly, b. 1765 d. 9 Oct 1843, dau. Stephen and Lois (Sargent) Kelly.

Abigail, b. 4 Apr 1782, d. 16 Dec 1801, m. 3 Apr 1800 John Cronk.
Stephen, b. 30 Jun 1783, d. 16 Jan 1784.
Anna, b. 25 Nov 1784, m. 3 Nov 1808 Charles Bancroft.
Lois, b. 18 Oct 1786 d. 29 Jan 1846, m. 12 Oct 1808 William Williams.
Elizabeth, b. 26 Nov 1788, d. 23 Sep 1806.
170 Stephen[6], 1791-1870.
Judith, b. 13 Jul 1794, m. 8 Nov 1819 Moses Hoyt.
171 John[6], b. 1798.
Hannah, b. 9 May 1800, m. 7 Apr 1821 Jacob Gale, Jr.

Sources: Amesbury MA census 1790, 1800, 1810. VR Amesbury MA. H83, K2.

80. **SYMMES[5] SAWYER** [see 34], b. 16 Jan 1766 Amesbury MA, d. 24 Dec 1845 Woodstock NH, m.(1) 16 Jan 1788 Lois Hoyt, b. 8 Oct 1767; m.(2) 31 May 1792 Dunbarton NH Ruth Page of Dunbarton NH, b. 15 Aug 1770 d. 27 Jun 1804, dau. Jeremiah and Sarah (Merrill) Page; m.(3) 2 Jan 1805 Elizabeth Hoyt of Sanbornton NH, b. 28 Mar 1783 d. 18 Jan 1853. Physician. Constable for Dunbarton NH 1789. Woodstock NH 1819. He bur. in Dunbarton NH.

John Jervais, adopted, b. 28 Apr 1798.
Ruth Page, b. 9 Jun 1804, d. 3 Sep 1804.
172 Sylvester[6], 1806-1837.
173 Symmes[6], 1807-1869.
Mary Ruth, b. 27 Dec 1809, d. 3 Mar 1881, m.(1) Martin Reed, m.(2) Eber Thayer.
Elizabeth, b. Nov 1811, d. 18 Oct 1839, m. 27 May 1832 Salmon Farrar.
Barnard, b. Nov 1811 Dunbarton NH. In Woodstock NH 1840.
Lois Ann, b. 6 Mar 1814.
174 Walter Harris[6], 1816-1889.
175 Moses Martin[6], 1818-1907.
176 John Page[6], 1824-1907.

Sources: Dunbarton NH census 1790,1800,1810.Woodstock NH census 1820, 1830, 1840. S81, B92, H83, R34, S75, G31, B83, N14, Leonard S. Sawyer rec

81. **WYBURD[5] (WIBERT) SAWYER** .[see 34], b. 17 Jan 1769 Amesbury MA, d. 2 May 1813 Hopkinton NH, m.(1) 2 Nov 1790 Amesbury MA Hannah Kelly, b. 19 Jan 1768 d. 16 Jun 1802, dau. Stephen and Lois (Sargent) Kelly; m.(2) 27 Feb 1803 Amesbury MA Elizabeth Williams, b. 14 Oct 1767, dau. William and Lydia Williams. B/land in Warner NH 1808.

177 John[6], 1791-1871.
Ruth, b. 2 Aug 1793, d. 5 Oct 1797.
Anna, b. 22 Sep 1795, d. 17 Jul 1826.
Ruth, b. 1 Sep 1798, m. 1 Apr 1819 Edward L. Sargent.
Hannah, b. 30 Sep 1801, d. 1 Apr 1864 Amesbury MA.
William, b. 12 Aug 1804 Amesbury MA.
Francis, b. 30 Jul 1806 Amesbury MA, d. 7 Nov 1843 Candia NH, m. 6 Sep 1829 Hampstead NH Phebe Little, b. 23 Mar 1811 d. 27 Apr 1880. Cooper. Joined church in Hampstead NH 1827, Portsmouth NH 1834. In Candia NH 1840. Wid. in Hampstead NH 1850. CH: Samuel Gordon Smith, b. 12 Sep 1830, d. 7 Feb 1851, unm; Ann Elizabeth, b. 14 Aug 1832, d. 31 Dec 1853, unm; Henry Little, b. 8 Jan 1835, d. 2 Aug 1843; Harriet Colby, b. 10 Apr 1837, d. 2 Apr 1886, m. 14 Aug 1862 Daniel L. Sawyer of Haverhill MA.
Abigail, b. 22 Sep 1809, m. in Haverhill MA Nathan Johnson.

Sources: Amesbury MA census 1800. Hopkinton NH census 1810. Portsmouth NH census 1830. Candia NH census 1840. Hampstead NH census 1850. VR Amesbury MA, Hopkinton NH. C50, K2, N9, C29, H84, L29, P59, N14, N38, H10.

82. **DANIEL$^5$ SAWYER** [see 36], bp. 10 Jun 1743 Wells ME, m. 30 Jun 1771 York ME Abigail Willson of York ME, b. ?, dau. Michael Willson. In Brookfield NH 1787, Middleton NH 1790, Brookfield NH 1810.

Daniel, b. 20 Sep 1772 Wells ME, m.(1) 30 Jul 1797 Wells ME Sarah Clark, b. ?; m.(2) 4 Mar 1804 Conway NH Betsey Abbott of Conway NH, b. ?. In Brookfield NH 1796.

178 Michael$^6$, 1774-1847.

John, b. 3 Jul 1776 Wells ME, d. Nov 1838 Wells ME. In Brookfield NH.

Isaac, b. 19 Apr 1778 Wells ME, d. 9 Jul 1834 Brookline MA.

179 Samuel$^6$, ca. 1781-1840.

180 Asa$^6$, 1787-1876.

181 Nathaniel$^6$, b. 1790.

Sources: Middleton NH census 1790. Brookfield NH census 1810. Salem MA census 1820, 1830. VR Wells ME, Conway NH, Brookline MA. T14, N5.

83. **NATHANIEL$^5$ SAWYER** [see 36], bp. 19 Oct 1760 Wells ME, d. 26 May 1835 Wells ME, m.(1) 24 Oct 1784 Lucy Clark of Wells ME, b. 1766 d. 2 Aug 1800; m.(2) 19 Mar 1801 Mary Gilpatrick of Wells ME, b. 6 Jul 1766 d. 13 May 1842. Revolutionary War: Pvt. in Capt. Samuel Sawyer's Company, Col. Patterson's Regiment. He bur. in Ocean View Cem., Wells ME.

Joshua, b. 29 Aug 1785 Wells ME, d. 18 Dec 1859 Wells ME, m. 28 Dec 1815 Mary Tinker of Waterboro ME, b. Feb 1786 d. 11 May 1857. Farmer. Will dated 1835.

182 Jotham$^6$, 1792-1865.

Sarah, b. 19 Oct 1795.

Frances, b. 28 Sep 1798.

Susannah, b. 20 Jul 1800.

Lucy, b. 27 Dec 1801, d. 15 Dec 1802.

Hannah, b. 1804, m. Stover Littlefield, who in 1842 was appointed executor of Mary's will.

Sources: Wells ME census 1800, 1810, 1820, 1830. VR Wells ME. T14, R17, H26, M5.

84. **JOSEPH$^5$ SAWYER**. [see 37], b. 18 Jun 1765 Ipswich MA, d. 11 Sep 1851 Litchfield ME, m.(1) 29 Sep 1891 Ipswich MA Susannah Day, b. 1767 d. 14 Oct 1829 Ipswich MA, dau. Isreal and Ruth Day; m.(2) 6 Nov 1831 Sarah (Clark) Averill, b. 1773 d. 31 May 1841. Lived in Fairfield or Pittston ME when he filed intention to m. Susannah; moved to Litchfield ME on wedding day and built a log cabin there. Captain in militia for six years.

Elizabeth, b. 13 Feb 1793, m. 2 Mar 1828 Josiah Jack.

Samuel, b. 27 Aug 1794 Litchfield ME, m. 2 Sep 1822 Milford NH Rachel Hay of Merrimac NH, b. 1780. In Merrimac NH 1830. CH: Lucy, b. ?, m. Thomas Carr; son, b. (1823-1825); Susan D., b. ca. 1825, m. 28 Mar 1853 Lowell MA John D. Mackey.

Susannah, b. 31 Oct 1796 d. 5 Dec 1832, m. Ambrose Case of Readfield ME.

Clarissa, b. 30 Sep 1798, m. 24 Feb 1822 Jesse Pike.

183 James Brown$^6$, 1800-1889.

John, b. 16 Feb 1802 Litchfield ME, d. 26 Aug 1848 Topsfield MA, m. 9 Feb 1829 Topsfield MA Sarah Averill, b. 23 Sep 1798.

Harriet, b. 5 Dec 1804, m. John Dennis.

Joseph, b. 26 Aug 1806 Litchfield ME, m. Sophia Beaucannon of New Brunswick ME, b. ?. In Calais ME 1850. Millwright.

Caroline, b. 23 Jan 1809, d. 20 Feb 1809.

Angeline, b. 16 Mar 1810, m. 5 Sep 1837 John Ray of Topsfield MA.

Sources: Litchfield ME census 1800, 1810, 1820, 1830, 1840, 1850. Merrimac NH census 1830, 1850. Topsfield MA census 1830, 1840. Calais ME census 1850. VR Ipswich MA, Topsfield MA. C46, N6, Robert L. Taylor rec.

85. **JOHN[5] SAWYER** [see 37], b. 15 Mar 1767 Ipswich MA, d. 23 Jul 1829 Boxford MA, m. 14 Apr 1803 Middleton MA Sarah Killam of Boxford MA, b. Nov 1779, dau. Thomas and Sarah (Fuller) Killam. S/land in Fairfield ME 1793. In Boxford MA 1804.

184 John[6], b. 1804.

Elizabeth, b. 22 Dec 1805, d. 2 Sep 1869, m. 17 Mar 1831 Capt. Samuel Kimball.

Sarah A., b. 16 Jul 1810, m. 11 Jan 1853 Samuel Lamson.

Charles Augustus, b. 28 Feb 1813 Boxford MA.

Sources: Amesbury MA census 1810. VR Ipswich MA, Middleton MA, Boxford MA. P34, M54, L3.

86. **GEORGE WHITEFIELD[5] SAWYER** [see 37], b. 1 Oct 1770 Ipswich MA, d. 23 Mar 1855 Boxford MA, m. 27 Mar 1800 Middleton MA Polly Killam of Boxford MA, b. 29 Aug 1774 d. 27 Sep 1860, dau. Thomas and Sarah (Fuller) Killam. Physician. B/S/land in Topsham ME 1798-1800. B/land in Ipswich MA 1806, 1808. Selectman for Boxford MA 1835, 1837, 1838.

Sarah, b. 27 Jan 1801, d. 22 Jan 1896, m. 28 Aug 1823 Aaron P. Lord.

185 George Whitefield[6], b. 1802.

Samuel, b. 7 Sep 1804 Boxford MA, d. 22 Jan 1893, m. 28 Nov 1833 Andover MA Cynthia Hutchinson of Andover MA, b. 14 Apr 1814 d. 10 Dec 1892, dau. Soloman and Lydia Hutchinson. Expressman. In Methuen MA 1850, Lawrence MA 1860. CH: Mary Elizabeth, b. 11 Nov 1836, d. 14 Sep 1839 Sanford ME; Mary Elizabeth, b. 8 Sep 1840, d. 5 Sep 1901, m. 15 Sep 1870 Joseph L. Fell; Ellen Frances, b. 5 Jul 1842, m. 2 Dec 1869 Lawrence MA Frank A. Blood.

James Brown, b. 14 Oct 1806 Boxford MA, d. 25 Aug 1847 Methuen MA, m. 3 Apr 1834 Danvers MA Rachel Matilda Potter of Ipswich MA, b. 20 Dec 1812 d. 6 Jan 1886. Trader. Wid. in Danvers MA 1850. CH: Mary Killam, b. 11 Feb 1841, m. 25 Feb 1863 Methuen MA George Henry Perkins; Louisa Potter, b. 11 Jul 1844, d. 28 Dec 1867, m. 1 Aug 1864 Danvers MA Orlando B. Millett.

186 Ebenezer[6], 1809-1892.

187 Thomas Killam[6], 1811-1895.

188 William[6], 1813-1900.

Sources: Ipswich MA census 1800. Boxford MA census 1810, 1820, 1830, 1840. Danvers MA census 1850. Methuen MA census 1850. Lawrence MA census 1860. VR Ipswich MA, Boxford MA, Middleton MA, Andover MA, Danvers MA, Methuen MA, Topsfield MA, SA/MA. P34, W13, W14, W39, Annette S. Meany rec.

87. **SAMUEL[5] SAWYER** [see 38], bp. 27 Apr 1735 Wells ME, d. 1 Aug 1779 in war, m. 21 Apr 1768 Mary Littlefield, b. ?. Revolutionary War: Captain, served from beginning, including eight months in Medford MA 1775 and in New York 1776. Wid. m. Borak Maxwell of Wells ME 1784. Probate record says Samuel d. Aug 1778.

189 Samuel[6], 1769-ca. 1802.

Mary, bp. 4 Feb 1770, d.y.

Eunice, b. 23 Jan 1771, d. 3 Apr 1812.

Mary, b. 3 Oct 1772.

Ebenezer, b. 7 Mar 1774 Wells ME.

Sources: VR Wells ME. T14, Y3, B67, P82k, D6.

88. **WILLIAM⁵ SAWYER** .[see 38], bp. 8 Nov 1740 Wells ME, d. 8 Jul 1825 Limington ME, m.(1) 29 Nov 1764 Mary Simpson of York ME, b. 16 Aug 1739 d. Feb 1823; m.(2) 30 Oct 1824 Hannah (Marriner) Dunn, wid. of Nathaniel, b. ? d. Oct 1835. Moved to Sawyer Mountain, Limington ME 1794, he bur. there. Wid. m. Benjamin Clay in Limington ME 1825.

Miriam, b. 15 Nov 1765, d. 8 Dec 1849, m. Andrew Pugsley of Cornish ME.
190 William$^6$, b. 1767.
Betsey, b. 5 Nov 1769, d. 29 Jul 1789, m. 15 Nov 1787 William Day, Jr.
191 Joseph$^6$, 1773-1833.
Mary, b. 15 May 1775, d. 31 Aug 1844, m. 2 Nov 1792 Nathan Cobb.
Lemuel, b. 8 Mar 1778 Wells ME. In Limington ME.
Hannah, b. 26 Apr 1780, d. 20 May 1858, m. 31 Mar 1796 Nathaniel Norton.
Lydia, b. 16 Sep 1782, m. 31 Mar 1822 Levi Cole of Porter ME.

Sources: Francisbore (Cornish) ME census 1790. Limington ME census 1800, 1810, 1820. T14, B67, T6, U1, N37.

89. **DANIEL$^5$ SAWYER** [see 39], b. 5 Mar 1744 Newbury MA, d. 1 Mar 1811 New Hampton NH, m. Martha _____, b. ca. 1742 d. 26 Jan 1833. In Newmarket NH 1767. B/land in Nottingham NH 1767. Will dated 15 Apr 1806.

192 Humphrey$^6$, ca. 1774-1839.
193 Ezra$^6$, 1778-1849.
194 James$^6$, 178?- ca. 1835.
Andrew Baker, b. ca. 1782 New Hampton NH, d. 2 Dec 1832 New Hampton NH. Will dated 21 Nov 1832. Bur. beside father.
Betsey, b. ?, m. _____ Plasted.
Sally, b. ?, m. _____ Whitten.

Sources: New Hampton NH census 1790, 1810, 1830. VR Newbury MA. P82i, N9.

90. **PHILLIPS$^5$ SAWYER** [see 39], b. 12 Apr 1746 Newbury MA, d. 31 Aug 1821 Weare NH, m. 22 Apr 1773 Lynn MA Mary Breed of Lynn MA, b. 15 Aug 1748, dau. Nathan and Mary (Basset) Breed. Cordwainer.

195 John $^6$, 1774-1841.
Judith, b. 3 Aug 1776 d. 1 Jul 1822, unm.
196 Ezra$^6$, 1779-1858.
Nabby, b. 16 Dec 1781, m. Jonathan Green.
Ruth, b. 17 Jul 1784, m. 5 Jul 1804 Weare NH Cheney Chase.
197 Nathan$^6$, 1787-1884.

Sources: Newbury MA census 1790. Weare NH census 1800, 1810, 1820, 1830, 1840, 1850, 1860, 1870. VR Newbury MA, Lynn MA. L31, E20, G30.

91. **JAMES$^5$ SAWYER** [see 39], b. 3 Nov 1750 Newbury MA, d. Freeport ME, m. 21 Sep 1775 Sarah Brown of Newbury MA, b. 3 Aug 1755, dau. John Brown. B/land in Freeport ME 1810, 1816, 1825. Note: His m. record says James of Royalsborough (Durham) ME.

Elizabeth, b. 14 May 1776, m.(I) 1800 Joseph Douglas, Jr.
198 John Brown$^6$, 1777-1863.
Theodata, b. 9 Feb 1779, m.(1) 1795 Amni Dunham, m.(2) 5 Jul 1827 William Jones.
Hannah, b. 20 Jun 1782, m. 29 Nov 1802 Ebenezer Gardiner.
James, b. 1 Nov 1785 Freeport ME.
199 Ezra$^6$, 1787-1848.

Stephen, b. 16 Sep 1789 Freeport ME, d. 24 Sep 1852 Durham ME, m. 10 Apr 1823 Diana Dillingham, b. Jul 1803 d. 16 Mar 1841. S/land in Freeport ME 1832, 1839. B/S/land in Durham ME 1839, 1842, 1846, 1849. CH: Hannah G., b. 28 May 1825, d. 1 Jul 1861 Durham ME; Helen L., b. 8 Jul 1827, d. 29 Oct 1864; Sarah E., b. 28 Aug 1831, d. 5 Aug 1902; Harriet J., b. 17 Aug 1834, d. 30 Dec 1893, m. 27 Feb 1872 Charles A. Cushing; Joanna S., b. 20 Mar 1837, d. 7 Mar 1863.

Sarah, b. 4 Jan 1793, m. 25 Sep 1812 David Trafton.

Elijah, b. 20 Mar 1801 Freeport ME, m.(I) 7 Jul 1822 Sarah Blethen of Lisbon ME, b. ?.

Sources: Freeport ME census 1790, 1800, 1810, 1830. Durham ME census 1840, 1850. VR Newbury MA, Freeport ME. R10a, E20, C94, David C. Young rec.

92. **ELIJAH$^5$ SAWYER** [see 39], b. 15 Jun 1762 Newbury MA, d. 28 Mar 1839 Newbury MA poorhouse, m. 25 May 1803 Newbury MA Miriam Brown, b. 10 Mar 1769 d. 24 Nov 1839, dau. Stephen and Miriam Brown.

William, b. ca. 1808 W. Newbury MA, d. 28 Jul 1839, m. 18 Apr 1839 New Durham NH Abigail Bean of Farmington ME, b. 5 Feb 1818, dau. James and Hannah (Roberts) Bean. He bur. in Quaker Burial Ground, W. Newbury MA. Wid. m. 1841 West Newbury MA Alfred Kelly.

Sources: Newbury MA census 1810, 1820. VR Newbury MA. T20, Nathalie S. Potts rec.

93. **HUMPHREY$^5$ SAWYER** [see 39], b. 12 Dec 1764 Newbury MA, d. 9 Jan 1820 Winchendon MA, m. Mary Hoag of Dover NH, b. ?, dau. Enoch and Judith (Varney) Hoag. Sievemaker. Sheriff.In Weare NH 1788.

200 James$^6$, 1793-1846.

Peace, b. 15 Nov 1797, unm.

201 Allen$^6$, 1803-1866.

Sources: Weare NH census 1800, 1810. VR Newbury MA, Winchendon MA.

94. **STEPHEN$^5$ SAWYER** [see 40], b. 8 Jun 1752 Dover NH, d. 30 Sep 1831 Dover NH, m. 4 Mar 1778 Mary Varney, b. 17 Aug 1756 d. 17 Jul 1843. Blacksmith. Town Clerk for Dover NH 1790, 1793, 1800, 1802, 1803, 1805.

Elizabeth, b. 12 Jan 1778, d. 14 Feb 1841, m. 1 May 1805 Abner Chase.

Nahum, b. 6 Nov 1779 Dover NH, drowned 7 May 1800 Newburyport MA.

Justin, b. 16 Jun 1781 Dover NH d. 7 Dec 1809 Boston MA, m. 1803 Phebe Holt, b. ?. CH: Mary V., b. 6 Dec 1803 Medford MA; Elizabeth Chase, b. 1809, d. Feb 1816 Salem MA.

Hosea, b. 25 May 1783 Dover NH, d. 17 May 1858 Dover NH, m. 15 Oct 1845 Elizabeth H. Hodgdon, b. 1815, dau. Benjamin and Sarah Hodgdon. Town Moderator 1810. Excommunicated from First Church of Dover NH 4 May 1834. Wid. m. _____ Rand 25 Nov 1862. CH: Laura A., b. 1847, d. 27 Feb 1852; Emma M., b. 1849, d. 15 Nov 1886, m. 28 Nov 1867 Frank P. Wentworth.

Walter, b. 1 Nov 1784 Dover NH, d. bef. Mar 1876, unm. Town Representative 1829.

Beniah, b. 6 Jul 1787 Dover NH, d. New York City. In Nantucket MA. Brother Levi appointed administrator of his estate 17 Oct 1835.

Ruth, b. 10 Sep 1789, d. bef. 1872. In Dover NH w/brother Levi 1860.

202 Levi$^6$, 1791-1868.

Edward, b. 2 Jul 1793 Dover NH, d. bef. 1835. In Salem NH. Brother Thomas appointed administrator of his estate.

Lydia, b. 20 Aug 1796, d. 9 Oct 1820.

203 Thomas Ellwood$^6$, 1798-1879.

Sources: Dover NH census 1790, 1800, 1810, 1830, 1850, 1860, 1870. VR Salem MA, Medford MA, SA/MA. Q2, P82i, V3, N5, N6, W26.

95. **TIMOTHY$^5$ SAWYER** [see 40], b. 5 Oct 1766 Dover NH, d. 1820 Wakefield NH, m. 5 May 1797 Wolfeboro NH Sarah Dearborn of Wakefield NH, b. 1773 d. 1861.

Nancy, b. 11 Oct 1797, d. 9 Aug 1798.

Alvah Haven, b. 14 Feb 1799 Wakefield NH, d. 23 May 1882 Wakefield NH. Blacksmith. Administrator of father's estate.

Charles, b. 28 Dec 1800, d. 4 Sep 1803.

204 Luther Dearborn$^6$, 1803-1884.

Sarah Ann, b. 5 Jun 1805, d. 8 Sep 1899, unm.

Lucy Maria, b. 14 Jul 1809, d. 12 May 1910, unm.

Sources: Wakefield NH census 1810, 1830, 1840, 1850, 1860. VR Wakefield NH. P82i.

96. **JACOB$^5$ SAWYER** [see 40], b. 1 Oct 1769 Dover NH, d. bef. 3 Nov 1846 Dover NH, m. 1 May 1800 Elizabeth Morrill of Maine, b. 15 Apr 1777 d. 6 Mar 1857, dau. Peter Jr. and Hannah (Winslow) Morrill. Town Moderator 1806. Will dated 5 Dec 1843. Wid. in Dover NH 1850.

Peter Morrill, b. 5 Jan 1801, d. 7 Jan 1802.

Sarah Ann, b. 17 Oct 1802, m. Oliver Foss.

205 John$^6$, 1804-1877.

Sources: Dover NH census 1800, 1810, 1820, 1830, 1840, 1850. VR Dover NH. S21, P82i, S70.

97. **ENOCH$^5$ SAWYER** [see 40], b. 4 Feb 1776 Dover NH, d. 11 Oct 1857 Alton NH, m. Eleanor Horn of Rochester NH, b. 13 Feb 1774 d. 1870. B/land in Alton NH 1798. Farmer, cooper, inn keeper, general store keeper. Wid. w/son Seth 1860, w/grandson Alonzo 1870.

Lavina, b. 28 Feb 1800, d. 4 Jul 1802.

206 Daniel$^6$, 1801-1869.

Sophia, b. 14 Nov 1803, m. 29 Mar 1826 Samuel Cate. Teacher in Alton NH.

207 Seth$^6$, 1806-1892.

Caroline, b. 20 Dec 1809, m. Judge Ira Mooney.

Sources: Alton NH census 1830, 1840, 1850, 1860, 1870. F17, M39, H94.

98. **SAMUEL$^5$ SAWYER** [see 41], b. 19 Jul 1751 Dover NH, d. 30 Apr 1827 Newburyport MA, m. Oct 1778 Durham NH Molly Bennet, b. 1757 d. 26 Apr 1838. Revolutionary War. In Lee NH 1790. May have res. in Newmarket NH. Had 9 CH?

Betsey, b. 16 Mar 1780, m. 24 Dec 1801 John Neal.

Nancy, b. 5 Feb 1782, m. 6 Nov 1802 Joseph Babson.

208 Jeremiah Hill$^6$, b. 1784.

Polly Nye, b. 18 Mar 1786.

Hannah, b. 1800, m. 3 Dec 1827 John Follansbee Sanborn.

Emeline, b. ?, m. 31 Oct 1839 Daniel C. Shaw.

Sources: Lee NH census 1790, 1800, 1810. B84, S8, N11.

99. **GEORGE$^5$ SAWYER** [see 41], b. 1 Aug 1758 Dover NH, d. 25 May 1813, m. 17 Feb 1785 Topsham ME Hannah Dain of Lisbon ME, b. ?, dau. John and Rachel (Bond) Dain of Connecticut. In Lisbon ME 1810. Wid. w/son Joseph 1820, 1840.

Ebenezer, b. 8 Oct 1785 Lisbon ME, d. 1785.

Mehitable, b. 13 Mar 1788, d. 1788.

209 Moses H.$^6$, 1789-1878.

210 Joseph$^6$, 1791-1882.

Hannah, b. 23 Apr 1794, m. 9 Apr 1815 Richard Merrill of Lewiston ME.
Jeremiah, b. 24 Oct 1796, d. 1807.
Ruth, b. 4 Dec 1798, d. 1804.

Sources: Lisbon ME census 1810, 1820, 1840. VR Topsham ME, No. Yarmouth ME. M36, M5, Beverly Strout rec, David S. Young rec.

100. **ZACCHEUS⁵ SAWYER** [see 41], b. 24 May 1760 Dover NH, d. Feb 1824 Strafford NH, m. Mary _____ of Nottingham NH, b. 1758 d. 30 Jul 1838. On Barrington NH tax list 1788.

Hulday (Huldah?), b. ?, m. 14 May 1804 Ebenezer Leathers, Jr.
Moses, b. ca. 1786 Barrington NH, m. Louisa _____, b. ca. 1810. Farmer. In Strafford NH 1822. Census says he had fol. CH during periods shown: 2 sons (1820-1825); 3 dau. (1825-1830); 1 dau. (1835-1840). Moses could neither read nor write; Louisa was deaf.
Bitfield, b. 1794 Barrington NH, d. 25 Feb 1862 Strafford NH, m.(1) 29 Jul 1824 Barrington NH Patience Brown of Barrington NH, b. ?; m.(2) 16 May 1859 Emily Arling of Rochester NH, b. 1816. CH: Mary A., b. ?. Neither Bitfield nor Mary could read or write. Wid. m. 8 Apr 1862 John Arlin.
211 Aaron⁶, 1803-ca. 1878.

Sources: Barrington NH census 1790, 1800, 1810. Strafford NH census 1830, 1840, 1850, 1860. VR Barrington NH, Strafford NH. N6, D10.

101. **STEPHEN⁵ SAWYER** [see 42], b. 12 Dec 1762 Amesbury MA, d. 12 Apr 1842 Hampden ME, m. 9 Nov 1793 Amesbury MA Deborah Farrington, b. 31 Oct 1769 d. 30 Aug 1838. Hampden ME 1820. Stephen w/son Amos in 1840.

212 Samuel⁶, 1797-1864.
Rachel, b. ?, m. John Holt.
Electa, b. ?, m. William Farrington.
Mary (Polly), b. ?, m. David Hewes.
213 Aaron⁶, 1803-1841.
214 Joseph Harvey⁶, 1805-1882.
215 Amos P.⁶, 1807-1877.
Eliza, b. 27 Mar 1810, d. 7 Sep 1893, m. Rev. B. D. Small.

Sources: Amesbury MA census 1800. Hampden ME census 1820, 1830, 1840. VR Amesbury MA. P20, D6, N21.

102. **JOSHUA⁵ SAWYER** [see 42], b. 23 Sep 1767 Amesbury MA, d. 2 Nov 1829 Hampstead NH, m. 23 Sep 1794 Dracut MA Abigail Patten, b. 15 Oct 1772 d. 4 Mar 1847, dau. John and Ruth (Pillsbury) Patten. Selectman for Hampstead NH 1810-1812. Abigail joined church in Hampstead NH 1797. Wid. moved to Concord NH, joined Unitarian Church 1831.

Ruth Pillsbury, b. 8 Aug 1795, m. 28 May 1818 Job Eaton of Hampstead NH.
216 John Patten⁶, 1797-1871.
Harriet, b. 8 Nov 1798, m. 27 Aug 1837 Philo Dow of Hampstead NH.
Aaron, b. 29 Aug 1801, d. 13 Apr 1803.
Abigail, b. 8 Oct 1803.
Sarah Clement, b. 5 Aug 1806, m. 23 Sep 1827 Warren L. Lane.
William Pecker, b. 16 Oct 1808 Hampstead NH.
Anna, b. 6 May 1810, d. 19 Aug 1815.
217 Joshua⁶, b. 1814.

Sources: Hampstead NH census 1800, 1810, 1820. VR Hampstead NH. N38, N7, B17, B18, R34, C50, N6.

103. **AARON[5] SAWYER** [see 42], b. 1773 (Kingston NH?), d. 25 Feb 1862 Amesbury MA, m. 25 Oct 1809 Sally Currier, b. 23 Sep 1787 d. 1 Jun 1838, dau. Seth and Ellis (Sargent) Currier. Farmer.

Alfred, b. 15 Feb 1810, d. Apr 1810.
Abbot, b. 9 Jul 1811.
Seth, b. 2 Jan 1814, d. 2 Feb 1814.
Anna, b. 5 Nov 1816, d. 20 Mar 1836.
Stephen, b. 12 Feb 1818, d. 7 Mar 1818.
218 Aaron[6], 1823-1899.
219 Amos[6], 1825-1922.
Andrew, b. 12 Nov 1829, d. 9 Apr 1833.

Sources: Amesbury MA census 1820, 1830, 1840, 1850. VR Amesbury MA. C93.

104. **BETFIELD[5] SAWYER** [see 43], b. 25 Mar 1774 Newton NH, d. 10 Sep 1835 Hill NH, m. 17 Jun 1793 Hannah Thompson of Kingston NH, b. 10 Jun 1776, dau. Thomas and Judith (Blaisdell) Thompson. In New Chester NH. He bur. in Hill NH.

David Colby, b. 9 May 1794 Newton NH, d. 28 Jun 1881 Manchester NH, m. 8 Jan 1824 Salisbury MA Mary W. Farmer of Andover MA, b. 1794 d. 31 Mar 1871. Lived w/nephew, Weare, in Manchester NH in later life. CH: Mary, b. May 1829, d. 30 Dec 1832; Luther, b. Nov 1831, d. 5 Jan 1833.
220 Thomas[6], 1796-1863.
Polly, b. 6 Mar 1797, d. 23 Dec 1797.
Hannah, b. 18 Oct 1798, m. Ebenezer Tucker of Andover MA.
Luther, b. 1 Jun 1801 Chester NH, d. 1856, unm.
Polly, b. 29 Aug 1804, d. 13 Aug 1852, m.(1) Daniel Loverin, m.(2) _____ Farnum.
Calvin, b. 3 Dec 1807, d. 23 Jan 1813.
Betsey, b. 9 Mar 1813, d. 23 Apr 1816.

Sources: New Chester NH census 1830. Hill NH census 1850, 1860. E2, S18.

105. **STEPHEN[5] SAWYER** [see 44], b. 15 Dec 1767 Newbury MA, d. 6 Apr 1844 Plaistow NH, m. 1789 Mary Heath of Hampstead NH, b. ?. In Springfield NH 1790, Greenfield NH 1800, Plaistow NH 1820. Wid. in Plaistow NH 1850.

Amos, b. 27 Apr 1790 Springfield NH.
Susannah, b. 19 Jun 1792, m. 7 Dec 1815 James Cross of Wilmot NH.
Fanny, b. 1793, m. Josiah Bly.
Polly, b. 7 Mar 1795, m. 7 Dec 1825 Plaistow NH George W. Flanders.
Rebecca. b. (1800-1810).
221 William[6], 1804-1860.
Laban, b. 1809 Springfield NH, m.(1) 30 Apr 1834 Haverhill MA Nancy H. Noyes of Pembroke MA, b. 22 Aug 1813, dau. John and Hannah Noyes; m.(2) Mary A._____ of Atkinson NH, b. 1813. Postmaster. In Atkinson NH 1840, Andover MA 1850. CH: Elbridge Bassett, b. 21 Dec 1834, d. 14 Feb 1835; Justin Cook, b. 6 Mar 1837, d. 15 Apr 1837; Ellen, b. 8 Dec 1838.
Nathaniel, b. 1813 Plaistow NH, m. Mary A. Holland, b. 1815 d. 15 Aug 1876. Veterinary doctor. In Plaistow NH 1860, 1870.
John, b. (1810-1820) Springfield NH.

Sources: Springfield NH census 1790, 1810. Greenfield NH 1800. Plaistow NH census 1820, 1840, 1850, 1860, 1870. Atkinson NH census 1840. Andover MA census 1850. VR Newbury MA, Plaistow NH, Hampstead NH, Haverhill MA. B27, A33, N40. N6.

106. **JOHN$^5$ SAWYER** [see 44], b. 3 May 1770 Newbury MA, m. Polly _____, b. ?. In Plaistow NH, Springfield NH 1794.

Polly, b. 10 Feb 1792, d. 18 Apr 1874, m. 9 Dec 1818 Simeon Peaslee of Plaistow NH.
Sally, b. 13 Jan 1796.
Lydia, b. 26 Dec 1797.
Susannah, b. 11 Aug 1800, m. 24 Oct 1826 Isaac McRobie of Danvers MA.
John, b. 29 Aug 1802 Springfield NH.
Betsey, b. 10 Mar 1806, m. Prescott Lovering.
222 Leonard$^6$, b. ca. 1821.

Sources: Springfield NH census 1800, 1810, 1820, 1830. VR Newbury MA, Plaistow NH, Lynn MA, SA/MA. N6.

107. **NATHANIEL$^5$ SAWYER** [see 44], b. 4 Nov 1780 Plaistow NH, m. 10 Jan 1805 Lydia Pierce of So. Hampton NH, b. ?. Wid. in Plaistow NH 1810.

223 Gilman$^6$, 1806-1875.
Melinda b. 11 Jan 1808, d. 18 Nov 1899, m. 13 Jan 1827 Calvin Eastman of Hawke (Danville) NH.

Sources: Plaistow NH census 1810. VR Plaistow NH, Danville NH. T20, N6.

108. **JACOB$^5$ SAWYER** [see 45], b. 8 Jan 1771 Newbury MA, d. 30 Jan 1843 W. Newbury MA, m. 1 Jan 1794 Newbury MA Judith Rogers, b. Oct 1772 d. 13 Sep 1847.

Hannah, b. 4 Sep 1794, d. 31 Oct 1870, m. 31 May 1813 Newbury MA Daniel Wentworth.
Enoch, b. 6 Feb 1797 Newbury MA.
Mary, b. 11 Jan 1802, m. 23 Jan 1825 Jonathan Longley of W. Newbury MA.
224 William$^6$, b. 1804.
225 Reuben$^6$, b. 1807.
Betsey, b. 23 Jan 1810.
Harriet, b. 13 Jun 1812, m. 30 Mar 1835 Warren Rogers.

Sources: Newbury MA census 1810, 1820, 1830, 1840. VR Newbury MA, Groveland MA, SA/MA. R34, M39.

109. **STEPHEN$^5$ SAWYER** [see 45], b. 25 Oct 1780 Newbury MA, d. 30 Oct 1874 W. Newbury MA, m.(I) 22 Sep 1810 Newbury MA Sarah Brown, b. 1789 d. 26 Nov 1871. Farmer.

Son, b. (1810-1815).
Daughter, b. (1810-1815).
Son, b. (1815-1820).
Henry W., b. ca. 1822 Newbury MA, d. W. Newbury MA, m. 10 Jun 1852 Newbury MA Harriet D. Moulton of Newbury MA, b. 26 Jun 1826, dau. Col. David and Diodemia (Spofford) Moulton. Quaker. Farmer. In Newbury MA 1850. He bur. Quaker Cem., W. Newbury MA. CH: Eleanor, b. 22 Apr 1856, d. 22 Apr 1857; Carrie E., b. 11 Feb 1858, m. 12 Jan 1887 Newburyport MA David H. Evans; Stephen, b. 12 May 1860, d. 13 Jul 1862; Henrietta M., b. 3 Jan 1864.

Sources: Newbury MA census 1820, 1830, 1840, 1850. VR Newbury MA. S65, Nathalie S. Potts rec.

110. **ENOCH$^5$ SAWYER** [see 46], b. 6 Jun 1767 Newbury MA, d. 26 Mar 1808 Newbury MA, m. 17 Oct 1793 Boston MA Judith Greenleaf of Boston MA, b. 12 Mar 1768 d. 2 Jul 1834. B/land in Waterford ME 16 Aug 1800. Judith B/land in Waterford ME 1809. Wid. in Newbury MA 1810.

Elizabeth, b. 27 Jun 1794, d. 16 Oct 1826, m. 7 Aug 1815 John Rollins of Newburyport MA.

Anna G., b. 27 Oct 1795, d. 29 Sep 1871, m. 28 Apr 1818 Amos Atkinson of Boston MA.
Edmund, b. 4 May 1798, d. Dec 1831 Marseilles, France.
Micajah, b. 24 Nov 1799, d. 30 Aug 1801.
Judith Greenleaf, b. 6 May 1801, d. 18 May 1835, m. William Parsons.
Eunice G., b. 24 Sep 1802, d. 27 Dec 1822.
Hannah Moody, b. 21 Jun 1806, d. 21 Aug 1872, m. 29 Apr 1830 Silas Titcomb of Portland ME.
Mary Sigourney, b. 31 May 1807, m. 12 Sep 1829 Moses P. Parish of Newburyport MA.
Enoch, b. Sep 1808, d. 24 Jul 1816.

Sources: Newbury MA census 1800, 1810. VR Newbury MA, Boston MA, SA/MA. R25, P5,G42.

111. **THOMAS[5] SAWYER** [see 47], b. 18 May 1783 Newburyport MA.
Thomas, b. ca. 1804.

Sources: VR Newburyport MA.

## SIXTH GENERATION

112. **NATHANIEL PEASLEE[6] SAWYER** [see 49], b. 19 Jun 1772 Haverhill MA, d. 30 Jun 1852 Hyde Park VT, m. Catherine Martin of New York, b. 1782 d. 1 Oct 1849. B/ land in Hyde Park VT 1799. Assistant Judge in Orleans City VT 1814, 1821, 1824.
Polly, b. 20 Nov 1798.
Sally, b. 23 Jul 1800.
William Peaslee, b. 10 Feb 1809 Hyde Park VT, d. 28 Jun 1852 Hyde Park VT, m. Adaline Goss of New Hampshire, b. Nov 1809 d. 28 Aug 1878. Attorney, farmer. CH: Julia A., b. 1835, m. 1 Nov 1859 John Crosby; Mary A., b. 1836, d. 1 Jun 1861; Sarah E., b. 29 Sep 1837, d. 24 Aug 1892, m. 28 Oct 1863 George L. Waterman; Isabella, b. 1839, m. 10 Oct 1861 William E. Mars.

Sources: Hyde Park VT census 1800, 1810, 1820, 1830, 1840, 1850. VR Haverhill MA, SA/VT. D11, W63, J6.

113. **JOSEPH[6] SAWYER** [see 49], b. 1786 Haverhill MA, d. 28 Dec 1857 Haverhill MA, m.(1) 31 Jan 1819 Haverhill MA Eliza C. Sawyer, b. ? d. 30 Oct 1838; m.(2) 14 Sep 1853 Haverhill MA Mary (Davis) Hodder of England, b. 1818, dau. Thomas and Mary Davis. Farmer, shoemaker.
Nathaniel F., b. ca. 1819 Haverhill MA, d. 7 Jul 1851 Haverhill MA, m. 31 Aug 1850 Newburyport MA Maria G. Hobbs of Milo ME, b. ?, dau. Reuben and Salomy Hobbs. Cordwainer.
Lydia, b. 1820, m. Charles Tufts.
Son, b. (1820-1825).
Daughter, b. (1825-1830).

Sources: Haverhill MA census 1820, 1830, 1840, 1850. VR Haverhill MA, SA/MA. M39.

114. **JOSHUA[6] SAWYER** [see 49], b. 23 Jul 1789 Haverhill MA, d. 16 Mar 1869 Hyde Park VT, m. Dec 1811 Mary Keeler b. 1796 d. 1892, dau. Aaron and Gloriana (Hubbell) Keeler. In Burlington VT 1809. Admitted to Bar, Orleans City VT 1810. State Attorney 1816-1823.
Maria, b. ?.
Victor Moreau, b. 1812 Hyde Park VT.
Lucien Bonaparte, b. 1816 Hyde Park VT, d. 1890, m.(1) ?; m.(2) Amanda Hooker, b. Jan 1832 d. 13 Apr 1860, dau. Hartwell and Cynthia Hooker; m. (3) 12 Feb 1862 Hinesburgh VT Lucia Irish, b.?. Clergyman.

William Norman, b. ca. 182? Hyde Park VT.
226 Edward Bertrand$^7$, 1828-1918.
Joshua Peaslee, b. 1835 Hyde Park Vt. Civil War: Enl. 12 Dec 1864 in U.S. Veteran Volunteers (Hancock Corps), Andover MA.
227 Franklin E.$^7$, 1837-1913.
Juliet, b. ?, m. 1 Jan 1843 William Frazier.
Ruth Peaslee, b. ?, m. Dr. Ira Metcalf.
Sources: Hyde Park VT census 1810, 1820, 1840, 1850. Morrisville VT census 1830. VR SA/VT. C4, H43, D11.

115. **ABEL$^6$ SAWYER** [see 50], b. 1 Sep 1771 Newbury MA, m. 13 Sep 1791 Newton NH Polly Clough of Hampstead NH, wid,. b.?. In Hampstead NH, Groveland MA 1850.
Rufus King, b. 28 May 1793, d. 13 Mar 1794.
Sources: Groveland MA census 1850. VR Newbury MA, Hampstead NH. M39.

116. **DAVID$^6$ SAWYER** [see 50], b. 4 Jul 1775 Newburyport MA, d. 27 May 1862 Deer Isle ME, m.(I) 2 Mar 1804 Deer Isle ME Rebecca Crockett, b. 1783 d. 29 Apr 1837. Will.
228 Nathan Wheeler$^7$, 1805-1881.
229 Admiral George$^7$, 1806-1891.
230 David$^7$, 1808-1884.
Mary W., b. 19 Nov 1810, d. 7 Sep 1874, m. 8 Oct 1839 Ezekiel Marshall.
Rebecca, b. 19 Nov 1810, d.y.
Rebecca Noyes, b. 5 Feb 1813, m. 29 May 1838 Samuel G. Barbour.
231 Mark Haskell$^7$, 1815-1890.
Abigail, b. 11 Jan 1819, m. 1844 James G. Bray.
Fanny, b. 12 May 1821, m. 1844 Mark H. Bray.
Abel, b. 17 Jan 1823 Deer Isle ME, d. ca. 1860, m. 25 Nov 1847 Martha B. Brown of Sedgwick ME, b. 7 Dec 1819 d. 15 Sep 1904, dau. Edward and Pamelia (Billings) Brown. Carpenter. Wid. in Sedgewick ME 1860. CH: Isadora A., b. 13 Nov 1850, m. 25 Nov 1880 Gilbert R. Currier.
Sources: Deer Isle ME census 1810, 1820, 1830, 1840, 1850, 1860. Sedgwick ME census 1850, 1860. VR Deer Isle ME. P82d.

117. **JONATHAN$^6$ SAWYER** [see 51], b. 27 Jul 1783 Hopkinton NH, d. 16 Apr 1860 Enfield NH, m. Sarah H._____, b. 1784 d. 18 Aug 1857.
Daughter, b. (1810-1815).
John R., b. 1817 Enfield NH, d. 6 Aug 1862 Canaan NH, m. Mary C._____, b.? d. 12 Nov 1866. CH: Matilda, adopted, b. 1841, d. 7 Nov 1858.
Sources: Enfield NH census 1810, 1820, 1830, 1840, 1850. W6.

118. **TRUMAN$^6$ SAWYER** [see 52], b. 10 Jan 1811 Hyde Park VT, d. 19 Jun 1864 Wolcott VT, m.(1) 6 Mar 1832 Sibel Wells, b. ?; m.(2) Lavina Davis, b. Jun 1830 d. 15 Apr 1864, dau. Nathan and Sally Davis. Blacksmith, farmer. In Johnson VT, Morristown VT, Wolcott VT 1850.
232 Nathan D.$^7$, b. 1849.
George W., b. Mar 1852 Wolcott VT, m. 2 Apr 1875 Walden VT Laura A. Hill of Woodbury VT, b. ?. Farmer. CH: Mamie A., b. Dec 1887, adopted, m. 30 Apr 1906 John A. Kennedy.
Asenath M., b. 1853, m. 14 Oct 1873 John R. Hill.
233 Charles Melvin$^7$, b. 1855.
Linda Annett, b. 24 Aug 1860, m. 7 Nov 1880 Wilber C. Schofield.

Ada Lavina, b. 13 Feb 1864.
Sources: Wolcott VT census 1850. VR SA/VT. C4.

119. **NOAH[6] SAWYER** [see 53], b. 6 Sep 1796 Enfield NH, d. 18 Aug 1882 Charlton MA, m. 26 Jun 1825 Laura Clark, of Hopkinton NH, b. 15 Feb 1803 d. 10 Jun 1874. Shoemaker. On Canaan NH tax list 1821. In Chelsea VT 1828, Canaan NH 1830, Hanover NH 1860.

Seraph, b. 15 Apr 1828, d. 17 Jan 1835.
Orvilla, b. Aug 1829, d. Feb 1830.
Algna, b. 1831.
Saloma, b. 1832.
234 Frank Clark[7], 1833-1906.
Stephen, b. 25 Jan 1835 Canaan NH, d. 30 Aug 1917 at County Farm, Haverhill NH, m. 7 Jan 1871 Mary E. Cilley, b. ?.
William W., b. 1845 Canaan NH.

Sources: Canaan NH census 1830, 1840, 1850. Hanover NH census 1860. N15, W6, N14, Family Bible.

120. **ABRAHAM[6] SAWYER** [see 54], b. 29 Aug 1785 Saco ME, m.(I) 14 Sep 1807 Elizabeth Sawyer of Saco ME, b. ca. 1786, dau. Joel and Mary (Warren) Sawyer. Farmer. In Saco 1810. War of 1812: Enl. 2 Jul 1814, deserted 5 Nov 1814.

235 Leason[7], 1807-1879.
Ellen, b. ca. 1808, d. 27 Feb 1881.
Katherine, b. ca. 1809, m. Daniel Knight.
236 Abraham[7], 1812-1877.
Betsey, b. ?, d. 1881, m. John Littlefield.

Sources: Saco ME census 1810. VR Saco ME.

121. **JOHN[6] SAWYER** [see 54], b. 20 May 1792 Saco ME, d. 24 Oct 1862 Augusta ME, m. 13 Dec 1812 Jane Thomas of New Hampshire, b. 25 Feb 1791 d. 31 May 1886.

237 Charles[7], 1813-1897.
Eliza Ann, b. 1 Apr 1815.
Jane, b. 17 Feb 1817, d. 29 May 1819.
238 James[7], 1818-1891.
Alfred, b. 29 Oct 1821 Saco ME, d. 26 Jan 1871 Wayne Village ME, m. 19 Sep 1845 Bowdoin ME Jane Becker, b. 1818 d. 25 Dec 1881. CH: Frances A., b. 16 Jun 1846.
John, b. 29 Oct 1823 Saco ME, m. Jun 1849 Boston MA Harriet E. Blake of Portland ME, b. 26 Jun 1823, dau. Thomas and Elizabeth (McClellend) Blake. Hackman. In Boston MA 1850, No. Yarmouth ME 1865. CH: Harriet Isabelle, b. 1 Feb 1850; Jennie Sophia, b. 15 May 1852; John Plumer, b. 1865, d. 16 Oct 1865.
Noah, b. 26 Aug 1824 Saco ME.
Zenas, b. 29 Jun 1826 Saco ME, lost at sea 1859, m. 8 Oct 1858 Boston MA Sophia Baker of Bowdoinham ME, b. 1833 d. 3 Oct 1878, dau. John and Mary Baker. Mariner.
Samuel, b. 3 Jul 1828 Saco ME.
239 George Francis[7], 1830-1886.
Jane, b. 20 Jul 1832, m. 3 Nov 1856 Boston MA Solon A. Whitcomb.

Sources: Saco ME census 1830. Augusta ME census 1850. Wayne ME census 1860. Bowdoin ME census 1850, 1860. Wayne Village ME census 1870. VR Saco ME, Bowdoin ME, Augusta ME, SA/ME, SA/MA. W39, M5, B49.

122. **DEANE[6] SAWYER** [see 54], b. 4 Jan 1797 Saco ME, d. 10 Jun 1859 Hiram ME, m. (1) 30 Nov 1815 Parsonsfield ME Nancy Brown, b. ? d. 1828; m.(2) 23 Oct 1828 Limington ME Sarah Harmon of Porter ME, b. 1806. War of 1812. In Parsonsfield ME 1820, Hiram ME 1834. Sarah granted pension on 3 Feb 1879.

240 Henry[7], 1816-1893.
Julia Ann, b. 25 Dec 1818, d. Jan 1892, m. 1839 James Tyler.
Clarissa, b. ca. 1829, d. 28 May 1892, m.(1) 17 Feb 1850 Henry Parker, m.(2) 1885 Cyrus B. Morrill.
Charles K., b. ca. 1834, d. 15 Apr 1900, m. 7 Oct 1856 Ann Mayberry.
241 Daniel P.[7], 1838-1886.
242 Ira C.[7], 1840-1906.
Lewis, b. 1842 Hiram ME, m. 7 May 1863 Hiram ME Emily W. Chase, b. 15 Sep 1844 d. 7 Apr 1900 Yarmouth ME, dau. Simon and Ann (York) Chase.

Sources: Parsonsfield ME census 1820, 1830. Hiram ME census 1840, 1850. VR Limington ME, Hiram ME. M5, B85, Will.

123. **DAVID[6] SAWYER** [see 55], b. 13 Jun 1771 Saco ME, d. 22 Feb 1805 at sea, m. 9 Jan 1791 York County ME Olive Holly of Saco ME, b. 10 Nov 1767. Mariner. Wid. in Saco ME 1810-1850.

John, b. 17 May 1791, d. 21 Feb 1805.
Aaron, b. 30 Mar 1793, d. 10 Apr 1816.
Olive, b. 21 Jan 1795.
Icy, b. 5 Sep 1797, d. 1 Oct 1800.
243 Nathaniel[7], 1800-1882.
George, b. 17 Mar 1804 Saco ME.

Sources: Saco ME census 1790, 1800, 1810, 1820, 1830, 1840, 1850. VR Saco ME. F38.

124. **JOEL[6] SAWYER** [see 56], b. 30 Aug 1772 Saco ME, d. 1852 Wilton ME, m. 16 Jan 1794 Susannah Pearl of Saco ME, b. 11 Mar 1771 d. 20 Nov 1838.

Sarah, b. 4 Jan 1794, m. 7 Nov 1811 Amos Jose.
Polly, b. 24 Jul 1796.
244 Isaac[7], b. 1798.
Ephraim Bryant, b. 9 Jul 1800 Saco ME, m.(1) 29 Apr 1820 Hannah Bryant, b. 4 Jun 1800 d. 6 Dec 1854; m.(2) Betsey _____, b. 1809. Lumberman. In Saco ME 1820, Standish ME 1840. CH: Son, b. (1820-1825); Son, b. (1825-1830); Daughter, b. (1825-1830).
Mary Simpson, b. 9 Feb 1802, m. 15 Jul 1827 Moses Meserve.
Abner Flanders, b. 13 Apr 1804, drowned 24 Jul 1806.
245 Henry H.[7], b. 1806.
Susannah, b. 14 May 1809, d. 13 Nov 1825.
Allison, b. 8 May 1811.
Charlotte, b. 30 Apr 1813, d. 19 May 1814.
Francis, b. 16 Dec 1816 Saco ME.

Sources: Saco ME census 1800, 1810, 1820, 1830, 1850. Standish ME census 1840. VR Saco ME. S1.

125. **ANDREW STACKPOLE[6] SAWYER** [see 56], b. 7 May 1779 Saco ME, d. 12 Jan 1855 m. Betsey Brown of Saco ME, b. 25 Sep 1789. In Effingham NH 1816, Saco ME 1820.

Apphia, b. 12 Aug 1806.
246 Joel[7], 1808-1895.
247 Edmund[7], 1809-1894.

248 Luther$^7$, 1811-1900.
249 Andrew S.$^7$, b. 1812.
Freeman, b. 2 Feb 1815 Saco ME, m. 4 May 1840 Kennebunkport ME Harriet N. Williams, b. 29 Jul 1812 d. 16 Jun 1841, dau. Charles and Abigail (Lord) Williams. Physician. In Indiana. CH: Harriet Newell, b. 11 Jun 1841.
Josiah Thomas, b. 19 Oct 1816 Saco ME, d. 3 Nov 1894 Bangor ME, m.(I) 27 Apr 1840 Hannah Curtis of Biddeford ME, b. 1817 d. 18 Aug 1887. Tinplater. In Bangor 1840, 1850, 1860. CH: Emma, b. 1843; Hannah, b. 1845.
Sarah Elizabeth, b. 15 Apr 1819, m. Oct 1837 Silas Ladd.
250 Arthur B.$^7$, 1821-1910.
Marshall, b. ca. 1823 Saco ME, d. 27 Feb 1848.
Daniel, b. ca. 1825 Saco ME, m. 9 Apr 1848 Rockland ME Eleanor Raymond of Vinalhaven ME, b. 1824 d. 8 Dec 1905, dau. John and Mary (Perry) Raymond. Tinplater. In Bangor ME 1850, Old Town ME 1870. CH: Emma F., b. 1851, m. 24 Nov 1877 Charles D. Gilbert; Sarah E., b. 1852; Anna A., b. 1859, m. Apr 1880 Ethan A. Allen.
Ruth, b. 1827, d. 28 Feb 1899, m. Charles Sinnott.
Gorham, b. ca. 1829 Saco ME, d.y.
Ira, b. ca. 1832 Saco ME.
Sources: Saco ME census 1820, 1830, 1840, 1850. Bangor ME census 1840, 1850, 1860. Old Town ME census 1870. VR Saco ME, Bangor ME, Rockland ME, Old Town ME. L1, L37.

126. **DANIEL$^6$ SAWYER** [see 56], b. 31 Jul 1792 Saco ME, d. 21 Oct 1876 Saco ME, m. (1) 18 Oct 1815 Saco ME Martha Sawyer, b. 10 Oct 1793 d. 21 Jun 1844, dau. John and Elizabeth Sawyer; m.(2) 13 Oct 1845 Effingham NH Huldah Hobbs of Eaton NH, b. 1803.
251 Albert$^7$, 1816-ca. 1880.
Mary E., b. 18 Mar 1818.
Jane, b. 23 Aug 1820, m. _____ Chick.
252 Daniel Franklin$^7$, 1846-1924.
Sources: Saco ME census 1820, 1830, 1840. VR Saco ME. P82k.

127. **TRISTRAM$^6$ SAWYER** [see 56], b. 10 Mar 1795 Saco ME, d. 26 Dec 1874 Saco ME, m. 7 May 1817 Scarboro ME Comfort Marston of Scarboro ME, b. 7 Jan 1794 d. 10 Sep 1856, dau. Simeon and Mehitable (Moulton) Marston. War of 1812: Pvt. in Lt. S. S. Fairfield's Company, Saco ME.
Sarah M., b. 28 Apr 1818.
Harriet, b. 21 Aug 1819, d. 4 Jan 1887 Biddeford ME. Had will.
253 Simeon$^7$, 1821-1898.
Cyrus, b. 19 Feb 1823 Saco ME d. 7 Feb 1878 Buxton ME, m.(1) Elizabeth P. Moulton of Saco ME, b. 15 Apr 1820 d. 29 Apr 1858, dau. Robert and Hannah (Pillsbury) Moulton; m.(2) 8 Jun 1860 Buxton ME Martha A. McQuillan of Gorham ME, b. 11 Nov 1828, dau. Joel and J. (Towle) McQuillan. Cordwainer. Will dated. 28 Jun 1879. He bur. in Tory Hill Cem., Buxton ME. CH: Viola E., b. 29 Apr 1851.
Mehitable, b. 23 Jul 1825, m. _____ Rumney.
254 James Lewis$^7$, 1828-1911.
255 Jason H.$^7$, 1830-1918
Alvin, b. 28 Apr 1832 Saco ME, d. bef. Oct 1871, m. 29 Dec 1858 Saco ME Mary B. Chadbourne, b. 1835. Blacksmith. In Saco ME 1850. Will dated. 17 Feb 1871. CH: Abbie May, b. 17 Sep 1863, m. 19 Sep 1863 Wakefield MA Willard E. Griffin.
Lucy, b. 22 May 1836, d. 22 Aug 1838.

Sources: Saco ME census 1820, 1830, 1840, 1850. Buxton ME census 1850, 1860, 1870. VR Saco ME, Scarboro ME, Gorham ME, Buxton ME, SA/ME, SA/MA. M5, P82k, M57.

128. **WILLIAM$^6$ SAWYER** [see 57], b. 28 Jul 1776 Saco ME, d. Mar 1812 at sea, m. 27 Nov 1803 Margaret Scammon of Saco ME, b. 17 Nov 1771 d. 19 Aug 1837, dau. Samuel and Sarah (Dimmatt) Scammon. Sea captain. Guardian appointed for minor CH 1819-1824. Wid. in Saco ME 1820, 1830.

256 William$^7$, b. 1803.
Sarah Frost, b. 6 Nov 1804, d. 25 Dec 1838.
Harriet, b. 12 Sep 1806, d. 21 Nov 1822.
257 Frederick William$^7$, 1810-1875.

Sources: Saco ME census 1810, 1820, 1830. VR Saco ME. N5, P82k.

129. **SAMUEL$^6$ SAWYER** [see 57], b. 1 Feb 1778 Saco ME, d. 23 Aug 1858 Saco ME, m.(1) 16 Mar 1806 Scarboro ME Grace Moulton of Scarboro ME, b. 19 Dec 1785 d. 29 Dec 1808, dau. Charles P. and Olive (Fabyan) Moulton: m.(2) 28 Nov 1810 Eunice Bradbury of Buxton ME, b. 27 Mar 1783 d. 6 Dec 1843, dau. Jabez and Sarah (Atkinson) Bradbury. He bur. in Tory Hill Cem., Buxton ME.

Jane, b. 28 Jun 1807, d. 30 Jul 1875, m. 12 Jun 1831 Jonathan Fogg.
Grace, b. 27 Oct 1811, d. 13 Oct 1858, m. 7 May 1835 _____.
William, b. 21 Feb 1814 Saco ME, m. 5 May 1841 Mary _____, b. ?
258 Horace$^7$, 1816-1900.
Sarah, b. 23 Mar 1818, d. 12 Jan 1874, m. 25 Nov 1848 _____.
Mary W., b. 1820, d. 1822.
Samuel Warren, b. 23 Jun 1823 Saco ME, m. 3 Jan 1877 Lynn MA Anna M. George of Bangor ME, b. 1853, dau. Nathan D. and Mary George. Merchant. In Saco ME 1850.

Sources: Saco ME census 1810, 1820, 1830, 1840, 1850. VR Saco ME, Scarboro ME, Buxton ME, SA/MA. M3, L8, W42, S1, M57.

130. **STEPHEN$^6$ SAWYER** [see 58], b. 11 Mar 1780 Saco ME, d. 2 Oct 1853 Saco ME, m.(I) 9 Feb 1805 Olive Sawyer of Saco ME, b. 20 Apr 1782 d. 21 Sep 1861, dau. William and Mary (Warren) Sawyer. Lumberman. B/S/land in Porter ME 1820, 1822. B/S/land in Lowell ME 1823, 1828. B/land in Baldwin ME 1832, Hiram ME 1834.

Gilbert, b. 7 Jan 1807 Saco ME, d. 14 Nov 1837 at sea, m. 22 Oct 1835 Biddeford ME Dorcas Jordan of Saco ME, b. 29 Sep 1813, dau. Rishworth and Mary (Sawyer) Jordan.
Miranda O., b. 14 Feb 1809, d. 22 Mar 1835, m. 18 Sep 1830 Tristram Jordan, Biddeford ME.Latter named executor of Olive's will 1861.
Lucy T., b. 18 Dec 1812, d. 6 Nov 1838, unm.
Lewis, b. 4 May 1814 Saco ME, d. 19 Oct 1907 Saco ME, m. Dorcas O. (Jordan) Sawyer of Saco ME, b. 29 Sep 1813, wid of brother Gilbert, dau. Rishworth and Mary (Sawyer) Jordan. Farmer. CH: Infant b. 6 Aug 1843, d. 7 Aug 1843; Lewis, b. 1844 d. 20 Feb 1847; Anna F., b. 1847, m. _____ Patterson; Ellen, b. 1847; Dorcas, b. 1851; Mary L., b. 1853.
259 Charles William$^7$, 1816-1858.
Mary, b. 30 Aug 1817, d. 21 Aug 1869 (1879?), unm.
Anna, b. 25 May 1819, d. 26 May 1896.
260 Stephen$^7$, 1820-1902.
261 James$^7$, 1822-1901.
Augustus, b. 7 Jan 1825 Saco ME, d. 3 Dec 1869, m. 17 Oct 1860 Saco ME Mary A. Barrows, b. ? d. 19 Aug 1863. In Biddeford ME 1850.

Sarah Leah, b. 5 Jun 1826, d. 25 Jun 1893.

Sources: Saco ME census 1810, 1820, 1830, 1840, 1850, 1860, 1880. Biddeford ME census 1850. ME 1880 census index. VR Saco ME, SA/ME. Y3, R10g, P82k, Carle Sawyer rec.

131. **MARK$^6$ SAWYER** [see 58], b. 13 Dec 1799 Saco ME, d. 15 Apr 1865 Saco ME, m. 21 Apr 1825 Saco ME Asenath Patterson, b. 27 Mar 1803 d.14 Jul 1866, dau. Abraham and Sarah (Sawyer) Patterson. Sea captain, farmer.

Cordelia, b. 1827, m. George Titcomb.
262 Horace Bacon$^7$, Rev., 1830-1893.
Sarah M., b. 1832, m. Edward Styles of Saco ME.
263 Greenleaf$^7$, 1835-1907.
Charles Evans, b. 1846 Saco ME, m.(1) Sarah E. Trickey of Saco ME, b. 1849, dau. Noah and Margery (Shaw) Trickey; m.(2) Almeda H. Ladd of Saco ME, b. 1845 d. 28 Mar 1910, dau. Andrew and Ann (Dearborn) Ladd. In Saco ME 1880. CH: Lena Margaret, b. 1877.

Sources: Saco ME census 1830, 1840, 1850, 1880. VR Saco ME, SA/ME. L30, P82k, F11, P69, S1.

132. **NOAH$^6$ SAWYER** [see 58], b. 20 Nov 1800 Saco ME, d. 22 Aug 1862 Saco ME, m. 27 Jan 1825 Saco ME Hannah Jacobs, b. 21 Dec 1807 d. 1885, dau. Moses and Mary Jacobs. War of 1812. Appointed guardian of brother Charles C., 1823. Wid. w/son Alonzo 1880.

Mary E., b. 2 Jul 1826.
Emily, b. 7 Aug 1828, d. 26 Oct 1828.
Marshall, b. 24 Apr 1830 Saco ME, d. 8 Dec 1831.
264 Noah$^7$, 1832-1899.
Louisa, b. 18 Jun 1835, d. 1863.
Dorcas A., b. 13 Nov 1837, d. 1867.
Melinda, b. 18 Oct 1840, d. 7 Mar 1887, m. 10 Feb 1864 Boston MA Enoch Lord.
265 Alonzo$^7$, 1843-1919.
Hannah, b. 1846, d. 4 Oct 1862.
266 Orrin$^7$, 1850-1920.

Sources: Saco ME census 1830, 1840, 1850, 1880. VR Saco ME, SA/ME, SA/MA. P82k, S1, D6.

133. **CHARLES C.$^6$ SAWYER** [see 58], b. 25 Mar 1805 Saco ME, d. 27 Sep 1864 Portland ME, m.(1) 16 Dec 1824 Saco ME Mary Maxwell of Biddeford ME, b. Sep 1806 d. 28 Apr 1860; m.(2) 24 Oct 1861 Boston MA Mary (Gardner) Averill of Springfield MA, b. 1824 d. 30 Jun 1895, wid. of Daniel, dau. Gideon and Melinda Gardner. B/S/land in Standish ME 1841. Lumberman. He bur. in Eastern Cem., Portland ME.

Horatio, b. 2 May 1825, d. 6 Dec 1838.
Leah, b. 2 Sep 1827.
Charles, b. 20 Jan 1829 Saco ME, m. Dorcas O. Jordan, b. ca. 1818 d. 19 May 1883. In Saco ME 1850.
Mary P., b. 25 Jun 1832, d. 7 Jun 1837.
Miranda P., b. 25 Jan 1836, d. 25 Apr 1864, m. 29 Sep 1858 Alonzo L. Berry.
Mary E., b. 13 Dec 1840, d. 25 Jul 1842.
267 Albert C.$^7$, b. 1844.

Sources: Saco ME census 1830, 1840, 1850. VR Saco ME. P82k, R10g, S1, M5, B99.

134. **AMOS B.[6] SAWYER** [see 59], b. 20 Jan 1795 Hopkinton NH, d. 12 Jun 1882 Concord NH, m. 18 Feb 1819 Martha Austin of Concord NH, b. 1792 d. 3 Dec 1886, dau. Andrew and Martha (Carter) Austin. Farmer. In Hopkinton NH 1820, Concord NH 1827.

Daughter, b. 1819.
268 John[7], 1821-1908.
Son, b. (1820-1825).
Mary, b. Oct 1833, d. 30 Apr 1880, unm.
Daughter, b. (1835-1840).

Sources: Hopkinton NH census 1820. Concord NH census 1840, 1850, 1860, 1880.

135. **JOHN[6] SAWYER** [see 59], b. Jun 1798 Hopkinton NH, d. 1 Oct 1888 Concord NH, m.(1) 6 May 1833 Phebe C. Elliot, b. 1801; m.(2) Hannah H. Hale of Franklin NH, b. 8 Dec 1823 d. 25 May 1899. Representative 1853.

Daughter, b. (1835-1840).
Warren P., b. ca. 1836 Concord NH.

Sources: Concord NH census 1840, 1850, 1860, 1870. B68.

136. **SAMUEL[6] SAWYER** [see 60], b. 8 May 1781 Newbury MA, d. 23 Nov 1815 Newbury MA, m. 17 Nov 1803 Newbury MA Sarah Chase of Sandown NH, b. 1786 d. 5 Dec 1859. Wid. in Newbury MA 1820, 1840; w/son in Bradford MA 1850.

Lydia Morse, b. 22 Aug 1804.
Alice Bartlett, b. 2 Oct 1805, m. 1839 Humphrey Hoyt.
Sarah, b. 25 Nov 1807, m. 1831 James M. Morse of Boston MA.
269 Samuel Chase[7], b. 1811.
Mary Elizabeth, b. 20 Apr 1813, d. 6 Mar 1818.

Sources: Newbury MA census 1810, 1820, 1840. Bradford MA census 1850. VR Newbury MA, Hampstead NH.

137. **EDMUND[6] SAWYER** [see 62], b. 2 Sep 1759 Hampstead NH, d. 20 Feb 1827 Warner NH, m. 30 Sep 1784 Mehitable (Mittie) Morrell of Warner NH, b. 3 Sep 1765 d. 25 Dec 1834 Henniker NH. Revolutionary War: Enl. 20 Jul 1777 in Webster's Company, Stickney's Regiment, fought at Bennington VT and Long Island NY.

Anna, b. 9 Jan 1790.
270 Jacob[7], 1794-1865.
Judith, b. 11 Feb 1796, m. 25 Dec 1817 Eliot Badger.
Daniel, Rev., b. 15 Mar 1797 Warner NH, d. 24 Aug 1888 Hopkinton NH, m. 21 May 1832 Nancy Johnson of Warner NH, b. 29 Dec 1802 d. 23 Mar 1892,dau. William Johnson. Minister, preached in Augusta ME, Portland ME, Boston MA, Medford MA, and Quincy MA. CH: Cornelia Maria, b. 1836, d. 4 Feb 1857, m. John Parker of Nashua NH.
Polly, b. 2 Jan 1799.
271 Edmund[7], 1802-1856.
Samuel Woods, b. 27 Mar 1804 Warner NH, d. 24 Nov 1804.
Mittie (Mehitable), b. 12 Sep 1805, m. 14 Nov 1832 Stephen K. Hoyt.
Dorcas, b. 7 Dec 1807, d. 14 Mar 1810.
Dorcas, b. 29 Nov 1810.

Sources: Warner NH census 1800,1810,1820. Lempster NH census 1850. Merrimac NH census 1860. H83, N11, N10, N6, H27, N9. Bonita Folck rec.

138. **MOSES⁶ SAWYER** [see 62], b. 27 Feb 1767 Hampstead NH, m.(1) 21 Oct 1783 Warner NH Lydia Rowell, b. ?; m.(2) 23 Apr 1799 Lavinia Kelly of Warner NH, b. ?.

Lavinia Bailey, b. 24 Jan 1800, m. 25 Oct 1818 Amos Flood.

272 Joseph[7], b. 1802.

Lois, b. 16 Sep 1804.

Deborah Page, b. 13 Sep 1807.

Moses, b. 9 Apr 1812 Warner NH, m. Anna _____, b. 1802. In Boscawen NH 1840. In Concord NH insane asylum 1860. CH: Mary B., b. 1843.

Judith Kelly, b. May 1818.

Sources: Warner NH census 1790, 1800, 1810, 1820, 1830, 1840. Boscawen NH census 1840, 1850. Concord NH census 1860. VR Warner NH.

139. **JOSEPH[6] SAWYER** [see 62], b. 2 Feb 1771 Hampstead NH, d. 30 Jul 1856 Newport NH, m. 20 Jun 1796 Dunbarton NH Ruth Page of Dunbarton NH, b. 7 Oct 1776 d. 18 Nov 1842. In Newport NH 1796.

Lydia P., b. 27 Nov 1799, m. Rev. John Wilcox.

William, b. 10 May 1803, d. 10 Feb 1805.

Edmund, b. 22 Dec 1805 Newport NH, d. insane, unm.

Laura, b. 30 Aug 1807, d. 6 Jun 1877, m.(1) Calvin Hurd, m.(2) 13 Dec 1844 Stoddard Tower.

273 Joseph[7], 1809-1857.

Uriah, b. 18 May 1813 Newport NH, m. Marilla Gunnison of Goshen NH, b. 1817. Owned a tannery in Goshen NH. Went to Broadhead WI. CH: Ellen M., b. 1838, m. 1 Oct 1857 Oliver Parker; Mary M., b. 1847; Annah, b. ?, d. at 18 yrs.

274 Langdon[7], 1815-1879.

275 John B.[7], b. 1817. Went to Wisconsin.

276 Benjamin F.[7], 1819-1879. Went to California.

Sources: Newport NH census 1800, 1810, 1820, 1830, 1840, 1850. Goshen NH census 1850. W33, C16, N14, N6, N3.

140. **RICHARD KELLY[6] SAWYER** [see 62], b. 25 Jun 1779 Warner NH, d. Oct 1838 Alexandria NH, m. 21 Sep 1800 Salisbury NH Mary B. Bean of Warner NH b. 6 Jun 1782 d. May 1860, dau. Phineas and Judith (Snow) Bean of Boscawen NH.

Lois, b. 19 Dec 1801 Newport NH, d. Jun 1862, m. 1827 William Abbott.

277 Phineas B.[7],1804-1853.

278 Jonathan B.[7], 1806-1848.

279 Moses[7], 1807-1876. Went to Iowa.

Ann C., b. 2 Sep 1809 Warner NH, d. Jan 1857, m. Joseph Sawyer.

Lorenda, b. 6 Feb 1813 Hill NH, d. Dec 1865, m. Ezekiel Sanborn.

Judith, b. 3 Jan 1818 Sanbornton NH, d. Dec 1865, m. Zackariah Scribner.

Mary E., b. 20 Oct 1823 Alexandria NH, m. 29 Apr 1847 Kendrick Prescott.

Elizabeth, b. ?, m. 1852 John Colgon.

Sources: Newport NH census 1810. Sanbornton NH census 1820. Alexandria NH census 1830. R34, W33, J3, N5, B40.

141. **SAMUEL[6] SAWYER** [see 63], b. 31 Jul 1771 Hampstead NH, d. 22 Jun 1848 Francestown NH, m.(1) 30 Dec 1794 New Boston NH Susannah Reed of Litchfield NH, b. 1774 d. 17 Jan 1815, dau. Zadoc Reed; m.(2) 22 May 1816 Eleanor Orr of Bedford NH, b. 1779 d. 21 Feb 1841, dau. Daniel Orr. On Bedford NH tax list 1817. In Goffstown NH, Antrim NH 1810, Bedford NH 1820. He bur. on Meeting House Hill, Francestown NH.

Lucy M., b. 23 Nov 1795, d. 2 Apr 1867, m. 11 Apr 1815 Thomas Carr.
Sally L., b. 24 Dec 1797, d. 9 Aug 1800.
Zadoc R., b. 3 Oct 1799, d. 10 Aug 1800.
Sally L., b. 24 Sep 1802, d. 2 Jan 1858, m. Samuel Murch of Quincy MA.
Maria N., b. 25 Aug 1804, d. 5 Mar 1876, unm.
280 William Reed[7], 1806-1897.
Abigail P., b. 3 Dec 1808, d. 29 Feb 1812 Francestown NH.
Mary W., b. 8 Jan 1810, m. 1834 Francis Merrion of Boston MA.
Nathaniel Nurse, b. 8 Jun 1812 Antrim NH, d. 18 Apr 1851 Windsor NH, m. 15 Mar 1842 Hillsboro NH Sally Bagley of Windsor NH, b. 1802. In Seminole War 3 years and wounded. In Windsor NH 1842.
281 George O.[7], b. 1818.
Jonathan M., b. 22 Mar 1820 Bedford NH, d. Oct 1873 Sterling MA, m. 23 Jul 1850 Boston MA Rebecca Lund of Milford NH, b. 1821. Farmer. In Boston MA (Ward 5) 1850, Sterling MA 1855. CH: Maria Alma, b. 17 Mar 1855, m. 22 Jun 1876 Westboro MA John P. Forbes.

Sources: Antrim NH census 1810. Bedford NH census 1820, 1830, 1840. Windsor NH census 1850. Boston (Ward 5) MA census 1850. VR Chelsea MA, SA/MA. L29, C6, C54, N9, N14.

142. **ENOCH[6] SAWYER** [see 63], b. 21 Feb 1777 Goffstown NH, d. 5 Mar 1840 Antrim NH, m. 1 Sep 1802 Lucy Simonds, b. 2 Jan 1784 d. 7 Jun 1853. Cooper. He bur. in Center Cem., Antrim NH. Wid. w/son Rodney 1830-1850.
282 Rodney[7], 1804-1886.
283 Reuben M.[7], 1805-1878.
284 Edmund M.[7], 1807-1894.
Enoch, b. 27 Aug 1812 Antrim NH, d. 4 Jun 1884 Hillsboro NH, m. 10 Dec 1835 Jemima Jones, b. 1807 d. 12 Sep 1888, dau. Benjamin and Polly (Adams) Jones. Farmer. In Hillsboro NH 1840-1870; Selectman for two years. CH: Lucy Emerline, b. 24 Apr 1838, d. 29 Dec 1902, m. 15 Jan 1867 Sylvester Atwood.
John Avril, b. 23 Apr 1818 Antrim NH, d. 12 May 1890 Leavenworth County KS, m. 1 Apr 1847 Antrim NH Betsey Robinson of Antrim NH, b. 8 Jan 1823 d. 8 Jul 1866. Blacksmith. In Francestown NH 1840, Stoddard NH 1850, Peterborough NH 1853. CH: Helen, b. 4 Apr 1848, d. 8 Jul 1848; Edward B., b. 5 Aug 1853, d. 29 Jul 1861; Nancy Emma, b. 9 Nov 1858, d. 5 Feb 1881, m. 7 Mar 1877 Kansas Joseph A. McCune.
Lucretia T., b. 9 Mar 1821, d. 2 Nov 1865, unm.

Sources: Antrim NH census 1810, 1820, 1830, 1840, 1850. Hillsboro NH census 1840, 1850, 1860, 1870. Francestown NH census 1840. Stoddard NH census 1850. L29, C54,N9, H93, Eleanor Robinson rec.

143. **TRISTRAM[6] SAWYER** [see 63], b. 31 Dec 1780 Goffstown NH, d. 11 Aug 1859 Hillsboro NH, m. Mar 1805 Antrim NH Mary Ann Templeton of Hillsboro NH, b. 14 Apr 1781 d. 22 Feb 1869. Carpenter. In Antrim NH 1794. Town Moderator for Antrim NH 1809. Deacon of Presbyterian Church 1816. Selectman for Antrim NH 1822. Wid. in Hillsboro NH 1860. Note: Death record says Tristram was b. in Derry NH.
285 Silas N.[7], 1805-1876.
Mary Ann, b. 14 Sep 1806, d. 4 Sep 1807.
Mary W., b. 5 Jun 1808, d. 23 Jul 1810.
Elizabeth, b. 17 Sep 1809, m. 24 May 1836 Andrew Mack of Orange MA.
Samuel, b. 8 May 1811, d. 3 Jul 1813.
Jane, b. 26 Dec 1812, d. 21 Feb 1899, m. 1 Jun 1842 Warren Foster.

Samuel, b. 30 Jun 1813, d.y.
Harriet N., b. 6 Aug 1814, d. 22 Feb 1863, unm.
286 John Nichols$^7$, 1816-1881.
Abby Whiton, b. 28 Dec 1817, m. 9 Dec 1847 John S. Burt.
Tristram, b. 3 Nov 1819 Antrim NH, d. 24 Jul 1872 Keene NH, m. 13 Apr 1848 Sarah J. Morrison of Henniker NH, b. 17 Sep 1823 d. 18 Nov 1871, dau. Samuel and Betsey (Goss) Morrison. Tristram and brother Edmund made reed organs and melodeons. He bur. Henniker NH. CH: Jesse Marion, b. 8 Dec 1852, m. 28 Nov 1876 Natick MA Frank E. Edwards.
287 Edmund$^7$, 1821-1873.
Frances Christie, b. 5 Oct 1825, d. 6 Sep 1913 Orange MA, unm.
Sources: Antrim NH 1810,1820, 1830. Hillsboro NH census 1840, 1850. 1860. Keene NH census 1870. L29, C54, N9, S31, N6.

144. **EDMUND$^6$ SAWYER** [see 63], b. 17 Sep 1782 Goffstown NH, d. 21 Dec 1873 Stockbridge VT, m. 14 Feb 1808 Royalton VT Jane Taggart of Hillsboro NH, b. 19 May 1782 d. 8 Jan 1874, dau. Joseph and Lydia Taggart. Joiner. In Antrim NH 1810, Stockbridge VT 1820, Nashua NH 1860.
288 Mark Woodbury$^7$, 1808-1871. Went to Illinois.
289 Joseph Taggart$^7$, b. 1810.
Abigail Martin, b. 8 Feb 1812, d. 1 Feb 1813.
Lydia Taggart, b. 19 Jan 1816.
Levi Parsons, b. 11 Nov 1819 Stockbridge VT, d. 28 Apr 1868 Nashua NH, m.(1) Elizabeth L. ____, b. ?; m.(2) 10 Jun 1858 Boston MA Susan E. Merriam of Boston MA, b. 29 Mar 1839 d. 14 Feb 1890, dau. Francis B. and Mary V. (Sawyer) Merriam. Dartmouth College graduate. Physician. Taught at Royalton Academy VT 1846-47. Civil War: Assistant Surgeon, 13th Regular NH Volunteer Infantry. CH: Mary Lizzie, b. 18 Nov 1865.
Cephas Washburn, b. 25 Feb 1825 Stockbridge VT, d. 14 Apr 1899 Stockbridge VT, m. 27 Oct 1853 Jefferson OH Anna R. Pengry of Mt. Holly VT, b. 6 Dec 1833, dau. Asabel and Lydia (Parker) Pengry. Farmer. CH: Ella May, b. 1 May 1856, m. 9 Oct 1878 George G. Page; Alice Adella, b. 2 Sep 1860 d. 25 Apr 1872; Hattie Vira, b. 27 May 1865, m. 29 Jun 1892 George E. Miner; Florence Almira, b. 17 Nov 1874, m. 2 Apr 1896 James B. Sargent.
Reuben Marsh, b. 5 Nov 1828 Stockbridge VT, d. 5 May 1898 Nashua NH, m. 17 Jun 1856 Almira Bowers of Hancock NH, b. 14 Oct 1832 d. 17 Jul 1906, dau. Mark and Selina (Foster) Bowers. Grocer. Councilman. In Nashua NH 1848. CH: Frank M., b. 21 Apr 1861, d. 18 Jul 1879.
Sources: Antrim NH census 1810. Stockbridge VT census 1820, 1830, 1840, 1850. Nashua NH census 1860, 1870. VR Stockbridge VT, SA/NH, SA/VT. L29, P43, P10, W62, P27, C18.

145. **JOSIAH$^6$ SAWYER** [see 64], b. 13 Dec 1760 So. Hampton NH, d. 14 Aug 1833 Gilford NH, m. 7 Mar 1784 of Gilmanton NH Martha Eastman of Gilmanton NH, b. 30 Jul 1760 d. 12 Mar 1841. Revolutionary War: Enl. from Deerfield NH in Captain S. Marston's Company, Colonel Waldron's Regiment. Will dated 4 Apr 1831. In Gilmanton NH 1790, Gilford NH 1820.
290 Josiah$^7$, 1785-1848.
Patty, b. 24 Nov 1787, d. 11 Oct 1819.
Miriam, b. 3 Dec 1789, d. 21 Mar 1831, m. 18 Mar 1810 Enoch Small.
Hannah, b. 21 Apr 1793, m. 19 Nov 1809 Reuben Leavitt.
291 Isaac Eastman$^7$, 1795-1850.

Isreal, b. 19 Jan 1797, d. 23 Mar 1797.
Sally, b. 24 Mar 1798, d. 1 Nov 1825.
John, b. 5 Aug 1800 Gilmanton NH.
292 Isreal$^7$, 1803-1843.
Sources: Gilmanton NH census 1790, 1810. Gilford NH census 1820, 1830. VR Gilmanton NH. N14, S80, N9, N11, P82i.

146. **JEREMIAH$^6$ SAWYER** [see 64], b. 1764 So. Hampton NH, d. 18 Mar 1833 Gilmanton NH, m. 11 Feb 1790 Brentwood NH Meribah Purrington, b. ? d. bef. 9 May 1837. In Deerfield NH 1776, Gilmanton NH 1798. He bur. in Belmont Cem., Gilmanton NH.
Anna, b. 22 Apr 1791.
Meribah, b. 13 Jan 1793, d. 1 Aug 1864.
293 John$^7$, 1794-1868.
294 Jeremiah$^7$, 1797-1857.
Lydia, b. 10 Apr 1798, m. 27 Mar 1825 Abner Jones of Epping NH.
Joshua, b. 2 May 1802 Gilmanton NH, m. 4 Mar 1830 Gilmanton NH Asenath M. Greene, b. 3 Jan 1809, dau. Jacob and Sally (Dow) Greene. CH: Anne, b. 1837, m. 27 Feb 1859 Robert C. Davis, Amesbury MA.
295 James$^7$, 1805-1864.
Polly, b. 2 Jan 1808, m. 25 Dec 1844 Nathan Clay of Thornton NH.
296 David$^7$, 1810-1887.
Sources: Gilmanton NH census 1810, 1830, 1850, 1860. VR Gilmanton NH. P82i, N14, R34, C45.

147. **DAVID$^6$ SAWYER** .[see 64], b. 14 Apr 1766 in NH, d. 21 Aug? 1845 Lee NH, m.(1) Hannah Palmer, b. 2 Feb 1765, dau. Joseph and Lydia (Glidden) Palmer; m.(2) 27 Aug 1806 Northwood NH Mary Knowles of Northwood NH, b. 27 Sep 1777 d. 1826, dau. Simeon and Deborah (Palmer) Knowles; m.(3) 12 Jul 1830 Durham NH Susan Chesley, b. 9 Jun 1776 d. 12 Feb 1871, dau. Benjamin and Deborah (Randall) Chesley. Clergyman. Surveyor of Highways for Deerfield NH 1803. Will dated 7 Apr 1835.
297 David$^7$, b. 1790.
298 Josiah$^7$, 1799-1881.
299 John$^7$, 1801-1878.
Hannah, b. ?, m. John Porter.
Luella, b. ?, m. _____ Conklin of Exeter NH.
300 Jefferson$^7$, 1817-1894.
Sources: Deerfield NH census 1790, 1800, 1810, 1820. Lee NH census 1830, 1840. VR Newmarket NH. P82i, H17, S68, H89.

148. **JOHN$^6$ SAWYER** [see 64], b. 30 Apr 1771 South Hampton NH, d. 23 Aug 1840 Andover NH, m. 2 Nov 1797 Mercy Brown, b. 17 Mar 1774 d. 27 Feb 1860, dau. Abba and Elizabeth (Leavitt) Brown. In Andover NH 1800, Franklin NH 1830. He bur. in Franklin NH.
John, b. 29 Apr 1798 Franklin NH, m.(1) 24 Nov 1825 Andover NH Mary F. Scribner, b. 1807; m.(2) 5 Jul 1865 Groton MA Frances B. (Trefry) Warner of Franklin NH, b. ?, dau. Jonas and Susannah Trefry. Shoemaker. In Clinton MA 1850. CH: Lucile E., b. 1846, m. 4 Jul 1863 Roxbury MA James H. Downs.
Betsey, b. 28 Jan 1802, d. 12 Nov 1870, m. 6 Dec 1824 James Simonds. [R34] says she m. James Morrison Jr. in Sanbornton NH.
Mercy, b. 12 Oct 1805, d. 24 Aug 1884, m. 13 Jan 1831 John Tilton.
301 Josiah$^7$, 1808-1880.

Moses, b. 15 Mar 1811, d. 17 Aug 1813. Joanna, b. 5 Mar 1815, d. 22 Mar 1849, m. 21 May 1839 Chandler Connor. Went to Illinois.

Moses, b. 28 Jan 1819, d. Apr 1846.

Sources: Andover NH census 1800, 1810, 1820. Franklin NH census 1830, 1840. Clinton MA census 1850. VR SA/MA. E2, N14, B91, N10, R34.

149. **ISREAL C.⁶ SAWYER** [see 64], b. 9 Jun 1773 So. Hampton NH, d. 184? Atkinson ME, m. 28 Feb 1797 Phebe Prescott of Raymond NH, b. 13 Sep 1775, dau. Ebenezer and Phebe (Eastman) Prescott.

302 Coffin$^7$, 1795-1838.

Lydia, b. 6 Dec 1799, d. 26 Apr 1802.

Phebe, b. 22 Feb 1802, d. 27 Jan 1865 East Corinth ME.

Ebenezer Prescott, b. 7 Feb 1804, d. 10 Feb 1832, unm.

Isreal, b. 27 Oct 1806, d. 27 Oct 1812.

David, b. 5 Mar 1809 Deerfield NH. In Atkinson ME.

303 Jeremiah E.$^7$, 1812-1852.

304 John C.$^7$, 1815-1872.

305 Tristram B.$^7$, 1822-1891.

Sources: Deerfield NH census 1800, 1810, 1820. Atkinson ME census 1830, 1840. C58, P76, N16, Coffin Sawyer rec.

150. **WILLIAM$^6$ SAWYER** [see 66], b. 8 Dec 1776 So. Hampton NH, d. 26 Nov 1824 Gilmanton NH, m. 18 Dec 1799 Molly Lane, b. 22 Feb 1778 d. 27 Jan 1835, dau. Noah and Mchitable (Burnham) Lane. Surveyor of Highways for Deerfield NH 1799, 1802, 1803; for Gilmanton NH 1815. Assessor, 1806. Selectman for Gilmanton NH 1819. Molly appointed administrator of William's estate 1825. Jabez Page appointed guardian of Judith, Noah, Timothy, Sally, and "Anne Elizabeth", 1832. Wid. w/son William 1830.

Thomas Jefferson, b. 13 Mar 1803 Deerfield NH. In Gilmanton NH 1825.

306 William$^7$, 1804-1857.

Eunice, b. 21 Mar 1806, m. 19 Mar 1826 Gilman D. Hunt.

Jonathan, b. 14 Nov 1807 Deerfield NH, d. 15 Nov 1831 Gilmanton NH.

Mary, b. 1812, d. 27 Sep 1831.

Sarah, b. 23 Oct 1813.

Judith, b. ?.

307 Noah$^7$, b. 1817.

308 Timothy Upham$^7$, b. 1819.

Elizabeth, b. 1 Sep 1821, m. 1 Jan 1843 Belmont NH Alfred C. Jacobs.

Sources: Deerfield NH census 1800, 1810. Gilmanton NH census 1820, 1830. VR Gilmanton NH. G9, N14, C58, N14,P82i, N6.

151. **ISREAL$^6$ SAWYER** [see 66], b. 17 Jul 1778 So. Hampton NH, d. 31 Jul 1831 W. Alton NH, m. 21 Oct 1813 Gilford NH Nancy Small of Alton NH, b. 2 Apr 1778 d. 6 Dec 1870, dau. Samuel Small of Gilmanton NH.

Sally, b. 1813, d. 24 Apr 1878, m. 29 Dec 1844 John Ricker.

Isreal, b. 10 Nov 1816 Gilmanton NH, d. 20 Nov 1895 Alton NH, m.(1) Matilda _____, b. ?; m.(2) 29 Apr 1859 (div. Dec 1863) Emily L. Smith, b. 1810. CH: Elvira Amanda, b. 16 Nov 1850, m. 12 May 1881 William A. Willard.

Sources: Gilmanton NH census 1810. Alton NH census 1830, 1860. 1870. VR Gilford NH, SA/NH. N6, N9, N10, N14.

152. **JOHN⁶ SAWYER** [see 67], b. 25 Oct 1772 Salisbury MA, d. 2 Sep 1850 So. Hampton NH, m.(1) 15 Aug 1799 Salisbury MA Betsey Creasey, b. ? d. 5 Apr 1800; m. (2)12 May 1804 Salisbury MA Hannah Perkins of Raymond NH, b. 1780 d. 1 Jun 1860.

John, b. 21 Apr 1805 Salisbury MA, d. 17 Mar 1850 So. Hampton NH, m. 10 Jan 1833 So. Hampton NH Ann Perkins of So. Hampton NH, b. ?. CH: Ann, b. 6 Apr 1835; Hannah Perkins, b. 13 Nov 1836, m. 10 Feb 1858 Charles Perry.

309 Benjamin[7], 1807-1895.

310 Thomas[7], 1809-1894.

Sources: So. Hampton NH census 1810, 1820, 1830, 1840, 1850. VR Salisbury MA. H84, P82g, T20.

153. **JEREMIAH[6] SAWYER** [see 67], b. 19 May 1777 Salisbury MA, d. 19 Apr 1854 Salisbury MA, m. 1 Aug 1804 Salisbury MA Betsey Fitts, b. 23 Feb 1780, dau. Joseph and Ruhmah (Judkins) Fitts. Farmer.

311 Enoch[7], b. 1806.

Moses Judkins, b. 26 Oct 1808 Salisbury MA, m. 22 Aug 1854 Salisbury MA Martha True Page of Gilmanton NH, b. 15 Sep 1804, dau. Winslow and Martha (True) Page.

Elizabeth, b. 15 Feb 1811.

312 Josiah[7], 1813-1882.

Sarah, b. 25 Jan 1816, m. Rev. William Douglas of Rhode Island.

313 Jeremiah Hayden[7], b. 1823.

Sources: Newburyport MA census 1800. Salisbury MA census 1810, 1820, 1830, 1840, 1850. VR Newburyport MA, Salisbury MA, SA/MA. F19, C16, H84.

154. **RICHARD[6] SAWYER** [see 68], b. 14 Dec 1776 So. Hampton NH, d. 28 Mar 1853 Vershire VT, m. 14 Feb 1803 Hampstead NH Anna Poore of Hampstead NH, b. 9 Jun 1777 d. 22 May 1865, dau. David and Phebe (Carleton) Poore. Farmer. In Corinth VT 1820, Vershire VT 1840.

Atalus, b. 17 Jan 1804, d. 26 Jul 1850, unm.

Brydone, b. 23 Jun 1805, d. 10 Apr 1831, unm.

Betsey, b. 26 Sep 1806, d. 23 Jul 1835, unm.

Marion, b. 23 Feb 1809, d. 29 Oct 1828, unm.

314 Mayo Greenleaf[7], 1810-1845.

Mary P., b. 15 Feb 1814, d. 5 Jun 1848, m. 1 Feb 1838 Alfred Lathrop.

Ann, b. 2 Nov 1815, d. 21 Nov 1842, m. 23 May 1839 Erastus Dickenson.

Susan, b. 5 Apr 1817, m. 3 Feb 1840 John Bragg.

Sarah, b. 12 Jan 1819, d. 25 Dec 1864, unm.

Caroline, b. 11 Feb 1821, unm.

Sources: Corinth VT census 1810, 1820. Vershire VT census 1840, 1850. VR Hampstead NH, SA/VT. H84, P59, D41.

155. **PLANT[6] SAWYER** [see 68], b. 19 Apr 1779 So. Hampton NH, d. 28 Feb 1840 Corinth VT, m. Ruth Eastman of Benton NH, b. 26 Jul 1785 d. 14 Jan 1864, dau. Obediah and Mehitable (Merrill) Eastman. Town Representative. He bur. in Corinth Center VT.

Ira, b. 6 Nov 1808, d. 26 Nov 1822.

Rosilla, b. 19 Aug 1812, m. Horace Richardson.

315 Otis[7], 1813-1882.

Almira, b. 3 Mar 1815, d. 7 Mar 1817.

316 Dana M.[7], 1817-1856.

Almira, b. 26 Sep 1819, m. 2 Aug 1838 Daniel Fitts of Washington VT.

Emeline, b. 9 Jan 1822, m. 28 Oct 1841 Hylas Dickey of Manchester NH.
Lucinda, b. 27 Sep 1826, m. 29 Mar 1849 Amos P. Collins.
317 Moreau$^7$, b. 1829.
Sources: Corinth VT census 1810, 1820. VR Newburyport MA. H84, R21.

156. **MOSES$^6$ SAWYER** [see 69], b. 11 Mar 1776 South Hampton NH, d. 26 Aug 1847 Ipswich MA, m. 6 Jul 1802 Boscawen NH Fanny Kimball, b. 9 Aug 1776 d. 13 May 1854. Dartmouth College 1799. Minister and teacher. Preached in Henniker NH 1802-1806, Congregational churches in Boscawen NH, Scarboro ME, Gloucester MA, and Saugus MA.
Caroline F., b. 28 May 1804, m. 5 Sep 1826 Rev. Daniel Fitz of Derry NH.
Livona, b. 18 May 1806, m. 1 Nov 1844 Capt. C. T. Bagley of Boston MA.
Cassandra, b. 24 Jun 1809, d. 23 Jun 1840, m. Rev. Jesse Lockwood.
Moses Kimball, b. 7 Jul 1812 Henniker NH, d. Jan 1875 Portland ME, m. 7 Oct 1844 Ipswich MA Caroline Kimball of Boscawen NH, b. 1820, dau. Benjamin T. Kimball. Merchant, currier. B/S/land in Portland ME 1859-1861. In Peabody MA, Concord NH. In Portland ME 1860, 1870. CH: Mary Frances, b. 23 Jul 1846; Louisa Kimball, b. 25 Aug 1847 Salisbury MA. Note: VR SA/MA says that Moses and Caroline were m. in Gloucester MA.
Sources: Henniker NH census 1810, 1820. Danvers MA census 1850. Portland ME census 1860, 1870. Ipswich MA, VR SA/MA, SA/ME. C59, M54, R10a, N6.

157. **ISAAC FITTS$^6$ SAWYER** [see 69], b. 9 Mar 1778 So. Hampton NH, d. 1 Feb 1846 Salisbury NH, m.(1) Apr 1800 Rebecca Pettengil of Salisbury NH, b. 25 Aug 1799 d. 9 Mar 1834; m.(2) 26 Dec 1837 Henniker NH Mehitable Colby of Bradford NH, b. 1792 d. 23 Apr 1847. Farmer.
Hannah, b. 3 Jan 1801, d. 31 Jan 1833, m. 28 Feb 1827 Royal Choate.
Fanny, b. 1 May 1803, d. 27 Apr 1887, m. 9 Feb 1831 Uri Perley.
David, b. 13 Jan 1806, d. 27 Apr 1827 Concord NH, unm.
Amanda Malvina, b. 21 Feb 1809, d. 19 Sep 1882, m. Thomas Wilson. Note: Gravestone in Salisbury NH says she was b. 14 Feb 1808 d. 13 Apr 1861.
318 Isaac Newton$^7$, 1811-1894.
Moses, b. 14 Sep 1813, d. 4 Nov 1841, unm.
319 Nathaniel$^7$, 1815-1885.
320 Daniel Fitts$^7$, 1820-1878.
321 Francis Brown$^7$, 1823-1907.
Sources: Salisbury NH census 1800, 1810, 1820, 1830, 1840. VR So. Hampton NH, Salisbury NH. N9, A31, P33, L29, B68.

158. **NATHANIEL$^6$ SAWYER** [see 69], b. 10 Apr 1784 Salisbury NH, d. 3 Oct 1853, m. 12 Sep 1821 Pamelia (Anderson) Bacon, b. ? d. 14 Mar 1886. Dartmouth College 1805. Lawyer. In Lexington KY, Chillicothe OH, and Cincinnati OH 1839.
Mary Ann, b. 27 Dec 1822, d. 16 Mar 1912, m. 25 May 1841 Ohio Henry O. Hotchkiss.
Dewitt Clinton, b. 25 Jul 1825, d. 25 Sep 1899, m. 1 Nov 1854 Catherine M. Smith, b. ?. Went to Ohio.
Sally Frances, b. 29 Dec 1829, m.(1) 5 Jun 1849 William Eliot, m.(2) 5 Apr 1859 Lebeus C. Chapin.
Nathaniel Isaac, b. 29 Oct 1832, m. 9 Jan 1861 Helen Wingate, b. ?. Went to Kentucky.
Sources: N5.

159. **GEORGE$^{6}$ SAWYER** [see 70], b. 10 Mar 1776 Newbury MA, d. 16 Feb 1847, m.(1) 4 Feb 1790 Judith Boardman of Salisbury MA, b. ? d. 3 Jan 1812; m.(2) 19 Dec 1822 Sarah Challis, b ?. W/son Joshua T. in 1840.

322 Matthias Plant$^{7}$, 1797-1879.

323 Moses Little$^{7}$, b. 1799.

William, b. 22 Aug 1801, d. at sea, unm.

George, b. 27 Nov 1805, d. at sea, unm.

Miriam, b. 11 Jul 1803.

Joshua Tilton, b. 11 Nov 1810 Salisbury MA, d. 7 Feb 1877 Pembroke NH, m. 18 Dec 1842 Salisbury MA Ann B. Cockran of Pembroke NH, b. 18 Mar 1813 d. 13 Feb 1879. Carpenter. In Suncook NH, Pembroke NH 1850, Concord NH 1870. CH: Quincy C., b. 23 May 1844, d. 3 Apr 1857; Sarah Ann, b. 4 Sep 1845, m. 19 Nov 1868 Milan D. Cummings; Caroline, b. 3 Mar 1849, d. 15 Mar 1849; Mary Little, b. 22 Nov 1851, d. 18 Aug 1852.

Sources: Salisbury MA census 1800, 1810, 1840. Pembroke NH census 1850, 1860. Concord NH census 1870. VR Newbury MA, Salisbury MA, SA/MA. L29, E20, H84, M39, N9, N6.

160. **MOSES$^{6}$ SAWYER** [see 72], b. 1 Dec 1795 So. Hampton NH, d. 6 Dec 1894 Corinth VT, m.(1) Susan Taplin, b. 1798 d. 24 Dec 1832; m.(2) 17 Feb 1835 Rebecca Hale, b. 1804 d. 14 Jan 1864.

Sarah Ann, b. 1823, d. 2 May 1824.

Mattison, b. 5 Mar 1825 Corinth VT.

324 Elbridge G.$^{7}$, b. 1827.

Sources: Corinth VT census 1830, 1840, 1850. VR SA/VT.

161. **JOSEPH$^{6}$ SAWYER** [see 72], b. 10 Nov 1797 So. Hampton NH, d. 19 Jan 1852 Moretown VT, m. 13 Jul 1823 Corinth VT Lovina Merrill, b. 1807. In Moretown VT 1830, 1840, 1850. Innkeeper, judge. Town representative, 1840-1841.

Joseph, b. 29 Apr 1824 Monkton VT, d. 23 Jun 1877 Waitsfield VT, m. 25 Feb 1852 Moretown VT Nancy M. Winslip of Moretown VT, b. Sep 1828 d. 17 Oct 1889, dau. Elijah and Sally (Chapman) Winslip. CH: Jennie Sabrina, b. 10 Jun 1853, m. 15 Aug 1875 Walter C. Lamphier; Mary A., b. 10 Oct 1855, m. 26 Jan 1875 Eugene E. Joslin.

325 William Merrill$^{7}$, b. 1827.

Emily Malvina, b. 14 Mar 1829.

Sarah W., b. ca. 1836.

Sources: Moretown VT census 1830, 1840, 1850. VR Moretown VT, SA/VT.

162. **JACOB M.$^{6}$ SAWYER** [see 72], b. 27 Sep 1801 So. Hampton NH, d. 23 Nov 1869 Corinth VT, m. 8 Dec 1825 Martha Orr, b. 1810 d. 15 Jan 1874, dau. John and Nancy (Mills) Orr. Farmer.

326 Edwin R.$^{7}$, b. 1828.

Hannah, b. 1830, m. 26 Nov 1850 Franklin Page.

Amanda W., b. 1836, m. 29 Dec 1857 Daniel Rowland.

Sources: Corinth VT census 1830, 1840, 1850. VR Corinth VT, SA/VT, SA/MA.

163. **GIDEON$^{6}$ SAWYER** [see 73], b. 1779 Northfield NH, d. 27 Mar 1854 Starksboro VT, m.(1) ?; m.(2) Polly _____ of Vermont, b. 1785 d. 26 Feb 1855. He bur. Mason Hill Cem., Starksboro VT.

327 Reuben$^{7}$, b. 1819.

Elizabeth A., b. 1822, d. 23 Jun 1842.

Martha J., b. ?, d. 29 Sep 1859.
Sources: Northfield NH census 1810, 1820. Starksboro VT census 1830, 1840, 1850. VR SA/VT.

164. **JOTHAM[6] (JONATHAN) SAWYER** [see 75], b. 1793 Northfield NH, m. Dorothy M. _____ of Vermont, b. 1803. In Stewartstown NH 1830, 1840, Columbia NH 1850.
Jotham, b. 1836 Stewartstown NH.
Mary H., b. 1839.
Peter E., b. 1841 Stewartstown NH.
Celestia, b. 1844.
Sources: Stewartstown NH census 1830, 1840. Columbia NH census 1850.

165. **JOSHUA[6] SAWYER** [see 76], b. 16 Oct 1775 Hampstead NH, d. Dorchester NH, m. 28 Feb 1804 Dorchester NH Abigail Piper, b. 1777 d. 10 Jan 1858 Dorchester NH, dau. Samuel Piper. Wid. w/son Joshua C. 1830, in Dorchester NH 1850.
Abigail, b. ?, m. 12 Jun 1825 Abel Bridgeman.
Mary P., b. 10 Jun 1806, d. 6 Jul 1867, m. 24 Aug 1826 Joshua H. Sanborn. [N6] says her name was Nancy.
Joshua C., b. ca. 1812 Dorchester NH, m. 9 Mar 1837 Dorchester NH Priscilla S. Wells, b. ?. CH: Priscilla W. b. 1843, m. 13 Mar 1862 Londonderry NH Reuben Flanders. In Dorchester NH 1830, 1860, Rumney NH 1850.
Sources: Dorchester NH census 1810, 1830, 1850, 1850. Rumney NH census 1850. R34, N14, S8, N6.

166. **JOHN[6] SAWYER** [see 76], b. 28 Apr 1783 Andover NH, d. 10 Apr 1860 Bath NH, m. (I) 24 Dec 1807 Dorchester NH Mary Piper of Salisbury NH, b. 17 May 1783 d. 25 Jan 1853. In Dorchester NH 1810-1850. He bur. in Swiftwater NH.
328 Hiram Dow[7], 1808-1883.
Hannah, b. ?, d. 11 Sep 1887, m. 11 Apr 1843 Daniel Carr.
Eliza, b. 19 Mar 1810, d. 21 Apr 1833.
Alice, b. 29 Sep 1812, d. 26 Dec 1833.
329 John[7], 1815-1867.
Benjamin Piper, b. 27 Jan 1821, d. 1 Jul 1827.
Noah Steven, b. 23 Jul 1823, d. 22 Jul 1826.
330 Noah Piper[7], 1828-1894.
Mary, b. 8 Jan 1831, m.(1) James Calder, m.(2) Milan Hebard.
Sources: Dorchester NH census 1810, 1820, 1830, 1840, 1850. VR Salisbury NH. N14, Merrill C. Sawyer rec.

167. **SAMUEL[6] SAWYER** [see 77], b. 30 Mar 1788 Salisbury NH, d. 12 Jul 1847 Claremont NH, m.(1) 13 Mar 1817 Salisbury NH Hannah Judkins of Salisbury NH, b. 8 Aug 1795 d. 18 May 1834, dau. Samuel and Abigail (Greeley) Judkins; m.(2) 5 Dec 1839 Claremont NH Huldah Johnson of Claremont NH, b. 1788 d. 12 May 1864. In Salisbury NH 1820, Franklin NH 1830. Wid. in Claremont NH 1850.
Hannah, b. 17 Jul 1819, m. 25 Sep 1860 John Angell.
Elizabeth Susan, b. 22 Feb 1825, d. 11 Apr 1869, m. 21 May 1843 Moses A. Young.
Mary Abby, b. 2 Jun 1830, m. 3 Sep 1850 George Foster of Stoddard NH.
331 Samuel Judkins[7], b. 1834.
Sources: Salisbury NH census 1820. Franklin NH census 1830. Claremont NH census 1850. N14, N9, G36, J25.

168. **MOSES⁶ SAWYER** [see 78], b. 28 Apr 1775 Newbury MA, d. 16 Sep 1843 Amesbury MA, m. 10 Feb 1808 Abigail Colby of Hopkinton NH, b. ? d. 22 Jul 1852, dau. David and Rebecca Colby.

Mary A., b. 22 Dec 1808, d. 1849, m. 23 Jan 1849 Newburyport MA John E. Lewis.
Sally C., b. 19 Apr 1810, d. 13 Sep 1820.
332 Leonard Colby[7], b. 1812.
Moses Bailey, b. 18 Feb 1816 Newbury MA. In Amesbury MA.
Abigail, b. 13 Aug 1817, m. 8 Jan 1835 Isaac Osgood.
333 Aaron C.[7], b. 1819.
John, b. 1 May 1821, d. 5 May 1821.
William, b. 20 Mar 1822, d. 24 Oct 1825.
334 Thomas Frederick[7], 1824-1900.
335 William[7], b. 1825.
Albert T., b. 9 Jan 1831, d. 22 Feb 1845.

Sources: Newbury MA census 1810, 1820, 1830. Amesbury MA census 1850. VR Newbury MA, Amesbury MA, SA/MA.

169. **WILLIAM[6] SAWYER** [see 78], b. 11 Jun 1777 Amesbury MA, d. 20 Feb 1828 Amesbury MA, m. 4 Oct 1798 Dorothy Richardson, b. 1771 d. 10 Nov 1833, dau. Joseph and Dorothy (Monroe) Richardson of Bradford MA.

336 Moses[7], 1800-1861.
337 William[7], 1805-1854.

Sources: Amesbury MA census 1800. VR Amesbury MA, SA/MA. V8

170. **STEPHEN[6] SAWYER** .[see 79], b. 27 Nov 1791 Amesbury MA, d. 4 Nov 1870 Concord NH, m.(1) 2 May 1821 Mary Currier, b. 26 Dec 1797 d. 13 Jan 1823 (bur. in Merrimac MA), dau. Nathan and Polly (Noyes) Currier; m.(2) 6 Dec 1823 Bedford NH Sally B. McQueston of Bedford NH, b. 10 Jul 1791 d. 31 Dec 1857, dau. William McQueston. Farmer. In Nashua NH 1850, 1860. In Concord NH 1870.

Caroline W., b. 17 Mar 1822, d. 8 Jan 1844, m. 19 Apr 1842 Henry Morse.
Luther Dimmick, b. 10 Sep 1826 Amesbury MA, d. 14 Jan 1892, m. 22 Jun 1853 Dracut MA Azubah T. Ames of Dracut MA, b. 1830, dau. Daniel and Mary Ames. Machinist. In Hamilton, Ontario.
Samuel Foster, b. 6 Jul 1828 Amesbury MA, d. 27 Aug 1860, m. 6 May 1850 Nashua NH Jane M. Hinman of Dorset VT, b. ?. In Nashua NH.
Mary E., b. 6 Dec 1829, d. 5 Feb 1900, m. 29 Jun 1855 Horatio Laws.
Stephen Payson, b. 13 Jan 1832 Amesbury MA, d. 13 Mar 1911 Muscatine, Iowa, m. 21 Jun 1853 Frances P. Gillett of Newport NH, b. 1 Sep 1832 d. 18 Mar 1897. In Hamilton, Ontario, Canada 1849; in 1871 went to Muscatine IA. seven CH, six b. in Hamilton, Canada, one b. in Muscatine IA.

Sources: Nashua NH census 1850, 1860. Concord NH census 1870. VR SA/MA. S84, N14, C93.

171. **JOHN[6] SAWYER** [see 79], b. 2 Feb 1798 Amesbury MA, m.(1) 3 Apr 1820 Amesbury MA Sophia Tucker, b. 9 Feb 1802 d. 5 Mar 1826, dau. Elisha and Mehitable Tucker; m.(2) 9 Apr 1827 Hannah Sargent of Amesbury MA, b. 21 Mar 1803, dau. Zebulon and Hannah (Sargent) Sargent. Farmer.

338 John Warren[7], 1824-1854.
Sophia E., b. 18 Oct 1828, m. 14 Dec 1849 Daniel H. Bradley.
339 Charles Washington[7], b. 1831.

Sources: Amesbury MA census 1820, 1830, 1840, 1850. VR Amesbury MA. S11.

172. **SYLVESTER[6] SAWYER** [see 80], b. 13 Mar 1806 Woodstock NH, d. 15 Oct 1837 Peeling NH, m. 1 Jan 1834 Sarah A. Clark of Canada, b. 8 Jan 1813 d. 31 Mar 1876, dau. Joshua and Mary (Colden) Clark. In Woodstock NH, Boston MA, Peeling NH. He bur. w/Clark family in Thornton Cem., Peeling NH.

Mary J., b. 3 Nov 1834, m. Truman Humphrey. Went to Wisconsin.
340 Charles Sylvester[7], 1837-1923.
Sources: C43, N9, K15.

173. **SYMMES[6] SAWYER** [see 80], b. 27 Jun 1807 Dunbarton NH, d. 4 Mar 1869 Woodstock NH m. 1 Mar 1838 Martha P. Fifield of Thornton NH, b. 12 May 1815 d. 23 Sep 1888, dau. Jonathan and Sarah (Pinkham) Fifield. Wid. in Woodstock NH 1870.

Sylvestrus, b. 21 Apr 1839, d. 1 May 1839.
William Hoyt, b. 23 Aug 1840, Woodstock NH d. 11 May 1920 Plymouth NH, m. 23 Jun 1875 Emma Ferrin, b. 15 Sep 1848 d. 10 Apr 1914, dau. Jonathan and Mary (Hall) Ferrin.In Plymouth NH 1875. No CH.
Danford, b. 10 Oct 1841, d. 20 Oct 1860, unm.
341 Sylvester George[7], 1842-1926.
Mary A., b. 12 Sep 1844, m. 20 Sep 1865 Augustus Cross.
Charles A., b. 19 Sep 1846 Woodstock NH, d. 30 Jul 1917 Woodstock NH, unm.
Daniel Hoyt, b. 22 May 1848 Woodstock NH, d. 1 Apr 1922 Plymouth NH, m. 25 Dec 1889 Annie J. Leonard of Iowa, b. 25 Dec 1863. Carpenter. In Plymouth NH 1889. No CH.
342 Almus B.[7], 1850-1913.
Emma Martha, b. 9 Feb 1855, d. 3 Dec 1932, m. 2 Mar 1878 Woodstock NH Thomas Gray.
Sources: Woodstock NH census 1850, 1860, 1870. VR SA/NH. N6, S81, G31, Leonard S. Sawyer rec.

174. **WALTER HARRIS[6] SAWYER** [see 80], b. 19 May 1816 Sanbornton NH, d. 22 Dec 1889 Woodstock NH, m. Sarah Ann Fifield of Thornton NH, b. 26 Dec 1822 d. 13 Apr 1909, dau. Jonathan and Sarah (Pinkham) Fifield.

Elizabeth Nichols, b. 28 Jul 1840, m. 28 Nov 1861 Albion Kendall.
343 Frank Roper[7], 1842-1911.
Julia A., b. ca. 1843, m. 27 Apr 1868 Woodstock NH Charles W. B. Davis. CH: Florence, b. 5 Aug 1863, no father listed.
344 George A.[7], 1845-1929.
Ruth R., b. ca. 1848.
W.Augustus, b. 15 Dec 1849 Woodstock NH, d. 17 Nov 1912, unm.
Mary R., b ?.
Wyman H., b. ca. 1853 Woodstock NH.
Sarah Ida, b. 23 Jun 1854, m. 26 Jun 1873 Amasa W. Avery.
Fred M., b. 1858 Woodstock NH, d. 4 Apr 1934 Plymouth NH, m.(1) 23 May 1885 Ida May Leavitt of Exeter NH, b. 16 Aug 1859 d. 11 Apr 1923, dau. Charles P. and Sarah M. (Dustin) Leavitt; m.(2) 14 Jun 1924 Rumney NH (later div.) Flora B. (Avery) Coffin of Ellsworth ME, b. 1889, dau. Bert H. and Laura (Ward) Avery. Janitor, farmer, coachman. In Laconia NH. In Plymouth NH 1908. CH: Lela Atwood, b. 3 Apr 1889.
Verna, b. 1860.
Ernest E., b. 17 Dec 1861 Woodstock NH, m.(1) 17 Apr 1889 Woodstock NH Emma C. Harquail, b. 1863 d. 2 Dec 1891, dau. John and Catherine (Carrie) Harquail of

Delhaven, New Brunswick; m.(2) 6 Jun 1894 Thornton NH, Cora B. Steele of Thornton NH, b. 1863.

Margery F., b. 1864, d. 21 Jun 1880.

Lula E., b. 1866, m. 15 Oct 1891 Franconia NH Marshall A. Bowles.

Sources: Woodstock NH census 1850, 1860, 1870. VR SA/NH. S81, M64, N6, E11.

175. **MOSES MARTIN$^6$ SAWYER** [see 80], b. 4 Sep 1818 Sanbornton NH, d. 4 Feb 1907 No. Woodstock NH, m. 23 Mar 1846 Manchester NH Susan C. Russell of Franconia NH, b. 22 Mar 1827 d. 5 May 1900, dau. Joseph and Abigail (Pinkham) Russell.

345 Eugene A.$^7$, 1850-1916.

346 Albert W.$^7$, 1853-1934.

Fred H., b. 10 Dec 1856, d. 17 Jul 1857.

Hattie A., b. 8 Aug 1859, d. 1 Jan 1937, m. 12 Dec 1876 Woodstock NH Willie Smith.

Henry Merton, b. 1 Mar 1863 Woodstock NH, d. 1 Jun 1947 WoodstockNH, m.(1) 29 May 1888 Northwood NH Myrtie Miller of Northwood NH, b. 20 Sep 1868 d. 18 Sep 1892, dau. Henry and Liza J. (Griffin) Miller; m.(2) 6 Jun 1895 Campton NH Mattie M. Foss of Thornton NH, b. 1865 d. 26 May 1932; m.(3) 23 Dec 1942 Gene McCarthy, b. ?. CH: Mary G., b. 16 Dec 1942, m. _____ Thompson of So. Weare NH.

Charles F., b. 12 Jul 1865 No. Woodstock NH, d. 30 May 1891, m. 1 Jan 1891 Belle P. Durgin Portsmouth NH, b. ca. 1872. In Northwood NH.

Emily R., b. 5 Apr 1868, d. 29 Dec 1906, m. 26 Apr 1888 Boston MA Frederick J. Goodwin.

Sources: Woodstock NH census 1850, 1860, 1870. VR SA/MA, SA/NH. S81, N6, N14, Leonard S. Sawyer rec.

176. **JOHN PAGE$^6$ SAWYER** [see 80], b. 1 Apr 1824 Woodstock NH, d. 19 Apr 1907 Haverhill NH, m. ca. 1850 Mary A. Johnson of Campton NH, b. 27 Jul 1825 d. 22 Aug 1890, dau. Jerry and Dolly (Moses) Johnson.

347 George F.$^7$, 1850-1917.

J. P. A., b. ca. 1853.

Carrie M., b. ca. 1858.

William Aldanis, b. 11 Dec 1861 Woodstock NH, d. 24 Jan 1906 Woodstock NH, unm.

Cora Isadore, b. Oct 1863, d. 28 Oct 1895, m. 8 Aug 1885 Rumney NH George Fisher.

Grace, b. ca. 1866.

Josephina, b. ca. 1868, m. 18 May 1887 Joseph Poitras.

Nellie G., b. ?, m. 13 Sep 1890 Groton MA George J. Wise.

Sources: Woodstock NH census 1860, 1870. VR SA/NH. H17, N6.

177. **JOHN$^6$ SAWYER** [see 81], b. 24 Sep 1791 Amesbury MA, d. 23 Jan 1871 Warner NH, m. 16 Jun 1814 Hopkinton NH Phebe Story of Hopkinton NH, b. 1793 d. 23 Aug 1865. He bur. in Webster NH.

Phebe Story, b. 22 Sep 1816.

348 Thomas W.$^7$, 1818-1884.

Sarah Burnham, b. 5 Feb 1823.

Elinor Nichols, b.8 Jun 1827 Boscawen NH.

Sources: Hopkinton NH census 1820. Warner NH census 1830, 1840, 1850, 1860, 1870. VR Hopkinton NH, Warner NH, Boscawen NH. N9.

178. **MICHAEL⁶ SAWYER** [see 82], bp.28 Aug 1774 Wells ME, d. 9 Jul 1847 Cambridge MA, m. 11 Feb 1802 Wells ME Ellse Littlefield of Kennebunk ME, b. 20 Sep 1781 d. 10 Dec 1863. In Brookfield NH 1796, 1810, 1830. Note: Census and tombstone both say Ellse.

349 Samuel⁷, 1803-1871.
350 Othniel⁷, 1818-1892.
Almira W., b. ?, m. 25 Dec 1831 Gilman Smith of Somersworth NH.
Amanda, b. ?, m. George Bragdon.
Martha A., b. ca. 1823, d. 11 May 1851.
Olive, b. ?, m. _____ Rich. Went to Michigan.
Eliza Jane, b. ?, m. N. T. Hooper.

Sources: Brookfield NH census 1810, 1820, 1830. VR Wells ME, Skowhegan ME, SA/ME, F34, N14. Gladys Wood rec, Bessie Folsom rec.

179. **SAMUEL⁶ SAWYER** [see 82], b. ca. 1781 Wells ME, d. 4 May 1840 Salem MA, m.(I) 28 Dec 1804 Polly Littlefield of Kennebunk ME, b. ?.

Daughter, b. (1804-1810).
Jane Chapman, b. 12 Jan 1812, m. 5 Sep 1837 Salem MA Asa A. Ward.
351 Asa⁷, b. 1813.
Nathaniel, b. ca. 1819 Salem MA, d. 11 Aug 1851 Salem MA.
Daughter, b. (1820-1825).

Sources: Salem MA census 1820, 1830. VR SA/MA. M17.

180 **ASA⁶ SAWYER** [see 82], b. 30 Aug 1787 Brookfield NH, d. 18 Aug 1876 Peabody MA, m. 9 Apr 1815 Salem MA Mary Chapman of Salem MA, b. 1790 d. 29 Jan 1843. Victualler. In Danvers MA.

Mary Jane, b. 5 Jan 1817, d. 7 Jul 1829.
352 Asa Wilson⁷, b. 1818.
Elizabeth M., b. 26 Sep 1820, d. 26 Feb 1885, unm.
George Washington, b. 25 Sep 1822 Danvers MA. Butcher. In Danvers MA 1850. Went to Nevada.
353 Thomas Hadley⁷, 1826-1905.
Mary Chapman, b. 23 Dec 1830, m. 18 May 1851 Danvers MA Benjamin M. Hills.

Sources: Danvers MA census 1820, 1830, 1840, 1850. VR Danvers MA, Salem MA. Paul B. Sawyer rec.

181. **NATHANIEL⁶ SAWYER** [see 82], b. 10 Mar 1790 Brookfield NH, m. 1 Jun 1817 Salem MA Mary Stevens of Salem MA, b. ?. In Salem MA 1820, Danvers MA 1830. Wid. in Salem MA 1850.

354 Nathaniel⁷, b. 1819.
Daniel Frye, b. 8 Mar 1822 Salem MA.
Samuel Miles, b. 25 Feb 1824 Danvers MA.
Isaac, b. 7 Nov 1828 Danvers MA.
Edward Augustus, b. 30 Jun 1831 Danvers MA.
Horace, b. 15 Jul 1833 Danvers MA.

Sources: Salem MA census 1820, 1850. Danvers MA census 1830. VR Salem MA, Danvers MA, Andover MA.

182. **JOTHAM⁶ SAWYER** [see 83], b. 4 Jul 1792 Wells ME, d. 31 Aug 1865 Belgrade ME, m.(1) 17 Feb 1830 Louisa Littlefield of Wells ME, b. 1806 d. 21 Jan 1834; m.(2) Mary Hill of

Belgrade ME, b. 1810 d. 10 May 1881. In Wells ME 1840, 1850, Belgrade ME 1860. He bur. in Wells ME.

Isabella, bp. 6 May 1830.
Nathaniel, bp. 13 Dec 1831, d. 23 May 1840.
Joseph Hill, b. 29 Sep 1836 Wells ME, d. 21 Aug 1906, m. Mary J._____, b. ?.
Charles Lincoln, b. 20 Jul 1839, d. 13 Dec 1861.
Mary L., b. 30 Sep 1841, d. 18 Feb 1844.
Ann M., b. 12 Jul 1844, d. 1 Sep 1847.

Sources: Wells ME census 1840, 1850. Belgrade ME census 1860. Livermore ME census 1860. VR Wells ME. T14, P82k.

183. **JAMES BROWN[6] SAWYER** [see 84], b. 6 Oct 1800 Litchfield ME, d. 12 Feb 1889 Gardiner ME, m. 24 Dec 1834 Litchfield ME Abiah Stinson of Bowdoin ME, b. 1804 d. 15 May 1887 Gardiner ME, dau. Rev. William and Abiah Stinson. James in Litchfield for 80 yrs.

William S., b. 19 Sep 1835 Litchfield ME, m. 30 Jun 1864 Bangor ME Helen M. Graves, b. ?. CH: Edna M., b. 23 Aug 1865.
355 Joseph[7], 1836-1913.
Sarah A., b. 10 Jul 1839, d. 13 Jun 1875.
Ellen, b. 11 Nov 1841, m. 27 Feb 1884 Daniel C. Palmer.
Susan A., b. 20 Feb 1848, m. 9 Sep 1875 E____ S. Brown.

Sources: VR Litchfield ME, Gardiner ME, SA/ME. C46.

184. **JOHN[6] SAWYER** [see 85], b. 19 Mar 1804 Boxford MA, m. 20 Sep 1842 Boxford MA Elizabeth N. Lamson of Salem MA, b. 30 Jun 1818, dau. Samuel and Sarah (Sleuman) Lamson. Farmer. Selectman for Boxford MA 1839.

John, b. 5 Jun 1843 Boxford MA d. 7 Aug 1864 Andersonville Prison GA.
Samuel Lamson, b. 20 Jun 1845 Boxford MA, d. 18 Feb 1910, m. 22 Dec 1869 Boxford MA Ellen Barnes of Boxford MA, b. 9 Apr 1846, dau. Benjamin and Dorcas F. (Kimball) Barnes. Bank President. State Representative 1891-1892. State Senator 1893-1894. In Danvers MA, Salem MA.
Sarah L., b. 20 Dec 1846, d. 26 Dec 1846.
Annie Elizabeth, b. 18 Jun 1848, m. 27 Oct 1880 Boxford MA Colonel Joseph F. Black.
Mary, b. 28 Feb 1855, unm.

Sources: VR Boxford MA, SA/MA. L3, P34.

185. **GEORGE WHITEFIELD[6] SAWYER** [see 86], b. 21 Aug 1802 Boxford MA, m. 6 Jun 1832 Billerica MA Elizabeth Walker of Bedford NH, b. 1802 d. 16 Jan 1899, dau. Robert Walker. Clothier, trader. B/land in Dexter ME 1832-36.

George Alonzo, b. 19 Feb 1833 Dexter ME.
Ellen ELIzabeth, b. 1834.
Sarah Adelaide, b. 1836.
Robert Henry, b. 1 May 1839, d. 1 Oct 1840.
Henry, b. 1 Feb 1841, d. 10 Aug 1841.
Bessie C., b. 1842.
Almira C., b. 22 Sep 1843, m. Luther C. Paine of Dover ME.
Charles Eben, b. 28 Nov 1845, d. 17 Oct 1863.
Mary Submit, b. 19 Mar 1848, d. 27 Jan 1899.
William Irving, b. 17 Jan 1849, d. 3 Aug 1852.

Sources: Dover-Foxcroft ME census 1840, 1850. VR Boxford MA, Billerica MA, SA/ME. W39, R10d, M5.

186. **EBENEZER⁶ SAWYER** [see 86], b. 4 Mar 1809 Boxford MA, d. 7 Sep 1892, m. 26 Sep 1833 Andover MA Susan McColister of Andover MA, b. 3 Mar 1802 d. 14 Aug 1881, dau. John and Mary (Moreland) McColister. Trader. In Methuen MA 1840-1860.

George Whitefield, b. Jul 1835 Methuen MA, d. 28 Jan 1901, m. 3 Nov 1859 Methuen MA Nancy E. Richardson of Methuen MA, b. 7 Oct 1831 d. 24 Jul 1901, dau. William and A____ Richardson. Trader. CH: William Monroe, b. 11 Jul 1860, d. 2 Aug 1860.

356 John E.[7], 1837-1906.

William Henry, b. 7 Dec 1845, d. 27 Oct 1850.

Sources: Methuen MA census 1850,1860. VR Andover MA, Methuen MA, Boxford MA, SA/MA. W39, Annette S. Manny rec.

187. **THOMAS KILLAM[6] SAWYER** [see 86], b. 28 Mar 1811 Boxford MA d. 22 Apr 1895, m. 25 Jan 1848 Salem MA Sophia Bridgeman Howe of Norwich VT, b. 12 Dec 1821 d. 28 Apr 1893, dau. Abijah and Martha (Bridgeman) Howe. Farmer. In Boxford MA 1860.

Thomas Killam, b. 5 Apr 1849 Boxford MA, m. 25 Jan 1873 Boxford MA Nellie Twesden of Lynn MA, b. 1849, dau. John B. and Elizabeth Twesden. Railroad conductor. In Nickerson KS. CH: Elizabeth, b. 1882.

357 James Bridgeman[7], 1850-1924.

Evie Sophia, b. 23 Nov 1853, m. 25 Jan 1873 Boxford MA Nelson E. Harris.

Susan Maria, b. 27 Oct 1855, m. 30 Jun 1881 Nathaniel L. Howe.

358 Isaac Howe[7], b. 1858.

Martha, b. 22 Feb 1862, d. 28 Apr 1869.

Annette, b. 12 Dec 1863, m. 23 Jun 1904 Frank A. Manny. Went to Michigan.

John Herbert, b. 11 Nov 1865, d. 21 Jun 1872.

Sources: Boxford MA census 1860. VR Boxford MA, Salem MA, SA/MA. H80, W39, V9. Annette S. Manny rec.

188. **WILLIAM[6] SAWYER** [see 86], b. 28 Oct 1813 Boxford MA, d. 24 Aug 1900 Georgetown MA, m. 17 Jul 1845 Boxford MA Mary Osgood Foster of Salem MA, b. 20 Apr 1825 d. 14 May 1904, dau. Jonas and Mary Foster. Box manufacturer.

William Foster, b. 20 Mar 1847 Boxford MA, m. 5 Jun 1873 Boxford MA Mary E. Barnes of Boxford MA, b. 27 Mar 1848, dau. Benjamin and Dorcas (Kimball) Barnes. Mason. In Georgetown MA 1880. CH: Franklin Lincoln, b. 22 Jan 1876, d. 24 Nov 1886; Elizabeth Barnes, b. 26 Oct 1882, unm.

Mary Elizabeth, b. 6 Sep 1850, d. 30 Nov 1881, m. 15 Oct 1873 Boxford MA George Lunt.

Sources: Georgetown MA census 1880. VR Boxford MA, SA/MA. P43, S65, W39, Annette S. Manny rec.

189. **SAMUEL[6] SAWYER** [see 87], b. 2 Feb 1769 Wells ME, d. bef. Apr 1802, m. 20 Oct 1791 Lucy Littlefield of Wells ME, b. 1770. Will probated 19 Apr 1802. Wid. in Wells ME 1810.

Elsie, b. 14 Oct 1793, m. 18 Jun 1812 Moses Perkins, Perkins Cove ME.

Clarissa, b. 14 Mar 1796, m. William Hutchings.

359 Samuel B.[7], 1798-1860.

Lucy, b. 27 Sep 1800.

Sources: Wells ME census 1800, 1810. VR Wells ME. P32, T14, P82k.

190. **WILLIAM[6] SAWYER** [see 88], b. 15 Jul 1767 Wells ME, d. Cornish ME, m. 17 May 1792 Wells ME Susanna Goodwin, b. ca. 1769 d. 15 Aug 1835. In Limington ME, Cornish ME. Note: Census says they had eight dau.

Mary, b. 9 Aug 1795, d. 27 Nov 1879, m. 29 Mar 1818 Nicholas Cobb of Limington ME.
Nancy, b. ca. 1799, m. 7 Jun 1819 Ephraim Gray of Cornish ME.
Samuel, b. ca. 1800, d.y.
Susanna, b. ca. 1803, m. 17 Mar 1823 William Merrill of Cornish ME.
Sarah, b. ca. 1807, d. 9 Feb 1880, m. 24 Dec 1825 Thomas Smith of Hiram ME.
360 William[7], 1810-1877.
Olive, b. ?, m. 12 Apr 1842 Cyrus Binford.
Sources: Cornish ME census 1810, 1820, 1830. T6, E13, N37, Mrs. Addie Small rec.

191. **JOSEPH[6] SAWYER** [see 88], b. 19 Jun 1773 Wells ME, d. 4 Sep 1833 Limerick ME, m. 31 Mar 1796 Mary Burk of Cornish ME, b. Oct 1771 d. 11 May 1860. Lived on Sawyer's Mountain, Limerick ME. Will dated 19 Aug 1833.
361 Lemuel B.[7], 1797-1882.
Betsey, b. 27 Feb 1798, d. 7 Apr 1892, m. 7 Sep 1817 Samuel Wentworth of Sebago ME.
Joseph B., b. 8 Jun 1799 Limington ME, d. 19 Oct 1877 Brownfield ME, m. 9 Oct 1831 Jane Ellis of Cornish ME, b. ?. B/S/land in Brownfield ME 1833-1835. CH: Harriet Ann, b. 11 Apr 1835, m. 18 Jul 1858 Daniel P. Sawyer; Mary J., b. 1843.
362 James B.[7], 1800-1886.
Joanna, b. 8 May 1802, d. Aug 1830.
Thomas, b. 27 Sep 1803, d. 1808.
363 Benjamin Thompson[7], 1806-1887.
Abraham, b. 14 Feb 1807, d. 1824.
Isaac, b. 5 Sep 1808, d. Dec 1819.
364 Jacob[7], 1810-1886.
Lydia Ann, b. 8 Dec 1811, d. 19 Feb 1868, m. 16 Apr 1845 Samuel Blake of Standish ME.
Jane B., b. 8 Jun 1813, d. 4 Jun 1908, m. 20 Jan 1842 Ivory Norton of Standish ME.
Mary, b. 27 Dec 1814, d. Dec 1819.
Zachariah, b. 14 Oct 1818 Limington ME, d. 16 Apr 1858, m. Maria R. Smith, b. ?. In Charlestown MA. CH: Cecelia Maria, b. 12 Jul 1851, m. 2 Dec 1873 Newton MA Samuel H. Hall.
365 Isaac[7], 1820-1887.
Sources: Limington ME census 1810, 1820, 1830. VR Brownfield ME, SA/MA. B49, T6A, N37, W26, R10c.

192. **HUMPHREY[6] SAWYER** [see 89], b. ca. 1774 Newbury MA, d. 6 Oct 1839 Plymouth NH, m. 1 Apr 1798 New Hampton NH Susannah Piper of Holderness NH, b. 2 Feb 1773 d. 7 Apr 1857 Nashua NH, dau. William and Susanna (Shepard) Piper. Appointed co-executor w/brother James of father's estate 16 Oct 1813. Wid. w/son Daniel 1850.
William P., b. ca. 1799 Holderness NH, m. Theodosia Shepard, b. ?, dau. William and Hannah (Hill) Shepard. In Ontona MN 1840. In Santa Barbara CA. CH: Ann T., b. 25 May 1823, d. 11 Mar 1848; Elizabeth A., b. ?, d. 26 Aug 1840; Laurentina, b. 1825, d. 3 Oct 1836; William F., b. 1836, d. 12 Oct 1837 Lowell MA.
366 Daniel[7], 1800-1858.
367 Humphrey[7], b. 1805.
Susan P., b. ?, m. 28 Aug 1828 Orlando Taylor.
Martha, b. ?, m. _____ Morrison.
Sources: Holderness NH census 1800, 1810, 1820. Plymouth NH census 1830, 1850. S81, P82i, F11A.

193. **EZRA⁶ SAWYER** [see 89], b. 1778 Newburyport MA, d. 1 Apr 1849 Woodstock NH, m. 21 Apr 1807 New Hampton NH Mary Smith, b. 1788. In Woodstock NH 1824. Wid. in Woodstock NH 1850, 1860 and bur. there.

Betsey Smith, b. 19 Jun 1807.
368 Elisha Smith[7], 1808-1894.
Sally Nuse, b. 15 Feb 1811.
Noah H., b. 1816 New Hampton NH, d. 22 Jun 1893 Ellsworth NH, unm. In Woodstock NH 1850-1870.
Frank, b. 1824 Woodstock NH, m. 12 Apr 1874 Boston MA Elizabeth Rafferty of Ireland, b. 1834. Teamster.
369 Elbridge Gerry[7], 1826-1918.
Andrew Baker, b. 31 May 1828 New Hampton NH, d. 9 Apr 1903 Thornton NH, unm.
Caroline T., b. 1830.

Sources: New Hampton NH census 1810, 1820. Woodstock NH census 1830, 1840, 1850, 1860, 1870. VR SA/MA. S81.

194. **JAMES[6] SAWYER** [see 89], b. 178? New Hampton NH, d. bef. 19 Nov 1835 New Hampton NH, m. 4 May 1802 New Hampton NH Polly Shepard of No. Holderness NH, b. 1782. Wid. appointed guardian of three dau 1836; in New Hampton NH 1840.

370 Daniel S.[7], b. ca. 1800.
Martha, b.?, m. 28 Nov 1844 Charlestown MA Asa Fairbanks.
Sally, b. ?.
Betsey A., b. ?, m. 14 Nov 1844 Charlestown MA Elijah Thompson.
Caroline, b. ?, m. 17 Sep 1902 Jonathan Smith.
John B., b. ?, New Hampton NH. Will dated 2 Sep 1840.
Note: census records say that James had the following CH during the periods indicated: 1 son, 5 dau. (1800-1810); 1 son, 3 dau. (1810-1820).

Sources: New Hampton NH census 1810, 1820, 1830, 1840. VR SA/MA. P82i, F11A.

195. **JOHN[6] SAWYER** [see 90], b. 25 Jun 1774 Lynn MA, d. 3 Jan 1841 Henniker NH, m. 4 Mar 1799 Weare NH Eunice Gove of Weare NH, b. 26 Mar 1781 d. 22 Apr 1876, dau. Daniel and Miriam (Cortland) Gove. Quaker. Town Representative 1812. Selectman for Henniker NH. Wid. in Weare NH w/son Moses.

Mary, b. 15 Mar 1800, m. 21 Oct 1820 Nathan Page of Danvers MA.
371 Moses[7], 1803-1892.
372 Nathan[7], 1806-1890.
373 Daniel[7], 1808-1885.
Albert, b. 6 Sep 1816 Henniker NH, d. 24 Jan 1833.

Sources: Henniker NH census 1800, 1810, 1820, 1830, 1840. VR Newbury NH. G30, C59.

196. **EZRA[6] SAWYER** [see 90], b. 4 Jul 1779 Newbury MA, d. 1858, m.(1) Anna Kelly of Deering NH, b. 1783 d. 1818, dau. Moses and Elizabeth (Fling) Kelly; m.(2) 28 Sep 1820 Weare NH Mary Green of Weare NH, b. 1791. In Weare NH 1810-1840.

Phillips, b. 24 Dec 1816 Weare NH, d. 24 Sep 1903 Weare NH, m. 25 Apr 1839 Weare NH Miriam Peasley of Weare NH, b. 16 Jun 1818 d. 8 Jan 1900, dau. Nathaniel and Sally (Patch) Peasley. Shoemaker. CH: Angeline G., b. Oct 1840, d. 14 Aug 1856; Caroline M., b. Mar 1842 d. 5 Oct 1871, m. 22 Jun 1857 Frederic Spiller.
Moses G., b. ?, unm.
Mary G., b. ca. 1822, m. 13 May 1847 James M. Eastman. Went to Boston MA.

Note: Census records say that Ezra had the following CH during the periods indicated: 2 sons, 3 dau. (1800-1810); 1 son (1810-1820); 1 son, 1 dau. (1820-1825).

Sources: Weare NH census 1810, 1820, 1830, 1840, 1850, 1860, 1870. VR Newbury MA, SA/NH. K2, L31, N9.

197. **NATHAN$^6$ SAWYER** [see 90], b. 30 Nov 1787 Newbury MA, d. 14 Dec 1884 Weare NH, m. 1817 Abigail Gove, b. 1 May 1798 d. 19 Jan 1881, dau. Obediah and Sarah (Nichols) Gove. Quaker. Farmer.

Frederick, b. ca. 1805.
Daughter, b. (1810-1820).
Sarah G., b. 28 Nov 1819, m. 9 Nov 1848 David Neale of Lynn MA.
Mary Ann, b. 8 Jun 1824, m. 10 Nov 1870 Daniel Johnson.

Sources: Weare NH census 1820, 1830, 1840, 1850, 1860, 1870. VR Newbury MA. G30, B84, N5.

198. **JOHN BROWN$^6$ SAWYER** [see 91], b. 19 Aug 1777 Freeport ME, d. 16 Jan 1863 Litchfield ME, m. 1803 Betsey Parker, b. 24 Dec 1783 d. 17 Jun 1864. In Litchfield ME 1801.

Hannah, b. 31 Jul 1804, m. 19 Apr 1828 Daniel Maxwell.
374 Enoch Parker$^7$, 1805-1884.
Ammi, b. 1 Oct 1807, d. 29 Oct 1835 Hallowell ME.
James, b. 14 Sep 1809, d. 1 Jan 1836 Hallowell ME.
Parmelia, b. 27 Mar 1811, d. 1871, m. 1841 Chelubia Bowman.
Page, b. 16 Jul 1813, lost at sea.
375 Cyrenius$^7$, 1815-1880.
Betsey P., b. 1 Feb 1818, m. Isley Osborn of West Gardiner ME.
Mary W., b. 21 Nov 1822, m. 12 Sep 1861 William T. Sinclair of Manchester ME.

Sources: Litchfield ME census 1810, 1820, 1830, 1840, 1850. Manchester ME census 1860. VR Litchfield ME, Gardiner ME. C46.

199. **EZRA$^6$ SAWYER** [see 90], b. 23 Dec 1787 Freeport ME, d. 22 Nov 1848 Topsham ME, m. Sarah Fields of Durham ME, b. 13 Oct 1794 d. 13 Nov 1863. In Lisbon ME 1820, Topsham ME 1830. Wid. in Topsham ME 1850.

Eunice L., b. 25 Apr 1814 Freeport ME, d. 17 Dec 1841.
Stephen F., b. 18 Mar 1816 Lewiston ME.
376 James E.$^7$, 1818-ca. 1864.
Ann F., b. 10 May 1820 Durham ME, m. 2 May 1842 Moses A. Gray.
377 Justus B.$^7$, 1823-1901.
Elijah P., b. 25 Dec 1825 Topsham ME, d. bef. 1866, m.(1) 1850 Julia Ann Parish of Somersworth NH, b. 5 Dec 1829 d. 9 Oct 1851, dau. Chester and Lucy (Bean) Parish of Gilmanton NH; m.(2) 16 Jan 1853 Wealthy Clara Parish of Somersworth NH, b. ?. Shoemaker. In Tamworth NH 1860. Wid. m. 7 Oct 1866 James Gilpatrick. CH: Fanny A., b. 1851, d. 15 May 1852; Clara E., b. 1855; Julia A., b. 1857, m. 24 Dec 1876 Lawrence MA Melvin E. Rugg.
378 Ezra$^7$, b. 1828.
Sarah D., b. 10 May 1831 Topsham ME, d. 5 Apr 1898, m. 13 Feb 1855 Silas Brackett.
Elizabeth F., b. 10 May 1831 Topsham ME, m. 23 May 1850 Elisha P. Mallet.
Hannah G., b. 30 May 1833 Topsham ME, m. 27 Apr 1851 John D. Manor of Freeport ME.
379 Charles H.$^7$, b. 1835.
Albert, b. 9 Feb 1838 Topsham ME, d. 13 Oct 1840.

Sources: Lisbon ME census 1820. Topsham ME census 1830, 1840, 1850. Tamworth NH census 1860. P5, N6, C99.

200. **JAMES⁶ SAWYER** [see 93], b. 7 Jun 1793 Weare NH, d. 4 Apr 1846, m.(1) Nancy Tewksbury, b. ?; m.(2) 8 Nov 1820 Weare NH Polly George of Weare NH, b. 1793 d. Feb 1856, dau. Elijah and Molly (Eastman) George. Farmer.

Eliza, b. 3 May 1814, d.y.
Lucy, b. 3 May 1814, d.y.
Esther B., b. 9 Sep 1821, d. 20 May 1842.
380 Humphrey$^7$, 1824-1904. Went to Wisconsin.
Mary Jane, b. 19 Mar 1826, d. 1832.
Charles, b. 11 Apr 1828, d. 1830.

Sources: Weare NH census 1830. VR Weare NH. L31.

201. **ALLEN$^6$ SAWYER** [see 93], b. 27 Jun 1803 Weare NH, d. 15 Apr 1866, m.(1) 19 Mar 1828 Anna Osborn of Loudon NH, b. ?; m.(2) 19 Nov 1845 Weare NH Mary B. Peasley of Henniker NH, b. 1820 d. 26 Feb 1882. Shoemaker. Quaker. Wid. in Weare NH 1870.

John Osborn, b. 12 Sep 1829, d. 1856.
Eliza L., b. 10 Oct 1830, d. Jul 1905, m. 10 Dec 1859 Concord NH David Warren Cogswell.
Mary Jane, b. 13 May 1832, m. 17 Nov 1852 John W. Hanson.
381 Lindley M.$^7$, 1833-1902.
Anna Maria, b. 3 May 1847, m. 13 Jun 1867 Charles A. Jones.
Hannah E., b. 12 May 1850, d.y.
Abbie E., b. 8 Sep 1854, d.y.
Abbie E., b. 27 Aug 1858, m. 28 Aug 1876 Lindley M. Farr.

Sources: Weare NH census 1830, 1840, 1850, 1860, 1870. VR SA/MA. H93, V2, S43, C48, N6.

202. **LEVI$^6$ SAWYER** [see 94], b. 11 Aug 1791 Dover NH, d. 23 Nov 1868 Dover NH, m. 5 Jul 1826 Amesbury MA Hannah G. Pinkham, b. 17 May 1804, dau. Paul and Rose (Austin) Pinkham. Blacksmith. On Garrison Hill, Dover NH.

Lydia, b. 12 Apr 1827, d. 3 May 1836.
Elizabeth Chase, b. 6 Sep 1829, d. 28 Apr 1836.
Joseph Browne, b. 20 Nov 1832 Dover NH, d. 18 Jul 1905 Dover NH, m. 7 Nov 1894 Springfield MA Addie M. Sturtevant of Springfield MA, b. 8 Oct 1853 d. 7 May 1811 Dover NH, dau. Warren (Warner C.?) and Nancy (Hurd) Sturtevant. Tailor. In Pittsburgh PA, returned to Dover NH 1888.
Lydia Elizabeth, b. 9 Jun 1837, d. 10 Mar 1896.
Levi Newell, b. 25 Feb 1842 Dover NH. Went to Chicago IL.

Sources: Dover NH census 1830, 1860. VR SA/NH. P82i, S44, S21, N9.

203. **THOMAS ELLWOOD$^6$ SAWYER** [see 94], b. 21 Nov 1798 Dover NH, d. 27 Feb 1879 Dover NH, m.(1) 27 Feb 1831 Elizabeth (Reynolds) Watson, b. 4 Feb 1813 d. 1 Dec 1847, dau. Oliver and Sarah (Hanson) Reynolds; m.(2) 15 Oct 1848 Elizabeth Moody of Parsonsfield ME, b. 20 Oct 1819 d. 11 Sep 1887, dau. Daniel K. and Elizabeth (Sargent) Moody. Lawyer, politician. Mayor of Dover NH.

Charles Walter, b. 19 May 1832 Dover NH, d. ca. 1864 in Civil War.
Mary Elizabeth, b. 8 Dec 1833, d. 9 Mar 1880, m. Alfred D. Hoit.
Ruth Ann, b. 8 Jul 1835, d. 19 Aug 1835.
Edward, b. 11 Jul 1836 Dover NH, d. 8 Oct 1916 St. Paul MN, m. 29 Nov 1859 Rochester NH Frances P. Kelly of Rochester NH, b. 4 Sep 1833 d. 1907, dau. Stephanus and

Abigail (Morse) Kelly. In Rochester NH 1860. He bur. Concord NH. CH: Elizabeth, b. ?, m. Charles Grant.

Sarah Ellen, b. 2 Jan 1838, d. 8 Jan 1842.

Thomas, b. 28 Oct 1840, d. 8 Aug 1842.

Ruth Ellen, b. 9 May 1843, d. 27 Aug 1848.

Son, b. 25 Nov 1847, d. same day.

382 William$^7$, 1849-1913.

Henry C., b. ca. 1852 Dover NH, d. 3 Jun 1904 Westboro MA, m. 14 Nov 1888 Boston MA Mary Burns of Pittsfield ME, b. 1859, dau. Eugene and Hannah Burns. In Dover NH 1860, Boston MA 1888. He bur. Dover NH.

Helen, b. ca. 1853, m. Nahum Yeaton.

383 Frederick$^7$, 1855-1929.

Sources: Dover NH census 1840, 1850, 1860. VR SA/MA, SA/NH. S68, M27, P82i, H95, K2, A20.

204. **LUTHER DEARBORN$^6$ SAWYER** .[see 95], b. 7 Mar 1803 Wakefield NH, d. 9 Jul 1884 Wakefield NH, m.(1) 1 Feb 1843 Lydia Hanson of Sandwich NH, b. 17 Apr 1815 d. 10 Apr 1854 and bur. in Hubbard Cem., East Sandwich NH; m.(2) 5 Dec 1856 Marblehead MA Mary B. Chamberlin of Marblehead MA, b. 1814, dau. Jason and Eleanor Chamberlin. Lawyer. Educated at Philips Exeter Academy, Bowdoin College. In Ossipee NH, Sandwich NH, Dover NH 1859.

384 Horatio G.$^7$, b. 1844.

William Hanson, b. 15 Jan 1845, d. 25 Sep 1846.

385 Frank D.$^7$, 1851-1930.

Sources: VR SA/MA. L30, H95, D10.

205. **JOHN$^6$ SAWYER** [see 96], b. 5 May 1804 Dover NH, d. 9 May 1877, m.(1) 18 Sep 1825 Lee NH Eunice Page of Parsonsfield ME, b. 2 Jul 1802 d. 23 Sep 1840; m.(2) 2 Sep 1841 Abigail Morrill, b. 29 Apr 1808 d. 6 Jan 1881. Farmer. Will dated 15 Oct 1857. Abigail appointed executrix of Jacob's will 1877. Wid. w/son Jacob M. 1880.

Sarah A., b. ca. 1829, d. 19 May 1849 Boston MA.

Hannah M., b. ?, m. _____ Furbish.

Mary H., b. ?, m. _____ Smith.

386 Enos H.$^7$, b. ca. 1832.

387 Jacob M.$^7$, b. 1847.

Sources: Dover NH census 1840, 1850, 1870, 1880. P82i, A22, T20.

206. **DANIEL$^6$ SAWYER** [see 97], b. 4 Oct 1801 Alton NH, d. 13 Sep 1869 Alton NH, m. 15 Nov 1826 Tamson Walker, b. 31 Oct 1805 d. 1874. Farmer. Selectman. Wid. w/son Alonzo.

388 Alonzo Haventon$^7$, 1827-1885.

Marinda Ellen, b. 3 Sep 1835, m. Jeremiah Jones of Alton NH.

Franklin Pierce, b. 3 Jun 1839 Alton NH, d. 3 Jan 1898 Alton NH, m. 1 Nov 1876 Lynn MA Jennie Farnham of Bristol NH, b. 1843 d. 1890. Shoemaker. He bur. in Alton NH.

Sources: Alton NH census 1830, 1840, 1850. 1860. VR SA/MA. G45, H94.

207. **SETH$^6$ SAWYER** [see 97], b. 28 Aug 1806 Alton NH, d. 4 Feb 1892 Alton NH, m.(1) 10 Jan 1830 Elizabeth Ann Wiggins of Alton NH, b. 7 Jul 1812 d. 27 May 1863, dau. Benjamin and Elizabeth (Chase) Stevens; m.(2) 5 Aug 1864 Sarah E. Stevens, b. 1828 d. 1869, dau. Joseph and Susan Gooch; m.(3) 2 Oct 1870 Middleton NH Lucy J. Tripper, b. 1837 d. 18 Jul 1880. Farmer. Baptist minister. School committee member.

Charles P., b. 7 Dec 1830, d. 10 Nov 1855.

Emiline R., b. 22 May 1833, d. 1909, m. Henry C. Avery.
Sources: Alton NH census 1830, 1840, 1850, 1860. Middleton NH census 1870. Hanover NH census 1850 (Charles P., student). VR Middleton NH. G45, N14, W44.

208. **JEREMIAH HILL$^{6}$ SAWYER** [see 98], b. 16 Feb 1784 Lee NH, d. Exeter NH, m. 21 Dec 1807 Jane Chase, b. 22 Feb 1787, dau. James and Abigail (Bickford) Chase. Painter. In Exeter NH 1821. May have res. in Newburyport MA.

Mary Jane, b. 2 Jul 1808, d. 20 Dec 1895, m. 6 Nov 1832 Andrew Baker.
389 Jeremiah$^{7}$, 1810-1876.
Samuel, b. ?, d.y.
390 William F.$^{7}$, 1813-1873.
391 Samuel J.$^{7}$, 1814-1850.
Lydia, b. ?, m. Henry Hook of Newmarket NH.
Abigail, b. 1 May 1821, m.(1) 1840 William H. Marshall, m.(2) 1846 Michael Teel.
392 Joseph B.$^{7}$, b. ca. 1828.

Sources: Lee NH census 1810. Exeter NH census 1820, 1830. C30, R6, C97.

209. **MOSES H.$^{6}$ SAWYER** [see 99], b. 12 Apr 1789 Lisbon ME, d. 12 Jul 1878, m. 15 Dec 1816 Elizabeth Tibbets of Brunswick ME, b. 15 Jan 1794 d. 24 Dec 1875. Mill owner. In Raymond ME, Lisbon ME.

Phebe, b. 15 Dec 1816, d. 29 Jan 1864, m.(I) 27 Aug 1841 Jeremiah Higgins.
393 George W.$^{7}$, 1819-1910.
Daughter, b. 21 Jan 1822, d. 7 Feb 1822.
James A., b. 4 Jan 1823 Raymond ME. In Lisbon ME.
Curtis G., b. 3 Dec 1827 Raymond ME, d. 8 Oct 1886 Bowdoinham ME, m.(1) 15 Dec 1856 Hannah D. Higgins of Webster ME, b. 19 Nov 1830 d. 6 Jan 1868, dau. Zaccheus and Mary (Totman) Higgins; m.(2) 1 Nov 1868 Bowdoinham ME Susan O. Higgins, b. 8 Mar 1830 d. 17 Dec 1901, dau. William and Sarah (Blanchard) Higgins. In Lisbon ME, Webster ME, Bowdoin ME.
Wesley, b. 20 Feb 1830 Raymond ME. In Chicago IL.
Samuel T., b. 1 Jan 1833 Raymond ME. In Lisbon ME.
394 Paschal Merrill$^{7}$, 1834-1890.

Sources: Raymond ME census 1820, 1830. Lisbon ME census 1840, 1850, 1860. VR Raymond ME, Bowdoinham ME, SA/ME. H47, Beverly Strout rec.

210. **JOSEPH$^{6}$ SAWYER** [see 99], b. 27 Sep 1791 Lisbon ME, d. 14 May 1882 Lisbon ME, m. Jan 1816 Mary Blanchard, b. ca. 1790 d. 6 Jun 1848. War of 1812.

Pauline B., b. 26 Jan 1817, m. 19 May 1842 Lewis Thompson.
395 Jeremiah$^{7}$, 1819-1906.
George, b. 17 Feb 1821 Lisbon ME.
Martha A., b. 17 Nov 1828, m. 1848 Lisbon ME William Haley.
Mary J., b. 17 Nov 1828.

Sources: Lisbon ME census 1810, 1820, 1830, 1840, 1850, 1860. VR Topsham ME. David C. Young rec.

211. **AARON$^{6}$ SAWYER** [see 100], b. ca. 1803 Barrington NH, d. yr ending 31 Mar 1878 Barrington NH, m. 7 Mar 1823 Strafford NH Anna Hanscom of Barrington NH, b. 1798 d. 26 Nov 1892. Farmer. In Strafford NH 1822, Farmington NH, Middleton NH.

Hannah, b. 1827, m. 13 Jun 1854 Benjamin Arlen.
396 Aaron$^{7}$, 1831-1917.

Eliza, b. ca. 1832.
Sally, b. ca. 1837.

Sources: Strafford NH census 1830. Farmington NH census 1840. Middleton NH census 1850. Barrington NH census 1860, 1870. VR Strafford NH, Barrington NH.

212. **SAMUEL[6] SAWYER** [see 101], b. 22 Jan 1797 West Amesbury MA, d. 8 Dec 1864 Hampden ME, m. 1825 Rebecca Hewes, b. ?.

Sarah, b. 1826, m. Daniel Patten.
Myra A., b. 1828, d. 1859, m. Richard Patten.
Electa, b. 1830, m. Joseph Miller. Went to Canada.
Charles A., b. 1832 Hampden ME.
Eliza, b. 1834, m. J. N. Batchelder.
Amos, b.?, d. at 21 yrs, unm.

Sources: Hampden ME census 1840, 1850. P20, P82f.

213. **AARON[6] SAWYER** [see 101], b. 1803 Hampden ME, d. bef. 23 Dec 1841 Hampden ME, m. 28 May 1835 Nancy Stoddard of Durham ME, b. ?. B/land in Hampden ME 1830, 1835. Wid. B/land from Stephen[5] [see 101] 1841. Wid. m. Rama Martin.

397 James T.[7], 1836-1909.
Margaret H., b. ca. 1837.
Edward H., b. 1839 Hampden ME. In Carmel ME 1850.

Sources: Hampden ME census 1840. Carmel ME census 1850. P31, P20, R10d, P82f.

214. **JOSEPH HARVEY[6] SAWYER** [see 101], b. 15 Jul 1805 Hampden ME, d. 21 May 1882, m. Jun 1828 Mary Patten of Hampden ME, b. 27 Jun 1807 d. 25 Oct 1882. Farmer. B/land in Exeter ME 1852.

398 George W.[7], 1829-1902.
Mary, b. 1832.
Elbridge W., b. 5 May 1833 Hampden ME, d. 26 Sep 1909 Brewer ME, m. Sarah T. Leonard, b. 1 Feb 1839 d. 13 Jul 1920, dau. Solon and Dolly (Patterson) Leonard. Wheelwright. In Brewer ME 1880. CH: Alice F., b. ca. 1871.
Rachel H., b. 1835.
Eliza A., b. 1837, m. Henry Smith.
Stephen S., b. 16 Feb 1840 Hampden ME, d. 28 Aug 1913 Hampden ME, m. 17 May 1899 Henrietta C. Bunker of Massachusetts, b. 29 Nov 1858, dau. William G. and Huldah (Staples) Bunker. Civil War. In Brewer ME 1880.
Harvey, b. Jul 1841 Hampden ME, d. 1 Jan 1892 Hampden ME, m.(1) Mary E. Gorton of Hampden ME, b. ? d. 8 Jul 1873, dau. James and Sibyl (Dudley) Gorton; m.(2) 2 Jan 1882 Ada E. Blake of Brewer ME, b. 24 Jun 1854 d. 8 Jan 1914, dau. Levi and Roxy (Jordan) Blake. Carpenter. CH: Edith M., b. ?; Ella Blake, b. 15 Dec 1882; Ella Harvey, b. 15 Sep 1886.
Aaron P., b. Dec 1843 Hampden ME, d. 27 Mar 1906, m. Ida E._____, b. Nov 1857 d. 27 Mar 1906. In Brewer ME.
Lydia T., b. 30 Apr 1844, d. 18 Jun 1921, m. 17 May 1899 Shadrack Smith. Went to Colorado.
Chauncy N., b. 3 Sep 1847 Hampden ME, d. 26 Apr 1918 Hampden ME.
Wilson Joseph, b. Sep 1850 Hampden ME, d. 9 Mar 1906 Bangor ME, m. 13 Nov 1875 Bangor ME Susan A. Moore of Bangor ME, b. Aug 1853. In Hampden ME 1880. CH: Mary T., b. 4 Nov 1878, d. 25 Jun 1892 Brewer ME; Louise W., b. Feb 1894.
Dora, b. ca. 1853, m. _____ Cowen.

Wilbur, b. Nov 1853 Hampden ME, m. 28 May 1892 Hampden ME Ella O. York, b. Nov 1854, dau. Isaiah C. and Lorinda (Patterson) York. In Brewer ME. CH: Lulu F., b. Jan 1896.
Louisa, b. ?.
Emily D., b. ?.
Flora, b. ?.
Sources: Hampden ME census 1830, 1840, 1850, 1860, 1870, 1880. ME 1880 census index. VR Hampden ME, Bangor ME, SA/ME. P20.

215. **AMOS P.$^{6}$ SAWYER** [see 101], b. 1807 Hampden ME, d. 1877, m. Betsey Sylvester of Elna ME, b. ca. 1810. Farmer, mill worker. B/land in Hampden ME 1830, 1835. Wid. w/son Frederick 1880.
399 John$^{7}$, 1840-1922.
Mary E., b. ca. 1842, m. Allen Carter of Hermon ME.
Melvina, b. ca. 1845, m. Charles Patterson.
400 Frederick$^{7}$, 1848-1911.
Sources: Hampden ME census 1840, 1850, 1880. VR SA/ME. P20, O2, P30, R10d.

216. **JOHN PATTEN$^{6}$ SAWYER** [see 102], b. 4 May 1797 Hampstead NH, d. 13 Nov 1871, m. 18 Nov 1824 Dracut MA Sally (Jones) Thissell of Dracut MA, b. 18 Oct 1803 d. 12 Dec 1880 Groton MA. In Hampstead NH 1830, Dracut MA 1840, 1850.
Aaron Jones, b. 21 Oct 1825 Hampstead NH, m.(1) ? in Groton MA; m.(2) 15 Mar 1888 Groton MA Lucy P. Lewis of Hillsboro NH, b. ca. 1821, dau. Nathaniel and Rachel Coolidge. In Dracut MA 1850.
Sarah Ann, b. 30 Oct 1827, d. 22 Mar 1830.
401 John Andrew$^{7}$, b. 1829.
Jerome Harris, b. 18 Mar 1832 Hampstead NH, m.(1) 3 Jul 1860 Haverhill MA Lizzie H. Wight of New York, b. 8 Mar 1828 d. 28 Oct 1863 Haverhill MA, dau. Eli and Fanny Wight; m.(2) 6 Oct 1867 Charlestown MA Sarah Drew of Charlestown MA, b. ca. 1829, dau. David and Olive Kelley. Machinist. No CH.
Joshua, b. ca. 1836 Hampstead NH. In Dracut MA 1850.
Mary A., b. 6 Apr 1841, d. 4 Sep 1861 in Lowell MA.
Lucy Ellen, b. ca. 1843, m. 22 Sep 1869 Milford MA Augustus Hamblet.
402 William Eaton$^{7}$, 1846-1919.
Sources: Hampstead NH census 1830. Dracut MA census 1840, 1850. VR Hampstead NH, Dracut MA, Haverhill MA, SA/MA. C48, H70, Alice M. Sawyer rec.

217. **JOSHUA$^{6}$ SAWYER** [see 102], b. 10 Jun 1814 Hampstead NH, m. 13 Nov 1839 Essex MA Lucy Emerson Burnham of Essex MA, b. 18 Jul 1815.
George Byron, adopted, b. 27 Jun 1838 Hampstead NH, m.(1) 6 Aug 1862 Plymouth NH Esther Spooner of Plymouth NH, b. ?, dau. Ephraim and Mary E. Spooner; m.(2) 21 Dec 1893 Framingham MA Sarah A. Mick of New Brunswick, Canada, b. 1855, dau. Thomas and Bethia (Bird) Mick. Lumber, jeweler. CH: Mary Esther, b. 25 Feb 1873.
Sources: VR SA/MA. B18, N7.

218. **AARON$^{6}$ SAWYER** [see 103], b. 11 Apr 1823 Amesbury MA, d. 1899 Amesbury MA, m. 26 Nov 1861 Amesbury MA Lois D. Jones of Salisbury MA, b. 1822 d. 1895, dau. Abel and Pauline Jones.
403 Harland Aaron$^{7}$, 1868-1929.
Sources: Amesbury MA census 1850. VR SA/MA. Joan Wernsdorfer rec.

219. **AMOS[6] SAWYER** [see 103], b. 12 Aug 1825 Amesbury MA, d. 14 Feb 1922 Haverhill MA, m. 12 Dec 1850 Amesbury MA Sarah Irene Ham of Dover NH, b. ?, dau. Ephraim and Sally Ham. Carriage maker. W/father 1850.

Ella Morton, b. 15 Sep 1851, d. 1948, m. James H. Choate.

Edgar Hamilton, b. 11 Aug 1853 Amesbury MA, m. 3 Apr 1879 Bradford MA Emma G. Gale of Bradford MA, b. 1858, dau. Moses H. and Ellen Gale.

Thomas Elwell, b. 7 Sep 1853.

Sources: Amesbury MA census 1850. VR Amesbury MA, Haverhill MA, SA/MA. H32.

220. **THOMAS[6] SAWYER** [see 104], b. 28 Jan 1796 New Chester NH, d. 14 Jan 1863 Hill NH, m. 19 Nov 1818 Joanna Scribner of Hanover NH, b. 5 Aug 1800 d. 11 Feb 1875. In New Chester NH 1830, Hill NH 1840.

404 Calvin[7], 1819-1868.

Betfield, b. 20 May 1821, d. 17 Jul 1838 Danbury NH.

Mary Ann, b. 29 May 1823, d. 4 Mar 1903, m. 13 Dec 1843 Horace Clay.

405 Meshack Weare[7], 1825-1895.

406 Thomas Warren[7], 1827-1873.

Betsey E., b. 20 Jan 1830, d. 11 Oct 1846.

Isobella Jane, b. 6 May 1832, d. 22 Feb 1886, m. 14 Aug 1852 James Parker.

407 Luther[7], 1834-1899.

Clement, b. 24 Apr 1837 Hill NH, d. 24 Sep 1930 Goffstown NH, m. 24 May 1876 Fannie A. Roberts of Hill NH, b. 12 Oct 1845 d. 12 Dec 1929, dau. Jonathan and Mercy (Allen) Roberts. Farmer. In Andover NH 1860, Goffstown NH 1867. On Goffstown NH tax list 1880. No CH.

Harvey Betfield, b. 4 Apr 1839 Hill NH, d. 8 Oct 1915 Manchester NH, m. 6 Apr 1870 Adelaide M. Drew of Alton NH, b. 5 Jun 1844 d. 4 Dec 1908, dau. George and Betsey (McDuffee) Drew. In Bedford NH. In Manchester NH 1870. CH: Bertha Ora, b. May 1871, d. 16 Aug 1871; Ethelene, b. 1879, d. 2 Feb 1880.

Orrin David, b. 11 Apr 1843 Hill NH, d. 3 Mar 1913 Manchester NH, m. 11 Apr 1868 Ellen Mary Rogers of Manchester NH, b. 26 Nov 1847 d. 21 Mar 1928, dau. William M. and Sarah (Gibbs) Rogers. Trader. CH: Lizzie Mable, b. 14 Jan 1870, d. 4 Oct 1870; Sanborn, stillborn 3 Oct 1871; Grace Ellen, b. 10 May 1873, m. 10 Jul 1891 Manchester NH Horace Prescott; Lillian Belle, b. 25 Sep 1876, m. 4 Jul 1897 William T. Woodman of Havana, Cuba; Alice Maud, b. 21 Nov 1878, d. 17 Feb 1879; Dora May, b. 5 Jun 1880, d. 29 Nov 1881; Gertrude Helen, b. 20 Feb 1884, d. 19 Sep 1906; Bertha Pearl, b. 6 Nov 1886, m. 30 Sep 1905 Sidney E. Gibson.

Viola, adopted, b. 20 Mar 1848 Danbury NH, d. 7 Nov 1920 Roxbury MA, m. 27 Nov 1871 Winchester MA Charles M. Grant.

Sources: New Chester NH census 1830. Hill NH census 1840, 1850, 1860. Andover NH census 1860. Goffstown NH census 1870. Manchester NH census 1870, 1880. VR SA/NH. S18, E2, N6, Jay Norwalk rec.

221. **WILLIAM[6] SAWYER** [see 105], b. 12 Aug 1804 Springfield NH, d. 8 Jan 1860 Haverhill MA, m. 15 Sep 1827 Eliza Noyes of Plaistow NH, b. 23 Jan 1807 d. 8 Jan 1860, dau. James and Polly (Webster) Noyes. Livery stableman. In Plaistow NH 1850.

Lucinda S., b. 1827, d. 6 Sep 1835.

William, b. ca. 1833 Haverhill MA, m. 27 Sep 1864 Boston MA Elizabeth A. Prescott of Newburyport MA, dau. David and Nancy Prescott, b. ?. In Chelsea MA. Eliza Jane, b. 1834, m. 1 Jan 1863 Haverhill MA Daniel Hunt.

Ira O., b. 17 Jan 1838 Haverhill MA, d. 22 Aug 1915, m. 29 Nov 1860 Haverhill MA Martha A. Farnham, b. 1838, dau. John and Mary Farnham. CH: Grace S., b. ?, m. _____ Foote.

408 Gayton P.[7], b. 1841.

Sources: Haverhill MA census 1850. VR Haverhill MA. N40. H32.

222. **LEONARD[6] SAWYER** [see 106], b. ca. 1821 Wilmot NH, m.(1) (I)3 Nov 1844 Lynn MA Dolly Jane Knight, b. ca. 1821 d. 11 Feb 1848 Lynn MA; m.(2) 29 Oct 1848 Lynn MA Caroline Choate of Lyndeboro NH, b. ca. 1821. Cordwainer.

Henry Eugene, b. 5 Nov 1845, d. 22 Mar 1846.
Charlotte Augusta, b. 24 Oct 1852, d. 30 Aug 1853 Lynn MA.
Walter Harold, b. 22 Jun 1854, d. 16 Jan 1857.
Walter C., b. ca. 1857 Lynn MA, m. 18 Nov 1880 Lynn MA Ada E. Keene.
Clinton Algernon, b. 25 May 1858 in Lynn MA.
Clarence Leslie, b. 25 May 1858, d. 17 Oct 1858.

Sources: Lynn MA census 1850. VR Lynn MA, SA/MA.

223. **GILMAN[6] SAWYER** [see 107], b. 23 Apr 1806 Plaistow NH, d. 3 Jun 1875 Manchester NH, m.(1) 25 Nov 1834 New London NH Lois Adams of New London NH, b. ?, dau. Solomon and Mary (Sargent) Adams; m.(2) Elmira A. Blood of Deering NH, b. 1812 d. 19 Jan 1872. Adopted by his aunt, Mrs. Ebenezer Noyes (Lydia Sawyer).

409 George Washington[7], 1835-1884.
Emily Adams, b. 7 Jul 1837.

Sources: Springfield NH census 1840, 1850, 1860. New London NH census 1870. L40, N16, A7.

224. **WILLIAM[6] SAWYER** [see 108], b. 2 Mar 1804 Newbury MA. In Groveland MA.

Charles H., b. ca. 1833, d. 1851.

Sources: VR Newbury MA, Groveland MA, SA/MA. M39.

225. **REUBEN[6] SAWYER** [see 108], b. 23 Feb 1807 Newbury MA, m. 21 Aug 1827 Bradford MA Betsey Hardy, b. 1804, dau. S. Hardy. Farmer, shoemaker. In Bradford MA. Groveland MA 1855.

Enoch, b. 2 Dec 1827 Bradford MA.
Adeline, b. 20 Jul 1829, m. 18 Aug 1850 Georgetown MA Alexander C. Richie.
Elbridge A., b. 22 Oct 1831 Bradford MA. In California 1853.
Rhoda A., b. 15 Jan 1834.
410 Reland W.[7], b. 1839.

Sources: VR Newbury MA, Bradford MA, SA/MA. M39.

## SEVENTH GENERATION

226. **EDWARD BERTRAND[7] SAWYER** [see 114], b. 16 Apr 1828 Hyde Park VT, d. 1918 Hyde Park VT, m.(1) Jun 1849 Susan Almira Pennock of Hardwick VT, b. 3 May 1831 d. 30 Jun 1865, dau. Isaac Pennock; m.(2) Aug 1866 Helen M. Pennock of Wolcott VT, b. Apr 1837. Civil War: Colonel in 1st Vermont Cavalry. Lawyer. Newspaper editor 1867.

Nellie M., b. May 1850, m. 5 Apr 1871 Fred Keeler.
411 Edward Bertrand[8], b. 1857.
Martha Helen, b. 3 Aug 1859, unm. Went to Boston MA.
Bertha Myra, b. 25 Nov 1861, d. 18 Mar 1886.
Alma Dorcas, b. 9 Jan 1868.

Clarence Parsons, b. 20 Feb 1871 Hyde Park VT, d. 1921 Hyde Park VT, m. 20 Feb 1895 Frances Warner of Quebec, Canada, b. 1867. Editor of a gazette. In Hardwich VT. CH: Helen Frances, b. 24 May 1896; Alene, b. 2 Aug 1905.

Lucy Etta, b. 10 Feb 1873, m. 27 Jul 1905 Charles S. Hager. Teacher.

Sources: Hyde Park VT census 1860, 1870, 1880. VR SA/VT. D11, C4, H42.

227. **FRANKLIN E.**[7] **SAWYER** [see 114], b. 1837 Hyde Park VT, d. 1913 Hyde Park VT, m.(1) 25 Nov 1874 Elizabeth M. Wood, b. 1847 d. 1888; m.(2) 29 Oct 1905 Alzada Preston Smith, b. 1837 d. 1917. Farmer. Civil War Sergeant.

Lawrence W., b. 1878 Hyde Park VT, d. 1908 Hyde Park VT, m. 31 Mar 1897 Amber F. Whitcomb, b. ?. Laborer. CH: Son, b. 20 Jan 1899, d. 20 Jan 1900.

Sources: VR SA/VT. D11, C4.

228. **NATHAN WHEELER**[7] **SAWYER** [see 116], b. 23 Jan 1805 Deer Isle ME, d. 24 Aug 1881 Deer Isle ME, m.(1) (I) 16 Sep 1828 Deer Isle ME Ruth Pickering, b. Sep 1805 d. 21 Apr 1871, dau. Samuel Pickering; m.(2) 4 Feb 1873 Fanny (Harvey) Grant, wid., b. ? d. 5 Feb 1880. Carpenter.

Harriet, b. 10 Mar 1830, d. 4 Jan 1871, m. Robert Pickering.

412 Nathan S.[8], 1832-1859.

Eliza P., b. 26 Jul 1833, d. 6 Aug 1872, m.(I) 14 Jul 1852 Charles Johnson.

Sources: Deer Isle ME census 1830, 1840, 1850. VR Deer Isle ME.

229. **ADMIRAL GEORGE**[7] **SAWYER** [see 116], b. 25 Jul 1806 Deer Isle ME, d. 27 May 1891 Deer Isle ME, m.(1) (I) 18 May 1828 Deer Isle ME Mary Cole, b. 1805 d. 24 May 1863; m.(2) 23 Feb 1864 Mary E. Foster, b. 1812 d. 1901, dau. Samuel and Mary (Howard) Foster. Mariner.

Mary, b. 28 Jul 1830, m. 16 Dec 1849 Moody P. Gray.

Abigail, b. 8 Feb 1832, m. 26 Jun 1855 Boston MA Rufus A. Junkins.

413 Admiral George[8], 1833-1907.

414 Benjamin C.[8], 1834-1897.

415 Caleb Parker[8], 1837-1908.

Abel B., b. 5 Jan 1840, d. 28 May 1841.

Gideon H., b. 26 Jul 1842, d. 20 Apr 1843.

Son, b. ?, d. 2 Aug 1844.

Sources: Deer Isle ME census 1830, 1840, 1850, 1860. VR Deer Isle ME, SA/MA.

230. **DAVID**[7] **SAWYER** [see 116], b. 7 Sep 1808 Deer Isle ME, d. 24 Sep 1884, m.(1) (I) 20 Jul 1830 Rachel Pressey, b. 1810 d. 3 Sep 1838; m.(2) 29 Oct 1839 Adeline Dunham, b. 1811.

David, b. 4 Jan 1831 Deer Isle ME, d. 11 Apr 1831.

Elbridge P., b. 23 Apr 1834 Deer Isle ME.

Joshua Pressey, b. 20 Sep 1837 Deer Isle ME, d. 30 Jun 1904 Castine ME, m. Henrietta N. Sullivan, b. 9 Nov 1846 d. 31 Mar 1918, dau. Daniel and Sarah (Bowden) Sullivan. Henrietta judged incompetent, Rowland Brown was appointed her guardian.

Infant, b. ?, d. 23 Jan 1838.

416 John Grindle[8], b. 1840.

Mary Elizabeth, b. 19 Sep 1841, m. 15 May 1875 George W. Howard.

Lucinda Blake, b. 1 Nov 1843, d. 15 Aug 1846.

Eliza Jane, b. 12 Aug 1845, d. 23 Aug 1848.

Henry Whitney, b. 20 Mar 1846 Castine ME, d. 21 Feb 1904, m. 19 Aug 1877 Mary H. Keeler, b. ?.

Lucretia Noyes, b. 6 Sep 1849, d. 11 Jun 1854.
417 Abner Jarvis[8], b. 1850.
Frances Whitney, b. 25 Jul 1854, m. 7 Jul 1875 Fall River MA Elisha Tripp.
Sources: Castine ME census 1840, 1850, 1860. VR Castine ME, Deer Isle ME, SA/ME, SA/MA.

231. **MARK HASKELL[7] SAWYER** [see 116], b. 30 May 1815 Deer Isle ME, d. 2 Oct 1890 Deer Isle ME, m.(1) 1 Jul 1834 Deer Isle ME Susan C. Bray, b. 1815, dau. Nathaniel and Lucy (Nason) Bray; m.(2) 11 Mar 1874 Sarah D. Eaton, b. ?. Note: He was listed as Noah H. in father's will.
Margaret, b. 5 Feb 1835. Susan M., b. Apr 1837, d. 15 Apr 1863, m. 7 Oct 1856 Benjamin C. Sawyer. See sister Nancy H., below.
James Bray, b. 11 Jun 1839 Deer Isle ME, d. 16 Dec 1902, m. 14 Feb 1864 Sophronia W. Ames, b. 17 Apr 1840 d. 20 May 1912.
Samuel Holbrook, b. 18 Apr 1840 Deer Isle ME.
Nancy H., b. 2 Aug 1843, d. 5 Jan 1906, m. 29 Mar 1864 Benjamin C. Sawyer.
Hezekiah, b. 27 Apr 1846 Deer Isle ME.
Lydia H., b. 1852, m. 8 Jan 1871 Ellis S. Gray.
418 William Martin[8], 1854-1878.
Sources: Deer Isle ME census 1840 1850, 1860. VR Deer Isle ME. P82d, Dorothy Guptill rec.

232. **NATHAN D.[7] SAWYER** [see 118], b. 1849 Wolcott VT, m.(1) 5 Nov 1870 Woodbury VT Lorrisa L. Rollins of Woodbury VT, b. 26 Nov 1848, dau. Alexander and Cynthia (Laird) Rollins; m.(2) 15 May 1906 _____. Carpenter, farmer. In Walden VT, Hardwick VT, Woodbury VT 1872.
Mattie M., b. 3 Feb 1872, d. 23 Oct 1872.
Walter Irvin, b. 2 Dec 1875 Walden VT, m. 17 Mar 1897 Mertie E. Orcutt, b. ?. In Hardwick VT. CH: Daughter, b. 31 Jul 1899.
Sources: VR SA/VT. R25.

233. **CHARLES MELVIN[7] SAWYER** [see 118], b. 2 Nov 1855 Morristown VT, m. 10 Sep 1883 Hardwick VT Julie M. Colburn of Wolcott VT, b. Aug 1864. Lumberman.
Carl, b. Jun 1884, d. 4 Oct 1885.
Neal W., b. 1 Jul 1886 Hardwick VT.
Georgia M., b. 10 Nov 1888, d. 30 Sep 1891.
Clyde T., b. 20 Jul 1891 Hardwick VT.
Daughter, b. 20 Jul 1893, d. 21 Jul 1893.
Jessie L., b. 19 Jan 1898 Hardwick VT.
Nora Lydia, b. 11 Mar 1900, d. 21 Jul 1902.
Earl Charles, b. 27 Oct 1902.
Sources: VR SA/VT.

234. **FRANK CLARK[7] SAWYER** [see 119], b. Oct 1833 Hanover NH, d. 29 May 1906 Charlton MA, m.(1) 27 Aug 1853 Concord NH Mary E. Nutter of Portsmouth NH, b. 1830 d. 5 Sep 1892 Leicester MA, dau. Benjamin and Mary (Hayman) Nutter; m.(2) 1 Oct 1894 Saugus MA Jennie E. (Lewis) Chase of Maine, b. ca. 1844, dau. John and Jane W. Lewis. Civil War: Enl. in Navy 17 Mar 1863, discharged 24 May 1864, reenlisted 1864-1865. Mill superintendent. In Canaan NH, Rochester NH, Portsmouth NH, Laconia NH, Charlton MA.
Edward James, b. 4 Sep 1865 Portsmouth NH, d. 21 May 1928 Worcester MA, m. (1) 5 Jun 1895 Worcester MA Harriet J. Morse of Worcester MA, b. 1865 d. 13 Aug 1913, dau. James H. and Mary E. (Spring) Morse; m.(2) 4 Sep 1915 Warner NH Eleanor (Hackett)

Golden of Elizabeth NJ, wid., b. ?, dau. of George and Mary (Bryer) Hackett. He bur. in Manchester NH.

Frank M., b. 15 Aug 1866, d. 16 Sep 1866.

Sources: Canaan NH census 1850. Rochester NH census 1860. VR SA/MA, SA/NH. N7, L38, N44.

235. **LEASON**$^{7}$ **SAWYER** [see 120], b. 1 Feb 1807 Saco ME, d. 17 Jan 1879 Portland ME, m.(1) 13 Jul 1835 Ellsworth ME Maria Curtis, b. 6 Mar 1811 d. 17 Aug 1839; m.(2) 12 Mar 1841 Lucinda M. Curtis, b. 14 Sep 1823 d. 3 Dec 1891. Shoemaker. B/land in Scarboro ME 1847. In Ellsworth ME 1835, Bluehill ME 1840, Scarboro ME 1850, Westbrook ME 1860.

Eliza A., b. 1 Sep 1836, d. 15 Dec 1874.

John, b. 30 Nov 1837, d. 12 Aug 1861.

James H., b. 6 Dec 1838 d. 6 Jul 1901 Auburn ME, m. 29 Jan 1867 Emily Smith, b. ?. CH: Grace, b. ?, m. Dr. Bragg; Marion, b. ?, m. Arthur Grey.

Maria, b. 12 May 1843, d. 4 Mar 1921, m. 26 May 1869 Cambridge MA Simon Hitchcock.

Nathaniel, b. 28 Feb 1844 Salmon Falls ME, d. 6 Dec 1929 Freeport ME, m. 28 Nov 1863 Lucetta Tyler of Buxton ME, b. 23 Apr 1846 d. 5 Jul 1922, dau. James and Julia (Sawyer) Tyler.

Ellen, b. 15 Sep 1846, d. 6 Oct 1887.

Jones, b. 8 Jul 1848, d. 1880 Burlington IA, m. Martha _____, b. ?. CH: Lizzie, b. ?; Ella, b. ?; Leason, b. ?.

Charles S., b. 12 Aug 1850 Scarboro ME, d. 30 Dec 1926. Went to Canada.

Georgia A., b. 6 Feb 1852, d. 22 Nov 1930, m. 29 Jun 1872 Gideon P. Lowell.

419 Gardner$^{8}$, 1856-1942.

Sources: Bluehill ME census 1840. Scarboro ME census 1850. Westbrook ME census 1860. Freeport ME census 1900. VR Buxton ME, SA/ME, SA/MA. R10a, P31, Myron Sawyer rec.

236. **ABRAHAM**$^{7}$ **SAWYER** [see 120], b. 1812 Saco ME, d. 20 Feb 1877 Portland ME, m. 27 Mar 1853 Newburyport MA Sarah Hooker of Newburyport MA, b. 1811, dau. Mary Hooker. Bur in Eastern Cem., Portland ME.

420 Warren$^{8}$, b. ?.

Sources: VR SA/MA. M5.

237. **CHARLES**$^{7}$ **SAWYER** [see 121], b. 4 Dec 1813 Saco ME, d. 8 Nov 1897 Newport ME, m. 16 Jan 1838 Augusta ME Elizabeth Plummer of Rochester NH, b. Jan 1815 d. 21 Nov 1904. Hotel keeper.

Louise, b. ca. 1839.

Ellen L., b. ca. 1841.

421 Charles H.$^{8}$, 1844-1913.

Ann A., b. 1846.

Sarah J., b. Apr 1847.

George E., b. 1848 Augusta ME.

Sumner F., b. Feb 1851 Augusta ME.

Elizabeth E., b. Aug 1854, d. 6 Nov 1855.

Carrie E., b. 1859.

Sources: Augusta ME census 1840, 1850. VR Saco ME, Augusta ME, SA/ME.

238. **JAMES**$^{7}$ **SAWYER** [see 121], b. 31 Dec 1818 Saco ME, d. 5 Nov 1891 Conway NH, m. Addie O._____, b. ?. Stableman.

422 James Walter$^{8}$, b. ca. 1847.

Sources: VR Saco ME, SA/NH.

239. **GEORGE FRANCIS$^{7}$ SAWYER** [see 121], b. 3 Aug 1830 Saco ME, d. 6 Feb 1886 Augusta ME, m.(1) 11 Apr 1855 Augusta ME Ann S. Bolton of Saco ME, b. 1833 d. 27 Apr 1882, dau. Walter Bolton; m.(2) 16 Jul 1883 Boston MA Elida H. McKenzie of Nova Scotia, Canada, b. ? d. Cambridge MA. Farmer, broker. In Augusta ME 1860, Vassalboro ME 1863, Taunton MA 1864, Cambridge MA 1882.

423 Arthur W.$^{8}$, b. 1863.

Sources: Augusta ME census 1860. Vassalboro ME census 1870. VR Saco ME, Augusta ME, SA/MA.

240. **HENRY$^{7}$ SAWYER** [see 122], b. 11 Jun 1816 Parsonsfield ME, d. 12 Jan 1893 Waterboro ME, m. 2 Aug 1840 Mary Guptill of Cornish ME, b. 11 May 1822 d. 6 Aug 1867, dau. Timothy and Anna Guptill. Farmer. On Cornish ME voting list 1838. B/land in Hiram ME 1847.

Emilie, b. 1840, d. Dec 1863.

424 Francis E.$^{8}$, 1842-1910.

Hezikiah, b. 18 Dec 1846 Cornish ME, d. 23 Jan 1920 Hiram ME. In Limington ME 1850.

Ervin, b. Jan 1848, d. Aug 1863.

Henry, b. 1849 Hiram ME, d. 5 Sep 1894, unm.

Mary A., b. 1851.

Elizabeth Hannah, b. 23 Dec 1852, d. 6 May 1924, m. Stephen Young.

Addison, b. 20 May 1855 Hiram ME, d. 30 Jun 1932 Limerick ME, m. 3 Dec 1895 Limerick ME Ada M. Watson of Limerick ME, b. 2 Jul 1860 d. 8 Oct 1957, dau. Nathaniel and Annie E. Watson. In Limerick and Cornish ME. Both bur. Limerick ME.

Priscilla, b. 1858, d. 24 May 1881.

Sarah A., b. 1860.

Emma G., b. 1865, d. 25 May 1881.

Sources: Hiram ME census 1850. Cornish ME census 1860, 1870. Limington ME census 1870. VR Parsonsfield ME, SA/ME. E13, C62, R10c, M5, Obit.

241. **DANIEL P.$^{7}$ SAWYER** [see 122], b. 1838 Hiram ME, d. 2 Nov 1886 Hiram ME, m. 18 Jul 1858 Limington ME Harriet A. Sawyer of Brownfield ME, b. 11 Apr 1835 d. 18 Sep 1908, dau. Joseph B. and Jane (Ellis) Sawyer. Farmer.

Elizabeth, b. Mar 1859, d. 31 Aug 1876 Brookline MA.

425 Albert Dean$^{8}$, 1860-1919.

Emily J., b. 22 Feb 1862, d. 22 Jul 1939, m.(1) 1881 Freedom NH Orrell Gilpatrick, m.(2) John E. Flye in Cornish ME.

Willis E., b. 5 May 1864 Hiram ME, m.(I) 19 Mar 1889 Porter ME Rosa V. Sawyer of Limerick ME, b. Feb 1872, dau. Jacob and Harriet (York) Sawyer [see 364]. Wid. m. 6 Nov 1901 Joseph A. Hill. CH: Justin Eugene, b. 14 Aug 1890, d. 30 Jan 1945, m. Lena Hill, b. ?; Harvey E., b. 2 Apr 1895, d. 8 Mar 1921 Limerick ME (suicide).

Elvira, b. 12 Feb 1867, d. 3 Feb 1934, m. 22 Jul 1882 Freedom NH Charles C. Wescott.

Lovina, b. 1868.

Ervin Daniel, b. ca. 1870 Hiram ME, d. 1910 Hiram ME, m. 11 Oct 1895 Limerick ME Abbie S. Fogg of Limerick ME, b. 1 May 1871 d. 1 Apr 1910, dau. Charles D. and Frances (McKusick) Fogg. Farmer. In Brownfield ME 1895. He bur. in Stanley Cem., So. Hiram ME. No CH.

Hattie F., b. 12 Sep 1871, m.(1) Elwood D. Harriman, m.(2) 12 Nov 1892 Conway NH Waldo H. Hanson.

Winifred, b. 1874.

Melvin L., b. 1877 Hiram ME, d. 20 Sep 1944 Hiram ME, m. 21 Jul 1906 Freedom NH Lucy B. Wakefield of Jay Bridge ME, b. 1889, dau. Sidney S. and Mattie W. (Whitten) Wakefield of Saco ME. He bur. in Stanley Cem., South Hiram ME. CH: Sylvia, b. 1909, m. 11 Apr 1926 Loren M. Brown of Raymond ME; Ethel B., b. 1911, m. 5 Dec 1928 Lawrence C. Brown of Raymond ME.

Weston, b. 1879 So. Hiram ME, m. 2 Jul 1904 Freedom NH Mary O'Lena Watkins of Providence RI, b. Nov 1887 d. 20 Apr 1910 Portland ME, dau. Samuel and Josephine (Cougster) Watkins (both mulatto). Farmer.

Sources: Hiram ME census 1860, 1870, ME 1880 census index. VR Limington ME, Raymond ME, Newfield ME, SA/ME. N6, C53, M5, W42, Robert L. Taylor rec.

242. **IRA C.$^{7}$ SAWYER** [see 122], b. 2 Mar 1840 Hiram ME, d. 12 Apr 1906 Springvale ME, m.(1) 15 Feb 1865 Bridgton ME Ellen Edes, b. ?; m.(2) Georgia Page of Harrison ME, b. Apr 1857 d. 1926. Physician/surgeon. In Naples ME 1879, Springvale ME 1885. He bur. in Riverside Cem., Springvale ME.

Florence M., b. 1879, d. 21 Feb 1896.

426 Claude E.$^{8}$, 1885-1948.

George B., b. 1890 Springvale ME, m.(1) (div.); m.(2) 25 Apr 1936 Stratham NH Irene French of Stratham NH, b. 1916, dau. John and Annie (O'Brien) French.

Sources: ME 1880 census index. VR Bridgton ME. E18, R10a.

243. **NATHANIEL$^{7}$ SAWYER** [see 123], b. 26 Feb 1800 Saco ME, d. 28 Jan 1882 Lisbon ME, m.(1) 11 Oct 1821 Buxton ME Nancy Harmon of Buxton ME, b. 12 Aug 1802; m.(2) 29 Mar 1829 Lisbon ME Harriet E. Norris of Conway NH, b. 27 Aug 1809 d. 14 Feb 1852, dau. Josiah and Hannah (Davis) Norris; m.(3) Hannah C._____, b. 8 Jan 1817 d. 24 Jun 1902. Hotel keeper. In Saco ME 1830-50. He bur. in cem. on Rt. 5, Hollis ME.

Mary Elizabeth, b. 30 Jun 1822.

427 Aaron$^{8}$, b. 1830.

Sarah J., b. 24 Oct 1831, m. Pelatiah Foss.

David, b. 2 Jan 1834, d. 10 Aug 1837.

George S., b. 3 Dec 1835, d. 19 Aug 1837.

428 Norris$^{8}$, 1838-1894.

George, b. 1 Oct 1839, d. 3 Aug 1840.

Edgecomb, b. 29 Nov 1840, d. 12 Dec 1842.

Sources: Saco ME census 1830, 1840, 1850. VR Saco ME. N28, S1, M5, Obit.

244. **ISAAC$^{7}$ SAWYER** [see 124], b. 24 Feb 1798 Saco ME, m. 30 Dec 1821 Sarah A. Hayford of Tamworth NH, b. 1795. War of 1812: Private in Captain Robert McLellan's Company, Portland ME. In Greenville ME 1827.

Sarah A., b. 1823.

Mary J., b. 7 Jun 1825.

429 Lewis$^{8}$,1827-1920.

Maria, b. 1830.

430 Charles George$^{8}$, 1832-1902.

Amanda, b. 1841.

Sources: Haskell Plantation (Greenville) ME census 1830. Greenville ME census 1840, 1850. VR Greenville ME, SA/ME. S1.

245. **HENRY H.$^{7}$ SAWYER** [see 124], b. 22 Mar 1806 Saco ME, m. 23 Mar 1828 Saco ME Hannah Patterson, b. 7 Mar 1808. Farmer. In Standish ME 1840.

Samuel, b. 1837 Saco ME, d. 24 May 1885 Auburn NH, m.(1) 1 Jan 1865 Franklin MA Caroline M. Lawrence of Wrentham MA, b. ca. 1840, dau. Addison and Olive Lawrence; m.(2) 25 Dec 1871 Portsmouth NH Mary E. Preble of Maine, b. ca. 1839, dau. Stephen and Julia Preble. In Standish ME, Wrentham MA. CH: Mary Olive, b. 3 Dec 1865; Sylvia L., b. 6 Oct 1867, m. 25 Dec 1895 Franklin MA Ernest C. Greenwood.

Sources: Saco ME census 1830. Standish ME census 1840. VR Saco ME, Franklin MA, SA/ME, SA/MA. S1.

246. **JOEL$^{7}$ SAWYER** [see 125], b. 22 Apr 1808 Saco ME, d. 14 Jun 1895 Greenville ME, m. Emily C. Woodman, b. 1815 d. 23 Dec 1896. Farmer. In Greenville ME 1840.

Franceah, b. 1834.
Emma, b. 1836, m. Samuel Scammon.
431 Archelous Woodman$^{8}$, 1838-1914.
Andrew T., b. 1840, d. 1863 in Civil War.
Hannah S., b. Feb 1842, m. 13 Feb 1864 Frank L. Sawyer.
432 Edmund Merritt$^{8}$, 1845-1922.
Isadore M., b. 1847, m. _____ Russell.
Eveline, b. Nov 1848.
433 Marshall O.$^{8}$, 1852-1917.
Mary A., b. Aug 1854.

Sources: Greenville ME census 1840, 1850, 1860, 1870. VR Saco ME, SA/ME. M5, H26.

247. **EDMUND$^{7}$ SAWYER** [see 125], b. 15 Sep 1809 Saco ME, d. 6 Jan 1894, m. Lavinia Snow of Milo ME, b. 1814. In Milford ME 1835, Kittery ME 1840, Medford ME 1860.

434 Marshall W.$^{8}$, b. 1839.
Helen Elizabeth, b. 1841.
Carolaide, b. 10 Mar 1849, d. 31 Jan 1898, m. 27 Nov 1872 William Walton. Elizabeth F., b. ?, m. I_____ G. Mayo.

Sources: Kittery ME census 1840, 1850. Medford ME census 1860. VR SA/ME.

248. **LUTHER L.$^{7}$ SAWYER** [see 125], b. 4 Mar 1811 Saco ME, d. 21 May 1900 Bangor ME, m. Lorinda Blanchard, b. 1816 d. 26 Mar 1886. Farmer. In Kittery ME 1840, Bangor ME 1860.

Alonzo J., b. 1838 Kittery ME, m. 4 Feb 1864 Old Town ME Celesta M. Turner, b.?. In Kittery ME 1850. Wid. m. 8 Aug 1886 George F. Lull.
Himan M., b. 1841 Kittery ME.
Alfred L., b. 1844 Kittery ME.
435 Seth H.$^{8}$, b. 1852.

Sources: Kittery ME census 1840, 1850. Bangor ME census 1860, 1870. VR Bangor ME, Old Town ME.

249. **ANDREW S.$^{7}$ SAWYER** [see 125], b. 5 Nov 1812 Saco ME, m.(I) 2 Nov 1835 Bangor ME Harriet Lombard of Gorham ME, b. 31 Jul 1807. B/land Orono ME 1833. In Medford ME 1835, Kittery ME 1840.

Roxanna, b. 1836.
436 Frank L.$^{8}$, 1839-1915.
437 Ether C. G.$^{8}$, 1841-1910.
438 Alfred Freeman$^{8}$, b. 1842.
Harriet R., b. 1844.
439 Andrew Fitzland$^{8}$, b. 1848.

Marietta, b. 1850.
Sources: Kittery ME census 1840, 1850. VR Gorham ME, Bangor ME, SA/ME. R10d.

250. **ARTHUR B.$^{7}$ SAWYER** [see 125], b. 10 Apr 1821 Saco ME, d. 22 Jun 1910 Greenville ME m.(1) 29 Aug 1847 Biddeford ME Eunice B. Lombard of Gorham ME, b. ?; m. (2) 7 May 1899 Greenville ME Huldah (Tidd) Gorham, b. Mar 1869, dau. William and Sarah (Nye) Tidd. Mason. In Kittery ME 1850, Medford ME 1880.

Helen A., b. 1848.
440 Henry P.$^{8}$, 1850-1909.
Caroline F., b. 14 Apr 1852.
441 John Greeley$^{8}$, b. 1855.
Marion R., b. 1859.
Nellie W., b. 19 Aug 1864.
Jennie L., b. 1869.

Sources: Kittery ME census 1850. ME census 1880 index. Greenville ME census 1890. VR Greenville ME, SA/ME. Henry's death certificate.

251. **ALBERT$^{7}$ SAWYER** [see 126], b. 1 Oct 1816 Saco ME, d. bef. 1880, m. 1 Sep 1840 Kennebunk ME Elizabeth Scammon, b. 1818 d. 1896. In Portland ME 1851, Cape Elizabeth ME 1870. He bur. in Bayview Cem., So. Portland ME. Wid. in Cape Elizabeth ME 1880.

George Addison, b. 1843, d. 1889.
Carrie A., b. 1848, d. 21 Feb 1924, m. Charles S. Blair.
442 Richard S.$^{8}$, 1852-1918.
William Hayden, b. 1854, d. 6 Aug 1854.
Mary Collins, b. 28 Jan 1857, d. 23 Jun 1942, m. Alfred M. Crook.
Warren J., b. Apr 1861, d. 12 Mar 1886.

Sources: Saco ME census 1840. Cape Elizabeth ME census 1870. VR Saco ME, Kennebunk ME, SA/ME. M5.

252. **DANIEL FRANKLIN$^{7}$ SAWYER** [see 126], b. 29 Jan 1846 Saco ME, d. 26 Feb 1924 Ossipee NH, m. Celia A. Shaw of Effingham NH, b. 1861 d. 14 Feb 1903, dau. Leonard W. and Sophronia (Stillings) Shaw. Farmer. In Effingham NH 1880, Ossipee NH 1893.

Daughter, stillborn 12 Sep 1884.
Dora F., b. ?, had son Hayes William, b. 27 Oct 1900, d. 13 Mar 1963, who m. Violet Brown.
George L., b. 6 Feb 1886 Effingham NH. In Haverhill MA?
443 Guy Llewelyn$^{8}$, 1887-1967.
Ruth A., b. 12 Oct 1893, d. 23 Oct 1979, m. Guy Libby of Freedom NH.

Sources: Effingham NH census 1880. VR Saco ME, SA/NH.

253. **SIMEON$^{7}$ SAWYER** [see 127], b. 12 Aug 1821 Saco ME, d. 30 Dec 1898 Saco ME, m. Nancy J. Brown of Saco ME, b. 23 Nov 1838 d. 23 Apr 1923. Brickmaker. Executor of sister Harriet's will. He bur. in Laurel Grove Cem., Saco ME.

Fred A., b. Nov 1872 Saco ME, m. 5 Apr 1905 Saco ME Gertrude D. Merrill of Buxton ME, b. 31 Dec 1880 d. 2 Apr 1916. dau. William J. and Phoebe (Nason) Merrill. In Augusta ME.

Sources: Saco ME census 1850. ME 1880 census index. VR Saco ME, SA/MA. P82k.

254. **JAMES LEWIS$^{7}$ SAWYER** [see 127], b. 16 Feb 1828 Saco ME, d. 26 Nov 1911 Buxton ME, m. 6 May 1855 Saco ME Margaret T. Marston of Canton ME, b. 9 Aug 1835 d. 13 Dec 1894,

dau. Joseph and Susan (Ellis) Marston. Blacksmith. In Saco ME 1850, Buxton ME 1860. He bur. in Tory Hill Cem., Buxton ME.

444 George A.[8], 1857-1888.

Sarah E., b. 22 Feb 1862, d. 1939.

Charles Lewis, b. 25 Jul 1868 Buxton ME, d. 1947 Buxton ME, m.(1) 24 Dec 1898 Buxton ME Cora B. Berry of Saco ME, b. 1872 d. 1906, dau. Edward and Harriet (Deering) Berry; m.(2) 25 Dec 1907 Georgia B. Bennett, b. 1877 d. 1951. Farmer. He bur. in Tory Hill Cem., Buxton ME.

445 Cyrus Elwyn[8], 1870-1937.

Sources: Saco ME census 1850. Buxton ME census 1860, 1870. ME 1880 census index. VR Saco ME, Buxton ME, SA/ME. M5, R17.

255. **JASON H.[7] SAWYER** [see 127], b. 24 Jan 1830 Saco ME, d. 31 Dec 1918 Saco ME, m.(1) 23 Feb 1851 Buxton ME Clarinda B. Marston of Hartford ME, b. 4 Aug 1828, dau. John and Mary J. (Hall) Marston; m.(2) 4 Jun 1868 Buxton ME Hannah C. Carle of Buxton ME, b. 11 May 1838 d. 20 Jul 1920, dau. George and Eunice (Watts) Carle.

George F., b. 1853, d. 26 Jan 1870.

Bertha M., b. 1872.

Edwin J., b. 1875 Saco ME, m. 26 Sep 1900 Biddeford ME Lilla E. Billings, b. 1878 d. 8 Nov 1904, dau. George P. and Maria (Ladd) Billings.

Son, b. 1880.

Sources: Saco ME census 1850, 1860, 1870. ME 1880 census index. VR Saco ME, Buxton ME. VR Biddeford ME, SA/ME. Robert L. Taylor rec.

256. **WILLIAM[7] SAWYER** [see 128], b. 12 Jun 1803 Saco ME, m. 6 Dec 1827 Esther Spencer, b. 6 Mar 1808. In Saco ME 1830-1850.

Elizabeth, b. 4 Feb 1830.

Lucy J., b. 8 May 1832.

Sarah, b. 1 Dec 1833.

Juliann, b. 3 Oct 1835, m 4 Feb 1864 Rollingsford NH Lorenzo D. Brackett.

Horatio, b. 12 Jul 1839 Saco ME. In Civil War one week.

Abigail F., b. 7 Oct 1841.

Ellen, b. 1844.

Martha, b. 1845.

William, b. 1848 Saco ME.

Sources: Saco ME census 1830, 1840, 1850. VR Saco ME. S1, N6.

257. **FREDERICK WILLIAM[7] SAWYER** [see 128], b. 22 Apr 1810 Saco ME, d. 6 Sep 1875, m. 18 Sep 1849 Caroline Beal Burgess of Sandwich MA, b. 1 Mar 1821, dau. Benjamin J. and Mary (Swift) Burgess. Lawyer. In Boston MA 1838, Cambridge MA.

Ella Burgess, b. 15 Aug 1850, drowned 15 Aug 1863.

Frederick Charles, b. 29 Jul 1853 Cambridge MA.

Rufus F. Burgess, b. 8 May 1860 Cambridge MA.

Sources: VR SA/MA. N5, B95.

258. **HORACE[7] SAWYER** [see 129], b. 28 Feb 1816 Saco ME, d. 14 May 1900, m. 22 Dec 1850 Scarboro ME Lydia J. Moulton of Scarboro ME, b. 17 Aug 1824 d. 10 Mar 1912, dau. Joshua and Lydia (Stone) Moulton. He bur. in Tory Hill Cem., Buxton ME.

Frederick Woodbury, b. 17 Jan 1854, d. 27 Aug 1888, unm.

Elmer Freedom, b. 3 Sep 1861, d. 22 Nov 1881.

446 Charles Oliver[8], 1865-1936.
Sources: Saco ME census 1850, 1860, 1870. VR Saco ME, SA/ME. M5, M57, M3.

259. **CHARLES WILLIAM[7] SAWYER** [see 130], b. 12 Mar 1816 Saco ME, d. 21 Jan 1858 Saco ME, m. 13 Dec 1837 Hannah Berry of Saco ME, b. ?. Lumberman, had mills in Saco and Biddeford ME. B/land in Scarboro ME 1864-1865.
447 Gilbert Augustus[8], 1838-1903.
Lucy T., b. 1 Mar 1840, d. 10 Nov 1894, m. 9 Mar 1859 Dorrance Littlefield.
448 John Quincy[8], 1841-1916.
449 Charles Henry[8], 1843-1916.
George Hopkins, b. 28 Oct 1845, d. 15 Aug 1846.
Martha H., b. 23 Jun 1847, m. Samuel Edgerly.
450 George Franklin[8], b. 1849.
James Rishworth, b. 4 Jul 1849 Saco ME.
451 Herbert[8], 1854-1905.
Sarah E., b. 16 Dec 1856, m. Oakes Drinkwater.
Sources: Saco ME census 1840, 1850. VR Saco ME, SA/ME. P82k.

260. **STEPHEN[7] SAWYER** [see 130], b. 5 May 1820 Saco ME, d. 28 Jun 1902 Saco ME, m.(1)29 Jan 1844 Pelham NH Louisa M. Butter of New Hampshire, b. 1823 d. 23 Apr 1853; m.(2) 7 Feb 1856 Saco ME Emily Cole, b. 16 Jun 1830 d. 24 Jun 1893, dau. Benjamin F.and Mary (Jacobs) Cole. Carpenter.
Clara A., b. 1849, d. 13 Sep 1850.
Orville B., b. 1857, d. 10 Sep 1858.
Sarah Lucy, b. 1859.
Benjamin F., b. 19 Oct 1865 Saco ME, d. 4 Jun 1919 Fairfield ME, m. 23 Dec 1896 Saco ME Mary G. Lord of Saco ME, b. Jun 1874 d. 3 Jul 1904, dau. Augustus and Lydia (Huff) Lord. Farmer.
Frederick A., b. Mar 1870 Saco ME, m. 29 Oct 1895 Saco ME Eva Deering of Saco ME, b. 1874, dau. George E. and Sarah (Cole) Deering. Carpenter. CH: Rodney M., b. 26 Oct 1896, d. 4 Feb 1897.
Sources: Saco ME census 1850. ME 1880 census index. VR Saco ME, SA/ME.

261. **JAMES[7] SAWYER** [see 130], b. 5 Jun 1822 Saco ME, d. 18 Dec 1901, m. 18 May 1847 Limington ME Sophia Foss of Limington ME, b. 1823 d. 23 Feb 1896, dau. John and Jane (Joy) Foss. Physician. In Biddeford ME 1850. Appointed guardian of brother Charles William 1859. Executor of brother Augustus' estate 1869. He bur. Biddeford ME.
452 Frank Haller[8], 1850-1918.
Sources: Biddeford ME census 1850. VR Saco ME, Limington ME, SA/ME. P82k, D37.

262. **HORACE BACON[7] SAWYER** [see 131], b. 16 Feb 1830 Saco ME, d. 23 Jun 1893 Havverhill MA, m. 31 Jul 1860 White River Junction VT Clarissa Carter. of Lebanon NH, b. 15 Mar 1841 d. 24 Apr 1910, dau. Horace B. and Ruth (Wood) Carter. Attended school of theology in Concord NH. Minister. In Putney VT, Wells ME 1862-1864, Wilmot NH 1870, Danbury NH, Albion ME, and Brunswick ME 1880-1887
Sarah A., b. 12 Dec 1861, d. in Putney VT.
George Mark, b. 1864 Wells ME, m. 30 Jul 1885 Boston MA Annie E. Galvin of Quincy MA, b. 1864, dau. Jerry and Hannah Galvin. Clerk.
Harvey Lincoln, b. 1867, d. 1888.
453 Clarence Evans[8], 1869-1941.

Clara Mabel, b. 1875, m. W_____ O. Capethorn of Natick MA.
Sources: Wilmot NH census 1870. ME 1880 census index. VR SA/ME, SA/MA. L30.

263. **GREENLEAF[7] SAWYER** [see 131], b. Jun 1835 Saco ME, d. 2 May 1907 Saco ME, m. Sarah G. Chick, b. 6 Aug 1837 d. 11 Nov 1911, dau. Sidney and Lettice (Chick) Chick.
454 Howard M.[8], b. 1860.
Ada, b. 1867.
Sources: Saco ME census 1870. VR SA/ME. L30.

264. **NOAH[7] SAWYER** [see 132], b. 18 Dec 1832 Saco ME, d. 26 Jan 1899 Bridgton ME, m. 27 May 1858 Biddeford ME Ruby F. Farnham of Sebago ME, b. 21 Sep 1832 d. 3 Aug 1918, dau. Alfred and Sarah (Ross) Farnham. In Bridgton ME 1860.
455 Marshall[8], 1859-1903.
Sarah A., b. 16 May 1860, d. 30 Apr 1919 Augusta ME State Hospital.
Carrie Louise, b. 24 Jan 1861, m. 20 Jul 1898 Ed. A. Pingree of Rhode Island.
Emma C., b. 7 Nov 1863, d. 11 Sep 1946, m. 19 Jul 1885 Everett Gove.
456 Howard B.[8], 1866-1895.
Charles Cook, b. 22 Dec 1871 Bridgton ME, d. New York City, m.(1) 25 Sep 1895 Bridgton ME Hattie M. Warren of Bridgton ME, b. 16 Oct 1874 d. 11 Dec 1917, dau. Henry and Mary Tabitha (Wentworth) Warren; m.(2) Ethel Clarisse _____, b. 1873. Clerk. CH: Ethel M., b. 5 May 1889 Pownal ME; Warren, b. 25 Jun 1896, d. 29 Jul 1896.
Sources: Bridgton ME census 1860, 1870. ME 1880 census index. VR Saco ME, Biddeford ME, Bridgton ME, Pownal ME, SA/ME. G30, R10a, W31.

265. **ALONZO[7] SAWYER** [see 132], b. 25 Jul 1843 Saco ME, d. 1919 Biddeford ME, m. Abby Grant of Wells ME, b. Jan 1848 d. 2 Jul 1932. Farmer. In Saco ME 1880.
Lizzie H., b. 26 Apr 1873, m. _____ Viles. Went to Colorado.
Mary A., b. 26 Dec 1874 d. 21 Nov 1923, m. _____ Littlefield of Saco ME.
Ethel B., b. 25 Dec 1876, d. 16 Nov 1914.
Fred, b. 22 Feb 1882 Saco ME, d. 8 Nov 1940, m. 26 Nov 1908 Lorna M. Ladd, b. ?. CH: Infant, stillborn 12 Mar 1910.
Harry, b. 21 Sep 1893, d. 24 Feb 1884.
Lester M., b. 1890 Saco ME, m. 9 Aug 1912 Portsmouth NH Mamie Ham of Saco ME, b. 1891, dau. Alpha and Jennie (Duncan) Ham.
Sources: Saco ME census 1880. VR SA/ME. P82k, M. E. Senior rec.

266. **ORRIN[7] SAWYER** [see 132], b. 5 Sep 1850 Saco ME, d. 2 May 1920 Saco ME, m. 3 Jun 1871 Alice Andrews of Saco ME, b. ?. Carpenter.
Eva, b. 1872.
Noah N., b. 1876 Saco ME, m. Emily Cole of Biddeford ME, b. ?.
Sources: ME census 1880 index. VR SA/ME.

267. **ALBERT C.[7] SAWYER** [see 133], b. 11 Apr 1844 Saco ME, m.(1) 12 Sep 1866 Jennie N. Frazier, b. 1845 d. 1 Oct 1881, dau. John Gilpatrick; m.(2) 5 Nov 1886 Boston MA Ella C. Mitchell of New Brunswick, Canada, b. ?, dau. John F. and Sarah E. Mitchell. Clerk. In Saco ME 1880.
Mary M., b. 1868, m. 30 Oct 1889 Boston MA Charles H. Mitchell.

Albert M., b. 1869 Saco ME, m. 21 Dec 1891 Boston MA Bessie Curtis of Boston MA, b. ca. 1874, dau. Charles R. and Mary A. Curtis. Salesman. In Saco ME 1880, Boston MA 1893. CH: Son, b. 23 Dec 1893.
Annie G., b. 1874, m. 7 Aug 1895 Boston MA Albert F. Paine.
Katy, b. Dec 1875.
Alice Mabel, b. Jan 1878.
Sources: Saco ME census 1870, 1880. VR Saco ME, SA/ME, SA/MA. B99.

268. **JOHN[7] SAWYER** [see 134], b. 13 Jan 1821 Hopkinton NH, d. 3 Dec 1908 Boscawen NH, m.(1) 23 Jan 1844 Polly E. Hoit of Concord NH, b. 23 Apr 1826 d. 19 Feb 1851; m.(2) 8 Oct 1863 Boscawen NH Charlotte H. Stone of Webster NH, b. 25 Feb 1839, dau. Peter and Ruth (Corser) Stone; m.(3) ?; m.(4) 6 Jun 1889 Elizabeth Stevens of Ireland, b. 1831. In Concord NH 1850.
Alonzo P., b. 7 May 1844, d. 26 Nov 1848.
457 Edwin[8], 1845-1915.
Sources: Concord NH census 1850. VR SA/NH. C79, A2, A3.

269. **SAMUEL CHASE[7] SAWYER** [see 136], b. 15 Oct 1811 Newbury MA, m. 7 May 1839 Haverhill MA Martha (Kimball) Ayer, Haverhill MA, b. ?. Shoe manufacturer. In Bradford MA.
458 Edward Ayer[8], b. 1839.
Martha F., b. Aug 1841, d. 2 Mar 1844.
Isobella, b. 30 Aug 1844, m. 9 Aug 1865 Bradford MA Hazen W. Swazey.
Helen Florence, b. 17 Sep 1847, d. 27 Mar 1848.
Emma Florence, b. 12 May 1851.
Carrie Elizabeth, b. 1 Oct 1853.
Martha Louise, b. 17 Feb 1856.
Lewis Warren, b. 25 Oct 1858 Bradford MA.
Bertha May, b. 10 May 1862.
Sources: VR Newbury MA, Haverhill MA, Bradford MA.

270. **JACOB[7] SAWYER** [see 137], b. 16 Jun 1794 Warner NH, d. 6 Dec 1865 Manchester NH, m. Apr 1820 Laura Bartlett of Warner NH, b. 13 Aug 1797 d. 9 Apr 1877, dau. Joseph and Susannah Bartlett. Railroad clerk. In Warner NH 1820, Henniker NH 1830, Manchester NH 1850.
Joseph Bartlett, b. 3 Oct 1823 Warner NH, d. 28 May 1897 Manchester NH, m. Rachel C. Barnes of England, b. 5 May 1835 d. 30 Dec 1900, dau. John and Mary (Dale) Campbell. Civil engineer. In Manchester NH 1870. CH: Daughter, stillborn 29 Oct 1861; Mary D., b. 16 Jul 1865, d. 26 Dec 1896, unm.; Sarah G., b. 18 Aug 1869, d. 15 Jul 1916, unm.
459 Henry Edmund[8], 1826-1906.
Edward, b. 24 Jun 1828 Henniker NH, m. 25 Feb 1864 Charlestown MA Frances Elizabeth Everett of Charlestown MA, b. 1837, dau. Horace and Julia (Dodd) Everett. Civil engineer. In Newton MA 1878. CH: Frances Everett, b. 18 Jun 1865, m. 25 Feb 1890 Newton MA Herbert G. Pratt.
460 John Marshall[8], b. 1831.
George Blagdon, b. 28 Feb 1834 Henniker NH, d. 19 Sep 1903 Wiscassett ME, m. 3 May 1859 Anna A. Lord of So. Berwick ME, b. 15 Jul 1836 d. 8 Aug 1920, dau. Oliver and Abigail (Goodwin) Lord. Lawyer. In Waldoboro ME 1860. CH: Annie L., b. 12 Mar 1860, d. Portland ME; Edith A., b. 17 Sep 1865; Helen F., b. 4 May 1867.
461 Jacob Herbert[8], b. 1837.
Sources: Warner NH census 1820. Henniker NH census 1830, 1840. Manchester NH census 1850. Waldoboro ME census 1860. VR SA/MA, SA/ME. A20.

271. **EDMUND[7] SAWYER** [see 137], b. 23 Apr 1802 Warner NH, d. 20 May 1856 Charlestown MA, m. 23 Feb 1836 Boston MA Rebecca Fairbanks, b. 5 Aug 1808 d. 30 Mar 1878, dau. Amos and Rebecca (Whitney) Fairbanks. Machinist. In Boston MA 1827. He bur. in Forest Hills Cem., Boston MA.

462 Charles Edmund[8], 1836-1904.
Eliza Rebecca, b. 11 Sep 1838.
Georgianna Frances, b. 12 Apr 1841, m. 26 Sep 1878 Boston MA Edward L. Perkins.
463 Horace Fairbanks[8], b. 1843.
Caroline Marion, b. 7 Nov 1846, d. 13 Jan 1865.
Sources: VR Boston MA, Harvard MA, SA/MA. F2.

272. **JOSEPH[7] SAWYER** [see 138], b. 18 Apr 1802 Warner NH, m. Anna C. Sawyer, b. 2 Sep 1809 d. Jan 1857 Minnesota. In Warner NH 1840-1850.

Florence, b. 1837, m. Isaac Sanborn. Went to Minnesota.
Mary L., b. 1840, m. Alfred Sanborn. Went to California.
Joseph A., b. 1847 Warner NH, m. 1881 Nellie Abbot of Minnesota, b. ?.
William F., b. 1850. Went to Minnesota.
Sources: Warner NH census 1840, 1850. B40.

273. **JOSEPH[7] SAWYER** [see 139], b. 10 Apr 1809 Newport NH, d. 13 Aug 1857 Newport NH, m. 6 Apr 1837 Newport NH Mary Colby of Hopkinton NH, b. 15 Aug 1812. Farmer.

Charles, b. ca. 1837.
Mary Jane, b. 31 Mar 1838, m. 10 Nov 1859 James W. Miller.
Augusta L., b. 31 Aug 1839, d. 25 Mar 1886, m. 25 Jun 1863 Edmund Wheeler.
464 Andrew Joseph[8], 1844-1932.
Sources: Newport NH census 1850. W32, W33, N6.

274. **LANGDON[7] SAWYER** [see 139], b. 7 Sep 1815 Newport NH, d. 8 Nov 1879 Springfield VT, m.(1) 20 Jun 1850 Marcia Smith of Springfield VT, b. 1 Sep 1821 d. 23 Mar 1862, dau. Hugh and Elizabeth Smith; m.(2) Sarah G. Gregg of Unity NH, b. ?. Physician. In Springfield VT 1844. B/land in Grafton VT 1868. Sarah B/land in Grafton VT 1873. He bur. in Summer Hill Cem., Springfield VT.

Frank Page, b. 12 Jan 1856, d. 28 Apr 1864.
Lizzie, b. ?, d. 8 Jan 1858.
Marcia, b. ?, d. 8 Jan 1858.
Twins, b. 1 Feb 1858, d. same day.
Helen Frances, b. 4 May 1865, m. 10 May 1884 George Earle.
Frederick Langdon, b. 12 Aug 1867 Unity NH. In Springfield VT.
William Gregg, b. 10 Jul 1869 Springfield VT.
George Thompson, b. 26 Apr 1871 Springfield VT.
Sources: VR SA/VT. W33, B26.

275. **JOHN B.[7] SAWYER** [see 139], b. 10 Sep 1817 Newport NH, m. Julia A. Copp, b. 25 May 1820. Farmer. In Decatur WI.

Laura, b. 11 Jul 1849, teacher in Lincoln NE.
Daniel, b. 4 Nov 1851, d. 1878.
Frank, b. 22 Feb 1853.
Nettie, b. 18 Mar 1854.
Langdon, b. 26 Jul 1857 Decatur WI.

Carrie, b. 11 Oct 1859.
William, b. 4 Sep 1861.
Julia, b. 10 Sep 1863.
Kittie, b. 18 Aug 1865.
Charles, b. 18 May 1868 Decatur WI.
Sources: W33.

276 **BENJAMIN F.[7] SAWYER** [see 139], b. 14 Dec 1819 Newport NH, d. Jan 1879, m. 24 Apr 1844 Goshen NH Lois Minerva Gunnison, b. 13 Nov 1823 d. 1878, dau. Samuel and Dorcas (Cutts) Gunnison. Farmer, teacher. In Goshen NH 1840, Newport NH 1850 -1860, Napa CA.
465 French Albert[8], 1845-1901.
Lydia Sophia, b. 30 Apr 1847, d. 5 Jan 1865.
Sources: Goshen NH census 1840. Newport NH census 1850, 1860, 1870. H78, W33, N3

277. **PHINEAS B.[7] SAWYER** [see 140], b. 4 Mar 1804 Newport NH, d. 9 May 1853 Hebron NH, m.(1) 25 Dec 1828 Hebron NH Relief Vickery, b.?; m.(2) 1836 Bristol NH Lydia Sanborn of No. Hampton NH, b. 2 Apr 1813, dau. John and Phebe (Sanborn) Sanborn. Drover. In Alexandria NH 1830, Hebron NH 1850.
Elizabeth, b. 1829, d. 1869. Went to Lemond MN.
George, b. 1831, d. 1835.
George P., b. 1838, d. 2 Jul 1863 Gettysburg PA. Civil War.
Sarah M., b. 1844, m. Mathew McCook of New Brunswick, Canada.
E.V., b. 1849.
Mary, b. 1850, d. 1878, m. 1877 Minnesota Ed James.
Sources: Alexandria NH census 1830, 1840, 1850. Also in Hebron NH census 1850. VR Hebron NH. B40.

278. **JONATHAN B.[7] SAWYER** [see 140], b. 27 Mar 1806 Sutton NH, d. 20 Mar 1848 Alexandria NH, m. 1837 Bristol NH Orpha Powell, b. 26 May 1811. In Alexandria NH 1840. Wid. in Alexandria NH 1850, later returned to Bristol NH and m. 12 Apr 1855 Daniel Sleeper.
466 Richard Kelly[8], 1839-1869.
Lois Ann, b. May 1842, d. 28 Aug 1843.
Sources: Alexandria NH census 1840, 1850. M64, N6.

279. **MOSES[7] SAWYER** [see 140], b. 15 Oct 1807 Sutton NH, d. 6 Mar 1876 Iowa, m. 14 Mar 1833 Hebron NH Catherine P. Ladd, b. ?. In Alexandria NH 1830, Bristol NH 1840, Hill NH 1850.
Ann Elizabeth, b. 1831 Hebron NH, d. 1835.
Charlotte E., b. 1833 Alexandria NH, d. 1834.
Laura A., b. 1838 Hebron NH, m. Richard Carr. Went to Iowa.
William, b. Bristol NH 1839. Went to Advance IA.
Mary A., b. May 1842 Sanbornton NH, m. Horatio Morrison. To Iowa.
Newell James, b. 1846 Sanbornton NH. Went to Advance IA.
Anna, b. 1858 Sanbornton NH, m. Henry Reynolds. Went to Iowa.
Sources: Alexandria NH census 1830. Bristol NH census 1840. Hill NH census 1850. R34, B40.

280. **WILLIAM REED[7] SAWYER** [see 141], b. 22 Dec 1806 Antrim NH, d. 14 Jan 1897 Francestown NH, m. 23 Jan 1835 Abby Stevens of Francestown NH, b. 25 Aug 1813 d. 21 Jan 1897. Farmer. On Bedford NH tax list 1829. In Francestown NH 1850, 1870.
Charles Franklin, b. 17 Mar 1836, d. 22 Jun 1858.
Susie Maria, b. 10 Jan 1842, m. 1 Feb 1866 Francestown NH Amasa Downes.

467 William Reed[8], 1846-1935.
Sources: Francestown NH census 1850, 1870. L29, N6, William Reed Sawyer rec.

281. **GEORGE O.[7] SAWYER** [see 141], b. 27 Jun 1818 Bedford NH, m. 25 Aug 1853 Boston MA Elizabeth G. Beard of Wilmington NH, b. 1819, dau. Edward Beard. Furniture manufacturer. In Boston MA 1850, Sterling MA 1859.

George Orr, b. 4 Jul 1854 Boston MA.

Frederick A., b. 12 Feb 1859 Sterling MA, m. 24 Sep 1890 Everett MA Annie L. Bramhall of Cambridge MA, b. ?. CH: Edith Elizabeth, b. 28 May 1893.

Samuel Edward, b. 12 Feb 1859 Sterling MA.

Sources: Boston MA (W5) census 1850. VR Chelsea MA, SA/MA. L29.

282. **RODNEY[7] SAWYER** [see 142], b. 10 Mar 1804 Antrim NH, d. 14 Feb 1886 Antrim NH, m. 29 Oct 1835 Sarah Hill, b. 1806 d. 11 Feb 1853. Cooper. Lived 10 yrs. in Bunker Hill IL. He bur. in Center Cem., Antrim NH.

Albert Rodney, b. 15 Dec 1838 Antrim NH, d. 21 May 1868 Bunker Hill IL, m. 1856 Sarah A. Wright, b.?. Graduated from medical school in Cincinnati OH. Civil War: Army Surgeon w/rank of Captain.

468 David H.[8], 1840-1882. Went to Illinois.

Sources: Antrim NH census 1830, 1840, 1850, 1870. L29, N9, Eleanor Robinson rec.

283. **REUBEN M.[7] SAWYER** [see 142], b. 31 Aug 1805 Antrim NH, d. 9 Jul 1878 Francestown NH, m. 18 May 1837 Windsor NH Mary Preston of Windsor NH, b. 14 Mar 1805 d. 1 Feb 1870, dau. Samuel and Rebecca (Gibson) Preston. Carpenter. In Windsor NH 1838, Antrim NH 1840, Francestown NH 1850.

Clarissa A., b. 20 Apr 1838, m. 21 Mar 1867 Garvin Sleeper of Francestown NH.

Henry H., b. 26 Dec 1840 Antrim NH, m. 5 Dec 1876 Antonia H. Savage of Waterville ME, b. ?. Teacher in Francestown NH. Merchant. In Boston MA.

Sources: Antrim NH census 1840. Francestown NH census 1850, 1860, 1870. VR Francestown NH. L29, C55, N6.

284. **EDMUND M.[7] SAWYER** [see 142], b. 17 Sep 1807 Antrim NH, d. 29 May 1894 Antrim NH, m. 19 Nov 1835 Nancy J. Steele, b. 19 May 1809 d. 16 Jun 1884, dau. Deacon Robert Steele. Blacksmith, farmer. In Bedford NH, Antrim NH. He bur. in North Branch Cem., Antrim NH.

469 Samuel Steele[8], 1836-1928.

Mary Frane, b. 18 Jun 1846, d. 24 Jan 1923, m. 20 Jun 1872 Antrim NH David Bryer.

Sources: Antrim NH census 1840, 1850, 1880. N6, H93, L29, N9.

285. **SILAS N.[7] SAWYER** [see 143], b. 19 Jun 1805 Antrim NH, d. 28 Mar 1876 Newport NH, m.(1) 4 Jun 1833 Lucy P. Moore of Hillsboro NH, b. 28 Jun 1811 d. 3 Apr 1863; m.(2) 11 May 1864 Sarah A. Hackett of Goshen NH, b. ?. Butcher. In Hillsboro NH 1840, 1860, 1870. In Lawrence MA 1850.

Abby, b. 1836 in Maine.

470 James M.[8], 1844-1892. Went to Illinois.

Lewis, b. ca. 1845 in Maine.

John W., b. 1864 Hillsboro NH, m.(1) ?; m.(2) 24 Jan 1893 Pelham NH Mary L. Bradley of Pelham NH, b. 1870, dau. George and Esther Bradley. In Crown Point NY, Worcester MA.

Sources: Hillsboro NH census 1840. Lawrence MA census 1850, 1860, 1870. B92, H93, L29.

286. **JOHN NICHOLS[7] SAWYER** [see 143], b. 1 Sep 1816 Antrim NH, d. 21 Jul 1881 Texas, m.(1) Frances Whitmore, b. ?; (2) 30 Sep 1851 Boston MA Susan Newall of Wakefield NH, b. ca. 1817. In Dennison TX.

John F., b. 6 Jun 1849. Went to San Francisco CA.

Herbert, b. ?.

Sources: VR SA/MA. L29.

287. **EDMUND[7] SAWYER** [see 143], b. 11 May 1821 Antrim NH, d. 21 Dec 1873, m. 12 Oct 1858 Louisa A. Wright, b. ? d. 16 Jul 1867. Piano tuner, furrier. In Charles River Village MA, built house in Dover MA 1872.

Jesse A., b. 22 Apr 1862, m. 22 Apr 1880 Boston MA Herbert Wilson.

Son, b. 26 Apr 1864.

Frederick, b. 6 Nov 1865 Boston MA.

Louisa A., b. 18 Jul 1867.

Sources: VR SA/MA. L29, S54.

288. **MARK WOODBURY[7] SAWYER** [see 144], b. 28 Sep 1808 Antrim NH, d. 7 Dec 1871 Palatine IL, m. 28 Mar 1832 Stockbridge VT Mary E. Whitcomb, b. 5 Aug 1812 d. 28 Nov 1895 Itaska IL, dau. James and Hannah (Blossom) Whitcomb. In Stockbridge VT.

Edmund Mark, b. 6 Mar 1840, d. 17 Aug 1898, m. 28 Nov 1865 Anna Rogers, b. ?. Went to Illinois.

Sources: VR Stockbridge VT, SA/VT. S92.

289. **JOSEPH TAGGART[7] SAWYER** [see 144], b. 31 Jul 1810 Antrim NH, m. 16 Jan 1838 Deering ME Frances Fisher of Deering NH, b. 1815. Civil War. In Stockbridge VT, in Nashua NH.

Jane F., b. 7 Nov 1838, d. 29 Aug 1882, unm.

Edmund Fisher, b. Sep 1844, d. 22 Sep 1846. He bur. Deering NH.

471 George Fisher[8], 1849-1906.

Sources: Nashua NH census 1850, 1860, 1870. VR Deering NH. P10, M5.

290. **JOSIAH[7] SAWYER** [see 145], b. 21 Mar 1785 Deerfield NH, d. 19 Apr 1848 Gilford NH, m.(1) 2 Apr 18?? Sally Rand, b. 19 Sep 1785 d. 3 Aug 1819; m.(2) 25 Aug 1822 Betsey Gove of Gilford NH, b. 27 Sep 1795 d. 6 Sep 1840. Preacher. In Tuftonboro NH 1810, Gilford NH 1830.

Polly, b. 8 Oct 1810, m. 31 Aug 1836 Increase W. Davis.

Philbrick R., b. 6 May 1812 Tuftonboro NH.

Sally Rand, b. 29 Jul 1816, m. 22 May 1836 Greenleaf Ambrose.

Sources: Tuftonboro NH census 1810. Gilford NH census 1830, 1840. G30, A19, H5, N9, N14. N6.

291. **ISAAC EASTMAN[7] SAWYER** [see 145], b. 20 Mar 1795 Gilmanton NH, d. 17 Nov 1850 Gilford NH, m. 25 Mar 1817 Barnstead NH Nancy Gilman, b. 20 Jan 1797 d. 18 May 1887. Farmer.

Joseph S., b. 1825, d. 21 Jan 1855, m. 14 Oct 1847 Mary Ann Bean, b. 1825. Laborer. CH: Viola, b. 11 Nov 1850. Note: Although I found record of Joseph S.'s birth, the fact that he is buried in the same Gilford plot as Issac Eastman suggests that he is probably the latter's son.

Mary, b. 1827, d. 31 Oct 1850.

Sources: Gilmanton NH census 1830, 1840, 1850. VR Gilmanton NH. N9, N14, B40.

292. **ISREAL$^7$ SAWYER** [see 145], b. 10 Mar 1803 Gilmanton NH, d. 26 Feb 1843 Gilford NH, m. 19 Aug 1827 Gilford NH Mariam Davis, b. 8 Jul 1803 d. Apr 1876, dau. Melcher and Anna (Jewell) Davis. In Gilford NH 1830. Bur. in McCoy Cem., Old Lakeshore Road, Gilford NH. Wid. m. 3 Nov 1846 Horace Bugbee.

472 Levi Davis$^8$, 1828-1903.
Selina Elvira, b. 26 Oct 1833, d. 30 Jan 1842.
Pamelia, b. 7 Jul 1835, d. 6 Mar 1875, m. _____ Bugbee.
John, b. 13 Dec 1837, d. 11 May 1841.
Albert, b. 17 Jan 1843, d. 26 May 1843.

Sources: Gilford NH census 1830, 1840. L29, N9, N14, N6.

293. **JOHN$^7$ SAWYER** [see 146], b. 22 Jun 1794 Gilmanton NH, d. 19 Jul 1868 Greensboro VT, m. Sarah Hill of Greensboro VT, b. 1794 d. 8 Aug 1866, dau. Peleg and Polly Hill. Farmer. In Greensboro VT 1820-1850. He bur. in Village Cem., Greensboro VT.

John Alvah, b. 19 Aug 1819 Greensboro VT, d. 19 Apr 1873 Greensboro VT, m. 22 Oct 1855 Greensboro VT Adelaide C. Penney of Greensboro VT, b. ?. Merchant, farmer. In Wolcott VT. CH: Alfred, b. 7 Nov 1860, d. 9 Mar 1861; Inez M., b. 20 Jul 1864, m. 24 Jun 1885 Boston MA George M. Page; Alice Genevieve, b. 22 Oct 1865.

473 William Badger$^8$, 1825-1893.

Sources: Greensboro VT census 1820, 1830, 1840, 1850. VR SA/VT.

294. **JEREMIAH$^7$ SAWYER** [see 146], b. 5 Feb 1797 Gilmanton NH, d. 13 Feb 1857 Greensboro VT, m.(1) 25 Jan 1819 Gilmanton NH Lydia Mudget of Gilmanton NH, b. 1799 d. 15 Nov 1847; m.(2) Almira_____, b. 1809. Farmer. In Greensboro VT 1820.

John C., b. 1829, d. Dec 1849.

Sources: Greensboro VT census 1820, 1830, 1840, 1850. VR Gilmanton NH, SA/VT. N14.

295. **JAMES$^7$ SAWYER** [see 146], b. 9 Nov 1805 Gilmanton NH, d. 6 Apr 1864 Gilmanton NH, m. 26 Mar 1833 Gilmanton NH Hannah Sanborn, b. 9 Apr 1808, dau. Coffin and Polly (Whicher) Sanborn.

474 Jeremiah Fellows$^8$, 1834-1863.
475 Charles S.$^8$, 1841-1927.

Sources: Gilmanton NH census 1840, 1850, 1860. VR Gilmanton NH. S8, R34, N14.

296. **DAVID$^7$ SAWYER** [see 146], b. 5 Mar 1810 Gilmanton NH, d. 3 Dec 1887 Belmont NH, m. Lucy C. Sleeper of Bristol NH, b. 27 Aug 1809 d. 3 Apr 1884, dau. Jesse and Betsey (Cummings) Sleeper. Appointed executor of mother's will 1837. In Gilmanton NH 1840-1860, Belmont NH 1870.

476 John R.$^8$, 1840-1909.
477 Nahum W.$^8$, 1844-1905.
Matilda O., b. 1847.

Sources: Gilmanton NH census 1840, 1850, 1860. Belmont NH census 1870. P82i.

297. **DAVID$^7$ SAWYER** [see 147], b. 1790 Deerfield NH, m. 1810 Northwood NH Deborah Knowles of Northwood NH, b. 1 Jul 1785, dau. Simeon and Deborah (Palmer) Knowles.

478 Gilman$^8$, 1812-1863.
Perry, b. 1813 Deerfield NH, d. 15 Jul 1861 Nottingham NH, m. 29 Nov 1840 Northwood NH Mary C. Knowles of Northwood NH, b. 28 Jul 1816 d. 30 Apr 1887, dau. Jonathan and Mary (Pillsbury) Knowles. Farmer. In Nottingham NH 1850. Wid. in Nottingham NH 1870.

Emeline, b. ?, m. 31 Oct 1839 Daniel C. Shaw.
Sources: Deerfield NH census 1810. Nottingham NH census 1850,1860, 1870. H89, C58.

298. **JOSIAH[7] SAWYER** [see 147], b. 1799 Deerfield NH, d. 13 Dec 1881 Lee NH, m. 21 Dec 1818 Joanna Sanborn of Kingston NH, b. Feb 1794 d. 9 Dec 1883. In Lee NH 1830-1870. He bur. in Brackett-Sawyer family cem., Lee NH.
Angelina A., b. Aug 1819, d. 29 Sep 1902, m. 4 Jan 1849 John Bunker of Newfields NH.
Almira, b. 1825, m. 9 Jan 1849 Edward Bartlett of Lee NH.
479 Franklin P.[8], 1833-1878.
Sources: Lee NH census 1830, 1840, 1850, 1860, 1870. P82i, N6, C58, N9, F20, T20.

299. **JOHN[7] SAWYER** [see 147], b. 16 Mar 1801 Deerfield NH, d. 5 Jan 1878 Deerfield NH, m. 19 Apr 1826 Lee NH Clarissa Chesley of Durham NH, b. 22 Nov 1801 d. 1 Sep 1874, dau. Thomas Chesley. Farmer. He bur. in Deerfield Parade NH.
Hannah S., b. 4 Apr 1827, m. 25 Jun 1846 Francis G. Bean.
480 Ezra A. J.[8], 1828-1886.
C. Josephine, b. 1831, d. 8 Jul 1844.
Sources: Deerfield NH census 1830, 1840, 1850, 1860. C58, T20, S68.

300. **JEFFERSON[7] SAWYER** [see 147], b. 1817 Deerfield NH, d. 1894 Lee NH, m. 29 Nov 1840 Northwood NH Elizabeth Jane Knowles of Northwood NH, b. 23 Feb 1818 d. 2 Oct 1895, dau. Jonathan and Mary (Pillsbury) Knowles. Farmer. Appointed executor of father's will 1845. In Lee NH 1850-1870. He bur. in Sawyer Cem., Lee NH.
Mary Francena, b. 4 Nov 1845, m. 10 Sep 1869 John Eaton.
Miriam A., b. 9 Dec 1846.
Francilla J., b. 5 Jul 1850, d. 12 Mar 1851.
Frances D., b. 5 Jul 1850, d. 25 Aug 1854.
Hattie B., b. 6 Dec 1856, d. 26 Feb 1919, m. _____ Hobbs.
Charles L., b. 28 Mar 1860 Lee NH, m. 16 Jan 1892 Olive H. Bennett of Gilford NH, b. ?. Went to Chicago IL.
Sources: Lee NH census 1850, 1860, 1870. C58, H89, P82i

301. **JOSIAH[7] SAWYER** [see 148], b. 6 Jun 1808 Andover NH, d. 20 Aug 1880, m.(1) 14 Jan 1836 Nancy Kittredge of Nelson NH, b. 14 Jun 1805 d. 13 Jan 1847, dau. Joshua and Beulah (Baker) Kittredge; m.(2) Sanbornton NH Betsey Hazen, b. 1808 d. 25 Nov 1881. In Franklin NH 1840, Andover NH 1850-1870.
Nancy Maria, b. 26 Dec 1836, d. 20 Oct 1852.
Juliana, b. 29 Mar 1838, d. 22 Feb 1841.
Joanna, b. 2 Aug 1840, d. 15 Apr 1841.
Victoria Rosilla, b. 18 Jan 1842, d. 7 Dec 1895, m. 11 Jan 1865 Henry H. Lewis.
481 George Washington[8], 1844-1914.
Sources: Franklin NH census 1840. Andover NH census 1850, 1860, 1870. E2, R34, N6.

302. **COFFIN[7] SAWYER** [see 149], b. 30 Oct 1795 Deerfield NH, d. 12 May 1838 Atkinson ME, m. 25 Sep 1823 Deerfield NH Huldah Seavey, b. 11 Apr 1796 d. 4 Jan 1882. B/land in Atkinson ME 1824. In Atkinson ME 1830. Wid. in Atkinson ME 1840-1850.
482 Ebenezer Prescott[8], 1824-1901.
Jane, b. 1836, m. William Greeley.
483 Stephen Shepard[8], 1837-1921.

Sources: Atkinson ME census 1830, 1840, 1850. VR SA/ME. P76, R10d, Coffin Sawyer rec, S. Shepard Sawyer rec., Lauri Cover rec.

303. **JEREMIAH E.[7] SAWYER** [see 149], b. 12 Apr 1812 Deerfield NH, d. 24 Mar 1852 Raymond NH, m. 30 May 1836 Atkinson ME Elizabeth P. Durgin of Nottingham NH, b. ?, d. 1834. Farmer. In Hudson MA.

Elisha P., b. 1837, d. 15 Jul 1857.
Charles H., b. ?, d. 24 Jul 1848 Hanscom MA.
Caroline A., b. 1847. Adopted by Uncle Tristram B. [see 305].

Sources: VR Hanscom MA, SA/MA. N9, P76, Coffin Sawyer rec.

304. **JOHN C.[7] SAWYER** [see 149], b. 15 Jun 1815 Deerfield NH, d. 26 Jul 1872, m. 1 Jan 1839 Betsey T. Harvey of Atkinson ME, b. 1823. Farmer. In Atkinson ME 1850-1860, E. Corinth ME 1870. Wid. w/Leonard H. 1880.

Asa H., b. 1840 Atkinson ME, d. 6 Apr 1864 in Texas.
484 Leonard H.[8], 1848-1923.
Charles H., b. ?.

Sources: Atkinson ME census 1850, 1860. East Corinth ME census 1870, 1880. VR Old Town ME. B40, P76, Coffin Sawyer rec., Robert L. Taylor rec.

305. **TRISTRAM B.[7] SAWYER** [see 149], b. 14 Dec 1822 Deerfield NH, d. 20 Jun 1891 Dexter ME, m. 9 Jun 1845 Dexter ME Mary B. Addison of Dexter ME, b. 1826 d. 17 Jun 1906, dau. David and Matilda (Preston) Addison. Dyer. In Atkinson ME. In Dexter ME 1850-1880.

Charles M., b. 16 Sep 1846 Dexter ME, d. 11 Nov 1914 Dexter ME, m. 7 Oct 1867 Agnes M. Wyman of Dexter ME, b. ?. CH: Mabel W., b. 31 Dec 1874.
Caroline A., adopted niece (dau. Jeremiah E.), b. 1847. [see 303].

Sources: Dexter ME census 1850, 1860, 1870. ME 1880 census index. VR SA/ME. C58, D4.

306. **WILLIAM[7] SAWYER** [see 150], b. 24 Aug 1804 Deerfield NH, d. 22 Oct 1857 Gilmanton NH, m. 29 Nov 1827 Gilmanton NH Betsey H. Connor of Gilmanton NH, b. 1800 d. 26 Sep 1857. In Deerfield NH 1830, Alton NH 1850. He bur. in Pine Grove Cem., Gilmanton NH.

Mary L., b. 1830.
Arthur W. S., b. 1833 Gilmanton NH, m. 14 Dec 1859 New Durham NH Georgianna L. Flanders of Alton NH, b. ca. 1843.
Clara C., b. Aug 1840, d. 18 May 1889.
Eunice, b. 1841.

Sources: Deerfield NH census 1830. Alton NH census 1850. VR Gilmanton NH. N14.

307. **NOAH[7] SAWYER** [see 150], b. 29 Jun 1817 Gilmanton NH, m. 9 Mar 1841 Adaline Flanders of Alton NH, b. ?, dau. Jedidiah and Lucy (Hatch) Flanders. Wid. remarried 1853.

Leander, b. 1844, d. yr. ending 31 Mar 1863.

Sources: VR Gilmanton NH.

308. **TIMOTHY UPHAM[7] SAWYER** [see 150], b. 13 Sep 1819 Gilmanton NH. Shoemaker. In Alton NH 1860, Gilmanton NH 1870.

Leander, b. 1841.

Sources: Alton NH census 1850, 1860. Gilmanton NH census 1870. VR Gilmanton NH.

309. **BENJAMIN⁷ SAWYER** [see 152], b. 11 Mar 1807 So. Hampton NH, d. 12 Jan 1895 So. Hampton NH, m. 3 Jan 1841 Salisbury MA Olive Jewell of Salisbury MA, b. 3 Jul 1809 d. 26 Oct 1884, dau. Joseph and Judith (Woodman) Jewell. Farmer.

Joseph James Jewell, b. 13 Sep 1848 Amesbury MA, d. 18 Oct 1925 Plaistow NH, m. 31 Oct 1877 Newburyport MA Elizabeth Evans of Salisbury MA, b. 8 May 1852 d. 15 Jun 1915, dau. Reuben and Mary (Sleeper) Evans. In So. Hampton NH 1860, Salisbury MA 1879. CH: Edith Marion, b. 3 Sep 1879.

Sources: So. Hampton NH census 1850, 1860, 1870. VR Salisbury MA, Plaistow NH, SA/MA.

310. **THOMAS[7] SAWYER** [see 152], b. 4 May 1809 So. Hampton NH, d. 28 Mar 1894 So. Hampton NH, m. Henrietta Brown, b. 16 Mar 1815 d. 4 Sep 1877, dau. Nathan and Nancy (Hoyt) Brown. Carpenter.

Charles Henry, b. 25 Nov 1837, d. bef. 1865, unm. Note: His b. record says his mother was Olivia, dau. of Nathan Brown.

Sarah E., b. 9 Jun 1839, m. 28 Feb 1860 Newton NH P. J. Ring.

485 George Henry[8], b. 1843.

Sources: South Hampton NH census 1840, 1850, 1860, 1870, 1880. B91, P82g, N6.

311. **ENOCH[7] SAWYER** [see 153], b. 20 Aug 1806 Newburyport MA, m. 21 Apr 1836 Salisbury MA Aphia Kelly, b. 7 Nov 1812, dau. Joseph and Betsey (Adams) Kelly. Shoemaker. In Salisbury MA 1840-1850. Wid. m. 28 Feb 1886 Amesbury MA Joshua Colby.

Susan Colby, b. 4 Mar 1837.

Joseph William, b. 4 Feb 1839, d. 6 Aug 1840.

486 Enoch[8], b. 1841.

Sources: Salisbury MA census 1840, 1850. VR Newburyport MA, Salisbury MA, SA/MA. K2.

312. **JOSIAH[7] SAWYER** [see 153], b. 16 Dec 1813 Salisbury MA, d. 10 Oct 1882 Salisbury MA, m. 5 Dec 1841 Montville ME Abigail Page of Gilmanton NH, b. 18 Oct 1814 d. 22 Mar 1905, dau. True and Abigail (Edgerly) Page. Ship owner. In Newburyport MA 1850. Note: Marriage is recorded in both Salisbury MA and Gilmanton NH.

487 Albert Page[8], b. 1842.

Sarah Abby, b. 10 Jun 1848.

Sources: Newburyport MA census 1850. VR Salisbury MA, Newburyport MA, Gilmanton NH. N14, E7, G36.

313. **JEREMIAH HAYDEN[7] SAWYER** [see 153], b. 2 Sep 1823 Newburyport MA, m.(1) Inez _____ of Amesbury MA, b. ?; m.(2) 31 Oct 1850 Newburyport MA Lydia O. Davis of Newburyport MA, b. 1830, dau. Nathaniel and Lydia Davis. Painter. Physician. In Newburyport MA 1850, Brentwood NH 1868.

Frank Hayden, b. 30 Jul 1852 Newburyport MA. In Brentwood NH 1868.

Sarah Little, b. 5 Dec 1860.

John S., b. 3 Apr 1868 Brentwood NH.

Sources: Newburyport MA census 1850. VR Newburyport MA, SA/MA.

314. **MAYO GREENLEAF[7] SAWYER** [see 154], b. 11 Dec 1810 Vershire VT, d. 11 Aug 1845 Chelsea VT, m. 1 Mar 1837 Haverhill NH Caroline Eastman of Haverhill NH, b. 3 Dec 1812 d. 18 Sep 1894 Bath NH.

488 Richard[8], 1839-1902.

Brydone, b. 26 Feb 1843, d. 24 Jan 1916, unm.

Sources: VR SA/NH, SA/VT. P59.

315. **OTIS[7] SAWYER** [see 155], b. 17 Feb 1813 Corinth VT, d. 31 Jul 1882 Irasburgh VT, m.(1) 27 Jul 1836 Corinth VT Mary A. Bickford, b. Feb 1813 d. 3 Nov 1842, dau. Paul and Charlotte Bickford; m.(2) 16 Oct 1843 Derby VT Caroline Rowe of Lyme NH, b. 1818. Farmer. In Newport VT 1840, 1860; St. Johnsbury VT 1850.

Ira F., b. 1837 in New York. In St. Johnsbury VT 1850.
Dana, b. 1839 in New York. In St. Johnsbury VT 1850.
Clara L., b. 1844, m. 4 Jul 1864 John N. Young.
Lucinda, b. 1845.
George A., b. 1855 Newport VT, m. 12 Sep 1889 Albany VT Alice L. Hunter of Albany VT, b. 4 Apr 1867, dau. Hiram M. and Lucy (Coburn) Hunter.
Ida M., b. 24 Apr 1859, m. 24 Jun 1888 Levi C. Bean.

Sources: Newport VT census 1840, 1860. St Johnsbury VT census 1850. VR SA/VT. R21, D41.

316. **DANA M.[7] SAWYER** [see 155], b. 14 Aug 1817 Corinth VT, d. 1856 Corinth VT, m. 23 Jun 1840 Corinth VT Sally Sanborn of Benton VT, b. 18 Feb 1818. Farmer.

Henry T., b. 1841 Corinth VT.
Emma V., b. 1845.

Sources: Corinth VT census 1840, 1850. VR SA/VT. R21.

317. **MOREAU[7] SAWYER** [see 155], b. 14 Jun 1829 Corinth VT, m. 20 Aug 1861 Craftsbury VT Helen R. Nelson of Craftsbury VT, b. Mar 1843 d. 1 Sep 1880, dau. Horace and Liza Nelson.

Lizzie Emeline, b. 13 Sep 1862, d. 10 Jul 1908, unm.
Nellie S., b. 1865, m. 23 Sep 1891 John J. Urie.
489 Martin S.[8], b. 1868.

Sources: VR SA/VT.

318. **ISAAC NEWTON[7] SAWYER** [see 157], b. 5 Apr 1811 Salisbury NH, d. 26 Nov 1894 Salisbury NH, m.(1) 22 Jan 1834 Plainfield NH Abigail M. Chellis of Plainfield NH, b. 30 Apr 1810 d. 15 Apr 1860; m.(2) 1 Jan 1861 Betsey Jane Hoitt of Lee NH, b. 26 Jan 1825 d. 13 Mar 1899, dau. Gorham W. and Abigail (Locke) Hoitt. Farmer.

Leander Newton, b. 13 Dec 1861 Salisbury NH, d. 15 Nov 1935 Concord NH, m. 1 Jan 1891 Elizabeth B. Rogers of Salisbury NH, b. 8 Jul 1862 d. 10 Dec 1930, dau. Charles C. and Martha J. (Putney) Rogers. In Durham NH. CH: Lucy H., b. 26 Oct 1891, d. 5 Jul 1975, m. 22 Jun 1916 Harry F. Twombly; Daughter, stillborn 4 Jan 1896; Daughter, stillborn 30 Jun 1898.
490 Gorham Hoitt[8], b. 1866.

Sources: Salisbury NH census 1840, 1850, 1860, 1870. VR SA/NH. N9, S68, S16, L35, Kay Sleeper rec.

319 **NATHANIEL[7] SAWYER** [see 157], b. 14 Sep 1815 Salisbury NH, d. 1 Dec 1885 Salisbury NH, m.(1) 2 May 1840 Lucy H. Wood, b. 6 Dec 1816 d. 19 Apr 1863, dau. of E_____ and Mary (Gerrish) Wood; m.(2) 23 Jan 1866 Mary Ann Wood, sister of Lucy, b. 23 Jul 1825 d. 29 Jan 1905. Farmer. Justice of the Peace 1855-1876.

Lucy Ann, b. 15 Oct 1841, d. 22 Jul 1880, m. 15 Oct 1873 Salisbury NH George Little.
Mary Rebecca, b. 22 Oct 1843, m. 31 Aug 1882 George Little of Webster NH.
491 Charles Henry[8], b. 1848.
Fanny Elizabeth, b. 20 Jun 1854, d. 31 Jan 1923 in Wisconsin.
Caroline Wood, b. 16 Jan 1857.
Martha Louise, b. 30 Oct 1859, m. 5 Sep 1883Dr.Frank Southwick.

Ann, b. 7 Dec 1860.
492 Edward Nathaniel[8], 1867-1936.
Sources: Salisbury NH census 1840, 1850, 1860, 1870. VR SA/NH. L29, D28, N9, S16, N6, Annette S. Manny rec.

320. **DANIEL FITTS[7] SAWYER** [see 157], b. 29 Feb 1820 Salisbury NH, d. 22 May 1878, m. 8 Jan 1846 Mary Ann DeMerret of Durham NH, b. 23 Oct 1815 d. 11 Nov 1863.
Sarah P., b.ca. 1844.
Nancy Rebecca, b. 12 Oct 1850, d. 14 Jan 1871.
Isaac Fitts, b. 16 Feb 1854 Salisbury NH. Res. w/"Thompson family" in 1870. Lawyer. In Cambridge MA.
Anna R., b. ?, adopted w/father's consent by Mary P. Thompson of Durham NH 1870.
Sources: Salisbury NH census 1850, 1860, 1870. S68, N9, P82i, S16.

321. **FRANCIS BROWN[7] SAWYER** [see 157], b. Apr 1823 Salisbury NH, d. 13 Jan 1907 Webster NH, m. 11 Sep 1851 Boscawen NH Ellen Little of Boscawen NH, b. 27 Feb 1833 d. 5 Oct 1870, dau. Enoch and Aphia Little. Farmer. Taught school in Concord NH 1847.
Mary Frances, b. 28 May 1853, d. 10 Mar 1921 Concord NH.
Sarah Ellen, b. 25 Dec 1858, d. 1946.
Emma Elvira, b. 10 Apr 1861, d. 19 Jan 1933.
493 Herman Little[8], 1865-1954.
Louisa Jane, b. 14 Jul 1868, d. 6 Jan 1870.
Sources: Boscawen NH census 1860. Webster NH census 1870. VR SA/NH. L29, N9, B68, S16, Jeanette Sawyer rec.

322. **MATTHIAS PLANT[7] SAWYER** [see 159], b. 6 Jun 1797 Salisbury MA, d. 24 Nov 1879 Minot ME, m.(1) 20 Jul 1818 Elizabeth Hackett, b. 1799 d. 23 May 1821; m. (2) 5 Sep 1822 Martha Allen of Minot ME, b. 1797 d. 7 Jul 1881. S/land in Minot ME 1830. He bur. in Center Hill Cem., Minot ME. Note: Judith B's m. record says her mother was Rebecca Allen.
Judith B., b. 26 Dec 1818, d. 1876, m. 5 Sep 1844 Aaron P. Woodman.
Joseph H., b. May 1821, d. 27 Jan 1822.
494 Joseph Plant[8], 1825-1910.
John Allen, b. 23 Jan 1828 Minot ME, m. 23 Sep 1857 Susan Griggs of Milton MA, b. ?. In Stoughton MA 1849. CH: Mattie, b. 8 Nov 1870.
495 Joshua Follansby[8], 1830-1919.
496 Seth Chandler[8], 1833.
Mary Little, b. 1 Jan 1836 Minot ME, d. 6 Jan 1910. Taught in Lewiston ME.
William Felton, b. 17 Apr 1838 Minot ME, m. 25 Nov 1871 Boston MA Sarah Waterman of Poland ME, b. 4 Dec 1837, dau. Benjamin and Irene (Emery) Waterman. Shoemaker. Civil War. In Holbrook MA, Randolph MA 1871.
497 George Franklin[8], b. 1840.
Eliza Hackett, b. 16 Jan 1844, d. 13 Jun 1851.
Sources: Minot ME census 1820, 1830, 1840, 1850. VR SA/MA, SA/ME. L29, M39, M5, Obit (Mary L.)

323. **MOSES LITTLE[7] SAWYER** [see 159], b. 5 Jun 1799 Salisbury MA, m. 24 Aug 1832 Haverhill MA Maria W. Quimby of Newbury MA, b. 1799 d. 7 Mar 1849. In Salisbury MA 1840, Methuen MA 1850.
Charles F., b. 1834, d. 29 Oct 1834.
Martha A., b. ca. 1835, m. 16 Sep 1867 Haverhill MA Warren A. Kimball.

Charles W., b. ca. 1836 Haverhill MA, m. 3 Jul 1864 Haverhill MA Susan Dodge of Salem MA, b. 1837, dau. Edward and Elizabeth Dodge. Clerk.

498 Daniel Long[8], 1837-1878.

George Edward, b. ?, d. in Civil War.

Sources: Salisbury MA census 1840. Methuen MA census 1850. VR Haverhill MA, Salisbury MA, SA/MA. L29

324. **ELBRIDGE G.[7] SAWYER** .[see 160], b. 21 Jul 1827 Corinth VT, m. 18 Dec 1850 Corinth VT Mary Adelaide Stevens, b. b. Aug 1830 d. 6 Mar 1885, dau. Samuel and Hannah Stevens. Farmer. In Corinth VT 1850, Topsham VT 1870.

Everett P., b. Jul 1856 Corinth VT, m. 21 Apr 1886 Ellen M. Page of Corinth VT, b. Sep 1864 d. 8 Jul 1902. In Topsham VT. CH: Evelyn P., b. 18 Sep 1895; Son, stillborn 26 Oct 1896.

Susan A., b. Jul 1858, m. 13 Oct 1880 George F. Butterfield.

May E., b. 1866, m. 27 Apr 1888 Moses A. Currier.

Sources: Corinth VT census 1850. Topsham VT census 1870. VR SA/VT.

325. **WILLIAM MERRILL[7] SAWYER** [see 161], b. 1 Aug 1827 Moretown VT, m. 27 Sep 1849 Moretown VT Sophia E. Walker of Bath NH, b. 1832 d. 11 May 1906, dau. Fred and Electa (Partridge) Walker. Saddler.

Joseph H., b. Mar 1852 Moretown VT, d. 24 Aug 1906, unm.

Charles M., b. 19 Sep 1859 Moretown VT, d. 23 Mar 1860.

499 William F.[8], b. 1860.

Sources: Moretown VT census 1850. VR SA/VT.

326. **EDWIN R.[7] SAWYER** [see 162], b. 1828 Corinth VT, m.(1) 28 Jun 1854 Corinth VT Mary Taplin of East Corinth VT, b. 1834 d. 20 Feb 1860, dau. John and Mary Taplin; m.(2) 23 May 1861 Boston MA Flora A. Holbrook of Truro MA, b. 1842, dau. Jesse and Mary Holbrook. Bookkeeper, coal dealer. In Boston MA and Somerville MA.

Edwin Holbrook, b. 5 Mar 1862 Boston MA.

Henry R., b. 20 Dec 1866 Boston MA, m. 26 Jun 1889 Somerville MA Sarah Jane Dodd of Boston MA, b. 1865, dau. George H. and Eliza A. Dodd.

Sources: VR SA/VT, SA/MA.

327. **REUBEN[7] SAWYER** [see 163], b. 1819 Northfield NH, m.(1) 23 Oct 1842 Starksboro VT Rosannah Stokes, b. 1826 d. 19 Apr 1846 (bur. in Starksboro VT); m.(2) 7 Mar 1847 Sherburne VT Lucy D. Irish, b. ?. In Starksboro VT 1850.

Reuben, b. 1846.

Sources: VR SA/VT.

328. **HIRAM DOW[7] SAWYER** [see 166], b. 20 Mar 1808 Dorchester NH, d. 23 Jul 1883 Bath NH, m. 7 Mar 1838 Joanna H. Johnson of Wentworth NH, b. 8 Apr 1819 d. 4 Aug 1893. In Dorchester NH, Bath NH after 1850.

Albert J., b. 7 Jan 1839 Dorchester NH, d. 27 Jun 1896 Manchester NH, m. 1 Jan 1872 Lebanon NH Mary J. Hix of Haverhill NH, b. ca. 1844. Lumber dealer. In Bath NH, Manchester NH.

500 George Alvah[8], 1840-1911.

501 William Henry[8], 1843-1926.

J. Westley, b. 3 Jun 1845, d.y.

Mary H., b. 10 Aug 1848, m. 8 Dec 1874 Joshua W. Sawyer of Worcester MA.

Hiram Sylvester, b. 16 Jul 1851, d. 30 Jun 1873.
Joanna, b. Jun 1856, d. 25 Mar 1863.
Jennie A., b. 16 Aug 1858, d. 17 Apr 1915, m. 27 Mar 1883 Lisbon NH Henry G. Marston.
502 Charles Wesley$^{8}$, b. 1864.
Sources: Dorchester NH census 1840, 1850. Bath NH census 1850, 1860, 1870. ME 1880 census index. W36, S16, N6.

329. **JOHN$^{7}$ SAWYER** [see 166], b. 7 Apr 1815 Dorchester NH, d. 14 Oct 1867, m. 1842 Louisa Johnson of Wentworth NH, b. 12 May 1816 d. 2 Mar 1907, dau. William and Hannah (Brown) Johnson. Farmer. In Rumney NH 1847, Bath NH 1866. Wid. in Bath NH 1870.
John Murray, b. 1843 Dorchester NH, unm.
Charles Newton, b. 1845 Dorchester NH, unm.
503 Joshua W.$^{8}$, b. 1849.
George H., b. 1852 Rumney NH, m. Abbie J._____, b. 1856. CH: Ella, b. 1878. In Bath NH 1880.
Amanda L., b. 1856, m.(1) 29 Jan 1883 Ezra A. Rodiman, m.(2) 1888 Charles M. Merrill.
Sources: Rumney NH census 1850. Bath NH census 1870. N6, C35.

330. **NOAH PIPER$^{7}$ SAWYER** [see 166], b. 26 Aug 1828 Dorchester NH, d. 30 Mar 1894 Center Haverhill NH, m. 14 Jul 1853 Ruth Clifford of Rumney NH, b. 30 Apr 1832 d. 23 Jan 1903, dau. Alden and Lydia Clifford. Miller. In Rumney NH 1854, Cabot VT, Ryegate VT, Haverhill NH. Bur. in Bath NH.
Lizzie, b. 30 Apr 1854, d. 23 Jun 1873, m. 28 Jan 1873 Harry Elliot.
504 Clifford John$^{8}$, 1861-1916.
Sources: VR SA/NH. N6, Merrill C. Sawyer rec.

331. **SAMUEL JUDKINS$^{7}$ SAWYER** [see 167], b. 13 May 1834 Salisbury NH, m. Jennie M. Dodge of Lisbon NH, b. ?. Civil War: Served in "Troop L," mustered 4 Oct 1862. In Claremont NH.
Daughter, b. 4 Feb 1858.
Ernest S., b. 27 Jun 1862 Claremont NH.
Sources: W2.

332. **LEONARD COLBY$^{7}$ SAWYER** [see 168], b. 11 Feb 1812 Newbury MA, m.(1) 31 Jan 1834 Newbury MA Hannah Morse of Newburyport MA, b. 3 Feb 1817; m.(2) 3 Aug 1865 Susan Brown, b. ?. Blacksmith. In Amesbury MA 1840-1850.
505 John Andrew J.$^{8}$, b. 1834.
Sally A., b. 3 Dec 1835.
Annette, b. 1836, m. 29 Nov 1854 Amesbury MA Joshua Grant.
Ann Elizabeth, b. 9 Nov 1837, m. 27 Jan 1857 Lynn MA Edward Hunter.
506 Ephraim Alvah$^{8}$, b. 1842.
Ellen (Ella) Maria, b. 15 Dec 1845, m. 28 Nov 1866 Newburyport MA William C. Tusan.
Hannah Frances, b. 25 Mar 1850, m. 7 Dec 1867 Amesbury MA Joseph A. Morrell. Note: In a second listing Hannah m. Joseph A. Newell.
Sources: Amesbury MA census 1840, 1850. VR Newbury MA, Amesbury MA, SA/MA.

333. **AARON C.$^{7}$ SAWYER** [see 168], b. 3 Jul 1819 Newbury MA, m. 22 Nov 1843 Amesbury MA Caroline Morse of Amesbury MA, b. ?. Painter. In Amesbury MA 1850.

Albert Lowell, b. 8 Sep 1846 Amesbury MA, m. 24 Dec 1872 Medford MA Anna C. Richards of Portland ME, b. ?, dau. Samuel and Sarah W. Richards. Druggist. CH: Carrie B., b. 30 Jun 1873.

Sources: Amesbury MA census 1850. VR Newbury MA.

334. **THOMAS FREDERICK**$^{7}$ **SAWYER** [see 168], b. 27 May 1824 Newbury MA, d. 25 Jan 1900 Chester NH, m.(1) 1 Jan 1850 Haverhill MA Priscilla W. Silloway, b. 1828 d.22 Nov 1863, dau. David and Nancy Silloway; m.(2) 6 Mar 1867 Billerica MA Eliza Clement of Billerica MA, b. 1828, dau. Henry and Eliza Allen; m.(3) 5 Feb 1894 Chester NH Hannah M. Marston of Chester NH, b. Apr 1848 d. 28 Feb 1931, dau. Samuel and Betsy Noyes. Blacksmith.

Otis L., b. 21 Sep 1850, m. 14 Dec 1881 Helen M. Fowler, b. ?.

Augustine Lee, b. 30 Apr 1857, d. 5 Jan 1860.

Austin Weed, b. 30 Apr 1857 Amesbury MA, m. 2 Jun 1888 Merrimac MA Josephine Villason of Amesbury MA, b. ca. 1862, dau. Franklin and Isabella Villason.

Sources: VR West Newbury MA, Haverhill MA, Amesbury MA, SA/MA, SA/NH. C31, N9.

335. **WILLIAM**$^{7}$ **SAWYER** [see 168], b. 27 Dec 1825 Newburyport MA, m.(1) 1 Dec 1850 Haverhill MA Lydia E. Elliot of Haverhill MA, b. 1830 d. 23 Jul 1860, dau. David and Abigail Elliot of Newton NH; m.(2) 11 Dec 1862 Haverhill MA Annette Elliot, sister of Lydia E., b. 1832 d. 4 Jan 1872; m.(3) 3 Jan 1873 Haverhill MA Hattie E. (Fox) Swan of Dracut MA, b. ca. 1837, dau. Nathaniel Fox; m.(4) 30 Jun 1874 Haverhill MA Abbie H. Williams of Hampstead NH, b. ca. 1830, dau. Jonathan and Filena Williams. Blacksmith, carriage maker.

Frank Howard, b. 11 Dec 1851, d. 3 Aug 1855 Amesbury MA.

George Elliot, b. 3 Jan 1854 Amesbury MA.

Abby Flora, b. 19 Sep 1856, m. 21 Jun 1876 Haverhill MA Charles Peaselee.

William, b. 16 Aug 1864 Haverhill MA.

Sources: Amesbury MA census 1850. VR Newbury MA, Haverhill MA, Amesbury MA, VR SA/MA.

336. **MOSES**$^{7}$ **SAWYER** [see 169], b. 4 Apr 1800 Amesbury MA, d. 7 May 1861 Amesbury MA, m. 7 Dec 1826 Hannah M. Rowell of New Hampshire, b. ?.

Amanda F., b. 1 Jan 1828, m. 30 Jan 1850 Haverhill MA Ezekiel Fowler.

507 Addison A.$^{8}$, b. 1834.

Elbridge G., b. ca. 1838 Amesbury MA, m. 12 Jun 1859 Newburyport MA Ann M. Dennett of Salisbury MA, b. 1839, dau. John and Louisa Dennett.

Albion Howard, b. 7 Jul 1842 Amesbury MA.

Sources: Amesbury MA census 1850. VR Amesbury MA, Haverhill MA.

337. **WILLIAM**$^{7}$ **SAWYER** [see 169], b. 22 Jan 1805 Amesbury MA, d. 8 Jan 1854 Amesbury MA, m. 7 Oct 1825 Joanna Pickett, b. ?. Shoemaker. In Bradford MA, Georgetown MA. Wid. in Georgetown MA 1850.

Mary Jane, b. 19 Nov 1825, m. 20 May 1846 Bradford MA Ariel K. Winter.

Sarah A., b. 26 Jul 1828, d. 15 Mar 1833.

Almira, b. 28 Jul 1831, d. 2 Mar 1833.

Sarah A., b. 7 Mar 1834 m. 26 Jul 1855 Georgetown MA Benjamin Farnum.

Charles H., b. 6 Jan 1836, m. 3 Jul 1859 Annie Leighton, b. ?. CH: Ella Chase, b. 16 Jan 1860 Georgetown MA.

Clarissa Almira, b. 21 Jan 1839, m. 29 Jan 1863 Perley Perley of New London NH.

William, b. 22 May 1843 Georgetown MA, m. 24 May Lynn MA Emma A. Biter of Lynn MA, b. 1847, dau. Samuel and Eliza Biter. Shoemaker. In Georgetown MA 1850. CH: Nellie Mabel, b. 25 Nov 1869, m. 6 Jun 1894 Lynn MA William F. Harrington.

Sources: Georgetown MA census 1850. VR Georgetown MA, Bradford MA, SA/MA.

338. **JOHN WARREN[7] SAWYER** [see 171], b. 16 Jun 1824 Amesbury MA, d. 18 Sep 1854 Haverhill MA, m. 25 Jul 1847 Haverhill MA Julia A. Burnham of Enfield NH, b. 1824 d. 21 Jan 1854, dau. David and Mary Burnham. Wheelright. In Andover MA, Lawrence MA.

Charles W., b. 25 Jun 1849, d. 2 Jun 1850 Haverhill MA.

Sources: VR Amesbury MA, Haverhill MA, SA/MA.

339. **CHARLES WASHINGTON[7] SAWYER** [see 171], b. 26 Apr 1831 Amesbury MA, m. 19 Sep 1852 Amesbury MA Sarah B. Clark of Cape Cod MA, b. 1833. Carriage maker.

508 Elmer Warren[8], b. 1854.

Charles Everett, b. 20 Jan 1860 Amesbury MA, m. 19 Jun 1884 Haverhill MA Addie F. Carr, b. ?.

Sources: Amesbury MA census 1850. VR SA/MA.

340. **CHARLES SYLVESTER[7] SAWYER** [see 172], b. 5 Dec 1837 Boston MA, d. 13 Nov 1923 Thornton NH, m.(1) Rhodie Merrill of Thornton NH, b. 1834 d. 1878, dau. Peter Merrill; m.(2) 9 Sep 1878 Rumney NH Fidelia (Dustin) Cheney of Westville NY, b. 3 Jun 1841 d. 16 Mar 1916, dau. Jonathan and Mary (Avery) Dustin. In Waterville NH 1880, Compton NH. He bur. in Blair Cem., Compton NH.

Delia, b. ca. 1854.

509 George S.[8], 1869-1927.

Mary, b. 1874.

Alta B., b. 1880, d. 12 Sep 1969, m. Charles Muzzey of Compton NH.

Lilla, b. 4 Jan 1882 d. 1 Dec 1971, m. 28 Apr 1906 William Fowler of No. Woodstock NH. Had dau., Gladys Irene, b. 23 Oct 1903 Manchester NH, adopted by James and Mary Minard [see 643].

Eda, b. 31 Mar 1884, m. Frank Steele of Thornton NH.

Eva, b. 31 Mar 1884, d. 1939, m. Horace Plummer of Thornton NH.

Sources: Waterville NH census 1880. VR SA/NH. C43, N9, Leonard S. Sawyer rec.

341. **SYLVESTER GEORGE[7] SAWYER** [see 173], b. 12 Dec 1842 Woodstock NH, d. 5 Jun 1926 Woodstock NH, m. 22 Sep 1869 Alma Elizabeth Smith of Woodstock NH, b. 18 May 1847 d. 8 Aug 1913, dau. Joseph and Mary (Vincent) Smith. Farmer.

Alice Emma, b. 26 Sep 1870, d. 7 Jan 1956, unm.

Cora May, b. 12 Mar 1873, d. 29 Jan 1955, m. 12 Nov 1896 Henry S. Brown.

510 Danford Lucien[8], 1875-1908.

511 Vincent Isaac[8], 1881-1950.

Harry Dean, b. 18 May 1884 Woodstock NH, d. 27 Apr 1950, m. 25 Mar 1915 Dover NH Ida Estelle Tilton of Nyack NY, b. ? d. Dec 1970, dau. Fred C. and Emelia F. (Bliss) Tilton. Farmer. CH: Elinor, b. 9 Apr 1923, m. 29 May 1948 Roland Ladd Osgood.

Charles Augustine, b. 10 Mar 1887 Woodstock NH, d. 15 May 1911, unm.

512 Howard Symmes[8], 1890-1959.

Sources: Woodstock NH census 1880. VR SA/NH. N6, R34, Leonard S. Sawyer rec., Lloyd V. Sawyer rec.

342. **ALMUS B.**$^{7}$ **SAWYER** [see 173], b. 13 Sep 1850 Woodstock NH, d. 9 Nov 1913 Woodstock NH, m. 1 Mar 1882 Sarah Isabell Lunnin of Boston MA, b. 1856 d. 1928. Farmer. Note: His d. record says he was b. 26 Jan 1850.

Isabella M., b. 23 May 1884, d. 10 Apr 1965, m. William Haskell.
Annie L. b. 20 Oct 1885, m. George Fadden of Thornton NH.
513 Frank Almus$^{8}$, 1890-1944.
Edward D., b. 26 Aug 1895 Woodstock NH, d. 10 Mar 1921, unm.

Sources: VR SA/NH. G31, Leonard S. Sawyer rec.

343. **FRANK ROPER**$^{7}$ **SAWYER** [see 174], b. 19 Jan 1842 Woodstock NH, d. 8 Sep 1911 Somerville MA, m. 1 Jan 1870 Olive Melinda Brown of Newport NH, b. 22 Jan 1850 d. 14 Jun 1920. Tanner. In Bristol NH 1868-1881, Enfield NH 1881-1887, Salem MA 1887-1902. Also in West Somerville MA.

Myra Clair, b. 16 Apr 1871, m. 4 Sep 1895 Salem MA Everett W. Durgin.
Mae Frances, b. 7 Dec 1873, m. 15 Nov 1894 Salem MA Eugene L. Pack.
Frank Roy, b. 25 May 1878 Bristol NH, m. 8 Aug 1904 So. Newbury NH Mary G. Gillingham of Newbury NH, b. 1881, dau. Benjamin F. and Martha A. (Fowler) Gillingham. Bank teller. In Boston MA, Somerville MA. CH: Virginia, b. ca. 1906, d. 9 Dec 1992, m. _____ Kendall.
Olive Maud, b. 8 Jun 1885.

Sources: VR SA/MA. M64, Obit (Virginia).

344. **GEORGE A.**$^{7}$ **SAWYER** [see 174], b. 20 Jul 1845 Woodstock NH, d. 11 Mar 1929 Franconia NH, m. 18 Nov 1869 Ella R. Brown of Claremont NH, b. 4 Aug 1848 d. 1 Nov 1924, dau. Albert W. and Hannah (Felch) Brown. In Woodstock NH 1870-1880, Franconia NH 1888.

Daisy W., b. 1873.
Laura M., 1876.
514 Arthur W.$^{8}$, b. 1879.

Sources: Woodstock NH census 1870. VR SA/NH.

345. **EUGENE A.**$^{7}$ **SAWYER** [see 175], b. 5 Apr 1850 Woodstock NH, d. 21 Aug 1916 Lincoln NH, m. Amy Macomber, b. ?.

Ralph E., b. ? Lincoln NH, m. Edith Tolman, b. ?. CH: Amy, b. ?, m. _____ Fisk.

Sources: VR SA/NH. Leonard S. Sawyer rec.

346. **ALBERT W.**$^{7}$ **SAWYER** [see 175], b. 21 Aug 1853 Woodstock NH, d. 16 Jul 1934 Woodstock NH, m.(1) 20 Nov 1873 Clara C. Snow of Thornton NH, b. 10 Aug 1851 d. 12 Jan 1919, dau. William T. and Lavina (Houston) Snow; m.(2) 5 Oct 1921 Eliza A. (Ford) Woodbury of Holden MA, b. ca. 1857 d. 25 Jan 1954, dau. George W. and Susan (Howe) Ford. Hotel keeper.

Bertha E., b. 28 Sep 1875, d. 17 Apr 1975, m.(1) 20 Nov 1895 Henry W. Currier, m.(2) Alfred Day.
515 Thomas Fenno$^{8}$, 1879-1971.
516 Joseph R.$^{8}$, 1881-1974.
Susie Linda, b. 5 Aug 1883, d. 1967, m. Edgar Anderson.

Sources: Woodstock NH census 1880. VR SA/NH. Leonard S. Sawyer rec.

347. **GEORGE F.**$^{7}$ **SAWYER** [see 176], b. 29 Oct 1850 Woodstock NH, d. 15 Sep 1917, m. 26 Apr 1890 Thornton NH (div. 28 May 1908) Lilla B. Merrill of Thornton NH, b. 1871.

Mabel, b. 28 Jun 1893, d. 28 Jan 1978, m. Walter L. Long.
517 Almon$^{8}$, 1895-1943.

Sources: VR SA/NH. Leonard S. Sawyer rec.

348. **THOMAS W.$^7$ SAWYER** [see 177], b. Oct 1818 Hopkinton NH, d. 1 Jul 1884 Warner NH, m. Sarah Ann Couch of Hopkinton NH, b. 30 Aug 1838 d. 29 Aug 1907, dau. James and Mary (Eastman) Couch. In Warner NH 1850-1870.

Charles H., b. 1853 Warner NH, m. 27 Apr 1904 Hopkinton NH Nellie M. Eastman of Salisbury NH, b. 18 May 1852 d. 7 Jul 1924, dau. Josiah and Electa (Libby) Sargent. Her 4th m. In Weare NH.

John F., b. 21 May 1857 Warner NH, d. 22 Jan 1898 Warner NH.

Mary Etta, b. 11 Aug 1859, d. 15 Oct 1885.

Sources: Warner NH census 1850, 1860, 1870. VR SA/NH. N9.

349. **SAMUEL$^7$ SAWYER** [see 178], b. 16 Jul 1803 Brookfield NH, d. 1 Nov 1871 Hermon ME, m.(1) 6 Jan 1825 Middleton NH Jane K. Whitehouse of Middleton NH, b. 29 Nov 1802 d. 18 Jun 1860; m.(2) 1 Jan 1861 Bangor ME Eliza H. Clement of Bucksport ME, b. 16 Sep 1806 d. 16 Jul 1876, dau. Abner and Amy (Lowell) Clement. Farmer. He bur. in Cambridge ME. Will dated 21 Jan 1861, probated Feb 1872.

518 Ivory C.$^8$, 1825-1898. Went to California.

Enos W., b. ca. 1830, m. 28 Feb 1853 Bangor ME Lydia A. Doane of Bangor ME, b. ?. In Hermon ME 1850, Bangor ME 1860.

519 Freeman C.$^8$, b. ca. 1832.

Adeline P., b. 1848.

Sources: Cambridge ME census 1840. Hermon ME census 1850. VR Middleton NH, Bangor ME. C50, Will, Lawrence A. Sawyer rec.

350. **OTHNIEL$^7$ SAWYER** [see 178], b. 7 Jun 1818 Brookfield NH, d. 27 Sep 1892 Cambridge ME, m. Betsey Ann Hilton of St. Albans ME, b. 25 Dec 1818 d. 25 Dec 1900, dau. Jonathan and Nancy (Stoddard) Hilton. Farmer. In Cambridge ME 1840.

Almira S., b. 9 Sep 1842, m. _____ Cole.

Sarah Jane, b. 23 Jan 1845, m. _____ Fields.

520 Albert$^8$, b. 1846-1927.

Almon Ithamas, b. 1850 Cambridge ME, d. 17 Oct 1875, unm.

Olive R., b. ca. 1851, m. _____ Barron.

James A., b. ca. 1852 Cambridge ME, d. 15 Feb 1875 in California.

521 Samuel$^8$, b. 1857.

Sources: Cambridge ME census 1840, 1850, 1860. R35, Gladys Wood rec., Bessie Folsom rec.

351. **ASA$^7$ SAWYER** [see 179], b. 16 Mar 1813 Salem MA, m.(1) 19 May 1836 Reading MA Mary Susan Buxton of Reading MA, b. Apr 1818 d. 31 Oct 1845, dau. Elijah and Mary Buxton; m.(2) 27 Dec 1845 Abby M. Ferguson of Shapleigh ME, b. ca. 1826. Lumber dealer. In Danvers MA 1840, Saugus MA 1850.

Susan A., b. 11 Feb 1837.

Mary A., b. 9 Dec 1838, m. 25 Feb 1863 Salem MA George A. Perkins.

Asa, b. 22 Jul 1841 Danvers MA, d. 6 Feb 1923 Lebanon NH, m.(1) 25 Nov 1862 Lawrence MA Susan G. Currier of Warner NH, b. ca. 1845, dau. John and Clara Currier; m.(2) 1 Aug 1870 Lawrence MA Susan B. Mace of Salem MA, b. 1 Sep 1848 d. 27 Mar 1919, dau. Joseph and Mary (Sawyer) Mace. Boxmaker. In Swampscott MA 1863, Lebanon NH 1870. CH: Florence Susan, b. 16 Nov 1863.

William, b. 10 May 1843, d. 1845.

Susan, b. 1844, d. 1849.

Albert, b. 16 Jul 1845, d. 29 Sep 1845.
Alice, b. 3 Oct 1846, m. 14 Jun 1892 Providence RI N_____ B. Upham.
William F., b. 11 Dec 1847 Danvers MA, m. 18 Apr 1869 Melrose MA Carrie Jones of Brewster MA, b. ca. 1849, dau. Benjamin and Caroline Brewster. Salesman. In Saugus MA 1850, Peabody MA 1885. CH: Alice Merrill, b. 8 Nov 1873; Edna Gertrude, b. 8 Jan 1885.
Albert E., b. 22 Dec 1849 Danvers MA, m. 24 Dec 1872 Lawrence MA Emma A. Lewis of Pelham NH, b. ca. 1853, dau. Henry and Ann Lewis.
Sources: Saugus MA census 1850. VR Reading MA, Danvers MA, SA/MA, SA/NH.

352. **ASA WILSON**$^{7}$ **SAWYER** [see 180], b. 19 Sep 1818 Danvers MA, m. 5 Apr 1845 Thompsonville CT Hannah Chase Wellman of Thompsonville CT, b. 5 Apr 1824, dau. Stephen and Charlotte (Rawlins) Wellman. Butcher. Commanded a light infantry company 1848. In Danvers MA 1850.
George Thomas, b. 24 Dec 1846 Danvers MA.
Channey R., b. 20 Sep 1847 Danvers MA.
Rollins Wellman, b. 24 Sep 1848 Danvers MA.
Sources: Danvers MA census 1850. VR Danvers MA, SA/MA. H14, W25, R25.

353. **THOMAS HADLEY**$^{7}$ **SAWYER** [see 180], b. 10 Dec 1826 Danvers MA, d. 8 Dec 1905 Peabody MA, m. 9 Dec 1847 Marblehead MA Lydia Messervey of Marblehead MA, b. Sep 1829 d. 6 Oct 1903, dau. Ambrose and Lydia Messervey. Butcher. In Danvers 1850.
522 Asa Chapman$^{8}$, 1849-1926.
Alice Messervey, b. 1 Feb 1855, m. 25 Dec 1873 Peabody MA Daniel Buxton.
Sources: Danvers MA census 1850. VR Danvers MA, Marblehead MA, SA/MA. Paul B. Sawyer rec.

354. **NATHANIEL**$^{7}$ **SAWYER** [see 181], b. 28 Jun 1819 Salem MA, m. 18 Oct 1838 Salem MA Mary A. Kehew of Salem MA, b. ?. Truckman. In Salem MA 1840-1850.
Nathaniel, b. 18 Sep 1837 Salem MA, m. 11 Oct 1858 Salem MA Augusta Kimball of Salem MA, b. 1839, dau. Joseph and Sarah Kimball. Carpenter.
Sarah Elizabeth, b. 3 Jan 1839, m. 19 Nov 1855 Lynn MA John Griffin.
Samuel, b. 9 Sep 1840, d. 24 Jan 1843.
523 Caleb$^{8}$, b. 1842.
John, b. 12 Jan 1844, d. 26 Feb 1844.
Mary Ellen, b. 25 Jan 1845, d. 20 Feb 1845.
Mary Ellen, b. Feb 1846.
Samuel Kehew, b. 1 Mar 1848 Salem MA, m. 22 Nov 1866 Salem MA Caroline A. Stevens of Salem MA, b. 1848, dau. George and Mary Stevens. Printer.
524 William Henry$^{8}$, b. 1850.
Sources: Salem MA census 1840, 1850. VR Salem MA, Danvers MA, SA/MA.

355. **JOSEPH**$^{7}$ **SAWYER** [see 183], b. 11 Nov 1836 Litchfield ME, d. 22 Nov 1913 Augusta ME, m. 3 Jan 1865 Gardiner ME Annie M. Stinson of Bath ME, b. ?. Painter. In Augusta ME.
Miriam F., b. 18 Oct 1865.
Lillian M., b. 15 Sep 1867, d. 25 Jul 1875.
James Brown, b. 23 Sep 1870 Litchfield ME, m. 18 Jun 1894 Augusta ME Harriet Gannett of Augusta ME, b. 2 Apr 1866 d. 8 Sep 1929, dau. Charles E. and Hannah (Fish) Gannett. In Somerville MA 1900.
525 Herbert B.$^{8}$, 1872-1921.

Joseph, b. 26 Jan 1875, d. 1888.
Sarah A., b. 30 Dec 1876.
Alice M., b. 1879.

Sources: ME 1880 census index, Somerville MA census 1900. VR Gardiner ME, SA/ME. C46, D37.

356. **JOHN E.[7] SAWYER** [see 186], b. 7 Feb 1837 Lowell MA, d.4 Apr 1906, m. (1) 13 Sep 1865 Methuen MA Charlotte E. Chase of New York, b. 26 Feb 1844 d. 30 Apr 1867, dau. Seth and Charlotte Chase; m.(2) 30 Dec 1869 Lawrence MA Mary D. Low of Warner NH, b. 1 Jan 1840 d. 30 Apr 1887, dau. Seth and Nebro (Davis) Low; m.(3) Annie M. _____ of Nova Scotia, b. 1842. Bookkeeper. In Methuen MA 1880.

Susan Emma, b. 20 Feb 1866, m. 8 Jul 1896 Joseph W. Emerson of Maine.
Charlotte E., b. 16 Nov 1870, m. 15 Feb 1894 Bennie E. Hill.
Nirha Jane, b. 31 May 1872, d. 19 Oct 1872.
William Henry, b. 30 May 1873 Methuen MA, m. 8 Jul 1897 Hattie M. Snell, b. ?. Newspaper editor. CH: Persis Low, b. 22 Jun 1902.
Ebenezer, b. 14 Jan 1875 Methuen MA, m. 14 Apr 1906 Lucy E. Crane. b. ?. Went to Omaha NE. CH: Charlotte Louise, b. 7 Feb 1909.
Nathaniel Low, b. 22 Sep 1876, d. 4 Aug 1877.
Edwin Low, b. 30 Oct 1877 Methuen MA, m. 20 Apr 1907 Margaret A. Hogg of Derry NH, b. ?. In Atlanta GA.
Perley Dana, b. 4 Feb 1879 Methuen MA.

Sources: Methuen MA census 1880. VR SA/MA. Annette S. Manny rec.

357. **JAMES BRIDGEMAN[7] SAWYER** [see 187], b. 12 Dec 1850 Boxford MA, d. 1924, m. 1 Dec 1881 Boxford MA Sarah E. Howe of Boxford MA, b. 8 Aug 1859, dau. Edward and Lydia Sanborn (Leavitt) Howe. Farmer, milkman. In Haverhill MA 1900.

George Edward, b. 12 Mar 1883 Boxford MA. Went to Seattle WN.
Thomas Horace, b. 26 Oct 1884, d. 22 Mar 1890.
Esther Howe, b. 9 Jul 1891, d. 3 Jun 1904.
James Earl, b. 30 Sep 1893, d. 8 Oct 1894.
Robert Hamilton, b. 27 Jul 1895 Haverhill MA, m. Dorothea B. Baker, b. ?.

Sources: Haverhill MA census 1900. VR SA/MA. Annette S. Manny rec.

358. **ISAAC HOWE[7] SAWYER** [see 187], b. 3 Apr 1858 Boxford MA, m. 15 Jan 1895 Quincy MA Bertha Colby of Boston MA, b. 24 Dec 1872, dau. William F. and Anna Colby. Shoe manufacturer. In St. Louis MO.

John Colby, b. 6 Sep 1896.
Aaron Everett, b. 6 Jul 1898.

Sources: VR SA/MA.

359. **SAMUEL B.[7] SAWYER** [see 189], b. 6 Jul 1798 Wells ME, d. 16 May 1860 Wells ME, m. 21 Apr 1874 Mary Littlefield, b. 1808.

526 Christopher B.[8], b. 1824.
Caroline, b. 14 May 1827.
Adeline, b. 1828, m. 13 Mar 1867 Eben C. Freeman.

Sources: Wells ME census 1820, 1830, 1840, 1850, 1860. N6, P82k, P32.

360. **WILLIAM[7] SAWYER** [see 190], b. ca. 1810 Cornish ME, d. 14 Dec 1877 Cornish ME, m.(1) 21 Sep 1837 Eliza Wentworth of Limington ME, b. 6 Apr 1816 d. 12 Oct 1860, dau.

Benjamin and Sally (Bryant) Wentworth; m.(2) 11 Feb 1861 Cornish ME Susan Barnes of Cornish ME, b. 15 Jan 1829 d. 4 Feb 1906, dau. Abraham and Jane (Estes) Barnes. Wid. m. Horace Wood of Saco ME.

Emily, b. 10 Aug 1838.

Samuel, b. 24 Nov 1839 Cornish ME.

Sarah J., b. 4 Sep 1842, d. 30 Jan 1844.

Benjamin W., b. 22 Apr 1844 Cornish ME, d. 8 Jan 1888 Cornish ME, m. 14 Jan 1884 Lydia A. (Haskell) Decker, wid., b. 1 Aug 1844 d. 2 Mar 1899, dau. Francis and Jemima (Nason) Haskell. Farmer. He bur. in Riverside Cem., Cornish ME. CH: Mabel Florence, b. 31 Aug 1886, m. William Guptill.

Charles, b. 5 May 1846, d. 22 Jan 1850.

Susan, b. 30 May 1848, d. 1 Jan 1850.

Franceah, b. 27 Apr 1850.

William, b. 1854 Cornish ME, d. 1936, m. 24 Jan 1878 Annie M. Grafton, b. ?. Railroad worker. No CH.

Adelle, b. ca. 1862, m.(I) 31 Aug 1878 Horace H. Libby.

Eliza, b. ca. 1864, m. 16 Nov 1880 Nathaniel Batties.

Ella, b. 1866, d. 1935, m. Frank Decker.

Margie, b. 1869, m. 25 Dec 1890 Frank Decker.

Ernest L., b. 29 Dec Feb 1871, d. 14 Jun 1892.

Sources: Cornish ME census 1840, 1850, 1860, 1870. VR SA/ME. W26, C62, N6, F34, P82k, Dorothy Guptill rec., Robert L. Taylor rec.

361. **LEMUEL B.[7] SAWYER** [see 191], b. 19 Jan 1797 Limington ME, d. 25 Sep 1882 Porter ME, m. 26 Mar 1820 Mary Berry of Limington ME, b. 4 Feb 1800 d. 26 May 1873, dau. Samuel and Mary (Anderson) Berry. In Porter ME 1830.

Samuel Berry, b. 8 Aug 1820 Limington ME, d. 23 Dec 1898 Wolfeboro NH, m. 20 Jun 1844 Susan Maleham of Wolfeboro NH, b. 28 Jul 1809 d. 10 Jun 1896, dau. William and Marylee (Tibbets) Maleham. Farmer. In Porter ME 1850-1870. He bur. Wolfeboro. CH: Harriet A., b. 1846, m. 13 Nov 1862 Wolfeboro NH Charles H. Tibbets; Emily A., b. 10 Jun 1847, d. 13 Dec 1918; Almira S., b. 19 Apr 1854, m. 13 Nov 1892 Nathaniel F. Avery.

527 Thomas Boothby[8], 1825-1885.

Sylvester B., b. 1827 Limington ME, d. 22 Oct 1908 So. Hiram ME. He bur. in Porter ME.

528 Isaac B.[8], 1829-1904.

Mary A., b. 22 May 1832, d. 29 May 1913, m. 15 May 1856 Hanson Libby.

Lydia A., b. 1835, m. 17 Feb 1870 Mark A. Young of Wolfeboro NH.

529 George Washington[8], 1837-1913.

Louisa, b. 27 Feb 1840, d. 21 Jan 1924, m. 18 Jan 1873 Benjamin Franklin Sawyer [see 531].

Almira, b. 1844, d. 7 Mar 1898, m. 13 Feb 1884 Tuftonboro NH Orrin Durgin.

Sarah B., b. 26 Jan 1846, d. 10 Mar 1898, m. 23 Dec 1848 Eldric Clemens.

Sources: Limington ME census 1820. Porter ME census 1830, 1840, 1850, 1860, 1870. Wolfeboro NH census 1850, 1860, 1870. VR Saco ME, Porter ME. Obit. L20, N6, T64, P66, T6A, T6, C3, Robert L. Taylor rec.

362. **JAMES B.[7] SAWYER** [see 191], b. 3 Dec 1800 Limington ME, d. 17 Jul 1886 Porter ME, m. 15 Sep 1822 Desire Cobb of Limington ME, b. 5 Jul 1800 d. 11 Sep 1884, dau. Andrew and Betsey (Irish) Cobb. Farmer. In Limington ME 1830, 1850, Porter ME 1880. Desire was in Brownfield ME 1840.

Ebenezer Cobb, b. 17 Feb 1823 Limington ME, d. 3 Mar 1851, m. 9 May 1843 Martha A. Rogers.
Sylvester Boothby, b. 7 Mar 1827 Limington ME, d. 22 Oct 1910.
William Bean, b. 7 Aug 1829 Limington ME, d. 24 Mar 1851 Boston MA.
James Birks, b. 7 Dec 1833 Limington ME.
Mary Ann Bangs, b. 16 Feb 1835, m. 5 May 1858 Andrew J. Richardson.
Francina Lorine, b. 15 Mar 1839, d. 6 Jan 1916, m.(1) Thomas Boothby Sawyer, m.(2) 24 Aug 1886 John Bradeen.

Sources: Limington ME census 1830, 1850. Brownfield ME census 1840. Porter ME census 1880. VR SA/ME. T6, R10g. Obit (Desire).

363. **BENJAMIN THOMPSON[7] SAWYER** [see 191], b. 30 Jul 1806 Limerick ME, d. 7 Feb 1887 Limerick ME, m. 24 Aug 1829 Limington ME Phebe S. Cobb, b. 28 Apr 1813 d. 11 Sep 1884, dau. Andrew and Betsey (Irish) Cobb. Trader. S/land to brother James B. 1833. In Brownfield ME 1830, Limerick ME 1840-1850.

530 William Henry[8], 1831-1908.
Clementine B., b. 12 Oct 1833, d. 6 Oct 1851.
531 Benjamin Franklin[8], 1835-1900.
Elizabeth Mary, b. 22 Nov 1852, d. 13 Apr 1895, m. 20 Dec 1876 John Fogg.

Sources: Brownfield ME census 1830. Limington ME census 1840,1850. VR Limington ME. R10c.

364. **JACOB[7] SAWYER** [see 191], b. 1 May 1810 Limington ME, d. 9 Aug 1886 Limington ME, m.(1) 24 Sep 1837 Scarboro ME Agnes H. Libby, b. 23 Nov 1808 d. 10 Nov 1871, dau. Henry and Margaret (Meserve) Libby; m.(2) 30 Mar 1875 Presque Isle ME Harriet E. York of Smyrna ME, b. 1 Jun 1847 d. 10 May 1917, dau. Daniel and Serena (Morrison) York. Civil War. In Brownfield ME, Limerick ME, Maysville ME. He bur. in Limerick ME.

George Washington, b. 10 Aug 1839, d. 22 Mar 1860.
Mary Jane, b. 6 Jun 1840, d. 3 Mar 1861.
Margaret L., b. ca. 1842, m. Emery Marean of Standish ME.
Maria Olive, b. ca. 1844, d.y.
Alfaretta, b. ca. 1848, d. 29 Jan 1882, m. (I) 27 Sep 1876 Soloman Hamilton Kilpatrick. CH: Jennie, b. 1866.
532 Oswald (Osro) Jacob[8], 1852-1930.
Daniel, b. ca. 1866 Ashland ME, m. 22 Sep 1900 Sarah Louise York.
Edwin L., b. 1870 Mayesville ME.
Rose Violet, b. 18 Feb 1872, d. 27 Sep 1938, m.(1)(I) 12 Mar 1889 Willis E. Sawyer [see 241}, m.(2) 6 Nov 1901 Joseph A. Hill.
Maria O., b. ca. 1874.
533 Clifford Leroy[8], 1876-1936.
Alta Gertrude, b. 11 Sep 1878, d. Dec 1965, m. 3 Oct 1914 Charles W. Pulsifer.
Ernest Andrew, b. 25 Sep 1882 Limerick ME, d. 24 Nov 1962 Buxton ME, m.(1) 18 Aug 1905 Limerick ME (div. 13 Feb 1912) Cordelia E. Herbert of New Brunswick, Canada, b. ca. 1886, dau. Joseph and Lizzie (Taylor) Herbert; m.(2) Etta May Roberts, b. ? d. 20 Mar 1932. He bur. in Tory Hill Cem., Buxton ME. CH: Winfred Ernest, b. 24 Apr 1906, d. 20 Jan 1973, m. 5 Sep 1929 Carrie Tibbets Berry.
Etta Mae, b. 1 Jun 1885, d. 24 Jan 1967.

Note: According to [P82k], Margaret L., Oswald J., and Alfaretta were all of unsound mind.

Sources: Brownfield ME census 1840. Limington ME census 1850, 1860, 1880. Maysville ME census 1870, 1880 census index. VR SA/ME, SA/MA. D37, L20, T6, N37, P82k, Clifford L. Sawyer rec., Winnifred Ahlquist rec.

365. **ISAAC[7] SAWYER** [see 191], b. 30 Aug 1820 Limington ME, d. 16 Apr 1887 Limerick ME, m. 4 Jul 1846 Salome Thompson of Newfield ME, b. 14 Aug 1826 d. 29 Oct 1907, dau. Stephen and Martha (Drew) Thompson. Civil War. B/land in Brownfield ME 1848.

Francis A., b. 14 Dec 1846 Limerick ME, d. 3 Oct 1920 Conway NH, m.(1) 19 Jan 1868 (div. 1876) Sarah Smith of Cornish ME, b. 8 Feb 1842 d. 1929, dau. Eli Smith; m.(2) (div. 1883) Lucy J. Roberts of Nova Scotia, b. 21 Sep 1844 d. 2 May 1929; m.(3) 1 May 1883 Lynn MA Mary D. Cotton of Troy MI, b. 19 Dec 1851 d. 30 Oct 1931, dau. James and Eliza Cotton. In Limington ME 1880, Lynn MA 1884. CH: Fanny, b. 1 Mar 1869, d. 1945, m. Richard Maddox; Eveline C., b. ca. 1877, m. 21 Sep 1895 Harrison Libby of Limerick ME; Emma, b. 18 Jun 1879, d. 19 Jan 1950, m. Frank Ward; Laura L., b. 14 Feb 1882, m.(1) 5 Jul 1903 Charles Berry of So. Cornish ME, m.(2) 1946 Rufus Emerson of Meredith NH; Elsie M., b. 27 Apr 1884, m. Ralph Purrington.

534 Autien W. S.[8], 1849-1918.

Wilbur Fisk, b. 20 Sep 1851 Limerick ME, d. 29 Apr 1941 Baldwin NY, m.(1) 9 May 1872 Holliston MA Addie Fallansbee of Holliston MA, b. 1853, dau. Melvin and Hannah Fallansbee; m.(2) Leonora Randall, b. 17 May 1867 d. 28 Mar 1937. CH: Randella C., b. 29 Jan 1905, m. Joseph Arzanna.

535 Walter Edgecomb[8], b. 1854.

Sources: Limerick ME census 1850, 1860, 1870, Limington ME census 1880 index. VR SA/MA. Will, M5, T6, R10g, T6A.

366. **DANIEL[7] SAWYER** [see 192], b. 1 Jun 1800 Holderness NH, d. 26 Dec 1858 Bridgewater NH, m. 27 Jan 1828 Boston MA Eleanor Robbins of Maine, b. 10 Feb 1798 d. 21 Apr 1870, dau. Oliver and Sarah Robbins. Miller. In Boston MA, Plymouth NH 1830, Holderness NH 1842, Bridgewater NH.

Ellen Amanda, b. 2 Aug 1829, d. 11 Nov 1893, m. 12 Sep 1849 Plymouth NH David M. Webster.

536 Daniel[8], 1835-1889.

Amelia B., b. 15 May 1841, m. 25 Dec 1882 James M. Vinal.

Sources: Plymouth NH census 1830. Holderness NH census 1850. VR SA/MA. S81, N6, Family Bible.

367. **HUMPHREY[7] SAWYER** [see 192], b. 1805 Holderness NH, m. 11 Apr 1828 Phebe M. Cummings of Hebron NH, b. 9 Oct 1808, dau. Andrew and Hannah (Crawford) Cummings. Carpenter. In Plymouth NH, Nashua NH.

537 Samuel Augustus[8], 1830-1897.

Oliver M., b. ca. 1839, d. Hastings MT, m.(1) 5 Feb 1860 Nashua NH (div. 7 Jun 1865) Carrie D. McFarlane of Trenton ME, b. 1839; m.(2) 8 Nov 1866 Lowell MA Mary E. (Crum) Vaughn of New Hampshire, b. 1834, dau. Eliphalet and Abby Crum. Laborer. In Nashua NH 1850. Civil War: Enl. 19 Apr 1861 Nashua NH, Co. E, mustered 2 May 1861 as Sgt., captured 14 Jul 1861, released 3 Jun 1862. CH: Martha A., b. 15 Nov 1860, m. 3 Jul 1877 Worcester MA Adolphus B. Chambers.

Martha Ann, b. ca. 1847.

Sources: Plymouth NH census 1830, 1840. Nashua NH census 1850, 1860. VR SA/MA, SA/NH. S81, C90, P10.

368. **ELISHA SMITH⁷ SAWYER** [see 193], b. 19 Dec 1808 New Hampton NH, d. 14 Oct 1894 Laconia NH, m. Susanna C. Woodbury of Dunbarton NH, b. 29 Mar 1814 d. 1 Jun 1897, dau. David and Mary (Colby) Woodbury. Farmer.

Sarah H., b. 6 Dec 1836.
Marsha E., b. 27 Oct 1838, m. 7 Jul 1863 Boston MA Charles J. Richardson.
Mary S., b. 7 May 1841.
Martha E., b. 9 Nov 1843.
Elisha W., b. 17 Feb 1846 New Hampton NH.
538 Kendrick Dana[8], 1848-1921.
Abbie O., b. 28 Nov 1852, m. 23 May 1871 Rufus P. Dow.
One child d. Jul 1847 in Sanbornton NH.

Sources: New Hampton NH census 1850. Gilford NH census 1870. VR SA/MA. H18, Family Bible, Margaret Sawyer rec.

369. **ELBRIDGE GERRY[7] SAWYER** [see 193], b. 3 Feb 1826 New Hampton NH, d. 2 Oct 1918 Plymouth NH, m. 23 Jul 1850 Julia Clifford Hanson of Gilmanton NH, b. 10 May 1830 d. 5 Mar 1920, dau. Jeremiah Hanson. Shoemaker. In New Hampton NH 1850-1860, Woodstock NH 1870-1880, Plymouth NH 1908.

Fidelia, b. Oct 1851, d. Aug 1853.
539 Elbridge Gerry[8], 1854-1921.
Albert Henry, b. 16 Sep 1855 No. Hampton NH, m. 15 Sep 1884 Thornton NH Emma Marden of Thornton NH, b. ?. In Campton NH and Woodstock NH. Note: [G6] says he m. Emma F. McCutcheon, dau. Frederick and Martha (Clark) McCutcheon.
Melissa, b. 10 Aug 1857, m.(1) James W. Piper, m.(2) P____ Craw.
Almon Libbey, b. 19 Aug 1859, d. 26 Sep 1881.
540 Leroy Alfred[8], 1861-1905.
Fanny Lillian, b. 14 Dec 1863, m. 9 Oct 1893 Leon C. Huse.
Julia Etta, b. 15 Oct 1865, m. 11 Oct 1890 Thornton NH Charles C. Griffin.
Leah Sophia, b. 15 Sep 1867, m. 13 Oct 1897 Plymouth NH Charles S. Tilton.
Alice Izetta, b. 22 Apr 1870, m. 1 Jun 1898 Alfred L. Brown.
Annie M., b. 1 Sep 1873, m. 25 Oct 1893 George Dolloff of Campton NH.
Rose Maude, b. 9 Aug 1877, d. 26 Nov 1878.

Sources: New Hampton NH census 1850, 1860. Woodstock NH census 1870, 1880. VR SA/NH. N6H, S81, H17, H96, J17.

370. **DANIEL S.[7] SAWYER** [see 194], b. ca. 1800, m. 7 Nov 1836 Sarah Hobb of Jackson ME, b. ca. 1802. In New Hampton NH, Orford NH.

Daniel, b. ca. 1840 Orford NH.

Sources: Orford NH census 1850.

371. **MOSES[7] SAWYER** [see 195], b. 26 Oct 1803 Henniker NH, d. 27 Jan 1892 No. Weare NH, m.(1) 23 Nov 1833 Rebecca B. Morrill of Seabrook NH, b. ? d. 2 Apr 1848; m.(2) 23 Jun 1852 Hannah (Bassett) Jones of Wolfeboro NH, b. 18 Mar 1815 d. 13 Mar 1889, wid. of Amos, dau. Daniel and Abigail (Bean) Bassett. Manufacturer (woolen mill). Quaker. Moses' house was a station on the "underground railway" during the days of slavery. In Starksboro VT 1822, E. Deering NH, Sallisbury MA 1829-1830, Weare NH 1831-1870.

John Edward, b. 17 Apr 1841, d. 1858.
541 Henry Abbott[8], 1853-1892.
Rebecca Ellen, b. 24 Jul 1857, m. J. Fred Smith. Went to New York.
Mary Elizabeth, b. 21 Sep 1860, d. 2 Apr 1893, unm.

Sources: Weare NH census 1840, 1850, 1860, 1870. B40, G30, C59, N5.

372. **NATHAN⁷ SAWYER** [see 195], b. 28 Apr 1806 Henniker NH, d. 5 Jul 1890 Henniker NH, m. 27 Oct 1831 Weare NH Anna Hodgdon of Weare NH, b. 20 Apr 1809 d. 7 Apr 1885, dau. Moses and Dorcas (Dow) Hodgdon. Quaker. Merchant. Selectman for Henniker NH.

Mary H., b. 15 May 1835, m. 7 May 1857 Nathan Page of Danvers MA.

Moses Hodgdon, b. 8 Jun 1839 Henniker NH, d. 13 Jul 1873 Henniker NH, m. (1) 12 Jan 1867 Emma F. Gove of Weare NH, b. 1 Aug 1847 d. 4 May 1867, dau. Peter and Charlotte (Sumner) Gove; m.(2) 10 Nov 1870 Eliza Smith of Henniker NH, b. 1846.

Sources: Henniker NH census 1840, 1850, 1860, 1870. G30, W38, C59, C16.

373. **DANIEL⁷ SAWYER** [see 195], b. 26 Jul 1808 Henniker NH, d. 6 Apr 1885 Weare NH, m. 16 Jun 1831 Weare NH Dorcas N. Hodgdon of Weare NH, b. 25 Jul 1811 d. 26 Apr 1882, dau. Moses and Dorcas (Dow) Hodgdon. Quaker. Wholesale grocer. Portland ME 1840, Weare NH 1850-1870.

Susan H., b. 2 Nov 1834, d. 24 Jan 1836.

542 Albert Hodgdon⁸, 1837-1899.

Oliver Dennett., b. 19 Nov 1839 Portland ME, d. 1 Jan 1921 Weare NH, m. 8 Oct 1884 Mary Jane Morgan of Hopkinton NH, b. Jun 1846 d. 16 May 1917, dau. Richard and Mary (Allen) Morgan. Quaker. Attended Colby Academy NH and Friends School, Providence RI. State senator 1886-1888.

Amelia H., b. 3 Feb 1848, m. 17 Aug 1871 John W. Whittle.

Sources: Portland ME census 1840. Weare NH census 1850, 1860, 1870. VR SA/NH. N6, C59, N9, W38.

374. **ENOCH PARKER⁷ SAWYER** [see 198], b. 17 Nov 1805 Litchfield ME, d. 1884 Chelsea MA, m. 9 Aug 1832 Skowhegan ME Mary T. Gardiner, b. 1811, dau. Ebenezer Gardiner. Cabinetmaker. In Hallowell ME 1832. B/land in Troy ME 1842, 1846, 1847. In Gray ME, Plymouth ME.

Melissa, b. 1 Feb 1834.

543 Granville Parker⁸, 1836-1900.

Hannah E., b. 1839. Went to Gray ME.

James F., b. 1840 Troy ME.

544 Byron P.⁸, b. 1844.

Mary E., b. 1849.

Sources: Troy ME census 1840, 1850, 1880. VR Hallowell ME. C46, P82e, J21

375. **CYRENIUS⁷ SAWYER** .[see 198], b. 1 Oct 1815 Litchfield ME, d. 28 Dec 1880 West Gardiner ME, m. 2 Oct 1851 Bowdoin ME Julia M. Cox, b. 1817 d. 19 Apr 1894, dau. Nathaniel and Marcia Cox. In Manchester NH 1860. Both bur. Howard Cem., W. Gardiner ME.

Edmund Page, b. 1 May 1853. Went to Minnesota.

Walter Guy, b. 30 Apr 1856 W. Gardiner ME, d. 7 Oct 1906 Gardiner ME.

Sources: Manchester ME census 1860. C46, M5.

376. **JAMES E.⁷ SAWYER** [see 199], b. 12 Apr 1818 Durham ME, d. ca. 1864, m. Lydia _____ of Dixfield ME, b. 10 Sep 1818. Wid. B/land in Brunswick ME 1864.

George Henry, b. 26 Nov 1841, d. 9 Jul 1843.

George Albion, b. 23 Sep 1843 Topsham ME, d. 3 Aug 1889 Portland ME, m. 26 Feb 1877 Portland ME Sadie A. Whraff of New Gloucester ME, b. ca. 1853. CH: Grace, b. 1876. In Portland ME 1880.

William H., b. 5 Feb 1845 Topsham ME. Civil War: Enl. 29 Sep 1862 in Co. D, 25th Regiment.
Melissa A., b. 26 Aug 1846, m. _____ Pushard.
James, b. ca. 1849, d.y.
Martha J., b. 30 Jun 1850, m. _____ Bennett.
Eugene A., b. 2 May 1852 Topsham ME, d. 2 Jun 1875, m. 24 Dec 1870 Litchfield ME Matilda C. Tapley of Litchfield ME, b. 11 Jul 1852, dau. Joseph and Betsey (Ridley) Tapley.
Emma T., b. 1854.
Sarah E., b. 7 Aug 1856.
Ella Laura, b. 10 Jan 1858.
James E., b. 13 Aug 1861 Brunswick ME, d. 1937 m.(1) 21 Nov 1892 Boston MA Jennie M. Merrill of No. Scituate MA, b. ca. 1862, dau. George and Deborah Merrill, m.(2) Henrietta C. _____, b. 1863 d. 1946. Mason. Both bur. Riverside Cemetery, Brunswick ME.

Sources: Portland ME census 1880. VR SA/ME, SA/MA. R10a, P82a, T1, M5.

377. **JUSTUS B.[7] SAWYER** [see 199], b. 4 Jan 1823 Lisbon ME, d. 17 Jul 1901 Auburn ME, m. 17 Nov 1844 Topsham ME Marcia J. Rodrick of Brunswick ME, b. ca. 1825. Writing teacher. Shoe manufacturer. Appointed guardian of brother James' minor CH 1869.
Charles H., b. 1846.
James H., b. 1850.
Mary E., b. 1852.
George W., b. 1854.
John R., b. 1858.
Frank H., b. 1859 Leeds ME.

Sources: Rollingsford NH census 1850. Leeds ME census 1860. VR Topsham ME. R10a, P82a.

378. **EZRA[7] SAWYER** [see 199], b. 23 Nov 1828 Topsham ME, m. 22 Nov 1854 Medford MA Mary E. Rich of Boston MA, b. 1836, dau. Charles H. Rich. Ship carpenter.
Charles A., b. 16 Sep 1855 Medford MA, d. 17 Aug 1857.
Ida M., b. 13 Jun 1857, d. 6 Sep 1857.
Ada M., b. 13 Jun 1857, d. 9 Sep 1857.
Child, b. 19 Dec 1858, d. 20 Dec 1858.

Sources: VR SA/MA.

379. **CHARLES H.[7] SAWYER** [see 199], b. 6 Oct 1835 Topsham ME, m. 3 May 1863 Matilda L. Prince of Brunswick ME, b. 18 Sep 1838. In Auburn ME 1880.
Alice W., b. 28 Jan 1864.
Solomon C., b. 18 Apr 1866 Brunswick ME.
Samuel, b. 1876 Brunswick ME

Sources: ME Census Index 1880.

380. **HUMPHREY[7] SAWYER** [see 200], b. 9 Mar 1824 Weare NH, d. 12 Nov 1904 Yakima WN, m. Boston MA Barbara Perry of Boston MA, b. 1827 d. 28 Jun 1892, dau. John and Lucy (Wood) Perry. Hardware dealer. In Wisconsin.
Charles Humphrey, b. ?, m. Debora Hill, b. ?.
Lucy Ella, b. 14 Jan 1849.
William Perry, b. 19 Sep 1851.
Mary Emma, b. 17 Jan 1853, d. 29 Mar 1870.

Sarah Helen, b. 18 Sep 1859, d. 13 Mar 1939, m. Frank Wilson.
Harriet Eliza, b. 6 Oct 1866.
Sources: VR SA/MA.

381. **LINDLEY M.⁷ SAWYER** [see 201], b. 25 Sep 1833 Weare NH, d. 16 Nov 1902 Weare NH, m. 28 Nov 1867 Weare NH Ellen R. Dickey of Manchester NH, b. 26 Feb 1842 d. 20 Nov 1921. Shoe manufacturer.
Allen Webster, b. 24 Feb 1869 Weare NH, m. 10 Jun 1903 So. Weare NH Emma J. Gould of Weare NH, b. 1869, dau. Jessie N. and Ellen (Haynes) Gould. CH: Gertrude, b. 21 Nov 1909, d. 4 Aug 1915.
Florence E., b. 28 Mar 1871, d. 16 Mar 1875.
Emma R., b. 19 Dec 1875, d. 27 Nov 1936, unm.
George M., b. 26 Aug 1877 Weare NH.
Son, stillborn 23 Jan 1879.
Gertrude E., b. 10 Nov 1879.
Sources: Weare NH census 1870. VR SA/NH.

382. **WILLIAM⁷ SAWYER** [see 203], b. 24 Jul 1849 Dover NH, d. 17 May 1913 Dover NH, m. 22 Sep 1882 Sarah Randall of Conway NH, b. 22 Aug 1851. Clerk. Mother willed him pew in Methodist Church, Dover NH 1887.
Jessie Maud, b. 14 Mar 1883, m. Benjamin P. Brierly of Stratham NH.
Edith Broughton, b. 28 Apr 1884.
545 Thomas Ellwood⁸, b. 1886.
Sources: VR SA/NH. S22, P82i, A19.

383. **FREDERICK⁷ SAWYER** [see 203], b. 7 Jan 1855 Dover NH, d. 14 Feb 1929 Dover NH, m.(1) Isobel _____, b. ?; m.(2) 24 Nov 1887 Nellie Cate of Wolfeboro NH, b. 12 Oct 1860, dau. John G. and Anna A. (Clarke) Cate. In Boston MA 1882. Went to Seattle WN.
Daughter, stillborn 7 May 1878.
Frederick, b. 30 Sep 1882 Boston MA.
Sources: VR SA/MA, SA/NH. R15, P82i.

384. **HORATIO G.⁷ SAWYER** [see 204], b. 1844 Ossipee NH, m. Matilda W. McGoldrick of Natchez MS, b. ?. Railroad engineer. In Sandwich NH 1860-1870, Wakefield NH 1880.
Harry L., b. ca. 1867 Sandwich NH.
John A., b. ca. 1869 Sandwich NH.
James R., b. 1871.
Carl Shurz, b. Jun 1877, d. 23 Aug 1877.
Jane Matilda, b. 26 Jun 1879.
Sources: Sandwich NH census 1860, 1870. Wakefield NH census 1880. N9.

385. **FRANK D.⁷ SAWYER** [see 204], b. 8 Feb 1851 Ossipee NH, d. 31 Dec 1930 Wolfboro NH, m. 3 Jun 1877 Biddeford ME Mary O. Seavey of Limington ME, b. Oct 1856 d. 30 Dec 1934, dau. Eastman P. and Eliza (Smith) Seavey. Merchant. In Dover NH, Wakefield NH.
Son, b. 18 Oct 1874, d.y.
Luther Eastman, b. 2 Jun 1878 East Wakefield NH.
Lydia E., b. 27 Aug 1879.
Daughter, b. 12 Dec 1882.
Sources: Dover NH census 1860, 1870. Wakefield NH census 1880. VR SA/ME, SA/NH.

386. **ENOS H.⁷ SAWYER** [see 205], b. ca. 1832 Dover NH, m. Martha Frances Hussey, b. 31 Dec 1832, dau. Paul and Mary (Wentworth) Hussey of No. Berwick ME. In Dover NH 1850.

Frank H., b. ca. 1854 No. Berwick ME, m.(1) 10 May 1876 Lynn MA Sarah E. Hammond of Lynn MA, b. 1855, dau. William and Emeline Hammond; m.(2) 22 Jul 1891 Lynn MA Mary E. Tyler of Wendell MA, b. 1856, dau. William and Charlotte Tyler. Shoe cutter.

Ellen F. b. 1856, m. 10 Jun 1875 Lynn MA Eugene M. Libby.

Sources: VR SA/MA. W26.

387. **JACOB M.⁷ SAWYER** [see 205], b. 1847 Dover NH, m. 11 Jan 1868 Maria D. Barber of Madbury NH, b. ca. 1845. Shoemaker. In Dover NH 1880.

Hattie M., b. ca. 1866.
Millard F., b. 23 Aug 1868 Dover NH.
Carrie R., b. 27 Mar 1870.
Frederick H., b. 4 Jan 1872 Dover NH.
Charles H., b. ca. 1873.
Jennie B., b. ca. 1875.
Ella B., b. ca. 1877.
Daughter, b. 6 May 1882.
Son, b. 13 Apr 1884 (10th CH?).

Sources: Dover NH census 1850, 1880.

388. **ALONZO HAVENTON⁷ SAWYER** .[see 206], b. 17 May 1827 Alton NH, d. 17 Jul 1885 Alton NH, m. 7 Nov 1850 Lebanon ME Martha J. Shapleigh of Lebanon ME, b. 17 Feb 1831 d. 18 May 1918, dau. Samuel and Eunice (Wentworth) Shapleigh. Trader, teacher. In Great Falls NH, Alton NH.

Frederick Shapleigh, b. 20 Jul 1853, d. 9 May 1872.

Sources: VR Lebanon ME, SA/NH. W26, S70, H94, G45.

389. **JEREMIAH⁷ SAWYER** [see 208], b. 14 Apr 1810 Lee NH, d. 26 Jan 1876 Newburyport MA, m.(1) Dec 1832 Susan Gilman Sherriff, b. 24 Oct 1806, dau. Benjamin P. and Martha (Gilman) Sherriff; m.(2) 4 Sep 1861 Amesbury MA Inez Evans of Salisbury MA, b. 4 Jul 1834, dau. John and Abigail (Smith) Evans. House painter. In Exeter NH, Amesbury MA, Cambridge MA 1847, Brentwood NH.

546 Howard Malcolm⁸, 1834-1902.
Anna Elizabeth, b. ?, d. at 5 years.
Sarah Ellen, b. 10 Jul 1837, m. 5 May 1861 Cambridge MA Charles H. Atwood of Cambridge MA.
Jeremiah Stow, b. ca. 1840.
Annie Mary, b. ca. 1842, m. 31 Dec 1863 Charles E. Wheeler.
John Sheriff, b. 27 Jun 1847 Cambridge MA. Civil War: Captain.
Child, b. ?, d. an infant.
Child, b. ?, d. an infant.

Sources: Cambridge MA census 1850. Brentwood NH census 1860. VR Amesbury MA, SA/MA. E25.

390. **WILLIAM F.⁷ SAWYER** [see 208], b. 1813 Lee NH, d. 25 Jun 1873 Exeter NH, m. Sarah Tuck of Brentwood NH, b. 1821 d. 18 Aug 1895, dau. William and Jane Tuck. Painter. In Exeter NH 1840, Pelham NH 1860.

Frederick W., b. 26 Aug 1841 Exeter NH, d. 17 Aug 1864 Woburn MA, m. 14 Jun 1862 Newton NH Harriet W. Sweet of Newton NH, b. ca. 1845.

Amelia, b. 1846.

547 Edward Warren$^{8}$, 1848-1897.

Emma J., b. 7 Mar 1856, d. 10 Jan 1872 Woburn MA.

Sources: Exeter NH census 1840, 1850. Pelham NH census 1860. VR Woburn MA. D10.

391. **SAMUEL J.$^{7}$ SAWYER** [see 208], b. 1814 Lee NH, d. 7 May 1850 Exeter NH, m. Lucy Otis, b. 1820.

Martha, b. 1838, d. 29 Jun 1853.

Otis, b. ca. 1839 Exeter NH, m. 2 Dec 1866 Boston MA Mary E. Marston of Exeter NH, b. ca. 1844, dau. William B. Marston. In So. Boston MA, Cambridge MA 1873. CH: Daughter, b. 16 Oct 1873.

Lucy A., b. ca. 1845, m. 21 Feb 1866 in Boston MA Henry Foster.

Munroe, b. ?.

Sources: VR SA/MA.

392. **JOSEPH B.$^{7}$ SAWYER** [see 208], b. 29 Aug 1828 Exeter NH, m. 8 Apr 1852 Hannah (Nash) Swett, b. ca. 1835.

Ellen J., b. 7 Feb 1855, m. 10 Apr 1875 Lynn MA Joseph C. Boyden.

Charles A., b. 15 Dec 1857 Exeter NH, d. 19 Aug 1909 Gardiner ME.

Joseph, b. 15 Dec 1859 Exeter NH.

Child, b. 1862, d. 12 Sep 1863.

Sources: Exeter NH census 1860. VR SA/MA, SA/ME.

393. **GEORGE W.$^{7}$ SAWYER** [see 209], b. 2 May 1819 Raymond ME, d. 9 May 1910 Lisbon ME, m.(1) 1841 Sarah M. Tibbetts, b. 1824 d. 18 Mar 1842; m.(2) Esther Julianne _____, b. 15 Sep 1818 d. 18 Jan 1890. Harness maker. In Lisbon ME after 1850.

Sarah E., b. 26 Feb 1842.

George William, b. 10 Mar 1847, d. 23 Aug 1850.

Philena R., b. 1848.

Eliza Eva, b. 7 Apr 1852.

William George, 3 Jul 1854 Lisbon ME, m. Anna M. Proctor of Lisbon ME, b. ca. 1860. CH: Linden W., b. 21 Sep 1878, d. 16 Feb 1893. In Lisbon ME 1880 w/grandfather.

Sources: Lisbon ME census 1850, 1860, 1870. ME 1880 census index. VR SA/ME. David C. Young rec., Beverly Strout rec.

394. **PASCHAL MERRILL$^{7}$ SAWYER** [see 209], b. 1834 Raymond ME, d. 1890 Poland ME, m.(1) Eliza _____, b. ca. 1825; m.(2) Portland ME Emma G. Ames of Norway ME, b. 1834; m.(3) 1 May 1859 Pownal ME Mrs. George P. Merrill of Portland ME, b. ?; m.(4) 5 Feb 1868 Sarah A. Wilbur of Freeport ME, b. 1841 d. 1905. Dentist. Civil War: Received pension 1882. In Lisbon ME, Yarmouth ME, Casco ME, Minot ME.

Frank C., b. Dec 1855 Norway ME, d. 1 Oct 1910 Otisfield ME, m. Sadie L. Philbrick of Durham ME, b. ?. Blacksmith. CH: Maude E., b. 7 Jan 1889.

Irving P., b. 1869 Casco ME, d. 1936. In Minot ME, Auburn ME.

Willie, b. 1870, d.y.

Estelle Means, b. 1872, d. 1953, m. Frederick H. Yeaton of Minot ME.

Elizabeth, b. 1872, d. at birth.

George Atwood, b. 25 Dec 1874 Casco ME, d. 2 Apr 1912 Minot ME, m. 25 Dec 1899 Grace L. Prescott of Farmington ME, b. ca. 1874 d. 1906, dau. George W. and Abbie (Bartlett) Prescott. Barber.

Sources: Yarmouth ME census 1860. Casco ME census 1870. ME 1880 census index. VR Portland ME, Pownal ME, SA/ME. R10a, D37. Obit.

395. **JEREMIAH$^{7}$ SAWYER** [see 210], b. 28 Oct 1819 Lisbon ME, d. 9 Nov 1906, m. Sarah B. Estes of Durham ME, b. 21 Jun 1818 d. 16 Mar 1905, dau. Isreal and Sarah (Baker or Bunker) Estes. In Lisbon ME 1850.

George K., b. 1843 Lisbon ME.

Dexter, b. 1847 Lisbon ME, d. 13 Jan 1907.

Coreden, b. 19 Sep 1850 Lisbon ME, d. 18 Nov 1920 No. Harpswell ME, m.(1) 28 Feb 1872 Boston MA Melissa Thayer of Chelsea MA, b. ca. 1853, dau. Luther and Melissa Thayer; m.(2) 5 Aug 1883 Marlboro MA Susan (Harvey) Thompson of Boylston MA, b. ca. 1855, dau. J_____W. and Eliza Harvey. Boxmaker.

Sources: Lisbon ME census 1850. VR SA/ME, SA/MA. E23.

396. **AARON$^{7}$ SAWYER** [see 210], b. 1831 Strafford NH, d. 15 Feb 1917 Dover NH, m. (1) Betsey _____, b. ? d. 25 Oct 1908; m.(2) 12 Sep 1857 Barrington NH Mary Ann Richardson of Barrington NH, b. ca. 1839. Farmer. In Middleton NH, Barrington NH, Lynn MA, Lawrence MA.

Levi, b. 30 Aug 1858 Lynn MA.

Lydia A., b. 14 Jun 1863, m. 13 Dec 1882 Cambridge MA George L. Carr.

Emma C., b. ?, m. 11 Nov 1885 Dover NH Charles Lord.

Sources: Middleton NH census 1850. VR Barrington NH, SA/MA, SA/NH.

397. **JAMES T.$^{7}$ SAWYER** [see 211], b. 21 Mar 1836 Hampden ME, d. 11 Oct 1909 Exeter NH, m. 22 Jan 1867 Bangor ME Lucy P. Stinson, b. ca. 1845. Engineer. Civil War: 1st Maine Regiment. In Exeter NH 1870.

Charles, b. ca. 1877, m. _____. Went to New Jersey. No CH.

548 Edward Kent$^{8}$, 1880-1967.

Sources: Exeter NH census 1870, 1880. VR SA/NH. P20, Lloyd C. Sawyer rec.

398. **GEORGE W.$^{7}$ SAWYER** [see 214], b. Apr 1829 Hampden ME, d. 9 Jun 1902 Hampden ME, m. Leana P. _____, b. Apr 1830. Farmer.

Eliza, b. 1856.

Abbie, b. 1858.

John P., b. 1859 Hampden ME.

Stephen L., b. 1860 Hampden ME.

Frances A., b. 1864.

Myra D., b. 1866.

Aldana, b. 1868.

Rachel, b. 1873.

Lois, b. 1875.

Sources: Hampden ME census 1860, 1870. ME 1880 census index. P20.

399. **JOHN$^{7}$ SAWYER** [see 215], b. 28 Feb 1840 Hampden ME, d. 8 Jan 1922 W. Hampden ME, m. Mary Lucinda Rundlett of Etna ME, b. 25 May 1847, dau. Joseph P. and Nancy (Sylvester) Rundlett. Civil War.

Edna A., b. ca. 1870.

Eliza M., b. ca. 1874.

Winfield A., b. ca. 1878 Hampden ME.
Sources: ME 1880 census index. VR SA/ME. P20, D37, O2.

400. **FREDERICK$^7$ SAWYER** [see 215], b. 3 Feb 1848 Hampden ME, d. 11 Nov 1911, W. Hampden ME, m. Julia York of Hampden ME, b. 15 Feb 1857 d. 18 Dec 1909 Bangor ME, dau. Isaiah C. and Lorinda (Patterson) York.
549 Arthur Benjamin$^8$, 1877-1943.
Sources: Hampden ME 1880 census index. VR SA/ME. P30, Marie Rines rec.

401. **JOHN ANDREW$^7$ SAWYER** [see 216], b. 6 Nov 1829 Hampstead NH, m. Mary J._____ of Henniker NH, b. ?. In Dracut MA, Lowell MA.
Fred H., b. 1860 Lowell MA, m.(1) ?; m.(2) 2 Nov 1924 Gilmanton Iron Works NH Laura S. Hanson of Malden MA, b. 1901, dau. Sidney and Laura M. (Nutter) Hanson of Strafford NH. Farmer. In Gilmanton NH.
Sources: Dracut MA census 1850.

402. **WILLIAM EATON$^7$ SAWYER** [see 216], b. 7 Feb 1846 Dracut MA, d. 14 Jan 1919 Lowell MA, m. 22 Sep 1875 Lowell MA Ella M. Stickney of New York, b. 20 Jan 1850 d. 12 May 1914, dau. Elvy and Lucia (Kellogg) Stickney. In Dracut MA 1850.
Clarence Kellogg, b. 6 Jun 1877 Lowell MA, unm.
Pansy, b. 1 May 1884, m. Joseph Cullinane.
550 William Augustine$^8$, 1884-1943.
Sources: Dracut MA census 1850. VR SA/MA. H70, C48, Alice M. Sawyer rec.

403. **HARLAND AARON$^7$ SAWYER** [see 218], b. 1868 Amesbury MA, d. 1929, m. 16 Nov 1892 New Haven VT Harriet E. Mason of Vergennes VT, b. 27 Aug 1865, dau. Charles Mason.
Harland Mason, b. 20 Jul 1897 Amesbury MA.
Lois, b. 1904, d. 1974, m. _____ Starke.
Sources: VR SA/MA, SA/VT. R24.

404. **CALVIN$^7$ SAWYER** [see 220], b. 26 Mar 1819 Hill NH, d. 13 Feb 1868 Kensington NH, m.(1) 30 May 1844 Plaistow NH Azubah H. Currier of Plaistow NH, b. 19 Nov 1810 d. 10 Oct 1852, dau. Stephen and Anna (Dow) Currier; m.(2) 27 Apr 1854 Mehitable Eaton, b. 1819 d. 18 Mar 1876. In Plaistow NH. He bur. in Plaistow NH.
551 Stephen Calvin$^8$, 1846-1934.
Annie M., b. 2 Apr 1849, d. 1 Jun 1849.
Walter G., b. 27 Mar 1851, d. 23 Nov 1859.
Ida M., b. 7 Jun 1856, d. 15 Feb 1935, m. 28 Aug 1876 Kensington NH Frank A. Mace.
Wesley Lincoln, b. 22 May 1860 Plaistow NH, d. 1927, m. 28 Nov 1889 Hattie Spink of E. Greenwich RI, b. ?. CH: Maud Gertrude, b. 19 Mar 1891, m. 6 Sep 1915 Adolph Ehrezeller of W. Roxbury MA; Margueritte Eaton, b. 30 May 1893, m. 14 Oct 1916 Alexander Allen of Needham MA.
Sources: Kensington NH census 1860. VR Haverhill MA. N6, P82g, C91, S17.

405. **MESHACK WEARE$^7$ SAWYER** [see 220], b. 17 Jul 1825 Hill NH, d. 23 Jul 1895 Plaistow NH, m. 17 Oct 1856 Concord NH Abby (Dow) Chase of W. Newbury MA, b. 5 Jun 1835 d. 27 Apr 1908, dau. Samuel S. and Eunice N. (Colby) Chase. Farmer. In Haverhill MA, Plaistow NH, Hill NH.
Mary Eunice, b. 27 Mar 1857, d. 9 Jun 1927, m. 25 Apr 1883 Charles Haseltine.
552 William Howard$^8$, 1858-1924.

Annie Isobelle, b. 19 Nov 1859, d. 11 Jul 1877.
553 Arthur Weare[8], 1861-1954.
Maud Abbie, b. 7 Feb 1864, m. 19 Nov 1886 Charles Boswell.

Sources: Hill NH census 1860, 1870. VR Plaistow NH, SA/MA, SA/NH. N6, C30, Mary (Haseltine) Sawyer rec.

406. **THOMAS WARREN[7] SAWYER** [see 220], b. 25 Nov 1827 Hill NH, drowned on 4 Feb 1873 Laconia NH, m.(1) Lucy Sleeper, b. 1832 d. 3 May 1856; m.(2) 12 Aug 1859 Nashua NH Mary E. Danforth of Danbury NH, b. 10 Apr 1837 d. 7 Feb 1863; m.(3) 25 May 1869 Abbie Morgan of E. Haverhill MA, b. 19 Oct 1834 d. 5 Apr 1881, dau. Moses and Lucy W. (Jeffers) Dunkley. In Tilton NH.

George Warren, b. 1853 Danbury NH, d. 16 Jul 1918 Exeter NH, m.(1) 20 Feb 1872 Amanda Sawyer of Hill NH, b. 1854, dau. Washington Sawyer; m.(2) 29 Sep 1889 Newburyport MA Delia Burke of Ireland, b. ca. 1867, dau. Daniel and Kate Burke. In Andover MA 1860, Amesbury MA 1889.
Charles H., b. 4 Apr 1856, d. 10 Aug 1856.
Charles Harvey, b. 4 Jun 1862 Hill NH, m. 9 Feb 1883 Concord NH Cora E. Hall of Tilton NH, b. 6 Sep 1858. CH: Estelle May, b. 7 Nov 1884.
Abbie Bella, b. 1871, m. 10 Oct 1893 Almon D. Page of Orange NJ.
554 Thomas Warren[8], b. 1873.

Sources: Danbury NH census 1850. Hill NH census 1860. Sanbornton NH census 1870, Tilton NH census 1880, Andover NH census 1860, 1870. VR Andover NH, SA/MA. M64, S18, Richard F. Sawyer rec.

407. **LUTHER[7] SAWYER** [see 220], b. 9 May 1834 Hill NH, d. 4 Jul 1899 Andover NH, m.(1) 19 Jan 1858 Danbury NH Susan A. Littlefield of Hill NH, b. 22 Sep 1839 d. 13 Dec 1886, dau. Jeremiah and Molly B. (Thurston) Littlefield; m.(2) 7 Nov 1888 Alzira Ordway of Auburn NH, b. 1834 d. 13 Mar 1896, dau. James and Dorothy (Trefethen) Severence. Farmer. In Hill NH 1860, Andover NH 1862. Note: Luther's m. record says he was b. in Kingston NH.

Bessie Ellen, b. 25 Feb 1859, d. 2 Aug 1892, m. 2 Oct 1881 George Eastman of Franklin NH.
Lewis Edgar, b. 27 Nov 1861 Hill NH, d. 3 Mar 1939, m.(1) 1888 Lizzie Perkins, b. ? d. Feb 1923; m.(2) 14 Jul 1924 Elizabeth Bennett, b. ? d. 9 Jun 1935.
Albert Eugene, b. 2 Jan 1863, d. 20 Dec 1865.
Orrin Leroy, b. 24 Apr 1865 Boscawen NH, d. 3 Nov 1910 Franklin NH, m. 19 Mar 1905 Franklin NH Minnie Sargent of Enosburg VT, b. 1867 d. 8 Apr 1931, her m.(2), dau. Charles and Elizabeth (Adams) Waterman. CH: Lewis Edgar, stillborn 31 Jul 1905; Clarissa Adams, b. 28 Nov 1909, adopted by Uncle Harvey and name changed to Orrine G., m. 1 Aug 1948 Guy Heath of Concord NH.
Harvey Calvin, b. 21 Jun 1868 Andover NH, d. 14 May 1948, m. 15 Aug 1894 Garuetta Goodhue of Northhampton NH, b. 1 May 1859 d. 26 Nov 1936, dau. James B. and Mary G. (Fisk) Goodhue. Minister. Preached in Andover Center NH 1893. In Charlestown NH. CH: Orrine G., adopted dau. of brother Orrin, b. 28 Nov 1909, m. 1 Aug 1948 Guy Heath of Concord NH.
Daisy Ada, b. 13 Jun 1873, d. 9 Jan 1966, m. 26 Jun 1894 George E. Eastman.
555 Luther Jere[8], 1877-1947.
Susan Mary, b. 6 Apr 1885, d. 3 Dec 1951, m. 6 Apr 1908 William B. Irwin of Fall River MA.

Sources: Hill NH census 1860. Andover NH census 1880. VR SA/NH. E2, H88, S18, R21, C60, Richard F. Sawyer rec

408. **GAYTON P.[7] SAWYER** .[see 221], b. 1841 Haverhill MA, m.(1) 27 Jan 1865 Haverhill MA Clarissa E. Frink of Haverhill MA, b. 9 Aug 1844 d. 15 Feb 1874, dau. Samuel and Sarah Frink; m.(2) 31 Mar 1877 Plaistow NH Marion Hollingworth, b. ?. Shoemaker. In Philadelphia PA 1868.

Eliza J., b. 30 Mar 1865, m. 24 Apr 1887 Haverhill MA Matthew Bamford.
William L., b. 1 Oct 1866 Haverhill MA, d. 23 Jul 1933 Newburyport MA, m. 30 Apr 1899 Manchester NH Florence Goodwin of Dover NH, b. 1873. In Exeter NH.
556 Gayton H.[8], b. 1868.
Elizabeth F., b. 25 Aug 1870, m. 1 Sep 1888 Haverhill MA Frank C. Wyman.
Clara, b. 1891, m. 25 Dec 1907 Llewelyn M. Dow.
Sources: VR Haverhill MA, SA/MA, SA/NH. D50.

409. **GEORGE WASHINGTON[7] SAWYER** [see 223], b. 24 Nov 1835 Springfield NH, d. 1 Jan 1884 Manchester NH, m. 3 Jan 1863 Mary A. Rider of Canada, b. 20 Feb 1836 d. 30 Sep 1916 dau. Abner and Judith (Cass) Rider. In Manchester NH, Grafton NH, Wilmot NH.

Mary Lois, b. 26 Apr 1869, m. 2 Sep 1888 Thomas F. Doyle.
George Henry, b. 10 Mar 1872 Manchester NH, d.y.
Jennie Blanche, b. 17 Jan 1874, m. 20 Oct 1896 Manchester NH Willard S. Smith.
557 Leon Eugene[8], 1876-1953.
Sources: Manchester NH census 1880. VR SA/NH. L40, N6, Family Bible, Curtis B. Sawyer rec.

410. **RELAND W.[7] SAWYER** [see 225], b. 3 May 1839 Groveland MA, m. 26 Jul 1867 Groveland MA Annie M. Chase of W. Newbury MA, b. ?, dau. Rufus H. and Sarah Chase. Shoemaker.

George A., b. 16 Nov 1868 Groveland MA.
Sources: VR Bradford MA, SA/MA.

## EIGHTH GENERATION

411. **EDWARD BERTRAND[8] SAWYER** [see 226], b. 1 Jan 1857 Hyde Park VT, m. _____ Peters, b. ?. Civil engineer. Went to Montrose CO.

Joshua, b. ?.
Sources: C4.

412. **NATHAN S.[8] SAWYER** [see 228], b. 19 Aug 1832 Deer Isle ME, d. 7 Jun 1859 Deer Isle ME, m. 27 Nov 1856 Deer Isle ME Sarah J. Redman, b. ?.

Samuel Pickering, b. 28 Sep 1857 Deer Isle ME, d. 30 Aug 1938 Buxton ME. He bur. in Troy Hill Cem. Buxton ME.
John Franklin, b. 15 Sep 1858 Deer Isle ME.
Note: Census says 2d CH was Nathan F., b. ca. 1859.
Sources: Deer Isle ME census 1850, 1860 (widow). VR Deer Isle ME. Nathan Wheeler Sawyer Bible rec.

413. **ADMIRAL GEORGE[8] SAWYER** [see 229], b. 12 Oct 1833 Deer Isle ME, d. 7 Jul 1907 Deer Isle ME, m. 3 Nov 1854 Deer Isle ME Lucy N. Pickering of Deer Isle ME, b. Dec 1835 d. 12 Aug 1901, dau. Richard and Keziah (Nason) Pickering.

Flovilla, b. 6 Aug 1856, m. 6 Aug 1877 Jason Greenlaw.
Jane L., b. 29 Mar 1858.

William B., b. 22 Sep 1860 Deer Isle ME, d. 2 Sep 1904, m. 7 May 1884 Portsmouth NH Emma F. Lang of Deering ME, b. Dec 1857 d. 1934. In Portland ME. CH: Ethel B., b. Dec 1885; George B., b. 27 Jul 1892, d. 2 Feb 1894.

Everett A., b. 23 Apr 1862, d. 1 Oct 1863.

George Washington, b. 14 Aug 1864 Deer Isle ME.

Antoinette (Nettie), b. 2 May 1867.

Isabell M., b. 24 Oct 1877, m. _____ Huckins.

Sources: Deer Isle ME census 1860, 1870, 1880, 1900. VR Deer Isle ME, Rockland ME

414. **BENJAMIN C.[8] SAWYER** [see 229], b. 22 Nov 1834 Deer Isle ME, d. 27 Mar 1897 Deer Isle ME, m.(1) 7 Oct 1856 Deer Isle ME Susan M. Sawyer of Deer Isle ME, b. Apr 1837 d. 15 Apr 1863; m.(2) 29 Mar 1864 Nancy H. Sawyer of Deer Isle ME, b. 2 Aug 1843 d. 5 Jan 1906. Both wives were dau. of Mark Haskell and Susan (Bray) Sawyer. [See 231].

Benjamin Frank, b. 9 Nov 1858 Deer Isle ME, d. 15 Aug 1904.

Hezikiah C., b. 14 May 1862 Deer Isle ME, d. 24 Feb 1932.

Susan Etta, b. 1 May 1865, m. 25 Dec 1927 Sumner Perkins.

Margery A., b. 22 Apr 1869, d. 3 Jun 1914 Bangor ME.

Sarah Dodge, b. 12 Feb 1879.

Sources: Deer Isle ME census 1860, ME 1880 census index. VR Deer Isle ME, SA/ME. P32.

415. **CALEB PARKER[8] SAWYER** [see 229], b. 4 Dec 1837 Deer Isle ME, d. 18 Oct 1908, m. 9 Mar 1860 Deer Isle ME Harriet Pickering of Deer Isle ME, b. 15 Sep 1842 d. 17 Oct 1889, dau. Richard and Keziah (Nason) Pickering. He bur. in Warren Cem., Deer Isle ME.

George H., b. 23 Sep 1860, d. 6 Nov 1860.

Ada Ella, b. 8 Apr 1862, d. 13 Jul 1864.

Burtman C., b. 4 Aug 1865 Deer Isle ME, m. 9 Jan 1891 Gloucester MA Ida Richardson of Gloucester MA, b. ca. 1865, dau. Nathan and Caroline (Allen) Richardson. Motorman.

558 Frederick Elwood[9], 1869-1940.

Daisy D., b. 23 Sep 1872, d. 25 Apr 1873.

Samuel James, b. 24 Oct 1877 Deer Isle ME, m. Lottie M. Thurlow, b. ?. Note: Listed as Tilden J., age 4, in ME 1880 census index.

Daisy D., b. 23 Nov 1883, m. 24 Dec 1901 Charles M. Spofford.

559 Arthur Copeland[9], b. 1887.

Sources: ME 1880 census index. VR Deer Isle ME, SA/ME.

416. **JOHN GRINDLE[8] SAWYER** [see 230], b. 18 Jan 1840 Castine ME, m. 14 Dec 1858 Mary L. Bowden, b. 2 Jun 1843 d. 26 May 1918, dau. John and Eunice Bowden. Fisherman.

Alice Maria, b. 30 Jul 1861, d. 18 Jun 1899, m. 26 Jun 1876 Eugene Thombs.

Elizabeth Margaret, b. 3 Aug 1863.

John Grindle, b. 28 Mar 1865 Castine ME, d. 24 Dec 1922 Castine ME, m. 7 May 1887 Jennie May Morey, b. Feb 1868 d. 24 Aug 1950. He bur. in Castine ME. CH: Guy, b. ?, d. 1887; Edith, b. ?, d. 1905; Beatrice Louise, b. 20 Aug 1893.

560 Charles Francis[9], b. 1867.

Lillian L., b. 9 Jan 1869, d. 30 Jan 1918, m. Peter J. McEwen.

Jennie S., b. 7 Dec 1871.

Walter William, b. Jun 1873 Castine ME, m. 2 Jan 1897 Castine ME Mabel D. Conny of Portsmouth NH, b. ?, dau. Frank and Frances (Williams) Conny.

Leon E., b. 3 Jul 1876 Castine ME, m. Alice Eva Buckmore of Machias ME, b. ?. In Boston MA. CH: James McBean, b. 14 Sep 1898, d. 11 Feb 1901.

Sarah L., b. 15 Jun 1879.

561 Russell Stanley[9], 1882-1942.
Sources: Castine ME census 1870. ME 1880 census index. VR Castine ME, SA/ME. M5.

417. **ABNER JARVIS[8] SAWYER** [see 230], b. 24 Nov 1850 Castine ME, m. 13 Apr 1873 Lucy E. Vane of Machias ME, b. 1859. In Castine ME 1880. Wid. m. Captain William D. Bennett of Bucksport ME.

William H., b. 5 Jan 1874 Castine ME, m. 12 Oct 1894 Castine ME Hattie Weed of Deer Isle ME, b. ca. 1875, dau. Ebenezer and Susan (Haskell) Weed. CH: Annie M., b. 5 Jul 1895; Daughter, b. 11 Sep 1897.
Margaret M., b. 1876, m. Charles E. Morey.
Annie M., b. 1879, m. _____ Bowden of Camden ME.
Catherine Davenport, b. 3 Jan 1881, m.(1)_____ Saunders, m.(2) Herman Dyer.
Raymond Keeler, b. 29 Apr 1884.
Burchett Cleveland, b. 6 May 1886.
Clarabelle, b. ?, m. Thomas Baker.

Sources: Castine ME census 1880. VR Castine ME, Bangor ME, Gardiner ME, SA/ME. Elizabeth C. Wescott rec.

418. **WILLIAM MARTIN[8] SAWYER** [see 231], b. 1854 Deer Isle ME, d. 17 Dec 1878, m. 15 Jan 1876 Martha Susan Stinson, b. ?.

William Martin, b. 18 Jun 1878 Deer Isle ME, d. 22 Mar 1948 Ash Point ME, m. 12 Nov 1899 Ina Adeline Dow of Tremont ME, b. 24 Jun 1883 d. 22 Aug 1932, dau. Daniel and Jennie M. (Ferrell) Dow. In Stonington ME. Both bur. Ash Point ME Cem. CH: Arlene Burnett, b. 9 Mar 1902, m. 15 Jun 1921 Earl Clifford Woodman.

Sources: VR Deer Isle ME, SA/ME. D4, M5.

419. **GARDNER[8] SAWYER** [see 235], b. 6 May 1856 Scarboro ME, d. 17 May 1942 Portland ME, m. 2 Jul 1884 Sylvia A. Wood, b. 15 Jan 1861 d. 19 Aug 1935. In Berwick ME, Westbrook ME.

562 Curtis Leonard[9], 1885-1952.
Everett Leason, b. 15 Dec 1886, d. 20 Aug 1969, unm. Bur. in Portland ME.
Fanny Lura, b. 20 Jun 1888, d. 29 Dec 1943, m. 1918 Robert Walker.
563 Gardner Edison[9], 1891-1982.
564 Walter Scott[9], 1896-1962.

Sources: VR SA/MA. Myron R. Sawyer rec.

420. **WARREN[8] SAWYER** [see 236], b. ca. 1855, m. ?.

Warren, b. ?.
Richard, b. ?.
Carrie, b. ?, m. George Blair.
Minnie, b. ?, m. Charles Crook.

Sources: VR SA/MA.

421. **CHARLES H.[8] SAWYER** [see 237], b. 2 Dec 1844 Augusta ME, d. 7 Aug 1913 Greenville ME, m. 1865 Elizabeth J. Littlefield, b. Apr 1845. Civil War. In Greenville ME 1880.

Carl I., b. 3 May 1871 Greenville ME, d. 16 Jun 1910 Roach River ME, m. 25 Oct 1894 Chester PA M. Bell Lackin, b. 1873, dau. Charles T. and E. (Tucker) Lackin. Hotel manager. Civil War.

Sources: ME 1880 census index. VR SA/ME. D37.

422. **JAMES WALTER[8] SAWYER** [see 238], b. ca. 1847 Boston MA, m.(1) 14 May 1868 Conway NH Jennie M. Charles, b. ca. 1851; m.(2) 12 Oct 1888 Tamworth NH (div. May 1913) Drusilla B. Harriman of Albany NH, b. ca. 1870. Farmer, veterinary. In Conway NH 1880.

Annie W., b. ca. 1869, m. 1 Jan 1884 George W. Eastman.
James Bailey, b. ca. 1870, m. 3 Oct 1888 Kate McGlynn, b. ?.
Grace M., b. ca. 1872.
565 Edward Walter[9], b. 1878.
Daughter, b. 28 Jul 1888.
Ralph, b. 14 Nov 1890, d. 30 Nov 1890.
Arthur R., b. 10 Nov 1892 Conway NH, d. 1943 Conway NH, m. 20 Dec 1914 Sarah A. Charles of Conway NH, b. ca. 1878 d. 1960.
Thomas C., b. 29 Dec 1894 Conway NH, m. 28 Feb 1931 Conway NH Leona L. Linscott of Brownfield ME, b. ?, dau. Herman and Adeline (Haynes) Linscott.

Sources: Conway NH census 1880. VR SA/NH, SA/MA.

423. **ARTHUR W.[8] SAWYER** [see 239], b. 11 May 1863 Orono ME, m. 15 Jul 1884 Boston MA Alice M. Davis of Boston MA, b. 1863, dau. William H. and Emma Davis. Clerk, printer. In Cambridge MA, Taunton MA. Note: VA SA/MA shows him b. in Cambridge MA 1863 and in Taunton MA 1864.

Harry M., b. 20 May 1887 Boston MA.
Walter R., b. 11 Jul 1893 Boston MA.

Sources: VR SA/MA.

424. **FRANCIS E.[8] SAWYER** [see 240], b. 20 Sep 1842 Cornish ME, d. 23 Nov 1910 Waterboro ME, m. 1 Jun 1870 Biddeford ME Emma L. Watson of Limerick ME, b. 4 May 1842 d. 2 May 1914. In Cornish ME, Limerick ME.

Ernest E., b. 20 Sep 1871 Limerick ME, d. 22 Jun 1943 Parsonsfield ME, m. 26 Nov 1899 Waterboro ME Mary A. Day of Limerick ME, b. Nov 1883, dau. James B. and Annie (Bridge) Day. Farmer.

Sources: ME 1880 census index. VR Biddeford ME, SA/ME. M5.

425. **ALBERT DEAN[8] SAWYER** [see 241], b. Oct 1860 South Hiram ME, d. 30 Jan 1919 Baldwin ME, m.(1) 7 Nov 1883 Ella L. Sanborn of Baldwin ME, b. 1865 d. 11 Aug 1897, dau. John F. and Alverah Sanborn; m.(2) 15 Jul 1899 Nancy W. York of Baldwin ME, b. Dec 1877 d. 5 Feb 1928. Railroad worker. In Conway NH. Wid. m. 1921 William Hoyt.

Edgar Dean, b. 7 Jan 1884, d. 1 Jan 1920.
Nancy, b. ?.
Herbert E., b. 5 Sep 1888, d. 15 Aug 1909 Conway NH.
Son, b. 27 Apr 1893.
Elsie M., b. 14 May 1900, d. 31 Aug 1975, m. 25 Feb 1917 William A. Day.
Lewis, b. 1903, d. 15 Jul 1906.

Sources: VR Baldwin ME, SA/ME, SA/NH. M8, Robert L. Taylor rec.

426. **CLAUDE E.[8] SAWYER** [see 242], b. 1885 Springvale ME, d. 1948 Springvale ME, m. 28 Nov 1907 Dover NH Ada Durgin of Alfred ME, b. 1884, dau. Frank and Mary Jane (Beal) Durgin. Horse trainer. In Emery Mills ME. He bur. in Riverside Cem., Springvale ME.

James, b. 1912 Springvale ME, m. 17 Jul 1933 Mary H. Fox, b. ?.

Sources: VR Dover NH.

427. **AARON[8] SAWYER** [see 243], b. 11 Jun 1830, d. Wilmington DE, m. 22 Mar 1854 Salem MA Emmeline Bennett of Norwich CT, b. 1835 d. 9 Jan 1868, dau. Abraham and Amelia (Jennings) Bennett. Shoemaker. In Bradford MA, Salem MA 1850.

Fred Bennett, b. 9 Jun 1856 Bradford MA, m. 29 Sep 1888 Edna Perkins, b. ?. Went to Iowa. No CH.

Sources: Salem MA census 1850, SA/MA. M55.

428. **NORRIS[8] SAWYER** [see 243], b. 9 Apr 1838 Saco ME, d. 25 May 1894 Chelsea MA, m. 23 Nov 1859 Salem MA Myra Averil of Frankfort ME, b. 3 Apr 1837, dau. Nathaniel and Mary (Spearing) Averil. Civil War. Shirt manufacturer. In Lynn MA 1850.

Harriet, b. 15 Jan 1863, m. 15 Dec 1888 George W. Fleet.

566 Frank Norris[9], b. 1864.

Sources: Saco ME census 1850. VR SA/MA. M55, A36.

429. **LEWIS[8] SAWYER** [see 244], b. 21 Mar 1827 Saco ME, d. 7 Jul 1920 Greenville ME, m.(1) 24 Oct 1855 Clarinda M. Davis, b. ?; m.(2) 23 Apr 1860 Bangor ME Elizabeth Young, b. 9 Mar 1828 d. 7 Jun 1915, dau. Thomas and Mary (Dyer) Young. Farmer. In Greenville ME 1880.

Ada M . b. 2 Jul 1864.

Clara, b. ca. 1866.

Annie E., b. ca. 1868.

Albert, b. ca. 1870 Greenville ME.

Sources: ME 1880 census index. VR Saco ME, Bangor ME, SA/ME.

430. **CHARLES GEORGE[8] SAWYER** [see 244], b. 13 Apr 1832 Greenville ME, d. 7 Oct 1902, m.(1)(I) 11 Jul 1856 Greenville ME Huldah J. Delano of Guilford, New Brunswick, Canada, b. 1832 d. 26 Jul 1866, dau. John Delano; m.(2) 1 Jan 1867 Portland ME Nellie Blake of Detroit MI, b. 7 Jun 1838 d. 24 Jul 1900, dau. Zebulon and Sarah (Durgin) Blake; m.(3) 29 Jul 1891 Dover NH Agnes M. Kneeland, b. 1856, dau. Patrick and Margaret Kneeland. Civil War. In Bangor ME, Wells ME, Wilton ME.

Lelia E., b. 6 Jan 1857.

567 Willard Eugene[9], b. 1859.

Ida Maria, b. 25 Nov 1861, m. 18 Oct 1884 Wilton NH Ruel W. Poor.

Charles Everett, b. 7 Jan 1864 Bangor ME, m. 14 Jan 1899 Livermore Falls ME Effie E. Newman, b. 1876, dau. S____ S. and Eva (Dodge) Locklin. Clerk. In E. Livermore ME. CH: Phyllis E., b. 18 May 1900. Note: His m. record says his mother was Ellen Davenport.

Sources: VR Greenville ME, SA/ME. W69, D37, M5.

431. **ARCHELOUS WOODMAN[8] SAWYER** .[see 246], b. 8 Mar 1838 Greenville ME, d. 23 Nov 1914 Turner ME, m.(1) Nellie V. Young, b. 1845 d. 1876; m.(2) 30 Sep 1877 TurnerME Ada I. Dow of Hebron ME, b. 12 Apr 1857 d. 15 Aug 1921 (suicide), dau. Alexander and Clarinda (Snell) Dow. Farmer. Civil War. In Turner ME 1878, Buckfield ME 1879. S/land in Buckfield ME 1881. He bur. in Turner ME.

Minnie, b. 1874.

Wilfred Andrew, b. 14 Sep 1878 Turner ME, d. 18 Jul 1974, unm.

Nellie L., b. 16 Dec 1879, d. 21 Jan 1966, m. 11 Mar 1902 William Hathaway.

George Low, b. 2 Feb 1882, d. 18 Dec 1930.

Mabel F., b. Jul 1884, d. 11 Jan 1966, m. 26 Jun 1909 Clarence H. Robinson.

Clara E., b. 6 Dec 1885, d. 30 Sep 1967, m. Leon Smith.

Edith I., b. 16 Dec 1886, d. 31 Oct 1982, m. 2 Jun 1904 Arthur G. Hayes.

568 Percival Gerald[9], 1888-1975.
Flora E., b. 24 Sep 1889, d. 6 Sep 1914 Turner ME.
569 Alexander Paine Dow[9], b. 1891.
Archelous Woodman, b. 11 Jun 1894 Buckfield ME, d. 30 Dec 1968 Mechanic Falls ME, m.(1) 10 Sep 1920 Richmond ME Anna Record of Buckfield ME, b. ?; m.(2) 1 Nov 1952 Mechanic Falls ME Frances Young, b. ?. He bur. in No. Auburn ME. No CH.
Emily A., b. 7 May 1899, m. 1 Dec 1916 Carroll L. Robinson.
Sources: Greenville ME census 1850. ME 1880 census index. VR Turner ME, SA/ME. D37, M5, R10c, Carolyn Small rec.

432. **EDMUND MERRITT[8] SAWYER** [see 246], b. 14 Jul 1845 Greenville ME, d. 14 Apr 1922 Turner ME, m. 19 May 1879 Hebron ME Mary E. Ashe of Turner ME, b. 21 Jun 1861 d. 25 Jun 1907, dau. Benjamin F. and Sarah (Keene) Ashe. In Turner ME 1884. In Lisbon Falls ME 1891. He bur. in Turner ME.
Arrobine, b. 1881, d. 1955, m. 1898 Diamond Berry.
570 Linwood Elmer[9], 1883-1944.
Harriet L., b. Sep 1884.
Marshall E., b. 16 Dec 1891, d. 26 May 1893.
Sources: Greenville ME census 1850. VR Turner Falls ME, Hebron ME, SA/ME. M5, Persis Chenery rec., Paul W. Sawyer rec.

433. **MARSHALL O.[8] SAWYER** [see 246], b. 7 Aug 1852 Greenville ME, d. 22 May 1917 Greenville ME, m. 23 Aug 1888 Portland ME Harriet E. Ashe of Turner ME, b. 12 Oct 1863, dau. Benjamin and Sarah (Keene) Ashe. In Greenville ME 1892.
571 Clifford Benjamin[9], 1892-1967.
Sources: VR Greenville ME, SA/ME.

434. **MARSHALL W.[8] SAWYER** [see 247], b. 1 Mar 1839 Milford ME, m. 24 Jun 1866 Old Town ME Lucy A. Willey of Milford ME, b. 1845, dau. William and Sena Willey.
572 Edmund M.[9], 1867-1897.
573 Frank W.[9], b. 1870.
Lula Belle, b. 29 Jul 1875, d. 2 Nov 1899.
Sources: Kittery ME census 1850. Milford ME census 1870. ME 1880 census index. VR Old Town ME, SA/ME. P30, M5.

435. **SETH H.[8] SAWYER** [see 248], b. 1852 Kittery or Bangor ME, m. 1 Jan 1885 Carrie L. Foye of Wiscasset ME, b. ?. Went to California.
574 Seth Harold[9], b. 1890.
Sources: VR SA/NH.

436. **FRANK L.[8] SAWYER** [see 249], b. 28 Jun 1839 Medford ME, d. 30 Aug 1915, m. 13 Feb 1864 Greenville ME Hannah S. Sawyer of Greenville ME, b. Feb 1842, dau. Joel and Emily C. (Woodman) Sawyer. Farmer. Civil War.
Herbert A., b. Mar 1865 Greenville ME.
Nettie A., b. ca. 1868.
Frank Melville, b. Aug 1869 Greenville ME, d. 1948, m. 12 Apr 1893 Portland ME Mary Lenora Kitteridge of St. Albans VT, b. Sep 1865 d. 1949, dau. George A. and Anna M. (McFarland) Kitteridge. CH: Catherine, b. Aug 1894.
575 Harry L.[9], b. 1872.
Louise, b. ?, m.(1) _____ Barney, m.(2) _____ Jackman.

Sources: Greenville ME census 1870, 1890. ME 1880 census index, VR Greenville ME. M5, D37, Paul Sawyer rec.

437. **ETHER C. G.[8] SAWYER** [see 249], b. May 1841 Medford ME, d. 2 Apr 1910 Medford ME, m. 21 Jul 1867 Orneville ME Sarah J. Johnson of Medford ME, b. Feb 1850. Woodsman. Civil War.

Gardner E., b. ca. 1868 Medford ME. Not shown in ME 1880 census index.

Frank E., b. 5 Nov 1871 Medford ME, m. 24 Dec 1898 Atkinson ME Bessie Strange of Bangor ME, b. Sep 1870, dau. Francis and Winnie (Ford) Strange. CH: Rowland E., b. Feb 1900, d. 1903.

Harold D., b. 28 Mar 1876 Medford ME, d. 1959 Warren ME, m.(1) 29 Nov 1899 Ethel R. Darling of Enfield ME, b. Jun 1882, dau. George W. and Hettie S. Darling; m.(2) Margaret Brown, b. 1889 d. 1968. Harnessmaker. He bur. in Sawyer Cem., Warren ME.

Lawrence C., b. Sep 1880 Medford ME.

Ola M., b. Apr 1883.

Eva A., b. Sep 1886.

Sources: Medford ME census 1870, 1900.ME 1880 census index, VR Medford ME, SA/ME. D37.

438. **ALFRED FREEMAN[8] SAWYER** [see 249], b. 1842 Kittery ME, m. 15 Sep 1867 Chester ME Jane E. Keene of Chester ME, b. 1844. Farmer.

Capitola J., b. 1868.

576 Thomas J.[9], b. 1869.

Alfred Freeman, b. 21 Dec 1872 Medford ME.

Harriet M., b. 14 Nov 1873.

Robert C., b. 1876 Medford ME.

Julia E., b. 1878.

Sources: Medford ME census 1860, 1870, 1880. VR Medford ME. P31.

439. **ANDREW FITZLAND[8] SAWYER** [see 249], b. Aug 1848 Orono ME, m. Sarah B. Littlefield of Medford ME, b. 1861. Farmer.

Anna F., b. 7 May 1878.

Clara Ella, b. 9 Apr 1880, m. 24 May 1903 Edwin P. Hichborn, Jr. Note: Listed as Afphia in ME 1880 census index.

Eunice F., b. Apr 1882.

Eula M., b. Nov 1884.

Omar Arthur, b. 26 Mar 1886 Medford ME.

Merlin Edward, b. Apr 1889 Medford ME.

Carrie E., b. 9 Apr 1895.

Gertrude Alice, b. 5 Jan 1897, d. 15 Aug 1897.

Sources: Maine 1880 census index. VR Medford ME, SA/ME. W31.

440. **HENRY P.[8] SAWYER** [see 250], b. 9 Jun 1850 Medford ME, d. 8 Jan 1909 Greenville ME, m. Louisa M. Davis of Stillwater ME, b. 30 May 1856 d. 3 May 1957. Carpenter. In Greenville ME 1880.

577 Stillman White[9], 1880-1960.

578 Fred J.[9], 1884-1951.

Florence E., b. 10 May 1886, d. 14 Nov 1972, m. Harley Budden.

Sources: Greenville ME census 1880. VR Greenville ME, SA/ME. Death certificate, Frances Richards rec.

441. **JOHN GREELEY⁸ SAWYER** [see 250], b. 1855 Medford ME, m. 22 Jan 1877 Enfield ME Nellie F. Buck of Lowell ME, b. Jul 1857. Merchant. In Greenville ME 1890.

Leslie Merton, b. 19 Aug 1878, d. 21 May 1921 Foxcroft ME.

Edith C., b. 29 Apr 1890.

Sources: ME 1880 census index, Greenville ME 1890 census. VR Greenville ME, SA/ME.

442. **RICHARD S.⁸ SAWYER** [see 251], b. 27 Sep 1852 Portland ME, d. 1918 Portland ME, m. 23 Nov 1878 Maria Hyer of Portland ME, b. Nov 1857 d. 27 Nov 1915, dau. Martin and Mary (Spellman) Hyer. Painter. At Cape Elizabeth ME 1880.

Claude B., b. 1877 Portland ME.

Albert L., b. 5 Apr 1880 Cape Elizabeth ME.

Blanche M., b. 16 Aug 1882, d. 17 Aug 1883.

Eva M., b. Nov 1884.

William Warren, b. 10 Aug 1887.

Elizabeth S., b. Jan 1895.

Mira Alberta, b. 21 Jun 1899.

Sources: Cape Elizabeth ME 1880 census. VR SA/ME, SA/MA. D9

443. **GUY LLEWELYN⁸ SAWYER** .[see 252], b. 26 Apr 1887 Effingham NH, d. 16 Apr 1967 Rochester NH, m.(1) 22 Jan 1907 Cora Colburn, b. 30 Sep 1887, dau. Robert and Anna (Burns) Colburn; m.(2) 13 May 1909 W. Newfield ME (div. 30 Oct 1925) Estella M. Cotton of Newfield ME, b. 1891, dau. Cyrus and Lucy (Long) Cotton; m.(3) Carolyn Watson, b. 31 May 1897 d. 24 Jan 1960. In Conway NH, Rochester NH.

Guy Ellsworth, b. 18 Jul 1914 Rochester NH, d. 31 Dec 1986 Rochester NH, m. (1) 3 Apr 1934 Rochester NH (later div) Verna M. Cutting of Effingham NH, b. 1918, dau. Verne and Edna E. (Gardellon) Cutting; m.(2) Florence Bogart of Lebanon ME, b. 20 Jul 1917 d. 6 Dec 1992, dau. Frank O. and Addie (Simpson) Bogart. CH: Guy Lawrence; Norma, m. _____ Rouleau, went to California; Robert L., m. Alice _____; Donna, b. 1945, m. James Black, to Farmington NH.

Nathaniel Haley, b. Jun 1928, m. Jul 1951 Marilyn Ames. CH: Christina, b. 25 May 1952; Lorna; Nathaniel Haley.

Philip Dunlap, b. 27 Jul 1932 Rochester NH, m. 17 Nov 1951 Louise DuFault, CH: Carol A., b. 1952, m. 1981 Fred M. Probst; Susan E., b. 1963, m. 20 Aug 1983 Peter Davidson.

Sources: VR SA/NH. Philip Dunlap Sawyer rec.

444. **GEORGE A.⁸ SAWYER** [see 254], b. 8 May 1857 Buxton ME, d. 4 Dec 1888 Buxton ME, m. Annie E. Atkinson, b. ?. In Portland ME. Bur. in Tory Hill Cem., Buxton ME. Wid. appointed guardian of Lillian B., 1888.

Lillian B., b. Jan 1883, d. 21 Mar 1891.

579 Lewis John⁹, 1885-1970.

Sources: P82g, R17, M5.

445. **CYRUS ELWYN⁸ SAWYER** [see 254], b. 6 Feb 1870 Buxton ME, d. 11 Jul 1937, m. 27 Jun 1894 Portland ME Mary Rachel Buckley of New Brunswick, Canada, b. 30 May 1870 d. 17 Jun 1950, dau. Joseph and Mary (Bullock) Buckley. Clerk. Bur. in Tory Hill Cem., Buxton ME.

Ethel Beatrice, b. 18 May 1895, d. 15 Oct 1974, m. Evans F. Carlson.

Alice Margaret, b. 9 Sep 1897, d. 6 Sep 1978, m. 7 Aug 1918 Henry Henderson.

580 Harold Lester⁹, b. 1899.

Hazel B., b. 14 Sep 1907, d. 8 Sep 1985, m. 17 Aug 1938 Victor E. Everett.

Sources: VR Portland ME, Buxton ME, SA/ME. M5, Harold Lester Sawyer rec.

446. **CHARLES OLIVER$^{8}$ SAWYER** [see 258], b. 18 Mar 1865 Saco ME, d. 23 Jul 1936 Biddeford ME, m. 31 May 1891 Buxton ME Hattie E. Smith of Buxton ME, b. 17 Feb 1863 d. 13 Oct 1933, dau. Thomas H. and Sarah (Porter) Smith. In Buxton ME. He bur. in Tory Hill Cem., Buxton ME.

Elmer Freedom, b. 26 Apr 1892 Saco ME, d. 19 Nov 1946 Saco ME, m. 30 Jun 1920 Gladys J. Thurston of Saco ME, b. ? d. Dec 1985. CH: Myrtle A., b. 18 Aug 1923, m. 30 Jun 1950 Robert Andrews. Went to North Dakota.

Dwight Leland, b. 17 Apr 1894 Saco ME, d. 9 Jan 1961 Saco ME, m. 30 Jun 1920 Florence P. Boothby of Cape Elizabeth ME, b. 4 Oct 1890. CH: Paulena B., b. 6 Feb 1922, d. 9 Feb 1922; Bina Elizabeth, b. 16 Apr 1923, unm., medical missionary in Thailand; Faith H., b. 31 Mar 1926, m.(1) 1 Feb 1948 Robert L. Moore, m.(2) 2 Jun 1960 Alf Eikaas; Marjorie J., b. 20 Aug 1929, m. Aug 1955 Fred Fitanides.

Horace, b. 29 Feb 1902 Saco ME, d. 1956 Old Orchard Beach ME, m. Marion Higgins, b. ?. In Biddeford ME.

Sources: VR Buxton ME, SA/ME. M5, Faith Eikaas rec.

447. **GILBERT AUGUSTUS$^{8}$ SAWYER** [see 259], b. 1 Jul 1838 Saco ME, d. 11 Aug 1903 Biddeford ME, m. 25 Jun 1859 Saco ME Annie C. Boulter of Standish ME, b. 18 May 1839 d. 2 Aug 1915, dau. William and Phebe (Cain) Boulter. Sawmill worker. In Limington ME 1860, Biddeford ME 1880.

581 Henry S.$^{9}$, 1864-1917.
Edith L., b. 1865.
Marcia E., b. 1869.
George H., b. 1872 Limington ME.
Gilbert Augustus, b. 20 Jun 1874 Limington ME.

Sources: Limington ME census 1860, 1870. Biddeford ME census 1880. VR Limington ME, SA/ME.

448. **JOHN QUINCY$^{8}$ SAWYER** [see 259], b. 10 Jan 1841 Saco ME, d. 19 Dec 1916 Biddeford ME, m.(1) Sarah E. Deering of Kennebunk ME, b. 10 Nov 1841 d. 22 Oct 1902, dau. Joshua and Abigail (Warren) Deering; m.(2) 6 Aug 1903 Annie L. Dolliff, b. ?. Adopted granddaughter Lucy Helen 7 May 1895. Merchant. In Somersworth NH 1870.

Charles E., b. Jun 1861 Saco ME, m.(1) 7 Dec 1881 Rose Cribbs of Nova Scotia, Canada, b. May 1859 d. 23 Jan 1899, dau. John and Sarah A. (Morrison) Cribbs; m.(2) 4 Oct 1899 Concord NH Fannie Mahoney of Saco ME, b. Jun 1859, dau. Daniel and Mary (McNutt) Mahoney. CH: Lucy Helen, b. 19 Jan 1883, adopted by grandparents.

Sources: Somersworth NH census 1870. VR Saco ME, SA/ME. P82k.

449. **CHARLES HENRY$^{8}$ SAWYER** [see 259], b. 10 Nov 1843 Saco ME, d. 8 Dec 1916 Biddeford ME, m. 27 Sep 1865 Biddeford ME Mary A. Lowell of Biddeford ME, b. ca. 1844, dau. Samuel Lowell. Druggist.

Frederick William, b. May 1867, m. Rena Carle, b. Aug 1882 d. 1966. CH: Carle F. of Portsmouth NH; Elizabeth, b. ca. 1912, d. 15 Nov 1993, m. Walter White; Theodore of Salem NH; Alan of Saco ME; Daughter.
Isabel, b. ca. 1868, d. 1961, m. Adney Fenderson.
Georgia, b. ca. 1870, d. 1956, m. Charles Innes.
Mary, b. 28 Feb 1880, d. 1938, unm.

Sources: VR Biddeford ME, SA/ME. Obit. (Elizabeth), Julian Sawyer rec., Elizabeth White rec., Carle Sawyer rec.

450. **GEORGE FRANKLIN[8] SAWYER** [see 259], b. 4 Jul 1849 Saco ME, m. Carrie C. Smith of Saco ME, b. Oct 1857. In Somersworth NH, Saco ME 1886.

Howard Berry, b. May 1886, m. 22 Oct 1907 Ella W. Cole.

Sources: Somersworth NH census 1870. ME 1880 census index. VR SA/ME.

451. **HERBERT[8] SAWYER** [see 259], b. 16 Feb 1854 Saco ME, d. 2 May 1905 Saco ME, m. Lovina H. Smith of Dayton ME, b. 1854.

Clarence F., b. Nov 1878 Saco ME, m. 10 Oct 1905 Alice M. Hyde, b. ?.
James H., b. Sep 1882 Saco ME.
Charlotte R., b. 13 Oct 1893, d. 4 Jan 1914 Saco ME.

Sources: Saco ME census 1880. VR SA/ME.

452. **FRANK HALLER[8] SAWYER** [see 261], b. 6 Mar 1850 Biddeford ME, d. 14 Apr 1918 Biddeford ME, m. Mary V. E. _____ of Wendell MA, b. 1851.

George L., b. 1875 Biddeford ME.
Frances Arline, b. 27 Sep 1894.

Sources: Biddeford ME census 1880. VR SA/ME, SA/MA.

453. **CLARENCE EVANS[8] SAWYER** [see 262], b. 7 Aug 1869 Wilmot NH, drowned in Casco Bay, Portland ME, 24 Feb 1941, m. 18 Aug 1896 Yarmouth ME Blanche M. Brown of Yarmouth ME, b. Feb 1870, dau. John F. and Mary (Lovell) Brown. In Brunswick ME, Portland ME.

582 Russell Fulton Brown[9], 1897-1972.
Lovell Brown, b. 29 Oct 1900, m. Mildred _____, b. ?. No CH.
Louisa B., b. ?, unm.
Clarence Evans, b. ?, unm. In Boston MA.

Sources: VR SA/ME. L30, Death certificate, Richard J. Sawyer rec.

454. **HOWARD M.[8] SAWYER** [see 263], b. May 1860 Saco ME, m. Elizabeth M. Cousins of Buxton ME, b. Feb 1867.

Maybell G., b. Aug 1886.
Bertha M., b. Feb 1888, m. P_____ N. Sylvester.
Ellsworth H., b. Jan 1890 Saco ME.
Ruby E., b. 11 Jan 1892.
Charles, b. 22 Jan 1899, d. 4 Apr 1900.

Sources: VR SA/ME.

455. **MARSHALL[8] SAWYER** [see 264], b. 30 Oct 1859 Bridgton ME, d. Feb 1903 McMinnville TN, m. Apr 1898 Cora Belle Staples of Auburn ME, b. 20 Mar 1869 d. 31 Mar 1949, dau. Charles and Henrietta (Stevens) Staples.

Arthur Howard, b. 15 Apr 1899 Bridgton ME.
Grace H., b. 16 Oct 1900.

Sources: Bridgton ME census 1860. Mary E. Senior rec., Robert L. Taylor rec.

456. **HOWARD B.[8] SAWYER** [see 264], b. 10 Mar 1866 Bridgton ME, d. 19 Jan 1895 So. Bridgton ME, m. Nellie L. Bennett, b. 16 Jan 1868 d. 28 Mar 1934. Mill operator, farmer. In Adams MA?

Myrtie B., b. 19 May 1888, d. 7 Feb 1889.
Clifford H., b. 29 Oct 1889, d. 11 Nov 1889.
Roger M., b. ?.
Sources: VR SA/ME. Robert L. Taylor rec.

457. **EDWIN[8] SAWYER** [see 268], b. 14 Aug 1845 Concord NH, d. 11 Aug 1915 Concord NH, m.(1) 16 Aug 1873 Georgia A. Runnell of Concord NH, b. 1854 d. 23 Dec 1896; m.(2) 26 Apr 1905 Penacook NH Emma V. Watson of Boscawen NH, b. 7 Feb 1872 d. 5 Oct 1918, dau. John A. and Sarah A. (Hart) Watson. Farmer.

Alonzo J., b. 1875 Concord NH.
Levi W., b. 1876 Concord NH, m. 25 Jul 1912 Warner NH Sarah E. L. Davis of Northfield NH, wid., b. 1885, dau. John P. and Sarah Watson. Farmer. In Warner NH.
Willie E., b. 25 Aug 1884, d. 28 Sep 1884.
Harry C., b. 29 Jun 1891, d. 2 Nov 1891.
Alice Mae, b. 21 Feb 1906, d. 23 Feb 1906.
Sources: Concord NH census 1850, 1860, 1870, 1880. VR SA/NH.

458. **EDWARD AYER[8] SAWYER** [see 269], b. 25 Jul 1839 Bradford MA, m. 3 Apr 1862 Boston MA Josephine A. Maynard of Boston MA, b. 13 Oct 1838, dau. Lambert and Luseba (Locke) Maynard. Shoemaker. In Boston MA, Sullivan NH.

Anna Florence, b. 11 May 1863, d. 22 Feb 1865.
Samuel Lambert, b. 27 Jan 1867 Boston MA.
Etta Josephine, b. 30 Mar 1870.
Sources: VR Bradford MA, SA/MA. S31, E16.

459. **HENRY EDMUND[8] SAWYER** [see 270], b. 14 Jul 1826 Warner NH, d. 21 Sep 1906 Randolph VT, m.(1) 27 Nov 1851 Julia A. French of Candia NH, b. 26 Jan 1824 d. 27 Nov 1875; m.(2) 13 May 1885 Weathersfield CT M. Helen (Rogers) Bunce of Rocky Hill CT, b. 1846, dau. Theodore B. Rogers. Dartmouth College graduate. Teacher. Principal of Francestown NH Academy, Henneker NH Academy, Concord NH High School 1857-1865. Also in Middletown CT, New Britain CT, Gill MA.

Julia Lillian, b. 1 Oct 1852.
William Henry, b. 29 Dec 1854, d. 24 Sep 1855.
Edmund French, b. 9 Sep 1858 Concord NH, m. 17 May 1883 Mary Stoddard of Albion NY, b. ?. Music critic, composer. In Boston MA, Wayland MA. CH: Caroline, b. 25 Feb 1895.
Sources: Hanover NH census 1850 (student). Concord NH census 1860. VR SA/MA. B68, C59.

460. **JOHN MARSHALL[8] SAWYER** [see 270], b. 14 Oct 1831 Henniker NH, m. 18 Aug 1863 Manchester NH Laura James of Pittsfield NH, b. ?. Manufacturer. In Lowell MA, Middletown CT, Holyoke MA 1863, Chicopee Falls MA 1864.

Bertha, b. May 1864.
Walter Howard, b. 21 May 1867 Middletown CT, d. 21 Dec 1923 Auburn MA, m. 23 Apr 1900 Helen Frances Hayes of Wellesley MA, b. ?. In Boston MA, Auburn MA. CH: Elizabeth Hayes, b. 21 Apr 1904, m. 21 Jan 1927 Stephen H. Palmer, Jr.
Mabel A., b. 16 Jul 1879.
Sources: VR SA/MA. C59.

461. **JACOB HERBERT[8] SAWYER** .[see 270], b. 10 Jun 1837 Henniker NH, m.(1) 9 Mar 1864 Rollinsford NH Elizabeth M. Wentworth of Somersworth NH, b. 28 Oct 1838, dau. William

T. and Lucinda (Ricker) Wentworth; m.(2) 14 Jun 1882 Boston MA Lucy M. Newhall of Boston MA, b. 1842, dau. John and Maria Newhall. Mill superintendant. In Lowell MA, Ware MA 1865, Boston MA, Wellesley MA.

William, b. 26 Oct 1865 Ware MA.

Henry B., b. 1871, d. 1950, m. 1906 Georgia Pope, b. ? In Boston MA. CH: Henry B., Avery, Elizabeth Wentworth, m. Charles Mixter.

Sources: VR SA/MA. A20, C59.

462. **CHARLES EDMUND[8] SAWYER** [see 271], b. 7 Dec 1836 Boston MA, d. 2 Oct 1904 Harvard MA, m. 25 Dec 1872 Harvard MA Sarah Maria Willard of Harvard MA, b. 9 Jan 1849 d. 11 Nov 1930, dau. Joseph and Sarah (Wetherbee) Willard. Card manufacturer, school superintendent. In Roxbury MA.

Perley Willard, b. 22 May 1873 Boston MA.

Herbert Edmund, b. 6 Oct 1878 Boston MA.

Florence Gertrude, b. 25 Mar 1880.

Joseph Kendall, b. 23 Apr 1885 Boston MA.

Charles Edmund, b. 4 Dec 1886 Boston MA.

Webster Morrell, b. 12 Oct 1893 Boston MA.

Sources: VR SA/MA. P63, Bonita Folch rec.

463. **HORACE FAIRBANKS[8] SAWYER** [see 271], b. 29 Dec 1843 Boston MA, m. 3 Jun 1872 Boston MA Mary E. Bracebridge of Boston MA, b. 1848, dau. James P. and Mehitable Bracebridge. Superintendent of a card company.

Arthur Bracebridge, b. 1875 Boston MA.

Sources: VR SA/MA.

464. **ANDREW JOSEPH[8] SAWYER** .[see 273], b. 6 Jul 1844 Newport NH, d. 2 Jan 1932 Newport NH, m. 18 Sep 1866 Marcia A. Humphrey of Croydon NH, b. 21 Jan 1842 d. 13 Aug 1909, dau. Piam and Alvira (Marsh) Humphrey. Farmer. Served three years in Civil War. In Croydon NH 1870, 1880.

Henry Joseph, b. 10 Nov 1867 Croydon NH, m. 8 Nov 1893 Meriden NH Della S. Davis of Sunapee NH, b. 1872.

Bertha E., b. 21 Jun 1869, m. 7 Nov 1900 Albert I. Barton.

Kittie Florence, b. 14 Feb 1871, m. 25 Sep 1895 Robert F. Martin.

Annie Marcia, b. 22 Sep 1872, m. 2 Dec 1897 Daniel S. Rowell.

Piam Drury, b. 29 Feb 1880 Croydon NH, d. 21 Apr 1932 Newport NH, m. 9 Nov 1910 Claremont NH Gladys P. Fitzgerald of New York, b. 1889, dau. James and Jennie L. (Armstrong) Fitzgerald. Lumberman.

Sources: Croydon NH census 1870, 1880. VR SA/NH. N6, M13.

465. **FRENCH ALBERT[8] SAWYER** [see 276], b. 30 Jan 1845 Newport NH, d. 24 Jan 1901 Concord NH, m. 18 Nov 1869 San Francisco CA Martha W. Holden of Concord NH, b ?. He bur. in Napa CA.

Hattie S., b. 22 Sep 1870, m. Adam P. Holden.

Benjamin F., b. 6 Apr 1872.

Lois M., b. 16 Jan 1874.

Sources: VR SA/NH. P85.

466. **RICHARD KELLY[8] SAWYER** [see 278], b. Oct 1839 Alexandria NH, d. 20 Mar 1869 Plymouth NH, m.(1) 22 Feb 1861 Plymouth NH Arianna Kidder, b. 29 Aug 1838 d. 12 Jan 1863;

m.(2) 7 Dec 1865 Almira R. (Corliss) Merrill of Grafton NH, b. 20 Dec 1838. In Bristol NH 1860, Plymouth NH 1864. Wid. m. 1872 Charles McQuesten, went to Canada.

Lurie Ann, b. 12 Dec 1862, d. 15 Mar 1869.

Frank R., b. 12 Mar 1869 Rumney NH, d. 7 Jul 1935 Laconia NH, m. 14 Nov 1894 Whitefield NH Addie M. Boutwell of Montpelier VT, b. 1870. In Jefferson NH, Plymouth NH, Laconia NH 1905.

Sources: Bristol NH census 1860. M64, S81, S74, M31

467. **WILLIAM REED$^8$ SAWYER** [see 280], b. 29 Jan 1846 Francestown NH, d. 2 Aug 1935 Lawrence MA, m.(1) Lawrence MA Ella F. Camp of Piermont NH, b. 1851 d. 10 Jul 1883 Lawrence MA, dau. Jonah and Emily M. Camp; m.(2) 20 Feb 1889 Sarah A. Camp of Manchester NH, b. ?. Carpenter. In Manchester NH, Lawrence MA 1889.

William Reed, b. ca. 1875 (Manchester NH?).

Ella Frances, b. Feb 1876, m.(1) _____ Muzzey; m.(2) _____ Post.

583 Charles Franklin$^9$, 1878-1961.

Abby May, b. 2 Nov 1880, d.y.

Son, b. 8 Jun 1883 Lawrence MA.

Emily Maria, b. Dec 1889, m. Peter Gulesian.

584 Samuel Stevens$^9$, b. 1891.

Lewis Francis, b. May 1892 Lawrence MA, m. _____ CH: Dorothy, b.?; Elizabeth, b. ?.

Joseph W., b. Jan 1894 Lawrence MA.

Dorothy H., b. 21 Sep 1895, m. Charles Masterman.

Sources: Manchester NH census 1880. VR SA/NH, SA/MA. William Reed Sawyer rec., Marion Sawyer rec.

468. **DAVID H.$^8$ SAWYER** [see 282], b. 13 Aug 1840 Antrim NH, d. 21 Jan 1882 Bunker Hill IL, m. 14 Jun 1864 Ann Wood of Venice NY, b. 21 Jan 1838 d. 9 Aug 1919. Furniture business. Deacon, Congregational Church.

Alberta Augusta, b. 27 Feb 1866, d. 14 May 1902.

Arthur Rodney, b. 26 Aug 1868.

Sources: L29

469. **SAMUEL STEELE$^8$ SAWYER** .[see 284], b. 8 Nov 1836 Bedford NH, d. 28 Jan 1928 Antrim NH, m.(1) 18 May 1861 Mary Day of Peterboro NH, b. 8 Sep 1838 d. 23 Aug 1916, dau. Robert and Lydia (Carr) Day; m.(2) 2 Jun 1919 Milford NH Delia F. Toddof Newbury MA, b. 18 Mar 1848 d. 10 Aug 1938, dau. John and Patty (Cheney) Morse. Farmer, real estate. Selectman for 10 years. Town Treasurer. In Antrim NH 1870, 1880. Member NH Legislature.

Willis Herbert, b. 6 Jan 1863 Antrim NH, d. 8 Apr 1927 Dorchester MA, m.(1) 1 Nov 1893 Boston MA Mabel Ladd of Dorchester MA, b. ?, dau. George O. and Patience Ladd; m.(2) Alice Woodward of Dorchester MA, b. ?. Graduate of Tufts College and a New York medical school.

Eva Louise, b. 31 Dec 1865, m. 24 Sep 1890 Watson Fearing.

Georgianna, b. 10 Apr 1867, d. 16 Jul 1911, m. 4 May 1887 Antrim NH John I. Nesmith.

Alice Bertha, b. 12 Dec 1869, m. 5 Jun 1901 Alfred E. Shaw.

585 Henry Gilbert$^9$, b. 1873.

Sources: Antrim NH census 1870, 1880. VR SA/MA, SA/NH. H93, L29.

470. **JAMES M.$^8$ SAWYER** [see 285], b. 4 Jun 1844 Newport NH, d. 28 Jul 1892, m. Jane Elizabeth Wilson, b. ? d. 1892. In Hillsboro NH, Freeport IL.

Mabel Moore, b. 1876, m. Franklin L. McVey.

Murray Gibson, b. 1886, Hillsboro NH, m. Sarah Fulton, b. ?. CH: Anne Fulton, b. 1907.
Florence, b. ?, d.y.

Sources: H93, N9.

471. **GEORGE FISHER[8] SAWYER** [see 289], b. 3 Feb 1849 Nashua NH, d. 8 Nov 1906 Nashua NH, m. 8 Oct 1873 Wilton NH Helen T. Law of Milford NH, b. 18 Jun 1852 d. 16 Feb 1926, dau. Thomas and Alma (MacIntosh) Law. Shipper.

Ora Frances, b. 16 Apr 1877.
Joseph Harrison, b. 5 Aug 1878 Nashua NH.
Helen Imogene, b. 23 Jun 1886.
Gertrude Evelyn, b. 31 May 1888.

Sources: VR SA/NH.

472. **LEVI DAVIS[8] SAWYER** [see 292], b. 26 Jan 1828 Gilford NH, d. 7 Jul 1903 Gilford NH, m. 1851 Mary A. Dame of Center Harbor NH, b. 29 Oct 1830 d. 8 Jun 1908, dau. Benjamin and Betsey (Goss) Dame. Farmer.

Luther C., b. 12 Aug 1852 Gilford NH, d. 30 Mar 1876 Gilford NH.
Ora Anna, b. 21 May 1859, d. 22 Jan 1943, m. 2 Feb 1884 Charles H. Gove of Gilford NH.
586 Ansel Bugbee[9], 1863-1933.
Ernest Perry, b. 6 Nov 1870 Gilford NH, m. 30 Sep 1897 Pittsfield NH Sadie Emma Adams of Tewksbury MA, b. 3 Apr 1876 d. 29 Oct 1935, dau. George W. and Julia (Ware) Adams. Farmer. CH: George Levi, b. 9 Mar 1900, d. 10 Mar 1900; Ruth Edna, b. 21 Apr 1907; Emma Ware, b. 18 Jul 1909.

Sources: Gilford NH census 1850, 1860. VR SA/NH. N9, G30, H23.

473. **WILLIAM BADGER[8] SAWYER** [see 293], b. 11 Jul 1825 Greensboro VT, d. 12 Apr 1893 Keene NH, m. Julia F. Wilson of Royalton VT, b. 12 May 1829. Farmer. In Greensboro VT 1850. He bur. in Tilton NH.

Julia Ella, b. 1854, d. 25 Jan 1857.
John G., b. 1859 Greensboro VT, m. 4 Jul 1885 Greensboro VT Alice N. Bradley of Brownington VT, b. ?. Laborer. CH: Grace, b. 15 Nov 1885.
Sarah W., b. 20 Nov 1864, m. 20 Nov 1893 Keene NH E. Alberton Hofses.
William S., b. 23 Jul 1868, d. 3 Aug 1888 Tilton NH.

Sources: Greensboro VT census 1850. VR SA/VT. N9, N6

474. **JEREMIAH FELLOWS[8] SAWYER** [see 295], b. 14 Sep 1834 Belmont NH, d. 15 May 1863 Belmont NH, m. 28 Jun 1857 Orpha C. Loomis of England, b. 20 Nov 1832. Died of wounds in Civil War.

587 George Edwin[9], 1857-1911.

Sources: Gilmanton NH census (includes Belmont) 1860. R34.

475. **CHARLES S.[8] SAWYER** [see 295], b. 16 Jan 1841 Belmont NH, d. 21 Oct 1927 Belmont NH, m.(1) 4 Sep 1862 Mary Ann Hutchins of Canterbury NH, b. 1840 d. 28 Apr 1871, dau. Reuben and Olive Hutchins; m.(2) 26 Mar 1874 Mary Ann Kilbourn of Salisbury NH, b. 9 May 1843 d. 19 May 1932, dau. Jedediah and Rebecca (Page) Kilbourn. Farmer.

Child, b. 7 Mar 1871, d. 7 May 1871.
Lucy Cummings, b. 19 Feb 1875.
Charles Roscoe, b. 9 Jan 1877, m. 23 Jan 1925 Laconia NH Helen R. (Atwood) Whitter of Littleton NH, wid., b. 1870, dau. Daniel W. and Julia H. (Brackett) Atwood. Farmer.

Sources: Belmont NH census 1870, 1880. VR SA/NH. R34.

476. **JOHN R.[8] SAWYER** [see 296], b. 22 Dec 1840 Belmont NH, d. 13 Apr 1909 Gilmanton NH, m. Mary J. Marsh of Gilmanton NH, b. 26 Jul 1852 d. 26 Apr 1935, dau. Richard and Hannah (Peaslee) Marsh. Farmer. He bur. Smith Meeting House Cem., Gilmanton NH.

588 David[9], 1873-1956.
Blanche, b. 12 Aug 1877, m. 1 Jun 1899 Walter H. Ayer.
John R., b. ca. 1880.

Sources: Gilmanton NH census 1850, 1860, 1880. VR SA/NH. N7, H89, N6.

477. **NAHUM W.[8] SAWYER** [see 296], b. 1844 Belmont NH, d. 1905, m. 6 Mar 1879 Octa Thompson of Belmont NH, b. 26 Sep 1857 d. 26 Apr 1931 Plymouth NH, dau. Isreal S. and Mary (Marsh) Thompson of Gilmanton NH. Farmer. In Enfield NH, California.

Walter M., b. 2 Jul 1880 Enfield NH, m.(1) 14 Jun 1905 Campton NH Ethel G. Palmer of Campton NH, b. 1880, dau. Christopher and Hannah (Pease) Palmer of Rumney NH; m.(2) 7 Oct 1908 Plymouth NH Lyle Fellows of Plymouth NH, b. 1882, dau. Chauncy A. and Jennie (Lyford) Fellows. Clerk. In Plymouth NH.
Edward Thompson, b. 24 Dec 1881, d. 20 Nov 1883.
Son, b. 22 Dec 1883.

Sources: VR Enfield NH. SA/NH.

478. **GILMAN[8] SAWYER** [see 297], b. 1812 Deerfield NH, d. 1863 So. Newmarket NH, m. Mary A. _____, b. ?. Carpenter. Wid. m. Luther Veasey.

Orrissa J., b. 1837, m. 23 Apr 1857 Exeter NH Joseph E. Lang.
Charles A., b. 1848 Newmarket NH, m. 16 Dec 1879 Manchester NH Lizzie Griffen of Concord NH, b. ?.
Ansel G., b. 1849 Newmarket NH.

Sources: Newmarket NH census 1840, 1850. VR Manchester NH. P82g, N6.

479. **FRANKLIN P.[8] SAWYER** [see 298], b. 1833 Lee NH, d. 18 Apr 1878 Lee NH, m.(1) 25 Feb 1850 Stratham NH Lydia Perkins of Greenland NH, b. May 1823 d. Sep 1861; m.(2) 16 Sep 1862 Addie DeMerritt of Nottingham NH, b. 1842 d. 15 Nov 1865; m. (3) 8 Feb 1868 Newmarket NH Sarah P. Fernald of Newmarket NH, b. ?. Will probated 1882. Wid. m. _____ Batchelder.

589 Frank P.[9], b. 1853.
590 Josiah F.[9], 1859-1908.
Flora A., b. 1869.

Sources: Lee NH census 1850, 1860, 1870. VR Stratham NH. N9, P82i

480. **EZRA A. J.[8] SAWYER** [see 299], b. 3 Nov 1828 Deerfield NH, d. 16 Dec 1886 Deerfield NH, m. 24 May 1853 Candia NH Sarah Collins Bean of Candia NH, b. 8 Apr 1830 d. 5 Mar 1906, dau. Joseph and Lydia (Collins) Bean. Farmer, teacher, tax collector, deputy sheriff, postmaster. He bur. in Deerfield Parade NH.

Frederick Bean, b. 16 Apr 1854 Deerfield NH, d. 1874 Dubuque IA, unm.
John Francis, b. 2 Mar 1856 Deerfield NH, m. Nellie E. Pierce, b. ?. In Dubuque IA 1874.
Mary L., b. 9 Sep 1859, d. 12 Sep 1859.
Mabel J., b. 11 Apr 1861, d. 31 Jan 1910, unm.

Sources: VR SA/NH. B40, H95, H3.

481. **GEORGE WASHINGTON[8] SAWYER** [see 301], b. 10 Oct 1844 Franklin NH, d. 18 Jul 1914 Franklin NH, m. 10 Aug 1869 Louise C. Barnes of Hillsboro NH, b. May 1849 d. 3 Jan 1924, dau. Augustus and Mary (Severence) Barnes. In Franklin Falls NH.

591 Augustus Barnes[9], 1870-1938.
Enos K., b. 24 Aug 1879 Franklin NH, d. 2 Mar 1833 Franklin NH, m. 28 Feb 1911 Somerville MA Mabel E. White of Charlestown MA, b. 1882, dau. Frank H. and Annie O. (Burbank) White.
Sources: Franklin Falls NH census 1880. VR SA/NH, SA/VT. B92, E2.

482. **EBENEZER PRESCOTT[8] SAWYER** [see 302], b. 2 Nov 1824 Atkinson ME, d. 7 Apr 1901 Dover-Foxcroft ME, m. 30 Nov 1845 Mary A. Sawyer, b. 1822. Farmer.
592 Josiah C.[9], 1848-1907.
George, b. Aug 1851, d. 23 Feb 1854.
Sources: Atkinson ME census 1850, 1860, 1870. Dover-Foxcroft ME census 1880 S. Shepard Sawyer rec., Robert L. Taylor rec.

483. **STEPHEN SHEPARD[8] SAWYER** .[see 302], b. 2 Nov 1837 Atkinson ME, d. 24 Jan 1921 Dover-Foxcroft ME, m. 2 Nov 1862 Elma E. Drewof Charleston ME, b. 16 Jan 1844 d. 18 Jan 1924. Civil War. He bur. in Atkinson ME.
Eliza Eva, b. 1864, m. Lionel Lincoln.
Minnie Delia, b. 1866, m. Walter Herrick.
593 Frank Leslie[9], 1869-1949.
Herbert Coffin, b. 1874 Atkinson ME, m.(1) Alice Leland, b. ?; m.(2) Eldora Black, b. ?. No CH.
Sources: Atkinson ME census 1880. VR SA/ME. D37, S. Shepard Sawyer rec., Lauri Cover rec.

484. **LEONARD H.[8] SAWYER** [see 304], b. 13 Feb 1848 Atkinson ME, d. 17 Mar 1923, m. Garland ME Maria A. Bean, b. 21 Dec 1850 d. 5 Mar 1939, dau. Carlos and Sarah (Grey) Bean of East Corinth ME. In East Corinth ME.
Harry C., b. 21 Mar 1874, d. 13 Apr 1874.
Lora F., b. 4 Jun 1876, d. 10 Jun 1919, m.(1) 7 Mar 1899 Tilton NH Livingston Rogers, m.(2) Aug 1908 Sidney Davis.
Annie M., b. 12 Feb 1879, d. 1 Jan 1950, m. Fred Burton of E. Corinth ME.
594 Charles Bean[9], 1886-1939.
595 Walter Leonard[9], b. 1890.
Sources: East Corinth ME census 1880. B40, N6.

485. **GEORGE HENRY[8] SAWYER** .[see 310], b. 15 Oct 1843 So. Hampton NH, m. 3 Mar 1866 So. Hampton NH Susan M. Fowler of Boxford MA, b. ?. In So. Hampton NH 1850, 1860, Newton NH 1880.
Lizzie A., b. 24 May 1868, m. 8 May 1886 Newton NH Amos E. Smart.
George Thomas, b. Aug 1874 So. Hampton NH.
Eva N., b. 7 Mar 1883.
Susie Annabel, b. 16 Dec 1888.
Sources: So. Hampton NH census 1850, 1860. Newton NH census 1880. VR So. Hampton NH. N6.

486. **ENOCH[8] SAWYER** [see 311], b. 27 Nov 1841 Salisbury MA, m. 20 Nov 1881 Exeter NH Adelaide A. (Pike) Getchell of Salisbury MA, b. 1844.
596 Enoch Earl[9], b. 1884.
Sources: VR Salisbury MA, SA/MA.

487. **ALBERT PAGE$^8$ SAWYER** [see 312], b. 8 Oct 1842 Salisbury MA, m. 15 Nov 1868 Newburyport MA Sarah Rebecca Collins, b. 15 Mar 1845, dau. Ephraim and Rebecca Collins. Insurance agent. In Newburyport MA.

Abbie Laura, b. 3 Jul 1869.
Albert Hayden, b. 8 May 1871 Newburyport MA.
Sarah Augusta, b. 4 Sep 1872.
Alice Adams, b. 13 Mar 1876.

Sources: VR Salisbury MA, Newburyport MA, SA/MA. A4, G36.

488. **RICHARD$^8$ SAWYER** [see 314], b. 26 Dec 1839 Vershire VT, d. 4 Oct 1902 Bath NH, m. 16 Apr 1868 Mary A. Howland of Eaton NH, b. 22 Oct 1842 d. 11 Jan 1926, dau. Stephen and Elsie (Demsey) Howland. Wid. in Lisbon NH 1880.

Danna Forest, b. 1 Dec 1871, d. 7 Apr 1874.
597 Tracy M.$^9$, 1878-1932.

Sources: Vershire VT census 1850. Bath NH census 1870. Lisbon NH census 1880. VR SA/NH, SA/VT. P59.

489. **MARTIN S.$^8$ SAWYER** [see 317], b. 1868 Craftsbury VT, m. 27 May 1896 Craftsbury VT Viola D. Allen of Craftsbury VT, b. ?. Merchant.

Day Moreau, b. 11 Aug 1898 Craftsbury VT.

Sources: VR SA/VT.

490. **GORHAM HOITT$^8$ SAWYER** [see 318], b. 15 Jun 1866 Salisbury NH, m. 20 Feb 1891 Alice M. Little of Salisbury NH, b. 4 Jul 1866. Farmer. In Durham NH 1889. Owned store in Durham NH 1897. In Lee NH 1923.

Lester Little, b. 16 Aug 1893 Durham NH, m.(1) 9 Jul 1917 Bellows Falls VT (later div.) Ethel H. Dame of Epping NH, b. 1887, dau. John R. and Annie (Emerson) Dame; m.(2) 3 Feb 1923 Dover NH Grace P. Longee of Conway NH, b. 1898, dau. Frank H. and Pauline Longee of Tamworth NH. Farmer. In Lee NH.
Charles Gorham, b. 20 Oct 1895 Durham NH.
Warren Dearborn, b. 14 Jan 1897 Durham NH, d. 17 Apr 1986 Newmarket NH, m. 1 Jun 1935 Lee NH Ruth M. Watson of Newmarket NH, b. 1916 d. 25 Feb 1993, dau. _____ and Helen Watson. Butcher. Selectman, tax collector, and road agent for Lee NH. CH: Warren Dearborn, b. ?.
John Thomas, b. 22 Aug 1900 Durham NH. Went to California.
Eugene Hoitt, b. 24 Jun 1904 Durham NH, m. Helen Kochelike of Philadelphia PA, b. ?. In Lee NH. CH: Gloria May, b. 5 Feb 1935, d. 30 Apr 1935 Lee NH.
Lena Alice, b. 1 Dec 1905, d. 4 Apr 1906.

Sources: VR SA/NH. S68, L34.

491. **CHARLES HENRY$^8$ SAWYER** [see 319], b. 4 Oct 1848 Salisbury NH, m. 23 Jan 1881 Eva M. Davidson, b. ?. In Missouri.

Fred Lewis McKay, b. 5 Apr 1888 Amherst NH. Went to Missouri.

Sources: Annette S. Manny rec.

492. **EDWARD NATHANIEL$^8$ SAWYER** [see 319], b. 29 Jun 1867 Salisbury NH, d. 6 Feb 1936 Concord NH, m. Amanda Henderson of Prince Edward Island, Canada, b. 1864. Farmer.

Charlotte M., b. 4 May 1899.

Nathaniel, b. 1903 Salisbury NH, d. 1985 Concord NH, m. 3 Aug 1929 Concord NH Pauline G. Davenport of Lakeport NH, b. 1902, dau. Harry N. and Bessie L. (Trover) Davenport. Salesman. In Concord NH.

Sources: VR SA/NH.

493. **HERMAN LITTLE⁸ SAWYER** [see 321], b. 25 Apr 1865 Webster NH, d. 27 Jan 1954, m. 15 Dec 1896 Stella Maude Burkert, b. ? d. 1 Mar 1939. Minister.

598 Raymond Burkert⁹, b. 1897.

Ruth Frances, b. 2 Oct 1913.

Sources: L29, Jeanette Sawyer rec.

494. **JOSEPH PLANT⁸ SAWYER** [see 322], b. 29 Oct 1825 Amesbury MA, d. 20 Jul 1910 Auburn ME, m.(1) 5 Oct 1854 Lucy Popham, b. ? d. Jul 1862, dau. Daniel Popham; m.(2) Julia Davis of Buckfield ME, b. ? d. Dec 1867; m.(3) 13 Apr 1869 Canton MA Margery Griggs of Stoughton MA, b. 1836, dau. Moses and Martha Griggs. Bookmaker.

Lillian, b. 12 Apr 1856, m. Feb 1881 Elisha McCollister.

Lucy, b. 8 Jun 1859, d. Nov 1872.

Frank E., b. 21 Oct 1865 Auburn ME, m. 17 Mar 1883 Lillian Tuttle, b. ?.

Elizabeth Woodman, b. 2 Dec 1866.

Sources: Auburn ME census 1860. VR Auburn ME, SA/ME, SA/MA. L29.

495. **JOSHUA FOLLANSBY⁸ SAWYER** [see 322], b. 1 Feb 1830 Minot ME, d. 5 Mar 1919 Minot ME, m. 7 Nov 1853 Abby Childs of Livermore ME, b. Jan 1829 d. 3 Jan 1911, dau. Abiza and Polly (Marston) Childs.

Eliza Hackett, b. 27 Dec 1854. Teacher.

599 Crosby Stuart⁹, b. 1857.

600 Claude Wilson⁹, b. 1866.

Sources: VR SA/ME. L29

496. **SETH CHANDLER⁸ SAWYER** [see 322], b. 15 Jul 1833 Minot ME, m. 28 Jan 1869 Meriel White of Randolph MA, b. ?. Post cutter. In Holbrook MA.

Annie, b. Aug 1869. Note: VR SA/MA says she was b. 5 Aug 1867.

Thomas White, b. 31 May 1870 Holbrook MA, m. 30 Nov 1870 Quincy MA Lillian A. Robinson of New York, b. ?, dau. Matthew and Marcilia Robinson.

Sources: VR SA/MA. L29.

497. **GEORGE FRANKLIN⁸ SAWYER** [see 322], b. 27 Jan 1840 Minot ME, m. Apr 1874 Mary Thompson, b. ?. Teacher. Civil War. Went to New York.

Harold Paine, b. Nov 1880 Minot ME.

Sources: L29.

498. **DANIEL LONG⁸ SAWYER** [see 323], b. 27 Jun 1837 Haverhill MA, d. 22 Jun 1878 Haverhill MA, m.(1) 9 Jan 1858 Groveland MA Helen F. Perry of Exeter NH, b. 1841 d. Aug 1858; m.(2) 14 Aug 1862 Groveland MA Harriet Colby Sawyerof Hampstead NH, b. 10 Apr 1837 d. 2 Apr 1886, dau. Francis and Phebe (Little) Sawyer of Portsmouth NH. Jeweler. Civil War. In Groveland MA 1855.

Helen Marie, b. 6 Jun 1863.

Anne E., b. 12 Jul 1865, d. 22 Aug 1873.

601 Frank Henry⁹, 1868-1910.

Mary Little, b. 28 Aug 1870, m. George W. Chase.

Frederick Olin, b. 4 Feb 1878 Haverhill MA. In Hampstead NH 1880.
Sources: VR Haverhill MA, Hampstead NH, SA/MA. L29, P59, H32, M39.

499. **WILLIAM F.[8] SAWYER** [see 325], b. 20 Dec 1860 Moretown VT, m. 6 Sep 1893 Cornelia H. Sawyer of New York, b. Jun 1874. Farmer.
Thomas Manning, adopted, b. Nov 1885.
Jessie, b. May 1895.
Grace Ione, b. 20 Nov 1903.
George Philip, b. 23 Oct 1906, m. Ruth C. _____, b. ?.
William Chester, b. 9 Jan 1908.
Sources: VR Moretown VT.

500. **GEORGE ALVAH[8] SAWYER** [see 328], b. 22 Oct 1840 Bath NH, d. 25 Sep 1911 Holden MA, m. 21 Nov 1861 Betsey Merrill McKean of Landaff NH, b. 27 Jul 1841 d. 5 Apr 1915. Lumber dealer.
Harry W., b. ca. 1864 Bath NH.
Susan G., b. 13 Apr 1872, m. 4 Jun 1890 Worcester MA George A. Ward.
Son, stillborn 29 Nov 1874.
Mabel, b. 17 Jun 1878.
Sources: Bath NH census 1850, 1860, 1870. M17.

501. **WILLIAM HENRY[8] SAWYER** [see 328], b. 8 Aug 1843 Bath NH, d. 30 Jul 1926 Worcester MA, m.(1) 4 Jan 1870 Woodstock CT Sylvania T. Child of Bath NH, b. 8 Sep 1841 d. 25 Sep 1872, dau. Lewis and Betsey Child; m.(2) 6 May 1874 Worcester MA Frances Anne Weld of Brooklyn CT, b. 13 Jul 1844 d. 26 Nov 1919; m.(3) (later div.) Marie L. Everett, b. ?. Lumber business. Alderman, Worcester MA 1888-1889.
Gertrude May, b. 13 Feb 1871, d. 29 Jan 1872.
Alice L., b. 30 Nov 1875, m. Ralph L. Morgan of Worcester MA.
Gertrude May, b. ?, m. Charles L. Morse of Worcester MA.
Anna Weld, b. 12 Sep 1877.
Helen J., b. 8 Oct 1879, m. Frank L. Lisle of Providence RI.
Lottie M., b. 3 Sep 1883.
602 William Henry[9], 1886-1945.
Sources: VR Woodstock CT, SA/MA. N9, Obit, John W. Sawyer rec

502. **CHARLES WESLEY[8] SAWYER**. [see 328], b. 4 Apr 1864 Bath NH, d. Concord NH, m. (1) 27 Feb 1884 Benton NH Luvie E. Marston of Benton NH, b. 3 Apr 1863 d. 11 Apr 1914, dau. Bartlett and Anna (Brown) Marston; m.(2) 21 Oct 1918 Concord NH Jenie M. Roby of Haverhill MA, b. 1861, dau. Nathan and Cordelia (Carr) Archer. Carpenter. In Bath NH 1884, Woodsville NH, Concord NH 1912.
Ethel G., b. 17 Jul 1884, m. James W. Spinney.
Eva M., b. 19 Nov 1887, m. 29 Jun 1913 Earl C. Whittier of Concord NH.
Earl Wesley, b. 24 Jan 1897 Haverhill NH, d. 24 Oct 1933 Dover NH. In Woodsville NH, Concord NH, Exeter NH.
Sources: VR SA/NH. W37, W36.

503. **JOSHUA W.[8] SAWYER** .[see 329], b. 1849 Rumney NH, m. 8 Dec 1874 Bath NH Mary H. Sawyer of Bath NH, b. 10 Aug 1848, dau. Hiram Dow and Joanna Sawyer. Carpenter.
Frank H., b. 11 May 1878 Worcester MA.
Bertha M., b. 6 Jul 1882.

Sources: VR SA/MA. N6.

504. **CLIFFORD JOHN[8] SAWYER** [see 330], b. 19 Sep 1861 Newbury VT, d. 26 Aug 1916 No. Haverhill NH, m.(1) 5 Sep 1888 Newbury VT Carrie B. Clark of Haverhill NH, b. 13 Jan 1868 d. 15 Dec 1910, dau. James B. and Drusilla (Bisbee) Clark; m.(2) 19 Sep 1911 Littleton NH Abbie L. (McCluer) Whiting of Amherst NH, b. 1862, dau. George A. and Lucy A. (Melendy) McCluer. In Center Haverhill NH. Note: (a) His b. is recorded in Ryegate VT; (b) his d. record says he was b. in Cabot VT.

Edna May, b. 29 May 1889, d. 3 Sep 1891.

James Noah, b. 24 Oct 1895 No. Haverhill NH, d. 19 Mar 1958, m. 27 Jun 1918 Mabel Weston, b. ?.

603 Everett Fowler[9], 1897-1944.

Sources: VR SA/NH. B69, W36, Merrill C. Sawyer rec.

505. **JOHN ANDREW J.[8] SAWYER** .[see 332], b. 20 Jul 1834 Amesbury MA, m.(1) 1855 Newburyport MA Adeline Locke of Seabrook NH, b. ?, dau. Herbert and Jane Locke; m.(2) 23 Nov 1864 Lynn MA Maud Gould of Prince Edward Island, Canada, b. 1844, dau. John and Charlotte Gould; m.(3) 16 Jun 1870 Boston MA Marcie F. Smalley of Falmouth MA, b. 1844, dau. Reuben and Marcia Smalley; m.(4) 13 Apr 1895 Lynn MA Emily F. Fish of Sandwich MA, b. 1839, dau. Isaiah and Caroline Fish. Blacksmith. In Amesbury MA 1850.

Jennie R. A., b. 11 Jul 1856, m. 31 Dec 1874 Lynn MA Richard Jacques.

Herbert Leonard, b. 10 Jul 1858 Lynn MA, m. 16 Nov 1884 Lynn MA Maggie S. Whittaker of New Brunswick, Canada, b. 1860, dau. Henry and Agnes Whittaker.

Frances Leona, b. 8 Apr 1862. So dated in VR.

Addie Marie, b. 10 Apr 1862. So dated in VR.

Emma Frances, b. 6 Apr 1863.

Sources: Amesbury MA census 1850. VR SA/MA.

506. **EPHRIAM ALVAH[8] SAWYER** [see 332], b. 1 Sep 1842 Amesbury MA, m.(1) 18 Jun 1863 Lynn MA Abbie M. Foss of Amesbury MA, b. 1842, dau. Isaac and Ann Foss; m. (2) 3 May 1873 Amesbury MA Annie E. Goodwin, b. 1842, dau. Willoughby and Margery Goodwin. Blacksmith. In Amesbury MA, Salisbury MA.

604 Fred Morse[9], b. 1863.

605 Burton Augustus[9], b. 1867.

Nellie Warren, b. 31 Aug 1871.

Sources: VR Amesbury MA, SA/MA.

507. **ADDISON A.[8] SAWYER** [see 336], b. 23 Aug 1834 Amesbury MA, m. 4 Sep 1859 Salisbury MA Adeline A. Brown of Salisbury MA, b. ?, dau. Enos and Nancy Brown. Trader.

Howard Brown, b. 27 Apr 1860 Amesbury MA.

Mary R., b. 20 Feb 1862.

Clara Allen, b. 9 Jan 1864.

Sources: VR Amesbury MA, SA/MA.

508. **ELMER WARREN[8] SAWYER** [see 339], b. 5 Oct 1854 Amesbury MA, m. Sarah M. Barlow of Exeter NH, b. ?.

John Elmer, b. 14 Oct 1880 Merrimac MA.

Sources: VR Amesbury MA, SA/MA.

509. **GEORGE S.[8] SAWYER** [see 340], b. 14 Apr 1869 Campton NH, d. 17 Mar 1927 Campton NH, m. 13 Oct 1897 Emma G. Clark of Wellington, Prince Edward Island, Canada, b. 12 Mar 1879 d. 30 Aug 1929, dau. Joseph and Isabelle (McHart) Clark. Farmer. In Thornton NH, Center Sandwich NH.

Charles Ephriam, b. 26 Mar 1899, d. 22 Jun 1900.
Raymond, b. 9 Oct 1900, d. 22 May 1901 Center Sandwich NH.
Elroy J., b. 1903 Sandwich NH, d. 1985, m. 22 Mar 1930 Barbara M. Broad of Thornton NH. Farmer.
Ruth, b. 1904, d. 1967, m. 15 Mar 1922 Alexander McDonald.
Isabelle, b. 1906, d. 26 May 1983, m. James McIsaac.
Medeline, b. ?, m. Maurice Avery of Plymouth NH.
Everett G., b. 8 Jul 1912, d. 12 Dec 1989, unm. In Thornton NH.

Sources: VR SA/NH. Obit (Everett), N13, Leonard S. Sawyer rec.

510. **DANFORD LUCIEN[8] SAWYER** [see 341], b. 27 Mar 1875 Woodstock NH, d. 30 Oct 1908 Candia NH, m. 1 Jun 1904 Hooksett NH Cora D. Lantry of Hooksett NH, b. 1884, dau. Richard A. and Maria H. (Durgin) Lantry. In Woodstock NH, Hooksett NH, Manchester NH. Note: His d. record says his name was Daniel L.

Ruth, b. 3 Feb 1905, d. 12 Aug 1935, m. Atherton Frost.
Danford Lucien, b. 20 Jul 1907, m. Ida _____. CH: Danford Lucien, m. Ruth Ann _____; Susan.

Sources: Leonard S. Sawyer rec.

511. **VINCENT ISAAC[8] SAWYER** [see 341], b. 31 Oct 1881 Woodstock NH, d. 9 Feb 1950 Woodstock NH, m. 21 Nov 1906 Woodstock NH Pauline A. Brown of Thornton NH, b. 22 May 1888 d. 7 Aug 1971, dau. George H. and Roana (Pollard) Brown. Highway supervisor.

Daughter, stillborn 27 Sep 1907.
Lloyd Vincent, b. 17 Nov 1908 Woodstock NH, m. 19 Oct 1932 Portsmouth NH Margaret W. Durgin of St. Johnsbury VT, b. 12 Feb 1912, dau. John and Elinor (Collins) Durgin. State highway engineer. In Concord NH. CH: Lloyd Vincent, b. 4 Apr 1937 Concord NH, m. 6 Feb 1965 Judith (Harper) Eastburn; Wendell Dean, b. 23 May 1940, m. 13 Feb 1971 Barbara Howlett Thomas; Roanne, b. 10 Oct 1941, m. 4 Feb 1961 Edward H. Sanborn; Mark Betts, b. 2 Dec 1951, m. 1 Jun 1985 Linda DuCharme.
Helen Annie, b. 26 Sep 1910, m. 26 Sep 1930 Robert Ricker.
Ethel Cora, b. 10 Jun 1912, m. 1 Sep 1936 Malcolm Darling.
Stanley Edward, stillborn 25 Nov 1922.

Sources: VR SA/NH. Lloyd V. Sawyer rec.

512. **HOWARD SYMMES[8] SAWYER** [see 341], b. 21 Aug 1890 Woodstock NH, d. 12 Mar 1959, m. 14 Jun 1923 Rose Veronica Eagan of Malden MA, b. 1 Jan 1889 d. 29 May 1967. Railroad clerk, state highway employee.

Leonard Sylvester, b. 14 Jun 1925, m. 7 Sep 1960 Caroline Eldora Smith of New Hampton NH. Lawyer. In Plymouth NH. CH: Edward Mark, b. 11 Jul 1969; Charles Leonard, b. 28 Jun 1970.

Sources: Leonard S. Sawyer rec.

513. **FRANK ALMUS[8] SAWYER** [see 342], b. 7 Sep 1890 Woodstock NH, d. 26 Dec 1944, m.(1) 5 Oct 1911 West Boylston MA (div. 30 Jun 1922) Hope R. _____, b. ?; m.(2) Rose M. (Bates) Vigneau, b. ?. In Wells River VT.

Edward F., b. 19 Jul 1924 Woodsville VT, d. 1976 California, m. Rita Rosenthal. CH: Pamela Rose, b. 1958; Stephen, b. 1962.
Doris Marie, b. 18 Aug 1927, m. 1955 Robert Tumulty.
Barbara A., b. 10 Nov 1932, m. 11 Oct 1952 William Emery.
Sources: VR SA/NH. Leonard S. Sawyer rec., Barbara Emery rec.

514. **ARTHUR W.$^8$ SAWYER** [see 344], b. 1879 Woodstock NH, m.(1) 19 May 1907 Portsmouth RI Elenor A. Chase of Prudence Island RI, b. ?., dau. Eugene and Elizabeth (Alderson) Chase; m.(2) 1 Jul 1914 Lisbon NH Anne E. Lewis of Plymouth MA, b, ?, dau. Arthur E. and Anne E. (Churchill) Lewis; m.(3) 15 Jun 1921 Littleton NH Charlotte Henderson of Newbury VT, b. 24 Jul 1898 d. 27 Oct 1982, dau. Joseph E. and Olga (Wilson) Henderson. Postmaster.
Arthur W., b. ?.
Elizabeth S., b. ?, m. _____ Gibson.
Sources: VR SA/NH.

515. **THOMAS FENNO$^8$ SAWYER** [see 346], b. 19 Jul 1879 Woodstock NH, d. 27 Jul 1971, m. 8 Oct 1902 Woodstock NH Alice M. Peaslee of Thornton NH, b. 1880 d. 14 Jul 1936, dau. Benjamin L. and Mary R. (Sellingham) Peaslee.
Raymond B., b. 1903 Woodstock NH, d. 1 Jul 1962 Woodstock NH, m. 14 May 1927 Thornton NH Elizabeth E. Kendall of Woodstock NH, b. 1907, dau. Jessie A. and Mabel R. (Willey) Kendall. Note: Elizabeth was a great-grandchild of Walter Harris$^6$ Sawyer [see 174]. CH: Derek P.; Harold R., b. 4 Jun 1929; Gerald B., b. 9 Nov 1932, d. 1985, m. 26 Dec 1951 (later div.) Arlene Foley.
Verne, b. ?.
Clara, b. ?.
Sources: VR SA/NH. Leonard S. Sawyer rec.

516. **JOSEPH R.$^8$ SAWYER** [see 346], b. 3 Nov 1881 Woodstock NH, d. 13 May 1974, m. Annie Willey, b. ?.
Clara, b. 1910, m. 6 Dec 1927 Nelson Haynes.
James, b. 1916, d. 6 Dec 1959, m. 28 Oct 1938 Marion Champagne. In Lincoln NH. CH: Joseph, b. 13 Jul 1939.
Albert W., b. 4 Feb 1925, d. 23 Oct 1943.
Sources: Leonard S. Sawyer rec.

517. **ALMON$^8$ SAWYER** [see 347], b. 4 Oct 1895 Woodstock NH, d. 4 May 1943, m. Jennie Haley, b. ?.
Arlene, b. 8 Mar 1919.
Alice.
Marguerita.
Alfred Paul.
Leroy.
Sources: Leonard S. Sawyer rec.

518. **IVORY C.$^8$ SAWYER** [see 349], b. 30 Nov 1825 Brookfield NH, d. 29 Jun 1898 Humbolt County CA, m. 3 Sep 1848 Stetson ME Caroline Higgins Wing of Levant ME, b. 15 Apr 1833 d. 8 Dec 1917, dau. William and Abigail (Higgins) Wing. Ivory left wife and CH in 1868 and went to California; Caroline div. him in 1874 and m. 27 Nov 1875 Andrew J. Marston.
Matilda Jane, b. 16 Oct 1849, d. 6 Jun 1930, m. 23 Jul 1865 Fred Jewett of Minnesota.
606 Asa Samuel$^9$, 1854-1931.

607 Orrin$^{9}$, 1856-1938.
Frank L., b. 2 Dec 1861, d. 17 Jul 1902 in mine accident, Washington State.
Sources: VR Bangor ME, SA/ME. Lawrence A. Sawyer rec.

519. **FREEMAN C.$^{8}$ SAWYER** [see 349], b. ca. 1832 Hermon ME, m.(1) 28 May 1854 Bangor ME Mary J. Austin of Bangor ME, b. ?; m.(2) Serena Banks, b. ?.
608 Charles Elmon$^{9}$, 1862-1917.
Sources: VR Bangor ME, SA/ME.

520. **ALBERT$^{8}$ SAWYER** [see 350], b. Dec 1846 Cambridge ME, d. 1927 Ripley ME, m. California Irena T. Smith, b. Nov 1853 d. 18 Mar 1902, dau. Erasmus and Elizabeth Smith. In Ripley ME 1880. He bur. in W. Ripley ME.
William A., b. ca. 1873 Ripley ME.
Georgie B., b. ca. 1878, m. ______ Brackett.
Elizabeth A., b. ca. 1879, m.(1) _____ Todd, m.(2) _____ Clark.
609 Othniel L.$^{9}$, 1881-1944.
Fannie M., b. Feb 1883, m. _____ Hemenway.
Albert E., b. Apr 1885 Ripley ME, m. Annie Stafford, b. ?.
Nellie B., b. May 1890, m. Edward Hight.
Edward, b. 25 Sep 1893.
Maurice C., b. 8 Feb 1896 Ripley ME, m. Mazie Dyer, b. ?.
Sources: Ripley ME census 1880. VR SA/ME. Bessie Folsom rec.

521. **SAMUEL$^{8}$ SAWYER** [see 350], b. Jun 1857 Cambridge ME, m. Nancy Anne Watson of Parkman ME, b. Jun 1865.
Bessie Edna, b. Mar 1886, m. 22 Oct 1904 Thomas W. Folsom.
Bertha L., b. Jul 1887, m. _____ Jewell.
Henry Clair, b. May 1889 Cambridge ME, m. Olive Harrington, b. ?.
Harold Leigh, b. 2 Jul 1892 Cambridge ME, m. Olive Holt, b. ?.
Ferne Christiana, b. 16 Mar 1896, m. _____ Kenny.
Daughter, stillborn 21 Sep 1898.
Margarite, b. ?, m. _____ Carter.
Sources: VR SA/ME. F23, Bessie Folsom rec.

522. **ASA CHAPMAN$^{8}$ SAWYER** [see 353], b. 28 Sep 1849 Danvers MA, d. 11 Jan 1926 Peabody MA, m. 25 May 1876 Marblehead MA Ellen Donahue of Ireland, b. 31 Dec 1854 d. 28 May 1925, dau. David and Mary Donahue. Butcher.
Florence C., b. 26 Jun 1876.
610 Thomas Hadley$^{9}$, 1878-1939.
611 Harry Arthur$^{9}$, 1880-1951.
Sources: VR SA/MA. Paul B. Sawyer rec.

523. **CALEB$^{8}$ SAWYER** [see 354], b. 3 Oct 1842 Salem MA, m. 13 Jun 1867 Salem MA Sarah D. Smith of Nova Scotia, Canada, b. 1845, dau. Josiah and Eliza Smith. Painter.
Mary Eliza, b. 26 Jun 1868.
Son, b. 7 Sep 1870.
Arthur, b. 6 Nov 1873 Salem MA.
Son, b. 11 Apr 1876.
Sources: VR Salem MA, SA/MA.

524. **WILLIAM HENRY⁸ SAWYER** [see 354], b. 27 Oct 1850 Salem MA, m. 19 Jan 1883 Peabody MA Sarah Butler of England, b. 1859. Carpenter.

Clarence, b. 5 Jul 1887 Salem MA.

Sources: VR SA/MA.

525. **HERBERT B.[8] SAWYER** [see 355], b. 6 May 1872 Litchfield ME, d. 1 Jun 1921 Augusta ME, m. Louise Estelle Hunt of Augusta ME, b. 1874. Real estate.

Herbert Hunt, b. 1904 Gardiner ME, m. 30 May 1933 Portsmouth NH Leona W. Martin of Hebron ME, b. 1907, dau. Henry and Mabel Whitman. Construction engineer. In Portland ME.

Sources: VR SA/ME.

526. **CHRISTOPHER B.[8] SAWYER** [see 359], b. 9 Jul 1824 Wells ME, m. 6 Sep 1846 Eliza Jane Perkins of York ME, b. 1826, dau. Moses and Elsie (Sawyer) Perkins. Sea captain.

612 Samuel B.[9], 1847-1927.

Christopher B., b. 1850, d. 1851.

Sources: Wells ME census 1850. VR SA/MA. P32.

527. **THOMAS BOOTHBY[8] SAWYER** [see 361], b. 4 Apr 1825 Porter ME, d. 23 May 1885 Cornish ME, m.(1) 10 May 1846 Lydia Mason, b. 3 Sep 1829 d. 21 Apr 1910; m.(2) Francina L. Sawyer of Limerick ME, b. 15 Mar 1839 d. 1916, dau. James B. and Desire (Cobb) Sawyer. Farmer. Wid. m. 24 Aug 1886 Conway NH John Bradeen. Note: 1880 census says Thomas and Francina were div.

Hannah J., b. 1847.

John R., b. 9 May 1852 Porter ME, d. 12 Oct 1863.

613 Martin R.[9], b. 1854.

Joseph S., b. 1855 Porter ME, d. 1887.

Ruth E., b. 1859, d. 6 Dec 1863. Bur. in Stanley Cem., Hebron ME.

614 Wilbur Thomas[9], b. 1861.

Sources: Porter ME census 1850, 1860, 1870, 1880. VR Porter ME. N6, R10c, F34, P66, C53.

528. **ISAAC B.[8] SAWYER** [see 361], b. 1829 Porter ME, d. 14 Mar 1904 Porter ME, m. 16 May 1854 Saco ME Olive Willard of Porter ME, b. ca. 1832 d. 9 Aug 1905. In Wolfeboro NH 1860. Blacksmith. Civil War: Company D, 6th NH Volunteers, 26 Oct 1861 - 17 Feb 1863. He bur. in Stanley Cem., Hiram ME.

Jannie J., b. 1857.

615 George F.[9], 1859-1908.

Charles, b. 1862 Wolfeboro NH, d. 25 Sep 1902 Porter ME, m. 15 Oct 1889 Conway NH Edna J. Green of Providence RI, b. 1868 d. 25 Jan 1890. In Porter ME 1870, 1880.

Horace C., b. 22 Feb 1865 Wolfeboro NH, d. 30 Aug 1943 Kezar Falls ME, m. 24 Dec 1885 Porter ME Nellie Stanley of Hiram ME, b. 25 Mar 1866 d. 16 Jan 1942. B/land in Bethel ME 1870. S/land in Bethel ME 1873.

Jason H., b. 1871 Porter ME.

Sources: Wolfeboro NH census 1860. Porter ME census 1870, 1880. VR Porter ME. T7, P8, M5, Will.

529. **GEORGE WASHINGTON[8] SAWYER** [see 361], b. 22 Oct 1837 Porter ME, d. 15 Jun 1913 Tuftonboro NH, m.(1) 1 May 1864 Christie C. Cate of Brookfield NH, b. 2 Jun 1842 d. 14 Jun 1908, dau. William T. and Betsey Cate; m.(2) 8 May 1913 Tuftonboro NH Nellie V. Moore of

Marblehead MA, wid., b. 1857, dau. John and Sarah (Wilford) Shattuck. In Tuftonboro NH 1880. Bur. in Beverly MA.

Martin Herbert, b. 3 Nov 1867 Tuftonboro NH, d. 20 Sep 1940, m. Nellie Moore, b. ?

Abbie, b. ?, unm.

Katie Marion, b. 27 Nov 1874, d. 3 Nov 1952, m.(1) 11 Jun 1894 Charles Hoyt, m.(2) Frank Stilling.

616 William Lemuel[9], 1876-1953.

Mary A., b. 1880.

Sources: Tuftonboro NH census 1880. VR SA/NH. P8, N6, Louise McDuffee rec.

530. **WILLIAM HENRY[8] SAWYER** [see 363], b. 5 Nov 1831 Limerick ME, d. 25 Apr 1908 Kennebunkport ME, m. 23 Nov 1859 Kennebunkport ME Eunice R. Brackett of So. Berwick ME, b. 21 Feb 1833 d. 23 Nov 1895, dau. Humphrey and Joanna Brackett. Physician. In Limerick ME 1860, Kennebunkport ME 1880. Both bur. Woodlawn Cem., Biddeford ME.

Mary C., b. 7 Nov 1863, d. 16 Jan 1871.

Charles P., b. 1865 Limerick ME, d. 1944, m. 10 Oct 1889 Chelsea MA Alice Thurkill of Canada, b. 1867 d. 1937, dau. William K. and Mary S. Thurkill. In Everett MA. Both bur. Woodlawn Cem., Biddeford ME.

Annie L., b. 17 Feb 1872, d. 1 Apr 1891.

William Brackett, b. 9 Jun 1873 Kennebunkport ME, m. 20 Apr 1894 Boston MA Belle Walker Jeffrey of Kennebunkport ME, b. ca. 1875, dau. Joseph W. and Louise Jeffrey. Jeweler. In Everett MA 1894. CH: Louise, b. 28 Apr 1894, m. _____ Smith; Elizabeth, b. ?, m. _____ Arms; Joseph Warren, b. Sep 1908, d. 25 Feb 1909.

Sources: Limerick ME census 1860, 1880. VR Kennebunkport ME, SA/ME, SA/MA. P82k.

531. **BENJAMIN FRANKLIN[8] SAWYER** [see 363], b. 19 Jan 1835 Limington ME, d. 10 Nov 1900 Wolfeboro NH, m. 18 Jan 1873 Limerick ME (1st cousin) [see 361] Louisa Sawyer of Porter ME, b. 27 Feb 1840 d. 21 Jan 1924, dau. Lemuel B. and Mary (Berry) Sawyer. In Limerick ME 1850, Wolfeboro NH 1890. He bur. in Lakeview Cem., Sanbornville NH.

Mary A., b. 30 Nov 1873, d. 3 Oct 1933, m. 6 May 1897 Walter Coppen.

617 Eugene Allen[9], 1875-1934.

Arthur Henry, b. 9 Dec 1877 Limerick ME, d. 1961, m. 1 Jun 1909 Clara Young, b. 1884 d. 1968. In Wolfeboro NH.

Sources: Limerick ME census 1850. ME 1880 census index. Wolfeboro NH census 1890. N9, N6, Robert L. Taylor rec.

532. **OSWALD (OSRO) JACOB[8] SAWYER** [see 364], b. 16 May 1852 Limington ME, d. 26 Aug 1930 Westbrook ME, m. ca. 1882 Emma M. Butler of Fort Fairfield ME, b. 1857 d. 1918. Laborer. In Limerick ME, Sebago Lake ME, Caribou ME, Standish ME. He bur. Sanbornville NH.

Agnes, b. May 1882, m. 4 Sep 1896 Ossipee NH Winthrop H. Shaw.

Rosie E., b. Apr 1886, m. Charles Sprague of Newfield ME.

Florence M., b. 1 Aug 1887, d. 12 Feb 1967, m. Albert C. Sanborn.

Harry L., b. 3 Oct 1889 Limerick ME, m. 29 Nov 1947 E. Rochester NH Gladys M. Morton of Bridgton ME, b. 1896, dau. Granville and Ida (Plummer) Green, her 2nd m. after a div. In Sebago Lake ME.

Reuben, b. 29 Dec 1892, d. 21 Dec 1966. Went to Texas.

Son, b. 20 Jun 1894.

Sources: VR SA/ME. M8, Robert L. Taylor rec.

533. **CLIFFORD LEROY$^8$ SAWYER** [see 364], b. 23 Mar 1876 Maysville ME, d. 4 Jan 1936 Farmington NH, m.(1) 3 Dec 1907 Limerick ME (div. 1928) Lucy Burnham Hoyt, b. Mar 1891 d. Feb 1967, dau. Charles L. and Alta E. (Chapman) Hoyt; m.(2) 10 Nov 1934 Farmington NH Minnie Charles Gilpatrick, b. 21 Mar 1881 d. 27 Dec 1963, dau. Oris and Emily J. (Sawyer) Gilpatrick. In Limerick ME, No. Conway NH, Farmington NH.

Clifford Leroy, b. 17 Aug 1908 d. 19 Oct 1976, m. Gladys I. Luce.

Forest Ellsworth, b. 15 Nov 1909 d. 13 Apr 1912 in fire, Limerick ME.

Sources: VR SA/NH. Clifford L. Sawyer rec.

534. **AUTIEN W. S.$^8$ SAWYER** [see 365], b. 20 May 1849 Limerick ME, d. 20 Jun 1918 Limerick ME, m. 25 Sep 1870 Boston MA Mary (Nellie) E. Dorsey of Roxbury MA, b. 10 Oct 1851 d. 13 Mar 1931, dau. Thomas and Margaret Dorsey. Plumber. In Limerick ME 1880. He bur. in Limerick Village Cem., Limerick ME.

Isaac H., b. 22 Sep 1871 Limerick ME d. 24 Jul 1917 Limerick ME, m. Georgia G. Stimson, b. 1877 d. 1956. Electrician. Both bur. Highland Cem. Limerick ME. CH: Henry Autien, b. 1903; Daniel Stimson, b. 1904, d. 1906; John Herbert, b. 1910.

Lulu N., b. 1 Jul 1875, d. 3 Nov 1934, m. Ebenezer Cobb.

Winfield Herbert, b. 13 Jan 1879 Limerick ME, d. 2 Jan 1970.

Sources: ME 1880 census index. VR SA/ME, SA/MA. M5, Marjory Perkins rec.

535. **WALTER EDGECOMB$^8$ SAWYER** [see 365], b. 20 Jun 1854 Limerick ME, m.(I) 19 Apr 1883 Lucy J. Roberts of Nova Scotia, Canada, b. 21 Sep 1844 d. 2 May 1929, div. from Walter's brother Francis A.. Clerk.

618 William Walter$^9$, b. 1885. Went to Pennsylvania.

Imogene Grover, b. 19 Sep 1887 d. 1965, m. 26 Nov 1906 David E. Parmenter.

Ethel, b. 28 Sep 1890, m. 20 Oct 1915 Llewellyn Cain. Went to California.

Isobel, b. 12 May 1894, m. 7 Mar 1910 Lawrence F. Stacy of Kezar Falls ME.

Sources: VR Cornish ME, SA/ME. P82k, T6, W42, E13.

536. **DANIEL$^8$ SAWYER** [see 366], b. 13 Jul 1835 Plymouth NH, d. 21 Jun 1889 Medford MA, m. 1865 Ellen A. Boothbay of Benton NH, b. ?. Machinist.

Edwin Webster, b. 6 Oct 1868 Dedham MA.

Louis W., b. ca. 1872 Hyde Park MA, m. 16 Nov 1891 Hyde Park MA Clara A. Barron, b. ca. 1872, dau. William and Eliza Barron.

Sources: VR SA/MA.

537. **SAMUEL AUGUSTUS$^8$ SAWYER** [see 367], b. 12 Mar 1830 Plymouth NH, d. 18 Sep 1897 Nashua NH, m. 16 May 1851 Mary N. Knapp of Sugar Hill NH, b. Sep 1829 d. 19 Jul 1913, dau. James and Rhoda (Howland) Knapp.

Mary E., b. ca. 1855, m. 26 Sep 1876 Nashua NH George B. Wood.

Minna, b. ca. 1856.

Jessie B., b. ca. 1858, m. 17 Nov 1881 Nashua NH Walter M. Libbey.

Samuel H., b. ca. 1869 Nashua NH.

Sources: Nashua NH census 1860, 1870. VR SA/NH. N6.

538. **KENDRICK DANA$^8$ SAWYER** [see 368], b. 25 May 1848 New Hampton NH, d. 8 Jun 1921 Laconia NH, m.(1) 29 Nov 1871 New Hampton NH Annie McNalley of Canada, b. 8 Dec 1852 d. 19 May 1884; m.(2) 12 Oct 1887 New Hampton NH Carrie H. Read of Attleboro MA, b. 1860. Machinist. In Gilford NH, Lake Village NH, Somerville MA, Laconia NH 1903.

Rockwell K., b. 9 Aug 1883, d. 17 Nov 1883.

619 Edmund Read[9], b. 1889.
Sources: VR SA/NH. Margaret Sawyer rec.

539. **ELBRIDGE GERRY[8] SAWYER** [see 369], b. 4 Jan 1854 No. Hampton NH, d. 26 Jan 1921 Hanover NH, m.(1) 24 Oct 1880 Thornton NH Alice Tourtelotte of Maxfield ME, b. 4 Jun 1865 d. 13 Feb 1915, dau. Orrin A. and Almeda (Emery) Tourtelotte; m.(2) 21 Sep 1915 Plymouth NH (div. 1916) Mary (Liesenfield) Sawyer of Boston MA, b. 3 Aug 1861 d. 29 Aug 1929, wid. of Elbridge's brother Leroy, dau. Anton and Lena (Korcher) Liesenfield of Germany. Lumber business. In Woodstock NH, Campton NH.
620 Leon Leroy[9], 1883-1910.
Anna S., stillborn 5 Dec 1885.
621 Omar Eugene[9], 1886-1925.
L. Roy, b. 30 Dec 1892 Plymouth NH, m. 22 Feb 1919 Lebanon NH Mabel Ammel of Hanover NH, b. 1892, dau. Edward and Effie (Labbie) Ammel, both of Canada. Railroad employee.
Daughter, b. 12 Feb 1896.
Sources: VR SA/NH. S81.

540. **LEROY ALFRED[8] SAWYER** [see 369], b. 27 Nov 1861 New Hampton NH, d. 20 Jan 1905 Plymouth NH, m. 19 Apr 1893 Plymouth NH Mary Liesenfield of Boston MA, b. 3 Aug 1861 d. 29 Aug 1929, dau. Anton and Lena (Korcher) Liesenfield of Germany. Butcher. In Woodstock NH. Wid. m. brother-in-law Elbridge Gerry 21 Sep 1915.
Edith Emily, b. 24 Apr 1899, d. 28 Apr 1899.
Leroy Alfred, b. 29 Jun 1901 Woodstock NH, d. 1967, m. Ethel M. _____ of Barre VT, b. 1900 d. 1 Jan 1992. In Laconia NH.
Sources: VR SA/NH. Obit (Ethel).

541. **HENRY ABBOTT[8] SAWYER** [see 371], b. 1 Aug 1853 Weare NH, d. 21 Dec 1892 No. Weare NH, m. 29 May 1878 Weare NH Elizabeth A. Matthews of Henniker NH, b. 27 Apr 1858 d. 4 May 1935, dau. Joseph H. and Adeline H. (Adams) Matthews.
622 Moses Hugh[9], b. 1881.
Sources: VR SA/NH. B84.

542. **ALBERT HODGDON[8] SAWYER** [see 373], b. 26 Oct 1837 Portland ME, d. 12 Jul 1899 Weare NH, m. Mary Ellen Boynton of Weare NH, b. 19 Mar 1840 d. 17 Aug 1892, dau. David and Lydia (Favor) Boynton.
623 Albert Oliver[9], 1861-1946.
Sources: Weare NH census 1860, 1870. B73, W38, George Carter Sawyer rec.

543. **GRANVILLE PARKER[8] SAWYER** [see 374], b. 5 Jun 1836 Troy ME, d. 19 Feb 1900, m.(1) 25 Dec 1864 Biddeford ME Frances M. Haley of Hollis ME, b. 1840 d. 16 May 1873; m.(2) 1 Aug 1875 Hallowell ME Sarah L. Palmer of Plymouth ME, b. 6 Feb 1851 d. 21 Jun 1916, dau. John and Louise (Hodgdon) Palmer. Farmer. In Plymouth ME 1880.
Frank H., b. 1873, d. 1 Feb 1874 in Hollis ME.
Leona M., b. May 1876.
Harry A., b. Dec 1878 (Plymouth ME?).
Laura L., b. 3 Dec 1884.
Sources: Plymouth ME census 1880. VR Biddeford ME, Hallowell ME, SA/ME. M5.

544. **BYRON P.[8] SAWYER** [see 374], b. 1844 Troy ME, m. 9 Oct 1868 Worcester MA Mary Delight Parker, b. 12 Aug 1847, dau. Charles E. and Mary A. (Moore) Parker. Shoemaker.

Nellie Alice, b. 30 Aug 1869, d. 30 Jul 1870.
Edward Parker, b. 9 Nov 1870.
Mary Estelle, b. 27 Jun 1872.
Charles Arthur, b. 9 Oct 1876.
Ethel Lorena, b. 1 May 1881.

Sources: VR SA/MA. J21.

545. **THOMAS ELLWOOD[8] SAWYER** [see 382], b. 15 Mar 1886 Dover NH, m. 10 Jun 1912 Franklin NH Alexana A. Rayno of Franklin NH, b. 1891, dau. John and Margaret (Gayette) Rayno. In Franklin NH. Clerk.

Thomas Ellwood, b. 5 Mar 1916 Franklin NH, m. 16 Dec 1945 Sunapee NH Phyllis A. Morgan of New London NH, b. 1 May 1920. In Nashua NH. CH: William Morgan, b. 4 Oct 1946 Nashua NH, m. 11 Apr 1969 Nashua NH Nancy Amburg of Maine, b. 7 Aug 1947; Susan Marilyn, twin, b. 15 Jan 1950, m. 7 Aug 1976 Richard Jackson; Joan Elizabeth, twin, b. 15 Jan 1950, m. 14 Jul 1972 Jeffrey C. Pitman; James Richard, twin, b. 29 May 1951; Thomas Robert, twin, b. 29 May 1951, m. 17 Apr 1982 Cheryl Barrell.
Richard Edward, b. 5 Sep 1917, m. 21 Sep 1954 Verial MacKay. Went to California.

Sources: P82i, Thomas E. Sawyer rec.

546. **HOWARD MALCOLM[8] SAWYER** [see 389], b. 19 Feb 1834 Exeter NH, d. 7 Sep 1902 Medford MA, m. 27 Nov 1859 Newburyport MA Mary Haskell Pettingill of Newburyport MA, b. 7 Aug 1838, dau. William H. and Hannah (Johnson) Pettingill. Manufacturer of waterproof clothing. In E. Cambridge MA 1847, Chicago IL, Medford MA.

Mary Ella, b. 17 Sep 1860, m. 14 Sep 1899 William F. Macey of Medford MA.
624 Charles Howard[9], b. 1862.
Susan Sherriff, b. 21 Nov 1866, d. 30 May 1868.
William Miner, b. 12 Mar 1870, d. 12 Dec 1870.
625 Lawrence Taylor[9], b. 1875.
Sarah Annie, b. 20 Mar 1878, m. 14 Sep 1899 John W. Emery, Medford MA.
626 Ralph Underwood[9], b. 1880.

Sources: VR SA/MA. P37.

547. **EDWARD WARREN[8] SAWYER** [see 390], b. 18 Jul 1848 Exeter NH, d. 19 Jun 1897 Concord NH, m. Mary Elizabeth Manney, b. ?. Civil War. Harvard College 1873. Physician. In Pelham NH, Chicago IL.

Philip Ayer, b. ?. In Chicago IL. Artist.
Edward Warren, b. ?. In Chicago IL.

Sources: Pelham NH census 1860.

548. **EDWARD KENT[8] SAWYER** [see 397], b. 20 May 1880 Exeter NH, d. 12 Jul 1967 Brunswick ME, m. 1907 Emma C. Fottler, b. 21 Dec 1880 d. 9 Nov 1985, dau. Stephen and Margaret C. (Williams) Fottler. In Boston MA.

Enid M., b. 2 Apr 1910, d. 29 Oct 1976.
Lloyd C., b. 16 Feb 1914 Boston MA, m. 1 Jan 1938 Evelyn L. Cameron. In Portland ME. CH: Edward Lloyd, b. 9 Jan 1939, m. Sandra _____; Martha A., b. 24 Oct 1943, m. _____ Thurlow.

Sources: Lloyd C. Sawyer rec.

549. **ARTHUR BENJAMIN⁸ SAWYER** [see 400], b. 5 May 1877 Hampden ME, d. 11 Jun 1943, m. 11 Dec 1901 Blanche Goodell of Hampden ME, b. 22 Dec 1876. Farmer.

Ralph Noble, b. 9 Oct 1902 Hampden ME, d. 15 Oct 1967 Newington NH, m. 20 Feb 1937 Portsmouth NH Margaret L. Rowell of Hampden ME, b. 18 Jun 1897 d. 16 May 1985 Newington NH, dau. Leroy and Elsie (Dunton) Rowell. Carpenter. CH: Marie, b. 31 May 1939, m. 24 Mar 1961 Richard Rines of New Hampshire.

Clarence, b. ?. Went to Camp Hill PA.

Sources: Marie Rines rec.

550. **WILLIAM AUGUSTINE⁸ SAWYER** [see 402], b. 1 May 1884 Lowell MA, d. 10 May 1943 Boston MA, m. 18 Apr 1911 Lowell MA Elizabeth Gertrude Barryof Wareham MA, b. 24 Sep 1888 d. 2 Dec 1970 Quincy MA.

Anna Evelyn, b. 1 Dec 1912, m. 29 Apr 1934 John P. O'Malley.

John Joseph, m. Alice Magner. CH: John Joseph; Janet Marie.

Gertrude Elizabeth, m. Lawrence Daley.

Dorothy Mae, m. Francis Lamb.

William Francis. No CH.

Sources: Alice M. Sawyer rec.

551. **STEPHEN CALVIN⁸ SAWYER** [see 404], b. 7 Mar 1846 Plaistow NH, d. 28 Dec 1934 Kensington NH, m. 27 Feb 1873 Phebe Maria Blake of Kensington NH, b. 17 Jun 1847 d. 8 Sep 1921, dau. Colonel John T. and Elizabeth (Moulton) Blake. Farmer, shoemaker. In Kensington NH 1854. Sexton for 45 years.

627 Roland Douglas⁹, 1874-1969.

Wesley Stephen, b. 6 Jan 1880 Kensington NH, d. 5 Jun 1958, unm. Lawyer. Went to New York City. Note: Listed as Harry Steven in 1880 census.

Mary Elizabeth Moulton, b. 10 Apr 1882, d. 20 Apr 1931, m. 2 Nov 1913 Edward S. Kingsbury.

Sources: Kensington NH census 1880. VR SA/NH. B49, Nathalie S. Potts rec.

552. **WILLIAM HOWARD⁸ SAWYER** [see 405], b. 8 Jun 1858 Hill NH, d. 29 Nov 1924 Plaistow NH, m. 13 Dec 1883 Merrimac MA Mary Ward Drake of West Newbury MA, b. 27 Oct 1858 d. 17 Feb 1923, dau. Samuel and Abigail (Drake) Drake. Groceryman. In E. Haverhill MA. Note: His d. certificate says he was b. 6 Jun 1858.

Annie Pearl, b. 20 Mar 1886, m.(1) 8 Sep 1910 George A. Carpenter, m.(2) Harley F Kendall.

Harold Herbert, b. 8 Aug 1892, d. 30 Jun 1941, m.(1) 20 Oct 1914 Alice Blanchard, b. ?; m.(2) Louise Cunningham, b. ?; m.(3) 1 Apr 1933 Marjorie Good, b. ?. CH: Lois E., b. 4 Aug 1933. Note: Called Harold Hazeltine in VR SA/MA.

Sources: VR Plaistow NH, SA/MA, SA/NH. S18, T11, Mary H. Sawyer rec.

553. **ARTHUR WEARE⁸ SAWYER** [see 405], b. 4 Nov 1861 Hill NH, d. Jan 1954, m.(1) 19 Nov 1890 (later div.) Mary Haseltine of Plaistow NH, b. 1861 d. 1938; m.(2) Mollie _____, b. ?. Farmer.

Annie Elizabeth, b. 21 Mar 1891, d. 1974, m. 25 Dec 1911 Ralph Sherbert.

Carl Haseltine, b. 13 Jul 1892, d. 27 Feb 1916, unm.

628 Allen Weare⁹, 1895-1981.

629 Sewall Chase⁹, 1897-1972.

Clement Scribner, b. 13 Nov 1904, d. 29 Jan 1905.

Sources: VR SA/NH. S18, Mary (Haseltine) Sawyer rec.

554. **THOMAS WARREN[8] SAWYER** [see 406], b. 4 Mar 1873 Tilton NH, m. 13 Dec 1902 Nellie King of Philadelphia PA, b. 16 Feb 1878. Toolmaker. In Athol MA, Beverly MA, Goffstown NH 1908.

Gloria S., b. 19 Feb 1904, d. 9 Jan 1995, m. Robert H. Kelly.

Flavia, b. 3 Nov 1909.

Warren King, b. 11 Aug 1915 Goffstown NH, m. 24 Sep 1936 Portsmouth NH Eugenia Pennewart of Chelsea MA, b. 1914, dau. Richard and Rosine (Rogers) Pennewart. Carpenter.

Sources: H1.

555. **LUTHER JERE[8] SAWYER** [see 407], b. 5 Mar 1877 Andover NH, d. 31 Jan 1947 Chelsea MA, m. 12 Mar 1902 Franklin NH Florence Buchanan of Franklin Falls MA, b. 22 Oct 1877 d. 12 Jun 1949, dau. William W. and Emma (Butterworth) Buchanan. Spanish American War: Enl. 11 May 1898 Company H, 1st New Hampshire Regiment; discharged 31 Oct 1898. In Westborough MA, Lexington MA, Walpole MA.

Melba Bessie, b. 6 May 1903, d. 6 Oct 1950, m. 17 May 1924 Foxboro MA Harold W. Willis.

Gladys Eva, b. 25 Mar 1906, m.(1) 21 Jun 1931 Joseph Snow, m.(2) Walter Fuller.

Daisy Ellen, b. 6 Feb 1912, d. 24 Sep 1966, m. 12 Jul 1933 Gustav T. Winroth.

Richard Francis, b. 26 Aug 1914 Walpole MA, m. 8 Sep 1940 Ruth Boggs, b. 6 Oct 1912. CH: Jeanne Leslie, b. 23 Jul 1946, m. 10 Aug 1968 George Wool.

Sources: H88, Richard J. Sawyer rec., Calvin Winroth rec.

556. **GAYTON H.[8] SAWYER** [see 408], b. 16 Mar 1868 Philadelphia PA, m. 11 Oct 1887 Haverhill MA Carrie L. Glover of Exeter NH, b. 1866, dau. Albert and Abbie Glover. Railroad brakeman.

William Gayton, b. 27 Jan 1893 Haverhill MA.

Sources: VR Haverhill MA, SA/MA.

557. **LEON EUGENE[8] SAWYER** [see 409], b. 7 Feb 1876 Manchester NH, d. 5 May 1953 Wilmot NH, m. 24 Feb 1904 Manchester NH Bessie M. Bell of Nova Scotia, Canada, b. 31 May 1882 d. 30 Nov 1966, dau. Leyman and Sarah Bell.

Mildred Inez, b. 16 Dec 1904, d. 31 Mar 1995, m. 26 Jun 1926 Clarence F. Howard.

Leon Randolph, b. 15 Jun 1907 Manchester NH, d. 8 Oct 1973 Indianapolis IN, m. 29 Aug 1933 Clara M. Lippa, b. 7 Mar 1906. In Wilmot NH, Boise ID, Denver CO. CH: Eleanora May, b. 26 Feb 1935, m. 1954 Guillermo Guzman: Nancy Judith, b. 21 Aug 1936, m. 27 Apr 1957 John W. Lottes; Leon Eugene, b. 5 Jun 1938 Wilmot NH, d. 29 Jan 1976 Wilmot NH, m. 17 Mar 1961 (later div.) Marilyn Lauka, b. 25 Aug 1939.

Lois Muriel, b. 20 Apr 1909, d. 8 Oct 1982, m. 2 Aug 1930 Robert K. Stanley.

Curtis Boyd, b. 22 Apr 1911 Wilmot NH, m. 27 Jun 1936 Littleton NH Doris I. Smith, b. 18 Oct 1910 d. 12 Nov 1984, dau. Samuel and Sylvia (Bean) Smith of Quebec, Canada. Horticulturalist. In Littleton NH, Concord MA, Hartford CT. CH: Donald Boyd, b. 4 Sep 1937 Wilmot NH, m. 15 Jun 1963 Linda M. Crofts; Judith Mae, b. 18 Aug 1943, m. 12 Mar 1966 Quentin E. Boyle.

Henry Rider, b. 27 Dec 1912 Wilmot NH, d. 11 Jan 1978, m. 22 Jun 1940 Eleanora D. Boston, b. 2 Apr 1913 d. 7 Aug 1978. In Dover NH. CH: Stephen Roy, b. 2 Aug 1942, m. 23 Jun 1967 Sally M. Benoit, b. 17 Mar 1944; Eugene Frank, b. 13 Oct 1947, m. 29 Jun 1974 Priscilla S. Pattee, b. 23 Mar 1948; Cheryl Lee, b. 17 May 1950, m. 5 Apr

1975 Aubrey E. Payne; David Nelson, b. 14 Dec 1952, m. 7 Oct 1978 Brenda M. Fessenden, b. 4 Jan 1955.

Blanche Arlene, b. 8 Dec 1914, d. 21 Sep 1989, m.(1) 15 May 1938 William Clapper, m.(2) James Currier.

Channing Pierce, b. 4 Apr 1918 Wilmot NH, d. 10 Mar 1982.

Janice Bell, b. 9 Feb 1921, m. 24 Feb 1943 Jules Nolon of Windsor CT.

Sources: VR Manchester NH. Obit (Blanche), Curtis B. Sawyer Rec.

## NINTH GENERATION

558. **FREDERICK ELWOOD[9] SAWYER** [see 415], b. 23 Nov 1869 Deer Isle ME, d. 6 Jan 1940, m. 9 Feb 1889 Lillie A. Jordan of Ellsworth ME, b. 5 Oct 1855 d. 2 Jun 1932. In Deer Isle ME, Stoneham ME.

630 Elwood Arnold[10], 1894-1966. (Listed as CH. no. 2.)

Sources: Stoneham ME census 1900.

559. **ARTHUR COPELAND[9] SAWYER** [see 415], b. Aug 1887 Seal Cove (Deer Isle) ME, m. (1) 20 Oct 1906 Center Lincolnville ME Leona Dunton of Vinalhaven ME, b. ?, dau. Ezalor A. and Lennie (McAlister) Dunton, b. ?; m.(2) Evelyn Aldrich, b. ?.

Fred Alford, b. 23 Dec 1906.

Sources: Maine 1880 census index.

560. **CHARLES FRANCIS[9] SAWYER** [see 416], b. 5 Aug 1867 Castine ME, m.(1) 25 May 1886 Cynthia Gray, b. ca. 1870 d. 13 Dec 1895; m.(2) Hattie E. Gray of Brooksville ME, b. 1876.

Charles C., b. Nov 1886 Brooksville ME.

Edward F., b. 18 Nov 1887.

Grace E., b. Aug 1888.

Addie E., b. 22 Oct 1896.

Alice May, b. 2 Oct 1897.

Sources: VR Castine ME, SA/ME.

561. **RUSSELL STANLEY[9] SAWYER** [see 416], b. 3 Sep 1882 Castine ME, d. 1942 Castine ME, m. Mattie Morey of Castine ME, b. 1885 d. 1957. He bur. in Castine ME.

Stanley E., b. 1905 Castine ME, m. 18 Jun 1929 Ellsworth ME Ella G. (Griffin) Batchelder of Brooklin ME, b. 1899, dau. Edward and Carrie (Smith) Griffin.

Sources: VR Ellsworth ME.

562. **CURTIS LEONARD[9] SAWYER** [see 419], b. 13 Jun 1885 Wilton ME, d. 7 May 1952 Portland ME, m. 11 Mar 1908 Katherine Mosher, b. 20 Mar 1886 d. 17 Nov 1945. In Worcester MA.

Harry Leason, b. 3 Nov 1908, m. 15 Oct 1932 Minnetta Leighton.

Iola, b. 7 Jul 1914, d. 3 Apr 1989, m. 26 Feb 1937 Victor Owens.

Charles Scott, b. 30 Mar 1916, d. 29 May 1976, m. 31 Mar 1941 Eleanor Pottle of Waltham MA.

Harriet A., b. 11 Aug 1918, m. 7 Sep 1938 Richard Buckley of Waltham MA.

Roscoe Wood, b. 5 Sep 1919, m. Frances Wisman.

Vondella C., b. 12 Apr 1926, m. 21 Jun 1947 Howard Doucette of Portland ME.

Sylvia W., b. 9 Dec 1928, m. 29 Jun 1946 Richard Thurston of Portland ME.

Sources: Obit (Iola), Myron R. Sawyer rec.

563. **GARDNER EDISON⁹ SAWYER** [see 419], b. 8 Jan 1891 Portland ME, d. 17 Apr 1982 Berwick ME, m. 27 Sep 1914 Jennie Webster of Prince Edward Island, Canada, b. 27 Jan 1891 d. 2 Dec 1981. World War I.

Norman, b. 28 Mar 1916, m. 21 Jul 1940 Roberta Priest.
James, b. Mar 1925, d. Mar 1925.
David, b. Mar 1925, d. Mar 1925, bur. at New Port Richie FL.

Sources: Myron R. Sawyer rec.

564. **WALTER SCOTT⁹ SAWYER** [see 419], 3 Oct 1896 Portland ME, d. 28 Mar 1962 Portland ME, m. 23 Jun 1820 Catherine M. Rollins of Rockland ME, b. 30 May 1896.

Walter Scott, b. 6 Mar 1922 Portland ME, m. 3 Dec 1945 Mary I. Murch of So. Windham ME, b. 10 Apr 1923. CH: Sandra Jean, b. 12 Feb 1947; Walter Scott, b. 12 Nov 1951; Candice Joan, b. 1 Dec 1953.
Myron Robert, b. 22 Jun 1930 Portland ME, m. 22 Aug 1959 Katherine Lynn Brown of Paoli PA, b. 10 Dec 1936. In Wilmington DE, New York. CH: Katherine Starrett, b. 27 Jun 1962; Robert Evans, b. 6 Aug 1967; Michael James, b. 13 Apr 1970.

Sources: Myron R. Sawyer rec.

565. **EDWARD WALTER⁹ SAWYER** [see 422], b. 15 Oct 1878 Conway NH, m. 24 Apr 1899 Annie Dinsmore of Conway, b. ca. 1881. Laborer.

George Edward, b. 20 Sep 1899 Bartlett NH, d. 8 Jan 1973.
Child, b. 1 Aug 1918, d. 3 Aug 1918.

Sources: VR SA/MA. N14.

566. **FRANK NORRIS⁹ SAWYER** [see 428], b. 7 Jul 1864 Lynn MA, m. 17 Feb 1885 Attie Van Blarcom of Marblehead MA, b. 3 Nov 1865. Machinist.

Florence K., b. 6 Jul 1887.
Harold Leonard, b. 31 Jan 1891 Lynn MA.
Helen Norris, b. 22 Dec 1895.

Sources: VR SA/MA.

567. **WILLARD EUGENE⁹ SAWYER** [see 430], b. 23 Aug 1859 Greenville ME, m. Lillian M. Whittier of Chesterville ME, b. Nov 1860, dau. Daniel E. and Caroline A. (Dyer) Whittier. Merchant. In Wilton ME.

Ralph Eugene, b. 25 Dec 1883, d.y.
631 Ralph Eugene¹⁰, b. 1885.
Earle Whittier, b. 17 Dec 1886 Wilton ME, m.(1) 10 Dec 1913 Pownal ME Edith Merrill, b. ?; m.(2) ?.
632 Willard Henry¹⁰, b. 1888.
Gladys W., b. 14 Apr 1891, d. 28 Jul 1891.
633 Philip Daniel¹⁰, b. 1895-1975.

Sources: VR Wilton ME, SA/ME. Barbara Wentworth rec.

568. **PERCIVAL GERALD⁹ SAWYER** [see 431], b. 13 May 1888 Buckfield ME, d. 30 Mar 1975 Orlando FL, m. 1 Jan 1916 Auburn ME Alice Williams, b. ?. He bur. in Auburn ME.

Russell, b. ?. In Turner ME.

Sources: Caroline Small rec.

569. **ALEXANDER PAINE DOW⁹ SAWYER** [see 431], b. 27 May 1891 Buckfield ME, m. 1 Dec 1922 Gladys Shaw, b. ?.

Gerald.
Alexander.
Sources: Carolyn Small rec.

570. **LINWOOD ELMER[9] SAWYER** [see 432], b. 19 May 1883 Greenville ME, d. 25 Aug 1944 Portland ME, m. Sep 1904 Grace Merrill of Minot ME, b. 23 Nov 1885, dau. William and Persis (Marshall) Merrill. In Hebron ME, Portland ME 1923.
Merritt W., b. 23 Oct 1905, d. 19 Jan 1907.
Persis Emily, b. 21 Jan 1907, m. May 1944 Clarence Chenery.
Louise G., b. 30 May 1909, m. Apr 1929 Herschal Nickerson.
Clifford Ashe, b. 23 Jun 1913 Hebron ME, m. 1933 Eleanor Leighton. On Peaks Island ME. CH: Allen Merritt, b. 21 Jun 1936; Clayton Ashe, b. 23 Jun 1937, unm, went to Mexico City; John Richard, b. 19 Nov 1940, d. 6 Nov 1974.
Elroy Linwood, b. 23 Aug 1915 Hebron ME, m. 1938 Evelyn Steeres.
Shirley M., b. 19 Aug 1923, m.(1) 1941 Robert Howe, m.(2) Orval H. Olson.
Marjorie J., b. 27 Jul 1927, m. 13 Aug 1952 John Russell.
Sources: Persis Chenery rec.

571. **CLIFFORD BENJAMIN[9] SAWYER** [see 433], b. 12 Aug 1892 Greenville ME, d. 9 Nov 1967, m. 14 Dec 1912 Lola B.Cole, b. 25 Aug 1891 d. 16 Feb 1978, dau. Charles and Dorothy (Bowker) Cole.
Hugh, b. 31 Oct 1913.
Charles M., b. 10 Sep 1918, m. Margaret McLeod, b. ?.
Paul W., b. 22 Jun 1920, m. Winifred R. Perry, b. ?.
Charlotte B., b. 15 Jun 1922, m. Robert H. Ware.
Sources: Paul W. Sawyer rec.

572. **EDMUND M.[9] SAWYER** [see 434], b. Aug 1867 Milford ME, d. 28 Apr 1897 Milford ME, m. Josephine Mabel Roberts, b. ?. He bur. in Old Town ME.
Ralph Marshall, b. 24 Dec 1894.
Frances M., b. 13 Apr 1896.
Son, b. 20 Apr 1897.
Sources: VR SA/ME.

573. **FRANK W.[9] SAWYER** [see 434], b. Jan 1870 Milford ME, m. Elizabeth Murphy of New York, b. Nov 1874. In Millinocket ME.
Wilbert, b. 1916, d. 1956, m. Esther Tardy.
Sources: Esther Sawyer rec.

574. **SETH HAROLD[9] SAWYER** [see 435], b. 1890 Leadville CO, m. 24 Dec 1917 Portsmouth NH Blanche May Gaghan of Lewiston ME, b. 1889, dau. William and Bridgett (McWilliam) Gaghan. Ship fitter. In Bath ME, Worcester MA.
William R., b. 1911, m. 23 Sep 1932 Jane E. Parreault.
Sources: VR SA/NH.

575. **HARRY L.[9] SAWYER** [see 436], b. Sep 1872 Greenville ME, m.(1) Derby VT (later div.) Emma C. Dailey of Dexter ME, b. Jul 1871; m.(2) 2 May 1921 Rochester NH Louise Perkins of Rochester NH, b. 1889, dau. Calvin and Fannie (Wescott) Perkins. Lumber merchant.

Reginald Lewis, b. 13 Jul 1897 Greenville ME, m. Frances O. Small of Bangor ME, b. ca. 1907 d. 19 Apr 1994, dau. Frank V. and Florence (Bradford) Small. CH: Kenneth Carleton, Francis Carleton, Eleanor m. Freeman Frost, Regina m. James Heckman.

Rachel, b. ?.

Ruth, b. ?.

Sources: VR SA/ME. Obit (Frances O.), Paul Sawyer rec.

576. **THOMAS J.[9] SAWYER** [see 438], b. 1869 Medford ME, m. 9 Sep 1897 Hermon ME Annie H. Silvester of Elna ME, b. 1879, dau. Sumner and Marella (Raymond) Silvester. Engineer.

Robert, b. 3 Jul 1898 Hermon ME.

Sources: VR SA/ME.

577. **STILLMAN WHITE[9] SAWYER** [see 440], b. 28 Feb 1880 Greenville ME, d. 22 Dec 1960, m.(1) Winifred Dunning of Prince Edward Island, Canada, b. 13 Jun 1880 d. 28 Mar 1913, dau. David and Elizabeth Dunning; m.(2) 25 Nov 1916 Bertie Mae MacGould of Dixmont ME, b. 26 Aug 1887 d. 14 Apr 1966.

Florence Estelle, b. 3 Jul 1905, d. 17 Jul 1975, m. 17 Jun 1927 Myron D. Tucker.

Sarah M., b. Jan 1910, d. 6 Jul 1910.

Oliver Stillman, twin, 18 Mar 1913 Greenville ME, d. 3 Nov 1982, m. 8 Apr 1938 Jeanette Audette. In Pomona CA. CH: Ernest Stillman, m. Jean Winkleplech; Richard Oliver, b. 3 Mar 1950, m. Elizabeth Cotter.

Son, b. 18 Mar 1913, d. 27 Mar 1913 (twin).

Erma Leola, b. 20 Sep 1917, m. 29 Jun 1940 Ernest B. Harvey.

Henry Edward, b. 23 Dec 1919, m. 29 Mar 1942 Elizabeth Thompson.

Virginia May, b. 1 Apr 1921, m. Lowell H. Osgood of Bangor ME.

Frances Ardis, b. 5 Nov 1924, m. 29 Jun 1946 John P. Richards.

Sources: VR SA/ME. Frances Richards rec.

578. **FRED J.[9] SAWYER** [see 440], b. 4 May 1884 Greenville ME, d. 8 Jul 1951, m.(1) Isabelle Files, b. ?; m.(2) Hazel _____, b. ?; m.(3) Ida _____, b. ?.

Kenneth.

Dorothy Budden.

Louisa Worster.

Madelina Jennings.

Sources: Paul Sawyer rec.

579. **LEWIS JOHN[9] SAWYER** [see 444], b. 7 Apr 1885 Buxton ME, d. 10 Nov 1970, m. Mary Susan Dyer of Saco ME, b. 30 Jan 18?? d. Dec 1961, dau. _____ and Georgia (Lane) Dyer. Optician. In Bangor ME.

Daughter, b. ?, d. 8 Aug 1904.

Allen Lewis, b. 24 Sep 1906.

Arthur A., b. 5 Oct 1907.

Lewis J., stillborn 16 Jul 1909.

Sources: VR SA/ME. M5.

580. **HAROLD LESTER[9] SAWYER** [see 445], b. 14 Feb 1899 Portland ME, m. 9 Feb 1921 Cora M. Hopkins, b. 18 Jun 1898 d. 31 Jul 1979. In So. Portland ME.

Herbert Hopkins, b. 13 Jul 1922, m. 3 Oct 1944 Barbara Leach.

Donald Lester, b. 17 Apr 1926, m. 24 Jul 1954 Mary J. Shorey.

Sources: Harold L. Sawyer rec.

581. **HENRY S.$^{9}$ SAWYER** [see 447], b. Jun 1864 Biddeford ME, d. 16 Apr 1917 Biddeford ME, m. 7 Jun 1885 Biddeford ME Margaret Gallant of New Brunswick, Canada, b. ?.

Edward, b. 6 Jul 1885 Biddeford ME.
Annie, b. 20 Oct 1886.
Grace, b. 5 Dec 1887.
John James, b. 18 Nov 1889 Biddeford ME.
Nellie, b. 26 Aug 1891, d. 18 May 1892 Biddeford ME.
Celia, b. 15 Jul 1899.

Sources: VR Biddeford ME, SA/ME.

582. **RUSSELL FULTON BROWN$^{9}$ SAWYER** [see 453], 20 Feb 1897 Brunswick ME, d. 2 Nov 1972 Portland ME, m. 23 Oct 1926 Danvers MA Marjory Jordan of So. Boston MA, b. 4 Nov 1901, dau. Arthur L. and Lucia (Tuttle) Jordan.

Richard J., b. 23 Apr 1928, m.(1) 14 Sep 1957 (later div.) Judith A. Davey; m.(2) ? (later div.). CH: Teresa Mae, b. 17 Apr 1958; Linda Louise, b. 8 Nov 1960; Russell Fulton Brown, b. 11 Aug 1963, d. 13 Aug 1963; Sandra Davey, b. 2 Sep 1964; Michael Jordan, b. 20 Nov 1965.

Sources: VR SA/ME. Richard J. Sawyer rec.

583. **CHARLES FRANKLIN$^{9}$ SAWYER** [see 467], b. 24 Jul 1878 Manchester NH, d. 19 Apr 1961 Lawrence MA, m. 15 Jun 1910 Agnes Robinson, b. 14 Aug 1879 d. 12 Apr 1944.

William Reed, b. 25 Dec 1914 Andover MA, d. 28 Oct 1990 Winchester MA, m. 24 Jul 1944 Norfolk VA Marion B. Hudson of Lawrence MA, b. 18 Jul 1915 d. 6 Feb 1990 Boston MA, dau. Jonathan and Clara Hudson of England. In Methuen MA. CH: Janice Marion, b. 14 Sep 1947, unm; William Reed, b. 26 Feb 1949 Lawrence MA, m. 21 Sep 1974 Barbara Gail Whitman of Middlebury VT, b. 12 Nov 1951. In St. Albans VT.
Alice Veronica, b. ?, unm. Went to Arizona.

Sources: William R. Sawyer rec., Marion Sawyer rec.

584. **SAMUEL STEVENS$^{9}$ SAWYER** [see 467], b. 7 Feb 1891 Lawrence MA, m. ?.

Joseph.
John.

Sources: William R. Sawyer rec.

585. **HENRY GILBERT$^{9}$ SAWYER** [see 469], b. 18 May 1873 Antrim NH, m. 8 Feb 1898 Emma L. Weichert, b. ?. Milk dealer. In Dorchester MA, Milton MA.

Mildred G., b. 24 Jan 1902.
Richard E., b. 28 Jan 1908.

Sources: VR Antrim NH.

586. **ANSEL BUGBEE$^{9}$ SAWYER** [see 472], b. 11 Aug 1863 Gilford NH, d. 29 Oct 1933 Gilford NH, m. 30 Sep 1886 Pittsfield NH Alice Julia Adams of Lowell MA, b. 31 Jan 1865. Farmer.

Ellen Caroline, b. 24 Jul 1887, d. 14 Sep 1966, m. 16 Aug 1917 Alfred W. Kingsbury.
Ezra (Emery) Ansel, b. 23 Sep 1888 Gilford NH, d. 5 Oct 1951, m. 30 May 1913 Erma Clough, b. ?. Farmer.
Clarence Everett, b. 27 Oct 1890 Gilford NH, d. 4 Apr 1968, m. 4 Jun 1927 Laconia NH Maud E. Sleeper of Lakeport NH, b. ca. 1890, dau. Charles E. and Ida A. (Goodwin) Sleeper.

Maurice Ware, b. 6 Jan 1893 Gilford NH, d. 4 Apr 1968, m. 17 Nov 1917 Gilford NH Rachel G. L. Crosby of Gilford NH, b. 1895 d. 31 Dec 1989, dau. George F. and Gertie (Ordway) Crosby. Farmer. CH: Malcolm M., b. 24 Apr 1919, m. Helen Louise Irwin; George A., b. 24 Jun 1921, m. Ruth Nolan; Chester Crosby, b. 9 Dec 1923 d. 22 Jun 1924; Richard A., b. 1 Apr 1928, m. Ruth W. _____; Edna, b. 22 Jun 1931, m. Gerald W. Wellbourn.

John Levi, b. 6 Jan 1898 Gilford NH, m. 11 Oct 1927 Katherine Sears, b. ?. Went to Illinois.

Esther Mary, b. 2 Nov 1899, m. 26 Mar 1925 Paul Alfred Southard.

James Adams, b. 30 Nov 1903 Gilford NH, d. 23 May 1986, m. 20 Apr 1925 Minnie Davis.

Sources: VR SA/NH. H23, N9, K14, Obit (Rachel), John Levi Sawyer rec., Minnie D. Sawyer rec, Ruth N. Sawyer rec.

587. **GEORGE EDWIN[9] SAWYER** [see 474], b. 13 Dec 1857 Belmont NH, d. 29 Sep 1911 Belmont NH, m. 1879 Mary Eunice Foster of No. Reading MA, b. ca. 1863, dau. Sumner and Elizabeth (Putnam) Foster. Farmer. In Gilmanton NH 1860, No. Reading MA 1880.

Elizabeth Belle, b. 9 Jul 1880, d. 17 Feb 1891.

634 Otto Edwin[10], b. 1884.

Sources: Gilmanton NH census 1860. North Reading MA census 1880. VR SA/MA. SA/NH. P43.

588. **DAVID[9] SAWYER** [see 476], b. 1 Sep 1873 Gilmanton NH, d. 25 Mar 1956, m. 19 Apr 1908 Gilmanton NH Betsey M. Knowles, b. 4 Oct 1885 d. 16 Apr 1961, dau. Rufus A. and Arabella J. (Moody) Knowles. Farmer. He bur. in Smith Meeting House Cem., Gilmanton NH.

Theodore Howard, b. 28 Mar 1909, d. same day.

John David, b. 1911 Gilmanton NH, m. 12 Jun 1934 Laconia NH Lillian Fay of Lakeport NH, b. 1909, dau. Park S. and Hattie (Merrill) Fay.

Barbara, m. Lyle Jenkins.

Sources: VR SA/NH. H89, N9.

589. **FRANK P.[9] SAWYER** [see 479], b. ca. 1853 Lee NH, m. 2 Jan 1878 Boston MA Lillian E. Purbeck of Boston MA, b. ca. 1853, dau. William and Mahala H. Purbeck. Machinist. In Lee NH 1860, Cambridge MA 1886.

Arthur Garfield, b. 12 Nov 1880 Boston MA.

Grace A., b. 1886.

Sources: Lee NH census 1860. Boston MA census 1880. VR SA/MA.

590. **JOSIAH F.[9] SAWYER** [see 479], b. 1859 Lee NH, d. 14 Jan 1908 Lee NH, m. 4 Mar 1883 Laura A. Gilman of Sandwich NH, b. 3 Mar 1859 d. 7 Jan 1889, dau. David and Sarah M. (Lewis) Gilman.

Charles L., b. 1 Jan 1885 Lee NH.

Sources: VR SA/NH. N9, P82i.

591. **AUGUSTUS BARNES[9] SAWYER** [see 481], b. 1870 Franklin NH, d. 1938 Franklin NH, m. 20 Jan 1904 Henniker NH Mary A. Emerson of Sanbornton NH, b. ?, dau. Jonathan and Sarah R. (Sweetzer) Emerson. Reporter, editor.

George W., b. 1905 Franklin NH, m. 17 Jun 1929 Masardis ME Ruth Greenlaw of Masardis ME, b. 1907, dau. George E. and Myrtie (Quincy) Greenlaw. Chemical engineer.

Parker E., b. 1907 Franklin NH, m. 13 Jul 1929 Franklin NH Olive M. Cutler of Livermore Falls ME, b. 1908, dau. Robert W. and Mary (Woodson) Cutler. Clerk.

Sources: VR Henniker NH.

592. **JOSIAH C.[9] SAWYER** [see 482], b. Mar 1848 Atkinson ME, d. 25 Sep 1907 Dover ME, m. 15 Oct 1871 Georgianna A. Labree of Parkman ME, b. 16 Jun 1848 d. 9 Dec 1922, dau. Luther and Scherina (Judkins) LaBree. In Dover ME 1880.

Cora Bell, b. 29 Aug 1873, d. 29 May 1916, m. 7 Apr 1892 Howland ME Foster Daniel Chamberlain.

Perley F., b. 1876, m. 24 Nov 1898 Dover ME Ethel Plummer of Dover ME, b. 1877, dau. George W. and Eddrannah (Hill) Plummer. No CH.

Clyde L., b. 1879 Dover ME, m. 1 May 1904 Nina B. Littlefield, b. ?.

635 Ora M.[10], b. 1881.

Sources: ME 1880 census index. VR SA/ME. S. Shepard Sawyer rec.

593. **FRANK LESLIE[9] SAWYER** [see 483], b. 6 Nov 1869 Atkinson ME, d. 10 Nov 1949 Dover-Foxcroft ME, m. 23 Nov 1899 Atkinson ME Avavesta Flanders of Garland ME, b. 27 Sep 1874 d. 9 Mar 1944, dau. H. A. and Sarah (Messor) Flanders.

Minnie Delia, b. 1901, d. Jan 1973, m. 1923 Leslie Colson.

Ethel Elma, b. 1905, d. 1 May 1983, unm.

Norman Herbert, b. 1908, d. 1980, m. Jul 1934 Olive McComb. CH: Gerald A.

Maude Leslie, b. 17 Jul 1910, d. 5 Oct 1981, m. 10 Aug 1933 John E. LaBree.

Stephen Shepard II, b. 1913, m. 15 May 1943 Alyce Davis. CH: Stephen Shepard III.

Sources: VR SA/ME. S. Shepard Sawyer rec, Lauri Cover rec.

594. **CHARLES BEAN[9] SAWYER** [see 484], b. 26 Oct 1886 East Corinth ME, d. 13 Aug 1939, m. Charlestown MA Daisy A. Libby, b. 31 May 1893, dau. John L. and Joan (Bussell) Libby. In Charlestown MA, Everett MA.

Lowell Leonard, b. 15 Jan 1914 Everett MA, m. 11 Oct 1939 Everett MA Marjory Matthews, b. in England.

Charles Libby, b. 2 Apr 1923, m. 24 Jan 1946 (later div.) Sonja Sreda. Went to California.

Roger Hugh, b. 11 Jul 1939.

Sources: B40.

595. **WALTER LEONARD[9] SAWYER** [see 484], b. 29 Aug 1890 E. Corinth ME, m. 1 Oct 1917 E. Wilton ME Gertrude Yeaton, b. 1 May 1894 d. Jun 1984, dau. Elias H. and Lula (Hosmer) Yeaton. In Bangor ME.

Charles Eastman, b. 29 Nov 1918 East Corinth ME, m. 9 Oct 1948 Brewer ME Alice Roberta (Barstow) Curran of Brewer ME, b. 21 Jun 1924. In Bangor ME.

Sources: B40.

596. **ENOCH EARL[9] SAWYER** [see 486], b. Dec 1884 Salisbury MA, m. 20 Jan 1906 Salisbury MA Ethel B. Follansby of Seabrook NH, b. 1890, dau. Preston C. and Blanche (Randall) Follansby.

Enoch Earl, b. 1906 Salisbury MA, m. 16 Sep 1933 Seabrook NH Ethel Jones.

Sources: VR Salisbury MA.

597. **TRACY M.[9] SAWYER** [see 488], b. 11 Apr 1878 Bath NH, d. 30 Dec 1932 Concord NH, m.(1) 25 Dec 1902 Haverhill NH Bessie L. Howland of Bath NH, b. 1 Feb 1882 d. 21 Nov 1918; m.(2) 30 Aug 1919 Woodville NH Minnie (Howland) Crosby of Ryegate VT, b. 11 Jun 1875 d. 2 Nov 1930. Both wives were dau. George and Mary (Chamberlin) Howland. In Haverhill NH, Milford MA, Bath NH.

Son, stillborn 2 Oct 1904.

Dana R., b. 1906 Bath NH, m. 30 Jul 1927 Woodville NH Pheobe Dion of Benton NH, b. 1907, dau. Peter and Florence (Brill) Dion.
Sources: VR Bath NH, Concord NH, SA/NH, SA/VT.

598. **RAYMOND BURKERT[9] SAWYER** [see 493], b. 16 Oct 1897, m. Aug 1824 Jeanette Ela, b. ?. In Pennsylvania.
Richard Ela, b. 10 Aug 1929, m. 22 Jun 1857 Janet Spencer.
Raymond Francis, b. 30 Aug 1932.
Sources: Jeanette Sawyer rec.

599. **CROSBY STUART[9] SAWYER** [see 495], b. 5 Mar 1857 W. Minot ME, m. 4 Nov 1879 Stoughton MA Carrie I. Deane of Stoughton MA, b. 1859, dau. Eli and Hepzibah Deane.
Helen Caroline, b. 18 Oct 1880.
Horace Deane, b. 1 May 1882 Stoughton MA.
Sources: VR SA/MA.

600. **CLAUDE WILSON[9] SAWYER** [see 495], b. 15 Oct 1866 W. Minot ME, m. 20 Mar 1895 Minot ME Vivian Thomas of Minot ME, b. 1878, dau. L. E. and Mary (Farris) Thomas.
Louise, b. 20 Feb 1896.
Matthias Plant, b. 1 Jun 1897 Minot ME.
Edward F., b. 24 Sep 1899 Minot ME.
Claude W., b. 18 May 1910, d. 5 Jun 1910.
Sources: VR SA/ME.

601. **FRANK HENRY[9] SAWYER** [see 498], b. 4 Feb 1868 Hampstead NH, d. Sep 1910 Haverhill MA, m. 18 Oct 1893 Haverhill MA Mabel E. Dean of Dedham MA, b. ca. 1873, dau. Albert and Emma (Ridley) Dean. Plumber.
Albert Francis, b. 8 Jul 1895 Haverhill MA.
Dana Dean, b. ?.
Eleanor R., b. ?.
Sources: VR SA/MA. H32.

602. **WILLIAM HENRY[9] SAWYER** [see 501], b. 4 Jun 1886 Worcester MA, d. 12 Sep 1945 Worcester MA, m. 19 Apr 1913 Leicester MA Dorothy Winslow of Leicester MA, b. 1890 d. 8 Aug 1954, dau. Samuel and Bertha (Russell) Winslow. In lumber business.
Dorothy Ann, b. 5 Mar 1914, m.(1)_____ Mayher, m.(2) Arthur Lowery, m.(3) Joseph Staples.
William Henry III, b. 5 Oct 1915 Worcester MA, m. 23 Jun 1939 Marjorie Carleton, b. 1915. Lumber business. CH: Joan, b. 1 Jan 1941; Judith, b. 4 Oct 1942; Polly, b. 4 Oct 1945; William Carleton, b. Feb 1949.
John Edward, b. 9 May 1917 Worcester MA, m. Anne W. Swift. CH: Katherine; John Winslow; Stephen.
Sources: Anne W. Sawyer rec., John W. Sawyer rec., William H. Sawyer III rec.

603. **EVERETT FOWLER[9] SAWYER** [see 504], b. 10 Jul 1897 No. Haverhill NH, d. 21 Aug 1944 No. Haverhill NH, m. 28 Nov 1918 Haverhill NH Dorothy Meader of Haverhill MA, b. 14 Jun 1897, dau. Moses A. and Kate (Child) Meader. In Woodstock CT.
Clifford Moses, b. 8 Nov 1919 Woodstock CT, m. 14 May 1955 Shirley Bruce.
Carolyn Eda, b. 6 Dec 1920, m. 17 Jul 1945 William Grass, Jr.
Carl Clinton, b. 16 Jul 1922 Woodstock CT.

Everett Fowler, b. 13 Jul 1924 Woodstock CT, m. 16 Sep 1951 Barbara Waterhouse.
Richard Paul, b. 15 May 1926 Woodstock CT, m. 2 Dec 1949 Marguerite Douglas.
Katherine Elizabeth, b. 16 Jul 1928, d. 16 Jul 1931.
Merrill Clark, b. 27 May 1932, m. 28 Oct 1954 Betty L. Elliot.
Sources: B69, N9, W36. Merrill Clark Sawyer rec.

604. **FRED MORSE[9] SAWYER** [see 506], b. 12 Jul 1863 Salisbury MA, m.(1) 19 Apr 1884 Lynn MA Agnes W. Doughty of Peabody MA, b. 1868, dau. David W. and Jane W. Doughty; m.(2) 30 Jun 1910 Nashua NH Elizabeth (MacDonald) Cochrane of Norwich CT, wid., b. 1866, dau. Donald and Josephine (Sanders) MacDonald. Carriage trimmer.
636 Ralph Doughty[10], b. 1885.
Donald, b. ?.
Esther, b. ?.
Sources: VR SA/MA. Myrtle F. Sawyer rec.

605. **BURTON AUGUSTUS[9] SAWYER** [see 506], b. 1 Nov 1867 Merrimac MA, m. 25 Dec 1886 Mary E. Taylor of Salem MA, b. 1870. Carriage painter. In Lynn MA.
Alvah Burton, b. 21 Feb 1888 Lynn MA.
Sources: VR SA/MA.

606. **ASA SAMUEL[9] SAWYER** [see 518], b. 19 Jan 1854 Springfield ME, d. 14 Sep 1931 Orono ME, m.(1)4 Jul 1874 Julia Ames of Bangor ME, b. 4 Mar 1853 d. 8 Feb 1893, dau. David D. and Betsey Ames; m.(2) 25 Dec 1897 Hattie M. Smith of Hermon ME, b. 25 Jan 1876 d. 21 Jul 1939, dau. Otis and Martha (Leighton) Smith. In Bangor ME, Orono ME.
George Ivory, b. 16 Nov 1875, d. 22 Apr 1876.
Nina Mae, b. 19 May 1877, d. 29 Aug 1916, m. William Nelson of Bangor ME.
637 Albert Lester[10], 1879-1949.
638 Asa Frank[10], 1881-1963.
639 David Ivory[10], 1883-1959.
Caroline E., b. 24 Apr 1884, d. 5 Oct 1957, m. 1 May 1902 Edward Moores of Lubec ME.
Myrtle C., b. 30 May 1886, m. 10 Jun 1905 Charles W. Mitchell.
Vera J., b. 11 Jan 1899, d. 17 Nov 1899 Orono ME.
Clayton Leonard, b. 5 Apr 1901 Orono ME, d. 21 Dec 1951 Washington DC, m. 27 Mar 1929 Phyllis Hannaford of Bradley ME, b. 4 Nov 1910. He bur. in Orono ME. CH: Rena J., b. 23 Jul 1931, m. 22 Nov 1951 Robert Bewink of Washington DC; Weston R., 1 Nov 1932, m. 26 Dec 1952 Marilyn Wilkins.
Gladys M., b. 25 Sep 1905, m. 16 Jul 1925 Leslie C. Woods of Bradley ME.
Sources: VR SA/ME. Gladys M. Woods rec, Lawrence A. Sawyer rec.

607. **ORRIN[9] SAWYER** [see 518], b. 9 Apr 1856 Hermon ME, d. 17 Jan 1938 Jackman ME, m. 8 Dec 1877 Viola Colby of Moose River ME, b. ca. 1862. He bur. in Jackman ME. In Holden ME 1880.
Ina B., b. 9 May 1879, d. 17 Jun 1934, m. Sanford Moore.
Lottie A., b. 1 Dec 1881, d. 6 Mar 1904, m. _____ Williams.
Leo J., b. 21 Mar 1884 Moose River ME, d. 9 May 1923, m. Blanche Moore.
Una Clara, b. 20 Mar 1885, m.(1) 9 Jun 1906 Chester H. Mills, m.(2) Elmer Hight.
Ula, b. 14 Feb 1887, d. 20 Oct 1934.
640 Ora Mandal[10], 1892-1967.
Leroy E., b. 8 Aug 1893, d. 31 Oct 1912 Moose River ME.
641 Reed A.[10], 1896-1954.

Byrdena, b. 11 Feb 1899, d. 22 Apr 1987, m. Owen McClintock.
Caroline, b. 6 Feb 1902, m. 9 Mar 1925 Levi Sawyer.
Freeman C., b. 13 Feb 1905 Moose River ME, d. 6 Nov 1974 Farmington ME, m. 14 Jan 1936 Frances Bonnell. He bur. in Stratton ME.
Alvira, d.y.
Queen, d.y.

Sources: Holden ME census 1880. VR Skowhegan ME, SA/ME. Ethelyn Nichols rec., Frances Sawyer rec.

608. **CHARLES ELMON**[9] **SAWYER** [see 519], b. 9 Sep 1862 Hermon ME, d. 25 Jun 1917 Hermon ME, m. Orah E. Nowell of Hermon ME, b. ?. Farmer.

Budd O., b. 27 Apr 1889 Hermon ME, m. Emily Veazie of Hermon ME, b. 15 Jan 1892 d. 24 Nov 1918, dau. Charles and Emma (Mansell) Veazie. CH: Willis Freeman, b, 25 Jan 1911, d. 8 May 1993, m. Helen Fowler.
Ralph M., b. 17 Dec 1899 Hermon ME. (7th CH.)

Sources: VR SA/ME. Obit (Willis).

609. **OTHNIEL L.**[9] **SAWYER** [see 520], b. 8 May 1881 Ripley ME, d. 1944, m.(1) Clara E. Graves of Sangerville ME, b. 10 Jun 1883 d. 31 Mar 1922, dau. Elmer and Ruth (Farrar) Graves; m.(2) Maude Roach, b. ?.

Maurice E., 17 Mar 1918 Ripley ME, d. 15 Jan 1987 Waterville ME, m. 28 Jan 1938 Palmyra ME Velma A. Neal In St. Albans ME.
Ralph, b. 1927, m. Kay Pierce of Pittsfield ME. In Pittsfield ME.
Harold E., b. 1930, m. Alta Yeo of Dexter ME. In Dexter ME.
Stanton, b. 1932, m. 20 May 1961 Carole Needham of Skowhegan ME. In Skowhegan ME.
Richard, b. 1935, m.(1) Donna Watson, m.(2) Mary K. Leavitt.
Arnold, b. 1937, m. Glenda York of Harmony ME. In Harmony ME.

Sources: VR Skowhegan ME, SA/ME. Obit, Bessie Folsom rec., Velma Sawyer rec.

610. **THOMAS HADLEY**[9] **SAWYER** [see 522], b. 17 Jan 1878 Peabody MA, d. 20 Dec 1939, m. 1898 Nellie Eaton. b. ?.

Ralph Eaton, b. 1899, d. 1943.

Sources: Paul B. Sawyer rec.

611. **HARRY ARTHUR**[9] **SAWYER** [see 522], b. 7 Jul 1880 Peabody MA, d. 5 Mar 1951 Boston MA, m. 21 Sep 1910 Boston MA Emily Grace Smith of Windham NH, b. 11 Dec 1887 d. 5 Sep 1972. He bur. in Newton Center MA.

Gretchen, b. 12 Jun 1912, d. 27 Jan 1981 in Florida.
John Asa, b. 17 Jan 1915, d. 1 Apr 1987 in Georgia.
Paul Barton, b. 25 Jul 1924 Springfield MA, m. 24 Nov 1951 Newton MA Sarah G. Nichols, b. 13 Jul 1929.

Sources: VR SA/MA. Paul B. Sawyer rec.

612. **SAMUEL B.**[9] **SAWYER** [see 526], b. 1847 Wells ME, d. 1927, m. 13 Dec 1870 Amesbury MA Elizabeth H. Ross of Amesbury MA, b. 12 May 1850 d. 19 Apr 1925, dau. Benjamin and Sarah Ross. Carriage maker.

Samuel Bailey, b. 3 Oct 1873 Salisbury MA.
Lizzie May, b. 30 Apr 1878.

Sources: VR SA/MA. P82k.

613. **MARTIN R.$^9$ SAWYER** [see 527], b. ca. 1854 Porter ME, m. 14 Apr 1877 Pembroke NH Martha A. Wainwright of Exeter NH, b. 1855, dau. Thomas Wainwright. Engineer. In Gilford NH 1881, Lawrence MA 1885.

Daughter, b. 12 Jun 1881.

Ralph W., b. 1885, m. 17 Jun 1908 Ethyl W. Dean, b. ?.

Sources: VR Pembroke MA.

614. **WILBUR THOMAS$^9$ SAWYER** [see 527], b. 1861 Porter ME, m.(1) 31 May 1880 Pembroke NH (div. 1905) Livisa Matthews of Henniker NH, b. 27 Apr 1858, dau. Joseph M. and Adeline (Adams) Matthews; m.(2) 23 May 1908 E. Andover NH (div. 1910) Lillian M. Reed of Merrimack NH, wid., b. 1864, dau. Sullivan and Nancy (Clapp) Nesmith; m.(3) 16 Oct 1914 Nashua NH Frances (Patterson) Veaner of Chester NH, b. 1864, dau. Charles and Harriet (Smith) Patterson. Carpenter. In Henniker NH, Warner NH, Peterboro NH, Andover NH, Boston MA.

642 Roscoe Wilbur$^{10}$, 1881-1950.

Florence L., b. Aug 1882, m. Wallace Main of Kittery ME.

Ethel M., b. 9 Sep 1885, m. John Geddings of Concord NH.

Elizabeth, b. 25 Apr 1889, m. Fred Erskin of Manchester NH.

Sources: VR SA/NH. Norman E. Sawyer rec.

615. **GEORGE F.$^9$ SAWYER** [see 528], b. 1859 Wolfeboro NH, d. 1908, m. Asenath J. Reeves, b. ?. In Porter ME 1870, Medford MA, Somerville MA 1892. Family bur. in Stanley Cem., So. Hiram ME.

Loring Franklin, b. 7 Mar 1886 Boston MA, d. 1924.

Harry, b. 5 Apr 1892, d. 1896.

Clifton, b. 1893, d. 1896.

Sources: Porter ME census 1870. VR SA/MA. M5, Will.

616. **WILLIAM LEMUEL$^9$ SAWYER** [see 529], b. 12 Apr 1876 Tuftonboro NH, d. 16 Apr 1953 Tuftonboro NH, m.(1) 3 Jun 1897 Bertha Trask of Beverly MA, b. 3 Jun 1879 d. 16 Jan 1926; m.(2) Martha Guppy, b. ?. In Beverly MA, Danvers MA.

Elizabeth Ellen, d.y.

Carrie Maud, m. Linwood Kimball.

Hollis William, d.y.

George Alonzo, d.y.

Louise, m.(1) Edward L. Stinnings, m.(2) Lloyd McDuffee.

Doris, d.y.

Elsie, d.y.

Viola, m. Frederick Harding.

Charles Jackson, b. ca. 1914, m. 18 Mar 1935 Doris Howard.

Mae Trask, m. Mark Winkley.

William Herbert, d.y.

Sources: P8, Louise McDuffee rec.

617. **EUGENE ALLEN$^9$ SAWYER** [see 531], b. 11 Jul 1875 Limerick ME, d. 26 Mar 1934 Franklin NH, m. 8 Oct 1898 (later div.) Mary Yeaton, b. ca. 1879, dau. John and Eunice (Block) Yeaton. Shoemaker. In Wolfeboro NH, Clinton MA, Franklin NH.

643 Harry Albert$^{10}$, 1899-1936.

Eunice, b. 1 May 1904 d. 4 Sep 1976, m.(1) Ernest Collins, m.(2) Edward Verville.

Allen, b. 10 Sep 1908, m.(1) Sophie Jones, m.(2) Pearl Britton.

Sources: VR SA/NH.

618. **WILLIAM WALTER⁹ SAWYER** [see 535], b. 9 Aug 1885 Limington ME, d. ca. 1970 Upper Darby PA, m.(1) Katherine Thorne of Reading MA, b. ?; m.(2) Mary Braun of Woburn MA, b. ?. In Conway NH, Woburn MA. Left Mary and went to Pennsylvania.

William.

Several other CH.

Sources: VR Limington ME, VR SA/ME.

619. **EDMUND READ⁹ SAWYER** [see 538], b. 24 Jul 1889 Lakeport NH, m.(1) 1 Sep 1928 Margaret McAvery, b. ?; m.(2) ?. In Jaffrey NH.

Kendrick Leonard.

Thomas Dean.

Ted B.

Sources: Margaret M. Sawyer rec., Ted B. Sawyer rec.

620. **LEON LEROY⁹ SAWYER** [see 539], b. 3 Feb 1883 Woodstock NH, d. 26 Aug 1910 No. Woodstock NH, m. 8 Nov 1902 Woodstock NH Emma M. Gilbert of Lancaster NH, b. 1882, dau. William and Jennie Gilbert. Fireman. In Littleton NH, Plymouth NH 1908.

Frank Alfred, b. 20 Dec 1902, d. 29 Dec 1902.

Harold A.

Carl Ray, b. 1 Sep 1905, d. 30 Mar 1910.

Marjorie P.

Ruby D.

Sources: VR SA/NH.

621. **OMAR EUGENE⁹ SAWYER** [see 539], b. 1886 Woodstock NH,d. 29 Dec 1925 Concord NH, m. 25 Feb 1909 Berlin NH Frances M. Houghton of Ireland, b. 1 May 1889 d. 24 Feb 1920, dau. John and Annie (Crossen) Houghton. Engineer. In Plymouth NH.

John Raymond, b. 1910 Plymouth NH, m. 15 Jun 1931 Durham NH Margaret H. O'Brien of Malden MA, b. 1910, dau. D_____ and Margaret (Murphy) O'Brien. Insurance agent.

Sources; VR SA/NH. S81.

622. **MOSES HUGH⁹ SAWYER** [see 541], b. 14 Feb 1881 Weare NH, d. ca. 1954, m. 4 Oct 1911 Wilton NH Carrie Neale Wheeler of Worcester MA, b. 12 Dec 1880 d. 1945, dau. Frank E. and Susan S. (Neale) Wheeler. Farmer.

Francis Edward, b. 27 Jul 1914, d. same day.

Elizabeth, b. 30 May 1916, m. 1949 John Mastalir.

Edward Wheeler, b. 10 Jul 1918, m. Barbara Simons.

Frederick Abbott, b. 13 May 1924, m. 1977 Joyce L Newman.

Dorothy, b. 3 Oct 1925, m. 13 Sep 1849 Ralph Dudley.

Sources: VR SA/NH. B84, Dorothy Barnes rec.

623. **ALBERT OLIVER⁹ SAWYER** [see 542], b. 18 May 1861 No. Weare NH, d. 19 Jun 1946 Weare NH, m. 14 Oct 1893 Weare NH Cornelia Carter of White River Junction VT, b. 27 Jun 1862 d. 30 Apr 1922, dau. James and Cornelia (Blaisdell) Carter.

Daniel Augustus, b. 17 Mar 1895 Weare NH, d. 1977.

Frank Nathan, b. 25 Dec 1896 No. Weare NH, d. 14 Sep 1975, m. 26 Jun 1926 Weare NH Verna E. Slack of Manchester NH b. ca. 1900 d. 23 Nov 1992, dau. George L. and Edith (Bates) Slack of Ontario, Canada. Executive secretary. CH: Joan, Frank Nathan.

644 George Carter¹⁰, 1899-1988.

Sources: VR SA/NH. George Carter Sawyer rec.

624. **CHARLES HOWARD⁹ SAWYER** [see 546], b. 19 Aug 1862 Cambridge MA, m. 7 Jul 1887 Medford MA Sarah L. Simms, b. 3 Jul 1863, dau. Alexander S. and Sarah (Livermore) Simms. Manufacturer. President of National Bank of Medford MA.

Howard Martin, b. 16 Mar 1890 Medford MA.

Winnifred, b. 21 Oct 1898.

Charles Lawrence, b. 7 Oct 1900 Medford MA.

Sources: VR SA/MA.

625. **LAWRENCE TAYLOR⁹ SAWYER** [see 546], b. 8 May 1875 W. Medford MA, m. 3 May 1906 Alice Louise Hurd, b. 13 Jul 1875, dau. Edward P. and Sarah L. (Pope) Hurd of Dorchester MA. Vice President of Sawyer Manufacturing Company. In Medford MA, W. Newton MA.

Edward Lawrence, b. 1 Jul 1907 Medford MA.

Sources: VR SA/MA. P37.

626. **RALPH UNDERWOOD⁹ SAWYER** [see 546], b. 8 Dec 1880 W. Medford MA, m. 1 Dec 1906 Marion Coburn of Medford MA, b. 15 Mar 1883, dau. Frank J. and Hannah C. (Haskins) Coburn.

John Coburn, b. 21 Feb 1908 Medford MA.

Sources: G24.

627. **ROLAND DOUGLAS⁹ SAWYER** [see 551], b. 8 Jan 1874 Kensington NH, d. 10 Oct 1969, m. 29 Jun 1898 Mary Locke Palmer of Ware MA, b. 32 Dec 1874 d. 4 Dec 1949, dau. Daniel Palmer. Minister, In Brockton MA, Hanson MA, Haverhill MA, Ware MA.

Ruth Elizabeth, b. 22 Jun 1899 d. 11 Sep 1982, m.(1) 29 May 1923 Seymour Getter; m.(2) John Schwill.

Rachel Nathalie, b. 12 May 1901, m. 26 Jul 1923 Harold Y. Smith of Marshfield MA.

Roland (Withrow) Darrow, b. 26 Dec 1902 Ware MA, d. 18 Feb 1983 Wentworth By The Sea NH, m.(1) Louise _____; m.(2) Margaret Burnett. In Southboro MA, Newcastle NH.

Robert Palmer, b. 24 Aug 1904 Ware MA, d. 7 Dec 1969, m.(1) 10 Mar 1922 Ruby Levolette of Ware MA; m.(2) Adelaide Hillard. In Kensington NH. CH: Robert Stephen, b. 29 Sep 1922 Kensington NH; Evelyn; Arlene Gilbert, b. 8 Nov 1924; Clement Calvin, b. 26 Mar 1927 Kensington NH, m. Natalie Jacques.

Rosalind Blake, b. 17 Jun 1906, m. 1936 J. C. B. Chetwynd of Las Vegas NV.

Ramona J., b. 16 Sep 1911, m. 1934 Rev. Joseph Barth of Alna ME.

Sources: Nathalie Potts rec.

628. **ALLEN WEARE⁹ SAWYER** [see 553], b. 23 Feb 1895 Plaistow NH, d. 5 Oct 1981 Melbourne FL, m.(1) 28 Apr 1917 Plaistow NH (later div.) Mildred E. Howe, b. 28 Apr 1900 d. 26 Dec 1972, adopted by Robert A. and Edith L. (Angell) Howe; m.(2) Nov 1950 Elizabeth Sims, b. ?. Poultryman. Note: Mildred's b. parents were Averill and Agnes (Ray) Aldrich.

Aldrich Weare, b. 13 Jul 1918 Haverhill MA, d. 2 Apr 1982 Hampstead NH, m. 19 Jul 1941 Kittery Point ME Victoria E. Jones of Haverhill MA, b. 14 Nov 1917, dau. Arthur H. and Victoria Elizabeth (Sylvester-Weeks) Jones. Machinist. In Plaistow NH, Newburyport MA. CH: Jean Carolyn, b. 19 Apr 1943, m. 25 Aug 1961 George Hickman; Martha Anne, b. 16 Nov 1945, m. 7 Aug 1980 Harold R. Lockard; Allen Weare II, b. 20 Feb 1949, in Raymond NH.

Mahlon Chase, b. 30 Mar 1920 Haverhill MA, m. 16 Jun 1950 Amesbury MA Evelyn R. Gadsby, b. 27 Mar 1922 d. Nov 1981. In Plaistow NH, Newburyport MA. CH: Judith D., b. 1 Dec 1951, m. 15 Feb 1975 Evan B. Sederquist.

Esther Marion, b. 29 Jan 1922, m.(1) 25 Oct 1941 Harold F. Chase, (2) Raymond R. Rickter.

Ruth Pearl, b. 21 Sep 1923, m. 29 May 1946 Donald R. Robinson.

Kenneth Allen, b. 6 Jun 1925 Haverhill MA, m. 10 Jun 1951 Monmouth NJ Alma Jiannine, b. 15 Jan 1923, dau. Philip and Amenin (Thorne) Jiannine. In New Jersey, Tucson AZ. CH: Kendy Jeannine, b. 16 Jan 1956.

Chester Robert, b. 6 Aug 1926 Haverhill MA, m. 28 Apr 1949 Gloria M. Cronshaw of Worcester MA, b. 8 Jul 1930. In Amesbury MA. CH: Roberta Ann, b. 24 Jan 1950, m. 22 Sep 1985 Richard Blaum; Patricia M. b. 27 Apr 1952, m. 17 May 1975 ?; Chester Robert, b. 3 Sep 1954, m. 22 Feb 1975 Linda Mercer, b. 19 Mar 1953.

Sources: VR Plaistow NH. S18, Martha Lochard rec.

629. **SEWALL CHASE[9] SAWYER** [see 553], b. 16 Feb 1897 Plaistow NH, d. 15 Nov 1972, m. 24 Dec 1923 Cleveland OH Florence Burnham, b. 19 May 1895 d. 13 Apr 1969. In Cleveland OH, Chicago IL.

Sewall Chase, b. 21 Aug 1930, m. 21 Nov 1959 Elspeth G. Henry.

Lawrence Weare, b. 5 Oct 1934, m. 8 Jun 1963 Audry N. Shafer.

Dale Burnham, b. 15 Aug 1937, m. 28 Aug 1965 Hannelore Reeder.

Sources: Mary (Haseltine) Sawyer rec.

## TENTH GENERATION

630. **ELWOOD ARNOLD[10] SAWYER** [see 558], b. 2 Mar 1894 Stoneham ME, d. 1966, m.(1) 16 Mar 1915 Estelle B. Reid, b. 2 Apr 1897; m.(2) Edith A. Blanchard of Rhode Island, b. 19 Mar 1897 d. 16 Oct 1990, dau. Everett and Alison E. (Scott) Blanchard. In Stonington ME.

Elizabeth A., b. 23 Oct 1915, m. 9 Feb 1935 Burtis D. Trundy.

Climena E., b. 24 Oct 1917, m. Emery A. Knight.

Elwood Vincent, b. 15 Aug 1921 Stonington ME, m. 4 Jul 1940 Ann G. Warren.

Frank Melvin Reid, b. 12 Jan 1924, d. 24 May 1926.

Sources: VR Stoneham ME, Obit (Edith).

631. **RALPH EUGENE[10] SAWYER** [see 567], b. 28 May 1885 Wilton ME, d. Portland ME, m. 28 Jun 1910 Phillips ME Grace M. Timberlake, b. ?.

Evelyn, m. Robert Waite.

Harold Timberlake, m. ?.

Ruth, b. ca. 1919.

Sources: VR Wilton ME. Barbara Wentworth rec.

632. **WILLARD HENRY[10] SAWYER** [see 567], b. 5 Sep 1888 Wilton ME, m. 26 Mar 1912 Pownal ME Avis R. Rand of Wilton ME, b. ?.

Barbara, m. _____ Wentworth.

Willard Henry, b. 9 Jan 1923, d. Nov 1944.

Joyce Anne, b. 21 Jun 1926, m. Russell N. Martin.

Sources: VR Wilton ME. Barbara Wentworth rec.

633. **PHILIP DANIEL[10] SAWYER** [see 567], b. 17 May 1895 Farmington ME, d. 1975 Temple ME, m.(1) 16 Aug 1917 Strong ME Wilma Ferris Dodge, b. ? d. 1950; m.(2) Lucy Farmer, b. ?.

Norman Eugene, b. 20 Nov 1919 Farmington ME, m. 4 Oct 1939 Skowhegan ME Phyllis A. York of Farmington ME, b. 1923, dau. Linwood J. and Lila (Mosher) York.

Thelma Marion.

Sources: VR Skowhegan ME.

634. **OTTO EDWIN[10] SAWYER** [see 587], b. 12 Apr 1884 Belmont NH, m. 4 Jun 1904 Belmont NH Daisy Patten of Lakeport NH, b. 1886, dau. Charles and Minnie (Smith) Patten. Farmer.

Ruth E., b. 23 Mar 1912, d. 10 Sep 1913.

Herbert Elliot, b. 21 Feb 1917, d. 4 Mar 1917.

Fred A., b. 1919 Belmont NH, m. 28 May 1936 Newmarket NH Bernadine (White) Canney (formerly div.) of Newmarket NH, b. 1914, dau. Harry and Clara (Kelley) White. Shoe worker.

Esther Eunice, b. 24 Sep 1920, d. 15 Mar 1921.

Sources: VR SA/NH.

635. **ORA M.[10] SAWYER** [see 592], b. Jul 1881 E. Dover ME, m. 1 May 1902 Elizabeth Hilton.

Eugene.

Monroe, m. Marguerite Rollins. No CH.

Sources: S. Shepard Sawyer rec.

636. **RALPH DOUGHTY[10] SAWYER** [see 604], b. 25 Oct 1885 Salisbury MA, m. Roselda Laferniere, b. ?. Carriage trimmer.

Frederick Doughty, b. 3 Mar 1907, d. 1965, m. Myrtle F. Delong.

Harry Alva, b. 26 Jan 1912, d. 1985, m. Alice Fleet.

Sources: VR SA/MA. Myrtle F. Sawyer rec.

637. **ALBERT LESTER[10] SAWYER** [see 606], b. 18 May 1879 Bangor ME, d. 30 Oct 1949, m. Aug 1905 Bessie E. Mitchell, b. 2 May 1887 d. 18 Oct 1955. In Old Town ME, Stillwater ME.

Hazel M., b. 28 Jan 1906, m. 7 Oct 1933 Stephen G. Morse of Milford ME.

Una Beryl, b. 17 Apr 1907, m. Irving C. Hinckley.

Albert Lester, b. 13 Oct 1908, d. 12 Oct 1967, m. 3 Jul 19?? Myrtie Bowley of Old Town ME.

Eva Marjory, b. 1 Sep 1911, d. 21 Feb 1967, m. 3 Sep 1932 Charles Pettis.

Winifred Eleanor, b. 26 Dec 1915, d. 30 Jul 1964, m. Colby Bracy.

Harold Arthur, b. 24 Mar 1919, d. May 1953, m. Catherine Hamilton of Hallowell ME. CH: Sue Ellen, b. 14 Sep 1952.

Sources: Lawrence A. Sawyer rec.

638. **ASA FRANK[10] SAWYER** [see 606], b. 25 Aug 1881 Bangor ME, d. 9 Apr 1963, m. (1) 10 Feb 1906 Maude Pratt, b. ?; m.(2) Charlotte Rawley of Portland ME, b. ?.

Willard.

Gladys Mae, b. 25 Oct 1921, m. 25 Feb 1941 Herbert Higgins of Portland ME.

Charlotte Amy, b. 23 Dec 1922.

Sources: Gladys Woods rec., Lawrence A. Sawyer rec.

639. **DAVID IVORY10 SAWYER** [see 606], b. 27 Feb 1883 Bangor ME, d. 2 Oct 1959, m. 27 Jun 1904 Lillian Staples of Orrington ME, b. 26 Oct 1882 d. 3 Aug 1960. On Swan's Island ME, Scarboro ME.

Elmer J., adopted, b. ca. 1910 Swan's Island ME, m. 20 Jan 1934 Newton NH Nellie B. Wilbur, dau. Harvey and Sadie (Bowley) Wilbur.

Wella, adopted.

Sources: Lawrence A. Sawyer rec, Gladys Woods rec.

640. **ORA MANDAL10 SAWYER** [see 607], b. 8 Mar 1892 Moose River ME, d. 24 Feb 1967 Skowhegan ME, m. 10 Feb 1914 Villa Wilson of Denniston ME, b. ?. He bur. Skowhegan ME.

Raynard Howell, b. 1 Aug 1914 d. 2 Oct 1982, m. 4 Oct 1941 Ella Erikainen.

Leith Rollo, b. 5 Mar 1916 Moose River ME, m.(1) 6 Jul 1940 Skowhegan ME (later div.) Thelma M. Linkletter of Cambridge ME, b. 1922 d. 26 Jul 1985, dau. Parker and Eva W. (Carle) Linkletter; m.(2) 4 Dec 1954 Skowhegan ME Lena A. Beane of Concord ME, b. 31 Mar 1929, dau. Granville and Florence Beane.

Harold Henry, b. 18 Aug 1917, d. 26 Sep 1917.

Ellsworth Milton, b. 4 Mar 1921, unm. Went to California.

Milford Eugene, b. 22 Jan 1923 Moose River ME, m. 7 Jul 1969 Ethelyn Ashby of Vasselboro ME, b. 23 Feb 1929.

Linwood Leo, b. 23 Mar 1924 Moose River ME, m. 30 Mar 1947 Skowhegan ME Ruth A. Tuscan, b. 23 Feb 1929, dau. Royce and Wyona H. (Simpson) Tuscan.

Glendon Leroy, b. 16 Feb 1929 Moose River ME, m.(1) 9 Oct 1954 (later div.) Loantha E. Ward of Guilford ME, b. 1935; m.(2) 4 Jul 1960 Bingham ME Joyce Demko of Bingham ME, b. 12 Sep 1937 d. 5 Aug 1976, dau. George J. and Mildred (MacFarland) Demko.

Sources: VR Skowhegan ME, SA/ME. Frances Sawyer rec.

641. **REED A.10 SAWYER** [see 607], b. 6 Feb 1896 Moose River ME, d. 22 Dec 1954 Skowhegan ME, m. Naomi P. Newton of Augusta ME, b. 9 Oct 1893 d. 8 Feb 1965, dau. Isaac and Jennie (Wilson) Newton. Carpenter.

Hollis Reed, m. Sylvia J. McKeon.

Sources: VT Skowhegan ME, SA/ME. Ethelyn Nichols rec.

642. **ROSCOE WILBUR10 SAWYER** [see 614], b. 1 Apr 1881 Henniker NH, d. Jan 1950 Unity NH, m. 20 Jan 1910 Nora A. Pletzner of Gilsum NH, b. 13 Jul 1892 d. 14 Jan 1934, dau. John A. and Emily (Howard) Pletzner. Farmer. In Lempster NH, Gilsum NH. He bur. in Goshen NH, his wife in Nash Corner Cem., Gilsum NH.

Norman Edward, b. 21 Jul 1911 Lempster NH, m. 19 Dec 1947 Keene NH Eva A. (Guptil) Martin of W. Baldwin ME, b. 4 Mar 1905. World War II. In Munsonville NH. No CH.

Edith Nora, b. 7 Apr 1913, m. 12 Nov 1932 Stillman D. Nash.

Herman, b. 30 Sep 1914 Lempster NH, m.(1) Frances Burquist of Everett MA, b. 9 Mar 1911 d. 24 Aug 1961, dau. Frank and Fanny (DeLong) Burquist; m. (2) 2 Jul 1962 Millicent A. Sells of New York, b. 1 Aug 1920, dau. Theodore and Louisa Smith. In W. Virginia. CH: David Oscar, stillborn 29 Oct 1946; Philip Andrew, adopted, b. 25 Sep 1949.

Ernest Roscoe, b. 21 Aug 1916 Lempster NH, m. Dorothy C. Howard of Keene NH, b. 8 Oct 1921, dau. John H. and Matilda (Sharkey) Howard. In Keene NH, Marlborough NH. CH: Vena Rae, b. 18 Jan 1943; Ernest Rosco, b. 17 Jan 1945, d. 1 Feb 1974; Leesa Marie, b. 28 Mar 1947.

Elsie, b. 1918, m.(1) Richard H. Pelkey, m.(2) James Bennet Graves, m.(3) Christopher A. Horne.

Helen May, b. 15 Feb 1920, m. Willard H. Bennet.

Clifford Ray, b. 2 Jan 1922 Gilsum NH, m. 23 Jul 1945 E. Lempster NH Maydeane Frye, b. 18 Apr 1924, dau. Harry and Ruth (Barton) Frye. World War II. In Hanover NH, Cornish NH. CH: Dana Ray, b. 17 Feb 1951; m. 15 Sep 1974 Linda Normand.

Harry George, b. 16 Jun 1923, d. 30 Jul 1923 Gilsum NH.

Sources: VR Henniker NH, Gilsum NH, SA/NH.

643. **HARRY ALBERT[10] SAWYER** [see 617], b. 25 Dec 1899 Wolfeboro NH, d. 16 May 1936 Watertown NY, m. 13 May 1922 Franklin NH Gladys Irene Minard of Manchester NH, b. 23 Oct 1903 d. 1 Oct 1985, adopted dau. James E. and Mary S. (Gardner) Minard. Note: Gladys' birth mother was Lilla Sawyer [see 340].

Clarence Eugene, b. 11 Oct 1922, d. 10 Apr 1984, m. Lorraine Thomas. CH: Clarence Eugene, b. 11 Nov 1946. m. Pamela McWeeney; Dale, b. 20 Jun 1949, m. Joseph DeMezzo.

Daughter, b. 8 Feb 1924, d. same day.

Sources: VR SA/NH. Clarence Eugene Sawyer rec.

644. **GEORGE CARTER[10] SAWYER** [see 623], b. 18 Dec 1899 Weare NH, d. 11 Sep 1988, m. 18 Jun 1921 E. Weare NH Eva M. Moore of Calais ME, b. 6 Feb 1897 d. 5 May 1970, dau. Frederick and Georgia (Hanson) Moore.

George M., b. 1 Nov 1932, m. 9 Oct 1960 Nancy Reade.

Sources: Obit, George Carter Sawyer rec.

# PART III

## ☙ THOMAS OF LANCASTER ❧

1. **THOMAS[1] SAWYER** was born in England ca. 1616[a], according to published genealogies. Upon his arrival in Massachusetts in 1636, he settled in Ipswich. In 1643 he moved to Rowley, where, known as the village blacksmith, he lived near his brother, Edward. In 1646 he moved west to Nashaway Plantation (now Lancaster), along with the Prescotts, Wilders, Houghtons, and two other families, thereby becoming one of the first six settlers in that area. Later that year (or in 1648) he married Mary Prescott[b]. Thomas and Mary had the large family shown below.

Very active during his lifetime, Thomas contributed much to the settlement and development of Lancaster, serving often as Prudential Manager. He was a selectman as late as 1685. In 1652 he was the third subscriber to the town and church covenant, and on 3 May 1654 was admitted as a freeman. He was a church member three years later. Not only a blacksmith, Thomas was a builder as well; with his father-in-law, John Prescott, he erected many saw mills and grist mills, two important sources of shelter and food in the wilderness of central Massachusetts. Like most early settlers he was also a part-time soldier, and the Sawyer home was one of five garrison houses where town inhabitants took refuge during Indian raids.

Hostile Indians were, of course, a serious problem in those early days. Among the incidents involving the Sawyer family was the so-called Great Massacre of 10 February 1676, when King Philip and some 1500 warriors attacked the town and killed or captured 50 of the residents -- one-sixth of the entire population[c]. Ephraim, son of Thomas, was one of those killed at Prescott's Garrison, in what is now the town of Clinton. So great was the devastation that the survivors left Lancaster and did not return for four years. The Sawyer family may have lived in Charlestown during the interim[d].

Thomas Sawyer lived most of his life in a house on a low-lying lot beside the Nashua River, bordering Narrow Lane in South Lancaster near the Atherton Bridge. Apparently he owned a fair amount of land, for in 1693 he gave to his son John 25 acres of "the second division upland," and in 1699 gave to his youngest son Nathaniel half of the upland and a house lot of 10 acres near Narrow Lane, the other half having previously been given to his son Thomas. In his will, moreover, dated 6 March 1706 and proved on 12 April 1720, he bequeathed 40 acres of land (along with a pair of young oxen, a mare, and 10 shillings) to Thomas and 10 acres (and five shillings) to each of his other sons, Joshua, James, Caleb and Nathaniel.

Thomas died in Lancaster on 12 September 1706 and was buried in the Old Settlers Burial Field, where his tombstone still stands. His wife was designated as the sole executor of his estate. On 12 April 1720, she being dead, son Thomas appeared in court for the purpose of adminstering the estate. In a letter to the court dated 28 December 1719, meanwhile, Mary (Sawyer) Wilder, oldest daughter, while excusing herself for not appearing in court on account of her "age and the extremity of the weather," requested an allowance from her father's estate in recompense for the

---

[a] His actual birthdate is not known, but his gravestone states that he died in 1706 at "about 90 years."

[b] Mary was the daughter of John Prescott, founder of Nashaway Plantation, and Mary Platt (sometimes written Platta or Platts). She was baptized in Sowerby, Halifax Parish, Yorkshire, England, on 24 February 1630 and died in April 1716.

[c] A bronze marker erected in South Lancaster reads: "Site of Thomas Sawyer's Garrison House. Between the Massacre of February 10, 1676 and the Abandonment of the Town the Inhabitants Took Refuge in the Stevens (Willard) and Sawyer Garrisons."

[d] Thomas[1] had bought "1 1/2 Aker, house, garden and piece of Marsh" in Charlestown on 6 October 1650.

care of her "father and Mother, whilst my brother Thomas was in Captivity the time they were with me 8 or 9 months and I was at the whole charge of my said father's burial." Whether she received the allowance is not recorded.

1. Thomas[1] and Mary had the following children:
2 Thomas[2], 1649-1736.
Ephraim, b. 16 Nov 1650, d. 10 Feb 1676 in the Great Massacre.
Marie (Mary), b. 4 Nov 1653, m. 24 Nov 1673 Nathaniel Wilder.
Elizabeth, b. 7 Jan 1654, d.y.
3 Joshua[2], 1656-1738.
4 James[2], 1657-1753.
5 Caleb[2], 1659-1755.
6 John[2], 1661-1705.
Elizabeth, b. 5 Jan 1664, d. 16 Jan 1745, m. 6 Feb 1788 James Hosmer.
Deborah, b. 1666, d. 17 May 1666.
7 Nathaniel[2], 1670-1756.
Martha, b. 10 Aug 1673, m. John Woods.
Hannah, b. ?, m. 15 Apr 1706 in Concord MA Joseph Blood of Groton MA [W21]. This dau. is not listed in Lancaster VR.

Sources: VR Lancaster MA. W72, G39, H75, W21, Will.

2. **THOMAS[2] SAWYER** [see 1], b. 2 May 1649 Lancaster MA, d. 5 Sep 1736 Lancaster MA, m.(1) 11 Aug 1670 Sarah Fairbanks, b. 9 Dec 1645 Dedham MA d. 2 Jan 1672, dau. John and Sarah (Fiske) Fairbanks; m.(2) 21 Aug 1672 Hannah Lewis of Lancaster MA, b. 18 Mar 1649, dau. William and Amy (Weld) Lewis; m.(3) 15 Jul 1718 Mary (Rice) White, wid. of Josiah, b. 4 Sep 1656 d. 22 Aug 1733 Sudbury MA, dau. Thomas and Mary (King) Rice of Sudbury MA; m.(4) 15 Dec 1733 Anna Ross, wid. of Thomas, b. ? d. Nov 1753. Blacksmith, millwright, and builder. He joined the First Church of Lancaster MA in 1718. His wid. joined the church at Sterling MA in 1745. His entire family is accounted for in his will.

On 26 October 1708, 59-year-old Thomas[2], his son Elias, 21, and one John Biglo (Bigelow) were captured by Indians and taken to Canada. When the party reached Montreal, Sawyer offered to erect a saw mill on the River Chambly on condition that the French governor obtain the release of the captives. Apparently there was little difficulty in arranging for the freedom of young Elias and Mr. Biglo, but for some reason the Indians were determined to put Thomas to death by slow torture. This may have been their way of paying tribute to him, for he was reputed to be a very brave man. In any event, a seeming miracle, probably arranged by the French governor, saved Thomas. He had already been tied to the stake when a friar appeared before the Indians and announced dramatically that he held the key to Purgatory in his hand. Unless they released their prisoner at once, he thundered, he would unlock the gate and throw them all in! The Indians, being superstitious, turned Thomas over to the French. He finished the saw mill as promised -- reportedly the first built in Canada -- before the year was out, and was sent home to Lancaster along with John Biglo. Elias Sawyer remained for some time in order to teach the Canadians the art of "sawing and keeping the mill in order, and then was dismissed with rich presents."[a]

Mary, b. 30 Nov 1671, d. 1766, m. Joshua Rice.
Bezaleel, b. 1673, d.y.
Hannah, b. 23 May 1675 Marlborough MA, d. 1 May 1765, m. Jonathan Moore.
8 William[3], 1679-1741.
9 Joseph[3], 1683-1737.

---

[a] His story appears in published histories of Lancaster, as well as in many Sawyer family histories. See Peter Whitney, *Worcester County Massachusetts History, Worcester MA 1793.*

10 Bezaleel[3], 1685-1760.
11 Elias[3], 1689-1752.
Sources: VR Lancaster MA. M19, F25, W21, W39, N27, K2, Will.

3. **JOSHUA[2] SAWYER** [see 1], b. 13 Mar 1656 Lancaster MA, d. 14 Jul 1738 Woburn MA, m. 2 Jan 1678 Concord MA Sarah (Wright) Potter of Concord MA, wid. of Samuel, b. 16 Feb 1653, dau. Deacon John and Priscilla Wright of Charlestown MA. In Woburn MA 1670. King Philip War: Member of Captain Henchman's Company, 1676. Signed petition in Marlborough MA 1677.

Abigail,b. 17 May 1679, d. 6 Jan 1707, m. 22 May 1699 John Converse.
Mary, b. ?, d. 1766, m. 19 Dec 1698 Robert Converse.
12 Joshua[3], 1684-1738.
Sarah, b. 4 Jul 1687, d. 1 Mar 1737, m. 1 Feb 1705 Lt. Thomas Reed.
Hannah, b. 25 Nov 1689, d. 18 Jun 1747, m. 30 Dec 1706 Josiah Converse.
Martha, b. 26 Apr 1692.
Elizabeth, b. 7 Nov 1698, d. 22 Jul 1764, m. 16 Dec 1718 Joseph Blodgett.
Sources: VR Lancaster MA, Concord MA. S52, M51, S60.

4. **JAMES[2] SAWYER** [see 1], b. 22 Jan 1657 Lancaster MA, d. 27 Jan 1753 Pomfret CT, m.(1) 4 Feb 1678 Concord MA Mary Marble, b. ? d. 20 Mar 1709; m.(2) Mary Prescott, b. ? d. 28 Dec 1763. Blacksmith. King Philip War: Enl. at Concord MA 24 Aug 1676; member of garrison 1691. Proprietor of Okoocangansett Plantation 1686. On Marlborough MA tax list 1688. B/land in Pomfret CT 1709 and built first grist mill on Bark Meadow Brook. Cornet in Windham CT militia 1710.

13 Ephraim[3], b. 1678.
James, b. 12 Jul 1686.
Mary, b. 17 Sep 1696, d. 17 Sep 1696 Marlborough MA.
Benjamin, b. 11 Feb 1698 Marlborough MA, d. 24 Sep 1761 Pomfret CT, m. 27 Jan 1721 Mary Elmar, b. ?. Settler of Pomfret CT. CH: Mary, b. 16 Apr 1723, m. 25 Aug 1742 Amariah Winchester; Sarah, b. 30 Jun 1724, m. 1 Nov 1744 Simon Carpenter; Hannah, b. ca. 1727, m. John Jeffords.
Cornelius, b. 30 Aug 1712, d. 25 Jan 1735.
Mary, b. 11 Sep 1714, m. 25 May 1735 John Atherton.
14 Jonas[3], 1716-1791.
Martha, b. 19 May 1719, m. 9 Nov 1745 Joseph White.
15 Joseph[3], 1721-1791.
Sarah, b. 9 Aug 1724, m. John Jones.
16 Thomas[3], b. 1726.
Sources: VR Lancaster MA, Pomfret CT. H65, N5.

5. **CALEB[2] SAWYER** [see 1], b. 20 Feb 1659 Lancaster MA, d. 12 Feb 1755 Harvard MA, m. 28 Dec 1687 Sarah Houghton, b. 17 Feb 1662 d. 15 Nov 1751, dau. Ralph and Jane (Stowe) Houghton. Selectman for Harvard MA 1737. His home, a garrison, was standing in the early 1900's.

John, b. 1688 Lancaster MA, d. 2 Oct 1731 Lancaster MA, m. Ruth ____, b. ?. CH: Sarah, b. ?, d. 21 Dec 1717; Damaris, b. 1 Apr 1725, m. 7 May 1751 Matthias Larkin; Dinah, b. 16 Feb 1728.
Abigail, b. 1689, d. 9 Apr 1778, m. 18 Nov 1730 Thomas Wright.
17 Jonathan[3], 1690-1746.
Hepsibah, b. 1692, m. 28 Jan 1719 Jabez Fairbanks, Jr.

Beulah, b. 1699, m. 23 Jun 1737 Ebenezer Taylor.
18 Seth[3], 1705-1768.
19 Joseph[3], 1709-1775.
Sources: VR Lancaster MA. N36, O1, F2.

6. **JOHN[2] SAWYER** [see 1], b. 6 Feb 1661 Lancaster MA, d. 1705 Lyme CT, m. 16 Jan 1686 Lancaster MA Mary Bull (Ball?) of Worcester MA, b. ? d. 27 Feb 1750. In Worcester MA, Saybrook CT, Lyme CT, Hebron CT.
20 Edward[3], 1687-1766.
21 Jacob[3], b. 1689.
Elizabeth, b. ? Lancaster MA.
22 Moses[3], ca. 1690-1732.
Joseph, b. ca. 1692 Lyme CT. In Hebron CT.
James, b. ca. 1696 Lyme CT. In Lyme, Hebron CT.
Mercy, b. ? Lyme CT.
John, b. ca. 1699 Lyme CT. In Hebron CT.
Oliver, b. ca. 1700 Lyme CT.
Sources: VR Lancaster MA, Lyme CT. P49, H37A.

7. **NATHANIEL[2] SAWYER** [see 1], b. 24 Nov 1670 Lancaster MA, d. 10 Nov 1756 Lancaster MA, m.(1) 1692 Mary _____, b. ?; m.(2) bef. 1724 Elizabeth _____, b. ? d. 28 Oct 1768. French and Indian War. S/land 1709, 1724, 1738, 1753.
23 Amos[3], 1693-1756.
24 Ephraim[3], 1694-1759.
25 Samuel[3], 1697-1784.
26 John[3], b. 1700.
27 Ezra[3], 1702-1765.
28 Nathaniel[3], b. 1706.
Mary, b. 1708, m. 17 Jan 1729 Hezikiah Gates.
29 Thomas[3], ca. 1711-1787.
Jonathan, b. ?, m. Thankful _____, b. ?.
30 Phineas[3], ca. 1713-1787.
Sources: VR Lancaster MA. W21, R10h.

## THIRD GENERATION

8. **WILLIAM[3] SAWYER** [see 2], b. 2 Feb 1679 Lancaster MA, d. 3 Feb 1741 Bolton MA, m. 1700 Mary Houghton of Woburn MA, b. 7 Feb 1679 d. 1 Apr 1752 Bolton MA, dau. John 2nd and Mary (Farrer) Houghton. William owned 300 acres in Bolton MA and is bur. in ground he gave to the town. Mary joined the Church of Lancaster 1711. Note: Bolton MA History says that William was also the father of Benjamin, Isreal, Joseph and Uriah, but these do not appear in the vital records.
Mary, b.?, m.(1) 27 Feb 1723 Abraham Willard, m.(2) Phineas Willard.
Hannah, b. ?, m.(1) 19 Jan 1727 John Snow, m.(2) Jonathan Powers.
Hepzibah, b. ?, m.(1) 25 Feb 1729 William Whitcomb, m.(2) Increase Powers.
31 Aholiab[4], ca. 1711.
32 William[4], 1711-1794.
33 Josiah[4], 1714-1805.
Thankful, b. 4 Apr 1717, d. 18 Mar 1782, m. 8 Apr 1735 Jonathan Fairbanks.
Martha, b. 5 Jul 1719, m. 13 May 1738 Charles Wilder.

David, b. 27 Aug 1721 Lancaster MA.
Abigail, b. 23 Aug 1724.
Sources: VR Lancaster MA, Bolton MA, Littleton MA. H76, H75, W37A, F2, P63.

9. **JOSEPH$^3$ SAWYER** [see 2], b. 1683 Lancaster MA, d. 10 Jul 1737 Lancaster MA, m.(1) Lancaster MA Sarah T. Beaman, b. 25 Jan 1681 d. 7 Mar 1718, dau. John and Priscilla (Thornton) Beaman and grandaughter of Bezaleel Beaman, one of the first settlers of Lancaster MA; m.(2) 10 Nov 1718 Lancaster MA Abigail Wilder, b.?. Blacksmith. Joined the First Church of Lancaster 1718. On 10 October 1733 he was a founder of the First Church of Harvard MA. Built Sawyer's Mill in 1721. He bur. in Old Settlers Burial Ground, Lancaster MA.

34 Joseph$^4$, ca. 1705-ca. 1743.
Sarah, b. 1707, m. 15 Dec 1726 Ephraim Houghton.
35 Thomas$^4$, 1710-1797.
Abner, b. 1711 Lancaster MA, d. 6 Dec 1758 Lancaster MA, m. 8 Apr 1736 in Lancaster MA Mary Wilder, b. ?, dau. Oliver and Mary (Fairbanks) Wilder. Wid. in Sterling MA 1790. He bur. in Chocksett Burial Ground, Lancaster MA. CH: Kezia, b. 2 Dec 1739, m.(1) 11 Dec 1760 Ezra Sawyer, m.(2) 1779 Ephraim Powers; Hannah, b. 11 Feb 1744, m. 2 Jul 1772 Jonathan Buttrick; Releaf, b. 29 Dec 1749, d. 31 Jul 1814, m. 20 Apr 1768 Richard Rand, went to Vermont; Mary, b. 13 Dec 1751, m. 5 Oct 1769 Abijah Houghton; Olive, b. 13 Apr 1754, d. 6 Oct 1756; Prudence, b. 26 Mar 1757, m. 18 Mar 1784 Josiah Randall.
Asenath, b. 1714, d.25 Feb 1753, m. 18 Jun 1735 Jonathan Osgood.
Mary, b. ca. 1717, d. 2 Dec 1794, m. 1 Jun 1737 Phineas Sawyer.
Sources: Sterling MA census 1790. VR Lancaster MA. M19, B84, W64.

10. **BEZALEEL$^3$ SAWYER** [see 2], b. 13 May 1685 Lancaster MA, d. 25 Aug 1760 Lancaster MA, m.(1) Eunice _____, b. 1687 d. 14 Mar 1713; m.(2) 4 Mar 1713 Judith White, b. 1694 d. 24 Mar 1774, dau. Josiah and Mary (Rice) White. Farmer. Constable, Town Treasurer. B/land in Clinton MA 1719 in part of Lancaster which became Sterling MA in 1781.

Infant, stillborn 1713.
Eunice, b. 27 Nov 1716, m.(1) Dr. John Dunsmore, m.(2) Samuel Gambell.
36 Josiah$^4$, 1718-1801.
37 Darius$^4$, 1720-1789.
38 Bezaleel$^4$, 1723-ca. 1785.
Hannah, b. 13 Sep 1725, d. 30 Jan 1727.
Hannah, b. 4 Jan 1728, d. 29 Jan 1770.
39 Moses$^4$, b. 1730.
40 Paul$^4$, 1733-1783.
Thomas, b. 4 Aug 1737 Lancaster MA, d. 1 Mar 1760 Lancaster MA, m. Anna Ross, b. 1736 d. 5 Nov 1753. He bur. in Old Settlers Burial Ground, Lancaster MA.
Mary, b.?, d. 1 Aug 1813, m. 16 Nov 1758 Concord MA Richard Baker.
Sources: VR Lancaster MA. M19, E16.

11. **ELIAS$^3$ SAWYER** [see 2], b. ca. 1689 Lancaster MA, d. 20 Nov 1752 Bolton MA, m. Beatrix. Houghton, b. 3 Sep 1685 d. 1770 Lunenburg MA, dau. Robert and Esther (Lippenwell) Houghton. Elias and his father were captured by Indians 1705 (see Thomas$^2$, above). He and Beatrix joined First Church of Lancaster MA, 1716. Both bur. in Old Settlers Burial Ground, Lancaster MA. Note: [C9] says that sons Elijah and Elisha were twins

Bette, b. 1712, d. Jul 1807, m. 19 Jan 1739 Thomas Carter.
41 Elijah$^4$, 1713-ca. 1790.

Thankful, b. 1715, d. 5 Dec 1755, m. 9 Feb 1731 Nathaniel Carter of Leominster MA.
42 Elisha$^{4}$, 1718-1786.
Prudence, b. 24 Sep 1726, d. 10 Jan 1747, m. 29 Mar 1744 James Carter.
Sources: VR Lancaster MA. M19, C9.

12. **JOSHUA$^{3}$ SAWYER** [see 3], b. 20 Jun 1684 Woburn MA, d. 1 Mar 1738 Woburn MA, m. 22 May 1706 Charlestown MA Mary Carter of Woburn MA, b. 17 Jul 1683 d. 23 Oct 1751 Charlestown MA, dau. Thomas and Margery (Whitmore) Carter. He bur. in First Burial Ground, Woburn MA.

Mary, b. 14 Sep 1706, d. 22 Nov 1783, m. 26 Aug 1736 Stephen Richardson.
Ruth, b. 6 Mar 1709, d. 15 Jun 1787, m. 1731 Joseph Wright.
Sarah, b. 3 Sep 1711.
43 Joshua$^{4}$, 1713-1767.
Abigail,b. 15 Nov 1714, m.(1) 1736 Abraham Annis, m.(2) 1754 John Childs.
44 John$^{4}$, 1716-1784.
45 James$^{4}$, 1718-1793.
Phebe, b. 3 Jan 1720, d. 18 Nov 1765, m. 14 Sep 1738 Samuel Tidd.
46 Benjamin$^{4}$, b. 1721.
47 Oliver$^{4}$, b. 1726.
48 Jonathan$^{4}$, 1728-1813.
Sources: VR Woburn MA. N5, F16.

13. **EPHRAIM$^{3}$ SAWYER** [see 4], b. 2 Dec 1678 Marlborough MA, m. 4 Jul 1700 Marlborough MA Elizabeth George, b. ?, dau. Joshua and Elizabeth George of Dorchester MA. In Mansfield CT 1708, Windham CT 1717. Granted rights at Falls of Willimantic River, Windham CT 1718.

James, b. 14 Apr 1701 Marlborough MA. In Mansfield CT?
49 Joshua$^{4}$, b. 1703.
Mary, b. 13 Dec 1704, d. 5 Dec 1758, m. Norwich CT 14 Oct 1724 Joseph Downer.
50 Jacob$^{4}$, 1706-1758.
51 Elijah$^{4}$, 1708-1792.
Bethy, b. 24 Aug 1711, d. Jan 1815, m. 1732 Aholiab Sawyer.
52 Jeduthan, b. 1713.
Sources: VR Mansfield CT, Windham CT, Marlborough MA. B38, W60, D52.

14. **JONAS$^{3}$ SAWYER** [see 4], b. 4 Sep 1716 Pomfret CT, d. 2 Nov 1791 Pomfret CT, m. 11 Nov 1746 Lydia Ross of Windom CT, b. 22 Mar 1728 d. 4 Sep 1781, dau. Joseph and Sarah (Utley) Ross. In Killingly CT 1755, Woodstock CT 1759.

53 James$^{4}$, 1747-1828.
54 Cornelius$^{4}$, b. 1748.
Sarah, b. 2 Jun 1751, m. 1 Feb 1770 John Wade of Putnam CT.
55 William$^{4}$, b. 1754.
Sybil, b. 10 Aug 1756, d. 8 Jan 1777.
Daughter, b. 2 Mar 1760.
Prescott, b. 20 Jul 1761 Woodstock CT, m. 16 Oct 1783 Anne Stoddard of Pomfret CT, b. 9 Jan 1763, dau. Ebenezer and Ann Stoddard. CH: Nancy, b. 16 Oct 1784; Chloe Stoddard, b. 16 Dec 1790.
Sources: Pomfret CT census 1800. Somers CT census 1810. VR Pomfret CT, Woodstock CT. B3, P58, C15.

15. **JOSEPH$^{3}$ SAWYER** [see 4], b. 5 Dec 1721 Pomfret CT, d. 5 Jan 1791 Reading VT, m. 21 Nov 1750 Hannah Hutchins, b. 6 Dec 1726 d. 4 Apr 1813, dau. Thomas and Sarah Hutchins.

Anna, b. 5 Oct 1751, d. 3 Aug 1786.

Joseph, b. 14 Apr 1753 Pomfret CT, d. 8 Apr 1846 Westmoreland NH, m. 18 Mar 1781 Reading VT Abigail Kendall, b.?, Revolutionary War: Enl. Dec 1775, served eight mos; enl. 1777, served one year CH: 2 dau, 3 sons.

56 John$^{4}$, 1755-1847. Went to New York.

Hannah, b. 5 Feb 1758, m. Thomas Hapgood of Reading VT.

57 Cornelius$^{4}$, 1760-1835.

58 Benjamin$^{4}$, 1763-1842.

Mary, b. 9 Aug 1765, d. 16 Aug 1843, m. 31 Mar 1785 Isaac Kimball.

Eleanor, b. 6 Jan 1769, d. 1813.

Sarah, b. 6 Jan 1769.

Sources: Westmoreland NH census 1790, 1800, 1820. VR Pomfret CT. D18, M54, P58.

16. **THOMAS$^{3}$ SAWYER** [see 4], b. 20 Nov 1726 Pomfret CT, m. 7 Nov 1751 Sarah Ross, b. ?. In Dudley MA 1758-1763, Wyoming Valley PA.

Olive, b. 7 Dec 1754, d.y.

Lemuel, b. 30 Nov 1758 Dudley MA.

Asa, b. 23 Apr 1761, d. in the Army.

Thomas, b. ?, d. in the Army.

Sarah, b. 12 May 1763, d. 16 Mar 1833, m. William Slocum.

Rhoda, b. ?, m. General John Swift.

Daniel, b. 30 Oct 1775, d. 18 Jan 1819, m. 2 Jul 1794 Theodosia P. Boughton, b. ?.

Sources: VR Pomfret CT, Dudley MA.

17. **JONATHAN$^{3}$ SAWYER** [see 5], b. 1690 Lancaster MA, d. 30 Sep 1746 Harvard MA, m. 1711 Elizabeth Wheelock, b. 1697 d. 8 Mar 1765, dau. Joseph and Elizabeth Wheelock of Lancaster MA. Captain of a militia company 1737.

59 Jonathan$^{4}$, 1715-1805.

Elizabeth, b. 6 Oct 1717, m. 16 Feb 1736 Joshua Moore.

60 Caleb$^{4}$, 1720-1815.

Lois, b. 9 Feb 1723, d. 12 Oct 1724.

61 Paul$^{4}$, ca. 1725-179?.

Olive, b. 29 May 1726, d. 1755, m. 25 Aug 1747 David Whitney.

Sarah, b. 30 Jul 1727, m. 12 Feb 1742 Gabriel Priest, Jr.

62 Manasseh$^{4}$, 1729-1808.

Lois, b. 6 Aug 1732, d. 12 Oct 1746.

Sources: N36, P46, J3.

18. **SETH$^{3}$ SAWYER** [see 5], b. 7 Jan 1704 Lancaster MA, d. 29 Mar 1768 Harvard MA, m.(1) 11 Jan 1726 Lancaster MA Dinah Farrar, b. 1704 d. 25 Oct 1727; m.(2) 12 Oct 1732 Harvard MA Hepsibah Whitney of Harvard MA, b. 1710 d. May 1797, dau. Richard and Elizabeth (Sawtelle) Whitney of Stowe MA. Selectman for Harvard MA 1755. Wid. in Harvard MA 1790.

John, b. 5 May 1734 Harvard MA, d. 22 Mar 1796 Harvard MA, m. 4 Feb 1761 Harvard MA Elizabeth Gates, b. 1 Oct 1736 d. 24 Oct 1822, dau. Jacob and Elizabeth Gates. Wid. in Harvard MA 1800. CH: Child, b. 1761, d. Sep 1761; Hepsibah, b. 2 Apr 1763; Relief, b. 5 Sep 1765, d. 8 Jan 1788; Elizabeth, b. 6 Nov 1767, m. 6 Jun 1786 Joseph Pratt; Seth, b. 22 Sep 1769, d. 15 Jun 1771; Dinah, b. 15 Nov 1771, d. 12 Jun 1825, m.

16 May 1799 John Pierce; Hannah, b. 2 Nov 1776, d. 13 Sep 1844, m. 11 Jun 1797 Leonard Whitcomb of Boxboro MA.
63 Caleb[4], 1737-1820.
Dinah, b. 11 Apr 1739, m. 17 Sep 1772 Nathan Agar.
Betty, b. 15 Nov 1741, m. 7 Jun 1771 Stephen Wilder.
64 Phinehas[4], b. 1746.
Sources: Harvard MA census 1790, 1800. VR Lancaster MA, Harvard MA. P46, N36.

19. **JOSEPH[3] SAWYER** [see 5], b. 1709 Lancaster MA, d. 9 May 1775 Harvard MA, m. 9 Mar 1732 Harvard MA Abigail Foskett of Harvard MA, b. Feb 1709 d. 30 Mar 1793 Boxboro MA. Note: I believe that Joseph is the son of Caleb[2], who lived and died in Harvard MA, where Joseph lived. All other Sawyers of the second generation were in Lancaster MA or Connecticut.
John, b. 17 Feb 1734 Harvard MA.
Abigail, b. 3 Oct 1735, d. 15 May 1740.
65 Oliver[4], b. 1738.
66 Joseph[4], Jr., b. 1741.
Lemuel, b. 15 May 1745, d. 30 Oct 1809, unm.
Mary, b. 15 May 1745.
Sarah, b. 17 Nov 1748, m. 19 Jun 1777 William Whitcomb of Bolton MA.
Sources: VR Lancaster MA, Harvard MA. N36.

20. **EDWARD[3] SAWYER** [see 6], b. 30 Mar 1687 Lancaster MA, d. 27 Mar 1766 Hebron CT, m. 3 Jul 1707 Lyme CT Elizabeth Mack of Hebron CT, b. 28 Oct 1687 Hebron CT d. 15 Mar 1750, dau. John and Sarah (Bagley) Mack. King Phillip War.
John, b. 3 Sep 1708 Hebron CT, d. 1 Jan 1794 Hebron CT, m. 10 May 1733 Barsheba Mann, b. 1702 d. 30 Jan 1795. CH: Rachell, b. 10 Feb 1734, m. 26 Mar 1752 Nathaniel Phelps; John, b. 6 Apr 1735, d. 16 Jan 1737; Mary, b. 25 Jun 1737, m. 14 Nov 1754 Jacob Ellis; Delight, b. 26 Mar 1739, m. 31 Jan 1759 Asher Merrill; Elizabeth, b. 7 May 1741, m. 11 Dec 1760 John Ellis; John, b. 15 Jun 1743,d. 1 Dec 1753.
Jonathan, b. 16 Sep 1710 Hebron CT, d. 10 Apr 1737 Hebron CT, m. 28 Jan 1731 Dorothy Post, b. 29 Jan 1708, dau. Stephen and Hannah (Hasmer) Post. Wid. m. 10 Mar 1743 Ronald Beakwith, Bolton CT. CH: Delight, b. 25 Mar 1737, d. 28 Mar 1737.
Edward, b. 19 Jan 1713, d. 1 Dec 1736.
67 Thomas[4], 1715-1785.
Elizabeth, b. 16 Jan 1717, d. 18 Jun 1804, m. 6 Jul 1738 Benjamin Bissel.
Mary, b. 23 Mar 1719, d. 5 Dec 1736.
68 Isaac[4], 1721-1786.
Lydia, b. 2 Nov 1723, m. 16 Aug 1744 Benjamin Beach.
Joseph, b. 27 Dec 1725, d. 27 Jan 1747.
Hannah, b. 9 Apr 1728, d. 27 Jan 1802, m. 7 Sep 1747 Jonathan Hutchinson.
Phebe, b. 5 Nov 1730, d. 30 Nov 1763, m. 26 May 1748 Benjamin Carter.
Sources: C9, P49, A25.

21. **JACOB[3] SAWYER** [see 6], b. ca. 1689 Lancaster MA, m. 22 Jun 1710 Lyme CT Martha Loomes, b. ?, dau. Stephen Loomes. Blacksmith. In Lyme CT.
Martha, b. 7 May 1711.
James, b. 7 Dec 1712 Lyme CT, d. 2 Jan 1795 East Haddam CT, m.(1) 30 Apr 1739 Colchester CT Hezadiah Bartlett, b. ?; m.(2) 20 Sep 1759 East Haddem CT Amy (Scoville) Rogers, wid. of Adam, b. 1711 d. 1 Feb 1793, dau. Benjamin and Amy Scoville. In Colchester CT, Bolton CT, East Haddam CT. CH: Sarah Ward, b. 24 Jul

1740; Eunice, b. 9 Jan 1743, m. 27 Jan 1762 Pierce Mohs; Hezadiah, b. ?, m. 29 Oct 1764 Isaiah Chapman.

Elias, b. ?.

69 Jacob$^4$, b. ca. 1720.

Sources: VR SA/CT. P49, J3, N5.

22. **MOSES$^3$ SAWYER** [see 6], b. ca. 1690, d. 7 Feb 1732 Hebron CT, m. 14 Feb 1717 Hebron CT Ruth Lewis, b. 1 Jan 1695, dau. Thomas and Sarah (Percival) Lewis.

Ruth, b. 28 Nov 1717, m. 10 Jun 1734 Aaron Fuller.

Sarah, b. 2 Feb 1720, d. 11 Sep 1774, m. 2 Apr 1747 Thomas Carter.

70 Nathan$^4$, 1722-ca. 1759.

Child, b. 24 Mar 1724, d. same day.

Moses, b. 19 Apr 1725, d. 30 Jul 1727.

Moses, b. 11 Apr 1728, d. 7 Feb 1732.

Mary, b. 31 Mar 1731, m. 14 Nov 1754 Jabez Ellis.

John, b. 31 Mar 1731, d. 4 Jun 1731.

Sources: VR SA/CT, Colchester CT. C9, M11, J3.

23. **AMOS$^3$ SAWYER** [see 7], b. 20 Jun 1693 Lancaster MA, d. 29 Dec 1756 Lancaster MA, m. 14 May 1719 Lancaster MA Abigail Houghton, b. 18 Apr 1689 d. 20 Nov 1753, dau. Robert and Esther (Lippenwell) Houghton. She bur. in Old Settlers Burial Ground, Lancaster MA.

Esther, b. 20 Apr 1720, d. 6 Sep 1720.

Abigail, b. 24 Apr 1721, d. 13 Nov 1812, m. 11 Dec 1740 Josiah Sawyer.

Amos, b. 1 Dec 1724, d. 26 Dec 1726.

Deborah, b. 25 Apr 1727, d. 2 Mar 1802, m. 29 Oct 1743 Darius Sawyer.

David, b. 29 Mar 1729, d. 3 Jun 1729.

71 Amos$^4$, 1733-1768.

Sources: VR Lancaster MA. H75, M19, Zelda Moore rec.

24. **EPHRAIM$^3$ SAWYER** [see 7], b. ca. 1694 Lancaster MA, d. 8 May 1759 Burlington VT, m.(1) 25 May 1719 Lancaster MA Eunice Houghton, b. 1 Mar 1696 d. 24 Jun 1748, dau. Jonas and Mary (Burnham) Houghton; m.(2) 23 Nov 1750 Sarah Richardson of Woburn MA, b. 1706 d. Feb 1794. Magistrate and Justice of the Peace at Sterling MA. Both joined Chocksett Church, Sterling MA, 1745. Ephriam signed petition in Lancaster MA 1746. Left a will. He bur. in Lakeview Cem., Burlington VT.

Mary, b. 1722, d. 8 May 1759, m. 29 Jun 1743 Nathaniel Wyman.

Eunice, b. 28 Feb 1725, d. 7 Sep 1760, m. 26 Dec 1744 Colonel Asa Whitcomb.

Katherine, b. 16 Jul 1727, m. 29 Apr 1756 Joseph Osgood.

72 Ephraim$^4$, 1729-1813.

Sources: VR Lancaster MA. N5, J3.

25. **SAMUEL$^3$ SAWYER** [see 7], b. 12 Feb 1697 Lancaster MA, d. 13 Jun 1784 Sterling MA, m. 20 Feb 1729 Lancaster MA Deborah Rugg, b. 11 Oct 1711 d. 17 Nov 1790, dau. Daniel and Elizabeth (Priest) Rugg. Indian Wars, 1722-25. CH were bp. in First Church of Lancaster MA until 1744, and in Chocksett Church, Sterling MA, after 13 Jan 1745. Owned Lot #2 in Petersham MA 1733. Signed petition in Lancaster MA 1746. Wid. in Sterling MA 1790.

Mary, b. 11 Feb 1730, m. 22 Jan 1752 Joseph Kilborn.

Azubah, b. 28 Aug 1732, d. 16 Sep 1756, m. 14 Mar 1753 Nathan Burpee.

Ruth, b. 10 Mar 1735, d. 9 Aug 1751.

Lucy, b. 8 Jul 1737, m. 27 Jan 1757 Jonas Brooks in Lancaster.

73 Samuel$^4$, 1740-ca. 1800.
74 Joshua$^4$, 1742-1817.
Deborah, b. 11 Oct 1744, m. 29 Nov 1764 Jonathan Wilder, Jr.
Martha, b. 3 Apr 1748, d. 30 Nov 1748.
Elizabeth, b. Sep 1750, m. 28 Dec 1769 Silas Wilder.
Ruth, b. 22 Feb 1754, m. 10 Jul 1722 David Jewett.
Sources: Sterling MA census 1790. VR Lancaster MA, Petersham MA. E16, C9, R30, J12, G38, N5.

26. **JOHN$^3$ SAWYER** [see 7], b. ca. 1700 Lancaster MA, m. 22 Nov 1722 Concord MA Sarah Joslyn, b. ca. 1704 d. ca. 1746, dau. Peter and Johannah (Whitcomb) Joslyn. Owned Lot #59 in Petersham MA 1733. John$^3$, John Jr., Deliverance and Benjamin were each allowed 100 acres in Maidstone VT 1774. In Petersham MA ca. 1742, Charlestown NH 1760, Piermont NH 1776.
Sarah, b. 13 Apr 1723, d. 17 Dec 1723.
Sarah, b. 20 Aug 1724, m. 27 Jun 1749 Barre Vt Ralph Rice.
Dorothy, b. 3 Mar 1726, m. 10 Jun 1745 Joseph Stevens of Petersham MA.
75 John$^4$, b. 1728.
Moses, b. 3 Nov 1730, d. 4 Dec 1730.
Aaron, b. 29 Aug 1731, d. 16 Sep 1731.
Nathaniel, b. 23 Apr 1733, d. 26 Apr 1733.
Damaris, b. 20 Sep 1734.
Joanna, b. 20 Sep 1734, d. 30 May 1735.
Benjamin, b. 21 Aug 1736 Lancaster MA. Witnessed will in Charlestown NH 1762. B/land in Haverhill NH and Bath NH 1764. B/land in Northumberland NH 1771.
Cornelius, b. 8 Dec 1738, d. 6 Apr 1740.
Mary, b. 8 Mar 1740, d. 13 Mar 1741.
Martha, 8 Mar 1740, d. 27 Mar 1741.
Peter, b. 31 Jan 1742 Petersham MA.
Nathaniel, b. 31 Jan 1742 Petersham MA.
Rebecca, b. 22 Apr 1744, d. 6 May 1745.
76 Deliverance (Dill), 1746-1835.
Sources: VR Lancaster MA, Piermont NH. N5, C74, H65.

27. **EZRA$^3$ SAWYER** [see 7], b. 1702 Lancaster MA, d. 23 Oct 1765 Sterling MA, m. 16 Jun 1725 Lancaster MA Rebecca Whitcomb of Bolton MA, b. 1708 d. 28 Jan 1792, dau. David and Mary (Haywood) Whitcomb. Indian Wars, 1723. Signed petition in Lancaster MA 1746. Town Treasurer for Lancaster MA. He bur. in Chocksett Burial Ground, Sterling MA.
Prudence, b. 29 Sep 1726, m. 6 Nov 1745 Joshua House.
Elizabeth, b. 2 Jul 1728, m. 31 Jan 1751 Tilly Richardson.
77 Ezra$^4$, 1730-1776.
Kezia, b. 27 Feb 1734, m. 1 Jun 1757 John May, Jr.
Rebekah, b. 24 Feb 1736, m. 7 Mar 1754 Levi Moore.
Cornelius, b. 9 May 1737, d. 23 May 1737.
Esther, b. 6 May 1739, d. 13 Apr 1832, m. 26 Mar 1760 Josiah Kendall, Jr.
78 Nathaniel, b. 1741.
Mary, b. 6 Dec 1742, d. 12 Apr 1774, m. 27 Apr 1763 Moses Sawyer.
John, b. 2 Jun 1747 Lancaster MA.
Manasseh, b. 23 Jul 1749 Lancaster MA, d. 6 Jan 1801 Sterling MA, m. 10 Jan 1768 Lucy Richardson, b. 13 Jun 1749 d. 24 Feb 1811. CH: Lucy,b. 8 Mar 1769, m. 8 Jul 1790

Josiah Houghton; Dolly, b. 26 Apr 1778, d. 19 Jan 1861, m. 16 Jan 1805 Wilder Carter; Catherine, b. ?, d. 1830, m. 15 May 1792 Levi Kilburn; two daughters, b. ?.

Sources: Sterling MA census 1790, 1800. VR Lancaster MA, Sterling MA. G38, W37A, M19, K3, C74, N5, C9, R30.

28. **NATHANIEL$^3$ SAWYER** [see 7], b. ca. 1706 Lancaster MA, d. Lancaster MA, m. 19 Mar 1735 Lancaster MA Mary Houghton, b. 19 Sep 1715 d. 28 Dec 1768, dau. Jonathan and Thankful (White) Houghton. Captain of Lancaster Company, Colonel Oliver Wilder's Regiment, marched to Fort William Henry 1757.

Oliver, b. 24 Jul 1735 Lancaster MA, d. 2 Jul 1770 Lancaster MA.
Mary, b. 24 Jan 1738, m. 22 Feb 1758 Phineas Carter.
Elizabeth, b. 5 Jul 1741, d. 3 Oct 1741.
Elizabeth, b. 24 Jul 1742, m. 29 Nov 1759 Levi Nichols.
79 Nathaniel$^4$, b. 1745.
Jonathan, b. 9 Aug 1747 Lancaster MA, killed by Indians 1777.
Relief, bp. 1 Apr 1750.
Thankful, b. 8 Oct 1752, d. 15 Aug 1835, m.(1) 1775 Isaac Clark, m.(2) Jonathan Heaton.

Sources: VR Lancaster MA. E16, W39, C9, B51, S31.

29. **THOMAS$^3$ SAWYER** [see 7], b. 1711 Lancaster MA, d. 20 Jul 1787 Sterling MA, m. 27 Apr 1737 Lancaster MA Abigail White, b. 26 Jun 1712 d. 6 Mar 1799 Princeton MA, dau. Josiah J. and Abigail (Whitcomb) White.

Nathaniel, b. 20 Nov 1737, d. 22 Nov 1737.
Betty, b. 29 Dec 1738, m. 26 Jan 1762 Asa Whitcomb.
Thomas, b. 29 Apr 1740, d. 28 Sep 1756.
Catherine, b. 27 Jan 1741, m. 9 Oct 1760 Isreal Moore.
Eunice, b. 27 Mar 1744, m. 26 Oct 1768 Silas Houghton.
James, b. 20 Nov 1745, d. 3 Oct 1756.
Josiah, b. 21 Nov 1748, d.y.
Abigail, b. 21 Nov 1748, m. 7 Jul 1772 Joseph Sever.
Sarah, b. 6 Aug 1751, d. 26 Sep 1756.
Cornelius, b. 10 Nov 1754 Lancaster MA, d. 5 Feb 1834 Sterling MA, m. 8 Feb 1776 Princeton MA Eunice Buss, b. 1753 d. 8 Jun 1821.

Sources: Sterling MA census 1790, 1810. VR Lancaster MA, Princeton MA. N27, W39, H88, N5.

30. **PHINEAS$^3$ SAWYER** [see 7], b. 1713 Lancaster MA, d. 20 Apr 1787 Fitchburg MA, m. 1 Jun 1737 Lancaster MA Mary Sawyer, b. ca. 1717 d. 2 Dec 1794, dau. Joseph and Sarah (Beaman) Sawyer. All CH bp. at First Church of Lancaster MA.

Susannah, bp. 9 Dec 1739, m. 29 Jun 1759 Hooker Osgood.
Beulah, bp. 16 Mar 1740, m. 19 Sep 1779 Lt. Samuel Prentice.
80 Phineas$^4$, 1742-1794.
Mary, bp. 2 Sep 1744, d. 20 Oct 1756.
Eunice, bp. 26 Jul 1747.
81 Joseph$^4$, 1749-1832.
82 Abner$^4$, bp. 1753.
Luke, bp. 14 Dec 1755, d. 10 Nov 1757.
Mary, bp. 4 Dec 1757, m. 12 Dec 1796 Fitchburg MA Daniel Putnam, Jr.
83 Luke$^4$, bp. 1762.

Sources: VR Lancaster MA, Fitchburg MA. S31, Gravestone.

## FOURTH GENERATION

31. **AHOLIAB[4] SAWYER** [see 8], bp. 1711 Lancaster MA, d. after 1764 Bolton MA, m. 1732 Elizabeth Sawyer of Mansfield CT, b. 2 Aug 1711 d. Jan 1815, dau. Ephraim and Elizabeth Sawyer. In Bolton MA, Windham CT 1735.

84 Joshua[5], 1732-1812.
85 Silvanus[5], b. 1734.
Submit, b. 17 Jun 1736.
Elizabeth, b. 25 Sep 1737, m. 25 May 1757 John Wheeler.
Mary, b. 30 Sep 1738.
86 Aholiab[5], 1742-1823.
Sibillah, b. 8 Mar 1744, m. 19 Jan 1769 Abel Piper.
Betty, b. 29 May 1747, m. 9 Feb 1769 George Nickless of Starks ME.
Ephraim, b. 20 Nov 1749 Bolton CT, m.(1) 3 Dec 1772 Winchendon MA Peggy Fisher of Winchendon MA, b. ?; m.(2) 16 Jan 1799 Templeton MA Sarah Houghton of Lancaster MA, b. 9 Nov 1756, dau. Phinehas and Ruth (Osgood) Houghton. In Templeton MA, Winchendon MA 1772. CH: Lucy, b. 28 Apr 1778.
87 Isreal[5], 1751-1832.
Susannah, b. 15 Feb 1754, m. James Snow.
88 George[5], 1757-1842.

Sources: VR Lancaster MA, Winchendon MA, Templeton MA. W32.

32. **WILLIAM[4] SAWYER** [see 8], bp. 18 Nov 1711 Lancaster MA, d. 14 Jul 1794 Bolton MA, m.(1) 25 Aug 1732 Hannah Whitcomb, b. 7 Feb 1713 d. 18 Jun 1747, dau. Hezekiah and Hannah (Green) Whitcomb; m.(2) 7 Jul 1748 Bolton MA Sarah (Smith) Sawtell, b. ? d. 23 Jan 1810, dau. Richard and Abigail Smith. Indian Wars: In Captain Ephraim Welder's Company 1748. Wid. w/son Joseph in 1800.

89 William[5], 1749-1794.
90 Josiah[5], 1751-1817.
Sarah, b. 15 Jul 1753, m. 24 Jun 1786 John Nurse.
91 Joseph[5], 1756-1828.
92 Benjamin[5], 1758-1844.
93 Barnabas[5], 1761-1848.
Levi, b. 21 Jan 1765 Bolton MA.
Daniel, b. 12 Sep 1767 Bolton MA.
94 Uri[5], 1770-1799.

Sources: Bolton MA census 1790, 1800. Madison ME census 1850. VR Bolton MA. W37A.

33. **JOSIAH[4] SAWYER** [see 8], b. 13 Aug 1714 Lancaster MA, d. 13 Jul 1805 Berlin MA, m.(I)(1) 28 Jul 1739 Sarah Fairbanks, b. 29 May 1719 d. 2 Apr 1761, dau. Jabez and Hepsibah (Sawyer) Fairbanks of Bolton MA; m.(2) 14 Jan 1764 Lancaster MA Mary Tucker,b. 14 Sep 1728 d. 25 Mar 1799, dau. Thomas and Mary (Divoll) Tucker. Joined First Church of Lancaster MA 1738.

Josiah, b. 24 Nov 1739, d.y.
95 William[5], 1740-1822.
Hannah, b. 25 Jan 1744, m. 20 Mar 1780 Timothy H. Curtis of Harvard MA.
Rebecca, b. 15 Feb 1746, m. 24 May 1763 John Wilder of Putney VT.
Sarah, b. 6 Feb 1748, m. 16 Oct 1766 William Wilder of Putney VT.
Aholiab, b. 1749.
96 Josiah[5], 1752-1808.

Levi, b. 10 Nov 1764, d. 9 Feb 1765.
97 Silas[5], 1766-1842.
Thomas, b. 9 Mar 1770, d. 14 May 1771.
Sources: Berlin MA census 1790, 1800. VR Lancaster MA, Berlin MA, Bolton MA. H76, F2.

34. **JOSEPH[4] SAWYER** [see 9], b. 1705 Lancaster MA, d. bef. 1743 Lancaster MA, m. 19 May 1731 Lancaster MA Tabitha Prescott, b. 8 Oct 1710, dau. John III and Dorothy (Howe) Prescott. Tabitha joined First Church of Lancaster MA 17 Feb 1740, m. Silas Brigham 1743. At Sawyer's Mill in that part of Lancaster which became Sterling MA.
98 Aaron[5], 1732-1774.
99 Moses[5], 1734-1805.
Sarah, b. 4 Mar 1736.
100 Joseph[5], b. 1738.
Tabitha, b. 1 Jun 1740.
Sources: VR Lancaster MA. F25, P76, B84.

35. **THOMAS[4] SAWYER** [see 9], b. 1710 Lancaster MA, d. 31 Mar 1797 Bolton MA, m. (1) 21 Oct 1736 Lancaster MA Elizabeth Osgood, b. 1710 d. 28 May 1761, dau. Hooker and Dorothy (Wood) Osgood; m.(2) 25 Mar 1762 Bolton MA Mary Houghton, b. 1719 d. 3 Oct 1800, dau. John and Mehitable (Wilson) Houghton. Thomas and Elizabeth joined First Church of Lancaster MA 1738. He bur. in South Cem., Bolton MA.
101 Abraham[5], 1737-1811.
102 Thomas[5], 1740-1796.
103 Abner[5], 1742-1779.
Hooker, b. 3 Nov 1744 Bolton MA, d. 12 Nov 1772 Bolton MA, m. 2 Oct 1766 Bolton MA Releaf Whitcomb, b. 14 Mar 1748. Wid. m. William Lincoln 1773. CH: Eunice, b. 7 Sep 1767, d. 21 Aug 1771; Mary, b. 21 Apr 1769, d. 20 Aug 1771; Releaf, b. ?.
Elizabeth, b. 12 Jun 1747, m. 12 May 1767 Eliakim Atherton.
Joseph, b. 7 Jul 1750, d. 26 Jul 1750.
Sources: Bolton MA census 1790. VR Lancaster MA, Bolton MA.

36. **JOSIAH[4] SAWYER** [see 10], b. 7 Nov 1718 Lancaster MA, d. 19 Mar 1801 Lancaster MA, m. 11 Dec 1740 Lancaster MA Abigail Sawyer, b. 24 Apr 1721 d. 13 Nov 1812, dau. Amos and Abigail (Houghton) Sawyer. Joined Chocksett Church, Sterling MA 1738; all CH were bp. there. Two CH d. Apr 1749.
Lucy, bp. 1 Oct 1749, m. 12 Jan 1768 Lancaster MA Silas Carter.
104 Lemuel[5], ca. 1749-1830.
Abigail, b. 1 Dec 1751, m. 1775 Nathaniel Haskell.
Eber, b. 1754 Lancaster MA, d. Scoharie NY. Revolutionary War.
Sabre, b. 27 Feb 1757, m.(I) 17 Jul 1782 Samuel Carey.
Hannah, b. 13 Jan 1760, m.(I) 30 Oct 1780 David McClellan Jr.
Jeduthan, b. 21 Aug 1763 Lancaster MA, m. 14 Sep 1802 Nabby Keyes of Winchester MA, b. ?. In New Braintree MA.
Jedidah, b. 5 Apr 1767, d. 14 Feb 1850, m. 8 Nov 1792 Daniel Keyes.
Sources: Lancaster MA census 1790. VR Lancaster MA. W39.

37. **DARIUS[4] SAWYER** [see 10], b. 4 Nov 1720 Lancaster MA, d. 13 Aug 1789 Lancaster MA, m.(I) 29 Oct 1743 Deborah Sawyer, b. 25 Apr 1727 d. 2 Mar 1802, dau. Amos and Abigail (Houghton) Sawyer. He bur. in Old Settlers Burial Ground, Lancaster MA.
Deborah, b. 20 Feb 1744, d. 16 Dec 1765, m. _____ Daught.

Darius, b. 18 Jul 1746 Lancaster MA, d. 20 Mar 1814 Chester VT, m.(I) 30 Aug 1770 Woodstock CT Sarah Geary, b. 21 Jan 1749, dau. Joseph and Ruth (Goodale) Geary. CH: Child, b. 8 Mar 1772, d. same day.

Olive, b. 8 May 1749, m. 8 Oct 1778 James Townsend.

Jude, b. 8 May 1751 Lancaster MA, d. 18 Dec 1843 Gardner MA, m. 26 Nov 1778 Westminster MA Phebe Keyes of Westminster MA b. 31 Jul 1752 d. 4 Jul 1837. Jude was one of the first settlers of Gardner MA. Death recorded in Hubbardston MA Feb 1844. Revolutionary War: Enl. Cambridge MA, private in Captain Elisha Jackson's Company, Colonel Bridges' Regiment; at Bennington VT, 1777. CH: Daughter, b. (1790-1800).

105 Jacob[5], 1756-1827.

Amos, b. 13 Aug 1758 Lancaster MA, d. 23 Aug 1843, m.(1) 22 Jun 1783 Lancaster MA Prudence Geary of Sterling MA, b. 1764 d. 11 Oct 1822; m.(2) 15 Mar 1825 Nancy Fuller, b. 1777 d. 29 Dec 1840, dau. James and Sarah Fuller. CH: Amos, b. 26 Aug 1789, d. 1 Nov 1792. Note: Census lists more CH, names and sex not given.

106 Abel[5], 1760-1836.

Esther, b. 4 Apr 1763, m. 7 Jul 1786 John Dollison.

107 Thomas[5] 1765-1829.

Bezaleel, b. 11 Feb 1768 Lancaster MA.

Sources: Halifax VT census 1790, 1800. Gardner MA census 1790, 1800, 1810, 1820, 1830, 1840. Lancaster MA census 1790, 1800, 1810, 1820, 1830, 1840. VR Lancaster MA, Westminster MA, SA/VT. M19.

38. **BEZALEEL[4] SAWYER** [see 10], b. 25 Mar 1723 Lancaster MA, d. ca. 1785 Jaffrey NH, m. 7 Dec 1751 Groton MA Lois Lawrence of Groton MA, b. 6 Sep 1726 d. 8 Jun 1803 Lancaster MA, dau. Nathaniel and Anna Lawrence. In Townsend MA 1761, Jaffrey 177?. Lot 9, Range 9, south of Gilmore Road, Jaffrey, was in family for three generations.

Hannah, b. 1746.

Eunice, b. 11 Mar 1753.

108 Bezaleel[5], 1754-1835.

Lois, b. 27 Jul 1755, m. Dennis Organ of Jaffrey NH.

Thomas, b. 10 Oct 1756, d. same day.

109 Rufus[5], 1760-1845.

110 Nathaniel[5], 1765-1852.

Martha, b. ?.

Judith, b. ?.

Sources: VR Groton MA. A27, G39, Will.

39. **MOSES[4] SAWYER** [see 10], b. 20 Aug 1730 Lancaster MA, m. Dinah _____, b. ?, who joined Chocksett Church, Sterling MA, 24 Sep 1758.

111 Paul[5], ca. 1753.

Judith, b. ca. 1755.

Ruth, b. ca. 1757.

Dinah, b. 3 Aug 1760.

Thomas, b. 5 Sep 1762 Lancaster MA, m. 6 Sep 1784 Wendell MA Ziliah Hare, b. ?.

Louisa, b. 10 Mar 1765.

Sources: Wendell MA census 1790. VR Wendell MA.

40. **PAUL[4] SAWYER** [see 10], b. 19 May 1733 Lancaster MA, d. 2 Jul 1783 Princeton MA, m. 7 Mar 1758 Lancaster MA Lois Houghton, b. 15 Aug 1731 d. 8 Jun 1803, dau. Isreal and

Martha (Wheelock) Houghton. French and Indian War: Enl. in Colonel Oliver Wilder's Regiment, went to Crown Point NY 1755. All CH were bp. at First Church of Lancaster MA. Wid. in Lancaster MA 1790.

112 Paul[5], 1759-1826.
Lois, b. 13 Jul 1760, m. 7 Apr 1780 Thomas Burdit.
Charlotte, b. 28 Mar 1762, d. 6 Nov 1810.
Judith, b. 13 Jan 1765.
Thomas, b. 9 Oct 1768, d. 21 Sep 1778.
113 Isreal[5], 1771-1847.
Beulah, b. 9 May 1773.

Sources: Lancaster MA census 1790. VR Lancaster MA.

41. **ELIJAH[4] SAWYER** [see 11], b. 1713 Lancaster MA, d. bef. 1790 Bolton MA, m. (1) Lucy _____, b. 1719 d. 31 May 1750; m.(2) Lydia _____, b. 4 Nov 1726 d. 2 May 1799. Wid. in Bolton MA 1790.

Katherine, b. 8 Sep 1743 Bolton MA, m. 1 Jun 1769 John Wilder.
Son, b. 2 Oct 1744 Bolton MA, d. 19 Oct 1744.
Elias, b. 11 Mar 1746 Bolton MA, m. 16 Jan 1772 Acton MA Ruth Haywood of Acton MA, b. 1745 d. 16 Aug 1838. CH: Mary, bp. 3 Jun 1786; Ruth, bp. 3 Jun 1786.
114 Calven[5], 1750-1802.

Sources: Bolton MA census 1790. Acton MA census 1790. VR Lancaster MA, Bolton MA, Acton MA.

42. **ELISHA[4] SAWYER** [see 11], b. 17 Aug 1718 Lancaster MA, d. 25 Aug 1786 Sterling MA, m.(1) 7 Jan 1740 Bolton MA Ruth White, b. 9 Feb 1716 d. 1755, dau. Josiah and Abigail (Whitcomb) White; m.(2) 8 Mar 1756 Susannah Huckof Bolton MA, b. ?. Ruth joined Chocksett Church, Sterling MA, 1742. Ch. were bp. there after 1745. Revolutionary War: 1st Lieutenant in Major John Carter's Company, Colonel Wilder's Regiment, 1762.

Prudence, b. 2 Oct 1741, d. 2 Jan 1818, m. 28 Apr 1774 Bolton MA Holman Priest.
115 Elisha[5], 1744-1810.
116 Jotham[5], 1745-1837.
117 Elias[5], 1747-1825.
Thankful, b. 1 Aug 1747, d. 20 May 1821, m. 8 Oct 1770 Daniel Norcross.
Ruth, b. 15 Mar 1750, m. 12 May 1770 Samuel Brooks.
Martha, b. 2 Nov 1752, d. 17 Dec 1816, m.(I) 23 Mar 1870 Philemon Whitcomb.
118 Thomas[5], 1757-1825.
Beatrix, b. 27 Oct 1758, m. 29 Dec 1785 John Wilder, Jr.
Susanna, b. 22 Jun 1760, m.(I) 10 Mar 1781 Nathan Wilder.
Hannah, b. 9 Jun 1765.
Elizabeth, b. 20 Nov 1767.

Sources: VR Lancaster MA, Bolton MA. E16, W39, N5.

43. **JOSHUA[4] SAWYER** [see 12], b. 5 May 1713 Woburn MA, d. 1767 Haverhill MA, m. 3 Feb 1736 Katherine Richardson, b. 6 Feb 1714 d. 4 Dec 1791 Atkinson NH, dau. James and Elizabeth Richardson of Woburn MA. Blacksmith. On Alarm list 1752. S/land in Plaistow NH 1763.

119 James[5], 1737-1801.
Katherine, b. 22 Jun 1740, m. 20 Nov 1760 Ezekiel Belnap.
120 Jesse[5], 1748-1817.
Joshua, b. ?, d. 28 Jun 1749.

Mary, b. 29 Aug 1750.
Sources: C29, V8.

44. **JOHN$^4$ SAWYER** [see 12], b. 31 Aug 1716 Woburn MA, d. 29 Jun 1784 Haverhill MA, m. Haverhill MA Abigail Thompson, b. 2 Feb 1718. Revolutionary War. B/land near Plaistow NH.

Abigail, b. 26 Feb 1739, d.y.
Sarah, b. 5 Nov 1742, d. 10 Jan 1832, m. 13 Aug 1761 Caleb Cushing.
John, b. 10 Mar 1744, d. 7 Aug 1746.
Abigail, b. 12 May 1745.
Phebe, b. 31 May 1747, m. 4 Sep 1766 Philip Clement.
121 John$^5$, 1749-1784.
122 Leonard$^5$, 1752-ca. 1783.
Susannah, b. 6 Apr 1754, m. 2 Jun 1772 Nathaniel Kimball.
123 Nathaniel$^5$, 1757-1819.
Anne, b. 23 Mar 1761, m. Nathan Follansbee of Canaan NH.
Sources: VR Woburn MA, Haverhill MA. C94, E20, C50.

45. **JAMES$^4$ SAWYER** [see 12], b. 22 Jun 1718 Woburn MA, d. 9 Oct 1793 Thetford VT, m. 8 May 1841 Elizabeth Wood, b. 18 Jun 1720 Thetford VT d. 8 Dec 1780. In Dunstable MA 1754-56. B/land in Dunstable MA 1760.

Sarah, b. 21 Jun 1742.
124 James$^5$, 1745-1821.
Elizabeth, b. 25 Feb 1747, m. 29 Nov 1764 Atkinson NH Jonathan Poor.
Abigail, b. 10 Mar 1749, m. 16 Sep 1773 Peter Dearborn.
Mary, b. 27 Dec 1754.
Bridget, b. 21 Dec 1756.
Sources: VR Dunstable MA. N6, N5.

46. **BENJAMIN$^4$ SAWYER** [see 12], b. 24 Nov 1721 Woburn MA, m. 30 Sep 1743 Phebe Jones, b. ?. In Haverhill MA 1745, Wilmington MA 1747, Salem MA 1750, Danvers MA 1753. B/land in Boothbay ME 1781. Committee member 1775 and 1781 in Boothbay ME.

Benjamin, b. 14 Feb 1745 Haverhill MA, m.(1) 10 Dec 1765 Danvers MA Hepzibah Leech, b. ? d. Dec 1768; m.(2) 1 May 1770 Danvers MA Mary Hasseltine, b. ?. CH: Hepzibah, b. 23 Jun 1766, m. 28 Dec 1789 John Underwood; dau., b. ?, d. Dec 1771.
Jonathan, b. 7 Jul 1746, d. 28 Dec 1747.
Jacob, b. 27 Oct 1747 Wilmington MA, d. 9 Mar 1821 Sawyer's Island ME, m.(1) 9 May 1780 Elizabeth (Linnekin) Herrington, wid. of Hezikiah, b. ? d. 7 Nov 1813, dau. Benjamin and Mary Linnekin; m.(2) ?. Blacksmith. Revolutionary War: Sergeant in Captain Benjamin Brown's Company, LTC. William Bond's 37th Regiment, eight months around Boston 1775. In Boothbay ME 1768. CH: Son, b. (1780-90); son, b. (1794-1800); son, b. (1810- 1820).
125 Jonathan$^5$, 1749-1809.
Joshua, b. 19 May 1750 Salem MA, d. bef. Sep 1785, m. 16 Apr 1772 Danvers MA Achaicus Emerson, b. ?. Shipwright. In Boothbay ME 1784. CH: Betty b. 27 Jul 1772.
126 Amos$^5$, 1753-1821.
Nathaniel, b. 7 Sep 1754 Danvers MA, d. in Ohio, m. 29 Nov 1773 Deliverance Lewis, b. ?. Went to Ohio 1787.
Phebe, b. 29 Mar 1756, m. Andrew Reed.
127 Aaron$^5$, b. 1758.
Betty, b. 2 Oct 1760.

Ebenezer, b. 8 Mar 1762, d. 11 Feb 1763.
128 Ebenezer[5], 1764-1840.
Sources:Boothbay ME census 1790, 1800, 1810, 1820. VR Wilmington MA, Danvers MA, Salem MA, Woburn MA, Haverhill MA. M3.

47. **OLIVER[4] SAWYER** [see 12], b. 14 Jul 1726 Woburn MA, d. Grafton NH, m. Sarah Bowditch, b. ?. In Haverhill MA 1790. Enl. in lst Company of Militia, Haverhill MA 1757.
Oliver, b. 13 Jan 1752, d. 15 Feb 1752.
Oliver, b. 8 Feb 1753, d. 28 Sep 1754.
129 William[5], 1754-1817.
Oliver, b. 12 Sep 1757 Haverhill MA, d. 28 Aug 1820 Bath NH, m.(I) 28 Sep 1776 Ruth Morgeridge of Atkinson NH, b. 1752 Atkinson NH. On Revolutionary War Roll at Atkinson NH. Surveyor of Highways for Bath NH 1805. Wid. in Bath NH 1830. CH: Hannah, b. 19 Mar 1786, d. 1887, m. 11 Apr 1843 Daniel Carr; Sally, b. 3 Oct 1787; Martha, b. 29 Aug 1790, d. 4 Oct 1796; Nancy, b. 1796, in Poorhouse 1850. Census says 5 dau. b. bef. 1790; 2 dau. b. (1790-1800); 1 son b. (1800-1810).
Sarah, b. 24 Apr 1760, m. 16 Aug 1787 Moses Nichols.
Hannah, b. 14 Jul 1761.
130 Timothy[5], 1763-183?.
Sources: Haverhill MA census 1790. Bath NH census 1790, 1800, 1810, 1820, 1830. VR Haverhill MA. C29.

48. **JONATHAN[4] SAWYER** [see 12], b. 19 Jul 1728 Woburn MA, d. 22 Jun 1813 Atkinson NH, m.(1) 5 Mar 1752 Sudbury MA Elizabeth Tenny, b. 1731 d. 27 Mar 1774, she bur. in Atkinson NH; m.(2) 20 Jul 1774 Atkinson NH Hannah Mullican, b. ? d. 16 Apr 1775, she bur. in Atkinson NH; m.(3) 22 Jan 1776 Boxford MA Hannah Johnson of Boxford MA, bp. 1 Jun 1740. Enl. in 1st Company of Militia, Haverhill MA 1757. B/S/land in Plaistow NH 1771, Atkinson NH 1771. In Atkinson NH 1772. On Revolutionary War Roll in Atkinson NH. Lived on Main Street near Atkinson Depot.
Elizabeth, b. 17 Nov 1752.
Bettee, b. 3 May 1754, m. 7 Feb 1771 Peter Dustin.
131 Jonathan[5], 1756-1829.
Mary, b. 19 Oct 1758, d. 1804, m. Captain Joseph Smith.
Abigail, b. 28 Sep 1760, d. 6 Oct 1845, m.(1) 27 Oct 1782 Dr. Beniah Clemment, m.(2) Ebenezer Hoyt.
132 Benjamin[5], 1762-1813.
133 Joshua[5], 1765-1843.
134 John[5], 1768-1854.
Sources: VR Atkinson NH, Haverhill MA. C50, H83, B27, C29, N9.

49. **JOSHUA[4] SAWYER** [see 13], b. 19 Jan 1703 Marlborough MA, m. 11 May 1735 Sarah Flint, b. ?. She was admitted to ____ Church, Windham CT, 23 Jan 1737. In Mansfield CT, Windham CT 1790. Note: 1790 census says Joshua had eight CH.
Ruth, bp. 27 Jan 1737, d. 9 May 1819, m.(1) 1754 Joseph Case, m.(2) ____ Huntington, m.(3) E____ Waterman.
Keziah, bp. 14 Jan 1739, m. 1 Apr 1765 Daniel Foster.
Rhoda, b. 23 Jan 1740, d. 14 Apr 1802.
Mary, b. 28 Feb 1742, m. 30 Dec 1762 Sylvanus Pingrey.
Beulah, b. 18 Nov 1744.
Elizabeth, b. 28 Dec 1746.

135 James[5], 1749-1838.
Sources: Windham CT census 1790. VR Mansfield CT, Windham CT. J6.

50. **JACOB[4] SAWYER** [see 13], b. 17 Dec 1706 Marlborough MA, d. 22 Aug 1758 Windham CT, m. 23 Sep 1730 Prudence Standish of Preston CT, b. 9 May 1711 d. 25 Dec 1769, dau. Isreal and Elizabeth (Richards) Standish.

Jemima, b. 4 Jul 1731, d.y.
Elizabeth, b. 13 Jan 1734.
Eunice, b. 22 May 1736, d. 1805, m. 12 Feb 1756 Benjamin Blackman.
Prudence, b. 30 Apr 1738.
136 Ephraim[5], 1740-1807.
Abigail, b. 29 Dec 1742.
Dinah, b. 20 Apr 1744, m. 2 Jun 1763 John Brown.
Jeremiah, b. 26 Jun 1746 Windham CT.
Jemima, b. 7 Mar 1749.
Cornelius, b. 6 Jul 1751 Windham CT.
137 Jacob Standish[5], 1754-1830.
Sources: VR Windham CT. N5, V9.

51. **ELIJAH[4] SAWYER** [see 13], b. 17 Oct 1708 Marlborough MA, d. 27 Jan 1792 Windham CT, m. 7 Mar 1733 Windham CT Hannah Terrill, b. 1716 d. 13 Nov 1801. She was admitted to _____ Church, Windham CT, 5 Sep 1742.

Elijah, b. 20 Apr 1734 Windham CT.
Anne, b. 28 Feb 1735, d. 29 Oct 1813, m. Feb 1755 Abishal Bingham.
Rebecca, b. 21 May 1737.
Jerusha, b. 16 Dec 1739, d. 1826, m. 1767 Joseph Coy.
Lydia, b. 17 Apr 1742, m. ca. 1770 Andrew Frink. She joined church at Windham CT, Sep 1766.
Matthias, b. 1 Jun 1744 Windham CT, m.(1) 5 Apr 1778 Delight Hill, b. 1737 d. 10 Sep 1800; m.(2) 11 Jul 1802 Windham CT Jerusha Fitch, b. ?, who was admitted to church on 25 Sep 1803.
Irene, b. 3 Sep 1746, m. 6 May 1773 Benjamin Jones of Coventry CT.
Deborah, b. 29 Jun 1749.
138 Asabel[5], 1751-1817.
James, b. 20 Mar 1753 Windham CT.
Ephraim, b. 20 Mar 1753 Windham CT.
139 Azariah[5], 1755-1829.
Hannah, b. 7 Jul 1759.
Rachel, b. 22 Mar 1761.
Sources: Windham CT census 1790, 1800, 1810. VR Windham CT. H6, S97, J3, Ann Bingham's Bible.

52. **JEDUTHAN[4] SAWYER** [see 13], b. 8 Oct 1713 Mansfield CT, m. 14 Apr 1738 Esther Marsh, b. 15 Jul 1714, dau. Ebenezer and Elizabeth (Gillet) Marsh. In Windham CT, Montague MA, Lebanon CT.

Esther, b. 5 Apr 1739.
Elizabeth, b. 22 Aug 1741.
Martha, b. ?.
Mary, b. 14 Mar 1746, m. 27 May 1767 Ephraim Jennings.
140 Elias[5], b. 1749.

Moses, b. 2 Feb 1754, d. 3 Feb 1759.
Sources: VR Montague MA, Mansfield CT. P78, S56, M13.

53. **JAMES[4] SAWYER** [see 14], b. 28 Aug 1747 Pomfret CT, d. 4 Feb 1828 Pomfret CT, m. 28 Feb 1771 Sarah Jones of Killingly CT, b. 12 Jul 1746 d. 2 Jan 1807, dau. John and Sarah (Sawyer) Jones. Revolutionary War: Private in Captain Nathaniel Wales' Company, Colonel J_____ Mason's Regiment, 13 Sep 1776 to 17 Oct 1776.

Child, b. ?, d. 26 Sep 1772.
Elizabeth, b. 13 Jan 1775, d. 28 Dec 1777.
Sarah, b. 30 Dec 1776, m. 20 Jun 1824 in Pomfret CT Albermarle Stone.
John Jonas, b. 31 Mar 1779, d. Apr 1793.
Lydia, b. 28 Aug 1781.
Mary, b. 3 Apr 1785, d. 9 May 1805.
141 Jonas[5], 1787-1876.
Zerniah, b. 28 Mar 1790, d. 24 Aug 1795.
James, b. 23 Oct 1794, d. 26 Aug 1795.
Sources: Pomfret CT census 1790, 1800, 1810. VR Pomfret CT. D6, B33, D13.

54. **CORNELIUS[4] SAWYER** [see 14], b. 20 Nov 1748 Pomfret CT, m.(1) 5 Nov 1772 Putnam CT Anne Williams, b. ?: m.(2) Caroline Ellis, b. ?. Revolutionary War. In Killingly CT, Stafford CT 1790.

Oliver William, b. 4 Nov 1773 Killingly CT, m. 4 May 1797 Lucinda Morse, b. ?.
Thomas Angell, b. 17 Apr 1776 Killingly CT.
Flavel, b. 11 Jan 1780.
Sibel, b. 25 May 1782.
Elizabeth, b. 13 Oct 1784.
Cornelius, b. 7 Oct 1788 Stafford CT.
Daughter, b. 24 Dec 1791.
Sources: Stafford CT census 1790. VR Windsor CT. B3.

55. **WILLIAM[4] SAWYER** [see 14], b. 11 Feb 1754 Pomfret CT, m. 28 Oct 1783 Pomfret CT Diadema Sanger, b. 27 Dec 1764, dau. John and Dorothy (Peake) Sanger. Revolutionary War. In Charlestown NH 1823.

Lucy, b. 14 Aug 1784, d. 1 Aug 1864, m. 13 Mar 1810 Joel Lewis.
142 Manley[5], 1786-1870.
Hilyard, b. 27 Mar 1789 Pomfret CT d. Mar 1870 Waterford VT, m. 5 Aug 1836 Wheelock VT Lydia Phillips, b. ?. In St. Johnsbury VT, Waterford VT.
John, b. 17 Jan 1792 Pomfret CT, d. 19 Nov 1882 Waterford VT. In St. Johnsbury VT, Waterford VT.
143 William[5], b. 1795.
Aelisa, b. 30 Jul 1797.
Lovey, b. 28 Mar 1803, d. 9 Jul 1807.
144 Philander[5], 1804-1895.
145 Ross[5], 1806-1883.
Dorothy, b. ca. 1807 Lyndon VT, d. 18 Aug 1865, m. 24 Nov 1831 Trueworthy Parker.
Calista, b. 8 Aug 1808 Waterford VT.
Sources: Waterford VT census 1810, 1850. St. Johnsbury VT census 1820. VR Pomfret CT, SA/VT. N11, J2, C15, S81, N8.

56. **JOHN[4] SAWYER** [see 15], b. 7 Sep 1755 Pomfret CT, d. 15 May 1847 Yates NY, m. 8 Nov 1780 Olive Weld, b. 26 Aug 1759 d. 23 Oct 1818. Revolutionary War: Sergeant for one year with "Colonel Durkee" of Connecticut. In Pomfret CT, Reading VT, Whitehall NY 1815, Ridgeway NY 1816, Yates NY 1824.

Morris, b. 16 Aug 1782, m. 25 Sep 1803 Sally Parker, b. ?. In New York.

Perin, b. 16 Oct 1783, d. 7 Aug 1785.

Elisha, b. 30 Sep 1785 Reading VT, d. 8 Dec 1868 Paxton IL, m. 11 Feb 1819 Deerfield NH Nancy Mudgett, b. 25 Jan 1788 d. 18 Apr 1864, dau. William and Rhoda (Willey) Mudgett. CH: Warren Elisha, b. 22 Dec 1819, d. 31 Mar 1897, m. Oct 1894 ElizaG. Sinclair. War of 1812. Went to Illinois.

Ella, b. 7 Dec 1787, m. 11 Dec 1819 Stephen Mudgett.

John, b. 30 May 1791 Reading VT.

Sources: Reading VT census 1790, 1800, 1810, 1820. VR SA/VT. N1A, M62, Mrs. Warren Sawyer rec.

57. **CORNELIUS[4] SAWYER** [see 15], b. 6 Feb 1760 Pomfret CT, d. 9 Feb 1835 Reading VT, m.(1) 22 May 1782 Redding CT Elles Forbes, b. 19 Nov 1760 d. 15 Dec 1825; m. (2)7 Feb 1827 Windsor VT Sarah Hulett, b. 1775. Revolutionary War: Enl. at Pomfret CT 1778 under "Colonel Smith." In Reading VT 1780. Wid. went to Cornish NH 1864.

146 Joshua[5], 1783-1854.

147 Joseph[5], 1785-1831.

Simon, b. 25 Dec 1786, d. 29 Nov 1805.

148 Thomas A.[5], 1789-1848.

Elles, b. 8 Nov 1792, d. 14 Jun 1866, m. 20 May 1819 Asa Morse.

149 Cornelius[5], 1797-1835.

James, b. 9 Dec 1799, d. 30 Jul 1822.

Polly, b. 1800, d. 9 Aug 1825.

Thankful, b. 13 Aug 1803, d. 3 Oct 1822.

Harriet, b. 1813, d. 25 Jan 1814.

Sources: Reading VT census 1790, 1800, 1810, 1820, 1830. C99, N1A, B3.

58. **BENJAMIN[4] SAWYER** [see 15], b. 3 Feb 1763 Pomfret CT, d. 12 Aug 1842 Reading VT, m. 12 Apr 1787 Reading VT Sarah York, 22 Dec 1765 d. 13 Apr 1835. Revolutionary War: 1st Lieutenant in Bedel's Regiment, VT Militia, 1777-1779.

John York, b. 7 Mar 1788 Reading VT, d. 1836, m. Ann Alice Gwinn, b. ?. War of 1812. Judge. Went to Illinois.

Anna, b. 4 Feb 1789, d. 1 Feb 1870, m. James W. Hall.

Daughter, b. ?, d. 1 Mar 1792 Reading VT.

150 Benjamin[5], 1793-1875.

Daughter, b. ?, d. 21 Dec 1796 Reading VT.

Sally, b. 3 Feb 1797, d. 20 Jan 1884, m. Elijah M. Marshall.

Nathan, b. 22 Aug 1799 Reading VT, m. Lucretta Moore, b. ?. Lawyer, preacher. Went to Illinois.

Hannah, b. 13 Feb 1802, d. 28 Nov 1887, m. 12 Apr 1825 Charles Buck.

Thomas Jefferson, b. 9 Jan 1804 Reading VT, d. 24 Jul 1899, m. 21 Sep 1831 New York City Caroline Fisher of Newton MA, b. ?. Studied theology at Middlebury College, ordained 1829. Harvard graduate 1850. Head of Tufts Theological School 1870. Went to New York, New Jersey.

Seth Thompson, b. 19 Aug 1806 Reading VT, d. 9 Feb 1895 Alton IL, m. 13 May 1847 Sarah Jane Smiley of Springfield VT, b. 4 Jul 1814 d. 26 Mar 1885. Attorney.

Emerline C., b. 16 Jan 1810, m. 6 Sep 1837 Dr. William G. Pierce.
Jonas Galusha, b. 8 Mar 1812, d. 26 Mar 1812.
Alles Lucinda, b. 11 Mar 1817.
Sources: Reading VT census 1790, 1800, 1810, 1820, 1830, 1840. VR SA/VT. D6, D18, C99, H41, N1A, N8.

59. **JONATHAN⁴ SAWYER** [see 17], b. 12 May 1715 Lancaster MA, d. 21 Feb 1805 Bolton MA, m. 30 Sep 1740 Harvard MA Elizabeth Whitney, b. 1710 d. 19 Jan 1815. In Harvard MA.
Lois, b. 26 Jul 1741, m. 9 Dec 1762 Thaddeus Hazen.
Peter, b. 27 Nov 1743, d. 18 Dec 1746.
Jonathan, b. 24 Nov 1745, d. 18 Dec 1746.
151 John[5], 1748-1812.
Adington, b. 27 Jan 1752 Bolton MA.
Sources: Bolton MA census 1790, 1800. VR Harvard MA, Bolton MA.

60. **CALEB[4] SAWYER** [see 17], b. 19 Jun 1720 Lancaster MA, d. 1815 Westmoreland NH, m. Lydia Reed, b. ? d. 27 Mar 1798. Revolutionary War. In Harvard MA, Leominster MA, Westmoreland NH 1766.
152 Caleb[5], Jr., 1741-1772.
Lydia, b. 8 Dec 1743, m. 6 Oct 1867 James Butterfield.
Abijah, b. 14 Aug 1744 Leominster MA.
Jonathan, b. 13 Dec 1747 Leominster MA, m. 28 Sep 1766 Sarah Battles, b. ?.
Betsey, b. 25 Oct 1750.
Sarah, b. 26 Aug 1752, m. 1768 Enos Burt.
153 Ephraim[5], 1756-1827.
154 Manasseh[5], 1759-1842.
Sources: VR Leominster MA. N36, J3.

61. **PAUL[4] SAWYER** [see 17], b. ca. 1725, d. ca. 179?, m. 3 Jul 1755 Bolton MA Ephe Houghton, b. ? d. 1825.
Arufas, b. 29 May 1756.
155 Jonathan[5], 1758-1833.
John, b. 31 Mar 1761.
156 Caleb[5], b. 1764.
Betty, b. 31 Dec 1766, d. 1830, unm.
Sources: Bolton Ma census 1790, Wid. 1800, 1810. VR Bolton MA.

62. **MANASSEH[4] SAWYER** [see 17], b. 1 Jun 1729 Lancaster MA, d. 24 Dec 1808 Harvard MA, m. 18 Feb 1756 Harvard MA Lydia Fairbanks, b. 16 Aug 1731 d. 31 Mar 1805, dau. Joseph and Mary (Brown) Fairbanks. Revolutionary War: At Lexington MA 1775; Surgeon, Captain James Fairbanks' Company, Colonel Asa Whitcomb's Regiment.
Jonathan, b. 9 Mar 1758 Harvard MA, d. 28 Apr 1776.
157 Jabez[5], 1759-1841.
Lydia, b. 30 Nov 1761 Harvard MA, m. 11 Sep 1783 James Bowers.
Rhoda, b. 30 Mar 1764 Harvard MA, m. 1 Feb 1791 Charles Warner.
Abijah, b. 12 Aug 1766 Harvard MA.
158 Manasseh[5], 1768-1856.
Joseph, b. 4 Apr 1771 Harvard MA.
159 Luther[5], 1773-1834.
Sources: Harvard MA census 1790, 1800. VR Harvard MA. N36, D6, P46.

63. **CALEB⁴ SAWYER** [see 18], b. 24 Jul 1737 Harvard MA, d. 6 May 1820 Harvard MA, m.(1) 9 Dec 1760 Harvard MA Relief Fairbanks of Harvard MA,b. 1 Dec 1739 d. 2 Dec 1764, dau. Joseph and Mary (Brown) Fairbanks; m.(2) 1 Dec 1766 Stow MA Sarah Patch of Stow MA, b. 1741 d. 19 Aug 1825. French and Indian War: In Colonel Oliver Wilder's Regiment 1755.

Seth, b. 22 Aug 1761, d. 27 Aug 1761.
Caleb, b. 2 Mar 1764, d. 7 Apr 1764.
160 Phineas[5], 1768-1820.
161 Jonathan[5], 1771-1817.

Sources: Harvard MA census 1790, 1800, 1810. VR Harvard MA, Stow MA. N36.

64. **PHINEHAS[4] SAWYER** [see 18], b. 25 Jul 1746 Harvard MA, m.(1) 14 Feb 1771 Harvard MA Hannah Whitcomb, b. 26 May 1747 d. 26 Nov 1807, dau. James and Hannah (Graves) Whitcomb; m.(2) 1809 Mary Gilmore, b. ?. A skillful mechanic; a rifle dated 1777, stamped with his name, is said to survive [N36].

162 Abel[5], b. 1771.
Seth, b. 18 Jun 1780, d. 24 Jan 1857 unm.
Lydia, b. 30 Sep 1787, m.(1) 30 Nov 1803 Francis Whitney, m.(2) 15 Apr 1807 Isaiah Whitney.

Sources: Harvard MA census 1790, 1800. VR Harvard MA. N36, W37A.

65. **OLIVER[4] SAWYER** [see 19], b. 1 May 1738 Harvard MA, d. Bethlehem NH, m. 22 Nov 1763 Harvard MA Abigail Townsend, b. ?.

Abigail, b. 30 Sep 1764, m. 17 Feb 1784 Bolton MA Daniel Daby.
Olivea, b. 25 Apr 1766, m. 24 Oct 1791 Bolton MA Samuel Hill, Jr.
163 Oliver[5], b. 1767.
Joshua, b. 16 Jun 1769 Harvard MA, m.(1) ?; m.(2) 8 Dec 1813 Mary Palmer of Littleton MA, b. ?. Owned 100 acres in Bethlehem NH 1800. CH: 2 dau, b. (1800-1810).
Relefe, b. 3 Feb 1771, m. 6 Apr 1795 Bolton MA Eleazar Russell.
Lucy, b. 24 Sep 1772, d. 1819, m. 20 Jan 1796 Boxboro MA John Conn.
John, b. 21 Apr 1776, d. 1778.
Ezra, b. 8 Nov 1779 Harvard MA, m. 28 Aug 1806 Betsy Griggs of Littleton MA, b. ?.

Sources: Boxboro MA census 1790. Bethlehem NH census 1800, 1810. VR Harvard MA, Westboro MA.

66. **JOSEPH[4] SAWYER** [see 19], b. 14 Jan 1741 Harvard MA, m. 28 Apr 1768 Northboro MA Sarah Townsend of Northboro MA, b. ?.

Mary, b. 30 Sep 1770, m. 1786 Oliver T. Davis.
164 William[5], 1772-1859.
Sarah, b. 21 May 1775, m. 11 May 1791 Jeremiah Laughton.
Betsey, b. 30 May 1779, m. _____ Pollard.

Sources: Boxborough MA census 1790. VR Harvard MA, Northboro MA.

67. **THOMAS[4] SAWYER** [see 20], b. 24 Jan 1715 Hebron CT, d. 8 Sep 1785 Orford NH, m. 16 Jun 1737 Hepsibah Dewey, b. 28 Dec 1715 d. 22 Mar 1792, dau. Nathaniel and Margaret (Burroughs) Dewey. In Orford NH 1766. B/S/land in Orford NH 1767, 1770. Selectman for Orford NH 1768. Church member 1770.

Susannah, b. 5 May 1738, d. 14 Apr 1739.
Elizabeth, b. 4 Oct 1739, d. 10 Jan 1740.
165 Jonathan[5], b. 1740.

166 Edward$^5$, 1743-1815.
Mary, b. 30 Dec 1744, m. 27 Apr 1770 Daniel Tillotson.
Hepsibah, b. 26 Mar 1747, m. 1768 Shubael Cross.
Joseph, b. 22 May 1749, d. 26 Nov 1749.
167 Ichabod$^5$, 1750-1826.
168 Abel$^5$, 1753-1845.
John, b. 9 Oct 1755 Hebron CT, d. 14 Oct 1858 Bangor ME, m. 16 Jul 1789 Pembroke MA Rebecca Hobart, b. ? d. 23 Dec 1836. Dartmouth College graduate 1785. Minister. In Penobscot County as missionary, founded theological seminary in Bangor ME. Revolutionary War. B/S/land in Dexter, Garland ME, 1813-1821. He bur. in Garland Cem., Bangor ME. CH: Rebecca, b. 10 May 1790, d. 28 Feb 1831, m. 22 Jun 1809 Stephen Kimball; Sarah, b. 7 Mar 1792, m. Samuel French of Garland ME; John, b. 24 Jul 1793 d. 2 May 1796; Hepsibah, b. 4 Jul 1795, d. 8 Aug 1825, m. 19 Oct 1823 Daniel Kimball; Cynthia, b. 10 Dec 1796.
Joseph, b. 5 Jul 1758 Hebron CT. In Orford NH.
Sources: Orford NH census 1790. Boothbay ME census 1800.Bangor ME census 1810 1820. Garland ME census 1840, 1850. VR Pembroke MA, Boothbay ME. N6, D34, H58A,

68. **ISAAC$^4$ SAWYER** [see 20], b. 17 Jul 1721 Hebron CT, d. 1786 Pittstown NY, m. (1) 14 Apr 1740 Susanna Gillet of Norwich CT, b. ?; m.(2) Hannah McFarland b. 1736 Ireland, d. 1781; m.(3) ?. Revolutionary War: 2nd Lieutenant in Captain Savage's Company, 25 Aug-3 Oct 1755.
Isaac, b. 24 Dec 1740, d.y.
Edward, b. 24 Dec 1740, d.y.
Susanna, b. 15 Apr 1742, m. 13 Oct 1760 Stephen Palmer.
Edward, b. 12 Oct 1743, d. 3 Mar 1750.
Lydia, b. 15 Aug 1745, d. 19 Sep 1838, m. 6 Oct 1768 Paul Brigham.
Joseph, b. 17 Jan 1747, drowned.
Prudence, b. 4 Mar 1749, m. 28 Mar 1768 Samuel Brown.
Benjamin, b. 12 Jun 1750 Hebron CT, m. 5 Nov 1769 Sarah Dewey of Hebron CT, b. 11 Jul 1745, dau. Roger and Patience (Rollo) Dewey. In Caanan NH 1782, 1790.
Caroline, b. 6 Jan 1752, m. 24 May 1775 William Bols.
Calvin, b. 3 Jul 1753 Hebron CT.
169 Conant Bagley$^5$, 1756-1838.
Elizabeth, b. 12 Jan 1768, m. 11 Aug 1888 Ebenezer Mudge. Went to New York.
Sally, b. 22 Jan 1769, m. 15 May 1789 Asa Forbes.
170 Isaac$^5$, 1770-1847.
Anna, b. 11 Jun 1775, d. 1838, m. 1799 John Forbes.
David, b. 1782 Hebron CT. Went to Canada.
Sources: VR Hebron CT. P49, D6, V9.

69. **JACOB$^4$ SAWYER** [see 21], b. ca. 1720 Lyme CT, m. 12 Jan 1743 Lyme CT Rose Bennet of Lyme CT. Mariner. Revolutionary War: On ship "Oliver Cromwell".
171 Jacob$^5$, 1745-1802.
Phebe, b. 10 Feb 1747, m. 22 Mar 1767 Thomas Rubey.
Rose, b. 10 Feb 1747.
Matthew, b. 30 Jan 1751.
John, b. 8 Feb 1753.
Asa, b. 30 Jul 1756.
Sources: VR Lyme CT.

70. **NATHAN⁴ SAWYER** [see 22], b. 1 Mar 1722 Hebron CT, d. bef. Mar 1759, m. 23 May 1745 May 1745 Colchester CT Desire Fuller of Colchester CT, b. 2 Feb 1723, dau. Samuel and Naomi (Rowley) Fuller. Wid. m. 8 Nov 1759 John Morey.
172 Samuel[5], 1746-1813.
Child, b. 1756, d. 25 Mar 1759 Colchester CT.
Sources: B3, F44.

71. **AMOS[4] SAWYER** [see 23], b. 30 Sep 1733 Lancaster MA, d. 25 Jan 1768 Lancaster MA, m. 9 Jan 1755 Lancaster MA Mary Rugg of Sterling MA, wid., b. 10 Oct 1734. All CH bp. at First Church of Lancaster MA.
Lydia, b. 19 Dec 1755, m. 13 Feb 1777 Jacob Wilder.
Releaf, b. 24 May 1756, d. 12 Jan 1757.
Releaf, b. 1 Dec 1758, d. 10 Jun 1839, m. 5 Mar 1778 Seth Fairbanks.
173 Calvin[5], 1760-1834.
174 Luther[5], 1762-1824.
Sarah, b. 7 Jun 1764.
Mary, b. 3 Dec 1766, m. 29 Jun 1786 Rufus Fletcher.
175 Amos[5], 1768-1845.
Sources: VR Lancaster MA. R30.

72. **EPHRAIM[4] SAWYER** [see 24], b. 20 Feb 1729 Lancaster MA, d. Feb 1813 So. Hero VT, m. 11 Jun 1752 Lancaster MA Susannah Richardson, bp. 22 Aug 1736, dau. Josiah and Dolly (Wilder) Richardson. French and Indian War: With Lt. General James Abercrombie at Ticonderoga NY Jul 1758. Revolutionary War: With Colonel John Whitcomb's Regiment of Minutemen at Lexington MA 19 Apr 1775; commanded Worcester County Regiment at Bunker Hill 1775, Saratoga 1777. He bur. in Lake View Cem., Burlington VT. Five sons served in the Revolutionary War.
176 Ephraim[5], b. 1753.
Dorothy, b. 6 Jun 1755, m. _____ Eldridge.
177 Josiah[5], 1757-1837.
John, b. 12 Sep 1759. Revolutionary War: Adjutant of Colonel John Brooks' 7th Massachusetts Regiment of Infantry. Original grantee of Grand Isle VT 1779, went there with family 1781.
178 James[5], 1761-1827.
Peter, b. 10 Aug 1763 Lancaster MA, d. 1827, m.(1) Nancy Stark, b. 1785, dau. John and Eunice (Adams) Stark; m.(2) 1817 Chloe Landon of Litchfield CT, b. 8 Mar 1775 d. 11 Mar 1859, dau. David and Chloe (Buell) Landon. Revolutionary War. In South Hero VT. Will dated 8 Nov 1827. CH: Sally Lucia, b. 2 Sep 1800, d. 22 Sep 1849, m. 18 Jan 1827 John Phelps; Nancy, b. 8 Jan 1818; Eunice, b. ?, m. 26 Feb 1824 Peter Corbin.
Susannah, b. 2 May 1765, m. _____ Bingham.
179 Daniel Greenleaf[5], 1767-1845.
Eunice, b. 16 Aug 1768, d. 10 Apr 1857 m. George W. Foster.
180 Artimus[5], b. 1771.
Abraham, b. 1773 South Hero VT.
Timothy, b. 1774 South Hero VT.
Sources: South Hero VT census 1790, 1800.VR Lancaster MA, Sterling MA, SA/VT. S20A, H41, D6, P40, L5.

73. **SAMUEL[4] SAWYER** [see 25], b. 2 Jan 1740 Lancaster MA, d. bef. 1800, m. 18 Jan 1768 Templeton MA Phebe Cooper of Lancaster MA, b. 12 Jan 1748 d. 6 Jul 1820, dau. Moses and

Phebe (Jewett) Cooper. Revolutionary War: Captain of Lancaster Company, Colonel John Whitcomb's Regiment, 1775. Wid. w/son Samuel 1800.

181 Cooper[5], 1768-1830.
182 Samuel[5], 1770-1848.
Martha, b. 30 Oct 1772, d. 1 Mar 1853, m. Ezra Sawyer.
Phebe, b. 1 Sep 1774, d. Jul 1793.
Putnam, b. 23 Aug 1776 Lancaster MA, d. 11 Oct 1843.
Ruth, b. 11 Nov 1778, d. Oct 1857, m. 17 Feb 1806 Jonas Houghton of Leominster MA. Note: [R30] says Ruth m. 29 May 1805.
Mary, b. 10 Nov 1781, d. 28 Mar 1864, m. 25 Mar 1807 Joseph Willard.
Moses, b. 27 Apr 1784 Sterling MA, d. 4 Jan 1870, unm.
Sally, b. 14 Feb 1787, d. Mar 1792.

Sources: Sterling MA census 1790, 1800. VR Templeton MA. P63, R30, B53, C8.

74. **JOSHUA[4] SAWYER** [see 25], b. 7 Mar 1742 Lancaster MA, d. 4 Dec 1817, m. 19 Jan 1769 Chocksett (Sterling?) MA Esther Jewett, b. 9 Jun 1745 d. 24 Dec 1828, dau. David and Esther Jewett. Revolutionary War: In Colonel Asa Whitcomb's Regiment 1775.

183 Solomon[5], 1770-1851.
Elizabeth, b. 17 Sep 1772, d. 14 Sep 1831 Ludlow VT.
Dolly, b. 6 Aug 1774, m. 2 Nov 1806 Abel Haild.
184 David[5], 1776-1844.
Eunice, b. 13 Feb 1779, d. 3 Dec 1800.
Esther, b. 25 Jan 1782.
Deborah, b. 30 Mar 1785.
Samuel, b. 30 Mar 1785 Sterling MA.

Sources: Sterling MA census 1790, 1800. VR Lancaster MA, SA/VT. J14, R30.

75. **JOHN[4] SAWYER** [see 26], b. 7 Aug 1728 Lancaster MA, m. Prudence _____, b.?. Revolutionary War: Enl. 22 Aug 1776. S/land in Lancaster MA 1763-68, Charlestown NH 1765. B/land in Bath NH 1765-69. In Charlestown NH 1760, Bath NH 1767, Piermont NH 1776.

Azubah, b. 2 Oct 1752 Charlestown NH, d. 26 Jul 1834, m. 24 Sep 1769 Sylvanus Heath.
185 Enos[5], 1754-1804.
Benjamin, b. 11 Feb 1757 Petersham NH, m. Polly Marsh, b. ?. Revolutionary War: Enl. in Colonel Timothy Bedel's NH Regiment, Bradford VT, 1775.
Lucy, b. 28 May 1759 Petersham NH.
186 John[5], b. 1761.
187 Silvanus[5], b. 1763.
Damaris, b. 14 Mar 1765.
Mary, b. 14 Sep 1767.

Sources: Charlestown NH census 1760. VR Lancaster MA, Charlestown NH, Petersham MA. N14.

76. **DELIVERANCE[4] SAWYER** [see 26], b. 11 Dec 1746 Lancaster MA, d. 1835 Starkey NY, m. Mercy Nash, b. ?. Revolutionary War: Private in Lieutenant E. Hall's Company of Rangers, Mar 1780 for eight months; Corporal in Lieutenant Ward Bayley's Company, Jun 1781 for four months; In Lieutenant Ward Bayley's Company, Mar 1782 to Dec 1782. Received 100 acres in Maidstone Vt 1774, B/land in Bath NH 1767 and 1769.

188 Deliverance[5] 1764-1863.
Eunice, b. ?, m. Lyman Morehouse.
Dorothy, b. 2 Apr 1791, d. 2 Apr 1834, m. 15 Mar 1810 Buell Newcomb.

Sources: Piermont NH census 1790. N1A, D6, N21.

77. **EZRA$^4$ SAWYER** [see 27], b. 18 Aug 1730 Lancaster MA, d. 4 Mar 1776 Dorchester MA, m. 11 Dec 1760 Sterling MA Kezia Sawyer, b. 12 Dec 1739 d. 1789, dau. Abner and Mary Sawyer. Revolutionary War: Private in Captain Samuel Sawyer's Company, Colonel John Whitcomb's Regiment, 19 Apr 1775. In Sterling MA. He bur. in Sterling MA. Wid. m. 23 May 1779 Ephraim Powers.

Abner, b. 8 Nov 1761, d. 10 Nov 1777 in Revolutionary War, Albany NY.
189 Ezra$^5$, 1764-1828.
190 Thomas$^5$, 1766-1825.
Nathaniel, b. 10 Sep 1769 Lancaster MA, d. 24 Mar 1835, unm.

Sources: VR Lancaster MA. P72, C8, D6.

78. **NATHANIEL$^4$ SAWYER** [see 27], b. 15 Mar 1741 Lancaster MA, m.(1) ?; m.(2) 28 Jun 1796 Boxboro MA Lucy (Stow) Whitcomb, wid of James W., b. 1745 d. 26 Dec 1834 Boxboro MA. In Boxboro MA.

Sally, b. ca. 1779, m.(I) 15 Mar 1801 Josiah Whitcomb.
Son, b. (1784-1790).
Son, b. (1784-1790).
Daughter, b. (1784-1790).

Sources: Boxboro MA census 1800, 1810, 1820. VR Lancaster MA, Boxboro MA.

79. **NATHANIEL$^4$ SAWYER** [see 28], b. 21 Feb 1745 Lancaster MA, m. 30 Oct 1771 Medway MA Catherine Ellis of Medway MA, b. 28 Sep 1748 d. 7 Sep 1839 Watertown MA, dau. Abner and Mary (Maccane) Ellis. Revolutionary War.

191 Oliver$^5$, 1772-1859.
Dolly, b. 8 Nov 1773, m. 6 Apr 1801 Josiah Whitcomb.
Mary, b. 12 Nov 1775, m. Cyrus Daniels.
192 Jonathan$^5$, 1778-1831.
Nathaniel, b. 8 Jan 1780 Lancaster MA.
Catherine, b. Mar 1782, m. Elijah Hill.
Cynthia, b. Mar 1784, m.(1) 7 Apr 1807 Eben Wheelock, m.(2) Asa Whitney.
193 Alpheus$^5$, 1786-1852.
194 John$^5$, b. 1788.

Sources: Lancaster MA census 1790. VR Lancaster MA, Medway MA. G20, E16.

80. **PHINEAS$^4$ SAWYER** [see 30], b. 28 Apr 1742 Lancaster MA, d. 9 Mar 1794 Fitchburg MA, m. 4 Jan 1774 Lancaster MA Mary Prescott of Lancaster MA, b. 24 Dec 1743 d. 15 Oct 1795, dau. John and Mary (White) Prescott. In Fitchburg MA: Constable 1780, Town Moderator 1786, Town Clerk 1790. All CH b. in Fitchburg MA.

Mary, b. 27 Sep 1774, d. 16 Jul 1856, m. 11 Feb 1796 Daniel Putnam.
Beulah, b. 27 Jun 1776, d. 1 Sep 1778.
Dorothy, b. 11 Mar 1779, d. 16 Apr 1847, m. 24 Feb 1801 Ephraim Kimball.
John, b. 11 Mar 1779, m. 23 Apr 1807 Groton MA Rebecca Stone of Groton MA, b.?, dau. Jonas and Rebecca (Fletcher) Stone. In Lunenburg MA.
Eunice, b. 15 May 1781, d. 28 Sep 1848, m.(I) 28 Sep 1805 Ensign Phillip Cowdin.
Sarah, b. 16 Jun 1783, d. 21 Feb 1853, m. 18 Nov 1805 Moses Smith.

Sources: Fitchburg MA census 1790. VR Lancaster MA, Groton MA. M54, F25, K16, D20, P76.

81. **JOSEPH$^4$ SAWYER** [see 30], bp. 31 Dec 1749 Lancaster MA, d. 26 Jan 1832 Bloomfield ME, m. 8 Sep 1774 Fitchburg MA Mary (Molly) Steward of Lunenburg MA, b. 8 Jun 1756 d. 13

Apr 1840, dau. Solomon Steward. Paid by the town of Fitchburg MA "for services" 1772. In Fitchburg MA: Surveyor of Highways 1780, Warden 1784. All CH b. in Fitchburg MA.

Polly, b.28 Feb 1775, m. 1 Jan 1798 Kendall Boutell, Jr.
Betsey, b. 6 Apr 1777, d. 30 Sep 1860, m. Levi Merrill.
Beulah, b. 4 Jul 1779, d. 6 Feb 1861, m. John Kimball.
Rebecca H., b. 5 Sep 1781.
Abigail, b. 25 Feb 1784, m.(I) 13 Aug 1708 Josiah Brown.
195 Joseph$^5$, 1786-1835.
196 Phineas$^5$, b. 1789.
197 Nathaniel$^5$, 1792-1832.
198 Osgood$^5$, 1799-1877.
Phafilena, b. 13 Jul 1801, m. 23 Feb 1823 Ichabod Rapell.

Sources: Fitchburg MA census 1790, 1800. Canaan ME census 1810. Bloomfield ME census 1820. Skowhegan ME census 1830. D20, M54, P13, William C. Moulton rec.

82. **ABNER$^4$ SAWYER** [see 30], b. 11 Mar 1753 Lancaster MA, d. Fitchburg MA, m. 27 Mar 1777 Fitchburg MA Elizabeth Perkins, b. ?. Surveyor of Highways in Fitchburg MA 1788. In Rindge MA 1797. All CH b. in Fitchburg MA.

Betsey, b. 9 Oct 1777, m. 11 Mar 1798 Thomas Cowdin.
Susannah, b. 28 May 1780, d.y.
Joseph, b. 23 Apr 1782. In Rindge NH.
Susannah, b. 3 Apr 1785, m. 30 May 1804 Horatio Hale.
Asenath, b. 4 Sep 1790, d. 3 Jun 1815.
Sophia, b. 4 May 1792. Taught school in Rindge NH, 1816-1818, received $8 for eight weeks. Missionary and teacher in Arkansas.

Sources: Fitchburg MA census 1790. Rindge NH census 1800. D20, S821, N6.

83. **LUKE$^4$ SAWYER** [see 30], b. 21 Nov 1762 Lancaster MA, d. Fitchburg MA, m. 27 Dec 1787 Fitchburg MA Polly Smith, b. 1764, dau. Benjamin and Ruth (Perry) Smith. All CH b. in Fitchburg MA.

199 Luke$^5$, 1793-1874.
Mary, b. 16 Nov 1795.
Ruth, b. 29 Dec 1797.
Abe, b. 29 May 1800. In Sherburne VT.

Sources: Fitchburg MA census 1790. D20.

## FIFTH GENERATION

84. **JOSHUA$^5$ SAWYER** [see 31], b. 9 Sep 1732 Lancaster MA (bp. 5 Nov 1732 Windham CT), d. 6 Jan 1812 Bolton MA, m. Thankful Whitcomb,b. 24 Jan 1739, dau. Simon and Thankful (Houghton) Whitcomb. Revolutionary War. In Bolton MA, Templeton MA 1770, Berlin MA.

Joshua, b. 18 Aug 1759 Bolton MA.
Betty, b. 14 Feb 1761.
200 Peter$^6$, 1765-1840.
Zilpah, b. 19 Mar 1766, m. 12 Mar 1786 Jonathan Holman, Jr.
James, b. 20 Feb 1767 Bolton MA. In Templeton MA.
Thankful, b. 17 Oct 1770.
Aholiab, b. 24 Apr 1773 Templeton MA.
Keziah, b. 27 Aug 1775.
Keturah, b. 16 Sep 1777.

Patience, b. 10 May 1782, d. 20 May 1845, m. 18 Sep 1806 Joseph Conant.
Sources: Berlin MA census 1800. VR Bolton MA, Templeton MA. A27, C24.

85. **SYLVANUS⁵ SAWYER** [see 31], b. 8 Jun 1734 Lancaster MA, d. Aug 1796 Madison ME, m. 14 Jul 1757 Bolton MA Susannah (Geary) Whitcomb, b. Mar 1734 d. Jan 1797, wid. of John, dau. Thomas and Phebe (Wyman) Geary. Went to Norridgewock ME 1774. B/land in Madison ME 1784.

John, b. 13 Feb 1758, drowned 4 Jul 1776.
201 Luke[6], 1760-1841.
Betsey, b. 20 Jan 1763, d. 7 Mar 1835.
Levi, b. 20 Feb 1765 Templeton MA, d. 5 Apr 1861 Madison ME. War of 1812: Private in Captain Joseph Patten's Company of Infantry, 2d Regiment. On Norridgewock ME tax list 1787. In Madison ME 1850, 1860.
Olive, b. 1766, d. 1857.
202 Sylvanus[6], 1768-1847
Joseph, b. 27 Aug 1770, d. Sep 1775.
203 Ephraim[6], 1772-1848.
Lucy, b. 29 Jan 1777, d. 16 Sep 1777.

Sources: Norridgewock ME census 1790. VR Bolton MA. W37A, A17, W21.

86. **AHOLIAB[5] SAWYER** [see 31], b. 27 May 1742 Bolton MA, d. 4 Jan 1823 Templeton MA, m. 5 Jun 1769 Bolton MA Barshebah Barrett, b. 2 Apr 1744 d. 28 Jan 1827, dau. Oliver and Hannah (Hunt) Barrett. Revolutionary War. Town Treasurer 1772-1774 and Selectman 1789, 1791, 1795 for Templeton MA.

Rebecca, b. 8 Dec 1770, m. 10 Mar 1791 Levi Barrett of Dublin NH.
Lucy, b. 29 Dec 1772, m. 6 Nov 1793 Asa Hosmer.
Catherine, b. 14 Mar 1775, m. 17 Apr 1796 Elisha Gregory.
Edward, b. 2 Feb 1778, d. 9 Sep 1806.
204 Joshua[6], 1780-1860.
Hannah, b. 14 Dec 1782, m. 14 Mar 1803 Phileman Robbins.
Polly, b. 30 Apr 1786, d.y.

Sources: Templeton MA census 1790, 1810, 1820. VR Bolton MA, Templeton MA. W70.

87. **ISREAL[5] SAWYER** [see 31], b. 9 Sep 1751 Bolton MA, d. 18 Jan 1832 Swanzey NH, m.(1) 25 Nov 1773 Bolton MA Beulah Willson, b. ?; m.(2) 22 Jul 1783 Putney VT Thankful Houghton, b. ?; m.(3) 20 Feb 1787 Dunstable MA Caty Woodward, b.?; m. (4) Anna Thompson,b. ca. 1771. Physician. Revolutionary War. In Bolton MA 1774, Putney VT 1777, Swanzey NH 1787.

Gardiner, b. 19 Apr 1774 Bolton MA. In Swanzey NH.
Beulah, b. 31 May 1777, d.y.
Elizabeth, b. 9 Dec 1779, m. 9 Mar 1812 Asa Whitcomb.
205 Elijah[6], b. 1783.
Archibald, b. 29 Dec 1791 Swanzey NH.
206 Josiah[6], 1796-1876.
207 William[6], 1797-1839.
Caty, b. 4 Dec 1799, m. 19 Mar 1838 George Nurse.
Polly, b. 1801, d. 3 Sep 1803.
Beulah, b. 5 Mar 1808.
Aholiab, b. 26 Jul 1809 Swanzey NH.

Sources: Swanzey NH census 1790, 1800, 1810, 1820, 1830. VR Putney VT, Dunstable MA, Bolton MA, Swanzey NH. N6, R7, G46.

88. **GEORGE[5] SAWYER** [see 31], b. 25 Nov 1757 Bolton MA, d. 30 Apr 1842 Mercer ME, m. 3 Jul 1786 Templeton MA Lucy Merritt,. b. 25 May 1762 d. 2 Mar 1832, dau. Noah and Sarah (Lee) Merritt. Revolutionary War: Lexington MA 1775, Seige of Boston 1776-1777. Town Moderator for Starks ME 1797-1805. In Mercer ME 1830, Smithfield ME 1840. He bur. in Mercer ME.

Henry, b. 9 Dec 1786, d. Sep 1788.
Betsey, b. 3 Feb 1789, d. 1848, m. 1812 Andrew Munsey.
208 Otis[6], 1792-1826.
209 Josiah[6], 1796-1873.
Lucy, b. 24 Dec 1799, m. _____ Bailey.
Sarah L., b. 20 Sep 1801, d. 1866, m. Jeremiah Boyden.
210 George[6], 1805-1857.

Sources: Starks ME census 1790, 1800, 1810. Mercer ME census 1830. Smithfield ME census 1840. VR Bolton MA, Templeton MA. D51, S68, N1A, L44.

89. **WILLIAM[5] SAWYER** [see 32], b. 26 Sep 1749 Bolton MA, d. 10 Oct 1794 Bolton MA, m. 22 Dec 1769 Bolton MA Kezia Moor, b. 15 Mar 1748. Revolutionary War: Captain, Colonel Ephraim Stearns' Regiment, 1787. Wid. in Bolton MA 1800.

Levi, b. 14 May 1769, d. 29 Mar 1771.
Zeresh, b. 17 Nov 1770.
Abigail, b. 30 Jan 1773.
Kezia, b. 20 Jun 1775, m. 12 Jun 1798 Luther Sawyer.
Polly, b. 1 Nov 1777, m. 1805 M_____ Whiting of Charlestown MA.
Charity, b. 24 Dec 1779.
William, b. 28 Mar 1782 Bolton MA.
211 Samuel[6], 1784-1826.
Josiah, b. 30 Mar 1786 Bolton MA.
Sarah, b. 15 Mar 1789.
Phineas, bp. 15 Mar 1789 Bolton MA.

Sources: Bolton MA census 1800. VR Bolton MA. N26, N36.

90. **JOSIAH[5] SAWYER** [see 32], b. 18 Aug 1751 Bolton MA, d. 9 Feb 1817 Bolton MA, m. 7 Dec 1774 Bolton MA Judith Ross, b. ?.

Sarah, b. 25 Mar 1775.
Judith, b. 24 Aug 1776, m. 15 Apr 1804 Peter Gates of Stow MA.
Achsah, b. 24 Oct 1778, d. 22 Feb 1837, m. 25 Jul 1799 William Munroe of Waterford ME.
Arrithusa, b. 15 Aug 1780, m. 3 Jan 1802 John Newton.
Josiah, b. 26 Sep 1782, d.y.
212 Daniel[6], b. 1784.
Josiah, b. 18 Aug 1786 Bolton MA.
Hannah, b. Nov 1788.
Betsey, b. 26 Sep 1791.
John, b. 10 Feb 1793 Bolton MA.

Sources: Bolton MA census 1790, 1800, 1810. VR Bolton MA.

91. **JOSEPH[5] SAWYER** [see 32], b. 8 Mar 1756 Bolton MA, d. 12 Mar 1828 Bolton MA, m. 31 Jul 1782 Bolton (or Berlin) MA Ruth Walcott, b. 1763 d. 10 Jun 1830. Revolutionary War. B/S/land in Waterford ME 1790, 1795.

Eunice, b. 10 Apr 1783, m. 8 Aug 1802 Nathan Cary.

Achsah, b. 4 Feb 1785.
213 Joseph$^6$, b. 1787.
Ruth, b. 15 Jun 1789, m. 7 Feb 1813 Robert Pekham.
Asenath, b. 4 Apr 1791, m. 11 May 1834 Joel B. Fuller.
Zilpah, b. 29 May 1795, d. 2 Sep 1852, m. 2 Mar 1818 Oliver Adams.
Sarah, b. 20 Jan 1797.
214 George$^6$, 1800-1876.
Joel, b. 24 Jul 1805 Bolton MA, m. 18 Feb 1830 Bolton MA Sarah Barrett, b. 5 Dec 1806. In Bolton MA 1840.
215 Nathan$^6$, b. 1807.
Sources: Bolton MA census 1790, 1800, 1810, 1820, 1830, 1840. VR Bolton MA, Berlin MA. R10c, A4.

92. **BENJAMIN$^5$ SAWYER** [see 32], b. 10 Sep 1758 Bolton MA d. 30 Mar 1844 Bolton MA, m. 6 Dec 1781 Bolton MA Rebecca Houghton, b. 24 Apr 1760 d. 22 Dec 1832, dau. Jonas and Rebecca (Nichols) Houghton. Revolutionary War.
Rebecca, b. 16 Mar 1782, m. 23 Nov 1807 David Ross.
216 Levi$^6$, 1783-1844.
217 Benjamin$^6$, b. 1785.
Betsey, b. 27 Apr 1786, d.y.
Jonah, Captain, b. 31 Aug 1787 Bolton MA, m.(1) 5 Nov 1822 Greenfield MA Adeline Griswold, b. ?; m.(2) 30 Jan 1828 Greenfield MA Rebecca Bowers, b. ?; m.(3) 26 Apr 1854 Springfield MA Nancy Pendleton, b.ca. 1805, dau. Joseph Robinson. In Greenfield MA 1840. CH: Son b. (1823-1825); dau., b. (1825-1830).
Sally, b. 27 Oct 1788, d. 3 Mar 1790.
William, b. 30 Apr 1792 Bolton MA.
218 John$^6$, b. 1794.
Lucy, b. 3 Oct 1795, d. 9 Feb 1861, m. 18 May 1825 Holloway Bailey.
Betsey, b. 6 Sep 1797, m. 27 May 1821 Abel Sawyer, Jr.
Cephas, b. 20 Aug 1800 Bolton MA.
Sally, b. 3 Jul 1804, d. 5 Jul 1804.
Sources: Bolton MA census 1790, 1800, 1810, 1820, 1830, 1840. Greenfield MA census 1840. VR Bolton MA, Greenfield MA, Leominster MA, SA/MA. H75, B5, N11.

93. **BARNABAS$^5$ SAWYER** [see 32], b. 1 Apr 1761 Bolton MA, d. 26 Jan 1848 Buxton ME, m.(1) 14 Dec 1778 Bolton MA Unity Houghton, b. 19 Sep 1762; m.(2) 19 Jun 1783 Bolton MA Lydia Whitcomb, b. 14 Feb 1766 d. 24 Aug 1818; m.(3) 23 Feb 1826 Hannah Butler, b. 12 Mar 1777 d. 1860, dau. Thomas and Bridget (Gerrish) Butler of Sanford ME. Revolutionary War: Fifer in Newton's Co., Stearns' Massachusetts Militia. Teacher in Buxton ME. B/land 1810 Bridgton ME and Otisfield ME. Wid. in Limington ME 1850.
Unity, b. 16 May 1780, d. 6 Apr 1818, m. _____ Burnell.
William, b. 8 Dec 1785, d. 5 Dec 1795.
Sally, b. 30 Jan 1788, d. 1 Jun 1814, m. 29 Nov 1809 Elijah Davis.
Lydia, b. 8 Nov 1793, d. 28 May 1810.
219 Barnabas Whitcomb$^6$, 1794-1858.
Silas, b. 25 Apr 1798, d. 4 May 1798.
Rebecca, b. 22 Mar 1799, d. 3 Nov 1874, m. 30 Nov 1817 Daniel Thompson.
Sources: Buxton ME census 1790, 1800, 1810, 1820, 1830, 1840. Widow in Limington ME 1850. VR Buxton ME, Saco ME. P82k, W26, S70, M5, R17, F21, R10g, B100, Barnabas' Bible.

94. **URI$^5$ SAWYER** [see 32], b. 19 May 1770 Bolton MA, d. 3 Jun 1799, m. 14 Feb 1791 Lancaster MA Lydia Pollard, b. ?. B/S/land in Waterford ME 1791-1793.

Uri, b. 1791 Bolton MA.
220 Seth$^6$, b. 1795.
Henry, b. 9 Jun 1797 Bolton MA.

Sources: VR Bolton MA, Lancaster MA. R10c.

95. **WILLIAM$^5$ SAWYER** [see 33], b. 5 Mar 1740 Bolton MA, d. 28 Feb 1822 Berlin MA, m. 18 Jan 1764 Bolton MA Hannah Barrett of Bolton MA, b. 19 Feb 1742 d. 2 Feb 1830, dau. Oliver and Hannah (Hunt) Barrett.

Abigail, b. 5 May 1765, d. 26 Dec 1852, m. 25 Oct 1785 Cotton Newton.
William, Jr., b. 6 Feb 1767 Bolton MA. In Berlin MA.
221 Amos$^6$, 1769-1842.
Mary, b. 8 Feb 1771, m. 22 Sep 1792 Rufus Howe.
222 Oliver$^6$, 1774-1851.
223 Asa$^6$, 1775-1845. Went to New Hampshire and Ohio.
224 Uriah$^6$, 1778-1862. Went to New Hampshire and Ohio.
Hannah, b. 14 Oct 1781, d. 1871, m. 28 Dec 1805 Robert Fosgate.
Levi, b. 2 May 1784 Berlin MA, d. 16 Mar 1844.

Sources: Berlin MA census 1790, 1810, 1820. VR Bolton MA, Berlin MA. H76, H80, L16.

96. **JOSIAH$^5$ SAWYER** [see 33], b. 8 Nov 1752 Bolton MA, d. 3 Jun 1808 Berlin MA, m.(1) 6 Aug 1770 Bolton MA Barshebah Moore of Putney VT, b.? d. 1778; m.(2) 10 Feb 1779 Bolton MA Persis Baker, b. 8 Jun 1759 d. 1785, dau. Samuel Baker; m.(3) 4 Jan 1786 Prudence Johnson of Leominster MA, b. 23 Jul 1759 d. 13 Jul 1826, dau. Asa and Tamar (Whitcomb) Johnson. Revolutionary War: Captain. Wid. in Berlin MA 1810, 1820.

225 Alvin$^6$, 1770-1842.
Eunice, b. 10 Nov 1774, d. 10 Mar 1863, m. 4 May 1793 Ephraim Babcock.
Bathsheba, b. 9 Mar 1778, d.y.
Bathsheba, b. 29 Feb 1780.
Susannah, b. 19 Nov 1781, d. 30 Aug 1818, m. 3 Oct 1803 Caleb Houghton.
226 Ira$^6$, 1787-1861.
Lucinda, b. 20 Apr 1789, d. 8 Mar 1875, m. 1 Dec 1808 Amory Carter.
227 Rufus$^6$, 1790-1865.
George, b. 6 Feb 1793 Berlin MA, m. 5 Jan 1816 Berlin MA Lucy Hoar, b. 9 Oct 1791. In Lancaster MA, Berlin MA, Northboro MA, Sutton MA. Went to Tennessee. CH: Son, b. (1816-1820); 3 dau. b. (1816-1820).
228 Asa$^6$, 1795-1861.
Persis, b. 18 Jun 1796, d. 1796.
Persis, b. 18 Jun 1798, m. 11 Apr 1822 William L. Howe of Marlboro MA.
Sarah, b. 12 Jul 1800, d. 27 Feb 1895, m. 17 Apr 1821 Lewis Carter.

Sources: Berlin MA census 1790, 1800, 1810, 1820. Northboro MA census 1830. Sutton MA census 1840. VR Berlin MA, Bolton MA, Lancaster MA. W39, C9, H76, V9.

97. **SILAS$^5$ SAWYER** [see 33], b. 5 Jul 1766 Bolton MA, d. 8 Nov 1842 Berlin MA, m. (1) 6 Jan 1785 Berlin MA Sarah Howe, b. 1 Mar 1767 d. 26 Jun 1832, dau. Phineas and Experience (Pollard) Howe; m.(2) 4 Jul 1833 Berlin MA Mary Barnard, b. ? d. 21 Dec 1840.

229 Thomas$^6$, 1785-1864.
230 Jonas$^6$, 1787-1827.
231 Abraham$^6$, 1789-1836.

Experience, b. 27 Jun 1791, d. 28 Dec 1829, m. 20 Oct 1814 Moses Greenleaf.
Phineas, b. 29 Nov 1793 Berlin MA. Went to Ohio.
Mary, b. 31 Mar 1798, d. 21 May 1819, m. 24 Dec 1817 Samuel Spofford.
Silas, b. 1 Oct 1800, d. 30 Jun 1805.

Sources: Berlin MA census 1790, 1800, 1810, 1820, 1830. VR Berlin MA. E16, H76, H75, G42, H80.

98. **AARON$^5$ SAWYER** [see 34], b. 13 May 1732 Lancaster MA, d. 15 Dec 1774 Lancaster MA, m. 25 Apr 1754 Sterling MA Abigail Moore, b. 27 Jan 1738 d. 19 Jul 1824, dau. Oliver and Abigail (Houghton) Moore. Founded Sawyer Mill, Boylston MA. In Sterling MA.

232 Aaron$^6$, 1756-1817.
233 Oliver$^6$, 1759-1838.
Parna, b. 16 Sep 1761, d. 20 May 1788, m.(1) 13 May 1779 Abraham Howe, m. (2) 6 Jan 1787 Andrew Kimball.
Abigail, b. 2 Jul 1764.
Dolly, b. 12 Nov 1767, d. 21 May 1782.
Submit, b. 5 Aug 1770, m. 31 Jul 1788 Silas Howe, Jr.
Silence, b. 23 Dec 1774, d. 26 Jun 1862, m. 18 Apr 1793 Stephen Hastings.

Sources: VR Lancaster MA, Shrewsbury MA. M54, F25, B93.

99. **MOSES$^5$ SAWYER** [see 34], b. 13 Jan 1734 Lancaster MA, d. 5 Oct 1805 Clinton MA, m.(1) 27 Apr 1763 Lancaster MA Mary Sawyer, b. 6 Dec 1742 d. 12 Apr 1774, dau. Ezra and Rebecca (Whitcomb) Sawyer; m.(2) 23 Apr 1777 Lancaster MA Betty Larkin, b. 1750 d. 21 Apr 1844. Held commission as lieutenant in British Army 1757. Revolutionary War: Lieutenant. Wid. bur. in Old Burial Ground, Lancaster MA.

234 Moses$^6$, 1764-1831.
Molly, b. 18 Jan 1766, m. 24 Sep 1788 Abijah Moore of Boylston MA.
Betty, b. 18 Apr 1768, d. 2 Mar 1852, m. 29 Sep 1796 Joseph Rice.
John, b. 16 Mar 1770 Lancaster MA.
Sarah, b. 10 May 1772, d. 2 Sep 1788.
Artimas, b. 2 Nov 1777 Lancaster MA, d. 1815 Marietta OH. Harvard graduate 1798. Professor, University of Ohio at Athens OH.
Joseph, b. 1 Jan 1780, d. 2 Oct 1805. Baptismal record says Jonas.
Nathaniel, b. 26 Apr 1782, d. 13 Feb 1788.
235 Peter$^6$, 1784-1831.
Ezra, b. 6 Dec 1785 Lancaster MA, d. 18 Jan 1825 Lancaster MA, unm.
Lusena, b. 14 Feb 1788, d. 25 Jun 1825, m. 3 Nov 1802 Ebenezer Wilder.
Katy, b. 13 Aug 1790, m. 3 May 1807 Stephen Wilder.
Achsah, b. 25 Dec 1794, m. 20 Sep 1813 Ephraim Hastings of Boylston MA.

Sources: Lancaster MA census 1790, 1800. VR Lancaster MA, SA/MA. F25, C8, E16.

100. **JOSEPH$^5$ SAWYER** [see 34], b. 23 Apr 1738 Lancaster MA, m. 20 Aug 1761 Lancaster MA Agnus Dunsmore .of Stow MA, b. 28 Jun 1735, dau. William and Jane Dunsmore. In Sterling MA.

Joseph, b. 6 Jun 1762 Lancaster MA, d. 1830, m. 3 Mar 1791 Sterling MA Eunice Moor of Sterling MA, b. 1761 d. Dec 1824. Graduate of Williams College. Minister in Leverett MA. CH: 3 sons b. (1790-1800); dau., b. (1790-1800); son, b. (1800-1810); son (1810-1820).
236 Ameriah$^6$, b. 1765.
237 William$^6$, 1768-1824.

238 Jabez⁶, 1770-1849.
Persis, b. 1 May 1773, d. 9 Feb 1851, m. 1812 William Fairbanks.
239 Aaron⁶, 1775-1846.
John, b. 15 Mar 1779 Lancaster MA.
Sources: Wendell MA census 1800. Boylston MA census 1800, 1810. VR Boylston MA, Shrewsbury MA, Royalston MA, Wendell MA, Lancaster MA.

101. **ABRAHAM⁵ SAWYER** [see 35], b. 19 Sep 1737 Bolton MA, d. 8 Feb 1811 (gravestone) or 18 Feb 1811 (d. certificate) Chester VT, m. 30 Apr 1761 Petersham MA ExperienceHorton of Petersham MA, b. 1743 d. 25 Jun 1833. In Templeton MA. In Rockingham VT 1775. He bur. in Brookside Cem., Chester VT.
Elizabeth, b. 13 Feb 1762, d. 4 May 1838, m. 6 Jun 1784 Josiah Heald.
Experience, b. 9 May 1764, d. 27 Aug 1825, m. 10 Sep 1786 David Davis.
Joseph, b. 2 May 1767, d. 27 Sep 1770.
Sarah, b. 4 Feb 1770, d. 4 Sep 1777.
Mary, b. 1 Nov 1771, d. 26 Nov 1771.
240 Joseph⁶, 1773-1843.
Aaron, b. 25 Jun 1775, d. 24 Aug 1777.
Mary, b. 9 Dec 1776, d. 3 Sep 1777.
Thomas, b. 18 Dec 1778, d. 4 Jun 1795.
Abraham, b. 22 Jun 1784 Chester VT, d. 10 Oct 1855 Chester VT, m. 3 Aug 1812 Westminster VT Mary Edgell, b. 1778 d. 1 Feb 1841. Miller.
Sources:Chester VT 1790, 1800, 1810, 1820, 1830, 1840, 1850. VR Bolton MA, Petersham MA, Templeton MA, Chester VT, SA/VT. P24, E8.

102. **THOMAS⁵ SAWYER** [see 35], b. 6 Feb 1740 Bolton MA, d. 12 Mar 1796 Manchester NY, m. 13 Sep 1762 Bolton MA Prudence Carter, b. 7 Jan 1746 Bolton MA d. 1818, dau. James and Prudence (Sawyer) Carter. Millwright. Revolutionary War: Sergeant at Lexington 1775, helped construct fort at Bunker Hill, commanded company at Rutland VT. In Templeton MA 1763, Winchendon MA 1771, Clarendon VT 1778, Leicester VT 1783.
241 Stephen⁶, 1764-1829.
Prudence, b. 14 Jan 1767, d. 13 Aug 1856, m. 14 Mar 1793 Jesse Walker.
Eunice, b. 2 May 1769, d. 1812, m. 22 Mar 1790 Peter White.
242 Hooker⁶, 1771-1843.
Lucy, b. 25 Feb 1774, d. 27 Jul 1871 Bolton MA.
243 Joseph⁶, 1777-1861.
Oliver, 14 Oct 1779 Clarendon VT, d. 29 Mar 1848 Manchester NY. In Leicester VT.
Thusebe, b. 3 Jun 1782, d. 9 Oct 1796.
Luke, b. 6 Jul 1785 Leicester VT, d. 13 Aug 1831 Manchester NY, m. 1809 Rhoda P. Cook. In Manchester NY. CH: Robert B., b. 29 Apr 1813, m. 8 Jul 1845 Caroline Webb, b. ?; Clotilda, b. 26 Mar 1816, m. Henry Lane; Thomas C., b. ?, d. 1851 Gilead MI.
Mark, b. 25 Feb 1788, d. 27 Jul 1790.
Sources: VR Bolton MA, Harvard MA, Winchester MA, SA/VT. W19.

103. **ABNER⁵ SAWYER** [see 35], b. 9 May 1742 Bolton MA, d. 4 Sep 1779 Templeton MA, m. 26 May 1763 Bolton MA Hannah Piper, b. 1744 d. 5 Feb 1836. Revolutionary War. Wid. m. 10 Sep 1787 in Philipston MA Isreal Lamb.
244 Silas⁶, 1764-1841.

Abner, b. 26 Aug 1766 Templeton MA, d. 16 Jul 1845 Fulton NY, m. 3 Apr 1792 Athol MA Eunice Haven, b. 20 Jul 1762 d. 26 Feb 1838, dau. John and Susanna (Drury) Haven. In Woodstock CT. CH b. 1793 Athol MA, d. 26 Jan 1795.

245 Thomas[6], 1768-1857.

Hannah, b. 21 Aprl 770, m. 1 Apr 1790 Jonas Lamb of Philipston MA.

Hooker, b. 5 Jun 1773 Templeton MA, m. 11 Jan 1795 Bolton MA Lucy Stratton of Bolton MA, b. 1773, dau. David and Dinah Stratton. In Marlboro MA, Boylston MA.

Dorothy, b. 12 Apr 1775, d. 8 May 1778.

Phebe, b. 15 Mar 1777, m. 9 Jan 1797 Isaac Lamb.

246 Phinehas Houghton[6], 1779-1845.

Sources: Boylston MA census 1800. West Boylston MA census 1810. VR Bolton MA, Templeton MA.

104. **LEMUEL[5] SAWYER** [see 36], b. 24 Oct 1749 Lancaster MA d. 25 Aug 1830 Plymouth VT, m. 10 Sep 1775 Lancaster MA Anna Pratt, b. Jul 1749 d. 25 Sep 1831. Revolutionary War: In Captain Thomas Gates' company, marched 19 April 1775 to Cambridge MA.

Betsy, b. 3 Apr 1776, d. 28 Jul 1832, m.(1) 5 Mar 1792 Ephraim Moore, m.(2) Solomon Morgan.

John, b. 4 Mar 1778, d. 3 Oct 1804.

247 Joseph[6], 1781-1845.

248 Emanuel[6], 1784-1853.

Abigail, b. 13 Oct 1785.

Ira, b. 23 Dec 1788 Plymouth VT, d. 25 Aug 1813 Plymouth VT.

Sources: Guildford VT census 1790. Plymouth VT census 1800, 1810. VR Lancaster MA, Plymouth VT, SA/VT. Early Families of Plymouth VT, G50, S49, D11.

105. **JACOB[5] SAWYER** [see 37], b. 22 Jun 1756 Lancaster (Sterling) MA, d. 21 Jul 1827 Ira VT, m. 4 Jul 1782 Shrewsbury MA Esther Coolidge of Shrewsbury MA, b. 1758 d. 27 Feb 1854. Revolutionary War. In Sudbury VT, Clarendon VT, Rutland VT.

249 Sherard[6], 1789-1877.

Sally, b. 29 Sep 1792, d. 6 Mar 1850, m. 20 Sep 1806 Luke Patrick.

250 Oliver[6], 1794-1852.

Esther, b. 1803.

Sources: Clarendon VT census 1790, 1810. Rutland VT census 1800. VR Lancaster MA, Shrewsbury MA, SA/VT. H13.

106. **ABEL[5] SAWYER** [see 37], b. 1 Nov 1760 Lancaster MA, d. 13 Nov 1836 Berlin VT, m. 27 Oct 1785 Shrewsbury MA Abigail Goldsberry, b. 1767 d. 1851. Blacksmith. In Revolutionary War seven years. Went to Berlin VT 1788. Wid. received pension Berlin VT 1 Jun 1840, w/son Moses 1840, 1850.

Moses Hastings, b. 1789 Hartland VT, d. 1861 Berlin VT. War of 1812.

John b. ?.

Rebecca, b. 4 Nov 1800, d. 13 Oct 1878 Barre VT, unm.

Phebe, b. 23 Oct 1804.

Mary, b. ?, m. 9 Mar 1823 David Boles.

Abel, b. 25 May 1809 Berlin VT. Blacksmith.

Sources: Hartland VT census 1790. Berlin VT census 1800, 1820, 1830, 1840, 1850, 1860. VR Lancaster MA, Bolton MA, Shrewsbury MA, SA/VT. N46, N11.

107. **THOMAS[5] SAWYER** [see 37], b. 21 Aug 1765 Lancaster MA, d. 19 Mar 1829 Lancaster MA, m. 1 Dec 1796 Lancaster MA Elizabeth White, b. 1766 d. 14 Feb 1799. In Bolton MA, Stow MA.

James, b. 14 Feb 1797, d. 8 Jan 1827.
Elizabeth, b. 7 Feb 1799.

Sources: VR Lancaster MA.

108. **BEZALEEL[5] SAWYER** [see 38], b. ca. 1754, d. 12 May 1835 Wentworth NH, m. 13 Apr 1786 Hollis NH Jerusha Williams of Pepperell MA, b. Apr 1762 d. 7 Aug 1846 Greensboro VT. Revolutionary War. Member of training band, Jaffrey NH 1784.In Pepperell MA, Groton NH. Wife in Groton NH 1830.

251 Jonas[6], 1789-1866.
Nancy, b. 1790, m. 1836 Amos Powers.
Joseph, b. ?.

Sources: Pepperell MA census 1790. Groton NH census 1800, 1810, 1830. D10, N1A, A27.

109. **RUFUS[5] SAWYER** [see 38], bp. 20 Jul 1760 Lancaster MA, d. 29 Sep 1845 Jaffrey NH, m.(1) 15 Mar 1793 Jaffrey NH Susannah Green, b. 1770 d. 15 Oct 1810; m. (2) 25 Nov 1811 Eunice Darling, b. 1772 d. 27 Jul 1834. Revolutionary War. Member of training band, Jaffrey NH 1784. Surveyor of Highways 1785, Constable 1789.

Susan, b. 31 Jan 1794, d. 13 May 1868, unm. Nurse.
Syrena, b. Jan 1796, d. 19 Feb 1800.
Sally, b. 1797, d. 4 Jul 1853, m. 31 Dec 1817 David Jaquith.
Edward, b. 1800, d. 11 Oct 1829.
Rufus, b. Feb 1802, d. 23 Mar 1802.
Adeline, b. 1807, d. 16 Jun 1878, m. 29 Nov 1829 Abraham Whitney.
252 Rufus[6], 1809-1869.
253 James D.[6], 1813-1867.
254 Levi, b. ca. 1815.

Sources: Jaffrey NH census 1790, 1800, 1820, 1830, 1840. A27, N12, N6.

110. **NATHANIEL[5] SAWYER** [see 38], b. ca. 1765 Groton MA, d. 18 Feb 1852 Middlesex VT, m. 25 Jan 1793 Polly Lawrence, b. ?. Member of training band, Jaffrey NH 1785.

Orra, b. ?.
255 George R.[6], 1796-1869.
Orinda, b. 1799, m. 2 Dec 1819 Jonathan Strong.
Mindwell, b. 1 Jan 1801, d. 4 Apr 1812.
Harmon, b. 1812 Acworth NH, d. 3 Oct 1876 Middlesex VT, m.(1) 13 Sep 1848 Moretown VT Lauthera Keyes, b. 1813; m(2) Sarah S. _____, b. 1819. Farmer. CH: Mary, b. 1850; Emily J., b. 1859, m.(1) ?, m.(2) 10 Jan 1881 Royal J. Stevens.

Sources: Acworth NH census 1790, 1800, 1810. Middlesex VT census 1820, 1830, 1840, 1850. VR SA/VT. A27, M38.

111. **PAUL[5] SAWYER** [see 39], b. ca. 1753 Lancaster MA, m. 1786 Wendell MA Sibil Huggins, b. ?. Revolutionary War: Served 8 years in 6th Massachusetts Regiment. Received 100 acres of land. In Genoa NY?

Uriah H., b. ?.
Bezaleel, b. ?.
Joseph, b. ?.
Elmira, b. ?, m. _____ Rummer.

Lovisa, b. ?, m. _____ Vinces.
Solana, b. ?, m. _____ Handy.
Sources: VR SA/ME. M7, N1a.

112. **PAUL[5] SAWYER** [see 40], b. 18 Mar 1759 Lancaster MA, d. 11 Oct 1826 Boston MA, m.(1) 23 May 1784 Lancaster MA Martha Wheelock, b. 1764 d. 10 May 1794, dau. Joseph and Alice (Page) Wheelock; m.(2) 24 Dec 1797 Boston MA Mehitable Haven, b. 7 Sep 1768 d. 7 Jan 1799; m.(3) 17 Oct 1801 Boston MA Keziah Hunnewell, b. 1768. In Lancaster MA 1790, Boston MA 1798. Martha bur. in Old Settlers Burial Ground, Lancaster MA.
256 Jonas[6] (or Joseph), b. 1793.
Alpha, b. ca. 1811, m. ?.
Susanna, b. ? m.(1) _____ Paul, m.(2) Isaac Everett.
Julia, b. ?.
Sources: Lancaster MA census 1790. VR Lancaster MA, Boston MA, Charlestown MA, SA/MA. B69, E27, H19.

113. **ISREAL[5] SAWYER** [see 40], b. 12 May 1771 Lancaster MA, d. 22 Jul 1847 Cambridge MA, m. 23 Mar 1796 Newton MA Mary (Polly) Hicks of Newton MA, b. 1771 d. 17 Dec 1855. In Lancaster MA, Concord MA, Newton MA.
John Hicks, b. 1797 Lancaster MA.
Susan H., b. 16 Feb 1799, d. 6 Jun 1875, m. 25 Jun 1822 William Bates.
Eliza, b. 27 Nov 1806, m. 22 Aug 1831 Acton MA Andrew Conant.
Mary Hicks, b. ?, m. 4 Oct 1824 John B. Russell.
(More CH?)
Sources: Lancaster MA census 1800. Concord MA census 1810. Newton MA census 1820, 1830. VR Lancaster MA, Concord MA, Newton MA. P1.

114. **CALVEN[5] SAWYER** [see 41], b. 15 May 1750 Bolton MA, d. 1802, m. 7 Jan 1772 Bolton MA Abigail Barrett, b. 8 Aug 1752 d. 26 Nov 1839, dau. Oliver and Hannah (Hunt) Barrett. Wid. w/son Elijah 1810, w/son Daniel 1820, 1830.
257 Elijah[6], b. 1773.
Calven, b. 25 Oct 1774 Bolton MA.
258 Luther[6], 1777-1826.
259 Daniel[6], 1781-1847.
260 Oliver[6], 1784-1836.
Abigail, b. 12 Aug 1786, d. 1850, m. 12 Aug 1804 Dr. Asaph Rice.
Catherine, b. 29 Nov 1788.
261 Elias[6], 1791-1849.
262 Silas[6], b. 1793-1856.
Sources: Bolton MA census 1790, 1810, 1820, 1830. VR Bolton MA. E16, J14.

115. **ELISHA[5] SAWYER** [see 42], b. 9 Feb 1744 Lancaster MA, d. 24 Mar 1810 Princeton MA, m.(1) 31 Oct 1765 Sterling MA Patience Bennett, b. ?, dau. Josiah and Hannah (Rice) Bennett; m.(2) 3 May 1770 Woburn MA Mary (Flagg) Belnap, wid. of William, b.?, dau. Zachariah and Mary (Gardner) Flagg.; m.(3) 14 Oct 1802 Sterling MA Mary Bowker, b. ? d. Oct 1822. Revolutionary War: In Captain Solomon Stuart's Company, Colonel Joseph Whitney's Regiment, at Bennington VT.
Paul, b. 20 Oct 1767 Lancaster MA, d. 28 Apr 1845 Royalton NY, m. Hannah Mudge of Lynn MA, b. 17 Feb 1767 d. 23 Aug 1828 Royalton NY, dau. John and Hannah

(Hutchinson) Mudge. B/land in Pymouth VT 1788. CH: Jane, b. 1797, d. 1 Mar 1860 Bridgewater VT; Child, d.y

263 William$^{6}$, 1771-1827.
264 Samuel Flagg$^{6}$, 1774-1853.
John, b. 11 Aug 1776, d. 1788.
265 Franklin$^{6}$, 1778-1869.
Elisha, b. 1780, d. 1784.
Joan, b. ?.
266 Charles$^{6}$, b. 1808.
Lois or Louis, b. ?.

Sources: Sterling MA census 1790, 1800. Plymouth VT census 1790, 1800, 1810. VR Sterling MA, Woburn MA. C8.

116. **JOTHAM$^{5}$ SAWYER** [see 42], b. 27 Apr 1745 Lancaster MA, m. 10 Feb 1837 Templeton MA, m. 9 Jan 1766 Sterling MA Dinah (Weeks) Goodale, wid., b. 2 Oct 1737 d. 28 Sep 1822, dau. John and Dinah Weeks and ward of Nathan Goodale. Farmer. Revolutionary War. W/son John 1830.

267 John$^{6}$, 1767-1842.
Dinah, b. 11 Jul 1768, m. Capt. Joseph Wilder, Jr.
Elizabeth, b. 13 Jun 1776, m.(I) 26 Nov 1804 Nathaniel Kendall.
Jotham, b. 6 Dec 1778 Templeton MA, d. 1856, m. 8 Jun 1805 Templeton MA Lucy Fisk, b. 14 Oct 1784, dau. Samuel and Sally Fisk. Templeton MA 1820. CH: Sally Fisk, b. 15 May 1805; Louisa Caroline, b. 25 May 1807, d. 1845, m. Seth Matoon of Ohio; son, b. (1810-1820); 2 dau., b. (1810-1820).
Job, b. 8 Apr 1781 Templeton MA, m. 10 Jan 1804 Templeton MA Becca(Dill) Upham of Templeton MA, b. ?. In Watertown MA.

Sources: Templeton MA census 1790, 1800, 1810, 1820, 1830. VR Templeton MA. W39, W20, B69, L16, E16.

117. **ELIAS$^{5}$ SAWYER** [see 42], b. 1 Aug 1747 Lancaster MA, d. 15 Dec 1825 Templeton MA, m.(I) 24 Feb 1774 Lancaster MA Hannah Farrow, b. 8 Sep 1753 d. 3 May 1841, dau. John and Mary Farrow. Revolutionary War. Built a mill in Templeton MA.

Prudence, b. 8 Jan 1775.
Hannah,b. 19 Mar 1777, m. 20 Feb 1799 James Badger of Athol MA.
268 Elias$^{6}$, 1778-1838.
Aaron, b. 5 Sep 1781 Templeton MA.
269 Elisha$^{6}$, b. 1783.
270 James$^{6}$, 1785-1858.
271 John$^{6}$, 1787-1856.
Elijah, b. 1 Jan 1789 Templeton MA.
Nabby, b. 3 Jul 1790, m. 30 Jun 1810 Ezra Willis.
Becca, b. 2 Oct 1792, m. 25 Dec 1811 Silas Jones of Roylaston MA.
Ephraim, b. 15 Jun 1794 Templeton MA.
272 Joseph$^{6}$, b. 1798.

Sources: Templeton MA census 1790, 1800, 1810, 1820. VR Lancaster MA, Templeton MA.

118. **THOMAS$^{5}$ SAWYER** [see 42], b. 7 Sep 1757 Sterling MA, d. 23 Apr 1825 Watertown NY, m. 12 Jan 1779 Lancaster MA Susanna Wilder, b. 13 Dec 1756 Halifax VT d. 30 Jul 1847, dau. Jotham and Phebe (Wheeler) Wilder. Revolutionary War. War of 1812. In Plymouth VT.

Elias, b. 9 Apr 1779 Sterling MA, m. Hannah Slafter, b. 1781, dau. Stephen and Hannah (Slafter) Slafter. In Plymouth VT 1800.
Thomas, b. 5 Jun 1780 Sterling MA, m. Eunice Fellows, b. ?. In Plymouth VT.
Sarah, b. 16 Nov 1781.
Elisha, b. 2 Dec 1783, d. 1785.
Jotham, b. 28 Oct 1785 Sterling MA, m. _____ Harper, b. ?. In Plymouth VT.
Susannah, b. 26 Dec 1787, d. 23 Jul 1836, m. 20 Sep 1803 Dunstable MA Joseph Wakefield.
273 Elisha$^6$, b. 1790.
Eunice, b. 28 Feb 1792, m. 13 Dec 1812 Joseph Wakefield of Dublin NH.
274 Joseph Wheeler$^6$, 1794-1874.
275 Jesse$^6$, b. 1796.
Ezra, b. 22 Apr 1798 Plymouth VT.
Sources: Saltash VT census 1790, 1800. VR Lancaster MA. S46, W4, D6, V9.

119. **JAMES$^5$ SAWYER** [see 43], b. 3 Dec 1737 Woburn MA, d. 5 Mar 1801 Berlin VT, m. 3 Jan 1760 Haverhill MA Lydia Flint of Plaistow NH, b. 4 May 1740 d. 16 Apr 1819, dau. Edward and Lydia (White) Flint of Salem MA. Farmer. Revolutionary War: Captain of Minute Men at Concord and Lexington, Col. James Frye's Regiment. B/S/land in Plaistow NH 1764. B/land in Berlin VT 1795. In Haverhill MA, Atkinson NH 1777, Berlin VT 1789.
276 Joshua$^6$, 1760-1840.
Edward, b. 11 Jan 1763 Haverhill MA, d. 3 May 1849 Berlin VT, unm. Revolutionary War: Enl. 15 Apr 1782 Atkinson NH. In Atkinson NH 1777, Landaff NH 40 yrs, Canada, Berlin VT. He bur. in Johnson Cem., Berlin VT.
277 James$^6$, 1765-1859.
278 Samuel$^6$, b. 1767.
Lydia, b. 22 Oct 1769, m.(1) _____ Green, m.(2) Col. L. Lamb.
279 Dudley$^6$, 1772-1855.
Polly, b.?, m. 30 Nov 1895 Oxford MA Thomas Davis of Montpelier VT.
Sarah, b. 14 Sep 1777, d. 11 Aug 1849, m.(1) 11 Feb 1798 William Hutchins, m.(2) Jonathan Shepard.
Sources: Berlin VT census 1790, 1800. VR Haverhill MA. D5, F11A, D6, D11, N46.

120. **JESSE$^5$ SAWYER** [see 120], b. 18 May 1748 Haverhill MA, d. 16 Oct 1817 Atkinson NH, m. 10 Nov 1768 Haverhill MA Judith Dustin, b. 20 Feb 1749 d. 15 Sep 1825, dau. Nathaniel and Triphena (Haseltine) Dustin. Blacksmith. S/land in Plaistow NH 1770. B/farm on Main Street, Atkinson NH 1773. Justice of the Peace 1774. Revolutionary War: At Valley Forge 1777-78.
Katherine, b. 29 Nov 1769, d. 30 Mar 1787.
280 Joshua$^6$, 1771-1830.
Rebecca, b. 14 Sep 1773, m. 21 Aug 1794 Joseph Jacques of Lynn MA
Lucy, b. 18 Jun 1777, d. Jan 1787.
Hannah, b. 17 Feb 1782, d. Jan 1787.
281 Amos$^6$, 1788-1857.
Sources: Atkinson NH census 1790, 1800, 1810. VR Haverhill MA. B27, Ruth L. Sawyer rec.

121. **JOHN$^5$ SAWYER** [see 44], b. 17 Nov 1749 Haverhill MA, d. 29 Jun 1784 Haverhill MA, m. 19 Dec 1769 Salem MA Hannah Mansfield, b. 1751 d. 9 Oct 1810. Died after leaping from Meeting House steeple. Wid. in Salem MA 1790.
Matthew, b. 12 Apr 1770, d. 4 Aug 1789.

John, b. 3 Nov 1771 Haverhill MA, m. 20 Sep 1794 Sarah Stackpole, b. ?, dau. Charles and Rachel (Pray) Stackpole of South Berwick ME.
Lydia, b. 1 May 1774, m. 27 Apr 1800 Samuel Buffum, Jr.
Nabby, b. 31 Mar 1776.
Sources: Salem MA census 1790. VR Haverhill MA. C29, S71.

122. **LEONARD$^5$ SAWYER** [see 44], b. 1 Jan 1752 Haverhill MA, d. bef. 1783, m. 14 Oct 1773 Danvers MA Mary Bixby, b. ?. Wid. m. 29 Jun 1783 John Brickett.
282 David$^6$, 1779-1859.
Sources: VR Haverhill MA, Danvers MA. E20.

123. **NATHANIEL$^5$ SAWYER** [see 44], b. 12 May 1757 Haverhill MA, d. 27 Mar 1819 Haverhill MA, m. 26 Nov 1802 Haverhill MA Mary Whittier, b. 30 Oct 1776 d. 20 Jul 1834, dau. Thomas and Mary (Dustin) Whittier. Wid. in Haverhill MA 1820, 1830.
Leonard, b. 8 Jan 1804 Haverhill MA, d. 31 Mar 1837, m. 18 Jun 1826 Haverhill MA Mary Smiley of Weare NH, b. Apr 1807 d. 25 Jul 1879, dau. Asa and Jane Smiley. CH: Mary K., b. 1827, d. 27 Sep 1866 Haverhill MA, unm; Elizabeth W., b. Aug 1829, d. 31 Dec 1875; Sarah Elizabeth, b. Jun 1831, d. 13 Jul 1832; Jane Frances, b. ca. 1832, m. 13 Feb 1860 New Hampshire Mark H. Thompson.
283 Thomas Whittier$^6$, 1805-ca. 1835.
Mary B., b. 25 Dec 1807, d. 17 Mar 1890, m. 1 Aug 1832 Benjamin Fisk.
Ruth W., b. 28 Oct 1809, m. 22 Feb 1831 James Mellon.
284 Harrison$^6$, b. 1811.
Harriet, b. 2 Jul 1819, d. 13 May 1833.
Sources: Haverhill MA census 1810, 1820, 1830, 1840, 1850.VR Haverhill MA. H32, W43.

124. **JAMES$^5$ SAWYER** [see 45], b. 14 Apr 1745 Woburn MA, d. 7 Feb 1821 Thetford VT, m. 3 Oct 1780 Hartford VT Elizabeth Dows, b. 28 Jan 1757 d. 1 Apr 1823, dau. Ebenezer and Elizabeth (Corey) Dows of Thetford VT.
Son, b. ?, d. 4 Jan 1783.
James, b. 2 Jul 1783 Thetford VT.
Molley, b. 17 Oct 1785, d. 28 Mar 1871 Norwich VT.
285 Ebenezer$^6$, b. 1787.
Thomas, b. 16 Jun 1791 Thetford VT.
Sources: Thetford VT census 1790, 1800, 1810, 1820. VR SA/VT. D50.

125. **JONATHAN$^5$ SAWYER** [see 46], b. 6 Mar 1749 Wilmington MA, d. 21 Oct 1809 Boothbay ME, m. 1764 Sarah Flint, b. 4 Nov 1752. Revolutionary War: At Lexington with a Minute Man company. In Danvers MA: Town Clerk, 1787; Selectman, 1780, 1782, 1785, 1787. Justice of the Peace. Clerk for Town Record 1794-1807. Wid. and family res. with son Jonathan.
Sarah, b. 9 Nov 1768, d. 8 Mar 1818.
Phebe, b. 30 Sep 1770, m. 1792 Joshua Hodgdon.
286 Jonathan$^6$, 1772-1845.
Anne, b. 2 Jan 1775 Danvers MA, m.(1) Edward Emerson, m.(2) John Poor.
Betty, b. 12 Mar 1780, d. 20 Feb 1802, m. George W. Merrill.
Clarissa, b. 22 Jan 1791, m. Amos Carlisle.
287 Alfred$^6$, 1794-1861.
Sources: Boothbay ME census 1790, 1800. VR Wilmington MA, Danvers MA. G41, J5, M29, H14, W38, M5.

126. **AMOS[5] SAWYER** [see 46], b. 15 Mar 1753 Danvers MA, d. 13 Jun 1821 Lancaster MA, m. 12 May 1774 Danvers MA Hannah Duston, b. 1 Jul 1754 d. 30 Dec 1830 Salem MA. Revolutionary War: In Captain Peter Coburn's Company of Dracut MA at Battle of Bunker Hill.

288 Amos[6], 1776-1851.

Hannah, b. 18 Jul 1778, d. 1848, unm.

Nancy, b. 9 Feb 1781, d. 27 Dec 1831, m. 24 Aug 1801 Farnham Plumer.

Harry, b. 23 Apr 1783, d. 10 Aug 1784.

Betsey, b. 4 Aug 1785, d. 12 Oct 1786.

Henry, b. 4 Sep 1787 Haverhill MA, d. 2 Apr 1817 Holmes Hole MA. In Salem MA.

Betsey, b. 21 Apr 1790, d. 2 Nov 1793 Beverly MA.

Eben, b. 2 Feb 1797 Haverhill MA, d. 23 Oct 1822 Lancaster MA, m. 9 Nov 1820 Lancaster MA Sarah Ann Thurston of Lancaster MA, b. 19 May 1799 d. 8 Jan 1881 Worcester MA, dau. Peter and Sally (Sweetsir) Thurston. He bur. in Middle Cem., Lancaster MA. CH: Sarah Ann, b. 3 Sep 1821, d. 8 Sep 1887, m. 14 Sep 1843 William H. Young, Leominster MA; Mary Thurston, b. 8 Nov 1822, d. May 1888, m. 14 May 1844 Herbert H. Stimpson.

Sources: Haverhill MA census 1790, 1800. Beverly MA census 1810. VR Danvers MA, Haverhill MA, SA/MA. P35, G47.

127. **AARON[5] SAWYER** [see 46], b. 11 Feb 1758 Danvers MA, m.(1) 27 Mar 1780 Edgecomb ME Sally Hodgson of Edgecomb ME. b. 1759; m.(2) 16 Mar 1795 Sarah Kent,b. ?. Revolutionary War: In Captain Isaac Davis' Company, Colonel McCash's Regiment 1777; in Colonel Jones' Regiment, General Heath, Pownalborough ME 20 Aug 1778.

289 Aaron[6], b. 1781.

290 Benjamin[6], b. 1783.

291 Joshua[6], b. 1785.

Sally, b. 1787, m. Samuel Milliken.

Jonathan, b. 1789 Boothbay ME.

Jacob, b. 1791 Boothbay ME, m. 5 Mar 1817 Boothbay ME Martha Linnaker of Boothbay ME, b. ?.

292 Stephen[6], 1794-1849.

293 Simeon[6], ca. 1803-1864.

John, b. ca. 1804, m. 9 Apr 1826 Nancy Fowler.

294 Samuel[6], b. 1808.

Hannah, b. ?.

Elizabeth, b. ?.

Sources: Boothbay ME census 1790. Mt. Desert ME census 1800, 1820. Kent Island ME census 1810. VR Danvers MA. G41, M7A, Richard M. Sawyer rec.

128. **EBENEZER[5] SAWYER** [see 46], b. 15 Aug 1764 Danvers MA, d. 26 Jan 1740 Deer Isle ME, m. Boothbay ME Martha Giles, b. 22 Jul 1759 d. 7 Jan 1842, dau. Joseph and Martha (Pinkham) Giles. Revolutionary War: Enlisted 1 Jul 1781 in Captain Lemont's Company, Colonel McCobb's Regiment, served near Penobscot ME. Wid. in Isle Haute ME 1840.

Betsey, b. 1781, d. 26 Jul 1854, m. 22 Sep 1810 Jacob Bacon.

Stephen, b. 1785 Boothbay ME.

Mary, b. 1787, m. 27 Oct 1807 William Yeaton.

295 Paul[6], 1790-1866.

296 Nathaniel[6], 1792-1870.

297 Ebenezer[6], 1803-1893.

Son, b. ?, d.y.

Phebe, b. ?, m. 16 Nov 1822 William Babbidge of Deer Isle ME.
Lydia, b. ?, m. 20 Mar 1823 George Allen of Deer Isle ME.

Sources: Boothbay ME census 1790. Deer Isle Me census 1800, 1810, 1820, 1830. Isle Haute ME census 1840. VR Danvers MA, Boothbay ME, Deer Isle ME, SA/MA. R15, J14, A27, G41, V7, Family Bible.

129. **WILLIAM**$^{5}$ **SAWYER** [see 47], b. 20 Sep 1754 Haverhill MA, d. 1 Jul 1817 Haverhill MA, m.(1) 9 Jul 1780 Haverhill MA Hannah Snow, b. 31 Mar 1753 d. 14 Jul 1790; m.(2) 27 Oct 1791 Haverhill MA Hannah (Brickett) Snow., wid. of Joseph, b. ? d. 1 Dec 1806; m.(3) 17 Sep 1807 Haverhill MA Bethiah W. Wyman of Nantucket MA, b. 1768 d. 11 May 1853 Haverhill MA. Revolutionary War. He bur. in Plaistow NH.

298 Peter$^{6}$, 1780-1835.
Susanna, b. 4 Dec 1781, d. 11 May 1782.
299 William$^{6}$, 1783-1830.
Susanna, b. 17 May 1784, d. 9 Feb 1827.
Betsey, b. 2 Aug 1785, m. John Pierce.
300 Leonard$^{6}$, 1787-1841.
Hannah, b. 5 Oct 1788, d. 19 Jul 1828, m. 12 Nov 1816 Isaac Howe, Jr.
Lydia, b. 16 Jun 1792, m. 25 Apr 1813 Timothy Smith of Charlestown MA.
James, b. 14 Mar 1800 Haverhill MA.

Sources: Haverhill MA census 1790, 1800. VR Haverhill MA. H90, D10, W72.

130. **TIMOTHY**$^{5}$ **SAWYER** [see 47], b. 8 Jan 1763 Haverhill MA, d. 183? Grafton NH, m. 26 Nov 1789 Haverhill MA Lucy Harriman, b. ?. Surveyor of Highways for Haverhill MA 1797. Wid. in Grafton NH 1840.

301 Ebenezer$^{6}$, b. 1791.
Nancy, b. 11 Oct 1797.
Lucy, b. 1800.
Timothy, b. ca. 1803 Grafton NH.
Sarah Ann, b. 5 Jun 1805.

Sources: Hollis NH census 1790. Grafton NH census 1800, 1810, 1820, 1830, 1840. VR Haverhill MA.

131. **JONATHAN**$^{5}$ **SAWYER** [see 48], b. 6 Oct 1756 Haverhill MA, d. 11 Dec 1829 Stockbridge VT, m. 28 Apr 1779 Jemima Webster, b. 1765 d. 6 Mar 1848. On Revolutionary War Roll at Atkinson NH: Enl. in May or Jun 1775, Private eight months in Captain Gilman's Company, Colonel Poor's NH Regiment, including Battle of Bunker Hill; enl. March 1776, Private one year in Captain Phillip Tilton's Company, Colonel Poor's NH Regiment, including Battle of Trenton; nine months in Captain Blanchard's Company, Colonel Preston's NH Regiment, including Battle of Saratoga. He bur. in South Hill Cem., Stockbridge VT. Wid. w/son Benjamin in New York 1846.

302 Isaac$^{6}$, 1779-1834.
Betsey, b. 25 Mar 1783, d. 16 May 1850, m. 30 Dec 1818 Nehemiah Chandler.
Rebecca, b. 19 Jan 1790, m. 17 Dec 1815 Russell G. Hurd.
Lucy, b. ?, m. 23 Nov 1815 Jonathan Collins.
Ephraim, b. ?.
303 Benjamin$^{6}$, b. 1801.
304 Eliphalet, 1802-1835.

Sources: Atkinson NH census 1790. Alstead NH census 1800, 1810. Stockbridge VT census 1820. VR Atkinson NH. N11, D11, C25.

132. **BENJAMIN[5] SAWYER** [see 48], b. 16 Nov 1762 Haverhill MA, d. 13 Feb 1813 Atkinson NH, m. 8 Nov 1787 Abigail Webster of Atkinson NH, b. 9 Jan 1768 d. 10 Nov 1862, dau. Jonathan Webster. Revolutionary War. Wid. m. Jesse Dart of Gilsum NH.

John, b. 20 Apr 1788 Atkinson NH, m. 10 Feb 1807 Hannah Watts, b. ?. Went west.
Sarah, b. 1 Feb 1790, m. 12 Feb 1811 Belding Dart.
Hannah, b. 1 May 1793, m.(1) 29 Mar 1812 John Raundy, m.(2) Lemuel Davis.
305 Jonathan[6], 1795-1880.
306 Benjamin[6], 1797-1884.
Rebecca, b. 22 Aug 1801, d. 19 Sep 1875, m. Cyrus Cheney of Westmoreland NH.
David, b. 28 Aug 1804, d. 13 Aug 1814 Alstead NH.
Elizabeth, b. 3 Apr 1807, d. 3 May 1875, m. 25 Dec 1828 Reuben Griffen of Marlow NH.
Amos, b. 3 Jan 1810 Gilsum NH, d. 13 May 1863 Boston MA, m.(1) LucyAnn (Sawyer) Austin, b. 22 May 1811 d. 6 Dec 1856, wid. of Samuel, dau. Eliakim and Hannah (Bailey) Sawyer; m.(2) 14 Oct 1849 Boston MA Elizabeth Rood, b. 1814; m.(3) Rhoda Griffin of Marlow NH, b. 1828 d. Jul 1859, dau. John and Patty (Tubbs) Griffin; m.(4) 24 Nov 1859 Peterborough NH Cemira F. Tubbs of Peterborough NH, b. 30 Mar 1824, dau. Abisha and P_____ Tubbs. Mechanic, carpenter. Wid. m. 12 Jan 1869 Amos Avery. CH: Lucy A., b. ca. 1844, m. 26 Jul 1870 Haverhill MA John C. Little; Mary L., b. ca. 1849, m. 8 Jun 1868 Boston MA Francis Dorman; Alice Justina, b. 2 Dec 1861, d. 5 Mar 1938, m. 1 Sep 1892 Gilmore W. Avery. Went to Illinois.

Sources: Atkinson NH census 1790. Alstead NH census 1810. Marlow NH census 1860. VR SA/NH, SA/MA. H36, K15, N14.

133. **JOSHUA[5] SAWYER** [see 48], b. 16 Apr 1765 Haverhill MA, d. 4 Mar 1843 New Sharon ME, m. Elizabeth Kimball .of Bradford MA, b. 1 Dec 1770 d. 27 Dec 1848, dau. Isaac and Bettie (Hall) Kimball. B/land in New Sharon ME. In Raby NH 1788. In New Sharon ME 1795. Both bur. Village Cem., New Sharon ME.

Son, b., (1784-1790).
307 Seth Kimball[6], 1788-1850.
308 Leonard[6], 1790-1828.
Daughter, b. (1790-1800).
309 Joshua[6], 1798-1878.
310 John Hovey[6], 1804-1880.
311 Isaac[6] 1805-1852.
312 Beniah C.[6], ?-?.

Sources: New Sharon ME census 1800, 1810, 1820, 1830, 1840. VR Raby NH, New Sharon ME. M54, M5, Jeanne Sawyer rec.

134. **JOHN[5] SAWYER** [see 48], b. 21 Jun 1768 Haverhill MA, d. 20 Mar 1854 Stockbridge VT, m. Elizabeth Withington, b. 28 Apr 1775 d. 16 Aug 1842, dau. William and Martha (Locke) Withington of New Hampshire. He bur. in So. Hill Cem., Stockbridge VT.

Martha, b. 23 Apr 1810, d. 15 Feb 1899, m. 26 Sep 1833 Silas Ranney. Went to Wisconsin.
Betsey Locke, b. 1814, d. 29 May 1851, m. 25 Apr 1833 Dr. Elijah C. Lamb.
313 John H.[6], 1816-1875.

Sources: Alstead NH census 1810. Stockbridge VT census 1830, 1840, 1850. VR Haverhill MA, Stockbridge VT, Middleton CT. L35.

135. **JAMES⁵ SAWYER** [see 49], b. 28 Oct 1749 Windham CT, d. Sep 1838 Weybridge VT, m. 9 Jul 1770 Windham CT Lucy Warner, b. 12 Jun 1748 d. 20 Sep 1809, dau. Isaac and Anne (Davis) Warner.
314 Daniel$^{6}$, 1770-1825.
315 Bela$^{6}$, 1773-1855.
Sources: Middlebury VT census 1800. VR SA/MA, SA/VT. D11.

136. **EPHRAIM$^{5}$ SAWYER** [see 50], b. 10 Feb 1740 Windham CT, d. 21 Oct 1807 Haddam CT, m. Haddam Neck CT Esther B. Smith of Haddam CT, b. 11 Mar 1740 d. 28 Sep 1822, dau. Lt. David and Dorothy (Brainerd) Smith. In Haddam CT 1763.
Esther, b. 1765, d. 6 Nov 1807.
316 David$^{6}$, 1767-1856.
Anna, b. 1769, d. 8 Oct 1841.
Erasmus, b. ca. 1772, m. 9 Oct 1797 East Haddam CT Esther Kelley, b. ?. Wid. in Haddam CT 1800. CH: Son, b. ?.
George Anson, b. ca. 1774 Haddam CT.
Sources: Haddam CT census 1790, 1800. B77.

137. **JACOB STANDISH$^{5}$ SAWYER** [see 50], b. 10 Apr 1754 Windham CT, d. 24 Sep 1830 Norwich VT, m. Jennie (Jemima)_____, b. ?. Admitted to church in Windham CT 21 Apr 1782.
Ralph, b. 21 Dec 1778 Windham CT. d. 8 Mar 1861 Norwich VT.
Erastus, b. 3 Feb 1781 Windham CT. In Norwich VT.
317 Cornelius$^{6}$, 1783-1860.
Jemima, b. 19 May 1785.
Abner, b. 24 Nov 1787 Windham CT. In Norwich VT.
Elijah Weston, b. 21 Mar 1790 Norwich CT, d. 1864, m. 21 Mar 1811 Hartford VT Sally Drake, b. ?. War of 1812. Wid. in Warren OH.
Sally, b. 29 Sep 1792, m. 21 Jan 1813 Cephas Harding.
Sources: Norwich VT census 1790, 1800, 1810, 1820, 1830. VR Windsor VT, SA/VT.

138. **ASABEL$^{5}$ SAWYER** [see 51], b. 21 May 1751 Windham CT, d. 29 Jul 1817 Windham CT, m.(1) Mary Roundy, b. ? d. May 1778, dau. Robert and Elizabeth (Green) Roundy; m.(2) Betsey Rindge, b. ?.
Philena, b. 10 Dec 1773, m. Solomon Main.
Rachel, b. 7 Dec 1777, d. 25 Oct 1851, m. Jonathan Fuller.
318 Elijah Rindge$^{6}$, 1787-1833.
Polly, b. ?, m. 1810 Dan Atwood. Went to Salt Lake City UT.
Sources: Windham CT census 1790, 1800, 1810. VR Windham CT. J3.

139. **AZARIAH$^{5}$ SAWYER** [see 51], b. 11 Sep 1755 Windham CT, d. 12 Dec 1829, m. 17 Apr 1781 Esther Sessions, b. 1763 d. 29 Jul 1843. Revolutionary War. In Windham CT 1800.
Katurah, b. ?.
Ardon, b. 1784, d. 27 Mar 1785.
Seymore, b. 1786, d. 16 Jul 1789.
Harriet, b. 1797, d. 18 Jul 1862.
Joseph, b. ca. 1800 Windham CT, m. 1 Oct 1843 Prudence Deming, b. ? d. 27 May 1879, dau. George and Keziah Deming.
Azariah, b. Jan 1802, d. 30 Jan 1802.
Child, b. 1 Jan 1804, d. 13 Jan 1804.
Sources: Windham CT census 1800.

140. **ELIAS⁵ SAWYER** [see 52], b. 16 May 1749 Windham CT, m. 22 Oct 1772 Chatham MA Margaret Stevenson, b. ?. Revolutionary War: Member of Minuteman company, 19 Apr 1775, Colonel Samuel Williams' Regiment. In Ashland MA, Montague CT 1773-1775.

Esther, b. 2 Dec 1773.

Elizabeth G., b. 21 May 1775, m. Chileab Smith, Jr.

John, b. 17 Nov 1776 Ashland MA.

Sources: VR Ashland MA, Montague CT. B3.

141. **JONAS⁵ SAWYER** [see 53], b. 23 Sep 1787 Pomfret CT, d. 22 Sep 1876 Pomfret CT, m. 14 Nov 1812 Huldah Holmes of Pomfret CT, b. 9 May 1792 d. 24 May 1873, dau. Ebenezer and Serena (Dresser) Holmes.

319 James Jonas⁶, 1813-1888.

320 Ebenezer Holmes⁶, 1815-1892. Went to Illinois.

321 Lucius Edwin⁶, 1817-1876. Went to Illinois.

Sarah Lucretia, b. 24 Dec 1820, d. 5 Jan 1899, m. 15 Apr 1840 Daniel Medbury.

Sources: Pomfret CT census 1830, 1840, 1850. VR Pomfret CT. G35, B69, D13, N8.

142. **MANLEY⁵ SAWYER** [see 55], b. 18 Nov 1786 Pomfret CT, d. 11 Apr 1870 Charlestown VT, m. 14 Aug 1808 Waterford VT Nancy Farrington, b. 1793 d. 13 Sep 1862. Farmer.

322 Willard⁶, 1808-1882.

323 Isaac P.⁶, 1810-1900.

Clark, b. ca. 1820 Charlestown VT, m. 1 Jan 1848 Louisa J. Clarage, b. ca. 1829, dau. Winthrop Clarage of Portsmouth NH. Wood carver. In North Bridgewater MA, Cambridge MA, Dedham MA. CH: Lillian C., b. 8 Dec 1848, m. 9 Jan 1877 Brockton MA Levi L. Curtis; Lizzie L., b. 29 Jan 1852; Annie May, b. 6 Jul 1864.

Delilah, b. 6 Mar 1827, d. 15 Oct 1845 Lowell MA.

Esther, b. 1837.

Sources: Waterford VT census 1810 .St. Johnsbury VT census 1820. Charlestown VT census 1830. Belchertown MA census 1840. Brighton MA census 1850. Cambridge MA census 1850. VR SA/VT, Lowell MA, SA/MA. K12.

143. **WILLIAM⁵ SAWYER** [see 55], b. 27 June 1795 Waterford VT, m. 25 Aug 1826 Littleton NH Tryphosa Lewis of Littleton NH, b. 20 Aug 1797 d. 31 Jul 1889, dau. James and Tryphosa Lewis.

Elvira, b. May 1822, d. 27 Dec 1889.

324 William A.⁶, 1826-1889.

Calvin, b. Sep 1827 Charleston VT, m. 25 Mar 1852 Charleston VT Emeline A. Lawrence, b. Sep 1830 d. 5 May 1908, dau. Albert and Sylvia (Hadley) Lawrence. CH: Ada, b. 4 Jul 1857, m. 7 Aug 1879 Marvin R. Delos.

325 Loren W.⁶, 1831-1876.

Benjamin Franklin, b. Feb 1833 Charlestown VT, m.(1) 16 Jun 1857 Plymouth NH Eunice E. Nutting, b. ?; m.(2) 10 Sep 1879 Charleston VT Rose L. Smith of Columbia VT, b. ?. Farmer. CH: Lula, b. 27 Sep 1884, m. 30 Dec 1903 Arthur A. Kittredge; son, stillborn 15 Aug 1889.

Sources: Charleston VT census 1840, 1850, 1860. VR SA/VT. S81.

144. **PHILANDER⁵ SAWYER** [see 55], b. 7 Sep 1804 Waterford VT, d. 3 Sep 1895 Barton VT, m. 17 Jan 1830 Coventry VT Keziah Briggs, b. 15 Feb 1805 d. 30 Nov 1887. Farmer. In Albany VT, Newport VT, Sutton VT.

Nathaniel P., b. 1830 Newport VT, m.(1) Jan 1862 Albany VT Ann Sylvester, b. 1837 d. 11 Feb 1901; m.(2) 20 Oct 1904 Derby VT Anna(Thompson) Woodbury, b. ?, dau. Levi S. and Jane (Hodgkin) Thompson. Farmer. Wid. m. Freeman Blake.

Arvilla, b. 1832, m. 17 Apr 1855 Wells Hyde.

Sources: Newport VT 1830, 1840. Sutton VT census 1850. VR SA/VT.

145. **ROSS⁵ SAWYER** [see 55], b. 20 Jan 1806 Waterford VT, d. 9 Sep 1883 Derby VT, m. 15 Nov 1831 Mary Spooner of Franconia NH, b. 1808. In Franconia NH, Columbia NH.

Elvira J., b. 1833.

Mary A., b. 1837.

326 Martin Calvin⁶, b. 1840.

Sources: Columbia NH census 1850, 1860, 1880.

146. **JOSHUA⁵ SAWYER** [see 57], b. 23 Sep 1783 Reading VT, d. 18 Jun 1854 Reading VT, m. 1 Feb 1816 Windsor VT Martha A. Stevens of New Hampshire, b. 1780 d. 3 May 1859. Farmer. War of 1812.

327 Simon Fobes⁶, 1816-1907.

328 Orrin Spaulding⁶, 1820-1895.

Martha Irin, b. 8 Sep 1822, d. 6 Feb 1857, unm.

Sources: Reading VT census 1820, 1830, 1840, 1850. VR SA/VT. J18.

147. **JOSEPH⁵ SAWYER** [see 57], b. 24 Mar 1785 Reading VT, d. 7 Feb 1831 Reading VT, m. 20 Apr 1807 Reading VT Anna Adams, b. 4 May 1790 d. 28 Sep 1870 Plymouth VT, dau. Joseph and Jerusha Adams.

Son, b. 10 Jan 1808, d. 13 Jan 1808.

Mary Adolyne, b. 21 Feb 1809.

Polly, b. 4 Dec 1810, d. 3 Apr 1813.

Amarillas, b. 8 Apr 1812.

Harriet, b. 8 Feb 1814, d. 8 Mar 1814.

Betsey, b. 23 Feb 1815, d. 11 Jan 1825.

Alice Lucinda, b. 11 Mar 1817, m. 20 Jan 1839 Gustavus A. Blood.

Joseph Allen, b. 1 Apr 1819, d. 4 Mar 1820.

Thankful R., b. 29 Dec 1821.

329 Joseph Albert⁶, b. 1823.

Emily Pauline, b. 19 Dec 1828.

Sources: Reading VT census 1810, 1820, 1830. VR SA/VT.

148. **THOMAS A.⁵ SAWYER** [see 57], b. 26 Sep 1789 Reading VT, d. 20 May 1848 Reading VT, m. 19 Dec 1819 Clarissa Bigelow, b. 12 Mar 1797 d. 27 Mar 1835, dau. Elisha and Wealtha (Gorton) Bigelow.

Jerome Osgood, b. 12 May 1822 Reading VT.

James Perkins, b. 3 Dec 1823 Reading VT.

Clarissa Malvina, b. 29 Aug 1825.

Cornelia Isadora, b. 4 Jan 1831.

Marcus Homer, b. 1 Jul 1833 Reading VT.

Helen Jane, b. 15 Mar 1835, d. Mar 1840.

Sources: Reading VT census 1830, 1840. VR SA/VT. H81, D11.

149. **CORNELIUS$^5$ SAWYER** [see 57], b. 27 Mar 1797 Reading VT, d. 20 Feb 1835 Reading VT, m.(1) Mary _____, b. 1801 d. 9 Aug 1825; m.(2) 10 Dec 1826 Charlotte (Peck) Thomas, b. 21 Sep 1800 d. 30 Dec 1883, dau. Daniel and Abigail Peck. Farmer.

330 Daniel Peck$^6$, 1827-1902.

Lucretia M., b. 4 Jan 1832, d. 15 Jan 1912.

Sources: Reading VT census 1830. VR SA/VT. C99.

150. **BENJAMIN$^5$ SAWYER** [see 58], b. 22 May 1793 Reading VT, d. 5 Apr 1875 Springfield VT, m. 19 Jun 1817 Marinda Whiting of Windsor VT, b. 1797 d. 12 Jun 1867, dau. Joseph and Azubah Whiting. Farmer. He bur. in Summer Hill Cem., Springfield VT.

Seloma Whiting, b. 12 Jul 1818, m. 16 Nov 1837 Hamlin Whitmore.

Nathan Winslow, b. 1819, d. 17 Jun 1830.

Benjamin Oscar, b. 29 Oct 1820 Reading VT, d. 23 Dec 1838 New York.

Harriet Marinda, b. 29 Aug 1822, d. 11 Jan 1835.

John York, b. 2 Nov 1824 Reading VT, d. 12 Feb 1912, m. 1851 Sarah J. Robbins, b. 21 Oct 1834 d. 28 Nov 1899. Civil War: Lieutenant in 31st Vermont Infantry. In Springfield VT. CH: Ann Jane, b. 16 Aug 1852, d. 1 Nov 1928, m. 1 Jan 1876 John Scribbens.

Sources: Reading VT census 1820, 1830, 1840, 1850. VR SA/VT. P84, D6.

151. **JOHN$^5$ SAWYER** [see 59], b. 31 Mar 1748 Bolton MA, d. 30 May 1812 Bolton MA, m.(1) 29 Nov 1770 Bolton MA Mary Moore, b. 25 Sep 1750 d. 8 Nov 1795; m.(2) 7 Nov 1798 Worcester MA Rhoda (Stone) Flagg of Worcester MA, b. 3 Aug 1754 d. 25 Sep 1801, dau. Jonathan and Ruth (Livermore) Stone; m.(3) 4 Oct 1802 Groton MA Ruth Carter of Groton MA, wid. of Phineas, b. 7 May 1762.

Mary, b. 23 Sep 1774, m. 6 Sep 1792 Silas Reed.

Betty, b. 8 Feb 1777.

John, Jr., b. 20 Jan 1779 Bolton MA, d. 8 Jan 1825 Templeton MA, m. 10 Nov 1811 Sarah Force of New Braintree MA, b. 1782 d. 1805. CH: Mary Wood, b. (1784-1795); Sarah Force, b. (1800-1810).

Lucy, b. 24 Nov 1780, m. 10 May 1798 Elijah Sawyer.

Nabby, b. 25 Jan 1783, m. in Bolton MA Simon Stone.

Peter, b. 21 May 1785 Bolton MA.

Sophia, b. 19 Oct 1788, m. 6 Oct 1805 Jabez B. Low.

Caty, b. 24 Jun 1792.

Betsey, b. 4 Jul 1805.

Sources:Bolton MA census 1790, 1800, 1810. Templeton MA census 1810, 1820. VR Bolton MA, Boston MA, Groton MA, Worcester MA, Templeton MA. B33, C9.

152. **CALEB$^5$ SAWYER** [see 60], b. 13 Jan 1741 Harvard MA, d. 10 Mar 1772 Swanzey NH, m. 1 Aug 1762 Leominster MA Sarah Rogers of Leominster MA, b. 4 Sep 1737, dau. Benjamin and Alice (Perley) Rogers. Farmer. Killed by sleigh. Wid. m. John Starkey. In Westmoreland NH.

331 Abijah$^6$, 1765-1823.

Sarah, b. 1 Feb 1767, m. 1 Nov 1789 Joshua Graves, Jr.

332 Samuel$^6$, 1768-1835.

Eunice, b. 6 May 1770, m. 9 May 1793 Isaac Benson, Jr.

Caleb, b. 4 Mar 1772 Swanzey NH. Went west. CH: 2 dau., b. (1794-1810); 2 sons, b. (1804-1810).

Sources: Springfield VT census 1820. VR Leominster MA. J3, R7, G34, C32, N6.

153. **EPHRAIM$^5$ SAWYER** [see 60], b. 19 Sep 1756 Leominster MA, d. 14 Oct 1827 New Haven VT, m.(1) 1779 Westmoreland NH Abigail _____, b. ? d. 1790 Whiting VT; m. (2) Susannah Farnham, b. ? d. 1792; m.(3) 3 Jun 1798 Mary F. Bowers, b. ?. Minister. Revolutionary War: Carleton's Company, Nichols' Regiment, at Bennington VT. In Westmoreland NH, Charlotte CT and Whiting VT. Had 16 CH, but only the following have been identified:

333 Ephraim$^6$, 1780-1830.
Polly, b. 1781, d. 1860, m. Josiah Metcalf.
Betsey, b. 1783, m. 24 Dec 1800 Caleb Pratt, Jr.
Naomi, b. 1785, d. 1821, m. Captain _____ Wiswell.
Isreal, b. 5 Apr 1787 Putney NH. In Whitney VT.

Sources: D11, V9, Gary Sawyer rec.

154. **MANASSEH$^5$ SAWYER** [see 60], b. 27 Mar 1759 Leominster MA, d. 24 Mar 1842 Potsdam NY, m.(1) 1 Mar 1779 Westmoreland NH Beulah Howe of Rutland MA, b. 7 Sep 1763, dau. Edward and Lois (Maynard) Howe; m.(2) 19 Aug 1804 Pittsfield MA Deborah Beach, b. ?. Revolutionary War: Sergeant in Putnam Rangers, Battle of Bennington, Stoney Point. In Westmoreland NH 1776, Londonderry VT 1793, Charlotte VT, Troy NY, Potsdam NY. According to census records, there were 11 CH.

334 Manasseh$^6$, 1783-1837.
335 Martin$^6$ b. ca. 1785.
336 Willard$^6$, b. ca. 1785.
337 George Rex$^6$, ca. 1787-1855.
Sally, b. (1784-1790).
3 Daughters, b. (1790-1800)

Sources: Charlotte VT census 1800, Ferrisburg VT census 1810, Potsdam NY census 1820. VR SA/VT. N12, H80, C8.

155. **JONATHAN$^5$ SAWYER** [see 61], b. 20 Sep 1758 Bolton MA, d. 29 May 1833 Henniker NH, m. Lydia Howe of Henniker NH, b. 10 Dec 1762 d. 26 Dec 1834, dau. Ezra and Phebe (Bush) Howe.

338 Rufus$^6$, 1783-1861.
Lydia, b. ?, m. 28 Oct 1810 Owen Perry.
Epha, b. ?.
339 Paul$^6$, b. 1789-1868.
Jabez, b. ca. 1792.
Infant, b. Aug 1794, d. 18 Aug 1794.
John, b. (1800-1810).
Jonathan, b. (1800-1810).
Rodney, b.. ca. 1800 Henniker NH, d. 2 Apr 1864 East Hamburg NY, m.(1) _____ Barber; m.(2) Jane Ann Paxton of Pennsylvania, b. 1808 d. 1889 Hamburg NY, dau. Aaron and Susanna Paxton. CH: Jonathan Barber, b. 5 Nov 1826, d. 20 Jun 1905, m. Eliza Rockwood, b. 25 Feb 1831 d. 6 Dec 1906, dau. Nathan and Anne (Ferguson) Rockwood; Daughter, b. ?; Hiram Rodney, b. Dec 1832, d. 1 May 1897; Mary Jane; Levi Aaron; Mary Ann; Emily Susan.

Sources: Henniker NH census 1790, 1800, 1810. H80, C59, Evelyn M. Sawyer rec.

156. **CALEB$^5$ SAWYER** [see 61], b. 20 Jan 1764 Bolton MA, m. 24 Jan 1787 Harvard MA Releaf Fairbanks, b. 26 Apr 1763 d. 27 Mar 1819. In Gardner MA, Ashburnham MA, Freedom NY.

Salley, b. 23 Mar 1788, m. 26 Dec 1811 Joseph Clark, Jr.

Eunice, b. 1 May 1791.
Caleb, b. 4 Apr 1793 Boston MA, m. 23 Sep 1820 Springfield VT Martha Stafford.
Betsey, b. 5 Jul 1795, m. 30 Mar 1820 Samuel Spafford.
Rufus, b. 5 Feb 1806 Gardner MA, d. 1888, m.(1) 28 Aug 1832 Auburn NY Huldah Kellogg, b. 12 Feb 1811 d. 13 Feb 1850; m.(2) Sabra E. Wood, b. ?. In Picton CA.
Lydia, b. 29 Jul 1807, d. 1886, m. 20 Jun 1837 Henry McCartey.

Sources: Bolton MA census 1790, Ashburnham MA census 1810, Freedon NY census 1830. VR Bolton MA, Harvard MA. D6.

157. **JABEZ⁵ SAWYER** [see 62],b.24 Dec 1759 Harvard MA, d. 21 Dec 1841 Fitchburg MA, m.(1) 29 Oct 1785 Harvard MA Ruth Wheeler of Harvard MA, b. ?; m.(2) 27 Oct 1787 Westminster MA Hannah Brooks of Westmoreland MA, b. 17 May 1766 d. 15 Dec 1846, dau. John and Eunice (Darby) Brooks. Revolutionary War. Surveyor of Highways for Fitchburg MA 1788.

Lydia, b. 16 Aug 1788, d. 3 Jan 1846, m. 17 Sep 1812 Ebenezer Thurston.
Levi, b. 2 Aug 1790, d. 5 Aug 1790.
340 Jabez$^6$, 1792-1824.
341 Asa$^6$, 1794-1881.
342 Manasseh$^6$, 1796-1836.
John, b. 2 Dec 1798 Fitchburg MA, m. 7 May 1824 Leominster MA Maria Lincoln of Leominster MA, b. ?. In Fitchburg MA.
343 Edward$^6$, b. 1804.
Charles B., b. 3 May 1808 Fitchburg MA, m. 1 Apr 1831 Eliza D. Haskell of Fitchburg MA, b. 1810. Farmer. CH: Harriet E., b. 1831, m. 2 Aug 1848 Leominster MA John W. Burns; Charlotte E., b. 1839, m. 16 Nov 1864 Fitchburg MA Edwin L. Hall; Isabel Fannie, b. 1843, m. 2 May 1866 Fitchburg MA Herbert C. Dean; Mary Anna, b. 13 Mar 1849.

Sources: Fitchburg MA census 1790, 1810, 1830, 1840, 1850, 1860. Leominster MA census 1840. VR Harvard MA, Fitchburg MA, Westminster MA, Leominster MA, SA/MA. D6, D20.

158. **MANASSEH⁵ SAWYER** [see 62], b. 6 Sep 1768 Harvard MA, d. 28 May 1856 Harvard MA, m. 23 Dec 1788 Bolton MA Mercy Mead of Harvard MA, b. 10 Jun 1769 d. 20 Feb 1849, dau. Samuel and Hannah (Willard) Mead. Farmer.

344 Jonathan$^6$, b. 1789.
Manasseh, b. 28 Jul 1791 Harvard MA, d. 5 Oct 1826 Harvard MA.
Rebeckah, b. 14 Nov 1793, d. 16 Sep 1798.
Nathaniel, b. 10 Dec 1795, d. 24 Mar 1818.
Mercy, b. 26 Dec 1798, m. 19 Oct 1822 Thomas Sprague Frost.
345 Josiah$^6$, 1802-1884.

Sources: Harvard MA census 1790, 1800, 1810, 1820, 1830, 1840, 1850. VR Harvard MA, Bolton MA. D6, N36, C98.

159. **LUTHER⁵ SAWYER** [see 62], b. 18 Apr 1773 Harvard MA, d. 5 Sep 1834 Harvard MA, m. 30 Nov 1797 Harvard MA Achsa Burnham of Bolton MA, b. 1 Oct 1772 d. 18 Apr 1852. Wid. in Harvard MA 1840, 1850.

Luke, b. 7 Dec 1798 Harvard MA.
Achsa, b. 5 Jul 1800, d. 27 Apr 1823.
Luther, b. 18 Jan 1802 Harvard MA.
Sophia, b. 27 Dec 1803.

Nahum, b. 1 Jun 1805 Harvard MA, m. Lucy _____, b. ?. Carpenter. CH: Lucy, b. 29 Oct 1839.
Mary, b. 13 Jun 1806, d. 1806.
Mary, b. 15 Jul 1808, m. 5 Apr 1827 Charles Grover.
346 Arad$^{6}$, 1808-1878.
Cephas, b. 10 Mar 1810 Harvard MA.
Lydia, b. 4 Dec 1811, d. 29 Jul 1872, m.(1) 30 Mar 1834 John Blanchard, m. (2) Joseph Fairbanks of Northboro MA.
Abner, b. 9 Oct 1813, d. 17 Jan 1814.
Permelia, b. 2 Dec 1815, m. 4 Apr 1843 Joshua L. Boynton.
Jabez, b. 4 Jan 1819 Harvard MA. Carpenter.

Sources: Harvard MA census 1800, 1810, 1820, 1830, 1840, 1850. VR Harvard MA, SA/MA. N36, F2, D6, B73.

160. **PHINEHAS$^{5}$ SAWYER** [see 63], b. 23 May 1768 Harvard MA, d. 14 Jan 1820 Marlborough MA, m. 17 May 1791 Harvard MA Hannah Whitney of Bolton MA, b. 23 Apr 1773 d. 5 Oct 1849, dau. Deacon Isreal and Hannah (Mead) Whitney. Wid. in Marlborough MA 1820 and 1830, went to Lowell MA and is bur. in Chelmsford MA. Note: See [C8] for a good write-up on Phinehas.

Hannah, b. 18 Mar 1792, d. 9 Aug 1817, m. 1 Jun 1815 Eliphonz Davis.
Eusebia, b. 9 Oct 1793,d. 4 Sep 1857, m. 3 Jul 1817 James Hickman.
Sarah, b. 6 Feb 1795, d. 23 Sep 1883, unm.
Sophia, b. 19 Jun 1797, d. 7 Feb 1884, m. 7 Apr 1816 William Brigham.
347 Alfred Ira$^{6}$, 1799-1849.
Eliza,b. 28 May 1802, d. 1 Jul 1860, m. 15 May 1839 Roswell Douglas.
Mary, b. 30 Sep 1804, d. 4 Jan 1885, m. 25 Apr 1830 Rev. Aaron Sargent of Malden MA.
Arethusa, b. 3 May 1806, d. 1882, m. 1 Jan 1849 Rev. James W. Mowry.
348 Zenas$^{6}$, 1808-1856.
349 Wesley$^{6}$, 1810-1878.
Francis Asbury, b. 11 Nov 1812 Marlborough MA, d. 16 Jun 1881, m. 7 May 1843 Martha Sawyer, b. ?. Appointed guardian of brother Alfred's CH 1850.
Edmund, b. 31 Aug 1815, d. 21 Mar 1816.
350 Jonathan$^{6}$, 1817-1891.

Sources: Marlborough MA census 1800, 1810, 1820, 1830. Dover NH census 1830, 1840, 1850. VR Harvard MA, Marlborough MA, Lowell MA. C8,P46, D36, S9, N36.

161. **JONATHAN$^{5}$ SAWYER** [see 63], b. 28 Jul 1771 Harvard MA, d. 9 Sep 1817 Harvard MA, m. 2 Jul 1794 Mary Priest, b. 25 Dec 1772 d. 10 Oct 1854, dau. John and Hannah Priest. Wid. in Harvard MA 1820.

Jonathan, b. 12 Feb 1796, d. 8 Jan 1802.
351 Caleb$^{6}$, 1798-1829.
Mary, b. 14 Feb 1800, d. 17 Jan 1802.
Lucy, b. 2 May 1805, d. 24 Mar 1830, m. 6 Nov 1828 Jacob Gutterson.
Wesley, b. 5 Oct 1807, d. 2 Dec 1809.
352 Luke$^{6}$, b. 1809.
Mary W., b. 6 Jun 1812, m. 23 Dec 1846 Sidney Bull.
Augustus Jonathan, b. 14 Aug 1816 Harvard MA, d. 1882, m. 17 Dec 1851 Madison NY Hannah Whitcomb Coolidge of New York, b. 1803 d. 5 Jul 1882. In Clinton MA 1850. Changed name from Jonathan to Augustus Jonathan 16 Aug 1836.

Sources: Harvard MA census 1800, 1810, 1820. Clinton MA 1850. VR Harvard MA, SA/MA. N36.

162. **ABEL$^5$ SAWYER** [see 64], b. 28 Dec 1771 Harvard MA, m. 19 Sep 1791 Billerica MA Molly Cutting of Boylston MA, b. ?. In Harvard MA.
353 James$^6$, b. 1793.
354 Abel$^6$, b. 1797.
355 Phineas$^6$, b. 1803.
Sources: Harvard MA census 1800 (w/father), 1810, 1820, 1830. VR Harvard MA, Boylston MA, Bolton MA. N36.

163. **OLIVER$^5$ SAWYER** [see 65], b. 15 Nov 1767 Harvard MA, m. Oct 1796 Shirley MA Mary Burt, b. 21 Aug 1775 d. 20 Aug 1859 Littleton MA, dau. Simeon and Mary (Clark) Burt of Lunenburg MA. Surveyor of Highways for Bethlehem NH 1804. Constable and Tax Collector for Bethlehem NH 1816. Also in Whitfield NH.
356 Alpheus$^6$, 1796-1887.
357 Oliver$^6$, b. 1798.
Josiah, b. 11 Mar 1800 Bethlehem NH, d. 14 Jan 1890 Tilton NH, m. 29 May 1823 Susan Fitzgerald of Gilmanton NH, b. ca. 1800. Shoemaker. On Bethlehem NH tax list 1822. CH: Son, b. (1820-1825); son, b. (1825-1830); son, b. (1830-1835); Isoline, b. ca. 1850.
Mary Ann, b. 13 Jun 1802, m. 16 Jan 1822 Bethlehem NH Simeon Bayley.
Emily, b. 9 Apr 1804, m. 11 Jun 1820 Baxter Bowman of Bethlehem NH.
Sources: Bethlehem NH census 1800, 1810, 1820, 1830, 1840. Whitfield NH census 1840, 1850. Sanbornton NH census 1860. Tilton NH census 1870. VR Lancaster MA, Shirley MA. J2, N6.

164. **WILLIAM$^5$ SAWYER** [see 66], b. 10 May 1772 Harvard MA, d. 12 Sep 1859 Littleton NH, m. 6 Mar 1805 Dolly Burt of Lunenburg MA, b. 14 Dec 1781 d. 17 Apr 1844, dau. Simeon and Mary (Clark) Burt. Farmer, cooper. On Lunenburg MA tax roll 1803. He bur. in Bethlehem NH.
358 William Hubbard$^6$, 1806-1880.
Dolly, b. 18 Jan 1808, d. 18 Aug 1865, m. 24 Nov 1831 Timothy L. Parker.
Sarah, b. 1810, m. 1830 John Crouch.
Eliza J., b. 1812, d. 1873, m. Alfred P. Foster. Went to Illinois.
Alpheus, b. ca. 1814 Bethlehem NH. Butcher. In Littleton NH 1850.
359 Eli Davis$^6$, 1815-1905.
Mary C., b. ?, m. _____ Jossiman.
Lydia Ann, b. 14 Mar 1826, d. 21 Mar 1863, m. 10 Jan 1846 Washington W. Howland.
Sources: Bethlehem NH census 1810, 1820, 1830, 1840. Dalton NH census 1850. Littleton NH census 1850. S80, N6, J2, D10, N5, G31.

165. **JONATHAN$^5$ SAWYER** [see 67], b. 6 Nov 1740 Hebron CT, d. Orford NH, m. 5 Jan 1772 Tabitha Palmer of Windham CT, b. 29 Jun 1754, dau. Jochabed and Phebe (Broughton) Palmer. In Orford NH 1766. B/land from father 1770. Revolutionary War.
Phebe, b. 22 Jul 1772, m. Joseph Wallace.
Jonathan, b. 29 Mar 1774 Orford NH, m. 1 Sep 1805 Orford NH Judith Jones, b. ?. CH: Son, b. (1794-1800); 2 sons b. (1800-1810); dau., b. 1800-1810).
Cynthia, b. 28 Feb 1776, d. 14 Oct 1795, m. 29 Mar 1895 Jonathan French.
360 Thomas$^6$, b. 1778.
361 Benjamin Carter$^6$, 1780-1831.
Mehitable, b. ?, m. 4 Oct 1810 John Emery.

George, b. 1787 Orford NH, d. 3 Aug 1823 Orford NH, intestate.
362 Leonard[6], 1790-1867.
Silence, b. ?, m. 31 May 1819 Nathaniel Niles.
Tabitha, b. ?.
Sources: Orford NH census 1790, 1800, 1810, 1820, 1830. H58A, D6, A8.

166. **EDWARD[5] SAWYER** [see 67], b. 9 Jan 1743 Hebron CT, d. 15 Sep 1815 intestate, m. 27 Aug 1771 Hannah Strong of Bolton CT, b. 15 Jul 1751, dau. Jonathan and Mary (Northam) Strong. Yoeman. Town Clerk for Piermont NH. B/land from father 1770.
Clarissa, b. 28 Jun 1772 d. 25 Dec 1842, m. 11 Mar 1793 Daniel Mason.
Hannah, b. 23 Aug 1774, d. 2 Jun 1861, m. 1796 Uri Chandler.
Elizabeth, b. 29 Apr 1778, d. 12 May 1812, m. 10 Mar 1800 Luke Chandler.
Lydia, b. 12 May 1783, m. 19 Mar 1804 William Hill.
363 Joseph[6], 1785-1858.
Edward, b. 12 Aug 1788 Piermont NH, d. 2 Feb 1855 Grand Blanc MI, m. 1 Jan 1818 Sheffield MA Almira Kellogg, b. 2 Feb 1800, dau. Thomas and Mary (Bushnell) Kellogg.
Sources: Piermont NH census 1790, 1800, 1810. D61, J2, P82c, H58A.

167. **ICHABOD[5] SAWYER** [see 67], b. 30 Sep 1750 Hebron CT, d. 9 Oct 1826 Orford NH, m. 20 Mar 1780 Ann Palmer, b. 1757 d. 7 Aug 1845. Revolutionary War: Enl. 20 Dec 1777 in Grafton NH for 3 mos., 11 days in Captain Joshua Hayward's Company.
Isaac, b. 20 Dec 1780 Orford NH.
Theda, b. 26 Dec 1782, d. Apr 1864, m. 18 Jun 1809 Captain Jeremiah Marston.
Bela, b. 16 Dec 1784 Orford NH, d. 8 May 1813 Orford NH, m. 26 Jan 1813 Abigail Robbins, b. ?. CH: Child, b. ?, d. 4 Oct 1815.
364 Jared[6], 1787-1869.
Anna, b. 28 Mar 1789, d. Aug 1862, m. 5 May 1814 Peter Marston.
Asenath, b. 11 May 1791, d. 18 Jun 1878, m. 2 May 1819 Edward Rugg.
Patty, b. 18 Feb 1794, d. 25 Sep 1867, m. 25 Dec 1814 Nathan Dewey.
365 Ichabod[6], b. 1796.
Child, b. ?, d. 2 Mar 1800.
Sources: Orford NH census 1790, 1800, 1810. D34, N12, N7, R30.

168. **ABEL[5] SAWYER** [see 67], b. 24 Jan 1753 Hebron CT, d. 29 Mar 1845 Orford NH, m. 14 Feb 1780 Thetford VT Mary Strong of Bolton CT, b. 25 Nov 1752 d. 15 Aug 1841, dau. Jonathan and Mary (Northam) Strong. Surgeon. Revolutionary War: Jun 1776-Jun 1777, "Green Mountain Boys," David Hobart's Regiment; reenlisted 1 Aug 1777 as substitute for brother Edward.
Abel, b. 13 Mar 1782, d. 30 Mar 1782.
Candice, b. 7 Aug 1783, m. 31 May 1804 Elam Brown.
366 Benning[6], 1785-1870.
Mary, b. 7 Feb 1788, m. 5 Mar 1818 James Hibbard.
367 Jonathan Strong[6], 1790-1858.
Sources: Orford NH census 1790, 1800, 1810, 1840. VR Orford NH. N11, D61, N12.

169. **CONANT BAGLEY[5] SAWYER** [see 68], b. 8 Apr 1756 Hebron CT, d. 18 Apr 1838 Norwich VT, m.(1) 25 May 1782 Norwich VT Deborah Robinson, b. 1757 d. 23 Jul 1787; m.(2) 24 Jan 1788 Norwich VT Roxalana Miller, b. 1755 d. 1795; m.(3) Norwich VT Ruth Boardman of Bolton CT, b. 8 Sep 1764 d. May 1813; m.(4) Mary G. McAllister, b. 1784 d. 1815; m.(5) 19 May

1816 Margaret (McAllister) Smith, b. 1763 d. 29 Mar 1838. Revolutionary War: Enl. 1777 Coventry CT for three years in Colonel John Chandler's Regiment. He bur. in West Norwich VT.

Armon, b. 20 Mar 1783, d. 20 Jan 1803 or 1805.
Phebe, b. 15 Aug 1784, m. 25 Sep 1806 John Henry.
368 Calvin$^6$, 1796-1883.
369 Oramel$^6$, 1798-1875.
Ruth, b. 13 May 1800.
370 Almon$^6$, 1803-1878.
Harriet, b. 12 Apr 1805, d. 1898, unm.
Milo, b. 17 Oct 1807 Norwich VT.
Edwin, b. 1816.
Edward, b. 1816, d. 11 Aug 1840.

Sources: Norwich VT census 1790, 1800, 1810, 1820, 1830. VR SA/VT. G16, Robert L. Taylor rec.

170. **ISAAC$^5$ SAWYER** [see 68], b. 22 Nov 1770 Hoosic NY, d. 30 Sep 1847 Jay NY, m. 20 Sep 1792 Monkton VT Mary Willoughby, b. 16 Mar 1772 d. 26 Aug 1849, dau. Joseph Willoughby. Minister. In Hebron CT, Rochester VT 1797, Monkton VT 1800.

Joseph Willoughby, b. 5 May 1794 Monkton VT, d. 26 Jun 1859 Whiting VT, m. (1) Sally Whitman of Fairfield VT, b.?; m.(2) Abigail Finch of Saratoga NY, b.?. Minister. Ordained in Hubbardston VT 1816. In Whiting VT 1822. Also in Brandon VT, Shaftsbury VT, Jay NY. He bur. in Whiting VT. CH: Mary, b. 6 Mar 1822, d. 8 Jul 1825; Sarah A., b. 1837, m. by her father 16 Mar 1858 to William W. Watts.
Asa, b. 29 Feb 1796 Monkton VT.
Susannah, b. 26 Feb 1797.
371 Reuben$^6$, 1798-1869.
William, b. 29 Dec 1799 Monkton VT, m. 23 May 1822 Brandon VT Lucy Merriam, b. ?.
372 John Fay$^6$, b. 1802.
Conant, b. 23 May 1805 Monkton VT, m. Jan 1829 Roxanna Cooper, b. ?. Minister, ordained Apr 1836 Braintree MA. In Shoreham VT.
373 Isaac M.$^6$, b. 1808.
Miles McFarland, b. 3 Sep 1810, d. 21 Jan 1861, m. 5 Jan 1832 Caroline E. Halstead, b. 8 Aug 1809 d. 27 Mar 1870. Arm amputated 1836. In Cornwall CT.

Sources: Monkton VT census 1800, 1810. VR SA/VT. D6.

171. **JACOB$^5$ SAWYER** [see 69], b. 12 Jun 1745 Lyme CT, d. 15 Apr 1802 Hartland CT, m. 16 Mar 1769 Sarah Rathbone of Lyme CT, b. 8 Mar 1744 d. 24 Dec 1822, dau. Daniel and Thankful (Higgins) Rathbone.

Diademia, b. 25 Dec 1769, m. 27 Nov 1809 Samuel Benjamin.
Thankful, b 25 Nov 1771, m. Isaac Blanchard.
Desire, b. 9 Mar 1774, d. 22 Oct 1785 in Hartland CT.
Sarah, b. 25 Jul 1776, m. _____ Gillett.
Lucy, b. 25 Jul 1776, m. 9 Jan 1797 Warren Higley.
374 Samuel$^6$, 1779-1837.
Mary, bp. 11 Apr 1781, d. 8 Mar 1850, m. 17 Feb 1812 Roswell White.
David, bp. 10 Aug 1783 Hartland CT, d. 1812 Granville MA, m. 1807 Marilda Parsons, b. 24 Nov 1788, dau. William and Vashi (Bissell) Parsons. In Granville MA. CH: Eliza, b. 18 Jan 1808; Julia, b. 24 Oct 1809; Clarissa, b. 4 Oct 18ll.
Desire, b. 1787.

Sources: Litchfield CT census 1790, Hartland CT census 1800, Wid. w/son David in Granville MA census 1810. VR Granville MA, SA/CT. W39, B3, Marshall W. McCoy rec.

172. **SAMUEL[5] SAWYER** [see 70], b. 1 Jan 1746 Colchester CT, d. 25 Aug 1813 Cornwall CT, m. 13 Apr 1769 Colchester CT Mary (Molly) Clark, b. 1 Jun 1749, dau. Alexander Clark. French and Indian War. Revolutionary War: Seriously wounded 1777. Res. on border between Cornwall and Kent CT.

Samuel, b. 3 Jan 1771 Cornwall CT, m.(1) Phebe Sackett, b. ?; m.(2) Currency _____ of Connecticut, b. 1787. Miller. In Cornwall CT 1800, Kent CT 1810, Alford MA 1850. CH: Sarah, b. ca. 1801.

Lois, b. 25 Feb 1773, d. 6 Mar 1773.

Mary, b. 20 Apr 1774.

Elizabeth, b. 8 Nov 1777, m. 31 Dec 1797 William Pierson of Derby CT.

Violette, b. 18 Jan 1781.

Nathan, b. 8 Nov 1783 Cornwall CT, m. Sarah Whitcomb, b. ?, dau. Hiram and Sarah (Dutton) Whitcomb, had six CH.

Matilda, b. 17 Sep 1786, m. Josiah Bonney.

Rodah, b. 18 Jun 1789, d. 12 Jan 1831, m. _____ Kinchell.

Sources:Cornwall CT census 1790, 1800, 1810, 1820, 1830. Kent CT census 1810. Alford CT census 1850. N1A, C9.

173. **CALVIN[5] SAWYER** [see 71], b. 29 Oct 1760 Lancaster MA, d. 4 Oct 1834 Worcester MA, m.(1) 24 Jul 1783 Lancaster MA Releaf Houghton of Lancaster MA, bp. 28 Apr 1754, dau. Abijah and Alice (Joslyn) Houghton; (2) 19 Sep 1793 Polly Britton of Shrewsbury MA, b. 11 Jun 1769 d. 30 Apr 1854, dau. Samuel and Ruth Britton. Revolutionary War. In Sterling MA 1783, Shrewsbury MA 1804. B/land in Baldwin ME 1803, 1816. S/land in Baldwin ME 1816.

Sally, b. 20 Feb 1783.

Calvin, b. 28 Mar 1784 Sterling MA. In Shrewsbury MA, Providence RI.

Sophia, b. 29 Jan 1786.

Susannah, b. 3 Feb 1788, m. 29 May 1808 Abijah Knight.

Lucy, b. 10 Dec 1789.

Henry, b. 19 Oct 1791 Shrewsbury MA. In Providence RI.

Dennis, b. 6 Apr 1794 Shrewsbury MA, m.(1) 25 Jun 1820 Shrewsbury MA Susan Rider, b. 1795 d. 5 Sep 1832 Shrewsbury MA, dau. Gideon Rider; m.(2) 4 Aug 1833 Walpole MA Sabra D. Parker of Walpole MA, b. ?.

375 Austin[6], b. 1796.

Releaf, b. 15 Jul 1798, m. 4 Dec 1817 Jonas Temple.

Eliza, b. 17 Aug 1804.

Ruth Parker, b. 16 Nov 1806, m. 29 Apr 1828 Joseph Temple.

376 Franklin Adams[6], b. 1809.

Caroline, b. 1812, m. 11 Sep 1832 Samuel Houghton.

Sources: Lancaster MA census 1790, 1800. Shrewsbury MA census 1810, 1820, 1830. Providence RI census 1830, 1840. VR Lancaster MA, Shrewsbury MA, Foxboro MA, Walpole MA, SA/MA. R30.

174. **LUTHER[5] SAWYER** [see 71], b. 21 Aug 1762 Lancaster MA, d. 2 Sep 1824 (suicide) Lancaster MA, m. 16 Jun 1785 Lancaster MA Zilpah Houghton of Lancaster MA, b. 6 Jun 1766, dau. Abijah and Alice (Joslyn) Houghton.

377 Eliakim[6], 1786-1858.

Zilpah, b. 30 Jan 1788.

Luther, b. 22 Sep 1792 Lancaster MA. In Sterling MA.
Cynthia, b. 15 Feb 1800, d. 1 Apr 1815.
Almy Ellery, b. 12 Nov 1805 Lancaster MA.
Sources: Lancaster MA census 1790. VR Lancaster MA. R30.

175. **AMOS$^5$ SAWYER** [see 71], b. 26 Aug 1768 Lancaster MA, d. 1 Jan 1845 Cambridge MA, m. 8 Apr 1793 Lancaster MA Polly Allen, b. ?.
Polly, b. 16 Nov 1795, d. 29 Mar 1864 Woburn MA.
Son, b. Sep 1798, d. 29 Oct 1798.
Amos, b. 21 Jul 1800 Lancaster MA.
378 Eusebius$^6$, b. 1803.
Eliza A., b. 21 Jul 1805.
Sources: Lancaster MA census 1800. Bolton MA census 1810. Cambridge MA census 1820. VR Lancaster MA.

176. **EPHRAIM$^5$ SAWYER** [see 72], b. 27 May 1753 Lancaster MA, m. 6 Mar 1775 Lancaster MA Mary Allen, b. 1755. Minister. Revolutionary War: In 11th Continental Infantry at Ticonderoga 1776. Rec. pension 1818. B/land in Grand Isle VT 1818.
379 Ephraim$^6$, 1778-1851. Went to Pennsylvania.
380 Allen$^6$, 1792-1851. Went to Iowa.
Polly, b. ?.
Sophia, b. ?.
Abram, b. ?.
Eunice, b. ?.
Susan, b. ?.
Charles, b. ?.
Henry, b. ?.
Sources: South Hero VT census 1790. Middle Hero VT census 1800. North Hero VT census 1810, 1820. VR Lancaster MA, SA/VT. H39, H43, H44, M35, Pat Chastain rec.

177. **JOSIAH$^5$ SAWYER** [see 72], b. 27 Jan 1757 Lancaster MA, d. 10 Mar 1837 Thetford VT, m. 8 May 1777 Lancaster MA Susannah Green, b. 20 Dec 1756 d. 30 Nov 1836, dau. Peter Green. Revolutionary War. In Clarendon VT 1783, Eaton, Canada 1798, Shrewsbury VT 1820. Also in Wallingford VT.
Son, d. at birth, 1778.
381 Peter Green$^6$, 1783-1867. Went to Canada.
382 Josiah$^6$, 1786-1839. Went to Canada.
Susannah, b. 20 Apr 1786, d. 3 Jan 1861, m.(1) James Lobdell, m.(2) Joseph B. Smith.
John, b. 30 Jun 1788 Wallingford VT, d. 10 Sep 1869, m. Theodocia Labaree, b. ?. CH: Lucretia, b. ?, m. 13 Dec 1842 Eaton, Canada, Wellington Osgood. In Eaton, Canada 1798.
Martha, b. 29 Jul 1792, d. 29 Apr 1846, m. Nathaniel Currier.
Abigail Smith, b. 15 Aug 1795, d. 2 Jun 1885, m. 3 Dec 1818 Eaton, Canada, Asa Alger.
383 Rufus$^6$, 1798-1874.
Sources: Shrewbury VT census 1820. VR Lancaster MA. D11, S5, Family Bible.

178. **JAMES$^5$ SAWYER** [see 72], b. 10 Dec 1761 Lancaster MA, d. 27 Mar 1827 Burlington VT, m. 29 Mar 1790 Clarendon VT Lydia Foster of Clarendon VT, b. 1772 d. 2 Sep 1853, dau. Benjamin and Rachel (Day) Foster. Merchant. Revolutionary War: Colonel, aide to Alexander Hamilton at Yorktown. Selectman and Town Clerk. Wid. rec. war pension in Burlington VT 1840.

In South Hero VT, Rutland VT, Brandon VT, Burlington VT. He bur. in Elmwood Cem., Burlington VT.

384 James Lucius$^6$, 1791-1850.

Frederick Augustus, b. 9 Sep 1792 Brandon VT, d. 1 May 1831 Burlington VT. War of 1812: Lieutenant in 11th Infantry Regiment at siege of Fort Eric (?), 30 Jul-17 Sep 1814.

Maria, b. 24 Sep 1794, d. 16 Aug 1796.

385 Horace Bucklin$^6$, 1797-1860.

Gamaleal B., b. 25 Mar 1801 Burlington VT, d. 10 Jul 1868 Burlington VT. Lawyer. Admitted to Bar, Chittenden City VT 1822. In New York. He bur. in Elmwood Cem., Burlington VT.

Mary Curtis, b. 19 Jul 1804, d. 23 Aug 1865.

Maria A., b. 23 Aug 1811, d. 16 Oct 1845, m. 23 Jan 1840 Charles Prentis.

George Foster, b. 25 Apr 1821 Burlington VT, d. 24 Jun 1852 Sardinia on Frigate *Cumberland* m. 14 Mar 1850 St. Albans VT Mary A. Houghton, b. 8 Sep 1823 d. 7 May 1906 St. Albans VT, dau. Abel and Emelia (Stebbins) Houghton. Purser, 28 years in Navy. He bur. in St. Albans VT.

Sources: Brandon VT census 1790. Burlington VT census 1800, 1810, 1820, 1840 (wid.). VR SA/VT. B78, D11, B48, H43.

179. **DANIEL GREENLEAF$^5$ SAWYER** [see 72], b. 1767 Lancaster MA, d. 2 Jan 1845 Grand Isle VT, m. 8 Jan 1794 Irene Ransom of New York, b. 3 Oct 1776 d. 25 Dec 1863, dau. Elisha and Irene (Wells) Ransom. Lawyer. Delegate from South Hero VT to Constitutional Convention 1814. Had 13 CH in census.

386 Jedediah S.$^5$, b. 1801.

Electa, b. ?, m. 4 Jun 1820 Henry Gregory.

Rowena, b. ?, m. 6 Nov 1839 Edward Moore.

(Additional CH?)

Sources: South Hero VT census 1800, 1810, 1830, 1840. VR SA/VT. D11.

180. **ARTIMUS$^5$ SAWYER** [see 72], b. 25 Jan 1771, m.(1) Mary C. Hopkins, b. ?; m. (2) Lucy Holton, b. ?. In South Hero VT, Brandon VT, Vergennes VT.

387 John C.$^6$, 1800-1853.

388 Roswell Hopkins$^6$, 1803-1875.

George Artimus, b. ?, m. Marie L. Skinner, b. ?.

Sources: Vergennes VT census 1800, 1810. D11.

181. **COOPER$^5$ SAWYER** [see 73], b. 14 Nov 1768 Lancaster MA, d. 10 Oct 1830 Templeton MA, m. 24 May 1801 Templeton MA Betsey Baldwin of Templeton MA, b. 23 Jul 1777 d. 31 Jan 1821, dau. Jonathan and Mary (Hunt) Baldwin. Selectman for Templeton MA.

Fidelia, b. 1802, unm (blind).

Cooper, b. ca. 1806, d. 1869, unm.

Betsey, b. ?, m. 10 Mar 1831 Charles Church of Templeton MA.

Eden, b. 1807 Templeton MA, d. 27 Dec 1839 Templeton MA, m. 10 Jan 1833 Templeton MA Eliza Forristell of Fitzwilliam NH, b. ?. CH: Child, b. 1839, d. 15 Oct 1839.

389 Samuel$^6$, b. 1814.

Sources: Templeton MA census 1790, 1800, 1810, 1820, 1830.VR Templeton MA. R30, B11.

182. **SAMUEL$^5$ SAWYER** [see 73], b. 11 Oct 1770 Lancaster MA, d. 23 Nov 1848 Sterling MA, m.(1) 29 Mar 1805 Lancaster MA Hepshibah Thurston of Lancaster MA, b. 1 Aug 1771 d. 31

Jul 1814, dau. Samuel and Priscilla (Burpee) Thurston; m.(I)(2) 10 Feb 1822 Sterling MA Azuba Roper, b. ca. 1786 d. 22 Nov 1854. Farmer.

Samuel Thurston, b. 17 Mar 1806 Sterling MA, d. 20 May 1874 Sterling MA, m. 25 Jun 1848 Abigail (Rollins) Tilson of Mt. Vernon NH, b. ca. 1809 d. 17 Jun 1875, dau. John and Mary Rollins. Farmer.

Daughter, b. (1805-1810).

390 Putnam[6], 1808-1875.

Reuben Holcom, b. 6 Jan 1811 Sterling MA.

Moses, b. 23 Oct 1813 Sterling MA, m. 12 Feb 1839 Betsey Sawyer Wilder, b. 11 Jan 1819, dau. Jonathan and Betsey (Roper) Wilder. Farmer, CH: Child, stillborn 22 Nov 1842; Samuel, b. 19 Nov 1843, d. 21 Nov 1843; Moses Wilder, b. 23 Sep 1845, d. 5 Oct 1845.

Sources: Sterling MA census 1800, 1810, 1820, 1830, 1840, 1850. VR Sterling MA, Lancaster MA, SA/MA. R30.

183 **SOLOMON[5] SAWYER** [see 74], b. 15 Aug 1770 Lancaster MA, d. 3 Jun 1851 Hubbardston MA, m. 24 May 1796 Gardner MA Abigail(Wilder) Wheeler, b. 25 Feb 1773, dau. Josiah and Lucy (Graves) Wilder.

Abigail, b. 23 Jul 1797.

Sally, b. 15 Feb 1800.

Eunice, b. 13 Dec 1801.

Josiah Wheeler, b. 25 Oct 1803 Sterling MA.

Melinda, b. 31 Aug 1806.

Luke, b. (1800-1810).

Silvia Ann, b. 17 Jan 1809, d. 8 Sep 1855 Hubbardston MA. Suicide.

Sources: Sterling MA census 1800, 1810. VR Gardner MA, SA/MA. R30, W32.

184. **DAVID[5] SAWYER** [see 74], b. 20 Nov 1776 Lancaster MA, d. 22 May 1844 Ludlow VT, m. 1 Mar 1808 Ludlow VT Martha Mayo, b. 1787 d. 15 Sep 1870. Wid. m. 1854 John Gilbert.

Daughter, b. (1808-1810).

Parker W., b. 10 Sep 1811 Peru VT, d. 25 Mar 1864 Ludlow VT, m. 13 Sep 1846 Mt. Holly VT Jane C. Andrews, b. May 1824 d. 29 Oct 1847, dau Jerial and Alinda (Parker) Andrews. Laborer.

Esther, b. (1810-1815), m. 29 Nov 1837 _____ Hill.

391 Anson J.[6], 1819-1897.

Sources: Ludlow VT census 1820, 1830, 1840, 1850. VR SA/VT. G8.

185. **ENOS[5] SAWYER** [see 75], b. 23 Nov 1754 Charlestown NH, d. 9 Oct 1804 Haverhill MA, m. 28 Jul 1791 Haverhill NH Debrah Silver of Haverhill NH, b. ? d. 183?. Revolutionary War: Enl. Timothy Bedel's NH Regiment 1775, served in Canada. In Piermont NH 1800. Wid. went to Fairlee VT.

392 Benjamin[6], 1791-1855.

393 Enos[6], 1793-1882.

Hannah, b. 9 Aug 1795.

Sources: Piermont NH census 1800. J2, N1A.

186. **JOHN[5] SAWYER** [see 75], b. 29 Sep 1761 Petersham NH, m. 30 Dec 1790 Newbury VT Betsey Heath, b. ?. Revolutionary War: Enl. 22 Aug 1776 w/father in Captain Strong's Company. In Newbury VT 1791, Topsham VT 1800.

Prudence, b. 28 May 1791, d. 18 Apr 1880, m. 7 Dec 1815 Hezikiah Felch.

Zebadiah, b. 22 Jul 1792 Newbury VT, d. 18 Apr 1850 Brattleboro VT, m.(1) 22 Aug 1816 Topsham VT Susan W. Hutchins, b. 1795 d. 26 Jul 1848; m.(2) 11 Apr 1850 Brattleboro VT Cordelia Allen, b. ?. In Orange VT 1830, 1840. CH: Augusta, b. ?, m. 13 Dec 1838 Frank S. Rogers; John H., b. Apr 1820, d. 23 Aug 1825; Susan, b. Jan 1824, d. 25 Jul 1825.

Elizabeth, b. 23 Jul 1793, m. 22 Aug 1816 John Richards.

Lydia, b. 25 Jul 1794, d. 9 Jan 1876, m. 4 Jul 1816 Charles Grow.

Azubah, b. 15 Aug 1795, m. 28 Mar 1820 Moulton Smith.

Mehitable, b. 5 Sep 1796.

394 Mark[6], 1799-1865.

Anna, b. 6 Jul 1800.

John, b. 15 Apr 1802 Topsham VT.

Mary, b. 2 Dec 1804.

Abigail, b. 7 Dec 1806, d. 15 Dec 1865.

Hazen, b. 2 Dec 1808.

Hannah, b. 26 Feb 1810.

Sources: Topsham VT census 1800, 1810, 1830. Orange VT 1830, 1840. VR SA/VT. D11.

187. **SILVANUS[5] SAWYER** [see 75], b. 31 May 1763 Petersham VT, m. Deliverance _____, b. ?. In Topsham VT 1790, 1820, 1830, In Newbury VT 1800.

Son, b. (1784-1790).

Daughter, b. (1784-1790).

Eleanor, b. 1795, d. 16 May 1865 Topsham VT.

Daughters (4), b. (1790-1800).

Lovina, b. 1801, m.(1) ?, m.(2) 17 Jun 1860 Lyman Bolton.

Sources: Topsham VT census 1790, 1820, 1830. Newbury VT census 1800. VR SA/VT.

188. **DELIVERANCE[5] SAWYER** [see 76], b. 1764, d. 1863, m.(1) Lucy Lord, b. ?; m. (2) 5 Jun 1805 Abigail Newcomb of New York, b. 25 Jun 1787 d. 29 Jan 1817, dau. Azariah and Rebecca (Bradley) Newcomb.

Adna, b. 14 Mar 1806 Haverhill MA, m. 31 Jan 1843 Elizabeth A. Marten, b. ?, dau. C_____ Marten of New York.

Orrel, b. 26 Jan 1808, m. 9 Oct 1827 Edmund Weatherby of New York.

Olive A., b. 12 Feb 1810, m. 3 Mar 1839 Edward Hotchkiss.

Cyrus, b. 22 Dec 1811 Haverhill MA, d. 21 Jan 1848, m. 3 Sep 1840 Harriet M. Woodworth.

Joseph N., b. 2 May 1813 Haverhill MA, d. 18 Dec 1813.

Abigail, b. 23 Jan 1816, d. Dec 1816.

Sources: N21, D6.

189. **EZRA[5] SAWYER** [see 77], b. 20 Mar 1764 Lancaster MA, d. 1 Feb 1828 Sterling MA, m. 20 Feb 1800 Sterling MA Martha Sawyer, b. 30 Oct 1772 d. 1 Mar 1853, dau. Samuel and Phebe Sawyer. Bought Lot 170 in Gardner MA 1808.

Daughter, b. (1794-1800).

395 Samuel[6], 1800-1869.

Ezra, b. 20 Feb 1804, d. 4 Oct 1806.

Martha, b. 28 Jan 1808, d. 31 Jul 1837, m. 15 Jan 1837 Augustus Hill.

Sources: Sterling MA census 1790, 1800, 1810. Lancaster MA census 1800. VR Lancaster MA. P33, R30.

190. **THOMAS[5] SAWYER** [see 77], b. 15 Apr 1766 Sterling MA, d. 16 Aug 1825 Sterling MA, m. 8 Jan 1789 Elizabeth Houghton, b. 1 Jan 1769 d. 10 Mar 1856. Wid. w/son Ezra 1830, w/son Luke 1840, 1850.

396 Ezra[6], 1794-1872.

397 Thomas[6], 1796-1846.

Amey, b. 25 Apr 1799, m. 3 Jun 1823 John d. Pratt.

Luke, b. 19 Aug 1801, d.y.

Susan Houghton, b. 20 Sep 1802, d. 11 Oct 1868.

Mary Elizabeth, b. 22 Mar 1806, d. 11 Dec 1889, m. 31 Mar 1835 Columbus Tyler. Note: this was the little girl John Roulstone had in mind when he wrote the well-known poem "Mary Had a Little Lamb." See *The Story of Mary's Little Lamb,* booklet published by Longfellow's Wayside Inn, Sudbury MA. Includes photos of Mary, her mother Elizabeth, and her brother Nathaniel. Mary and husband were in charge of an insane asylum in Somerville MA for 30 years.

398 Nathaniel[6], b. 1808.

399 Luke R.[6], b. 1814.

Sources:Sterling MA census 1790, 1800, 1810, 1820, 1840, 1850. VR Sterling MA. J21, G20, B85, C8, H34, D6.

191. **OLIVER[5] SAWYER** [see 79], b. May 1772 Lancaster MA, d. 16 Jun 1859 Westminster VT, m. 15 Feb 1801 Lancaster MA Mary (Polly) Wilder, b. 1779 d. 6 Nov 1853, dau. Samuel and Sarah (Ballard) Wilder. He bur. in Old East Parish Cem., Westminster VT.

Sally, b. 9 Aug 1801, m. 20 Oct 1824 Jacob Chapin, Jr.

Mary, b. 21 Feb 1805, m. 23 Jan 1829 Ashel Thayer, Jr.

Louisa, b. 2 May 1806, m. 14 Aug 1827 Rufus Howard.

Merrick, b. 2 Feb 1808 Heath MA, d. 21 May 1900 Belleville, Ontario, m.(1) 1834 Esther Holden of Ontario, b. 3 Aug 1812 d. 8 Feb 1840, dau. James and Esther (Call) Holden; m.(2) 1842 Almira Lyon of Ontario, b. ?. Teacher, druggist. CH: Mary E., b. ?, m. John H. Holden.

Almira, b. 9 Oct 1809, d. 6 Dec 1898, m. 17 Oct 1832 Ira Goodhue.

Josephine, b. 12 Aug 1811.

Sarah, b. 11 Feb 1813, d. 1 Mar 1813.

Anthony, b. 7 Jan 1814 Heath MA.

Sarah, b. 22 Mar 1817, d. 22 Mar 1817.

Catherine, b. 21 Mar 1818.

Martha, b. 3 Apr 1820, m. 4 Feb 1847 Westminster VT Thomas Burnell.

Sources: Heath MA census 1810, 1820, 1830, 1840. Westminster VT census 1850. VR Lancaster MA, Heath MA. F22, D6, D11.

192. **JONATHAN[5] SAWYER** [see 79], b. Mar 1778 Sterling MA, d. 17 Aug 1831 Brockton MA, m. 1819 Boston MA Mary Crane Wilder. of Braintree MA, b. Nov 1796. He bur. Boston MA. In Medford MA 1830.

400 George[6], b. 1822.

401 Warren[6], b. 1825.

Mary Elizabeth, b. Sep 1826, m. 26 Nov 1859 North Bridgewater MA Jonathan R. Perkins.

Sources: Medford MA census 1830, 1850. VR Cambridge MA, Medford MA, Brockton MA, SA/MA.

193. **ALPHEUS[5] SAWYER** [see 79], b. 27 Jun 1786 Lancaster MA, d. 5 Oct 1852, m. 3 Dec 1807 Leominster MA Betsey Damon of So. Reading MA, b. 27 Mar 1788 d. 25 Jul 1851, dau. Thomas and Betsey Damon.

402 Leander[6], b. 1810.
Lucretia M., b. 15 Oct 1820, d. 12 Apr 1839.
Jonathan, b. 1825 Acton MA, m. 17 Mar 1863 Elizabeth Johnson of Worcester MA, b. 1839.
Martha, b. 1831, m. 12 Dec 1854 in Shrewsbury MA Cheney Reed.

Sources: Acton MA census 1830. Shrewsbury MA census 1840. VR Leominster MA, SA/MA.

194 **JOHN[5] SAWYER** [see 79], b. Oct 1788 Lancaster MA, m.(1) Sarah _____, b. ? d. 11 Nov 1836; m.(2) 13 Sep 1837 Sudbury MA Lydia P. (Bickford) Dodge, b. ?. Trader, farmer. In Watertown MA, Waltham MA 1820, Sudbury MA 1830.

403 John[6], 1815-1888.
404 Samuel[6], 1817-1851.
Caroline, b. 28 Nov 1819, d. 3 Oct 1820.
405 George Washington[6], b. 1821.
406 Andrew Jackson[6], b. 1832.
Caroline, b. ca. 1839, m. 19 Jul 1857 Bolton MA Richmond Hosmer.
James Madison, b. 11 Jul 1843 Sudbury MA, m. 23 Apr 1867 Waltham MA Jennie Edgarton of Harvard MA, b. ca. 1845, dau. John and Mary Edgarton. Barber.
407 Thomas Jefferson[6], b. 1845.
408 Edward M[6], 1847-1936.
Lydia Ann, b. 7 Oct 1849, m. 26 Jan 1874 Acton MA Henry C. Jones.
409 Franklin Pierce[6], b. 1852

Sources: Waltham MA census 1820. Sudbury MA census 1830, 1840, 1850. VR Lancaster MA, Sudbury MA, Waltham MA, Stowe MA, SA/MA. H86, Herbert Sawyer rec.

195. **JOSEPH[5] SAWYER** [see 81], b. 8 May 1786 Fitchburg MA, d. 6 Apr 1835, m. 25 Mar 1812 Skowhegan ME Deborah Mendel of Fairfield ME, b. 1790. In Fairfield ME 1813, Bloomfield ME 1820, Skowhegan ME 1830. Wid. in Skowhegan ME 1840, 1850.

Mary M., b. 21 Jan 1813, m.(I) 30 May 1836 Maximilian S. Webb.
John Mendel, b. 30 Dec 1814 Fairfield ME. In Bloomfield ME.
Deborah, b. 28 Feb 1818, m. 16 Oct 1843 George B. Folsom.
Lydia M., b. 19 Mar 1821.
Seth M., b. 6 Jan 1823 Bloomfield ME.
J_____ H. son, b. 1832 Bloomfield ME.

Sources: Bloomfield ME census 1820.Skowhegan ME census 1830, 1840, 1850. VR Fitchburg MA, Skowhegan ME. F23, D9.

196. **PHINEAS[5] SAWYER** [see 81], b. 1 Feb 1789 Fitchburg MA, m.(1) 16 Sep 1813 Leominster MA Sally Woods, b. 1787 d. 29 Jul 1822 Boston MA; m.(2) Maria _____,b. ?; m.(3) 29 May 1849 Skowhegan ME Persis Mitchell, b. 1795. Census lists seven CH.

Joseph Woods, b. 14 May 1814 Fitchburg MA, m.(I)(1) ?; m.(2) 28 Feb 1867 Boston MA Annie J. Griggs of Boston MA, b. ca. 1830, dau. Robert L. and Jeanette Griggs. Mason. In Skowhegan ME, Boston MA.
Caroline W., b. 20 Jul 1828.

Sources: Fitchburg MA census 1830. Skowhegan ME census 1850, 1860. VR Leominster MA, Skowhegan ME, Bangor ME, SA/MA. D20.

197. **NATHANIEL$^5$ SAWYER** [see 81], b. 21 Jun 1792 Fitchburg MA, d. 11 Dec 1832 Sebec ME, m. 20 Dec 1815 Betsey Davidson, b. 25 Dec 1795 d. 29 Sep 1885 Sebec ME, dau. John and Jerusha (Cook) Davidson. In Skowhegan ME. Wid. w/dau. Frances, m. 1838 _____ Springer.

Harriet Newell, b. 14 Feb 1817, m. 4 Apr 1861 Amesbury MA Joseph Kingsbury.
410 Nathaniel Osgood$^6$, b. 1821.
Charles Augustine, b. 17 Apr 1822, unm.
Frances Ann, b. 14 Oct 1824, d. 15 Oct 1898, m. Sumner Hutchinson.
411 William Gustavus$^6$, 1827-1896.
412 John Kimball$^6$, 1829-1863.
Mary Elizabeth, b. 12 May 1832, d. 6 Sep 1854, unm.

Sources: Sebec ME census 1830. VR Fitchburg MA, Skowhegan ME, SA/ME. P82f, William C. Moulton rec.

198. **OSGOOD$^5$ SAWYER** [see 81], b. 1799 Fitchburg MA, d. 18 Apr 1877 Skowhegan ME, m. (I) 5 Aug 1835 Skowhegan ME Miranda Soule of New Portland ME, b. 19 Jul 1809 d. 2 Feb 1904.

Franklin Russell, b. 18 May 1836 Skowhegan ME.
413 Simeon Matthew$^6$, 1841-1930.

Sources: Skowhegan ME census 1850, 1860, 1870. VR Skowhegan ME, SA/ME. R18.

199. **LUKE$^5$ SAWYER** [see 83], b.23 Sep 1793 Fitchburg MA, d. 8 Apr 1874 Sherburne VT, m. 1 Apr 1846 Esther Avery of Sherburne VT, b. 9 May 1818 VT d. 6 Jan 1904 Bridgewater VT, dau. Abijah and Lydia (Lamb) Avery.

414 William Pearson$^6$, b. 1850.
Lydia Maria, b. 14 Aug 1853, m. Francis Fuller.

Sources: VR SA/VT. A37, D20.

## SIXTH GENERATION

200. **PETER$^6$ SAWYER** [see 84], b. 3 May 1765 Bolton MA, d. 18 Oct 1840 Bolton MA, m. 22 Feb 1786 Bolton MA Sarah Whitcomb, b. 1753 d. 27 Nov 1838. In Bolton MA 1787, Templeton MA, Brattleboro VT.

415 Joshua$^7$, b. 1787.
Hannah, b. 18 May 1793, d. 26 Oct 1802.

Sources: Bolton MA census 1800, 1810, 1820, 1830. VR Bolton MA.

201. **LUKE$^6$ SAWYER** [see 85], b. 24 Jun 1760 Templeton MA, d. 8 Apr 1841 Starks ME, m. 24 Aug 1784 Pownalboro ME Rachel Greenleaf of Pownalboro ME, b. 7 Apr 1763 d. 6 Oct 1852, dau. Joseph and Dorcas (Gray) Greenleaf. Revolutionary War: Enl. 1777. In Norridgewock ME 1776, Starks ME 1785. He bur. Starks ME. Wid. in Starks ME 1850.

416 John$^7$, 1785-1884.
Martha, b. 26 Oct 1787, d. 2 Feb 1868, m. John Greenleaf.
Susannah, b. 29 Nov 1789, d. 19 Jun 1865, m. 30 Mar 1809 James Manter.
Keturah, b. 22 May 1792, d. 22 Feb 1841, m. 9 Aug 1812 John Moore.
417 Luke$^7$, 1795-1878.
418 Imri$^7$, 1799-1886.
Asenath, b. 2 Dec 1802, d. 13 Feb 1889, m.(1)_____ Robinson, m.(2) Joshua Greenleaf.
419 Columbus$^7$, b. 1804.

Sources: Starks ME census 1790, 1800, 1810, 1820, 1830, 1840, 1850. VR Starks ME, Wiscasett ME, Anson ME. H15, G42, F21, A17, D6.

202. **SYLVANUS[6] SAWYER** [see 85], b. 7 Nov 1768 Norridgewock ME, d. 7 Jul 1847 Madison ME, m. 1802 Sally Crosby, b. 1786. Wid. in Madison ME 1850.

420 Jefferson[7], 1805-1846.
421 Luke[7], 1810-1881.
422 Sylvanus Ripley[7], b. 1814.
423 Almon H.[7], 1819-1902.
Sarah D., b. ca. 1826, m. 2 Apr 1846 Randolph MA Horace Daggett.
(More CH?)

Sources: Madison ME census 1820, 1830, 1840, 1850, 1860. VR SA/MA, SA/ME. A17.

203. **EPHRAIM[6] SAWYER** [see 85], b. 18 Dec 1772 Barnardston MA, d. 9 May 1848, m. 25 May 1800 Norridgewock ME Elizabeth B. Williams of Anson ME, b. 25 Mar 1784 d. 19 Dec 1871, dau. Lemuel and Anna (Hilton) Williams. Justice of the Peace. In Norridgewock ME 1803, Enden ME 1810, New Portland ME 1830.

424 William[7], 1803-1897.
Sophronia, b. 1 Jan 1806, d. 1854, m.(1) Hiram Hill, m.(2) Asa Knowles.
Emeline, b. 23 Jan 1810, m. David Butler.
Ann W., b. 9 Oct 1812, d. 9 Oct 1878, m. 31 Oct 1843 Joseph M. Dennis.
Albinia, b. 5 Feb 1815, d. 10 Dec 1883, m. 15 Nov 1836 Southwich W. Smith.
Viola F., b. 5 Apr 1818, d. 10 Aug 1901, m. 6 Sep 1838 Abram C. Richardson.
Ephraim G., b. 1820, d. 13 Oct 1829.
Eliza Britton, b. 29 Jan 1824, d. 20 Apr 1893, m. 28 Jun 1849 Benjamin Adams.

Sources: Anson ME census 1800. Embden ME census 1810, 1820. New Portland ME census 1830, 1840, 1850, 1860. VR Norridgewock ME, Anson ME. A4, W54, D6, W5A.

204. **JOSHUA[6] SAWYER** [see 86], b. 18 Mar 1780 Templeton MA, d. 1860, m. 9 Apr 1812 Templeton MA Sally Simonds, b. ?. Farmer. Note: Templeton MA VR lists a Ruth as mother of the last six CH, but according to the 1850 census Joshua was still m. to Sally.

425 Edwin[7], b. 1812.
426 Joshua[7], 1814-1863.
427 Luke[7], b. 1816.
428 George[7], 1818-1863.
Hannah, b. 11 Feb 1821, m. 19 May 1859 Hubbardston MA Jesse Craven.
429 William[7], b. 2 Dec 1822.
430 Oliver[7], b. 18 Dec 1825.
Lucy, b. 14 Feb 1828, m. 8 Sep 1870 Templeton MA Charles Nourse.
Charles Edward, b. 22 Jan 1830 Templeton MA, d. 21 Mar 1873, m. 1 Jan 1865 Barre MA Sarah Parlin of Barre MA, b. 25 Aug 1844, dau. David and Melinda Parlin. Machinest, inventor. In Templeton MA 1850, Petersham MA 1870. CH: Charles Parlin, b. 10 Feb 1866, d. 5 Sep 1866; Jennie Gertrude b. 4 Sep 1871.
James, b. 28 Sep 1832 Templeton MA, m. 30 Apr 1863 New Ipswich NH Mary E. Harding of Winchendon MA, b. ?. Chair manufacturer. In Templeton MA 1850. CH: Lillian M., b. 24 Dec 1865, m. 25 Apr 1889 Gardner MA Charles H. Hartshorn; Mary Bell, b. 14 Jul 1869.

Sources: Templeton MA census 1820, 1830, 1840, 1850. Petersham MA census 1870. VR Templeton MA, SA/MA. P13.

205. **ELIJAH$^6$ SAWYER** [see 87], b. 27 Nov 1783 (Putney VT?), m.(1)2 Dec 1804 Mary Ramsdell, b. 1786 d. 8 Mar 1843, dau. Aquila Ramsdell, b. ?; m.(2) Mary Baxter, b. ?. Justice of the Peace, Clerk of Courts.

Thankful, b. 15 Feb 1805, m. 23 Oct 1827 Swanzey NH William Sebastian.
431 Jerome$^7$, b. 1807.
Esther Brown, b. 20 Aug 1811, d. 8 Jan 1899, m.(I) 30 Jul 1839 Samuel K. Tyler.
Elijah Houghton, b. 11 Feb 1814 Swanzey NH.
Selick Osborn, b. 26 Nov 1817 Swanzey NH.
George Gardner Byron, b. 28 Nov 1820 Swanzey NH (census). Birth record shows name as Thomas Gordon.
Mary Catherine, b. 3 Mar 1823.

Sources: Swanzey NH census 1820, 1830, 1850, 1860. Keene NH census 1840. VR Swanzey NH. B85, R7, G46, G30. N6.

206. **JOSIAH$^6$ SAWYER** [see 87],b. 19 May 1796 Swanzey NH, d. 5 Jul 1876 Keene NH, m. 29 Mar 1820 Jane Wheeler of Keene NH, b. Feb 1799 d. 26 Dec 1863. Innkeeper.

432 William W.$^7$, 1821-1895.
433 Nelson Newton$^7$, 1823-1872.
434 George Gordon$^7$, 1825-1901.
Mary J., b. 1 Jan 1829, d. 5 Feb 1908, unm.
Josiah, b. 1833, d. 11 Feb 1836.
Fanny J. A., b. 1836, d. 27 Aug 1887.
Sarah E., b. 31 Mar 1840, d. 23 Jan 1922, unm.

Sources:West Keene NH census 1820, 1830, 1840. Keene NH census 1860, 1870. VR Swanzey NH. W32, G46.

207. **WILLIAM$^6$ SAWYER** [see 87], b. 26 Nov 1797 Swanzey NH, d. 29 Aug 1839 Waltham MA, m. 7 Dec 1817 Waltham MA Rosina Bridges, b. ?. Wid. in Waltham MA 1840.

Adaline, b. 30 May 1819, d. 13 Sep 1820.
435 William Isaac$^7$, 1821-1892.
Adaline M., b. 19 Oct 1822.
Harriet Newell, b. 19 Aug 1824.
Mary Louisa, b. 27 Feb 1827.
436 Charles H.$^7$, ca. 1834-1916.
Ann Maria, b. 27 Sep 1835, d. 26 Jun 1837.
Ellen Maria, b. 3 Aug 1839.

Sources: Waltham MA census 1820, 1830, 1840. VR Waltham MA.

208. **OTIS$^6$ SAWYER** [see 88], b. 19 Apr 1792 Starks ME, d. 12 Feb 1826 Starks ME, m. 1816 Mahala Leathers, b. ?. Note: Death record of son Otis says his mother's last name was Holmes.

Henry, b. 4 Jan 1817, d. 3 Mar 1845.
Louisa, b. 20 May 1819, d. Oct 1873, m. Giles Cunnoff.
Hannah, b. 24 Sep 1821, m. Nicholas Rogers.
437 Alden$^7$, b. 1824.
438 Otis$^7$, 1826-1914.

Sources: Starks ME census 1820. VR SA/ME.

209. **JOSIAH$^6$ SAWYER** [see 88], b. 12 Aug 1796 Starks ME, d. 27 Oct 1873 Smithfield ME, m. 3 Mar 1823 Sarah Boston, b. 1807. War of 1812. Wid. w/son George in Norridgewock ME 1880.

Son, b. ?.
Betsey, b. 1830.
Thelence, b. 1831.
Caroline Augusta, b. 1837, m. Sep 1863 Ephraim Bigelow.
439 George Aholiab$^{7}$, b. 1839.
Sources: Mercer ME census 1830. Smithfield ME census 1840, 1850. Norridgewock ME census 1880. H81.

210. **GEORGE$^{6}$ SAWYER** [see 88], b. 1805 Starks ME, d. 1857, m. Sarah _____, b. 1807. In Smithfield ME 1840, 1850.
440 Roloson B.$^{7}$, b. 1847.
Sources: Smithfield ME census 1840, 1850.

211. **SAMUEL$^{6}$ SAWYER** [see 89], b. 5 Jun 1784, d. 20 Sep 1826, m. 30 Mar 1815 Martha Roper, b. 22 May 1790 d. 10 May 1845.
Martha Jewett, b. 25 Sep 1817, m. Levi Kilburn.
441 Solon$^{7}$, b. 1821.
Sources: VR Bolton MA, Sterling MA. R26.

212. **DANIEL$^{6}$ SAWYER** [see 90], b. 29 Aug 1784 Bolton MA, m. 31 Mar 1811 Katherine Jackson of Dedham MA, b. 10 Apr 1788 d. 20 Jan 1862 Berlin MA. Farmer. In Tolland CT 1840.
Hannah, b.2 Feb 1812, d. 19 Dec 1866, m. 25 Nov 1833 Henry Coburn.
442 Josiah$^{7}$, b. 1813.
443 Daniel Jackson$^{7}$, 1814-1891.
Katherine, b. 9 Feb 1816, m. 23 May 1836 William Coburn.
444 David$^{7}$, 1817-1846.
Miriam, b. 11 Sep 1819.
Cephas, b. 27 Aug 1821, d. 13 Nov 1821.
Betsey, b. 11 Jul 1822, d. 12 Jan 1862 Berlin MA, unm.
445 George Fairbanks$^{7}$, b. 1824.
Otis Erastus, b. 28 Aug 1826 Bolton MA, m. 27 Apr 1853 Lancaster MA Sarah J. Smith of Boston MA, b. 1835, dau. Oliver and Salina E. Smith. Shoemaker.
Janson, b. 21 Oct 1828 Bolton MA. In Tolland CT 1850.
Sources: Bolton MA census 1810, 1820, 1830. Tolland CT census 1840, 1850. VR Bolton MA, Berlin MA, SA/MA. G24.

213. **JOSEPH$^{6}$ SAWYER** [see 91], b. 15 Mar 1787 Bolton MA, m.(I) 7 Jan 1816 Bolton MA Abigail Bender of Marlboro MA, b. 18 May 1787 d. 12 Oct 1856, dau. Peter and Abigail (Brigham) Bender. Trader.
Caroline Downs, b. 27 Feb 1818, m. 3 May 1836 Asa Holman, Jr.
Abigail B., b. 9 Nov 1819, m. 15 Oct 1840 Oliver Barrett, Jr.
Sarah, b. 13 Apr 1821, d. 15 Mar 1889, m. 12 Sep 1865 Bolton MA William Reed.
446 Frederick Adolphus$^{7}$, 1822-1891.
Louisa Green, b. 6 Oct 1824, m. 6 Apr 1851 Bolton MA Frederick H. Crocker.
Ann Barbara, b. 7 Oct 1826, m. 22 Jun 1852 Bolton MA Daniel S. Richardson.
Eleanor, b. 7 Apr 1828, m. 15 Oct 1857 Bolton MA Humphrey Cummings.
Joseph Henry, b. 19 Oct 1829 Bolton MA.
Sources: Bolton MA census 1820, 1830, 1840, 1850. VR Bolton MA, SA/MA. B84.

214. **GEORGE⁶ SAWYER** [see 91], b. 23 Jan 1800 Bolton MA, d. 2 Aug 1876 Epping NH, m.(1) 23 May 1823 Bolton MA Sarah Whitney, b. 8 Oct 1799 d. 27 Mar 1836 Medford MA; m.(2) 7 Aug 1836 Bolton MA Abigail Shedd of Medford MA, b. 22 Nov 1809 d. 19 Jan 1840 West Medford MA, dau. Thomas and Abigail (Greenleaf) Shedd; m.(3) 31 May 1840 Haverhill MA Mary Elizabeth Wilson of Portland ME, b. 1816 d. 1 Feb 1857 Epping NH; m.(4) 21 Apr 1857 Sarah Holt, b. 1812. Baker. In Medford MA 1836, Epping NH 1846.

Lucy Permelia Whitney, b. 30 Jan 1826, m. 14 Sep 1856 Alonzo Atherton.
Susannah Newall Whitney, b. 28 Nov 1827, m. 15 Oct 1851 Albert Gale.
Nathan Corey, b. 28 Feb 1829, d. 29 Aug 1829.
Eunice Corey, b. 29 Sep 1830, d. 15 Apr 1864, m. 1850 David G. Young.
447 Isaiah Whitney[7], 1833-1864.
Sarah Whitney, b. 4 Sep 1837, d. 29 Apr 1919, m. 24 Apr 1862 John T. Sawin.
448 George[7], 1841-1870.
Abby G., b. 11 Jul 1842.
Mary Elizabeth, b. 28 Nov 1843.
449 Nathan Corey[7], b. 1845.
Charles E., b. 1848, d. 3 Aug 1893, unm.
Laura E., b. Feb 1850.
450 Alonzo Charles[7], b. 1852.

Sources: Epping NH census 1850, 1860, 1870. VR Bolton MA, Cambridge MA, SA/MA. P46, N28, B33, S34, D9.

215. **NATHAN[6] SAWYER** [see 91], b. 18 May 1807 Bolton MA, m. 18 May 1830 MA Lucinda Pollard, b. ?. In Bolton MA 1840.

Josephine, b. 2 Jan 1832.
Amory Pollard, b. 30 Oct 1833 Bolton MA, d. 1860. Harvard Graduate 1858.
451 John Henry[7], b. 1836.

Sources: Bolton MA census 1840. VR Bolton MA.

216. **LEVI[6] SAWYER** [see 92], b. 1 Oct 1783 Bolton MA, d. 13 Mar 1844 Bolton MA, m. 8 Nov 1818 Bolton MA Hannah Nourse, b. 5 Aug 1797 d. 1 Nov 1824. Physician. War of 1812: Enl. 14 Nov 1811.

Zilparah, b. 31 Aug 1819.
452 Sterling Kenisky[7], b. 1821.
Rufus, b. 31 Dec 1823 Bolton MA.

Sources: Bolton MA census 1820, 1830, 1840. VR Bolton MA. N1A, Barnabas Sawyer's Bible.

217. **BENJAMIN[6] SAWYER** [see 92], b. 19 Feb 1785 Bolton MA, m. 9 Jun 1818 Greenfield MA Charlotte Griswald, b. 2 Jun 1787. In Northfield MA.

Rebecca, b. 2 Mar 1819.
453 Benjamin[7], b. 1821.
Charlotte G., b. 24 May 1823.
Lucy B., b. 4 Mar 1825, d. 2 May 1825.
Lucy B., b. 15 Feb 1826, m. 17 Jan 1847 Moses S. Chapin.
John T., b. 12 Nov 1827 Northfield MA, m. 25 Feb 1857 Susan H. Hunt of Vermont, b. ca. 1828, dau. Salmon Hunt. Miller. In Shelburne MA. CH: Son, b. 19 Feb 1858.
Cephas L., b. Aug 1837 Northfield MA, d. 14 Aug 1880 Athol MA, m. 21 Jan 1864 Northhampton MA Ellen A. Wood of Westfield MA, b. ?, dau. Samuel and Augusta Wood. Baker. In Greenfield MA. CH: Mary E., b. ca. 1872, m. 14 Jul 1889 Warwick MA William E. Mayo.

Sources: VR Greenfield MA, Northfield MA. D12.

218. **JOHN[6] SAWYER** [see 92], b. 17 Feb 1794 Bolton MA, m. 4 Nov 1821 Bolton MA Abigail Moore, b. 26 Jan 1801 d. 1858. In Bolton MA 1840.

Henrietta H., b. 15 Nov 1823, d. 22 Jul 1847.

454 John Francis[7], b. 1825.

Charles Augustus, b. 27 Dec 1829 Bolton MA, d. 19 Nov 1866, m. 23 May 1861 Fannie S. Kidder, b. 5 Feb 1836 d. 1 Dec 1921 Sterling MA, dau. Jedidiah and Martha (Kendall) Kidder of Hudson MA. Wid. m. 9 Jun 1867 George A. Tripp.

James Moore, b. 14 Sep 1834 Bolton MA. Civil War: 39th Regiment, 18 Aug 1862-18 Jul 1865.

Sources: Bolton MA census 1830, 1840. VR Bolton MA. K3, F2, S74.

219. **BARNABAS WHITCOMB[6] SAWYER** [see 93], b. 23 Oct 1794 Buxton ME, d. 5 Dec 1858 Buxton ME, m. 19 Oct 1815 Huldah Richardsonof Baldwin ME, b. 11 Jul 1791 d. 19 Feb 1884, dau. Joseph and Mary (Carpenter) Richardson. Farmer, music teacher. War of 1812.

Lucy W., b. 25 Sep 1816, d. 30 May 1892, m. 21 Jun 1856 Buxton ME Abram B. Anderson.

455 Silas Whitcomb[7], b. 1818.

456 William[7], b. 1820-1897.

Levi Loring, b. 18 Jul 1822 Buxton ME, d. 27 Nov 1851 Buxton ME, m. 16 Aug 1849 Lowell MA Lydia B. Dearborn of Compton NH, b. ca. 1821, dau. Henry and Abigail Dearborn. In Lowell MA 1850.

Phineas Ingalls, b. 15 Apr 1824, d. 13 Feb 1825.

Sarah M., b. 28 Nov 1826, m. 19 Apr 1868 Samuel Putney of Chelmsford MA.

Joseph R., b. 10 Nov 1827 Buxton ME, d. 8 Apr 1899 Buxton ME. Civil War: Company C, 27th Maine Infantry.

Nathaniel W., b. 27 Jun 1830 Buxton ME, m.(1) 8 Feb 1856 Buxton ME Hannah Martin, b. 4 May 1827 d. 22 Feb 1884; m.(2) 18 Oct 1884 Buxton ME Sarah M. Hutchinson of Buxton ME, b. 23 Aug 1841 d. 17 Dec 1915, dau. Benjamin and Mary (Merrill) Hutchinson. Both wives bur. in Buxton ME. CH: Alice M., adopted, b. 4 May 1864, d. 12 Feb 1884, m. George A. Anderson; Aldana W., b. 31 Mar 1886.

Stephen H. b. 4 Nov 1832 Buxton ME, m.(1) 1 Jan 1856 Conway NH Adelia M. Hazelton, b. ?; m.(2) Charlotte Woods of Buffalo NY, b. ?.

Sources: Buxton ME census 1820, 1830, 1840, 1850. Lowell MA census 1850. VR Lowell MA, Buxton ME, Saco ME, Lowell MA, SA/MA. V8, M3, R17, M5, P82k, Family Bible.

220. **SETH[6] SAWYER** [see 94], b. 14 Jan 1795 Bolton MA, m. Susan P. Frost of Bolton MA, b. 12 Dec 1807. Victualler. In Charlestown MA 1850.

457 Seth F.[7], b. ca. 1829.

Susan F., b. 1831, m. 21 Jan 1858 Charlestown MA Gershom Burnham.

458 Charles W.[7], b. 1833.

459 Jefferson[7], b. 1835.

Josephine, b. Aug 1836, d. 29 Sep 1837.

George W., b. 1838 Charlestown MA, m. 29 Apr 1861 Charlestown Ellen E. Robinson of Concord MA, b. 1821, dau. Henry and Myra (Conant) Robinson. Carpenter. CH: Anna F., b. 21 Jul 1862; Emma Josephine, b. 24 Oct 1864.

Albert G., b. 1840 Charlestown MA, m. 25 Jan 1866 Charlestown MA Hannah M. Lewis of Charlestown MA, b. 1839, dau. Seth and Sarah Lewis. Engineer. In Everett MA. CH:

Alice Gertrude, b. 8 Jun 1867, m. 1 Jan 1893 Somerville MA George R. Totman; daughter, b. 24 Jul 1874.

Alice E, b. 1845, m. 10 Feb 1876 Somerville MA Thomas C. Brown.

William Frederick, b. 30 Oct 1847 Charlestown MA, d. 17 May 1929 Bristol ME, m.(1) Annie M. Wentworth of Lebanon ME, b. Feb 1847 d. 7 Oct 1885, dau. H____ G. Wentworth; m.(2) 23 Nov 1870 Royalston MA E. Helen Bryant of Troy NH, b. 1840, dau. Lucian and Charlotte P. Bryant; m.(3) 11 Oct 1921 Lyme NH Annie F. B. Bryant of Exeter NH, b. 1856, dau. John C. and Caroline A. (Sweet) Burnham. Druggist. In Boston MA, Athol MA 1870. CH: William Prince, b. 25 Oct 1879, d. Sep 1945, unm., lawyer.

Ella F., b. 1850.

Herbert, b. 22 Jan 1852, d. 31 Aug 1852.

Sources: Charlestown MA census 1840, 1850. VR Chelsea MA, Bristol ME, SA/MA. W72.

221. **AMOS⁶ SAWYER** [see 95], b. 17 Mar 1769 Bolton MA, d. 3 Oct 1842 Berlin MA, m. 3 Aug 1792 Berlin MA Persis Howe of Marlborough MA, b. 8 Jun 1769 d. 25 Sep 1850 Berlin MA, dau. Joseph and Persis (Rice) Howe. Town Clerk, Selectman for Berlin MA. Representative to the General Court.

460 Amory[7], 1793-1831.

Lucy, b. 13 Dec 1794, m. 3 Apr 1816 Hollis Eager of Marlborough MA.

461 William A.[7], b. 1796.

Polly, b. 12 Feb 1798, d. 25 Apr 1845, m. 28 Jan 1821 Benjamin F. Spofford.

Betsey, b. 6 Aug 1799, d. 1833, m. 17 Dec 1817 Abel Howe of Berlin MA.

Franklin, b. 3 Sep 1801, d. 26 Jun 1809.

Joseph, b. 3 Sep 1801, d. 3 Jul 1809.

462 Amos[7], 1808-1866.

Franklin, b. 3 Nov 1809, d. 10 Oct 1847, unm.

Joseph, b. 3 Nov 1809, d. 30 Sep 1825.

Sources: Berlin MA census 1800, 1810, 1820, 1830, 1840. Northboro MA census 1840.

222. **OLIVER[6] SAWYER** [see 95], b. 17 Apr 1774 Bolton MA, d. 15 Apr 1851 Berlin MA, m.(1) 16 Oct 1800 Northboro MA Lucy Fairbanks of Northboro MA, b. 1781 d. 22 Apr 1804; m.(2) 3 Apr 1811 Northboro MA Sophira Rice of Northboro MA, b. 13 Jan 1785 d. 1 Sep 1841, dau. Seth and Sarah (Brigham) Rice. Farmer. Deacon, First Church of Berlin MA.

Lewis, b. 2 Feb 1812, d. 8 Feb 1856, unm.

463 Oliver Barrett[7], b. 1816.

Lucy Fairbanks, b. 9 Sep 1819, d. 30 Dec 1847, m. 8 Jan 1845 Stephen Sawyer of Worcester MA.

Sophia Rice, b. 9 Sep 1819, d. 24 Oct 1873, unm.

Sources: Berlin MA census 1810, 1820, 1830, 1840, 1850. VR Berlin MA, Northboro MA. H76, B84.

223. **ASA[6] SAWYER** [see 95], b. 2 Aug 1775 Bolton MA, d. 1845 Brimfield OH, m. 19 Jun 1800 Berlin MA Eunice Bruce, b. 1779, dau. John and Martha (Moore) Bruce. On Jaffrey NH tax list, 1803-1817. In Berlin MA, Jaffrey NH 1810, Ohio 1817.

Levi, bp. 28 Jun 1801 Berlin MA, d. 22 Feb 1836 Berlin MA.

464 Asa[7], 1802-1881.

William, bp. 10 Feb 1805 Berlin MA, m.(1) 24 May 1829 Almira Priest, b. Brimfield OH; m.(2) 19 May 1835 Harriet Babcock, b. ?. In Jaffrey NH.

Sophia, bp. 8 Feb 1807, m. 29 Nov 1827 Oliver H. Sawyer.

Alvin, bp. 22 Oct 1809 Berlin MA. In Jaffrey NH, Brimfield OH.
Luke, bp. 6 Oct 1816 Berlin MA. In Jaffrey NH, Brimfield OH.
Lucy, bp. 6 Oct 1816.

Sources: Jaffrey NH census 1810. VR Berlin MA, Jaffrey NH, SA/NH. A27.

224. **URIAH$^6$ SAWYER** [see 95], b. 24 May 1778 Bolton MA, d. 5 Aug 1862 Brimfield OH, m. 2 Feb 1803 Berlin MA Sally Spafford of Berlin MA, b. 1 Aug 1781 d. 1863, dau. Deacon John and Esther (Taylor) Spafford. On Jaffrey NH tax list 1802-1817. War of 1812. In Berlin MA, Jaffrey NH, Brimfield OH 1817.

Oliver H., b. 21 Apr 1804 Jaffrey NH, m. 29 Nov 1827 Sophia Sawyer, b. 1807. In Brimfield OH.
Henry, b. 8 Apr 1806, d. 19 Jul 1882, m. Susan Hall, b. ?. Went to Brimfield OH.
Lockhart, b. 1808, d. 15 Sep 1830.
Uriah, b. 14 Jul 1810, m. 3 Jul 1836 Caroline Pike, b. ?. Went to Brimfield OH.
William B., b. ?.
Benjamin F., b. ?.
Sally, b. ?, m. John Walker.
Hannah, b. ?.

Sources: VR Berlin MA. A27.

225. **ALVIN$^6$ SAWYER** [see 96], b. 30 Oct 1770 Berlin MA, d. 14 Jan 1842 Berlin MA, m.(1) 13 Feb 1794 Berlin MA Sarah Goddard, b. ? d. 14 Nov 1806, dau. James Goddard; m.(2) 19 Oct 1808 Berlin MA Sally Newton of Northboro MA, b. 1778 d. 22 Jul 1848 Worcester MA, dau. Ezekiel and Tabitha Newton.

Lucy, b. 16 Mar 1795, d. 17 May 1878, m.(1) 3 Apr 1816 Amory Sawyer, m.(2) 1835 Moses Greenleaf.
Zilpah, b. 3 Feb 1797, d. 11 Oct 1875 West Boylston MA, unm.
Levi, b. 7 Apr 1799, d. 9 Feb 1836, unm.
465 Eli$^7$, 1801-1870.
Alvin, b. 8 Sep 1803 Berlin MA, d. 4 Nov 1856 Newfields NH, m.(1) 13 Apr 1828 Waltham MA Lucy Bigelow of Sherborn MA, b. 18 Jul 1806 d. 18 May 1831, dau. Solomon and Lydia (Haven) Bigelow; m.(2) 3 Apr 1847 Dover NH Annie J. Tarleton of Dover NH, b. 1823. Engineer. In Portsmouth NH 1850.
466 Josiah$^7$, 1810-1885.
467 George William$^7$, 1811-1881.
468 Stephen$^7$, b. 1813.
Sally Newton, b. 1815, m. Julius Clarke of Worcester MA.
Susannah H., b. 25 Apr 1819, d. 31 Dec 1872, m. 25 Apr 1844 Leonard Brigham.

Sources: Berlin MA census 1800, 1810, 1820, 1830, 1840. VR Berlin MA, Worcester MA, Waltham MA. G42, H76, B84.

226. **IRA$^6$ SAWYER** [see 96], b. 31 Oct 1787 Berlin MA, d. 30 Aug 1861 Berlin MA, m. 15 Jan 1811 Bolton MA Abigail Hastings of Bolton MA, b. 24 Mar 1788 d. 24 Oct 1869, dau. William Hastings. In Bolton MA 1820, 1840, Berlin MA 1830.

469 William$^7$, b. 1812.
470 Josiah Ellsworth$^7$, 1814-1890.
Mary Ann, b. 11 Dec 1815, d. 4 Jan 1892, m. 10 Apr 1839 George William Sawyer.
471 Hartwell$^7$, 1818-1898.
Ira Johnson, b. 31 Dec 1819 Berlin MA, d. 1852, m.(1) 27 May 1846 Lancaster MA Abigail M. Houghton, b. 15 Aug 1821 d. 24 Aug 1849, dau. Lewis Houghton (SA/MA say she

was dau. Caleb and Abigail [Merriam] Houghton); m.(2) Clinton MA Irene G. Sargent of New Hampshire, b. 15 Aug 1821 d. 24 Aug 1849, dau. James and Nancy Sargent. Farmer. In Lancaster MA. CH: Susan Abby, b. 27 Nov 1847, d. 11 Aug 1848; William Henry, b. 2 Mar 1852, d. 18 Mar 1853; Abby Susan, b. 18 Mar 1854; Emma, b. 17 Oct 1856, d. 1942.

Charles F., b. 19 Mar 1822, d. 26 Dec 1851 Bolton MA, unm.

Sarah J., b. 18 Jan 1824, d. 6 Oct 1887, m. 22 Dec 1845 Amory A. Bartlett.

472 Benjamin Hastings$^7$, 1826-1903.

George Quincy, b. 26 Aug 1828 Berlin MA, d. 10 Jan 1887 Hudson MA, m. 16 Jan 1851 Lunenburg MA Marilla Saunderson of Lunenburg MA, b. 1831. Comb maker. In Clinton MA.

473 Oliver$^7$, b. 1830.

Sources: Bolton MA census 1820, 1840, Berlin MA census 1830. Clinton MA census 1850. VR Berlin MA, Lancaster MA, Bolton MA, SA/MA. C9, W39.

227. **RUFUS$^6$ SAWYER** [see 96], b. 22 Sep 1790 Berlin MA, d. 12 Apr 1865 Berlin MA, m. 12 Feb 1813 Berlin MA Sereph Bartlett, b. 8 Oct 1792 d. 3 Dec 1863, dau. Adam Bartlett.

474 Alden$^7$, 1813-1889.

Elmira, b. 11 Jul 1815, d. 25 Apr 1890, m. 14 Oct 1834 Horace Bigelow.

475 Isreal$^7$, 1817-1881.

Lucinda, b. 5 Aug 1819, d. 27 Oct 1840, m. 26 Feb 1840 Isreal Moore.

476 Edwin$^7$, 1821-1891.

Eli, b. 22 May 1823 Berlin MA, d. 16 Jul 1906 Clinton MA, m. 27 Nov 1845 Berlin MA Sarah E. (Goss) Carter of Lancaster MA, wid. of Rufus, b. 19 Jun 1810 d. 4 Nov 1855, dau. John and Mary (Fuller) Goss. Stone mason. CH: Lucinda A., b. 6 May 1847; Orin Rufus, b. 1 Feb 1850, d. 19 Sep 1851; Sarah A., b. 24 Nov 1851, m. 13 Dec 1892 Clinton MA Carl Lehnert.

477 Addison A.$^7$, 1825-1893.

Joseph B., b. 2 Jun 1827 Berlin MA, m.(1) ?; m.(2) 23 Mar 1852 Berlin MA Elena Randall of Enfield MA, b. 1 Jun 1810 d. 2 Jun 1883, dau. Titus C. and Patty (Davison) Randall. Farmer. In South Hadley MA. No CH.

Jonathan Orrison, b. 26 Jul 1829 Berlin MA, m. 10 Feb 1856 Methuen MA Alice A. Currier of Methuen MA, b. ca. 1829, dau. Asa and Sarah Currier.

478 Rufus Curtis$^7$, 1832-1903.

Dexter, b. ca. 1837 Berlin MA.

Sources: Berlin MA census 1820, 1830, 1840, 1850. Clinton MA census 1850. VR Berlin MA, SA/MA. H81.

228. **ASA$^6$ SAWYER** [see 96], b. 25 Sep 1795 Berlin MA, d. 30 Aug 1861 Bolton MA, m. 3 Nov 1814 Berlin MA Emma Bailey, b. 27 Oct 1790 d. 6 Apr 1880, dau. Stephen and Sally (Crosby) Bailey.

Fanny W., b. 17 Jul 1815, d. 18 Aug 1830.

Winthrop Bailey, b. 3 Jun 1817 Berlin MA, d. 30 Apr 1865 Berlin MA, m. ?. Minister. CH: Margaret Bailey, b. ?; Winthrop Bailey, b. ?. Changed last name to Bailey. Went to Long Island NY.

Theodore Wilder, b. 14 Feb 1819 Berlin MA, d. Apr 1869 Berlin MA, m. 22 Mar 1842 Marlborough MA Lucinda Rice of Marlborough MA, b. 11 Jul 1821 d. 16 Dec 1893, dau. Levi and Lucinda (Bigelow) Rice. Farmer, cordwainer. Civil War. In Marlborough MA. CH: Henrietta Estella, b. 24 Sep 1843, d. 19 Apr 1844; Henrietta Estella, b. 20 Apr 1845, d. 2 Nov 1846; Matthew Bailey, b. 19 Aug 1846, d. 7 Oct 1846; Theodore Burrett,

b. 28 Dec 1847, d. 27 May 1849; Effie Ginevra, b. 22 Apr 1850, m. 5 Apr 1869 Marlborough MA Theodore Temple; Emma L., b. ca. 1852, m. 25 May 1870 Marlborough MA Newton A. Mills.

Humphrey Whiton, b. 14 Jan 1822 Berlin MA.

Emma B., b. 13 Nov 1826, d. 4 Sep 1831.

Henrietta E., b. 3 Sep 1829, d. 24 May 1834.

Sources: Berlin MA census 1820, 1830, 1840, 1850. VR Berlin MA, Marlborough MA, SA/MA. B5, E16, W39.

229. **THOMAS[6] SAWYER** [see 97], b. 10 Jun 1785 Berlin MA, d. 13 Jun 1864 Berlin MA, m.(1) 16 Apr 1809 Sarah Bigelow, b. 12 Feb 1791 d. 9 Feb 1833; m.(2) 17 Jul 1836 Hannah (Lawrence) Warner of Salem MA, b. 16 Sep 1776 d. 21 May 1849. Cooper.

Silas, b. 15 Jul 1811 Berlin MA, d. 9 Feb 1906 Berlin MA, m.(1) 16 Apr 1835 Berlin MA Lucy W. Holman. of Bolton MA, b. 19 Jun 1816 d. 10 Jul 1848, dau. Amory and Lucy (Whitcomb) Holman; m.(2) 31 Oct 1849 Shirley MA Mary L. Holman of Bolton MA, b. 20 Oct 1826 d. 31 Dec 1905, dau. Amory and Lucy (Whitcomb) Holman. Farmer. CH: Ellen Frances, b. 29 Apr 1836, d. 18 Oct 1863, m. 31 Aug 1856 Berlin MA Samuel W. Moore; Lavinia Kittredge, b. 30 Mar 1838, m. 26 Nov 1851 Berlin MA George H. Cutting.

479 Abel[7], 1813-1853.

Mary Bigelow, b. 19 Aug 1815, d. 19 Nov 1892, m. 7 May 1835 Berlin MA Albert Babcock.

Sarah H., b. 18 May 1818, m.(1) 4 Dec 1836 Amos Sawyer, m.(2) 27 Apr 1870 Henry D. Coburn.

Betsey, b. 21 Mar 1820, d. 21 Mar 1872, m. 18 Nov 1840 Boylston MA Eldridge Wheeler.

Clarissa, b. 20 Apr 1822, d. 16 Aug 1854, m. 18 Mar 1846 Berlin MA William P. Keyes. Lucy, b. 22 Feb 1824, m. 27 Nov 1845 Berlin MA James Boyd.

Sources: Berlin MA census 1810, 1820, 1840, 1850. VR Berlin MA, Shirley MA, SA/MA. W39, E16, W32, H81.

230. **JONAS[6] SAWYER** [see 97], b. 1 Jul 1787 Berlin MA, d. 1 May 1827 Berlin MA, m. 22 Oct 1809 Berlin MA Euseba Bailey, b. 11 Jun 1787 d. 27 Feb 1821 Pelham NH, dau. Stephen and Sally (Crosby) Bailey.

Eliza, b. 30 Jun 1811, m. 24 Jan 1830 Abram Bigelow.

Jonas, b. 26 Apr 1812 Berlin MA, d. 21 Jul 1894 Berlin MA, m. 4 Apr 1880 Berlin MA Mary Angeline Wheeler of Bolton MA, b. 14 Aug 1832, dau. Jonathan and Phebe (Kimmens) Wheeler. Farmer.

Silvina, b. 4 Jul 1813, d. 29 Jul 1837.

Sally Howe, b. 23 May 1815.

Stephen B., b. 23 May 1821 Berlin MA, m.(1) 4 Sep 1842 Westboro MA Lucy A. M. Stone of Westboro MA, b. ?; m.(2) 28 Apr 1874 Berlin MA Mary Bruso of Montreal, Canada, b. 1849. Farmer. CH: Francis Jerome, b. 11 Nov 1845 Bangor ME, d. 10 Mar 1852.

Sources: Berlin MA census 1810. VR Berlin MA, Westboro MA. B5, W39, H81.

231. **ABRAHAM[6] SAWYER** [see 97], b. 26 Jun 1789 Berlin MA, d. 28 Apr 1836 Berlin MA, m. 5 Nov 1816 Northboro MA Abigail Keyes of Northboro MA, b. 1791 d. 7 Aug 1830.

Davis, b. 18 May 1817, d. 5 Dec 1841.

Roswell, b. 29 Nov 1818, d. 6 Jul 1843.

Curtis, b. 17 Aug 1820 Berlin MA, d. 4 Mar 1851 Berlin MA, m. 31 Mar 1845 Northboro MA Sarah A. Crosby of Northboro MA, b. ?, dau. Walter Crosby. Shoemaker.

Sarah M., b. 17 Mar 1822, m. Sidney Harris of Clinton MA.
James K., b. 8 Oct 1824, d. 15 Sep 1844.
Harriet, b. 20 Feb 1829, d. 9 May 1833.
Sources: Berlin MA census 1820, 1830, 1850. Marlborough MA census 1850. VR Berlin MA, Northboro MA, SA/MA.

232. **AARON$^6$ SAWYER** [see 98], b. 24 Aug 1756 Lancaster MA, d. 31 Apr 1817 Boylston MA, m. 25 Mar 1779 Lancaster MA Kezia Richardson, b. 11 Aug 1765. In Shrewsbury MA 1782, Boylston MA.
Dolly, b. 11 Jul 1782, m. 21 Jun 1803 Caleb Kendall.
Elizabeth, b. 17 Jan 1784, m. 21 Jun 1803 Hezikiah Gibbs.
480 Aaron$^7$, 1785-1849.
481 Joseph$^7$, 1787-1847.
James, b. 1791 Boylston MA, d. 3 Dec 1823 Pearington MO.
Ezra, b. 12 Oct 1793, d. 12 Sep 1813.
Sources: VR Lancaster MA, Boylston MA, Shrewsbury MA. W32, M19, C86.

233. **OLIVER$^6$ SAWYER** [see 98], b. 2 Feb 1759 Lancaster MA, d. 31 Dec 1838 Boylston MA, m. 23 Feb 1785 Shrewsbury MA Patty Hinds of West Boylston MA, b. 29 Sep 1760 d. 31 Mar 1836, dau. Benjamin and Elizabeth (Temple) Hinds of West Boylston MA. S/land in Baldwin ME 1785.
Patty, b. 18 Apr 1786, m. 25 May 1807 Joshua Kendall.
482 Oliver$^7$, 1788-1824.
Abigail, b. 5 Dec 1791, m. 21 Sep 1815 Pitt Moore.
Sources: Boylston MA census 1800. VR Shrewsbury MA, Boylston MA. R19, H55.

234. **MOSES$^6$ SAWYER** [see 99], b. 29 May 1764 Lancaster MA, d. 12 Mar 1831 So. Lancaster MA, m. 18 Jul 1792 Lancaster MA Elizabeth Divol, b. 20 Mar 1765 d. 20 Nov 1849 Lancaster MA, dau. John and Elizabeth (Beaman) Divol. He bur. in Middle Cem., Lancaster MA.
Sally, b. 7 May 1793, d. 6 Mar 1894, m. 13 May 1841 Flavel Case.
483 Charles$^7$, b. 1795.
Henry, b. 31 Aug 1797 Lancaster MA, d. 17 Jun 1876, m.(1) 2 Sep 1826 Katherine Burnett of Warwick MA, b. ? d. 12 Nov 1840; m.(2) 11 Nov 1852 Sterling MA Cornelia S. (Wilder) Smith of Sterling MA, wid. of N____, b. 8 Jun 1820 d. 25 Mar 1883, dau. Calvin and Hannah (Newton) Wilder. Tinware manufacturer. In Lancaster MA 1840, Sterling MA 1850, Boylston MA. CH: Franklin, b. 3 Feb 1828, d. 2 Jul 1829; Katherine Amelia, b. 11 May 1830, d. 12 Oct 1870, m. 2 Aug 1855 Boston MA John Waltherin; Almeda Augusta, b. 23 Mar 1832, d. 26 Jul 1833; AugustaA., b. 1835; Mary E., b. 2 Jul 1854, m. 16 Sep 1886 Ira B. Brush; Charles Henry, b. 1856, d. 4 Jan 1859.
John, b. 24 Dec 1810 Lancaster MA, m. 2 Mar 1845 Roxbury MA Mary C. Clarke of Sanbornton NH, b. 1821, dau. Samuel and Martha (Thompson) Clarke. Active abolitionist. In Boston MA 1850. No CH.
Sources: Lancaster MA census 1800, 1810, 1820, 1830, 1840. Sterling MA census 1850. Boston MA census 1850. VR Lancaster MA, Clinton MA, Roxbury MA, SA/MA.

235. **PETER$^6$ SAWYER** [see 99], b. 25 Jan 1784 Lancaster MA, d. 2 Jun 1831 Lancaster (Clinton) MA, m. 21 May 1807 Lancaster MA Mary H. Sawyer, b. 1786 d. 12 Dec 1828.
Son, b. 2 Mar 1808, d. 14 Mar 1808.
Evelina, b. 16 May 1809, d. 23 Jun 1835.
484 Peter$^7$, b. 1811.

Ezra, b. 8 Jul 1814, d. 27 Aug 1833.
Moses Elias, b. 12 Jun 1817 Lancaster MA, d. 16 Jun 1857.
Frederick Charles, b. 14 Dec 1819 Lancaster MA.
Marietta Hayward, b. 10 Jun 1820.
Elmirick, b. 31 Mar 1822, d. 15 Jan 1832.
Child, b. 1826, d. 10 Sep 1829.
Sources: Lancaster MA census 1810, 1820, 1830. VR Lancaster MA. F25.

236. **AMERIAH$^6$ SAWYER** [see 100], b. 14 Oct 1765 Lancaster MA, d. bef. 1830, m.(1) 18 Feb 1794 Shrewsbury MA Sarah Moore, b. ? d. 3 Feb 1817; m.(2) 10 May 1827 Royalston MA Eunice Taft, b. ?. In Boylston MA 1800, 1810. Wid. in Wendell MA 1830, 1840.
Lucy, b. 1 Oct 1795, d. 9 Jun 1819.
Ruth, b. 23 Sep 1797.
Persis, b. 1 Nov 1799, d. 3 Aug 1803.
Sarah, b. 13 Apr 1802, d. 1830, m. 2 Nov 1824 Peter Parker of Royalston MA.
Ameriah, b. 28 Jul 1804, d. 1804.
Ameriah, b. 12 Feb 1807 Boylston MA, d. 8 Nov 1831. In Wendell MA.
Joseph, b. 23 Aug 1809, d. 9 Mar 1829.
Arunah. b. 23 Dec 1811.
Sources: Boylston MA census 1800, 1810. Wendell MA census 1830, 1840. VR Boylston MA, Shrewsbury MA, Royalston MA, Wendell MA.

237. **WILLIAM$^6$ SAWYER** [see 100], b. 4 Feb 1768 Lancaster MA, d. 19 Sep 1824 Shrewsbury MA, m. 12 Jul 1798 Boylston MA Abigail (Nabby) Siles, b. 1782 d. 22 Feb 1839. In Boylston MA, Northboro MA 1800.
Nabby, b. 28 Dec 1798, m. 9 Mar 1817 Joseph P. Carey.
John, b. 2 Oct 1800 Northboro MA, d. 2 Oct 1854 Millbury MA.
2 dau., b. ?.
Benjamin, b. ca. 1809, d. 8 Mar 1851 Worcester MA.
Sources: Northboro MA census 1800. VR Boylston MA, Northboro MA. M42, C8.

238. **JABEZ$^6$ SAWYER** [see 100], b. 13 Oct 1770 Lancaster MA, d. 28 Jan 1849 Wendell MA, m. 23 Feb 1798 Athol MA Jemima Carruth of Gerry MA, b. 1779 d. Apr 1833. In Wendell MA.
485 Jabez$^7$, 1799-1888.
486 Asabel$^7$, b. 1801.
Jemima, b. 24 Aug 1803.
Levina, b. 22 Nov 1808, m. 4 Feb 1834 George B. Richardson.
Lydia C., b. 5 Mar 1815.
Sarah, b. 10 Aug 1818.
Sources: Wendell MA census 1800, 1810, 1820, 1830, 1850. VR Athol MA, SA/MA.

239. **AARON$^6$ SAWYER** [see 100], b. 6 Oct 1775 Sterling MA, d. 18 Mar 1846 Wendell MA, m. 1 May 1800 Boylston MA Patience Fairbanks of Sterling MA, b. 12 Jul 1779 d. 14 Feb 1864 Chestertown NY. Wid. in Hinsdale MA w/son Aaron 1850.
487 Lyman$^7$, b. ca. 1800.
488 Aaron$^7$, 1803-1862.
489 Milton$^7$, 1811-1889.
Sources: New Salem MA census 1830, 1840. Hinsdale MA census 1850. VR New Salem MA, Boylston MA. F27.

240. **JOSEPH⁶ SAWYER** [see 101], b. 5 Aug 1773 Templeton MA, d. 14 Mar 1843 Chester VT, m.(1) 31 Dec 1797 Abigail Mann, b. 1779 d. 14 Jan 1806; m.(2) 14 Feb 1808 Westminster VT Dorcas Edgell, b. 1781 d. 22 May 1853. Wid. w/son Silas 1850.

490 Thomas$^7$, b. 1799.
Betsey, b. 11 May 1801, d. 10 Jul 1884, m. Sep 1819 Thomas Williams.
Mary Laurenza, b. 1808, d. 11 May 1813.
Abigail Mann, b. 1811, d. 8 Apr 1813.
Dorcas P., b. 27 Mar 1814, d. 8 Jan 1881, m. 22 Oct 1834 Walter Richardson.
491 Silas S.$^7$, b. 1815.
Joseph Franklin, b. 6 Nov 1824, d. 29 Aug 1825.

Sources: Chester VT census 1800, 1810, 1820, 1830, 1840, 1850. VR Chester VT, SA/VT. D11, A20.

241. **STEPHEN$^6$ SAWYER** [see 102], b. 4 Oct 1764 Templeton MA, d. 11 Nov 1829 Leicester VT, m. 1787 No. Milford CT Eunice Averill, b. 2 May 1769 d. 8 Mar 1848.

Earl, b. 24 Mar 1789 Leicester VT, d. 4 Jul 1866 Freedom NY, m. 5 Feb 1811 Leicester VT Polly Davis, b. 1792 d. 1871. CH: James A., b. 22 Feb 1812; Eunice, b. 1813, d. 1878; Ebenezer Davis, b. 6 Oct 1825, d. 20 Jun 1902, m. 31 Jul 1854 Lavinia Trowbridge; John, b. ca. 1828; Ellen, b. 17 Feb 1830, d. 30 Mar 1852; Martha, b. ca. 1832; Herman, b. ca. 1834.
Lucy, b. ?, m. 17 Sep 1818 Stephen Sparks, Jr.
Sarah, b. ?, m. 11 Jul 1818 James Irish.
James, b. 1794, d. 15 Aug 1799.
Stephen, b. Feb 1795, b. 10 May 1798.
Ezra, b. 1796.
492 Ebenezer$^7$, 1797-1869.
Lorain, b. ca. 1802.
Mary, b. ca. 1804.
Marilla, b. 17 Jul 1807, d. 5 Jul 1895, m. 4 Jul 1835 Gregory Metcalf.
Betsey, b. 27 Mar 1810, d. 1882. m. _____ Metcalf.
493 Harrison$^7$, 1813-1894.

Sources: Leicester VT census 1790, 1800, 1810, 1820. VR SA/VT. D11, Ethel L. Morris rec., Ron Sawyer rec.

242. **HOOKER$^6$ SAWYER** [see 102], b. 11 Jun 1771 Winchendon MA, d. 1843 Springfield OH, m.(1) Polly Rhodes, b. 1775 d. 1824; m.(2) Lucy Nobles, b. ?. In Clarendon VT 1783, Salisbury VT 1794. In Manchester NY.

Althy, b. 2 Feb 1794.
Thomas C., b. 1811 Manchester NY, d. 1835, m. Mary Benham, b. 1812 d. 1894. CH: Frances Carter, b. 1834, d. 1899; Henry, b. 1819, d. 1883, m. Eliza Brown.

Sources: VR SA/VT. J3, Bonita Folck rec.

243. **JOSEPH$^6$ SAWYER** [see 102], b. 30 Mar 1777 Winchendon MA, d. 25 Sep 1861 Manchester NY, m.(1) 1802 Desire Root, b. ?, dau. Joseph and Tryphena (Moseley) Root; m.(2) 25 Dec 1807 Anna Coates, b. ? d. 28 Oct 1878. In Clarendon VT, Salisbury VT, Manchester NY.

494 Henry$^7$, 1803-1870.
Theuseba, b. 1806, m. _____ Southworth.
Desire, b. 23 Oct 1809, d. 26 Nov 1877, m. 30 Jan 1830 Thomas J. McLouth.
Adeline, b. 15 Dec 1811, d. 25 Mar 1857.
Joseph Norris, b. 4 Apr 1814, d. 16 Mar 1880, m. 6 Oct 1843 Caroline Johnson, b. ?.

(More CH b. in New York.)
Sources: D34, Ron Sawyer rec.

244. **SILAS[6] SAWYER** [see 103], b. 6 Mar 1764 Templeton MA, d. 21 Nov 1841 Phillipston MA, m.(1) 14 Dec 1785 Templeton MA Mary Ross, b. 1766 d. 13 Jul 1823; m. (2) 14 Dec 1823 Phillipston MA Elizabeth Cole, b. 1763 d. 9 Mar 1840; m.(3) 11 May 1841 Phillipston MA Grace Howe, b. 1775 d. 26 Nov 1861.

Abner, b. 26 Jul 1786 Templeton MA, d. Calais ME, m.(1) 16 Nov 1808 Phillipston MA Phebe Cole, b. ?; m.(2) 1843 Rebecca Nutting, b. 1790. Trader. CH: Child, b. 1809 d. 1809; Child, b. 1810 d. 1810; Salome A., b. 7 Feb 1811, m. Manly B. Townsend; Mary L., b. 16 Jan 1814, d. 29 Sep 1849, m. 1837 Joseph A. Lee. Calais ME census lists the following children for the periods shown: dau., b. (1800-1810); dau., b. (1810-1815); son, b. (1820-1825); son, b. (1825-1830).
Hannah, b. 18 Aug 1787, d. 8 Apr 1789.
Polly, b. 13 Feb 1789, d. 18 Apr 1790.
Polly, b. 21 Oct 1790, m. 1 Dec 1834 Marvin Wesson.
Betsey, b. 15 Sep 1792.
Lydia, b. 8 Jan 1794, m. 27 Dec 1814 Daniel Thompson.
Lucy, b. 19 Feb 1797, d. 6 Dec 1831, m. 20 Apr 1818 Marvin Wesson.
495 Silas[7], b. 1799.
496 Thomas[7], b. 1801.
Nancy, b. 10 Apr 1803, d. 2 Sep 1803.
Abigail, b. 24 Sep 1805.
497 George Washington[7], 1807-1888.
Dorothy, b. 7 Jul 1811, m. 17 Apr 1834 Foster Willis.

Sources: Petersham MA census 1800. Gerry MA census 1810. Phillipston MA census 1820, 1830, 1840. Calais ME census 1830, 1840. VR Templeton MA, Phillipston MA. H43.

245. **THOMAS[6] SAWYER** [see 103], b. 29 Mar 1768 Templeton MA, d. 6 Aug 1857 Brooks ME, m. 1 Jan 1788 Bolton MA Olive Priest of Bolton MA, b. 1764 d. 1 Oct 1842 Brooks ME. In Prospect ME 1817, Brooks ME. Thomas joined Brooks church 1812, Olive in 1818.

Dolly, b. 13 Nov 1788.
498 Thomas[7], b. 1790.
Olive, b. 27 May 1792.
499 Abner[7], b. 1794.
500 Phineas[7], 1802-1843.

Sources: Brooks ME census 1820, 1830, 1840. VR Templeton MA, Bolton MA, Brooks ME, SA/NH. R10e. Obit (Olive, Sr.).

246. **PHINEHAS HOUGHTON[6] SAWYER** [see 103], b. 1 Oct 1779 Templeton MA, d. 25 Oct 1845 Whittingham VT, m. 15 Feb 1803 Templeton MA Rebekah Orcutt of Templeton MA, b. 15 Feb 1784 d. 19 Dec 1869, dau. Jonathan and Mary Orcutt. In Whittingham VT 1803.

501 Houghton[7], 1805-1872.
Mary H., b. 2 Feb 1808, m. Foster Willis.
Emory, b. 7 Apr 1812 Whittingham VT, d. 5 May 1857 Brattleboro VT, m.(1) Maria J. _____, b. 1816 d. 30 Jun 1846; m.(2) 10 Apr 1849 Whittingham VT Ann D. Godfrey, b. 1815. Miller. CH: Laura J., b. 1846.
Abner, b. 29 Dec 1818 Whittingham VT, m. 16 Dec 1847 Harriet E. Calkins, b. ?. In Savannah GA.

George Henry, b. 15 Aug 1823 Whittingham VT, d. 8 Mar 1871 Brattleboro VT, m.(1) ?; m.(2) 6 Dec 1868 Brattleboro VT Harriet Reed, b. ?. Produce dealer. In Boston MA, California 1849, Milwaukee WI, Brattleboro VT. CH: Laurette, b. 21 Oct 1870, d. 27 Feb 1871.

Sources:Whittingham VT census 1810, 1820, 1830, 1840. Brattleboro VT census 1840, 1850. VR Templeton MA, Brattleboro VT, SA/VT.

247. **JOSEPH[6] SAWYER** [see 104], b. 17 Dec 1781 Plymouth VT, d. 1 Jan 1845 Plymouth VT, m. 11 Oct 1802 Catherine E. Coolidge of Vermont, b. 4 Apr 1784 d. 24 Sep 1862, dau. John and Hannah (Priest) Coolidge.

Hannah C., b. Jan 1803, d. 31 Mar 1886, m. 31 Dec 1823 Moses Hall.

John Coolidge, b. 17 Mar 1805, d. 16 Apr 1812.

Joseph C., b. 1808, d. 16 Apr 1812.

502 Paul[7], 1811-1899.

Calvin Coolidge, b. 22 Apr 1812 Plymouth VT, d. 3 Feb 1893, m. 11 Nov 1838 Plymouth VT Clarissa Sumner of Plymouth VT, b. 9 Jun 1816 d. 2 Jun 1909, dau. Justus and Elizabeth (Thompson) Sumner. Farmer. In Plymouth VT 1850. CH: Daniel C., b. 28 Aug 1839, d. 1843; Son, b. 26 Dec 1843, d.y; Sarah, adopted, b. 5 Dec 1843, m. A. Petty; Katherine E., b. 29 Apr 1846, d. 16 Dec 1924; Alice Ann, b. 27 Mar 1849, d. 11 May 1938, m. 6 Dec 1869 Frank Josselyn; Hattie, b. 1852, m. 10 Aug 1878 Fred H. Bagley.

Mary C., b. 1 Sep 1814, d. 14 Dec 1899, m. 9 Oct 1834 Edwin Spear.

503 Joseph E.[7], 1817-1896.

Anna Pratt, b. 16 Apr 1819, d. 5 Jun 1909, m. 14 Oct 1841 Alpheus N. Earle.

Sally, b. ca. 1823, d. 11 May 1842.

Harriet E., b. 22 Mar 1825, d. 28 Dec 1906, m. 20 Mar 1845 Rufus Earl.

Martha, b. ?, m. Fred McCollum.

Sources: Plymouth VT census 1810, 1820, 1830, 1840, 1850. VR Plymouth VT, SA/VT. C75, D6, Early Families of Plymouth VT.

248. **EMANUEL[6] SAWYER** [see 104], b. 2 Jun 1784 Plymouth VT, d. 28 Jun 1853 Plymouth VT, m.(1) Submit Foster, b. 1782 d.23 Dec 1830; m.(2) 20 Dec 1832 Reading VT Tryphena Nichols, b. 1800 d. 23 Mar 1842; m.(3) 17 Oct 1842 Bridgewater VT Jane Paul, b. 1797 d. 1 Mar 1860, dau. Jeremiah and Jane (Starbridge) Paul. Farmer, Justice of the Peace.

Laura, b. 27 May 1805, m. 25 Dec 1824 Jesse Robinson.

Horace, b. 3 Jan 1807 Plymouth VT, m.?. In Bridgewater VT 1830.

Claraca, b., 1 May 1809.

504 Ira[7], 1811-1892.

Betsey, b. 19 May 1813.

Leaffy, b. 29 Jul 1815, m. 25 Nov 1835 Ira Angell.

505 Addison Foster[7], 1818-1895.

Orpha, b. 14 Jul 1820, d. 6 May 1885, m. 23 Apr 1840 Ziba A. Marsh.

John W., b. 10 May 1822 Plymouth VT, d. 12 Jun 1900 Bridgewater VT, m. 22 Sep 1850 Hartland VT Lucy Williams, b. ?, dau. Aden and Lucinda (Childs) Williams.

Martha J., b. 1835, d. 8 Feb 1874.

Homer Webster, b. Nov 1837, d. 16 Sep 1853.

Levi, b. Feb 1842, d. 1 Nov 1853.

Sources: Plymouth VT census 1810, 1820, 1830. Bridgewater VT census 1850. VR Taunton MA, SA/VT. D11, Early Families of Plymouth VT.

249. **SHERARD⁶ SAWYER** [see 105], b. 11 Jan 1789 Clarendon VT, d. 18 Mar 1877 Middlesex VT, m.(1) Catherine Stratton, b. 1790 d. 11 Apr 1865; m.(2) Abigail Finch of New York, b. Dec 1795 d. 9 Dec 1872. Farmer.

Loiya A., b. 1817, d. 11 Jan 1844.
Mary Ann, b. 1820, d. 9 Dec 1848 Corinth VT.
506 James Edward[7], 1827-1882.
Melissa, b. 1831.

Sources: Ira Vt census 1820. Pittsford VT census 1830. Cornwall VT census 1840, 1850. VR SA/VT. D11.

250. **OLIVER[6] SAWYER** [see 105], b. 1794 Clarendon VT, d. 4 Oct 1852 Sudbury VT, m. 24 Mar 1816 Shrewbury VT Mehitable Wheeler of Alstead NH, b. 1788 d. 9 Nov 1860 Sudbury VT. Farmer. He bur. in Wallace Cem., Sudbury VT.

507 James A.[7], 1823-1855.
508 Sherard[7], 1825-1879.
Dilpha, b. 1834.
Henry M., b. 18 Apr 1848, d. 8 Jul 1871.

Sources: Shrewsbury VT census 1820. Ira VT census 1830. Sudbury VT census 1840, 1850. VR SA/VT. H13, N14.

251. **JONAS[6] SAWYER** [see 108], b. 4 Aug 1789 Pepperell MA, d. 31 Mar 1866 Wentworth NH, m.(1) 3 Oct 1808 Rumney NH Polly Bailey, b. 7 Dec 1790 d. 13 Mar 1859; m.(2) Polly Clifford of Wentworth NH, b. 21 Sep 1803 d. 11 Nov 1886, dau. S_____ and R_____ (Smith) Clifford. Farmer.

Mary, b. 1811, d. 9 Apr 1853, m. 1829 Samuel Foster of Rumney NH.
509 Rufus[7], 1813-1860.
Rosswell Frank, b. 1815, d. 3 Jan 1847 Rumney NH, m. 1 Jan 1834 Permelia Whitcher of Wentworth NH, b. ?, dau. Aaron Whitcher. CH: Amelda Ann, b. 1839; Martha Bailey, b. 1840.
Hannah Bailey, b. 1817, m. 4 May 1847 Levi P. Keyes of Lowell MA.
510 Richard Bailey[7], b. 1820.
Sally Cheever, b. 1822, m. 3 Jul 1839 Bristol NH Jason Copp.
James Sidney, b. 1830 Wentworth NH, m. 15 May 1850 Lawrence MA Laura A. Keyes of Benton NH, b. ca. 1828, dau. John and Laura Keyes.

Sources: Groton MA census 1810. Wentworth NH census 1840, 1850, 1860. VR Lowell MA, SA/MA. P57, M39, N9, S81, N6.

252. **RUFUS[6] SAWYER** [see 109], b. 1809 Jaffrey NH, d. 10 Sep 1869 Jaffrey NH, m. 13 Dec 1831 Alstead NH Elmira Livermore of Alstead NH, b. 29 Oct 1801 d. 31 Aug 1872.

Emily, b. 1835, m. 15 Feb 1855 Jaffrey NH Anson William Jewett.
William L., b. 5 Feb 1838 Jaffrey NH, d. 19 Dec 1912 Jaffrey NH, m. Emily A. Boyce of Richmond NH, b. ?, dau. Robert and Rebecca (Bowen) Boyce. In Winchendon MA.

Sources: Jaffrey NH census 1850, 1860, 1870. A27, N14.

253. **JAMES D.[6] SAWYER** [see 109], b. 2 Jan 1813 Jaffrey NH, d. 26 Sep 1867 Jaffrey NH, m. 5 Dec 1839 Betsey P. Livermore of Alstead NH, b. 1819 d. 31 Jul 1872. Wid. in Jaffrey NH 1870.

511 James Henry[7], 1843-1881.
Sarah Lizzie, b. 29 Oct 1850, m. 14 Nov 1869 Benjamin F. Lawrence.
George E., b. 8 Jul 1861, d. 9 Jan 1877.

Sources: Jaffrey NH census 1840, 1850, 1860, 1870. N6.

254. **LEVI[6] SAWYER** [see 109], b. ca. 1815 in Jaffrey NH, m.(1) 11 Jun 1840 Susan Abigail Hinds of Milton MA, b. ?; m.(2) Lorinda A. _____, b. ca. 1817. Truckman, watchman. In Jaffrey NH, Milton MA, Auburn ME 1860.

512 Edward Howard[7], 1841-1914.

Frederick H., b. ca. 1842 (Milton MA?), m. Augusta H. Dore, b. ?. In Auburn ME 1860.

Charles F., b. ca. 1844 (Milton MA?), m.(1) 1 Dec 1865 Hannah C. Messer of Lewiston ME, b. ?; m.(2) 1870 Windham ME by Rev. E. H. Libby Margaret M. Jordan, b. 9 Nov 1842. CH: Alma, b. ca. 1872.

Syrena, b. 1857.

Sources: Auburn ME census 1860. VR Milton MA, Auburn ME, SA/ME.

255. **GEORGE R.[6] SAWYER** [see 110], b. 1796 Acworth NH, d. 5 Sep 1869 Middlesex VT, m.(1) 8 Jan 1821 Middlesex VT Betsey Putnam of New Hampshire, b. 1796 d. 14 Mar 1858; m.(2) 27 Feb 1860 Middlesex VT Eldulia (West) Roberts, b. 1802 d. 25 Oct 1874, dau. _____ West. Farmer.

513 Nathaniel P.[7], 1823-1899.

Polly, b. 23 Feb 1824.

Chester, b. 23 Feb 1824 Middlesex VT, d. 14 Sep 1898 Cabot VT, m. 11 Mar 1850 Marshfield VT Harriet Spenser of New York, b. 1823. Farmer.

Lucia J., b. 25 Jul 1825.

514 Russell[7], b. 1827.

515 Gardner[7], b. 1829.

Calvin P., b. 25 Mar 1830 Middlesex VT, m.(1) 11 Nov 1855 Charlestown VT Ann M. Proctor of Chelmsford MA, b. ca. 1833, dau. Willard and Maria Proctor; m.(2) 3 Dec 1862 New Ipswich NH Lucy Maria Reed of New Ipswich NH, b. 27 May 1842 Charlestown NY; m.(3) Experience _____, b. ?. Farmer. B/land in Belfast ME.

516 Hiram Allen[7], 1832-1893.

Harriet, b. 12 Oct 1833.

Ann M., b. 1840, m. 25 Oct 1858 George Spencer.

Sources: Middlesex VT census 1830, 1840, 1850. Cabot VT census 1850. VR SA/VT.

256. **JONAS[6] SAWYER (or Joseph)** [see 112], b. 6 Sep 1793 Lancaster MA, m. 24 Nov 1825 Susan Christian Passenger of Dorchester MA, b. ?. In Boston MA.

Henry Hendley, b. 15 Sep 1826 Boston MA.

Sources: VR Dorchester MA, SA/MA. B33.

257. **ELIJAH[6] SAWYER** [see 114], b. 25 Jan 1773 Bolton MA, d. Bolton MA, m.(1) 10 May 1798 Bolton MA Lucy Sawyer, b. 24 Nov 1780, dau. John and Mary(Moore) Sawyer; m.(2) 26 Sep 1802 Bolton MA Dorcas Tombs, b. ?. Blacksmith. Wid. m. Apr 1815 Elijah Stearns.

Lucy, b. 31 Mar 1799, d. 10 Jan 1827, m. 18 May 1825 Halloway Bailey.

517 America[7], 1803-1884.

Elijah, b. 29 Aug 1805 Bolton MA, d. bef. 1871, m. 11 Nov 1832 Leominster MA Martha H. Joslyn, b. 1808. Tin manufacturer. CH: Lucy Caroline, b. 22 Sep 1833; Francina Eliza, b. 20 Dec 1834, d. 29 Jul 1836; Clara Elizabeth b. 9 Apr 1841, m. 6 Jun 1864 Fitchburg MA Albert T. B. Ames; Abby Lizette, b. 2 Aug 1844, m. 17 Nov 1864 Fitchburg MA Boardman Parkhurst; Frederick Elijah, b. 9 Nov 1849, d. Oct 1850.

518 Warren[7], 1806-1862.

Dorcas, b. 3 Aug 1810.

Sources: Bolton MA census 1800, 1810. Lancaster MA census 1840, 1850. VR Bolton MA, Leominster MA, SA/MA. V2.

258. **LUTHER[6] SAWYER** [see 114], b. 6 Feb 1777 Bolton MA, d. 1826 Bolton MA, m. 12 Jun 1798 Bolton MA Kezia Sawyer, b. 20 Jun 1775 d. 27 Oct 1848 Cambridge MA, dau. William and Kezia (Moore) Sawyer.

Zeresh, b. 12 Dec 1798.

William Steadman, b. 31 Dec 1800 Bolton MA.

Abigail, b. 14 Sep 1802, d. 25 Dec 1863, m. 12 Apr 1829 Ezekiel H. Higgins.

Samuel, b. 21 Jul 1804 Bolton MA, d. 19 Oct 1847 Cambridge MA, m.(I)8 Jun 1828 Groton MA Amelia Dalrymple, b. 1807 d. 19 Oct 1840. In Cambridge MA. CH b. ?, d. 19 Jul 1829.

Luther, b. 9 Nov 1808 Bolton MA.

Sources:Bolton MA census 1810, 1820. VR Bolton MA, Cambridge MA, Groton MA. H47.

259. **DANIEL[6] SAWYER** [see 114], b. 1 Nov 1781 Bolton MA, d. 4 Nov 1847 Bolton MA, m.(1) 24 May 1809 Bolton MA Rachel Jewett, b. 27 Feb 1783 d. 12 Nov 1843; m.(2) 19 Jun 1845 Lancaster MA Mary Whitney, b. 24 Oct 1785 d. 31 Dec 1848. Wheelwright.

Catherine, b. 29 Aug 1810, d. 7 Nov 1862, m. 7 Jun 1838 Jonathan Whitcomb.

519 Alfred[7], 1812-1897. Went to New Hampshire and Illinois.

Emily, b. 26 Jun 1815, d. 15 Dec 1874, m. 28 Apr 1841 Reuben Newton.

520 Edwin[7], 1817-1885.

Sources: Bolton MA census 1820, 1830, 1840. VR Bolton MA, SA/MA. J14, L16.

260. **OLIVER[6] SAWYER** [see 114], b. 3 Feb 1784 Bolton MA, d. 25 Mar 1836 Bolton MA, m.(1) 12 Apr 1809 Bolton MA Polly Whitcomb, b. ?; m.(2) 8 May 1821 Bolton MA Azubah Holman, b. 26 Feb 1786 d. 4 Jun 1839. Blacksmith.

Horace, b. 22 Feb 1811 Bolton MA.

Roxana, b. 3 May 1812, m. 3 Apr 1833 John H. Wood.

521 Oliver[7], b. 1818.

Sources: Bolton MA census 1810, 1820, 1830. VR Bolton MA.

261. **ELIAS[6] SAWYER** [see 114], b. 9 Oct 1791 Bolton MA, d. 16 Jan 1849 Lancaster MA, m. 19 Oct 1815 Nancy Ballard of Lancaster MA, b. 11 Sep 1792 d. 16 Dec 1849 Sterling MA, dau. John and Anna (Phelps) Ballard. Blacksmith, mechanic.

Charles Ballard, b. 26 Nov 1816 Lancaster MA, m. Sabrina L. Hawkins of Vergennes VT, b. 1823. Coppersmith. In Taunton MA 1850. CH: Louise M., b. 1845, m. 14 Feb 1867 Providence RI James J. Ford; Loraine Elizabeth, b. 15 Jul 1848, d. 9 Apr 1850 Taunton MA; Frances, b. 20 Feb 1854; Lizzie B., b. 19 Jun 1857; Hattie J., b. 24 Apr 1859; Emma C., b. 19 May 1861.

Mary Ann, b. 21 Nov 1820, d. 8 Jan 1846, m. 12 Apr 1843 James Chandler.

Emeline Amanda, b. 18 Sep 1822, m. 4 Feb 1847 Worcester MA Isaac Willard.

Abigail Barrett, b. 26 Nov 1824, d. 3 Oct 1842.

Louisa Augusta, b. 28 Nov 1827, d. 14 Jan 1844.

Francine E., b. 24 Sep 1832, d. 2 Sep 1833.

Frederick H., b. 24 Sep 1832, d. 9 May 1834.

Sources: Lancaster MA census 1820, 1830. Taunton MA census 1850. VR SA/MA. F5, C25, P63.

262. **SILAS[6] SAWYER** [see 114], b. 26 Nov 1793 Bolton MA, d. 24 Mar 1856 Lancaster MA, m. 9 Nov 1818 Bolton MA Sally Farnsworth, b. 2 Jul 1796 d. 15 Dec 1887, dau. Benjamin and Sally (Haskell) Farnsworth. Wheelwright.

522 Anthony Lane[7], b. 1821.

Francis Augustus, b. 18 Mar 1823 Bolton MA, d. 10 Jun 1846.

Lucy Ann, b. 9 Aug 1825, d. 28 Oct 1829.

Martha Salome, adopted, b. ?.

Sources: Bolton MA census 1820. Lancaster MA census 1830, 1840, 1850. VR Bolton MA.

263. **WILLIAM[6] SAWYER** [see 115], b. 13 Apr 1771 Lancaster MA, d. 28 Mar 1827, m. 30 Jan 1800 Lancaster MA Nancy Carter, b. 28 Jul 1777 d. 21 Jul 1844 Lancaster MA, dau. Levi and Silence (Beaman) Carter. In Orange MA 1801. Wid. in Sterling MA 1830, 1840.

Eliza, b. 26 May 1801, d. 1865, m. George Smith of Boston MA.

Mary, b. 27 Mar 1803, d. 12 Apr 1877, m. 27 Apr 1834 Alvin Haley.

Nancy, b. 12 Jan 1806, m. Mar 1828 Hiram Davis of Sterling MA.

Franklin, b. 1 Jul 1808, d. 24 May 1812.

Susan, b. 7 Feb 1813, d. 1881, m. 2 Sep 1838 Isaac Pulsifer of Boston MA.

William Franklin, b. 7 Dec 1814 Sterling MA, d. Aug 1868, m.(1) 17 Apr 1845 Fitchburg MA Nancy B. Ordway of Fitchburg MA, b. 1808; m.(2) 6 Sep 1866 Boston MA Susan (Haraden) Wilder of Wiscasset ME, b. 1828, dau. Thomas and Nancy Haraden. Chairmaker, farmer. CH: Charles S., b. 24 Jun 1858, d. 7 Aug 1858.

Caroline Augusta, b. 2 Aug 1819, d. 23 Mar 1886.

Sources: Sterling MA census 1810, 1820, 1830, 1840, 1850. VR Lancaster MA, Fitchburg MA. C9.

264. **SAMUEL FLAGG[6] SAWYER** [see 115], b. 20 Feb 1774 Sterling MA, d. 16 Apr 1853 Cambridge, m. 16 Feb 1800 Cambridge MA Patience (Sanger) Leonard, b. 30 Aug 1778. Mason. In Sterling MA. Selectman for Cambridge MA 1823-25.

Samuel, b. 20 Mar 1804 Cambridge MA, d. 4 Jan 1859 Cambridge MA, m. 21 Nov 1833 Lucy Tufts, b. Charlestown MA 1807, dau. Isaac and Lucy (Green) Tufts. Harvard Medical School 1831. Physician. In Fairhaven MA, San Francisco CA 1849-53. CH: Mary Ann Browner, b. 8 Mar 1835; Lucy, b. 5 Oct 1836; Caroline L., b. 7 Sep 1838; Ellen M., b. 16 Apr 1840; Martha E., b. 18 Jun 1842; Evelyn Augusta, b. 11 May 1844, m. 26 Oct 1887 Somerville MA Augustus A. Whitney.

Mary Ann, b. 15 Jan 1806, m. 26 Mar 1835 Jere Browner.

Louisa, b. 7 Apr 1808, m. 16 Nov 1836 William Thurston of Rhode Island.

Martha, b. 25 Feb 1810, m. 28 Sep 1841 Hubbard Lawrence.

Caroline, b. 19 Jul 1812, d. 23 Sep 1818.

John James, b. 29 Jul 1814 Cambridge MA, m.(1) 16 Oct 1850 Somerville MA Anna Morse Tufts of Somerville MA, b. 1816 d. 5 Sep 1871, dau. Isaac and Lucy (Green) Tufts; m.(2) 16 Dec 1873 Somerville MA Louisa Tufts of Charlestown MA, b. 1812, dau. Isaac and Lucy (Green) Tufts. Clerk of Court. Mexican War: US Navy. In Somerville MA.

Lucy Downing, b. 29 Sep 1816, d. 4 Oct 1872.

Sources: Cambridge MA census 1810, 1820, 1830, 1840, 1850. VR Cambridge MA, SA/MA.

265. **FRANKLIN[6] SAWYER** [see 115], b. 15 Jan 1778 Sterling MA, d. 1869 Kansas, m. 20 Feb 1806 Cambridge MA Mary Hastings, b. 1 Oct 1786 d. 31 May 1853. Mason.

Mary Elizabeth, b. 30 Sep 1807, m. 15 Oct 1830 Hannable Wright.

523 Franklin[7], 1809-1851.

Evelina, b. 9 Sep 1811, d. 22 Feb 1838, m. 29 Oct 1832 Thomas Atkinson.
Ann Lucretia, b. 5 Sep 1814, d. 21 May 1840.
Eliza Jane, b. 18 Apr 1817.
Caroline A., b. 19 May 1819, m. 4 Aug 1846 Charles Ingersoll.

Sources: Cambridge MA census 1810, 1820, 1830, 1840, 1850. VR Cambridge MA, SA/MA. C8, A20, P1, A38.

266. **CHARLES$^6$ SAWYER** [see 115], b. 1808 Princeton MA, m. 12 Sep 1833 Princeton MA Margaret C. Maynard of Groton VT, b. 1811. Farmer, spinner.

524 Alphonso Brooks$^7$, b. 1837.
Sophronia R., b. 10 Jan 1840, m. 18 Oct 1870 Holden MA Stephen N. Hubbard.
Charles Jason, b. 29 Jul 1850 Holden MA.

Sources: Holden MA census 1840, 1850. VR Holden MA, Princeton MA, SA/MA.

267. **JOHN$^6$ SAWYER** [see 116], b. 21 Feb 1767 Lancaster MA, d. 25 Feb 1842 Templeton MA, m. 8 Jan 1793 Templeton MA Phebe Knight of Sterling MA, b. 2 Mar 1768 d. 8 Mar 1852, dau. Ebenezer and Prudence Knight. Farmer.

Paul, b. 19 Jan 1794 Templeton MA.
Betsey, b. 9 Aug 1795, d. 23 Jun 1839, unm.
John, b. 7 Sep 1797, d. 1797.
Silas, b. 14 Mar 1799 Templeton MA, d. Nov 1817 Charlestown MA.
Talmon, b. 5 Nov 1800, d. 16 Oct 1810.
Jotham, b. 25 Apr 1802 Templeton MA.
Ebenezer, b. 30 Apr 1804 Templeton MA.
525 John$^7$, b. 1805.
Phebe, b. 29 Jul 1810, d. 4 Jan 1852 Templeton MA.

Sources: Templeton MA census 1800, 1810, 1820, 1830, 1840. VR Templeton MA, SA/MA.

268. **ELIAS$^6$ SAWYER** [see 117], b. 3 Nov 1778 Templeton MA, d. 23 Oct 1838, m. 30 Nov 1809 Heath MA Harriet L. Williams of Heath MA, b. 6 May 1787 d. 11 Apr 1829. In Heath MA, Charlemont MA. Tombstone on Mohawk Trail near Route 2.

526 Elijah$^7$, b. 1819.
More unnamed children listed in 1820 census.

Sources: Heath MA census 1810, Charlemont MA census 1820. VR Heath MA, Charlemont MA.

269. **ELISHA$^6$ SAWYER** [see 117], b. 10 May 1783 Templeton MA, m. 22 Jan 1811 Phillipston MA Esther Bruce of Phillipston MA, b. ?. Farmer.

Adaline Bruce,b. 1812, m. 11 Apr 1836 Richard Fry of Athol MA.
Julia Fisher, b. 1818, m. 6 Jul 1847 Templeton MA Charles Leland.
Elijah Harrington, b. 1819 Templeton MA, d. 9 Nov 1851 Michigan, m. 6 Jan 1843 Dana MA Sophia E. Blackman of Dana MA, b. 6 Jan 1819. Wheelwright.
527 Elisha Emery$^7$, b. 1822.

Sources: Templeton MA census 1820, 1830, 1840, 1850. Dana MA census 1850. VR Templeton MA, Phillipston MA, Dana MA, SA/MA.

270. **JAMES$^6$ SAWYER** [see 117], b. 17 May 1785 Templeton MA, d. 26 Mar 1858 Templeton MA, m. 28 Nov 1813 Templeton MA Seraph Baldwin of Templeton MA, b. 31 Jan 1793, dau. Eden and Abigail W. (Force) Baldwin. Carpenter, millwright.

Addison, b. 1814, d. 17 Feb 1814.
Sherlock, b. ?, d. 9 Feb 1816.

Seraph W., b. 7 Dec 1815, m. Joel Whitney of Sterling MA.
Rebecca, b. 19 Aug 1818, m. Thomson Way of Worcester MA.
James, b. 1820, d. 28 Mar 1822.
James Sullivan, b. 11 Nov 1821 Templeton MA, d. 5 Dec 1853, m. 2 Apr 1850 Brattleboro VT Marie Divol of Winchendon MA, b. ?. Carpenter, architect. In Templeton MA.
528 Eden Baldwin[7], b. 1823. Went to Texas.
Louisa H., b. 23 Oct 1825, m. 6 Apr 1856 Edward Greenwood of Gardner MA.
Mary A., b. 5 Nov 1827.
Christopher Columbus, b. 3 Apr 1829, m. Martha Brown, b. ?.
Adelaide R., b. 13 Nov 1831.
Sources: Templeton MA census 1820, 1850. VR Templeton MA, SA/MA. B11.

271. **JOHN[6] SAWYER** [see 117], b. 24 Mar 1787 Templeton MA, d. 28 Oct 1856 Templeton MA, m.(1) 28 Mar 1802 Templeton MA Asenath Fairbanks, b. ?; m.(2) 11 Feb 1811 Templeton MA Lucy Balcomb, b. 178?. Farmer.
Joel, b. 31 Jan 1808, d. 9 Jan 1811.
529 Joseph Balcomb[7], b. 1819.
Sylvanus, b. 15 Apr 1822 Templeton MA, d. 13 Oct 1895 Fitchburg MA, unm. Inventor. In Fitchburg MA 1851-1855. Worked in Augusta ME.
530 Addison Monroe[7], 1827-1890.
More unnamed children listed in census.
Sources: Templeton MA census 1820, 1830, 1850. VR Templeton MA SA/MA. L18, A20.

272. **JOSEPH[6] SAWYER** [see 117], b. 2 Feb 1798 Templeton MA, d. Fitchburg MA, m. 26 Dec 1820 Royalston MA Jerusha Blanchard of Royalston MA, b. ?. Mechanic.
531 Sylvester[7], 1822-1895.
Frances R., b. 1824, d. 4 Jul 1882, m. 14 Dec 1842 George Colburn.
More unnamed children listed in census.
Sources: Royalston MA census 1830, 1840, 1850. VR Templeton MA, Royalston MA.

273. **ELISHA[6] SAWYER** [see 118], b. 16 Feb 1790 Plymouth VT, m. 26 Dec 1822 Rutland VT Sally Palmer, b. ?. In Benson VT 1830.
Henry, b. 1823.
More unnamed children listed in census.
Sources: Benson VT census 1830. VR SA/VT.

274. **JOSEPH WHEELER[6] SAWYER** [see 118], b. 7 Mar 1794 Plymouth VT, d. 8 Dec 1874 Watertown NY,m. 25 Oct 1818 Mary Roper, b. 21 Oct 1797 d. 12 Apr 1873.
Elvira M., b. 22 Aug 1820, d. 20 Aug 1843, unm.
Melissa E., b. 8 Aug 1822, d. 1850, m. Dr. William T. Clark.
Laurentus Thomas, b. 25 Nov 1824, m. 13 Dec 1858 Carriane Tollman.
Mariette, b. 15 Jul 1826, d. 6 May 1881, m. 25 Feb 1846 Aaron O. Sawyer.
Charlotte Maria, b. 19 Jun 1830, d. 10 Nov 1851, unm.
Fanny L., b. 12 Nov 1832, d. 4 Jan 1883, m. 22 Sep 1858 George W. Hammond.
Joseph B., b. 16 Jun 1838, d. 21 Jul 1838.
Sources: C8, D6.

275. **JESSIE[6] SAWYER** [see 118], b. 24 May 1796 Plymouth VT, m. 1819 Elizabeth Goodell, b. 17 Mar 1794. In Utica NY.

Lorenzo, b. 23 May 1820, d. 7 Sep 1891, m. 10 Mar 1857 Jennie (Jones) Aldrich, b. ?. Went to San Francisco CA.

William J., b. 1829 Watertown NY, m. 25 Dec 1856 Monson MA Jane F. Bradford of Monson MA, b. ca. 1827, dau. Otis and Betsey Bradford. In Massachusetts.

Sources: SA/MA. N5.

276. **JOSHUA[6] SAWYER** [see 119], b. 25 Nov 1760 Haverhill MA, d. 24 Feb 1840 Dorset VT, m. Margarette _____, b. 1778 d. 22 Jan 1830. In Atkinson NH, Berlin VT. Dorset VT 1830. He bur. in Maple Hill Cem., Dorset VT.

Catherine S., b. 1809, d. 12 Feb 1848.

Mehitable, b. ca. 1810.

532 Joshua[7], 1816-1888.

2 daughters, b. ?.

Sources: Dorset VT census 1830. VR Haverhill MA, Manchester VT, SA/VT.

277. **JAMES[6] SAWYER** [see 119], b. Jan 1765 Haverhill MA, d. 11 Jul 1859 Berlin VT, m. 2 Jun 1805 Berlin VT Anne Howe, b. 21 Feb 1780 d. 1 Aug 1819, dau. Elisha and Anna (Holliston) Howe. Farmer. B/land in Berlin VT 1794. Brother Edward res. w/James in Berlin VT 1841.

James J., b. 12 Apr 1806 Berlin VT, d. 8 Nov 1835 Berlin VT. CH: Dau. b. (1825-1830).

Lydia, b. 10 Feb 1808, d. 17 Jun 1881.

Sally, b. 1 Feb 1812, d. 4 Jan 1880, unm.

Edward Flint, b. 20 Mar 1814 Berlin VT, d. 9 Jul 1861.

Solomon W., b. 26 Nov 1816 Berlin VT, d. in mill accident 22 Apr 1872 Milford NH, m. 31 Jan 1848 Hillsboro NH Eliza M. Marcy, b. 29 Oct 1820 d. 4 Mar 1905. Millwright. Went to Milford NH from Hillsboro NH. CH: Amy Lizzie, b. 19 Oct 1849, d. 13 Mar 1896, m. 27 Aug 1872 George Bryant; dau, b. 30 Aug 1851 Hillsboro NH; Edward Norman, b. 18 Jan 1858, d. 17 Jun 1864.

533 Norman Davis[7], 1819-1885.

Sources: Berlin VT census 1790, 1800, 1810, 1820, 1830, 1840, 1850. Johnson VT census 1830. VR SA/VT. J7, H80, B69, N46, James' Bible, Norman D. Sawyer rec.

278. **SAMUEL[6] SAWYER** [see 119], b. 19 Apr 1767 Haverhill MA, m. 7 May 1793 Alstead NH Sarah Wheelock of Alstead NH, b. ca. 1775. Gold/silversmith. In Atkinson NH, Alstead NH, Surrey NH 1800. Wid. in Surrey NH 1820.

Sally, b. 27 Sep 1795, m. 4 Feb 1812 John T. Wilcox of New York.

Happy, b. 27 Nov 1797, m. 13 Oct 1816 Peter Joslin, Jr.

Samuel, b. 219 Feb 1799 Alstead NH. Went to New York City.

Betsey, b. 16 May 1801, d. 14 Apr 1806.

James, b. 11 Sep 1803, d. 1823.

Maria, b. 31 Dec 1805, d. 11 Jan 1806.

Amos, b. 6 Jan 1807 Surrey NH.

Sources: Surrey NH census 1800, 1810, 1820. VR Haverhill MA. N14, K15, N6.

279. **DUDLEY[6] SAWYER** [see 119], b. 31 May 1772 Haverhill MA, d. 3 Apr 1855 Ann Arbor MI, m. 15 Nov 1801 Berlin VT Olive Field of New Hampshire, b. 31 Jan 1781, dau. Bennett and Elizabeth (Pierce) Field. In Atkinson NH, Berlin VT.

Leander, b. 1810 (Berlin VT?), d. 1874, m. 1836 Harriet P. Leonard, b. ?.

Sources: VR Haverhill MA, SA/VT. D6, P50.

280. **JOSHUA⁶ SAWYER** [see 120], b. 11 Jul 1771 Atkinson NH, d. 19 May 1830 Concord NH (suicide), m. 23 Oct 1792 Abigail. Belnap of Atkinson NH, b. 1771 d. 28 Jan 1853. Tavern owner. Town Moderator for Atkinson NH 1814. He bur. Old North Cem., Concord NH.

Judith, b. 30 Jan 1795, d. 30 Feb 1795.
534 Jonathan Ayer[7], 1799-1840.
535 Jesse L.[7], b. 1802.
Joseph Sprague, b. 9 May 1806, d. 20 May 1806.

Sources: Atkinson NH census 1810. VR Concord NH, Haverhill MA, SA/MA.

281. **AMOS[6] SAWYER** [see 120], b. 15 Jun 1788 Atkinson NH, d. 5 May 1857 Atkinson NH, m. 26 Dec 1822 Atkinson NH, Mary R. Webster of Atkinson NH, b. 2 Apr 1789 d. 18 Nov 1857, dau. Joseph and Sarah (Bailey) Webster. Farmer, wheelwright. War of 1812. Justice of the Peace. Town Moderator. Selectman, 1827, 1831, 1833-35. Will dated 9 Mar 1853.

536 Jesse Augustus[7], 1823-1915.
537 Alanson Mason[7], 1825-1895.

Sources: Atkinson NH census 1820, 1830, 1840, 1850. M39, N9, N14, P82g, Ruth L. Sawyer rec.

282. **DAVID[6] SAWYER** [see 122], b. Sep 1779 Bradford MA, d. 26 Jul 1859 Haverhill MA, m. 29 Jun 1800 Sally Wood of Bradford MA, b. 4 Aug 1784 d. 9 Oct 1874, dau. Samuel and Lucy Wood. Shoemaker.

538 Leonard[7], ca. 1808.
539 Moses W.[7], b. ca. 1810.
540 Richard[7], b. 1814.
Annie R., b. ca. 1829, m. 16 Dec 1856 Boston MA Joseph C. Brook.
Six more unnamed children in census.

Sources: Bradford MA census 1810. Haverhill MA census 1830, 1840. SA/MA.

283. **THOMAS WHITTIER[6] SAWYER** [see 123], b. 13 Dec 1805 Haverhill MA, d. before 1835 Haverhill MA, m. 3 Jul 1828 Haverhill MA Eunice Maria Greenough, b.?. Wid. m. Harrison Sawyer 1835.

Albert J., b. ca. 1829, m. 27 Nov 1850 Boston MA Maria H. Fernald of Boston MA, b. ca. 1826, dau. Oliver Fernald. Bookkeeper.

Sources: Haverhill MA census 1850. VR Haverhill MA, SA/MA.

284. **HARRISON[6] SAWYER** [see 123], b. 9 Dec 1811 Haverhill MA, m.(1) 24 Nov 1835 Haverhill MA Eunice (Greenough) Sawyer, wid. of Harrison's brother Thomas, b. 1811 d. 30 Nov 1860, dau. Moses and Eunice Greenough; m.(2) 29 Apr 1863 Newburyport MA Abbie Knapp Livingston of Newburyport MA, b. 1824,. dau. Alexander and Abigail Livingston. Shoe cutter. In Haverhill MA 1850.

Albert Livingston, b. 24 Jul 1864, d. 1933, unm.

Sources: Haverhill MA census 1850. VR Haverhill MA, SA/MA. H32.

285. **EBENEZER[6] SAWYER** [see 124], b. 10 Oct 1787 Thetford VT, m.(1) 17 Mar 1824 Vershire VT Laura Paine of Vershire VT, b. 18 Aug 1809, dau. Jesse and Polly (Robinson) Paine; m.(2) Mary Bartlett, b. 24 Sep 1785 d. 28 Mar 1871, dau. Ebenezer and Mary Bartlett. War of 1812. In Thetford VT 1830, Hartford VT 1850.

James, b. 26 Dec 1824 Thetford VT, d. 4 Feb 1881 Vineland NJ, m. 17 May 1858 Lucy Dunham, b. 8 Oct 1826 d. 30 Dec 1897.
Laury Ann, b. 5 May 1826.
Elizabeth, b. 17 Oct 1827, d. 12 Dec 1853 Boston MA.

Mary, b. 26 Oct 1829.
Harriet, b. 28 Feb 1832.
John, b. 1834 (Thetford VT?). In Hartford VT 1850.
Sources: Thetford VT census 1830. Hartford VT census 1850. VR SA/VT. P2, J18.

286. **JONATHAN$^6$ SAWYER** [see 125], b. 5 Nov 1772 Danvers MA, d. 1845 Levant ME, m. 23 Dec 1803 Martha Reed, b. 26 Oct 1770 d. 3 Jul 1812, dau. Joseph and Sarah (Wylie) Reed. Blacksmith. In Boothbay ME 1800, 1810. W/nephew Alfred in Montville ME 1840.
Betsey, b. 15 Oct 1804, d. in Camden ME.
Sarah, b. 2 Apr 1806, d. in New York.
Mary H., b. 28 Sep 1807, d. 17 Apr 1892 Brewster ME.
541 Joseph Reed$^7$, 1809-1884.
542 Warren$^7$, b. 1811.
Sources: Boothbay ME census 1800, 1810. Montville ME census 1840. VR Danvers MA. G41, M29.

287. **ALFRED$^6$ SAWYER** [see 125], b. 11 Jan 1794 Danvers MA, d. 6 Jun 1861 Montville ME, m. 17 Aug 1821 Knox ME Sarah M. Evans of Gilmanton NH, b. 1796 d. 31 Mar 1895, dau. Ephraim and Polly (Batchelder) Evans. Merchant. War of 1812. B/land in Knox ME 1821. In Montville ME 1840. Will dated 19 Apr 1861. He bur. Halldale Cem., Montville ME. Wid. went to Freedom ME.
Laura M., b. 1824.
543 Ephraim E.$^7$, b. 1825-1909.
Hannah T., b. ca. 1827, m. _____ McLaughlin.
Alfred, b. ca. 1829 Montville ME, m. 1 Jan 1857 Boston MA Elizabeth Oakman of Marshfield MA, b. ca. 1839. Carpenter.
Phebe G., b. 1833, m. Asa M. Gowen.
Eloise R., b. Apr 1834, d. 26 Aug 1863, m. Aaron C. Plummer.
Winfield Scott, b. 1838, d. 19 Aug 1865, unm.
Sources: Montville ME census 1840, 1850. VR SA/MA, SA/ME. G41, P82j, M5.

288. **AMOS$^6$ SAWYER** [see 126], b. 6 Jun 1776 Haverhill MA, d. 14 Sep 1851 Salem MA, m.(1) 7 June 1798 Ipswich MA Mary Appleton of Ipswich MA, b. 2 Dec 1772 d. 25 Aug 1829 Salem MA, dau. Samuel and Mary (White) Appleton; m.(2) Hannah _____, b. ca. 1784. Goldsmith.
Appleton, b. 5 Apr 1799, d. 1825 at sea.
544 Leverett$^7$, 1801-1839.
Augustus, b. 8 Jul 1804, d. 21 Sep 1805 Charlestown MA.
Augustus, b. 23 Jan 1809, d. 5 Nov 1827.
Mary E., b. 30 Jan 1812.
Sources: Beverly MA census 1810. Salem MA census 1820, 1830, 1840, 1850. VR Salem MA, Beverly MA, Ipswich MA, Haverhill MA, Boston MA, SA/MA. E20.

289. **AARON$^6$ SAWYER** [see 127], b. 1781 Boothbay ME, m.(1) 1 Jul 1805 Boothbay ME Abigail Kenney, b. 1783 d. 20 Jul 1806; m.(2) Rosanna Dodge of Isleboro ME, b. 1791 d. 1869 Bangor ME. Tanner. B/S/land in Belfast ME 1816. In Isleboro ME, Belfast ME, Bangor ME.
545 Benjamin W.$^7$, 1811-1865.
Helen, b. 1834, d. 4 Jul 1915 Bangor ME.
Sources: Isleboro ME census 1810. Bangor ME census 1840. VR SA/ME. R10e, G41.

290. **BENJAMIN[6] SAWYER** [see 127], b. 1783 Boothbay ME, m.(1) 30 Oct 1810 Mima Wines, b. ? d. 8 Sep 1817; m.(2) 12 Jan 1819 Charlotte (Long) Wilde of Newport NH, b. 10 Nov 1797. Dartmouth College 1808. Minister. In Cape Elizabeth ME 1813.

546 Benjamin Edwards[7], 1811-1879.
Ann Maria, b. 1 Mar 1813, d. 11 Oct 1895, m. 31 Jan 1833 Orlando S. Patten.
Henry Homes, b. 25 Jul 1815 Amesbury MA. In Salisbury MA 1850. Teacher.
Mima W., b. 8 Nov 1819, d. 17 Jan 1865, m. 8 Nov 1841 John Q. Evans.
Mary W., b. 29 Dec 1820, m. 22 Oct 1840 Alfred Clough.
Ezra Worthen, b. 23 Sep 1823 Amesbury MA, d. 18 Apr 1851. Clerk.
Sarah, b. 3 May 1826, m. 30 Oct 1848 Salisbury MA Felix D. Parry.
Mary G. W., b. 9 Feb 1830.
Charlotte A., b. 28 Jun 1832.

Sources: Amesbury MA census 1820. Salisbury MA census 1840, 1850. VR Amesbury MA, SA/MA. E25, G41, B17.

291. **JOSHUA[6] SAWYER** [see 127], b. 1785 Boothbay ME, m. 22 Nov 1808 Mt. Desert ME Abigail Milliken, b. Jul 1787 d. 2 May 1862, dau. Samuel and Susannah Milliken. Farmer.

Joshua, b. 5 Mar 1810, d.y.
Sophronia, b. 28 Sep 1811, m. Lewis Freeman.
547 Jacob[7], 1813-1897.
Eliza, b. 18 Jun 1815, m. George Pierce.
548 Benjamin[7], 1817-1892.
Willard, b. 6 Mar 1819 Mt. Desert ME, lost at sea.
Edward, b. 4 Jan 1821 Mt. Desert ME.
Joshua, b. 15 Dec 1822 Mt. Desert ME.
William Penn, b. 23 Sep 1825 Mt. Desert ME, d. 8 Jun 1899 Tremont ME, m. 4 Jul 1855 Tremont ME Nancy S. Newman, b. 1839. Ship carpenter. He bur. in Tremont ME. CH: Addy M., b. 1859, m. 21 Aug 1884 Tremont ME P_____ Kittredge; Phebe M., b. 1862.
549 Caleb Hodgdon[7], 1828-1902.
Julia A., b. 1830, d. 1 Jul 1846.

Sources: Mt. Desert ME census 1810, 1820, 1830, 1840. Tremont ME census 1850, 1870. VR Saco ME, Rockland ME, SA/MA, SA/ME. L30, G41.

292. **STEPHEN[6] SAWYER** [see 127], b. 4 Jul 1794 Mt. Desert ME, d. 17 Jul 1849 Boothbay ME, m. 15 Jul 1820 Abigail Anderson of Wiscasset ME, b. 17 Oct 1798 d. 13 Dec 1870. Sea captain. Wid. in Boothbay ME 1850.

Wilmot, b. 25 Feb 1821, d. 23 Mar 1821.
Louisa, b. 19 Sep 1822, d. 1895, m. Robert Day of Damariscotta ME.
Stephen, b. 24 Aug 1824, d. 4 Feb 1830.
Simeon, b. 19 Sep 1826 Boothbay ME, d. California, m. 27 Jun 1868 Bristol-Nobleboro ME Mary E. Day of Damariscotta ME, b. ?. In Gold Rush 1849.
Abigail, b. 7 Oct 1828.
Stephen, b. 5 Oct 1831 Boothbay ME.
Sarah E., b. 15 Dec 1833, m. Elias H. Fisk of Newcastle ME.
Henry C., b. 27 Feb 1836 Boothbay ME, d. San Francisco CA, m. Abbie E._____, b. ?. Ship builder. CH: Flora E., b. 26 Aug 1863; Edith A., b. 4 Jan 1865.
550 William M.[7], 1838-1906.
Mary Eliza, b. 30 Jun 1841, d. 1926, m. 1863 Benjamin S. Reed.

Sources: Boothbay ME census 1830, 1840, 1850. VR Boothbay ME, Edgecomb ME, Bristol ME. G41, M29.

293. **SIMEON⁶ SAWYER** [see 127], b. 1803 Kent Isle ME, d. 17 Dec 1864, m.(1) Eliza Butler of Boothbay ME, b. ?; m.(2) 4 May 1854 Charlestown MA Lydia D. (Butler) Blaisdell of Mt. Desert ME, b. ca. 1813, dau. George and Lydia Butler. Master mariner.

Lydia B., b. 22 Apr 1827, m. 21 Aug 1851 Charlestown MA Alexander Hodgdon.
Simeon, b. 2 Oct 1828 Boothbay ME.
John M., b. 11 Nov 1830 Boothbay ME, d. Jan 1865 at sea, m. 26 Apr 1855 Charlestown MA Phebe R. Hodgdon of Boothbay ME, b. 29 Jan 1828 d. 8 Aug 1907, dau. Tyler and Jerusha (Parsons) Hodgdon. Sea captain. Wid. m. Wilmot Lewis. CH: George W., b. 21 Jun 1856, d. 24 Dec 1875; Melvin, b. 5 Jun 1859, d. 8 May 1864.
Sarah, b. 10 May 1832.
Clarissa A., b. 5 Nov 1834, m. 27 Jan 1856 Charlestown MA Charles Fernald.
Eliza A., b. 25 Mar 1837, m. 19 Apr 1859 Charlestown MA Silas A. Yuill(?).
Mary Butler, b. 4 Nov 1838, d. 14 Dec 1911, m. 5 Feb 1862 Somerville MA Loring Goodell.
William, b. 22 Dec 1840 Boothbay ME,
Alexander, b. 25 Sep 1842 Boothbay ME.
Martha E., b. 12 Apr 1844, m. 18 Jan 1866 Somerville MA William F. Tuttle.
Wilmot, b. 6 May 1846, d.y.
Lenora H., b. 17 Oct 1849 Boothbay ME, m. 11 Nov 1869 Boston MA Edgar W. Savalow.
Eupherna, b. ca. 1852.

Sources: Mt. Desert ME census 1830. Boothbay ME census 1840, 1850, 1860, VR Boothbay ME, Woodstock CT, SA/MA.

294. **SAMUEL⁶ SAWYER** [see 127],b. 1808 Kents Isle ME, m.(1) Lydia _____, b. 1805 d. 13 Apr 1851; m.(2) 25 Feb 1853 Boothbay ME Martha Farnham, b. ?; m.(3) 23 Jul 1872 Salem MA Eliza A. Buzzell of Malden MA or Deerfield NH, b. ca. 1832, dau. William and Hannah _____ (her m.(2), no maiden name given). Sea captain, carpenter. Built first tannery in Boothbay ME. In Mt. Desert ME 1830, Boothbay ME 1840, Chelsea MA 1872.

Lydia A., b. 2 Nov 1826.
Samuel, b. 21 Sep 1828 Boothbay ME, d. 21 Jun 1851 at sea.
Robert A., b. 21 Jun 1830 Boothbay ME, d. 19 Oct 1856.
Lucy H., b. 22 Apr 1832, m. 7 Apr 1852 Boston MA Nicholas H. Habig.
George B., b. 5 Jun 1834, d. 16 Feb 1839.
Alvira R., b. 10 Oct 1836, m. 16 Jan 1859 Boston MA Joseph A. Tuten.
Louisa, b. Oct 1839.
Franklin, b. 27 Oct 1840 Boothbay ME, d. 19 Mar 1862 in Civil War: Private, Company G, 5th Maine Regiment.
Alden L., b. 13 Jul 1844, d. 19 Oct 1856.
Jessie L. (f), b. 6 Mar 1873.

Sources: Mt. Desert ME census 1830. Boothbay ME census 1840, 1850. VR Boothbay ME, SA/MA. G41.

295. **PAUL⁶ SAWYER** [see 128], b. 1790 Boothbay ME, d. 5 Oct 1866 North Haven ME, m. 20 May 1816 Vinalhaven ME Diadena Cooper, b. 1798. Sea captain. In Vinalhaven ME 1820, North Haven ME 1850.

551 Stephen⁷, b. 1816.
552 William Yeaton⁷, 1818-1903.
553 Walter S.⁷, 1822-1900.
Knott, b. 1828 Vinalhaven ME.

Barbary, b. 1834.
554 Reuben Freeman$^7$, b. 1837.
555 Horace M.$^7$, 1839-1907.
Sources: Vinalhaven ME census 1820, 1830, 1840. North Haven ME census 1850. VR Vinalhaven ME, SA/ME. B23.

296. **NATHANIEL$^6$ SAWYER** [see 128], b. 18 Nov 1792 Boothbay ME, d. 26 Nov 1870 Isleboro ME, m. 28 Dec 1815 Deer Isle ME Sarah Grover, b. 16 Sep 1794 d. 14 Feb 1871. Shipbuilder. B/land in Belmont ME 1839.
William, b. 24 Mar 1817, d. 22 Apr 1817.
Eliza B., b. 28 Aug 1818, m. 9 Jan 1836 David Collins II.
556 Paul$^7$, 1820-1888.
Amelia, b. 14 Jan 1826, m. William Collins.
Matilda T., b. 1 Sep 1827, m. 3 Jan 1847 Gamaliel R. Pendleton.
Nathan, b. 1 Sep 1827, d.y.
557 George Washington$^7$,b. 1828.
Sarah M., b. 10 Jul 1832, m.(1) 16 Jan 1851 Rodolphus Pendleton, m.(2) 1873 Leonard Martin.
558 Elbridge Blanchard$^7$, 1834-1873.
Mary A., b. 3 Mar 1837, m. Charles A. Coburn.
Lydia A., b. 3 Mar 1837, m. Stephen B. Coombs.
Sources: Deer Isle Me census 1820, 1830. Belmont ME census 1840. Isleboro ME census 1850. VR Deer Isle ME, SA/ME. R10b, P26, L30.

297. **EBENEZER$^6$ SAWYER** [see 128], b. 13 Jul 1803 Deer Isle ME, d. 5 Apr 1893 Searsport ME, m. 24 Jul 1826 Elcey Kempton, b. 1 Nov 1807 d. 23 Apr 1882, dau. Charles and Lucy (Stinson) Kempton. Ship carpenter. He bur. in cem. between Searsport and Belfast ME.
559 Charles Kempton$^7$, 1827-1878.
560 Stephen$^7$, 1828-1891.
Elcey, b. 13 Jan 1831, d. 27 Jan 1896, m. Lincoln Gilkey.
Artimus T., b. 7 Nov 1833 Deer Isle ME, d. 16 Aug 1857, m. Aberine (Gilkey) Towle, b. 1837 d. 1922, dau. Isaac and Martha Gilkey. In Searsport ME. Wid. in Searsport ME 1860. He bur. in cem. between Searsport and Belfast ME.
561 Eben A.$^7$, 1836-1905.
562 William Babbidge$^7$, 1839-1910.
Elizabeth M., b. 8 Oct 1841, m. Alonzo Hanson.
Phebe B., b. 12 Jan 1844, d. 22 May 1937, m. George A. Darling.
Sources: Deer Isle ME census 1830, 1840. Searsport ME census 1850. ME 1880 census index. VR Deer Isle Me, SA/ME. Family Bible, Jane McCormick rec.

298. **PETER$^6$ SAWYER** [see 129], b. 17 Nov 1780 Haverhill MA, d. 11 Apr 1835 Haverhill MA, m. 30 Apr 1809 Charlotte Chickering, b. 25 May 1782 d. 30 Jun 1847, dau. John and Sarah (Webster) Chickering. Wheelwright. Charlotte joined church in Charlestown MA 8 Nov 1812. Wid. in Charlestown MA 1840 and bur. there in Old Burial Ground.
Maria, b. 11 Oct 1809, d. 22 Dec 1827.
Sarah Webster, b. 1 Oct 1811, d. 1826.
Charlotte, b. 28 Oct 1813, m. 30 Nov 1837 Hosea Whitney.
William Bainbridge, b. 13 Mar 1816 Charlestown MA.
Elizabeth Ann, b. 6 Jun 1818, d. 4 Feb 1821.
Martha C., b. ca. 1821, m. 6 Aug 1855 Charlestown MA Franklin Holmes.

563 Otis Vinal[6], b. 1822. Mary Ann Tufts, b. 28 Aug 1824, d. 3 Feb 1827.
John Chickering, b. Sep 1828, d. 27 Mar 1830.
Sources: Charlestown MA census 1810, 1820, 1830, 1840. VR Haverhill MA, Charlestown MA, SA/MA. H90, C34, W72, P46.

299. **WILLIAM[6] SAWYER** [see 129], b. 3 Mar 1783 Haverhill MA, d. 12 May 1830 Charlestown MA, m. 20 Sep 1807 Susannah Thompson of Charlestown MA, b. 24 Mar 1791 d. 9 Jan 1886. Dry goods dealer. B/land in Unity ME 1829, S/land to son William 1830. Wid. in Charlestown MA 1830.
564 William[7], 1807-1852.
Susan Lavinia, b. 12 Sep 1809, unm.
Mary Thompson, b. 7 Jan 1812, d. 25 Mar 1860, unm.
Harriet E., b. 29 Sep 1814, m. 1 Sep 1835 David S. Messinger.
565 Timothy Thompson[7], b. 1817.
Lydia Ann, b. 4 May 1821, d. 2 Sep 1823.
Frances Ann, b. 4 Jul 1826, d. 9 Sep 1906, m. 22 Mar 1849 Abraham Prichard.
Sarah M., b. 2 May 1829, d. 15 Oct 1885, unm.
Hannah F., b. ?, m. 19 Dec 1906 George G. Lee.
Sources: Charlestown MA census 1810, 1820, 1830. W72, S19, H90, D6, T14A, R10e.

300. **LEONARD[6] SAWYER** [see 129], b. 12 Jan 1787 Haverhill MA, d. 24 Jun 1841 Haverhill MA, m.(I) 25 May 1812 Haverhill MA Abigail Brickett, b. Apr 1788 d. 26 Mar 1876, dau. John and Abigail (Haseltine) Brickett.
566 James Brickett[7], b. 1812.
Abigail, b. 8 Sep 1814, d. 5 Feb 1844, m. 10 Oct 1839 Nathan Johnson.
Leonard, b. 15 Aug 1816 Haverhill MA.
Susan B., b. 12 Sep 1821, m. 25 Oct 1842 Samuel Beach.
567 William F.[7], b. 1821.
Charles, b. 16 Aug1823 Haverhill MA, d. 11 Feb 1853 Haverhill MA, m. 1 May 1844 Lowell MA Clarina Amanda Jennings of Leeds ME, b. 13 Feb 1823 d. 4 Mar 1911, dau. Lewis and Abigail (Foster) Jennings. Machinist/RR. CH: Clarina Adelea, b. 4 Nov 1847, d. Mar 1931, m. 26 Dec 1872 John Wesley Reed.
568 Joseph Warren[7], 1826-1885.
Sources: Lowell MA census 1850. VR Haverhill MA, Lowell MA, SA/MA. S35, Wilfred M. Sawyer rec.

301. **EBENEZER[6] SAWYER** [see 130], b. ca. 1791 (Grafton NH?), m. Lucretia_____ of Massachusetts, b. 1797.
Lucretia, b. ca. 1831.
Jefferson, b. ca. 1835 Grafton NH.
Franklin, b. ca. 1840 Grafton NH.
Mary, b. ca. 1844.
Sources: Grafton NH census 1850.

302. **ISAAC[6] SAWYER** [see 131], b. 22 Feb 1779 Atkinson NH, d. 31 Oct 1834 Stockbridge VT, m.(1) 20 Mar 1809 Stockbridge VT Charlotte Green, wid., b. 1779 d. 27 Apr 1816; m.(2) 6 Nov 1816 Stockbridge VT Polly L. Belcher of New Hampshire, b. 1784 d. 7 Aug 1857.
2 dau., b. (1810-1815).
1 son, b. (1815-1820).
569 Samuel B.[7], 1818-1875.

1 dau., b. (1830-1835).

Sources: Stockbridge VT census 1820, 1830. VR Stockbridge VT, SA/VT.

303. **BENJAMIN[6] SAWYER** [see 131], b. 1801 Alstead NH, m. 11 Jul 1822 Stockbridge VT Eliza Richardson, b. ?. In Atkinson NH, Stockbridge VT 1830, Norfolk NY 1839.

Alvah Carlos, b. 14 Apr 1823.
Esther Richarson, b. 15 Aug 1824.
Russell Hurd, b. 20 Jun 1826.
Calista Jemima, b. Feb 1828.
Thirza, b. 16 Mar 1830.
Leonard, b. Jul 1831, d. 21 Feb 1834.
Isabella, b. Nov 1834, d. May 1836.
Marilla Eleanor, b. 19 May 1842 Norfolk NY.

Sources: Stockbridge VT census 1830. VR SA/VT.

304. **ELIPHALET[6] SAWYER** [see 131], b. 1802 Alstead NH, d. 1 Apr 1835 Stockbridge VT, m. Persis Barr (or Gould) of New York, b. ? d. 30 Jun 1859. He bur. in South Hill Cem., Stockbridge VT. Wid. m. Elijah Lamb 1843.

Mary A., b. 2 Mar 1820, d. 10 Dec 1889, m. Andrew Littlefield.
Priscilla, b. 27 Nov 1825, d. 16 Apr 1896, m. 16 Oct 1843 Dr. Ezekiel Lamb.
Henry C., b. ca. 1829, m. 16 Aug 1853 Nina Bagley, b. ?.
Emily L., b. 2 Jan 1831, d. 22 Jun 1916, m. 29 Jan 1855 Dr. Edwin J. Farr.
Arabella M., b. 14 Jan 1833, d. 14 Mar 1900, m.(1) David Joslyn, m.(2) Isaac Monroe.
Olive, b. 1835, d. 26 Sep 1859 in Brattleboro VT asylum.

Sources: Stockbridge VT census 1830. VR SA/VT. N1A, D41, Kathryn L. Brassington rec.

305. **JONATHAN[6] SAWYER** [see 132], b. 25 Dec 1795 Alstead NH, d. 18 Mar 1880 Alstead NH, m.(1) 20 Feb 1823 Charlestown NH Harriet Dwinnell of Surrey NH, b. 11 Jul 1801 d. 15 Feb 1840, dau. Michael Dwinell; m.(2) 4 May 1841 Sally Griffen of Marlow NH, b. 29 Jul 1800 d. 24 Feb 1845, dau. Patrick and Rachel Griffin; m.(3) 27 Jan 1849 Elmira B. Davis of New Ipswich NH, b. Jul 1804 d. 4 May 1883. Note: Son Benjamin's m. record says Jonathan was b. in Wilton NH.

570 Willard Jonathan[7], 1824-1908.
John Warner, b. 28 Jul 1826 Alstead NH, d. 28 Apr 1915 Amherst NH, m. 25 Nov 1852 Marlborough NH Evelina F. Brigham of Alstead NH, b. 11 Apr 1829 d. 23 Feb 1901, dau. Aaron and Susan (Proctor) Brigham. Carpenter. In Keene NH 1860, Marlborough NH 1865. CH: Lestina Amanda, b. 16 Jul 1855, m.(1) 16 Apr 1876 Charles E. Richardson, m.(2) 7 May 1896 George E. Holbrook.
Emily Abigail, b. 4 Mar 1828, d. 12 Jul 1892, m. 5 Oct 1853 Levi P. Town.
571 Amos Augustus[7], 1829-1912.
572 David Webster[7], 1832-1911.
Harriet C., b. 26 Oct 1834, d. 30 Oct 1920, m. 1 Jan 1861 Joseph White.
573 Benjamin Franklin[7], 1836-1923.
Rebecca, b. ?, d. 1858, m. Russell Hurd of Maine.

Sources: Alstead NH census 1830, 1840, 1850, 1860, 1870. Keene NH census 1860, 1870, 1880. Marlborough NH census 1870. VR Gilsum NH. N14, K15, Kenneth E. Sawyer rec.

306. **BENJAMIN[6] SAWYER** [see 132], b. 28 Oct 1797 Atkinson NH, d. 16 Feb 1884 Hampstead NH, m. 1825 Priscilla Gibson, b. 4 May 1804 Nashua NH. Carpenter. Joined church in Hampstead NH 1 May 1842.

Belinda Ann, b. 15 Feb 1826, d. 5 May 1850.
Benjamin K., b. 23 Aug 1828, d. 19 Apr 1833.
Caroline P., b. 26 Dec 1831, d. 23 May 1833.
Francis Henry, b. 21 May 1834, d. 5 May 1907, unm. Selectman for Hampstead NH 1887-1888.
574 Horace Reuben$^7$, 1836-1891.
Sarah Elizabeth, b. 4 Apr 1839, d. 2 Nov 1901, m. 4 Jul 1865 Sandown NH John P. Hunkins of Concord NH.
Lucy A., b. ca. 1846, m. 26 Jul 1870 Hampstead NH John C. Little.
Sources: Hampstead NH census 1830, 1840, 1850, 1860, 1870. VR Hampstead NH. N6, N38, N14.

307. **SETH KIMBALL$^6$ SAWYER** [see 133], b. 31 Mar 1788 Raby NH, d. 13 Oct 1850 New Sharon ME, m. 1 Apr 1813 Jemima Paine Dyer of Truro MA, b. 1791 d. 16 Oct 1856. In Haverhill MA, New Sharon ME.
Betsey, b. 8 Mar 1814, d. 23 Jul 1829.
Mary Knowles, b. 31 Jul 1816, d. 28 May 1894, m.(1) 1838 Cornelius Butler, m.(2) Reuben Morton.
575 Charles B.$^7$, 1818-1901.
Hannah Lombard, b. 18 Jan 1820, d. 11 Sep 1845, m. 10 Dec 1839 Benjamin S. Kelly.
576 Thomas D.$^7$, 1822-1862.
Seth Kimball, b. 22 May 1825 New Sharon ME, d. 24 Feb 1902, m. 4 Jan 1860 Norridgewock ME Elsie M. Mitchell, b. 1841 d. 14 Feb 1891. Both bur. Village Cem., New Sharon ME.
577 Caleb D.$^7$, 1825-1907.
Betsey, b. 1828, m. 21 Oct 1845 Michael Scully.
Emily E., b. Jul 1831, d. 14 Nov 1850.
Sources: New Sharon ME census 1820, 1830, 1840, 1850. VR Raby (Enfield) NH, Truro MA, Sharon ME, Norridgewock ME. M5, Jeanne Sawyer rec.

308. **LEONARD$^6$ SAWYER** [see 133], b. May 1790 New Hampshire, d. 12 Dec 1828 New Sharon ME, m. 24 Sep 1816 Lydia Fellows of New Hampshire, b. 1796 d. 26 Sep 1844. Wid. in New Sharon ME 1830, 1840.
Charlotte, b. 5 Oct 1817.
Truman, b. 15 Feb 1820 New Sharon ME, d. 2 Dec 1895 Skowhegan ME, m. 1 Jan 1848 Norridgewok ME Elizabeth M. Anderson, b. 1827 d. 20 Jan 1899. Carpenter, seaman. In Norridgewock ME. CH: Angie, b. ca. 1854; Juliette, b. Jul 1859.
Martha, b. 5 Mar 1822.
Louise, b. 24 Mar 1824, d. 12 Apr 1825.
Hiram, b. 26 Sep 1826 New Sharon ME. Millwright. In Skowhegan ME 1850.
Lydia, b. 3 Jun 1828.
Sources: New Sharon ME census 1820, 1830, 1840. VR New Sharon ME, SA/ME.

309. **JOSHUA$^6$ SAWYER** [see 133], b. 1798 New Sharon ME, d. 1878, m.(1) Abigail Riggs, b. 1798 d. 14 Aug 1851; m.(2) Mary A_____, b. ? d. 1800 d. 16 May 1886. Farmer. In New Sharon ME 1830-1860. Both wives bur. Village Cem., New Sharon ME.
Daughter, b. ca. 1820.
Nelson, b. May 1822 New Sharon ME, d. 30 Apr 1864, m.(1) Feb 1852 Thirza Coburn, b. Aug 1832 d. 4 Feb 1858, dau. Thaddeus and Hannah (Greenleaf) Coburn; m.(2) 27 Nov 1858 Dorcas Greenleaf of New Sharon ME, b. ca. 1828. He bur. Weeks Mills Cem., New Sharon ME. CH: Emma M., b. 1854.

James, b. 1825, d. 18 May 1855 New Sharon ME.
Julia Ann, b. 1827, d. 1 Jul 1846.
Lewis, b. 1830 New Sharon ME, d. Castle Hill ME. In Australia.
Emerson, b. 1833 New Sharon ME. In New Sharon ME 1850.
578 Jotham S.[7], 1834-1873.
579 Jefferson[7], b. 1837.
Louisa, b. 1839.
Sources: New Sharon ME census 1830, 1840, 1850, 1860. M5, Clark J. Sawyer rec.

310. **JOHN HOVEY[6] SAWYER** [see 133], b. ca. 1804 New Sharon ME, d. 2 Feb 1880, m. Louisa W. Waugh of Starks ME, m. 1807 d. 23 Mar 1887. Merchant, hotel keeper. In Norridgewock ME. Wid. w/son Russell 1880.
Sarah M., b. 1831, d. 30 Oct 1851.
580 Russell F.[7], 1834-1914.
Annette, b. ca. 1835, m. 10 Dec 1859 John H. Burgess.
581 Henry K.[7], 1837-1922.
John K., b. ca. 1845, d. 5 Aug 1850.
Sources: Norridgewock ME census 1840, 1850, 1860, 1880. VR SA/ME. B95, M25, Jeanne Sawyer rec.

311. **ISAAC[6] SAWYER** [see 133], b. 5 Sep 1805, d. 26 Sep 1852 New Sharon ME, m. 11 Oct 1827 New Sharon ME Sarah Bean, b. 12 Oct 1803 d. 13 Jun 1890 in California. He bur. Village Cem., New Sharon ME.
Isaac Madison, b. 7 May 1829 New Sharon ME, d. 9 Mar 1877 New Sharon ME.
Sarah Elizabeth, b. 14 May 1831, d. 9 Aug 1927, m. 1853 Jacob Track. Went to Arizona.
Leonard Franklin, b. 6 Jan 1837, d. 25 Jan 1851.
John W., b. 16 Aug 1839 New Sharon ME, d. 1863 New Sharon ME.
Roxanna D., b. 25 Jun 1841, d. 12 Apr 1925, m. Samuel Owens. Went to California.
Anna Marie, b. 4 Jan 1844, d. 19 Aug 1929, m. 24 Jul 1864 William W. Batch. Went to California.
Martha Adams, b. 16 Apr 1846, d. 25 Apr 1929, m. 16 Nov 1863 Daniel Lewis. Went to California.
Sources: New Sharon ME census 1830, 1840, 1850, 1860. VR SA/ME. B40, M5.

312. **BENIAH C.[6] SAWYER** [see 133], b. New Sharon ME, m. 26 Nov 1829 Abigail Bradley of New Sharon ME, b. ? d. 9 Oct 1846.
Edwin, b. ?, d. 9 Aug 1845.
Sources: VR SA/ME.

313. **JOHN H.[6] SAWYER** [see 134], b. 11 Oct 1816 Stockbridge VT, d. 20 Feb 1875 Stockbridge VT, m.(1) 18 Jun 1839 Stockbridge VT Sylvia A. Pratt, b. 1817 d. 25 Nov 1843; m.(2) 23 Apr 1844 Stockbridge VT Emily D. Davis, b. ?. His d. also recorded in Pittsfield VT.
Norman Royce, b. 14 Jul 1840 Stockbridge VT.
Sewall F., b. 1 Sep 1843 Stockbridge VT, m. Abigail _____, b. ?. Farmer. CH: Adeline M., b. 4 Feb 1869.
Nathan S., b. Oct 1846, d. 10 Feb 1847.
Sarah Jane Browning, adopted, b. 1848, d. 7 Apr 1855.
Sources: VR Stockbridge VT, SA/VT. D6.

314. **DANIEL[6] SAWYER** [see 135], b. 17 Oct 1770 Windham CT, d. 16 Oct 1825, m. 5 Feb 1795 Windham CT Charlotte Denison, b. 20 Apr 1773.
Juliette, b. 26 Jan 1796, d. 11 Oct 1796.
Susannah D., b. 4 Dec 1798, d. 15 Apr 1843, m. 3 Jan 1819 Henry Bachus.
Lucy W., b. 17 Aug 1800, m. 12 Feb 1821 Henry Reed.
Charlotte E., b. 18 Jul 1803.
Prudence Davis, b. 10 Oct 1805.
Nancy M., b. 5 May 1809.
James Denison, b. 17 Sep 1813 Windham CT, d. 12 Jan 1877 Buffalo NY, m. 29 Mar 1841 Charlotte O. Field, b. ?. CH b. in New York.
Sources: Windham CT census 1800, 1810. VR Windham CT. B12, B3.

315. **BELA[6] SAWYER** [see 135], b. 1773 Windham CT, d. 4 May 1855 Middlebury CT, m. Litchfield CT Lydia Johnson of Litchfield CT, b. 7 Jul 1771 d. 12 Aug 1862, dau. James Johnson. Farmer.
Liddy, b. ?.
Anna, b. ?, m. 28 Apr 1825 Charles Abbey.
582 Chester[7], b. 1795.
583 George[7], 1800-1863.
Julia, b. 1805, d. 1 Jan 1840.
584 William[7], 1815-1898.
Edmund, b. 1817 Middlebury VT, d. 8 Mar 1856 Middlebury VT.
More unnamed children listed in census.
Sources: Middlebury VT census 1800, 1810, 1820, 1830, 1840, 1850. VR SA/VT. D6, J3.

316. **DAVID[6] SAWYER** [see 136], b. Jul 1767 Haddam CT, d. 20 Mar 1856 Tinmouth VT, m.(1) 1790 Mary Woodruff, b. 1772 d. 18 Jun 1840 Pittsford VT, dau. Noah and Mary (Cadwell) Woodruff; m.(2) Electa _____, b. 1784 d. Aug 1859. He bur. in Public Cem., Tinmouth VT.
Noah Woodruff, b.8 May 1797 Tinmouth VT, d. 27 Mar 1870 Tinmouth VT, m.(1) 7 Nov 1819 Tinmouth VT Olive Barker, b. 6 Nov 1802 d. 19 May 1837; m.(2) 22 Aug 1837 Tabitha W. Clark, b. 14 Feb 1810 d. 1 May 1894, dau. Theophilus and Lydia (Bingham) Clark. Merchant. Mayflower desc. CH: Mary Woodruff, b. 27 Mar 1821, d. 18 Jun 1899, m. 24 May 1842 William Gray; Noah Barker, b. 31 Jul 1826, d. 31 Aug 1842; Olive Barker, b. 10 Mar 1833, d. 2 Nov 1913, m. 4 Sep 1851 Henry Martyn Stone; Theophilus Clark, b. 10 Jun 1838 d. 8 Mar 1839.
585 David[7], 1807-1859.
Prudence, b. ?, m. 6 Jul 1819 Peter Rogers.
Daughter, b. ?.
Sources: Tinmouth VT census 1800, 1810, 1820, 1830, 1840, 1850. C99.

317. **CORNELIUS[6] SAWYER** [see 137], b. 5 May 1783 Windham CT, d. 20 Feb 1860 Norwich VT, m. Olive Johnson, b. 1785 d. 23 May 1852, dau. James and Olive Johnson. Farmer.
586 James Johnson[7], 1803-1861.
Emerline, b. 8 Feb 1808, m. 9 Jul 1867 Timothy Rogers.
Olive Alvira, b. 16 Feb 1810, m. 1 Jan 1828 Silas Smutt.
587 George Milton[7], 1813-1894.
Arvilla, b. 17 May 1817, m. 24 Dec 1835 E_____ S. Sargent.
588 Ralph[7], b. 1820.
Sources: Norwich VT census 1810, 1820, 1830, 1840, 1850. VR SA/VT.

318. **ELIJAH RINDGE$^6$ SAWYER** [see 138], b. 31 Oct 1787 Windham CT, d. 8 Jan 1833 Windham CT, m. 24 Oct 1811 Windham CT Fanny Spencer, b. 1791 d. 1831.

Child, b. Feb 1812, d. 26 Aug 1812.
Elizabeth, b. 25 Jan 1813.
Edith, b. 21 Nov 1815, d. 25 Apr 1888, m. 12 May 1834 Nelson Hollister.
Mary, b. Nov 1817, m. James Prentice.
Lucy, b. 9 Mar 1819, d. 1845.
Samuel, b. 1821 Windham CT.
Albert, b. 1823 Windham CT, m. 22 Sep 1846 Grafton MA Clarissa J. Pinkham, b. ca. 1826, dau. Joseph and Sarah Pinkham.
George, b. 1825 Windham CT.
589 Andrew$^7$, b. 1830.
William, b. 18 Aug 1830, d. 18 Feb 1831.

Sources: Windham CT census 1830. Springfield MA census 1850. VR Windham CT, Grafton MA, SA/MA. C14.

319. **JAMES JONAS$^6$ SAWYER** [see 141], b. 29 Jun 1813 Pomfret CT, d. 29 Jan 1888, m. 1 Jan 1843 Sophia Harsen, b. ?. Farmer, artist. In New York City, Pomfret CT 1850.

James H., b. 1843 Pomfret CT. Civil War: Enl. 4 Aug 1862 Woodstock CT, captured 1863, discharged 1865. In New York City, Niles MI.
Virgilia, b. 29 Jan 1845, m. 9 Jan 1867 Clarendon M. Greene.
Catherine J., b. 1 Sep 1847.

Sources: Pomfret CT census 1850. VR Pomfret CT. G35, B69.

320. **EBENEZER HOLMES$^6$ SAWYER** [see 141], b. 7 Sep 1815 Pomfret CT, d. 4 Jun 1892 Waterman IL m.(1) 1 Nov 1842 Pomfret CT Ruby King, b. 10 Mar 1814 d. 22 Nov 1859; m.(2) 5 May 1858 Illinois Mary Ann Pearl, b. 30 Jun 1827 d. 10 Apr 1894. In Pomfret CT 1845, Southbridge CT 1846, Monson IL, Pierce IL.

Martius King, b. 18 May 1845 Pomfret CT m. 1 Mar 1870 Elizabeth E. Conkey, b. ?. In Illinois.
Cassius Clay, b. 14 May 1846 Southbridge CT. In Illinois.
Huldah Serena, b. 24 Nov 1848.
Charlotte Pearl, b. 2 May 1859, d. 16 Jun 1859.
Ella Pearl, b. 12 Feb 1861.
Mary Sylvia Emma, b. 8 Jun 1867.

Sources: G35, K9, Beverly Christell rec.

321. **LUCIUS EDWIN$^6$ SAWYER** [see 141], b. 27 Apr 1817 Pomfret CT, d. 4 Mar 1876 Chebouse IL, m.(1) 7 Mar 1843 Woodstock CT Patience S. Carpenter of Putnam CT, b. 29 May 1821 d. 29 Jun 1868, dau. Amos Carpenter; m.(2) 1869 MaryA. Williams of Illinois, b. ?. Laborer. In Thompson CT 1850.

590 Thomas Sylvester$^7$, b. 1844.
Jonas Newton, b. 1846, d. 28 Jul 1847.
Sarah C., b. 12 Nov 1850, d. 13 Apr 1883, m. Oct 1870 Eugene Rockwell.

Sources: Thompson CT census 1850. VR Woodstock CT. D13, C5, D6, H68, G35.

322. **WILLARD$^6$ SAWYER** [see 142], b. 1808 Brighton VT, d. 25 Apr 1882 Charleston VT, m. Leantha Pingay of Hanover VT, b. 1810 d. 4 Feb 1889. Farmer.

Susan, b. 17 Dec 1838, d. 2 May 1903 Stewartstown NH, unm.

Willard, b. 1839 Charleston VT, m. Augusta _____ of Charleston VT, b. ?. CH: Son, b. 19 Jun 1863.
Mary E., b. 1841, m. 27 Mar 1859 Elisha Foster.
Eunice Augusta, b. 12 Jul 1844, m. 24 Oct 1861 Derby VT James F. Morrell.
Lemira E., b. 1845, d. 27 Oct 1862.
Electa, b. 1846, d. 27 Oct 1862.
Harriet, b. 1848.
591 Luther Henry$^7$, 1850-1905.
Martha M., b. 1851, d. 24 Jan 1863.
Sources: Charleston VT census 1840, 1850. VR SA/VT. N6, S50.

323. **ISAAC P.$^6$ SAWYER** [see 142], b. 1810 Waterford VT, d. 20 Nov 1900 Claremont NH, m. 13 Dec 1840 Lowell MA Susan E. Varnum of Candia NH, b. 7 Mar 1822, dau. Josiah and Lucy (Rowe) Varnum. Blacksmith. In Cambridge MA, Lowell MA, Harvard MA 1850, St. Johnsbury VT 1860. Note: VR SA/VT says Susan Norman.
592 Henry Porter$^7$, 1844-1924.
Mary J., b. 1 May 1846, d. 24 Jul 1846 Lowell MA.
Delia A., b. 1848, d. 12 Nov 1865 St. Johnsbury VT.
Ellen Morse, b. 25 Mar 1850, m.(1) 15 Jun 1869 William Alexander, m.(2) 23 Nov 1888 Wallace Clark.
Charles E., b. 1855 Brighton VT, m. 15 Aug 1876 Carrie M. Willard of Worcester MA, b. 1853. Blacksmith. In Lebanon NH, St. Albans VT. CH: Etta, b. 10 Aug 1877.
Lucera Elmira, b. 1857, m.(1) 24 Nov 1877 Frank E. Thompson; m.(2) 30 Mar? Morris N. Cone.
Sources: Harvard MA census 1850. St. Johnsbury VT census 1860. VR Lowell MA, SA/VT, SA/MA. V4, N6.

324. **WILLIAM A.$^6$ SAWYER** [see 143], b. 8 Jul 1826 Waterford VT, d. 29 Nov 1889 Derby VT, m. 1850 Derby VT Mary Harvey of Charleston VT, b. 1830. Cooper.
593 Amos C.$^7$, b. 1851.
Julia B., b. 1852, m. 8 Feb 1877 Charles Streeter, Jr.
Ambrose, b. 26 Feb 1854, d. 5 Jun 1855.
Adney, b. 10 Jun 1859 Charleston VT, m.(1) 9 Dec 1883 Barton VT Fanny L. Robinson of Maine, b. 1861 d. 24 Dec 1883; m.(2) Hillsboro NH Mary Whitaker of Goshen NH, b. 12 Dec 1866 d. 29 Nov 1926, dau. Henry P. and Eliza (Dow) Whitaker. Farmer. In Barton VT 1883, Milford VT 1893. CH: Nina Bell, b. 25 Feb 1886; Winifred Alice, b. 13 Aug 1889; Ida Adeline, b. 24 Aug 1891.
Arthur A., b. 14 Sep 1861 Charleston VT.
594 Elwyn$^7$, b. 1863.
Sources: Charleston VT census 1850, 1860, 1870. VR SA/VT.

325. **LOREN W.$^6$ SAWYER** [see 143], b. 1831 Charleston VT, d. 16 Jun 1876 Charleston VT, m. Emily L. Parlin, b. 1835, dau. Amos and Nancy Parlin. Farmer. Wid. m. 5 Jan 1881 Richard Mapledon.
595 Arthur D.$^7$, b. 1858.
Elmer Abel, b. 1 Feb 1863, d. 19 Sep 1865.
Sources: Charleston VT census 1850. VR SA/VT.

326. **MARTIN CALVIN[6] SAWYER** [see 145], b. 1840 Franconia NH, m.(1) 14 Jan 1865 Eliza M. Kelsea of Columbia NH, b. 1848; m.(2) 21 Dec 1869 Martha J. Pilbro of Columbia NH, b. Oct 1850, dau. William Pilbro. In Columbia NH.
596 Charles Graham[7], b. 1867.
Henry F., b. 1875 Columbia NH.
Sources: Columbia NH census 1880.

327. **SIMON FOBES[6] SAWYER** [see 146], b. 16 Nov 1816 Reading VT, d. 13 Nov 1907 Sherburne VT, m.(1) 31 Jan 1856 Clarendon VT BetseyJane Taylor, b. Jun 1836 d. 22 Jan 1858, dau. Orin and Christiana Taylor; m.(2) 11 Jul 1858 Mary L. Talbert of Rutland VT, b. Dec 1822 d. 13 Feb 1905. Farmer. In Sherburne VT.
Lyman W., b. ca. 1851 Sherburne VT.
Lonuda (?), b. 1853.
597 Cornelius Simon[7], b. 1859.
Orrin, b. 21 Jul 1861, d. 14 Jul 1867.
Sources: VR SA/VT.

328. **ORRIN SPAULDING[6] SAWYER** [see 146], b. 4 Jun 1820 Reading VT, d. 5 Apr 1895 Chester VT, m. 7 Mar 1850 Cavendish VT Sophronia Wheelock of Cavendish VT, b. 24 Sep 1817 d. 5 Jun 1889, dau. Joseph D. Wheelock. Farmer.
598 James Orrin[7], 1851-1936.
Charles Edwin, b. 1852 Reading VT, m. 10 Oct 1893 Melrose MA GraceEllen Duncley of Charlestown MA, b. ca. 1871, dau. Nathan S. and Martha E. (Warren) Duncley. Carpenter. CH: Mildred W., b. 10 Jun 1897; Geraldine, b. 2 Nov 1905.
Frank Albert, b. 31 Aug 1853 Reading VT.
Mary Alma, b. 26 Nov 1854, unm.
Caroline, b. 31 Oct 1856, m. 10 Mar 1874 Marshall T. Weeden.
Frances, b. 31 Oct 1856, m. 16 May 1883 Holyoke MA Frank H. Haskell.
Julia S., b. 1859, m. and went west.
Jacob E., b. 1861 Reading VT.
Clarence, b. 1864 Reading VT.
Sources: Reading VT census 1850. VR Reading VT, SA/VT, SA/MA. Katherine Keene rec.

329. **JOSEPH ALBERT[6] SAWYER**. [see 147], b. 16 Oct 1823 Reading VT, m. Miranda S. Mills, b. ?.
Henry W., b. 1858 Reading VT, m.(1) ?, m.(2) 5 Nov 1891 Lulie Blagg, b. ?.
Sources: VR SA/VT.

330. **DANIEL PECK[6] SAWYER** [see 149], b. 18 Oct 1827 Reading VT, d. 15 Mar 1902 Reading VT, m.(1) 9 Jun 1851 Windsor VT Arabella Ruggles of Windsor VT, b. 11 Jan 1824 d. 17 Sep 1890, dau. Samuel and Arabella (Huggins) Ruggles; m.(2) 15 Jun 1891 FrancesM. Hewlett, b. Apr 1832. Farmer. Note: [R31] says Arabella was dau. Samuel and Flora (Hoisington) Ruggles.
George Washington, b. 22 Feb 1852, d. 24 Jul 1861.
Flora A., b. 20 Oct 1853, d. 6 Aug 1854.
Otis Cornelius, b. 21 Nov 1855 Reading VT, m. 2 Feb 1887 Mary(Stimpson) Barrett of Springfield VT, b. ?. Merchant. In Sharon VT. CH: Maude Bell, b. 26 Nov 1891, d. 14 Apr 1892; Harold Stimpson, b. 30 Jul 1893, d. 29 Dec 1895.
John Edward, b. 1 Mar 1859, d. 28 Dec 1861.
Mary Elizabeth, b. 25 May 1861, m. 7 Sep 1887 Gardiner ME Edgar L. Fisher.

Ned E., b. 27 Feb 1864 Reading VT, d. 4 Oct 1902 (suicide) Reading VT, m. 6 Oct 1889 Reading VT Mary I. Corey of Marlborough NH, b. 1870, dau. Amos and Ellen (Sperry) Corey. Poultry dealer. Wid. m. 1905 Reading VT Herbert A. Davis. CH: Ida Pearl, b. 21 Feb 1890; Inez, b. 4 Oct 1892, d. 9 Oct 1892; Irene, b. 4 Oct 1892, d. 11 Nov 1892; Hazel Mabel, b. 11 Jul 1898.

Sources: Reading VT census 1860, 1870. VR SA/VT. C99, R31, Ruggles family Bible.

331. **ABIJAH$^6$ SAWYER** [see 152], b. 24 Sep 1765 Swanzey NH, d. 28 Mar 1823 Swanzey NH, m. 26 Nov 1783 Meletiah Graves, b. 20 Jan 1766 d. 7 Nov 1837, dau. Joshua and Lydia (Woodcock) Graves. Cooper.

599 Henry$^7$, 1784-1877.
Hannah, b. 12 Jan 1786, m. 7 Jan 1806 Abraham Day. Went to Pennsylvania.
Joshua, b. 10 Feb 1789, d. 10 Sep 1789.
Hephzibah, b. 5 May 1791, d. 14 Sep 1795.
Abijah, b. 5 May 1791, d. same day.
Rhoda, b. 5 Jul 1793, d. 2 Mar 1803.
Daughter, b. 31 Aug 1795, d. same day.
Caleb, b. 5 Dec 1796, d. 8 Feb 1801.
Lydia, b. 14 Jun 1799, d. 3 Mar 1803.
600 Joshua$^7$, 1801-1899.
Lydia, b. 31 Jul 1804, m. James Hosley.
601 Caleb$^7$, 1806-1881.

Sources: Swanzey NH census 1790, 1800, 1810, 1820. G34, R7, D6, J3.

332. **SAMUEL$^6$ SAWYER** [see 152], b. 1 Sep 1768 Swanzey NH, d. 1835 Swanzey NH, m. 23 Nov 1790 Shirley MA Ruhamah (Harrington) Hazen of Swanzey NH, wid. of Paul, b. 5 Sep 1762 d. 1849, dau. Thaddeus and Thankful (Dodge) Harrington.

602 Samuel$^7$, 1791-1863.

Sources: R7, H39, A20.

333. **EPHRAIM$^6$ SAWYER** [see 153], b. 1780 Westmoreland NH, d. 1830, m. Rutland VT Polly Packs, b. ?. Farmer, blacksmith. In Whiting VT, Crown Point NY 1817.

Chauncy P., b. ca. 1812 Whiting VT, m. Martha Bigelow, b. ?. In Ticonderoga NY. CH: Jennie, b. ca. 1855, m. 16 May 1870 Albert J. Gibbs.
Mary, b. ca. 1813, d. 1888, m. 1831 Asabel Bailey. Went to Wisconsin.
Ephraim P., b. ca. 1814. Went to Pennsylvania.
Philetus Horace, b. 22 Sep 1816, d. 29 Mar 1900, m. 1841 Melvinia Hadley, b. ?. Went to Wisconsin.
Alonzo J., b. 1818.
Andrew, b. 1820.

Sources: A20.

334. **MANASSEH$^6$ SAWYER** [see 154], b. 6 Sep 1783 Westmoreland NH, d. 25 Jul 1837 Georgia Plains VT, m.(1) Azubah Chamberlin, b. ?, dau. Ebenezer and Martha (Howe) Chamberlin; m.(2) 1805 Chloe Hall of Croyden NH, b. 1787 d. 17 Aug 1869, dau. James and Huldah (Cooper) Hall. Minister. In Canada, Georgia Plains VT 1830.

Azubah, b. 13 Mar 1802, m. 28 Dec 1820 William Carpenter. Went to New York.
Melinda Haven, b. ca. 1806, d. 1883, m.(1) 1825 Joshua Lewis, m.(2) Joshua Crosby.
603 James H.$^7$, 1807-1850.
Huldah Cooper, b. ca. 1812, m. Amory Weeks.

Carlton, b. ca. 1814, m. Delilah _____ . Went to California.
604 Lyman$^7$, ca. 1820-1860.
Belmira, b. ca. 1828, m. Truman Godfrey.
Sources: Georgia Plains VT census 1830. H80, C5, Frederick W. Sawyer III rec.

335. **MARTIN$^6$ SAWYER** [see 154], b. 1783 Westmoreland NH, m. Eunice A. Tinker, b.?. In Lyme CT.
605 Elisha Maturin$^7$, b. 1814.
Sources: H80, B77.

336. **WILLARD$^6$ SAWYER** [see 154], b. ca. 1785 Westmoreland NH, m. ?.
Charles, b. ?.
James, b. ?.
Sources: H80, C8.

337. **GEORGE REX$^6$ SAWYER** [see 154], b. ca. 1787 Westmoreland NH, d. 1855 Potsdam NY, m. 28 Feb 1816 Ferrisburg VT Hannah Taft, b. 1795.
William H., b. 15 Oct 1826, m. 22 Sep 1854 Marion H. Clark, b. ?.
Ann, b. ?.
(5 more dau?)
Sources: VR SA/VT.

338. **RUFUS$^6$ SAWYER** [see 155], b. 14 Sep 1783 Henniker NH, d. 7 May 1861 Henniker NH, m. 30 Jun 1808 Polly Howe of Henniker NH, b. ?, dau. William and Lydia (Whitman) Howe.
William H., b. 21 Mar 1813 Henniker NH, d. 25 Sep 1872 Weare NH, m. 1 May 1836 Emily A. Felch of Weare NH, b. 7 May 1810, d. 18 Aug 1872. Farmer. Captain of rifle company in Henniker NH. In Weare NH. CH: Melvina, b. 23 Apr 1838, d. 7 May 1838; Emily A., b. 8 Jun 1839, m. 25 Oct 1857 Wallace A. Dow; William, b. 8 Sep 1840, d. 6 Aug 1841; Delia, b. 31 Aug 1842, d. 31 Aug 1842; Melvina, b. 22 Apr 1843, d. 9 May 1843; Willis, b. 25 Jan 1845, d. 7 Feb 1845; Orman, b. 28 Aug 1846, d. 15 Sep 1846; Flora, b. ?; Lonora, b. 1848, m. _____ Smith; Ada, b. 14 May 1851, d. 3 Sep 1853; Ellen May, b. 1856.
Rufus, b. 1815 Henniker NH, m. Mary S. Clark of Newport, b. 1815. Captain of rifle Company in Henniker NH.
Lydia, b ?, d. 12 Sep 1846, m. _____ Bruce.
Sources: Henniker NH census 1810, 1820, 1830, 1840, 1850, 1860, Hopkinton NH census 1850, Concord NH census 1860. Weare NH census 1870. C59, H80.

339. **PAUL$^6$ SAWYER** [see 155], b. 19 Jan 1789 Henniker NH, d. 23 Jan 1868, m. 24 Mar 1814 Sally Howe, b. 1792, dau. William and Lydia (Whitman) Howe. Wid. w/son James M. in Newbury NH.
William H., b. 8 Apr 1815 Henniker NH, d. 3 Feb 1893 Newbury NH, m. 15 Dec 1840 Abigail Rowe, b. 1820. CH: Helen J., b. 1841, m. 13 Oct 1869 Boston MA Alstead W. Brownell; Mary Frances, b. 1852, m. 21 Nov 1874 Manchester NH Auren M. Lewis.
Daughter, b. (1810-1820).
606 James Madison$^7$, 1822-1885.
Sources: Henniker NH census 1820, 1830, Newbury NH census 1840, 1850, 1860. C59, H80.

340. **JABEZ$^6$ SAWYER** [see 157], b. 10 Sep 1792 Harvard MA, d. 28 Jul 1824 Fitchburg MA, m. 8 Apr 1819 Fitchburg MA Susan O. Thurston of Fitchburg MA, b. 2 Dec 1789 d. 18 Mar 1858,

dau. Stephen and Mary (Osgood) Thurston. Wid. in Fitchburg MA 1830, w/brother-in-law John 1850.

Samuel Thurston, b. 22 Dec 1819, d. 6 Jan 1843.

Mary O., b. 3 Dec 1821, m. 5 Dec 1844 George Litchfield.

Jabez, b. 5 Oct 1824 Fitchburg MA, d. 16 Mar 1852 Fitchburg MA, m. 8 Mar 1849 Grafton VT Lucy Holmes of Vermont, b. ca. 1821. Mason. In Fitchburg MA 1850 w/Uncle John.

Sources: Fitchburg MA census 1820, 1830, 1850. VR SA/VT. D20.

341. **ASA$^{6}$ SAWYER** [see 157], b. 22 Oct 1794 Fitchburg MA, d. 1881 Harvard MA, m. (1) 15 Sep 1818 Nancy Thurston of Fitchburg MA, b. 10 Apr 1797 d. 23 Apr 1821, dau. John and Elizabeth Thurston; m.(2) 22 Jan 1823 Princeton MA Betsey Keyes of Princeton MA, b. 20 Sep 1799.

Nancy, b. 6 Oct 1819, m. 30 Jun 1842 John B. Davis of Holliston MA.

Henry, b. 26 Mar 1825, d. 8 Sep 1825.

607 Henry Edward$^{7}$, b. 1827.

Eveline E., b. 3 Nov 1828, m. 11 May 1848 Fitchburg MA Silas Waters.

Lydia E., b. 14 Aug 1830, d. 30 Aug 1849.

Maria, b. 21 Jul 1832 Fitchburg MA, m. 6 Sep 1854 Fitchburg MA Francis F. Farrar.

608 Charles K.$^{7}$, b. 1835.

Alvin Manasseh, b. 8 Aug 1839 Fitchburg MA, m. 24 Sep 1863 Lempster NH Sarah Augusta Collins of Lempster NH, b. 1841. Teacher, farmer. In New Ipswich NH 1860, Harvard MA 1870. CH: Fannie Etta, b. 17 Sep 1869. Note: VR SA/MA says Alvin and Sarah m. 21 Sep 1863 Fitchburg MA.

Sources: Fitchburg MA census 1820, 1830, 1840, 1870. New Ipswich NH census 1860. VR Fitchburg MA, Princeton MA, Harvard MA. B51, N36, D20.

342. **MANASSEH$^{6}$ SAWYER** [see 157], b. 26 Dec 1796 Fitchburg MA, d. 30 Oct 1836 Fitchburg MA, m.(I) 1 Jun 1822 Leominster MA Dorothy Lincoln of Fitchburg MA, b. ?. Town constable 1827. Selectman for Fitchburg MA. Wid. in Fitchburg MA 1840, 1850.

Abigail L., b. 23 Aug 1824, d. 22 Aug 1825.

Thomas Lincoln, b. 6 Jun 1826, d. 17 Jun 1848.

John Snow, b. 9 Sep 1831 Fitchburg MA, m. 29 Dec 1857 Boston MA Sarah L. Pratt of Fitchburg MA, b. ca. 1833, dau. Levi Pratt. Merchant. CH: Emma, b. 21 Jun 1865, d. 7 Nov 1916, m. 2 Apr 1896 George McQuesten; Harriet L., b ca. 1868, m. 1 Jun 1892 Cambridge MA Wendell Brown; Anna Gertrude, b. 8 Aug 1870, m. 1 May 1893 Cambridge MA Atherton Loring.

Sources: Fitchburg MA census 1840, 1850. VR Leominster MA, SA/MA. M31, D20, P61.

343. **EDWARD$^{6}$ SAWYER** [see 157], b. 7 Mar 1804 Fitchburg MA, m. 25 Oct 1827 Leominster MA Mary Lincoln of Leominster MA, b. 1810. Shoemaker. In Ashburnham MA 1830, 1840.

Abigail M., b. 8 Jun 1830, d. 2 Mar 1838.

609 Charles Edward$^{7}$, ca. 1836-1903.

610 Henry Lincoln$^{7}$, 1840-1906.

Mary Nichols, bp. 8 Feb 1845.

Laura Maria, b. 8 Feb 1845, m. 28 Aug 1866 Edward Moore.

Sources: Ashburnham MA census 1830, 1840, 1850. VR Ashburnham MA, Leominster MA, SA/MA. D61, D20.

344. **JONATHAN$^6$ SAWYER** [see 158], b. 26 Jul 1789 Harvard MA, m.(1) Eliza _____, b. 1794 d. 28 May 1818; m.(2) 30 May 1839 Harvard MA Adaline Hildreth, b. ?.

Rebecca, b. 3 Jul 1817, d. 8 Aug 1817.

Jonathan E., b. 1818, d. 26 Sep 1844.

Sources: Harvard MA census 1840, 1850 (w/father.) VR Harvard MA.

345. **JOSIAH$^6$ SAWYER** [see 158], b. 9 Dec 1802 Harvard MA, d. 2 Mar 1884, m.(1) 1 Apr 1827 Harvard MA Agatha H. Gardiner, b. Mar 1809 d. 11 Jun 1828, dau. Moses Gardiner; m.(2) 18 Apr 1829 Boston MA Mary D. Sanger of Hopkinton MA, b. 16 Aug 1809, dau. Jedediah and Mary (Dench) Sanger. Shoe manufacturer.

Gardner, b. 1828.

Ellen Mary, b. 9 Apr 1834, unm.

611 Albert Josiah$^7$, b. 1840.

Sources: Harvard MA census 1830. Cambridge MA census 1850. VR Harvard MA.

346. **ARAD$^6$ SAWYER** [see 159], b. 15 Jul 1808 Harvard MA, d. 24 May 1878 Harvard MA, m. 1 Nov 1831 Lucy P. Farwell of Harvard MA, b. 18 May 1804 d. 20 Dec 1879. Farmer.

Arathusa Farwell, b. 16 May 1832, m. 5 Jan 1852 Harvard MA James Atherton.

George Luther, b. 15 May 1839 Harvard MA, m. 2 Jun 1861 Harvard MA Sarah Maria Frost of Harvard, b. 1839, dau. Thomas and Mercy (Sawyer) Frost. Carpenter.

Lucy, E., b. 1841.

Sarah Stetson, b. 18 Nov 1845, m. 29 Nov 1871 Harvard MA Charles Atherton.

612 Alfred Augustus$^7$, b. 1849.

Sources: Harvard MA census 1840. VR Harvard MA, SA/MA.

347. **ALFRED IRA$^6$ SAWYER** [see 160], b. 6 Oct 1799 Harvard MA, d. 1 Aug 1849 Dover NH, m. 22 Sep 1829 Lowell MA Nancy Davis, b. 1800 d. 14 Apr 1840. His name was changed from Ira to Alfred Ira in Dover NH 1824. Operated grist mill in Dover NH 1824. Brother Francis Asbury appointed guardian of his CH 1850.

Hannah, b. 1830, m. 24 Oct 1852 in Lowell MA Cyrus M. Battles.

613 Charles Alfred$^7$, b. 1837.

Sources: Dover NH census 1830, 1840. VR Marlboro MA, Lowell MA. P82i.

348. **ZENAS$^6$ SAWYER** [see 160], b. 25 Dec 1808 Marlborough MA, d. 20 Feb 1856 Boston Ma, m. 13 Nov 1837 Rochester NH Sophronia Brackett of Maine, b. 22 Sep 1812, d. 27 Aug 1879. Flannel maker. In Dover NH 1843. Helped brother run mill in Dover NH 1850.

Sophronia, b. 1842, m. 25 Dec 1862 Lowell MA Arthur Wright.

Ellen, b. 1843, m. 25 Feb 1862 Lowell MA George A. Brigham.

Amanda, b. 19 Sep 1847, m. 7 Jul 1874 George H. Manning.

Walter M., b. 1852 Dover NH, m. 12 Jul 1877 Lowell MA Jennie H. Read of Massachusetts, b. 1855, dau. William M. and Hannah J. Read. Bank Teller.

Sources: Dover NH census 1850. SA/MA. M10, B74.

349. **WESLEY$^6$ SAWYER** [see 160], b. 2 Feb 1810 Marlborough MA, d. 1878, m. 20 Sep 1835 Lowell MA Mary M. Patten of Candia NH, b. 25 Jul 1810. Fisherman, machinest. In Dover NH 1840, Dracutt MA 1850, Lowell MA 1856.

Alfred Patten, b. 20 Aug 1856 Lowell MA, m. 15 Dec 1886 Lowell MA Addie L. Gibson of Wakefield MA, b. ca. 1858, dau. Moses and Hattie Gibson. Clerk. In Chelmsford MA. CH: Mary W., b. ?, school teacher in Brookline MA.

Sources: Dover NH census 1840. Dracut MA census 1850. VR Lowell MA, SA/MA. M48.

350. **JONATHAN$^6$ SAWYER** [see 160], b. 17 Jun 1817 Marlborough NH, d. 20 Jun 1891 Dover NH, m. 25 Jun 1839 Woodstock VT Martha Perkins of Barnard VT, b. 17 May 1816 d. 19 Jan 1896, dau. Cyrus and Martha (Childs) Perkins. Attended school in Lowell MA. Superintendent of a woolen mill in New York. W/brother Zenas, took over Dover Mills when Alfred Ira died. In Dover NH 1851. Will dated 24 May 1890.

614 Charles Henry$^7$, 1840-1908.

Mary Elizabeth, b. 28 Oct 1842, d. 26 Feb 1899, unm.

Francis Asbury, b. 5 Mar 1845 Dover NH, d. 23 Dec 1889, m. 10 Sep 1884 Emma K. Smith, b. ?. CH: Eleanor G., adopted, b.?.

Roswell Douglas, b. 14 Mar 1848 Dover NH, d. 1894 Rome, Italy, m. 18 Sep 1879 Edwina D. Lowe of St. Louis MO, b. ?. Artist. In New York City.

Martha Frances, b. 3 Mar 1851, m. 10 Sep 1878 Winfield S. Bradley.

Alice May, b. 24 Jul 1853, m. 29 Jan 1894 Fred W. Payne of Boston MA.

615 Frederick Jonathan$^7$, 1860-1902.

Sources: Watertown NY census 1840. Dover NH census 1860, 1870. P82i, H95.

351. **CALEB$^6$ SAWYER** [see 161], b. 13 Apr 1798 Harvard MA, d. 30 May 1829 Harvard MA, m. 14 Aug 1819 Harvard MA Lydia Sprague, b. 10 Feb 1800.

616 Jonathan$^7$, b. 1820.

Andrew Jackson, b. 3 Nov 1821 Harvard MA, d. 5 Sep 1851 Leominster MA, unm.

Henry Harrison, b. 27 Sep 1823 Harvard MA.

Sarah E., b. 1826.

Sources: VR Harvard MA, Leominster MA, SA/MA.

352. **LUKE$^6$ SAWYER** [see 161], b. 18 Oct 1809 Harvard MA, m.(1) 9 Sep 1834 Harvard MA Mercy B. Whitcomb of Waterford ME, b. Jan 1811 d. 12 Aug 1849; m.(2) 1 Oct 1850 Marlborough MA Caroline (Temple) Smith of Marlborough MA, b. ca. 1812, dau. Jonas and Betsey Temple. Farmer. In Waterford ME, Harvard MA 1840, 1850.

Wilbur Fisher, b. ca. 1835 Harvard MA, m. 15 Mar 1870 Harvard MA Abby C. Smith of Marl-borough MA, b. 1844, dau. Abner and Caroline (Temple) Smith.

Mary L., b. Oct 1838, d. 30 Jul 1845.

Wesley Caleb, b. 26 Aug 1839 Harvard MA. Harvard College 1861. Civil War: wounded 1862. In Wisconsin.

Caroline L., b. Nov 1842, d. 18 Jul 1843.

Martin Aubra, b. 24 Jun 1845, d. 18 Aug 1849 Harvard MA.

John P., b. Jan 1847, d. 15 Aug 1849 Harvard MA.

Seth Augustus, b. 24 Jun 1849, d. 6 Oct 1855 Harvard MA.

Sources: Harvard MA census 1840, 1850. VR Harvard MA, SA/MA. C8.

353. **JAMES$^6$ SAWYER** [see 162], b. 1 Jul 1793 Harvard MA, m. 17 Jun 1817 Harvard MA Naomi Whitney, b. 28 Apr 1797. In Harvard MA 1820, Boxboro MA 1830.

Alvira, b. 22 Jan 1819, d. 11 Feb 1882, m. 1837 John M. Danforth.

Alvin, b. 13 Mar 1822, d. 21 Aug 1849 Boxboro MA.

Alma, b. 1 Sep 1826, d. 7 Oct 1826.

Alzaman, b. 5 Jan 1828 Bolton MA. In Harvard MA.

Julia Ann, b. 12 Feb 1831, m. 6 Sep 1870 Boxboro MA John B. Thompson.

Marshall, b. 3 Aug 1833 Harvard MA. In Clinton MA.

Sources: Harvard MA census 1820. Boxboro MA census 1830, 1840, 1850. Clinton MA census 1850. VR Harvard MA, SA/MA. P46, M25.

354. **ABEL⁶ SAWYER** [see 162], b. 3 Jan 1797 Harvard MA, m. 27 May 1821 Bolton MA Betsey Sawyer, b. 6 Sep 1797, dau. Benjamin and Rebecca (Houghton) Sawyer.
Cephas, b. 3 Feb 1822 Harvard MA.
Adna, b. 11 Feb 1824 Harvard MA.
2 sons, b. (1825-1830).
2 dau., b. (1825-1830).
Sources: Harvard MA census 1830. VR Harvard MA, Bolton MA.

355. **PHINEAS⁶ SAWYER** [see 162], b. 13 Sep 1803 Harvard MA, m. 17 Aug 1824 Harvard MA Nancy Wheeler, b. ?.
617 Evander Erastus⁷, b. 1825.
Frances, b. ca. 1832, m. 10 Oct 1850 Sterling MA Ervin W. Stuart.
Lucy Ann Maria, b. 11 May 1836, m. 8 Aug 1853 Waltham MA Samuel H. Gault.
618 Edrick⁷, b. 1838.
Sources: Waltham MA census 1840. VR Harvard MA, Waltham MA, SA/MA.

356. **ALPHEUS⁶ SAWYER** [see 163], b. 19 Oct 1796 Shirley MA, d. 16 Apr 1887 Whitefield NH, m. 8 Feb 1819 Bethlehem NH Charlotte Shattuck of Bradford NH, b. 29 Dec 1795, dau. Sherman and Hannah Shattuck. Farmer. On Bethlehem NH tax roll 1818.
Mary B., b. 25 Jul 1819, m. Jan 1847 G____ W. Cole of Manchester NH.
Franklin B., b. 19 Apr 1823 Whitefield NH, d. 24 Dec 1883 Bethlehem NH, m. 30 Nov 1853 Juliette G. Blanding, b. ?. CH: Mary Maria, b. 1855, m. 19 Feb 1885 Springfield MA George H. Hill; Martha, b. 1858.
619 Cyril A.⁷, b. 1825.
John B., b. 8 Apr 1835, d. 25 Mar 1838.
Sources: Littleton NH census 1830. Whitefield NH census 1840, 1850, 1860, 1870. Bethlehem NH census 1870. VR SA/MA. C24, S33.

357. **OLIVER⁶ SAWYER** [see 163], b. 10 May 1798 Bethlehem NH, m. 20 Mar 1817 Bethlehem NH Lillis Palmer, b. 1793. In Littleton NH 1816. Res. w/dau. Martha in Lancaster NH 1870.
620 Oliver Putnam S.⁷, b. 1818.
621 George⁷, 1822-1896.
Mary B., b. 29 Apr 1826, m. 18 Feb 1844 Whitefield NH George W. Smith.
Martha Ann, b. 12 Oct 1837, m. Charles Gotham.
Sources: Whitefield NH census 1820, 1830, 1840, 1850. Lancaster NH census 1870. N6.

358. **WILLIAM HUBBARD⁶ SAWYER** [see 164], b. 22 Feb 1806 Bethlehem NH, d. 2 Jan 1880, m. Mehitable Cole, b. 1816 d. 17 Feb 1882. Joiner. In Whitefield NH 1870.
622 Evarts W.⁷, 1836-1903.
Marianna B., b. 1839, m. 29 Jun 1864 Nathaniel Libby of Bethlehem NH.
623 Samuel Cole⁷, 1845-1915.
Sources: Whitefield NH census 1840, 1850, 1860, 1870. J2, N5.

359. **ELI DAVIS⁶ SAWYER** [see 164], b. 4 Jun 1815 Bethlehem NH, d. 29 Nov 1905 Littleton NH, m. 19 Dec 1848 Sarah O. Pierce of Bethlehem NH, b. 22 Feb 1830 d. 27 Jun 1912, dau. John and Rebecca (Cushman) Pierce. Hotel keeper. Selectman for Littleton NH 1863-1866.
Elmer G., b. 25 Nov 1849, d. 12 Oct 1850.

John Pierce, b. 11 Oct 1851 Bethlehem NH, m.(1) 9 Sep 1882 Boston MA Carrie E. (Swift) Towne of Locke Mills (?), b. 1858, dau. John and Christian Swift; m.(2) 1884 Nellie Dooling, b. ?; m.(3) 3 May 1897 Ida M. Tucker of Portsmouth NH, b. 1873. In Boston MA, Texas, Baton Rouge LA, Rollinsford NH 1897.
Frank Pierce, b. 28 Jun 1854, d. 6 Feb 1855.
Hattie Grace, b. 30 Oct 1857, m.(1) 10 Jun 1875 Fred A. Tilton, m.(2) T____ P. Lindsey.
Charles Martin Tuttle, b. 18 Feb 1865 Littleton NH, m. 30 Sep 1888 Annie F. Harper, b. ?. Lawyer. In Fort Payne AL. CH: Sarah Pierce, b. ?; Hattie Grace, b. ?.
624 William Henry$^7$, 1867-1947.
Sources: Bethlehem NH census 1850. Littleton NH census 1860, 1870, VR SA/MA, SA/NH. N6, V2, J2, P43.

360. **THOMAS$^6$ SAWYER** [see 165], b. 16 Mar 1778 Orford NH, m. 8 Nov 1803 Orford NH Asenath Sargent, b. 1782, dau. Timothy and Asenath (Tillotson) Sargent. Vershire VT 1840.
625 Timothy$^7$, 1805-1869.
Thomas, b. 6 Jul 1807 Orford NH.
Cynthia, b. 29 Nov 1811.
Eliza, b. 6 Mar 1814.
Mehitable, b. 14 Aug 1817, d. ?.
Mehitable Emery, b. 1819.
Sources: Vershire VT census 1840. N7, S10.

361. **BENJAMIN CARTER$^6$ SAWYER** [see 165], b. 16 Mar 1780 Orford NH, d. 13 May 1831 Orford NH intestate, m. 1 Oct 1807 Orford NH Mindwell Sargent, b. 1 Aug 1788 d. 16 Aug 1846.
Benjamin Carter, b. 26 Oct 1808 Orford NH.
John Henry, b. 17 Apr 1810 Orford NH, m. 10 Feb 1835 Lebanon NH May A. Estabrook of Lebanon NH, b. ?. In Washington VT 1835, Haverhill NH 1840.
Adeline, b. 15 Oct 1812.
626 Hiram$^7$, 1814-1888.
Joseph, b. 27 Nov 1816 Orford NH.
Lewis, b. 23 Jan 1819 Orford NH. Highway surveyor 1841. In Benton NH.
Abigail, b. 13 Feb 1824, d. 3 Feb 1827.
Solomon, b. ca. 1826 Orford NH.
Sources: Orford NH census 1820, 1830. P82c, D6, H58A, N7.

362. **LEONARD$^6$ SAWYER** [see 165], b. 1790 Orford NH, d. 1867, m. Lucy (Truesdell) Drake, b. ?. In Orford NH 1860.
Abby, b. 1810, m. 6 Jan 1851 Boston MA Charles F. Hills.
Martha, b. 1816.
Tabitha, b. 1819, m. 8 Apr 1868 Leonard H. Morey.
Elizabeth, b. 1820.
Charles, b. 1823 Orford NH, d. 1862 Orford NH, m. Tabitha Morey, b. ? d. 1889.
627 George$^7$, b. 1824.
Leonard, b. ?. Went to California.
Lucy, b. 1832.
Hannah, b. 1836.
Note: One CH d. 1823.
Sources: Orford NH census 1830, 1840, 1850, 1860. VR SA/MA. K12, N6.

363. **JOSEPH⁶ SAWYER** [see 166], b. 11 Oct 1785 Piermont NH, d. 4 Jul 1858, m. 29 Nov 1829 Mary Dale, b. 27 Oct 1803 d. 1 Feb 1885 Pontiac MI, dau. Moses and Lucy (Poor) Dale. Judge. Wid. in Cambridge City MI 1859, Piermont NH 1860.

Mary Dale, b. 22 Aug 1830, m. 23 Oct 1856 John Calloway.
Elizabeth, b. 4 Nov 1832, unm. Went to Indiana.
Catherine Lucy, b. 24 May 1834, d. 1921, m. 19 Aug 1856 Charles F. Kimball. Went to Michigan.
Elenor Merrill, b. 16 Jul 1835, d. 1901, m. 27 Dec 1870 Evan Hughes. Went to Indiana.
Isabella, b. 9 Dec 1840, d. 12 May 1877, m. 3 Sep 1862 Abram Schult.
Gilenda Poore, b. 10 Jan 1844, d. 1 Nov 1934, m. 1 Nov 1866 James Newby.
Joseph Edward, b. 1 Jan 1847 Piermont NH, d. 1 Dec 1916 Pontiac MI, m. 1877 Elizabeth Satterlee, b. ?. Lawyer. Had 5 CH.

Sources: Piermont NH census 1830, 1840, 1850, 1860. D10, P51A, P59.

364. **JARED⁶ SAWYER** [see 167], b. 27 Mar 1787 Orford NH, d. 15 Jun 1869 Lyme NH, m. 20 Oct 1815 Orford NH Cynthia Dewey, b. 17 Nov 1794 d. 1 Mar 1862. Farmer. Joined church in Orford NH 15 Apr 1827.

Sarah Ann, b. 1816, d. 12 Dec 1857, m. 21 Jan 1840 John Richardson.
Bradley, b. 1820, d. 7 Oct 1839.
Bela, b. 10 Aug 1825 Orford NH, d. 16 Oct 1904, m. Orford NH Deborah Joselyn of Lyme NH, b. 9 Dec 1827 d. 8 Feb 1917, dau. Freeman and Abigail (Bowman) Joselyn. Town Clerk, Selectman for Lyme NH. CH: Arthur H., b. 6 Feb 1854, d. 12 Oct 1889, unm. In Lyme NH 1870.
More unnamed children listed in census.

Sources: Orford NH census 1830, 1840, 1860. Lyme NH census 1870. D34, N7, N6.

365. **ICHABOD⁶ SAWYER** [see 167], b. 3 May 1796 Orford NH, m. 15 Jun 1827 Beverly MA Anna Woodbury of Danvers MA, b. ca. 1805. Currier. S/land in Maine 1829.

Anna P., b. 31 Nov 1829, d. 12 Jun 1847.
John Woodbury, b. 14 Nov 1832, d. 5 Sep 1833.
John Woodbury, b. 5 Nov 1835 Danvers MA, m. 8 Feb 1871 Danvers MA Mary E. Proctor, b. 1839, dau. Edward J. and Mary Ann (Woodbury) Proctor. Harvard College 1859. Physician. In Danvers MA 1850, Salem MA 1867-81, Providence RI 1871.
Asenath Augusta, b. 11 Jul 1838.

Sources: Danvers MA census 1830, 1840, 1850. VR Danvers MA. R10c.

366. **BENNING⁶ SAWYER** [see 168], b. 27 Jul 1785 Orford NH, d. 17 Nov 1870 Thetford VT, m. 25 Dec 1808 Lydia Thompson, b. 11 Dec 1785 d. 16 Mar 1866. Dartmouth College. In Lyme NH 1830.

628 John Thompson⁷, 1810-1894.
Abigail D., b. 26 Dec 1811, d. 27 Mar 1812.
Benning Wentworth, b. 14 Jul 1813 Orford NH, m. 1834 Melissa Rice, b. ?. In Lyme NH.
Caleb Abel, b. 6 Mar 1815, m. 4 Jul 1833 Clarissa Harvey, b. ?. Went to Iowa.
Eliza A., b. 31 Jan 1818, d. 5 Mar 1897, m. 16 Sep 1846 Abner B. Hosford.
Edmund Freeman, b. 21 Apr 1820 Lyme NH, m. 7 May 1851 Sarah E. Carpenter of Strafford VT, b. 3 May 1832. Mechanic. CH: Effie, b. 22 Feb 1861.
629 Albert Edward⁷, 1822-1893.
Lydia L., b. 15 Jul 1824, m. 29 Apr 1846 Willard White.
Sarah J., b. 20 Dec 1826, m. 2 Jan 1851 Hilliard White.

Sources: Orford NH census 1810. Lyme NH census 1830, 1840, 1850, 1860, 1870. VR. SA/VT. D11, H72, John Freeman Sawyer rec.

367. **JONATHAN STRONG[6] SAWYER** [see 168], b. 7 Apr 1790 Orford NH, d. 11 Mar 1858, m. May 1813 Orford NH Ruth Phelps, b. 1788 d. 1863. In Orford NH 1840.

Ruth, b. Sep 1815, d. 11 May 1829.

Jonathan N., b. 1823 Orford NH, m. 1 Jan 1850 in VT Cordelia M. Metcalf, b. ?. CH: Abigail A., b. 1852.

Abigail, b. 1828, m. 6 Oct 1851 Harold Glines.

Child, b. ?, d. 1833.

Charles, b. ca. 1813, m. 30 Jan 1844 (div. 1861) Lyme NH Elizabeth G. Dimmock, b. 1822. In Orford NH. CH: Ellen, b. 1845; George W., b. Apr 1849 Orford NH, d. 19 Feb 1913 Bangor ME, m. Sarah O. _____ b. 1855, CH: Jennie E. b. ca. 1874; AugustaM. b. ?, m. 14 Sep 1869 Isaac E McAllister.

More unnamed children listed in census.

Sources: Orford NH census 1840, 1850, 1860. ME 1880 census index. VR SA/ ME, SA/NH. N6, N7, H58A.

368. **CALVIN[6] SAWYER** [see 169], b. 27 Nov 1796 Norwich VT, d. 12 May 1883, m. 17 Jan 1822 Chelsea VT Fanny Hatch of Preston CT, b. 9 Dec 1799 d. 4 Aug 1889, dau. Joseph and Betsey (Weeden) Hatch. Farmer.

Lucius Carlton, b. 11 Dec 1822, d. 2 Jan 1844.

630 Charles Curtis[7], 1825-1907.

Edith Maria, b. 19 Aug 1828.

Milo S., b. 11 Nov 1830 Norwich VT, d. 2 Oct 1861.

Margaret Ellen, b. 10 Jun 1832, d. 27 Dec 1851.

631 John W.[7], b. 1836.

Joseph C., b. 13 Jul 1838 Norwich VT, m. 20 Dec 1810 in Vermont Ellen M. Chase of Hartford VT, b. 1841. In Norwich VT 1850.

Catherine F., b. 1842, d. 21 Feb 1852.

Sources: Norwich VT census 1830, 1840, 1850. VR SA/VT. G14, Robert L. Taylor rec.

369. **ORAMEL[6] SAWYER** [see 169], b. 8 May 1798 Norwich VT, d. 2 Oct 1875, m.(1) 8 Nov 1824 Royalton VT Alvira Parkhurst of Royalton VT b. 31 Mar 1798 d. 3 Nov 1825, dau. Joseph and Meriam (Burroughs) Parkhurst; m.(2) 27 Feb 1827 Hartford VT Charlotte Poor of Massachusetts, b. 1796 d. 29 Mar 1873. Farmer, saddler, postmaster, town representative, Selectman for Royalton VT.

Alvira, b. 27 Oct 1825, d. 31 Aug 1908, m. 14 Jun 1860 Joseph Root. Went to Pennsylvania.

Charlotte, b. 11 Dec 1828, d. 7 Oct 1874, m. 1 Jan 1856 General Alonzo Jackman.

632 Charles Edward[7], 1830-1879.

Sources: Royalton VT census 1840, 1850. VR SA/VT. L42.

370. **ALMON[6] SAWYER** [see 169], b. 5 Aug 1803 Norwich VT, d. 20 Oct 1878 Cincinnati OH, m. 23 Oct 1828 Charlotte N. Libby of Limington ME, b. 17 Nov 1807 d. 28 Apr 1888, dau. Abner and Anna (Harding) Libby. In Exeter NH 1830. Bur. in Spring Grove Cem., Cincinnati OH.

Augustus J., b. 28 Aug 1829 Cincinnati OH, d. 17 Feb 1900, m. 9 Jan 1853 Marie Chard.

Francis O., b. 22 Dec 1833, d. 21 Oct 1915.

Charlotte Anna, b. 4 May 1842, d. 8 May 1922.

Sources: Exeter NH census 1830. T6A, Family Bible.

371. **REUBEN[6] SAWYER** [see 170], b. 11 Mar 1798 Monkton VT, d. 29 Jun 1869 Leyden NY, m.(1) 9 Sep 1819 West Haven VT Laura Wyman, b. 1799 d. 25 Jul 1847; m.(2) 26 Jul 1848 Brandon VT Eliza Barber, b. 1807 d. 21 Nov 1875 East Hubbardston VT. Minister. In Brandon VT 1820, West Haven VT 1830, New London VT 1840, Chester VT 1850.

William C., b. 1816, d. 7 Jan 1826.
Samantha, b. 1820, m. 23 Oct 1855 John D. Lord. Went to New York.
Artimas W., b. 182? Brandon VT. Minister, teacher.
Edward, b. 1829 West Haven VT. Physician. In Chester VT 1850.
Caroline M., b. 1830, d. 26 Nov 1861 Hinesburgh VT.
Newton H., b. 1831 W.Haven VT, d. 7 Apr 1883. Postmaster for Chester VT 1850.
Frances A., b. 1836.
633 Everett R.[7], b. 1839.

Sources: Brandon VT census 1820. W. Haven VT census 1830. New London NH census 1840. Chester VT census 1850. VR SA/VT. D34, L39.

371. **JOHN FAY[6] SAWYER** [see 170], b. 2 Jun 1802 Monkton VT, m. 25 Mar 1823 Brandon VT Mary Gilbert, b. ?.

John G., b. ca. 1825 Brandon VT, m.(1) ?; m.(2) 27 Jun 1855 Plainfield MA Eliza A. Shaw of Plainfield MA, b. ca. 1828, dau. Josiah and Lydia Shaw. In Albion NY.

Sources: VR SA/MA.

372. **ISAAC M.[6] SAWYER** [see 170], b. 1808 Monkton VT, m. Hannah N. Buell of Vermont, b. 1809. Baptist minister. In Amesbury MA 1848.

Edward A., b. 1831 (Monkton VT?). In Nantucket MA 1850.
Lois B., b. 1834.
634 Isaac[7], b. 1837.
Mary Ellen, b. 27 Jun 1848.

Sources: Nantucket MA census 1850. VR SA/VT, SA/MA. P65.

373. **SAMUEL[6] SAWYER** [see 171], b. 11 Apr 1779 Hartland CT, d. 29 Jun 1837 Granville MA, m. Adah _____, b. ?.

Adah Elnora, b. 1807, d. 2 Mar 1808.
Sarah M., b. 1809, d. 7 Jan 1810.
635 Samuel[7], b. ca. 1814.

Sources: Granville MA census 1810, 1820, Lyme CT census 1840, 1850. VR SA/CT. Marshall W. McCoy rec.

374. **AUSTIN[6] SAWYER** [see 173], b. 4 Jun 1796 Shrewsbury MA, m. 29 Aug 1816 Shrewsbury MA Susannah Temple, b. ?, dau. Joseph S. Temple.

Clarissa Relief, b. 15 Jan 1817.
Ann, b. ca. 1818, m. 20 Jun 1838 in Mendon MA Artimus Keith.
Daughter, b. (1820-1825).
Daughter, b. (1825-1830).
Leander H., b. 23 Sep 1826 Burrillville RI, m. Huldah Mowry of Uxbridge MA, b. 15 Sep 1824, dau. Gideon and Anne (Dennis) Mowry. Wheelwright. In Uxbridge MA 1850. CH: Philena T., b. 23 Sep 1848.

Sources: Shrewsbury MA census 1820. Providence RI census 1830. Smithfield RI census 1840. Uxbridge MA census 1850. VR Shrewsbury MA, Mendon MA, Uxbridge MA, SA/MA.

375. **FRANKLIN ADAMS[6] SAWYER** [see 173], b. 11 Jul 1809 Shrewsbury MA, m.(1) 8 Sep 1833 Uxbridge MA Hannah Prentis of Hopkinton MA, b. ca. 1811 d. 28 Aug 1849, dau. Abner and Hannah Prentis; m.(2) 9 Oct 1850 Shrewsbury MA Ann (Munroe) Harrington of Shrewsbury MA, b. ?, dau. Abraham and Sally Munroe. Bootmaker. In Shrewsbury MA 1850.

Susan R., b. ca. 1835, m. 1858 in Wisconsin Francis H. Harrington.

George C., b. ca. 1838 Shrewsbury MA, m. 27 Nov 1866 Milford MA Jennie A. Wales of Milford MA, b. 5 May 1842, dau. Thomas and Lucy (Fairbanks) Wales. Bootmaker. Civil War: Enl. 21 Jun 1861; deserted 1 Jul 1862; discharged 9 Dec 1862. In Shrewsbury MA 1850.

Hannah J., b. 29 Jan 1846, d. 28 Aug 1847.

Sources: Shrewsbury MA census 1850. VR Hopkinton MA, Uxbridge MA, SA/MA.

377. **ELIAKIM[6] SAWYER** [see 174], b. 22 Jan 1786 Lancaster MA, d. 5 Jan 1858, m. 3 Jul 1810 Sterling MA Hannah Bailey of Sterling MA, b. 13 Oct 1784, dau. Shubal and Hannah (Whitmore) Bailey. In Sterling MA, Warwick MA, Boston MA 1811, Lancaster MA 1812.

Helen Ann Byron, b. 15 May 1807, adopted by Dr. Isreal Atherton.

Lucy Ann, b. 22 May 1811, d. 6 Dec 1856, m.(1) Samuel Austin, m.(2) Amos Sawyer.

Eliakim, b. 7 Dec 1812 Lancaster MA, m. 17 Feb 1839 Boston MA (div. Jun 1859) Louisa _____, b. ?. Mason. In Warwick MA, Boston MA 1850. No CH. Note: Census says wife was Nancy.

Cynthia, b. 1815, d. 9 Apr 1816 Templeton MA.

Samuel Ward, b. ca. 1817 Warwick MA.

George M., b. ca. 1818 Warwick MA.

636 Charles Bailey[7], 1819-1896.

637 George M.[7], b. ca. 1822.

Sources: Boston MA census 1850. VR Sterling MA, SA/MA. B5, R30.

378. **EUSEBIUS[6] SAWYER** [see 176], b. 3 Jul 1803 Lancaster MA, m. Deborah _____, b. ca. 1802. Soap boiler. In Concord MA, Cambridge MA.

Jesse Lee, b. 26 Oct 1822 Concord MA, m. 29 Oct 1848 Cambridge MA Olivia A. Abbot of Salem MA, b. 1831, dau. Erastus Abbot. Painter. In Cambridge MA 1850. CH: Adelaide, b. 23 Feb 1850; Olivia C., b. 12 Dec 1851; Alice W., b. 16 May 1854; Grace B., b. 20 May 1856; Evelyn Barker, b. 2 Jun 1859.

George Eusebius, b. 11 Jun 1825. Painter. In Cambridge MA.

Daniel Allen, b. 23 Jun 1827, d. 26 Nov 1843.

Caroline Brooks, b. 18 Jul 1829, m. 31 Dec 1849 Cambridge MA Albert Goodman.

Edward Howard, b. 11 Aug 1831 Cambridge MA, m. 5 Feb 1856 Boston MA Henrietta M. Marsh of Dedham MA, b. 1836, dau. Henry Marsh. Driver. CH: Edna, b. 20 Aug 1860; E. Lillian, b. ca. 1862, m. 10 Apr 1883 Boston MA William P. Cook.

Charles Augustus, b. 5 Sep 1833 Cambridge MA, m. 15 Sep 1875 Boston MA Mary A. King of Providence RI, b. 1850, dau. Bela and Mary King. Painter, soap boiler. In Cambridge MA 1850.

Minerva Hoyt, b. 25 Aug 1835, m. 5 Jun 1859 Cambridge MA Thomas Howe.

William Henry, b. 30 Nov 1837 Cambridge MA, m. 17 Nov 1869 Keene NH Emma F. Pike, b. 1844. In Keene NH 1870.

Ellen D., b. 1839, m. 20 Dec 1837 Cambridge MA Edward T. Fairfield.

638 Thomas Parker[7], b. ca. 1840.

Albert V., b. ca. 1842 Cambridge MA.

Sources: Cambridge MA census 1830, 1840, 1850. Keene NH census 1870. VR Cambridge MA, Keene NH, SA/MA.

379. **EPHRAIM[6] SAWYER** [see 176], b. 3 Apr 1778 South Hero VT, d. 21 Mar 1851 in Pennsylvania m. Mary Stearns, b. ?. Minister.
639 John[7], 1815-1865. Went to Pennsylvania.
Sources: V2.

380. **ALLEN[6] SAWYER** [see 176], b. 1 Jul 1792 So. Hero VT, d. 1851 Clermont IA m. 1815 Clarissa Hazen, b. 1795 d. 1890.
Charles Pinkney, b. 25 Jun 1816. Went to Iowa.
Sarah H., b. 2 Jun 1818.
Daniel, b. 30 Apr 1820 No. Hero VT, d. 11 Jul 1888 Plum Valley NB, m. 1840 Sarah Hazen, b. 1 May 1820 d. 1 Apr 1856, dau. Solomon and Sally (Knight) Hazen. Sarah bur. in Jerusalem Cem., No. Hero VT.
Ephraim, b. (1820-1825).
Alcesta, b. 6 Nov 1822. Went to Iowa.
James Lucius, b. 4 Jul 1825. Went to Iowa.
Mary, b. 18 Apr 1828. Went to New York.
George Washington, b. 1831, d. 1851. Went to Iowa.
Harriet D., b. 29 May 1833. Went to Iowa.
640 Iram Allen[7], 1839-1909.
Sources: North Hero VT 1820, 1830, 1840. VR SA/VT. H39.

381. **PETER GREEN[6] SAWYER** [see 177], b. 8 May 1783 Clarendon VT, d. Jun 1867 Sawyerville, Quebec, Canada, m. 11 Sep 1803 Polly Hall of Canada, b. 9 Jan 1785 d. 22 May 1864. In Newport, Canada.
Polly, b. 29 May 1804, d. 1879, m. 25 Jul 1819 Eaton, Quebec, Canada, John Bennett Heard.
641 Artemus[7], 1809-1889.
Emma, b. 15 Jan 1817, d. 8 Jan 1858?. m. 17 Sep 1838 Eaton, Quebec, Canada, George R. Picard.
642 Charles C.[7], 1822-1907.
Jerome, b. 19 Jun 1834, m. 20 Dec 1864 Margaret S. Cairnes, b. ?.
Sources: VR Wallingford VT. S5, D11, Sawyer Bible in Eaton, Quebec, Canada.

382. **JOSIAH[6] SAWYER** [see 177], b. 20 Apr 1786 Clarendon VT, d. 22 Oct 1839 Sawyerville, Quebec, Canada, m. Nancy Rice, b. ?.
Ephraim A., b. ?, m. 17 Mar 1846 Adeline A. Cummings, b. ?.
Sources: VR Clarendon VT. D11, S5, Sawyer Bible in Eaton, Quebec, Canada.

383. **RUFUS[6] SAWYER** [see 177], b. 24 Apr 1798 Eaton, Quebec, Canada, d. 9 Sep 1874, m. 26 Aug 1823 Ruth Alger, b. ?.
Rollin Augustus, b. ?, m. Martha E. Linn, b. ?.
Sources: S5.

384. **JAMES LUCIUS[6] SAWYER** [see 178], b. 9 Apr 1791 Clarendon VT, d. Nov 1850 New York, m. 1827 Julia Barr Kemp, b. Jun 1800 d. 1851. Lawyer. Admitted to bar Sep 1812. In Burlington VT, New York 1829.
Helen Lydia, b. 6 Aug 1830.
643 James Lucius[7], b. 1836.
Sources: VR SA/VT. S66, D11.

385. **HORACE BUCKLIN[6] SAWYER** [see 178], b. 22 Feb 1797 Burlington VT, d. 14 Feb 1860, m. 5 Nov 1833 Roxalana (Shaler) Wadsworth, b. ?. War of 1812: Enl. US Navy 4 Jun 1812; taken prisoner on Lake Champlain; in Halifax, Nova Scotia for one year; on *"Old Ironsides"* when she was captured. Note: For details see Vermont Quarterly Gazette, vol. I, pg. 581.

George W., b. 1823, d. 15 Aug 1838.
George Augustus, b. 9 Mar 1839 Burlington VT.
Emilie, b. ?, m. 19 Nov 1863 John W. Moore.

Sources: VR SA/VT. H43, D60, J18.

386. **JEDEDIAH S.[6] SAWYER** [see 179], b. 1801 So. Hero VT, m. 17 Apr 1826 Harriet Weeks, b. 27 Jun 1806, dau. Amos and Sabra (Boardman) Weeks.

Amos Weeks, b. 1 Jun 1825, d. 12 Dec 1855.
Harry, b. 12 May 1827 So. Hero VT, m. Minerva Parsons, b. ?.
Caroline, b. 20 Mar 1829.
Sophia M., b. 28 Jan 1831, m. Rev. William Coffin.
644 Albert Butler[7], b. 1837. Went to Illinois.
Harriet M., b. 11 Sep 1838, d. 13 Nov 1839.
Maria L., b. 20 Aug 1840. Went to Illinois.
Ellen M., b. 2 Oct 1843. Went to Illinois.
John, b. 8 Apr 1848, d. 1870.
Emma A., b. 17 Jun 1851, m. Zenophon L. Wardell. Went to Illinois.

Sources: So.Hero VT census 1830. Milton VT census 1840. VR SA/VT. L5.

387. **JOHN C.[6] SAWYER** [see 180], b. 17 Jan 1800 Brandon VT, d. 1 Apr 1853 Sudbury VT, m.(1) Lois R. _____, b. 1811 d. 15 Nov 1832 (VR); m.(2) Eliza B. _____, b. 1814 d. 10 Feb 1842. Merchant, farmer. In Brandon VT 1830. Note: Lois's d. is recorded in Sudbury VT as 15 Nov 1837.

645 David L.[7], 1835-1875.
John C., b. 1842 Sudbury VT.

Sources: Brandon VT census 1830, 1840, 1850. VR SA/VT. B78.

388. **ROSWELL HOPKINS[6] SAWYER** [see 180], b. 25 Apr 1803 Vergennes VT, d. 29 Jan 1875 New York, m.(1) 26 Nov 1832 LucretiaMiner, b. 17 Feb 1811 d. 30 Sep 1846, dau. William W. and Elizabeth (Lounsberry) Miner; m.(2) 24 Feb 1848 Sarah Miner, b. 7 Feb 1809 d. 28 Feb 1865.

Mary Elizabeth, b. 24 Aug 1833, m. 30 Jul 1851 Thomas D. Skinner.
Roswell Miner, b. 1 Jul 1836, d. 26 Dec 1866. Lawyer.
William Artemus, b. 23 May 1840, d. 12 May 1879.
Lucretia Miner, b. 23 May 1844, m. 23 May 1867 Benjamin T. Kissam.
Horace Miner, b. 18 Jul 1849, d. 5 Sep 1893.
Sarah Miner, b. 24 Mar 1851.

Sources: S29.

389. **SAMUEL[6] SAWYER** [see 181], b. 1814 Templeton MA, m. 17 Dec 1846 Templeton MA Harriet L. Bryant of Templeton MA, b. ca. 1823, dau. Nathan and Tabitah Bryant. Farmer. In Templeton MA 1850.

646 Charles C.[7], b. 1850.

Sources: Templeton MA census 1850. VR Templeton MA. B11.

390. **PUTNAM[6] SAWYER** [see 182], b. 21 Apr 1808, Sterling MA, d. 25 Sep 1875, m. (I) 1 May 1841 Eliza Kendall of Mason NH, b. ca. 1815. Farmer.

William, b. ca. 1841 Sterling MA.

Samuel Kendall, b. 10 Dec 1843 Sterling MA, m. 29 Apr 1879 Northfield MA Delia Minerva Stearns of Northfield MA, b. 7 Mar 1854 d. 7 Aug 1889, dau. A. D. and Delia Stearns. In Sterling MA 1850.

Mary, b. 1 Apr 1848.

Martha P., b. 1851, m. 10 Aug 1870 in Clinton MA Lorenzo Brockway.

George P., b. 1856, d. 15 May 1875, m. 5 Sep 1874 Anna C. Taylor.

Frederick A., b. 26 May 1862 Sterling MA, m.(1) 25 Nov 1895 Brookline NH Alice Rockwood of Brookline NH, b. ca. 1862; m.(2) 25 Apr 1884 Boston MA Ella A. Leonard of New Brunswick, Canada, b. 1864, dau. John and Asenath Leonard. Fish dealer.

Hattie Eliza, b. 22 Mar 1866.

Sources: Sterling MA census 1850. VR Brookline NH, Sterling MA, SA/MA. R30, N14.

391. **ANSON J.[6] SAWYER** [see 184], b. Oct 1819 Ludlow VT, d. 7 Jun 1897 Ludlow VT, m.(1) Elizabeth A. Hall of Springfield VT, b. 1826 d. 10 Mar 1871, dau. Samuel and Betsey Hall; m.(2) 26 Jan 1876 Mary E. Herrick, b. ?. Farmer.

George Anson, b. 1854 Ludlow VT, m. 14 Feb 1883 Charlestown NH Anna Louise Butterfield of Andover VT, b. 1856, dau. Henry and Louisa Butterfield. Innkeeper. In Chester VT, Windsor VT 1887. CH: Louise Abbie, b. 22 Oct 1888, m. 29 Jan 1908 Lewis A. Allen.

Vettie A., b. 15 Nov 1863, m. 11 Jan 1883 Wallace E. Hemmingway.

Sources: VR SA/VT.

392. **BENJAMIN[6] SAWYER** [see 185], b. 16 Oct 1791 Piermont NH, d. 23 Feb 1855 Littleton NH, m. 16 Jan 1820 Bradford VT Lydia Prouty of Bradford VT, b. Apr 1801 d. Oct 1870 Fairlee VT. Farmer. In Fairlee VT 1820, Littleton VT 1830.

Phebe Jane, b. 4 Jun 1821, d. 12 Mar 1893, m. 21 Nov 1849 Littleton NH John D. Chandler.

Emeline, b. 21 Dec 1824, d. 12 Feb 1899, m. Dec 1850 Fairlee VT Eben Whiting.

Ira Caswell, b. 2 Mar 1827 Littleton NH, m. Mar 1857 Fanny Dyke, b. ?.

Benjamin, b. 14 Sep 1829 Littleton NH, d. 6 Dec 1904 Littleton NH, m. 9 Dec 1854 Dalton NH Sophronia Carter of Wolcott VT, b. 2 Jul 1830 d. 30 Apr 1914, dau. Jeremiah and Diantha (Moffet) Carter. Farmer. CH: Benjamin, b. 8 Apr 1856, d. 6 Nov 1882, unm; Sophronia, b. 5 Nov 1857, m. 4 Jul 1876 Willard R. Humphrey; Edna, b. 24 Aug 1859, d. 14 Mar 1881; Ella, b. 25 Apr 1860, m. 14 Apr 1881 Harvey Howland.

Sources: Fairlee VT census 1820. Littleton NH census 1830, 1840, 1850, 1870. Dalton NH census 1860. VR SA/VT. J2, D6, J18, N6.

393. **ENOS[6] SAWYER** [see 185], b. 12 Feb 1793 Piermont NH, d. 27 Oct 1882 Fairlee VT, m. 28 Dec 1823 Fairlee VT Martha Follet, b. 21 Jan 1804 d. 9 Dec 1856. War of 1812. He bur. in Fairlee VT. Note: [D41] says Enos d. 29 Oct 1883.

Hannah Marie, b. 26 Dec 1824, m. 1 Jan 1850 Charlestown MA William B. Eastman.

Martha J., b. 26 Dec 1825, d. 9 Jun 1826.

Nancy J., b. 11 Jan 1827, d. 9 Jun 1832.

Martha A., b. 22 Jul 1828, d. 31 Dec 1912, m. Daniel Freeman.

Adaline W., b. 19 Aug 1830, d. 6 Apr 1843.

Mary P., b. 12 Oct 1831, d. 14 May 1856.

Azubah E., b. 20 Dec 1832, d. 4 Nov 1856.

Harriet K., b. 13 Nov 1834.
Ira E., b. 4 Nov 1837, d. 14 Apr 1842.
Lucius W., b. 13 May 1839 Fairlee VT, d. 4 May 1901 Fairlee VT.
Elliot F., b. 10 Apr 1842, d. 8 Apr 1909 Littleton NH, unm. Civil War.
647 Amos Blanchard[7], 1843-1912.
Sources: Fairlee VT census 1830, 1840, 1850. VR SA/VT, SA/MA, SA/NH. J2, D11, H43, C50.

394. **MARK[6] SAWYER** [see 186], b. 29 Jan 1799 Topsham VT, d. 9 Mar 1865 Topsham VT, m. 26 Jun 1823 Abigail Bayley, b. ?, dau. Abner and Hannah (White) Bayley. Farmer. Wid. m. ca. 1869 Joseph Blodgett.
Anna, b. 22 Sep 1825, d. 10 Jun 1837.
Jacob B., b. 17 Sep 1827, d. 5 Jun 1863 in Civil War.
M____ W., b. ca. 1831, m. 2 Jun 1874 Sarah A. White.
John, b. 1836 Topsham VT, d. 20 Jul 1913 Topsham VT, m. 1 Jan 1866 Topsham VT Clara E. Dickey of Topsham VT, b. 1849 d. 15 Jun 1877, dau. T_____ J. and Lydia Dickey. Farmer. Civil War: Company H, 11th Regiment, VT Volunteers. CH: Son, b. 30 Sep 1867, d. 30 Sep 1867; Carrie E., b. 1871, m. 8 Sep 1898 Cornish VT Harmon J. Locke; Daughter, b. 25 Jan 1876, d. 24 Mar 1876.
Sources: VR SA/VT. C84.

395. **SAMUEL[6] SAWYER** [see 189], b. 13 Nov 1800 Sterling MA, d. 29 Dec 1869 Sterling MA, m. 20 Nov 1823 Sterling MA Eunice Houghton of Sterling MA, b. 17 Dec 1802 d. 18 Jan 1885, dau. Manesseh and Eunice (Kendall) Houghton.
Jane Elizabeth, b. 15 Dec 1824, m. 18 Oct 1855 Sterling MA George Goss.
648 Ezra[7], b. 1827.
649 Frederick Augustus[7], 1832-1895.
Mary, b. 20 Jan 1834.
650 Henry Samuel[7], b. 1843.
Sources: Sterling MA census 1820, 1830, 1840, 1850. VR SA/MA. K3, R30, H75, G20.

396 **EZRA[6] SAWYER** [see 190], b. 22 Jul 1794 Sterling MA, d. 15 Apr 1872, m.(1) 7 Feb 1821 Sterling MA Eliza Houghton of Lancaster MA, b. 22 May 1794 d. 15 May 1851, dau. Oliver and Abigail (Hovey) Houghton; m.(2) 30 Nov 1853 Fitchburg MA Sophronia (Liscomb) Crosby of Hinsdale NH, b. 1810, dau. Lemuel and Submit Liscomb. Master mason. In Newton MA 1821, Clinton MA 1850.
651 Edmund Houghton[7], 1821-1879.
Henry Hovey, b. 18 Apr 1824, d. 30 Jan 1842.
652 Ezra Thomas[7], b. 1827.
653 Francis Oliver[7], 1829-1904.
654 Nathaniel Chandler[7], 1831-1910.
Sarah Elizabeth, b. 7 Aug 1833, m. 20 Oct 1852 Hingham MA Watson Gore.
Eliza Ann, b. 31 Dec 1838, m. 5 Jun 1860 Dr. Orin Warren.
Sources: Clinton MA census 1850. VR SA/MA. W12, H80, J20, D6, M19, G20, F25.

397. **THOMAS[6] SAWYER** [see 190], b. 18 Oct 1796 Sterling MA, d. 10 Jun 1846 Sterling MA, m. 4 Jul 1819 Lancaster MA Polly Wright of Lancaster MA, b. 1792 d. 3 Feb 1864. He bur. in Middle Cem., Sterling MA. Wid. in Clinton MA 1850.
Mary C., b. 13 May 1820, d. 15 Oct 1903.
Martha W., b. 20 Oct 1825, m. 2 Oct 1865 Somerville MA Clark Ranney.
Elizabeth E., b. Jan 1828.

Emory Thomas, b. 19 Mar 1835 Sterling MA, d. 22 Mar 1864 Clinton MA.
Sources: Clinton MA census 1850. VR Lancaster MA. G20.

398. **NATHANIEL[6] SAWYER** [see 190], b. 2 Sep 1808 Sterling MA, m. 15 Mar 1847 Emily Clark, b. ?.

Henry N., b. 11 Feb 1848 Sterling MA.
Mary E., b. 28 Aug 1850.
Joseph, b. 7 Dec 1852 Sterling MA.
Edmund, b. 6 Jul 1856 Sterling MA.

Sources: G20.

399. **LUKE R.[6] SAWYER** [see 190], b. 23 Jan 1814 Sterling MA, m. 1 May 1844 Sterling MA Martha Burpee of Sterling MA, b. 1820, dau. John and Betsey Burpee. Farmer.

Henry Francis, b. 15 Feb 1845 Sterling MA, m. 16 May 1842 Clinton MA Margaret Jane Blanchard of Harvard MA, b. ca. 1860, dau. John and Elizabeth Blanchard. Engineer. In Malden MA. CH: Son, b. 30 Dec 1894.
Christopher Thomas, b. 23 Aug 1848 Sterling MA, d. 10 Nov 1853.
Anna E., b. 30 Sep 1850.
Charles Addison, b. 6 Sep 1855 Sterling MA, m. 21 Oct 1885 Nantucket MA Alice Coggeshall of Nantucket MA, b. 23 Aug 1861, dau. Charles and Phebe (Swain) Coggeshall. In Malden MA. CH: Edith H., b. 20 Aug 1886.
Martha C., b. 29 Oct 1857.

Sources: Sterling MA census 1850. VR Sterling MA, SA/MA. C57.

400. **GEORGE[6] SAWYER** [see 192], b. 26 Jul 1822 Boston MA, m.(1) 15 Nov 1843 Medford MA Susan Eames of Brockton MA, b. 1821 d. 19 Dec 1863; m.(2) 9 Sep 1874 Boston MA Lois G. Knight of Naples ME, b. 21 Aug 1824 d. 4 Sep 1910, dau. Nathaniel and Hannah (Mugford) Knight. Shoe manufacturer. In Medford MA 1850, North Bridgewater MA 1853.

Susan Frances, b. 20 May 1845, d. 8 Sep 1846.
Helen L., b. 2 Jan 1847, m. 15 Sep 1867 No. Bridgewater MA Charles Dalton.
Martha B., b. 24 Nov 1848, m. 18 Sep 1870 No. Bridgewater MA Thomas Childs.
655 George Carroll[7], b. 1851.
Hattie Marie, b. 20 Jun 1853.
Mary Abbie, b. 22 Jun 1855, m. 30 Oct 1878 Brockton MA George H. Hinkley.

Sources: Medford MA census 1850. VR Medford MA, Brockton MA, SA/MA. K13, K12, T19.

401. **WARREN[6] SAWYER** [see 192], b. 23 May 1825 Boston MA, m.(1) 1848 Medford MA Mary E. Fuller of Medford MA, b. 26 Jul 1826 d. 30 Aug 1852; m.(2) 16 Nov 1853 Boston MA Rachel Alphia Fuller of Westminster MA, b. 28 Jul 1824 d. 14 Oct 1872, dau. Milton Fuller; m.(3) 27 Jan 1880 Boston MA Ellen R. White, b. 22 Oct 1843, dau. Henry B. and Priscilla P. White; m.(4) Mary Tilton, b. 28 May 1829; m.(5) Lucy J. Allen, b. 17 Nov 1836. Merchant, Bank president. In Cambridge MA, Medford MA 1851.

Fanny Fuller, b. 15 Oct 1851, m. 27 Apr 1880 Boston MA Walter L. Hayes.
Herbert, b. 26 Nov 1855 Cambridge MA.
Mary Cummings, b. 28 Mar 1864.

Sources: VR Cambridge MA, Medford MA, SA/MA. G20.

402. **LEANDER[6] SAWYER** [see 193], b. 1810 Lancaster MA, m.(1) 15 Apr 1834 Shrewsbury MA Eunice Sophronia Allen of Shrewsbury MA, b. 21 Mar 1807 d. 1850 Shrewsbury MA, dau.

Liberty and Mary Allen; m.(2) Abigail M. (Brigham) Green, wid. of James, b. 4 Feb 1812 d. 24 Jan 1885, dau. John and Sarah (Fay) Brigham. Shoemaker. In Shrewsbury MA.

Everett Leander, b. 10 May 1835 Shrewsbury MA.
Appleton, b. 1837, d. 19 Feb 1839.
Marion Sophronia, b. 24 Jan 1839.
Appleton Lohrstein, b. 29 Mar 1841 Shrewsbury MA, m. 10 Oct 1865 Worcester MA Sarah C. Whittemore of Shrewsbury MA, b. ca. 1841, dau. William W. and Eunice Whittemore.
Caroline Pauline, b. 19 Nov 1842, m. 17 Jun 1873 Worcester MA Herbert L. Savage.
Henry Adolphus, b. 5 Oct 1845, d. 3 Sep 1846.
Abigail Martin, b. 28 Apr 1852, d. 18 Mar 1898, m. 16 Sep 1883 Edmond W. Shepard.

Sources: Shrewsbury MA census 1840, 1850. VR Shrewsbury MA, SA/MA. E16, B44, F11A, C8, B84.

403. **JOHN[6] SAWYER** [see 194], b. 19 Jan 1815 Watertown MA, d. 5 Sep 1888 Stratford NH, m.(1) 7 Apr 1836 Hopkinton MA Fanny V. Fitch, b. 23 Jan 1809 d. 8 Aug 1844, dau. Elijah and Mary (Valentine) Fitch; m.(2) 20 Nov 1844 Hopkinton MA Jane Hotchkiss, b. 1823, dau. Ira H. and Charlotte Hotchkiss. Shoemaker. In Hopkinton MA, Acton MA, Stow MA, New York 1858.

Francena, b. 6 Jan 1837.
Isobell, b. 14 Apr 1840, m. 8 Jul 1862 Foxboro MA James W. Leonard.
Anna, b. 20 May 1842, m. 1 Aug 1868 Foxboro MA Lorenzo Wallace.
Arthur Tappan, b. 6 Jul 1844, d. 13 Jul 1846.
Arabella, b. 20 Sep 1845, d. 15 Mar 1851 Stow MA.
John Arthur, b. 1847, d. 12 Jan 1851 Stow MA.
656 Judson Cherubini[7], b. 1849.
657 Webber[7], b. ca. 1851.
Samuel, b. 1853, d. 5 Sep 1874.
Emma, b. ca. 1858, m. 18 May 1877 Osmore Howe.
Ann, b. 1860.
George S., b. 1862.
Nellie, b. ?, m. 18 Dec 1879 Stratford NH James L. Day.

Sources: Stow MA census 1850. VR Hopkinton MA, Acton MA, Stowe MA, SA/VT, SA/MA. V1, N6.

404. **SAMUEL[6] SAWYER** [see 194], b. 14 Sep 1817 Waltham MA, d. 1 Apr 1851 Sudbury MA, m. 18 Aug 1839 Hopkinton MA Eliza Howe, b. ?. In Sudbury MA, Hopkinton MA.

Ira J., b. 24 Jan 1845 Hopkinton MA.

Sources: Hopkinton MA census 1840. VR Hopkinton MA, SA/MA.

405. **GEORGE WASHINGTON[6] SAWYER** [see 194], b. 8 Sep 1821 Waltham MA, m.(1) 11 Oct 1840 Hopkinton MA Betsey Merritt of Framingham MA, b. ?; m.(2) 12 Jan 1879 Ashland MA Katie E. Barber of New York, b. ca. 1839, dau. John and Rachel Barber, her m.(2). Shoemaker. Civil War: Corporal, enl. 9 Sep 1 1861 Acton MA.

George E., b. 1842 Acton MA.
Sarah A., b. 1844, m.(1) 13 Oct 1861 Albert Edmonds, m.(2) 1868 Lucien Francis.
Mary Elizabeth, b. May 1846, d. 27 Sep 1847.
Martha T., b. 8 Jun 1848, d. 30 Aug 1848.
Alfred, b. ca. 1849 Acton MA, m. 19 Oct 1871 Acton MA Lucy Ann Walker of Sudbury MA, b. ca. 1850, dau. Abijah and Mary Walker. Shoemaker, baggagemaster. In Acton MA 1850, Sudbury MA 1876, Taunton MA 1894. CH: Emma May, b. 3 Mar 1876, m. 4

Sep 1888 Taunton MA Samuel L. Fairbanks; son, b. 27 Mar 1894. Note: Since Emma was only 12, her parents gave permission for her to marry.

Eva Louise, b. 27 Sep 1852, m. 25 Jul 1874 Newton MA Marcus O. Lane.

Albert Howard, b. 28 Jan 1858 Acton MA, m. 28 Nov 1877 New Bedford MA Eve S. Dunbar of Westport MA, b. ca. 1875, dau. David and Rebecca Dunbar. In Cambridge MA.

Mary Elizabeth, b. 16 Aug 1860, m.(1) 4 Feb 1880 Taunton MA Walter E. Cook, m.(2) 23 May 1891 Ira T. Chappell.

Sources: Acton MA census 1850. VR Hopkinton MA, Acton MA, SA/MA. P38.

406. **ANDREW JACKSON⁶ SAWYER** [see 194], b. 1832 Sudbury MA, m. 28 Oct 1854 Lowell MA Berintha W. Hood of Amherst NH, b. ?, dau. David G. and Margaret Hood. Shoemaker. Civil War: Sergeant, enl. 25 Aug 1862 Acton MA. In Sudbury MA 1850, Hopkinton MA 1854.

William E., b. 1857 Hastings NY, m. 17 Sep 1881 Milford MA Almira J. Butterfield-Puffer of Lowell MA, b. ca. 1851, dau. James and Almira (Cheever) Butterfield, her m.(2).

Sources: Sudbury MA census 1850. VR Sudbury MA, Acton MA, SA/MA. P38.

407. **THOMAS JEFFERSON⁶ SAWYER** [see 194], b. 10 Apr 1845 Sudbury MA, m. 13 Jan 1869 Waltham MA Katherine Wellington of New York City, b. 1845, dau. Thomas J. and Martha Wellington. Farmer, carpenter. In Acton MA.

Daughter, b. 16 Oct 1869.

Alice Maude, b. 21 Sep 1873, m. 3 Jun 1893 W. Acton MA Leonard F. Leavitt.

Harry W., b. 6 Aug 1875 Acton MA, m. 24 Mar 1895 Maynard MA Alice Mead of England, b. ca. 1876, dau. Mark and Sarah (Gunstone) Mead. Clerk.

Clara Luella, b. 23 Aug 1877.

Eva, b. 7 Jun 1880.

Jennie Blanche, b 3 Aug 1882.

658 Chester Arthur⁷, b. 1884.

Daughter, stillborn 27 Apr 1887.

Sources: VR SA/MA.

408. **EDWARD M.⁶ SAWYER** [see 194], b. 25 May 1847 Sudbury MA, d. 5 Oct 1936 Concord NH, m.(1) Marlboro MA (later div.) Ellen L. Webber, b. 14 Jul 1853 d. 3 Oct 1924, dau. John and Rhoda (Simpson) Webber; m.(2) 30 Dec 1875 Carrie Maynard, b. ?. Farmer. In Epsom NH, Maynard MA.

Herbert M., b. 6 Aug 1887 Maynard MA.

Sources: VR SA/MA, SA/NH. N9.

409. **FRANKLIN PIERCE⁶ SAWYER** [see 194], b. 9 Dec 1852 Sudbury MA, m. 15 Oct 1877 Clinton MA Harriet E. Turner of W. Boylston MA, b. 1856, dau. Asa and Isabella Turner. Barber, florist.

659 Herbert Leroy⁷, 1880-1953.

Sources: VR SA/MA.

410. **NATHANIEL OSGOOD⁶ SAWYER** [see 197], b. 30 Apr 1821 Skowhegan ME, m.(1) 17 Jan 1849 Amesbury MA Julia A. Sargent of Amesbury MA, b. 10 Jul 1819 d. 10 Aug 1863, dau. Willis and Hannah (Clement) Sargent; m.(2) 9 Oct 1864 Amesbury MA Sophia A. Morse of Amesbury MA, b. 1826 d. 28 Aug 1865, dau. John and Dorothy (Flint) Morse; m.(3) 9 Feb 1867

Amesbury MA Mary J. Osborn of Pittsfield MA, b. 1832, dau. Green and Mehitable Osborn. Tinworker. In Amesbury MA 1850.

Nathaniel Osgood, b. 27 Dec 1849 Amesbury MA.
Edwin A., b. 6 Oct 1856 Amesbury MA.
Arthur Willis, b. 10 Feb 1863 Amesbury MA.
Herbert Sumner, b. 13 Jan 1868 Amesbury MA.

Sources: Amesbury MA census 1850. VR Skowhegan ME, Amesbury MA, Haverhill MA, SA/MA. S10.

411. **WILLIAM GUSTAVUS$^6$ SAWYER** [see 197], b. 22 Feb 1827 Skowhegan ME, d. 24 Nov 1896 Mattamiscontis ME, m. 1 Jan 1851 Silena H. Roberts, b. 12 Sep 1830 d. 14 Sep 1889, dau. Jonathan Roberts. Farmer.

Albert G., b. 1852 Mattamiscontis ME, m.(1) 21 Jun 1874 Dover-Foxcroft ME Flora J. Bean of Guilford ME, b. 17 Jun 1853 d. 7 Jul 1886; m.(2) Sarah Jane Johnson, b. 10 Feb 1852 d. 9 Apr 1930, dau. Sylvester and Betsey Johnson. In Medford MA.
Harriet E., b. 1853, m. 18 Sep 1889 Boston MA Ernest C. Lint.
660 William H.$^7$, 1854-1946.
Addie L., b. 1858, m. Daniel Scanlon.
661 Herbert Jonathan$^7$, 1862-1948.
662 Frank O.$^7$, 1866-1954.
Maude, b. 25 Jul 1873, d. 1952, m. _____ Sanborn.

Sources: Mattamiscontis ME census 1850, 1860, 1870. ME 1880 census index. VR SA/ME, SA/MA. D51, Joann E. Sawyer rec.

412. **JOHN KIMBALL$^6$ SAWYER** [see 197], b. 23 Jul 1829 Sebec ME, d. 2 Jul 1863 Gettysburg PA, m. 12 Aug 1850 Union ME Chloe Elvira Ware of Union ME, b. 26 Jun 1828, dau. Jabez and Chloe (Titus) Ware. Tinsmith. Civil War. In Union ME, Amesbury MA 1854, Salisbury MA 1857, Northport ME 1860. Wid. m. 16 Sep 1866 Benjamin R. Field.

Deborah E., b. 30 Dec 1851, d. 24 Apr 1942, m.(1) Charles M. Skinner, m.(2) Pelham C. Morrill.
663 Charles Horace$^7$, 1854-1934.
Frances A., b. 24 Oct 1857.
Harriet A., b. 1 Jul 1860, d. 1944, m. 11 Dec 1886 Amesbury MA Norman Scott.

Sources: Northport ME census 1860. P82j, W10, William C. Moulton rec, Esther Sawyer rec.

413. **SIMEON MATTHEW$^6$ SAWYER** [see 198], b. 18 Oct 1841 Skowhegan ME, d. 12 Sep 1930 Skowhegan ME, m. 24 Dec 1867 Skowhegan ME Addie Durrell, b. 5 Mar 1844 d. 31 Mar 1927, dau. Elkansk and Susan (Parker) Durrell. Printer. Civil War: Company K, 21st Maine Infantry.

George Otis, b. ca. 1868 Skowhegan ME.

Sources: VR Skowhegan ME, SA/ME. M7a, Obit (says Simeon died 1922).

414. **WILLIAM PEARSON$^6$ SAWYER** [see 199], b. 14 Jul 1850 Sherburne VT, m. 2 Sep 1875 Elzina Jewett Ayers of Waterbury VT, b. Nov 1845. Farmer, tanner. In Sherburne VT 1890.

Franklin Luke, b. 11 Jun 1876 Sherburne VT, m. 9 Oct 1897 Bridgewater VT Sarah A. Batchelder of Stockbridge VT, b. ?. Farmer. CH: Flora Bessie, b. 11 Mar 1899, d. 27 Sep 1899.
Edith Lucinda, b. 30 Jun 1878, d. 15 Feb 1881.
Ethel Viola, b. 20 May 1881, m. 20 Apr 1902 Ludlow VT William Hiram Deumas.
664 Clarence Fayette$^7$, 1885-1950.

Arthur Harold, b. 7 Aug 1888 Waterbury VT.

Sources: Sherburne VT census 1880, 1890. VR SA/VT. A37.

## SEVENTH GENERATION

415. **JOSHUA[7] SAWYER** [see 200], b. 19 Aug 1787 Brattleboro VT, d. 5 Jul 1854 Bolton MA, m. 20 Feb 1810 Acton MA Esther C. (Parker) Davis of Acton MA, b. 179?, dau. Joshua and Louisa Parker. W/son Joshua 1850 in Bolton MA. Wid. m. 22 Mar 1855 Deacon Jonathan Nourse.

Joshua Elbridge, b. 29 Sep 1818 Bolton MA, m. 22 Apr 1841 Bolton MA Susannah Nourse, b. 20 Mar 1816. Farmer. In Bolton MA 1850, Lawrence MA.

Avery Davis, b. 23 Dec 1819 Bolton MA, m. 23 Sep 1849 Bolton MA Ann Genette Wheeler of Bolton MA, b. 11 Sep 1823 d. 10 Mar 1852, dau. Caleb and Dolly Wheeler. Stage driver. In Lawrence MA, Chelmsford MA 1852. CH: Francis W., b. Jan 1852, d. 29 Aug 1853 Bolton MA.

Sources: Bolton MA census 1810, 1820, 1840, 1850. VR Acton MA, Bolton MA, Lancaster MA, SA/MA.

416. **JOHN[7] SAWYER** [see 201], b. 21 Jul 1785 Norridgewock ME, d. 12 Dec 1884 Starks ME, m. Mary McKenzie, b. ?.

Mary, b. 19 Dec 1806.
665 Levi Greenleaf[8], b. 1808.
Amanda, b. 14 Sep 1810, m.(1) William Grey, m.(2) Isaac Grey.
Saladen, b. 9 Oct 1812, d. 30 Apr 1816.
Emily J., b. 6 Aug 1814.
666 John P.[8], ca. 1817-1858.
Olive P., b. 12 May 1819.
Melinda, b. 1820.
667 William M.[8], 1821-1907.
668 Thomas McKechnie[8], b. ca. 1828.

Sources: Starks ME census 1810, 1820, 1830, 1840. VA SA/MA. D51, Ruby Collins rec.

417. **LUKE[7] SAWYER** [see 201], b. 9 Jun 1795 Starks ME, d. 3 Oct 1878 Madison ME, m. 22 May 1817 Nancy Metcalf, b. 9 Apr 1795 d. 1878. War of 1812: Private in Captain James Collins' Company, Wiscasset ME.

Rachel Greenleaf, b. 30 Sep 1817, d. 8 Mar 1904, m. 5 May 1840 Benjamin Marshall.
Calvin M., b. 1822 Anson ME, d. 7 Dec 1905, m. 14 Jan 1845 Anson ME Celia Hilton, b. 1823 d. 1 Jan 1898, dau. Eben Hilton. Farmer. CH: Emma F., b. 1852, m. James W. Perkins.
669 Luke Fulsom[8], 1826-1922.
Betsey M., b. 1835, m. 17 May 1857 Seth H. Fletcher of Madison ME.
Mary C., b. 1835.

Sources: Anson ME census 1820, 1830, 1840, 1850. Augusta ME census 1850. Madison ME census 1860, 1870, 1880. VR Anson ME.

418. **IMRI[7] SAWYER** [see 201], b. 15 Aug 1799 Starks ME, d. 1 Aug 1886, m. Rachel Greenleaf, b. 14 Aug 1803 d. 26 Jan 1891, dau. John and Anna (Roberts) Greenleaf.

Keturah, b. 14 Mar 1823, m. 28 Dec 1847 Gideon A. Gilman.
Rose A., b. 21 Oct 1824, d. 8 Sep 1847, unm.
Elmira V., b. 4 Jul 1826, d. 8 Oct 1849, unm.
Rachel, b. 28 Sep 1828, m. 16 Aug 1844 Warren Gray.

670 Luke Greenleaf[8], 1830-1920.
John Greenleaf, b. 31 Jan 1833 Starks ME, d. 19 Jan 1894 Starks ME, unm.
671 Stephen Greenleaf[8], 1835-1894.
Fanny G., b. 28 Mar 1837, d. 25 Aug 1893, m. 7 Apr 1854 Almon H. Sawyer of Madison ME [see 423].
Johannas H., b. 25 Mar 1839 Starks ME, d. 22 Jan 1862, unm.
Vesta A., b. 27 Apr 1842, d. 4 Aug 1895, m. 31 Mar 1861 Josiah Bacon.
Anthony Greenleaf, b. 21 Mar 1844 Starks ME, d. 13 Sep 1920 Starks ME, m. 21 Aug 1878 Ella N. Taylor, b. Oct 1857. Farmer, Selectman.
672 Augustus Imri[8], 1846-1914.
Sources: Starks ME census 1830, 1840, 1850. VR SA/ME. G42.

419. **COLUMBUS[7] SAWYER** [see 201], b. 2 Jul 1804 Starks ME, m. Basheba _____, b. 1811.
Caroline H., b. 1833.
James H., b. 1835 Starks ME.
Annett M., b. 1840.
Jonas M., b. 1840 Starks ME.
Vilettey, b. 1843.
Sources: Starks ME census 1830, 1840, 1850.

420. **JEFFERSON[7] SAWYER** [see 202], b. 23 Mar 1805 Madison ME, d. 12 Oct 1846 Madison ME, m. Lydia Crosby of Gardiner ME, b. 5 May 1804 d. Mar 1846. In Norridgewock ME 1830.
Diachama B., b. 9 Nov 1825, d. 23 May 1885, m. ____ Howard.
Elizabeth M., b. 1827, d. 20 Jan 1899 Skowhegan ME.
673 David[8], 1830-1898.
Ephraim, b. 20 Oct 1832 Norridgewock ME, d. 13 Feb 1901, m. 15 Dec 1858 Sharon ME Adelaide Benson, b. 20 May 1839 d. 1915, dau. Russell and Abigail (Dunbar) Benson. Carriage maker. In Madison ME, Waterville ME, Sidney ME, Auburn ME. Both bur. Lakeview Cem. Oakland ME. CH: Edmund A., b. 18 Jan 1860, d. 7 Sep 1867; Elizabeth A., b. 23 Jan 1869. m. 20 Sep 1899 George E. Martin.
Darius, b. 21 Feb 1837 Madison ME, d. 13 Dec 1862 Fredericksburg VA, m. 8 Oct 1855 Lewiston ME Roxilanna M. Cole, b. ?. Carriage maker. Civil War. In Madison ME.
Lydia, b. 10 Mar 1839, d. 15 Jul 1866, m. ____ Walker.
Harriet Hale, b. 7 Mar 1842, m. 25 Dec 1861 Portland ME Barnabas Shailer.
Sources: Norridgewock ME census 1830. Madison ME census 1850, 1860. Sidney ME census 1870. Auburn ME census 1880. VR SA/ME. M5, D61, Family Bible (Dr. Carl Sawyer), Obit (David).

421. **LUKE[7] SAWYER** [see 202], b. 1810 Madison ME, d. 29 Nov 1881 Madison ME, m. Mary Robbins, b. Apr 1810 Madison ME d. 31 May 1910 Skowhegan ME, dau. Isaac Robbins. Brick mason.
Alvah, b. 1836 Madison ME.
674 Charles P.[8], 1840-1904.
Sources: Madison ME census 1840, 1850. VR Skowhegan ME, SA/ME. Deacon Ezra Dinsmore's diary (Luke's death).

422. **SYLVANUS RIPLEY[7] SAWYER** [see 202], b. 1814 Madison ME, m. 12 Oct 1841 Anson ME Martha G. Messor of Madison ME, b. Jan 1824 d. 2 May 1881. In Madison ME 1842, Waterville ME 1850. Wheelwright.

Helen, b. 9 Aug 1842.

Llewellyn, b. 3 Jul 1843 Madison ME. Civil War: Court-martial record of Private Llewellyn Sawyer, 5th Maine Battery, says he was sentenced to two years imprisonment at hard labor for desertion. President Lincoln's pardon 8 Feb 1865 is in the National Archives.

James A., b. 17 Jun 1846 Madison ME, m. 5 Dec 1872 Portland ME Annie J. Jewett of Portland ME, m. ?.

David, b. 27 Jan 1849 Madison or Waterville ME, m. Lucetta _____, b. ?.

Sources: Waterville ME census 1850. VR Anson ME, Gardiner ME. M5.

423. **ALMON H.[7] SAWYER** [see 202], b. Dec 1819 Madison ME, d. 18 May 1902 Madison ME, m. 7 Apr 1854 Fanny G. Sawyer, b. 28 Mar 1837 d. 25 Aug 1893, dau. Imri and Rachel (Greenleaf) Sawyer. [see 418]

675 Warren Grey[8], b. 1855.

Rose Ann, b. 1856.

Sylvanus B., b. ca. 1858 Madison ME.

Robert, b. ca. 1862 Madison ME.

Susan, b. 1867.

Lilla, b. 1869.

Sources: Madison ME census 1860, 1870. VR SA/ME.

424. **WILLIAM[7] SAWYER** [see 203], b. 3 Sep 1803 Embden ME, d. 21 Aug 1897, m.(1) Fidelia Hill of New Portland ME, b. ? d. 1836; m.(2) 1849 Emily Churchill, b. 6 May 1819, dau. Tobias and Jane (Everett) Churchill.

Eugene W., b. 1836 New Portland ME, m.(1) ?; m.(2) ?; m.(3) 4 Sep 1894 Laconia NH Ellen L. Pendleton of Boston MA, b. 1848. In Chicago IL.

Fidelia, b. 11 Jun 1850, m. Frank Davis Sawyer.

Emily, b. 7 May 1852.

Sources: New Portland ME census 1850, 1860. ME 1880 census index. VR Laconia NH, SA/MA. C42, W54.

425. **EDWIN[7] SAWYER** [see 204], b. 8 Dec 1812 Templeton MA, m.(1) 14 Sep 1845 Providence RI Lydia Manchester of Johnston RI, b. 2 Apr 1821 d. 10 Jun 1855, dau. William and Elizabeth Manchester; m.(2) 12 Mar 1856 Templeton MA Hannah (Wakefield) Greenwood, b. 29 Aug 1820, dau. James Wakefield. Chair maker.

Edwin F., b. ca. 1846, m. 7 Oct 1886 New Bedford MA Anna T. Howard of New Bedford MA, b. 27 Nov 1856, dau. Azel and Julia (Mason) Howard. In Newton MA. No CH.

Sources: Templeton MA census 1850. VR Templeton MA, SA/MA, SA/RI. W4.

426. **JOSHUA[7] SAWYER** [see 204], b. 23 Oct 1814 Templeton MA, d. 1863, m. 1 Jul 1839 Templeton MA Angeline Partridge, b. 1819 d. 1869, dau Ezekiel and Anna Partridge. Wid. m. 10 Jun 1869 Templeton MA Thomas Greenwood.

Edward, b. 5 Dec 1840 Templeton MA, d. 21 Dec 1891, m.(1) 19 Jun 1866 Bridgewater MA Emma W. Batchelder of Cambridge MA, b. 24 Dec 1839 d. 21 Jan 1873, dau. Dr. Joseph and Anna (Wellington) Batchelder; m.(2) 6 Jan 1876 Bridgwater MA Clara F. Parsons of Taunton MA, b. ca. 1842, dau. Lloyd and Juliner Parsons. Harvard College 1865. Physician. In New Ipswich NH 1860, Bridgwater MA 1871. CH: Anna Wellington, b. 6 Oct 1867, m. 16 Oct 1890 Bridgewater MA Frank Cooper; Edith A., b. 12 Oct 1868 Newton MA; May Edward b. 7 Aug 1871 of Templeton MA.

Mary Newall, b. 14 Dec 1844, d. 1931, m. 28 Dec 1865 Templeton MA Francis Leland.

Sources: Templeton MA census 1840, 1850. New Ipswich NH census 1860. VR Templeton MA, SA/MA.

427. **LUKE[7] SAWYER** [see 204], b. 27 Feb 1816 Templeton MA, m. 20 May 1847 Hubbardston MA Lois Warren of Hubbardston MA, b. 1818, dau. Ebenezer and Hepzibah Warren. Chair manufacturer. On Hubbardston MA tax list 1867.

676 Samuel Warren[8], 1848-1934.

Ella Jane, b. 24 Jun 1853, m. 10 Oct 1872 Gardner MA Warren Kendall.

Sources: Hubbardston MA census 1850. VR Templeton MA, Hubbardston MA, SA/MA. S96, Elizabeth W. Sawyer rec.

428. **GEORGE[7] SAWYER** [see 204], b. 28 Jul 1818 Templeton MA, d. 14 Oct 1863, m. 11 Nov 1851 Templeton MA Betsey Pierce Sawyer of Athol MA, b. 21 Oct 1823, dau. Nathaniel and Sally (Underwood) Sawyer. Lumber manufacturer.

Flora Belle, b. 27 Nov 1853, m. 26 Nov 1879 Templeton MA Schuyler Melendy.

Sally Emma, b. 26 May 1857.

Son, b. 11 Feb 1861, d. 17 Feb 1861.

George Scott, b. 9 May 1863 Templeton MA.

Sources: Templeton MA census 1850. VR Templeton MA, SA/MA. P46.

429. **WILLIAM[7] SAWYER** [see 204], b. 2 Dec 1822 Templeton MA, m. 22 Dec 1853 Templeton MA Julia Ann Wiley of Winchendon MA, b. ca. 1831, dau. David and Charlotte Wiley. Farmer.

William Gerad, b. 5 Oct 1854 Templeton MA.

Son, b. 5 Dec 1863.

Sources: VR Templeton MA, SA/MA.

430. **OLIVER[7] SAWYER** [see 204], b. 18 Dec 1825 Templeton MA, m. 18 Jun 1863 Winchendon MA Almira A. Johnson of Chester MA, b. ca. 1833. Chair manufacturer.

Oliver Johnson, b. 11 Feb 1865 Templeton MA.

William Wyman, b. 5 Oct 1866 Templeton MA.

Daughter, b. 29 Dec 1871.

Sources: VR Templeton MA, SA/MA.

431. **JEROME[7] SAWYER** [see 205], b. 3 Feb 1807 Swanzey NH, m. 28 Nov 1830 Abigail Varney of Hallowell ME, b. 1805. Painter. In Swanzey NH 1850.

Leroy Milton, b. 1 Mar 1831 Swanzey NH.

Evaline Arville, b. 22 Mar 1833, m. 31 Aug 1852 Rockingham VT Benjamin Wilson.

Son, b. 21 Sep 1834 Winchester NH.

Jerome, b. 12 Sep 1836 Swanzey NH.

George Hodges, b. 19 Apr 1838 Swanzey NH.

Charles, b. 20 Dec 1842 Swanzey NH.

Julia A., b. 1844.

Sources: Swanzey NH census 1840, 1850. VR Swanzey NH. R7.

432. **WILLIAM W.[7] SAWYER** [see 206], b. 25 Mar 1821 Keene NH, d. 28 Jul 1895 Keene NH, m.(1) Arvilla Carpenter of Surry NH, b. 14 Feb 1819 d. 6 Sep 1848, dau. Ezra Carpenter; m.(2) 21 Dec 1862 Mary Jane Pierce of Hartland VT, b. 1834 d. 31 May 1909 Cambridge MA, dau. John Pierce. Fireman.

William Henry, b. 15 Aug 1871 Keene NH.

Sources: Keene NH census 1870, 1890. VR SA/NH. G46, K15, C5.

433. **NELSON NEWTON⁷ SAWYER** [see 206], b. 21 Feb 1823 Keene NH, d. 1 Nov 1872 Concord NH, m. 22 Nov 1846 Jemima Nims of Sullivan NH, b. 20 Aug 1824 d. 24 Dec 1898 Keene NH, dau. Asabel and Mary (Heaton) Nims. Carpenter. In Keene NH 1850.

Charles Carroll, b. 27 Jul 1848 Keene NH, d. 4 Jul 1876 Holyoke MA.
Elizabeth Jane, b. 17 Sep 1852, d. 5 Apr 1923 Keene NH, unm.
Mary Helen, b. 13 Feb 1855, m. 29 Jan 1874 Elbridge A. Shaw.
Frank Newton, b. 31 Aug 1859, d. 22 Mar 1861.
George Perry, b. 15 Apr 1869, d. 3 Apr 1876.

Sources: Keene NH census 1850, 1860, 1870. VR SA/NH. G46, N6.

434. **GEORGE GORDON⁷ SAWYER** [see 206], b. 25 Dec 1825 Keene NH, d. 12 Dec 1901 Keene NH, m. 18 Oct 1854 Helen M. Shelley of Keene NH, b. 29 Jan 1829 d. 16 Jun 1917, dau. Joseph and Lois (Leonard) Shelley. Clerk.

Fred Josiah, b. 1 May 1858 Keene NH, d. 4 Nov 1898, m. 5 Nov 1885 Taunton MA Cora Luella Palmer of Taunton MA, b. ca. 1858, dau. Abel Jr. and Laura A. Palmer. Druggist. CH: Laura D., b. 7 Mar 1890.
Jennie Eloise, b. 21 Jan 1861, d. 29 Feb 1864.
Joseph Frank, b. 7 Feb 1864, d. 6 Mar 1864.

Sources: Keene NH census 1850, 1860, 1870. VR Keene NH, SA/MA, SA/NH. G46, K15.

435. **WILLIAM ISAAC⁷ SAWYER** [see 207], b. 17 Mar 1821 Waltham MA, d. 14 Feb 1892 Swanzey NH, m. 6 Jan 1848 Waltham MA Maria Parker, b. ?.

Leonard, b. 25 Apr 1848 Waltham MA.

Sources: VR Waltham MA, SA/MA.

436. **CHARLES H.⁷ SAWYER** [see 207], b. ca. 1834 Waltham MA, d. 12 Apr 1916, m. 1 Jul 1858 Needham MA Florinda Goding of Livermore ME, b. 11 Jun 1829 d. 18 Mar 1913, dau. Luke and Harriet Goding. Trader. Civil War: Bugler. In Waltham MA, Newton Lower Falls MA, Needham MA 1863.

677 Charles Millet⁸, 1860-1930.
Jennie A., b. 25 Dec 1863, m. 2 Dec 1890 Wellesley MA Frank Barron.

Sources: VR SA/MA. G15, Mrs. Walter T. Sawyer rec.

437. **ALDEN⁷ SAWYER** [see 208], b. Jan 1824 Starks ME, m. 23 Sep 1863 Amanda A. Leathers, b. 1832. Shoemaker. In Smithfield ME.

Henry F., b. 1856 Smithfield ME, m. 25 Dec 1884 Medfield MA Rose E. Holmes of Smithfield ME, b. ca. 1860, dau. Ebenezer and Louisa Holmes. Bookkeeper. In Medfield MA. CH: Leola, b. 2 Nov 1887.
Nellie, b. 1859.

Sources: VR SA/ME, SA/MA.

438. **OTIS⁷ SAWYER** [see 208], b. 2 Apr 1826 Starks ME, d. 4 Mar 1914 Smithfield ME, m. 1 Jul 1860 Maria C. Pattee of Mercer ME, b. 30 Nov 1836 d. 27 Feb 1914, dau. Asa and Clarissa (Leathers) Pattee. In Smithfield ME.

Charles J., b. 1862 Smithfield ME, m. 16 Jan 1892 Farmington ME Nettie L. Whitehouse of Boothbay ME, b. ?, dau. George W. and Marita (Tibbetts) Whitehouse. In Smithfield ME.

Harvey L., b. ca. 1863 Smithfield ME, d. 4 Apr 1914, m. 7 Jun 1887 Dedham MA Myrtie M. Walton of Norridgewock ME, b. ca. 1862, dau. Isaiah and Angie (Stafford) Walton. Straw maker.

Sources: VR SA/ME, SA/MA.

439. **GEORGE AHOLIAB$^{7}$ SAWYER** [see 209], b. Dec 1839 Smithfield ME, m. 18 Jun 1865 Fairfield ME Laura W. Decker of Smithfield ME, b. 1845 d. 10 Oct 1911, dau. Kendall and Mercy (Ellis) Decker. Farmer. In Norridgewock ME.

Howard George, b. 19 Oct 1866 Norridgewock ME, m. 21 Sep 1899 Framingham MA Mary E. Lincoln of Portland ME, b. 11 Feb 1866, dau. Royal and Harriet (McLellen) Lincoln. In Medford MA. No CH.

Annie L., b. 9 Jan 1874, m. Leland S. Merrill.

Sources: ME 1880 census index. VR SA/ME. L25.

440. **ROLOSON B.$^{7}$ SAWYER** [see 210], b. 1847 Smithfield ME, m. Laura Porter of Ipswich MA, b. 1861. Civil War. In Norridgewock ME.

678 Chester Porter$^{8}$, b. 1881.

Ernest P., b. 31 Jul 1885 Norridgewock ME.

George, b. 1894 Norridgewock ME, m. 20 Nov 1915 Marion Stevens, b. ?.

Son, b. 2 Jul 1895.

Sources: VR SA/ME. M7A, M40.

441. **SOLON$^{7}$ SAWYER** [see 211], b. Sep 1821 Sterling MA, m. 21 Apr 1842 Nancy Fletcher Hinds of Lancaster MA, b. 1821. Laborer, farmer. In Sterling MA 1850.

George F., b. 15 Feb 1845 Sterling MA.

Edward Hinds, b. 21 Aug 1854 Sterling MA.

Sources: Sterling MA census 1850. VR Bolton MA, SA/MA. R26.

442. **JOSIAH$^{7}$ SAWYER** [see 212], b. 3 Feb 1813 Bolton MA, m. 7 Mar 1835 Sutton MA Fatima Maynard of Sutton MA, b. 1812. Laborer. In Northboro MA 1840, Tolland CT 1850.

Louisa J., b. 1836, m. 26 Nov 1852 Calvin Smith.

679 Daniel H.$^{8}$, b. 1837.

Josiah G., b. ca. 1842 Northboro MA, m. 27 Sep 1868 Clinton MA Lucy E. Lawton, b. ca. 1849, dau. Stillman and Emma L. Lawton. Shoemaker. In Tolland CT 1850.

Catherine A., b. 1844, m. 14 Jul 1874 W. Boylston MA George Brigham.

680 Henry Elwin$^{8}$, b. 1849.

Sources: Northboro MA census 1840, Tolland CT census 1850. VR Bolton MA, Tolland CT, SA/MA.

443. **DANIEL JACKSON$^{7}$ SAWYER** [see 212], b. 5 Sep 1814 Bolton MA, d. 1891, m. Anna Marie Richards of Brighton MA, b. 1819. In Waltham MA 1840, Berlin MA 1850.

George Richard, b. ca. 1839 Waltham MA.

681 Daniel W.$^{8}$, b. ca. 1846.

682 John A.$^{8}$, b. 1847.

Charles A., b. 1848 Waltham or Berlin MA.

William F., b. 1858 Bolton MA, m. 22 Oct 1891 Nashua NH Inez (White) Sawyer of Niagra NY, b. 1856, wid of William's brother John A., dau. John and Elizabeth White. Laborer. In Groton MA 1892. CH: Blanche, b. 24 Mar 1892.

Carrie M., b. ?, m. 8 Mar 1894 Wesley Ritchey.

Sources: Waltham MA census 1840. Berlin MA census 1850. VR Bolton MA, Waltham MA, SA/MA.

444. **DAVID[7] SAWYER** [see 212], b. 6 Oct 1817 Bolton MA, d. 5 Nov 1846 Leominster MA, m. 14 Nov 1843 Leominster MA Lorina Kilborn of Lunenburg MA, b. 1817 d. 26 Oct 1846 Lunenburg MA.

David Sumner, b. 11 Sep 1844 Leominster MA, d. 30 Jan 1871 Berlin MA, m. 30 Oct 1870 Clinton MA Emma C. Beamon of Sterling MA, b. ca. 1848, dau. Elroy and Eunice Beaman. Civil War: 25th Regiment, Massachusetts Volunteers. Shoemaker. NOTE: He is listed in VR SA/MA as Sumner Russell.

William Clesson, b. 1 Jan 1846, d. 16 Feb 1848.

Sources: VR Bolton MA, Leominster MA, SA/MA.

445. **GEORGE FAIRBANKS[7] SAWYER** [see 212], b. 15 Apr 1824 Bolton MA, m.(1) Lavinia Porter of Glastonbury CT, b. 1825; m.(2) Arabella _____, b. ?. Soldier, shoemaker. In Tolland CT 1850, Berlin MA 1857, Spencer MA, Bolton MA 1863.

Ann M., b. ca. 1845, m. 7 Sep 1863 Bolton MA George W. Pratt.

George H., b. ca. 1847, d.y.

Betsey A., b. ca. 1849, m. 1 Feb 1868 Concord MA James Mouton.

Alma L., b. 30 Jan 1853, d. 10 Dec 1871 Nashua NH.

Arabella, b. 4 Jul 1857, d. 3 Dec 1872 Nashua NH.

Daughter, b. 1 Jul 1860.

George C., b. 3 Mar 1863 Bolton MA, d. 13 Mar 1928 Nashua NH, m. 28 May 1887 Pepperell MA Josephine Barnes of New York, b. 1868.

Sources: Tolland CT census 1850. VR Tolland CT, Nashua NH, Berlin MA, SA/NH, SA/MA.

446. **FREDERICK ADOLPHUS[7] SAWYER** [see 213], b. 12 Dec 1822 Bolton MA, d. 31 Jul 1891 Tennessee, m.(1) 1854 Delia E. Gray of Nashua NH, b. 1829 d. 1873 (bur. in Nashua NH); m.(2) Mary Mansfield, b. ?. Harvard College 1844. Taught school in Gardiner ME 1844-1847, Wiscassett ME 1847-1851, Lowell MA 1852, Wakefield MA 1853-1855, Boston MA 1855-1859. Head of State Normal School, Charleston SC, went north at outbreak of Civil War, returned in 1865. US Senator from South Carolina 1868-1873.

Maria Louise, b. 22 Jul 1856.

Clara Cooper, b. 15 Oct 1857.

George Carpenter, b. 2 Sep 1860 Cambridge MA, m. 3 Jun 1890 Chelsea MA Louise Carlton of Somerville MA, b. ca. 1865, dau. Joseph and Mary Carlton. Merchant, printer. In Quincy MA, Chelsea MA, Somerville MA. CH: Adeline Genevieve, b. 5 Jun 1893; Edith May, b. 12 Feb 1895.

Sources: Chelsea MA census 1890. VR SA/MA.

447. **ISAIAH WHITNEY[7] SAWYER** [see 214], b. 25 Jan 1833 Medford MA, d. 25 Mar 1864, m. 23 Mar 1856 Boston MA Lucy A. Leavitt of Exeter NH, b. 9 Feb 1831, dau. William P. and Lucy (Libby) Leavitt. Baker, painter. In Boston MA, Epping NH, Malden MA.

Charles Atherton, b. 13 Mar 1858 Medford MA, m.(1) 14 Mar 1882 Watertown MA Ida M. Bangs, b. at sea, dau. Perez and Lydia A. Bangs; m.(2) 5 Aug 1896 Nashua NH Ida J. Copp of E. Boston MA, b. 29 May 1871. No CH.

Isaiah Whitney, b. 22 Nov 1860 Medford MA, m. 4 Sep 1890 Malden MA Ida B. Tufts of Chelsea MA, b. 6 Oct 1866, dau. Isaac G. and Areanna Tufts. In Malden MA. No CH.

683 William Phillips[8], b. 1863.

Sources: SA/MA. N28.

448. **GEORGE⁷ SAWYER** [see 214], b. 28 Feb 1841 Haverhill MA, d. 14 Sep 1870 Raymond NH, m. 2 Mar 1870 Nellie M. Smith of Raymond NH, b. 14 Nov 1850 d. 5 Aug 1916, dau. Abraham B. and Hannah (Tilton) Smith. Railroad brakeman. Civil War. Grave has a soldier's marker.

George B., b. 17 Mar 1871 Raymond NH, m. 4 Jul 1917 Raymond NH Alice M. Magoon of Manchester NH, b. ?, dau. Nathan W. and Mary J. (Dearborn) Magoon. Real estate.

Sources: Epping NH census 1850. Concord NH census 1870. Raymond NH census 1880. VR SA/NH. N9.

449. **NATHAN COREY⁷ SAWYER** [see 214], b. 28 Dec 1845 Haverhill MA, m. Henrietta Emma Stone of Charlestown MA, b. 19 Jan 1843, dau. Charles and Eliza A. (Flagg) Stone. In Epping NH, Somerville MA, Charlestown MA.

George, b. 1 May 1871 Charlestown MA.

Sources: VR Haverhill MA, SA/MA. B33.

450. **ALONZO CHARLES⁷ SAWYER** [see 214], b. ca. 1852 Epping NH, m. 23 May 1887 Boston MA Jennie E. MacDonald of Boston MA, b. ca. 1865, dau. William J. and Jennie MacDonald. Packer. In Cambridge MA 1893.

Charles W., b. 8 Apr 1887 Boston MA.
Georgianna Evaline, b. 16 Sep 1888.
Ida Viola, b. 21 Aug 1893.

Sources: VR SA/MA.

451. **JOHN HENRY⁷ SAWYER** [see 215], b. 15 Jul 1836 Bolton MA, m. 6 Jun 1806 Bolton MA Sophia Whitcomb of Bolton MA, b. ca. 1838, dau. E____ A. and Persis (Hildreth) Whitcomb. Farmer.

Mary Phebe, b. 8 Jun 1867.
684 Amory Pollard⁸, b. 1869.
Margaret Louise, b. 24 Feb 1871, m. 25 Oct 1895 Bolton MA Charles Powers.
Edith Lucinda, b. 6 Dec 1873.
Ruth Walcott, b. 14 Apr 1876.
Esther W., b. 25 Oct 1878.

Sources: VR SA/MA. Dorothy W. Purdy rec.

452. **STERLING KENISKY⁷ SAWYER** [see 216], b. 20 Nov 1821 Bolton MA, m. Sarah B. Whitcomb of Bolton MA, b. ?. Farmer.

Alice Jane, b. 20 Feb 1848.
685 Charles H.⁸, b. 1855.
Mary Lincoln, b. 24 Sep 1861.

Sources: VR Bolton MA, SA/MA.

453. **BENJAMIN⁷ SAWYER** [see 217], b. 11 Sep 1821 Northfield MA, d. Greenfield MA, m. 2 Feb 1853 Greenfield MA Martha E. Wells, b. ca. 1819 Deerfield MA, her m.(2). B/farm in 1858. Farmer.

Edward G., b. 7 Dec 1853 Greenfield MA, m. 29 May 1883 Athol MA Nettie E. Decker, b. ?, dau. Christopher and Mary Decker. Shoemaker.
Daughter, b. 4 Sep 1856.

Sources: VR SA/MA. T13.

454. **JOHN FRANCIS[7] SAWYER** [see 218], b. 1 Nov 1825 Bolton MA, m. 27 Oct 1853 Bolton MA Achsah Barrett of Bolton MA, b. 24 May 1827, dau. Oliver and Lucy Barrett. Farmer.
Son, b. 6 Dec 1857.
Daughter, b. 25 Dec 1861.
Charles James, b. 7 Oct 1866 Bolton MA, m. 11 Feb 1891 Swampscot MA Nellie F. Foster of Swampscot MA, b. ?, adopted dau. of Ida Foster. Box manufacturer. In Hudson MA 1892. CH: Hazel Barrett, b. 9 Mar 1892.
Lucy Henrietta, b. 11 Jul 1869.
Sources: VR Bolton MA, SA/MA. F2.

455. **SILAS WHITCOMB[7] SAWYER** [see 219], b. 8 Oct 1818 Buxton ME, m. 13 Nov 1842 Lowell MA Charity Scott of Greensboro VT, b. ?. Manufacturer. In Lowell MA, Greensboro VT.
Francis E., b. 14 Nov 1844 Lowell MA. Civil War. In Greensboro VT.
Charles A., b. 1846 Greensboro VT, d. 24 Nov 1903 Lakeport NH, unm. Civil War. In Lakeport NH 1870.
Ella Marzette, b. 1 Jul 1848, d.y.
Ella M., b. 13 Dec 1851, d. 13 Aug 1881, m. 1 Feb 1874 Center Harbor NH Albert M. Huckins.
Silas Whitcomb, b. 14 Nov 1861, d. 15 Mar 1862.
Eva Jane, b. 7 Jul 1863, m. 7 May 1864 Dracut MA Charles Blake.
Rosetta M., b. ?, m. 16 Nov 1881 George Grimes.
Sources: Lakeport NH census 1870. VR Buxton ME, Lowell MA, SA/MA, SA/NH. N6, V8, B49, H18, Family Bible.

456. **WILLIAM[7] SAWYER** [see 219], b. 28 Sep 1820 Buxton ME, d. 23 Apr 1897 Buxton ME, m. Almira Smith of Cornish ME, b. 1831 d. 4 Nov 1880, dau. Simon and Patience (Ridlon) Smith. Carpenter.
James Carpenter, b. 12 Aug 1852, d. 18 Sep 1854. Bur. in Moore Cem., Standish ME.
Frank, b. 23 Oct 1855 Lovell ME. In Stow ME 1860, Buxton ME 1880.
686 Stephen William[8], b. 1862.
Jessie A., b. 13 Apr 1867, d. 17 Jul 1882.
Anto Nellie, b. 22 Dec 1872, m. Edward C. Hall of Buxton ME.
Sources: Stow ME census 1860. ME 1880 census index. VR SA/ME. M5.

457. **SETH F.[7] SAWYER** [see 220], b. ca. 1829 Charlestown MA, m. 3 Feb 1859 Charlestown MA Helen G. Johnson of Charlestown MA, b. ca. 1840, dau. David and Hannah Johnson. Cook. In Chelsea MA, Charlestown MA 1867.
Olive Josephine, b. 14 Mar 1867.
Son, b. 8 Dec 1871.
Arthur Ernest, b. 18 Apr 1874 Charlestown MA.
Sources: VR Chelsea MA, SA/MA.

458. **CHARLES W.[7] SAWYER** [see 220], b. 28 Feb 1833 Charlestown MA, m. 30 Oct 1856 Charlestown MA Julia A. Heal of Belmont ME, b. ? d. Sep 1894, dau. William and Emily Heal. Postoffice clerk. In Cambridge MA, Concord MA 1868, Somerville MA 1873.
Edward R., b. 30 Oct 1868 Concord MA. In Somerville MA.
Sources: VR Rockland ME, SA/MA. S7.

459. **JEFFERSON[7] SAWYER** [see 220], b. 1835 Charlestown MA, m.(1) 4 Dec 1862 Charlestown MA Elizabeth J. Mellen of Charlestown MA, b. 1839, dau. Thomas C. and Rebecca

Mellen; m.(2) Jane Ann ____ of South Boston MA (Scotland?), b. ?. US Navy, engineer. In Medford MA 1870, Boston MA 1874.

Charles Herbert, b. 1 Nov 1863 Charlestown MA.
Jefferson Edwin, b. 22 Oct 1870 Medford MA.
Grace Susan, b. 22 Jan 1872.
Frederick, b. 18 Jun 1874 Boston MA.
Elsie May, b. 1 Jul 1878.
George C., b. 1880 Boston MA.
Margaret Duffins, b. 22 Mar 1885.

Sources: Medford MA census 1880. VR SA/MA.

460. **AMORY$^7$ SAWYER** [see 221], b. 4 Jul 1793 Berlin MA, d. 7 Sep 1831 Berlin MA, m. 3 Apr 1816 Berlin MA Lucy Sawyer, b. 16 Mar 1795 d. 17 May 1878, dau. Alvin and Sarah Sawyer. Carpenter. Wid. m. Moses Greenleaf of Bolton MA.

Zilpah H., b. 27 Jan 1819, m. 21 Sep 1842 Edward Bliss.
Amory Bardwell, b. 8 Aug 1821 Berlin MA, m. 29 Nov 1849 Berlin MA Lucinda M. Coffron of Goshen NH, b. 27 Mar 1823 d. 3 Jul 1851, dau. Benjamin Coffron. Shoemaker. In Berlin MA 1850.
Lucy M., b. 22 Sep 1823, d. 19 Jun 1885, m. 27 Sep 1840 Henry H. Bliss.
Martha A., b. 11 Sep 1827, d. 24 Nov 1882, unm.

Sources: Berlin MA census 1820, 1830, 1850. VR Berlin MA, SA/MA. H76, G42.

461. **WILLIAM A.$^7$ SAWYER** [see 221], b. 30 Jul 1796 Berlin MA, m.(1) 7 Jun 1821 Berlin MA Zilpah Howe, b. 17 Aug 1802 d. 20 Oct 1844, dau. Ephraim and Hannah (Barnes) Howe; m.(2) 27 Oct 1847 Northboro MA Mary (Harrington) Allen of Shrewsbury MA, b. ?, wid. of Ethan of Worcester MA, dau. Warren and Martha Harrington. Millwright. In Berlin MA 1830, Northboro MA 1840, Grafton MA 1851. Went to California.

Lucinda H., b. 1 Apr 1822, m. 7 Oct 1845 Charles Eager.
Lucy, b. 3 Jan 1828, m. 28 May 1846 Stephen S. Eager.
Martha L., b. 17 Jan 1835.
William, b. 4 Oct 1851 Grafton MA. Went to California.

Sources: Berlin MA census 1830. Northboro MA census 1840. VR Berlin MA, Northboro MA, SA/MA. H76, H80.

462. **AMOS$^7$ SAWYER** [see 221], b. 10 Mar 1808 Berlin MA, d. 15 Aug 1866 Berlin MA, m. 4 Dec 1836 Berlin MA Sarah H. Sawyer of Berlin MA, b. 18 May 1818, dau. Thomas and Sarah (Bigelow) Sawyer. Stage driver. Wid. m. Henry D. Coburn.

Mary Adella, b. 5 Nov 1837, d. 8 Jun 1862, m. 6 Sep 1855 Boston MA William B. Carter of Georgia.
Margiana M., b. 1 Jan 1840, d. 21 Mar 1883, m. 12 Aug 1860 Lorren Arnold.
Joseph Marshall, b. 8 Nov 1841, d. 28 Feb 1843.
Sarah Grace, b. 18 Feb 1844, m. 26 Feb 1862 Hudson MA Oscar Holt.
Augusta E., b. 22 Jan 1846, d. 2 Aug 1868, m. 1 Jan 1867 Hudson MA Warren Peters.
Frederick Amos, b. 28 Jun 1848, d. 30 Sep 1851 Berlin MA.
Lucy Sophia, 13 Aug 1850, d. 29 Jan 1884, m. 24 Nov 1870 Berlin MA Warren S. Howe.
Joseph Amos, b. ?, d. 1853.
Lucinda Frances, b. 5 May 1852, d. 15 Jan 1866.
Franklin Amos, b. 14 Sep 1853 Berlin MA, d. 18 Mar 1856 Berlin MA.
687 Lewis Amos$^8$, 1856-1880.
Chester Albert, b. 22 Nov 1857 Berlin MA.

Cora Agnes, b. 11 Nov 1858, d. 15 Apr 1859.
688 Silas Abel[8], b. 1860.
Sources: Berlin MA census 1840, 1850. VR Berlin MA, SA/MA. H76, C9, W39.

463. **OLIVER BARRETT[7] SAWYER** [see 222], b. 5 Jun 1816 Berlin MA, m. 12 Apr 1842 Shrewsbury MA Angeline A. Baldwin of Shrewsbury MA, b. 26 Apr 1819, dau. Henry and Mary (Goddard) Baldwin. Trader. Joined church in West Boylston MA 1847.
689 Henry Oliver[8], b. 1844.
690 Walter Barrett[8], b. 1852.
Sources: West Boylston MA census 1850. VR Berlin MA, Shrewsbury MA, SA/MA. B11.

464. **ASA[7] SAWYER** [see 223], bp. 10 Oct 1802 Berlin MA, d. 4 Nov 1881, m. Caroline A. Lincoln of Brimfield OH, b. ?. In Jaffrey NH, Brimfield OH.
Henry D., b. ?.
Sources: VR SA/MA.

465. **ELI[7] SAWYER** [see 225], b. 7 Jan 1801 Berlin MA, d. 10 Mar 1870 Berlin MA, m. 6 Apr 1828 Newton or Stow MA Azubah Morseman, b. 1797 d. 21 Sep 1884. In West Newton MA, Berlin MA 1840.
Sarah G., b. 13 Jun 1829, d. 30 Dec 1865.
Amory, b. 14 Apr 1831, d. 13 Jun 1850.
William Greenough, b. 5 May 1833 West Newton MA, d. 19 May 1870 Berlin MA, m. 24 Nov 1869 Berlin MA Ellen L. Keyes, b. 9 Nov 1839. Farmer.
Levi, b. 30 Nov 1835, d. 31 May 1837.
Eli, b. 1838 Berlin MA, m. 4 Jan 1867 Berlin MA Margianna Johnson of Greenwich MA, b. ? d. 1877. Shoemaker. Joined church in Westboro MA 1871.
Sources: Berlin MA census 1840, 1850. VR Berlin MA, Newton MA, Stow MA, SA/MA.

466. **JOSIAH[7] SAWYER** [see 225], b. 25 Mar 1810 Berlin MA, d. 2 Jul 1885 Berlin MA, m. 31 Oct 1834 Berlin MA Arrissa Moore, b. 12 Jun 1811 d. 1 Jan 1899.
Henry Joseph, b. 7 Dec 1841 Berlin MA, m. 24 Mar 1866 Berlin MA Elizabeth M. Miller of Clinton MA, b. ?, dau. Charles and Matilda Miller. Farmer.
Edward Newton., b. 3 Mar 1844 Berlin MA, m.(1) 16 May 1876 Berlin MA Sarah H. Dow of Weare NH, b. 13 Apr 1848 d. 10 Apr 1888, dau. Greely and Lydia E. Dow; m.(2) Bolton MA Ellen F. Barrett, b. ?, adopted dau. of Elbridge Sawyer. Farmer. CH: Ella D., b. 10 Jan 1886, d. 16 Jan 1886; Lewis Josiah, b. 5 May 1887, d. same day
Sarah Arrissa, b. 5 Sep 1849, m. 17 Feb 1880 Berlin MA Elias L. Wheeler.
Sources: Berlin MA census 1840, 1850. VR Berlin MA, SA/MA. W32.

467. **GEORGE WILLIAM[7] SAWYER** [see 225], b. 11 Oct 1811 Berlin MA, d. 10 Jun 1881 Berlin MA, m. 10 Mar 1839 Bolton MA Mary Ann Sawyer of Bolton MA, b. 11 Dec 1815 d. 4 Jan 1892, dau. Ira and Abigail (Hastings) Sawyer. Shoemaker, farmer.
Martha C., b. 25 Aug 1842, d. 18 Oct 1844.
Mary Elizabeth, b. 3 Jan 1845, d. 6 Jan 1845.
William Hastings, b. 22 May 1846, d. 29 Sep 1864, unm.
Winthrop G., b. 14 Nov 1847 Berlin MA, m. 8 Sep 1875 Detroit MI Louise R. Nicholson of Detroit MI, b. 15 Jan 1854. CH: Bertha L., b. 4 Sep 1881; Elvin Wilfred, b. 21 Aug 188?, d. 26 Nov 1886.
Martha Ann, b. 7 May 1850, d. 12 Oct 1864. Note: SA/MA says Alice Viola b. 7 May 1850.

691 Charles Marshall[8], b. 1852.
Sources: Berlin MA census 1840, 1850. VR Berlin MA, Bolton MA.

468. **STEPHEN[7] SAWYER** [see 225], b. 23 Feb 1813 Berlin MA, m.(1) 8 Jan 1845 Berlin MA Lucy Fairbanks Sawyer, b. 9 Sep 1819 d. 30 Dec 1847, dau. Oliver and Sophira (Rice) Sawyer; m.(2) 29 Dec 1857 Worcester or Northbridge MA Mary W. Bigelow of Northbridge MA, b. 5 Jul 1827, dau. Silas and Silence (Pierce) Bigelow. Merchant. In Worcester MA.

Francis Jerome, b. 1846, d. 20 Mar 1852 Berlin MA.
Lucy Fairbanks, b. 29 Dec 1847.
Mary Sophia, b. 1 Nov 1858.
Hattie Louisa, b. 26 Sep 1862.
Daughter, b. 6 Nov 1867.
Stephen, b. 29 Oct 1868 Worcester MA.
Grace M., b. 6 Mar 1871.

Sources: VR Berlin, MA, Worcester MA, SA/MA. P43, H81.

469. **WILLIAM[7] SAWYER** [see 226], b. 5 Oct 1812 Berlin MA, m.(1) 19 May 1835 Berlin MA Harriet Babcock, b. ?, dau. Josiah and Betsey (Bowman) Babcock; m.(2) 5 Oct 1862 Clinton MA Eunice P. Sawyer [her m.(3)] of Nelson NH, b. ?; m.(3) 12 Feb 1874 Clinton MA Cornelia Chamberlain of Manchester VT, b. ca. 1830. Builder. In Sutton MA 1830, Clinton MA, Worcester MA.

William, b. 27 Nov 1838 Worcester MA.
Harriet E., b. 26 Aug 1845, m. 1 Nov 1866 Clinton MA John W. Townsend.
Ella Frances, b. 16 Oct 1854.

Sources: Sutton MA census 1840. VR Grafton MA, Sutton MA, SA/MA. W21, W39.

470. **JOSIAH ELLSWORTH[7] SAWYER** [see 226], b. 10 Jan 1814 Berlin MA, d. 15 May 1890 Berlin MA, m. 8 Sep 1841 Berlin MA Eunice S. Babcock of Berlin MA, b. 30 Mar 1817. Carpenter.

Abbie Theresa, b. 8 Mar 1843, d. 9 Dec 1907, m. 8 Mar 1868 Berlin MA Francis Copeland.
692 Frank Loring[8], b. 1858.

Sources: Berlin MA census 1850. VR Berlin MA. SA/MA. C76.

471. **HARTWELL[7] SAWYER** [see 226], b. 6 Jan 1818 Berlin MA, d. 5 Mar 1898 Berlin MA, m. 3 May 1842 Berlin MA (also recorded in Bolton MA) Zilpah Maria Bartlett, b. 4 Dec 1822 d. 6 Oct 1888, dau. Daniel Bartlett. Carpenter.

Harriet M., b. 28 Aug 1844, d. 21 Nov 1899, m. 19 Nov 1865 Berlin MA William T. Babcock.
693 Ivers Hartwell[8], 1847-1907.

Sources: Berlin MA census 1850. VR Berlin MA, Bolton MA, SA/MA.

472. **BENJAMIN HASTINGS[7] SAWYER** [see 226], b. 7 Aug 1826 Berlin MA, d. 3 Jul 1903, m. 23 Nov 1851 Berlin MA Sophia P. Rice of Northboro MA, b. 1 Feb 1832 d. 24 Jun 1897, dau. Luther Rice. Farmer.

Mary D., b. 9 Oct 1852, d. 4 Nov 1918, m. 30 Apr 1870 Clinton MA John Reed.
Arthur L., b. 15 Mar 1856 Berlin MA, m. 16 May 1884 Berlin MA Mary Grace Bliss of Berlin MA, b. 4 Jan 1863. Farmer.
Jane M., b. 14 Jun 1859, d. 30 May 1883.

Elmer Ernest b. 26 Sep 1862 Bolton MA, d. 3 Jul 1889 Worcester MA, m. 12 Aug 1885 Worcester MA Mary J. Holland of Port Jervis NY, b. ca. 1863, dau. George and Margaret Holland. Milk dealer. Wid. m. 4 Aug 1892 Worcester MA Herbert F. Divelly.

Herbert Benjamin, b. 24 Mar 1871 Berlin MA, d. 1943, m. Alice S. _____, b. 1872, d. 1951.

Sources: VR Berlin MA, SA/MA. W21, W39, Gravestone.

473. **OLIVER$^7$ SAWYER** [see 226], b. 27 May 1830 Berlin MA, m.(1) 13 Jan 1851 Berlin MA Lydia Ann Carter of Boylston MA, b. 16 Jan 1834 d. 20 Apr 1877, dau. Leonard and Ann (Brigham) Carter; m.(2) 1 Jan 1879 Hudson MA Martha (Moore) Bemis of Northboro MA, b. 1830, dau. Joseph and Phebe S. Moore. Cordwainer.

Lewis Neville, b. 28 Feb 1855 Berlin MA, m. 20 May 1877 Hudson MA Elizabeth O. Fosgate of Berlin MA, b. 23 May 1853, dau. John G. and Martha (Rice) Fosgate. Shoemaker. In Hudson MA 1879. CH: Laura Agnes, b. 20 Apr 1879; Martha Beatrice, b. 29 Jun 1883.

Laura Ann, b. 2 Sep 1861, d. 10 Sep 1866.

Edgar Oliver, b. 18 May 1869 Hudson MA, m. 2 Jun 1892 Fitchburg MA Barbara Downie, b. ca. 1863 in Scotland, dau. John and Margaret Downie.

Bertha Florence, b. 10 Nov 1874.

Sources: VR Berlin MA, SA/MA. B84, C9, W39.

474. **ALDEN$^7$ SAWYER** [see 227], b. 24 Mar 1813 Berlin MA, d. 28 Mar 1889 Berlin MA, m. 17 Nov 1842 Berlin MA Persis Gleason of Lunenburg VT, b. 17 Oct 1816 d. 4 Sep 1874 Berlin MA, dau. Joseph and Abigail (Howe) Gleason. Farmer.

694 Joseph Henry$^8$, b. 1845.

Alden Wesley, b. 9 Jul 1849, d. 31 Oct 1869.

Charles N., b. 16 Jan 1852 Lunenburg VT.

Persis Abigail, b. 25 May 1856, d. 24 Feb 1870.

Jane Isabell, b. 24 May 1859.

Sources: Berlin MA census 1850. VR Berlin MA, SA/MA. H80.

475. **ISREAL$^7$ SAWYER** [see 227], b. 12 Oct 1817 Berlin MA, d. 5 Dec 1881 Berlin MA, m. 15 Apr 1842 Groton MA Louisa Smith of Lunenburg VT, b. 30 Jul 1817 d. 19 Nov 1883, dau. Asa and Ede Smith. Shoemaker.

Sarah Louisa, b. 16 Apr 1843, m. 2 Jan 1869 Berlin MA Silas E. Jones.

Clara E., b. 22 Sep 1845, m. 29 Aug 1868 Theodore Guertin of Lancaster MA.

Emily A., b. 9 Oct 1848.

Adin Augustus, b. 3 Oct 1854 Berlin MA, d. 17 Nov 1893 Clinton MA, m. 9 May 1877 Berlin MA Ellen E. Wheeler of Berlin MA, b. 21 Jun 1854, dau. Elisha T. and Elizabeth (Frye) Wheeler. Clerk.

Sources: Berlin MA census 1850. VR Berlin MA, Groton MA, SA/MA.

476. **EDWIN$^7$ SAWYER** [see 227], b. 16 Sep 1821 Berlin MA, d. 19 Nov 1891 Berlin MA, m. 3 Jan 1848 Berlin MA Emily P. Hartwell of Berlin MA, b. 28 Jun 1829 d. 12 Mar 1892, dau. Leonard and Abigail (Pierce) Hartwell. Shoemaker.

Alice Viola, b. 10 Jan 1850, d. 19 May 1867.

Edwin Erving, b. 8 Dec 1855 Carterville MA, m. 17 Oct 1877 Berlin MA Lizzie A. Johnson of Berlin MA, b. 3 Sep 1856, dau. George and Harriet Johnson. Bookkeeper. In Marlborough MA. CH: Alice Maud, b. 4 Sep 1886, d. Dec 1886.

Sources: Berlin MA census 1850. VR Berlin MA, SA/MA.

477. **ADDISON A.⁷ SAWYER** [see 227], b. 6 Apr 1825 Berlin MA, d. 4 Mar 1893 Reading MA, m. 6 Apr 1851 Berlin MA Elizabeth Brigham of Bridgton ME, b. 26 Sep 1825 d. 14 Apr 1903, dau. Aaron and Asenath (Corsley) Brigham. Cabinetmaker. In Clinton MA 1850. He bur. in Forest Dale Cem., Malden MA.

695 Eugene N.[8], 1852-1902.

Jennie Maria, b. 23 Aug 1858, m. 29 Jan 1888 Malden MA George W. Wilkinson.

Euleyetta, b. 16 Nov 1859, d. 16 May 1937, unm.

Sources: Clinton MA census 1850. VR Berlin MA, SA/MA. B84.

478. **RUFUS CURTIS[7] SAWYER** [see 227], b. 8 Oct 1832 Berlin MA, d. 4 Oct 1903 Hudson MA, m. 19 Oct 1852 Berlin MA Catherine Fuller of Ludlow MA, b. 19 Oct 1835, dau. Samuel and Catherine (Bliss) Fuller. M. also recorded in Lancaster MA. Shoemaker. Civil War.

Emma L., b. 29 May 1853 d. 14 Jan 1884, m. 28 Aug 1875 Hudson MA John F. Elliot. CH: Grace, b. 15 Mar 1873.

Lizzie S., b. 19 May 1855, m. Robert Lackey. CH: Maude Eveline, b. 24 Jan 1872.

696 Samuel Rufus[8], b. 1857.

James Curtis, b. 16 Jul 1861 Berlin MA, m.(1) 16 Jul 1884 Hudson MA Mabel Rockwell of Nova Scotia, b. ca. 1862; m.(2) 8 Jan 1895 Marlborough MA Josie Young of Oakland MA, b. ca. 1861, dau. George and Anne F. Young. Shoemaker. No CH.

697 Loren Everett[8], b. 1864.

Charlotte Louise, b. 1 May 1868, d. 14 Jan 1885.

Sources: VR Berlin MA, SA/MA. B52, F44, W39.

479. **ABEL[7] SAWYER** [see 229], b. 20 May 1813 Berlin MA, d. 16 Mar 1853 Clinton MA, m. 12 Nov 1846 Lancaster MA Lucy Goss, b. 28 Sep 1816 d. 8 Mar 1870, dau. John and Mary Goss. Stable keeper. In West Boylston MA, Clinton MA 1850.

698 Francis Goss[8], b. 1848.

Sources: Clinton MA census 1850. VR Berlin MA, Lancaster MA, SA/MA. W39.

480. **AARON[7] SAWYER** [see 232], b. 1 Oct 1785 Boylston MA, d. 11 Dec 1849 Millbury MA, m. Margaret _____, b. ?. Wid. in Millbury MA 1850.

Son, b. (1810-1815).

Daughter, b. (1810-1815).

699 Frederick William[8], 1819-1872.

Margaret, b. 1821, m. 25 Jan 1845 Timothy B. Allen.

Lydia A., b. 13 Nov 1825, d. 19 Feb 1863, m. 22 May 1855 Charles D. Moore.

Sources: Sutton MA census 1830. Millbury MA census 1840, 1850. VR Boylston MA, Shrewsbury MA, Millbury MA, Woodstock CT, SA/MA. M42.

481. **JOSEPH[7] SAWYER** [see 232], b. 7 Aug 1787 Boylston MA, d. 4 Mar 1847 Holden MA, m. 16 Oct 1808 Boylston MA Lucy Kendall of Boylston MA, b. 1790 d. 3 Jun 1861, dau. Caleb and Lucy Kendall. Wid. in Clinton MA 1850.

700 Caleb Kendall[8], b. 1810.

701 Joseph Thomas[8], b. 1811.

Ezra, b. 1 Sep 1813, d. 2 Nov 1813.

Ezra, b. 27 Jul 1815 Boylston MA, m.(1) 13 Apr 1842 Holden MA Eliza Winn, b. ?, dau. Francis Winn of Holden MA; m.(2) 1881 Worcester MA Harriet Newell of Worcester MA, b. 1832, dau. Sanford M. and Susan (Woodcock) Newell. Machinist. In Holden MA, Worcester MA 1850. CH: Emma F., b. May 1843, d. 6 Sep 1843.

Lucy, b. 3 Sep 1817, m. 3 Jul 1839 Joseph Wood.
Emily Kendall, b. 6 Jun 1819, d. 18 Apr 1820.
Emily Kendall, b. 26 Mar 1821, m. 15 May 1844 Henry Eddy.
James Henry, b. 1823 Boylston MA.
702 Charles H.[8], b. 1825.
Abigail E., b. 31 Oct 1826.
Myra J., b. 8 Jan 1830, d. 9 Jun 1861.
Frances M., b. 1832, d. 21 Dec 1833.

Sources: Boylston MA census 1810, 1820. Holden MA census 1830, 1840. Clinton MA census 1850. VR Boylston MA, Holden MA, Worcester MA. E6.

482. **OLIVER[7] SAWYER** [see 233], b. 15 Jun 1788 Boylston MA, d. 1 Aug 1824 Boylston MA, m. 18 Sep 1816 Boylston MA Harriet Bush, b. ?. Wid. m. 1803 Boylston MA I_____ Goulding.

Alfred, b. 7 Dec 1816 Boylston MA, d. 14 Nov 1870, m. 20 Mar 1841 Boylston MA Sarah E. Goss of Lancaster MA, b. 4 Feb 1818 d. 31 Jan 1886. Farmer. In Holden MA 1850. CH: John William, b. 5 Dec 1843, d. 5 Feb 1844; Harriet, b. 9 Nov 1845, m. 1 Jan 1873 Sterling MA Lucian L. Mears; Sarah Greenwood, b. 3 Aug 1852, d. 14 Sep 1853.
Harriet, b. 10 Nov 1818, m. 2 Jun 1841 Thomas White.

Sources: Holden MA census 1850. VR Boylston MA, SA/MA. W39.

483. **CHARLES[7] SAWYER** [see 234], b. 2 Nov 1795 Lancaster MA, m. 28 Nov 1822 Lancaster MA Eliza Joslyn, b. 5 Jul 1799, dau. Jonas and Betsey (Beaman) Joslyn. Comb maker. In Lancaster MA 1850.

Sarah Elizabeth, b. 3 Sep 1823, d. 22 Apr 1827.
Martha Sophia, b. 1 Apr 1825, d. 28 Nov 1831.
Charles Francis, b. 22 Jan 1827, d. 8 May 1831.
Sarah E., b. 5 May 1829, d. 17 Sep 1832.
703 George Moses[8], 1831-1911. Went to Illinois.
Eliza, b. 28 Nov 1832, m. 24 Aug 1852 Lancaster MA Eustis H. Smith.
Child, b. 30 Nov 1834, d. 4 Dec 1834.
John Henry, b. 16 Jan 1838 Lancaster MA.

Sources: Lancaster MA census 1840, 1850. VR Lancaster MA. G8.

484. **PETER[7] SAWYER** [see 235], b. 18 Nov 1811 Lancaster MA, m. 6 Oct 1835 Grafton MA Jane May of Grafton MA, b. 1813. Carpenter. In Clinton MA 1850.

Alonzo Peter, b. 18 Nov 1848 Lancaster MA.
Laura Jane, b. 14 Oct 1850.

Sources: Clinton MA census 1850. VR Grafton MA, Lancaster MA, SA/MA.

485. **JABEZ[7] SAWYER** [see 238], b. May 1799 Wendell MA, d. 28 Apr 1888, m. 2 Dec 1830 Wendell MA Sally B. Pierce of Petersham MA, b. 15 Dec 1800, dau. William and Julia/Lydia? (Lincoln) Pierce. In Littleton MA 1835, Arlington MA 1837, Wendell MA 1850.

Emily, b. 23 Oct 1831, d. 13 Dec 1831.
Maria A., b. 18 May 1833, m. 24 Aug 1858 Wendell MA Rev. Charles F. Forbes.
Asabel W., b. 14 Jul 1835 Wendell MA, m.(1) 1 Dec 1869 Littleton MA Angelia Robbins of Littleton MA, b. 17 Aug 1844 d. 9 Jul 1871, dau. Nehemiah and Mary Robbins; m.(2) 14 May 1873 New Salem MA Helen Almeda Freeman of New Salem MA, b. ca. 1843 d. Littleton MA, dau. William Freeman. Mechanic. In Arlington MA, Wendell MA

1850, Littleton MA. CH: Son, b. 7 Oct 1878, d. 17 Oct 1878; Helen Angelia, b. 30 Jun 1881.

William H., b. 8 Oct 1837 Arlington MA. In Wendell MA 1850.

704 Charles Orville[8], b. 1842-1920.

Sources: Wendell MA census 1850. VR Wendell MA, SA/MA. P43.

486. **ASABEL[7] SAWYER** [see 238], b. 19 Apr 1801 Wendell MA, m. Hannah Stratton, b. ?. Mechanic. In Northfield MA 1830, 1840. Selectman, 1828, 1829, 1846. Representative to the General Court 1837.

Elvira, b. 13 Dec 1819.

Hannah Wright, b. 1 Apr 1821.

705 Harris Stratton[8], b. 1823.

Lucy, b. 29 Nov 1824, m. 24 May 1848 Northfield MA Elisha Shelton.

Martha, b. 13 Dec 1826, m. 1 Jan 1850 Northfield MA Cobb Alexander.

Asabel, b. 27 Sep 1828 Northfield MA, d.y.

Albert, b. 21 Sep 1830 Northfield MA, m.(1) 30 Nov 1854 Fitchburg MA Nancy Brown of Fitchburg MA, b. 15 Feb 1830, d. 22 Oct 1861, dau. Asa and Nancy Brown; m.(2) 19 Nov 1862 Fitchburg MA Caroline M. Lazell of Ware MA, b. 15 Aug 1829 d. 31 Oct 1885, dau. Reuben and Mary (Bowdoin) Lazell; m.(3) 24 Oct 1888 Orange MA Marcia A. (Titus) Wood of Vermont, b. ca. 1833, dau. Sumner and Sophronia Titus. Machinist.

Ellen A., b. 7 May 1836, m. 7 May 1857 Greenfield MA Edwin A. Stratham.

Asabel, b. 17 Nov 1843 Northfield MA. Civil War: Mustered 11 Oct 1862, 27th Infantry Regiment.

Sources: Northfield MA census 1830, 1840. VR SA/MA. D12, T8.

487. **LYMAN[7] SAWYER** [see 239], b. 6 Oct 1800 Sterling MA, m. 2 Sep 1827 New Salem MA Julia A. Osgood of New Salem MA, b. 24 Jul 1816. Carpenter, farmer.

706 Charles L.[8], b. 1828.

Julia L., b. 17 Apr 1833, m. 28 Nov 1850 Wendell MA Edwin R. Crosby.

Helen M., b. 17 Aug 1835, d. 26 Apr 1838.

Patience M., b. 5 Oct 1838, d. 27 Dec 1838.

Helen M., b. 8 Aug 1841, m. 15 Oct 1867 Fitchburg MA George E. Priest.

707 Erastus O.[8], b. 1843.

Henry Walter, b. 17 Sep 1849 Wendell MA, m. 23 Oct 1872 Erving MA Ella E. Thompson of Fryeburg ME, b. 1850, dau. A_____ P. and Sarah Thompson. Mechanic.

Sources: New Salem MA census 1830. Erving MA census 1840. Wendell MA census 1850. VR New Salem MA, Erving MA, Wendell MA, SA/MA. W39.

488. **AARON[7] SAWYER** [see 239], b. 3 May 1803 Sterling MA, d. 28 Jun 1862 Chicago IL, m. 8 Jan 1827 Laura Thayer, b. 3 Dec 1808 d. 12 Jan 1890. Farmer. Owned tavern, store, mill in Cummington MA. In New Salem MA 1834-1840, Hinsdale NY 1850, Ellensburg NY, Chicago IL.

708 Franklin[8], b. 1833.

709 William Harrison[8], 1835-1915.

Edwin, b. ca. 1839 Hinsdale MA, d. in New York. In Ellenburg NY.

Leander, b. ca. 1844 Hinsdale MA. CH: 4 dau.

Sources: Hinsdale MA census 1850. VR New Salem MA, SA/MA. F27, Beatrice E. Sawyer rec.

489. **MILTON[7] SAWYER** [see 239], b. 14 Mar 1811 New Salem MA, d. 4 Mar 1889 Glen Falls NY, m. 25 Dec 1833 Thankful French of Wendell MA, b. 16 Jun 1816 d. 23 Jul 1889.

Farmer, blacksmith. In Wendell MA, Athol MA, Plainfield MA, Cummington MA, West Hawley NY.

George Milton, b. 21 Mar 1838, d. 21 Jan 1915, m. Sep 1861 Emma C. Drake, b. ?.
Martha M., b. 16 Jul 1839, d. 23 Mar 1845.
Lydia Ellen, b. 10 Apr 1843, d. 29 Jun 1847.
Martha Lucy, b. 19 May 1847, d. 29 Aug 1879.
Ellen A., b. 4 Jun 1849, d. 18 Jan 1883.
Joseph Edward, b. 31 Mar 1851, d. 23 Aug 1919.
Charles French, b. 21 Sep 1853, d. 30 Nov 1880, m. 1875 Eleanor C. Jones, b. ?.
Dwight Henry, b. 4 Jun 1856, d. 7 Sep 1942, m. 4 Mar 1886 Helen Kerwin, b. ?.

Sources: Athol MA census 1840. VR SA/MA. F27, D6.

490. **THOMAS$^7$ SAWYER** [see 240], b. 23 Mar 1799 Chester VT, m. 18 Jan 1826 Alvira Davis, b. 1806. Manufacturer.

Joseph Franklin, b. 25 Nov 1826 Chester VT, m. Isadora Amanda Rand, b. 6 Apr 1831, dau. Chester and Patty (Osgood) Rand. Manufacturer. In Chester VT 1850.
Thomas Ransom, b. 1831 Chester VT, m. 14 Feb 1855 Chester VT Delia M. Aiken of Windham VT, b. ?. Mechanic. In Chester VT 1850. CH: Helen A., b. 25 Apr 1861.
Emma E., b. 1842, d. 12 May 1862.

Sources: Chester VT census 1830, 1840, 1850. VR SA/VT.

491. **SILAS S.$^7$ SAWYER** [see 240], b. 1815 Chester VT, m. 5 May 1842 Chester VT Julia Sargent of Rutland VT, b. 13 Feb 1821, dau. Ezra and Betsey (Putnam) Sargent. Farmer. In Chester VT 1850.

710 George Silas$^8$, b. 1843.
Walter Putnam, b. 11 Sep 1846 Chester VT.

Sources: Chester VT census 1850. VR SA/VT. S9, A20.

492. **EBENEZER$^7$ SAWYER** [see 241], b. 1797 Leicester VT, d. 18 Apr 1869 Leicester VT, m.(1) 14 Mar 1827 Leicester VT Maria Guilford, b. 1804 d. 12 May 1842; m.(2) Mary A. Dow, b. 1815 d. 7 Aug 1865. He bur. in Brookside Cem., Leicester VT.

Augusta Maria, b. 12 May 1828, d. 17 Sep 1833.
Mary Ellen, b. 1832, d. 11 Nov 1835.
Augustus, b. 2 Jan 1833, d. 24 Nov 1857.
Jane, b. 1837.
711 Francis E.$^8$, b. 1845.
712 Stephen E.$^8$, 1847-1877.
Augusta Maria, b. 19 Feb 1851, d. 17 Nov 1864.

Sources: Leicester VT census 1830, 1840, 1850, 1860. VR SA/VT. D11.

493. **HARRISON$^7$ SAWYER** [see 241], b. 20 Sep 1813 Leicester VT, d. 23 Sep 1894 Chicago IL, m. 5 Aug 1841 Brandon VT Ellen M. Wood, b. 3 Oct 1816 d. 3 Feb 1902. In Brandon VT 1843, Lake Geneva WI 1857, Chicago IL 1870.

Wallace Stephen, b. 17 Oct 1843, d. 7 Aug 1899, m. 20 Sep 1879 Nellie Quincannon, b. ?.
Henry E., b. 21 Mar 1846, d. 25 Aug 1863.
Jane, b. 14 Jun 1850, d. 19 Apr 1930, m.(1) Adolf Fleisher, m.(2) David Grover.
Mary Eunice, b. 12 May 1852, d. 14 Feb 1895, m. 27 Jun 1871 Benjamin Libby.
Ella Wood, b. 14 Nov 1857, d. 9 Oct 1934, m. 24 Nov 1881 Stephen Chantrell.
Emma E., b. 12 Oct 1858, d. 3 Jan 1877.

Sources: Obit (Wallace), Ethel L. Morris rec.

494. **HENRY[7] SAWYER** [see 243], b. 25 Apr 1803 Winchendon MA, d. 9 Dec 1870 Winchendon MA, m. Susannah S. Dewey of Connecticut, b. 11 Sep 1806 d. 7 Jan 1889, dau. John and Olive (Hovey) Dewey. In Manchester NY.

Cordelia, b. 2 Dec 1831, d. 27 Sep 1902.

Joseph Howard, b. 19 Mar 1833, d. 5 Nov 1854.

William Henry, b. 26 Oct 1834 Winchendon MA, d. 27 Sep 1920, m. 19 May 1875 Helen J. Pratt, b. ?.

Frances M., b. 4 Aug 1836, d. 21 Aug 1837.

Edwin Dewey, b. 30 Nov 1839, d. 18 Mar 1845.

Mary Louise, b. 24 Sep 1844, m. 19 Sep 1883 James M. Hudnut.

Sources: VR SA/MA.

495. **SILAS[7] SAWYER** [see 244], b. 12 Jan 1799 Templeton MA, m.(I) 1 Dec 1820 Phillipston MA Mercy Whitcomb, b. ca. 1800, dau. Silas and Abigail Baker. Farmer. In Phillipston MA.

Charlotte Augusta, b. 2 Dec 1821, d. 17 May 1878, m. 29 Dec 1842 Edward Powers.

Milla Wright, b. 30 Nov 1825, d. 21 Aug 1826.

Daughter, b. 24 Dec 1826, d. same day.

713 Jonathan Whitcomb[8], b. 1827.

Milly Wright, b. 25 Dec 1829, m. 7 Sep 1851 Phillipston MA Leonard F. Baker.

Mary Ross, b. 5 Jan 1832, m. 5 May 1857 Athol MA Pliney F. Fuller.

Sources: Phillipston MA census 1830, 1840, 1850. VR Phillipston MA, SA/MA. P73.

496. **THOMAS[7] SAWYER** [see 244], b. 12 Jan 1801 Phillipston MA, m. Maria Dyer, b. 1805, dau. Jonas Dyer. Tradesman. In Calais ME.

Abba M., b. 4 Jan 1834.

Albert Henry, b. 15 Aug 1835 Calais ME, m. Lydia Knight, b. ?.

Caroline D., b. 25 May 1837.

Emily D., b. 19 Oct 1840.

Mary E., b. 3 Feb 1846.

Sources: Calais ME census 1840, 1850. VR Calais ME.

497. **GEORGE WASHINGTON[7] SAWYER** [see 244], b. 8 Jul 1807 Phillipston MA, d. 1888, m. 17 Feb 1829 Phillipston MA Sally White, b. 2 Nov 1807 d. 8 Jan 1874, dau. Abel and Sarah (Wood) White. Farmer.

Henrietta, b. 14 Dec 1829.

Child, b. 1 Feb 1831, d. same day.

Serena, b. 11 Apr 1832, d. 31 Dec 1861.

Christopher Columbus, b. 17 Mar 1834 Phillipston MA, m. Mary Underhill of Indianapolis IN, b. 20 Jun 1844. Farmer. Civil War: Captain.

Betsey Burdell, b. 27 Aug 1836, d. ca. 1915, m. 10 Sep 1858 Templeton MA Ephram Wyman Stone.

Sarah White, b. 21 May 1839, d. 13 Nov 1841.

Dorothy, b. 21 May 1841, m. Eliphalet W. Clark. Went to Colorado.

Abner Washington, b. 8 Jun 1842 Phillipston MA, m. 29 Oct 1867 Orange MA Olive Ward of Orange MA, b. ca. 1841, dau. John S. and Olive Ward. In Cleveland OH. CH: Julia Ward, b. 18 Apr 1869; Carrie Eliza, b. 30 Nov 1871; Sally White, b. Jun 18??; Olive, b. Sep 1878.

George A., b. 9 Jun 1843, d.y.

George S., b. 11 May 1845 Phillipston MA.

Sarah White, b. 16 Oct 1847, m. 12 Oct 1869 Gardner MA Albert G. Bushnell.
Julia L., b. 8 Mar 1850, m. 31 May 1874 Templeton MA Thomas E. Ryan.
Sources: Phillipston MA census 1830, 1840. Templeton MA census 1850. VR Phillipston MA, SA/MA. B33, V8, W62.

498. **THOMAS[7] SAWYER** [see 245], b. 23 May 1790 Bolton MA, m. 13 Dec 1821 Claremont NH Mercy Thorndike of Claremont NH, b. ?. In Brooks ME 1820: Mercy B/land 1822-1824; Thomas B/land 1827, 1841, 1844.
Sarah T., b. ca. 1825.
714 Edward Augustus Thorndike[8], b. ca. 1828.
1 dau., b . (1825-1830).
Sources: Brooks ME census 1830, 1840. VR Bolton MA, Brooks ME, SA/NH, SA/MA. N14, R10e, M5.

499. **ABNER[7] SAWYER** [see 245], b. 27 Oct 1794 Bolton MA, m. 24 Aug 1814 Lucy Crary of Prospect ME, b. 1793 d. 14 Feb 1887. Ship carpenter. Lucy joined church in Brooks ME 1826, left 1849. B/land in Brooks ME 1842. Lucy B/land in Brooks ME 1845. Will.
Charles, b. 12 Oct 1815, d. 2 Sep 1816.
715 Emery[8], 1818-1882.
Hannah, b. 16 Jul 1820, d. 16 Jan 1821.
Andrew, b. 19 Nov 1822, d. 17 Sep 1825.
Abner, b. 21 Jul 1824, d. 21 Mar 1845.
Lucy A., b. 8 Jun 1827, d. 6 Apr 1837.
Andrew, b. 28 Apr 1829 Brooks ME. In Searsport ME. Declared of unsound mind 2 Sep 1884.
Cyril Pearl, b. 15 Aug 1833, d. 22 Mar 1835.
Charles, b. ca. 1835 Searsport ME.
Sources: Brooks ME census 1820, 1830, 1840. Searsport ME census 1850, VR Bolton MA, Brooks ME. R10e, P82j.

500. **PHINEAS[7] SAWYER** [see 245], b. 1802 Brooks ME, d. 26 Nov 1843 Brooks ME, m. 15 Jan 1823 Jackson ME Mary Jane Cram of New Hampshire, b. 1803. They both joined church in Brooks ME 1836. Wid. B/land in Brooks ME 1840, Searsport 1850.
Isreal Lamb, b. 10 Aug 1823 Brooks ME, d. 14 Dec 1846 Lowell MA, unm.
Edwin Beaman, b. 11 Mar 1825 Brooks ME, d. 14 Jul 1863 Searsport ME, m. Zilpah Long, b. ca. 1834. Wid. m. 6 May 1866. CH: Alice G., b. ca. 1854, m. 20 Jun 1888 Boston MA George E. Martin; Elizabeth L., b. ?., adopted and changed name to Perkins; Jessie M., b. ca. 1865, m. 11 Nov 1888 Lynn MA Oliver S. Chapman.
Thomas W., b. 29 Jul 1826 Brooks ME, m. 1850 Harriet E. Fields, b. 1830. Carpenter. In Searsport ME 1850. Ch: Lucy M., b. 1851, m. 6 Jun 1872 Boston MA Charles F. Pease; Harriet F., b. 27 Apr 1855, m. 27 Jun 1883 Boston MA Henry A. Browne.
Mary Ellen, b. 16 Feb 1831, m. 11 Nov 1862 Boston MA Edward R. Eaton.
Sources: Brooks ME census 1830, 1840. Searsport ME census 1850. VR Brooks ME, Lowell MA, SA/MA. P82j, R10e, M5.

501. **HOUGHTON[7] SAWYER** [see 246], b. 30 Jun 1805 Whitingham VT, d. 2 Sep 1872 Whitingham VT, m. 1830 Almeda Brown of Phillipston MA, b. 5 Mar 1808 d. 1 Jan 1893, dau. Nathan and Mary Brown. Farmer.
Martha Almeda, b. 3 Sep 1831, d. 20 Aug 1852.
716 John Wesley[8], b. 1832.

Keziah Rebecca, b. 21 Jun 1834, d. 10 Nov 1855.
Elizabeth, b. 3 Nov 1836, d. 13 Jun 1857.
Faustina, b. 23 Jul 1839, d. 30 Jan 1857.
Mary Jane, b. 9 May 1842, m. 24 Jun 1863 Springfield MA Gustavus Foster.
Charles Houghton, b. 18 Apr 1844, d. 6 Apr 1857.
Harriet Marie, b. 17 Sep 1847, d. 9 Dec 1868.
Martha Almeda, b. 1852, m. 13 Oct 1874 Lucius Murray of Boston MA.

Sources: Whitingham VT census 1840, 1850. VR SA/VT, SA/MA. C4.

502. **PAUL$^7$ SAWYER** [see 247], b. 20 Mar 1811 Plymouth VT, d. 22 Oct 1899, m. 17 Dec 1835 Plymouth VT Mary Barrett of Cavendish VT. b. 10 Sep 1814 d. 23 Mar 1905, dau. Robert and Abigail (Smith) Barrett. Cobbler. Deaf and dumb as result of childhood disease.

Ellen, b. ?, unm.
Caroline, b. ?, m. William Hall.
717 Joseph S.$^8$, 1838-1927.
Hannah, b. ca. 1841, d. 4 Jun 1843.
Luella A., b. 25 Jan 1844, m. 6 Sep 1869 Jonathan J. Hall. Went to Wisconsin.
Charles C., b. Oct 1847, d. 23 Mar 1864 New Orleans LA. Civil War.
Millie M., b. Apr 1858, d. 15 Sep 1864.

Sources: VR Plymouth VT, SA/VT. Early Families of Plymouth VT, Richard E. Sawyer rec.

503. **JOSEPH E.$^7$ SAWYER** [see 247], b. 18 Feb 1817 Plymouth VT, d. 4 Mar 1896, m. 1 Mar 1842 Granville VT Sophia King of Plymouth VT, b. 1823 d. 15 Jan 1889, dau. Ira and Betsey King. Farmer.

Anna M., b. 1848, m.(1) 27 Oct 1867 Thomas Baldwin, m.(2) 30 Nov 1882 Myron Dimick.
718 Alden S.$^8$, 1854-1892.
Mary E., b. 27 Dec 1865, m. 4 Dec 1894 Earl Bean.

Sources: D11, D40, Sawyer family Bible, Ada C. Durwood rec.

504. **IRA$^7$ SAWYER** [see 248], b. 16 Feb 1811 Plymouth VT, d. 11 Jan 1892 Bridgewater VT, m. Sarah A. Topliff, b. Oct 1815 d. 11 Sep 1873, dau. James and Sarah Topliff. Farmer.

Mary E., b. ca. 1837.
James E., b. 1842 Bridgewater VT, m. 4 Jun 1863 Martha A. Blanchard, b. ?. Farmer.

Sources: Bridgewater VT census 1850. VR SA/VT.

505. **ADDISON FOSTER$^7$ SAWYER** [see 248], b. 1 Nov 1818 Plymouth VT, d. 8 Feb 1895 Woodstock VT, m.(1) 3 Dec 1840 Reading VT Adella Kellog, b. 24 Jun 1821 d. 24 Apr 1848, dau. Chester and Mary (Stone) Kellogg, m.(2) 1 May 1853 Bridgewater VT AmandaM. Spaulding of Royalton VT, b. 18 Jan 1821 d. 2 Oct 1907, dau. Azel and Lucinda (Brown) Spaulding. Laborer. In Bridgewater VT, Hartland VT 1850, Woodstock VT.

Horace A., b. 6 Apr 1842 Bridgewater VT d. 2 Feb 1904, m. 15 Dec 1873 Ellen A. Young, b. ?. Civil War.
719 Foster Fordyce$^8$, 1844-1915.
Webster L., b. Feb 1855 Woodstock VT, m. 23 Feb 1875 Woodstock VT Olive O. Churchill, b. 15 Nov 1851, dau. Zebedee and Orlena (Boutwell) Churchill. Farmer. CH: Dora E., b. 21 Dec 1875, d. 7 May 1893.
720 William Ware$^8$, 1856-1914.
721 Frank Freeman$^8$, b. 1857.
Amanda M., b. 22 Jan 1858.
722 Frederick Alonzo$^8$, b. 1860.

Sources: Hartland VT census 1850. VR SA/VT. H70, S63, Sawyer family Bible, Pauline Sawyer rec.

506. **JAMES EDWARD⁷ SAWYER** [see 249], b. 19 Aug 1827 Pittsford VT, d. 19 Jun 1882 Whiting VT, m. 6 Oct 1857 Cornwall VT Mary M. French of East Windsor CT, b. 13 Sep 1836 d. 17 Jul 1872. Farmer. In Cornwall VT.

723 Albert Edward⁸, 1859-1939.
George A., b. 6 Aug 1861, d. 13 Jun 1868.
Lona M., b. 1864, d. 3 Jun 1874.
Katie Estelle, b. 3 Apr 1866, m. 3 Jul 1894 Brandon VT Willard H. Nott.
Fred Allen, b. 1868 Whiting VT, m. 2 Apr 1907 Eva E. Walker, b. ?. Farmer.
Elizabeth M., b. 18 Feb 1871, d. 12 Jul 1889.
Harriet Elsie, b. 2 Jul 1876, m. 30 Oct 1902 Pittsford VT Arthur E. Bowen.
Edward James, b. 23 Jan 1881 Whiting VT, m. 8 Nov 1905 Rutland VT Myrtle B. Halliday of Brandon VT, b. ?. Clerk. CH: Katherine Gladys, b. 31 Mar 1906.

Sources: Cornwall VT census 1850, 1860. VR SA/VT.

507. **JAMES A.⁷ SAWYER** [see 250], b. 1823 Shrewsbury VT, d. 8 Aug 1855 Sudbury VT, m. Zilpah _____, b. ?. Wid. m. 1860 Sudbury VT A. C. Ackerman.

Henry M., b. 15 Apr 1849 Sudbury VT, d. 6 Jul 1874 Sudbury VT. Farmer.

Sources: VR SA/VT.

508. **SHERARD⁷ SAWYER** [see 250], b. 18 May 1825 Pittsford VT, d. 20 Nov 1879 Sudbury VT, m. Jane A. Cahee, b. 17 Dec 1829 d. 18 Dec 1904, dau. Robert and Lucy (Calhoon) Cahee. Wid. m. 1881 A_____ Horton.

724 Wallace John⁸, 1846-1912.
George, b. 1849 Sudbury VT.
Roscoe Oliver, b. 1850 Sudbury VT, m. 18 Nov 1874 Brandon VT Alma E. Rich, b. 1852.
Robert A., b. 1852, m. 30 Oct 1876 Ella Gardner, b. ?.
Leamon, b. 1855 Sudbury VT, d. 31 Mar 1907 Hubbardton VT, m. 10 Mar 1880 Sudbury VT Celestia (Arnold) Haven, b. ?. Farmer.
Sherard, b. 7 Jun 1860 Sudbury VT.
Frank E., b. 27 Jun 1864 Sudbury VT, d. 16 Nov 1914, m. 6 Apr 1892 Sudbury VT Carrie Clark of Rutland VT, b. ?. Farmer.

Sources: Sudbury VT census 1850. VR SA/VT, SA/MA.

509. **RUFUS⁷ SAWYER** [see 251], b. 27 Aug 1813 Groton NH, d. 25 Jul 1860 Rumney NH, m. 2 Mar 1835 Mary J. Colburn of Compton NH, b. 24 Aug 1815 d. 1 Oct 1886, dau. Peter Colburn.

Sarah Jane, b. 1835.
725 James Albert⁸, 1837-1920.
Benjamin F., b. Nov 1838, d. 4 Feb 1843 Lowell MA.
Betsey C., b. 1840.
Amanda, b. 1842, m. 19 Jun 1861 Charles Merrill of Rumney NH.

Sources: Wentworth NH census 1840, 1850, 1860. N9, M39.

510. **RICHARD BAILEY⁷ SAWYER** [see 251], b. 1820 Groton NH, m. 9 Mar 1844 Springfield MA Rosette Keyes, b. ?. Laborer. In Wentworth NH, Lowell MA.

Rosette, b. 1845.
Charles F., b. 12 Jan 1847 Lowell MA.
Melissa A., b. 11 Nov 184?.

Sources: VR SA/MA. M39.

511. **JAMES HENRY[7] SAWYER** [see 253], b. 1843 Jaffrey NH, d. 11 Apr 1881, m. 10 Sep 1865 Winchendon MA Flora Ellen Larkin of Clinton MA, b. 1847. Grocer. In Winchendon MA.

Fred Henry, b. 27 Aug 1866 Jaffrey NH, m. 23 Sep 1888 Hudson MA Charity G. Russell of Hudson MA, b. ca. 1870, dau. John and Ellen (Mason) Russell.

Sources: VR SA/MA.

512. **EDWARD HOWARD[7] SAWYER** [see 254], b. 1 Aug 1841 Milton MA, d. 2 May 1914 Auburn ME, m. 4 May 1870 in Cambridge MA Eliza M. Nash of Auburn ME, b. 16 Oct 1847 d. 7 Jul 1927, dau. Lemuel and Elizabeth Nash. Expressman, engineer. In Cambridge MA 1873, Auburn ME 1876. He bur. in Mt. Auburn Cem., Auburn ME.

726 Harry L.[8], 1872-1965.
727 Leland Frederick[8], 1873-1942.
Mabel L., b. 20 Jan 1876, d. 1 Apr 1964, m. Melvin Hersey.
728 Alfred Garfield[8], b. 1882.
Charles Everett, b. 9 Feb 1887, d. 20 Oct 1934.

Sources: ME census 1880 index. VR Auburn ME, SA/ME, SA/MA. Leah Sawyer rec., Greenfield Sawyer rec.

513. **NATHANIEL P.[7] SAWYER** [see 255], b. 3 May 1823 Middlesex VT, d. 10 Jul 1899 Craftsbury VT, m. 28 Jan 1844 Middlesex VT Mary A. Houghton, b. 1827. Farmer. In Stowe VT.

729 George R.[8], b. 1849.
Alice A., b. 1853.
Burt W., b. 12 May 1861 Stowe VT, m. 21 Dec 1883 St. Johnsbury VT Mattie A. Penney, b. Nov 1864. Farmer. In Swanton VT, St. Johnsbury VT.
Daniel H., b. 26 Nov 1864 Stowe VT.
Arthur H., b. 1877 Craftsbury VT, m. 10 Apr 1902 Lettie M. Wells, b. ?. In Wolcott VT 1903. CH: Dau., b. 14 Apr 1903.

Sources: Stowe VT census 1850, 1860. VR SA/VT.

514. **RUSSELL[7] SAWYER** [see 255], b. 4 Sep 1827 Middlesex VT, m. 13 Feb 1851 Montpelier VT Caroline Steele of Middlesex VT, b. ?. Farmer. Town Representative 1880.

730 Charles H.[8], b. 1852.
Ella M., b. 1854, m. 14 Jan 1872 George L. Chamberlin.
Hattie L., b. 1857, m. 4 Jul 1880 George H. Hale.
Carrie C., b. 27 Jan 1863, d. same yr.
Frank H., b. 5 Jan 1865 Middlesex VT, m. 1 Sep 1888 Pluma E. Bruce, b. May 1863. Farmer. In Moretown VT.
Addie, b. 26 Apr 1867, m. 18 Oct 1887 Dow S. Phillips.

Sources: Middlesex VT census 1860. VR SA/VT.

515. **GARDNER[7] SAWYER** [see 255], b. 15 Jul 1829 Middlesex VT, m. 25 Nov 1851 Cabot VT Adeline Mary Spenser of Marshfield VT, b. Sep 1829 d. 6 May 1900 Montpelier VT. dau. Austin and Mary Spenser. Farmer. In Middlesex VT 1870.

Orvis A., b. 1854 Middlesex VT, m. 13 Nov 1880 Emma L. Hill, b. ?. In Berlin VT. CH: Dau., b. 18 May 1896, d. 21 May 1896.
Betsey Jane, b. 12 Jun 1857, m. 25 Aug 1877 Myron Long.
Myra A., b. 24 May 1864, m. 6 Aug 1885 Enoch E. Richardson.
May Evelyn, b. 7 Sep 1868, m. 7 Aug 1895 Michael D. Kelley.

Sources: Middlesex VT census 1870. VR SA/VT.

516. **HIRAM ALLEN[7] SAWYER** [see 255], b. 5 Nov 1832 Middlesex VT, d. 16 Apr 1893 Middlesex VT, m. Jane Spenser of Cabot VT, b. Jul 1833 d. 15 Mar 1900, dau. Austin and Mary Spenser. Farmer.

Arthur, b. 17 Oct 1859, d. 30 Jan 1860.

Henry R., b. 20 Oct 1861 d. 22 Nov 1878.

Don Putnam, b. 31 May 1863 Middlesex VT, m. 29 Sep 1886 Montpelier VT Clara Gertrude Holden, b. 27 Oct 1862. Farmer. In Cabot VT.

Sources: Middlesex VT census 1850. Cabot VT census 1860. VR SA/VT. P85.

517. **AMERICA[7] SAWYER** [see 257], b. 9 Aug 1803 Bolton MA, d. 20 Dec 1884 Lancaster MA, m. 11 Oct 1830 Lancaster MA Lucy H. Baldwin, b. 13 Jul 1811 d. 6 Dec 1858, dau. Oliver and Lucy (Hosley) Baldwin. In Lancaster MA 1840.

Henry Oliver, b. 4 Mar 1834, d. 24 Mar 1835.

Lucy Hosley, b. 6 Mar 1835, m. 10 Mar 1864 Shrewsbury MA James W. Lewis.

Lucinda Matilda, b. 27 Apr 1837.

Child, b. ?, d. 18 Oct 1840.

Oliver Baldwin, b. 16 Dec 1839 Lancaster MA, m. Jennie M. Taylor of Lancaster MA, b.?. Farmer. CH: Nellie E., b. 26 Nov 1866, m. 29 May 1887 Hudson MA Warren A. Baker.

George Alfred, b. 10 Aug 1842 Lancaster MA. Mechanic. In East Princeton MA.

Alber (*sic*) America, b. 23 Jan 1844 Lancaster MA.

Marietta C., b. 31 Dec 1846, m. 11 Nov 1872 Wayland MA Everett W. Perkins.

Elliot Elijah, b. 27 Dec 1850 Lancaster MA, m. 26 Mar 1874 Northboro MA Mary Ellen Mentzer of Northboro MA, b. 1851, dau. Cyrus and Mary (Fay) Mentzer. Merchant. In Putnam CT, Worcester MA 1874. Wid. m. Watrous Garnsey. CH: child, b. 29 Dec 1874.

Sources: Lancaster MA census 1840, 1850. VR SA/MA.

518. **WARREN[7] SAWYER** [see 257], b. 5 Jun 1806 Bolton MA, d. 16 May 1862 Starksboro VT, m. Mariah Houston of New Hampshire, b. May 1810 d. 19 Sep 1864, dau. Samuel and Phebe Houston. Lawyer. In Acworth NH, Starksboro VT.

731 Elijah L.[8], b. 1836.

Sarah F., b. 1837.

Philander M., b. 1839, m. 5 Apr 1860 Leonard T. Hill.

Emma, b. 1855, m. 9 Mar 1871 Lincoln VT Joel Chase Atkins.

Sources: Starksboro NH census 1840, 1850. VR SA/VT.

519. **ALFRED[7] SAWYER** [see 259], b. 27 Jan 1812 Bolton MA, d. 25 Dec 1897 Sycamore IL, m. 17 May 1837 Peacham VT Margaret Hendry of Peacham VT, b. ca. 1816. Machinist. In Winchendon MA 1850, Dorchester NH 1854, Illinois 1858.

Amory Watson, b. 19 Aug 1839 Bolton MA, m. Sycamore IL Martha J. Conant, b. ?. In Chicago IL.

Laura Jeanett, b. 13 Mar 1843, m. Philander M. Alden.

Susan S., b. 20 Jan 1852, d. 22 May 1854 Winchendon MA.

Lucien Hendry, b. 30 Jun 1854, m. Mary McCullough, b. ?.

Sources: Winchendon MA census 1850. VR SA/MA. J14.

520. **EDWIN[7] SAWYER** [see 259], b. 20 Jul 1817 Bolton MA, d. 20 Jul 1885 Watertown MA, m. 3 Mar 1850 Stowe MA Sarah B. Wright of Boxboro MA, b. ? d. 8 Feb 1902. Sash maker.

Herbert H., b. 6 Jul 1857 Watertown MA, m. 18 Jun 1883 Watertown MA Alice Tourtelotte of Oxford MA, b. 22 Jul 1855, dau. William H. and Mercy (Cromstock) Tourtelotte. In Watertown MA. CH: Minnie T., b. 26 Oct 1884.

Sources: VR Bolton MA, Watertown MA, SA/MA. J14.

521. **OLIVER⁷ SAWYER** [see 260], b. 13 Dec 1818 Bolton MA, m. 23 Feb 1841 Bolton MA Sophia Nourse of Bolton MA, b. ?. Blacksmith.

Ellen Sophia, b. 12 Jan 1842, m. 3 Oct 1865 Watertown MA Charles Adams.

Sarah Louisa, b. 20 Aug 1843, d. 5 Sep 1848 Bolton MA.

Horace Griffin, b. 20 Jul 1846 Bolton MA, m. 25 Aug 1875 Newton MA Ruth E. Wheaton of Calais ME, b. 1843, dau. William H. and Harriet Wheaton. Clerk.

Walter Whitcomb, b. 8 Jul 1848 Bolton MA, d. 15 Aug 1858 Vasselboro ME.

Sources: VR Bolton MA, Sterling MA, SA/MA.

522. **ANTHONY LANE⁷ SAWYER** [see 262], b. 1 May 1821 Bolton MA, m. 19 Oct 1843 Waltham MA Edith B. Haven, b. ?, dau. Luther and Lydia (Bacon) Haven. Wheelwright. In Lancaster MA.

732 Francis Haven⁸, b. 1849.

Sources: VR Waltham MA, SA/MA. S56.

523. **FRANKLIN⁷ SAWYER** [see 265], b. 25 Jun 1809 Cambridge MA, d. 18 Nov 1851 Cambridge MA, m. 1 Jun 1834 New Orleans LA Sarah M. Loring of Boston MA, b. 9 Dec 1813 d. 4 Jan 1867, dau. Braddock and Sarah (Shattuck) Loring of New Orleans LA. Lawyer. In Detroit MI 1831, New Orleans LA 1843, Cambridge MA 1850.

Sarah E., b. 23 Jan 1835, d. 25 Jan 1835.

Emily C., b. 19 Feb 1836, d. 1862 New Orleans LA.

Loring, b. 2 Nov 1837. Civil War: Killed in Second Battle of Bull Run, July 1861.

Frank, b. 15 Jun 1839, d. 31 Oct 1840.

Frank Hastings, b. 14 Apr 1841 New Orleans LA. In Cambridge MA.

John Talbot, b. 4 Feb 1843 New Orleans LA, m. 1877 Elizabeth McKnight, b. ?. In Cambridge MA.

Sarah, b. 30 Jan 1844, m. Charles McKnight of New Orleans LA.

Howard, b. 9 Nov 1850 Cambridge MA.

Sources: Cambridge MA census 1850. VR SA/MA. C8, P61, A20.

524. **ALPHONSO BROOKS⁷ SAWYER** [see 266], b. 28 Mar 1837 Holden MA, m. 1 Feb 1865 Holden MA Mary Bryant of Rutland VT, b. ca. 1862, dau. William and Mary Bryant. Bootmaker. Civil War: Enl. 19 Apr 1861 Company B, 3rd Battalion, ?. In Holden MA.

Charles Wesley, b. 10 Jan 1869 Holden MA.

Sources: Holden MA census 1840, 1850. VR Holden MA, SA/MA. E24.

525. **JOHN⁷ SAWYER** [see 267], b. 1 Feb 1805 Templeton MA, m.(1) 26 Nov 1827 Sterling MA Mary Whiting of Sterling MA, b. 1807 d. 23 Jul 1831; m.(2) 23 May 1833 Sterling MA Lucy Cobleigh, b. ?. In Templeton MA 1840.

Annis Marie, b. 21 Mar 1829, d. 21 May 1831.

Silas M., b. 10 Mar 1830, d. 24 May 1831.

Ann Mary, b. 12 Jul 1831, m. 14 Jun 1855 Templeton MA David P. Sheldon.

Peter Cobleigh, b. 14 Mar 1834 Templeton MA, m. 13 Aug 1857 Templeton MA Ellen A. Merritt of Hubbardston MA, b. 1837, dau. Warren L. Merritt. In Oakham MA. CH: Anna C., b. 1870, m. 14 Oct 1891 Holyoke MA Royce C. Strickland.

Ellen Maria, b. 24 Jul 1836, m. 31 Dec 1855 Templeton MA Calvin D. Smith.
Paul Knight, b. 17 Oct 1839 Templeton MA.
Lucy Fedelia, b. 1841.

Sources: Templeton MA census 1830, 1840. VR Templeton MA, Sterling MA, SA/MA.

526. **ELIJAH⁷ SAWYER** [see 268], b. 4 Nov 1819 Charlemont MA, m. 25 Nov 1838 Rutland VT Abigail Cleveland, b. 3 Jul 1820, dau. Chester and Polly (Townsend) Cleveland. In Rutland VT.

Mary J., b. 27 Oct 1840, m. 1883 Lyman Pike.
Willard William, b. 28 Oct 1842, m. Annie Lewis, b.?. Went to Illinois.

Sources: C48.

527. **ELISHA EMERY⁷ SAWYER** [see 269], b. 1822 Templeton MA, m. 2 Nov 1848 Templeton MA Mary E. Church of Templeton MA, b. 1825, dau. Joshua and Betsey Church. Farmer.

Emory Curtis, b. 29 Jun 1850 Templeton MA, m. 1 Jun 1878 Warren MA Delia McTighe of New Jersey, b. 1854, dau. John and Bridgett McTighe. Lawyer. In Warren MA 1880. CH: Mary Cady, b. 14 Feb 1880.
Abby Ann, b. 23 Aug 1857, d. 14 Sep 1857.

Sources: Templeton MA census 1850. Warren MA census 1880. VR SA/MA.

528. **EDEN BALDWIN⁷ SAWYER** [see 270], b. 19 Nov 1823 Templeton MA, m. 23 Aug 1859 Templeton MA Emma A. Brown of Hinsdale NH, b. 1842, dau. Henry E. Brown. Farmer, carpenter. Went to Texas.

Henry Eden, b. 19 Oct 1860.
Flora Louisa, b. 20 Aug 1864.

Sources: VR SA/MA. B11.

529. **JOSEPH BALCOMB⁷ SAWYER** [see 271], b. 21 Oct 1819 Templeton MA, m. 21 Jan 1859 Westminster MA (also recorded in Templeton MA) Martha Jane Lewis of Lancaster MA, b. 15 Oct 1830, dau. Levi and Abigail (Ballard) Lewis. Manufacturer, inventor.

Warren Francis, b. 25 Mar 1860, d. 30 Jun 1860.
Burnside Ellsworth, b. 10 Oct 1861 Templeton MA.
Lewis Joseph, b. 10 Jun 1863. Pastor of a Seattle WN church.
Albert Harris, b. 23 Jun 1868 Templeton MA.
Frank Hastings, b. 28 Sep 1869 Templeton MA.

Sources: VR SA/MA. L18.

530. **ADDISON MONROE⁷ SAWYER** [see 271], b. 14 Aug 1827 Templeton MA, d. 23 Jan 1890 Athol MA, m.(1) 23 Oct 1854 Petersham MA Harriet E. Blackmor of Dana MA, b. 28 Sep 1834 d. 23 Jul 1876, dau. Hosea and Sarah Blackmor; m.(2) 8 Aug 1877 Athol MA Mary E. Stevens of Guilford VT, b. 19 Aug 1844, dau. Darwin H. and Harriet (Andrews) Stevens. Inventor. In Athol MA 1860, Fitchburg MA 1861.

Aurora H., b. 13 Aug 1855, d. 21 Mar 1864.
Lana Estelle, b. 31 Aug 1861, d. 6 Aug 1868.
Charles Addison, b. 11 Jan 1864, d. 21 Mar 1890.
Ambrose Monroe, b. 23 Jul 1876, d. 2 Apr 1888.

Sources: Athol MA census 1860. VR SA/MA. C17, B25, S49.

531. **SYLVESTER⁷ SAWYER** [see 272], b. 28 Nov 1822 Templeton MA, d. 1895 Fitchburg MA, m.(1) 27 Jun 1843 Athol MA Esther Bigelow of Athol MA, b. 27 Nov 1821 d. 11 Mar 1846, dau. Abel and Hannnah Bigelow; m.(2) 22 Oct 1846 Royalston MA Minerva Simonds of Bedford MA, b. 1821, dau. Benjamin and Elizabeth Simonds. Cabinet maker. In Royalston MA 1850, Fitchburg MA 1852.

George, b. 10 Oct 1848 Royalston MA.

Sources: Royalston MA census 1850. VR Athol MA, Royalston MA, SA/MA. H81, K16.

532. **JOSHUA⁷ SAWYER** [see 276], b. Oct 1816 Whitefield NH, d. 23 Dec 1888 Duxbury VT, m.(1) 2 Oct 1849 Dorset VT Jane Kent, b. ?; m.(2) Eunice Hunt of Wells VT, b. Oct 1827 d. 2 Jul 1882, dau. Amos and Rosanna Hunt. Marble worker. In Dorset VT 1850, Northfield VT 1860.

Warren J., b. 1851, d. 1866.
733 Charles D.⁸, b. 1853.
Fannie, b. 1856.
Abba, b. 4 Feb 1858, d. 7 Dec 1884.
734 Fred K.⁸, 1860-1944.
Ella E., b. 24 May 1863, m. 1 Nov 1884 Williamstown VT Lewis N. Ellis.
Emma E., b. 1868, m. 20 Sep 1892 Harlan H. Slack.

Sources: Dorset VT census 1850, Northfield VT census 1860. VR SA/VT. John J. Sawyer rec.

533. **NORMAN DAVIS⁷ SAWYER** [see 277], b. 10 Feb 1819 Berlin VT, d. 2 Sep 1885 Berlin VT, m. 10 Jul 1862 West Berlin VT (later div) Wealthy Holden of Woodbury VT, b. 31 Oct 1833 d. 2 Apr 1928, dau. Jabez P. and Jeana (Powers) Holden. Farmer.

Anna Electa, b. 17 May 1863, d. 1950, m. 10 Jun 1896 Milton D. Drew.
Mary Elizabeth, b. 24 Jun 1865, d. 25 Sep 1905. Seamstress.
James, b. 8 Apr 1867, d. 1940.
735 Edward Solomon⁸, 1869-1900.
Norman Davis, b. 15 Feb 1872 Berlin VT, d. 25 Apr 1943 Arlington MA, m. 9 Nov 1910 Boston MA Sarah M. Ellison of New Brunswick, Canada, b. 13 Jan 1887 d. 1 Mar 1974, dau. David and Sarah (Knaves) Ellison. He bur. Mt. Pleasant Cem., Arlington MA. CH: Norman Davis, b. 7 Nov 1916, unm.

Sources: Berlin VT census 1850, 1860. VR SA/VT. Norman Davis Sawyer rec.

534. **JONATHAN AYER⁷ SAWYER** [see 280], b. 26 Jan 1799 Atkinson NH, d. 26 Jul 1840 Haverhill MA, m. 21 Mar 1822 Pembroke NH Abigail Hoit of Pembroke NH, b. 1798. In Concord NH 1830, Haverhill MA 1840.

Mary Ann, b. 12 Nov 1822, m. 20 Jan 1850 Haverhill MA Daniel D. Flanders.
Charles Hutchins, b. 14 Jun 1824 Concord NH. In Haverhill MA.
Sarah Elizabeth, b. 1830, m. 26 Jan 1850 Haverhill MA George Dawson.

Sources: Concord NH census 1830. Haverhill MA census 1840. VR Haverhill MA, Pembroke NH, SA/MA.

535. **JESSE L.⁷ SAWYER** [see 280], b. 14 Jul 1802 Atkinson NH, m. 6 Dec 1825 Haverhill MA Sarah B. LeBosquet of Portland ME, b. ?. Trader. B/S/land in Andover ME 1825, 1830-1848. B/S/land in Freeport ME 1828, 1830.

Sarah Olivia, b. 1827, m. 2 Jun 1853 Haverhill MA Nathaniel B. Currier. [M39] says Sarah m. Nathaniel Byron Webster.
Caroline M., b. 1829, m. 1 Nov 1855 in Haverhill MA Charles A. Morse.
Edwin H., b. 1831 Atkinson NH, m. 24 Feb 1857 Hattie Collum of Meadville PA. In Haverhill MA 1850.

Mary L., b. 1833, d. 31 Jul 1839 Boston MA.
Sources: Haverhill MA census 1850. VR Haverhill MA, SA/MA. R10a, M39.

536. **JESSE AUGUSTUS$^7$ SAWYER** [see 281], b. 4 Nov 1823 Atkinson NH, d. 14 Feb 1915 Atkinson NH, m. 13 Nov 1851 Haverhill MA Elizabeth Bradley Noyes of Atkinson NH, b. 30 Mar 1828 d. 25 Dec 1911, dau. Asa and Sophia (Bradley) Noyes. Farmer.
Charles A., b. 4 Oct 1852, d. 30 Jan 1879 Atkinson NH.
736 Herbert Noyes$^8$, 1860-1946.
Sources: Atkinson NH census 1860, 1870. VR Haverhill MA, SA/NH. N40. M39, N9, Ruth L. Sawyer rec.

537. **ALANSON MASON$^7$ SAWYER** [see 281], b. 19 Dec 1825 Atkinson NH, d. 27 Mar 1895 Atkinson NH, m. 14 Apr 1853 Haverhill MA Caroline R. Noyes of Atkinson NH, b. 26 Jun 1830 d. 11 Sep 1916, dau. Asa and Sophia (Bradley) Noyes. Farmer. Town Clerk 1852-54.
Mary Sophia, b. 5 May 1854, d. 28 Nov 1936, m. 29 Nov 1877 Atkinson NH George Cross of Exeter NH.
737 George Alanson$^8$, 1864-1945.
Eugene Edson, b. 24 Mar 1866 Atkinson NH, d. 2 Mar 1949 Atkinson NH, m. 13 Dec 1919 New York City Mabel Tourtillotte of Woodstock NH, b. 1897 d. 1949, dau. Josiah and Laura A. (Barron) Tourtillotte. Dairy farmer. No CH.
Sources: Atkinson NH census 1860, 1870. VR Haverhill MA, SA/NH. M39, N9, B27, N40.

538. **LEONARD$^7$ SAWYER** [see 282], b. ca. 1808 Bradford MA, m. 27 Oct 1833 Haverhill MA Rachel Dix of Tewksbury MA, b. ca. 1807. Shoemaker. In Haverhill MA 1850.
738 Leonard$^8$, b. ca. 1835.
Rachel, b. Jan 1838, d. 15 Jul 1842.
Lucretia, b. ca. 1840.
Rachel, b. ca. 1844, m. 7 May 1865 in Lynn MA Joseph A. Dow.
Lettie C., b. ca. 1845, m.(1) 3 Jun 1871 Mason Severence, m.(2) 15 Dec 1880 Daniel Dwinnell.
David, b. 24 Nov 1850, d. 27 Jan 1851 Haverhill MA.
Sources: Haverhill MA census 1850. VR Haverhill MA, SA/MA.

539. **MOSES W.$^7$ SAWYER** [see 282], b. ca. 1810 Massachusetts, m. 2 Jan 1831 Haverhill MA Mary Bailey, b. 1809, dau. Nathan Bailey. In Haverhill MA 1832, Malden MA 1850.
739 Charles Henry$^8$, b. 1832.
George Albert, b. 5 Jan 1834 Haverhill MA. In Malden MA 1850.
Sources: Malden MA census 1850. VR Haverhill MA, SA/MA. M39.

540. **RICHARD$^7$ SAWYER** [see 282], b. ca. 1814 Amesbury MA, m. 30 Apr 1834 West Newbury MA Mary W. Durgin, b. 1816. Shoemaker. In West Newbury MA 1850.
Lois Ann, b. ca. 1836, m. 3 Jun 1858 in Bradford MA Benjamin Perry.
Mary F., b. ca. 1837.
740 Nowell Fisher$^8$, b. ca. 1839.
741 Moses Sargent$^8$, b. ca. 1843.
Nicolas Durgin, b. 22 Jun 1848 West Newbury MA, d. 29 Apr 1917 Laconia NH, m. 24 Nov 1881 Bradford MA Ellen Augusta Eastman of Penacook NH, b. 25 Jul 1849 d. 13 Nov 1930 Laconia NH, dau. Luke and Sarah (Chandler) Eastman. In Concord NH.
Sources: West Newbury MA census 1850. VR West Newbury MA, SA/MA.

541. **JOSEPH REED[7] SAWYER** [see 286], b. 11 Mar 1809 Boothbay ME, d. 1 Oct 1884 Old Town ME, m. 27 Nov 1839 Sarah R. Haskell of Greene ME, b. 19 Sep 1820 d. 20 Mar 1906, dau. Job and Hannah (Cutler) Haskell. Cooper. B/land in Levant ME 1836, 1842. In Old Town ME 1864.

Georgianna C., b. 1 Aug 1840, d. 1911, m. 5 Aug 1856 William Manley.
Hudson, b. 6 Jul 1842 Old Town ME, d. 10 Nov 1904 Togus ME, m. 2 Oct 1865 Bridgton ME Frances A. Crane, b. Sep 1844. Clergyman. In Dexter ME, Augusta ME 1875, Ft. Fairfield ME 1880. He bur. in Boulder CO. CH: Edna M., b. 1868; Amy E., b. 1871; Helen E., b. 7 Oct 1876.
742 Andrew Chesley[8], b. 1844.
Joseph Warren, b. 24 Apr 1846, d. 29 Jan 1847.
743 Joseph Warren[8], 1848-1902.
Ada F., b. 18 Oct 1854, m. 30 Jun 1879 Charles McCulloch.
Martha H., b. 6 Dec 1856, d. 1 Aug 1863.
744 Charles Haskell[8], b. 1863.

Sources: Levant ME census 1840, 1850. Ft. Fairfield ME census 1880. VR Levant ME, Bridgton ME, Hallowell ME, SA/ME. G41, L30, R10d.

542. **WARREN[7] SAWYER** [see 286], b. 1811 Levant ME, d. Calais ME, m. Sarah _____, b. 1814. Carpenter. In Calais ME 1850.

Lorrinda, b. 20 Jul 1832.
Ann Marie, b. 20 Aug 1834.
745 Joseph Warren[8], b. 1834.
Phebe, b. 12 Jan 1838.
Alfred, b. ca. 1841 Calais ME.
746 Stillman Osgood[8], 1842-1917.
Trunzina, b. 8 Apr 1845.
Martha E., b. 10 Dec 1847, m. 18 Nov 1865 George W. Turner.

Sources: Calais ME census 1850. VR Calais ME, SA/ME.

543. **EPHRAIM E.[7] SAWYER** [see 287], b. Dec 1825 Montville ME, d. 30 Mar 1909 Montville ME, m. Rhoda A. Choate, b. Sep 1839 d. 23 Feb 1905, dau. Robert and Sophronia Choate. Both bur. Halldale Cem., Montville ME.

Ida B., b. 1873.
Robert, b. Feb 1874 Montville ME.
Bertha L., b. 1875, d. 11 Apr 1888.

Sources: ME census 1880 index. VR Montville ME. M5.

544. **LEVERETT[7] SAWYER** [see 288], b. 8 Dec 1801 Beverly MA, d. 22 Sep 1839 Salem MA, m. 26 Jan 1830 Salem MA Martha A. Kehew, b. ?. Watchmaker. B/land in Salem MA 1833. Wid. in Salem MA 1840, 1850.

747 Leverett Augustus[8], 1830-1899.
Mary A., b. 1831.
Emerline C., b. 1833.
George Carlton, b. 24 Dec 1834 Salem MA, m. 29 Jul 1858 Mary A. Gorham, b. 16 Apr 1832. Harvard College 1855. In Utica NY. CH: William Gorham, b. 10 May 1860, d. 20 Jun 1876.
Ellen, b. 1836.
Martha A., b. 1837.
Nathaniel A., b. ca. 1839 Salem MA.

Sources: Salem MA census 1830, 1840, 1850. VR Salem MA. C73.

545. **BENJAMIN W.[7] SAWYER** [see 289], b. 6 Jul 1811 Belfast ME, d. 13 Sep 1865 Rockland ME, m.(1) 13 Aug 1836 Bangor ME Nancy J. Robinson of Newcastle ME, b. 1818 d. 15 Oct 1864. Carpenter, furniture dealer. B/land in Bangor ME 1834. In Thomaston ME 1840, Rockland ME 1850.

Frederick M., b. 20 Feb 1839 Bangor ME. Civil War: Officer, 5th New York Cavalry. Sailor.

Charles Farwell, b. 26 Jan 1842 Rockland ME, d. 1900 Denver CO, m.(1) 26 Jul 1869 Charlestown MA Carrie M. Hoyt of Wisconsin, b. ?, dau. George and Susan Hoyt; m.(2) 30 Dec 1882 Antoinette (Shedd) Surbridge, b. 25 Sep 1847, dau. William B. and Chaphira (Dunham) Shedd. Clerk. Civil War: Officer, 4th Maine Regiment. In Thomaston ME, Rockland ME.

Helen L., b. 29 Oct 1844, d. 1917, m. 1863 William Wright.

Sources: Thomaston ME census 1840. Rockland ME census 1850, 1860. VR Bristol ME, Bangor ME, SA/MA. R10d, S34, E3.

546. **BENJAMIN EDWARD[7] SAWYER** [see 290], b. 11 Aug 1811 Cape Elizabeth ME, d. 2 Aug 1879 Haverhill MA, m.(1) 14 Jul 1833 Bedford NH Lucy Cordelia Noyes of Newport NH, b. 27 Aug 1813 d. 6 Oct 1849, dau. Moses and Lucy (Wilcox) Noyes; m.(2) 17 Oct 1850 Concord MA Mary Smith of Sudbury MA, b. 1824 d. 3 Jan 1851 Concord MA, dau. William R. and Elizabeth S. Smith; m.(3) 16 Sep 1851 Boston MA Sarah Foster of Hanover NH, b. ca. 181?, dau. Richard and Irene Foster. Physician. In Boscawen NH 1840, Concord MA 1850. He bur. in Concord MA.

Annie Maria, b. 24 Mar 1836, m. 15 Aug 1860 Haverhill MA Samuel M. Downes.

Ellen Augusta, b. 7 Jun 1839, m. 16 Oct 1859 Haverhill MA Robert Ingalls.

Benjamin Addison, b. 6 Mar 1843 Boscawen NH, d. Haverhill MA, m. Elizabeth M. George, b. ?, dau. Washington George. Civil War. Harvard College 1865. Physician. Concord MA 1850. Commanded GAR Post in Duxbury MA 1885. In Bradford MA. CH: Annie Frances, b. 12 Sep 1869, d. 6 Oct 1935, librarian.

Lucy C., b. 27 Oct 1846, d. 3 Aug 1848.

Charles Milton, b. 25 Feb 1849 Concord MA, m.(1) 14 Nov 1870 Haverhill MA L. Helen Kitfield of Manchester MA, b. ca. 1849, dau. Henry and Lucy Kitfield; m.(2) 14 Jun 1882 Haverhill MA Martha J. Littlefield of Kennebec ME, b. 1860, dau. David and Mary Littlefield. Physician.

Sources: Boscawen NH census 1840. Concord MA census 1850. VR Bedford NH, Concord MA, SA/MA. N40.

547. **JACOB[7] SAWYER** [see 291], b. 26 Jul 1813 Mt. Desert ME, d. 28 Apr 1897 Tremont ME, m. Caroline E. Briggs of Bradford ME, b. 24 Feb 1822 d. Jul 1894, dau. William and Betsey (Forbes) Briggs. Mechanic. B/land in Bradford ME 1840, Tremont ME 1850.

Salem T., b. 10 Feb 1840 Tremont ME, d. 1870, m. 29 Jun 1868 Charlestown MA Clara A. White of Charlestown MA, b. 1848, dau. George W. and Harriet White. Insurance agent. In Charlestown MA 1870. CH: Alice M., b. 23 Aug 1870.

748 Lewis Freeman[8], 1842-1919.

Emmons K., b. 1844 Tremont ME, d. 22 May 1858.

Julia C. b. 24 Sep 1846, m. Whitcomb Richardson.

Rosabell, b. Sep 1849, m. 5 Jul 1873 Boston MA William A. Abbott.

Elizabeth P., b. 9 Jun 1853, m. 16 May 1878 Clinton MA Robert E. Achorn.

Sophronia F., b. 10 May 1855, m. 8 May 1888 Henry White of Marlboro MA.

Son, b. 22 Oct 1857, d. 30 Oct 1857.

749 Joshua A.[8], 1859-1932.

Carrie C., b. 27 Nov 1863, m. 28 Dec 1892 Marlboro MA Charles H. Welsh.

Sources: Tremont ME census 1850, 1860, 1870. Charlestown MA census 1870. VR Tremont ME, SA/ME, SA/MA. P82d, Family Bible, James L. Sawyer rec., Harvey M. Sawyer rec.

548. **BENJAMIN[7] SAWYER** [see 291], b. 5 May 1817 Mt. Desert ME, d. 24 Nov 1892 Tremont ME, m. 23 Apr 1857 Charlotte Dodge of Mt. Desert ME, b. 1829. Ship carpenter. In Mt. Desert ME 1839, Tremont ME 1860.

Clara D., b. 1858.

Caroline, b. 1859.

Emily J., b. 21 Jul 1861, d. 29 Jan 1922 Tremont ME, unm.

Eva L., b. 1864.

William E., b. ca. 1867 Tremont ME.

Sources: Tremont ME census 1860, 1870. VR SA/ME.

549. **CALEB HODGDON[7] SAWYER** [see 291], b. Jul 1828 Mt. Desert ME, d. 26 Apr 1902 Tremont ME, m. 16 Mar 1853 Tremont ME Clarissa D. Pray of Mt. Desert ME, b. 17 Dec 1832 d. 24 Apr 1919, dau. Eben and Charlotte (Flyde) Pray. Sea captain. Wid. in Tremont ME 1910.

Amanda T., b. 1853, d. 1921, m. LLewellyn Norwood.

Phebe G., b. 1856, d. 1886, m. Will Brown.

750 Emmons Pray[8], 1859-1928.

Charles Raymond, b. Jul 1861 Tremont ME, m. 8 Jun 1899 Tremont ME Lizzie M. (Harper) Norwood, wid., b. 1857, dau. Nehemiah and Sophronia (Langdon) Harper. Seaman. In Rockland ME. He bur. in Seal Cove ME.

Eben Pray, b. 1865 Tremont ME, d. 1938, m. 29 Nov 1902 Pittsfield NH Mary J. Prentiss of Canada, b. 1878, dau. Robert and Mary Prentiss. In Hastings ME, Lincoln ME.

Herbert Lee, b. 1870, d. 1952, unm. Bur. in Seal Cove ME.

Sources: Tremont ME census 1860, 1870. ME census 1880 index. VR Tremont ME, SA/ME. M8, Richard M. Sawyer rec.

550. **WILLIAM M.[7] SAWYER** [see 292], b. 29 Jun 1838 Boothbay ME, d. 17 Aug 1906, m.(1) Angelina Jack, b. 1837 d. 1885; m.(2) 24 Dec 1887 Portland ME Aldania Blake, b. Jun 1841. Merchant. Owned wharf.

751 William Elmer[8], 1863-1941.

752 Melvin D.[8], 1865-1910.

Sources: VR Boothbay ME, SA/ME. G41, M5.

551. **STEPHEN[7] SAWYER** [see 295], b. 1816 Vinalhaven ME, m. 4 Dec 1839 Lydia Webster, b. ?. Fisherman. In Vinalhaven ME 1840, North Haven ME 1850.

Alonzo, b. ca. 1840 Vinalhaven ME. In North Haven ME.

Ora, b. 1843 Vinalhaven ME.

753 Miles J.[8], b. 1847.

Hudson, b. ca. 1849 North Haven ME.

Eliza J., b. 18 Jul 1855, m. 27 Dec 1873 Francis P. Cooper.

Frank B. C., b. 1 Aug 1859, d. 23 Jan 1860.

Charles S., b. ca. 1867 North Haven ME.

Sources: Vinalhaven ME census 1840. North Haven ME census 1850, 1860, 1870. VR Vinalhaven ME, Camden ME, SA/ME.

552. **WILLIAM YEATON[7] SAWYER** [see 295], b. 18 Aug 1818 Vinalhaven ME, d. 22 Mar 1903, m.(1) 27 Dec 1849 Lucinda Frye of Montville ME, b. 14 Apr 1826 d. 18 Mar 1852, dau. Amos and Mercy (Collier) Frye; m.(2) 30 Oct 1854 Rockland ME Harriet Newell Perley of Freedom ME, b. 21 Oct 1822 d. 8 Aug 1894, dau. John and Mary (Spaulding) Perley. Ship carpenter. B/land in Northport ME 1849. In Unity ME 1848, 1858, Thomaston ME 1856, Hampden ME 1870.

754 Roscoe Oscar[8], 1848-1925.
755 Trueman Irons[8], b. 1856.
Leslie Horace, b. 24 Jun 1858 North Haven Island ME, d. Fairbanks, Alaska, unm.
Foster Perley, b. 16 Oct 1860 Unity ME, m. Agnes M. Sharpe, b.?.
Jennie May, b. 25 Apr 1862, d. 12 Nov 1864.
Hattie May, b. 8 Jan 1864, m. 19 Jan 1886 James E. Garland.

Sources: Hampden ME census 1870. VR Dixmont ME, Bangor ME. R10e, P33, B23.

553. **WALTER S.[7] SAWYER** [see 295], b. Oct 1822 Vinalhaven ME, d. 4 Apr 1900 Rockland ME, m. 2 Dec 1857 Casselda Frye, b. 3 Mar 1829 d. 31 Jan 1894, dau. Amos and Mercy (Collier) Frye. In North Haven ME, Camden ME 1860, Rockland ME 1865.

Corilla, b. 1852.
Alpheus, b. 1853.
Ralph S., b. 9 Aug 1855, d. 20 Jan 1894.
Paul, b. 21 Jun 1859 Camden ME. In Rockland ME 1865.
Alice B., b. 9 Jul 1865.

Sources: Camden ME census 1860. VR Camden ME, Rockland ME, SA/ME. B23.

554. **REUBEN FREEMAN[7] SAWYER** [see 295], b. 1837 Vinalhaven ME, m. 1 Jan 1864 Rockport ME Lucy Jane Haskell of Deer Isle ME, b. 1835. Carpenter. In Rockport ME 1869, North Haven ME 1880.

Carrie Bell, b. 1869, m. 21 May 1890 Beverly MA James Henry Owen.
Sarah Elizabeth, b. 1871, m. 11 Jan 1893 Beverly MA George W. Rowell.
Walter A., b. 1873 North Haven ME.
Edith E., b. 4 Aug 1875, d. 28 May 1923, m. 16 Jul 1902 Boston MA Forest W. Howe.
Augusta, b. 1878.
Frederick Packard, b. 8 Nov 1882 North Haven ME.

Sources: ME census 1880 index. VR Rockland ME, SA/MA. H80.

555. **HORACE M.[7] SAWYER** [see 295], b. 25 Jan 1839 Vinalhaven ME, d. 17 Nov 1907 North Haven ME.

Janice, b. 1862.
William S., b. Apr 1890.

Sources: North Haven ME census 1870.

556. **PAUL[7] SAWYER** [see 296], b. 23 Aug 1820 Deer Isle ME, d. 30 Jan 1888 Bangor ME, m.(I) 25 May 1849 Lovina E. Rea, b. 4 Apr 1832 d. 13 Sep 1913, dau. John and Lovina C. (Coombs) Rea. Sea captain. B/land in Isleboro ME 1846. In Isleboro ME 1850, Stockton ME 1870, Bangor ME 1880.

Druzetta C., b. 24 Nov 1849, d. 1859.
756 William Nathaniel[8], 1852-1915.
Arvilla E., b. 16 May 1857, m. William H. Margesson.
Florence S., b. 3 Feb 1861, d. 1871.

Sources: Isleboro Me census 1850, 1860. Stockton ME census 1870. ME 1880 census index. VR Bangor ME, SA/ME. R10d, L30.

557. **GEORGE WASHINGTON$^7$ SAWYER** [see 296], b. 30 Oct 1828 Deer Isle ME, m.(1) Drizetta Sprague, b. 1829; m.(2) Arvilla Davis, b. ?. Mariner. In Isleboro ME 1850, Brewer ME 1857.

Joseph W., b. ca. 1857 Brewer ME, m. 18 Oct 1888 Boston MA Annie E. Wood of Braintree MA, b. 6 Nov 1859 d. 27 Feb 1922, dau. William and Hannah (French) Wood. Rope maker. In Boston MA.

William P., b. ca. 1859 Brewer ME, m. 15 Jan 1890 Boston MA Zoa E. Veazie of Isleboro ME, b. ca. 1859, dau. William F. and Deborah Veazie. In Boston MA.

Lulu S., b. ca. 1863, m. 7 Apr 1886 Cambridge MA Ernest Benson.

Sources: Isleboro ME census 1850. VR SA/MA. L30.

558. **ELBRIDGE BLANCHARD$^7$ SAWYER** [see 296], b. 15 Aug 1834 Deer Isle ME, d. 27 Aug 1873 Camden ME, m. Hope T. Clark, b. ?. In Isleboro ME.

Charles R., b. ca. 1867 Isleboro ME, m. 1 Oct 1899 Norridgewock ME Tina Maude Miller of Norridgewock ME, b. ca. 1881, dau. Charles R. and Harriet (Rogers) Miller.

Sources: VR Camden ME, SA/ME. L30.

559. **CHARLES KEMPTON$^7$ SAWYER** [see 297], b. 5 Apr 1827 Deer Isle ME, d. 23 Aug 1878 Searsport ME, m. 7 Aug 1852 Hannah Jane Colson of Searsport ME, b. 12 Mar 1833 d. 12 Sep 1908, dau. Josiah and Lydia (Staples) Colson. Sea captain. Town Clerk 1855. He bur. in Elmwood Cem., Searsport ME.

Georgiana Phoebe, b. 26 Apr 1855, d. 9 Nov 1927, m. 20 May 1878 William Richardson Gilkey.

Emily Tewksbury, b. 29 Nov 1862, d. 21 Mar 1926, m. 13 May 1882 Benjamin F. Colcord.

757 Charles Orlando$^8$, 1864-1930.

Sources: Searsport ME census 1870. VR SA/ME. P82j, P26, M5, Jane McCormick rec.

560. **STEPHEN$^7$ SAWYER** [see 297], b. 5 Dec 1828 Deer Isle ME, d. 16 Jul 1891 Presque Isle ME, m.(1) 16 Feb 1858 Elizabeth T. Kempton, b. May 1832 d. 30 Nov 1871, dau. Stephen and Mehitable (Rooks) Kempton; m.(2) 23 Sep 1873 Elizabeth J. Treat of Bradford ME, b. 10 Aug 1837 d. 17 Aug 1911, dau. Richard and Eliza (Matthews) Treat. Mariner. Listed in both Presque Isle and Searsport ME census 1880. He bur. in Presque Isle ME.

Willie, b. 13 Dec 1858, d. 29 May 1859.

758 Edwin Leslie$^8$, 1860-1928.

759 Hiram Blaisdell$^8$, 1867-1912.

Elizabeth, b. 12 Aug 1869, d. 30 Aug 1871.

Stephen, b. Sep 1871 Searsport ME, d. 2 Mar 1886.

Sources: Searsport ME census 1870. ME 1880 census index. VR SA/ME. M5, Jane McCormick rec.

561. **EBEN A.$^7$ SAWYER** [see 297], b. 7 Mar 1836 Deer Isle ME, d. 2 Jan 1905 Portland ME, m.(1) 30 Sep 1861 Nellie F. Hall, b. May 1841 d. 22 Jul 1889; m.(2) 16 Nov 1893 Portland ME Ada A. (McGorman) Sidensparker of New Brunswick, Canada, wid., b. May 1867 d. 1931, dau. Frank and Catherine (Phair) McGorman. Sailmaker. He bur. Sawyer Cem., Warren ME.

Elcey, b. 14 May 1898, d. 30 Jun 1977, unm.

Eben A., b. 3 Aug 1901, d. 26 Jul 1985, m.(1) Caroline Annis, b. ?; m.(2) 1955 Matilda Messi, b. ?. He bur. near Warren ME.

Sources: Portland ME census 1860, 1870. VR Portland ME, SA/ME. D51, M8, M5, Family Bible, Jane McCormick rec.

562. **WILLIAM BABBIDGE[7] SAWYER** [see 297], b. 23 Apr 1839 Deer Isle ME, d. 14 Sep 1910 Searsport ME, m. Abbie F. Palmer of Sedgwick ME, b. Jun 1847 d. 14 Mar 1926, dau. Charles and Jane (Colson) Palmer. Carpenter. Civil War. In Searsport ME 1880.

William H., b. 1866 Deer Isle ME, m. 19 Jan 1893 Boston MA Harriet M. Cary, b. 1863 Hampden MA, dau. William and Sarah E. Cary. Clerk.

Ralph Palmer, b. 1867 Deer Isle ME, d. 5 May 1891, unm. Went to Savannah GA.

Harvey Stone, b. Aug 1868 Deer Isle ME, d. 4 Jan 1930 Searsport ME.

Jennie E., b. 1872, m. Fred Shute.

Arthur M., b. Apr 1874, d. 1949, unm.

Eben E., b. 3 Mar 1876, d. 22 Nov 1922 Bangor ME, unm.

Frederick K., b. 2 Jun 1879 Searsport ME, d. 3 Oct 1960, m. 12 Jul 1911 Harwichport MA Sarah Lucile Grinnell, b. ?, dau. William and Ann Ross (Gilkey) Grinnell. In Searsport ME 1914. Dentist. CH: Mildred Lucile, b. 30 Mar 1914, m. 13 Dec 1945 John J. Connors; Ruth Ann, b. 18 Nov 1919, m. 14 Sep 1946 James E. Grambart.

Sources: ME 1880 census index. VR Waldo County ME, SA/ME, SA/MA. M7A, Family Bible, Jane McCormick rec.

563. **OTIS VINAL[7] SAWYER** [see 298], b. 31 Dec 1822 Charlestown MA, m. Charlotte E. Lincoln of Cohasset MA, b. 30 Jul 1839. In Needham MA 1844.

Manfred, b. 29 Jun 1842 Charlestown MA.

Charlotte M., b. ?, m. Luther Allen Kingsbury.

Harriet Elizabeth, b. ?, m. Ezra C. Dudley.

Sources: VR SA/MA. C44, L25.

564. **WILLIAM[7] SAWYER** [see 299], b. 15 Dec 1807 Charlestown MA, d. 24 May 1852 Waltham MA, m. 14 Dec 1834 Susan M. Gibbs of Charlestown MA, b. 15 Apr 1817 d. 13 Feb 1895. Harvard College 1828. Lawyer. In Cambridge MA, Waltham MA 1851. Killed with dau. Susan in railroad accident.

Susan E., b. 16 Dec 1836, d. 24 May 1852.

Hannah M., b. ca. 1839, m. Alonzo G. Conley.

May C., b. 15 Mar 1841.

Georgianna T., b. 15 Mar 1846, m. 12 Dec 1872 Charlestown MA Benjamin F. Stearns.

Julia Frances, b. 8 Jun 1849.

760 William[8], b. 1851-1922.

Sources: VR Charlestown MA, SA/MA. T14A.

565. **TIMOTHY THOMPSON[7] SAWYER** [see 299], b. 7 Jan 1817 Charlestown MA, m. 1 Sep 1834 Mary Stockman of Hampton NH, b. 25 Mar 1820. Member of the New England Historic Genealogical Society 1854. Mayor of Charlestown MA 1855-57. State senator 1858. President of Warren Institute for Savings, Charlestown MA, 1881-87. In Cambridge MA.

Maria Josephine, b. 1841, d. 1 Jun 1878, m. 10 Jun 1863 Thomas Richardson.

Mary C., b. 25 Oct 1842.

761 Timothy Thompson[8], b. 1848.

Annie M., b. 1851, m. 1 Dec 1881 Boston MA Calvin P. Sampson.

Edith K., b. 8 Mar 1858, m. 11 Jun 1885 Boston MA Horace H. Stevens.

Sources: VR Cambridge MA, SA/MA. N5, S19, H90, T14A.

566. **JAMES BRICKETT[7] SAWYER** [see 300], b. 28 Nov 1812 Haverhill MA, m. 31 May 1842 Haverhill MA Betsey Jane Davis of Chester NH, b. ?. Wheelwright. In Haverhill MA 1850.

762 Horace James[8], 1843-1920.
Eveline Davis, b. 3 Jun 1845, d. 12 Dec 1850 Haverhill MA.
Isadora Frances, b. 14 Feb 1848, d. 22 Nov 1848.
763 Frank[8], b. 1849.

Sources: Haverhill MA census 1850. VR Haverhill MA, SA/MA.

567. **WILLIAM F.[7] SAWYER** [see 300], b. 12 Sep 1821 Haverhill MA, m. 27 Nov 1845 Clarissa F. Hilton of Deerfield NH, b. 22 Nov 1801 d. 1 Sep 1874. Trader. In Portsmouth NH 1860, Boston MA 1867.

Leonard, b. Apr 1846, d. 27 Aug 1847 Bangor ME.
William Edward, b. 5 Mar 1850 Deerfield NH, m. 30 Nov 1869 Boston MA Martha McPhail, b. ca. 1850 Prince Edward Isle, Canada, dau. John A. and Mary A. McPhail. Reporter. In Portsmouth NH, Chicago IL.
Charles, b. ca. 1851, d. 1 Aug 1861 Portsmouth NH.
George W., b. 28 Oct 1861 Portsmouth NH.
Charlena Bryant, b. 11 Sep 1867.

Sources: Portsmouth NH census 1860. VR SA/MA.

568. **JOSEPH WARREN[7] SAWYER** [see 300], b. 24 Apr 1826 Haverhill MA, d. 21 Mar 1885 Richmond, Quebec, Canada, m. (I) 15 Jul 1847 Martha A. Paterson of Saco ME, b. 27 Apr 1827 d. 19 Mar 1898. Machinist. In Lowell MA 1848, Haverhill MA 1860.

Ida J., b. ca. 1849.
764 Charles E.[8], 1853-1923.

Sources: Haverhill MA census 1860. Wilfred M. Sawyer rec.

569. **SAMUEL B.[7] SAWYER** [see 302], b. 29 Jun 1818 Stockbridge VT, d. 7 Feb 1875 Stockbridge VT, m. 3 Jan 1843 Stockbridge VT Elizabeth Holland, b. May 1823 d. 3 Jan 1885, dau. Elihu and Lucy (Whitcomb) Holland.

Roberta S., b. 1843, m. 23 Feb 1864 Woodstock VT Preston Rand.
765 Romain A.[8], b. 1845.
766 Elihu L.[8],b. 1856.
Harris H., b. 11 Sep 1860, d. 2 Jul 1867.

Sources: Stockbridge VT census 1850. VR Stockbridge VT, Oakham MA, SA/VT, SA/MA. H38, B44.

570. **WILLARD JONATHAN[7] SAWYER** [see 305], b. 14 Apr 1824 Alstead NH, d. 30 Aug 1908 Concord NH, m. 31 Mar 1850 Boston MA Martha A. Burrell of Chester NH, b. 13 Nov 1829 d. 20 Sep 1907, dau. Elijah (or Micajah) Burrell. Carpenter. In Wakefield MA, Keene NH 1870.

Charles Willard, b. ca. 1852 (Wakefield MA?). In Keene NH 1870.
Hattie Perkins, b. ca. 1857, m. 2 Oct 1879 Keene NH Fred S. Hastings.
Mary Elizabeth, b. 5 Nov 1858, d. 29 May 1884.
Edward Franklin, b. Nov 1860, d. 11 Oct 1884.

Sources: Keene NH census 1870. VR SA/MA, SA/NH. N14, N9, N6.

571. **AMOS AUGUSTUS[7] SAWYER** [see 305], b. 19 Jul 1829 Alstead NH, d. 15 Apr 1912 Goffstown NH, m.(1) 26 May 1853 Lydia Buss of Vermont, b. 4 Sep 1831 d. 6 Oct 1891, dau. Nathan and Arvilla (Nay) Buss; m.(2) 27 Jul 1893 Peterborough NH Hattie B. Nichols of Perryville AL, b. ?. In Alstead NH 1860, Peterborough NH 1870.

Arvilla Harriet, b. ca. 1856., m. George Augustus Ayers.

Arthur Augustus, b. 16 Sep 1870 Peterborough NH, d. 1931 Hartford VT, m. 1897 Edith M. Roberts, b. 1864 d. 1933, dau. William and Mary (Huntoon) Roberts. Meat dealer. In White River Junction VT.

Sources: Alstead NH census 1860. Peterbororough NH census 1870, 1880. VR SA/VT.

572. **DAVID WEBSTER**[7] **SAWYER** [see 305], b. 20 Jun 1832 Alstead NH, d. 1 Sep 1911 Concord NH, m.(1) 11 May 1854 Marinda A. Kidder of Alstead NH, b. 10 Jan 1832 d. 1 Oct 1873, dau. Nelson and Sophia (George) Kidder; m.(2) 13 Jan 1876 Laura A. (Parkhurst) Tupper of Rindge NH, b. 10 May 1841 d. 2 Aug 1900, dau. Luke Parkhurst. Farmer. In Alstead NH 1860. He bur. in Alstead NH.

767 Albert Franklin[8], 1855-1925.

Abigail A., b. 1 Oct 1857, m. 20 Aug 1874 Frederick O. Pitcher. Note: [N6] says Nellie W., dau of David, m. 20 Aug 1874 Fred O. Pitcher.

Fred George, b. 8 Oct 1860 Alstead NH, d. in Chicago IL, m. 24 Jan 1885 Lilla G. Garland of Manchester NH, b. 1861.

Carrie E., b. 24 Jun 1862, m. 4 Feb 1886 Lucius Parker.

Willard Nelson, b. 10 Apr 1864 Alstead NH, d. Winchendon MA, m. 4 Jun 1887 Mary E. Sawtelle of Greenville NH, b. 1869, dau. Lyman K. Sawtelle. Mechanic. In East Jaffrey NH. CH: Nettie M., b. 10 Mar 1888.

768 John Wesley[8], 1866-1935.

769 Joseph Amos[8], 1869-1931.

Arthur Henry, b. 23 Jun 1871 Alstead NH.

Ralph Webster, b. 12 Jun 1877, d. 12 Jul 1877.

Lenora Maud, b. 23 Jun 1878, m. 7 Jan 1911 Frank E. Jewett.

Sources: Alstead NH census 1860, 1880. N9, N14, S31, N6, S74, P52, Kenneth E. Sawyer rec.

573. **BENJAMIN FRANKLIN**[7] **SAWYER** [see 305], b. 24 Oct 1836 Alstead NH, d. 19 Jul 1923 Keene NH, m.(1) 7 Jun 1860 Cynthia Buss of Peterborough NH, b. 6 Sep 1837 d. 5 Aug 1901, dau. Nathan B. and Arvilla Buss; m.(2) 3 Apr 1912 Manchester NH (div. 23 Mar 1915) Jennie B. (Anderson) Shattuck of Manchester NH, b. 1856, dau. David B. and Christian (Smith) Anderson, both of Scotland. Builder. In Boston MA, Keene NH 1880.

Frank Buss, b. 22 Nov 1874 Manchester NH, m. 5 Sep 1900 Keene NH Ona I. Edwards of Keene NH, b. 1875, dau. William Edwards. Bank teller.

Sources: NH 1880 census index. VR SA/NH.

574. **HORACE REUBEN**[7] **SAWYER** [see 306], b. 6 Jun 1836 Hampstead NH, d. 17 Jul 1891 Hampstead NH, m. 20 Aug 1862 Windham NH Almira W. Bailey of Salem NH, b. 11 Mar 1840. Shoemaker. Civil War: 11th NH Regiment, 13 Aug 1862-4 Jan 1865; wounded in mine explosion. Town Clerk for Hampstead NH 1866-1870.

Clarence Leon, b. 25 May 1866 Hampstead NH, m. Annie Graham of Prince Edward Isle, Canada, b. 24 April 1862 d. 25 Oct 1904 Boston MA, dau. John and Margaret (McLean) Graham.

Annie L., b. 7 Jul 1867, m. 7 Sep 1890 John E. Mills.

Edward G., b. 10 Mar 1871 Hampstead NH, d. Haverhill MA, m. Annie Hooper, b. ?. No CH.

Sources: Hampstead NH census 1880. VR Hampstead NH.

575. **CHARLES B.**[7] **SAWYER** [see 307], b. 13 Jul 1818 New Sharon ME, d. 6 Jun 1901 New Sharon ME, m.(1) 16 Jan 1845 Hallowell ME Abigail Chandler of Lowell MA, b. ? d. 11 Mar

1851; m.(2) 8 Feb 1852 Starks ME Clara S. Boynton of Mercer ME, b. 10 Sep 1830 d. 22 Apr 1918, dau. William and Betsey (Bumpers) Boynton. In New Sharon ME 1850, 1870, Starks ME 1860. He bur. Village Cem., New Sharon ME.

Alden Eugene, b. 7 Aug 1853 New Sharon ME, d. 17 Nov 1921 Waterville ME, m. (1) 14 Apr 1877 Augusta ME Jennie H. Phelps, b. ?; m.(2) 14 Mar 1882 Canton ME Mary Emma Young of East Livermore ME, b. 1859, dau. George G. and Martha Young. Veterinary, hotel keeper, salesman. In Mt. Vernon ME, Norton MA 1883.

Mary Emma, b. 8 Nov 1855, d. 1930, m. _____ Thing.

William Greenleaf, b. 1858 Starks ME, m. 22 Apr 1889 Norton MA Abby N. (Tinkham) Anthony of Norton MA, b. 1844, dau. Ebenezer and Adeline (Arnold) Tinkham. In New Sharon ME, Waltham MA.

Charles A., b. 1862 Starks ME. In New Sharon ME.

Herbert G., b. 1864 Starks ME. In New Sharon ME.

James P., b. 1867 Starks ME. In New Sharon ME.

Henry Augustus, b. May 1869 New Sharon ME, d. Farmington ME, m. 9 Oct 1900 Mabel E. Bangs, b. ?. CH: Evangelyn M., b. ?.

Sources: New Sharon ME census 1850, 1870, 1880. Starks ME census 1860, ME 1880 census index. VR Bangor ME, Augusta ME, SA/ME, SA/MA. C25, B73, M5, Jeanne Sawyer rec.

576. **THOMAS D.$^{7}$ SAWYER** [see 307], b. 1822 New Sharon ME, d. 2 Dec 1862 Fredericksburg VA, m. 11 Apr 1846 Hannah Dyer of Truro MA, b. 15 Aug 1826 d. 3 Dec 1873, dau. Thomas and Ruth (Collins) Dyer. Farmer. Civil War: Company G., 16th Maine Infantry.

Cornelius B., b. 19 Aug 1847 New Sharon ME.

Emily E., b. 17 Apr 1849, d. 1915, m. Luther Brown.

770 Seth C.$^{8}$, 1851-1916.

771 Benjamin F.$^{8}$, 1853-1909.

772 Edward$^{8}$, 1855-1928.

Fred, b. 13 Nov 1855 New Sharon ME.

Lewis H., b. 12 Mar 1857 New Sharon ME, d. Starks ME, m. Dora M. Dyer of Topsham ME, b. ?. CH: Blanch, b. 11 Apr 1890; Daughter, b. 6 Feb 1894.

773 Charles H.$^{8}$, 1860-1914.

Isabell, b. 12 Oct 1862, m. Oct 1878 Charles U. Davis.

Sources: New Sharon ME census 1850. VR New Sharon ME, Truro MA, SA/ME. Jeanne Sawyer rec.

577. **CALEB D.$^{7}$ SAWYER** [see 307], b. 22 May 1825 New Sharon ME, d. 6 Jan 1907 New Sharon ME, m. Emily A. Knowles of Wilton ME, b. 30 Jun 1831 d. 6 Jun 1913, dau. Ezekiel Knowles. Both bur. Village Cem., New Sharon ME.

774 Albert$^{8}$, 1854-1915.

Elisha, b. 14 Mar 1856 New Sharon ME.

Eliza, b. 15 Mar 1857, d. 30 Nov 1874.

Katie, b. 18 Jul 1861, d. 21 Apr 1881, m. 6 Nov 1880 Boston MA D_____C. Briggs.

Sources: New Sharon ME census 1860, 1870. VR SA/ME. M5, Jeanne Sawyer rec.

578. **JOTHAM S.$^{7}$ SAWYER** [see 309], b. 1834 New Sharon ME, d. 1873 Castle Hill ME, m.(1) Henrietta Dudley, b. ?; m.(2) Adeline F. _____, b. 1842 d. 1864 Castle Hill ME; m.(3) Ann Thomson of Gardiner ME, b. 1850. In Castle Hill ME 1870, Mapleton ME.

Henrietta C., b. 1861-1881 Castle Hill ME.

Eugene, b. 1863, d. 1866 Castle Hill Me.

775 Truman$^{8}$, b. 1869.

776 Howard[8], b. 1870.
777 Winfield[8], 1872-1916.
Sources: Castle Hill ME census 1870. VR New Sharon ME, SA/ME. Charles A. Sawyer rec.

579. **JEFFERSON[7] SAWYER** [see 309], b. Feb 1837 New Sharon ME, m.(1) Olive C. Dudley of China ME, b. 1844 d. 1870 Castle Hill ME; m.(2) 22 Feb 1871 New Sharon ME Annie A. Storer, b.?; m.(3) Jennie H. Bryant of Easton ME, b. 17 Jul 1851 d. 24 Jan 1944. Storekeeper. In New Sharon ME 1850, Castle Hill ME 1870.
778 Milton J.[8], 1863-1908.
Charles Wesley, b. 15 Nov 1865 New Sharon ME, d. Sep 1955, m. Nellie E. Dalkin, b. ?, dau. Levi and Maria (Penely) Dalkin. In Chesterville ME, Methuen MA, Salem MA.
Emma Louisa, b. 6 Jul 1868, m. George W. Dimock.
779 John Bryant[8], 1884-1984.
Mabelle, b. Jan 1888, d. 1962, m. Ralph Doe.
Lynn, b. ?, d. @ 2 yrs.
Louise Frances, b. 15 Jan 1891, d. 1988, unm. Teacher.
Sources: New Sharon ME census 1850. Castle Hill ME census 1870. VR New Sharon ME, SA/ME. Charles A. Sawyer rec., Charles J. Sawyer rec., John B. Sawyer rec.

580. **RUSSELL F.[7] SAWYER** [see 310], b. Aug 1834 New Sharon ME, d. 22 Feb 1914 Norridgewock ME, m. 1 Jan 1857 Skowhegan ME Louisa Jane Pishon of Fairfield ME, b. ?. In Norridgewock ME 1880.
John H. b. ca. 1857. In Norridgewock ME 1880.
Sources: ME 1880 census index. VR Skowhegan ME, Norridgewock ME, SA/ME.

581. **HENRY K.[7] SAWYER** [see 310], b. 19 Sep 1837 Norridgewock ME, d. 29 Mar 1922 Norridgewock ME, m. 1 Jan 1866 Skowhegan ME Elizabeth H. Warren of Skowhegan ME, b. 1 Jan 1841 d. 5 Jan 1922, dau. William and Mary (Badger) Warren. Hotelkeeper.
780 Charles H.[8], b. 1868.
William, b. ?
Sources: ME census 1880 index. VR Showhegan ME, SA/ME. M7A.

582. **CHESTER[7] SAWYER** [see 315], b. 1795 Middlebury VT, m. 24 May 1825 Waitsfield VT Lucinda Steward, b. 22 Feb 1809, dau. Moses and Lois Steward. Farmer. In Middlebury VT 1830, Westfield VT 1840, Waitsfield VT 1850.
Rodney (or Rodman), b. ca. 1830 Middlebury VT. Farmer.
Moses, b. ca. 1832.
Juliann, b. 1834.
Mary A., b. 1836.
Lucinda, b. 1838.
Edward (or Edmond), b. ca. 1840 Westfield VT.
Sources: Middlebury VT census 1830. Westfield VT census 1840. Waitsfield VT census 1850. VR SA/VT. J22.

583. **GEORGE[7] SAWYER** [see 315], b. 1800 Middlebury VT, d. 26 Oct 1863 Middlebury VT, m. 15 Feb 1825 Middlebury VT Betsey Hodgkins, b. 1803. Carpenter.
Lucia Jane, b. 25 Jul 1825, d. 10 Apr 1845.
George M., b. 1829 Middlebury VT. Carpenter.
Anne M., b. ?, m. 25 Oct 1858 George Spencer.
Sources: Middlebury VT census 1830, 1840, 1850. VR SA/VT.

584. **WILLIAM[7] SAWYER** [see 315], b. Feb 1815 Middlebury VT, d. Sep 1898 Palo Alto County, Iowa, m. 31 May 1846 Middlebury VT Emma Willard Champlin, b. 3 Dec 1820, dau. Paul and Esther (Evarts) Champlin. Carpenter. In Middlebury VT 1850.

Mary, b. 1848.
Laura DeEtta, b. 10 Oct 1850, m. Orville O. Williams.
Ella, b. ?.
Frank, b. ?.

Sources: Middlebury VT census 1850. VR SA/VT. Nancy C. Leach rec.

585. **DAVID[7] SAWYER** [see 316], b. 25 Sep 1807 Tinmouth VT, d. 31 Dec 1859 Moire NY, m. 1831 Danby VT Lucretia Stafford, b. 1813 d. 3 Dec 1893. In Danby VT 1837, New York 1843. He bur. in Danby VT.

781 Anson David[8], 1832-1879.
Child, b. ?, d. 11 Dec 1833.
782 Henry Arthur[8], 1834-1899.
Persis L., b. 3 Dec 1835, d. Oct 1911.
Melinda, b. 1 Aug 1837, d. 9 Aug 1846.
783 Palmer Stafford[8], 1839-1904.
Noah Barker, b. 20 Sep 1848 in New York.

Sources: C99.

586. **JAMES JOHNSON[7] SAWYER** [see 317], b. 3 Nov 1803 Norwich VT, d. 16 Mar 1861 Thetford VT, m. Anna Isley, b. 21 Feb 1804 d. 8 May 1869, dau. W. and Rachel Isley. In Thetford VT 1830. He bur. in Pleasant Ridge Cem., Thetford VT.

Olive, b. 1829, d. 19 Sep 1846.
Ralph, b. 1834 Thetford VT.
784 Aaron B.[8], b. 1835.
James, b. 19 Jul 1837 Thetford VT.
Abigail, b. 14 Jul 1841, m. 1 May 1879 A____ O. Austin.
785 Richard[8], 1844-1887.

Sources: Thetford VT census 1830. VR SA/VT. D11.

587. **GEORGE MILTON[7] SAWYER** [see 317], b. 15 Apr 1813 Norwich VT, d. 12 Feb 1894 Norwich VT, m.(1) 8 Apr 1835 Norwich VT Mary A. Corser of Thetford VT, b. 21 Jun 1815 d. 9 Sep 1865, dau. Jonathan and Rhoda Corser; m.(2) 23 Feb 1865 Randolph VT Sarah J. (Campbell) Dutton, b. ?, dau. Robert and Huldah Campbell. Farmer. In Sutton NH.

Melissa L., b. 3 Feb 1836, d. 30 Jun 1890, m.(1) 8 Mar 1853 James Flichnor, m.(2) 1 Apr 1860 Franklin Blodgett.
Helen C., b. 6 Apr 1838 New Hampshire, m. 1863 Ambrose B. Currier.
Candais M., b. 17 Mar 1840, d. 13 Feb 1866, m. 19 Jun 1863 Richard Pixley.
Washington Sprague, b. Feb 1842, d. 6 Aug 1843.
Lucia A. J., b. 12 Mar 1844, m. 12 Oct 1865 Homer E. Slack.
Martha L., b. 26 Jun 1846, m. 24 Nov 1864 Ransom A. Slack.
Albert Sprague, b. 3 Jun 1848, d. 19 Jan 1863.
Marcia, b. ?, d.y.
Clarissa M., b. 2 Sep 1851, m. 18 Feb 1872 John Real.
George Washington, b. 11 Jan 1854 Norwich VT.
Robert Milton, b. 1866, d. 3 Oct 1870.

Sources: Norwich VT census 1850. VR SA/VT. T12, C79, P54, N6.

588. **RALPH$^7$ SAWYER** [see 317], b. 6 Dec 1820 Norwich VT, m.(1) 8 Feb 1842 Lebanon NH Maria G. Swett of Errol NH, b. 22 Nov 1822 d. 13 Nov 1874, dau. Jesse and Sally (Downing) Swett; m.(2) 21 Mar 1882 Concord NH Frances B. Carlton of Sanbornton NH, b. 1837, dau. J. M. and M. (Gilman) Carlton. Peddler. In Plymouth NH 1850, Colebrook NH 1860, Peterborough NH 1870.

Child, b. ?, d. 7 Aug 1843.

Orvilla Matilda, b. 8 May 1843, d. Nov 1863, m. 16 Nov 1858 Colebrook NH Samuel Sargent.

Almiron La Forest, b. 18 Aug 1847, d. 1866.

786 Orin A.$^8$, b. 1850.

Almira S. F., b. 1850.

Ina, b. 5 Jun 1854, m. 25 Dec 1872 Charles H. Noone of Boston MA.

Sources: Plymouth NH census 1850. Colebrook NH census 1860. Peterborough NH census 1870, 1880. C79, M50, S72. N6.

589. **ANDREW$^7$ SAWYER** [see 318], b. 18 Aug 1830 Windham CT, m. 11 Jan 1854 Belchertown MA Mary C. Filer of Belchertown MA, b. ca. 1834, dau. H. T. Filer. Clerk. In Norwich CT 1850, Bridgeport CT 1890. Member Congregational Church, Bridgeport CT, 1890-1894.

787 Walter W.$^8$, b.?.

Sources: Norwich CT census 1850. Bridgeport CT census 1890. VR Windham CT, SA/CT. A20, D13.

590. **THOMAS SYLVESTER$^7$ SAWYER** [see 321], b. 9 Nov 1844 Woodstock CT, m. 18 Jun 1867 Woodstock CT Adelaide Barnes, b. ?.

Lucius Clyde, b. 9 Nov 1868 Woodstock CT.

Patience Aileen, b. 19 Feb 1871, m. 25 Aug 1903 Erastus Topping.

Roy, b. 12 Nov 1874 Woodstock CT, m. 11 Dec 1903 Margaret McDonald.

Clifford, b. 7 Apr 1882 Woodstock CT, m. 10 Aug 1904 Zelma Zoe Walker, b. ?.

Sources: VR Woodstock CT.

591. **LUTHER HENRY$^7$ SAWYER** [see 322], b. 1850 Charleston VT, d. 30 Jun 1905 Brighton VT, m. 3 Jul 1875 Charleston VT Rose (Batchelder) Skinner of Brighton VT, b. 16 Oct 1851. Farmer. In Morgan VT, Brighton VT.

788 Edwin Chester$^8$, b. 1884.

Leonard E., b. 15 Feb 1886, d. 19 Sep 1886.

Flossie Veda, b. 5 Sep 1888, m. 5 Sep 1907 Lyndon VT Henry P. Cole.

Sources: VR SA/VT. P41.

592. **HENRY PORTER$^7$ SAWYER** [see 323], b. 22 Sep 1844 Cambridge MA, d. 5 Apr 1924 Marlow NH, m.(1) 10 Nov 1875 Lowell MA Sarah Jane (McIntire) Hodgdon of Massachusetts, b. 1847 d. 31 Oct 1881 Lebanon NH, dau. John O. and Eliza McIntire; m. (2) 31 Mar 1884 Arvilla (Morrison) Bruce of Fairlee VT, b. 1855 d. 31 Aug 1889, dau. Cyrus Morrisson. Blacksmith. In Lebanon NH, Claremont NH.

789 Albert Henry$^8$, b. 1885.

Fred C., b. 12 Sep 1886 Strafford VT, d. 7 Oct 1918 Alstead NH, unm.

Arvilla, b. 9 Jan 1889, d. 6 Nov 1889.

Sources: VR SA/MA, SA/NH.

593. **AMOS C.[7] SAWYER** [see 324], b. Feb 1851 Charleston VT, m. 4 Mar 1874 Emma E. Greenleaf of Derby VT, b. 4 Mar 1850, dau. Charles and Maria (Traversy) Greenleaf. Farmer. In Morgan VT.

Charles Merle, b. 21 Jul 1875 Morgan VT.
Norman Ernest, b. 11 Mar 1877 Charleston VT.

Sources: VR SA/VT. G42.

594. **ELWYN[7] SAWYER** [see 324], b. 1863 Charleston VT, m. 18 Apr 1895 Derby VT Ellen Lunderville of Derby VT, b. ?. Laborer. In Derby VT.

Wallace Jasper, b. 3 May 1898.
Son, b. 28 May 1901.
Chester Nelson, b. 28 Oct 1903.

Sources: SA/VT.

595. **ARTHUR D.[7] SAWYER** [see 325], b. 1858 Charleston VT, m. 8 Jun 1893 Lucy (Cole) Nourse of Derby VT, b. ?. Farmer. In Derby VT.

Chester A., b. 22 Dec 1894.

Sources: VR SA/VT.

596. **CHARLES GRAHAM[7] SAWYER** [see 326], b. 14 Feb 1867 Columbia NH, m. 1 May 1889 Derby VT Clara Baseford of Canada, b. ?. Railroad fireman. In Newport VT, Derby VT, Barton VT 1905.

Fred, b. 22 Aug 1890.
Guy Raymond, b. 21 Jan 1894.
Earl, b. Jun 1900, d. 24 Mar 1905.

Sources: VR SA/VT.

597. **CORNELIUS SIMON[7] SAWYER** [see 327], b. 16 Jun 1859 Sherburne VT, m. 16 Jun 1880 Rutland VT Hattie Mogt of Rutland VT, b. ?. Farmer. In East Rutland VT.

Orrin J., b. 16 Dec 1881.
Daughter, b. 19 Oct 1884.

Sources: VR SA/VT.

598. **JAMES ORRIN[7] SAWYER** [see 328], b. 30 Jan 1851 Reading VT, d. 1936 Chester VT m. 1 May 1878 Chester VT Flora E. Weston of Cavendish VT, b. 26 May 1857 d. 1935. In Andover VT 1882.

Daughter, b. ?, d. 19 Sep 1880.
790 Charles Eugene[8], 1882-1960.
Ruth Marion, b. 1 Sep 1885, d. 1968, unm.
Nellie Grace, b. 21 May 1887, d. 12 Jun 1887.

Sources: VR SA/VT. Katherine Keene rec., Lucy Sawyer rec.

599. **HENRY[7] SAWYER** [see 331], b. 29 Feb 1784 Swanzey NH, d. 28 Sep 1877 Swanzey NH, m.(1) 28 Apr 1808 Rebecca Bailey, b. 4 Apr 1784 d. 17 Jul 1816; m.(2) 20 Jul 1817 Cynthia Bailey (Rebecca's sister), b. 19 Aug 1796 d. 24 Jan 1840. Farmer.

Albert, b. 28 Feb 1809, d. 28 Mar 1809.
Almira, b. 10 Jun 1810, d. 23 May 1879, unm.
Clarissa, b. 2 May 1812, d. 13 Dec 1898, m. 31 Jan 1830 Virgil Woodcock.
791 Amos Bailey[8], 1814-1864.
Rebecca, b. 9 Feb 1819, d. 28 Aug 1846, m. 17 Apr 1838 Hiram Peabody.

Abijah, b. 20 Apr 1821 Swanzey NH.
Joshua Bradley, b. 9 Mar 1823 Swanzey NH, d. 25 Nov 1873 Winchendon MA, m. 19 Oct 1847 Winchendon MA Elvira Sibley of Winchendon MA, b. 7 Jun 1822 d. 4 Jan 1896, dau. Joel Sibley. Lumber manufacturer. In Gardner MA, Winchendon MA 1850. CH: Daughter, stillborn 21 May 1861.
Cynthia B., b. 2 Jun 1826, d. 15 Jul 1827.
Cynthia J., b. 26 Jun 1828, d. 21 Feb 1875, m. Isaac Boynton.
792 Henry$^8$, 1832-1867.
Sources: Swanzey NH census 1820, 1830. Winchendon MA census 1850. VR Winchendon MA, SA/MA. R7, C32, P22.

600. **JOSHUA$^7$ SAWYER** [see 331], b. 21 Jul 1801 Swanzey NH, d. 15 May 1839 Swanzey NH, m. 31 Mar 1830 Lucinda Olcott, b. 25 Jun 1806 d. 27 Jul 1840. Wid. in Swanzey NH 1840.
Lydia H., b. 1 Jul 1831, m. 4 May 1852 James Ward of Bradford CT.
Joshua, b. 7 Jul 1833, d. 22 Dec 1835.
Emily E., b. 27 Jun 1836, d. 14 Aug 1851.
Joshua Abijah, b. 3 Jul 1839 Swanzey NH, d. 28 Jan 1932, m. 1 Jan 1868 Laura Engle, b. ?. Went to Oklahoma.
Sources: Swanzey NH census 1830, 1840. R7, S31, N6.

601. **CALEB$^7$ SAWYER** [see 331], b. 9 Sep 1806 Swanzey NH, d. 14 Mar 1881, m. 4 May 1829 Hannah Olcott, b. 1 Nov 1808 d. 14 Mar 1881. Farmer. In Swanzey NH 1850. Went west. Note: CH of Joshua were living with Caleb in 1850 census. [See 600].
Caleb Abijah, b. 7 Apr 1842 Swanzey NH, m. 1 Jan 1867 Elgin MN Aurora E. Rollins of Corinth VT, b. 23 Sep 1845, dau. Laban and Nancy (Colby) Rollins.
Martin Luther, b. 22 Feb 1846 Swanzey NH.
Sources: Swanzey NH census 1830, 1840, 1850. R7, S31.

602. **SAMUEL$^7$ SAWYER** [see 332], b. 1791 (Swanzey NH?), d. 1863, m. 1814 Abigail Smith, b. ?. In Palmyra NY.
Samuel William, b. 1821, d. 1914, m. 1845 Hannah Nelson, b. ?.
Mary Jane, b. 1827.
Sources: R7, H39. Mary J. Turner rec.

603. **JAMES H.$^7$ SAWYER** [see 334], b. 22 Jul 1807 Vermont, d. 30 Apr 1850, m. 17 Jun 1831 Hannah Mann of Surry ME, b. 29 May 1809 d. 27 Mar 1888, dau. Nathan and Mary (Young) Mann. In Sedgwick ME 1832, 1840, Bluehill ME 1833, Surry ME 1834. He bur. in Village Cem., Verona ME. Wid. in Wetmore Isle ME 1850. Wid. m. 9 Oct 1861 Joseph Lawrence. She bur. Leache's Point ME.
793 Lyman A.$^8$, 1832-1907.
794 James Carlton$^8$, 1833-1907.
Hannah Maria, b. 4 Sep 1834, d. 20 Feb 1923, m. 16 Oct 1860 Willis Bowden.
Edwin, b. ca. 1836 Sedgwick ME. In Wetmore Isle ME 1850.
Eliza, b. 15 May 1838, m. 4 Mar 1856 Seldon Bowden.
Ahira, b. 28 Mar 1842, d. 10 Apr 1861.
795 John Wesley$^8$, 1844-1904.
796 Joseph W.$^8$, 1847-1901.
Chloe B., b. 9 Jul 1849, m. 23 Jul 1864 George Lawrence.
Sources: Sedgewick ME census 1840. Wetmore Isle ME census 1850. VR Sedgwick ME, Orland ME. Frederick W. Sawyer III rec., James L. Sawyer rec., Elizabeth Wescott rec.

604. **LYMAN[7] SAWYER** [see 334], b. ca. 1820 Canada, d. 17 May 1860 Milton VT, m. Mary A. Miner, b. Feb 1827 d. 9 Oct 1860, dau. Lyndon Miner. In Georgia VT 1850.

Mary, b. 1845.

Charles A., b. 1846 Georgia VT, m. 27 Dec 1865 Georgia VT Agnes A. Shonian, b. ?. In Georgia VT 1850, Milton VT.

Richard, b. ca. 1849 Canada. In Georgia VT 1850.

797 George W.[8], 1852-1904.

Sources: Georgia VT census 1850. VR SA/VT.

605. **ELISHA MATURIN[7] SAWYER** [see 335], b. 4 Jul 1814 Lyme CT, m. 27 Mar 1842 Ursula Brainard of Haddom CT, b. 3 Jul 1814, dau. Caleb and Abigail (Griswald) Brainard. Farmer.

Sarah T., b. 4 Jan 1843, d. 8 Nov 1843.

Ann M., b. 17 Sep 1845, m. 7 Oct 1868 William Parkinson of Norwich CT.

Mary E., b. 13 Nov 1848, m. 20 Nov 1867 Martin Stanbly of Norwich CT.

Ellen A., b. Apr 1851, m. 19 Jun 1873 Walter Atkinson of Norwich CT.

798 Leander Price[8], b. 1854.

Sarah L., b. 18 Oct 1854, m. 5 Dec 1879 Frederick Turner of New York.

Sources: B77.

606. **JAMES MADISON[7] SAWYER** [see 339], b. 10 Nov 1822 Henniker NH, d. 3 Apr 1885 Grafton NH, m. 6 May 1845 Jane T. Clark of Newbury NH, b. 24 May 1820 d. 31 Mar 1885, dau. Abraham C. and Susan (Farmer) Clark. In Newbury NH, Nashua NH.

799 Madison Paul[8], b. 1846.

Sources: Newbury NH census 1850, 1860. Nashua NH census 1880. H16.

607. **HENRY EDWARD[7] SAWYER** [see 341], b. 19 Feb 1827 Fitchburg MA, m. 15 Dec 1852 Royalston MA Mary E. Wilson of Acton MA, b. ca. 1829, dau. Benjamin and Marilla Wilson. Millwright. In Fitchburg MA 1850.

Son, b. 23 Jan 1854, d. same day.

Francis Asa, b. 29 Mar 1855 Fitchburg MA.

Sources: Fitchburg MA census 1850. VR SA/MA. D20.

608. **CHARLES K.[7] SAWYER** [see 341], b. 14 Jul 1835 Fitchburg MA, m. 11 Mar 1858 Fitchburg MA Caroline L. Russell of Fitchburg MA, b. Nov 1833, dau. Charles and Sarah Russell. Farmer.

Sarah Lydia, b. 27 Dec 1858, m. 13 Sep 1888 Fitchburg MA John W. Jigger.

James Russell, b. 15 May 1862 Fitchburg MA, m. 21 Oct 1886 Fitchburg MA Mary L. Wilmouth of Fitchburg MA, b. 1862, dau. John and Mary Wilmouth. Farmer, fireman.

Mary Abby, b. 4 Dec 1869.

Carrie A., b. 1870, m. 4 Feb 1891 Fitchburg MA Walter B. Wightman.

Sources: Fitchburg MA census 1860, 1870, 1880. VR SA/MA. D20.

609. **CHARLES EDWARD[7] SAWYER** [see 343], b. 7 Aug 1836 Ashburnham MA, d. 28 May 1903 Springfield OH, m. 26 Nov 1856 Ashburnham MA Maria Jane Petts of New York, b. 5 Jan 1837 d. 26 Aug 1917, dau. John Petts. Carpenter. In Ashburnham MA 1850, Surry NH.

Frank E., b. 8 Nov 1860, m. 9 Aug 1888 Bertha F. Pierce, b. ?.

Herbert L., b. 7 Jan 1863, m. 9 Jul 1891 Fanny Rowe, b. ?.

Annie M., b. 6 Dec 1868.

John, b. 19 Mar 1871, d. 20 Jul 1871.
Sources: Ashburnham MA census 1850. VR SA/MA. K15, D20.

610. **HENRY LINCOLN[7] SAWYER** [scc 343], b. May 1840 Ashburnham MA, d. 23 Jul 1906 Framingham MA, m.(1) 6 Apr 1864 Acton MA Lucy A. Fuller of Strafford VT, b. 1838, dau. Alden and Sarah (Faulkner) Fuller; m.(2)9 Dec 1886 Natick MA Emma L. Drury of Natick MA, b. Sep 1859, dau. William D. and Elsie P. (Tyler) Drury. Hardware dealer. In Framingham MA 1880.
Etta May, b. 15 Feb 1865, unm.
Harry, b. 1869 Framingham MA, d.y.
Lulu, b. 9 Jul 1872, m. Richard Valentine.
Helen Lucile, b. 8 Sep 1893.
Ralph Henry b. 30 Jan 1895 Framingham MA, m. Elizabeth Nichols.
Marion D., b. Oct 1898, d. 10 Apr 1986, m. 12 Dec 1927 William J. Marshall.
Sources: Framingham MA census 1870, 1880. VR Ashburnham MA, Framingham MA, SA/MA. Jean Hulme rec.

611. **ALBERT JOSIAH[7] SAWYER** [see 345], b. 5 Oct 1840 Cambridge MA, m. 2 Mar 1862 Emma B. Carrier of Hartford CT, b. 8 Feb 1845, dau. Salmon and Betsey (Bullock) Carrier. Dentist.
Frederick Albert, b. 14 Jan 1869 Cambridge MA, m. 1 Jun 1898 Boston MA Grace Edna Dean of Boston MA, b. 7 Nov 1875, dau. Frederick B. and Anna B. (Loud) Dean. In Arlington MA.
Edith Lillian, b. 22 Feb 1875, m. 15 Jun 1899 Harrison G. Bourne.
Arthur Harold, b. 26 Apr 1879 Cambridge MA.
Sources: VR SA/MA. G35.

612. **ALFRED AUGUSTUS[7] SAWYER** [see 346], b. 12 Sep 1849 Harvard MA, m. 20 Nov 1873 Harvard MA Emma L. Houghton of Harvard MA, b. ca. 1850, dau. Charles W. and Sally (Willard) Houghton.
Guy Frank, b. 29 Oct 1874 Harvard MA.
Sources: VR SA/MA.

613. **CHARLES ALFRED[7] SAWYER** [see 347], b. 1837 Dover NH, m. 15 Jan 1862 Concord MA Josephine Josslyn of Quincy MA, b. 1835, dau. Nathan and Eliza Josslyn. Farmer.
Alfred Henry, b. 13 Jun 1867 Concord MA.
Sources: VR SA/MA.

614. **CHARLES HENRY[7] SAWYER** [see 350], b. 30 Mar 1840 Watertown NY, d. 18 Jan 1908 Dover NH, m. 8 Feb 1865 Susan E. Cowan of Dover NH, b. 13 Aug 1839 d. 20 Apr 1899, dau. Dr. James W. and Elizabeth (Hodgdon) Cowan. President of Dover Mills. Entered politics in 1881, appointed Colonel on the Governor's military staff. Governor of New Hampshire, 1887-1889.
800 William Davis[8], b. 1866.
801 Charles Francis[8], b. 1869-1939.
802 James Cowan[8], b. 1872.
Edward, b. 24 Jul 1874 Dover NH, m. 28 Apr 1906 Leslie Tobey of Boston MA, b. ?, dau. Phineas Sprague Tobey. Yale graduate 1898. Lawyer. President and Treasurer of Atlantic Insulated Wire Cable Co. In Stamford CT.
Elizabeth Coffin, b. 8 Mar 1880.
Sources: Dover NH census 1850, 1860, 1870, 1880. VR SA/NH. W38, H95, P82i.

615. **FREDERICK JONATHAN[7] SAWYER** [see 350], b. Jul 1860 Dover NH, d. 28 Nov 1902 New Bedford MA, m. 19 Aug 1881 Isabella Doatson of New Bedford MA, b. 1860. Electrical engineer. In Boston MA. He bur. in Dover NH.

Frederick Rollins, b. 30 Sep 1882 Boston MA, m.(1) ?, wife died; m.(2) 8 Jan 1932 Greenville ME Dorothy N. Robinson of Edgecomb ME, b. 1900, dau. Dr. Arthur and Florence (Philbrick) Robinson of Brookline MA. In Malden MA.

Gordon Blake, b. ?.

Sources: VR SA/MA, SA/NH. P82i.

616. **JONATHAN[7] SAWYER** [see 351], b. 17 Jul 1820 Harvard MA, m. 28 Apr 1850 Lancaster MA Elizabeth Ball of Bolton MA, b. ca. 1828, dau. William and Elizabeth Ball. Painter. In Clinton MA.

George Farley, b. 22 Sep 1851 Clinton MA, d. 1 Jan 1852.

Emeline F., b. 1853, m. 22 Aug 1875 Marlborough MA Edward F. Goodwin.

Abby Frances, b. 11 Sep 1857, m. 8 May 1883 Hudson MA Albert A. Gilson.

Laurietta, b. 25 Jul 1859.

Frederick A., b. Jan 1861, d. 1 Sep 1861 Clinton MA.

Sources: VR SA/MA.

617. **EVANDER ERASTUS[7] SAWYER** [see 355], b. 1825 Harvard MA, m. 27 Dec 1846 Waltham MA Sarah E. Underwood of Cambridge MA, b. 1825, dau. Abraham and Emily Underwood. Carpenter. Civil War: 17 Oct 1862-2 Sep 1863. In Waltham MA, Princeton MA.

Charles, b. 1847, d. 22 Nov 1849.

Elizabeth F., b. 23 Nov 1850, m. 8 Dec 1869 William Edson of Fitchburg MA.

William Evander, b. 12 Mar 1852 Waltham MA.

Ona A., b. 30 Oct 1858.

Elmer Ellsworth, b. 9 Oct 1861 Waltham MA.

Ada, b. 1 Jun 1863.

Henry Sydney, b. 5 Jun 1866 East Princeton MA, m. 24 Jul 1889 Leominster MA May B. Richards of Shirley MA, b. ca. 1869, dau. John and Jennie Richards.

Mabel, b. 20 Oct 1868, m. 23 Nov 1890 Fitchburg MA Henry F. Penniman.

Sources: VR Waltham MA, SA/MA. B51, E8, P29.

618. **EDRICK[7] SAWYER** [see 355], b. 24 Nov 1838 Waltham MA, m. Mary Augusta Stuart of Sterling MA, b. 22 Apr 1841. Mechanic. In Princeton MA. Wid. m. Byron Allen.

Ervin Whitmore, b. 23 Aug 1865 Princeton MA, m. 5 Feb 1885 West Boylston MA Katie M. Melville of Charlestown MA, b. ca. 1857, dau Thomas R. and Abbie (Robertson) Melville. Potter. CH: Marguerite, b. 24 Jun 1886.

Nancy, b. 10 Jun 1870.

Gala Pamelia, b. 3 May 1872, m. 30 May 1889 Fitchburg MA Archer E. Temple.

Charles, b. ?.

Lena, b. ?.

Sources: VR SA/MA. W39.

619. **CYRIL A.[7] SAWYER** [see 356], b. 20 Nov 1825 Whitefield NH, m. Esther Smith of Canada, b. ?. Millwright. In Whitefield NH 1860.

Elbe, b. ca. 1856.

Sources: Whitefield NH census 1850, 1860. S33.

620. **OLIVER PUTNAM S.[7] SAWYER** [see 357], b. 29 May 1818 Whitefield NH, m. Rebecca G. Hicks, b. 1828 d. 6 May 1904, dau. Benjamin Hicks. In Whitefield NH 1860, Jefferson NH 1880. Wid. m. 7 Sep 1881 Whitefield NH Cyrus B. Gould.

803 Frank T.[8], b. 1849.

Sources: Whitefield NH census 1850, 1860. Jefferson NH census 1880. N6.

621. **GEORGE[7] SAWYER** [see 357], b. 25 May 1822 Whitefield NH, d. 24 Mar 1896 Whitefield NH, m. Hannah G. Hicks of Jefferson NH, b. ?. In Whitefield NH 1880.

804 George Madison[8], 1855-1897.

Katie M., b. 1868, m. 26 Nov 1885 Whitefield NH Frank Warner.

Sources: Whitefield NH census 1850, 1860, 1880. N6.

622. **EVARTS W.[7] SAWYER** [see 358], b. 18 May 1836 Bethlehem NH, d. 27 Jul 1903 Whitefield NH m. 4 Aug 1858 Martha Kimball of Bath NH, b. 12 Feb 1839 d. 16 May 1912, dau. George K. and Elizabeth (Gordon) Kimball.

George E., b. 1860 Dalton NH, m. 18 Oct 1884 Bertha E. Fiske of Sugar Hill NH, b. 4 May 1864 d. 31 May 1928, dau. Sullivan and Carry (Russell) Fiske.

Julia E., b. 1864, m.(I) 25 Dec 1883 Whitefield NH Cyrus J Colby.

Mary A., b. 1869, m. 10 May 1893 Whitefield NH Charles S. Kilgore.

Daughter, b. 1877, d. 23 Mar 1880.

Sources: Whitefield NH census 1850, 1870. Dalton NH census 1860. VR SA/NH. N6.

623 **SAMUEL COLE[7] SAWYER** [see 358], b. 21 Aug 1845 Bethlehem NH, d. 15 Dec 1915 Littleton NH, m. 6 May 1868 Eliza J. Burns of Whitefield NH, b. 5 Apr 1847. Dentist. In Lakeport (Laconia) NH, Gilford NH 1770, Littleton NH 1873, 1880, Lisbon NH.

Fred Burns, b. 7 Sep 1870 Lakeport NH, d. 12 Jan 1913 Franklin NH, m. 23 Dec 1895 Bradford VT Sarah Greenleaf of Middlebury VT, b. 1864 d. 7 Apr 1931 Los Angeles CA (bur. in Littleton NH). Dentist. In Lisbon NH, Littleton NH. CH: Dau., b. 27 May 1891; Samuel Greenleaf, b. 2 Jul 1898, d. 17 May 1899.

Gertrude Prince, b. 18 Sep 1884.

Sources: Gilford NH census 1870. Littleton NH census 1880. VR SA/NH. J2.

624. **WILLIAM HENRY[7] SAWYER** [see 359], b. 18 Aug 1867 Littleton NH, d. 1947 Concord NH, m.(1) 18 Nov 1891 Carrie B. Lane of Littleton NH, b. 6 Apr 1867 d. Mar 1941, dau. Benjamin Franklin and Julia (Farr) Lane; m.(2) 1945 Anne H. Stephens, b. ?. Lawyer, Chief Justice of Superior Court of New Hampshire. All CH b. in Concord NH.

805 Howard Pierce[8], b. 1892.

Helen Lane, b. 13 Mar 1895, d. 10 Nov 1992, m. 1922 Max A. Norton.

Marion Farr, b. 22 Jul 1896, m. Eugene E. Gannon.

806 Robert Cushman[8], 1899-1987.

Charles Murray, b. 1906 Concord NH, d. 1982 Hanover NH, m. 10 Jun 1933 Concord NH Germaine B. Scully of Concord NH, b. 1905, dau. James and Catherine (Jordan) Scully. CH: Charles M, b. ?; Sylvia, b. ?.

Sources: B68, J2, S84, Obit (Helen), Howard Pierce Sawyer rec.

624. **TIMOTHY[7] SAWYER** [see 360], b. 29 Aug 1805 Orford NH, d. 11 Mar 1869 Richford VT, m. Esther Hill, b. Jul 1808 d. 21 Dec 1863, dau. Moses and Charlotte Hill. Shoemaker. In Berkshire VT 1840, Enosburg VT 1860.

Harlow Timothy, b. ca. 1835, Berkshire VT. In Enosburg VT.

Charlotte, b. ca. 1837.

Eliza L., b. 1845, m. 11 Feb 1866 John Allard.
Emerline A., b. 1846.
Timothy C., b. 1852 Berkshire VT. In Enosburg VT.
Sources: Berkshire VT census 1840, 1850. Enosbury VT census 1860.

626. **HIRAM[7] SAWYER** [see 361], b. 21 Aug 1814 Orford NH, d. 24 Nov 1888, m. 14 Feb 1837 Barbara Ann Wilson, b. 6 Oct 1819 d. 1 Oct 1905. In Haverhill NH 1840.
Daughter, b. (1835-1840).
Alvah Littlefield, b. 16 Sep 1854, d. 5 Feb 1925 Michigan, m. 13 Apr 1880 Josephine S. Ingalls, b. 9 Mar 1857 d. 10 Dec 1932.
Sources: Haverhill NH census 1840. H58A, D6.

627. **GEORGE[7] SAWYER** [see 362], b. 1824 Orford NH, m. 28 May 1851 Boston MA Ann Edmundson of Boston MA, b. ca. 1827. Railroad engineer. In Boston MA 1852, North Bridgewater MA.
Walter Leonard, b. 11 Jul 1852 Boston MA, m. 27 Nov 1878 Hattie Cummings of London, England, b. 1852, dau. Alexander and Catherine Cummings. Railroad worker.
Mary Jane, b. ca. 1853, m. 3 Oct 1879 William Keith.
807 Charles R.[8], b. ca. 1855.
George, b. 18 Nov 1857 North Bridgewater MA.
Edwin Edmundson, b. 8 Jun 1861 North Bridgewater MA.
Edward Hill, b. 8 Jan 1861 North Bridgewater MA, d. 21 Jul 1861.
Arthur B., b. 29 Sep 1864, d. 9 Sep 1865.
808 Hermon French[8], b. 1866.
Sources: VR SA/MA. K12, E9.

628. **JOHN THOMPSON[7] SAWYER** [see 366], b. 9 Apr 1810 Orford NH, d. 16 Oct 1894, m. 19 Feb 1832 Nancy Folsom Norris of Hanover NH, b. 14 Jul 1814 d. 13 Nov 1876, dau. Josiah and Polly (Adams) Norris. Wheelwright. In Orford NH 1840, Lyme NH 1850.
Mary Norris, b. 18 Jul 1833, d. 11 Aug 1848.
809 Freeman John[8], 1836-1906.
810 Charles Henry[8], b. 1839.
George Addison, b. 14 May 1844, d. 10 Apr 1845. Bur. in Thetford VT.
Nancy Ellen, b. 27 Dec 1846, d.y.
Mary Almy, b. 17 Sep 1849, d. 14 Mar 1875. Bur. in Thetford VT.
Myra Bell, b. 26 Dec 1851.
Sources: Orford NH census 1840. Lyme NH census 1850, 1860, 1870. VR SA/VT. D11.

629. **ALBERT EDWARD[7] SAWYER** [see 366], b. 31 Jul 1822 Lyme NH, d. 9 Mar 1893 Lyme NH, m.(1) Aug 1859 Grace A. Carpenter of Strafford VT, b. 1834; m.(2) 19 May 1880 Esther (Carpenter) Winslow of Strafford VT, b. 29 Oct 1829 d. 26 Nov 1912, dau. Nathan and S. (Chamberlin) Carpenter. Farmer.
Willard E., b. 3 Jan 1863, d. 30 Apr 1884 (suicide).
Fanny Gertrude, b. 1867, m. 1 Feb 1891 Lyme NH R. Seabrey Alden.
Sources: Lyme NH census 1850, 1860, 1870.

630. **CHARLES CURTIS[7] SAWYER** [see 368], b. 25 May 1825 Norwich VT, d. 29 Dec 1907 Norwich VT, m. Elizabeth Garland, b. 1829. In Manchester NH 1850, Norwich VT 1860.
Charles A., b. 1850.
Sources: Manchester NH census 1850. Norwich VT Census 1860.

631. **JOHN W.[7] SAWYER** [see 368], b. 29 May 1836 Norwich VT, m. 29 Nov 1860 Hartland VT Sarah G. Short of Norwich VT, b. ?. Harness maker. In Hartland VT 1870.

Ida L., b. Sep 1861.

Ed, b. 24 Aug 1873 Hartland VT.

Sources: Hartland VT census 1870. VR SA/VT.

632. **CHARLES EDWARD[7] SAWYER** [see 369], b. 1 Jun 1830 Royalton VT, d. 31 May 1879 Randolph VT, m.(1) 11 Nov 1856 Royalton VT Mary J. Corbin of Royalton VT, b. 3 Dec 1833 d. 24 Apr 1867, dau. Franklin and Abilena (Clapp) Corbin; m.(2) 8 Sep 1869 Randolph VT Clara M. Washburn of Randolph VT, b. 10 Oct 1842, dau. Levi and Prudentia (Flint) Washburn. He bur. in Old Christ Church Cem., Bethel VT.

Emma Louise, b. 28 Sep 1858, m. 30 Aug 1887 Boston MA Frank W. Eldredge.

George Edward, b. 23 Sep 1859 Bethel VT. Went to New York City.

Henry Melville, b. 9 Dec 1861 Bethel VT, m. 19 Apr 1908 Winthrop MA Susan Alice Wadsworth, b. ?. CH: Mary M., b. ?, m. 13 Feb 1874 Rutland VT William E. Smith.

Hattie May, b. 26 Nov 1863.

Alice Cora, b. 28 Jun 1871, m. 15 Nov 1899 John S. Smith.

Sources: VR SA/VT, SA/MA. L42.

633. **EVERETT R.[7] SAWYER** [see 371], b. 1839, m. 21 Dec 1871 his niece Sarah E. Lord, b. 22 Nov 1843, dau. John Dewey and Samantha (Sawyer) Lord. Minister. In Chester VT, Sandy Hill NY, New London NH.

Willoughby Lord, b. ?, m. Edith Lorman, b. ?.

Sources: Chester VT census 1850. D34, L39.

634. **ISAAC[7] SAWYER** [see 373], b. 1837 Wakefield MA, m.(1) 4 Jul 1858 Estelle Erskine Porter of Lowell MA, b. 3 Apr 1838, dau. Charles C. and Caroline (Patch) Porter; m.(2) 12 Mar 1882 Mary E. Coburn of Leicester VT, b. 24 Aug 1841 d. 30 Apr 1906, dau. Orin and Harriet (Parkhurst) Coburn. Dentist. In Nantucket MA 1850, Manchester NH 1865, Brandon VT 1882.

Isaac Erskine, b. 18 Oct 1865, m. 18 Oct 1893 Holyoke MA Maria L. Kirtland of Westbrook CT, b. ca. 1869, dau. Edwin and Edwina (Magna) Kirtland. CH: Lucy Erskine, b. 15 Jul 1897.

Charles Porter, b. 17 Oct 1868 Manchester NH, m. Maria L. Ouillette, b. ?.

Sources: Nantucket MA census 1850. VR SA/MA, SA/VT. P65, G24.

635. **SAMUEL[7] SAWYER** [see 374], b. ca. 1814 Lyme CT, m. 4 Jun 1837 Frances A. Gulliver of Lyme CT, b. ca. 1823. Farmer.

Charles, b. ca. 1838, d. 4 Mar 1873. Civil War: Enl. 2 Jan 1864, discharged w/disability.

John M., b. ca. 1842 Lyme CT. Civil War: 21 Sep 1861-1 Dec 1862.

James, b. ca. 1844 Lyme CT.

William, b. ca. 1846 Lyme CT.

Samuel, b. ca. 1849 Lyme Ct.

Sources: Lyme CT census 1840, 1850.

636. **CHARLES BAILEY[7] SAWYER** [see 377], b. 7 Aug 1819 Warwick MA, d. 1896 Chicago IL, m.(1) 28 Nov 1844 Sterling MA Mary W. Kendall, b. ca. 1821, dau. Harvey and Silba Kendall; m.(2) 31 Jul 1851 Boston MA Elizabeth E. Turner of Lyme NH, b. ?. Merchant.

811 Charles Adrian[8], b. 1854.

Twins, b. ?, d. at birth.

Sources: VR Sterling MA.

637. **GEORGE M.[7] SAWYER** [see 377], b. ca. 1822 Warwick MA, m. 14 Feb 1859 Cambridge MA Adeline A. Mackey of Sharon MA, b. ca. 1831, dau. Samuel and Julia Mackey. Blacksmith, provision dealer.

George E., b. 4 Feb 1860 Warwick MA.

Elizabeth P., b. 13 Mar 1862, m. 1 Jun 1892 Boston MA Edward B. Coffin.

Sources: VR SA/MA.

638. **THOMAS PARKER[7] SAWYER** [see 378], b. ca. 1840 Cambridge MA, m. 24 Feb 1859 Cambridge MA Elizabeth Marie Jay of Lawrence MA, b. 1841, dau. Isaac and Sophia Jay. Soap boiler.

812 George E.[8], b. 1862.

Charles A., b. 23 Dec 1864 Cambridge MA, m. Mary A. _____ of Rhode Island, b. ?. Painter. CH: Jessie Alice, b. 14 May 1884.

Sources: VR Cambridge MA, SA/MA.

639. **JOHN[7] SAWYER** [see 379], b. 1815 Wilkes Barre PA, d. 1865, m. Amy Leipham of Bavaria, Germany, b. ?. In Dimock PA, Washington PA.

Frances E., b. ?, d. 1848 m. Clark B. Hall of Manchester NH.

Catherine, b. ?, m. Will C. Brenton.

Hattie E., b. ?, m. Albert P. Smith.

Stephen D., b. ?.

John W., b. ?.

Andrew J., b. 8 Jun 1859 Washington PA, d. 28 Feb 1930 Manchester NH, m. 3 Sep 1890 Elizabeth Small of Newmarket NH, b. 2 Jul 1861 d. 15 Mar 1921, dau. William B. and Ellen M. (French) Small. In Newmarket NH 1883-1888. CH: Marion, b. 10 Dec 1894.

Margery Isobel, b. ?, m. Dr. O. H. Johnson of Manchester NH.

Dora, b. ?, m. Walter Seymour of New Jersey.

Sources: C31, S84.

440. **IRAM ALLEN[7] SAWYER** [see 380], b. 16 Feb 1839 North Hero VT, d. 9 May 1909 Keokuk IA, m. 6 Oct 1864 Mary C. Irwin, b. 6 Sep 1842 d. 20 Jun 1903, dau. Stephen and Elizabeth (Nichols) Irwin.

Ellen Nichols, b. 16 Oct 1866, d. 7 Jun 1955, m. 5 Jun 1891 Thomas Board.

Hazen Irwin, b. 10 Oct 1868, m. ?.

Sources: J11.

641. **ARTEMUS[7] SAWYER** [see 381], b. 11 Feb 1809 Vergennes VT, d. 13 Jan 1889, m. 27 Sep 1832 Eaton, Quebec, Canada, Betsey Sunbury, b. 20 Aug 1809 d. 15 Sep 1892.

Cornelia Ann, b. 16 Jan 1833, d. 10 Nov 1923, m. 24 Dec 1850 Eaton, Quebec, William Clough.

Tyler Hurd Wellington, b. 20 Jan 1835 Eaton, Quebec, d. 16 Jul 1899 Stark NH, m. Charlotte R. Robbins of Lancaster NH, b. 6 Apr 1845 d. 26 May 1927, dau. Samuel and Hannah (Rowell) Robbins. Farmer. In Dummer NH, Groveton NH, Stark NH. CH: Nellie J., b. ?, m. 19 Sep 1884 Dummer NH Charles J. Pratt; Judith F., b. ca. 1866; Ida L., b. 1871; Ezra W., b. Apr 1873, d. 28 May 1881; Mary E., b. ca. 1877; Henry Sidney, b. Apr 1880 d. 22 May 1881; Howard William, b. 6 Jun 1881 Dummer NH, m.(1) 12 Apr 1903 Colebrook NH Bessie Bailey of East Colebrook NH, b. 1887 d. 18 Mar 1905, dau. George W. and Lizzie (Annis) Bailey, m.(2) 26 Oct 1905 Lancaster NH Bessie

(Armington) McKelcey of Randolph NH, b. 1880, dau. William and Hattie Armington. CH: Jerry W., b. 23 Sep 1888, d. 8 May 1889.
Calvin, b. ?, d. at birth.
813 Charles S. D.[8], b. 1839.
James, b. 17 Nov 1842 Eaton, Quebec.
Henry A., b. 11 Sep 1843, d. 28 Dec ____, m. 1864 Carrie Grover, b. ?.
Calvin C., b. 30 Jan 1845 Eaton, Quebec, Canada, d. 26 Sep 1909, m. 15 Dec 1868 Haverhill NH Mary N. Morley, b. ?. Went to California.
Mary E., b. 3 Apr 1847, d. 14 May 1906.
814 William W.[8], 1849-1930.
Sources: S5, Sylvia Sawyer rec.

642. **CHARLES C.[7] SAWYER** [see 381], b. 6 Mar 1822 Newport, Canada, d. 3 Aug 1907 Sutton NH, m. 15 Feb 1842 Hannah LaBree of Canada, b. 12 Sep 1821 Canada d. 24 Jan 1901, dau. Henry and Harriet (Chambers) LaBree. In Sutton NH 1880, Greenfield NH 1887. He bur. in Greenfield NH.
815 Henry Elsor[8], 1842-1896.
Harriet J., b. 4 Apr 1844, d. 13 May 1873, m. 3 Apr 1865 Emanuel Jordan.
Emma C., b. 9 Jan 1846, d. 29 Mar 1870.
George Theodore, b. 26 Jun 1848 Newport, Canada, d. 7 Sep 1928 Warner NH, m.(1) 15 Jan 1876 Sutton NH Mary Burns, b. 1859 d. 28 Jul 1878; m.(2) 7 Jul 1877 Mary K. Bigger of Switzerland, b. 1864 d. 1953. Spanish-American War. In Warner NH 1908. CH: Freda Laura, b. 1895, d. 17 Oct 1895; Son, b. ?; 2 dau., b. ?.
Polly T., b. 30 Dec 1851, d. 23 Jan 1853.
816 Joseph Jerome[8], 1853-1944.
Charles Edwin, b. 26 Sep 1857 Newport, Canada, m.(1) 2 Oct 1880 Concord NH (div. 13 Jul 1892) Hattie E. Sargent of Warner NH, b. 1860; m.(2) 22 Dec 1894 Flora M. Eastman of Groton MA, b. 1871. In Sutton NH, Concord NH. CH: Edith M., b. Aug 1899, d. 29 Apr 1900.
Sources: Sutton NH census 1880. VR SA/NH. S5, N9, Paul A. Sawyer rec.

643. **JAMES LUCIUS[7] SAWYER** [see 384], b. 18 Sep 1836, m. Jemima A. Howard, b. 1834 d. 21 Mar 1905 Ludlow VT. In Iowa.
817 Thomas E.[8], b. 1859.
Sources: SA/VT.

644. **ALBERT BUTLER[7] SAWYER** [see 386], b. 3 Jan 1837 South Hero VT, m. Fanny Wardell, b. ?. In Olney IL.
Harriet, b. ?.
Margo, b. ?.
818 Albert Butler[8], 1887-1988.
Gertrude, b. ?.
Sources: VR SA/VT.

645. **DAVID L.[7] SAWYER** [see 387], b. 31 Aug 1835 Sudbury VT, d. 28 Mar 1875 Sudbury VT, m. 1 Dec 1859 Brandon VT Mary E. Nelson, b. 23 Sep 1837 d. 21 Mar 1901 Enosburg VT. Farmer.
819 Daniel R.[8], 1862-1906.
Lois L., b. 23 Apr 1871, d. 2 Apr 1872.
820 Fred J.[8], 1872-1913.

Sources: VR SA/VT.

646. **CHARLES C.[7] SAWYER** [see 389], b. 15 Apr 1850 Templeton MA, m. 14 Oct 1883 Mary Agnes Haverty of Ireland, b. 1865. In Winchendon MA.

William Henry, b. 30 Jan 1885 Winchendon MA.

Sources: VR SA/MA.

647. **AMOS BLANCHARD[7] SAWYER** [see 393], b. 15 May 1843 Fairlee VT, d. 13 Mar 1912 Bradford VT, m. 27 Nov 1888 Nancy Avery of Topsham VT, b. 30 Aug 1861 d. 13 Apr 1937. Laborer. Civil War.

Amos Blanchard, b. 15 Jan 1896 Bradford VT, d. 1958, m. 12 May 1920 Orford NH Menta M. Woodward of Lyme NH, b. 1895, dau. Herbert and Jennie (Coburn) Woodward.

Sources: Fairlee VT census 1850. H43.

648. **EZRA[7] SAWYER** [see 395], b. 8 Apr 1827 Sterling MA, d. Sterling MA, m. 21 Feb 1880 Emma Gilbeaux of New Orleans LA, b. ca. 1855. Farmer. Civil War: 53d Regiment of Massachusetts Volunteers. In Leominster MA, Brentwood NH 1902.

Samuel, b. 23 Jul 1884 Sterling MA.

Ann, b. ?, m. 29 Sep 1900 George W. Lourie of Brentwood NH.

Aldonia May, b. 1 May 1894.

Doris E., b. 11 Feb 1898, d. 2 Feb 1902 Brentwood NH.

Charles F., b. 1902 Brentwood NH, m. Pauline Temple, b. ?, dau Archer and Gaila (Sawyer) Temple.

Sources: VR SA/MA, SA/NH. G20, N6, Sharon R. Sawyer rec.

649. **FREDERICK AUGUSTUS[7] SAWYER** [see 395], b. 4 Apr 1832 Sterling MA, d. 10 Feb 1895 Wareham MA, m. 29 Jul 1856 Colraine MA Helen M. Deane of Colraine MA, b. 1826, dau. Dr. Christopher and Sarah (Ross) Deane. Harvard College 1856. Physician. Civil War: Surgeon, Massachusetts Volunteers, 19 Nov 1862-14 Aug 1863. In Sterling MA 1857, Greenfield MA 1862, Wareham MA.

Frederick Deane, b. 8 Sep 1857, d. 2 Mar 1861.

Sarah H., b. 12 Aug 1859, d. 1859.

Charles Packard, b. 6 Aug 1862 Greenfield MA. In Wareham MA.

Fanny Austin, b. 23 Apr 1867.

Sources: VR SA/MA. G20, R30, T13.

650. **HENRY SAMUEL[7] SAWYER** [see 395], b. 15 Jul 1843 Sterling MA, m. 3 Oct 1866 Sterling MA Mary L. Burpee of Sterling MA, b. 20 Apr 1845, dau. James and Eunice (Goss) Burpee. Attended Appleton Academy, New Ipswich NH. Teacher, farmer. In Sterling MA, Harvard MA.

821 Arthur Henry[8], b. 1868.

Mabel Jane, b. 19 Dec 1870. Teacher.

Ezra Warren, b. 17 Dec 1872 Sterling MA, m. Mary F. Priest of Sterling MA, b. ?, dau. Henry Harrison Priest.

Elsie Eunice, b. 26 Sep 1877. Teacher.

William Francis, b. 20 Sep 1887 Sterling MA.

Sources: VR SA/MA. G20, R30.

651. **EDMUND HOUGHTON[7] SAWYER** [see 396], b. 16 Nov 1821 Newton MA, d. 26 Nov 1879, m.(1) 4 Oct 1848 Brattleboro VT Mary A. Farnsworth of Brattleboro VT, b. 1826 d. 3 May

1851 Brattleboro VT, dau. Eleazer Farnsworth; m.(2) 1853 Sarah T. Hinckley of Norwich NY, b. 4 Jun 1827, dau. Joel and Hannah (Cummins) Hinckley. Bank president, member Massachusetts Legislature. In Brattleboro VT 1840, Easthampton MA 1849.

Henry H., b. 1849 Easthampton MA.

William Brewster, b. 1854 Easthampton MA, m. 29 Sep 1880 Easthampton MA Emma Jane Nichols of Belchertown MA, b. 1828, dau. Edwin and Miranda (Holley) Nichols. Harvard graduate 1879. Physician.

Edmund Houghton, b. 1856 Easthampton MA.

Mary, b. ?.

822 Edmund Hinckley$^{8}$, b. 1862.

Sources: Brattleboro VT census 1840. Easthampton MA census 1850. VR SA/VT, SA/MA. G20, C1, J20.

652. **EZRA THOMAS$^{7}$ SAWYER** [see 396], b. 4 Jan 1827 Sterling MA, m.(1) 24 Jul 1850 Caroline W. Howe of Bolton MA, b. 1829, dau. Moses and Eunice Howe; m.(2) 29 Apr 1885 Easthampton MA Mary E. Braisled [her m.(2)], b. ca. 1845, dau. David and Harriet _____. Engineer.

Frank Ezra, b. 14 Sep 1851 Piermont NH.

Sources: VR SA/MA.

653. **FRANCIS OLIVER$^{7}$ SAWYER** [see 396], b. 30 Jul 1829 Lancaster MA, d. 26 Jan 1904, m. 29 Dec 1852 Lancaster MA Matilda Warren of Boston MA, b. 1832 d. 25 Mar 1876, dau. Thomas B. and Sally Warren. In Burlington VT 1856.

823 Henry T.$^{8}$, b. 1856.

Sources: VR SA/MA.

654. **NATHANIEL CHANDLER$^{7}$ SAWYER** [see 396], b. 15 Aug 1831 Sterling MA, d. 25 Oct 1910 Brattleboro VT, m. 4 Mar 1856 Clinton MA Martha Palmer of Hallowell ME, b. 8 Apr 1835 d. 3 Dec 1919, dau. John and Martha Palmer. Banker. Civil War: Enl. 21 Jul 1863; Colonel, Paymaster, US Volunteers. In Washington DC 1883, Plymouth MA 1907, Brattleboro VT 1909.

George Edwin, b. 28 Apr 1869 Brattleboro VT, m. Genevieve Trust, b. ? d. 5 Dec 1898. In Buffalo NY.

Sources: VR SA/VT, SA/MA. H45, C1.

655. **GEORGE CARROLL$^{7}$ SAWYER** [see 400], b. 27 Mar 1851 Medford MA, m. 28 Jun 1876 Brockton MA Emma B. Millet of W. Bridgewater MA, b. ca. 1852, dau. Aaron and Myra Millett. Shoemaker.

Mildred Alice, b. 11 Aug 1881.

Carroll Eames, b. 3 Oct 1885 Brockton MA.

George Warren, b. 23 May 1894 Brockton MA.

Sources: VR SA/MA.

656. **JUDSON CHERUBINI$^{7}$ SAWYER** [see 403], b. 10 Jul 1849 Acton MA, m. 23 Jun 1873 Medway MA Georgianna Frances Lawrence of Medway MA, b. ca. 1855, dau. George Lawrence. Bootmaker.

Ralph Forest, b. 18 Mar 1874 Medway MA.

Varnum Eugene, b. 12 Jul 1877 Medway MA.

Roy Lawrence, b. 4 Jun 1885 Medway MA.

Sources: VR SA/MA.

657. **WEBBER$^7$ SAWYER** [see 403], b. 25 Sep 1851 Stow MA, m. 14 Dec 1875 Milton MA Caroline E. Kendall of Milton MA, b. ca. 1848, dau. Edward S. Kendall. Straw worker. In Stratford NH 1870, Medfield MA 1883.

William Clayton, b. 29 Jun 1883 Medfield MA.

Bessie Emeline, b. 21 Nov 1885.

Sources: Stratford NH census 1870. VR SA/MA.

658. **CHESTER ARTHUR$^7$ SAWYER** [see 407], b. 12 Jan 1884 Acton MA, m. 14 Oct 1901 Nashua NH Esther (Wellington) McKelvie of South Boston MA, b. ?, dau. Andrew and Esther (Wright) Wellington. Railroad trainman. In Fitchburg MA, Waltham MA.

Elmer W., b. 1912 South Acton MA, m. 31 Jul 1935 Derry NH Stella M. Halkest of Baltimore MD, b. 1915, dau. Carl M. and Ella F. (Ballard) Halkest. In Waltham MA.

Sources: VR Nashua NH, SA/MA.

659. **HERBERT LEROY$^7$ SAWYER** [see 409], b. 10 Jun 1880 Clinton MA, d. 1953 Leominster MA, m.(1) Grace Haywood of So. Acton MA, b. ?; m.(2) 1906 Sarah F. Floyd of Jacksonville FL, b. ? d. 1921; m.(3) 1923 Agnes M. Bill of Brooklyn NY, b. ?. Florist, innkeeper.

Herbert Leroy, b. 20 Sep 1908, m. 1932 Jane D. Hyde.

Sources: Herbert L. Sawyer rec.

660. **WILLIAM H.$^7$ SAWYER** [see 411], b. 26 Feb 1854 Mattamiscontis ME, d. 5 Jul 1946 Bangor ME, m.(1) (I) Sep 1876 Lincoln ME (later div.) Abbie L. Plumley of Lincoln ME, b. 30 Oct 1853 d. 1 Jan 1912, dau. David S. and Abigail (Lord) Plumley; m.(2) ca. 1896 Isabell Beatham of Chester ME, b. 4 Mar 1865 d. 17 Apr 1942. Laborer. In Bangor ME.

Daughter, b. 15 Jul 1897.

Bradley William, b. 15 Apr 1899 Bangor ME.

Sources: Mattamiscontis ME census 1860. VR SA/ME.

661. **HERBERT JONATHAN$^7$ SAWYER** [see 411], b. 5 Apr 1862 Mattamiscontis, d. 6 Jan 1948 Orrington ME, m. Nellie May (Clement) Ryan, b. 1869 d. 9 Feb 1930, dau. James Clement. He bur. in Lincoln ME.

Herbert Raymond, b. 29 Sep 1903 Lincoln Me, m. Lucille M Harris, b. 30 Aug 1909. dau. Percy and Sadie (Harriman) Harris. Railroad worker.

Sources: VR Ellsworth ME. Jo Ann E. Sawyer rec.

662. **FRANK O.$^7$ SAWYER** [see 411], b. May 1866 Mattamiscontis ME, d. 1954, m. Ruby Marie Spencer of Lincoln ME, b. 9 May 1872 d. 10 Nov 1909 Bangor ME, dau. George W. and Lydia M. (Darling) Spencer. In Mattawamkeag ME.

Harry A., b. Nov 1890 (Mattamiscontis ME?).

Lottie Mary, b. 14 Jul 1892.

Fay E., b. 22 Mar 1896.

Sources: VR SA/ME.

663. **CHARLES HORACE$^7$ SAWYER** [see 412], b. 4 Feb 1854 Amesbury MA, d. 20 Jul 1934, m. 29 May 1882 Dexter ME Isabella Dickson of Manchester NH, b. 12 Nov 1854 d. 22 Jan 1919 Vasselboro ME, dau. John and Marion (Young) Dickson. In Northport ME, Sangerville ME.

824 John Kimball$^8$, b. 1885.

Sources: SA/ME. Esther Sawyer rec.

664. **CLARENCE FAYETTE⁷ SAWYER** [see 414], b. 31 Oct 1885 Sherburne VT, d. 25 Apr 1950 Bridgewater VT, m. 8 Mar 1909 Lebanon VT Eva Peck of Springfield VT, b. 15 Feb 189? d. 24 Dec 1976, dau. Sidney Peck of Ludlow VT.

Ellsworth Gordon, b. ?, d. 1975 Hanover NH, m. Verna G. Mosher of Canada, b. ? d. 1977.

Sources: Ellsworth Sawyer rec.

## EIGHTH GENERATION

665. **LEVI GREENLEAF[8] SAWYER** [see 416], b. 6 Oct 1808 Starks ME, m.(1) Deborah _____, b. ? d. 25 Jan 1843; m.(2) Elvira Greenleaf, b. 10 Oct 1812 d. 14 Nov 1889, dau. William and Sally (Lander) Greenleaf. In Starks ME 1850.

Landon, b. 10 Jun 1837 Starks ME.

James Franklin, b. 5 Dec 1839 Starks ME, d. 31 Jul 1921 at Old Soldiers Home, m. 23 Sep 1862 Sharon MA Addie F. Skinner of Canton MA, b. ?, dau. William S. and Nabby Skinner. Mariner. He bur. in Starks ME

Deborah, b. 14 Nov 1841.

Eloisa E., b. 1847, m. James V. Greaton.

Benjamin Allen, b. 12 Jun 1850 Starks ME, d. 11 May 1948 Skowhegan ME, m. (1) Maora F. Wood of Starks ME, b. 19 Mar 1848 d. 24 Nov 1925 Skowhegan ME, dau. James and Anna (Greenleaf) Wood; m.(2) 1 Jan 1926 Skowhegan ME Mary A. Harris of Woolwich ME, b. ?, dau. Charles and Mary E. (Walker) Harris; m.(3) ?.

Esther E., b. 30 Aug 1853, m. 14 Aug 1872 R____ D. Trask.

Sources: Starks ME census 1840, 1850. VR Skowhegan ME, SA/ME, SA/MA. G42.

666. **JOHN P.[8] SAWYER** [see 416], b. 4 Mar 1817 Starks ME, d. ca. 1858, m. 10 Dec 1838 Industry ME Lois Lovell of Vienna ME, b. ?. Will dated 1858.

Nancy, b. 19 Oct 1839.

Charles Franklin, b. 18 Jan 1842 Starks ME.

Llewellyn Augustus, b. 12 Apr 1845 Starks ME. In Brewer ME.

Sources: P82h.

667. **WILLIAM M.[8] SAWYER** [see 416], b. 8 Aug 1821 Starks ME, d. 21 Jul 1907 Vienna ME, m. Jane F. Lane of Vienna ME, b. Feb 1830, dau. Nathan and Harriet (Healy) Lane. In Concord ME 1860 (Concordville ?), Vienna ME 1880.

John Harvey, b. 29 Nov 1850 Vienna ME.

William LaForest, b. 31 May 1857 Vienna ME, d. 1 May 1905 Vienna ME, m. 30 May 1887 Boston MA Gertrude Ida Stickney of Charlestown MA, b. 1868, dau. Lyman and Emma Stickney. Shoemaker. In Brockton MA. CH: Leona G., b. 21 Oct 1887; William Carroll, b. 23 Nov 1891.

Silas H., b. 9 Jan 1859 Vienna ME.

M. Hattie, b. 4 Jan 1861.

Charles D., b. 1 Feb 1862 Vienna ME.

Lizzie D., b. 9 Dec 1864.

Jennie R., b. 26 May 1867.

Coryden A., b. ca. 1869 Vienna ME, m. 25 Apr 1894 West Bridgewater MA Sarah Leavitt of Bridgewater MA, b. ca. 1876, dau. Ivory and Mariba Leavitt.

Angienette, b. ca. 1871.

Sources: Concord ME census 1860. ME 1880 census index. VR SA/MA.

668. **THOMAS MCKECHNIE[8] SAWYER** [see 416], b. ca. 1828 Starks ME, m. 19 Sep 1858 Dorchester MA Georgianna Morrill of Nashua NH, b. ca. 1840, dau. Micajah and Sarah Morrill. Clerk. In Boston MA.

Edgar, b. 25 Jun 1860 Boston MA.

Sources: VR SA/MA.

669. **LUKE FULSOM[8] SAWYER** [see 417], b. 12 Nov 1826 Madison ME, d. 22 Apr 1922 Madison WI, m. 11 Nov 1856 Paulina D. Gray, b. 25 Aug 1833 d. 29 Jun 1880. Farmer. In Ottawa KS.

Nellie, b. 1859.

Delos Luke, b. 15 Apr 1861, m. 7 Mar 1883 Emma V. Allman.

Sources: VR Anson ME.

670. **LUKE GREENLEAF[8] SAWYER** [see 418], b. 6 Dec 1830 Starks ME, d. 11 Feb 1920 Dover-Foxcroft ME, m. 5 Aug 1860 Alice McKenney, b. 12 Jul 1840 d. 9 Sep 1897, dau. Cyrus McKenney. In Madison ME.

Lorin C., b. 18 Sep 1863 Starks ME, m. 12 Mar 1882 Vesta L. Bennett, b. Mar 1863. In Dover-Foxcroft ME 1900. CH: Alice L., b. Jan 1883; Inez, b. Jul 1885.

Sources: Dover-Foxcroft ME census 1900. VR SA/ME.

671. **STEPHEN GREENLEAF[8] SAWYER** [see 418], b. 14 Feb 1835 Starks ME, d. 5 Feb 1894 Starks ME, m. 15 May 1867 Joan Furbish, b. ?. Carpenter.

Fannie A., b. 11 Jan 1865.

William R., b. 19 Apr 1878 Starks ME.

Hattie K., b. 5 Mar 1883, d. 12 Nov 1886.

Sources: ME 1880 census index. VR SA/ME.

672. **AUGUSTUS IMRI[8] SAWYER** [see 418], b. 11 Dec 1846 Starks ME, d. 3 Feb 1914 Skowhegan ME, m. 24 Jun 1872 Skowhegan ME Rose E. Durrell of Skowhegan ME, b. 15 Jun 1852 d. 9 Nov 1939, dau. George W. and Rose (Cleveland) Durrell. Merchant. In Skowhegan ME 1880.

Albert E., b. Apr 1878, d. 8 May 1906, unm.

Kattie F., b. Oct 1882, m. 14 Aug 1907.

Sources: ME 1880 census index. VR Skowhegan ME, SA/ME. C48, G42.

673. **DAVID[8] SAWYER** [see 420], b. 3 May 1830 Norridgewock ME, d. 18 Jan 1898 Hartland ME, m.(1) Martha A. Bowman of Hartland ME, b. 13 Oct 1835 d. 3 Feb 1892, dau. T_____J. and Mary Ann (Rose) Bowman; m.(2) 6 Aug 1894 Palmyra ME Sarah R. Jackson, b. 1870, dau. Edward and Millicent Jackson of Canada. Carriage maker. In Madison ME 1850. He bur. in Palmyra ME.

David, b. Mar 1851, d. 1 Sep 1852.

825 Frederick Randolph[9], 1852-1921.

Mary Isadora, b. 1 Nov 1854, d. 7 Feb 1892, unm.

Ann M., b. 1857.

Lodie Persis, b. Feb 1859, d. 3 May 1860.

George W., b. 16 Apr 1861 Oakland ME, d. 6 Jul 1911 Detroit ME, m. 17 May 1893 Hartland ME Sarah J. Walker of New Brunswick, Canada, b. Aug 1873, dau Edward Walker.

Mabel, b. 1864.

Lilly P., b. 26 Mar 1865, m. 14 Nov 1883 Lincoln Merrick.

David I., b. ca. 1869 Hartland ME.
Ernest S., b. Oct 1870, d. 3 Feb 1872.
Millie, b. 11 Nov 1894.
Sources: Madison ME census 1850, VR SA/ME. M36, M5, Death certificate.

674. **CHARLES P.[8] SAWYER** [see 421], b. 1840 Madison ME, d. 7 Nov 1904 Skowhegan ME, m. 25 Dec 1860 Frances O. Williams of Madison ME, b. 7 Jul 1841 d. 7 Oct 1901, dau. Morrill and Fatma (Albee) Williams. Dentist. In Dexter ME.
Alvin, b. 6 Dec 1861.
826 Frederick O.[9], 1862-1951.
Ralph W., b. 29 Jan 1870 Dexter ME.
Sources: ME 1880 census index. VR Skowhegan ME, SA/ME.

675. **WARREN GREY[8] SAWYER** [see 423], b. 15 Feb 1855 Madison ME, m. 15 Apr 1885 Nellie A. Young of Starks ME, b. 30 Jul 1864, dau. Reuben and Lauretta A. (Folsom) Young. Physician.
Herbert Leslie, b. 20 Aug 1886 Madison ME, m. 29 Jul 1914 Emma I. Brown of Atkinson ME, b. 19 Oct 1890. President of Colby Junior College. Charter member, Society of Mayflower Descendents.
Sources: VR SA/MA, F24, D4.

676. **SAMUEL WARREN[8] SAWYER** [see 427], b. 18 Sep 1848 Hubbardston MA, d. 1934 Gardner MA, m.(1) 22 Feb 1873 New Ipswich NH Laura Townsend of Fitzwilliam MA, b. 17 Jun 1853; m.(2) 23 Oct 1888 Fitchburg MA Annie McLean of Troy NY, b. ca. 1856, dau. Felix and Nancy McLean; m.(3) ca. 1915 Hattie Folger, b. ?. In Gardner MA, Nantucket MA.
Fred Warren, b. 1874 Nashua NH, d. 1962 Norwich CT, m. 1909 Mary E. Bastey, b. 1881 d. 1965. Electrical engineer. CH: Elizabeth Warren, b. 1912, teacher.
Henry Clinton, b. ?, d. 1918, unm.
Warren Folger, b. 1917 Nantucket MA, m. Eleanor Tomlinson. In Montana.
William Thomas, b. 1918 Nantucket MA, m(1) Mary Carter Grove; m(2) Mary Elizabeth Lutz. In Maryland.
Sources: VR Hubbardston MA, SA/MA. C9, Elizabeth W. Sawyer rec.

677. **CHARLES MILLET[8] SAWYER** [see 436], b. 3 Aug 1860 Waltham MA, d. Nov 1930, m. 26 Nov 1885 Newton MA Laura A. Moody of Chelsea MA, b. ca. 1860, dau. Nathaniel and Eliza Moody. Salesman.
Gerald Francis, b. 10 Dec 1889, d. 13 Jan 1897.
Marshall Moody, b. 18 Jul 1891, d. 9 Jun 1983.
Sources: VR SA/MA. G15, Mrs. Walter J. Sawyer rec.

678. **CHESTER PORTER[8] SAWYER** [see 440], b. 9 Jan 1881 Smithfield ME, m. 10 Jun 1903 Jennie Leavitt, b. 29 Sep 1882, dau. Horace C. and Lydia (Merrow) Leavitt. In Norridgewock ME.
William Leavitt, b. 16 Mar 1917.
Sources: M40.

679. **DANIEL H.[8] SAWYER** [see 442], b. 19 Feb 1837 Northboro MA, m. 19 Jul 1860 Berlin MA Angelina E. (Bigelow) Felton of Marlborough MA, wid., b. 14 Jun 1843, dau. Lambert A. and Harriet (Bliss) Bigelow. In Worcester MA, Berlin MA, Hudson MA, Bolton MA 1863. Shoemaker.
Lida Adelle, b. 28 Mar 1863.

827 Bertice Felton[9], b. 1868.
Sources: VR Berlin MA, SA/MA. F14, N44, H81.

680. **HENRY ELWIN[8] SAWYER** [see 442], b. ca. 1849 Tolland CT, m.(1) 16 Apr 1872 Lynn MA Lizzie Hitchings of Saugus MA, b. ?, dau. Rosswell Hitchings; m.(2) 26 Jan 1880 Douglas MA Mary Jennie Landry of Nashua NH, b. ca. 1856, dau. John Landry. Blacksmith, teamster. In Tolland CT 1850, Shrewsbury MA, Lynn MA 1872, Douglas MA 1880, Worcester MA 1887.

George Albert, b. 28 Sep 1884 Worcester MA.
Sophronia J., b. 2 Jan 1887.
Grace F., b. 20 Oct 1893.

Sources: Tolland CT census 1850. Douglas MA census 1880. VR SA/MA.

681. **DANIEL W.[8] SAWYER** [see 443], b. ca. 1846 Waltham MA, m.(1) 23 Dec 1869 Hudson MA Mary C. Brown of Harvard MA, b. ca. 1851, dau. S.H. and Catherine (Gates) Brown; m.(2) 26 Dec 1879 Boston MA Delia King of Calais ME, b. ca. 1857, dau. Lewis L. and Sarah King. Clerk, shoemaker

Fred Garfield, b. 30 Jun 1880 Cambridge MA.
Herbert, b. 23 Sep 1881 Cambridge MA.
Chester, b. 13 Apr 1891 Chelsea MA.

Sources: VR SA/MA.

682. **JOHN A.[8] SAWYER** [see 443], b. ca. 1847 Brighton MA, m. 8 Apr 1877 Shirley MA Inez F. White of Niagra NY, b. ca. 1844, dau. John and Elizabeth White. Farmer. In Brighton MA 1850, Pepperell MA 1878.

Clara Richard, b. 8 Mar 1878.
Frederick Richard, b. 26 Nov 1879.

Sources: Brighton MA census 1850. VR SA/MA.

683. **WILLIAM PHILLIPS[8] SAWYER** [see 447], b. 7 Oct 1863 Medford MA, m. 1892 Alma Cashman of Nova Scotia, Canada, b. ?. Butcher. In Boston MA.

William Thomas, b. 29 Jan 1893 East Boston MA.
Charles E., b. 15 Sep 1895 East Boston MA.
Marie, b. 5 Jan 1899.

Sources: VR SA/MA.

684. **AMORY POLLARD[8] SAWYER** [see 451], b. 28 Jun 1869 Bolton MA, m. 28 Sep 1890 Illinois Mary E. Z. Woods, b. ?, her m.(2).

Amory Pollard, b. ?, d. in France, World War I.
Helen L., b. ?, m. ____ Kjellberg.
John Henry, b. ?.
Dorothy Walcott, b. ?, m. ____ Purdy.
Donald Whitcomb, b. ?. unm.

Sources: VR SA/MA. Dorothy W. Purdy rec.

685. **CHARLES H.[8] SAWYER** [see 452], b. 11 Jul 1855 Bolton MA, m. 31 Aug 1880 Bolton MA Mary E. L. Bowers of Clinton MA, b. ca. 1862, dau. Thomas O. and Achsah Bowers. Farmer.

L____ H. (dau.). b. 1881.
George Kenisky, b. 25 Aug 1885 Bolton MA.

Sources: VR Bolton MA, SA/MA.

686. **STEPHEN WILLIAM$^8$ SAWYER** [see 456], b. 21 Jun 1862 Lovell ME, m. 6 Dec 1886 Hollis ME Eliza J. Burbank of Athens ME, b. Feb 1858. In Buxton ME.

828 Frank William$^9$, 1887-1968.
Dora M., b. Oct 1889, d. 24 Apr 1920, State Hospital, Augusta ME.
Clarence E., b. 1892, d. 16 Nov 1988 Westbrook ME.
Laura E., b. 19 Jun 1896, m. _____ Moulton.
Lamont D., b. 22 Apr 1900. Went to New York.

Sources: VR SA/ME. D51.

687. **LEWIS AMOS$^8$ SAWYER** [see 462], b. 11 Jan 1856 Berlin MA, d. 23 Jul 1880 Berlin MA, m. 20 Jul 1876 Berlin MA Lucinda Boyd Hebard of Brookfield MA, b. 1853 d. 1893, dau. Adrion B. Hebard. Butcher. In Southboro MA, Concord MA 1878.

Winifred Bates (male), b. 17 Jan 1877 Southboro MA.
Robert Lewis, b. 13 Nov 1878 Concord MA.

Sources: VR Berlin MA, SA/MA. H76.

688. **SILAS ABEL$^8$ SAWYER** [see 462], b. 15 Oct 1860 Berlin MA, m. 5 Jan 1889 Maynard MA Kate Jane Rouse of Stow MA, b. ca. 1868, dau. Thomas and Katie Rouse. Teamster.

Chester Amos, b. ca. 1889 Maynard MA.
Silas Oscar, b. 4 Jul 1891 Maynard MA.

Sources: VR Berlin MA, SA/MA. W39.

689. **HENRY OLIVER$^8$ SAWYER** [see 463], b. 10 Jun 1844 Berlin MA, m.(1) 1 Jan 1866 Clinton MA Flora A. Weatherbee of Putney VT, b. ca. 1848, dau. James and Laura Weatherbee; m.(2) 1 May 1890 West Boylston MA Martha W. Warner of West Boylston MA, b. ca. 1859, dau. Waters W. and Mandora (Goodale) Warner. Merchant.

829 Henry Lewis$^9$, b. 1868.
Angie Flora, b. 1871, m. 14 Sep 1892 West Boylston MA Frank M. Prescott.
Cora Anabell, b. 5 Dec 1882.

Sources: VR SA/MA.

690. **WALTER BARRETT$^8$ SAWYER** [see 463], b. 16 May 1852 West Boylston MA, m. 21 Jan 1872 Vernon VT Louise M. Hubbard of Southbridge MA, b. ?. Merchant.

Sarah Lillian, b. 7 May 1875.
Ella Louise, b. 9 Jul 1879.
Arthur Hubbard, b. 22 Apr 1882 West Boylston MA.
Lewis Walter, b. 12 Oct 1885 West Boylston MA.

Sources: VR SA/MA.

691. **CHARLES MARSHALL$^8$ SAWYER** [see 467], b. 21 Apr 1852 Berlin MA, m. 19 Nov 1879 Berlin MA Julia I. Bassett of Worcester MA, b. 28 Oct 1854. Farmer. In Clinton MA.

Florence Martha, b. 6 Apr 1884.
Hazel Isabel, b. 30 Jun 1886.
Marjory L., b. 21 Oct 1888.
Hermon Loren, b. 30 Dec 1890 Berlin MA.
Beatrice G., b. 30 Aug 1892.
William George, b. 19 Feb 1895 Berlin MA.

Sources: SA/MA. W39, B85.

692. **FRANK LORING[8] SAWYER** [see 470], b. 11 Aug 1858 Berlin MA, m. 1 Jan 1885 Boston MA Helen M. Stevens of Boston MA, b. ca. 1862, dau. Albert G. and Mary Stevens. Bookkeeper. In Jamaica Plain MA, Boston MA 1895.

Loring Ellsworth, b. 17 Jun 1886 Boston MA.
Eunice Mary, b. ?.
Laura H., b. 1891.
Wesley Stevens, b. 26 Jul 1895.

Sources: VR Berlin MA, SA/MA. W39.

693. **IVERS HARTWELL[8] SAWYER** [see 471], b. 13 Jul 1847 Berlin MA, d. 9 Feb 1907 Berlin MA, m. 14 Jun 1871 Berlin MA Abbie M. Farwell of Harvard MA, b. 22 Jan 1853, dau. George and Maria (Worate) Farwell. Farmer.

Elcia Grace, b. 5 Dec 1871, d. 1 Jul 1892, unm. In Worcester MA.
Ivers Ellsworth, b. 22 Apr 1874 Berlin MA, m. 21 Sep 1899 Berlin MA Jennie E. Cameron of Vermont, b. 1875.
George Hartwell, b. 8 May 1876 Berlin MA.
Perley Bartlett, b. 1 Oct 1878 Berlin MA, m. 31 Oct 1906 Florence M. Sawyer, b. ?.
Ethel Maria, b. 15 May 1881.
Son, b. 5 Oct 1883, d. same day.
Hattie Worster, b. 21 Mar 1886.
Elcia Grace, b. 21 Aug 1892.

Sources: VR Berlin MA, SA/MA. W39.

694. **JOSEPH HENRY[8] SAWYER** [see 474], b. 19 Sep 1845 Berlin MA, m. 13 Jun 1869 Hudson MA Abbie L. Greene of Berlin MA, b. 26 Nov 1849, dau. Edward and Louisa (Hartwell) Greene. Farmer, shoemaker.

830 Walter Alden[9], b. 1880.
831 Carl Eugene[9], b. 1882.
Louisa Persis, b. 26 Feb 1883.
Lucy May, b. 28 Nov 1887.
Ralph H., b. 5 May 1892, d. 17 Aug 1892.

Sources: VR Berlin MA, SA/MA. E16.

695. **EUGENE N.[8] SAWYER** [see 477], b. 23 Feb 1852 Reading MA, d. 4 Dec 1902, m. 13 Nov 1879 Reading MA Hattie Parker of Reading MA, b. ca. 1852, dau. Jerome and Harriet A. Parker. Bookkeeper. In Malden MA.

Marion, b. 13 Jul 1882.
Percy Parker, b. 13 Aug 1884 Malden MA.
Child, b. ?, d.y.

Sources: VR SA/MA. B84.

696. **SAMUEL RUFUS[8] SAWYER** [see 478], b. 3 Apr 1857 Berlin MA, m. 19 Sep 1883 Ellen Susan Stone of Northboro MA, b. 8 Jun 1859. Accountant.

Elsie Stone, b. 10 Jun 1888, d. 22 Aug 1912, m. Aug 1911 George A. Theobald.
Samuel Hermon, b. 15 Sep 1889, m. 12 Oct 1910 Florence Gertrude Dow, b. ?. CH: Thelma Ellen, b. 15 Oct 1911; Myrtle Gertrude, b. 5 Apr 1914.
Marion Fuller, b. 29 Apr 1898.

Sources: VR SA/MA. F44, B32.

697. **LOREN EVERETT[8] SAWYER** [see 478], b. 1 Apr 1864 Berlin MA, m. 31 Mar 1887 Millis MA Lucy B. Bullard of Medway MA, b. ca. 1862, dau. Cyrus and Alvira F. (Cass) Bullard. In Millis MA 1893.

Cyrus E., b. ca. 1888.
Rufus E., b. ca. 1890.
Elvira C., b. ca. 1891.
Lottie Louise, b. 18 Sep 1893.
Doldie, b. ca. 1895.
Grace, b. ca. 1897.
Mary, b. ca. 1898.
Charles L., b. ca. 1900 Medway MA.

Sources: VR SA/MA. F44, W39.

698. **FRANCIS GOSS[8] SAWYER** [see 479], b. 21 Jun 1848 Lancaster MA, m. 5 Jun 1878 Clinton MA Lora G. Morse of Northbridge MA, b. 1860, dau. Henry and Sarah Morse.Farmer.

Lora Genevieve, b. 14 Mar 1879.
Goss, b. 10 Oct 1880 Lancaster MA.
Clifton, b. 4 Nov 1886 Clinton MA.

Sources: VR SA/MA.

699. **FREDERICK WILLIAM[8] SAWYER** [see 480], b. 10 Feb 1819 Boylston MA, d. 13 Jun 1872, m.(1) 16 Jan 1851 LucyAnn Sprague of Worcester MA, b. 1833; m.(2) Harriet Saulsbury of Nova Scotia, Canada, b. 1844 d. 2 Dec 1871 Millbury MA. Mechanic. In Millbury MA.

Freeman Henry, b. 3 Apr 1866 Millbury MA.
Lillie Jane, b. 11 Oct 1869.
Minnie, b. 13 Sep 1871.

Sources: VR SA/MA. M42.

700. **CALEB KENDALL[8] SAWYER** [see 481], b. 21 Mar 1810 Boylston MA, m. 3 Oct 1837 Holden MA Nancy E. Howe of Holden MA, b. ?. Manufacturer. In Holden MA, Northboro MA 1837, Clinton MA.

832 Edgar Franklin[9], b. 1837.
Agnes Nancy, b. 25 Sep 1839, m. 26 Jun 1878 Clinton MA Asabel B. Winslow.
Lucy A., b. ca. 1842, m. 2 Mar 1865 Fitchburg MA John Edward Morse.
Infant, b. ?, d. 31 Jul 1844 Bolton MA.
Helen E., b. ca. 1846, m. 4 Jun 1874 Townsend MA Ambrose Stickney.
Joseph Wilson, b. 30 Jan 1851 Clinton MA.

Sources: VR Boylston MA, Holden MA, Northboro MA, SA/MA.

701. **JOSEPH THOMAS[8] SAWYER** [see 481], b. 28 Nov 1811 Boylston MA, m. 7 Jan 1834 Holden MA Eliza R. Howe of Holden MA, b. 11 Aug 1812 d. 17 Jun 1892, dau. Jasper and Nancy (Wilson) Howe. Weaver. In Holden MA, Lancaster MA, Clinton MA 1850.

Frances H., b. 31 Aug 1835.
Oscar F., b. 20 Mar 1838, d. 5 Apr 1860.
George Thomas, b. 8 Mar 1847 Lancaster MA.

Sources: Clinton MA census 1850. VR Boylston MA, Holden MA, Lancaster MA, SA/MA. H80.

702. **CHARLES H.[8] SAWYER** [see 481], b. 1825 Boylston MA, m. 3 Nov 1847 Hollis MA Rosine F. Sheldon of Fitchburg MA, b. ?, dau. Zachariah and Betsey Sheldon. Carpenter, machinist. In Worcester MA 1850.

Herbert Pliney, b. 1853 Worcester MA, m. 1 Jan 1878 Clinton MA Ida F. Bartlett of Bolton MA, b. ca. 1855, dau. Jonas B. and Sophronia Bartlett. Machinist.

Charles E., b. ca. 1856 Worcester MA, m. 12 Jan 1881 Spencer MA Emma Bimus of Spencer MA, b. ca. 1851, dau. Joshua and Lucille Bimus.

Frank A., b. ca. 1858 Holden MA, m. 13 May 1884 Clinton MA Clara E. Harrington, b. 1856, dau. Stephen J. and Amelia Harrington.

Eva, b. 7 Aug 1859.

Sources: Worcester MA census 1850, VR Lancaster MA, Holden MA, SA/MA.

703. **GEORGE MOSES[8] SAWYER** [see 483], b. 10 Jan 1831 Lancaster MA, d. 9 Jan 1911 Illinois, m. 18 Oct 1854 Putnam CT (also rec. in Boston MA) Adeline Gilbert of Putnam CT, b. 22 May 1835 d. 31 Jan 1920, dau. Horace and Sally (Hall) Gilbert. All CH b. in Illinois.

John Henry, b. 17 Apr 1857, m. 19 Apr 1880 Ella E. Hesselgrane, b. ?.

William Gilbert, b. 17 Nov 1859, d. 3 Aug 1908, unm.

Sarah Eliza, b. 22 Feb 1861.

Charles Horace, b. 2 Dec 1864, d. 11 Oct 1865.

Edward Joslyn, b. 8 Jan 1872, m. 12 Nov 1895 Minnie E. Webster, b. ?.

Sources: VR Lancaster MA, SA/MA. G8, W54.

705. **CHARLES ORVILLE[8] SAWYER** [see 485], b. 11 Mar 1842 Wendell MA, d. 30 Dec 1920 Illinois, m. 27 Aug 1873 Mary Eaton Gunn of Montague MA, b. ?. Teacher. In Wendell MA 1850, Orange MA, New Salem MA 1876.

Son, b. 17 Jul 1874.

Leroy Robinson, b. 11 Aug 1876.

Vera J., b. Oct 1880.

Alice Persis, b. Jul 1883.

Sources: Wendell MA census 1850. VR Wendell MA, SA/MA. P50A.

705. **HARRIS STRATTON[8] SAWYER** [see 486], b. 6 Jan 1823 Northfield MA, m.(1) 20 Jan 1846 Brattleboro VT Lucy M. Williams of Deerfield MA, b. ?; m.(2) 14 Oct 1874 Feeding Hills (Agawam) MA Mary F. Hamilton of Palmer MA, b. 12 Jan 1836, dau. Jacob and Fanny (Robinson) Hamilton. Bootmaker, farmer. In Northfield MA, Montague MA.

Albert E., b. 18 Nov 1846 Montague MA, m. 14 Dec 1868 Montague MA Althera Caswell of Montague MA, b. ca. 1845, dau. Solomon and Susan Caswell. In Northfield MA. CH: Alice M., b. ca. 1871, m. 18 Nov 1891 Greenfield MA Henry B. Marsh.

Son, b. 10 Dec 1847.

Alma G., b. 1848, m. 28 Dec 1867 in Montague MA Larkin E. Fisher.

Alice, b. 25 Dec 1851, m. 23 Sep 1872 Montague MA Albert A. Patten.

Lucy Ella, b. 17 Dec 1854, m. 30 Apr 1876 Colrain MA Charles W. Smith.

Sanford, b. 24 Dec 1857 Montague MA, m. 11 Mar 1886 Agawam MA Martha C. Roberts of Agawam MA, b. ca. 1845, dau. William and Sophronia Roberts. Farmer.

Dwight Howard, b. 28 Sep 1859 Montague MA.

Sources: Montague MA census 1850. VR Montague MA, SA/MA. T13.

706. **CHARLES L.[8] SAWYER** [see 487], b. Sep 1828 New Salem MA, m.(1) 2 Jan 1851 Wendell MA Clarissa R. Clark of Wendell MA, b. 1828 d. 23 Mar 1852, dau. Ender and Nancy Clark; m.(2) Eveline Clark of Brattleboro VT, b. ?. Livery stable. In New Salem MA, Erving MA, Wendell MA 1850, Greenfield MA 1860.

Daughter, b. 23 Mar 1852.

Fanny C., b. 25 Oct 1858.

Edward Eugene, b. 5 Aug 1860 Greenfield MA.
Charles H., b. 22 Sep 1862 Greenfield MA, m. 27 Nov 1884 Annie P. Turner of Erving MA, b. 1861. In Orange MA.
Sources: Wendell MA census 1850. Greenfield MA census 1860. VR SA/MA.

707. **ERASTUS O.[8] SAWYER** [see 487], b. 8 Sep 1843 Erving MA, m. 9 Nov 1867 Orange MA Ellen A. Turner of Orange MA, b. 1840, dau. John and Almira Turner. Mechanic.
Walter A., b. 21 Jun 1870 Orange MA.
Grace C., b. 13 Feb 1882.
Sources: Wendell MA census 1850. Orange MA census 1870. VR SA/MA.

708. **FRANKLIN[8] SAWYER** [see 488], b. 1833 Salem MA, m. 2 Jul 1857 Hinsdale MA Ellen M. Miller, b. 1834, dau. James Miller.
Robert, b. ?.
Fred, b. ?.
Mary, b. ?, m. John P. Lydiard of Chicago IL.
Sources: VR SA/MA.

709. **WILLIAM HARRISON[8] SAWYER** [see 488], b. 9 Sep 1835 New Salem MA, d. 25 May 1915 Ellenburg NY, m. 4 Mar 1884 Ellenburg NY Mary Elizabeth Allen, b. 15 Jul 1859 d. 14 Jan 1896, dau. Heman C. and Mary A. Allen. In Boston MA.
Harry Allen, b. 18 Apr 1885 Ellenburg NY, d. 27 Dec 1950 Canton NY, m. 17 Jul 1912 Adeline M. Garlick, b. 11 Aug 1887 d. 25 Jun 1959. CH: William Harry, b. 29 Apr 1913, m. 5 Oct 1946 Helen E. Smith, b. ?; John Edwin, b. 18 Jul 1914, d. 9 Jun 1961, m. Ruth Barton, b. ?; Dr. Janet Ruth, b. 21 Mar 1924; Beatrice Elizabeth, b. 1915.
Sources: VR New Salem MA. A16, Beatrice E. Sawyer rec.

710. **GEORGE SILAS[8] SAWYER** [see 491], b. 11 Sep 1843 Chester VT, m. Phoebe C. Hubbard, b. ?. In Mt. Pulaski IL, Oak Park IL.
Donald H., b. 1879, d. 1941, m. 1929 Harriet E. Merrian, b. ?.
George L., b. ?.
Fred S., b. ?.
Note: All three sons went to Seattle and Spokane WA 1910.
Sources: VR SA/VT. A20.

711. **FRANCIS E.[8] SAWYER** [see 492], b. 1845 Leicester VT, m. 31 Mar 1870 Addie J. Allen of Ohio, b. ?, d. 15 Dec 1920 Rutland VT, dau. Noel Allen. Farmer.
Frederick E., b. 24 Jan 1871 Leicester VT.
Augustus Allen, b. 6 Aug 1872 Leicester VT.
Sources: VR Leicester VT, SA/VT.

712. **STEPHEN E.[8] SAWYER** [see 492], b. 1847 Leicester VT, d. 20 Mar 1877 Leicester VT, m. 9 Mar 1870 Leicester VT Moana H. Jenny, b. 1851 d. 17 Feb 1871, dau. E_____ B. and Sarah (Kelsey) Jenny. Farmer.
Irvin J., b. 11 Feb 1871 Leicester VT, d. Leicester VT. Farmer.
Sources: VR Leicester VT, SA/VT.

713. **JONATHAN WHITCOMB[8] SAWYER** [see 495], b. 31 Oct 1827 Phillipston MA, m. 15 May 1859 Athol MA Martha J. Smith of Athol MA, b. 1840, dau. Adin H. and Mary Smith. Farmer.

Mary J., b. 1862, m. 2 Jan 1885 Athol MA Lemuel S. Smith.
Orrin, b. 2 Oct 1863 Athol MA, m. 28 May 1888 Orange MA Ada Edith Hardy of Winchendon MA, b. 1870, dau. Rufus and Hattie Hardy.
Everett, b. 30 Jan 1869 Athol MA.
Sources: VR SA/MA.

714. **EDWARD AUGUSTUS THORNDIKE⁸ SAWYER** [see 498], b. ca. 1828 Brooks ME, m. 21 Feb 1849 Boston MA Sarah Ann Tidd of Woburn MA, b. ca. 1828, dau. Eben and Catherine (Thompson) Tidd. Printer, clockmaker. In Woburn MA, Boston MA.
Augusta M., b. May 1849, d. 19 Mar 1850.
833 Frederick L.[9], b. ca. 1850.
Frank A., b. 26 Feb 1854 Boston MA, m. 24 Jun 1878 Methuen MA Jennie H. Lucas of Methuen MA, b. ca. 1854, dau. Peter J. and Mary Lucas. Baker. In Lawrence MA 1882. CH: Daughter, b. 28 Mar 1882.
Kate Isobel, b. 28 Apr 1856.
Edward Thorndike, b. 20 May 1861 Woburn MA, d. 24 Jul 1940, m. 15 Oct 1882 Chelmsford MA Cora Mae Fadden of St. Albans VT, b. 6 Jul 1859 d. 16 Nov 1942 dau. Isaiah and Emily Fadden. Machinist. In Lowell MA, Boston MA 1886. CH: Nettie M., b. 28 May 1883; Gertie Mae, b. 12 Dec 1884, d. 6 Feb 1956; Emma Idella, b. 3 May 1886, d. 29 May 1963, m. 1904 Harry Rockwood Howe; Harry Thorndike, b. 28 Feb 1889, d. 20 May 1910; Jenny, b. ?; Clara Louise, b. 7 Sep 1897, m. 1930 George Patz.
834 Augustus Thorndike[9], b. 1862.
Sources: VR Woburn MA, SA/MA.

715. **EMERY[8] SAWYER** [see 499], b. 6 Mar 1818 Brooks ME, d. 11 Jan 1882, m. 7 Sep 1841 Margaret A. Cochran of Monmouth ME, b. 16 Dec 1816 d. 22 May 1901, dau. James and Jane (More) Cochran. Lawyer. In Searsport ME 1843, Thomaston ME 1846.
James E., b. 1841 Searsport ME, m. 9 Mar 1862 Searsport ME Lucy A. Sargent of Searsport ME, b. ?. In Machias ME 1863. CH: Lucy S., b. 10 Nov 1863, d. 22 Apr 1874 Providence RI, bur. in Mt. Hope Cem., Searsport ME.
Lucy G., b. 1844, d.y.
Sarah L., b. 12 May 1846, d. 20 Jul 1904 Searsport ME.
Sources: VR Rockland ME. M52, P82j.

716. **JOHN WESLEY[8] SAWYER** [see 501], b. 11 Oct 1832 Whitingham VT, d. Whitingham VT, m. 17 Oct 1855 Calista D. Gillette of Wilmington VT, b. 16 Apr 1833 d. 20 Sep 1878, dau. Walter and Britana (Whitney) Gillette. Miller, lumberman. In Gardner MA, Templeton MA, Brooklyn NY, Whitingham VT.
Nellie Callista, b. 1857, m. 12 Dec 1889 Wallace Cook of Brattleboro VT.
Charles Wesley, b. 13 Sep 1859, d. 2 Jan 1880, unm.
835 Harry Waters[9], b. 1863.
836 Lincoln Houghton[9], b. 1865.
Clara Salerina,b. 13 Dec 1867, m. 11 Mar 1891 Elbert J. Roberts.
Son, b. 1868, d. 18 Nov 1869.
Son, b. 16 Sep 1869, d. 18 Sep 1869.
Sources: VR SA/VT.

717. **JOSEPH S.[8] SAWYER** [see 502], b. 25 Nov 1838 Plymouth VT, d. 25 Jun 1927, m. 20 Dec 1863 Plymouth VT Ellen A. Madden of Sherburne VT, b. 22 Mar 1844 d. 18 Feb 1900, dau. Michael and Mary Madden. Farmer. In Pomfret VT 1870.

Mary Anna, b. 31 Aug 1864, m.(1) 29 Dec 1883 Edwin W. Tarbell, m.(2) Harley Matherson.

837 Charles J.[9], 1865-1952.

Chennie M., b. Mar 1870 Plymouth VT, m. 6 Mar 1893 Plymouth VT Eva J. Brown, b. 13 Oct 1873 d. 7 Jun 1929. Machinist. CH: Son, b. 15 Apr 1901; Harold Everett, b. 29 Feb 1902, m. Laura Strart (Stuart?), b.?.

Son, b. Feb 1873, d. 23 Feb 1873.

Henry E., b. ca. 1877, m. 21 Jul 1906 Anna A. Blanchard, b. ?. No CH.

Sources: Pomfret VT census 1870. VR SA/VT. Early Families of Plymouth VT.

718. **ALDEN S.[8] SAWYER** [see 503], b. 8 Feb 1854 Granville VT, d. 28 Nov 1892 Reading VT, m.(1) 3 Jul 1877 Cornish NH Ada S. Dodge of Weathersfield VT, b. 1857 d. 1877, dau. Ariel and Susan Dodge; m.(2) Ellen Brown, b. ?. Teamster. In Plymouth VT, Shrewsbury VT 1890.

Henry A., b. 10 Apr 1878, d. 23 Apr 1893.

Edson I., b. 6 Aug 1879, d. 1905.

Arthur Lorenzo, b. 3 Sep 1880, d. same day.

Gertrude E., b. 25 Jun 1882, m. 11 Jan 1900 Manchester NH Arthur L. Brooks.

Minnie A., b. 1 May 1884, d. 1939, m. 10 Sep 1902 Weathersfield VT Will H. Gardner.

838 John Clifford[9], 1886-1944.

Grace S., b. 4 Sep 1890, d. 9 May 1891.

Bessie Allen, b. 9 Nov 1891, m. 26 Feb 1908 William C. Peoples.

Roy Alden, b. 2 May 1893, d. 1895.

Sources: Shrewbury VT census 1890. VR SA/VT. D49, N6, Ada C. Durwood rec.

719. **FOSTER FORDYCE[8] SAWYER** [see 505], b. 10 Nov 1844 Bridgewater VT, d. 1915 Bridgewater VT, m. 18 Nov 1869 Bridgewater VT Aldana L. Stevens of Bridgewater VT, b. May 1850 d. 8 Mar 1915. Farmer.

Albert H., b. 9 Feb 1872 Bridgewater VT, d. 1934, m. 11 Oct 1894 Sarah J. Porter, b. ?.

Adella Rena, b. 5 Jul 1873, d. 25 Jun 1948, m.(1) 27 Aug 1889 Charles J. Bador, m.(2) Henry Clogston.

Anna Jesse, b. 16 Mar 1875, m. 30 Jul 1898 Royalston VT Norman S. Hunt.

839 Clayton Foster[9], 1882-1964.

Sources: Bridgewater VT census 1850. VR SA/VT. H70, Pauline Sawyer family Bible.

720. **WILLIAM WARE[8] SAWYER** [see 505], b. 10 Sep 1855 Woodstock VT, d. 6 Apr 1914 Billerica MA, m. 27 Dec 1881 Windsor VT (also rec. in Lebanon VT) Anna Fay Wyatt of Woodstock VT, b. 1856. Railroad worker. In Windsor VT, Keene NH.

Lee William, b. 11 Feb 1884 Windsor VT, m. 24 Nov 1915 Keene NH Florence M. Houghton of Keene NH, b. ?, dau. Hollis and Marcia (Carlisle) Houghton. Machinist. In Keene NH.

Walter Addison, b. 1 Sep 1885 Windsor VT, m. 15 Sep 1915 Keene NH Ethel A. King of Marlow VT, b. 1890, dau. Lewis S. and Mattie (Matthews) King. Jeweler. In Keene NH.

Lewis Fisk, b. 9 Jul 1887 Windsor VT, m. 18 Sep 1913 in Keene NH Grace L. Fairbanks of Keene NH, b. 1888, dau. Arthur L. and Lelia (Gates) Fairbanks.

Sybil, b. 1 Sep 1889.

Sydney Joseph, b. 1 Sep 1889 Windsor VT, d. 17 Jun 1934 Keene NH (suicide), b. 8 Oct 1913 Keene NH Sarah Annie Hutchinson of Keene NH, b. 1893, dau. Robert E. and Margaret J. (Magee) Hutchinson. Plumber. In Greenfield MA.

Sources: VR Keene NH, SA/NH, SA/VT.

721. **FRANK FREEMAN[8] SAWYER** [see 505], b. Jun 1857 Woodstock VT, m. 5 Aug 1898 Woodstock VT, Mrs. Annie L. Giles of Hartland VT, b. ?. Farmer. In Hartland VT, Woodstock VT 1898.

Fred A., b. 20 Mar 1899, d. 7 Apr 1911 Hanover NH.
Nettie May, b. 2 Sep 1900.
Lewis Frank, b. 8 Sep 1903.
Ida Laura, b. 8 Jun 1907.

Sources: VR SA/NH, SA/VT. H70.

722. **FREDERICK ALONZO[8] SAWYER** [see 505], b. 26 Jun 1860 Woodstock VT, m. 28 Nov 1888 Pomfret VT Lora Etta Newton of Cornish NH, b. Feb 1871. Farmer. In Barnard VT 1888.

Arthur Leon, b. 8 Aug 1889 Pomfret VT, m. Marcia Perry of Woodstock VT, b. ?. CH: Gordon Frederick, b. Jan 1926, d. June 1927 Hanover NH.
Florence E., b. 30 Jan 1891.
Flora E., b. 1 Jul 1894.
Horace A., b. Jul 1898.
Charles Frederick, b. 16 Jun 1907.

Sources: VR SA/VT. H70, B24.

723. **ALBERT EDWARD[8] SAWYER** [see 507], b. 28 Aug 1859 Pittsford VT, d. 13 Sep 1939 Bellows Falls VT, m. 5 Aug 1887 Lucia E. Jenkins of Springfield VT, b. 9 Dec 1864 d. 27 Nov 1913. Farmer. In Chester VT, Rockingham VT.

Lena L., b. 16 Feb 1888.
Thomas J., b. 4 Jan 1892.
Helen Marcella, b. 20 Dec 1894.

Sources: VR SA/VT.

724. **WALLACE JOHN[8] SAWYER** [see 508], b. 8 Nov 1846 Sudbury VT, d. 11 Aug 1912 Sudbury VT, m. 17 Nov 1870 Brandon VT Esther E. Ketcham of Whiting VT, b. 24 May 1845 d. 21 Feb 1937, dau. Platt and Susan (Washer) Ketcham. Farmer.

840 William Ketcham[9], 1872-1950.
Mabel S., b. 18 Mar 1878, d. 8 Apr 1951.
Arthur Ernest, b. 27 Oct 1882 Sudbury VT, m. Julia F. Bissett, b. ?. CH: Doris, b. 30 Jan 1916, m. Thomas Whittaker.

Sources: VR SA/VT. K5, D41.

725. **JAMES ALBERT[8] SAWYER** [see 509], b. 7 Jan 1837 Wentworth NH, d. 7 Aug 1920, m. 1 Jan 1861 Warren NH Sarah E. Blodgett, b. 23 May 1841 d. 6 Jan 1916, dau. Gerid and Priscilla (Noyes) Blodgett. In North Haverhill NH 1870.

Frank L., b. ca. 1862 Haverhill NH. In Woodstock NH 1880.
Rufus N., b. 2 Sep 1863 Rumney NH, d. 17 Jun 1923 Lisbon NH, m. 14 Dec 1901 Woodsville NH Alice (Dodge) Rowe of Lyman NH, wid. and divorcee, b. 18 Oct 1863 d. 21 Feb 1928, dau. Moody B. and Sally Dodge. Blacksmith. In Haverhill NH, Woodsville NH, Lisbon NH.
Abbie D., b. 1865, m. 17 Apr 1884 West Fairlee VT.
Carrie L., b. ca. 1868, m. 29 Nov 1888 George H. Gilman.
Elvah J., b. 1871, m. 16 Sep 1889 Haverhill NH Peter Campbell.
841 Benjamin Franklin[9], b. 1873.

Laura B., b. ca. 1876.
Ernest O., b. 31 Mar 1879 Haverhill NH.

Sources: North Haverhill NH census 1870, Woodsville NH census 1880. VR Warren NH, SA/NH. N6, W37.

726. **HARRY L.[8] SAWYER** [see 512], b. 27 Jun 1872 Cambridge MA, d. Aug 1965, m. Elvie H. Johnson of Biddeford ME, b. ?. In Auburn ME, Lewiston ME.

Helen, b. ?, m. ____ Howard.
Leroy Albert, b. 4 Dec 1892 Lewiston ME.
Lyndon, b. 28 Feb 1895, d. 2 Sep 1895.
Elvie, b. 2 Apr 1898.
Dorothy E., b. ca. 1904, d. 26 Apr 1987, m. 4 Apr 1929 Robert P. Reed.
Gladys, m. ____ Moulton.
Florence, m. ____ Burns.

Sources: VR SA/ME. Obit (Dorothy), Greenfield Sawyer rec.

727. **LELAND FREDERICK[8] SAWYER** [see 512], b. 5 Jun 1873 Cambridge MA, d. 30 Sep 1942, m. Anna E. Coburn of Carthage ME, b. 22 May 1883 d. 2 Mar 1922 Portland ME, dau. Greenfield and Dorcas (White) Coburn. In Carthage ME, Portland ME. He bur. in Carthage ME.

Edward Preston, b. Sep 1909,. d. 12 Oct 1909.
Leland Frederick, b. 11 Jun 1911, d. Jul 1935.
Chester A., b. 8 Sep 1914, m. 22 May 1937 Leah M. Week, b. ?.
Greenfield Coburn, b. 28 Feb 1918.

Sources: VR Cambridge MA, SA/ME.

728. **ALFRED GARFIELD[8] SAWYER** [see 512], b. 5 May 1882 Auburn ME, m. 20 Oct 1902 Emma Rogers of Lewiston ME, b. 1881. In Bangor ME.

Alfred Carlton, b. 21 Apr 1904, d. 16 Jun 1985, m. Ethelyn Rogers, b. ?.
Gertrude M., b. 7 Nov 1907, d. 6 Oct 1967.
George Edmund, b. 4 Feb 1912, d. 12 Aug 1969, m. 22 Dec 1934 Hortense L. Clement, b. ?.
Helen, b. 31 Jul 1917, m. Claude Morneault.

Sources: Greenfield Sawyer rec.

729. **GEORGE R.[8] SAWYER** [see 513], b. Dec 1849 Stowe VT, m. 2 Nov 1870 Stowe Vt Emma C. Fuller of Stowe VT, b. 7 Sep 1852 d. 18 Jul 1903, dau. Seth and Pamelia (Bingham) Fuller of Hartford VT. Farmer.

Nathaniel S., b. 3 Jul 1871 Stowe VT, m. 11 Mar 1890 Bertha E. Murray b. ?.
Hattie May, b. 25 Jun 1878, m. 17 Sep 1895 Wolcott VT Benoni S. Morey.

Sources: F44.

730. **CHARLES H.[8] SAWYER** [see 514], b. 1852 Middlesex VT, m. 8 Mar 1874 Moretown VT Martha L. McElery, b. 1850 d. 28 Dec 1904. In Moretown VT.

842 Carl R.[9], b. 1875.

Sources: VR SA/VT.

731. **ELIJAH L.[8] SAWYER** [see 518], b. 1836 Acworth NH, m.(1) Christiana Russell of Sudbury VT, b. 1839 d. 22 Mar 1879, dau. Joseph and Margaret Russell; m.(2) 25 Dec 1880 Jennie Blanchard, b. ?. Farmer. In Starksboro VT 1850.

Florence Attoile, b. 5 Mar 1859, m. 20 Mar 1878 Charles W. Gilley.

Theresa, b. 1861, d. 4 Jul 1862.
Joseph Warren, b. 24 Jul 1873 Starksboro VT.
Mabel, b. 28 May 1876, d. 22 Mar 1877.
Sources: Starksboro VT census 1850. VR SA/VT.

732. **FRANCIS HAVEN⁸ SAWYER** [see 522], b. 23 Apr 1849 Lancaster MA, m. 14 Aug 1872 Frances A. Moore of Sterling MA, b. 15 Apr 1848, dau. William and Sarah A. (Howard) Moore of Lancaster MA. Clerk. In Clinton MA 1877.
William Frank, b. 27 Dec 1874 Lancaster MA. In Clinton MA.
Edith Moore, b. 15 Jun 1877.
Sources: VR SA/MA. H79.

733. **CHARLES D.[8] SAWYER** [see 532], b. Apr 1853 Dorset VT, m. 19 Oct 1885 Northfield VT Alma L. Rich of Berlin VT, b. May 1856. Marble cutter.
Clemis Leon (f), b. 2 Aug 1886.
Harold F., b. 13 Oct 1888.
Don Edward, b. 12 Jun 1890.
Marjorie E., b. 15 Oct 1894.
Sources: VR SA/VT. John J. Sawyer, Jr rec.

734. **FRED K.[8] SAWYER** [see 532], b. 13 Aug 1860 Northfield VT, d. 1944 Northfield VT, m. 23 Jan 1886 Northfield VT Gertrude S. Simons of Wilmington (or Williamstown) VT, b. 7 Dec 1865 d. 1927, dau. Charles and Sarah L. Simons. He bur. in Elmwood Cem., Northfield VT.
843 John Joshua[9], 1890-1970.
Roy Simons, b. 7 Jan 1895, d. 19 Sep 1904.
Ray Hartwell, b. 7 Jan 1895, d. 6 Oct 1895.
844 Ralph Albert[9], b. 1903.
Sources: VR SA/VT. R9, Richard Sawyer rec., John J. Sawyer, Jr rec.

735. **EDWARD SOLOMON[8] SAWYER** [see 533], b. 3 Apr 1869 Berlin VT, d. 7 Dec 1900 Montpelier VT, m. 19 Mar 1896 Ellen Ada Baker of Berlin VT, b. ?. Electrician.
Harold B., b. 13 Sep 1896, lost at sea 1927.
Doris Ellen, b. 26 Aug 1897, d. 1932, m. Frederick Los Kamp.
Ruth, b. 3 Mar 1900.
Sources: VR SA/VT.

736. **HERBERT NOYES[8] SAWYER** [see 536], b. 6 Jul 1860 Atkinson NH, d. Jan 1946 Atkinson NH, m. 17 Oct 1886 N. Grace Pettengill, b. 25 Aug 1866 d. 14 Dec 1954. Dairy farmer.
845 Arthur Herbert[9], 1889-1974.
Clifford Augustus, b. 30 Aug 1894 Atkinson NH, d. Nov 1858 Atkinson NH, m. (1) 25 Nov 1920 Atkinson NH Marion E. Bridgeham of Haverhill MA, b. 6 Aug 1893 d. 24 Dec 1933, dau. Justin R. and Nellie F. (Noyes) Bridgeham; m.(2) 15 Aug 1936 Mabel E. Frost, b. 20 Nov 1905. Farmer.
Sources: B27.

737. **GEORGE ALANSON[8] SAWYER** [see 537], b. 24 May 1864 Atkinson NH, d. 5 Oct 1945 Atkinson NH, m. 8 Oct 1890 Lillie E. Noyes of Hampstead NH, b. 11 Jun 1865 d. 10 Feb 1925, dau. Captain Edward R. and Elvira P. (Noyes) Noyes. Dairy farmer.
Ruth Lillian, b. 5 Jan 1895, unm. Town Clerk for Atkinson NH 1943-1969.
846 Ralph Alanson[9], b. 1895.

Sources: N40, N9, Ruth L. Sawyer rec.

738. **LEONARD[8] SAWYER** [see 538], b. ca. 1835 Haverhill MA, m. 26 Feb 1862 Haverhill MA Lydia Stevens of Haverhill MA, b. 1841, dau. William and Lois Stevens. Shoemaker. In Haverhill MA 1850.

Florence, b. 30 Aug 1864.
Abbie J., b. 10 Dec 1865, m. 14 Jan 1885 Newburyport MA Fred Huntington.
George E., b. 27 May 1867 Haverhill MA.
Daisy, b. 26 Oct 1869.

Sources: Haverhill MA census 1850. VR Haverhill MA, SA/MA.

739. **CHARLES HENRY[8] SAWYER** [see 539], b. 17 Jul 1832 Haverhill MA, m. 27 May 1869 Danvers MA Lydia A. (Hunt) Hoyt of Moultonboro NH, b. ca. 1842, dau. Nathaniel and Eliza Hunt. Mechanic. In Malden MA 1850.

Louis C., b. ca. 1875 Danvers MA, m. 30 Nov 1893 Everett MA Belle L. Bean of Maine, b. ca. 1874, dau. Roscoe G. and Abbie Bean. Insurance salesman.

Sources: Malden MA census 1850. VR Haverhill MA, SA/MA.

740. **NOWELL FISHER[8] SAWYER** [see 540], b. ca. 1839 West Newbury MA, m.(1) 17 Nov 1867 Bradford MA Isabelle Fowler of Salisbury MA, b. 14 Apr 1842, dau. Obediah? and Abby (Barnard) Fowler; m.(2) 26 Jun 1873 Bradford MA Ella Georgianna Anderson of Freeport ME, b. 1849, dau. George and Bertha Anderson. Machinist.

Herbert Richard, b. 10 Dec 1868.
Richard Herbert, b. 21 Feb 1870 Bradford MA, d. 24 Aug 1945 Haverhill MA, m. Elizabeth ____, b. ?.
Georgianna Bell, b. 30 Jan 1876.
Mollie F., b. ?.
Fred, b. 13 May 1878 Bradford MA.
Marguerita, b. 19 Jun 1882.
Philip Nowell, b. 26 Sep 1883 Bradford MA.
Wallace L., b. 4 Sep 1885 Bradford MA, d. Jan 1950 Haverhill MA, m. Gertrude Clark, b. ?

Sources: VR Bradford MA, SA/MA.

741. **MOSES SARGENT[8] SAWYER** [see 540], b. ca. 1843 West Newbury MA, m.(1) 17 Jun 1869 Bradford MA Ellen Dennison of Groveland MA, b. 28 Aug 1849 d. 1870, dau. Charles and Hannah Dennison; m.(2) 7 Jul 1873 Bradford MA Elizabeth McKeene of New Sharon ME, b. 1852, dau. Jedidiah and Dora M. McKeene. Shoemaker.

Child, b. ?, d.y.
Richard Warren, b. 5 Dec 1884 Bradford MA.
Lois Trask, b. 18 Oct 1886.

Sources: West Newbury MA census 1850. VR Bradford MA, SA/MA. B12.

742. **ANDREW CHESLEY[8] SAWYER** [see 541], b. 22 Mar 1844 Levant ME, m. 18 Jul 1871 Bangor ME Ella E. Pendleton of Bangor ME, b. 4 May 1852, dau. Benjamin E. (descendant of John and Priscilla Alden) and Abigail (Trickey) Pendleton. Shoe manufacturer. Civil War. In Bangor ME 1864, 1880.

Howard Field, b. 18 Nov 1872 Bangor ME, m. 7 Oct 1896 Bangor ME Blanche Clayton of Hampden ME, b. 1873, dau. William and Laura (Knowles) Clayton. Treasurer of a shoe company. CH: Elizabeth, b. 30 Jun 1897.

847 Rowland Judson[9], 1873-1944.

848 Harold Chesley[9], 1880-1916.
Edith M., b. 19 May 1885.
Mabel L., b. 20 Jul 1887.
Sources: ME 1880 census index. VR Bangor ME, SA/ME. P26.

743. **JOSEPH WARREN[8] SAWYER** [see 541], b. 14 Apr 1848 Levant ME, d. 16 Dec 1902 Old Town ME, m. 6 Jan 1872 Old Town ME Ella F. Pratt of Old Town ME, b. Oct 1851, dau. Samuel and Lucy Pratt. Liveryman. In Old Town ME 1872.
Fred H., b. Oct 1872 Old Town ME, m. 5 Feb 1898 Greenville ME Sarah Alice Woodman of LaGrange ME, b. ca. 1875, dau. Henry C. and Marie (McLillan) Woodman. Liveryman.
Sources: ME 1880 census index. VR Old Town ME, SA/ME.

744. **CHARLES HASKELL[8] SAWYER** [see 541], b. 14 Apr 1863 Levant ME, m. Mary A. Davis of Augusta ME, b. Feb 1865. In Old Town ME, Foxcroft ME.
Gertrude, b. Nov 1888.
Clifford D., b. 5 Jul 1898 Foxcroft ME.
Sources: VR SA/ME.

745. **JOSEPH WARREN[8] SAWYER** [see 542], b. 20 Aug 1834 Calais ME, m. 4 Apr 1857 Ellen Jay, b. ca. 1835 d. 11 Dec 1902. In Calais ME 1860.
Thomas W., b. ca. 1858 Calais ME.
George H., b. May 1860, d. 9 Aug 1900.
Sources: Calais ME census 1860.

746. **STILLMAN OSGOOD[8] SAWYER** [see 542], b. 5 Dec 1842 Calais ME, d. 30 Nov 1917, m. 12 Feb 1866 Mary A. Hutchins of Calais ME, b. ?. Carpenter. Civil War. He bur. in Fairfield ME.
Joseph W., b. Dec 1866 Calais ME, m. 19 Apr 1899 A. Venice Mitchell of Unity ME, b. Dec 1876, dau. C_____E. and Lucy (Foss) Mitchell. Carpenter.
Nina E., b. 1872.
Sources: Calais ME census 1870. ME 1880 census index. VR SA/ME. M7A.

747. **LEVERETT AUGUSTUS[8] SAWYER** [see 544], b. 13 Jul 1830 Salem MA, d. 2 Feb 1899 Manchester NH, m.(1) ?; m.(2) 8 Jul 1869 Fitzwilliam NH Salome Ripley of Montague MA, b. ca. 1842; m.(3) Rebecca ____ of Ellsworth ME, b. ?. Agent. In New York City, Boston MA 1875.
849 Leverett Augustus[9], b. 1862.
Sources: VR SA/MA, SA/NH.

748. **LEWIS FREEMAN[8] SAWYER** [see 547], b. 9 Dec 1842 Tremont ME, d. 16 Sep 1919 Cranberry Isles ME, m. ca. 1870 Vienna B. Dix of Tremont ME, b. 1848. Lighthouse keeper.
Heber G., b. 1871 Tremont ME, d. 1927 Tremont ME, m. 1 Aug 1898 Eden ME Hattie I. Hodgdon of Tremont ME, b. 1873 d. 1950.
Leah J., b. 16 Apr 1874.
Sources: Tremont ME census 1870, ME 1880 census index. VR SA/ME.

749. **JOSHUA A.[8] SAWYER** [see 547], b. 26 Jan 1859 Tremont ME d. 19 Dec 1932, m. 1889 Alberta T. Hodgdon of Seal Cove ME, b. 1869. Farmer, carpenter. In Bernard ME.
850 Henry W.[9], b. 1890.
851 Chester J.[9], b. 1892.

Rena Marion, b. 12 Jun 1894, d. 3 Feb 1967, m. William Andrew Clark.
George Richard, b. 7 May 1896, d. 13 Oct 1918.
Charles Welsh, b. 26 Jun 1898, m. Evelyn Hopkins, b. ?. In Southwest Harbor ME.
852 Ralph R.[9], b. 1900.
Dorothy M., b. 25 Mar 1901, m. Hershal Allen Gay. Went to New York.
Sources: VR SA/ME. M8, Family Bible, Katherine Bowker rec.

750. **EMMONS PRAY[8] SAWYER** [see 549], b. Mar 1859 Tremont ME, d. 1928, m. 10 Sep 1883 Mary L. Dodge of Tremont ME, b. 1861 d. 1937, dau. Benjamin and Lucinda Dodge. Sea captain. In Southwest Harbor ME 1910. He bur. in Southwest Harbor ME.
Helen L., b. 28 Oct 1884, d. 1967, unm.
Marie M., b. Feb 1886, d. 21 Jan 1911, unm. In Southwest Harbor ME.
Marion S., b. 2 Aug 1888, d. 2 Nov 1986, unm.
853 Paul Alger[9], 1891-1971.
Edward Emmons, b. 9 Jun 1895, d. 1917 Hebron ME. unm.
Malcolm Raymond, b. 1904 Southwest Harbor ME, d. 1971 Ellsworth ME, m. Hazel M. Beal, b. 1908. Carpenter.
Sources: VR Ellsworth ME, SA/ME. M8, Obit, Richard M. Sawyer rec.

751. **WILLIAM ELMER[8] SAWYER** [see 550], b. 15 Jun 1863 Boothbay ME, d. 1941 Boothbay ME, m. 22 Dec 1890 Minnie Gove of Newcastle ME, b. Nov 1871 d. 1937. Sea captain. In ice business 1905. In Newcastle ME. Bur. in Center Cem., Boothbay ME.
Angie Ray, b. 18 Mar 1892, d. 12 Jun 1971, m. Frank Williams.
Valeria E., b. 31 Aug 1893.
Elmer F., b. 8 Jul 1894 Boothbay ME, d. 28 Jul 1915.
Sources: VR SA/ME. G41.

752. **MELVIN D.[8] SAWYER** [see 550], b. 14 Aug 1865 Boothbay ME, d. 4 Feb 1910 Boothbay ME, m. 1 Jan 1889 Boothbay ME Evelyn M. Reed of Boothbay ME, b. Jan 1872 d. 1960. Note: VR says her first name was Eire.
Frank W., b. Oct 1889 Boothbay Harbor ME, m. 18 Jan 1930 Portsmouth NH Mary Y. Cyr of Portland ME, b. 1901, dau. Cyr M. and Cedulic Cyr.
Stephen, b. 3 Nov 1892 Boothbay ME.
Paul, b. 1905.
Sources: VR SA/ME. M5, M29.

753. **MILES J.[8] SAWYER** [see 551], b. 1847 North Haven ME, m. Julia Merrick of Vinalhaven ME, b. ?. Carpenter.
Lottie A., b. 1869.
Allen Veranus, b. 26 Aug 1873 North Haven ME, d. 7 Jun 1954, m.(1) 12 Oct 1893 North Haven ME Angie A. Carver of Deer Isle ME, b. ?, m.(2) Rosalind E. Snowdeal, b. 1880 d. 1948. Mariner. He bur. Ash Point Cem., Ash Point ME. CH: Evelyn B., b. 2 May 1894; Randall W., b. 8 Mar 1896, d. May 1896; Julia E., b. 21 Mar 1898; Margery G., b. 2 Jan 1900; child, b. ?, d.y.
Sources: VR SA/ME. M5.

754. **ROSCOE OSCAR[8] SAWYER** [see 552], b. 21 Oct 1848 Unity ME, d. 25 Apr 1925, m. Sarah .E. Duffey of Bangor ME, b. 10 Dec 1848 d. 19 Sep 1917, dau. Bernard and Catherine (Brown) Duffy. Stevedore. In Gardiner ME 1880.
Mary E., b. 1871, d. 19 Apr 1882.

William Bernard, b. Feb 1877, d. 8 Dec 1937.
Virginia M., b. 9 Oct 1881, d. 29 May 1959.
Irving Roscoe, b. 2 Aug 1883 Gardiner ME, d. 11 Dec 1970.
Sources: ME 1880 census index, Gardiner ME 1890. VR Gardiner ME, SA/ME. P33, M7A, David Sawyer rec.

755. **TRUEMAN IRONS[8] SAWYER** [see 552], b. 31 Oct 1856 Thomaston ME (at sea), m. (1) 5 Apr 1884 (later div.) Marcia Belle Eldridge of Etna ME, b. 14 Feb 1863, dau. Thompson and Sarah (Eldridge) Eldridge; m.(2) 8 Jan 1906 Portsmouth NH Mary E. Murphy of Newcastle ME, b. 1873, dau. John and Mary (Cusick) Murphy of Ireland. Joiner. In Dixmont ME, Portland ME.
Homer Benson, b. 11 Aug 1884 Dixmont ME.
Harriet Merle, b. 10 Jan 1886.
William Leslie, b. 23 Oct 1887 Dixmont ME, m. Myrtle Stevens of Troy ME, b. ?. CH: Homer Irving, b. ca. 1928 Newport ME, m. 25 Jun 1958 Skowhegan ME Shirley M. Steward of Skowhegan ME, b. 1931, dau. William and Elise (Littlefield) Steward.
Irving Trueman, b. 13 Apr 1894 Dixmont ME.
Casta Agnes, b. 25 Mar 1896.
Kneeland Arthur, b. 16 Feb 1900.
Sources: VR Skowhegan ME, SA/ME. P33.

756. **WILLIAM NATHANIEL[8] SAWYER** [see 556], b. 28 Mar 1852 Isleboro ME, d. 28 Nov 1915 Bangor ME, m. 25 Nov 1875 Bangor ME Carrie M. Fenno of Boston MA, b. ?. Construction worker. In Bangor ME 1880.
Ina May, b. 15 Nov 1876, m. 1897 Nealy Barrows.
Winfield Fenno, b. 25 Nov 1890 Bangor ME.
Sources: ME 1880 census index. VR Bangor ME, SA/ME.

757. **CHARLES ORLANDO[8] SAWYER** [see 559], b. 15 Jan 1864 Searsport ME, d. 15 Mar 1930 Searsport ME, m. 13 Nov 1893 Searsport ME Clara May Carver of Searsport ME, b. 13 Feb 1872 d. 27 Nov 1934, dau. Caleb F. and Clara (Colcord) Carver. Hardware dealer. He bur. in Elmwood Cem., Searsport ME.
Franklin Carver, b. 11 May 1903, d. 26 Oct 1905.
Clara Elizabeth, b. 4 Oct 1907, d. 1 Sep 1984, unm.
Charles Kempton, b. 26 Mar 1912, d. 24 Jan 1992, m. 3 May 1939 Nina D. McKeen, b. ?.
Sources: VR SA/ME. M5, Obit (Charles), Jane McCormick rec.

758. **EDWIN LESLIE[8] SAWYER** [see 560], b. 28 Mar 1860 Searsport ME, d. 21 Dec 1928, m. 1 Jan 1890 Almont MI Nellie Anderson of Almont MI, b. 14 Feb 1863 d. 29 Aug 1949, dau. William and Janet (Shepherd) Anderson.
Jessie, b. 30 Nov 1890, d. 17 Jan 1971, m. 1 Jan 1910 Ralph Bishop.
Nellie Maria, b. 16 Apr 1898, d. 2 Apr 1977, m. 11 Oct 1924 Colin McCormick.
Leslie Edwin, b. 20 Nov 1901, d. 3 Oct 1986, m. 9 Sep 1924 June Clark.
Sources: Jane McCormick rec.

759. **HIRAM BLAISDELL[8] SAWYER** [see 560], b. 9 Jul 1867 Searsport ME, d. 23 Nov 1912 Portland ME, m. 2 Aug 1893 Presque Isle ME Evelyn M. Whitney of Presque Isle ME, b. 1875, dau. Charles and Ruth (Cunningham) Whitney. In Portland ME 1899.
Daughter, b. 26 Mar 1894, d. 27 Mar 1894.

Stephen Whitney, b. 12 Feb 1895 Presque Isle ME, m.(1) 29 Jul 1924 Gladys E. Pride, b. ? d. 24 Aug 1968; m.(2) 1968 Sarah R. Stinneford, b. ?. CH: Florence Evelyn, b. 22 Sep 1925, m. 17 Jun 1948 Furber S. Roberts.

Alice Evelyn, b. 9 May 1896, d. 6 Aug 1935, m. 6 Dec 1925 Thomas Cloonan.

Herbert Calkens, b. 13 May 1899 Portland ME, d. 27 Sep 1967.

Sources: VR SA/ME. Jane McCormick rec.

760. **WILLIAM⁸ SAWYER** [see 564], b. 14 Mar 1851 Charlestown MA, d. 22 Jun 1922 Brighton MA, m. 14 Jun 1877 Melrose MA Sarah Bemis Summers of Melrose MA, b. 24 Sep 1855 d. Apr 1943 Medford MA, dau. Samuel and Nancy (Bemis) Summers. Bookkeeper.

William, b. 5 Jan 1878 Charlestown MA, d. 11 Jan 1958 Medford MA, m. 12 Jun 1907 Somerville MA Carrie Isabel Lincoln of Cambridge MA, b. 30 Oct 1879 d. Jan 1973. CH: Mabel Irene, b. 12 Apr 1908, d. 21 Dec 1973.

Susan Ellen, b. 3 Jul 1879, d. Oct 1922, m. 3 Feb 1904 Charlestown MA Albert Crosby.

George Summers, b. 12 Feb 1890 Charlestown MA, d. 11 Sep 1959 Pennsylvania, m. 26 Aug 1920 Marguerite Hoffhers, b. ?.

Sources: VR SA/MA. D55, William Beyer rec.

761. **TIMOTHY THOMPSON⁸ SAWYER** [see 565], b. 19 Jul 1848 Cambridge MA, m. 28 Nov 1871 Florence A. Denio of Boston MA, b. Jun 1850 d. 28 Nov 1888, dau. Sylvanus and Mary A. (Rice) Denio. Bank president.

Clifford Denis, b. 19 May 1873, m. 14 Jul 1903 in Auburn ME Gertrude B. Hersey of Boston MA, b. ?.

Mary Thompson, b. 6 Feb 1877.

Sources: VR Cambridge MA, SA/MA. D31, H90.

762. **HORACE JAMES⁸ SAWYER** [see 566], b. 16 Jul 1843 Haverhill MA, d. 8 Jul 1920 Rye NH, m. 5 Nov 1868 Haverhill MA Susan M. Jenness of Rye NH, b. 30 May 1848 d. 6 Feb 1934, dau. Sheridan and E. (Batchelder) Jenness. Selectman for Rye NH 1899-1901.

Anna Knox, b. 1 Oct 1869, m. 24 Apr 1902 Joseph Watt.

Edward, b. 11 Jan 1872 Rye NH.

Horace Russell, b. 12 Apr 1876 Rye NH, m.(1) 10 Oct 1900 Mary Whidden of Portsmouth NH, b. 14 Aug 1877 d. 20 Sep 1922, dau. Charles S. and Alice M. (Jenness) Whidden; m.(2) 9 Oct 1923 Rye NH Agnes E. (Emerson) Perkins of Bradford NH, b. 1884, dau. Fred and Mary (Duff) Emerson.

Mildred, b. 19 Jan 1889.

Sources: Rye NH census 1880. VR Rye NH, SA/NH. P16.

763. **FRANK⁸ SAWYER** [see 566], b. 2 Dec 1849 Haverhill MA, m. 3 Sep 1873 Groveland MA, Angenette J. Hopkinson of Georgetown MA, b. 1855, dau. Joseph W. and Carrie Hopkinson. Railroad conductor. In Bradford MA 1873.

Son, stillborn 29 Dec 1873.

854 George Francis⁹, 1876-1933.

Fred Mighill, b. 10 Jul 1878. No CH.

John Fairfield, b. 2 Sep 1880 Lowell MA, m. 24 Apr 1907 Reading MA Louisa S. Holden, b. ?.

855 Harry Leonard⁹, b. 1897.

Russell, adopted, b. ?

Sources: VR Haverhill MA, Lowell MA, SA/MA, SA/NH. Harry L. Sawyer, Jr rec.

764. **CHARLES E.[8] SAWYER** [see 568], b. 16 Jan 1853 Longuell, Lower Canada, d. 26 Aug 1923 Rivere Du Loup, Quebec, Canada, m. 20 Nov 1880 Katherine A. McGarry, b. ? d. 26 Feb 1915. In Haverhill MA 1861, Sherbrook Canada 1863, Portland ME 1872, Canada 1874.

Charles E., b. 27 Dec 1880, d. 18 Jun 1940.
Son, b. 20 Jan 1883, d. 23 Jan 1883.
856 William Michael[9], 1884-1946.
Frank, b. 2 Apr 1886, d. 9 Feb 1894.
George, b. 4 Jun 1888, d. 1 Feb 1894.
Frederick, b. 13 Aug 1890, d. 19 May 1937.
Ethel, b. 13 Jul 1892, m. Thomas Walsh.
Edward James, b. 9 Feb 1894.
Frances, b. 28 Aug 1895.
George, b. 21 Oct 1897.

Sources: Wilfred M. Sawyer rec.

765. **ROMAIN A.[8] SAWYER** [see 569], b. 1845 Stockbridge VT, m. 19 Jun 1869 Lowell MA Ellen F. Goodwin of Maine, b. 1851, dau. Edwin and Jane Goodwin. Machinist. In Worcester MA.

857 Arthur H.[9], b. 1873.
Bessie Edith, b. 26 Mar 1890, m. Clyde Hunt of Stockbridge VT.

Sources: VR SA/MA. H38.

766. **ELIHU L.[8] SAWYER** [see 569], b. 1856 Stockbridge VT, m. 2 Mar 1878 Stockbridge VT Katie S. Whitcomb of Stockbridge VT, b. ?. Physician. In Oakham MA, Exeter NH.

Elizabeth H., b. May 1879, d. 3 Jan 1885.
Alpha Reuben, b. 3 Oct 1881 (Oakham MA?).
Inez L., b. 12 Jun 1887.

Sources: VR SA/VT, SA/MA. W71.

767. **ALBERT FRANKLIN[8] SAWYER** [see 572], b. 18 Nov 1855 East Alstead NH, d. 9 May 1925 Manchester NH, m.(1) 18 Nov 1878 Hooksett NH Alice J. Putnam of Hooksett NH, b. 1855 d. 10 May 1895; m.(2) Laura A. Niles of New York, b. 23 May 1856 d. 17 Dec 1930, dau. Palmer and Ann (Reynolds) Niles of Vermont. Carpenter. In Manchester NH 1875.

Albert H., b. 7 Nov 1883 Manchester NH, m. 31 Aug 1908 Orford NH Grace C. Snow of Orford NH, b. 1883, dau. Herbert W. and Abbie S. (Giffin) Snow. Machinist. In Beverly MA.
Earl Frank, b. 9 May 1891, d. 20 Feb 1915, unm.
Carrie Niles, b. 26 May 1898, d. 8 Sep 1912.

Sources: VR SA/NH.

768. **JOHN WESLEY[8] SAWYER** [see 572], b. 10 Jun 1866 Alstead NH, d. 23 Aug 1935 Manchester NH m. 17 Oct 1888 Troy NH Mabel Alice Nims of Winchendon MA, b. 29 May 1869, dau. Samuel H. and Lavinia (Holt) Nims. Hostler. In Winchendon MA, Keene NH, Manchester NH 1902.

858 Kenneth Earl[9], 1892-1971.
859 Robert Nims[9], 1894-1971.

Sources: VR SA/MA, SA/NH. S31, Edgar Allard rec.

769. **JOSEPH AMOS[8] SAWYER** [see 572], b. 14 Jun 1869 Alstead NH, d. 17 Aug 1931 Jaffrey NH, m. 22 Sep 1892 Winchendon MA Lorie E. Flagg of Winchendon MA, b. ca. 1869, dau. Levi and Locia (Arnold) Flagg. Engineer. In Jaffrey NH 1921.

Arnold David, b. 24 Jul 1893 Winchendon MA.
Sources: VR SA/MA, SA/NH. A27.

770. **SETH C.[8] SAWYER** [see 576], b. 24 Mar 1851 New Sharon ME, d. 10 Mar 1916 Centerville ME, m.(1) Industry ME Cynthia Foster, b. ?; m.(2) 14 Feb 1880 Ella Georgia Jeffers, b. Feb 1865 d. 30 Dec 1923. In Strong ME. He bur. in Riverside Cem., Centerville ME.
Lillian, b. 18 Jan 1882, d. 15 Oct 1882.
Clinton W., b. Dec 1889 New Sharon ME. In Strong ME.
Sources: VR SA/ME. Jeanne Sawyer rec.

771. **BENJAMIN F.[8] SAWYER** [see 576], b. 9 Aug 1853 New Sharon ME, d. 14 Aug 1909 Gorham ME, m. 21 Aug 1889 Sarah (Allen) McKeen of New Brunswick, Canada, b. 16 Jan 1855 d. 6 Nov 1920 Skowhegan ME. Farmer.
Bessie, b. ?.
Fred, b. 26 May 1892 New Sharon ME.
Arthur L., b. 1 Aug 1895 New Sharon ME.
Ella Grace, b. 22 Jun 1899.
Sources: VR SA/ME. Jeanne Sawyer rec.

772. **EDWARD[8] SAWYER** [see 576], b. 13 Nov 1855 New Sharon ME, d. 1928 Farmington ME, m.(1) 3 Oct 1875 New Sharon ME Mary E. Chapman of New Sharon ME, b. ?; m.(2) Althea Bates, b. ? d. 16 Oct 1885; m.(3) 2 Jan 1886 New Sharon ME Leonora M. Hosmer of Farmington ME, b. 4 Jun 1867 d. 21 Sep 1895, dau. Leonard and Ruth (Welch) Hosmer; m.(4) 30 Dec 1896 New Sharon ME Elmira (Parlin) Gilbert, b. 1862, dau. Nathan and Mary (Fairbanks or Furbish) Parlin. Farmer. He bur. in Weeks Mill Cem., New Sharon ME.
Susie A., b. 1877.
Mabel, b. ?, d. at five mos.
Francis, b. 20 May 1895 Farmington ME.
Earle D., b. 20 May 1895, d. 30 Oct 1918.
Orland, b. 30 Sep 1899.
Sources: ME 1880 census index. VR New Sharon ME, Vienna ME, SA/ME. Jeanne Sawyer rec.

773. **CHARLES H.[8] SAWYER** [see 576], b. 19 Jun 1860 New Sharon ME, d. 22 Mar 1914 New Sharon ME (suicide), m.(1) 5 Mar 1892 Vienna ME Emma M. Austin of Vienna ME, b. ?, dau. Alexander and Fanny (Grant) Austin; m.(2) 16 Mar 1895 Vienna ME Nellie (Dalkens) Cramer of Chesterville ME, b. 20 Jun 1866 d. 15 Jun 1907, dau. Levi and Martha (Penley) Dalkens. Farmer. He bur. Weeks Mills Cem., New Sharon ME.
Henry C., b. 28 Jan 1896, d. 7 Feb 1896.
Ralph T., b. 29 Jan 1897 Chesterville ME.
Elizabeth, b. 27 Oct 1905, d. 9 Mar 1906.
Sources: VR New Sharon ME, Vienna ME, SA/ME. M5, Jeanne Sawyer rec.

774. **ALBERT[8] SAWYER** [see 577], b. 10 Nov 1854 New Sharon ME, d. 27 Sep 1915 New Sharon ME, m. Angie Brann, b. Apr 1858 d. 5 Mar 1888. In New Sharon ME. Both bur. Village Cem., New Sharon ME.
860 Arthur Burtt[9], 1881-1970.
Sources: VR New Sharon ME, SA/ME. M5, Jeanne Sawyer rec.

775. **TRUMAN[8] SAWYER** [see 578], b. Jan 1869 Castle Hill ME, m. 21 Apr 1894 Presque Isle ME Clara T. Ross of Mapleton ME, b. Dec 1870, dau. Alexander and Margaret (Hilace) Ross. Carpenter. In Thomaston ME, Mapleton ME.

861 Maurice Truman[9], 1897-1993.

Charlie A., b. 9 Sep 1898 Mapleton ME, d. 20 Mar 1992 Concord NH, m.(1) 4 Sep 1920 Flora M. Ross of Presque Isle ME, b. ?, dau. James and Blanche (Rowe) Ross; m.(2) Mabel Preble, b. ?.

Nellie, b. 23 Oct 1899, m. 27 Aug 1925 Errol L. Buker.

Lawrence A., b. 18 Aug 1903 Presque Isle ME, m. 24 Jan 1925 Portsmouth NH Helen Poland of Friendship ME, b. 1905, dau. Harry and Jennie (Hathorn) Poland. In Thomaston ME.

Elwood R., b. 13 Dec 1904.

Sources: VR Skowhegan ME, Portsmouth NH, SA/ME. Obit (Charlie A.), Nellie Buker rec., Charlie A. Sawyer rec.

776. **HOWARD[8] SAWYER** [see 578], b. 22 Mar 1870 Castle Hill ME, m. Mary Adams, b. ?. In Garland ME.

Elvis S., b. 26 Jan 1907, d. 5 Feb 1994, m. Lewis Hall.

Merna, m. ____ Dorr.

Wilma, unm.

Leta

Ervin, m. ____ Titcomb.

Sources: Obit (Elvis), Charlie A. Sawyer rec., Ivan H. Sawyer rec.

777. **WINFIELD[8] SAWYER** [see 578], b. Jan 1872 Mapleton ME, d. 12 May 1916 Bangor ME, m. 28 Nov 1894 Presque Isle ME Alice E. Griffin of Mapleton ME, b. Oct 1872, dau. Albert and Mary (Waldron) Griffin. Farmer. In Mapleton ME 1880.

John Henry, b. 22 Jul 1897 Mapleton ME.

862 Ivan H.[9], 1898-1989.

Sources: ME 1880 census index. VR SA/ME. Charlie A. Sawyer rec.

778. **MILTON J.[8] SAWYER** [see 579], b. 28 Dec 1863 New Sharon ME, d. 4 Jul 1908 Methuen MA, m.(1) 15 Jul 1888 Harvard MA Hattie York of Boston MA, b. ?, dau. Henry A. and Mary York; m.(2) 1 Jan 1894 Emma Hall of England, b. 19 Feb 1866 d. 3 Apr 1943. Salesman. He bur. in New Sharon ME.

Elizabeth Margaret, b. 17 Nov 1894, m. Albert Jackson.

Olive Marion, b. 14 Jun 1896, m.(1) Ralph Kimball, m.(2) Stanley Crocker.

Harold Arthur, b. 23 or 25 May 1898 Methuen MA.

Walter Wesley, b. 27 Apr 1899, d. 1939, unm.

Ruth Hall, b. 27 Sep 1902, m. Raymond I. Knightly.

Lyman Milton, b. 25 Sep 1904, d. 1958.

Sources: VR SA/MA. Clark J. Sawyer rec., Louise Knightly rec.

779. **JOHN BRYANT[8] SAWYER** [see 579], b. 10 Sep 1884 Easton ME, d. 29 May 1984, m. Elinor Clark, b. 20 Mar 1893 d. 13 Nov 1983. Lawyer. In Wakefield MA

Clark Jefferson., b. 23 Jan 1917 Wakefield MA, m. Lilianne Wilbur, b. 2 May 1923. In North Reading MA.

Alan Reed, b. 18 Jul 1919 Wakefield MA, m. Erika Heininger, b. ?. In Vancouver BC, Canada.

Janet Bryant, b. ?, m. Joseph Sheridan. Went to Washington DC.

Carol Louise, b. ?, m. in Redland CA (later div.) ____ Osborn.
Sources: Nellie M. Buker rec., John B. Sawyer rec.

780. **CHARLES H.$^{8}$ SAWYER** [see 581], b. 1868 Norridgewock ME, m. 23 Sep 1896 Norridgewock ME Mary L. Anderson of California, b. 1870, dau. Elijah M. and Mary O. (Loring) Anderson. Artist.

Harold B., b. ?, d. Jul 1980, m. Milicent M. ____, b. ?.
Sources: VR SA/ME. Milicent M. Sawyer rec.

781. **ANSON DAVID$^{8}$ SAWYER** [see 585], b. 13 Feb 1832 Tinmouth VT, d. 29 Mar 1879 Osborn KS, m. 31 Jul 1866 Phebe E. Goffe, b. 12 Dec 1845, dau. Isaac C. and Elizabeth (Crawford) Goffe.

Miles Standish, b. 1 Mar 1868 Tinmouth VT, m. 6 Apr 1893 Julia E. Harlow, b. ?. In Rutland VT. CH: Dorothy, b. 27 Dec 1893.
Oliver H., b. 18 Jun 1878 Tinmouth VT.
Sources: C99.

782. **HENRY ARTHUR$^{8}$ SAWYER** [see 585], b. 19 Mar 1834 Tinmouth VT, d. 6 Oct 1899 Rutland VT, m. 15 May 1866 Julia A. Putnam of Ludlow VT, b. 15 Nov 1841 d. 19 Oct 1908, dau. James and Sarah A. (Mason) Putnam. Book merchant. In Moira NY 1843, Boston MA 1852, Rutland VT 1861.

Daughter, stillborn 29 Nov 1867.
863 James Putnam$^{9}$, b. 1873.
Mary Lucretia, b. 21 Dec 1874, d. 12 Jul 1911, m. 5 Jun 1901 Henry W. Hudson of New York.
David Henry, b. 6 Sep 1878, d. 19 Dec 1910.
Sources: VR SA/VT. C99.

783. **PALMER STAFFORD$^{8}$ SAWYER** [see 585], b. 1 Jul 1839 Tinmouth VT, d. 20 May 1904 Rutland VT, m. Harriet M. Spencer of Moriah NY, b. ca. 1840. In Rutland VT 1867.

Harriet M., b. 1862, m. 8 Mar 1888 E____ A. Savery.
Herbert D., b. 24 Apr 1867, m. Edith Sager, b. ?. In Boston MA. CH: Henry Stafford, b. 15 Jun 1905.
Fred H., b. 21 Aug 1875 Rutland VT, d. 8 Dec 1947 Rutland VT, m. Noel ____. CH: Addie Allen, b. ?, d; 15 Dec 1920.
Sources: VR SA/VT. D11.

784. **AARON B.$^{8}$ SAWYER** [see 586], b. 28 Dec 1835 Thetford VT, m. Betsey W. Howe, Haverhill MA, b. Jan 1833 d. 21 Jun 1905 Thetford VT, dau. William Howe. Farmer.

Charles A., b. 25 Apr 1856, d. 11 Jun 1872.
Allen A., b. 1858 Thetford VT, m. 4 Feb 1882 Marcia F. Johnson of Thetford VT, b. ?. Miner. In Hartford VT 1891. CH: Lottie Annie, b. 19 Nov 1891, d. 19 Jun 1894.
Eugene Nelson, b. 27 Aug 1860 Thetford VT, d. 25 Dec 1937, m. 27 Mar 1882 Thetford VT Roxy Avery, b. Nov 1864. Farmer. In Thetford VT 1900. CH: Son, b. 1 Mar 1884; dau., b. 4 Dec 1886; Alice Mary, b. 14 Aug 1898.
Olive A., b. 1 Oct 1861.
864 George Washington$^{9}$, 1863-1902.
Lucy A., b. 5 Nov 1865, m. 12 Nov 1884 Luther W. Roberts.
Nellie, b. 6 Dec 1867, d. 16 Apr 1879.
Abigail E., b. 21 May 1871, m. 1 Nov 1893 Albert E. Nutbrown.

865 Charles F.[9], b. 1873.
Sources: Thetford VT census 1900. VR SA/VT. G30.

785. **RICHARD[8] SAWYER** [see 586], b. 1844 Thetford VT, d. 19 Jun 1887 Thetford VT, m. 27 Aug 1867 Thetford VT Mary A. Colby of Thetford VT, b. Oct 1848. Farmer.

Lyman M., b. 6 Oct 1870 Thetford VT, d. 10 May 1932 Hanover NH.

Ernest Edward, b. 1871 Thetford VT, m.(1) 9 Sep 1893 Wentworth NH Mary M. Dimond of Groton VT, b. 1878; m.(2) 20 Aug 1903 Brighton ME (div. 11 Jan 1913) Lula M. (Dimick) Littlefield, b. 1877, dau. William and Mattie (Hawking) Dimick; m.(3) 26 Aug 1914 Wentworth NH Alta (Browne) Burnham b. 1867 Dorchester NH, dau. Joseph and Nancy (Batchelder) Browne. Miner. In Groton NH, Conway NH, Rumney NH. CH: Nellie May, b. 2 Apr 1895; son, b. 17 Dec 1899, d. 19 Dec 1899; son, b. 23 Feb 1911 Conway NH, d. same day.

Flora B., b. 2 Mar 1877, m. 29 May 1903 Ernest B. Cross.

Mary J., b. ca. 1879.

Nettie M., b. Nov 1881, m. 14 Nov 1900 Charles H. Badger.

866 Philip M.[9], b. 1882.
Sources: Thetford VT census 1870, 1880. VR SA/VT. N6.

786. **ORIN A.[8] SAWYER** [see 588], b. 1850 Plymouth NH, m. 7 Apr 1870 Mary S. Farrell of New York City, b. 1850, dau. James Farrell. Overseer. In Peterborough NH, Lowell MA 1872.

Elmer, b. ca. 1871.

Myron, b. 2 Apr 1872.

Nettie M., b. 28 Sep 1874, m. 7 Aug 1893 Lowell MA Fred L. Roberts.

Evelyn Inez, b. 5 May 1878.

Sources: Plymouth NH census 1850. Peterborough NH census 1870. VR SA/MA.

787. **WALTER W.[8] SAWYER** [see 589], b. ?, m. Alice Merrison, b. ?. In Bridgeport CT, Troy NY, San Francisco CA.

Harold M., b. 1882 Troy NY, d. 1951 San Francisco CA, m. 1913 Eleanor Ecob, b. ?. No CH.

Sources: A20.

788. **EDWIN CHESTER[8] SAWYER** [see 591], b. 24 Jan 1884 Morgan VT, m. East Charleston VT Bernice E. Taylor, b. 16 Dec 1887, dau. Harry A. and Mary Ellen (Morrell) Taylor. In Brighton VT, North Stratford NH.

Leonard Bertram, b. 22 Feb 1910.

Sources: VR SA/VT.

789. **ALBERT HENRY[8] SAWYER** [see 592], b. 15 Feb 1885 Lebanon NH, m. 18 Dec 1913 New Haven CT Jessie L. Howard of Keene NH, b. 1898, dau. George M. and Eunice (Rumerill) Howard. In Marlow NH, Keene NH.

Frederick Leroy, b. ?, m. Dorothy Efantis, b. ?.

Lillian, b. ?, m. ____ Gagliarducci.

Sources: Lillian Gagliarducci rec.

790. **CHARLES EUGENE[8] SAWYER** [see 598], b. 19 Mar 1882 Andover VT, d. 1960, m.(1) 1 Jan 1907 Andover VT Sadie L. Cutler, b. ? d. 1925; m.(2) 1930 Lucy S. Gleason, b. ?. In Springfield VT.

Katherine E., b. 2 Oct 1906, m. 1941 A. Edwin Keene.

Carlton James, b. 1909, d. 1970, m. Olga Harmon, b. ?.
Gerald Eugene, b. 1911, d. 1981, m. 1936 Theodore Johnson.
Philip Charles, b. 1915, d. 1919.
Mary L., b. 1919, m.(1) 1940 Alfred Booska, m.(2) 1970 Robert Keller.
Genevieve R., b. 1921, m. 1941 Bernard Eldredge. To Staunton VA.
Phyllis, b. 1931, m. Marshall Parker.
Kenneth Wayne, b. 1932, m. Suzanne M. Amblo.

Sources: VR SA/VT. Lucy Sawyer rec., Katherine Keene rec.

791. **AMOS BAILEY$^{8}$ SAWYER** [see 599], b. 22 Feb 1814 Troy NH, d. 9 May 1864 Swanzey NH, m. 18 Nov 1847 Dorothy Davis of Fitzwilliam NH, b. 27 Apr 1824, dau. Chauncey and Eunice (Knight) Davis. Miller. In Fitzwilliam NH, Swanzey NH 1860. Wid. m. 14 Jun 1865 Otis Hayden.

Albert Henry, b. 29 Feb 1849 Swanzey NH, d. 24 Jul 1890 Fitzwilliam NH, m. 25 Dec 1873 Clara Emma Hale of Massachusetts, b. 8 Oct 1854 d. 13 Apr 1883. Stonecutter. CH: Gertrude E. b. ca. 1876, m. 12 Jul 1892 Troy NH Wilbur L. Blossom.

Sources: Fitzwilliam NH census 1850, 1880. Swanzey NH census 1860. R7, N6.

792. **HENRY$^{8}$ SAWYER** [see 599], b. 27 Apr 1832 Swanzey NH, d. 24 Feb 1867 Winchendon MA, m. 3 Aug 1853 Winchester MA Keziah Jane Small of Ashburnham MA, b. 25 Nov 1832, d. 9 Mar 1919, dau. Joseph Small. Laborer.

867 Walter Henry$^{9}$, 1854-1933.
Edwin James, b. 3 Aug 1863 Winchendon MA.
Ellen Jane, b. 3 Aug 1863, d. 9 Mar 1868.

Sources: VR SA/MA. Bradley Sawyer rec.

793. **LYMAN A.$^{8}$ SAWYER** [see 603], b. 14 Apr 1832 Sedgwick ME, d. 23 Aug 1907, m. (I) 29 Apr 1854 Maria Cordelia Blake, b. 25 Apr 1836 d. 22 Nov 1879, dau. Daniel and Christiana (Colson) Blake. Mariner. Civil War: Captain. In Wetmore Isle ME 1850, Brooksville ME 1860, Orland ME 1870. He bur. in Leaches Point ME.

868 Frank Lyman$^{9}$, b. 1855.
Rose L., b. 8 Aug 1858, d. 15 Nov 1937, m. 12 May 1877 Conrad T. Ames.

Sources: Wetmore Isle ME census 1850. Brooksville ME census 1860. Orland ME census 1870. VR Orland ME. M7A, Elizabeth Wescott rec.

794. **JAMES CARLTON$^{8}$ SAWYER** [see 603], b. 17 Jul 1833 Blue Hill ME, d. 7 Oct 1907 Bucksport ME, m.(1) Martha B. Bowden, b. ca. 1834 d. 13 Jul 1874; m.(2) 19 May 1875 Emma F. Hutchings of Ellsworth ME, b. 19 Nov 1849 d. 28 Oct 1924, dau. James Cook and Emaline (Lawrence) Hutchings. Mariner. Civil War: Enl. Co. D, 1st Maine Cavalry, Sep 1861 Orland ME. In Wetmore Isle ME 1850, Orland ME 1870, Bucksport ME 1900.

869 Carlton Augustus$^{9}$, 1866-1938.
870 Ira (Ahira) Hiram$^{9}$, 1868-1895.
James Ulysses, b. ca. 1872 Orland ME, d. 5 Jun 1907, m. 2 May 1897 Boothbay Harbor ME Willette Williams, wid., b. ca. 1860, dau. Wilmot ____. Laborer. CH: Alice F., b. 9 Jan 1898, d. 15 Feb 1898 Boothbay Harbor ME.
Lyman E., b. 8 Mar 1876 Orland ME, d. 13 Apr 1932 Bangor ME. Tanner.
Arthur M., b. ca. 1878 Orland ME. Butcher.
Martha A., b. 1880, d. 1911, m. Herbert L. Redman.
871 Albina Hall$^{9}$, 1885-1965.
Bertha B., b. Aug 1888, d. 1911, m. Walter S. Gross.

Lillian F. b. ?, m. William W. Durfee.

Sources: Wetmore Isle ME census 1850, 1860. Orland ME census 1870. ME 1880 census index. Bucksport ME census 1900. VR Orland ME, SA/ME. M8, M7A, James L. Sawyer rec., Frederick W. Sawyer III rec.

795. **JOHN WESLEY[8] SAWYER** [see 603], b. 5 Aug 1844 Wetmore Isle ME, d. 12 Apr 1904 Bar Harbor ME, m. 23 May 1878 Orland ME Minnie Nancy Hutchings of Orland ME, b. 12 Feb 1862 d. 19 Dec 1937, dau. James C. and Emeline (Lawrence) Hutchings. Sea captain. In Wetmore Isle ME 1850, Orland ME 1870, Garland ME 1883, Bucksport ME 1886, Eden ME 1910. Wid. m. Patrick Haley.

Edwin John, b. June 1879 Orland ME. Trucker.

Chloe J., b. Sep 1880, m. David A. Young.

872 Frederick Wesley[9], 1883-1942.

873 Raymond Leslie[9], b. 1886.

874 William R.[9], 1888-1964.

Sources: Wetmore Isle ME census 1850, 1860. Orland ME census 1870, ME 1880 census index. Eden ME census 1910. M8. Frederick W. Sawyer III rec.

796. **JOSEPH W.[8] SAWYER** [see 603], b. Aug 1847 Wetmore Isle ME, d. 19 May 1901 South Portland ME, m.(1) 4 Oct 1868 Nellie L. Colson, b. 1847; m.(2) AddieJ. ____, b. 1852; m.(3)(I) 27 Mar 1885 Cape Elizabeth ME Hattie A. Paige of Bucksport ME, b. ?. In Wetmore Isle ME 1850, Bucksport ME 1870, So. Portland ME 1899.

Willie F., b. Dec 1869 Bucksport ME, d. 1941, m. Mary S. Phillips, b. 1869 d. 1929. In Eden ME 1910. He bur. in North Ellsworth ME. CH: Mamie, b. ?, d. @ 3 yrs.

Fred W., b. ca. 1877 Bucksport ME.

Flora E., b. ca. 1878.

Addie G., b. 19 Aug 1886, d. 26 Sep 1886.

Mildred W., b. Mar 1890.

Bertha A., b. Nov 1894.

Esther Miriam, b. 3 Sep 1897.

Ivy M., b. 30 Jul 1899.

Sources: Wetmore Isle ME census 1850, 1860. Bucksport ME census 1870. ME 1880 census index. VR Cape Elizabeth ME, Orland ME, SA/ME. Frederick W. Sawyer III rec.

797. **GEORGE W.[8] SAWYER** [see 604], b. ca. 1852 Georgia VT, d. 29 May 1904 Tewksbury MA, m. 9 Aug 1873 Lowell MA Josephine E. Boyden of Georgia VT, b. 22 Apr 1853 d. 10 Oct 1886, dau. Edgar and Olive (Miner) Boyden. Farmer.

Edward, b. 13 Dec 1875, d. 7 Sep 1877.

875 Charles Henry[9], 1879-1962.

Mary Eliza, b. 22 Sep 1882, unm.

Sources: VR SA/VT. W58.

798. **LEANDER PRICE[8] SAWYER** [see 605], b. 18 Oct 1854 Lyme CT, m. 4 Jun 1877 Lydia Jennie Flint of Lyme CT, b. 12 Apr 1858 d. 7 Jan 1922, dau. William H. and Catherine (Flynn) Flint. In Milford CT.

Mabel I., b. 27 Aug 1877, m. Benjamin F. King.

William Flint, b. Jul 1885, m. Gertrude H. Webb, b. ?.

Ethel M., b. 6 Feb 1887, m. 25 Jun 1912 Everett M. Spicer.

Sources: B89, B77.

799. **MADISON PAUL[8] SAWYER** [see 606], b. 6 Aug 1846 Newbury NH, m. 27 Apr 1876 Harriet E. Hapgood, b. 14 Jul 1840, dau. George and Marcia (McGraw) Hapgood. Miller.

George Hapgood, b. 20 Nov 1879 Nashua NH.
James Madison, b. 13 Feb 1883 Nashua NH.
Kittie Clark, b. 2 Sep 1884, d. 30 May 1885.

Sources: ME 1880 census index. VR Nashua NH. H16.

800. **WILLIAM DAVIS[8] SAWYER** [see 614], b. 22 Nov 1866 Dover NH, m. 12 Nov 1890 Susan G. Hall of Dover NH, b. 1866, dau. Joshua G. and Susan E. Hall. Yale graduate 1889. Lawyer, manufacturing (Sawyer Mills, Dover NH). In New York City.

Jonathan, b. 24 Aug 1891 Dover NH.
Elizabeth Bigelow, b. 24 Jan 1898, d. 20 Jun 1988 Durham NH.

Sources: P82i, W38. Obit (Elizabeth).

801. **CHARLES FRANCIS[8] SAWYER** [see 614], b. 16 Jan 1869 Dover NH, d. 27 Dec 1839 Dalton MA, m. 29 Jan 1895 Honolulu HI Gertrude C. Severence of San Francisco CA, b. ?, dau. Hon. Henry W. and Hannah (Childs) Severence. Yale graduate. Lawyer. Woolen manufacturer, Dover Mills. In Dalton MA 1910.

Henry Severence, b. 15 Aug 1907, d. 21 Feb 1991, m. Helen Kelsey, b.?

Sources: Dalton MA census 1910. W38. Obit (Henry).

802. **JAMES COWAN[8] SAWYER** [see 614], b. 30 Mar 1872 Dover NH, m. 10 Jun 1897 Mary P. Frost of Dover NH, b. 18 Sep 1871, dau. George S. and Martha (Low) Frost. Yale graduate 1894. Lawyer. Treasurer, Phillips Academy, Andover MA. In Durham NH.

George Frost, b. 25 Jun 1902 Boston MA, d. 16 Jan 1992 Durham NH, m. 26 Sep 1931 Claremont NH Isabella Deane (Jones) Frye, b. 1907, dau. Thomas W. and Katherine D. Jones. In Andover MA.
Charles Henry, b. 20 Oct 1906.

Sources: F32, W38, Obit (George F.), George F. Sawyer rec.

803. **FRANK T.[8] SAWYER** [see 620], b. 1849 Whitefield NH, m. 1 Jul 1870 Whitefield (div. 2 Nov 1897) Addie A. Hicks of Jefferson NH, b. 1854. Farmer. In Carroll NH, Lancaster NH, Jefferson NH 1880, Lynn MA.

876 Fred Weston[9], b. 1871.
Frank N., b. 1874 Jefferson NH.
George F., b. 1877 Jefferson NH, m. 15 Jun 1907 in Littleton NH Annie Tibbetts of Stewartston NH, b. 1879, dau. Seth. and Isobell Tibbetts. Jeweler. In Groveton NH. CH: Isobel, b. ?, m. 29 May 1931 Hunter S. Kingsbury.
Morris D., b. 1880 Jefferson NH.

Sources: Jefferson NH census 1880. VR SA/NH.

804. **GEORGE MADISON[8] SAWYER** [see 621], b. 1855 Whitefield NH, d. 18 Aug 1897 Whitefield NH, m. 1875 Addie Leona Grant of Jefferson NH, b. 1861.

Burt W., b. 1877 Whitefield NH, m. 4 Jan 1898 (div. Sep 1918) Mina L. Morse of Lancaster NH, b. 1878. CH: Daughter, b. 21 Dec 1898; Ralph Morse, b. 17 Feb 1908, d. 2 Mar 1908; Gertrude, b. ca. 1911, d. 26 Nov 1993, m. 1940 Milton H. Driggs.
Son, stillborn 25 Jul 1885.
Maud Alice, b. 14 Nov 1889, d. 11 Apr 1903.
Hazel J., b. 27 May 1894.

Sources: Whitefield NH census 1860, 1880. VR SA/NH. Obit (Gertrude).

805. **HOWARD PIERCE[8] SAWYER** [see 624], b. 13 Aug 1892 Concord NH, m.(1) 6 Nov 1920 Detroit MI Mary Gerrish Willard, b. 17 Nov 1892, dau. Everett W. and Lizzie (Gerrish) Willard; m.(2) ?.

Howard Pierce, b. 2 Mar 1923.

Elizabeth Lane, b. 23 Apr 1927.

Sources: Howard Pierce Sawyer rec.

806. **ROBERT CUSHMAN[8] SAWYER** [see 624], b. 13 Mar 1899 Concord NH, d. 1987 Ossipee NH, m. 1 Jul 1924 Berlin NH Phyllis G. Hodgdon of Berlin NH, b. 1899, dau. Wilfred A. and Alice (Goebel) Hodgdon. In Haverhill NH. He bur. in Ossipee NH.

Jean Allerton, b. Jul 1925, m. John ____.

Robert Cushman, b. 18 Feb 1927.

William H., b. 7 Mar 1929, d. 10 Mar 1929.

Sources: VR SA/NH.

807. **CHARLES R.[8] SAWYER** [see 627], b. ca. 1855 Boston MA, m. 11 Oct 1879 Somerset MA Mary Belle Richardson of Braintree MA, b. 1862, dau. John and Olive W. Richardson. Engineer. In Braintree MA 1880.

Charles Hermon, b. 7 Feb 1880 Braintree MA.

Everett Richardson, b. 2 Sep 1881 Boston MA.

Sources: VR SA/MA.

808. **HERMON FRENCH[8] SAWYER** [see 627], b. 27 Nov 1866 Boston MA, m. 30 Oct 1893 Whitman MA Ella Edwards of Stoneham MA, b. 27 Nov 1866 d. 15 Oct 1914 Boston MA, dau. Frank W. and Carrie E. (French) Edwards. Railroad engineer. In Brockton MA.

Harold Edwards, b. 17 Jun 1894 Whitman MA, m.(1) ? (div.); m.(2) 27 Jun 1924 Marlborough NH Adaline M. Coutts of Marlborough NH, b. 1893, dau. David and Mary (Middleton) Coutts (both b. in Scotland).

Sources: VR SA/MA. E9.

809. **FREEMAN JOHN[8] SAWYER** [see 628], b. 11 May 1836 Lyme NH, d. 16 May 1906 Canton MA, m. 10 May 1860 Augusta Miriam Pitcher of Canton MA, b. 4 Feb 1842 d. 26 Oct 1921. Butcher. In Stoughton MA, Mansfield MA, Canton MA, Foxboro MA.

877 Henry Freeman[9], 1862-1922.

James Thompson, b. 6 May 1863, d. 7 Oct 1863.

878 James Almond[9], 1865-1945.

879 John Davis[9], 1867-1951.

Augusta, b. 8 Dec 1869, d. Feb 1936, m. 27 Nov 1889 Canton MA George Capen.

Sarah Norris, b. 27 Jul 1872, d. 4 Oct 1933, m. 25 Apr 1900 Harry Morton.

Flora Rebecca, b. 18 Mar 1877, d. 27 Jun 1930, m. 13 Apr 1895 Canton MA Ralph Richards.

880 Frederick Benning[9], 1878-1946.

881 Nathaniel French[9], 1880-1933.

Annie Miriam, b. 11 Apr 1881, d. 17 Aug 1958, m. 12 Jun 1900 Coburn S. Owen.

Sources: VR Lyme NH, SA/MA. John Sawyer rec., Robert E. Sawyer rec.

810. **CHARLES HENRY[8] SAWYER** [see 628], b. 16 May 1839 Lyme NH, m. 29 Nov 1860 Haverhill MA Cornelia B. Atwood of Haverhill MA, b. 1839, dau. Moses and Ruth Atwood. Butcher. In Canton MA, Mansfield MA.

Charles Freeman, b. 2 Apr 1862 Canton MA. Butcher.
Son, b. 9 Dec 1864.
Mary Nettie, b. 20 Apr 1867.
Sources: VR Haverhill MA, SA/MA.

811. **CHARLES ADRIAN[8] SAWYER** [see 636], b. 6 Dec 1854 Dorchester MA, m. 3 Dec 1879 Boston MA Florence C. Ames of Boston MA, b. 1856, dau. Seth C. and Abbey E. Ames. Mayflower Descendent No. 68898. In Chicago IL.
Charles A., b. 17 Oct 1880, d. in infancy.
Charles Adrian, b. 19 Aug 1881.
Abbie E., b. 17 Dec 1883, d. May 1884.
Clifton A., b. 9 May 1885.
Emerson G., b. 23 Sep 1895.
Harold T., b. 8 Jun 1900.
Sources: VR SA/MA. Charles B. Sawyer rec.

812. **GEORGE E.[8] SAWYER** [see 638], b. 27 Feb 1862 Cambridge MA, m.(1) 25 Sep 1883 Cambridge MA Harriet Marston of Brighton MA, b. 1863, dau. John H. and Elizabeth Marston; m.(2) 27 May 1891 Medford MA Frances W. Debbins of Melrose MA, b. ?, dau. William and Mary Debbins. Painter. In Medford MA 1891.
George, b. 21 Jun 1885 Brighton MA. Painter.
Charles A., b. 16 Aug 1892 Medford MA.
George Eusebius, b. 4 Oct 1893 Medford MA.
Sources: VR Cambridge MA, SA/MA.

813. **CHARLES S. D.[8] SAWYER** [see 641], b. 7 Feb 1839, m.(1) Hannah LaBeree, b. ?; m.(2) Lucy L. Degoosh, b. ?. In West Fairlee VT.
Charles, b. 26 Sep 1851 Bradford VT.
Jennie B., b. 1871, m. 4 Jan 1897 George H. Woods.
Sources; VR SA/VT.

814. **WILLIAM W.[8] SAWYER** [see 641], b. 23 May 1849 Eaton, Canada, d. 29 Apr 1930 Beecher Falls VT, m. 28 Jul 1870 Eaton, Canada, Jane L. Farnum, b. 29 Nov 1850 d. 20 Mar 1928. In Beecher Falls VT, Wisconsin. He bur. in Halls Stream, Quebec, Canada.
Stella Eldora, b. 29 Jun 1871, d. 1953, m. 2 Dec 1894 Nathan Beecher.
882 Marvin Artemus[9], 1873-1956.
Sources: D41, S5, Sylvia Sawyer rec.

815. **HENRY ELSOR[8] SAWYER** [see 642], b. 27 Nov 1842 Newport, Canada, d. 24 Jan 1896 Colebrook NH, m. 20 Jul 1867 Mary Landry, b. ?
Annie M., b. ?, m. 10 Mar 1896 Fred A. Lee of Colebrook NH.
Charles Henry, b. 14 Aug 1882 Nashua NH.
Sources: VR SA/NH.

816. **JOSEPH JEROME[8] SAWYER** [see 642], b. 28 Nov 1853 in Canada, d. 14 Jul 1944, m. 27 Nov 1875 Eliza Burns of Sherbrook, Canada, b. ca. 1853. Farmer. In Sutton NH, Bennington NH.
883 Charles John[9], 1878-1969.
Bertha M., b. ?, m. 7 Apr 1896 Emil Roth.
Lena, b. ?.

Nellie, b. ?

Edwin F., b. 1 Mar 1886 Sutton NH, d. Bennington NH, m.(1) 31 Mar 1906 Antrim NH Eva Parker of Canada, b. ca. 1887, dau. Alex Parker; m.(2) Margaret ____, b. ?; m.(3) Blanche Nault, b. ?. No CH.

George Theodore, b. 15 Nov 1887 Bennington NH. In New Haven CT. CH: Son, b. ?; 2 dau., b. ?.

Esther A., b. 13 Aug 1890.

884 Harry Joseph$^9$, 1893-1970.

Arthur W., b. 1 May 1896 Bennington NH, d. Bennington NH, m. 17 May 1936 Margaret E. Powers of Hancock NH, b. 1896. He bur. in Bennington NH. No CH.

Sources: VR SA/NH. N6, Paul A. Sawyer rec.

**817. THOMAS E.$^8$ SAWYER** [see 643], b. 1859 in Iowa, m.(1) ?; m.(2) 7 Jun 1898 Adelaide G. (Harris) Smith of Ludlow VT, b. ?. In Peru VT 1900.

Daughter, b. 17 Jul 1900.

Dorothy Jane, b. 3 Oct 1901.

Child, b. ?.

Helen Elizabeth, b. 1 Mar 1905.

Earl Synfort, b. 29 Apr 1907.

Sources: Peru VT census 1900. VR SA/VT.

818. **ALBERT BUTLER$^8$ SAWYER** [see 644], b. 1887 in Illinois, d. 1988, m. Agnes Porter, b.?.

Albert, b. ?.

Margaret Ellen, b. ?, m. Charles L. Block.

John Porter, b. ?.

Thomas, b. ?

Sources: L5.

819. **DANIEL R.$^8$ SAWYER** [see 645], b. Jun 1862 Sudbury VT, d. 24 Aug 1906 Fair Haven VT, m. 16 Apr 1889 Sudbury VT Nancy Hyde of Sudbury VT, b. Feb 1867 d. 1948. Hotel keeper.

David L., b. Oct 1891 Sudbury VT.

Curtis J., b. Sep 1893 Sudbury VT.

Marjorie L., b. 10 Jul 1901.

Helen Alice, b. 11 Apr 1908.

Sources: VR SA/VT.

820. **FRED J.$^8$ SAWYER** [see 645], b. 7 Dec 1872 Sudbury VT, d. 31 Oct 1913 Boscawen NH, m. 12 Apr 1892 Lebanon NH Mary A. Willey of Sharon VT, b. Apr 1872, dau. Hiram A. and Ellen E. (Joyce) Willey. Undertaker. In Sharon VT, Enosbury VT, Norwich VT, Burlington VT.

Byron Otis, b. 30 Aug 1896.

Cecil H., b. May 1897. In Jaffrey NH.

Roy C., b. 4 Jun 1898, d. 19 Dec 1949.

Sources: VR SA/NH. B26.

821. **ARTHUR HENRY$^8$ SAWYER** [see 650], b. 19 Jul 1868 Harvard MA, m. 14 Feb 1900 Alice Harriman, b. ?.

Edris H., b. ?.

Norman E., b. ?.

Sources: Diane Melone rec.

822. **EDMUND HINCKLEY[8] SAWYER** [see 651], b. 17 Nov 1862 Easthampton MA, m. 8 Feb 1889 Northhampton MA Susie E. Winslow of Enfield MA, b. 1861, dau. Joseph K. and Emily B. (Smith) Winslow. Contractor.

Winslow Brewster, b. 23 Jan 1891 Easthampton MA.

Harold Edmund, b. 8 Jun 1894 Easthampton MA.

Sources: VR SA/MA.

823. **HENRY T.[8] SAWYER** [see 653], b. 1856 Burlington VT, m. 20 Oct 1884 Springfield MA Martha C. Sawyer of Sterling MA, b. 29 Oct 1857, dau. Luke R. and Martha (Burpee) Sawyer. Clerk, brick manufacturer. In Malden MA, Boylston MA 1893.

Luke E., b. 22 Sep 1887 Malden MA.

Ruth Sterling, b. 23 Jan 1893 Boylston MA.

Sources: VR SA/MA.

824. **JOHN KIMBALL[8] SAWYER** [see 663], b. 9 Apr 1885 Sangerville ME, m. 18 Jan 1911 Guilford ME Bessie M. Seekins of Dover ME, b. 30 Oct 1885 d. 19 Jun 1958, dau. George H. and Ada (Harris) Seekins. In Waterville ME.

Gladstone Vincent, b. 10 Feb 1913 Sangerville ME, m. 2 Apr 1944 Esther Briggs, b. 16 Nov 19__, dau. Leo and Bertha Briggs. No CH.

George Horace, b. 5 Feb 1920, m. 9 Oct 1948 Dorothy M. Blue, b. 9 Oct 1924. CH: John Kimball, b. 30 Mar 1950; Pamela M., b. 31 Dec 1952.

Sources: Esther Sawyer rec.

## NINTH GENERATION

825. **FREDERICK RANDOLPH[9] SAWYER** [see 673], b. Jul 1852 Hartland ME, d. 1921, m. Hannah Augusta Dore, b. Sep 1852 d. 1926, dau. Caleb Dore. Cabinet maker. In Athens ME 1880 w/son.

Carl Dore, b. 30 Jan 1879 Athens ME, d. 6 Feb 1970 Providence RI, m. 9 Jun 1910 Ethel Gertrude Stevens, b. 9 Mar 1888 d. 24 Feb 1939. CH: Norma Alberta, b. 17 Mar 1911, m. 24 Oct 1938 Oscar Paul Hammer; Carl Stevens, b. 5 Oct 1912, m. 19 Jun 1943 Gertrude Doliber; Fred Albert, b. 25 Jun 1914, d. 7 Jan 1986, m. 16 Jan 1953 Audrey Winsor; Ethel Augusta, b. 29 Jan 1916, d. Jun 1947; Paula, b. 26 Dec 1920, m. 5 Dec 1942 George W. Fisher: Jacquelyn Dore, b. 14 Aug 1926, m. 2 Apr 1946 George E. Sinkinson.

Sources: ME 1880 census index. Family Bible (Carl S. Sawyer).

826. **FREDERICK O.[9] SAWYER** [see 674], b. 21 Mar 1862 Madison ME, d. 9 Mar 1951 Skowhegan ME, m. Ellen Goodrich of Dexter ME, b. 6 Jul 1862 d. 25 Nov 1955. In Skowhegan ME.

Fancher Goodrich, b. 7 Jul 1889, m. 17 Dec 1912 Herbert L. Swett.

Sources: VR Skowhegan ME, SA/ME.

827. **BERTICE FELTON[9] SAWYER** [see 679], b. 20 Apr 1868 Hudson MA, m. 26 Sep 1893 Worcester MA Cora Edna Perry of Putnam CT, b. 24 May 1863, dau. Elisha F. and Mary J. (Randall) Perry. Bank teller. In Worcester MA.

Everett P., b. 29 Sep 1894 Worcester MA.

Hazel A., b. 16 Feb 1896.

Irving P., b. 28 Apr 1897 Worcester MA.

Myrtle F., b. 13 Aug 1898.
Mary Elizabeth, b. 22 Feb 1900.
Bertice R., b. 23 Jul 1901 Worcester MA.
Sources: VR SA/MA. N44.

828. **FRANK WILLIAM**[9] **SAWYER** [see 686], b. 26 Oct 1887 Buxton ME, d. 21 Jul 1968 Augusta ME, m. Ella M. Mayberry, b. ? d. 11 Feb 1939, dau. Andrew and Hannah (Strout) Mayberry. In Westbrook ME. He bur. in Augusta ME.
Edith, b. 21 Jan 1910, m.(1) Fred Gooch, m.(2) Lewis Taylor.
Earl Lamont, b. 17 May 1913 Westbrook ME, d. 27 Oct 1979 Kingsport TN, m. 12 Feb 1939 Portsmouth NH Gladys M. Burnell, b. 28 Apr 1910. CH: Ernest Carl, b. 19 Feb 1941, d. Feb 1941; Clifford Earl, b. 31 Dec 1943, m. 27 Sep 1969 Donna L. Wood; Suzanna Ada, m. John Thurston.
Robert, b. 6 Sep 1914 Westbrook ME, d. 25 Dec 1979, m. Adelaide McFarland. CH: Frank, Robert, Douglas, Sharon, Francine.
Carroll, b. 1921, d. 4 May 1941.
Frank William, b. ca. 1925, d. 196_.
Sources: Gladys B. Sawyer rec.

829. **HENRY LEWIS**[9] **SAWYER** [see 689], b. 15 Oct 1868 W. Boylston MA, m. 20 Jun 1894 Worcester MA Nellie E. Baker of Rutland MA, b. 1 Jul 1870, dau. John E. and Sarah E. (Forbes) Baker. Merchant. In Fitchburg MA.
Ralph Henry, b. 28 Jul 1895 West Boylston MA.
Dorothy H., b. 17 Mar 1900.
Sources: VR SA/MA. W39.

830. **WALTER ALDEN**[9] **SAWYER** [see 694], b. 28 Jun 1880 Berlin MA, m. Mary E. Mahan, Leominster MA, b. ?. Clerk. In Clinton MA.
Walter, b. 1905.
Harold F., b. 1909 Clinton MA, d. 1957, m. 22 May 1937 Salem NH Marie A. Gauthier of Chicopee MA, b. 1913, dau. Joseph and Caroline (Turcotte) Gauthier. In Putnam CT.
William, b. 1911, d. 1958.
Kenneth, b. 1913.
Eleanor, b. 1915.
Sources: VR Berlin MA. Kathy Medeiros rec.

831. **CARL EUGENE**[9] **SAWYER** [see 694], b. 5 Mar 1882 Berlin MA, m. Sep 1905 Gertrude Alice Rice of Westboro MA, b. 8 Jul 1884, dau. Samuel W. and Jennie (Moore) Rice.
C. Eugene, b. 15 Aug 1911 in New York.
Dorothy, b. 27 Jan 1913.
Virginia, b. 14 Feb 1921.
Sources: VR Berlin MA. E16.

832. **EDGAR FRANKLIN**[9] **SAWYER** [see 700], b. 10 Dec 1837 Northboro MA, m. 2 May 1867 Clinton MA Margaret A. Neat of Lexington MA, b. ca. 1846, dau. William and Johanna Neat. Painter.
Etta Mabel, b. 3 Dec 1868.
Jasper E., b. 25 Jun 1883 Clinton MA, m. 12 Sep 1908 East Jaffrey NH Alta M. Pierce of East Jaffrey NH, b. 23 Nov 1879, dau. Clark M. and Mary E. (Coffin) Pierce. CH: Barbara P., b. 2 Mar 1914.

Sources: VR Northboro MA, SA/MA.

833. **FREDERICK L.[9] SAWYER** [see 714], b. ca. 1850 Boston MA, m. 27 Nov 1873 Woburn MA Sarah O. Bell of Woburn MA, b. ca. 1855, dau. James and Sarah Bell. Harness maker.

Charles Frederick, b. 6 Aug 1876 Woburn MA.

Sources: VR SA/MA.

834. **AUGUSTUS THORNDIKE[9] SAWYER** [see 714], b. 24 Nov 1862 Woburn MA, m. 5 Sep 1894 Woburn MA Harriet Elizabeth Page of Woburn MA, b. ca. 1869, dau. Theophelus F. and Etta R. Page. Grocer. In Somerville MA.

Stanley Phillips, b. 1904, d. 1983. m. Grace Isobell Deane, b. 1903 d. 1978. CH: Paul Stanley, b. 1945.

Sources: VR SA/MA. Paul S. Sawyer rec.

835. **HARRY WATERS[9] SAWYER** [see 716], b. 17 Jul 1863 Whitingham VT, m. Grace E. Strong, b. ?. In South Dakota.

Pierre, b. ?.

Sources: VR SA/VT.

836. **LINCOLN HOUGHTON[9] SAWYER** [see 716], b. 10 Jun 1865 Whitingham VT, m. 15 Oct 1890 Charlemont MA Clara. V. Negus of Charlemont MA, b. 1865, dau. Elliot A. and Clarissa E. Negus. Manufacturer.

Vesta S., b. 2 Aug 1897.

Houghton Negus, b. 3 May 1900 Whitingham VT.

Elliot Lincoln, b. 4 Nov 1904.

Sources: VR SA/VT, SA/MA.

837. **CHARLES J.[9] SAWYER** [see 717], b. 25 Dec 1865 Plymouth VT, d. 29 Oct 1952, m. 10 May 1897 Plymouth VT Maude E. Hall, b. 14 May 1871 d. 11 Aug 1965, dau. William and Caroline (Sawyer) Hall. Machinist, painter.

Evan Henry, b. Apr 1902 Plymouth VT, d. 1 Jul 1943, m. EllaChowin. CH: Richard Evan, b. 11 Jun 1925, m. Mary Williams; Edmund Arthur, b. 8 Dec 1927, m. Norma Longe; June Elizabeth, b. 20 Apr 1929, m. Ralph Waters; Zelda ,Ann, b. 4 Sep 1931, m. James Oldenburg; Paul Charles, b. 19 Nov 1933, m. GlennaHickory; Robert Leander, b. 22 Sep 1936, m. Jeannette Perkins; Donald Elton, b. 5 May 1939, m. Katherine McBain; James Clayton, b. 25 Nov 1941, m. ?

Raymond Leslie, b. 17 Feb 1905, d. 15 Mar 1906.

Marjorie Maude, b. 20 Apr 1907, m. 2 Jun 1928 Mellen Bigelow.

Kenneth Leroy, b. 17 Jan 1910, m. 6 Sep 1939 Mildred Prior, b. ?.

Marion May, b. 26 Jul 1917, m. 12 May 1940 Robert Ladeau.

Sources: VR SA/VT. Early Families of Plymouth VT, Richard E. Sawyer rec., Robert L. Sawyer rec.

838. **JOHN CLIFFORD[9]** [see 718], b. 23 Apr 1886 Shrewsbury VT, d. 13 Jul 1944 Claremont NH, m. 29 Jan 1906 Reading VT Elsie Matthews, b. ?. In Reading VT.

Ada Cynthia, b. 9 Nov 1907, m. Hugh Durwood, Jr.

Arthur Allen, b. 7 Oct 1908, d. 1971, m. Ruth Hardy.

Madelene, b. 1910, d. 1976, m. Louis Costello.

Helen, b. 1912, m. Howard Weld.

Alden E., b. 1914, d. 1975, m. Janice Knapp.

Sources: Ada Durwood rec.

Lena, b. 3 Jul 1890.
Mamie R., b. 28 Feb 1892.
Willard L., b. 28 Feb 1894, d. 22 Apr 1896.
Norman Wilton, b. 22 Dec 1900.
Sources: Lebanon NH census 1900. VR SA/NH, SA/VT.

865 . **CHARLES F.$^9$ SAWYER** [see 781], b. 15 Apr 1873 Thetford VT, m. Thetford VT Florence Clough of Thetford VT, b. 1886. Painter. In Lebanon NH.
Harry Burdette, b. 1908, m. 22 Jun 1929 Ruth M. Cody, b. ?.
Sylvia I., b. ca. 1918, d. 5 Jan 1990, m. Ernest H. Ashford.
Sources: VR SA/VT. Obit (Sylvia).

866 . **PHILIP M.$^9$ SAWYER** [see 782], b. 23 May 1882 Thetford VT, m.(1) 23 Nov 1904 Conway NH (div. 21 Dec 1906) Minnie B. Knox of Albany NH, b. 1888, dau. Irving and Stella L. (Douglas) Knox; m.(2) 21 Mar 1907 Conway NH Lucy M. Williams of New Brunswick, Canada, b. 1887, dau. Thomas and Grace (Graham) Williams. Farmer. In Conway NH.
Archie V., b. 2 Mar 1908.
Raymond P., b. 1910 Conway NH, m. 26 Nov 1931 Enfield NH Clara E. Nixon of Springfield NH, dau. William and Jennie S. (Williams) Nixon. Mechanic. In Thetford VT. CH: Son, stillborn 28 Jul 1912.
Sources: VR SA/NH, SA/VT.

867 . **WALTER HENRY$^9$ SAWYER** [see 789], b. 13 Sep 1854 Winchendon MA, d. 1933 Winchendon MA, m. 3 May 1876 Winchendon MA L. Emma Winch of Winchendon MA, b. 1854 d. 1947, dau. Aaron and Caroline Winch.
885 Henry D$^{10}$. 1883-1965.
Sources: VR SA/MA. Bradley Sawyer rec.

868. **FRANK LYMAN$^9$ SAWYER** [see 790], b. 10 Feb 1855 Brooksville ME, m. Flora (Blake) Wilson, b. Oct 1852, adopted dau. Moses and Martha (Bates) Blake. In Brooksville ME 1880.
Martha F., b. 5 Sep 1876.
Irl, adopted, b. Aug 1887.
Sources: ME 1880 census index. M8, B49, Elizabeth Wescott rec.

869. **CARLTON AUGUSTUS$^9$ SAWYER** [see 790], b. 5 Aug 1866 Orland ME, d. 18 Nov 1938 Orland ME, m. 7 Aug 1887 Ella V. Butler, b. 1865 d. 1940. Farmer.
Ralph, b. ca. 1889 Orland ME.
Sources: VR Orland ME, SA/ME.

870. **IRA (AHIRA) HIRAM$^9$ SAWYER** [see 791], b. Apr 1868 Orland ME, d. 16 May 1895 Tremont ME, m. Carrie E. Richards of Camden ME, b. 22 Jun 1868 d. 17 Apr 1894, dau. Henry and Angie Richards. In Bucksport ME. He bur. Benson Cem., Tremont ME.
886 Ralph E.$^{10}$, 1888-1952.
Harold Leroy, b. 26 Sep 1892, d. 19 Sep 1910 Bucksport ME.
Sources: VR Orland ME, SA/ME.

871. **ALBINA HALL$^9$ SAWYER** [see 791], b. 11 Jun 1885 Orland ME, d. 1965 Bucksport ME, m. Myrtle E. Quimby of Bucksport ME, b. 1887 d. 1951. Seaman. In Verona ME. He bur. at Silver Lake, Bucksport ME.

Allie Leroy, b. 18 Oct 1905, d. 1962, m. Charlotte E. Brooks, b. ?.
Florence E., b. 30 Jun 1907.
Walter E., b. 26 Jul 1909, d. 18 Nov 1911.
Ernest E., b. 1919, killed in a mill 1940.
Richard, b. 13 Oct 1924, d. 15 Mar 1992, m. Irene Dow.
Virginia, m. ____ Bowden.
Marjorie, m. ____ Hanscom.
Sources: VR SA/ME. M8, Obit (Richard), Elizabeth Wescott rec.

872. **FREDERICK WESLEY⁹ SAWYER** [see 792], b. 6 Jun 1883 Orland ME, d. 25 Nov 1942 Hartford CT, m. 11 Nov 1909 Bar Harbor ME Grace Mabel Wescott of Malden MA, b. 6 Nov 1883 d. 26 May 1921, dau. Charles D. and Adelia (Wescott) Roach, adopted by George and Lucy Wescott. Teamster. He bur. in Malden MA.
Loring Wescott, b. 4 Aug 1912.
Frederick Wesley, b. 26 Oct 1913, d. 14 Jan 1978, m. 1930 Frances Colpitts, b. ?.
Lawrence Hall, b. 16 Apr 1916.
Sources: Frederick W. Sawyer III rec.

873. **RAYMOND LESLIE⁹ SAWYER** [see 792], b. 18 Jun 1886 Bucksport ME, m. Alice L. Liscomb, b. ?. Driver. In Eden ME 1910.
R. Carlton.
Sources: M8, Elizabeth Wescott rec.

874. **WILLIAM R.⁹ SAWYER** [see 792], b. 25 Jul 1888 Bucksport ME, d. Jan 1964, m. Etta____ b. ?. Hostler. In Eden ME 1910.
George.
William.
Raymond.
John.
Douglas.
Flora.
Phyllis.
Sources: M8, Elizabeth Wescott rec.

875. **CHARLES HENRY⁹ SAWYER** [see 794], b. 19 Jun 1879 Georgia VT, d. 19 May 1962, m. 5 Oct 1904 Georgia VT Jennie E. Carpenter, b. ?, dau. Solomon and Grace (Lincoln) Carpenter. In Castleton VT, North Hebron NY. He bur. in Center Shaftsbury VT.
Harry Charles, b. 12 Jun 1905 No. Hebron NY, d. 1983 Keene NH, m.(1) Helen (Morgan) Porter; m.(2) Mildred ____. In Springfield VT.
Dorothy, b. ?, m. Carl Frasier.
Sources: VR SA/VT. W58, Joan Sawyer rec.

876. **FRED WESTON⁹ SAWYER** [see 800], b. 24 Mar 1871 Whitefield NH, m. 5 Jun 1895 Fannie Lindley of Almont, Canada, b. 1876. Grocer. In Lancaster NH, Lyndon VT 1901.
Arthur Weston, b. 23 Mar 1898 Lancaster NH, m.(1) ?, (div.); m.(2) 21 May 1935 Salem NH Emily Mae Hartman of Bronx NY, b. 1910, dau. Frank and Emily M. Hartman, both b. in Germany. In Lawrence MA.
Ethel Alice, b. 21 Jul 1899, m. ____ Plumber.
Raymond Morris, b. 1 Apr 1901.
Ruth Lena, b. 24 Oct 1903, m. ____ Marcory.

Norman T.
Dorothy, m. ____ Keogh.
Sources: VR SA/VT. Dorothy Keogh rec.

877. **HENRY FREEMAN[9] SAWYER** [see 806], b. 23 Feb 1862 Stoughton MA, d. 24 Sep 1922, m. Annie Eastman, b. 1862 d. 1923.
George F., b. 1885, d. 1938, m. Annie E. Crawford, b.?
Marion, b. ?, m. Norman Rogers.
Harold, b. ?, m. Hannah Porter, b. ?.
Sources: John Sawyer rec.

878. **JAMES ALMOND[9] SAWYER** [see 806], b. 16 Apr 1865 Mansfield MA, d. 1945, m.(1) 18 Feb 1888 Canton MA Belle Nichols of Providence RI, b. ?, dau. Thaddeus and Selena (Hilting) Nichols; m.(2) 16 Apr 1892 Boston MA Mary Maber of New Brunswick, Canada, b. 1874, dau. Clarissa (Lamb) Maber. Tinsmith.
Doris, b. ?.
James Almond, b. ?.
Edwin, b. ?.
Clara, b. ?.
Amey, b. ?.
Marion, b. ?.
Mildred, b. ?.
Gertrude Bell, b. 7 Dec 1892.
Sources: VR SA/MA. John Sawyer rec.

879. **JOHN DAVIS[9] SAWYER** [see 806], b. 30 Sep 1867 Canton MA, d. 1 Nov 1951, m. (1) Alice J. Eastwood, b. ? d. 4 Dec 1898; m.(2) Feb 1900 Ruth A Wasson of Providence RI, b. ?. In Pawtucket RI.
Ann E., b. 18 Jul 1888.
Grace P., b. ?.
John Davis, b. ?, m. Ruth M. Dexter.
Sources: John Sawyer rec.

880. **FREDERICK BENNING[9] SAWYER** [see 806], b. 19 (May or Aug) 1878 Canton MA, d. 19 Feb 1946 m. 4 Jun 1899 Daisy Emily Owen, b. 19 Jul 1876 d. 24 Oct 1942. Hardware salesman.
Frederick Benning, b. 4 Jan 1900, d. 8 Jan 1966, m. 23 Jun 1928 Gladys Evelyn Springer, b.?.
Freeman John, b. 8 Nov 1901, m. 31 Dec 1925 Ruth Erma Chandler, b. ?.
Dorothy Owen, B. 9 Jan 1903, m. 19 Sep 1953 William L. Sullivan.
William Cutler, b. 20 Apr 1904, d. 30 Mar 1984, m. 1 Jun 1934 Elizabeth Taber, b. ?.
Robert Emerson, b. 18 Dec 1905, m. 3 Dec 1925 Gladys Irene Boutelle, b. ?.
Alice Mary, b. 7 Sep 1908, d. 20 Jul 1969.
Sources: VR SA/MA. Robert E. Sawyer rec., Priscilla Hilton rec.

881. **NATHANIEL FRENCH[9] SAWYER** [see 806], b. 3 Jan 1880 Canton MA, d. 25 Jan 1933, m. Bessie May Sanborn of Monroe NH, b. ? d. 21 Dec 1972.
Herbert, b. 2 Sep 1908, d. 12 Oct 1976.
Nathaniel French, b. ca. 1910, d. 4 Nov 1954.
Priscilla, b. 9 Apr 1918, m. Carl Hilton.
Caroline, b. 1922, d. 10 Jul 1973.

Sources: Priscilla Hilton rec.

882. **MARVIN ARTEMUS[9] SAWYER** [see 811], b. 15 Jan 1873 Main WI, d. 9 Jan 1956 Concord NH, m.(1) 17 Aug 1895 Mary Eva Van Dyke, b. ? d. 26 Feb 1900; m.(2) 30 Sep 1903 Alice Frances Yates, b. 1885 d. 8 Jan 1938. Hotel clerk. In Canaan VT. He bur. in Canaan VT.

Kenneth Van Dyke, b. 10 Jul 1896 West Stewartstown NH, d. 24 Aug 1971 m.(1) ?; m.(2) 9 Jan 1926 Portsmouth NH Hazel Seeley Clayton of Canada, b. 1896, dau. M. and Della (Parks) Seeley.

Freda Eva, b. 16 Nov 1904, m. 16 Mar 1926 Carl Blom.

Eda Marion, b. 28 Dec 1906, m. 18 Mar 1929 Alison Bowen.

Nellie Birdena, b. 19 Sep 1908, m. 14 Aug 1929 Howard Pomeroy.

Fannie Betsey, b. 5 Dec 1911, d. 20 Feb 1990, m. Jun 1966 Benjamin Freeman.

Billie Artemus, b. 23 Mar 1914, d. 18 Sep 1985, m.(1) 31 Jul 1937 Shirley R. Bryan, m.(2) Margaret Elizabeth Merry.

Cleo Cromwell, b. 22 Jul 1916, d. 26 Nov 1975, m. Aug 1937 Mary K. Booth.

Stella Eloise, b. 24 Sep 1918, m. 1 May 1943 Louis Sillari.

Sources: D41, Sylvia Sawyer rec.

883. **CHARLES JOHN[9] SAWYER** [see 813], b. 6 Oct 1878 Sutton NH, d. 28 Jan 1969, m.(1) 1901 Leominster MA Sarah J. ____, b. ?; m.(2) 17 Jan 1916 Concord NH Vera Pearl Coleman of Fitzwilliam NH, b. ca. 1889, dau. Martin W. and Margaret F. (Grant) Coleman. In Concord NH.

Mildred, b. ?, m. Carroll White.

Carroll, b. ?. Went to Maryland.

Philip J., b. ?.

Sources: VR SA/NH. Philip J. Sawyer rec., Paul A. Sawyer rec.

884. **HARRY JOSEPH[9] SAWYER** [see 813], b. 1 May 1893 Bennington NH, d. 1970, m. 11 Aug 1919 Manchester NH Lillian Dustin of Manchester NH, b. 1899 d. 1968, dau. Fred A. and Lucy E. (Howard) Dustin. In Franklin NH, Barre VT. He bur. in Woodsville NH.

Daughter, b. 29 Sep 1925, d. same day.

Margaret L., b. 2 Jan 1930, d. 23 Dec 1934.

Paul A.

Richard.

Sources: VR SA/NH. Paul A. Sawyer rec.

## TENTH GENERATION

885. **HENRY D.[10] SAWYER** [see 866], b. 1883 Winchendon MA, d. 1965, m. Maude Taft, b. 1888 d. 1967.

Bradley T.

Sources: Bradley Sawyer rec.

886. **RALPH E. [10] SAWYER** [see 869], b. 6 Jul 1888 Bucksport ME, d. 1952 Bucksport ME, m.(1) Blanche G. Heath of Verona ME, b. 1894 d. 1940; m.(2) Ethel ____, b. ?. He bur. at Silver Lake, Bucksport ME.

Child, stillborn 19 May 1911.

Maynard Wallace, b. 1916 Bucksport ME, d. 1956, m. 1941 Adelma I. Paschal. In Bangor ME.

Daughter, stillborn 28 Oct 1918.

Sources: VR SA/ME. James L. Sawyer rec.

## PART IV

# ꧁ JAMES OF GLOUCESTER ꧂

1. **JAMES[1] SAWER** (later Sawyer) of Gloucester, Massachusetts, is the ancestor of many Sawyers living in northern New England today. There are several theories concerning his lineage, none of them proven. One suggestion is that James[1] was one of the three children who are said to have come to the New World with Edward[1]. It is true that the latter's will, recorded on 31 March 1674, mentions only his sons John and Ezekiel, (Part I) and his "wife," but it was not unusual at that time for a father to give some of his children money or land during his lifetime, and then to limit their inheritance or even omit them from his will altogether on the basis of their having already received their due share of his estate. William[1] seems to have done this. Furthermore, although James[1] did not name a son Edward, he had a grandson of that name who called one of his own sons Ezekiel [see 16]. It is also true that James[1]'s first child, a daughter, was named Mary, as were the wife and daughter of Edward[1]. Would it not have been natural for James[1] to name his first daughter after his own mother and sister? Finally, in 1669, before moving to Gloucester, James[1] bought a home in Ipswich, where both Edward[1] and Thomas[1] lived before they moved to Rowley.

Taking all this into consideration, I feel it possible that Edward[1] and James[1] may have been father and son, even though there is no provable link between them.[a] What is certain, is that James[1] first married a Martha, of whom little is known except that she and he "acknowledged" a mortgage in April 1670 for the house he bought in Ipswich. There is also record of a life-support agreement with Thomas and Joannah Smith of Ipswich, entered into by James[1] though later unfulfilled; since such agreements usually involved family members, it is conceivable that the Smiths were Martha's family.

By the time James[1] moved to Gloucester, he was married to Sarah Bray, a daughter of Thomas and Mary (Wilson) Bray of Gloucester, who was born in 1651 and died on 24 April 1727. In 1688 he received a grant of six acres of land on the west side of the Annasquam River and lived there. He was a weaver, a selectman in 1696, and died on 31 May 1703, six days after signing his will. His widow was living with their son, Abraham, in the family home in 1726.

1. **JAMES[1] SAWER** had the following children:
Mary, b. 1672, d. 17 Dec 1717, m. 5 Dec 1699 William Ring.
2 Thomas[2], 1674-1711.
3 John[2], ca. 1676-1760.
4 Nathaniel[2], 1677-1741.
Abraham, b. 5 Nov 1680, d. 1751, unm.
Sarah, b. 19 Jun 1683, d. 26 Aug 1724, m. 1 Apr 1708 John Mariner.
5 Isaac[2], 1684-1772.
6 Jacob[2], 1687-1767.
7 James[2], 1691-1776.

Sources: VR Gloucester MA. C65, W13, Essex deeds, P82b, Essex Co. Qtrly Court rec, E20, C97, Early Settlers of Essex, L30, B1, B2.

2. **THOMAS[2] SAWYER** [see 1], b. ca. 1674 Ipswich MA, d. 12 Jan 1711 Gloucester MA, m.(1) 17 Feb 1690 Hannah Millett, b. ? d. 15 Sep 1690, dau. John Millett; m. (2) 18 Nov 1691 Hannah (Verry) Foster, b. Mar 1653, dau. Thomas and Hannah (Giles) Verry. Hannah Foster had 10 CH by first marriage. B/home of second wife, located at the harbor. On list in Gloucester MA 1704.

---

[a] For an excellent discussion with a different conclusion, see D29A.

John, b. 13 Sep 1690, d. 14 Sep 1690.
8 James[3], 1692-1730.
Francis, b. 11 Dec 1694, d. 8 Aug 1695.
Sources: VR Gloucester MA. B1.

3. **JOHN[2] SAWYER** [see 1], b. ca. 1676 Ipswich MA, d. 23 Feb 1760 Cape Elizabeth ME, m. 20 Feb 1701 Gloucester MA Rebecca Stanford, b. 1677 d. 23 Aug 1755, dau. Robert Stanford. All CH were b. in Gloucester MA. John settled on the neck opposite Portland ME, on Cape Elizabeth, where he owned a ferry for many years. Proprietor of First Church of Falmouth ME. In Falmouth ME 1719. S/land in Falmouth ME 1749. He bur. on Meeting House Hill, South Portland ME.

Sarah, b. 26 Nov 1701, m.(1) 1720 William Roberts, m.(2) 1726 Robert Brooks.
9 John[3], b. 1704.
Mary, b. 16 Jul 1706, d. 10 May 1796, m.(1) Stephen Randall, m.(2) Nathaniel Jordan.
Job, b. 9 Oct 1708, d. 26 Aug 1792 Falmouth ME, m.(1) (I) 2 Mar 1735 Marion Hanscom, b. ?; m.(2) (I) 20 Oct 1753 Mary Mayo, b. ?. Husbandman. In Falmouth ME. On alarm list Cape Elizabeth Company, 29 Apr 1757. CH: Marian, b. ?, m. 1 Jun 1767 Jacob Randall; Hannah, b. 18 Dec 1737.
10 Joseph[3], 1711-1800.
11 Jonathan[3], b. 1713.
Rebecca, b. 21 Mar 1716, m. Samuel Skilling.
12 Daniel[3], b. 1718-1811.
Bethiah, b. 30 Sep 1722, d. 30 Mar 1764, unm.
Sources: VR Gloucester MA, Portland ME, SA/ME. B1, P82a, R10a, G23, J23, W56, C23, S35, W52.

4. **NATHANIEL[2] SAWYER** [see 1], b. 29 Oct 1677 Gloucester MA, d. 11 Apr 1741 Gloucester MA, m. 4 Nov 1706 Hannah Parker, b. ?. Mentioned in will of Edmund Chamberlain, Boston MA 1696. On list in Gloucester MA 1704.

Hannah, b. 11 Apr 1708, m. 13 Oct 1735 Joseph Parker.
Sarah, b. 15 Jul 1710, m. 25 Dec 1732 Jonathan Sawyer.
Mary, b. 8 Mar 1712, m. 6 Jan 1735 Jonathan Haskell.
Abigail, b. 7 Oct 1713, d. 24 Oct 1738.
Nathaniel, bp. 21 Aug 1715 Gloucester MA.
13 John[3], b. 1717.
14 Parker[3], 1719-1750.
Lydia, b. 5 Apr 1721, m. 6 May 1741 Samuel Parsons, Jr.
Marsey, b. 17 Sep 1723.
Deborah, b. 13 Mar 1726, m. 29 Nov 1750 Stephen Randall.
Sources: VR Gloucester MA. B1, C97, L27.

5. **ISAAC[2] SAWYER** [see 1], b. 14 Feb 1684 Gloucester MA, d. 13 Feb 1772 Falmouth ME, m. 19 Mar 1706 Gloucester MA Martha (Haskell) Bond, wid., b. 25 Aug 1686, dau. Benjamin and Emma (Graves) Haskell of Gloucester MA. In Falmouth ME 1724. B/land on Falmouth Neck ME 1726. Original founder of First Parish Church, Falmouth Neck ME, 8 Mar 1727. All CH were b. in Gloucester MA.

15 Isaac[3], 1707-1748.
16 Edward[3], b. 1709.
17 Thomas[3], 1711-1765.
Martha, b. 5 Jul 1714, m. Benjamin Stevens.

18 Abraham[3], 1717-ca. 1774.
Judith, b. 27 May 1719, d. 18 May 1722.
Elizabeth, b. 21 Apr 1722, m.(1) Samuel Staples, m.(2) 1762_____ Jinks.
Judith, b. 20 Aug 1724, m. 2 Nov 1742 Zackariah Brackett.
Sources: VR Gloucester MA. B1, W57, K10A, W56, B74, R10a, E20, Leonard F. Tibbetts rec.

6. **JACOB[2] SAWYER** [see 1], b. 24 Feb 1687 Gloucester MA, d. 18 Apr 1767 Cape Elizabeth ME, m. 2 Feb 1716 Sarah Wallis of Beverly MA, bp. 25 Feb 1694, dau. Joseph and Mary (Stanford) Wallis of Gloucester MA. In Falmouth ME 1728. S/land 1760-1762.
Deborah, b. 7 Jan 1717 Gloucester MA, d. 20 Sep 1807, m. 27 Oct 1734 John York.
19 Jacob[3], 1719-1800.
20 Josiah[3],1721-1783.
21 Samuel[3], 1723-1781.
Sarah, b. 23 Apr 1725, m.(I) 10 Jan 1741 Falmouth ME Joshua Strout.
Jeremiah, b. 14 May 1728 Falmouth ME, d. bef. 19 May 1806, m.(1) (I) 11 Aug 1750 Elizabeth Horton, b. ?; m.(2) 22 Aug 1760 Hannah Yeaton of Falmouth ME, b. 1730 d. 4 Mar 1812. Cooper. Private in Captain Loring Cushing's Cape Elizabeth Company, 29 Apr 1757. CH: Dau., b. (1774-1784).
22 Solomon[3], b. 1730.
23 William[3], 1735-1767.
Sources:Cape Elizabeth ME census 1790, 1800. VR Gloucester MA, SA/ME. R10a, K10A, W57, P18, S35, C97.

7. **JAMES[2] SAWYER** [see 1], b. 18 Nov 1691 Gloucester MA, d. 1776 Gloucester MA, m. 23 Dec 1714 Hannah Babson, b. 22 Dec 1695 d. 9 Sep 1747, dau. Richard and Mary Babson. Sailmaker.
24 James[3], 1715-1746.
Hannah, b. 9 Mar 1717, d. 7 Feb 1803, m. 15 Jul 1739 Michael Webber.
Rachel, b. 17 Dec 1718, m. 22 Nov 1739 John Parsons, 3rd.
Eunice, b. 28 Mar 1722, d. Apr 1727.
25 David[3], 1726-1752.
Eunice, b. 11 Oct 1727, m.(1) 26 Apr 1748 John Andrews, m.(2) 23 May 1779 Abraham Davis.
Jemima, b. 1730, d. 4 Mar 1776, m.(1) 15 Sep 1763 Samuel Morehead, m.(2) 2 Jan 1777 Thomas Pulsifer, Jr.
Mary, b. 6 Mar 1732, m. 16 Apr 1752 Andrew Parsons.
26 Abraham[3], 1737-1815.
Sources: VR Gloucester MA. C23, E20, C97.

## THIRD GENERATION

8. **JAMES[3] SAWYER** [see 2], b. 23 Sep 1692 Gloucester MA, d. 1 Nov 1730 Gloucester MA, m. 30 Nov 1714 Elinor Ellery of Gloucester MA, b. 30 Jun 1691, dau. William and Mary (Coyt) Ellery. Wid. m. James Edgerly 15 Aug 1732.
27 Thomas[4], b. 1716.
Mary, b. 28 Jun 1720, d. 13 Apr 1752.
28 James[4], 1722-1760.
Sources: VR Gloucester MA. B1, M33, F16.

9. **JOHN$^3$ SAWYER** [see 3], b. 24 Jun 1704 Gloucester MA, d. Gorham ME, m. 4 Jul 1726 Sarah Robinson of Falmouth ME, b. 26 Jan 1709, dau. Abraham and Sarah (York) Robinson. Husbandman. At Cape Elizabeth ME 1719. B/land in Falmouth 1730. In Gorham ME 1754. Revolutionary War: Served in 1st Army Corps (Hancock). He alive in 1778. Sarah alive in 1777.

John, b. 22 Dec 1726, d. 26 Dec 1728.
Sarah, b. 19 Nov 1727, m. Joseph Hatch.
Mary, b. 8 Sep 1731, m. 6 Apr 1751 Samuel Yeaton, Jr.
Rebecca, b. 13 Jun 1735, m. 24 Jan 1755 John Phinney, Jr.
29 Jonathan$^4$, 1736-1789.
30 David$^4$, b. 1737.
31 Joel$^4$,b. ca. 1750-1825.

Sources: VR Falmouth ME. K10A, P51, S67, D4.

10. **JOSEPH$^3$ SAWYER** [see 3], b. 7 May 1711 Gloucester MA, d. 31 Mar 1800 Cape Elizabeth ME, m. 1733 Joanna Cobb, b. 1716 d. 26 Nov 1784, dau. Ebenezer and Mary (Vaugh) Cobb. Private in Captain Loring Cushing's Cape Elizabeth Company, 29 Apr 1757. B/S land in Cape Elizabeth 1761-1786. Selectman for Cape Elizabeth ME 1772. Revolutionary War: Lieutenant on 21 Oct 1774. Appointed Special Justice to Court of Common Pleas and to Superior Court. He bur. in yard near North Meeting House, Cape Elizabeth ME.

32 Ebenezer$^4$, 1734-1795.
Mary, b. 15 Apr 1741 d. 1810, m.(I) 6 Apr 1761 Stephen Yeaton of Poland ME.
33 Jabez$^4$, 1743-1816.
34 John$^4$, 1745-1805.
Rachel, b. 16 Jun 1749, m.(1) 22 Nov 1770 Ebenezer Cobb Jr, m. (2) John Emery.
35 James$^4$, b. 1751.
Mercy, b. 14 Nov 1753, d. 21 Mar 1834, m. 14 Oct 1773 Joshua Dyer of Cape Elizabeth ME.
Lemuel, b. 23 Feb 1756 Cape Elizabeth ME. In Durham ME 1777.
Rebecca, b. 13 Oct 1760, m. 25 Jun 1778 John Skillings of Cape Elizabeth ME.

Sources: Cape Elizabeth ME census 1790. VR Cape Elizabeth ME, SA/ME. S69, L30, R10a.

11. **JONATHAN$^3$ SAWYER** [see 3], b. 18 Sep 1713 Gloucester MA, m. 25 Dec 1732 Sarah Sawyer of Gloucester MA, b. 15 Jul 1710, dau. Nathaniel and Hannah (Parker) Sawyer. Mariner. In Falmouth ME. On alarm list of Cape Elizabeth Company 29 Apr 1757.

Abigail, b. ca. 1736, m. 2 Nov 1754 Samuel Bradbury.
36 Jonathan$^4$, 1745-1824.
Deborah, b. 6 Nov 1749, d. 1 Sep 1807, m. 10 Apr 1770 Benjamin Fickett.

Sources: VR Gloucester MA. K10A, R10a, Robert L. Taylor rec.

12. **DANIEL$^3$ SAWYER** [see 3], b. 17 Sep 1718 Gloucester MA, d. 7 Jan 1811 Cape Elizabeth ME, m.(I) 15 Dec 1739 Sarah Woodbury of Beverly MA, b. 3 Jul 1722, dau. Joshua and Sarah Woodbury. Cordwainer. B/land in Falmouth 1731. Sergeant in Captain Loring Cushing's Cape Elizabeth Company, 29 Apr 1757.

Isaac, b. 1741 Cape Elizabeth ME.
37 Daniel$^4$, b. 1743.
38 Joshua$^4$, ca. 1745-1802.
39 John$^4$, ca. 1747-1832.
40 Nathaniel$^4$, 1749-1821.
Sarah, b. ca. 1751, d. 1802, m. Thomas Kelley of Jonesport ME.
Rebecca, b. ca. 1753.

Anna, bp. 1755, m. Isaac Lovett of Milbridge ME.
41 Peter[4], bap. 1757.
Sources: Cape Elizabeth ME census 1790, 1800. P18, L30, U1, Joshua Woodbury's will.

13. **JOHN[3] SAWYER** [see 4], b. 3 Apr 1717 Gloucester MA, m. 28 Nov 1745 Salisbury MA Martha Hubbard of Salisbury MA, b. 1716 d. 19 Feb 1811 Turner ME. B/S/land in New Gloucester 1748-1790. In New Gloucester ME 1763. Revolutionary War.
Martha, b. 3 Nov 1746, d.y.
Mary, b. 30 Aug 1748, m. 26 Dec 176? Judah Merrill.
Martha, b. 10 Jul 1750 d. 10 Jul 1829, m. Jacob Stevens.
Hannah, b. 15 Jun 1753, m. 9 Nov 1775 Jabez Merrill.
John, b. 17 Sep 1755 Gloucester MA.
Dorcas Hubbard, b. 31 Dec 1757, d. 10 Jun 1782, m. 10 Sep 1779 Benjamin Merrill.
42 Nathaniel[4], 1760-1828.
43 Parker[4], 1763-1800.
Sources: VR Gloucester MA, Salisbury MA. R10a, M38A, Obit.

14. **PARKER[3] SAWYER** [see 4], b. 2 Apr 1719 Gloucester MA, d. 1750, m. 10 Nov 1742 Comfort Haskell, b. 28 May 1717 d. 6 Sep 1809.
William, b. 14 Oct 1743, d. Sep 1758.
44 Jonathan Haskell[4], b. 1745.
Comfort, b.13 Aug 1747, m. 25 Mar 1766 Nathaniel Haskell, Jr.
Tammy, b. 8 Sep 1749, m. 8 Dec 1772 Enos Dodge.
Parker, b. 15 May 1751 Gloucester MA.
Sources: VR Gloucester MA. B1, B2, D40.

15 **ISAAC[3] SAWYER** [see 5], b. 22 Jun 1707 Gloucester MA, d. 1748 Falmouth ME, m. 1731 Sarah Brackett, b. 1 Mar 1709. Isaac was at meeting of First Parish Church of Falmouth ME 1727, joined 1733. Wid. m. Jonathan Morse 1754.
45 Zackariah[4], 1733-ca. 1820.
46 Anthony[4], 1735-1804.
Amie, b. 1737, m. Ebenezer Hilton.
Hannah Brackett, b. 1739, m. 2 Apr 1759 Daniel Morse.
47 Obediah[4], b. ca. 1741-1820.
Ann, b. 3 Apr 1740, m. 26 Mar 1764 Amos Knight.
Sarah, b. 1743, m. 1772 Daniel Bailey.
Isaac, b. ca. 1745, d. 24 Mar 1776 Falmouth ME.
48 Benjamin[4], 1746-ca. 1818.
49 Thomas[4], b. 1748.
Sources: VR Gloucester MA. K10A, P68, P82k, P18, B74, T19.

16. **EDWARD[3] SAWYER** [see 5], b. 5 Apr 1709 Gloucester MA, m.(I) 5 Jan 1734 Abigail Pitman, b. ?. Joined First Parish Church of Falmouth ME 1735. Member of Captain James Millis' Company, Falmouth Neck, 10 May 1757. Appointed Parish Sexton in 1759. S/land to brother Thomas 1762. On Falmouth ME tax list Nov 1766.
Edward, b. 1735 Old Falmouth ME.
Abigail, b. 1738.
50 Stephen[4], b. 1740.
51 Ezekiel[4], 1742-1828.
Sources: VR Gloucester MA, SA/ME. B1, K10A, R10a.

17. **THOMAS$^3$ SAWYER** [see 5], b. 12 Oct 1711 Gloucester MA, d. 1765 Falmouth ME, m. 7 Jul 1737 Hampton Falls NH Mehitable Blake of Hampton NH, b. 11 May 1720, dau. Jasper and Susan (Brackett) Blake. Joiner. Both joined First Parish Church of Falmouth 1738. B/land in No. Yarmouth from brother Abraham 1764. Wid. on Falmouth ME tax list Nov 1766, m.(I) 20 Jan 1769 Edmund Titcomb.

Mehitable, b. 1737, m. 8 Apr 1756 Henry Knight, Jr.
Anna, b. 8 Apr 1740, m. 26 Mar 1761 Amos Knight.
52 Jonathan$^4$, ca. 1741-ca. 1817.
Jerusha, b. 1745, m. 1764 Joseph Challice.
53 Isaac$^4$, ca. 1749-1818.
Hannah, b. ?, m. 12 May 1773 Joseph Titcomb.

Sources: VR Gloucester MA, Falmouth ME. P18, R10a, P82k, B49, T21A, K10A, M36.

18. **ABRAHAM$^3$ SAWYER** [see 5], b. 8 Mar 1717 Gloucester MA, d. bef. 1774, m.(1) 13 Jan 1743 Scarboro ME Elizabeth Graffam, b. ?; m.(2) 12 Nov 1754 Prudence Farr, b. ?. Joined First Parish Church of Falmouth ME 1737. Member of Falmouth Company at Siege of Louisburg, Nova Scotia, 1745. Granted land in present town of Standish ME. At Cape Elizabeth ME. S/land in Falmouth 1755. S/land in North Yarmouth 1762.

Reuben, b. 1746 Cape Elizabeth ME. Sea captain.
54 Enoch$^4$, bp. 1748.
Child, b. 1752.

Sources: VR Gloucester MA. B1, K10A, S22A, R10a.

19. **JACOB$^3$ SAWYER** [see 6], b. 20 May 1719 Gloucester MA, d. 31 May 1800 Cape Elizabeth ME, m.(1) Marcy _____, b. ?; m.(2) 25 Sep 1761 Mary Butler, b. ?. Private in Captain Loring Cushing's Cape Elizabeth Company, 29 Apr 1757. B/land from father 1762.

Olive, b. 25 Dec 1745, m. 19 Nov 1767 Jacob York.
Marcy, b. 7 Apr 1748.
Lucy, b. 7 Jul 1751.
55 Jacob$^4$, 1755-1832.

Sources: Cape Elizabeth ME census 1790. VR Gloucester MA. R10a.

20. **JOSIAH$^3$ SAWYER** [see 6], b. 30 May 1721 Gloucester MA, d. bef. 1783, m.(1) (I) 8 Dec 1743 Cape Elizabeth ME Phebe Strout, b. ca. 1725, dau. Joseph Strout; m.(2) 24 Mar 1765 Cape Elizabeth ME Abigail (Allen) Jordan, b. ?, wid. of William. Cordwainer. Corporal in Captain Loring Cushing's Cape Elizabeth Company 27 Apr 1757. Received land grant in Washington County 1764.

Sarah, b. 1744, d. 1774, m. 29 Nov 1764 Stephen Hutchinson.
56 Benjamin$^4$, 1744-1834.
Phebe, b. 10 Apr 1750, d. 21 Aug 1819, m. 11 Aug 1768 Ezra Jordan.
57 Josiah$^4$, 1763-1842.
Mary, b. ?.

Sources: VR Gloucester MA. K10A, R10a, P18, C97.

21. **SAMUEL$^3$ SAWYER** [see 6], b. 28 Mar 1723 Gloucester MA, d. 20 Oct 1781 Cape Elizabeth ME, m. 16 Nov 1750 Mary Wallis, b. 20 Aug 1730 d. 18 Jul 1808, dau. John and Patience (Hodgkins) Wallis. Private in Captain Loring Cushing's Cape Elizabeth Company, 19 Apr 1757. Surveyor of Highways for Cape Elizabeth ME 1766. S/land to Mary, wid. of brother William, 1770. He bur. in yard near North Meeting House, Cape Elizabeth ME.

58 Samuel[4], b.ca. 1751.
Mary, b. 28 Jul 1754, m. 1 Mar 1782 John Proctor, Cape Elizabeth ME.
Abigail, b. 27 Dec 1756, m. Thomas Stanford.
Ephraim, b. 2 May 1761 Cape Elizabeth ME, m. 17 Oct 1784 Phebe Dyer, b. ?, dau. James and Mary (Marriner) Dyer. CH: Mary, b. ?.
59 James[4], 1763-1845.
Sarah, b. 12 Feb 1766, m. _____ White.
William, b. 8 Feb 1768 Cape Elizabeth ME.
Patience, b. 4 Apr 1770, m. 1 May 1794 Isaac Blake of New Gloucester ME.
Hannah, b. 14 Jul 1774, m. Henry Parsons.
Sources: VR Cape Elizabeth ME, Falmouth ME, Portland ME. R10a, Robert L. Taylor rec.

22. **SOLOMON[3] SAWYER** [see 6], b. Sep 1730 Falmouth ME, m.(1) 16 Sep 1752 Ruth Bangs, b. 28 Sep 1731, dau. Ebenezer and Anna (Sears) Bangs; m.(2) 17 May 1765 Lydia (Small) Horn, b. 26 Oct 1729 d. 1826, dau. John and Hannah (Barnaby) Small of Provincetown MA. Private in Captain Loring Cushing's Cape Elizabeth Company 29 Apr 1757. Revolutionary War. At Cape Elizabeth ME, Gorham ME 1770, No. Yarmouth 1790. B/S/land 1774-1807. Wid. on Chebeaque Island 1810.
60 Solomon[4], 1757-1836.
Anna, b. 1770, m. 2 Dec 1790 John Hamilton.
Ruth, b. 1774, m. 27 Nov 1794 Ambrose Hamilton.
Sources:No. Yarmouth census 1790. Chebeaque Island census 1810. VR Falmouth ME, No. Yarmouth ME. K10A, U1, R10a, D9, K1A, D57.

23. **WILLIAM[3] SAWYER** [see 6], b. 19 Apr 1735 Falmouth ME, d. 1767 Cape Elizabeth ME, m.(I) 3 Feb 1759 Mary Mayo, b. ?. Wid. rec. land from Jacob, Jr. 1769. Wid. at Cape Elizabeth ME 1790.
61 Elisha[4], b. ca. 1764-1823.
Sources: Cape Elizabeth census 1790. R10a.

24. **JAMES[3] SAWYER** [see 7], b. 20 Oct 1715 Gloucester MA, d. 16 Jul 1746 Gloucester MA, m. 13 Mar 1739 Deborah Webber, b. 2 Nov 1717, dau. Michael and Sarah (Green) Webber. Wid. m. James Bishop, 1751.
62 James[4], b. 1740.
Deborah, b. 10 Nov 1741, d. 17 Jul 1746.
Sarah, b. 15 Apr 1743, d. 13 Jul 1834, m. 13 Dec 1763 Stover Sayward.
Hannah, b. 26 Aug 1744, m. 26 Mar 1764 Ebenezer Marble.
Benjamin, bp. 7 Apr 1746, d. 1 May 1746.
Sources: VR Gloucester MA. E20, B1.

25. **DAVID[3] SAWYER** [see 7], b. 13 Sep 1726 Gloucester MA, d. Nov 1752 Gloucester MA, m.(I) 16 Aug 1746 Martha Boynton, b. 26 Oct 1726.
Martha, b. 7 May 1747, m. 11 Dec 1766 John Davis.
Hannah, b. 7 May 1747, d. 9 Sep 1747.
David, b. 17 May 1749, d. Apr 1751.
63 David[4], 1751-1795.
64 James, bp.1753-1807.
Sources: VR Gloucester MA. B2, B1.

26. **ABRAHAM³ SAWYER** [see 7], b. 6 Mar 1737 Gloucester MA, d. 4 Apr 1815 New Gloucester ME, m. 13 Apr 1758 Mary Sayward of Gloucester MA, b. 1 Sep 1735 d. 23 May 1815, dau. Henry and Abigail Sayward. B/land in New Gloucester ME 1779 and 1782. Sailmaker.

Abraham, b. 19 Feb 1759, d. 1759.
65 Abraham⁴, 1760-1856.
James, bp. 12 Jun 1763 Gloucester MA, m.(1) 23 Feb 1786 Gloucester MA BetseyHough, b. 1764 d. 6 Aug 1833; m.(2) 16 Jul 1834 Gloucester MA Judith Morgan, b. ? d. 1845.
Molle, bp. 1 Sep 1765, m. 12 Feb 1789 Samuel Morehead.
66 Moses⁴, 1768-1839.
Hannah, bp. 6 Oct 1771, d. 17 Sep 1856, unm.
Nabby, b. 5 Aug 1774, d. 21 Dec 1851, m. 18 Sep 1796 David Ingersoll.
John, b. Sep 1776, d. 20 Nov 1849, unm.

Sources: Gloucester MA census 1790, 1800. VR Gloucester MA. B1, C23, A38, C97.

## FOURTH GENERATION

27. **THOMAS⁴ SAWYER** [see 8], b. 7 Jun 1716 Gloucester MA, m. ?.

Thomas, b. 12 Oct 1740 Gloucester MA.

Sources: VR Gloucester MA.

28. **JAMES⁴ SAWYER** [see 8], bp. 26 Aug 1722 Gloucester MA, d. 16 May 1760 Gloucester MA. m. 13 Feb 1743 Hannah Williams, b. 17 Dec 1723.

Jemima, bp. 5 Jun 1743, m. 15 Sep 1763 Samuel Morehead.
Hannah, b. 26 Aug 1750.
Thomas, b. 19 Aug 1753 Gloucester MA.
Molly, b. 27 Jul 1755, m. 17 Jun 1776 John Brooks.
Elinor, b. 28 Sep 1760 (after father's death).

Sources: VR Gloucester MA. B1.

29. **JONATHAN⁴ SAWYER** [see 9], b. 22 Oct 1736 Falmouth ME, d. Nov 1789 Gorham ME, m. 17 Oct 1763 Martha Rich, bp. 2 Dec 1744 Truro MA d. 13 Aug 1813, dau. Lemuel and Elizabeth (Harding) Rich. In Captain John Smith's Company 1760. Lt. and captain in Captain W. Stewart's Company. Revolutionary War. B/land in Gorham 1762. In Otisfield ME 1786. CH all moved to Otisfield ME ca. 1800.

Elizabeth, b. 12 Mar 1765, d. 31 Jan 1842, m. 13 Jan 1785 John Lombard.
Martha, b. 5 Jun 1767, d. 13 Jul 1839, m. 11 Jun 1790 John Millet.
John, b. 8 May 1769 Gorham ME, d. 28 Nov 1837 Otisfield ME, m. 4 Oct 1792 Hannah Edwards of Gorham ME, b. 1773 d. 5 Mar 1858, dau. Richard and Hannah (Lothrop) Edwards. Wid. with dau. in West Poland ME 1850 and bur. there. CH: Sarah, b. 4 Feb 1794, d. 18 May 1816; Hannah, b. 22 Jul 1796, d. Feb 1873, m. 7 Apr 1817 Eliphalet Dunn; Martha, b. 2 Sep 1799, d. 2 Aug 1852, m. 6 Mar 1828 John H. Faunce; Polly, b. 19 May 1802, d. 13 Feb 1892, m. Simeon Dunn.
67 David⁵, 1771-1811.
68 Barnabas⁵, 1773-1862.
Sarah, b. 25 Sep 1775 d. 6 Nov 1852, m. 27 Oct 1793 Benjamin Stevens.
Mary, b. 13 Apr 1778, m. Jeremiah Styles.
Deliverance, b. 15 Apr 1780, d. 27 Dec 1840, m. 20 Mar 1811 Levi Sargent.
69 Jonathan⁵, 1782-1861.
Eunice, b. 20 Apr 1785, m. Richard Lombard.
70 Samuel⁵, 1787-1864.

Sources: Otisfield ME census 1800, 1810. VR Otisfield ME, Gorham ME. P51, D6, M45, S67.

30. **DAVID$^4$ SAWYER** [see 9], b. 1737 Cape Elizabeth ME. In Gorham ME. Revolutionary War: Capt John Small's Company, Ruggles Regiment.

71 David$^5$, 1764-ca. 1804.

Sources: Gorham ME census 1790. VR Gorham ME. U1.

31. **JOEL$^4$ SAWYER** [see 9], b. ca. 1750, d. 11 Feb 1825 Gorham ME, m. 14 Oct 1773 Cape Elizabeth ME Elizabeth Stone, b. ? d. 31 Oct 1823. Revolutionary War: Joined Captain Stuart's Company, Colonel Edmund Phinney's Regiment 15 Jul 1775. B/S/ land in Gorham 1773-1800. Set off land to brother Jonathan in 1786.

Eunice, b. 19 Feb 1775, d. 29 Nov 1850, m. 14 Mar 1798 Rufus Harmon.

Polly, b. 22 May 1778, d. 19 Jul 1840, m. 3 Dec 1797 Daniel Moody of Standish ME.

Betsey, b. 22 Jul 1783, d. 1871, m. 25 Sep 1808 William Moody of Standish ME.

Dorcas, b. 29 Mar 1786, d. 1814, m. 19 Feb 1809 Enoch Moody of Standish ME.

Wealthy, b. ca. 1788, m. 19 Oct 1809 Stephen Lowell of Standish ME.

72 Isaac$^5$, 1793-1880.

73 Charles$^5$, 1804-1886.

Sources: Gorham ME census 1790, 1800, 1810, 1820. VR Gorham ME. R10a, M3, D6, H25.

32. **EBENEZER$^4$ SAWYER** [see 10], b. 27 Jan 1734 Cape Elizabeth ME, d. 7 Apr 1795 Cape Elizabeth ME, m.(1) 27 Feb 1757 Falmouth ME by Rev. Ephraim Clark Susan Yeaton, b. 1738 d. 16 Apr 1775, dau. Samuel and Susannah (Lang) Yeaton; m.(2) 11 Feb 1776 Hannah Small, b. 1736 d. 5 Nov 1812. Cordwainer. First four CH were b. in Falmouth ME. Corporal in Captain Loring Cushing's Cape Elizabeth Company, 29 Apr 1757. Surveyor of Highways for Cape Elizabeth ME 1766.

74 Ebenezer$^5$, 1757-1842.

75 Joseph$^5$, 1760-1848.

76 Samuel$^5$, b. 1762.

Joanna, b. 17 Aug 1764, m. 3 Feb 1784 Nathaniel Jordan, 3rd.

77 Reuben$^5$, 1766-1794.

Susanna, b. 15 Sep 1768, d. 27 Jul 1837, m. 24 Aug 1790 Isaac Small.

78 Nathan$^5$, 1771-1838.

Katherine, b. 2 Oct 1773, m. 5 Mar 1797 Stephenson Robinson.

79 James$^5$, 1777-1831.

Sources: Cape Elizabeth ME census 1790. VR Cape Elizabeth ME, Falmouth ME. M3, Lucy P. S. Thompson rec.

33. **JABEZ$^4$ SAWYER** [see 10], b. 31 Dec 1743 Cape Elizabeth ME, d. 19 Apr 1816 Buxton ME, m. 8 Mar 1765 Mary Pennell of Falmouth ME, b. ? d. 10 Mar 1814, dau. Thomas and Hannah (Brooks) Pennell. Settled Blue Hill ME 1765, returned to Cape Elizabeth ME when Indians became troublesome. Res. beside brother John in Buxton ME 1777. Revolutionary War.

Rebecca, b. 15 Jul 1765, d. 12 Sep 1819, m. 3 Jan 1788 Joseph Hobson.

Mary, b. 28 Oct 1766, d. 13 May 1802, m. 10 Oct 1790 William Elwell.

80 Jabez$^5$, 1768-1848.

81 Thomas Pennell$^5$, 1770-1818.

Joanna, b. 14 Jun 1772, d. Dec 1854, m. 12 Aug 1794 Joseph Hanson.

82 Joseph$^5$, 1774-1846.

83 James Thornton$^5$, 1776-1842.

Sarah, b. 30 Oct 1777, d. 7 Feb 1856, m. 5 Oct 1797 Isaac Deering.

84 William$^5$, 1779-1853.
Mercy, b. 27 Oct 1780, d. 26 Dec 1781.
Lydia, b. 18 Jun 1782, d. 27 Apr 1865, m. 12 Jan 1809 John Lord.
Mercy, b. 18 Jul 1784, d. 1 Jun 1870, m. 13 Nov 1817 John Knight of Westbrook ME.
85 Ebenezer$^5$, 1786-1835.
Sources: Buxton Me census 1790, 1800, 1801. VR Buxton ME. R17, Mercy (Sawyer) Knight rec.

34. **JOHN$^4$ SAWYER** [see 10], b. 24 Dec 1745 Cape Elizabeth ME, d. 30 Dec 1805 Buxton ME, m. 20 Jan 1768 Blue Hill ME Isabella Martin, b. 27 Sep 1749 d. 6 Dec 1839, dau. David and Hannah (Brooks) Martin. Revolutionary War: Joined Continental Army 1776, served two years as lieutenant and quartermaster. B/land in Standish ME 1782. In Buxton ME beside brother Jabez. He bur. in Tory Hill Cem., Buxton ME. Wid. in Buxton ME 1810, 1820, 1830.
Sarah, b. 1769, m.(1) 14 Feb 1788 Thomas Strout, m.(2) 14 Mar 1805 Samuel Stanford.
Hannah, b. 1 Sep 1771, m. 3 Feb 1799 Stephen Leighton of Limerick ME.
Molly, b. Jun 1772, d. 21 Oct 1857, m. 14 Mar 1793 Jeremiah Deering of Scarboro ME.
86 John$^5$, 1775-1849.
87 Robert$^5$, 1777-1834.
88 Lemuel$^5$, 1778-1851.
Abigail, b. 27 Oct 1782, m. 3 Dec 1801 John Deering of Scarboro ME.
89 David$^5$, 1784-1864.
Rachel, b. 29 Aug 1790, m. 16 Mar 1809 John Dunnell.
Joanna, b. 29 Aug 1790, d.y.
Sources: Buxton ME census 1810, 1820, 1830. VR Buxton ME. F21, M5, D6, W52, R17, Paul Coffin rec., Ruby Dunnell rec.

35. **JAMES$^4$ SAWYER** [see 10], b. 9 Jun 1751 Cape Elizabeth ME, m. 2 Jan 1773 Cape Elizabeth ME Margaret Jordan, b. ?. In Royalborough (Durham) ME 1783.
90 James$^5$, 1774-ca. 1806.
Sources: VR Cape Elizabeth ME.

36. **JONATHAN$^4$ SAWYER** [see 11], b. 1745 Cape Elizabeth ME, d. 7 May 1824 Cape Elizabeth ME, m. 25 Jan 1775 Cape Elizabeth ME Rebecca Parker, b. ?. Yoeman, rigger.
91 Joseph Parker$^5$, ca. 1775-1817.
92 Benjamin Franklin$^5$, ca. 1777-1834.
93 David$^5$, 1778-1834.
94 Lemuel$^5$, 1779-1835.
95 Elisha$^5$, 1781-1833.
Jonathan, b. ca. 1783 Cape Elizabeth ME d. Feb 1814 on a prison ship in England, m. 9 Aug 1806 Joanna Gammon, b. ?. CH: Joseph, b. 14 Mar 1810 d. 22 Oct 1824; Almira, b. 26 Feb 1812, m. 5 Jul 1835 George Webster; Martha Ann, b. 28 Mar 1814 d. 14 Dec 1842, m. William Cox.
96 John$^5$, 1786-1831.
Sources: Cape Elizabeth census 1790, 1800, 1810, 1820. VR Cape Elizabeth ME. R10a.

37. **DANIEL$^4$ SAWYER** [see 12], b. 1743 Cape Elizabeth ME, m.(1) 1 May 1766 Cape Elizabeth ME Miriam Jackson of Falmouth ME, b. ?; m.(2) 14 Dec 1772 Cape Elizabeth ME Lorania Cushing of Cape Elizabeth ME, b. 20 Dec 1735, dau. Jeremiah and Mary Cushing of Provincetown MA.
97 Daniel$^5$, b. (1767-1774).
Lorania, b. 16 Oct 1773, m. 29 Aug 1793 Isreal Stanford.

Sources: Cape Elizabeth ME census 1790, 1800, 1810. C94, C3A.

38. **JOSHUA$^4$ SAWYER** [see 12], b. ca. 1745 Cape Elizabeth ME, d. Jan 1802 Limington ME, m.(1) 2 May 1765 Rachel Dyer, b. ?; m.(2) (I) 5 May 1778 Sarah (Roberts) Bollen, wid. of Jonathan, b. ? d. Dec 1836. Cordwainer. Heir to Daniel Small of Truro MA, received land in Limington ME; settled on bank of Saco River in East Limington ME 1775. B/land 1791 in Cape Elizabeth ME.

Rebecca, b. 12 Jun 1772, d. 7 Feb 1858, m. 27 Mar 1793 Thomas Spencer.
Rachel, b. ca. 1776, m. 31 Mar 1796 Freathy Spencer.
Phebe, b. ?, d. Jun 1802, unm.
98 Joshua$^5$, 1791-1848.

Sources: Limington ME census 1790, 1800. VR Limington ME. T6, U1, R10a.

39. **JOHN$^4$ SAWYER** [see 12], b. ca. 1747 Cape Elizabeth ME, d. 1832 Jonesport ME, m. 3 Mar 1770 Wiscasset ME Mary Jordan of Steuben ME, b. ?, dau. Ebenezer and Rebecca (Brown) Jordan of Steuben ME. Settled Sawyer's Cove 1775. Revolutionary War: Corporal in Captain Reuben Dyer's Co., Colonel Benjamin Foster's Regiment 1777.

Rebecca, b. 1771, m. 1787 Nehemiah Sawyer of Jonesport ME.
Sarah, b. 1773, m.(I) 21 Mar 1805 Sewall Labaree.
John, b. 1775 Jonesport ME, d. 1854 Jonesport ME, m. 30 Mar 1800 Limington ME Mary Sawyer of Limington ME, b. 27 Jun 1775, dau. Nathaniel and Mary (Strout) Sawyer. Farmer. CH: Nathaniel, b. 26 Apr 1801, d. 14 May 1873, unm; Mary, b. 20 May 1803, d. 1868, m. 27 Apr 1820 Joshua Walker; Margaret, b. 25 May 1808, m.(1) Abijah W. Cummings, m.(2) John Richardson.
Elizabeth, b. 1777, m. Jesse Brown.
Dorcas, b. 1779, m. 26 Aug 1802 David Kelley.
Mary, b. 1781, m. 15 Jan 1797 Thomas Kelley.
Margaret N., b. 25 Apr 1783, d. 14 Dec 1871, m.(1) 18 Nov 1800 Ami Beal, m.(2) Nathaniel Beal.
99 Ebenezer Jordan$^5$, b. ca. 1785.
Hannah, b. 1788, m. Thomas Oliver.
100 Daniel Jordan$^5$, 1791-1879.

Sources: Jonesport ME census 1790, 1800, 1810, 1820. VR Machias ME, D91, Leonard F. Tibbetts rec., Mrs. Ed Ames rec.

40. **NATHANIEL$^4$ SAWYER** [see 12], b. 4 Jul 1749 Cape Elizabeth ME, d. 4 Jun 1821 Limington ME, m.(1) (I) 9 Apr 1774 Mary Strout, b. ? d. 26 Sep 1791 dau. Joseph and Sarah (Mayo) Strout; m.(2) 12 Jan 1792 Buxton ME Shuah Small, wid. of Issac, b. 28 Feb 1765 d. 29 Jun 1857, dau. Joshua and Susanna (Kennard) Small. Heir to Daniel Small of Truro MA, received land in Limington ME 1777, settled 30 acres (Range B). Bur. in East Limington ME.

Mary, b. 27 Jun 1775, m. 13 Apr 1800 John Sawyer. [See 39]
101 Daniel$^5$, 1776-1841.
Joseph, b. 24 Dec 1778, d. 13 Nov 1779.
102 Nathaniel$^5$, 1781-1857.
Ebenezer, b. 7 Aug 1783 Limington ME, d. 25 Aug 1812 Limington ME.
103 John$^5$, 1792-1871.
104 Peter$^5$, 1794-1876.
Susannah, b. 18 Oct 1796, d. 29 Aug 1870, m. 24 Sep 1820 Henry Small.
105 Samuel$^5$, 1799-1860.
Sally, b. 4 Aug 1800.

106 Joseph$^5$, 1802-1874.
107 Ephraim$^5$, 1804-1887.
Sources: Limington ME census 1790, 1800, 1810, 1820. T6A, T6, N39, P82a, U1, Robert L. Taylor rec.

41. **PETER$^4$ SAWYER** [see 12], bp. 1757 Cape Elizabeth ME, m.(I) Cape Elizabeth ME Margaret Fairbanks, b. ?. Heir to Daniel Small of Truro MA, received land in Limington ME 1777.
108 Peter$^5$, b. 1782.
David Fairbanks, b. 6 Aug 1784 Cape Elizabeth ME.
Deborah, b. 25 Feb 1787.
Ebenezer, b. 24 Jun 1789 Cape Elizabeth ME.
109 John$^5$, 1791-ca. 1827.
Nathaniel, b. 29 Jun 1794 Cape Elizabeth ME.
110 Ephraim$^5$, 1797-1872.
Sources: Cape Elizabeth ME census 1790, 1800, 1810, 1820. VR Cape Elizabeth ME. R10a, U1.

42. **NATHANIEL$^4$ SAWYER** [see 13], b. 1 May 1760 Gloucester MA, d. 18 Jan 1828 Danville ME, m. 16 Jan 1783 New Gloucester ME Sarah Morgan of Gloucester MA, b. 24 Dec 1762 d. 4 Jun 1828. Settled in Pejepscot Claim ca. 1788.
111 Solomon Morgan$^5$, 1784-1861.
Molly, b. 12 Mar 1786, d. 6 Nov 1788.
John, b. 13 Mar 1787, d. 14 Mar 1787.
Sally, b. 10 Sep 1790, d. 18 Jun 1808.
Polly, b. 8 Sep 1793, m. Dec 1823 Daniel Dill.
Patty, b. 14 Dec 1799, d. Apr 1800.
Lydia, b. 23 Jul 1801.
Sources: Pejepscot ME census 1800, Danville ME census 1820. VR Gloucester MA, New Gloucester ME. R10a, M4A, Robert L. Taylor rec., Mrs. Willis Hayes rec.

43. **PARKER$^4$ SAWYER** [see 13], b. 27 Dec 1763 Gloucester MA, d. 15 Sep 1800 New Gloucester ME, m. 17 Nov 1791 Gray ME Nancy Libby of Gray ME, b. ?, dau. Daniel and Sarah (Doughty) Libby. B/S/land in No. Yarmouth ME 1790-1802. Wid. m. Thomas Dutton.
112 Daniel$^5$, b. 1792.
Clarissa, b. 1793, d. 9 Mar 1865, m. 25 Apr 1824 Joseph McIntire.
113 John$^5$, 1795-1864.
Sources: New Gloucester MA census 1800. VR Gloucester MA, New Gloucester ME, SA/ME. Mrs. Willis D. Hayes rec., Robert L. Taylor rec.

44. **JONATHAN HASKELL$^4$ SAWYER** [see 14], b. Aug 1745 Gloucester MA, m. 12 Mar 1767 Gloucester MA Dorcas Parsons, b. 14 Mar 1743.
Dorcas, b. 13 Aug 1769, d. 29 Sep 1825, m. 29 Dec 1789 Jonathan Brown, Jr.
George Parsons, b. 17 Nov 1771, d.y.
George Parsons, b. 14 Nov 1773 Gloucester MA, m. 7 Apr 1797 Gloucester MA Judith Hubbard, b. ?. CH: Eliza Low, b. 5 Apr 1799; Sarah Hubbard, b. 4 Feb 1804 d. 20 Oct 1890 Poultney VT; Caroline S., b. 26 Jun 1814, m. 26 Nov 1846 Stephen Tolman, Dorchester MA; George Parsons, b. 20 Jan 1817, d. same day; Mary L., b. 5 Dec 1823, m. 9 Dec 1844 Gardner Parks.
Judith Wyer, b. 16 Mar 1776, d. 10 Aug 1815, m. 10 Apr 1798 John Dexter.
Sources: Boston MA census 1830. VR SA/MA, SA/VT. E20, D36, P12, L35.

45. **ZACKARIAH⁴ SAWYER** [see 15], bp. 27 Aug 1733 Cape Elizabeth ME, d. bef. 1820 m.(1) 27 Aug 1754 Sarah Knight, b. 1735, dau. Henry and Priscilla (Merrill) Knight; m.(2) May 1784 Susannah (Watson) Skillings of Gorham ME, wid. of Isaac, b. 3 Feb 1746 d. 7 Nov 1834, dau. Eliphalet and Elizabeth (Phinney) Watson. Joined First Parish Church of Falmouth ME 1752. B/S/land 1765-1803. On Falmouth tax list 1766. In Gorham ME 1784. Wid. w/son Nathan 1820, 1830.

Child, b. 1752.
Hannah, b. 1755, d. 10 May 1794, m. 1778 Samuel Knight.
114 Isaac$^5$, 1759-ca. 1850.
115 Nathan$^5$, 1764-1837.
116 Zackariah$^5$, Jr., 1767-ca. 1840.
117 Jonathan$^5$, 1768-1838.
Amos, b. 14 Oct 1770, lost at sea.
118 Brackett$^5$, 1775-1851.
Mark, b. ?, d.y.
119 Levi$^5$, 1786-1855.

Sources: Gorham ME census 1790, 1800, Falmouth ME census 1810, 1820, 1830. VR Gorham ME. K10A, R10a, B74, T19, D4, Robert L. Taylor rec.

46. **ANTHONY$^4$ SAWYER** [see 15], b. 21 Jan 1735 Falmouth ME, d. 21 Jun 1804 Falmouth ME, m. 7 Nov 1755 Susanna Marston, b. ca. 1738 d. 31 Aug 1819. French and Indian War. On Falmouth ME tax list Nov 1766. B/S land in Falmouth 1765-1803. He bur. in E. Deering ME.

120 Thomas$^5$, 1758-1833.
121 John$^5$, 1760-1842.
122 William$^5$, 1763-1825.
Sarah, b. 1 Jun 1765, d. 12 Feb 1839, m. 5 Feb 1784 Peter Brackett.
123 Ephraim$^5$, 1767-1814.
Jane, b. 29 Mar 1769, d. 5 Apr 1836, m. 11 Nov 1790 Amos Knight of Wayne ME.
Anthony, b. 8 Apr 1770 Falmouth ME, d. 14 Aug 1827 Portland ME, m. 28 Nov 1799 by Rev. Caleb Bradley in Westbrook ME Joanna Berry,b. 15 Nov 1772. CH: Dau., b. (1794-1800); two sons b. (1800-1810).
124 Daniel$^5$, b. 1772.
125 Asa$^5$, 1777-1858.
126 Joseph$^5$, 1779-1858.
127 Robert$^5$, 1783-1831.

Sources: Falmouth ME census 1790, 1800. Portland ME census 1810. K10A, R10a, D9, D74, T19, Obit, David Young rec.

47. **OBEDIAH$^4$ SAWYER** [see 15], b. 1741 Falmouth ME, d. 20 Dec 1820, m.(1) 1 Apr 1766 Anna Snow, b. ?, dau. John and Abigail Snow; m.(2) 9 Mar 1778 Judith Pollard, b. ?. Uncle Thomas Brackett appointed guardian of Obediah in 1755. On Falmouth ME tax list Nov 1766. Joined First Parish Church of Falmouth 30 Aug 1767. Land on which he lived was conveyed to son Samuel 1808 by dau. Susanna Knight and husband.

Thomas, bp. 30 Aug 1767 Falmouth ME, m. 8 Mar 1807 Westbrook ME Esther Johnson, b. ?. In Otisfield ME 1803.
128 John$^5$, bp. 1768.
129 Samuel$^5$, 1770-1841.
130 Joshua$^5$, ca. 1774-1806.

Obediah, Jr., b. (1784-1790) Falmouth ME, m. 4 Nov 1807 Harriet Pond, b. 19 Mar 1789, dau. Moses and Anne Pond. Wid. m. Thomas Neal Paine, went to Malden MA. CH: Son, b. (1808-1810).

Anne, b. ?, m. 9 Jun 1791 Thomas Merrill.

Susannah, b. ?, m. 2 Feb 1797 Henry Knight.

Sources: Falmouth ME census 1790, 1800, 1810. VR Falmouth ME. T19, P82k.

48. **BENJAMIN[4] SAWYER** [see 15], b. Feb 1746 Falmouth ME, d. bef. 1818 Falmouth ME, m. 1 Aug 1771 Miriam Sawyer, b. ?. Bricklayer. Joined First Parish Church in Falmouth ME 22 Nov 1772. Wid. in Westbrook ME 1820, 1830.

131 Thomas, Jr.[5], 1772-1852.

Amey b. 21 May 1775, m. 20 May 1800 Joshua Sawyer of Durham ME.

132 Zebulon[5], 1778-ca. 1832.

Miriam, b. ?, m. 6 Sep 1812 John Baker.

Sarah, b. ?, unm.

Anna, b. ca. 1786, d. 27 Jun 1861, unm. In New Gloucester ME.

Hannah, b. ca. 1789, d. 27 Sep 1870, m. 15 Mar 1810 Samuel Sawyer of Durham ME.

Sources: Falmouth ME census 1790, 1800, 1810. Wid. Westbrook ME census 1820, 1830. P18, K10A, R10a.

49. **THOMAS[4] SAWYER** [see 15], b. Mar 1748 Falmouth ME, d. Falmouth ME, m. 31 Mar 1767 Falmouth ME Eunice Knight, b. ?, dau. Henry and Priscilla (Merrill) Knight. Joined First Parish Church of Falmouth ME 15 May 1768. Heirs of Eunice S/land in 1805.

Thomas, bp. 13 Jul 1768 Falmouth ME.

133 Benjamin[5], 1769-1825.

Eunice, bp. 1772, d. 4 Apr 1820, m. 17 Jun 1790 John Huston.

134 Ebenezer Hilton[5], 1774-1850.

135 Samuel[5], b. 1777.

Hannah, b. 18 Feb 1783.

Dorcas, b. 1788, d. 1808.

Sarah, b. ?.

George, b. 1790, d. 13 Jun 1808.

Sources: Falmouth ME census 1790. VR Falmouth ME, SA/MA. R10a, K10A, B74, T19, David Young rec.

50. **STEPHEN[4] SAWYER** [see 16], b. 1740 Falmouth ME, m. 1 Jul 1761 Deliverance Barton, b. ?. Member of Captain James Milk's Company, Falmouth Neck 1757. On Falmouth ME tax list Nov 1766.

Molly, b. 29 Jun 1766.

William, b. 11 Sep 1768 Old Falmouth ME.

Sources: VR Falmouth ME.

51. **EZEKIEL[4] SAWYER** [see 16], b. 1742 Falmouth ME, d. 1828 Portland ME, m.(1) (I) 29 Mar 1766 Brunswick ME Sarah Hinkley, b. ?; m.(2) 4 Dec 1783 Margaret Coffin of Portland ME, b. ?. Served in Captain Benjamin Waite's Company, Colonel Waldron's Regiment, Feb/Mar 1760. B/S/land Portland 1771-1799. Joined First Parish Church of Falmouth, 5 Nov 1791. In Brunswick ME, Standish ME.

136 Edward[5], 1767-ca. 1807.

Martha, b. 2 Jun 1771 Standish ME, bp. Falmouth ME, m. 22 Dec 1792 Joseph Clark of Cape Elizabeth ME.

Sarah, b. 15 Aug 1773, m. 26 May 1804 Henry Pearson.
Hannah, b. 24 Aug 1786, m.(1) 31 May 1804 William Mulloy, m.(2) 31 May 1809 David Boyd of Portland ME.
Nancy, b. 3 Oct 1787, m. 24 Oct 1804 John Sisk.
Dorcas, b. 16 Nov 1789, m. 28 Dec 1806 Isreal Linnell.
137 William$^5$, 1793-1869.
Sophia, b. 7 May 1797, m. 2 Apr 1815 Samuel H. Bell.
Sources: Portland ME census 1790, 1800, 1810, 1820. VR Brunswick ME, Portland ME, Standish ME. R10a, G35A, Obit.

52. **JONATHAN$^4$ SAWYER** [see 17], b. ca. 1741 Falmouth ME, d. ca. 1817, m. 24 Jun 1766 Falmouth ME Mary Morse, b. ?. On Falmouth ME tax list 1766. Revolutionary War: Enl. Captain Samuel Knight's Company 1776. Wid. w/son Jonathan 1820.
Rebecca, b. 12 Jul 1767.
Anna, b. 12 Mar 1769.
Hannah, b. 8 Apr 1770, m. 29 Dec 1797 Abner Lowell.
Son, b. (1774-1784).
138 Jonathan$^5$, b. (1775-1784).
Son, b. (1784-1790).
Son, b. (1784-1790).
Sources: Falmouth ME census 1800, 1810, 1820. VR Farmington ME, Hallowell ME. K10A, R10a, L45.

53. **ISAAC$^4$ SAWYER** [see 17], b. ca. 1749 Falmouth ME, d. 29 Oct 1818 Falmouth ME, m. Susanna Sawyer, b. ca. 1756, dau. Anthony and Susannah (Marston) Sawyer. Housewright, merchant. B/S land in Westbrook ME.
Susannah, b. ca. 1779, m. 18 Dec 1800 Thomas Sawyer, Jr.
139 Henry$^5$ (Holmes), (1780-1790)-ca. 1846.
Jane, b. ?, m. Joseph Stevens.
Lucy, b. ?, m. 27 Nov 1806 Elisha Higgins.
Margaret, b. ?, m. 13 Jan 1803 Isaiah Woodford.
Charlotte, b. ?, m. 3 Jan 1816 Joseph Cox.
Isaac, b. (1790-1800)) Old Falmouth ME. Yoeman. B/S/land 1816, 1823.
140 Mark$^5$, 1794-1852.
Sources: Falmouth ME census 1790, 1800. VR Gloucester MA. K10A, R10a, D11.

54. **ENOCH$^4$ SAWYER** [see 18], bp. 1748 Cape Elizabeth ME, d. 181? No. Yarmouth ME, m. 1 Dec 1772 Cumberland ME Mary Sanborn, b. ?, dau. Paul Sanborn. In Cumberland ME. B/S/land in No. Yarmouth 1774-1801. Wid. w/son Reuben in No. Yarmouth ME 1820, Cumberland ME 1830.
Betsey, b. ?, m. 27 Oct 1795 Jabez True.
Abigail, b. ?, m. 31 Jan 1799 David Buxton.
Nathaniel, b. ?. Sailor in West Indies.
Eunice, b. ?, m. 21 Nov 1799 Isreal True.
Apphia, b. ?, m. 21 Feb 1811 Samuel Winslow.
141 Reuben$^5$, ca. 1785-1848.
Polly, b. 22 Feb 1788 d. 12 Mar 1873 m. 1 Nov 1813 Jonathan Cushing.
Joanna, b. ca. 1790, d. 18 Dec 1837 Cumberland ME.
142 Asa$^5$, b. ca. 1792.

Sources: North Yarmouth ME census 1810, 1820. Cumberland ME census 1830. VR North Yarmouth ME. R10a.

55. **JACOB$^4$ SAWYER** [see 19], b. 4 Jul 1755 Cape Elizabeth ME, d. 10 Dec 1832 Durham ME, m.(1) 18 Apr 1782 Cape Elizabeth ME Sarah Hatch, b. 1755 d. 14 Mar 1797; m.(2) 12 Mar 1798 Durham ME Hannah Roberts, b. 1760 d. 12 Feb 1799; m.(3) 2 Dec 1801 Durham ME Esther Hibbard, b. 1778 d. 10 Dec 1861. Revolutionary War: Enl. at Cape Elizabeth in Captain Daniel Strout's Company for six months 1775; Captain William Crockett's Company for nine months 1776; and Captain Joshua Jordan's Company for three and one-half months 1779. Pew owner in Congregational Church, Falmouth ME. B/land in Durham ME 1793. He bur. in Harmony Grove Cem., Durham ME. Wid. w/dau. Olive 1860.

Joseph, b. 1783 Cape Elizabeth ME. In Durham ME.
John Cushing, b. 16 Feb 1791 Durham ME.
Mary, b. 25 Jan 1799, d. 1 Jan 1841, m. 4 Dec 1817 Levi Bragdon.
Jacob, b. 21 Oct 1802, d. 15 Jan 1804.
Olive, b. 7 Jan 1806, d. 9 Jan 1872, m. 1830 Lemuel Turner.
Marcy, b. 1808, m. 25 Oct 1833 Nathaniel Mirch.
143 Merrick D.$^5$, 1809-1894.
James Hibbard, b. 7 Sep 1811 Durham ME, d. 22 Nov 1893 Buxton ME, m. Mary G. Moulton, b. 7 Dec 1818 d. 3 Feb 1860, dau. Joshua and Lydia (Stone) Moulton.Teacher. CH: Two, d.y.
David Blethen, b. Dec 1819 Durham ME, m. 23 Sep 1845 Lisbon ME Charlotte A. Gerrish of Lisbon ME, b. 1830, dau. Joshua and Charlotte (Sudlem) Gerrish. Physician. In Poland ME 1854. In Mechanic Falls ME, So. Paris ME, Lewiston ME. CH: Hattie, b. 1854.
Esther, b. ca. 1820.
Joseph R. b. (1820-1825).

Sources:Durham ME census 1800, 1810, 1820, 1830. Minot ME census 1850. Poland ME census 1860. Norway ME census 1870. VR Durham ME, Lisbon ME, SA/ME. R10a, S69, D9, N1A.

56. **BENJAMIN$^4$ SAWYER** [see 20], b. ca. 1744 Cape Elizabeth ME, d. 19 May 1834 Freeport ME, m.(1) (I) 11 Nov 1769 Mary Webber, b. ?; m.(2) 24 Sep 1773 Cape Elizabeth ME Catherine Mariner, b. 27 Feb 1753 d. 10 May 1843, dau. Joseph and Abigail (Hanscom) Mariner. Tanner. Captain in Revolutionary War. Deed proves parentage.

Phebe, b. 11 Dec 1771, d. 17 Mar 1851 m.(I) 1792 Benning Wentworth. Went to Ohio.
Polly, b. 10 Apr 1780, m. 14 Nov 1799 Abraham Mitchell of Kittery ME.
Hezikiah, b. (1780-1784), m.(I) 1801 Polly Woden b. 1779, d. 4 Feb 1853. Laborer. Wid. in Freeport ME 1820, w/son Benjamin 1850. CH: Catherine, b. ca. 1804, d. 24 Jul 1882 unm, in Rockland ME; Mary, b. (1800-1810), m. Philip Eastman; Benjamin W., b. ca. 1809, unm, in Rockland ME.
Sarah, b. ?.
Charlotte, b. ?.
Mary,b.?.
Hannah, b. ?, m. 1826 Asa Brown.

Sources: Freeport ME census 1790, 1800, 1810, 1820, 1830, 1850. R10a, N5, S70, W26.

57. **JOSIAH$^4$ SAWYER** [see 20], b. ca. 1763 Cape Elizabeth ME, d. Mar 1843 Steuben ME, m. 1785 Elizabeth Brown, b. ?, dau. Jessie and Lydia (Smith) Brown. Revolutionary War: Enl. 13 Apr 1781 for three years in Captain Haskell's Company, Colonel Noyes' 4th Regiment, 1st Brigade. After the war, he settled near river in what is now Milbridge ME. In Steuben ME 1833.

144 Josiah$^{5}$, 1787-1875.
145 William$^{5}$, b. 1791.
146 George B.$^{5}$, 1793-1853.
Lydia, b. 29 Jul 1795, m. Josiah Grindle.
Sally, b. 12 Jun 1798, m.(I) 19 Nov 1821 Josiah Wallace.
147 John G.$^{5}$, b. 1800.
Hannah, b. 1802, m.(1) 3 Aug 1825 Henry Dyer, m.(2) Edmund French.
Jane, b. 1804, m.(I) 20 May 1821 Thomas Strout.

Sources: Harrington ME census 1790, 1800, 1810, 1820, 1830. Steuben ME census 1840. VR Harrington ME, SA/ME. N1A, M7, M43.

58. **SAMUEL$^{4}$ SAWYER** [see 21], b. ca. 1750 Cape Elizabeth ME, d. bef. 1807, m. 5 Jul 1775 Hannah Horn, b. ?.
John, b. ?.
Abigail, b. ?, m.(I) 16 Jun 1811 Royal Talbot.

Sources: Portland ME census 1790. VR Cape Elizabeth ME. R10a.

59. **JAMES$^{4}$ SAWYER** [see 21], b. 4 Aug 1763 Cape Elizabeth ME, d. 14 Mar 1845 Portland ME, m.(1) 1 Jun 1786 Portland ME Elizabeth Brackett, b. 4 May 1766 d. 25 Jun 1799; m.(2) 30 May 1802 Portland ME Elizabeth Manchester, b. 1778 d. 7 Aug 1855. Mariner. B/S/land Cape Elizabeth ME 1799-1832. He bur. in Eastern Cem., Portland ME. Elizabeth bur. Torrington Point ME.
Jane B., b. 30 Oct 1787.
Thomas Brackett, b. 18 Jul 1789 Portland ME, d. 25 Oct 1815 Boston MA, m. ?. B/land Portland ME 1810. CH: George W., b. Oct 1814, d. 20 Sep 1815.
William, b. 6 Sep 1805, d. 17 Sep 1805.
Elizabeth B., b. 12 Sep 1809.
Lydia Waite, b. 20 Jan 1820, d. 13 Nov 1838.

Sources: Portland ME census 1790, 1800, 1810. VR Portland ME. P69, R10a, M5.

60. **SOLOMON$^{4}$ SAWYER** [see 22], b. 1757 Cape Elizabeth ME, d. 1836 Cumberland ME, m. 10 Oct 1779 Gorham ME Phebe Strout of Cape Elizabeth ME, b. ?. Revolutionary War. B/42 acres of land on Chebeaque Isle 6 Nov 1807. In Gorham ME, No. Yarmouth ME, Cumberland ME.
148 Solomon$^{5}$, 1782-1835.
Anne, b. 1788.
Becca, b. 1789, d.y.
Ruth, b. 1793.
Rebecca, b. 1795.
149 Jacob$^{5}$, b. 1797.
Deborah, b. 1799.

Sources: North Yarmouth ME census 1790, 1810, 1820. Cumberland ME census 1830. VR North Yarmouth. R10a, C78, F21.

61. **ELISHA$^{4}$ SAWYER** [see 23], b. ca. 1764 Falmouth ME, d. 4 Sep 1823 Pownal ME, m. 28 Jun 1786 Falmouth ME Elizabeth Dunbar, b. 1765. On Pownal ME tax list 1808. B/S/land in Pownal ME 1815. Wid. w/son Elisha 1830, 1840, 1850.
150 William$^{5}$, 1787-1839.
Apha, b. 9 Jan 1789, m.(I) 1805 Francis Duran.
151 Nathaniel$^{5}$, 1791-1838.

152 Enos$^5$, 1792-1846.
Peter, b. 16 Jul 1795 Freeport ME. In Pownal ME.
Rhoda, b. ca. 1796, d. 19 Oct 1853.
Samuel Dunbar, b. 16 Jan 1798 Freeport ME. In Pownal ME.
153 Elisha$^5$, b. 1812.
Jane, b. ?.
Sources: Falmouth ME census 1790. Freeport ME census 1800. Pownal ME census 1810, 1820, 1830, 1840, 1850. VR Freeport ME. R10a.

62. **JAMES$^4$ SAWYER** [see 24], b. 14 Mar 1740 Gloucester MA, m. 26 Oct 1762 Anne Davis, b. 24 Sep 1744.
James, b. 29 Aug 1763, d. 26 Nov 1784 at sea.
Anna, b. 10 Sep 1765.
David, b. 25 Jan 1768 Gloucester MA, d. 11 Aug 1819 Boston MA, m. Mary Holdon, b. 1772 d. 29 May 1802. CH: Delia, b. 27 Jun 1798, d. 14 Oct 1870, m. 28 Nov 1815 Ezekiel D. Cushing.
Betsey, b. 12 Oct 1783.
Deborah, b. 12 Oct 1783.
Robert Steward, bp. 24 May 1787.
James, b. 11 Sep 1788, d. 5 Jan 1811 at sea.
Sources: Gloucester MA census 1790. VR Gloucester MA.

63. **DAVID$^4$ SAWYER** [see 25], b. 30 Sep 1751 Gloucester MA, d. 14 May 1795 Gloucester MA, m. 20 Dec 1770 Gloucester MA Sarah Ingersoll, b. 25 May 1753.
Sally, b. 27 Mar 1771, d. 25 Apr 1773.
David, b. 20 Jul 1774 Gloucester MA, m. 18 Aug 1810 Harriet Shackleford, b. ?.
Sergeant, b. 1 Feb 1778, d. 11 Dec 1805.
Sally, b. Sep 1794.
Polly, b. Sep 1794.
Sources: VR Gloucester MA.

64. **JAMES$^4$ SAWYER** [see 25], bp. 1 Jul 1753 Gloucester MA, d. 14 Jun 1807 Gloucester MA, m.(I) 29 May 1776 Gloucester MA Deborah Newman, b. 9 Apr 1757 d. 26 Aug 1837 Boston MA, dau. Robert Newman (who hung the lantern in the Old North Church). Revolutionary War.
154 James$^5$, 1778-1858.
David, b. 26 Jun 1785 Gloucester MA, d. 2 May 1822 Charlestown MA.
155 Robert Stewart$^5$, 1796-1841.
156 William Newman$^5$, 1799-1862.
Charlotte, b. 19 Apr 1802 Gloucester MA, m. 20 Sep 1827 Gloucester MA Aaron Jaquith.
Sources: Gloucester MA census 1790, 1800, 1810 (wid.).VR Gloucester MA, Boston MA. B2, D50.

65. **ABRAHAM$^4$ SAWYER** [see 26], b. 28 Sep 1760 Gloucester MA, d. 3 May 1856, m. 26 Sep 1784 Gloucester MA Rachel Dolliver, b. 10 Feb 1758 d. 26 Sep 1843, dau. Paul Dolliver. Sailmaker.
Rachel D., b. 6 Dec 1786, m.(1) 12 Oct 1811 Sam Elwell of No. Yarmouth ME, m.(2) 17 Apr 1825 Cyrus Stevens.
157 Charles$^5$, 1788-1821.
Harriet, b. 17 Jan 1793, d. 3 Nov 1872, m. 10 Nov 1823 Major General John Webber of New Gloucester ME.

Sources: Gloucester MA census 1790, 1800. VR Gloucester MA. B1, C23.

66. **MOSES⁴ SAWYER** [see 26], b. 6 Jul 1768 Gloucester MA, d. 16 Nov 1839 New Gloucester ME, m. Gloucester MA 11 Nov 1795 Dorothy (Dolly) Babson, b. 2 Oct 1768 d. 1 Feb 1843 (or 1845). Sailmaker. B/S/land in New Gloucester 1803-1828. He bur. in Pineland Memorial Cem., New Gloucester ME.

158 Moses[5], 1795-1861.
Susan B., b. 17 Sep 1797, d. 8 Sep 1852.
Dorothy B., b. 30 Oct 1799, d. 17 Jun 1836, m. 3 Feb 1825 David K. Littlefield.
Mary, b. 5 Dec 1801, d. 3 Jul 1854.
Sally W., b. 3 Mar 1803, d. 30 Jun 1862, m. 17 May 1825 Thomas Morse.
James, b. 20 Sep 1805 New Gloucester ME.
Lydia B., b. 12 Jun 1808, d. 4 Dec 1856.
Betsey P., b. 13 Nov 1810, d. 18 Jun 1890.

Sources: New Gloucester ME census 1800, 1810, 1820, 1830. VR Gloucester MA, New Gloucester ME. E20, M5, C97.

## FIFTH GENERATION

67. **DAVID[5] SAWYER** [see 29], b. 27 Mar 1771 Gorham ME, d. 21 Dec 1811 Otisfield ME, m. 22 May 1806 Hebron ME Mary Greeley, b. 27 May 1783 d. 11 Mar 1858, dau. John and Elizabeth (Thompson) Greeley. B/land in Otisfield ME 1805-1811. Wid. m. 29 Dec 1817 David Jordan. She S/land in Otisfield ME 1832.

Barnabas, b. 14 Jan 1807 Otisfield ME, killed by falling tree 6 Feb 1832.
Harriet, b. 23 Mar 1809 Otisfield ME, d. 2 Apr 1880, m.(1) 28 Dec 1828 David Andrews, m.(2) David Jordan.
159 David[6], 1811-1879.

Sources: Otisfield ME census 1800, 1810. VR Otisfield ME, Hebron ME. R10a, S67.

68. **BARNABAS[5] SAWYER** [see 29], b. 26 Mar 1773 Gorham ME, d. 10 Apr 1862 Harrison ME, m.(I) 2 Feb 1797 Otisfield ME Sarah Rich, b. 4 Apr 1775 d. 15 Mar 1868, dau. Ezekiel and Sarah (Stevens) Rich. B/S/land in Norway ME, Hebron ME, Waterford ME.

Betsey, b. 3 Jun 1798, d. 15 Jun 1831, m. 29 Nov 1820 John Lombard.
Martha, b. 31 Mar 1800, d. 1883, unm. Ran a boarding house in Lawrence MA.
Jerusha A., b. 31 Jul 1802, d. 15 Jul 1837 m. 26 Sep 1822 Isaac Clark.
Jonathan, b. 28 Aug 1804 Otisfield ME, m.(1) 18 Nov 1830 Huldah Jackson of Otisfield ME, b. 10 Jul 1812 d. 10 Mar 1864; m.(2) 21 Aug 1864 Jane Holt, b. ?. In Norway ME 1840, Township #5 1850, Oxford ME 1870. CH: Clarissa, b. 1839.
David Mendum, b. 20 Feb 1806 Otisfield ME, d. 24 Apr 1864 Tunnel City WI, m. 3 Mar 1834 Julia Adams of Andover ME, b. 2 Sep 1816 d. 12 Dec 1911, dau. Enoch and Lucy (Strickland) Adams. Went to College Grant NH. CH: Emeline, b. 17 Nov 1842, m. 19 Jun 1862 Elijah Davenport; Martha J., b. 20 Jul 1845, m. 8 May 1869 William S. Wyman; Pauline, b. Feb 1850.
160 Daniel Barnabas[6], 1818-1899.
Sarah J., b. 1819.
Mary Delia., b. 1821, m. 17 Sep 1844 Lowell MA Josiah M. Tarr.
Eunice W., b. 1822, d. 1883. Went to Missouri.

Sources: Otisfield ME census 1800, 1810, 1820. Norway ME census 1840. Lawrence MA census 1850. Harrison ME census 1860. VR Otisfield ME, Windham ME, Gorham ME, Lowell MA, SA/MA. S67, L7, D6.

69. **JONATHAN[5] SAWYER** [see 29], b. 16 Jul 1782 Gorham ME, d. 29 May 1861, m. 25 Aug 1808 Lucretia Goss, b. 1786 d. 2 Jan 1881. B/S/land 1810, 1841.

161 William[6], 1809-1897.

Jonathan, b. 12 Feb 1811 Otisfield ME, m. 4 Nov 1845 Minot ME Emily Campbell, b. ?. CH: Clara M., b. 1847; Lavile, b. 1849.

Betsey, b. 25 Apr 1813.

162 Ebenezer E. H.[6], b. 1815.

Ann, b. 22 _____ 1817, m. Stanley Stiles.

Joel S., b. 20 Jul 1819, d. 8 Jan 1901, unm.

David K., b. 26 Jul 1822, d. 2 Jun 1851.

Mary W., b. 16 Mar 1827, d. 1 May 1892, m. Melzor Brown.

Sources: Otisfield ME census 1810, 1820. Batchelder's Grant ME census 1830, 1840. Stoneham ME census 1850, 1860, 1870. VR Minot ME, Stoneham ME, SA/ME. R10a, Obit, Will, Dan Barker rec.

70. **SAMUEL[5] SAWYER** [see 29], b. 7 Jun 1787 Gorham ME, d. 1864, m. 20 Apr 1808 Otisfield ME Releaf Moore, b. 11 Feb 1791 d. 1869, dau. Jonathan and Releaf (Nutting) Moore.

163 Samuel[6], 1808-1861.

Releaf, b. 1809.

Henry Moore, b. 30 Jun 1811 Otisfield ME, d. 8 Mar 1848, m. 27 Nov 1834 Sweden ME Abigail Parker of Stoneham ME, b. 18 Mar 1818 d. 19 Sep 1895. In Lovell ME, Stoneham ME 1834, Portland ME 1846. CH: Lydia, b. 13 Oct 1835, m. 7 Mar 1863 Zaccheus Gammon; Henrietta, b. 17 Apr 1837, d. 7 Feb 1849; Martha A., b. 27 Apr 1839; Sarah A., b. 5 Apr 1841; Abby Parker, b. 19 Jan 1846; Phosa, b. ?.

164 David[6], 1815-1886.

165 Abel M.[6], b. 1819.

Harriet A., b. 1829.

166 Hosea H.[6], 1830-1896.

Sources: Otisfield ME census 1810, Batchelder's Grant ME census 1830, 1840, Lovell ME census 1850, 1860. VR Gorham ME, Otisfield ME, SA/ME. R10a.

71. **DAVID[5] SAWYER** [see 30], b. 13 Mar 1764 Gorham ME, d. bef. 1804, m.(I) 14 Jan 1790 Scarboro ME Sarah Shute of Scarboro ME, b. ?, dau. William and Hannah (Carter) Shute. David was an illegitimate son of David and Mary McCorson. Sarah received land in Scarboro ME from Hannah Shute 1795. Wid. m. 12 May 1804 Timothy Berry.

167 Levi[6], ca. 1797-1874.

Betsey, b. ca. 1800, m. 23 Nov 1820 Joshua Mendum Libby.

Sources: Gorham ME census 1790. S2, L20, R10a, Pension Application of Timothy Berry, Robert L. Taylor rec.

72. **ISAAC[5] SAWYER** [see 31], b. 22 Apr 1793 Gorham ME, d. 1880 Garland ME, m. 19 Feb 1817 Gorham ME Eleanor Wescott of Garland ME, b. 21 Mar 1795 d. 1868. War of 1812. B/S/land in Gorham 1824-1836.

168 Marshall H.[6], 1818-1905.

Sarah, b. 14 Jul 1820, d. 2 Sep 1913.

Harriet, b. 3 Jul 1822, d. May 1910.

169 Reuben Wescott[6], 1824-1892.

Albion P., b. 18 Dec 1826 Thorndike ME, d. 20 Aug 1912 Gorham ME, m. 17 Jan 1854 Limington ME Eliza C. Gilkey of Limington ME, b. 17 Jun 1833 d. 7 Nov 1913, dau.

Reuben and Phebe (Marr) Gilkey. Civil War. Merchant. In Gorham ME, Portland ME. He bur. in Lewis Cem. West Gorham ME. CH: Eleanor, b. ?; Reuben, b. 1855 d. 1855; Isaac M., b. 1856, d. 1862; Phebe, b. 1861, d. 1870; Mildred G., b. 3 Aug 1877, d. ?.

Abigail, b. 7 Jan 1833 d. 2 Dec 1913, m. 28 Oct 1853 Ellsworth ME James Simpson.

Sources: Gorham ME census 1820. Thorndike ME census 1840. Garland ME census 1850, 1880 (with Reuben). VR Gorham ME. SA/ME. R10a, D6, H26, U1, D9, Guy S. Sawyer rec., Richard M. Sawyer rec.

73. **CHARLES[5] SAWYER** [see 31], b. 8 Sep 1804 Gorham ME, d. 8 Feb 1886 Atkinson ME, m.(1) 8 Oct 1829 Emily Reed of Cumberland ME, b. 1809; m.(2) 28 Mar 1867 Susan Harmmond, b. ?. B/S/land in Peru ME 1838-1847.

170 Frances Newell[6], 1831-1899.

Sophia L., b. 1834.

Louisa G., b. 1840.

Sources: Cumberland ME census 1830. Peru ME census 1840, 1850. Exeter ME census 1860. VR Cumberland ME, SA/ME. R10a.

74. **EBENEZER[5] SAWYER** [see 32], b. 16 Dec 1757 Falmouth ME, d. 10 Apr 1842 Limington ME, m.(1) (I) 10 Jul 1779 Abigail Small of Cape Elizabeth ME, b. 21 Jul 1760, dau. Michael and Hannah (Higgins) Small; m.(2) 5 May 1822 Lydia Clay of Buxton ME, b. Jun 1784 d. 1847, dau. Benjamin Clay. Revolutionary War: Private in Captain Mayberry's Company, Colonel Tupper's Regiment. At Cape Elizabeth ME 1765. In Limington ME 1784. He bur. in Clark Cem., Limington ME.

Lemuel, b. 1781 Limington ME, d. 5 Oct 1850 Phillips ME, unm. Cooper. War of 1812. In Phillips ME 1830.

171 James[6], 1784-1852.

Abigail, b. 1787, d. 14 May 1877, m.(I) 29 Jan 1810 John A. Libby of Scarboro ME.

Susan, b. 1789, unm. In Phillips ME.

Anna, b. Jan 1791, d. 29 Apr 1860, m.(I) 26 Dec 1813 William P. Marr.

Elmira, b. Apr 1793, d. 11 Nov 1881, m. 10 Oct 1819 James Marr. Went to Wisconsin.

172 Michael[6], 1795-1876.

Harriet, b. Jun 1800, d. 17 Jun 1864, m. 13 Oct 1829 Carl Goodwin of Hiram ME.

Ebenezer, b. 12 Dec 1801 Limington ME, d. 12 Oct 1888 Phillips ME, m. 9 Jan 1830 Sarah P. Davenport, b. 17 Nov 1805 d. 17 Nov 1886. Farmer.

173 Stephen[6], 1804-1877.

Sources: Limington ME census 1790, 1800, 1810, 1820, 1830, 1840. Phillips ME census 1830, 1840. 1850. T6, F21, N39, T6A.

75. **JOSEPH[5] SAWYER** [see 32], b. 2 Mar 1760 Falmouth ME, d. 12 Nov 1848 Steuben ME, m.(1) 3 Nov 1786 Cape Elizabeth ME Sarah Dyer, b. 12 Dec 1765 d. 18 Dec 1804, dau. Henry and Betty (Simonton) Dyer; m.(2) 1 Sep 1806 Addison ME Mary Took, b. 26 Dec 1771 d. 13 Mar 1852. W/son Daniel in 1840. B/land in Steuben ME 17961814. He bur. Sawyer Cem., Steuben ME.

Susannah, b. 1 Oct 1787, d. 16 Dec 1869, m. Nathaniel Ingersoll.

Betsey, b. 16 Feb 1789, d. Feb 1832.

174 Joseph[6], b. 1790.

175 Henry[6], 1791-1865.

Abigail, b. 12 Dec 1793, m. _____ Dyer.

Sally, b. 1 Apr 1795, m. Ambrose Coffin.

Catherine, b. 7 Feb 1797, m. Amos Allen.

176 Ebenezer[6], 1799-1876.

177 Lemuel Baker$^6$, 1802-1890.
Annie, b. 14 Feb 1804.
178 Daniel L.$^6$, 1808-1881.
Anna L., b. 9 Dec 1812, d. 1839.
Sources: Steuben ME census 1790, 1800, 1810, 1820, 1830, 1840. VR Steuben, ME, SA/ME. R10a, L30, A38, M43g, M5, S44, Obit (Sally), Charles L. Sawyer rec.

76. **SAMUEL$^5$ SAWYER** [see 32], b. 26 Mar 1762 Falmouth ME, d. Baldwin ME, m.(1) 2 Oct 1783 Cape Elizabeth ME Abigail Dyer, b. 25 Mar 1762, dau. Benjamin Dyer; m. (2) 23 Nov 1790 Nancy Cobb, b. ?. Joiner. Revolutionary War. In Limington ME 1786, Baldwin ME 1795. Selectman for Limington ME 1792, Baldwin ME 1812. B/S/ land 1802-1822. He bur. in Sawyer Cem., Baldwin ME. Wid. w/son Nathan 1840.
Benjamin, b. 22 Aug 1784, d. 27 Feb 1810.
179 Nathan$^6$, 1786-1866.
180 Ebenezer$^6$, 1789-1877.
Isabella S., b. 2 Aug 1792, d. 6 Jun 1827, m. 3 Nov 1811 Ezekiel Milliken of Baldwin ME.
Catherine, b. 7 Jul 1794, d. 1835, m. 25 Oct 1825 Solomon Anderson.
Sources: Limington ME census 1790. Baldwin ME census 1800, 1820, 1830, 1840. VR Baldwin ME. R10a, T6, Y3, M5, N40.

77. **REUBEN$^5$ SAWYER** [see 32], b. 31 Jul 1766 Falmouth ME, d. 21 Nov 1794 Freeport ME, m. 18 Nov 1789 Cape Elizabeth ME Deborah Small, b. 1764 d. 3 Nov 1822, dau. Edward and Abigail (Jordan) Small. Mariner. At Cape Elizabeth ME, Pownalboro ME. B/S/land Freeport ME 1793. Wid. m. Ebenezer Roberts of Durham ME.
Reuben, b. 1792 Cape Elizabeth ME, d. 23 Dec 1823 Portland ME, m. 13 Nov 1817 Phebe Ilsley of Portland ME, b. 1794 d. 15 Aug 1822. Cabinetmaker. He bur. in Eastern Cem., Portland ME. CH: Jane I., b. 18 Jul 1818, d. 10 Sep 1819; Susan, b. 18 Jul 1818, d. 19 Jul 1818; Phebe Newman, b. 2 Jan 1820, d. 15 Aug 1820. Note: According to Portland cemetery records, Reuben d. 1822.
181 Nathan$^6$, 1794-1824.
Sources: Portland ME census 1820. VR Cape Elizabeth ME, Portland ME. L20, Lucy P. S. Thompson rec.

78. **NATHAN$^5$ SAWYER** [see 32], b. 6 Feb 1771 Cape Elizabeth ME, d. 20 Jun 1838 Cape Elizabeth ME, m.(1) Abigail Dyer of Steuben ME, b. 24 Jul 1776 Steuben ME d. 1 Jan 1807, dau. Henry and Betty (Simonton) Dyer; m.(2) 26 Aug 1807 Minot ME Susannah Yeaton, b. 1776 d. 2 May 1851. He bur. Pleasant Hill Cem., So. Portland ME. Gravestone says he d. 20 May 1828. Wid. w/sons Ebenezer 1840, Simon 1850.
Reuben, b. 30 Nov 1796, d. 5 Aug 1824 Baton Rouge LA.
182 Asa$^6$, b. 1798.
183 Nathan$^6$, b. 1799.
Lemuel Dyer, b. 8 May 1801 Cape Elizabeth ME, m. 15 Nov 1842 Cherryfield ME Love M. Patten of Cherryfield ME, b. 25 Nov 1815 d. 30 Jul 1893, dau. John and Pamelia (Leighton) Patten. Harnessmaker. CH: Sarah Waite, b. 29 Nov 1845, d. 16 Dec 1870, m. W. T. Hill.
184 Andrew Simonton$^6$, 1802-1871.
Sally, b. 5 Apr 1805.
Abigail, b. 10 Dec 1806.
Ezekiel Dyer, b. 10 Dec 1806, d. 23 Feb 1807.
Mary, b. 6 Jul 1808.

185 Ebenezer[6], 1811-1884.
Joanna, b. 19 Mar 1813, d. 9 Jun 1879, m. 25 Nov 1842 Alvin Fickett.
186 Simon Cutter[6], 1816-1887.
Susan S., b. 23 Nov 1818, d. 22 Jan 1840.
Sources: Steuben ME census 1800. Cape Elizabeth ME census 1820, 1830, 1840, 1850. VR Steuben ME, Cape Elizabeth ME, Minot ME. Cherryfield ME. Obit.

79. **JAMES[5] SAWYER** [see 32], b. 15 Feb 1777 Cape Elizabeth ME, d. 29 Jan 1831 Gardiner ME, m. 3 Jul 1805 Scarboro ME Octavia Libby of Scarboro ME, b. 21 Jun 1787 d. 8 May 1857 in Wisconsin, dau. Reuben and Mercy (Marr) Libby. Farmer. Demaris, James M., Catherine, Mercy L. M. all bur. in Mt. Hope Cem., Bangor ME.
Almira, b. 23 Nov 1805, d. 30 Nov 1883, m. Heatherly Robinson.
Demaris, b. 8 Dec 1806, d. 12 Dec 1849.
Samuel, b. 13 Aug 1808, d. 1810.
James M., b. 26 Aug 1810, d. 27 Nov 1836.
Abigail, b. 6 Jul 1811, d. 19 Dec 1860.
187 Emerson M.[6], 1813-1898.
Catherine, b. 13 Jun 1815, d. 27 Mar 1908.
Mary Ann, b. 25 Sep 1817, d.y.
188 Stillman Higgins[6], 1819-1896.
189 Rufus H.[6], 1822-1889.
Mercy L. M., b. 10 Mar 1824, d. 23 Aug 1838.
Olive Ann, b. 13 Aug 1827, d. 14 Jun 1907, m. 2 Nov 1851 Howard W. Brooks.
Sources: Gardiner ME census 1830. Wid. in Bangor ME census 1840. VR SA/MA. S23, L20, Will, Olive Brooks Cooper rec.

80. **JABEZ[5] SAWYER** [see 33], b. 23 Jun 1768 Buxton ME, d. 26 Jan 1848 Hollis ME, m. 7 Nov 1793 Elizabeth Hanson, b. 12 Nov 1773 d. 16 Jun 1841, dau. Phineas and Hannah (Norton) Hanson. Received pension for father's service in the Revolutionary War. War of 1812.
Phineas H., b. 25 Aug 1794, d. Aug 1794.
Jabez, b. Jul 1796, d. Jul 1796.
Jabez, b. 16 Jun 1797, d. Jan 1802.
Hannah, b. 6 Apr 1799, d. 1886, m. 1 Dec 1817 Samuel Hobson.
Phineas Hanson, b. 6 May 1801, d. 8 Oct 1826.
Mary, b. 27 Aug 1803, m. 10 Apr 1828 Oliver Smith.
190 Alvin[6], b. 1805.
John, b. 9 Feb 1808 Buxton ME, killed by train in West Buxton ME 15 Mar 1870, m.(1) Sarah P. Smith of Waterboro ME, b. Mar 1810 d. 31 Jul 1853; m.(2) Fanny (Cousins) Hanson, wid., b. 3 Jan 1810 d. 26 Apr 1883. Lumberman. John and Sarah bur. Greenwood Cem., Biddeford ME. CH: Frances M., b. 9 Sep 1833, m. 22 Aug 1855 Billings A. Hodsdon; Amelia A., b. 23 Dec 1835 d. 27 Apr 1907, m. Henry Anthoine; Susan L., b. 9 Dec 1838, m. Fred Yates of Biddeford ME; Mary H., b. 8 Mar 1841.
191 Enoch McDonald[6], 1810-1884.
Thomas Bradbury, b. Feb 1813, d. 24 Aug 1825.
Deborah, b. 20 Apr 1816, d. 12 Mar 1899, m. 1837 Joseph Cousins.
Sources: Buxton ME census 1810, 1820, 1830, 1840. Biddeford ME census 1850. VR Buxton ME, SA/ME. F21, L30, Mercy (Sawyer) Knight rec., Ruby H. Dunnell rec.

81. **THOMAS PENNELL[5] SAWYER** [see 33], b. 5 Apr 1770 Buxton ME, d. 21 Jan 1818 Buxton ME, m. 26 Dec 1793 Cape Elizabeth ME Mercy Cobb, b. 5 Oct 1773 d. 16 Jul 1830, dau. Ebenezer and Rachel (Sawyer) Cobb. Wid. in Buxton ME 1820.

Ebenezer, b. 11 Oct 1794, d. 14 Oct 1794.
Rachel, b. 9 Feb 1796, unm.
192 Ebenezer[6], b. 1798.
Joanna, b. 4 Feb 1800, d. 4 Jan 1833.
William, b. 27 Jul 1802, d. Aug 1802.
Jabez, b. 2 Oct 1803, d. 7 Nov 1803.
William, b. 4 Nov 1804, d. 9 Apr 1807.
Priscilla D., b. 31 Mar 1807, m.(I) 25 Jul 1835 Nathaniel Johnson of Westbrook ME.
Mary, b. 17 Apr 1810, m. 6 Sep 1827 Joseph Hanson of Buxton ME.
Cyrena, b. 10 May 1814, d. 12 Mar 1855, m.(I) 5 Feb 1832 Joseph Deering.

Sources: Buxton ME census 1810, 1820. VR Buxton ME. L30, R17, Mercy (Sawyer) Knight rec., Ruby Dunnell rec.

82. **JOSEPH[5] SAWYER** [see 33], b. Apr 1774 Buxton ME, d. 1846 Elliotsville ME, m. (1) 17 Sep 1803 Joanna Cobb, b. 14 May 1775 d. 3 Sep 1825, dau. Ebenezer and Rachel (Sawyer) Cobb: m.(2) 11 Mar 1827 Mary Ridlon, b. 15 Oct 1785, dau. Ebenezer and Sarah (Hancock) Ridlon. He and brother Ebenezer built a shingle mill at Elliotsville Plantation 1828.

Eliza, b. 9 Dec 1804, d. 24 Jan 1892, m. 27 Oct 1830 Isaac Stevens of Sweden ME.
193 John Emery[6], 1807-1866.
James, b. 5 Jul 1809, d.y.
Ethelinda, b. 7 Apr 1812, d. 24 Sep 1814.
Joseph Stillman, b. 2 Apr 1815 Buxton ME, d. 25 May 1885, m. 1 Jan 1843 Elliotsville ME Olive MacIntire of New Hampshire, b. 1820 d. 4 Apr 1888. Lumberman. CH: Dianna E., b. 31 Dec 1843, d. 8 Feb 1877, m. 10 Jan 1869 William Stevens; Mary Jane, b. 7 Jun 1847, d. 6 Aug 1870, m. Samuel Morrill; Lucinda M., b. 27 Jun 1849, d. 27 Dec 1887, m. Daniel Carson; Ann E., b. 11 Jun 1856, d. 5 May 1915, m. 2 Jan 1878 Charles E. Stevens of Monson ME.
Mary, b. 17 Oct 1817, d. 19 Oct 1817.
194 Phineas Hanson[6], 1828-1910.

Sources: Buxton ME census 1810, 1820. Elliotsville ME census 1830, 1840, 1850. VR Bangor ME. L30, Mercy (Sawyer) Knight rec., Delia Libby rec.

83. **JAMES THORNTON[5] SAWYER** [see 33], b. 25 Jan 1776 Buxton ME, d. 22 Sep 1842 Bridgton ME, m.(1) 31 Jan 1799 Elizabeth Merrill of Buxton ME, b. 6 Nov 1781 d. 23 Mar 1808, dau. Samuel and Anna (Eaton) Merrill; m.(2) (I) 18 Jun 1809 Scarboro ME Abigail Milliken, b. 1780 d. 1 Jan 1862, dau. Joseph and Sarah (Foster) Milliken. Farmer. B/S/land in Fryeburg ME 1831-1832. He bur. in W. Bridgton ME Cem. Wid. w/son James 1860.

195 Samuel[6], 1799-1874,
Hannah, b. 7 May 1803, d. 3 Feb 1885, m.(1) (I) 9 Jul 1818 Christopher Dyer of Cape Elizabeth ME, m.(2) 10 Oct 1841 Luther Douglass of Denmark ME.
Mary Ann, b. 27 Jun 1805, d. 21 May 1881, m. 20 Sep 1822 Daniel Douglass of Denmark ME.
Eliza, b. 27 Nov 1807, d. 11 Dec 1840, m. 30 Jul 1824 Luther Douglass of Denmark ME.
Clara, b. 27 Nov 1807, d. 27 Oct 1808.
Eunice, b. 13 Feb 1810, m. 2 Dec 1838 Albert Jose of Saco ME.
Child, b. 13 Feb 1810, d. at birth.
196 James Thornton[6], 1811-1896.

Ellen, b. ?, m. Jefferson Cole.

Rebecca, b. Nov 1819, d. 20 Mar 1846, unm.

Sources: Buxton ME census 1810. Fryeburg ME census 1820, 1830, 1840. Sweden ME census 1860. VR Buxton ME. R10a, L30, Mercy (Sawyer) Knight rec., Robert L. Taylor rec.

84. **WILLIAM[5] SAWYER** [see 33], b. 27 Jun 1779 Buxton ME, d. 28 Sep 1853 Hollis ME, m. 10 Aug 1806 Buxton ME Betsey Knight of Buxton ME, b. 17 Dec 1776 d. 18 Dec 1853, dau. Samuel and Hannah (Whitten) Knight. Surveyor. B/land in Fryeburg ME 1826.

Ebenezer, b. 6 Jun 1807 Buxton ME, d. 19 Aug 1853 Hollis ME, m. 2 Sep 1830 Sarah Haley, b. 1813 d. 2 Oct 1885, dau. Joseph and Mary (Gilpatrick) Haley. Probate record says he d. 10 Aug 1853. Wid. went to Saco ME. CH: Mary E., b. 1831, d. 8 Dec 1886, m. Samuel D. Hobson of Buxton ME; Helen M., b. 1837, m. 15 Jan 1865 Joseph Tarbox, went to Illinois; Joseph Haley, b. 1839, d. 5 Feb 1863, unm; Sarah O., b. 1843, d. 17 May 1898; Julia A., b. 1848; Alma, b. ?; Clara E., b. ca. 1851.

197 William[6], 1809-1892.

Samuel, b. 16 Sep 1811 Buxton ME, d. 30 Mar 1864 Hollis ME, m. 28 Jun 1837 Elizabeth Atkinson of Hollis ME, b. ? d. 26 Dec 1870, dau. James and Polly Atkinson. Lumberman. CH: Algenon Sidney, b. 1838, d. 11 Oct 1864, unm; Anna A., b. 1841, m. 30 Dec 1874 Malachi Martin; twins, b. ? d. at 2 days.

Mary, b. 28 Apr 1814, d. 4 Dec 1817.

Mercy, b. 22 Feb 1817, d. 4 Dec 1817.

Eliza, b. 26 Jan 1819, d. 2 Mar 1901, m. 17 Nov 1841 Jeremiah Mason of Saco ME.

Sources: Buxton ME census 1810, 1820. Hollis ME census 1830, 1840, 1850, 1860. VR Buxton ME, Hollis ME. R10a, P82a, R17, L30, T19, Mercy (Sawyer) Knight rec., Sarah M. Hodson rec.

85. **EBENEZER[5] SAWYER** [see 33], b. 10 Mar 1786 Buxton ME, d. 5 Apr 1835 Elliotsville ME, m.(I) 28 Aug 1813 Buxton ME Betsey Knight of Westbrook ME, b. ?, dau. Nathaniel and Ruth (Elden) Knight. Had six fingers on each hand and six toes on each foot. B/S/land 1817-1826. At Elliotsville Plantation in 1828 with brother Joseph to construct a shingle mill.

Washington, b. 1812 Buxton ME. In Elliotsville ME 1828.

198 Jabez[6], b. 1814.

199 Nathaniel Knight[6], 1816-1888.

Thomas Pennell, b. 6 Jun 1818 Buxton ME, d. 27 Apr 1883, m. 29 Jun 1856

200 Ebenezer[6], 1820-1848.

Mary J., b. 24 Aug 1822, d. 11 Dec 1899, m. 31 Dec 1859 Isaac Deering Sawyer.

201 Lafayette W.[6], b. ca. 1825.

Ruth K., b. ca. 1826.

Isaac, b. 1828 Buxton ME. In Elliotsville ME 1828.

John Knight, b. 1832 Elliotsville ME, m. 6 Dec 1857 Brooklin ME Emma B. Herrick, b. 1834. Carpenter. CH: Fanny, b. 1859.

Sources: Buxton ME census 1820. Elliotsville ME 1830. Sedgwick ME census 1850. Brooklin ME census 1860. VR Brooklin ME. L30, R17, R10a, Mercy (Sawyer) Knight rec.

86. **JOHN[5] SAWYER** [see 34], b. 4 Oct 1775 Buxton ME, d. 6 May 1849 Standish ME, m. 2 Jun 1799 Standish ME Grace Jenkins of Scarboro ME, b. 19 Dec 1776 d. 16 Feb 1853, dau. Dennis Jenkins. Lived beside brother David on Standish Neck. S/land 1817. He bur. in Harding Cem., Standish ME.

202 John[6], 1800-1870.

Dennis J., b. 27 Jan 1805 Standish ME, d. 22 Oct 1838 Raymond ME, m. ?. CH: Elizabeth A., b. 30 Jan 1839.

203 Lemuel$^6$, 1807-1888.
204 Thomas$^6$, 1810-1858.
Sources: Standish ME census 1800, 1810, 1820, 1830, 1840. VR Raymond ME. R10a, M3, D6.

87. **ROBERT$^5$ SAWYER** [see 34], b. 12 Oct 1777 Buxton ME, d. 20 Dec 1834 Buxton ME, m. 25 Dec 1800 Lydia Townsend of Phippsburg ME, b. 24 Mar 1785 d. 11 Jun 1869, dau. Isaac and Nancy (Goodwin) Townsend. Wid. in Buxton ME 1840, 1850.

Robert, b. 14 Jan 1803, m. and had one child. Left New England.
Child, b. 14 Jul 1804, d. same day.
Nancy, b. 15 Dec 1805, d.y.
Hannah, b. 26 Jun 1806, d.y.
Polly, b. Nov 1807, d. 14 Jan 1835, unm.
Abigail, b. 24 Jul 1809, d. 6 Jun 1893, m. 1832 Asa Davis.
Isabella, b. 14 May 1811, m. Ivory Hill.
Joanna, b. 26 May 1813, m. 30 Nov 1846 Reuben Maynard of Lincolnville ME.
Sally, b. 14 Feb 1815 d. 15 Apr 1904, m.(1) 26 Jun 1853 Joseph Sands, m.(2) John Foster.
205 John$^6$, 1816-1903.
Eliza A., b. 19 Nov 1818 d. 3 May 1861, m. Aaron Hanson of Hollis ME.
David, b. 14 Jul 1820 Baldwin ME, d. 11 Jul 1861 Hollis ME, m.(I) 20 Sep 1845 Cordelia A. Harmon of Hollis ME, b. 19 Mar 1824 d. 19 Feb 1910, dau. Benjamin and Rebecca Harmon. Merchant. CH: Caroline A., b. 1847; Rebecca H., b. 1849, m. _____ Eaton, went to Nashua NH; Harriet G., b. 1852; Ellen C., b. 1855, d. 1940, m. 19 Sep 1882 Charles A. Getchell; Mary, b. 1860, m. _____ Bickford.
206 Isaac Scammon$^6$, 1822-1890.
Daughter, b. 24 Jul 1823, d. same day.
Hannah, b. 24 Mar 1824, m. David Stackpole.
Nancy, b. 18 Oct 1826, d. 8 Apr 1904, unm.
207 Joseph H.$^6$, 1828-1886.
Sources: Phippsburg ME census 1820. Buxton ME census 1830, 1840, 1850. Limington ME census 1850. Hollis ME census 1860. VR Buxton ME. R17, W31, M5, Margaret (Anderson) Plummer Bible, Obit (Sally).

88. **LEMUEL$^5$ SAWYER** [see 34], b. 1778 Buxton ME, d. 15 Dec 1851 Buxton ME, m. 9 Feb 1809 Lovie (Dunnell) Lane, wid. of L_____ Lane, b. 1774 d. 24 Dec 1862. He bur. in Buxton Lower Corner Cem. Wid. w/son in 1860.

Anna, adopted, b. 22 Dec 1803, d. 16 Jul 1826.
Mehitable W., b. 17 Jul 1809, d. Nov 1878, m. 18 Mar 1835 James M. Ridlon.
John, b. 10 Jul 1811 Buxton ME, d. 31 Mar 1863 Buxton ME, m. 24 Nov 1836 Buxton ME Kezia Lane of Hiram ME, b. 6 Mar 1817 d. 27 Jan 1859, dau. Daniel and Kezia (Hascomb) Lane. CH: Lovie Ann, b. 30 Apr 1836, m. 15 Aug 1858 Daniel J. Love of Wells ME; Eliza L., b. 25 Apr 1841; Almira F., b. 22 Oct 1843.
208 Lemuel$^6$, 1813-1901.
Susan D., b. 29 Feb 1816, d. 8 Feb 1847, m. 24 Jun 1841 David Emery. CH: Susan D., b. 4 Feb 1847, adopted by grandparents Lemuel and Lovie.
Joanna, b. 30 Jul 1819, d. Dec 1901, m. 20 Mar 1859 John Peter Shur.
Lovie A., b. 19 Jan 1822, d. 20 Apr 1848.
Sally, b. 11 Oct 1824, d. 1 Feb 1909, m. 13 May 1849 Leavitt Smith.
Mary Ann, b. 11 Jan 1828, d. 7 Mar 1905, m. 7 Nov 1863 Asa Dunnell.
Sources: Buxton ME census 1810, 1820, 1830, 1840, 1850, 1860. VR Buxton ME. M5, P82k.

89. **DAVID[5] SAWYER** [see 34], b. 27 May 1784 Buxton ME, d. 24 May 1864 Standish ME, m. 4 Jan 1807 Hannah Milliken of Saco ME, b. 7 Nov 1786 Saco ME d. 12 Jul 1879, dau. Isaiah and Eunice (Nason) Milliken. War of 1812. Lived beside brother John on Standish Neck. He bur. in Harding Cem., Standish ME.

Isabel, b. 29 Oct 1807, d. 30 Apr 1888, m. 8 Jan 1840 John Leighton.
209 Henry M.[6], b. 1810.
David, b. 24 Nov 1811, d. 12 Oct 1815.
Hannah L., b. 5 Sep 1813, d. 21 Nov 1871, m. 14 Sep 1838 Curtis Merrill.
Eunice M., b. 22 Jun 1817, d. 23 Nov 1855, m. 19 Mar 1840 Hiram Ellis of Portland ME.
David, b. 21 Oct 1819, d. 8 Jun 1821.
210 John Isaiah[6], 1822-1915.
Mary M., b. 28 Jun 1825, d. 15 Mar 1898, m. 10 Dec 1853 William Green.
Isaiah M., b. 28 Dec 1827, d. 10 Oct 1828.
Eliza A., b. 22 Jul 1830, m. 18 Nov 1850 Marshall Libby of Gorham ME.
Ellen J., b. 2 Apr 1833 d. 16 Mar 1892, m. 3 Feb 1852 William Webster.

Sources: Standish ME census 1820, 1830, 1840, 1850. VR SA/MA. H26, L20, S1, Nettie Dimmock rec.

90. **JAMES[5] SAWYER** [see 35], b. 28 Aug 1774 Royalborough ME, d. bef. 1806, m. Mary Stanford, b. Aug 1779 d. 13 Aug 1863. In Durham ME, Portland ME.

William, b. 9 Mar 1799 Cape Elizabeth ME.
Mary, b. 4 Jul 1803.

Sources: Portland ME census 1800. VR Cape Elizabeth ME. R10a, M5.

91. **JOSEPH PARKER[5] SAWYER** [see 36], b. 1775 Cape Elizabeth ME, d. 6 Dec 1817 Boston MA, m.(I) 6 May 1798 Lydia Allen, b. 12 Jul 1782, dau. David and Elizabeth Allen. Master of schooner *Solon.* At Cape Elizabeth ME 1800, 1810. B/land Cape Elizabeth ME 1807. Lydia, (wid.), Lydia Jr. and Joseph P. Jr. B/S/land 1819 and 1835. Wid. in Chelsea MA 1850.

Lydia, b. 3 Mar 1801, m. George Collins.
211 Joseph Parker[6], b. 1813.

Sources: Cape Elizabeth ME census 1800, 1810. Chelsea MA census 1850. VR Cape Elizabeth ME, SA/MA. R10a.

92. **BENJAMIN FRANKLIN[5] SAWYER** [see 36], b. ca. 1777, d. 1 Mar 1834 Boston MA, m. (1) 25 Mar 1801 Boston MA Marcy Rogers of Mansfield MA, b. ca. 1771 d. 19 May 1828; m.(2) 20 Nov 1828 Elizabeth Copeland Newcomb, b. ca. 1801 d. 24 Feb 1830.

212 Benjamin Franklin[6], b. 1801.
213 Nathaniel[6], b. 1804.
Willard B., b. ca. 1808, d. 18 Feb 1825 in Mansfield MA.
214 Gorham[6], 1811-1865.
Henderson, b. ca. 1814.
Gilbert, b. ca. 1818.
Joshua, b. ca. 1822 Boston MA, m. Eliza R. _____, b. ca. 1828. Blacksmith.
Guild, b. ?, d. 27 Apr 1836 at sea.
Elizabeth Copeland, b. ca. 1829.
Ellen, b. ca. 1832, d. 21 Sep 1835.

Sources: Boston MA census 1820. VR Mansfield MA, Boston MA, SA/MA. S89.

93. **DAVID[5] SAWYER** [see 36], b. 3 Jun 1778, d. 8 Dec 1834 Cape Elizabeth ME, m. 3 Nov 1799 Cape Elizabeth ME Betsey Allen, b. 21 Feb 1782 d. 4 May 1843, dau. John and Ruth (Lee)

Allen. Mate on ship *Philadelphia*. B/land in Cape Elizabeth ME 1807. He bur. in Mt. Pleasant Cem., So. Portland ME.

Eliza, b. 1 Sep 1800, d. 1864, m.(1) 1820 William Stanwood, m.(2) Steve Hubbard.
Ruth A., b. 22 May 1802, d. 1891, m. 3 Dec 1823 John Waterhouse, Jr.
Martha, b. 4 Jul 1804, d. 5 Dec 1845, m. 1834 Perez Tilson.
215 Abel[6], 1806-1872.
Sarah, b. 2 Sep 1808, d. 1889, m.(I) 4 Sep 1830 Eben M. Plummer of Boston MA.
Sophia B., b. 2 Dec 1810, d. 1882, m.(I) 30 Apr 1832 Charles Collins.
Mary P., b. 13 Apr 1813, d. 1882, m. 1832 Edward C. Tilson.
216 David A.[6], 1816-1900.
217 Frederick W.[6], 1818-1858.
Ethan A., b. 5 Apr 1820 Cape Elizabeth ME, m.(I) 30 Apr 1842 Esther Ann Proctor, b. 1822. Joiner. In Portland ME 1850. CH: Harriet F., b. 1843; Mary, b. 1847.
218 Alvin George[6], 1823-1889.

Sources: Cape Elizabeth ME census 1800, 1820, 1830. Portland ME census 1850. VR Cape Elizabeth ME, SA/MA. R10a, S15, Elizabeth Mullin rec.

94. **LEMUEL[5] SAWYER** [see 36], b. 19 Jul 1779 Cape Elizabeth ME, d. 27 May 1835 Portland ME, m.(1) 1 Nov 1801 Eleanor Presson, b. 1782 d. 27 Nov 1804; m.(2) 10 Nov 1805 Elizabeth (Betsey) Haggerty, b. ? d. 24 Jun 1809; m.(3) 7 Dec 1809 Sophia (Blanchard) Prince, wid. of David, b. 1787 d. 10 Aug 1851, dau. Seth and Hepzibah Blanchard. Sea captain. In Portland ME, Standish ME. Wid. m._____Holmes and went to Bath ME. Note: Newspaper says Lemuel d. bef. 14 Jan 1835.

Twins, b. ?, d. 28 Nov 1804.
Eleanor P., b. 3 Aug 1806.
Lemuel, b. 22 Sep 1808 Cape Elizabeth ME.
Benjamin Franklin, b. 21 Sep 1810,d. 24 Dec 1812.
219 Benjamin Franklin[6], b. ca. 1813.

Sources: VR Cape Elizabeth ME, SA/MA. R10a, Obit, Robert L. Taylor rec., David Young rec.

95. **ELISHA[5] SAWYER** [see 36], b. ca. 1781 Cape Elizabeth ME, d. 10 Apr 1833 New York, m. 21 Jun 1801 Cape Elizabeth ME Eleanor Lee, b. 14 Jul 1783, dau. Downing and Eleanor Lee. Mariner. B/S/land 1806-1817.

Rebecca, b. 8 Sep 1801.
Eleanor, b. 3 Oct 1803.
Loisa, b. 23 Aug 1805.
Downing Lee, b. 15 Apr 1808 Cape Elizabeth ME. In New York.
Elizabeth S., b. 3 Apr 1811.
William Lee, b. 3 Dec 1812 Cape Elizabeth ME. In New York.
Ann Mariah, b. 3 Dec 1815.
Elisha Parker, b. 6 Jan 1818, d. 21 Sep 1819 Cape Elizabeth.

Sources: Cape Elizabeth ME census 1810, 1820. VR Cape Elizabeth ME, Boston MA.

96. **JOHN[5] SAWYER** [see 36], b. 10 Aug 1786 Cape Elizabeth ME, d. 22 Dec 1831 at sea, m. 20 Nov 1805 Fanny L. Homer, b. 19 Jan 1790 d. 22 Mar 1869. Sea captain out of Portland ME on Brig *SUPERB*. (For an account of the loss of this ship see *Boston Transcript*, 20 Jan 1832). Wid. in Portland ME 1840.

John, b. 16 Jan 1807 Cape Elizabeth ME, d. 7 Dec 1839 Belfast ME, m. Martha Pray, b. ?. Blockmaker. In Bath ME.

Thomas Tandy, b. 11 Jan 1809 Cape Elizabeth ME, d. 1 Feb 1891 Portland ME, m.(1) (I) 21 Jul 1832 Caroline P. Plummer, b. 1814 d. 14 Feb 1867, dau. John and Eleanor (Haskell) Plummer; m.(2) 28 May 1868 Lucy N. Haskell, b. 28 May 1844 d. 11 Feb 1920. Cooper, coal dealer. CH: Sarah E., b. 1838.

220 Samuel Homer[6], 1811-1886.

Frances, b. 11 Jan 1813, d. 9 Oct 1839, m. 1832 Ezra Jewell.

221 Thorndike Homer[6], 1815-1893.

222 Horace Austin[6], 1817-1889.

223 Andrew Scott[6], 1820-1909.

Charles Owen, b. 10 Jan 1823 Cape Elizabeth ME, d. Charlestown MA, m. Elizabeth D. _____, b. ca. 1823. Clerk. S/land in Cape Elizabeth to brother Andrew 1852. In Charlestown MA census 1865. Wid. in Portland 1890.

224 Ellis Merrill[6], 1826-1863.

225 William Chadwick[6], 1828-1914.

Elizabeth Homer, b. 31 Aug 1830, d. 9 Jul 1897, m. Eben Corey.

Sources: Cape Elizabeth ME census 1810. Portland ME census 1820, 1840, 1850. New Gloucester ME census 1830. VR SA/ME. R10a, M5, S15, M8, George F. Sawyer rec.

97. **DANIEL[5] SAWYER** [see 37], b. (1767-1774) Cape Elizabeth ME, m. Almira Stanford, b. (1760-1770).

226 Ephraim, b. (1794-1800).

Miriam, b. (1794-1800).

Sources: Cape Elizabeth ME census 1810, 1820. R10a.

98. **JOSHUA[5] SAWYER** [see 38], b. 1791 Limington ME, d. 6 Jan 1848 Limington ME, m. 28 Dec 1815 Mary Sinclair of Waterboro ME, b. 4 Dec 1795 d. 20 Jun 1884. In Harrison ME, Bridgton ME. He bur. in Sawyer's Plot, Limington ME. Wid in Limington ME 1850.

Benjamin Sinclair, b. 6 Aug 1816 Limington ME, d. 5 Nov 1900 Parsonsfield ME, m. 7 Mar 1852 Margaret D. Hasty, b. 11 Oct 1828 d. 15 Dec 1887. In Limerick ME. CH: Edward Franklin, b. 24 Sep 1852, d. 15 Oct 1854; Albert B., b. 4 Aug 1859 d. 18 Sep 1865; Elizabeth May, b. 9 Oct 1866, d. 2 Jul 1955.

Sarah S., b. 31 Jul 1820, d. 19 Feb 1902, m. 23 Oct 1845 Daniel Whitmore.

Samuel S., b. 8 Sep 1823 Waterboro ME, d. 1 Feb 1884 Boston MA, m. 2 Nov 1845 New Bedford MA Sarah Chick of Limington ME, b. 18 May 1821 d. 24 Mar 1899, dau. John and Mary Chick. Carpenter. CH: Henrietta A., b. 22 Oct 1848, d. 28 Mar 1938, m. 2 Aug 1865 John Hutchinson Burnham.

Eunice, b. 2 Dec 1824, d. 5 Sep 1894, unm.

John Henry, b. 27 Apr 1827 Limington ME.

Charles L., b. 19 Dec 1829 Limington ME.

Joshua, b. 3 Mar 1832 Limington ME, d. 10 Sep 1864 Plymouth MA, m. Boston MA Elizabeth Phinney. b. ca. 1836, dau. Benjamin and Elizabeth Phinney. Railroad engineer.

Mary Peavey, b. 3 Aug 1834, d. 8 Jun 1903, m. 15 Nov 1855 Benjamin Haskell.

227 William Woodbury[6], b. 1839.

Sources: Waterboro ME census 1820. Limington ME census 1840, 1850. Limerick ME census 1850, 1860. Fall River MA census 1850. VR New Bedford MA, SA/MA. T6A, P82a, R10a, Robert L. Taylor rec.

99. **EBENEZER JORDAN[5] SAWYER** [see 39], b. 1785 Jonesport ME, m.(1) Hannah Strout, b.?; m.(2) Elra Cox of Columbia ME, b. 5 Mar 1795 Columbia ME, dau. Edward and Sarah Cox.

Phebe A., b. 4 Nov 1807, d. 24 Jan 1850, m. (I) 20 Sep 1826 Samuel Kelley.
Jane, b. 29 Apr 1810.
John Woodbury, b. 1812, d. 183?, unm.
Hannah, b. 19 Oct 1816.
228 Ebenezer Jones[6], 1818-1890.
229 Joseph Cutler[6], 1821-1898.
Sophia R., b. 11 Jan 1824, d. 1 Apr 1890, m. William C. Wilson.
Mary J., b. 23 Feb 1826, m. Eben Robins.

Sources: Jonesport ME census 1810, 1820, 1830, 1840, 1850. VR Jonesport ME. Mrs. Edward Ames rec., Leonard F. Tibbett rec.

100. **DANIEL JORDAN[5] SAWYER** [see 39], b. 1 May 1791 Jonesport ME, d. 6 Dec 1879, m.(1) Lois White, b. ?, dau. Tilly and Tamson (Willey) White; m.(2) 22 Nov 1820 Mary Bagley of Montville ME, b. 10 May 1801 d. 15 May 1861, dau. James and Abigail (Cromwell) Bagley. Boat builder. War of 1812. S/land 1820.

Lois White, b. 6 Jun 1821, d. 12 Nov 1904, m. 1 Dec 1836 Edward Mansfield.
230 Daniel James[6], 1824-1909.
Levi Bagley, b. 24 Mar 1826 Jonesboro ME, d. 14 May 1891, m.(I) 21 Jul 1876 Addison ME Jane B. Leighton, b. 1826, dau. Robert and Margaret (Barfield) Leighton. Sea captain and boat builder. CH: Francesca T., b. 21 May 1847 d. 11 Jan 1938, m. 1866 Thomas Drisko; Ida May, b. 1854, m. Luthor Howland, went to Iowa.
Rebecca, b. 21 Sep 1828, d. 17 May 1910, m. 1848 Daniel Hall.
Lydia B., b. 8 Dec 1833, d. 14 Mar 1919, m. Darius Kelley.
Ann B., b. 3 Feb 1836 d. 28 Apr 1868, m. 14 Aug 1858 Jeremiah Johnson.
Mary A., b. 21 May 1838, d. 13 Jun 1907, m. James Dobbins.
231 Edward Mansfield[6], 1841-1924.
Frances E., b. 4 Oct 1844, d. 7 Apr 1926, m. 28 Oct 1861 Oscar Brown.

Sources: Jonesport ME census 1830, 1840, 1850. Jonesboro ME census 1850. VR Jonesboro ME, SA/ME. M8A, Leonard F. Tibbett rec.

101. **DANIEL[5] SAWYER** [see 40], b. 26 Nov 1776 Limington ME, d. 20 Jan 1841 Monroe ME, m.(I) 3 Jan 1803 Polly Chadbourne of Sanford ME, b. 2 Aug 1780 d. 24 Jan 1843, dau. Rev. John and Elizabeth (Grant) Chadbourne. Cordwainer. In Monroe ME 1822. He bur. in East Dixmont ME. Note: Obit says he d. 26 Jan 1841.

232 John Chadbourne[6], 1804-1875.
233 Nathaniel[6], 1806-1883.
Mary, b. 1810, m. _____ Chapman.
Daniel G., b. 1816 Monroe ME, d. 4 Nov 1885 Old Town ME, m.(1) (I) 2 Sep 1837 Bangor ME Emily Basten, b. ? d. 1873; m.(2) 4 May 1873 Old Town ME Susan Hopkins of Milford ME, b. ?. Merchant. No CH.
234 Ephraim[6], 1822-1898.
Allen J., b. 19 Jul 1825 Monroe ME, d. 12 Feb 1898 Old Town ME, m.(I) 28 Apr 1862 Hannah W. Farnham of Newburgh ME, b.?. Merchant. Selectman.
Elsie J., b. ca. 1829, d. 15 Oct 1844.

Sources: Limington ME census 1810. Monroe ME census 1830, 1840. Old Town ME census 1850. VR Old Town ME, SA/ME. T6A, N5, P30, U1. Obit (Daniel).

102. **NATHANIEL[5] SAWYER** [see 40], b. 3 Mar 1781 Limington ME, d. 6 Jun 1857 Baldwin ME, m.(I) 4 Dec 1809 Sarah Small of Limington ME, b. 13 Jun 1786 d. 14 Jan 1854, dau. Isaac

and Shuah (Small) Small. In Limington ME 1811, Conway NH 1813, Limington ME 1816, Baldwin ME 1819-1850. Tanner. He bur. in Sawyer's Cem., Baldwin ME.

Hannah B., b. 4 Aug 1811, d. 12 Mar 1815.

Ebenezer, b. 23 Oct 1813 Conway NH, d. 12 Aug 1899 Baldwin ME, m. 31 Jan 1838 Zana C. Small, b. 1816 d. 24 Oct 1882. Farmer. Selectman for Baldwin ME 1856. CH: Susan H., b. Jan 1840, d. 24 Nov 1856; Mary A., b. 1842, d. 6 Nov 1856; Anna D., b. 20 Aug 1843, d. 18 May 1846; Isaac, b. 17 Oct 1846, d. 21 Sep 1847; Isabella, b. ?, d. 8 Nov 1856; Emily J., b. 4 Dec 1850, d. 25 Nov 1933, m. 12 Jan 1881 Lynn MA Frank Brown.

Isaac Newton, b. 16 May 1816 Limington ME, d. 2 Aug 1849 Ohio. In Baldwin ME.

Mary Brown, b. 18 Jan 1819, m. 7 Nov 1841 Stephen Brown, Baldwin ME.

Nathaniel, b. 23 Oct 1821 Baldwin ME, lost at sea 12 Sep 1857.

Hannah, b. 17 Jul 1824, d. 8 Jun 1832.

David, b. 16 Feb 1828, d. 17 Feb 1828.

Joshua, b. 16 Jun 1829, d. 16 Jun 1829.

Sources: Baldwin ME census 1820, 1830, 1840, 1850. VR Baldwin ME. E16, C62, V8, R10a, M5, T6, N39.

103. **JOHN[5] SAWYER** [see 40], b. 7 Nov 1792 Limington ME, d. 20 Apr 1871 Limington ME, m. 26 Oct 1817 Sarah Fogg of Brownfield ME, b. 26 May 1794 d. 15 Jul 1855, dau. Charles Fogg. Farmer. B/S/land 1823-1843.

235 Charles Fogg[6], 1818-1892.

236 Isaac[6], 1821-1891.

Louisa, b. 1825, m. 15 Sep 1854 Luther Whitney of Standish ME.

Samuel, b. 30 Oct 1828 Limington ME, d. 3 Apr 1906 Limington ME, m. Sarah A. Libby, b. 24 Jun 1839 d. 25 Oct 1880, dau. Nathaniel and Sally (Davis) Libby. Farmer. In Biddeford ME. He bur. in East Limington ME. CH: Annie, b. 10 Oct 1851.

Edwin, b. 1831 Limington ME.

Sources: Limington ME census 1820, 1830, 1840, 1850. R10g, T6A, W42, L22, N39.

104. **PETER[5] SAWYER** [see 40], b. 10 Jun 1794 Limington ME, d. 9 Mar 1876 Bridgton ME, m.(I) 20 Feb 1814 Sarah Small of Limington ME, b. 4 Dec 1796 d. 29 Aug 1870, dau. Jacob Small. S/land Bridgton ME 1862.

Josiah, b. 2 Mar 1815, d. 3 Jan 1816.

237 Jacob Small[6], 1816-1859.

Mary Small, b. 31 Aug 1818, d. 1896 Boston MA, m.(1) (I) 26 Jul 1835 Amos Thomas, m.(2) 29 Aug 1840 Ira Allen, m.(3) Greeley H. Johnson.

Josiah Small, b. 31 Jul 1821 Limington ME. In Maysville (Presque Isle) ME.

Nathaniel S., b. 31 Mar 1823, d. 27 Apr 1823.

Sally Susan, b. 15 Apr 1824.

Eliza S., b. 27 Mar 1826, d. 6 Mar 1901, m. 5 Dec 1844 John A. Winslow of Portland ME.

Arvilla M., b. 21 Aug 1829, d. 16 Jan 1912, m. 26 Mar 1846 Samuel Williams of Portland ME.

238 Alonzo Green[6], 1831-1894.

239 John Lorenzo[6], 1831-1904.

Aramantha Augusta, b. 9 Aug 1833, d. 21 Jan 1901, m.(1) 5 Aug 1857 Ambrose C. Burnham, m.(2) 10 Jul 1852 Benjamin C. Fogg of Standish ME.

240 Peter Wilson[6], 1835-1902.

Edmund W., b. 17 Apr 1839, d.y.

Frances J., b. 13 Jan 1842, d. 30 Oct 1928, m. 5 Feb 1860 Josiah Sanborn of Baldwin ME.

Sources: Limington ME census 1820, 1830, 1840, 1850. Bridgton ME census 1860. VR Limington ME. R10a, T6, T6A, N39, P41, S8, Robert L. Taylor rec.

105. **SAMUEL$^5$ SAWYER** [see 40], b. 1 May 1799 Limington ME, d. 1 Mar 1860 Limington ME, m. 14 May 1837 Susan Foss of Limington ME, b. 9 Mar 1809 d. 4 Dec 1885, dau. Elias and Susannah (Hagens) Foss. B/S/land 1833-1843 in Standish ME. He bur. in North Limington ME.

Shuah Ann, b. 23 Feb 1838, d. 22 Aug 1881, m. 10 Aug 1870 Stephen Libby of Limerick ME.

Susan Jane, b. 17 Dec 1841, d. 28 Apr 1843.

241 William Hayes$^6$, 1846-1937.

Sources: Limington ME census 1840. R10a, T6, L20, N39, Will, Nancy Welch rec.

106. **JOSEPH$^5$ SAWYER** [see 40], b. 4 Oct 1802 Limington ME, d. 2 Jun 1874, m. Elizabeth Dunphy of New Brunswick, Canada, b. 14 Nov 1810 d. 14 Dec 1856. In Maysville (Presque Isle) ME.

Thomas W., b. 6 Jun 1834, d. 17 Dec 1856.

242 Ephraim Alonzo$^6$, 1836-1909.

Elizabeth, b. ?, drowned at 8 years.

William John, b. ca. 1846, d. 1864 in Andersonville Prison, Georgia.

Sources: VR SA/ME. T6, Neil G. Sawyer rec.

107. **EPHRAIM$^5$ SAWYER** [see 40], b. 29 Oct 1804 Limington ME, d. 25 Sep 1887 Phillips ME, m.(I) 6 Jun 1835 Eliza Small of Gray ME, b. 19 Jan 1806 d. 22 Dec 1882, dau. George Small. He bur. in East Madrid ME. Both bur. Wing Cem., Phillips ME.

Ellis E. B., b. 14 May 1836 Limington ME. Printer. In Phillips ME, Camp Point, IL.

Joseph L., b. Apr 1839, d. 12 Feb 1862 in Civil War.

George Small, b. Jan 1841. Went to Nevada.

Charlotte S., b. 26 May 1843, d. 18 Feb 1873, m. Ezra H. McKeen of Phillips ME.

Henry Clinton, b. 15 May 1845 Phillips ME. Went to Illinois.

243 Albert$^6$ (Prince), b. 1847.

Sources: Phillips ME census 1850, 1860. T6, M5.

108. **PETER$^5$ SAWYER** [see 41], b. 1 May 1782 Cape Elizabeth ME, m. 9 Jun 1803 Harriet Short, b. 1786 d. 14 Oct 1814.

George P., b. 4 Mar 1804 Cape Elizabeth ME, m. 7 Feb 1826 Mary Stanford of Cape Elizabeth ME, b. ?. CH: Harriet, b. 10 Aug 1827, m. 13 Oct 1844 Jeremiah P. Strout; Mary E., b. 31 Mar 1829.

244 David Fairbanks$^6$, b. 1806.

Margaret F., b. 28 Mar 1808, d. 29 Jul 1894, m. 1 Jan 1829 Solomon T. Corser of Portland ME.

Harriet, b. 31 May 1809.

Sarah, b. 3 Sep 1811.

Sources; Cape Elizabeth ME census 1810. VR Cape Elizabeth ME. C79.

109. **JOHN$^5$ SAWYER** [see 41], b. 29 Aug 1791 Cape Elizabeth ME, d. bef. Sep 1827, m. 5 Jul 1812 Hannah Simonton of Cape Elizabeth ME, b. 1790 d. 9 Mar 1865. Hannah w/son Ebenezer in Portland ME 1850.

245 Ebenezer F.$^6$, 1814-1865.

246 John Graham$^6$, 1815-1863.

George E., b. ca. 1816 Cape Elizabeth ME.

Sources: Portland ME census 1850. R10a, M5.

110. **EPHRAIM$^5$ SAWYER** [see 41], b. 5 Oct 1797 Cape Elizabeth ME, d. 1872 Portland ME, m. 9 Feb 1822 So. Portland ME Charlotte G. Dyer, b. 1801 d. 1871. B/S/land in Cape Elizabeth ME 1829-1862. He bur. in Pleasant Hill Cem., Portland ME.

Peter, b. 18 May 1823 Cape Elizabeth ME, d. 1 May 1845.
George E., b. 19 Sep 1826 Cape Elizabeth ME, d. 19 Sep 1853.
Catherine D., b. 18 Jul 1829, d. 11 Apr 1905.
Mary E., b. 20 Sep 1831, d. 20 Jul 1860.
Margaret F., b. 20 Sep 1838, m.(I) 11 Mar 1861 Edward Flint of Bridgton ME.

Sources: Cape Elizabeth ME census 1830, 1840, 1850, 1860, 1870. VR Cape Elizabeth ME. R10a.

111. **SOLOMON MORGAN$^5$ SAWYER** [see 42], b. 24 Apr 1784 New Gloucester ME, d. 24 Sep 1861 Danville ME, m. 29 Jan 1810 Danville ME Hannah (Gowell) Curtis, wid. of William, b. 30 May 1788 Lebanon ME d. 1 Jun 1871, dau. John Gowell. S/land 1832. He bur. in Old Fitz Yard, near Danville Corner, Auburn ME.

247 John W.$^6$, 1811-1870.
248 Nathaniel$^6$, 1812-1881.
Solomon, b. 14 Jul 1815 Danville ME, d. 11 Apr 1841.
Sarah, b. 15 Feb 1819, m. 23 Feb 1858 Simon Webster.
249 William$^6$, 1823-1904.
250 George Washington Royal$^6$, 1826-1875.

Sources: Danville ME census 1820, 1830, 1840, 1850, 1860. VR Danville ME, Auburn ME. R10a, D51, Robert L. Taylor rec., Margaret Sawyer rec.

112. **DANIEL$^5$ SAWYER** [see 43], b. 1792 New Gloucester ME, m. Tabathy Jacobs of Mt. Vernon ME, b. 1800.

251 Parker$^6$, b. 1831.
Esther A., b. 30 Nov 1833, d. 24 Apr 1922 Clinton MA, unm.
John Jacob, b. 8 Aug 1835, m. 26 Sep 1858 Helen Dunham of Detroit ME, b. ?.

Sources: Mt. Vernon ME census 1830, 1840. Detroit ME census 1850, 1860. VR SA/ME.

113. **JOHN$^5$ SAWYER** [see 43], b. Jun 1795 New Gloucester ME, d. 30 Nov 1864 New Gloucester ME, m.(1) Minot ME Mary Ann Merrill, b. ? d. 1826; m.(2) 21 Apr 1832 Gray ME Irene Foster, b. 1810 d. 30 Nov 1887, dau. Moses Foster. War of 1812. B/S/land in New Gloucester ME and Gray ME 1817-1842. Wid. went to Gorham ME, received pension 10 Feb 1879.

252 Parker Libby$^6$, 1833-1887.
Eliza J., b. 1837, d. 1916, m. Joseph H. Colburn.
Clarissa, b. 1840, m. Charles Gore.
Mary A., b. 1843, d. 30 Apr 1864.
Lydia, b. 1846, m. George Gore.
Abby F., b. 1848, m. Edwin Goodwin.
Nancy L., b. 1849, m. Greeley Fogg.

Sources: Gray ME census 1840. New Gloucester ME census 1850. Westbrook ME census 1860. R10a, Mrs. Willis Hayes rec.

114. **ISAAC$^5$ SAWYER** [see 45], b. 3 Jan 1759 Falmouth ME, d. bef. 1850 Westbrook ME. Wife unk. Revolutionary War. Member of Congregational Church, Westbrook ME 1799. Brother Zachariah S/land to Isaac 1814. W/son Ebenezer B. 1840.

Son, b. (1784-1794).
Daughter, b. (1784-1794).
253 Isaac$^{6}$, 1798-1873.
Daughter, b. (1804-1810).
Ebenezer B., b. 1807, d. 7 Apr 1884, m. 2 Jun 1833 Rhoda North, b. 1811 d. 4 Jan 1879. Tinplater. CH: Ellen E., b. 1834, m. Stephen Isley.
Son, b. (1810-1820).
254 Charles S.$^{6}$, b. 1817.

Sources: Falmouth ME census 1800, 1810. Westbrook ME census 1820, 1830, 1840, 1850. VR Westbrook ME, Deering ME. F21, M3, R10a, B74.

115. **NATHAN$^{5}$ SAWYER** [see 45], b. ca. 1764 Old Falmouth ME, d. bef. 1837 Portland ME, m. 17 Mar 1796 Gorham ME Tabitha Skilling, b. 23 Nov 1770, dau. Isaac and Susanna (Watson) Skilling. B/S/land in Falmouth ME 1803-1837. Wid. m. James Wright.
Almira, b. 27 Apr 1801, d. 6 Nov 1888, m. 25 Dec 1820 James Knight.
Levi, b. 27 Sep 1806 Old Falmouth ME. In Westbrook ME.
Mary E., b. 25 Aug 1812.
255 John Skilling$^{6}$, 1815-1897.

Sources: Falmouth ME census 1800, 1810. Westbrook ME census 1820, 1830. VR Gorham ME, SA/ME. R10a, B74, D4, T19.

116. **ZACKARIAH$^{5}$ SAWYER** [see 45], bp. 1 Nov 1767 Falmouth ME, d. bef. 1840, m. 17 Jan 1797 Portland ME Sarah Thompson of Falmouth ME, b. ?. B/S/land in Westbrook ME 1818-1823.
Nathaniel. b. 25 Sep 1797 Westbrook ME.
Amos, b. 18 Oct 1798 Falmouth ME, d. 11 Mar 1879 Pownal ME, m. 19 Nov 1826 Pownal ME Miriam Brown, b. ca. 1804 d. 30 Dec 1890. He bur. in Lake Cemetery, No. Pownal ME. CH: Frances E., b. ca. 1842.
William, b. 1 Aug 1800, d.y.
Hiram, b. 10 Feb 1802 Falmouth ME, d. 1 Jun 1893 Deering ME, m. 15 May 1828 Westbrook ME Augusta Stevens, b. 20 Apr 1800 d. 8 Jun 1889, dau. Isaac and Mehitable (Knight) Stevens. Stove dealer. CH: Dorcas Ellen, b. 1831, d. 21 Apr 1910, unm; Harriet A., b. 1831.
Joanna, b. 8 Jan 1804.
Sarah, b. 15 Jul 1806.
Zackariah, b. 15 Mar 1808 Old Falmouth ME.
Hannah, b. 16 Apr 1810.
Jane, b. 17 Jun 1812.
Dorcas, b. 2 Jul 1814.
William, b. 29 Jul 1816 Old Falmouth ME.
Harriet, b. 23 Feb 1818.

Sources: Falmouth ME census 1800, 1810. Westbrook ME census 1820, 1830, 1840, 1850. New Gloucester ME census 1830. Pownal ME census 1840, 1850, 1860. VR Westbrook ME, Pownal ME, Portland ME. K10A, R10a, B74. T19, M5.

117. **JONATHAN$^{5}$ SAWYER** [see 45], b. 10 Mar 1768 Falmouth ME, d. 11 Jun 1838 Portland ME, m.(1) 6 Feb 1794 Miriam Stevens, b. 11 Jun 1769 d. 2 Dec 1803, dau. Joshua Stevens; m.(2) 14 Feb 1808 Sarah (Tobey) Cox of Portland ME, b. ca. 1768 d. 24 Jan 1821; m.(3) 15 Feb 1823 Elizabeth Noyes, b. 1769 d. 17 Mar 1855. He bur. in Pine Grove Cem., Portland ME. Wid. w/son Frederick 1850.
Harriot, b. 31 Oct 1794, d. 4 Oct 1802.

Lewis, b. 18 Sep 1801 Falmouth ME, d. 1847, m. Lydia A. Lamb, b. ?.
Son, b. 1802, d. 1804.
256 Frederick$^{6}$, 1809-1858.
Lucy A., b. 4 Oct 1811, d. 8 Jan 1849.
Lemuel C., b. 7 Mar 1813, d. 17 Oct 1814.

Sources: Falmouth ME census 1800, 1810. Westbrook ME census 1820, 1830, 1850. D9, B74, Robert L. Taylor rec.

118. **BRACKETT$^{5}$ SAWYER** [see 45], b. 4 Mar 1775 Falmouth ME, d. 21 Apr 1851 East Deering ME, m. 10 Jan 1805 Westbrook ME Elizabeth Webb of Westbrook ME, b. 3 Sep 1782 d. 21 Sep 1864. Housewright. B/land Falmouth ME 1807. He bur. in George St. Cem., E. Deering ME.

Son, b. (1805-1810).
Martha Bradbury, b. 6 Feb 1810, d. 1887. B/S/land in Westbrook ME 1851.
Mary Ann, b. 13 Jul 1811, d. 9 Sep 1813.
257 Harrison$^{6}$, b. 1814.
258 Brackett$^{6}$, 1817-1890.
Charlotte, b. 26 Dec 1818, d. 20 Sep 1825.

Sources: Falmouth ME census 1810. Westbrook ME census 1820, 1830, 1840, 1850. K10A, R10a, B74, M5, Robert L. Taylor rec.

119. **LEVI$^{5}$ SAWYER** [see 45], b. 13 May 1786 Gorham ME, d. 25 Nov 1855 Portland ME, m. 27 Nov 1808 Sarah Stockman of Portland ME, b. 1786 d. 21 Apr 1858. Bricklayer, trader. War of 1812: Quartermaster Sergeant in Captain Phineas Varnum's Company of Artillery, Major Lemuel Weeks' Battalion, Defense of Portland ME, 7 Sep-27 Oct 1814. B/S/land 1808-1859. He bur. Western Cem., Portland ME.

William Henry, b. 27 Aug 1809 Portland ME.
259 Mark Harris$^{6}$, 1812-1853.
Louisa A., b. 21 Jan 1814, m _____ Claridge.
Susan, b. 5 Nov 1816, m. Moses Jewett.
Charles Edward, b. 3 May 1819 Portland ME, d. 27 Sep 1864, m. 15 Jul 1843 Portland ME Frances Winslow Weeks of No. Yarmouth ME, b. 12 Jun 1819, dau. Ezra and Hannah (Merrill) Weeks. In Portland ME, Malden MA. Wid. m. 27 Jan 1869 Malden MA John F. Foss. CH: Georgianna, b. 5 Jan 1844, m. 24 Jul 1873 Jacques Smolders; Fanny L., b. 1 Aug 1851, m. 17 Aug 1870 Malden MA John McLaughlin.
Sarah E., b. 24 Jul 1823, d. 9 Jun 1851, m. Clement Pennell.
Levi, b. 1 Jul 1826, d. 4 Nov 1846 Portland ME.

Sources: Portland ME census 1810, 1820, 1830. VR Portland ME, SA/MA. R10a, M5, B74, P69, W20.

120. **THOMAS$^{5}$ SAWYER** [see 46], b. 14 Jul 1758 Falmouth ME, d. 11 Apr 1833 Westbrook ME, m.(1) 31 Jan 1784 Susanna Barton, b. 1765 d. 6 Feb 1805 E. Deering ME; m.(2) 31 May 1806 Durham ME Mary David, b. 1782. Revolutionary War: Captain. In Falmouth ME. He bur. Westbrook ME. Wid. m. Moses Roberts.

Dorcas, b. 1783, d. 23 Jun 1803.
Thomas, b. 15 Dec 1785, d. 21 Apr 1807.
George, b. 1790, d. 13 Jun 1808.
Daniel, b. ca. 1798, d. 17 Oct 1820.
Susan M., b. ca. 1807.
260 Aaron G.$^{6}$, 1812-1895.

Jane, b. 1816, d. 1900, m. Stanley Covell.

Daniel W., b. 24 Aug 1819 Westbrook ME, d. 12 Jan 1889 Boothbay ME, m.(1) 13 Jan 1842 No. Yarmouth ME Sarah R. McKenney, b. 1814 d. 1 Jul 1848; m. (2) 28 Jan 1851 Hollis ME Hannah C. Locke of Hollis ME, b. 1 Aug 1819 d. 11 Jul 1868, dau. Caleb and Sarah (Clarke) Locke; m.(3) 11 Aug 1869 Somersworth NH Caroline E. (Smith) Smith of Monmouth ME, b. 3 Feb 1820 d. 5 Jun 1886, wid. of Thomas J., dau. Erastus and Mary Smith; m.(4) 1888 Boothbay ME Fannie S. McIntyre of Boothbay ME, b. 22 Aug 1865 d. 1922. In Portland ME 1850, Hollis ME 1851. Sailmaker, bank cashier. Bur. Westbrook ME. CH: Sarah M., b. 17 Jan 1848, m. Byron Matthews; Ella M., b. 5 Jan 1853, d. 29 Nov 1855; Florence M., b. 16 Feb 1858, d. 16 Aug 1883.

Sources: Falmouth ME census 1790, 1800. Westbrook ME census 1820, 1830. Portland ME census 1850. Boothbay ME census 1860. VR Portland ME, Boothbay ME, SA/ME. D9, M8A, G41, R10a, L34, F21, M5, David Young rec.

121. **JOHN[5] SAWYER** [see 46], b. 13 Nov 1760 Falmouth ME, d. 6 Dec 1842 Westbrook ME, m. 22 Apr 1790 Abigail Graves of Portland ME, b. 13 Aug 1765 d. 10 Mar 1848. Revolutionary War. B/S/land 1795-1820. He bur. Pine Grove Cem., E. Deering ME.

Susannah, b. 1794, d. 16 Jan 1800.

Nabby, b. 1796, d. 25 Jan 1800.

John, b. Aug 1801, d. 2 Oct 1802.

261 Joel[6], 1805-1874.

Dorcas, b. ?.

Sources: Falmouth ME census 1800, 1810. Westbrook ME census 1820, 1830, 1840. R10a, F21.

122. **WILLIAM[5] SAWYER** [see 46], b. 1763 Falmouth ME, d. 14 May 1825 East Deering ME, m. 1793 Tabitha Graves, b. 11 Dec 1768 d. 6 Dec 1857, dau. Crispus Graves. B/S/land 1791-1819. Wid. in Westbrook ME census 1830-1850. He bur. in E. Deering ME.

William, b. 1794 Westbrook ME. Laborer.

262 Joseph M.[6], 1795-1875.

Crispus, b. 28 Mar 1804 Falmouth ME, d. 24 Aug 1873 Portland ME.

Daughter, b. (1804-1810).

Sources: Falmouth ME census 1800, 1810. Westbrook ME census 1820. R10a, M3, M5.

123. **EPHRAIM[5] SAWYER** [see 46], b. 6 Sep 1767 Falmouth ME, d. 12 Apr 1814 Back Cove in Portland ME, m. 3 Feb 1799 Portland ME Abigail Ingersoll of Cape Elizabeth ME, b. 1775 d. 11 Nov 1851. Sea captain. Wid. in Falmouth ME 1820, w/son Edwin in Portland ME 1850.

Daughter, b. (1790-1800).

Charles, b. 1801, d. 17 Sep 1822.

Eliza, b. 1803, d. 17 Jul 1874.

Mary R., b. 1807, d. 10 Sep 1904 in Bath ME.

Son, b. (1800-1810).

Daughter, b. (1800-1810).

263 Edwin A.[6], 1810-1896.

Sources: Falmouth ME census 1800, 1810. R10a, K10A, B74, M5, Obit.

124. **DANIEL[5] SAWYER** [see 46], b. 31 May 1772 Falmouth ME, m. 21 Oct 1804 Sandwich NH Bridget Blanchard of Sandwich NH, b. ?. In Eaton NH 1800. Wid. w/son Asa 1840.

264 Asa[6], b. 1806.

Daughter, b. (1800-1810).

Sources: Eaton NH census 1800, 1810. K10A, B74.

125. **ASA$^5$ SAWYER** [see 46], bp. 8 Jun 1777 Falmouth ME, d. 27 Jun 1858 No. Deering ME, m. 26 Apr 1801 Falmouth ME Sarah Knight, b. 1779 d. 1 Jan 1851, dau. Samuel and Hannah (Sawyer) Knight. Heirs B/land in Westbrook ME 1861.

Hannah, b. Apr 1801, d. 27 Feb 1882, m. 1 Apr 1832 Amasa Sawyer [see 133].
Nancy Y., b. ca. 1803, d. 16 Jul 1824.
Abba, b. ca. 1804, m. 25 Jun 1844 Solomon Foster.
265 James$^6$, 1808-1852.
Lucy, b. 1810, m.(1) William Foss, m.(2) Daniel Bradbury.
Rebecca, b. 1812, d. 10 Aug 1873, m. 28 Oct 1840 Adam Purves of Gray ME.
266 Simeon$^6$, 1814-1886.
267 George$^6$, 1817-1874.
Caroline, b. 1820, d. 1891.
Mary P., b. ?, m. 7 Dec 1845 Falmouth ME Josiah C. Cobb.

Sources: Falmouth ME census 1810. Westbrook ME census 1820, 1830, 1840, 1850. R10a, K10A, M3, B74, T19, Theodore L. Sawyer rec., David Young rec.

126. **JOSEPH$^5$ SAWYER** [see 46], b. 28 Sep 1779 Deering ME, d. 12 Apr 1858 Portland ME, m. 4 Sep 1804 Charlotte Hill, b. 19 Jan 1774 d. 25 Jun 1825. Sea captain. W/dau. Catherine 1850.

Catherine, b. 5 May 1805, d. 24 Jan 1894, m. 10 Nov 1831 Daniel Knight of Alfred ME.
Marston, b. 16 Nov 1806, d. 14 Feb 1808.
268 John Hill$^6$, 1809-1898.
Sarah, b. 28 Nov 1811, d. 25 Jul 1877, m. John Emery.

Sources: Portland ME census 1810, 1820. Limerick ME census 1850. VR Falmouth ME. K10A, B74.

127. **ROBERT$^5$ SAWYER** [see 46], b. 18 Feb 1783 Falmouth ME, d. 28 Dec 1833 Westbrook ME, m. 21 Oct 1804 Falmouth ME Betsey Sawyer, b. 1781 d. 25 Jun 1861. B/S/land in Raymond ME.

Robert, b. ca. 1805 Falmouth ME. In Raymond ME.
Daughter, b. (1800-1810).
Daughter, b. (1800-1810).
Son, b. (1810-1820).

Sources: Falmouth ME census 1810. Westbrook ME census 1820, 1830. VR SA/MA. B74, K10A, M5.

128. **JOHN$^5$ SAWYER** [see 47], bp. 13 Jul 1768 Falmouth ME, m.(1) Otisfield ME Mary Hancock, b. ? d. 28 Mar 1799, dau. Joseph and Jerusha (Whiting) Hancock; m.(2) ca. 1807 Betsey (Davis) Hayden of Gray ME, b. ca. 1782. B/S/land Otisfield ME and Gorham ME 1793-1807. Wid. w/son Daniel H. 1850.

269 Isaac$^6$, 1789-1853.
Anna, b. 1793, m. _____ Jordan. Went to Buckfield ME.
Sophia, b. 1795, d. 14 Sep 1871, m. 2 Dec 1819 Colonel Thomas Edes, Jr.
Abigail, b. 1798, m. 8 Dec 1825 Luther Scribner.
Jane, b. 1808.
270 David$^6$, 1812-1898.
271 Jonas$^6$, b. 1814.
272 Daniel H., 1820-1911.
273 James$^6$, b. 1822.

Sources; Otisfield ME census 1800. Madison ME 1820, 1830. VR Otisfield ME, SA/ME. R10a, K10A, S67, B40.

129. **SAMUEL$^5$ SAWYER** [see 47], b. ca. 1770 Falmouth ME, d. 28 May 1841 New Gloucester ME, m. 15 Mar 1810 Hannah Sawyer, b. ca. 1789, d. 27 Sep 1870, dau. Benjamin and Miriam (Sawyer) Sawyer. A male, 90-100 yrs. old lived with Samuel 1830. S/land in Falmouth ME 1812, Durham 1815-1819, Minot ME 1833-1841. Wid. in Portland ME 1850, 1860.

274 John R.$^6$, 1814-1889.
Sophronia, b. ca. 1815.
Son, b. (1815-1820).
Daughter, b. (1815-1820).
Joshua, b. ca. 1824.
Eliza A., b. ca. 1828, m. 13 Aug 1856 James D. Sawyer.
Rebecca, b. 1830, d. 1905, m. 26 Nov 1851 Joshua Lewis Sawyer of Durham ME.
Amos, b. 1831 Minot ME.
Frances, b. 1833, d. 26 Feb 1838.

Sources: Durham ME census 1820. Minot ME census 1830. New Gloucester ME census 1840. Portland ME census 1850, 1860. M5, R10a (deed #65/410 proves parentage), T19.

130. **JOSHUA$^5$ SAWYER** [see 47], b. ca. 1774 Falmouth ME, d. 22 May 1806 Falmouth ME, m. 20 May 1800 Emma Sawyer, b. 21 May 1775, dau. Benjamin and Miriam (Sawyer) Sawyer. Wid. m. _____ Hall.

275 Joseph Grant$^6$, 1801-1888.

Sources: Falmouth ME census 1800. Benjamin's will, Robert L. Taylor rec.

131. **THOMAS$^5$ SAWYER, Jr.** [see 48], b. 29 Nov 1772 Falmouth ME, d. 25 Nov 1852 Westbrook ME, m. 18 Dec 1800 Westbrook ME Susannah Sawyer, b. ca. 1779 d. 1855, dau. Isaac and Susannah Sawyer. Revolutionary War. B/S/land in Westbrook ME.

Susan, b. 1803.
Son, b. (1800-1810). (Zebulon K. ?)
Son, b. (1800-1810).
Daughter, b. (1800-1810).
Thomas, b. ca. 1812 Falmouth ME, d. 8 Jul 1879 Deering ME, m. Tryphena _____ of New Hampshire. CH: Mary E., b. Jun 1861, d. 29 Sep 1882. In Falmouth ME 1850. S/land in Westbrook ME 1866.
Daughter, b. (1810-1815).
Daughter, b. (1820-1825).
Daughter, b. (1825-1830).

Sources: Falmouth ME census 1810. Westbrook ME census 1820, 1830, 1840, 1850. VR Westbrook ME. R10a, K10A, H26.

132. **ZEBULON$^5$ SAWYER** [see 48], b. 6 Sep 1778 Falmouth ME, d. bef. 20 Dec 1832, m. 4 Oct 1804 Lyman ME Rebecca Ford of Lyman ME, b. ?. Combmaker. Rebecca w/son Benjamin 1830, 1840.

Benjamin, b. ca. 1805, d. 22 Aug 1878. Ship carpenter. B/S/land 1842.
Emily, b. ca. 1809, m. Sep 1831 Samuel Parsons.
Daughter, b. (1800-1810).
Son, b. (1810-1820).
Daughter, b. (1810-1820).
Daughter, b. (1810-1820).

Elizabeth A., b. (1810-1820), m. 15 Nov 1840 Isaiah Frank.
Sources: Falmouth ME census 1810. Westbrook ME 1820, 1830, 1840, 1850. K10A, R10a.

133. **BENJAMIN[5] SAWYER** [see 49], b. 14 Dec 1769 Falmouth ME, d. 23 Dec 1825 Westbrook ME, m. 26 Jan 1797 Portland ME Rebecca Barbour of Falmouth ME, b. 26 Jul 1776 d. 3 Oct 1852, dau. Adam and Betsey (Knight) Barbour. Bricklayer. B/S/ land in Falmouth ME. Wid. w/son Lewis 1840.

276 Lewis Bean[6], 1798-1858.
Eunice, b. 26 May 1801, d. 9 Sep 1820.
Mary B., b. 5 May 1803, d. 25 May 1825, m. Stephen Morse.
Son, b. 1804, d. 1810.
Amasa, b. 15 Jan 1808 Westbrook ME, d. 8 Nov 1877 Deering ME, m. 1 Apr 1832 Westbrook ME Hannah Sawyer of Westbrook ME, b. Apr 1801 d. 22 Feb 1882, dau. Asa and Sarah (Knight) Sawyer. Shoemaker. B/S/land 1859 and 1861. CH: Nancy C., b. 1833.

Sources: Falmouth ME census 1800, 1810. Westbrook ME census 1820, 1840, 1850, 1860. VR Portland ME, Deering ME. R10a, Theodora Hoyt Sawyer rec.

134. **EBENEZER HILTON[5] SAWYER** [see 49], b. 11 Apr 1774 Falmouth ME, d. 11 Jul 1850 Otisfield ME, m.(1) ?; m.(2) 19 May 1806 Falmouth ME Elizabeth (Bailey) Walker, b. 19 Dec 1775 d. 19 Jun 1870, wid. of George. Cordwainer. B/S/land 1805-1833. He bur. Blue Hill Cem., Otisfield ME.

277 Jeremiah[6], 1796-1880.
George W., b. 7 Apr 1807 Otisfield ME. Went to North Carolina.
Josiah B., b. 1 Jun 1809, m.(I) 18 May 1833 Elizabeth Barnes, b. 5 Aug 1803 d. 1850. In Yarmouth ME, Biddeford ME, Portland ME. Went to Iowa. CH: Ellen S., b. 9 Apr 1834; Rebecca B., b. 22 Aug 1836; Sarah A., b. 6 Nov 1838.
Francis, b, 21 Oct 1811 Otisfield ME.
Charles, b. 5 Oct 1812, d. 15 Jan 1831.
Elias, b. 22 Sep 1814 Otisfield ME.
Rebecca, b. 19 Oct 1817, d. 15 Jan 1901, m. 19 Oct 1837 Daniel Holden. Went to Wisconsin.
William B., b. 1819, d. in France.
278 Lewis H.[6], b. 1821.
Mary, b. 3 Aug 1823, d. 6 Dec 1898, m. _____ Parker.

Sources: Falmouth ME census 1800. Otisfield ME census 1810, 1820, 1830, 1840, 1860. VR Westbrook ME, Otisfield ME. S67, M5, R10a.

135. **SAMUEL[5] SAWYER** [see 49], b. 16 Nov 1777 Falmouth ME, m. 23 Nov 1800 Portland ME Nabby Cobb of Portland ME, b. ?. Joiner. B/S/land 1800-1805.

Smith Cobb, b. 180? Portland ME. S/land in Portland ME 1834.
Son, b. (1800-1810).
Son, b. (1800-1810).
Daughter, b. (1800-1810).

Sources: Falmouth ME census 1810. R10a, K10A.

136. **EDWARD[5] SAWYER** [see 51], b. 30 May 1767 Westbrook ME, d. bef. 1807, m. Abigail Curtis of Harpswell ME, b. 1771. In Standish ME, Portland ME, Topsham ME, Thompsonboro (Lisbon) ME. He received land in Harspwell 1793 from John Ross estate. Wid. m. 8 Aug 1807 John Owens.

Sarah, b. 30 Jul 1791.
Jane, b. 17 Jul 1793.
279 Daniel C.[6], 1795-1872.
Hannah, b. 30 Jul 1797.
Patience, b. 1 Sep 1799, m. 1 Dec 1822 Nicholas Sparks.
Paul C., b. 24 Apr 1805 Topsham ME, m. 7 Nov 1832 Harriet Harrison, b. ?. In Bath ME. CH: Son, b. (1825-1830).
280 Edward[6], 1805-1877.
281 Stephen C., 1806-1892.
Sources: Thompsonboro (Lisbon) ME census 1800. Bath 1840. VR Topsham ME, SA/ME. G35A, R10a.

137. **WILLIAM[5] SAWYER** [see 51], b. 24 Feb 1793 Falmouth ME, d. bef. 1869 Portland ME, m. 13 Jul 1813 Hannah Boynton, b. 1795 d. 22 Mar 1856, dau. Theophilus Boynton. Ropemaker. B/S/land 1827-1868.
Charles Augustus, b. 1 May 1814, d. 18 Jun 1827.
Harriet B., b. 8 Jan 1816, d. 6 Jan 1910, m. 4 Sep 1843 Rev. William A. Thompson.
282 Albion[6], 1823-1903.
Nathaniel Crockett, b. 19 Mar 1829 Portland ME, d. 10 Sep 1883 Deering ME. In Boston MA.
Angelina S., b. 5 Jan 1832, m. Jonas Hamilton.
Sources: Portland ME census 1820, 1830, 1840, 1850. VR Portland ME. M5, K10A, P69, R10a, Thos. Hamilton rec.

138. **JONATHAN[5] SAWYER** [see 52], b. ca. 1779 Falmouth ME, m. 30 Mar 1807 Windham ME Anna (Mary) Cobb of Falmouth ME, b. 31 Jun 1788. B/land in Windham ME 1803, S/land 1846.
Dorcas, b. ca. 1810.
Mary, b. 1813, d. 19 Jan 1864, m. Levi Bailey.
Hannah C., b. ?, m. 15 Jan 1837 Alvin Leighton.
283 Sumner P.[6], 1819-1899.
284 William F.[6], 1824-1904.
Andrew J., b. 1829, d. 13 Sep 1865.
285 Francis E.[6], 1830-1911.
More unnamed children listed in census.
Sources: Falmouth ME census 1810. Westbrook ME census 1820, 1830, 1840. VR Windham ME, SA/ME. R10a, M3, L9, Clyde M. Sawyer rec.

139. **HENRY[5] SAWYER** (Holmes) [see 53], b. ca. 1787 Portland ME, d. 1846, m. 30 Nov 1819 Falmouth ME Lois Noyes of Falmouth ME, b. ca. 1788 d. 27 Jul 1873. B/land in Westbrook ME 1820, 1822. His death is mentioned in a deed.
286 Simon M., 1820-1899.
Sources: Westbrook ME census 1820. Wid. in Portland ME census 1850, 1860. VR SA/ME. R10a, N40, David Young rec.

140. **MARK[5] SAWYER** [see 53], b. 1794 Eastport ME, d. 21 Apr 1852 Leominster MA, m. 24 Oct 1815 Falmouth ME Abigail Jackson of Lewiston ME, b. 3 Dec 1796, dau. Eli and Hannah (McKenney) Jackson. Combmaker. War of 1812.
287 Nelson[6], b. 1813-1864.

Mark P., b. 1830 Westbrook ME, d. 11 Feb 1863 Portland ME, m. Hannah E. Lord of No. Yarmouth ME, b. Oct 1836 d. 24 Jul 1909, dau. Samuel D. and Anne C. (Lunt) Lord. Combmaker. In Hollister MA, Clinton MA. CH: Mary Alice, b. 5 Feb 1856; Anna Clemens, b. 28 Nov 1859.

Philip W., b. ca. 1841, m. Mary E. McRulne of Dorchester MA, b. ?. Ch: Grace Woodford, b. 14 Jun 1866, m. 3 Mar 1886 Boston MA Walter H. Jackson.

288 Charles W.[6], b. 1844.

More unnamed children listed in census.

Sources: Westbrook Me census 1820, 1830, 1840, 1850. VR SA/ME, SA/MA. M5, Obit, Robert L. Taylor rec.

141. **REUBEN[5] SAWYER** [see 54], b. ca. 1785 Cumberland ME, d. 12 Mar 1848 Cumberland ME, m.(1) 13 Oct 1808 No. Yarmouth ME Betsey Wyman of No. Yarmouth ME, b. Mar 1787 d. 17 May 1816; m.(2) 28 Nov 1816 No. Yarmouth ME Olive Shaw of No. Yarmouth ME, b. 15 Jan 1792 d. 16 May 1831; m.(3) 13 Sep 1831 No. Yarmouth ME Susan Hill, b. ? d. 15 Feb 1837; m.(4) 5 Feb 1838 Jane C. Wilson, b. 20 Jun 1796 d. 22 Dec 1846. Farmer. He bur. Cumberland Center Cem.

289 Josiah Wyman[7], 1810-1894.

Mary, b. 28 Nov 1812, m. John Skilling Sawyer.

290 James[6], 1815-1891.

291 Joseph[6], 1818-1897.

Elizabeth, b. 7 Feb 1820, m. 1848 Joscph Sturdivant.

292 Asa[6], 1822-1910.

293 John Shaw[6], 1825-1909.

Huldah, b. 5 Jul 1828, d. 5 Apr 1843.

Albert, b. 21 Oct 1832.

Olive Susan, b. 31 Aug 1834, d. 5 Apr 1843.

Sources: No. Yarmouth ME census 1810, 1820. Cumberland ME census 1830, 1840. VR Cumberland ME, No. Yarmouth ME, SA/ME. G6, R10a, W10, David Young rec., Robert L. Taylor rec.

142. **ASA[5] SAWYER**, [see 54], b. ca. 1792 Cumberland ME, m. 20 Feb 1817 Cumberland ME Huldah Blanchard of Cumberland ME, b. 10 Aug 1795, dau. Nicholas and Sara (Gray) Blanchard. Wid. m. William Cary of Turner ME.

Mary Ann, b. ca. 1818, m. Horace Bradford of Turner ME.

James Gray, b. ca. 1820 Cumberland ME.

Asa, b. ca. 1822 North Yarmouth ME.

Luther, b. ca. 1824 Cumberland ME.

Ellen, b. ca. 1826.

Augusta, b. ca. 1828.

Sources: No. Yarmouth ME census 1820. Cumberland ME census 1840. VR No. Yarmouth ME, Cumberland ME. J. Crawford Hartman rec.

143. **MERRICK D.[5] SAWYER** [see 55], b. 18 Jul 1809 Durham ME, d. 4 Jan 1894 Thomaston ME, m.(1) Eliza H. _____, b. 1809 d. 1858; m.(2) 1 Jun 1859 Portland ME Louise Jane Chadbourne, b. Sep 1825 d. 10 Apr 1886, dau. John and Mehitable (Knight) Chadbourne. Stonecutter. B/S/land. In Palmyra ME, Portland ME. Wid. bur. Deering ME.

David Henry, Rev., b. 27 Jan 1836 Foxcroft ME, d. 3 Oct 1921 W. Medway MA, m. Emily M. Nickerson, b. 1834 d. 1921. Minister. In Wiscasset ME 1877. CH: Edith May, b. 1877.

James W., b. 16 Sep 1838 Portland ME, m. 11 Apr 1864 Portland ME Julia A. Swett of Boothbay ME, b. Sep 1839 d. 3 Jan 1893, dau. Harvey and Sarah (Greenleaf) Swett. Architect. On Chebeaque Island ME. CH: Clara Augusta, b. 18 Jul 1869, d. 15 Mar 1935, m. 9 Nov 1889 Amos Perkins Lord.

John W., b. 27 Jul 1842 Portland ME.

Mary E., b. 24 May 1844.

Marion, b. ca. 1865.

Frank C., b. ca. 1870.

Sources: Palmyra ME census 1840. Portland ME 1850, 1860, 1870. Wiscasset ME census 1880. ME 1880 census index. VR Portland ME, SA/ME. R10a, M5, S69, P32.

144. **JOSIAH$^5$ SAWYER** [see 57], b. 28 Mar 1787 Harrington ME, d. 1875, m. 12 Jul 1810 Sedgewick ME Rebecca Grindle of Sedgewick ME, b. 18 Sep 1790 d. 1862, dau. John and Joanna (Hotchkins) Grindle. Fisherman. B/land in Steuben and Harrington ME 1808.

294 George$^6$, 1813-1899.

295 Charles N.$^6$, b. 1816.

William, 2nd, b. (1810-1820).

Elbridge G., b. 25 Feb 1825 Harrington ME, d. 17 Mar 1886 d. Milbridge ME, m.(1) (I) 14 Oct 1846 Harrington ME Diana Turner of Harpswell ME, b. 27 Sep 1826 d. 6 Aug 1864, dau. Solon and Sarah (Pinkham) Turner; m.(2) Delia _____, b. ?; m.(3) 16 May 1870 Mary A. Ray of Harrington ME, b. 1827 d. 5 Apr 1901, dau. John and Jerusha (Evod) Ray. Fisherman. He bur. Wyman Cem., Milbridge ME. CH: Adreanna, b. 30 Sep 1848, d. 1849; Lenora, b. 8 Jul 1851, m. 30 May 1870 Lester Flagg; L. Diana, b. 1 Jul 1853, m.(1) 18 Jul 1874 John Robinson, m.(2) 21 Mar 1890 Adinoram Tracey; Sarah Lucinda, b. 23 Jul 1855, m. 5 Sep 1881 Beverly MA John W. Hanson; Addie, b. 6 Apr 1859, d. 19 Feb 1873.

296 Eben$^6$, 1828-1863.

297 Philo L.$^6$, 1830-1908.

Temperance, b. ?, d. 18 Sep 1894, m.(1) John Stevens, m.(2) Eliott Plummer, m.(3) John Bunker.

Louise, b. ?.

Joanna, b. ?, m. 22 Jan 1840 Joel Leighton.

Helen, b. ?, m. 17 Jun 1849 Daniel Chipman.

Rebecca, b. 1836, d. 6 Feb 1886, m. 18 Jan 1856 Tyler Robinson.

Sources: Harrington ME census 1810, 1830. Steuben ME census 1820, 1840, 1850. ME 1880 census index. VR Harrington ME, SA/ME, SA/MA. R10f, M49, M43, C26, M5, Leonard F. Tibbetts rec.

145. **WILLIAM$^5$ SAWYER** [see 57], b. 2 Dec 1791 Harrington ME, m. 22 Feb 1809 Sarah Dyer of Steuben ME, b. 8 May 1792, dau. Andrew and Ruth (Brown) Dyer. In Harrington ME, Milbridge ME.

Andrew D., b. 30 Jun 1809 Harrington ME.

William, b. 10 Aug 1810 Harrington ME.

Achsah, b. 22 Aug 1811, m. 24 Dec 1828 William Brackett.

Lydia, b. 31 Jan 1814, d.y.

Elizabeth, b. 15 Oct 1815.

Cyndulia, b. 24 May 1817.

Mary, b. 1 Dec 1819, m. 19 Feb 1835 John D. Sawyer.

Elmira, b. 24 Jan 1823.

Lydia, b. 24 Jan 1823.

Sources: Harrington ME census 1810, 1820, 1830. VR Harrington ME. Leonard F. Tibbetts rec.

146. **GEORGE B.$^5$ SAWYER** [see 57], b. 1 Mar 1793 Harrington ME, d. 17 Dec 1853 Milbridge ME, m. Nov 1815 Milbridge ME Mary A. Roberts of Cape Elizabeth ME, b. 21 Mar 1797 d. 23 Sep 1886, dau. Vincent and Sarah (Sawyer) Roberts. Ship carpenter. War 1812. In Harrington ME, Cherryfield ME. B/land in Harrington ME 1818.

Catherine, b. 1816, m.(I) 3 Feb 1838 Moses Wallace.
298 Joseph Warren$^6$, 1818-1898.
299 William Roberts, 1821-1887.
300 Stillman D.$^6$, 1822-1854.
301 Emery W.$^6$, 1825-1883.
George, b. ca. 1827.
Josiah, b. ?. Lost at sea.
302 Franklin$^6$, 1830-1895.
303 David$^6$, 1833-1895.
Mary Ann, b. 1838, m.(1) 23 Nov 1856 Melville H. Nash, m.(2) Isaac McCallum.
Phebe, b. ca. 1841, m. 14 Jun 1860 Myrick Preble.

Sources: Harrington ME census 1820, 1830. Cherryfield ME census 1840. Milbridge ME census 1850. VR Harrington ME, SA/ME. F21, R10f, M5, D6, M43.

147. **JOHN G.$^5$ SAWYER** [see 57], b. 1800 Harrington ME, m.(I) 27 Jan 1823 Lydia B. Dyer, b. 1802, dau. Andrew and Ruth (Brown) Dyer. Carpenter. Births of their CH are recorded in both Portland ME and Cape Elizabeth ME.

304 Josiah Handy$^6$, b. 1825.
Rebecca J., b. 30 Apr 1827.
Mary C., b. 4 Mar 1830, d. 29 May 1905, m. _____ Hinkley.
Sarah M., b. 16 Aug 1832, m. Charles Chambers.
John W., b. 12 Mar 1836 Cape Elizabeth ME.
Martha A. C., b. 16 Feb 1839.

Sources: Portland ME census 1840. Jonesboro ME census 1850. VR SA/ME. P69, M43.

148. **SOLOMON$^5$ SAWYER** [see 60], b. 1782 Gorham ME (or No. Yarmouth ME), d. 11 Jan 1835, m. 28 Apr 1808 No. Yarmouth ME Anna B. Chandler of No. Yarmouth ME, b. ?. In No. Yarmouth ME, Chebeaque Isle ME, Cumberland ME. S/land 1819.

305 Edmund Chandler$^6$ 1809-1881.
Phebe, b. 1813, d. 1896, m.(1) James Henley, m.(2) David Hill.
Anne, b. 1816, d. 1841, m. David Hill.
Ruth, b. 1822, d. 1841.
306 Jacob E.$^6$, ca. 1825-1887.

Sources: VR Cumberland ME, No. Yarmouth ME. R10a, K1A.

149. **JACOB$^5$ SAWYER** [see 60], b. 1797 Chebeaque ME, m. Sarah _____, b. ?. In Falmouth ME.

Jeremiah, b. 14 May 1828 Falmouth ME, m. 30 Mar 1851 Laura Tinney, b. ?.
Solomon, b. Sep 1830 Falmouth ME.
William, b. 12 Apr 1835 Falmouth ME.

Sources: VR Yarmouth ME, Falmouth ME.

150. **WILLIAM[5] SAWYER** [see 61], b. 19 Jan 1787 Freeport ME, d. 22 Feb 1839 Medford MA, m.(1) 2 Apr 1812 Hannah Knight, b. ?; m.(2) 30 Jan 1833 Portland ME Saloma Hanson of Portland ME, b. 1792 d. 28 Jan 1839.

William Bainbridge, b. 11 Mar 1815 Pownal ME.
Mary S., b. 29 Aug 1817, m. 4 Feb 1840 Medford MA James Pierce.
Elizabeth Jane, b. 21 Sep 1820, m. 18 Feb 1841 Medford MA Rufus Ventriss.
Almira J., b. ca. 1828, m. 16 Jan 1853 Medford MA James Pierce.

Sources: Pownal ME census 1820, Cumberland ME census 1830. VR Pownal ME, Medford MA, SA/ME.

151. **NATHANIEL[5] SAWYER** [see 61], b. 16 Mar 1791 Freeport ME, d. 8 May 1838, m. Abigail Fickett, b. ?. In Pownal ME 1813, Freeport ME 1820. Wid. in Portland ME 1840.

Eliza, b. 30 Nov 1813, d. 8 Apr 1839, m. _____ Hamilton.
307 Abner J.[6], b. 1815.
Apphia, b. 6 Dec 1818.
Nathaniel, b. 26 May 1821, d. 4 Jun 1828 in Raymond ME.
Nathan, b. 31 May 1824 Portland ME.
George, b. 7 May 1827 Portland ME, d. 28 Oct 1850, m. 19 Sep 1848 Elizabeth W. Varney of Windham ME, b. ?.
William H., b. 14 Apr 1829.
Mary J., b. 12 Jun 1832.

Sources: Freeport ME census 1820. Portland ME census 1840. VR Pownal ME, Windham ME. R10a, Dr. B. H. Sawyer rec.

152. **ENOS[5] SAWYER** [see 61], b. 27 Oct 1792 Freeport ME, d. 9 Sep 1846 Old Town ME, m. 8 Nov 1814 Pownal ME Clarissa Brown of Stillwater ME, b. 1791 d. 4 Nov 1886. War 1812. B/S/land in Pownal ME 1813-1829. Wid. in Old Town ME 1850, w/son Enos 1880.

308 Sewall Brown[6], b. 1817.
Elisha, b. 1819, m.(I) 3 Dec 1846 Matilda Clendenion, b. ?. Went West.
Almira B., b. 1821, m.(I) 28 Jul 1838 William Burlingame.
Jane, b. 1825, m. William Cousins.
309 Enos[6], 1827-1907.
Elizabeth A., b. 1832, m. 18 Sep 1855 Luther H. Averill.
Mahala B., b. 1834, m. (I) 29 Apr 1857 James Burke.

Sources: Pownal ME census 1820, 1830. Old Town ME census 1850, 1880. VR Pownal ME. H26, R10a.

153. **ELISHA[5] SAWYER** [see 61], b. 1812 Pownal ME, d. Old Town ME, m. 19 Apr 1832 Pownal ME Dorcas Haskell of Pownal ME, b. 1815.

310 Joseph D., 1832-1894.
311 Horace C., 1834-1902.
Pauline H., b. 1835, m. 6 Oct 1850 Joseph F. Cobb.
Lucinda, b. 1839, m. 30 Mar 1856 James W. Dutton.
William H., b. Sep 1840, d. 5 Dec 1895, m. 28 Nov 1885 Old Town ME Annie C. Goodwin of Old Town ME, b. 1862. In Orono ME, Bradley ME.
312 Arthur G., 1843-1917.
Addison B., b. 1848. In Orono ME.
Ella J. b. 1850.
Abby A., b. 1855, m. 4 Dec 1874 Lewellyn Decker.

Sources: Pownal ME census 1840, 1860. Orono ME census 1850. VR Old Town ME, SA/ME. P82f.

154. **JAMES$^5$ SAWYER** [see 64], b. 1 Feb 1778 Gloucester MA, d. 21 Feb 1858 Gloucester MA, m. 27 Nov 1802 Gloucester MA Lydia Morgan, b. 26 Dec 1779 d. bef. 1830. In Gloucester MA.

313 James$^6$, b. 1803.
314 William Morgan$^6$, 1805-1845.
Lydia Ann, b. 3 Mar 1807.
Warren Thaxter, b. 7 Oct 1809, d. 22 Sep 1849, m. ?.
315 Charles$^6$, b. 1811.
George, b. 21 Jul 1816 Gloucester MA, m.(1) 15 Aug 1838 Gloucester MA Clarissa T. Barrett, b. 5 Jan 1819 d. 9 Dec 1855, dau. John and Clarissa Barrett; m.(2) 11 Jan 1857 Worcester MA Mary (Rust) Chapman of Gloucester MA, b. 18 Aug 1823, dau. Benjamin and Lydia Rust. Fisherman. CH: Julia Ann, b. 22 Dec 1838, d. 8 Oct 1911, m. 15 Jun 1857 Manchester MA James Ingersoll; Alexander S., b. 10 Nov 1841, d. 22 Jul 1845; Clara B., b. ca. 1849, m. 24 Dec 1871 Gloucester MA Daniel Mead.

Sources: Gloucester MA census 1810, 1820, 1830, 1840, 1850 w/son George. VR Gloucester MA, SA/MA. A38, R35.

155. **ROBERT STEWART$^5$ SAWYER** [see 64], b. 5 Jul 1796 Gloucester MA, d. 3 Oct 1841 Cape Cod MA, m. 17 Oct 1820 Gloucester MA Lydia Douglas, b. 10 Aug 1800.

316 Robert$^6$, b. 1822.
Lydia, b. 1 Feb 1825, m. 16 Sep 1844 Gloucester MA William Carter.
317 David$^6$, b. 1828.
318 Aaron I.$^6$, b. 1830.
Charlotte, b. 20 Feb 1833, m. 25 Jun 1855 Gloucester MA George H. Bacon.
Thomas D., b. 9 May 1836 Gloucester MA, m. 24 Jul 1861 Gloucester MA Caroline E. Tarr of Gloucester MA, b. 1843, dau. Frederick and Rachel Tarr.
319 George Washington, b. 1839.

Sources: Gloucester MA census 1830, 1840, 1850 (wid.). VR Gloucester MA, SA/MA. B2, B16.

156. **WILLIAM NEWMAN$^5$ SAWYER** [see 64], b. 24 Dec 1799 Gloucester MA, d. 1 Jan 1862 Lexington MA, m. 8 Aug 1819 Ellen Whyte, b. 1 Jan 1802 Chester, England, d. 1874. Sea captain. Descendant of Gov. Winthrop.

320 Joseph$^6$, 1823-1901.
Ellen N., b. 1826, m. 14 May 1848 Chelsea MA Franklin Schoff.
William Newman, b. 9 Nov 1832 Chelsea MA, m. 28 May 1854 Chelsea MA Mary E. Brown of Boston MA, b. 1833, dau. Francis and Elizabeth Brown. CH: Mary Newman, b. 1 Sep 1869. In Newtonville MA.
Deborah, b. 9 Nov 1832, m. 12 Oct 1853 Gloucester MA Frederick G. Monson.
Martha T., b. 22 May 1839.
George W., b. 11 Sep 1841, d. 12 Jun 1844 Concord MA.
Ann M., b. 1845.

Sources: Chelsea MA census 1840, 1850. VR Gloucester MA, SA/MA.

157. **CHARLES$^5$ SAWYER** [see 65], b. 1 Jan 1788 Gloucester MA, d. 11 Aug 1821 Gloucester MA, m. 28 May 1812 Sally Corliss of No. Yarmouth ME, b. 24 Aug 1792 d. 1 Dec 1857, dau. Ebenezer and Lydia (Elwell) Corliss. B/land in No. Yarmouth ME 1820. He bur. in Gloucester MA.

321 Charles$^6$, 1813-1867.
Samuel Elwell, b. 25 Nov 1815 Gloucester MA, d. 15 Dec 1889 Boston MA, m. Abbie J. Mead, b. ?. Had dry goods business at 50 Milk St., Boston MA. B/land 1884 and deeded it to Gloucester MA. He bur. Gloucester MA.
Sources: Gloucester MA census 1820. VR Gloucester MA, Boston MA. R10a.

158. **MOSES$^5$ SAWYER** [see 66], b. 14 Oct 1795 Gloucester MA, d. 14 Oct 1861 New Gloucester ME, m. 20 Jan 1841 Mary B. Morse of New Gloucester ME, b. 1813, dau. Joseph and Abigail (Knight) Morse of Gray ME. S/land in New Gloucester ME 1854.
322 Joseph M., b. 1842.
Charles Boothby, b. 20 Oct 1855 New Gloucester ME.
Sources: New Gloucester ME census 1850, 1860. VR New Gloucester ME. T19, R10a.

## SIXTH GENERATION

159. **DAVID$^6$ SAWYER** [see 67], b. 1 Jun 1811 Otisfield ME, d. 8 Nov 1879 Harrison ME, m. 21 Apr 1840 Otisfield ME Edna Brackett of Harrison ME, b. 11 Jul 1821 d. 12 Aug 1896, dau. Enoch and Araminta (Caswell) Brackett. He bur. Bolster Mills Cem., Harrison ME.
323 Fernald J.$^7$, 1841-1912.
David A., b. 1 Jan 1846, d. 21 Nov 1860.
Harriet J., b. 3 Sep 1850, d. 22 Jun 1925, unm.
Lizzie M., b. 21 Nov 1857, d. 6 Sep 1935, unm.
Sources: Harrison ME census 1850, 1860. VR Otisfield ME, SA/ME.

160. **DANIEL BARNABAS$^6$ SAWYER** [see 68], b. 20 Nov 1818 Otisfield ME, d. 23 Jun 1899, m. Fannie L. Brackett of Harrison ME, b. 28 Jan 1823 d. 11 Feb 1903, dau. Enoch and Araminta (Caswell) Brackett. B/S/land 1842, 1845 in Waterford ME. He bur. in No. Yarmouth ME.
324 David E.$^7$, b. 1840.
325 George L.$^7$, 1844-1921.
Elizabeth N., b. 28 Oct 1846, m. 11 Jan 1877 James A. Hall of Windham ME.
Sarah D., b. 1850.
Mary D., b. 23 May 1854.
326 Daniel Millard, b. 1856.
Joel B., b. 11 Jul 1858 Gorham ME.
327 John Rich$^7$, b. 1860.
Angeline F., b. 16 Jan 1863, d. 25 Oct 1892, m.(I) 17 Nov 1888 Clarence L. Fogg.
Sources: Township No. 5 census 1850. Gorham ME census 1860. Westbrook ME census 1870. VR Gorham ME, SA/ME. R10a, M5, L7, B74, W42.

161. **WILLIAM$^6$ SAWYER** [see 69], b. 24 Jul 1809 Otisfield ME, d. 24 Jan 1897 Waterford ME, m.(1) Nancy M._____, b. ?; m.(2) Caroline McAllister of Stoneham ME, b. 1818 d. 8 Jun 1889, dau. John and Lydia (Evans) McAllister. B/S/land in Stoneham ME 1845.
Lydia, b. 16 Oct 1843, m._____ Gammon.
328 Cushman John$^7$, 1846-1910.
Eunice E., b. 18 May 1848, d. 4 Aug 1895, m._____McAllister.
Angenette, b. 14 May 1852, m._____ Brooks.
Georgiette, b. 15 Jul 1859, m. 29 May 1875 Walter B. Johnson.
Sources: Stoneham ME census 1850, 1860, 1870. ME 1880 census index. VR Stoneham ME, SA/ME. N6, Caroline's Will.

162. **EBENEZER E. H.[6] SAWYER** [see 69], b. 10 Jun 1815 Otisfield ME, m. 16 Oct 1843 Elizabeth Campbell of Minot ME, b. 1824. B/land in Stoneham ME 1849.

Huldah A., b. 1845.

Eliza, b. 1847.

Lewis W., b. 1849.

Sources: Stoneham ME census 1850. VR Stoneham ME. R10c.

163. **SAMUEL[6] SAWYER** [see 70], b. 5 Oct 1808 Otisfield ME, d. 1861, m. 30 Mar 1834 Sweden ME Olive Bryant, b. ?. S/land in Stoneham ME 1848.

Martha A., b. 27 Aug 1836, d. bef. 1873, m. Horace D. Eastman.

Rufus P., b. ca. 1846, m. 11 Sep 1879 Boston MA Rebecca F. Webber of Readville ME, b. 1849, dau. George and Rebecca H. Webber. Physician. In Fryeburg ME and Woodstock ME.

Sources: VR SA/ME, SA/MA. R10c, R21.

164. **DAVID[6] SAWYER** [see 70], b. 1815 Otisfield ME, d. 9 Apr 1886 Fryeburg ME, m.(I) 5 Nov 1842 Betsey Eastman, b. 14 Aug 1820. B/land in Stoneham ME. B/S/land in Lovell ME 1847-1855.

Barnet Walker, b. 8 Sep 1843 Lovell ME, d. 26 Nov 1923 Bartlett NH, m. Drusilla Watson of Lovell ME, b. 9 June 1845 d. 10 Oct 1918, dau. Thomas and Mary J. (Stearns) Watson. Civil War. In Fryeburg ME, Bartlett NH. CH: Mary E., b. 1867, m. 2 Nov 1893 Sandwich NH Charles E. Blanchard; H. Robinson, b. Jun 1877, d. 17 Jan 1914, unm.

329 Edward Seldon[7], b. 1847.

Lewis Warren, b. 10 Dec 1850 Lovell ME, d. bef. 1886, m. 29 Dec 1875 Lynn MA Florence N. Ireson of Lynn MA, b. 1855, dau. John J. and P. M. Ireson. In Fryeburg ME, Portland ME. CH: Mabel F., b. 20 Oct 1877; Alice L., b. 1879, d. 6 Dec 1885.

Georgianna, b. 6 Aug 1854, d. bef. 1886, m._____ Tasker.

Colby, b. 6 Aug 1854, d.y.

Sources: Lovell ME census 1850, 1860. Fryeburg ME census 1870, 1880. Portland ME census 1880. ME 1880 census index. Bartlett NH census 1890. VR Lovell ME, Portland ME, SA/MA, SA/NH. N6, R21, R10c.

165. **ABEL M.[6] SAWYER** [see 70], b. 1819 Otisfield ME, m.(1) Phesa Gammon, b. 1811 d. 16 Sep 1863; m.(2) Elizabeth M. Shaw, b. 17 May 1825, dau. Ebenezer and Anne (Morton) Shaw. Farmer. In Stoneham ME, Lovell ME, Fryeburg ME. B/S/land in Stoneham ME 1847-1856, Lovell ME 1847-1853.

Isaac Mc., b. 1843 Stoneham ME.

Sources: Stoneham ME census 1850. Lovell ME census 1860. Fryeburg ME census 1870. R10c, F11, Nancy Welch rec.

166. **HOSEA H.[6] SAWYER** [see 70], b. 1830 Batchelder's Grant ME, d. 19 Dec 1896 Lovell ME, m. Amanda M. Harriman of Madison ME, b. 1838. In Lovell ME, Porter ME, Wid. in Porter ME 1880.

Mary E. b. 1866.

Walter P., b. 1873 Kezar Falls ME, m.(1) 31 Mar 1894 Camden ME Mary E. Blood of Bucksport ME, b. 1874, dau. Oliver and Olivia (Ames) Blood; m.(2) 6 Nov 1904 Nashua NH Rebecca M. Howard of West Dennis MA, b. 1882, dau. Alexander and Lucy S. (Crowell) Howard; m.(3) 26 Jun 1923 Derry NH Sarah (Burgess) Dellatorre of

Nova Scotia, Canada, wid., b. 1880, dau. John and Eliza (Barron) Burgess. Salesman. In Bucksport ME, New Bedford MA, Portland ME. CH: Child, b. 15 Sep 1894.

Sources: Porter ME census 1870, 1880. VR Derry NH, Nashua NH, SA/ME.

167. **LEVI⁶ SAWYER** [see 71], b. ca. 1797 Gorham ME, d. 10 Mar 1874 Porter ME, m. 4 Dec 1817 Hiram ME Mary Leathers (of Limerick ME?), b. ca. 1800 d. 11 Feb 1885. Cooper. War 1812: Enl. at Bridgton ME, served as private in Captain Ingall's Company, LTC J. E. Foxcroft's Regiment, Defense of Portland ME, 13 Sep 1814-24 Sep 1814. B/S/land in Hiram ME 1817-1818. In Limerick ME, Cornish ME, Hiram ME, Effingham NH, Porter ME. He bur. in Porter ME Cem. Wid. w/son Henry 1880.

330 Christopher C.[7], 1818-1898.
Sewall, b. 1822, d. 1840 Porter ME.
331 William T.[7], 1824-1904.
Jason G., b. 1825 Porter ME, d. 25 Feb 1905, m. 24 Oct 1848 Lebanon ME Hannah Brown, b. 1837. In Porter ME, Lebanon ME. B/S/land in Porter ME 1851.
Bennett, b. 1832 Porter ME, m. Alice McCoy, b. ?.
332 Henry H.[7], 1834-1909.
Mary J., b. 1835, m. Ephraim Winters.
Clarindy, b. 1837, d. 8 Mar 1908, m. 14 Jul 1860 Daniel J. Fox.
Rose Ann, b. 1838, m. Oliver Peters.
Mehitable, b. ?, d.y.

Sources: Porter ME census 1830, 1840, 1850, 1860, 1870, 1880 wid. w/Henry H. VR Hiram ME, Limerick ME, Lebanon ME, SA/ME. R10c, N1A, M5, Peleg Wadsworth marriage rec., Lulu Wentworth rec., Kendal Willard Sawyer rec.

168. **MARSHALL H.[6] SAWYER** [see 72], b. 22 Feb 1818 Thorndike ME, d. 6 Jan 1905 Greene ME, m. 27 Feb 1867 Buxton ME Araxine Wilkins of Greene ME, b. 31 Jul 1831 d. 13 May 1899, dau. David and Dorcas (Hill) Wilkins. Farmer. In Bangor ME, Greene ME.

Alice M., b. 2 Feb 1868, m. 3 Jun 1896 Fred H. Marr.
333 Edward Payson[7], 1869-1953.
Annie Mabel, b. 12 May 1870.
Lyndon Wilkins, b. 24 Nov 1871, unm.
334 John Marshall[7], 1874-1946.
Mary Ellen, b. 1 Oct 1876, m. Harry Wilkie.

Sources: Bangor ME census 1850. Greene ME census 1880. ME 1880 census index. VR Buxton ME, SA/ME. M60, Richard M. Sawyer rec., Laura E. Sawyer rec.

169. **REUBEN WESCOTT[6] SAWYER** [see 72], b. 21 Oct 1824 Thorndike ME, d. 14 Jan 1892 Garland ME, m. 11 Jul 1862 Addie Blackstone of Blanchard ME, b. 19 Dec 1840 d. 15 Jun 1922, dau. Benjamin Blackstone. Farmer. In Garland ME.

Almont, b. 28 Jan 1864 Blanchard ME, d. 5 Oct 1949, m. 11 Mar 1897 Mattie Farrell of Ellsworth ME, b. 1875, dau. James T. and Lucinda (Chaney) Farrell. Merchant.
Lillian G., b. 25 Mar 1866, d. 26 Mar 1949, m. 19 Oct 1889 Hiram Floyd.
335 Henry Stanton[7], 1863-1966.
Nellie B., b. 16 Jul 1872, m. 16 Jul 1896 Rev. T. W. Harwood.
Hattie M., b. 21 Sep 1874, m. Arthur Jackson.
Roscoe M., b. 6 Mar 1877 Garland ME, d. 14 Mar 1920 Exeter ME, m. Marion Hobart, b. ?. Optometrist. In No. Abington MA.

Sources: Garland ME census 1870, 1880. ME 1880 census index. VR SA/ME. D6, C76, Guy S. Sawyer rec.

170. **FRANCIS NEWELL$^6$ SAWYER** [see 73], b. 1831 Cumberland ME, d. 21 Jul 1899 Charlestown MA, m. 12 Jul 1862 Sarah E. Morgan of Cumberland ME, b. 1835 d. 2 Apr 1897, dau. John S. and Mary (Smith) Morgan. Farmer. In Atkinson ME.

Clinton E., b. ca. 1863, d. 1937, m. 11 Mar 1896 Dexter ME Victoria Jeanette Fernald of Concord NH, b. 28 Apr 1865 d. 1940, dau. Jacob E. and Laura L. (Champion) Fernald. Dentist. No CH.

Emily R., b. ca. 1865.

Charles F., b. Dec 1867 Atkinson ME, m. 5 Jul 1894 Deering ME Ada W. H. Motley of Portland ME, b. ?, dau. William and Elizabeth Motley. Druggist. In Bangor ME. CH: Daughter, b. 17 Oct 1895.

Grace L., b. 1872.

Florence M., b. 1875.

Frank Pearl, b. 6 Jun 1877 Atkinson ME.

Sources: Atkinson ME census 1880. ME 1880 census index. VR SA/ME. P31, W55A.

171. **JAMES$^6$ SAWYER** [see 74], b. 15 Jan 1784 Limington ME, d. 23 Apr 1852 Buxton ME, m.(1) (I) 14 Apr 1805 Elizabeth Gray of Limington ME, b. ?; m.(2) 1 May 1851 Eliza Atkinson of Buxton ME, b. 1791 d. 24 Sep 1855. Minister. War of 1812. In Conway NH 1818, Brownfield ME 1821, Porter ME 1826. B/land in Porter ME 1825.

Abigail, b. 7 Oct 1805, m. 29 Mar 1827 Eben F. Goodwin.

Betsey, b. 27 Mar 1808, m. 7 Apr 1827 Porter ME Luther Fox.

Louisa (Leorina), b. 2 Dec 1812, d. 16 May 1903 Freedom NH, unm.

Sally F., b. 19 Feb 1815, m. 4 Sep 1836 _____ of Porter ME.

Harriet, b. 30 Mar 1818.

James V., b. 10 Sep 1821 Brownfield ME, d. 6 Oct 1841 in Florida.

Samuel H., b. 7 Sep 1823 Brownfield ME, d. 2 May 1847 Somersworth NH.

336 Thomas James$^7$, 1826-1896.

Sources: Porter ME census 1830. VR Porter ME. T6A, R10c, P82e, N39.

172. **MICHAEL$^6$ SAWYER** [see 74], b. 7 Jun 1795 Limington ME, d. 28 Oct 1876 Limington ME, m. 6 Dec 1827 Margery Morton of Jackson ME, b. 28 Apr 1802 d. 22 Mar 1884, dau. Ebenezer and Betsey (Boodey) Morton. Farmer. War of 1812: Private in Captain Solomon Strout's Company, Saco ME. S/land in Baldwin ME 1817.

Abigail A., b. 12 Feb 1829, d. 24 Aug 1908, unm.

Eliza J., b. 10 Jan 1831, d. 25 Nov 1919, m. 1 Feb 1852 Thomas J. Sawyer of Vermont.

Margery A., b. 4 Sep 1832, d. 6 Mar 1910, m. Nov 1853 George Bragdon.

Soloma M., b. 20 Dec 1834, d. 22 Jul 1882, m.(1) Levi Haskell, m.(2) Frank Stone.

Harriet A., b. 27 Dec 1837, m. 27 Dec 1861 Josiah Lewis.

Mary Ellen, b. 15 Mar 1840, d. 31 Jan 1912, m. 2 May 1865 Gardiner Estes.

337 Melville Henry$^7$, 1843-1899.

Martha F., b. 14 Aug 1846, m. 11 Dec 1868 Stephen Emery of Standish ME.

Sources: Limington ME census 1840, 1850. VR SA/ME. R10a, T6A, N40, C19.

173. **STEPHEN$^6$ SAWYER** [see 74], b. 29 Oct 1804 Limington ME, d. 11 Oct 1877 Madrid ME, m. 26 Apr 1827 Phillips ME Mehitable T. Davenport of Phillips ME, b. 11 Aug 1809 d. 12 Jul 1880, dau. Isaac and Hannah (Greeley) Davenport. Baptist Minister. Wid. w/son Newell H. 1880.

Susanna, b. Jan 1828, d. 22 May 1849.

Isaac Davenport, b. 16 Feb 1830, d. 18 Mar 1891, m. 22 Jun 1856 Olive W. Ridlon of Gorham ME, b. 25 Sep 1832 d. 16 Sep 1915, dau. Amos and Elizabeth (Berry) Ridlon. Civil War. In Gorham ME, Standish ME. He bur. Evergreen Cem., Portland ME.

338 William M.$^7$, 1837-1863.

339 Newall H.$^7$, 1845-1912.

340 Delbert N.$^7$, 1848-1875.

Susan A., b. ca. 1853, d. 6 May 1869.

Ladora G., b. ca. 1856.

Sources: Phillips ME census 1830, 1840, 1850. Madrid ME 1870, 1880. VR SA/ME. T6A, G6, R16, M7A, N8 (William Asa Sawyer's Letter), Obit, Robert L. Taylor rec., Nancy Welch rec.

174. **JOSEPH$^6$ SAWYER** [see 75], b. 12 Apr 1790 Steuben ME, m.(1) 7 Oct 1818 Wealthy Dyer of Addison ME, b. ?; m.(2) 24 Feb 1833 Mary Yeaton of Addison ME, b. 1808. In Addison ME. B/land in Addison ME 1818.

341 Luther S.$^7$, 1823-1898.

Ellery T., b. 5 May 1829 Addison ME, d. 15 Jun 1902 Addison ME, m. Emerline C._____, b. 1832. Caulker. CH: Lillian, b. 1859; Carrie H., b. Jul 1859.

342 Joseph D.$^7$, b. 1832.

Rebecca, b. 1834.

343 George M.$^7$, b. 1835.

344 William Augustus$^7$, b. 1838.

Catherine, b. 1841.

Mary E., b. 1845.

Marie C., b. 1847.

More unnamed children listed in census.

Sources: Addison ME census 1820, 1830, 1840, 1850, 1860. VR Steuben ME. R10f.

175. **HENRY$^6$ SAWYER** [see 75], b. 12 Nov 1791 Steuben ME, d. 22 Feb 1865 Augusta ME, m. 17 Jul 1814 Cynthia Foster, b. 1794 d. 9 May 1866, dau. James Foster. Carpenter.

Joshua Dyer, b. 25 Feb 1815 Sullivan ME.

Maria Hill, b. 28 Dec 1816, m. 10 May 1836 George B. Hoyt of Vassalboro ME.

Joseph Henry, b. 6 Nov 1821 Sullivan ME.

Henry Ebenezer, b. 24 Oct 1824, d. 18 Oct 1850.

Frances L., b. 1830, d. 10 Nov 1835.

George Llewellyn, b. Feb 1835, d. 30 Nov 1835.

Sources: Sullivan ME census 1820. Augusta ME census 1830, 1840, 1850. VR Augusta ME. M5.

176. **EBENEZER$^6$ SAWYER** [see 75], b. 20 Dec 1799 Stueben ME, d. 2 Sep 1863 Augusta ME, m.(1) (I) 26 Mar 1823 Frances Wass of Addison ME, b. 1804 d. 19 Jul 1864; m. (2) 4 Jun 1867 Augusta ME Lucy W. Hamblin, b. 26 Jun 1827 d. 29 May 1913, dau. Lewis and Susan (Williams) Hamblin.

345 Lemuel B.$^7$, b. 1824.

William W., b. 1827 Augusta ME.

Rebecca M., b. 1828, m. 5 May 1852 Charles W. Butler of E. Boston MA.

Silvina Susan, b. Jan 1829, m. 26 Oct 1854 Josiah W. Bangs.

346 Enos D.$^7$, 1839-1907.

Emma S., b. 1840, m. 1 Feb 1865 Joseph H. Hobson.

Georgianna B., b. Nov 1846, d. 17 Jul 1853.

Sources: Augusta ME census 1830, 1840, 1850. VR Augusta ME, Bristol ME, SA/ME. D57, A26.

177. **LEMUEL BAKER[6] SAWYER** [see 75], b. 23 Feb 1802 Steuben ME, d. 2 Mar 1890 Steuben ME, m.(1) 18 Mar 1828 Steuben ME Sophronia Handy, b. 24 Mar 1808 d. 17 Sep 1868; m.(2) (I) 30 Nov 1870 Sarah A. Brown, b. 11 Nov 1837 d. 21 Oct 1914, dau. Amos T. and Mersey (Higgins) Brown. Joiner. In Steuben ME. He bur. Sawyer Cem., Steuben ME.

Elmira D., b. 1835, m. 26 Oct 1881 Temple C. Coffin.
Lemuel B., b. 24 Nov 1871, d. 2 Oct 1897, unm. Lost at sea.
347 Charles Addison[7], 1878-1968.

Sources: Steuben ME census 1830, 1840, 1850, 1880. ME 1880 census index. VR Steuben ME, SA/ME. M5, Lemuel's family Bible.

178. **DANIEL L.[6] SAWYER** [see 75], b. 15 Feb 1808 Steuben ME, d. 1881 Steuben ME, m. 3 Nov 1842 Gouldsboro ME Maria A. Moore of Steuben ME, b. 15 Dec 1815. Joiner. In Steuben ME. He bur. Sawyer Cem., Steuben ME.

Charles A., b. 5 Aug 1843, d. 11 Jul 1845.
Olivette, b. 6 Oct 1844, d. same day.
Susan J., b. 30 Nov 1845, d. 23 Dec 1864.
Mary A., b. 25 Jul 1847, m. _____ Perry.
Sophronia E., b. 11 Feb 1850, m.(I) 1 Jan 1874 Winthrop J. Smith.
Joseph Henry, b. 29 Sep 1851, m. 22 Aug 1880 Westboro MA Persis K. Moore of Steuben ME, b. 1856, dau. Henry D. and Elvira Moore. Merchant. In Westboro MA.
Jenette, b. 3 Jul 1853.

Sources: Steuben ME 1850, 1880. ME 1880 census index. VR Steuben ME, Gouldsboro ME, SA/MA. M5.

179. **NATHAN[6] SAWYER** [see 76], b. 25 Mar 1786 Cape Elizabeth ME, d. 17 Jun 1866 Baldwin ME, m.(1) 12 Aug 1810 Joanna Dyer of Cape Elizabeth ME, b. 1788 d. 24 Mar 1842; m.(2) 15 Jan 1843 Windham ME Betsey Mayo of Windham ME, b. 1790 d. 8 Nov 1864; m.(3) 3 Mar 1865 Betsey (Clark) Marr, wid. of Eleazer, b. ca. 1793 d. 8 Nov 1866. War of 1812: Corporal in Captain B. Bodwell's Company, Portland ME. Selectman for Baldwin ME 1818. In Limington ME, Portland ME, Baldwin ME. He bur. in Sapling Hill Cem., Gorham ME.

Eliza A., b. 14 Jul 1811.
348 Benjamin[7], 1813-1884.
349 Christopher Dyer[7], 1815-1867.
Samuel, b. ca. 1828.

Sources: Portland ME census 1810. Baldwin ME census 1860. VR Baldwin ME, SA/ME. T6, C62, Robert L. Taylor rec.

180. **EBENEZER[6] SAWYER** [see 76], b. 14 Dec 1789 Limington ME, d. 10 Oct 1877, m. (1) 9 Jan 1814 Limington ME Mary Parker of Baldwin ME, b. ? d. 6 Mar 1849; m.(2) 13 Dec 1849 Jerusha Dyer of Limington ME, b. Feb 1797 d. 29 Jan 1884. Farmer. In War of 1812. B/S/land 1822-1857. Wid. received pension 6 Jan 1879.

Louise Dyer, b. 19 May 1814, m. 26 Dec 1833 Albert Sanborn.
350 Thomas Jefferson[7], b. 1815.
Eliza A., b. 17 Jul 1820, d. 16 Jan 1897, m. 8 Aug 1843 Daniel Thompson Richardson of Baldwin ME.
Mary M., b. 3 Aug 1823, m. 18 Nov 1841 Stephen Brown.

Sources: Baldwin ME census 1820, 1830, 1840, 1850, 1860. VR Baldwin ME. T6, R10a, N1A, V8, S8.

181. **NATHAN$^6$ SAWYER** [see 77], b. 30 Jul 1794 Pownalborough ME, d. 8 Sep 1824 Portland ME, m. 22 Apr 1817 Falmouth ME Harriet Little of Newbury MA, b. 7 Jan 1798 d. 22 Feb 1881, dau. Stephen and Rebecca (Dodge) Little. Bookbinder. In Boston MA. He bur. Portland ME. Wid. remarried.
351 Stephen Little$^7$, 1817-1860.
352 Nathan$^7$, 1819-1889.
353 Reuben S.$^7$, 1822-1863.
Sources: VR Portland ME. L29, V9, Lucy S. Thompson rec.

182. **ASA$^6$ SAWYER** [see 78], b. 20 Mar 1798 Steuben ME, m. 3 Oct 1824 Belfast ME Ann Whittier, b. ?. Saddler. In Bangor ME. B/land in Bangor ME 1827. S/land in Medford MA to brother Nathan 1830.
354 Henry Moses$^7$, b. 1825.
John Augustus, b. 12 Nov 1826, d. 24 Apr 1827.
355 John Hathaway$^7$, b. 1828.
Sources: VR Bangor ME. R10d.

183. **NATHAN$^6$ SAWYER** [see 78], b. 23 Apr 1799 Steuben ME, m. 16 Oct 1825 Lydia Dyer of Portland ME, b. 1804. Blacksmith. In Dedham MA, Medford MA. B/land in Medford MA from brother Asa 1830.
Albert Franklin, b. 9 Sep 1827 Medford MA. Physician.
Angelia C., b. 4 Nov 1831, m. 24 Jun 1856 Charles Brainard of Melrose MA.
Mary J., b. 1832, m. 23 Nov 1852 Medford MA George A. Tucker.
Sources: Medford MA census 1830, 1850. VR Steuben ME, Medford MA, SA/MA. R10a, D1.

184. **ANDREW SIMONTON$^6$ SAWYER** [see 78], b. 12 Aug 1802 Cape Elizabeth ME, d. 25 Sep 1871 Portland ME, m. 30 Dec 1825 Falmouth ME Mary Ann Buckman, b. 1806. Shoemaker. B/S/land 1846-1854 Portland ME, Windham ME 1865, Westbrook ME 1870.
Samuel Waite, b. 6 Feb 1827, d. 28 Sep 1837.
Adelaide Christian, b. 28 Jun 1829, d. 7 Mar 1849.
356 Charles Howard$^7$, 1837-1902.
John Erving, b. 14 May 1840, d. 8 Dec 1841.
Ella M., b. 1847, m. 30 Oct 1880 Bartlett S. Emery.
Sources: Lynn MA census 1850. Portland ME 1860. VR Portland ME, SA/ME. P69, M5, R10a.

185. **EBENEZER$^6$ SAWYER** [see 78], b. 31 Jan 1811 Cape Elizabeth ME, d. 27 Feb 1884 So. Portland ME, m. 1 Mar 1842 Gardiner ME Catherine F. Libby of Gardiner ME, b. 9 Feb 1820 d. 20 Jul 1903, dau. Cyprus and Sarah Libby. Farmer. He bur. in Bayview Cem., So. Portland ME.
357 Nathan I.$^7$, b. 1843.
George Gilbert, b. 17 Oct 1844 Cape Elizabeth ME, d. 31 Jul 1915 Cape Elizabeth ME, m. 15 Oct 1868 Portland ME Almeda A. Dyer, b. 26 Jan 1846 d. 1918, dau. Greeley H. and Mary W. (Quimby) Dyer. U. S. Customs employee. CH: Beatrice E., b. 27 Jan 1874, d. 27 Sep 1956.
Anne M., b. 13 May 1846, d. 19 Jan 1922.
Ebenezer W., b. 20 Dec 1847 Cape Elizabeth ME, d. 3 Aug 1881.
Cyprus L., b. 16 Jul 1850, d. 19 Dec 1857.
Frank P., b. 30 Apr 1853 Cape Elizabeth ME. Went to Wisconsin.
Addie Mary, b. 17 Jan 1856, d. 17 Jan 1877.
Sources: Cape Elizabeth ME census 1840, 1850, 1860, 1870. VR Cape Elizabeth ME, Gardiner ME, Portland ME, SA/ME. Obit (Lewiston Journal), Dr. B. H. Sawyer rec.

186. **SIMON CUTTER⁶ SAWYER** [see 78], b. 15 Jan 1816 Cape Elizabeth ME, d. 14 Nov 1887 Cape Elizabeth ME, m. 15 Mar 1842 Emily Fickett, b. 15 Sep 1823 d. 20 May 1888. Farmer. He bur. Bayview Cem., So. Portland ME.

358 Melville F.$^7$, 1840-1907.

Charles, b. 1852 Cape Elizabeth ME.

Sources: Cape Elizabeth ME census 1850, 1870, 1880. ME 1880 census index. VR Cape Elizabeth ME, SA/ME. C89, M5, M7A, Dr. B. H. Sawyer rec.

187. **EMERSON M.$^6$ SAWYER** [see 79], b. 26 Apr 1813 Bangor ME, d. 1898, m. 8 Nov 1842 Bangor ME Sarah Patterson, b. ?. Farmer. In Hampden ME.

Frances E., b. 1845.
James C., b. 1846 Hampden ME.
Rufus D., b. 1848 Hampden ME.
Edward B., b. 1850 Hampden ME.

Sources: VR Bangor ME. D51.

188. **STILLMAN HIGGINS$^6$ SAWYER** [see 79], b. 2 Nov 1819 Bangor ME, d. 14 May 1896 in Wisconsin, m.(1) 24 Oct 1844 Bangor ME Lucy J. Fogg, b. ca. 1825 d. 1855; m. (2) 11 Oct 1855 Mary M. Fogg, b. 1835, Sister of Lucy J. Had a harness shop.

Georgianna, b. ca. 1843.
Edna a., b. ca. 1844.
Charles M., b. ca. 1846.

359 Frederick T.$^7$, b. 1849.

Sources: VR Bangor ME. W42.

189. **RUFUS H.$^6$ SAWYER** [see 79], b. 8 Apr 1822 Bangor ME, d. 25 Nov 1889 Gardiner ME, m. 23 Jan 1851 Bangor ME Hannah A. Colby of Bangor ME, b. 3 Nov 1831 d. 14 Mar 1911, dau. Edward W. and Mary J. (Fogg) Colby. Houseware dealer. In Gardiner ME.

Edward, b. Sep 1851, d. 1 Mar 1853.
James Edward, b. 1852, d. 1 Mar 1853.
Ida J., b. 12 Oct 1854, d. 1866.
Elnora Lizette, b. 20 Jul 1856, d.y.
Clara E., b. Feb 1861.

360 Frederick A.$^7$, b. 1867.

Aga B. (dau.), b. 13 Mar 1869.

Sources: Gardiner ME census 1860. VR Gardiner ME, Bangor ME, SA/ME.

190. **ALVIN$^6$ SAWYER** [see 80], b. 9 Dec 1805 Buxton ME, m.(I) 20 Sep 1829 Eliza Moulton, b. 1810. Lumberman. In Hollis ME, Buxton ME. B/part of lumber mill.

Hannah A., b. 15 Aug 1830.
Aramartha D., b. 11 Jun 1832.
Matilda, b. 1833.
Mary E., b. 28 Feb 1835, d. 8 Oct 1836.
Alvin B., b. 31 May 1837, d.y.
Mary E., b. 17 Oct 1839, d. 13 Jun 1841.
Mary M., b. 1843, d.y.
Daniel D., b. 1845, drowned in Saco River.
Julia, b. 1847.
Evelyn, b. 1850, m. 3 Apr 1875 William Lord.

Alvin, b. 1854 Hollis ME.
Jessie M., b. 1857.
Charles, b. 1859 Hollis ME.
Note: One dau. m._____ Moore.
Sources: Hollis ME census 1830, 1850, 1860. Buxton ME census 1840. VR Hollis ME. R10g.

191. **ENOCH McDONALD[6] SAWYER** [see 80], b. 28 Mar 1810 Buxton ME, d. 20 Oct 1884 Steep Falls ME, m. Hannah Norton of Buxton ME, b. 1813 d. 7 Jul 1870, dau. Phineas Norton. In Standish ME.
Phineas S., b. 18 Feb 1839 Standish ME, d. 19 Dec 1901.
Caroline C., b. 3 Sep 1841, d. 30 Jul 1897.
Hannah, b. 1843.
Charles F., b. Oct 1846, d. 14 Apr 1849.
Sources: Standish ME census 1840, 1850, 1860. VR Buxton ME. L30.

192. **EBENEZER[6] SAWYER** [see 81], b. 12 Feb 1798 Buxton ME, m.(1) 15 Mar 1821 Scarborough ME Mary Deering of Buxton ME, b. 25 Jun 1798 d. 2 Jul 1853, dau. Isaac and Sarah (Sawyer) Deering; m.(2) 11 Jan 1854 Buxton ME Hannah Leavitt, b. 17 Sep 1797 d. 1877, dau. William and Mary (Cobb) Leavitt. Farmer. In Buxton ME.
361 Thomas Pennell[7], 1822-1897.
Isaac Deering, b. 15 Sep 1823, d. 5 Sep 1825.
Sally D., b. 15 Oct 1825, d. 20 Apr 1913 in Gorham ME.
362 Isaac Deering[7], 1827-1864.
Mercy, b. 9 Jul 1829, d. 14 Aug 1864, m. _____ Blake.
Mary Frances, b. ?, d. 6 Oct 1836.
Samuel, b. 27 Aug 1834, d. Sep 1835.
Samuel, b. 1 Oct 1836, d. 6 Oct 1836.
Frances Mary, b. 1838, m. 16 Feb 1859 Edward H. Child.
Lydia A., b. 17 Oct 1839, m. 30 Aug 1861 William H. Harmon of Bridgton ME.
363 Freeman Cheney[7], b. 1843.
Sources: Buxton ME census 1830, 1840, 1850. VR Buxton ME, Scarborough ME, SA/ME. P82k, L30, E11, Obit (Sally).

193. **JOHN EMERY[6] SAWYER** [see 82], b. 26 Feb 1807 Buxton ME, d. 1866 Elliotsville ME, m.(1) 4 Jun 1835 Elliotsville ME Diana Drake, b. 18 Feb 1811 d. 1841, dau. John and Martha (Packard) Drake; m.(2) 1847 Elliotsville ME Geraldine (Drake) Thompson, wid. of Samuel, b. 17 Jun 1819 d. 22 Feb 1860, dau. John and Martha (Packard) Drake. Lumberman. In Elliotsville ME.
Josephine M., b. 23 Sep 1847, d. Sep 1914, m. 28 Sep 1864 Richard C. Davis.
Geraldine V., b. 11 Sep 1849, d. 23 Aug 1852.
Marianna, b. 23 Jan 1852, d. 30 Sep 1923, m. 11 May 1872 James S. Leeman.
364 John Emery[7], 1854-1912.
Albra W., b. 13 Jan 1857, d. 8 Jul 1882.
Carrie, b. 21 Feb 1860, d. 14 Aug 1933, m. 6 May 1890 Ward S. Williams.
Laura J., b. 21 Feb 1860, m. 19 Mar 1882 Ole Thompson.
Sources: Elliotsville ME census 1840, 1850, 1860. T11, Delia Libby rec.

194. **PHINEAS HANSON[6] SAWYER** [see 82], b. 7 Feb 1828 Buxton ME, d. 3 May 1910 Jackson MN, m. 22 Mar 1851 Adeline W. Drake of Paris ME, b. 28 Jun 1828 d. 28 Sep 1907, dau. Stephen and Martha (Hicks) Drake. Tailor. Civil War: Served in Captain I. W. Case's Company,

22nd Maine Infantry, 10 Sep 1862-14 Aug 1863. In Elliotsville ME, Monson ME 1865, Minnesota 1871.

George Hanson, b. 14 Jul 1852, d. 1 Jan 1937, m. 26 Oct 1879 Frances Russell, b. ?.
Lucy A., b. 31 Jul 1854, d. 14 May 1941, m. Mar 1890 Jay D. Baughman.
Charles H., b. 22 Feb 1858, d. 1 Mar 1939, m. 2 Jun 1886 Annie Russell, b. ?.
Albert, b. 27 Jul 1860, d. 25 Apr 1947, m. 26 Dec 1898 Elsie L. Trenhaile, b. ?.
Ether, b. 22 Oct 1862, d. 11 Nov 1952, m. 9 Mar 1898 Arthur Baughman.
Fred Drake, b. 22 Dec 1865, d. 3 Dec 1957, m. 8 Dec 1897 Josephine Peterson, b. ?

Sources: Elliotsville ME census 1850.

195. **SAMUEL[6] SAWYER** [see 83], b. 7 Aug 1799 Fryeburg ME, d. 9 Oct 1874 Jackson NH, m. 9 Nov 1819 Cape Elizabeth ME Priscilla Dyer of Cape Elizabeth ME, b. 1790 d. 7 Oct 1865. Farmer. In Fryeburg ME, Bridgton ME. B/S/land in Fryeburg ME 1820-1853, S/land in Bridgton to son Samuel 1851. He bur. W. Bridgton ME.

Joseph Dyer, b. 17 Jun 1820 Fryeburg ME, d. 20 Feb 1906 Bridgton ME, m. Rebecca Warren of Fryeburg ME, b. 28 Nov 1815 d. 8 Apr 1903, dau. Caleb and Rebecca (Harndon) Warren. Farmer. S/land to brother Benjamin F. CH: Clarissa E., b. 10 Mar 1845, m.(1) George H. Taylor, m.(2) J. H. Harndon; Cordelia W., b. 10 Mar 1848, d. 29 Jan 1883, m. 15 Oct 1867 Aaron Cross.

365 Nathan Freeman[7], 1822-1903.
366 Samuel Merrill[7], 1825-1881.
367 Benjamin Franklin[7], 1829-1903.

Sources: Fryeburg ME census 1830, 1840. Bridgton ME census 1850, 1860. VR Bridgton ME, Fryeburg ME, Cape Elizabeth ME. R10a, R10c, N6, W12, Eliza Sawyer Mason rec.

196. **JAMES THORNTON[6] SAWYER** [see 83], b. 17 Oct 1811 Buxton ME, d. 4 Feb 1896 Sweden ME, m. 9 Oct 1842 Mary Jane Adams of Moultonboro NH, b. 9 May 1822, dau. Stephen and Betsey (Warren) Adams. In Sweden ME. S/land in Sweden ME 1852.

James S., b. 16 Aug 1843 Sweden ME, d. 8 Aug 1864 in Civil War.
Son, b. 5 Nov 1844, d. 7 Nov 1844.
Julia M., b. 12 Nov 1845, d. 17 Feb 1911, m. 14 Feb 1865 Samuel Libby.
Asa Lyman, b. 28 Dec 1846 Sweden ME, d. 3 Aug 1915 Sweden ME, m. 29 Aug 1894 No. Conway NH Florence Emerson of Harrison ME, b. 1870, dau. Samuel A. and Etta (Whitehouse) Emerson. No CH.
Cynthia Ann, b. 28 Jan 1849, d. 21 Oct 1864.
Theodate Helen, b. 11 May 1851, m. William H. Morrison.
368 Stephen Eugene[7], 1853-1921.
Thomas Almon, b. 29 Jun 1855 Sweden ME.
Henry Walter, b. 15 Dec 1858, d. 21 Sep 1859.

Sources: Sweden ME census 1850, 1860. VR SA/ME. R10c, L20, C89, Asa's will, Robert L. Taylor rec.

197. **WILLIAM[6] SAWYER** [see 84], b. 1 Apr 1809 Buxton ME, d. 29 Jan 1892 Buxton ME, m.(1) 31 Oct 1830 Susan P. Dyer of Hollis ME, b. 1808 d. 11 Feb 1833; m.(2) (I) 3 Oct 1835 Mary Earl of Hollis ME, b. Sep 1813 d. 15 Jun 1893, dau. Joshua and Mary Earl. Grocer. In Standish ME, Buxton ME. He bur. Tory Hill Cem., Buxton ME.

Blanche, b. 1831, d. 24 Feb 1833.
Charles Henry, b. 9 Jun 1837 Buxton ME, d. 27 Mar 1880, m. 7 Aug 1859 Buxton ME Martha Ellen Brown, b. 1836. Inventor.
369 Albert G.[7], 1842-1905.

Eliza A., b. 1846.

Sources: Buxton ME census 1840, 1850, 1860. VR Buxton ME, SA/ME. M5, P82k, R10g, Mercy S. Knight rec.

198. **JABEZ$^6$ SAWYER** [see 85], b. 9 Sep 1814 Buxton ME, m.(1) Roxanna Briggs, b. 1810 d. 17 Apr 1857; m.(2) Harriet _____, b. ?. B/S/land in Mexico ME 1854. In Sumner ME, Hartford ME, Mexico ME. Wid. bur. Hartford ME.

Solomon Briggs, b. 1836 Sumner ME.
Elizabeth, b. 1838, d. 10 Dec 1856.
Lydia E., b. 1841, d. 28 May 1858.
Philip L., b. 1846 Sumner ME.
Edward E., b. 22 Apr 1848, d. 4 Jul 1895, m. ?.
Lucy, b. 1850.
370 Frank Davis $^7$, b. 1852.
Lavins, b. 1857.
Harriet, b. 1860.

Sources: Sumner ME census 1850. Mexico ME census 1860. VR SA/ME. M5, R10c, D51.

199. **NATHANIEL KNIGHT$^6$ SAWYER** [see 85], b. 14 May 1816 Buxton ME, d. 30 Mar 1888 Jacksonville FL, m. Sophia H. Watson, b. 2 Sep 1818, dau. Samuel and Apphia (Herrick) Watson. Editor. Purchased newspaper and edited until 1872. In Sedgwick ME, California, Ellsworth ME, Florida.

Henry Kittridge, b. 10 Aug 1844, d. 22 Mar 1846.
Augustus Eben, b. ca. 1848 Sedgwick ME, m. Sarah A. Stearns of Calais ME, b. 1848, dau Mary A. Stearns. In Ellsworth ME. Wid. in Calais ME 1880. CH: Alice W., b. 1875; Mary Stearns, b. 17 Aug 1879.
Henry W., b. ca. 1851.
George Bancroft, b. Sep 1858, d. 22 Sep 1858 Ellsworth ME.
Charles Frederick, b. Jun 1861, d. 20 Jun 1861 Ellsworth ME.

Sources: Ellsworth ME census 1860. VR Ellsworth ME. D15, P82k, Elizabeth Wescott rec.

200. **EBENEZER$^6$ SAWYER** [see 85], b. 19 Jul 1820 Buxton ME, d. 5 Jan 1848 Sedgwick ME, m. Sophie _____, b. 1818.

Eben A., b. 1848.

Sources: Sedgwick ME census 1850 (wid.). VR Sedgwick ME.

201. **LAFAYETTE W.$^6$ SAWYER** [see 85], b. ca. 1825 Buxton ME, m.(1) (I) 10 Nov 1849 No. Yarmouth ME Sarah A. Maxfield of No. Yarmouth ME, b. ?; m.(2) 29 Jan 1854 Abigail (Gooch) Parsons, b. 7 May 1826, dau. _____Gooch. Cordwainer. S/land in No. Yarmouth ME 1856, B/land in Gray ME 1869.

Reuben Kinsman, b. 19 Sep 1850 No. Yarmouth ME, m. 9 May 1878 E. Ellen Flagg of Needham MA, b. ?, dau. William and Martha B. Flagg. In Boston MA. Lucy A., b. 1855.

Sources: Sumner ME census 1850. VR North Yarmouth ME, SA/MA. C78, R10a.

202. **JOHN$^6$ SAWYER** [see 86], b. 11 Jul 1800 Standish ME, d. 18 Oct 1870 Casco ME. m. 19 Jun 1825 Rebecca Longley of Waterford ME, b. 28 Aug 1802 d. 24 Feb 1879, dau. Eli and Mary (Whitcomb) Longley. Innkeeper. In So. Windham ME, Raymond ME (with his father-in-law), Casco ME. B/S/land in Windham ME 1825-1831. B/land in Raymond ME 1831-1840.

371 Franklin$^7$, 1826-1888.

372 Hamilton John$^7$, 1828-1898.
Mary Grace, b. 7 Jun 1831, m. 30 Jun 1856 George Walker of Casco ME.
373 Charles Carroll$^7$, 1833-1904.
Caroline Peabody, b. 20 Oct 1835, d. 25 Apr 1872, m. Nov 1858 Alvan Jordan of Raymond ME.
Whitman, b. 10 Jun 1838 Raymond ME, d. 20 Jan 1904 Portland ME, m. 4 Dec 1865 Maria L. (Fulton) Dingley of Limington ME, wid. of Sumner, b. 8 Nov 1838 d. 8 Nov 1936, dau. Elijah and Lucy (Abbott) Fulton. Civil War: 10 Sep 1862-20 Aug 1865. He bur. Evergreen Cem., Portland ME. CH: Nellie Maria, adopted, b. ?, m. C. H. Gifford.
Sarah Brooks, b. 1 May 1840, d. Aug 1916, m. 25 Apr 1862 Jesse F. Holden.
Jane Lamson, b. 17 Jun 1842, m.(1) John Tukey, m.(2) William H. Bickford.
Sources: Raymond ME census 1830, 1840, 1850, 1860. VR Raymond ME. P85, D6, L30, R10a.

203. **LEMUEL$^6$ SAWYER** [see 86], b. 18 Jul 1807 Standish ME, d. 12 Aug 1888 Standish ME, m. Oct 1832 Esther Purinton of Standish ME, b. 30 Jan 1807 d. 11 Dec 1880, dau. Meshack and Sarah (Gerish) Purinton. Farmer. B/land in Standish 1830-1836.
Sarah A., b. 8 Jul 1833, d. 21 Dec 1859, m. George E. Mead of Bridgton ME.
374 Dennis Jenkins$^7$, 1835-1912.
Maria H., b. 11 Sep 1836, m. 9 Nov 1851 John Barts Winslow.
375 Ellery Foxcroft$^7$, 1838-1876.
376 John Purington$^7$, 1839-1917.
Emily F., b. 21 Apr 1842, d. 13 Mar 1888, m. 1870 Charles A. Nichols.
377 Alfred Stanford$^7$, b. 1844.
Harriet L., b. 1 Jul 1847, d. 27 Dec 1850.
Marietta, b. 27 Jun 1850, m. Samuel C. Richards.
Eugene M., b. Oct 1859 Standish ME.
Sources: Standish ME census 1840, 1850, 1860. VR Standish ME, SA/ME. L30, R10a.

204. **THOMAS$^6$ SAWYER** [see 86], b. 23 May 1810 Standish ME, d. 8 May 1858 Bonny Eagle ME, m.(1) (I) 14 Aug 1831 Standish ME Esther Green of Buxton ME, b. 1808 d. 29 Jan 1834, bur. in Came Family Cem., Buxton ME; m.(2) 1 Mar 1835 Mary Hutcherson of Standish ME, b. 30 Mar 1814 Standish ME d. 30 Oct 1891, bur. in Maplewood Cem., Standish ME, dau. Matthias and Nancy (White) Hutcherson. Shoemaker. B/land in Standish ME 1844. He bur. in Emery Cem., Bonnie Eagle ME.
Octavia, b. 1832.
Esther, b. Jan 1834, d. 29 May 1837.
378 Thomas C.$^7$, 1838-1914.
379 William Pitt$^7$, 1840-1916.
Esther M., b. 1844, d. 1923, m. 4 Jul 1862 Gideon Smith of Hollis ME.
380 Matthias H.$^7$, 1847-1927.
Louisa Mary, b. 1851, d. 1927, m. 29 Apr 1866 Charles Rumney of Hollis ME.
Charles W., b. 1857 Standish ME, m. Emma C. Sawyer of Hollis ME, b. 1859, dau. John Lorenzo and Mary A. (Boulter) Sawyer. Went West. CH: Elsie V., b. 1879. See [239].
Sources: Standish ME census 1840, 1850, 1860 Wid. ME 1880 census index. VR SA/ME. F37, R10a, F11, M5, Mary E. Jackson rec.

205. **JOHN$^6$ SAWYER** [see 87], b. 26 Nov 1816 Baldwin ME, d. 18 Nov 1903 Hollis ME, m.(1) 12 Nov 1837 Hannah Edgecomb of Hollis ME, b. 11 Feb 1820 d. 21 Dec 1839, dau. Robert and Elizabeth (Seamon) Edgecomb; m.(2) 12 Nov 1841 Lydia Ridlon of Standish ME, b. 24 Jun 1818 d. 20 Aug 1878, dau. Robert and Sally (Cozens) Ridlon; m.(3) 10 Jan 1882 Elzina (Boothby)

Libby of Hollis ME, wid. of Joshua, b. 23 Feb 1819 d. 3 Jan 1905 Standish ME, dau. Thomas and Sally (Dyer) Boothby. In Saco ME, Rochester NH.

Betsey, b. 1838, m. 29 Oct 1854 William Dunnell of Buxton ME.
Sally M., b. 2 Nov 1842, d. 27 Apr 1924, m. Edward Whitehouse.
Hannah, b. 1843, d. 27 Oct 1861, unm.
Lydia Ellen, b. 9 May 1846, m. 30 Sep 1860 Gideon Ridlon, Sr.
Harriet C., b. 9 May 1846, d. 5 Jun 1920, m. Thomas C. Sawyer of Standish ME.
381 Robert G.$^7$, b. 1848.
Mary A., b. 1850, unm.
Julia, b. 1852, unm.
Cornelia, b. 1854, m. 29 Mar 1875 John F. Roberts.
Nicholas E., b. 1856 Hollis ME, d. 1927, m.(1) 29 Nov 1876 Alma J. Sawyer, b. 17 Oct 1856 d. 21 Jan 1918, dau. John Lorenzo and Mary Ann (Boulter) Sawyer; m.(2) Emma M. Breil, b. 1878. He bur. in Standish ME. See [239].
John L., b. 5 Jun 1858 Hollis ME, d. 28 Feb 1936 Rochester NH, m. Martha Rose Ricker, b. ?. In W. Buxton ME, Rochester NH.
Frances, b. 1860, d. 27 Oct 1861.
382 Frank$^7$, 1861-1936.

Sources: Hollis ME census 1850, 1860. Tamworth NH census 1870. VR SA/MA. R17, R16, M5.

206. **ISAAC SCAMMON$^6$ SAWYER** [see 87], b. 25 May 1822 Buxton ME, d. 11 Jan 1890 Buxton ME, m.(1) (I) 8 Aug 1841 Catherine Crockett of Buxton ME, b. 1824 d. 8 Dec 1864, dau. Daniel and Olive (Smith) Crockett; m.(2) 18 Nov 1865 Effingham NH Mary J. (Brown) Moulton of Parsonsfield ME, b. 1836 d. 9 Nov 1887. Farmer. He bur. in Hillcrest Cem., Hollis ME. Obit says he d. 11 Jan 1889, probate rec. say 7 Jan 1890 and 11 Jan 1890.

Freeman H. C., b. 25 May 1843 Buxton ME, d. 13 Dec 1862 in Civil War.
Isaac M., b. 2 Nov 1846, d. 7 May 1848.
383 Elbridge L.$^7$, 1846-1878.
Milton, b. ca. 1847.
Harriet C., b. 20 Oct 1849, d. 2 Aug 1851.
384 George Almon$^7$, b. 1851.
385 Marshall Pierce$^7$, 1853-1895.
Hattie A., b. 27 Nov 1855.
Isaac M., b. 21 Jan 1858 Buxton ME, m. 1 Sep 1881 Buxton ME Carrie A. Keene of Winslow ME, b. ?.
Nellie, b. Feb 1860, d. 5 Aug 1863.
Franklin H., b. 1861, d. 22 Nov 1862 in Hollis ME.
Alice Webster, b. 31 Jul 1868, m. 3 Feb 1892 Arlington MA William Prince.
Charles Freeman, b. 3 May 1870 Buxton ME.
Florence C., b. 26 Feb 1873, m. 27 Dec 1892 Arlington MA James McCarthy.
Georgia W., b. ca. 1876.

Sources: Buxton ME census 1840, 1850. Hollis ME census 1860. West Buxton ME census 1880. ME 1880 census index. VR Saco ME, Buxton ME, Winslow ME, SA/MA. P92a, M5, Obit (Isaac Scammon), Robert L. Taylor rec.

207. **JOSEPH H.$^6$ SAWYER** [see 87], b. 22 Jun 1828 Buxton ME, d. 6 Feb 1886 Portland ME, m.(I) 3 Feb 1849 Mary E. Tarbox of Hollis ME, b. 1829 d. 4 Oct 1899, dau. Gilbert Tarbox. Carpenter. In Hollis ME, So. Portland ME. B/land in Portland 1866.

386 Ansel G.$^7$, 1856-1913.
Anna Celia, b. ca. 1858, d. 12 Apr 1863.

J. Fred, b. 1861, d. 4 Apr 1863.
Josie M., b. 4 May 1863, d. 26 Jun 1896.
Sources: Hollis ME 1850, 1860. VR Buxton ME, Hollis ME, SA/ME. R17, R10a, P82k.

208. **LEMUEL[6] SAWYER** [see 88], b. 19 Sep 1813 Buxton ME, d. 11 Sep 1901 Buxton ME, m. 3 Feb 1842 Mary A. (Berry) Elwell, b. 1820 d. 3 Sep 1885, dau. Jabez and Anna Berry. In Buxton ME. He bur. Tory Hill Cem., Buxton ME.
Emily, b. 27 Jun 1844, m. 24 Jun 1865 Leonard Darling of Boston MA.
387 George Edwin[7], 1850-1936.
Luella, b. 8 Jul 1854, m. 4 Jul 1889 Edwin A. Harmon.
Daughter, b. 15 Feb 1856, d. 17 Feb 1856.
Sources: VR Buxton ME. R17, M5.

209. **HENRY M.[6] SAWYER** [see 89], b. 19 Apr 1810 Standish ME, m. 24 Jun 1838 Minot ME Priscilla Jackson, b. 1809. Stonemason. In Minot ME, Poland ME.
Albert E., b. Feb 1842 Standish ME, d. 27 May 1906 Mechanics Falls ME, m. Mary E. Verrill of Mechanics Falls ME, b. 1846 d. 13 Oct 1912, dau. Eben and Abigail (French) Verrill.
Sources: Poland ME census 1850, 1860. VR Minot ME, SA/ME. R28, Nettie Dimock rec.

210. **JOHN ISAIAH[6] SAWYER** [see 89], b. 3 May 1822 Standish ME, d. 20 Feb 1915 Hebron ME, m. 15 Apr 1847 Cynthis C. Parker of Standish ME, b. 27 Jan 1828 d. 1 Apr 1900, dau. Aaron and Abigail (Walker) Parker. Farmer. Civil War: Company D, 9th Maine Regiment. In Minot ME. He bur. Minot ME.
388 George Wesley[7], 1848-1927.
389 Curtis B. Merrill[7], 1849-1925.
Susanna, b. 5 May 1851, d. 1 Jul 1900.
Sources: Minot ME 1860, 1880. ME 1880 census index. VR SA/ME. M7A, M5, R28, Nettie Dimock rec.

211. **JOSEPH PARKER[6] SAWYER** [see 91], b. 1813 Cape Elizabeth ME, m.(1) 17 Nov 1836 Mary A. Armstrong of Cape Elizabeth ME, b. 1813 d. 10 Mar 1854; m.(2) 29 Oct 1854 Portland ME Louisa B. Ross of Bath, b. ?; m.(3) 14 Jul 1864 Medford MA Pemelia G. Waite of Newton MA, b. 1836, dau. Warren and Abigail (Fernald) Waite. Cooper. In Chelsea MA.
Matthew A., b. 1846 Chelsea MA.
Anna Louisa, b. 4 Dec 1850, d. 1 Dec 1852 Chelsea MA.
William M., b. 26 Jul 1855, d. 17 Sep 1855 Chelsea MA.
Edwin Clifford, b. 4 Dec 1857 Chelsea MA
Sources: Chelsea MA census 1850. VR SA/MA.

212. **BENJAMIN FRANKLIN[6] SAWYER** [see 92], b. 28 Dec 1801 Boston MA, m.(1) Margaret _____, b. ?; m.(2) 6 May 1854 Boston MA Elizabeth P. Blood of Bucksport ME, b. 1811. Messenger.
390 Franklin[7], ca. 1828.
Sources: VR SA/MA.

213. **NATHANIEL[6] SAWYER** [see 92], b. ca. 1804 Boston MA, m. 13 Jun 1830 Eliza A. Morrison. Innkeeper.

Nathaniel, b. ca. 1833, m.(1) ?; m.(2) ?; m.(3) 11 Nov 1893 Canton MA Sarah Ann (Whiting) Jackman of Canton MA, b. 1832, dau. Nathaniel and Betsey (Ripley) Whiting.

Sources: Boston MA census 1840. Brookline ME census 1850. VR Boston MA, Newton MA, SA/MA.

214. **GORHAM[6] SAWYER** [see 92], b. 25 May 1811 Boston MA, d. 10 Jan 1865 Philadelphia PA, m. 11 Apr 1829 Boston MA Susan Parkerson of Norwich, England, b. 1815 d. 26 Feb 1834 Boston MA, dau. John Parkerson.

391 Edward Gorham[7], 1829-1915.

Sources: VR SA/MA.

215. **ABEL[6] SAWYER** [see 93], b. 10 Aug 1806 Cape Elizabeth ME, d. 23 Dec 1872 Portland ME, m.(1) (I) 11 Dec 1830 Rebecca J. Miller, b. 1806 d. 8 Oct 1834; m. (2) Sarah A. Given, b. 1812 d. 23 May 1889. Mariner. S/land in Portland ME 1860. Rebecca bur. in Mt. Pleasant Cem., So. Portland ME. He bur. in Evergreen Cem., Portland ME.

John Given, b. 19 Nov 1837, d. Jun 1857 at sea on ship *William M. Rogers.*

Sarah W., b. 5 Jun 1840, d. 1892.

Harriet G., b. 14 Jun 1842.

Clement S., b. May 1844, d. 22 Aug 1845.

392 Abel Hargrave[7], 1846-1912.

Robert G., b. 1848 Portland ME.

Child, b. 1 May 1850, d. 9 May 1850.

Sophia C., b. 1854.

Sources: Portland ME census 1840, 1850. VR Portland ME. R10a, M5, S15.

216. **DAVID A.[6] SAWYER** [see 93], b. 11 Jan 1816 Cape Elizabeth ME, d. 1900 Greenwood ME, m.(I) 27 Mar 1838 Mary Ann Healey, b. 1820. Joiner. B/S/land in Greenwood ME 1861-1873.

Caroline A., b. 23 Mar 1840.

John W., b. 30 Jun 1844 Cape Elizabeth ME.

Winfield L., b. Jun 1847, d. 10 Mar 1851.

Eliza H., b. 1849, m. 28 Sep 1875 Quincy MA Erastus L. Metcalf.

Mary W., b. 1854.

Stephen, b. 1855 Cape Elizabeth ME.

Horace P., b. 1856 Cape Elizabeth ME, d. 20 Oct 1925, m. 29 Jul 1880 Franklin MA Hattie A. Frost of Franklin MA, b. ?, dau. William O. and Caroline Frost. Painter. In Norway ME, Franklin MA, Medfield MA.

Sources: Thomaston ME census 1840. Cape Elizabeth ME census 1850. Greemwood ME census 1870. VR SA/ME, SA/MA. R10c, T21.

217. **FREDERICK W.[6] SAWYER** [see 93], b. 5 Feb 1818 Cape Elizabeth ME, d. 21 Dec 1858, m. 13 Oct 1843 Sarah Elmira Thomas of Thomaston ME, b. 24 Oct 1824 d. 22 Dec 1865, dau. Edward and Melinda (Tilson) Thomas. B/S/land in Cape Elizabeth ME 1848-1860. He bur. in Mt. Pleasant Cem., So. Portland ME.

Edward T., b. 9 Jul 1845 Cape Elizabeth ME, m. Bessie Gray, b. ?.

Cora L., b. Dec 1846, d. 1861.

Clarence F., b. Dec 1846 Cape Elizabeth ME.

Emma Tilson, b. 28 Jun 1851, d. 8 Mar 1936, m. 24 Dec 1874 Lewis Hanniford.

Sophia C., b. 28 Jun 1853, m. 1877 Fred Dupree.

Sources: Cape Elizabeth ME census 1850, 1860 (wid.). R10a, Elizabeth Mullins rec.

218. **ALVIN GEORGE[6] SAWYER** [see 93], b. 1 Apr 1823 Cape Elizabeth ME, d. 7 Jul 1889 Winchester MA, m. 19 Sep 1848 Elizabeth W. Varney of Windham ME, b. 15 Jul 1823 d. 3 Sep 1882, dau. Ezekiel Varney. Mariner, cooper. California Gold Rush 1849-1851. B/land in Cape Elizabeth ME 1848, 1859. In Chelsea MA, Charlestown MA.

George W., b. 1850, d. 26 Nov 1850.
Eca A., b. 11 Apr 1852. Went to California.
393 Henry Holmes, b. 1854.
Harriette V., b. 29 Jun 1863, m. 5 Feb 1889 Boston MA George R. Goulding.

Sources: Portland ME census 1850. VR SA/MA. R10a, M5.

219. **BENJAMIN FRANKLIN[6] SAWYER** [see 94], b. ca. 1813 Portland ME, m.(1) (I) 7 Dec 1833 Portland ME Abba H. Harris, b. 1813; m.(2) 18 Mar 1857 Mansfield MA Elizabeth H. Osgood of Hiram ME, b. 1823, dau. James Osgood. Attorney. B/S/land 18341854. In New York City, Portland ME, Boston MA, Mansfield MA.

Benjamin Franklin, b. ca. 1836 Portland ME.
Henry, b. ca. 1839 Portland ME.
Mary, b. ca. 1841.
Cornelia, b. ca. 1845.
Eva, b. ca. 1847.
James William J., b. 6 Mar 1854 Mansfield MA.

Sources: Portland ME census 1840. Boston MA census 1850. VR Portland ME, SA/MA. R10a.

220. **SAMUEL HOMER[6] SAWYER** [see 96], b. 12 Jun 1811 Cape Elizabeth ME, d. 2 Jan 1886 Charlestown MA, m. 28 Sep 1835 Portland ME Eleanor (Ellen) Forsyth of Portland ME, b. Apr 1818 d. 30 Jul 1899 Cumberland ME, dau. Thomas and Sarah (Pray) Forsyth. Trader. B/S/land in Bangor ME 1834, Portland ME 1856-1869. In Gray ME, Bangor ME, Portland ME.

George H., b. 29 Apr 1836, d. 24 Aug 1858 New Orleans of yellow fever.

Sources: Gray ME census 1840. Portland ME census 1850, 1860. VR Bangor ME, SA/ME. R10a, R10d.

221. **THORNDIKE HOMER[6] SAWYER** [see 96], b. 8 Mar 1815 Portland ME, d. 28 Aug 1893 Portland ME, m. 24 May 1838 Wealthy B. Peterson of Portland ME, b. 1819. Salesman, clerk. Added Homer to name 1845. Civil War: Company H, 1st Massachusetts Infantry, Chelsea MA; received pension. In Gray ME, Portland ME, Cambridge MA.

Wealthy M., b. 1839.
William H., b. 1841 Portland ME. In Cambridge MA 1850.
Maria W., b. 1842, m. 26 Nov 1862 Boston MA Asa Williams.
Ada H., b. 1849, m. 23 Mar 1869 Boston MA Albert Lindsay Burgess.

Sources: Gray ME census 1840. Cambridge MA census 1850. VR SA/ME, SA/MA. P69, M7A.

222. **HORACE AUSTIN[6] SAWYER** [see 96], b. 26 May 1817 Portland ME, d. 10 Dec 1889 Lynn MA, m. 16 Jun 1844 Sarah Hale of Waterford ME, b. 1823 d. 20 Oct 1887. Cooper. In Waterford ME, Chelsea MA.

394 Horace Austin[7], b. 1845.
Frances J., b. 24 Sep 1846, m. 3 Jun 1869 Boston MA Charles E. Stone.
395 Walter Scott[7], b. 1849.
396 George Frederick[7], 1852-1915.

Sources: Chelsea MA census 1850. VR Chelsea MA, SA/MA. D6, S15, B33, Ernest A. Sawyer rec.

223. **ANDREW SCOTT[6] SAWYER** [see 96], b. 22 Aug 1820 New Gloucester ME, d. 11 Feb 1909 So. Portland ME, m.(1) Kate Given, b. 14 Mar 1824; m.(2) 3 Jan 1850 Caroline E. Stanwood, b. ?, dau. Philip and Rebecca (Given) Stanwood; m.(3) Catherine E. Stanwood, b. 14 Mar 1824 d. 22 Oct 1905, dau. Philip and Caroline (Trumbull) Stanwood. Gardener. B/land from brother Thomas T. in 1867. Sawyer Street in Cape Elizabeth named for Andrew. Appointed guardian of brother Ellis Merrill's CH.

Martha A., b. 1848.
Edward, b. 1850 Cape Elizabeth ME.

Sources: Cape Elizabeth ME census 1850. VR Cape Elizabeth ME, SA/ME. R10a, B57.

224. **ELLIS MERRILL[6] SAWYER** [see 96], b. 24 Feb 1826 Cape Elizabeth ME, d. 27 Nov 1863 in Civil War, m. 20 Aug 1847 Phebe C. Ingersoll, b. 1826. Civil War: Held rank of Major. Brother Andrew appointed guardian of his CH. Wid. in Cape Elizabeth ME 1870.

Martha A., b. 27 May 1848, d. 7 May 1860.
Edward E., b. 30 Dec 1849, d. 9 Jun 1865.
Isaac J., b. 1 Mar 1852, m.(I) 29 Apr 1878 Viola P. Shorey.
Elizabeth L., b. 16 Apr 1854, d. 1930, m. John Milliken.
397 Frank Augustus[7], b. 1856.
Josephine, b. 7 Jan 1860, d. 31 May 1860.
Albert Clinton, b. 6 Oct 1861 Cape Elizabeth ME.

Sources: Cape Elizabeth ME census 1850, 1870 (wid.). VR Cape Elizabeth ME. R10a, Ernest A. Sawyer rec.

225. **WILLIAM CHADWICK[6] SAWYER** [see 96], b. 8 Apr 1828 Cape Elizabeth ME, d. 15 Feb 1914 Portland ME, m. 15 Dec 1859 Portland ME Mary E. Blunt, b. Oct 1830 d. 22 Aug 1905, dau. William and Lelia (Hadock) Blunt. Lawyer. In Portland ME. He bur. Evergreen Cem., Portland ME.

William Theodore, b. 20 Sep 1859 Portland ME, d. 9 Oct 1936 Portland ME, m.(1) (I) 12 Jun 1884 Nellie E. Rumball of Harrington ME, b. 1864 d. 9 Mar 1910; m.(2) Annie L. Truman, b. ?. B/S/land in Woodstock ME. All bur. in Evergreen Cem., Portland ME.
Mary L., b. 1861, d. 28 Feb 1865.
Ellis Merrill, b. 2 Feb 1864, d. 11 Aug 1899.
Henry Thomas Woodford, b. 2 Nov 1868 Portland ME, d. 13 Jan 1947, m.(1) Laura _____, b. ?; m.(2) Alice M. _____, b. ?.

Sources: Portland ME census 1850. VR SA/ME. R10c.

226. **EPHRAIM[6] SAWYER** [see 97], b. (1794-1800) Cape Elizabeth ME, m. 26 Jun 1822 Almira Stanford, b. ?. B/S/land in Cape Elizabeth ME 1833-1861.

Son, b. (1825-1830).
398 Daniel M.[7], 1827-1905.
Mary S., b. 24 Mar 1830.
Ruth N., b. 3 Jul 1832.

Sources: Cape Elizabeth ME census 1830, 1840. VR South Portland ME. R10a.

227. **WILLIAM WOODBURY[6] SAWYER** [see 98], b. 31 Aug 1839 Limington ME, m.(1) Sarah Fitz, b. 19 Nov 1838, dau. Josiah and Sarah (Morgan) Fitz; m.(2) 12 Jun 1869 Hyde Park MA Elizabeth Batten of England, b. 1849, dau. Joseph and Esther Batten. Carpenter. In Lawrence MA, Boston MA.

William Woodbury, b. 27 Jul 1870 Boston MA.

Sources: Boston MA census 1870. VR SA/MA. F19, Robert L. Taylor rec.

228. **EBENEZER JONES[6] SAWYER** [see 99], b. 20 Mar 1818 Jonesboro ME, d. 20 Jul 1890 Machiasport ME, m. 27 Jan 1841 Machias ME Lucinda C. Sprague, b. 14 Aug 1822 d. 17 Jul 1880, dau. Stephen and Mary E. (Crocker) Sprague. Sea captain.

John Fairfield, b. 24 Dec 1841 Machiasport ME, d. 15 Apr 1911, m. 21 Sep 1863 Machiasport ME Susan A. Hooper, b. 20 Jan 1845 d. 6 May 1916, dau. Joseph and Clarissa (Palmer) Hooper.

George E., b. 1844 Machiasport ME.

Frances A., b. 1846, m. 17 Aug 1864 A____ F. Means.

Stephen E., b. 1848 Machiasport ME, d. 1903, m. 18 Jan 1873 Ada Gates, b. 1856 d. 26 Dec 1893.

399 William E.[7], 1850-1881.

Mary E. R., b. 1852, m. 1 Jan 1876 Boston MA James S. McIntyre.

Charles B., b. 1855 Machiasport ME, d. 1920, m. Mary F. Denham, b. ?.

Emma J., b. 25 Aug 1857, d. 14 Sep 1859.

Antoinette, b. 1859, m. 1 Feb 1890 Waltham MA Roscoe Green Ricker.

Warren E., b. 1861 Machiasport ME, m. Annie _____, b. ?.

Carrie G., b. 5 Sep 1863, d. 19 Dec 1865.

Walter B., b. Feb 1865, d. 23 Aug 1889.

Sources: Machiasport ME census 1850. VR SA/ME, SA/MA. D51, M29, Leonard F. Tibbetts rec.

229. **JOSEPH CUTLER[6] SAWYER** [see 99], b. 11 Jun 1821 Jonesboro ME, d. 24 Aug 1898, m. Sarah E Aldrich of Gouldsboro ME, b. 18 Apr 1828 d. 22 Apr 1883, dau. Ezdrich and Sarah Aldrich. In Jonesport ME.

Stephen J., b. 1850 Jonesboro ME.

Joseph E., b. Mar 1851, d. 13 Feb 1883.

Asa E., b. 27 Dec 1852 Jonesboro ME, d 27 Jun 1921 Calais ME, m. 24 May 1899 Calais ME Maggie B. Falls of Calais ME, b. 1877, dau. Andrew and Sarah (Watson) Falls. Sailor.

Nathaniel, b. 1855 Jonesboro ME.

Ezra Wilbur, b. 24 Nov 1857 Jonesboro ME, d. 24 Feb 1939, m. 9 Jun 1883 Etta F. Crowley of Addison ME, b. 1858, CH: Bessie Emma, b. 16 Apr 1889. Coast Guard.

400 John F.[7], 1859-1923.

Mary C., b. 1863, m. 5 Sep 1885 Chelsea MA Albert Murray.

401 Daniel James[7], 1866-1912.

Eliza G., b. 12 Nov 1867, d. 18 Sep 1892, unm.

Sources: Jonesport ME census 1850, 1860. VR SA/MA, SA/NH. Leonard F. Tibbett rec.

230. **DANIEL JAMES[6] SAWYER** [see 100], b. 2 Apr 1824 Jonesboro ME, d. 10 Jun 1909 Calais ME, m. 5 Jun 1858 Emeline P. Glover, b. 14 Apr 1836 d. 2 Jul 1902, dau. Rev. William and Emeline (Packard) Glover. Merchant. In Jonesport ME.

William Franklin, b. 1861, adopted.

Daniel Dodge, b. 9 May 1868, adopted, d. 20 Feb 1943, m. 22 Jan 1889 Delia Dunbar, b. ?. Both bur. Davis/Fairview Cem., Jefferson ME. CH: Emeline, b. 29 Oct 1898.

Sources: VR SA/ME. M5, Leonard F. Tibbetts rec.

231. **EDWARD MANSFIELD[6] SAWYER** [see 100], b. 26 Mar 1841 Jonesboro ME, d. 15 Feb 1924, m. 1865 Frances B. Hall of Addison ME, b. 20 Jan 1845 d. 17 Oct 1916, dau. Simeon and Mary A. (Franklin) Hall. In Harrington ME, Jonesport ME.

Mary A., b. 13 Mar 1866, d. 19 Mar 1916, m. 26 Jan 1889 Oscar W. Look.
Edward Burton, b. Jul 1869 Jonesport ME, d. 1936, m. 30 Mar 1892 Columbia Falls ME Josephine A. Bowles of Columbia Falls ME, b. Jan 1869, dau. George A. and Leona (Moss) Bowles.
402 John Vassar$^{7}$, 1878-1958.
Simeon Hall, b. 4 Mar 1880 Jonesport ME, d. 26 Aug 1912, unm.
Sources: Jonesport ME census 1880. ME 1880 census index. VR SA/ME. Leonard F. Tibbetts rec.

232. **JOHN CHADBOURNE$^{6}$ SAWYER** [see 101], b. 12 Mar 1804 Limington ME, d. 8 Mar 1875 W. Ellsworth ME, m .(I) 17 Mar 1828 Elizabeth B. Gilman of Jackson ME, b. 14 Mar 1806 d. 4 Jul 1888, dau. Enoch and Olive Gilman. Farmer, Minister. B/land in Dixmont ME 1826. He bur. Forest Hill Cem., Old Town ME.
Eliza I., b. ca. 1830, m. Joseph Jackson.
403 John Henry$^{7}$, 1833-1914.
Vesta Y., b. 1834, m. 13 Apr 1863 Medfield MA Robert H. Bruce.
404 Enoch C.$^{7}$, 1837-1915.
Olive Mary, b. 20 Jul 1839, d. 22 Nov 1915, m. John Seavey.
Maria A., b. 1842.
Delana Augusta, b. 1844, m.(I) 10 Jun 1863 Charles H. Cutler of Limington ME.
Thaddeus A., b. 1847 Monroe ME.
Sources: Jackson ME census 1840. Monroe ME census 1850. VR SA/ME, SA/MA. R10d, T6A, T6.

233. **NATHANIEL$^{6}$ SAWYER** [see 101], b. 12 Nov 1806 Limington ME, d. 14 Sep 1883 Monroe ME, m. 18 Mar 1829 Mary York of Dixmont ME, b. 23 May 1807 d. 16 Dec 1896, dau. Deacon Joseph York. Farmer. B/land in Dixmont ME 1826, Jackson ME 1840.
405 Charles Henry$^{7}$, 1829-1903.
David Mark, b. 3 May 1832, d. 31 Jul 1833.
Joseph Bailey, b. 22 Nov 1834, d. 29 Jul 1841.
Roscoe Gilman, b. 22 Dec 1836, d. 18 Jul 1841.
406 Daniel Roscoe$^{7}$, 1840-1920.
Mary Elizabeth, b. 1 Dec 1842, d. 1923, m. 5 Dec 1866 Fred A. Bean.
Lucretia M., b. 3 May 1845, m.(I) 24 Jan 1865 Thomas Patten of Hampden ME.
Katherine, b. 4 May 1848, d. 5 Feb 1917, m. 11 Jan 1871 Nathaniel Green.
Emma M., b. 18 Dec 1851, d. 18 Dec 1855.
Sources: Dixmont ME census 1840, 1850, 1880. ME 1880 census index. M7A, R10d, T6A, T6, D51, B40, Family Bible.

234. **EPHRAIM$^{6}$ SAWYER** [see 101], b. 21 Apr 1822 Monroe ME, d. 21 Apr 1898 Old Town ME, m. 5 Mar 1849 Providence RI Abby P. Woods of Revere MA, b. 24 Apr 1828 d. 9 Mar 1907, dau. Thomas and Lydia (Pratt) Woods. Shoemaker. In Chelsea MA, Old Town ME.
Emma I., b. 16 Oct 1849.
William H., b. 1856 Chelsea MA.
Franklin N., b. 1858 Old Town ME, m. 1 Aug 1883 Ware MA Carrie E. Lyon of Lawrence MA, b. 1860, dau. Calvin and Cynthia Lyon.
Hattie E., b. 1867.
Lydia, b. 1874.
Sources: Chelsea MA census 1850. Old Town ME 1860, 1870, 1880. ME 1880 census index. VR Rhode Island, SA/MA, SA/ME. T6, N40, S40.

235. **CHARLES FOGG⁶ SAWYER** [see 103], b. 25 Nov 1818 Limington ME, d. 8 Jul 1892 Limington ME, m. 29 Feb 1841 Westbrook ME Caroline (Graffam) Elwell of Westbrook ME, b. 1816 d. 24 Mar 1878, dau. Peter and Mary (Mason) Graffam. Farmer. In Limington ME, Standish ME.

Elizabeth, b. Jun 1841, d. 26 Oct 1866, m.(I) 4 Jun 1862 John E. Thompson.

Bradford, b. 4 Nov 1843 Limington ME, d.26 May 1919 Buxton ME, m. 19 Mar 1874 Mary Ellen Usher of Hollis ME, b. 18 Jan 1845 d. 3 Jan 1912. In Baldwin ME, Brownfield ME, Standish ME. He bur. Highland Cem., Buxton ME. CH: Mary E., b. 3 Dec 1875; Maud, b. 1877; Sarah L., b. 27 Jul 1885.

George R., b. 1846 Limington ME.

Sarah L., b. May 1847, d. 2 May 1874, m. John E Thompson.

407 Charles Lauriston⁷, 1849-1930.

John H., b. 1852 Limington ME, d. 1921. In Standish ME 1880.

Sources: Limington ME census 1850, 1860. Standish ME census 1870, 1880. ME 1880 census index. VR SA/ME. T6, L22, N40.

236. **ISAAC⁶ SAWYER** [see 103], b. ca. 1821 Limington ME, d. 21 Jan 1891 Limington ME, m. 5 Apr 1855 Mary E. Boothby, b. 16 Jan 1835 d. 26 Jan 1891, dau. John and Mary (Small) Boothby. Millman.

Edwin, b. 8 May 1856 Limington ME, d. 26 Apr 1926 Portland ME, m. 7 Feb 1885 Lizzie J. Bean of Gorham ME, b. 22 Nov 1860 d. 9 Feb 1906. He bur. in E. Limington ME.

Jennie, b. 1860.

Fred, b. 1863 Limington ME.

Ida B., b. 4 Oct 1864, d. 5 Sep 1946 Westbrook ME, m.(1) George M. Berry, m.(2) John McKeen, m.(3) 1885 Cyrus E Staples of Westbrook ME.

Sources: Limington ME census 1850, 1860, 1870. T6A, T6, N40.

237. **JACOB SMALL⁶ SAWYER** [see 104], b. 16 Oct 1816 Limington ME, d. 14 Oct 1859 Eaton NH, m. 6 Sep 1840 Maria Wallis of Sandwich NH, b. ? d. 23 Sep 1881 Freedom NH. Wid. in Eaton NH 1860.

408 Edmund P.⁷, 1841-1915.

Mary E., b. 1843, d. 18 Jan 1869, m. John M. Giles.

409 Josiah C.⁷, b. 1845.

Maria J., b. 1848, m. 19 Apr 1869 Lynn MA Benjamin Caswell.

Welthie A., b. 1852.

Sarah F., b. 1854.

Susan, b. 1855.

Sources: Limington ME census 1850. Eaton NH census 1860 (wid.). VR SA/MA. T6.

238. **ALONZO GREEN⁶ SAWYER** [see 104], b. 8 May 1831 Limington ME, d. 18 Jul 1894 Morgan VT, m.(1) 7 Mar 1855 Sylvinia A. Burnham of Standish ME, b. 1834 d. 12 Feb 1864, dau. Perley Foster Burnham; m.(2) 6 Mar 1869 Lancaster NH Alma Jane Avery of E. Haven VT, b. 1848, dau. Joel A. and Mary J. Avery. Cooper. In Bridgton ME, Morgan VT. Sylvinia and son were bur. in Burnham Cem., Standish ME.

410 Edgar Howard⁷, 1856-1922.

LaFontaine, b. 22 Sep 1862, d. 6 Feb 1863.

Henry R., b. 25 Jul 1871, d. 17 Aug 1889 Morgan VT.

Eldon Avery, b. 25 Dec 1876 Bridgton ME, d. 6 Jan 1904 Newport VT, m. 27 Nov 1902 Charleston VT Bessie I. Piper, b. ?. Laborer. CH: Daughter, b. 10 Jun 1903.

Mary S., b. 1879, m. 27 Feb 1896 John Eley.

Sources: Morgan VT census 1880. VR SA/VT. T6, M5.

239. **JOHN LORENZO[6] SAWYER** [see 104], b. 8 May 1831 Limington ME, d. 13 Jan 1904 Standish ME, m. 25 May 1854 Mary Ann Boulter of Standish ME, b. ?. In Minneapolis MN for 14 years. He bur. in Standish Cem., Standish ME.

Alma J., b. 17 Oct 1856, d. 21 Jan 1918, m. 29 Nov 1876 Nicholas E. Sawyer. See [205].
John K., b. ?. Physician. Went to Washington DC.
Emma C., b. 1859, m. Charles W. Sawyer of Minnesota [see 204].

Sources: T6.

240. **PETER WILSON[6] SAWYER** [see 104], b. 19 Nov 1835 Limington ME, d. 16 Mar 1902 Sebago ME, m. 12 Aug 1855 Mary Jewett of Sebago ME, b. May 1840 d. 30 Jan 1906. B/Land in Bridgton ME 1862.

Ella M., b. 6 Feb 1857, d. 12 Aug 1858.
Frances Mary, b. 25 Nov 1858, d. 24 Oct 1913 Sebago ME, m.(1) _____ Whitney; m.(2) Florella Wentworth.
Charles W., b. 24 Nov 1864, d. 12 Jun 1875.
Alice M., b. 24 Jun 1867, d. 1934, m. 24 Dec 1887 John H. Lombard of Portland ME.
411 Charles Frank[7], 1879-1954.

Sources: Sebago ME census 1860, 1870, 1880, 1900. ME 1880 census index. R10a, M5, H20, Family Bible, Robert L. Taylor rec.

241. **WILLIAM HAYES[6] SAWYER** [see 105], b. 30 May 1846 Limington ME, d. 22 Sep 1937 Limington ME, m. 11 Jan 1868 Cornish ME Ida T. Bragdon of Biddeford ME, b. 18 Mar 1850 d. 27 Feb 1935, dau. Hiram and Caroline (Dimock) Bragdon. He bur. in No. Limington ME.

Florence M., b. 24 Oct 1868, d. 6 Sep 1890.
412 Samuel Guy[7], 1871-1956.
Edmund Carroll, b. 20 Jun 1880 Limington ME, d. 1942, m. Nellie P. Palmer of E. Machias ME, b. 2 Dec 1899 d. 22 Jun 1988, dau. James A. and Caroline (Hanscom) Palmer. No CH.
William Hayes, b. 4 Feb 1892 Limington ME.

Sources: Limington ME census 1880. ME 1880 census index. VR SA/ME. C62, T6, N40, Nancy Welch rec.

242. **EPHRAIM ALONZO[6] SAWYER** [see 106], b. 2 Apr 1836 Maysville ME, d. 6 Jun 1909 Presque Isle ME, m. 22 Jun 1862 Sarah A. Todd of Ludlow ME, b. 20 Feb 1842 d. 28 Apr 1926, dau. Alfred and Mary (Towne) Todd. Farmer. He bur. in Greenridge Cem., Caribou ME.

Alice M., b. 16 Feb 1864, d. 2 Mar 1924, m. James H. Parker.
Mary E., b. 12 Dec 1865, d. 23 Oct 1943, m. 25 Dec 1884 Frank L. Johnson.
413 Fred B.[7], 1868-1945.
414 Joseph Wallace[7], 1870-1944.
Nellie G., b. 26 Sep 1873, d. 13 Jan 1955, m. Elijah Bishop.
Charles E., b. 15 Feb 1877, d. 1 Jan 1905.
Bertha Lois, b. 16 Jun 1881, d. 7 May 1944, m. 6 Jul 1903 William Gallup.
Kate F., b. 11 Nov 1887, d. Jul 1977, m. William Smith.

Sources: Maysville ME census 1880. ME 1880 census index. VR SA/ME. M5, Neil G. Sawyer rec.

243. **ALBERT[6] SAWYER** (Prince) [see 107], b. 23 Jun 1847 Phillips ME, m. Elvira _____, b. 1848.

Victor E., b. 1872 Phillips ME.

Prince E., b. 1874 Phillips ME.
Sources: Phillips ME census 1880. ME 1880 census index.

244. **DAVID FAIRBANKS$^6$ SAWYER** [see 108], b. 13 Jan 1806 Cape Elizabeth ME, m. 5 May 1825 Sarah Robards, b. ?.
415 Charles W.$^7$, 1826-1904.
416 George F., b. 1832-1894.
Sources: VR Cape Elizabeth ME.

245. **EBENEZER F.$^6$ SAWYER** [see 109], b. ca. 1814 Cape Elizabeth ME, d. 14 Jan 1865 Portland ME, m. 3 Jan 1837 Portland ME Martha Ann Parrott, b. 1813 d. 7 Apr 1895, dau. Ephraim and Anne (Dyer) Parrott. Ship builder. B/land from brother.
Hannah L., b. 24 Oct 1837.
Martha E., b. 28 Jan 1838, d. 29 May 1863.
Ebenezer F., b. 15 Feb 1841 Portland ME.
Annie E., b. 14 Feb 1844, d. 26 Apr 1853.
Augusta Deborah, b. 10 Sep 1846, m. Thomas Hart Benton.
Mary A., b. 13 May 1849.
Sources: Portland ME census 1840, 1850, 1860. VR Portland ME. P69, M5, C82, C83.

246. **JOHN GRAHAM$^6$ SAWYER** [see 109], b. ca. 1815 Portland ME, d. 31 Oct 1863 Augusta ME, m. 18 Jul 1840 (later div.) Harriet Jane Edgecomb of Portland ME, b. ?, dau. Noah and Betsey Edgecomb; she m. 1858 Albert C. Dawes. Secretary of State. S/land to brother on Cape Elizabeth ME 1845. He bur. In Eastern Cem., Augusta ME.
Charles Henry, b. 24 Jun 1841 Portland ME, m. 29 Oct 1867 Lucy Haight, b. 6 Mar 1844, dau. Fletcher M. Haight. Went to San Francisco CA.
Harriet A., b. 6 Feb 1846, m. 8 Sep 1870 Newton MA Albert D. Holmes.
Sources: Augusta ME census 1850. VR Gardner ME, SA/MA. R10a, D61.

247. **JOHN W.$^6$ SAWYER** [see 111], b. 6 Jan 1811 Danville ME, d. 19 Jan 1870 New Gloucester ME, m. 18 Apr 1833 Danville ME Sophronia Royal of Danville ME, b. 17 Dec 1807 d. 10 Aug 1870, dau. Samuel and Martha (Riggs) Royal. Farmer. B/S/land in Danville ME. He bur. in Upper Gloucester ME.
417 Winthrop R.$^7$, 1834-1918.
Martha H., b. 1837, d. 30 Jul 1853.
Salome F., b. 1840.
Charles, b. 1 Apr 1842 Danville ME, d. 3 Nov 1915 Auburn ME, m. 17 Apr 1889 Sarah L. Dinsmore, b. ? d. 1901.
Priscilla, b. 1844.
Alonzo, b. 3 Dec 1847 Danville ME, d. 9 Mar 1920 Yarmouth ME, m.(I) 22 Dec 1868 Frances E. Small of Lewiston ME, b. ?. CH: Child, b. Jul 1874, d. 15 Aug 1874.
John, b. 1849, d. 14 Jan 1850.
Sources: Danville ME census 1840, 1850, New Gloucester ME census 1860. VR Danville ME, SA/ME. R10a, Gravestone (Alonzo), Robert L. Taylor rec.

248. **NATHANIEL$^6$ SAWYER** [see 111], b. 18 Nov 1812 Danville ME, d. 12 Jan 1881 New Gloucester ME, m. 24 Jan 1842 Danville ME Lydia Waterhouse, b. 1 May d. 29 Sep 1896, dau. Joseph and Lydia (Parker) Waterhouse. In Danville ME, So. Auburn ME. B/land in Danville ME 1839. Most of this family is bur. in Hill Cem., White's Corner, New Gloucester ME.
Mary A., b. 26 Jan 1843, m. Joseph Ficket.

418 Joseph William.$^{7}$, 1844-1929.

Hiram G., b. 29 Sep 1846 Danville ME, d. 9 Mar 1895 Gray ME, m. 23 Apr 1865 Lewiston ME Mary R. Neal of Roxbury MA, b. 1848 d. 28 Oct 1939, dau. Margaret Neal. In Auburn ME. CH: Hattie M., b. 9 Oct 1870; Annie, b. 1874.

Lydia C., b. 19 Jan 1849, d. 1940, m. Charles Bangs.

John S., b. 10 Jun 1852, d. 13 Dec 1870.

Martha H., b. 7 Nov 1853, d. 14 Feb 1914, m. Frank King.

419 Horatio M.$^{7}$, 1856-1945.

Lillie A., b. 8 Oct 1859, m. William Snow.

Simon W., b. 22 Jul 1862 So. Auburn ME, d. 8 Jan 1944, m.(1) Martha J. Little of Ireland, b. 20 Jun 1862 d. 20 Nov 1922, dau. John Little; m.(2) 16 Dec 1931 Portsmouth NH Estelle (Leighton) Gowell of Augusta ME, b. 1872, dau. Andrew and Susan (Jackson) Leighton. Farmer, Butcher. In Lebanon NH, Gray ME. CH: Harold, stillborn 9 Nov 1891: Earl Victor, b. 20 Jan 1894, d. 1 Sep 1896.

Sources: Danville ME census 1850, 1860. Auburn ME census 1870, 1880. ME 1880 census index. VR Danville ME, Auburn ME, SA/ME. R10a, Gravestone. Margaret Sawyer rec.

249. **WILLIAM$^{6}$ SAWYER** [see 111], b. 8 May 1823 Danville ME, d. 2 Aug 1904 Mechanics Falls ME, m. 6 Jun 1845 Sarah Chase, b. 18 Aug 1823 d. 10 Feb 1864, dau. Jonathan and Hannah (Jordan) Chase. B/S/land in Danville ME 1848.

Elizabeth, b. 1848.

Hannah, b. 1849.

420 James Franklin$^{7}$, b. 1854.

421 George E.$^{7}$, 1856-1882.

Sources: Danville ME census 1850, 1860. VR Danville ME. R10a, C30.

250. **GEORGE WASHINGTON ROYAL$^{6}$ SAWYER** [see 111], b. 5 May 1826 Danville ME, d. 7 Dec 1875, m. 11 Jan 1855 New Gloucester ME Asenath Witham of Alfred ME, b. 14 Feb 1830 d. 27 Nov 1921. Peddler. In New Gloucester ME, Poland ME, Gray ME. Asenath B/S/land 1863-1870.

Sarah Caroline, b. 19 Dec 1855.

Fred Herbert, b. 22 Feb 1858 Danville ME, m. 24 Jan 1880 Gray ME Carrie A. (Small) Carlton, b. ?, dau. Isaac Small. In Poland ME, Gray ME. CH: Josephine, b. Oct 1881; Blanche, b. Mar 1887.

Emma E., b. 1864.

Lenora, b. 6 Jan 1870, d. 6 Jan 1945, m. 25 Dec 1888 John Milton Sawyer [see 422].

Eldora, b. 6 Jan 1870.

Sources: Gray ME census 1880 (wid.). VR New Gloucester ME, Auburn ME, Danville ME. M5, R10a.

251. **PARKER$^{6}$ SAWYER** [see 112], b. 2 Jun 1831 Mt. Vernon ME, m. Rebecca V. Norton of New Brunswick, Canada, b. 29 Dec 1837 d. 8 May 1909 Detroit ME, dau. Reuben and Margaret (Dinsmore) Norton. Farmer. In Detroit ME.

Lillian, b. 1858.

George W., b. 1860 Detroit ME.

Sources: Detroit ME census 1850. VR SA/ME.

252. **PARKER LIBBY$^{6}$ SAWYER** [see 113], b. Jun 1833 Gray ME, d. 21 Feb 1887 Gray ME, m. 13 Nov 1859 Sarah J. Rand of New Gloucester ME, b. 22 Mar 1842 d. 2 May 1915, dau. David and Eunice (Verrill) Rand. Coal merchant. In New Gloucester ME, Auburn ME.

John, b. 10 Apr 1862, d. 10 Feb 1863.

422 John Milton[7], 1863-1920.

Lewis Edwin, b. 13 Aug 1865 Gray ME, d. 20 Aug 1930, m. 2 Jul 1892 Portland ME Alice Morey of Auburn ME, b. 1875, dau. Charles and Laura Morey. Laborer. In New Gloucester ME, Portland ME, Gray ME. CH: Lewella L., b. 17 Dec 1892, d. 2 Feb 1893; Sadie E., b. May 1895, unm; Lewis E., b. 9 Oct 1898, d. 26 Feb 1899; Augustus Edwin, b. 31 Jul 1901, d. 13 Oct 1962; Irving J., b. 3 Mar 1904, m. 6 Nov 1926 Nellie Buckley; Harvey E., b. 12 Oct 1907; Louise, b. 3 Jan 1909, m. Clifford Ireland; Gladys, m. Peter Miller.

Annie M., b. 14 Mar 1867, d. 13 Mar 1951, m. 24 Dec 1887 Fred W. Fitz.

Florence I., b. 6 Mar 1868, d. 1893, m. 6 Jul 1892 Portsmouth NH John Batchelder.

Carolyn E., b. 20 Feb 1873, d. 1902, m. 17 May 1890 William Haskell.

Parker Leroy, b. 21 Jul 1877 New Gloucester ME, unm.

Sadie B., b. 15 Mar 1881, m. 24 Nov 1904 George E. Farnham.

Stephen David, b. 5 May 1883, d. 19 Dec 1863, m. 5 Oct 1910 Vesta Jordan, b. ?.

Albert E., b. Oct 1888, m. Lucy Mack of Portland ME, b. ?. CH: Ella May, b. Jan 1915, d. 21 Apr 1915.

Sources: New Gloucester ME census 1850, 1870, 1880. Auburn ME census 1860. ME 1880 census index. VR Portland ME, SA/ME. R28.

253. **ISAAC[6] SAWYER** [see 114], b. 1798 Falmouth ME. d. 25 Mar 1873 Portland ME, m. Esther A. Murray of Conway NH, b. 1801 d. 27 Nov 1861. Tinplater. In Westbrook ME, Portland ME.

William A., b. 1824, d. 18 Sep 1848 in Mexican War.

423 Francis M.[7], 1826-1894.

Martha, b. 1831, m. Lylander Townsend.

424 Alonzo W.[7], 1833-1897.

Joel Murray, b. 20 Jan 1836 Portland ME, d. 12 Dec 1917 Portland ME, m.(1) (I) 18 Jun 1859 Ann E. Knight of Falmouth ME, b. ?; m.(2) 8 Aug 1862 Sarah Jane Bartlett, b. 1 Mar 1840 d. 30 May 1909 So. Portland ME, dau. Alexander and Clarice (Jackson) Bartlett. Civil War. CH: Hattie E., b. ?, m. 4 May 1883 Dover NH Jason L. Hale.

Sources: Westbrook ME census 1830. Portland ME census 1840, 1850, 1860. VR SA/ME. P69, M5.

254. **CHARLES S.[6] SAWYER** [see 114], b. 1817 Westbrook ME, m. 1843 Mary A. G. Witham of Danville ME, b. ?. Tinplater. In Westbrook ME. B/land in Westbrook ME 1845, 1847.

Charles E., b. 1844 Westbrook ME.

Alfred A., b. 1847 Westbrook ME.

Sources: Westbrook ME census 1850, 1860. R10a.

255. **JOHN SKILLING[6] SAWYER** [see 115], b. 1 Nov 1815 Westbrook ME, d. 26 Mar 1897 Westbrook ME, m.(1) Mary E. Sawyer of Cumberland ME, b. 28 Nov 1812, dau. Reuben and Betsey (Wyman) Sawyer; m.(2) Sarah A. Knight, b. 12 Oct 1844 d. 22 Jun 1923, dau. Elmira Knight. Farmer. B/land from Reuben Sawyer's estate. In Westbrook ME.

Levi E., b. 11 Dec 1869 Westbrook ME, d. 20 Sep 1884.

Cora S., b. 1871, d. 1946, m. William R. Burke.

Arthur W., b. 30 Dec 1873 Westbrook ME, d. 1 Jul 1933.

Sources: Westbrook ME census 1850, 1860. ME 1880 census index. VR SA/ME. R10a, Gravestone.

256. **FREDERICK[6] SAWYER** [see 117], b. 24 Apr 1809 Westbrook ME, d. 21 Dec 1858 Westbrook ME, m. 11 Jun 1837 Harriet E. Merrill of Conway NH, b. 11 Mar 1810 d. 15 Nov 1900 Danbury NH, dau. Samuel and Dorcas (Eastman) Merrill. Shoemaker. S/land in Westbrook 1852. In Westbrook ME.

Eliza N., b. 9 Dec 1838, d. 26 Jun 1839.
425 William Kimball[7], b. 1840.
Eliza N., b. 9 Sep 1842, m. 8 Mar 1868 Conway NH Edward P. Eastman.
Sarah F., b. 14 Mar 1845, d. 6 Oct 1865. Had dau. Harriet E., b. ?.
Elmira M., b. 1 Nov 1848, d. 12 Dec 1849.
Frederick Elmer, b. 11 Jun 1851 Westbrook ME, d. 26 Jan 1928, unm. In Rochester NH.

Sources: Westbrook ME census 1840, 1850. VR Westbrook ME, SA/NH. R10a, C63, M5.

257. **HARRISON[6] SAWYER** [see 118], b. 9 Mar 1814 East Deering ME, m.(I) 23 Jan 1841 Frances Ellen Stevens of Portland ME, b. ca. 1826. Joiner. S/land 1863. In Portland ME, East Boston MA.

426 Michael S.[7], b. 1841.
Martha E., b. ca. 1843.
Child, b. Apr 1844, d. 13 Jun 1844.
427 Howard Dewolf[7], b. 1846.
Harrison, b. 10 Aug 1847 Portland ME, m. 18 Nov 1872 Boston MA Jane L. Warnick of New Brunswick, Canada, b. ca. 1853, dau. John and Mary A. Warnick. Clerk. In Boston MA.

Sources: Portland ME census 1850. VR SA/MA. P69, R10a, Robert L. Taylor rec.

258. **BRACKETT[6] SAWYER** [see 118], b. 22 May 1817 East Deering ME, d. 22 Dec 1890 Deering ME, m. 2 Dec 1846 Aurelia Wentworth of Casco ME, b. 31 Jan 1826 d. 9 May 1904, dau. William and Mehitable (Bryant) Wentworth. Shoemaker. In Westbrook ME. He bur. in Pine Grove Cem., Deering ME.

Charlotte E., b. 7 Sep 1847, d. 1939, m. 15 Jun 1873 Boston MA John Irvin.
Charles Edward, b. 1 Jun 1850, d. 7 Mar 1910 Westbrook ME, bur. Pine Grove Cem., Deering ME.
Barthana (female), b. 13 Dec 1853.

Sources: Westbrook ME census 1850. VR SA/ME, SA/MA. W26.

259. **MARK HARRIS[6] SAWYER** [see 119], b. 24 Mar 1812 Portland ME, d. 9 Mar 1853 Portland ME, m. Martha N._____ of England, b. 1819. Seaman. In Portland ME. Wid. m. (I) 14 Nov 1858 Cape Elizabeth ME Abia Chamberlain.

Eliza R., b. 5 Aug 1837, m. Robertson Dyer, Jr.
Helen A., b. 27 Mar 1840.
Charles Lemuel, b. 4 Apr 1842 Portland ME, m. 11 Jan 1872 Nancy C. Smith, b. ?. CH: Charles A., b. Jul 1873, d. 1 Sep 1873.
Mark Harris, b. 19 May 1843, d.y.
Mark Harris, b. 31 Jul 1844 Portland ME, d. 14 Aug 1918 Harrison ME, m. 7 May 1869 Portland ME Maria McRonald of Cape Elizabeth ME, b. Sep 1850 d. 9 May 1907, dau. Edgar J. and Mary (Dresser) McRonald. Civil War. Received a pension 1882.
Josephine E., b. 27 Apr 1846, d.y.
E. Josephine, b. 19 May 1847.

Sources: Portland ME census 1840, 1850. VR Cape Elizabeth ME, Portland ME, SA/ME. H26.

260. **AARON G.$^6$ SAWYER** [see 120], b. 1812 Falmouth ME, d. 30 Sep 1895 Mendon VT, m. Philena Rowe of Windsor VT, b. 1826 d. 28 Nov 1887 Mendon VT, dau. Harris and Susan Rowe. Farmer. In Pittsfield ME, Sherburne VT. His death recorded in Rutland VT also.

Susan A., b. 1844.
Isaac E., b. 1845 Falmouth ME.
Samuel H., b. 4 Aug 1849 Pittsfield ME, d. 17 Apr 1911 Mendon VT, m. 1 Jan 1880 Mendon VT Etta Temple, b. ?. Lumberman. CH: Son, b. ?, d. 23 Sep 1881.

Sources: Sherburne VT census 1850. VR SA/VT.

261. **JOEL$^6$ SAWYER** [see 121], b. Jan 1805 Westbrook ME, d. 2 Jul 1874 Westbrook ME, m. 1 Jan 1837 Anna Knight, b. 7 May 1807 d. 7 Mar 1896, dau. Amos and Jane (Sawyer) Knight. Farmer. B/land 1845 Westbrook ME.

John F., b. Jan 1840 Westbrook ME, d. 27 Jun 1905 Westbrook ME.

Sources: Westbrook ME census 1850. R10a. T19. M8.

262. **JOSEPH M.$^6$ SAWYER** [see 122], b. Aug 1795 Falmouth ME, d. 1 Jun 1875 East Deering ME, m. 18 Nov 1832 Dorcas Whittam, b. 1801 d. 15 Dec 1856. He bur. St. George Cem., E. Deering ME.

Joseph Merrill, b. 10 Oct 1832, d. 27 Sep 1835.
David N., b. 1837 Westbrook ME.
Sarah J., b. 1838.
Mary E. J., b. 1842, m. 4 Jan 1873 Boston MA Ammi C. Chick.

Sources: Westbrook ME census 1830, 1840, 1850. VR SA/ME, SA/MA. M5.

263. **EDWIN A.$^6$ SAWYER** [see 123], b. Jan 1810 Falmouth ME, d. 21 Dec 1896 Portland ME, m.(I) 1 Jan 1833 Emily A. Stevens, b. 1817 d. 1 Apr 1845. Confectioner. In Portland ME. His sister, Mary R. w/Edwin 1850. CH bur. in Eastern Cem., Portland ME.

Edwin Augustus, b. 5 Jul 1834, d. 12 Dec 1851.
428 Benjamin Leonard$^7$, 1840-1927.
Joseph Annis, b. 17 Jul 1843, d. 22 Jan 1860.
Emily E., b. 8 Feb 1845, d. 16 Jun 1845.
Edwin A., b. 1851, d. 1884.

Sources: Portland ME census 1840, 1850. VR SA/ME. P69, M5.

264. **ASA$^6$ SAWYER** [see 124], b. 6 Jan 1806 Eaton NH, d. 1858 Eaton NH, m. 10 Dec 1826 Eaton NH Nancy Drew of Newfield ME, b. 3 Mar 1807 d. 9 Nov 1893, dau. Clement and Anna (Tibbetts) Drew. Farmer. In Eaton NH. Wid. w/son Loren 1860, w/son Sylvanus 1870.

Anna, b. 1830.
429 Daniel C.$^7$, 1832-1903.
430 Loren D.$^7$, b. 1835.
Eliza J., b. 1837, m. 4 May 1862 Conway NH Joseph E. Shackford..
Emily T., b. 1841.
Mary F., b. 1843, m. 11 Mar 1860 Eaton NH John M. Giles.
Sabrina E., b. 1846.
Sylvanus A., b. 12 Feb 1848 Eaton NH, d. 19 Feb 1909 Conway NH, m.(1) ?; m. (2) 9 Feb 1909 Conway NH Ella (Tripp) Thurston of Porter ME, b. 1853, dau. Thomas and Susan (Lenscott) Tripp. Merchant.
431 Irvin A.$^7$, 1851-1932

Sources: Eaton NH census 1830, 1840, 1850, 1860 (wid.) 1870. VR SA/NH. K10A, N14, N6.

265. **JAMES[6] SAWYER** [see 125], b. 1808 Westbrook ME, d. 1852 Portland ME, m. Mary C. Todd, b. 1 Jan 1804 d. 12 Feb 1886. Joiner. B/S/land 1840-1861. He bur. in Evergreen Cem., Portland ME.

Lucy M., b. 5 Apr 1833, d. 24 Dec 1911, unm.
Margaret J., b. 28 Nov 1834, d. 1915, m. 17 Feb 1861 James Greenhalgh. VR give her b. as both 1834 and 1835.
Florentine C., b. 28 Aug 1836, m.(1) 4 Nov 1862 Joseph Walker, m.(2) Alexander Parker.
Frederick Augustus, b. 15 Jul 1838 Portland ME, m. 28 Nov 1867 Portland ME Mary Hamblin, b. ?.
Agnes M., b. 28 Aug 1840, d. 4 Dec 1841.
James Edward, b. 13 Jun 1844 Portland ME, d. 30 Nov 1931 Portland ME, m. 11 Dec 1872 Haverhill MA Marie Irene Allard of New Hampshire, b. Mar 1849 d. 1918 Wells ME, dau. John M. and Mesa (Clark) Allard. He bur. in Evergreen Cem., Portland ME. CH: Ethel P., b. 11 Mar 1883, m. John A. Carianns; Son, b. ?; Alice G., b. 12 Jan 1889, d. 17 Aug 1889; Frank Emery, b. 1891, d. 1892.
George Horace, b. 5 Aug 1846 Portland ME, d. 1913 Portland ME, m. 26 Nov 1874 Falmouth ME Mary A. Bailey of Falmouth ME, b. Dec 1849 Falmouth ME d. 1940, dau. Charles A. and Abbie Bailey. Carriage maker. In Falmouth ME 1878, Westbrook ME 1887. He bur. in Evergreen Cem., Portland ME. CH: Clarence, b. 15 Jul 1878, d. 18 Jan 1885; Florence A., b. 13 Sep 1887.

Sources: Portland ME census 1840, 1850. VR Portland ME, Falmouth ME, SA/ME, SA/MA. R10a.

266. **SIMEON[6] SAWYER** [see 125], b. 19 Jun 1814 Westbrook ME, d. 7 Feb 1886 Westbrook ME, m. 30 Jun 1840 Sophia Knight Sawyer, b. 16 Jun 1823 d. 17 Mar 1910 Westbrook ME, dau. Lewis Bean and Faronia (Knight) Sawyer. Carpenter. B/S/land 1841-1870. He bur. in Evergreen Cem., Portland ME.

432 Leander L.[7], b. 1843.
433 Eugene Willis[7], 1855-1926.

Sources: Westbrook ME census 1850, 1860. VR Deering ME, SA/ME, SA/MA. R10a, Theodore L. Sawyer rec.

267. **GEORGE[6] SAWYER** [see 125], b. 11 May 1817 Old Falmouth ME, d. 7 Oct 1874, m. Elizabeth E. Abbott, b. 6 Jun 1828 d. 9 Feb 1909. Carpenter. S/land 1841, 1843. Note: VR says George II.

Adalaide, b. 1 Mar 1850, d. 21 Jun 1871, m. _____ Walker.
Almenia, b. 1852, d. 1930.
434 Frank H.[7], 1854-1927.
Ella A., b. 1860, d. 1932, m. Charles Jackson.

Sources: Westbrook ME census 1850, 1860. VR SA/ME. R10a, P69.

268. **JOHN HILL[6] SAWYER** [see 126], b. 1 Jan 1809 Portland ME, d. 20 Feb 1898 Boston MA, m. 10 Apr 1831 Portland ME Hannah L. Weeks of Minot ME, b. 27 Feb 1816 d. 7 Mar 1899, dau. Philip and Martha (Hodgkins) Weeks. Mariner.

John Marston, b. 20 Oct 1831 Portland ME, d. 20 Aug 1864 Portland ME. Mariner.
Charlotte Augusta, b. 29 Jun 1835, d. 7 Feb 1914 Portland ME.
435 Edward Henry[7], 1837-1905.
436 Philip Weeks[7], 1840-1905.

Joseph Emery , b. 24 May 1842 Portland ME, d. 22 Feb 1922 Togus ME, m.(1) 10 Oct 1863 Portland ME Fanny Hawkes of Portland ME, b. ?; m.(2) 29 Apr 1883 Boston MA Elizabeth Gilbert of Phippsburg ME, b. 1845, dau. Caleb and Eliza Gilbert. Carpenter.
Martha Ellen, b. 4 Feb 1845, d. 7 Aug 1847 Portland ME.
Samuel Sargent, b. 6 Dec 1846 Portland ME, d. 28 Feb 1912 Boston MA, m. 11 Oct 1866 Boston MA Nellie O. Staples of Portland ME, b. ?.
437 Hadwin[7], 1850-1923.
Martha Ellen, b. 9 Sep 1852, d. 18 Dec 1934, m. 27 Jan 1872 Portland ME John Frank Mitchell.
Isabell Merrill, b. 3 Nov 1854.
Hannah, b. 30 Oct 1855, d. 12 Nov 1940 Boston MA.
Mary Ella, b. 9 Aug 1859, d. 21 May 1942.
George Washington, b. 21 Feb 1862, d. 24 Aug 1864 Portland ME.

Sources: Portland ME census 1840, 1850, 1860. Freeport ME census 1880. ME 1880 census index. VR Portland ME, Cape Elizabeth ME, SA/ME, SA/MA. P69, M5.

269. **ISAAC[6] SAWYER** [see 128], b. 18 Sep 1789 Falmouth ME, d. 6 Mar 1853 Augusta ME, m. 11 Dec 1808 Gardiner ME Diana Guabert, b. 23 Jun 1786 d. 6 Nov 1854. Blacksmith. In Hallowell ME 1813. B/S/land 1810-1836.

438 Robert[7], b. 1809.
Margaret, b. 23 Dec 1810, m. 19 Oct 1830 David Goodwin.
Catherine, b. 13 May 1812, m.(I) 23 Sep 1832 Henry Winslow.
439 Isaac[7], 1813-1851.
Mary J., b. 17 Oct 1815, m. 3 Oct 1834 Joseph Patterson.
440 William W.[7], b. 1817.
Diana R., b. 9 Mar 1819, m. 1840 Jones Smith.
Hannah, b. 2 Jul 1820, d. 1848, m. 10 Jun 1841 Isaac Smith.
Frances E., b. 27 Apr 1823, m. 7 Nov 1849 Alden Buttrick.
George Addison, b. Nov 1824, d. 30 Jan 1825.
441 George Addison[7], b. 1826.

Sources: Dresden ME census 1810. Hallowell ME census 1820, 1830, 1840, 1850. VR Hallowell ME, Gardiner ME, Augusta ME, Lowell MA. R10a, M4.

270. **DAVID[6] SAWYER** [see 128], b. 1 Apr 1812 Madison ME, d. 11 Oct 1898 Madison ME, m. 14 Mar 1841 Harmony ME Phebe Bucky of Madison ME, b. 1809. Farmer.

Corydon T., b. 20 Nov 1841, d. 30 Apr 1918.
John S., b. 1846, d. 24 Aug 1930.
Delia N., b. 1847.
Ann D., b. 1850.
Abby B., b. 1855.

Sources: VR Skowhegan ME, Madison ME, SA/ME. Death certificate.

271. **JONAS[6] SAWYER** [see 128], b. 1814 Madison ME, m.(1) 27 Dec 1836 Betsey Waterman, b. 1811 d. 9 Nov 1853; m.(2) 7 Feb 1855 Anson ME Hepsibah Hilton, b. 3 Jun 1828 d. 28 Jan 1917, dau. Edgar and Betsey Hilton. Carpenter.

Sarah W., b. ca. 1840.
Emily D., b. ca. 1846.
Frank Jr., b. ca. 1854.
Betsey, b. ca. 1858.
Olive B., b. ca. 1862.

Sources: Madison ME census 1840, 1850, 1860. VR Anson ME, SA/ME. D9.

272. **DANIEL H.[6] SAWYER** [see 128], b. 31 Jan 1820 Madison ME, d. 14 Jan 1911 Madison ME, m. Elvira Daggett, b. 1822.

442 Charles H.[7], 1847-1914.
Ida, b. 1850.
Frank, b. 1856.
Elizabeth, b. 1858.

Sources: Madison ME census 1850, 1860. VR SA/MA.

273. **JAMES[6] SAWYER** [see 128], b. 1822 Madison ME, m. 23 May 1847 Emily Bacon, b. Sep 1825, d. Jul 1909. Farmer.

Warren, b. 1848.
443 Elmer Ellsworth[7], 1851-1924.

Sources: Madison Me census 1850, 1860 (wid.). Somerset Co., Maine Marriages.

274. **JOHN R.[6] SAWYER** [see 129], b. 1814, d. 22 Feb 1889 Deering ME, m.(1)24 Sep 1837 Westbrook ME Mary A. Young, b. 1816 d. 14 Nov 1852; m.(2) Caroline D._____, b. ca. 1825 d. 26 Sep 1861. Wheelwright. B/S/land in Minot ME 1836, S/land in New Gloucester ME. He bur. Pine Grove Cem., Portland ME.

John Edwin, b. 12 May 1842 Westbrook ME, m. 1866 Lucy A. Brazier, b. Nov 1842, dau. Enoch and Phebe (Ilsley) Brazier. Merchant. B/S/land 1866-1868 w/father. CH: Alice B., b. 5 Mar 1872; Helen B., b. 22 Apr 1882.
Mary H., b. 1848, m. Alfred R. Houston.
Abby D., b. 1856.
Herbert A., b. 1869, d. 1895.

Sources: Westbrook ME census 1840, 1850, 1860. VR SA/ME. R10a.

275. **JOSEPH GRANT[6] SAWYER** [see 130], b. ca. 1801 Falmouth ME, d. 14 Jul 1888 Deering ME, m. 31 Mar 1825 Durham ME Eunice P. Knight of Falmouth ME, b. 3 Jun 1805 d. 6 May 1866, dau. Amos and Betsey (Knight) Knight. Farmer. In Durham ME with Uncle Samuel, Minot ME, Yarmouth ME.

Joshua Lewis, b. 25 Aug 1827 Minot ME, d. 20 Jul 1911 Portland ME, m. 26 Nov 1851 Rebecca S. Sawyer, b. 1830 d. 1905, dau. Samuel and Hannah (Sawyer) Sawyer. Carriage maker. Civil War. In Durham ME, Portland ME, Yarmouth ME. S/land in Yarmouth to brother Amos 1866. Agreed to care for parents for life. CH: Clara E., b. 19 May 1853, d. 19 Nov 1889; Joseph Eugene, b. Jul 1856, d. 3 Oct 1857; Minerva, b. 30 Jan 1864; Harry L., b. 30 Nov 1871 Portland ME, d. 9 May 1939.
Emma, b. ?.
Amos Knight, b. ca. 1832 Durham ME, d. 1916, m. 23 Apr 1860 Marcia Keen of Calais ME, b. ca. 1838 d. 1922. In Denmark ME, Portland ME. S/land to his father 1858.
Eunice Ellen, b. ca. 1836, m. 1 Jun 1856 James O. Durgan.
Almira K., b. ca. 1838, m. 17 Dec 1862 Josiah M. Walker.

Sources: Durham ME census 1840, 1850, 1860. VR Durham ME, SA/ME. R10a, M7A, M5.

276. **LEWIS BEAN[6] SAWYER** [see 133], b. 5 Jul 1798 Falmouth ME, d. 4 Jan 1858 Westbrook ME, m.(1) 26 Feb 1822 Faronia Knight, b. 1796 d. 27 Dec 1827, dau. Richard and Abigail (Cilley) Knight; m.(2) 2 Dec 1830 Comfort P. Lang of Portland ME, b. 2 Dec 1809 d. 1878, dau. William and Anna (Norris) Lang. Shoemaker. Will lists heirs.

Sophia Knight, b. 16 Jun 1823, d. 17 Mar 1910, m. 30 Jun 1840 Simeon Sawyer.

Fanny E. b. 21 Dec 1827, d. 15 Apr 1864, m. Horace F. Milliken.
444 Alonzo Willard[7], b. ca. 1835-1864.
Angelina, b. 1841, m. Rufus Rand.
Louisa, b. 1846, m. _____ Reed.
Sources: Westbrook ME census 1830, 1840, 1850, 1860 (wid.). R10a, T19, M47, P76, M55, Theodore L. Sawyer rec.

277. **JEREMIAH[6] SAWYER** [see 134], b. 11 Feb 1796 Cape Elizabeth ME, d. 20 Jan 1880 Otisfield ME, m. 28 Oct 1819 Westbrook ME Lydia Morrill of Westbrook ME, b. 28 Aug 1798 d. 7 Mar 1878. Cordwainer. B/S/land 1824-1838. He bur. in Blue Hill Cem., Otisfield ME.
445 Rufus M.[7],b. 1820.
446 Nathaniel K.[7], 1822-1904.
Julia A., b. 12 Oct 1823, d. 22 Dec 1852, m. 26 May 1843 Mark Knight, Jr.
Sarah E., b. 11 Aug 1834, d. 28 Sep 1888, m. 12 May 1857 Henry P. Spurr.
Sources: Otisfield ME census 1820, 1830, 1840, 1850, 1860. VR Westbrook ME, Otisfield ME. R10a, Robert L. Taylor rec.

278. **LEWIS H.[6] SAWYER** [see 134], b. 26 Jul 1821 Otisfield ME, m. 13 Jul 1846 Mary Holden of Otisfield ME, b. 26 May 1827, dau. Ronald and Dorcas (Plumber) Holden. Shoemaker. B/S/land 1849-1861. Town Clerk, 1851-55, 1859-63. Town Treasurer, 1855, 1859-61. Went to Nebraska.
Harriet E., b. 5 Oct 1847, m. 1867 Samuel M. Holden.
Wyman Parker, b. 14 Jun 1849 Otisfield ME.
George Evans, b. 7 May 1853 Otisfield ME.
Ida M., b. 22 Mar 1857.
Abby S., b. 21 Nov 1859.
Sources: Otisfield ME census 1850. VR Otisfield ME. P85.

279. **DANIEL C.[6] SAWYER** [see 136], b. 21 Jul 1795 Topsham ME, d. 30 Dec 1872 Harpswell ME, m. Anna Purington Ridley of Harpswell ME, b. ca. 1797 d. 9 Dec 1872, dau. Mark and Abigail (Webber) Ridley. Fisherman. Anna B/S/land 1833-1870. He bur. in Cranberry Horn Cem., Harpswell ME.
447 Oliver P.[7], 1817-1867.
Mary Ann, b. 14 Aug 1820, m. 3 Sep 1856 Lyman Doyle.
Abigail (or Albina),b. ca. 1825, m. Harmon Orr of Brunswick ME.
Sources: Harpswell ME census 1820, 1830, 1840, 1850, 1860. VR Topsham ME. R10a, M5, R16.

280. **EDWARD[6] SAWYER** [see 136], b. 24 Apr 1805 Topsham ME, d. 20 Nov 1877 Deering ME, m. 18 May 1828 Eliza F. Beals of Portland ME, b. 1804 d. 4 Aug 1877, dau. Joseph Beals. Bricklayer. He bur. Evergreen Cem., Portland ME.
Eliza, b. 1830.
George F. b. Jan 1832 Westbrook ME, d. 18 Dec 1902 in Gorham ME, m. Emeline Abbott Nason, b. Jan 1842, dau. Isaiah and Harriet (Manchester) Nason. Civil War. No CH.
Mary E. b. 1834.
448 Joseph E.[7], 1837-1916.
Sophia V., b. 1845, d. 1867.
Henry W., b. 1848, d. 2 Sep 1848.
Sources: Westbrook ME census 1830, 1840, 1850. VR Topsham ME, SA/ME.

281. **STEPHEN C.[6] SAWYER** [see 136], b. Feb 1806 Topsham ME, d. 20 Jan 1892 Bath ME, m. 26 Apr 1829 Bath ME Sarah A. Owen of Bath ME, b. Aug 1809 d. 11 Oct 1898, dau. Philip and Clarissa H. (Cook) Owen. Painter.

Mary F., b. 24 Jun 1831.
449 Charles Edwin[7], b. 1834.
Louisa F., b. 22 Feb 1837.
Addison, b. 1839 Bath ME. Civil War.
William R., b. 23 May 1843 Bath ME, d. 25 Feb 1912 Bath ME, m. 6 Aug 1871 Bath ME Anna R. Hallahan of Ireland, b. ?. CH: Emma, b. ?; Louisa, b. Jan 1876.

Sources: Hallowell ME census 1830. Bath ME census 1840, 1850. VR SA/ME. R20.

282. **ALBION[6] SAWYER** [see 137], b. 3 Oct 1823 Portland ME, d. 1903 Dorchester MA, m. 11 Jun 1863 Boston MA Lucy Ann Hill of Dorchester MA, b. ca. 1837, dau. George and Mary Hill.

450 Charles Winthrop[7], 1868-1943.

Sources: VR SA/MA. Albion T. Sawyer rec.

283. **SUMNER P.[6] SAWYER** [see 138], b. 17 Aug 1819 Westbrook ME, d. 6 Feb 1899 Westbrook ME, m. 13 Aug 1848 Scarboro ME Sarah E. Kilbourne of Scarboro ME, b. 1826 d. 1876. Farmer. S/land in Westbrook ME 1870.

Mary E., b. ca. 1851.
John E., b. 1853 Westbrook ME, m. 25 Jun 1899 Windham ME Jennie G. Lord of Portland ME, b. 22 Jul 1869 d. 26 Dec 1921, dau. Isreal (Isaiah ?) and Mary (Graffam) Lord.
Anna, b. ca. 1856.
451 Charles P.[7], 1859-1922.

Sources: Westbrook ME census 1860. VR SA/ME. R10a.

284. **WILLIAM F.[6] SAWYER** [see 138], b. 1824 Windham ME, d. 1 Feb 1904 Westbrook ME, m.(I) 13 Dec 1845 Windham ME Eunice R. (Bodge) Hawkes of Windham Me, b. 5 Mar 1820 d. 28 Nov 1898, dau. Thomas and Betsey (Mayberry) Bodge. B/S/land in Windham ME 1848-1868.

Eunice E., b. 1847, d. 28 Oct 1849.
Ella M., b. 1850.
John Edgar F.., b. 1857 Windham ME, d. 1885, m. 26 Apr 1885 Windham ME Gertrude F. Gowen of Westbrook ME, b. ?.
Zelia, b. Mar 1852, d. 2 Sep 1860.

Sources: VR Windham ME, SA/ME. R10a, H30.

285. **FRANCIS E.[6] SAWYER** [see 138], b. 27 Dec 1830 Westbrook ME, d. 14 Mar 1911 So. Windham ME, m. Mary Ann Hawkes of Windham ME, b. 27 Jan 1833 d. 25 Jul 1908, dau. Ebenezer and Dorcas (Cobb) Hawkes. Brickmaker.

452 Levi Willis[7], 1857-1932.
453 Walter H.[7], 1863-1929.
454 Eugene J.[7], 1865-1943.
Ferdinand, b. 6 Sep 1868 Windham ME, d. 26 Sep 1960, m. 26 Aug 1896 Windham ME Kate A. Elder of Windham ME, b. 1868, dau. Joseph G. and Callie (Cobb) Elder. No CH.
455 George W.[7], 1871-1918.
456 Frank Sanford[7], 1875-1951.

Sources: Windham ME census 1880. ME 1880 census index. VR Windham ME, SA/ME. Theodora Hoyt Sawyer rec., Kay Soldier rec., Clyde M. Sawyer rec.

286. **SIMON M.[6] SAWYER** [see 139], b. 3 Mar 1820, d. 30 Oct 1899, m.(I) 12 Jan 1843 Almira J. Richards of Falmouth ME, b. Oct 1824 d. 14 Aug 1901, dau. Samuel and Alphia (Lunt) Richards. Carpenter. In Saco ME, Portland ME. B/S/land in Portland ME 1852.

Bertha A., b. 1845, d. 23 Nov 1846. Bur. in Merrill Cem., Falmouth ME.

Frederick W., b. 16 Nov 1850 Portland ME.

Walter C., b. 1859 Portland ME.

Harriet F., b. 31 Jul 1861.

Willie R., b. 20 Apr 1866, d. 4 Sep 1867.

Sources: Portland ME census 1850. VR SA/ME. R10a, M5.

287. **NELSON[6] SAWYER** [see 140], b. 1813, d. 1864 Westbrook ME, m. 29 Apr 1838 Abigail M. Weston, b. 1816 d. 1892. Combmaker. In Bluehill ME 1830, Westbrook ME 1840, 1850. He bur. Saccarappa Cem., Westbrook ME.

Elizabeth, b. 1832, d. 1902, m. 13 Jan 1857 Clinton MA John E. Knight.

Kendall Boyd, b. ca. 1839 Westbrook ME, m. 16 Jun 1864 Marlborough MA Mary A. Holyoke of Marlborough MA, b. 1842, dau. Edward and Angeline (Toombs) Holyoke. Grocer. In Clinton MA. CH: William P., b. 4 Apr 1866 Clinton MA; Marion Louise, b. 22 Sep 1868; Herbert Houston, b. 20 Apr 1870 Fitchburg MA.

Sources: Bluehill ME census 1830. Westbrook ME census 1840, 1850. VR SA/ME, SA/MA. M5.

288. **CHARLES W.[6] SAWYER** [see 140], b. ca. 1844 Westbrook ME, m. Nellie _____, b. ca. 1848 d. 6 Oct 1887.

Charles, b. 9 May 1876 Portland ME.

Arthur, b. 26 Jul 1877 Portland ME.

Sources: VR SA/ME.

289. **JOSIAH WYMAN[6] SAWYER** [see 141], b. 18 Aug 1810 Cumberland ME, d. 19 Aug 1894 Alna ME, m. 25 Aug 1839 Cumberland ME Harriet Sturdivant, b. 11 Jun 1819 d. 4 Dec 1890, dau. Ephraim and Rachel (Drinkwater) Sturdivant.

Laura Alberta, b. 27 May 1840, m. 18 May 1863 Myrick Simpson of Newcastle NH.

Amanda M., b. 23 May 1842, d. 27 Dec 1871, m. 31 Jan 1869 Charlestown MA Charles J. Eaton.

Mary C., b. 29 Apr 1847, d. 2 Jan 1851.

Edwin A., b. 17 Apr 1849, d. 28 Sep 1849.

Clarence Melville, b. 25 Oct 1850 Alna ME, m. 1 Jan 1877 Lois J. Doughty, b. 17 Apr 1852, dau. Benjamin F. and Mary (Wilson) Doughty. CH: Mary W., b. 19 Apr 1879.

Sources: Alna ME census 1880. ME 1880 census index. G6.

290. **JAMES[6] SAWYER** [see 141], b. 18 Jan 1815 Cumberland ME, d. 19 Feb 1891 No. Yarmouth ME, m. 20 Jul 1841 Elizabeth L. Merrill of Cumberland ME, b. 4 Feb 1815 d. 11 May 1889. Sea captain. B/S/land in Buxton ME 1846, B/land in Cumberland ME 1848 and No. Yarmouth ME 1849. He bur. in Walnut Hill Cem., No. Yarmouth ME.

James Lincoln, b. 1844, d. 17 Jul 1847.

Charles Howard, b. 16 Sep 1847 North Yarmouth ME, d. 27 Oct 1922 No. Yarmouth ME, m. Ella F. Sweetsir, b. 9 Dec 1859 d. 27 Apr 1912. Sea captain. He bur. in Walnut Hill Cem., No. Yarmouth ME.

Georgianna L., b. 10 Nov 1850, d. 1877.

457 James Alexander[7], b. 1852.
Sources: North Yarmouth ME census 1850, 1860. VR North Yarmouth ME, SA/ME, SA/MA. M5, R10a. T19.

291. **JOSEPH[6] SAWYER** [see 141], b. 26 Jan 1818 No. Yarmouth ME, d. 16 Jun 1897, m.(1) 7 Aug 1842 Olive Merrill, b. 1823 d. 1888; m.(2) (first cousin) Sarah Elizabeth Abbott, b. 20 Feb 1831 d. 1896, dau. Moses and Mary (Shaw) Abbott.

Gilbert W., b. 1844, d. 21 Jan 1860.
Olive L., b. 2 Jun 1847, d. 10 Jan 1860.
458 Wesley[7], 1849-1934.
Emerson M., b. 6 Mar 1851, d. 9 Jan 1860.
459 Carleton[7], 1855-1924.
Albert, b. 1860, d. 1928, unm.
460 Edward Irving[7], b. 186?.

Sources: Cumberland ME census 1850, 1860. VR Cumberland ME.

292. **ASA[6] SAWYER** [see 141], b. 9 Aug 1822 Cumberland ME, d. 19 Dec 1910 Cumberland ME, m. 7 Feb 1854 Alna ME Eliza S. Clough of Alna ME, b. 26 Feb 1835 d. 22 Mar 1913, dau. Daniel and Elizabeth (Stevens) Clough. B/S/land 1849-1869.

Horace Eugene, b. 25 Nov 1854 Alna ME, m. 1890 Emily Harmon of Windsor CT, b. ?.
461 Fred Leland[7], b. 1858.
Alice M., b. 14 May 1862, m. Frank Daughty.
Edith Maud, b. 14 Nov 1870, m. Springfield MA James Alexander Sawyer.

Sources: Alna ME census 1850. Cumberland ME census 1880. ME 1880 census index. VR SA/ME. R10a, G6, S64.

293. **JOHN SHAW[6] SAWYER** [see 141], b. 25 May 1825 Cumberland ME, d. 9 Jan 1909 Cumberland ME, m. 1 May 1856 Abigail P. Ware, b. 30 Jun 1832 d. 24 Apr 1897, dau. David and Elizabeth (Haywood) Ware.

Alberta, b. 4 Jul 1857.
Reuben, b. 17 Nov 1860 Cumberland ME.
Harvey, b. 22 Sep 1862 Cumberland ME.
David, b. 4 Apr 1864, d. 13 Oct 1881.
Charles, b. 10 Jan 1866 Cumberland ME.
Orrin G., b. 13 May 1870 Cumberland ME.
Annie B., b. 28 Jul 1872, m. 24 Jun 1892 Christian Peterson of Yarmouth ME.
Child, b. 11 Oct 1874, d. 20 May 1875.

Sources: Cumberland ME census 1860, 1880. ME 1880 census index. VR Cumberland ME, SA/ME. W10.

294. **GEORGE[6] SAWYER** [see 144], b. 1813 Milbridge ME, d. 16 Jul 1899 Machiasport ME, m.(1) 21 Nov 1835 Mary A. Leighton, b. ?; m.(2) (I) 12 Nov 1844 Caroline W. Dyer, b. 1828. Sea captain.

Fairfield, b. 1842 Milbridge ME, m. Susan A. Hooper of Machiasport ME, b. 17 Dec 1844. Sea captain.

Sources: Steuben ME census 1840. Milbridge ME census 1850. VR Steuben ME. SA/ME.

295. **CHARLES N.[6] SAWYER** [see 144], b. 1816 Cherryfield ME, m. 24 Dec 1844 Penobscot ME Abigail D. Leach of Penobscot ME, b. 11 Nov 1826, dau. George and Betsey (Dorr) Leach. Shoemaker. In Bluehill ME, Brewer ME.

Mary L., b. 22 Oct 1845.
George Henry, b. 20 Nov 1846 Brewer ME.
462 Charles William$^{7}$, 1848-1933.
Frederick Augustus, b. 8 Jul 1851 Brewer ME.
Hattie B., b. 1856.
Henry Albert, b. 1860 Brewer ME, m. 1 Jun 1885 Lynn MA Nellie A. Ireson of Biddeford ME, b. 1862, dau. George M. and Eliza J. Ireson. Bookkeeper.
Alice B., b. 25 Jun 1865.
Alvin B., b. 25 Jun 1865 Brewer ME.

Sources: Brewer ME census 1850, 1860, 1870. VR Brewer ME, SA/MA.

296. **EBEN$^{6}$ SAWYER** [see 144], b. 1828 Harrington ME, d. 30 Aug 1863 Milbridge ME, m.(1) 22 Nov 1852 Caroline Ray, b. 5 Dec 1827 d. 5 Nov 1853; m.(2) 4 Aug 1855 Martha H. Dyer of Milbridge ME, b. Apr 1830 d. 18 Aug 1902, dau. Asa and Sallie (Yeaton) Dyer. Carpenter.

James R., b. 12 Sep 1853, d. 26 Jul 1854.
Caroline, b. 1857, m.(I) 21 Jan 1878 Raymond Gay.
463 Asa D.$^{7}$,1859-1901.
Fred A., b. Oct 1860 Milbridge ME, d. 18 Oct 1910 Lubec ME, m. Lettie M. Rich, b. ?. Carpenter. In Bangor ME. CH: Mabel Rich, b. 27 Jul 1889; Marjorie Frances, b. 12 May 1892.

Sources: Milbridge ME census 1850, 1860. VR Ellsworth ME, Bangor ME, SA/ME.

297. **PHILO L.$^{6}$ SAWYER** [see 144], b. Jan 1830 Steuben ME, d. 1908 Milbridge ME, m.(1) 31 Oct 1852 Milbridge ME Sarah H. Robinson, b. 1834 d. 1862; m.(2) 16 Mar 1864 Emma W. Farnsworth of Addison ME, b. Dec 1843 d. 11 Dec 1910 Milbridge ME. Mariner. He bur. Evergreen Cem., Milbridge ME.

Raymond, b. 1856 Milbridge ME.
Sarah, b. 1864.
Elinor, b. 1867.
Maude L., b. 4 Aug 1873.

Sources: Milbridge ME census 1860, 1880. ME 1880 census index. VR SA/ME. M5.

298. **JOSEPH WARREN$^{6}$ SAWYER** [see 146], b. 26 Nov 1818 Harrington ME, d. 11 Jan 1898 Milbridge ME, m. Mary J. Wallace of Milbridge ME, b. 26 Nov 1822 d. 7 Jan 1882. Sea captain.

Matilda, b. 14 Jul 1846, d. 1925, m.(I) 13 Jul 1863 George R. Smith.
464 Warren$^{7}$, 1850-1914.
Janette, b. 7 Sep 1852, d. 27 Jan 1899, m. 19 Jul 1884 Edwin L. Wallace.
Augustus, b. Sep 1853, d. 3 Mar 1854.
Emma G., b. 1855, d. 7 Jan 1882, m. 24 Aug 1878 Edwin L. Wallace.
Martha N., b. 2 Oct 1857, d. 5 Oct 1877, unm.
Arthur, b. 28 Dec 1860 Milbridge ME, d. 20 Jun 1911.
465 Elmer Eben$^{7}$, 1862-1917.
466 Alonzo$^{7}$, 1864-1939.

Sources: Milbridge ME census 1850. VR SA/ME. M5, A38.

299. **WILLIAM ROBERTS$^{6}$ SAWYER** [see 146], b. 22 Dec 1821 Harrington ME, d. 16 Jul 1887, m. 11 Nov 1844 Lucy A. Gay, b. 5 Oct 1826 d. 25 Apr 1902. Sea captain.

Theresa R., b. 8 Nov 1846, d. 31 Dec 1911, m.(I) 25 Aug 1875 Handy Hinkley.

Harriet V., b. 29 Dec 1846, d. 4 Feb 1884, m. 4 May 1867 Frank M. Hopkins.
Irving E., b. 1851 Milbridge ME, d. lost at sea 26 Feb 1879, m. 10 Jun 1876 Milbridge ME Ida B. Allen of Gouldsboro ME, b. ?. CH: Geneva, b. 1878.
Willis L., b. 10 Jun 1857 Milbridge ME, d. 4 Nov 1875.
467 George A.[7], 1859-1936.
Nellie, b. 1864.
Sources: Milbridge ME census 1850. M5, Theodora Hoyt Sawyer rec.

300. **STILLMAN D.[6] SAWYER** [see 146], b. Dec 1822 Harrington ME, d. 31 May 1854 Milbridge ME, m. 19 Dec 1844 Nancy V. Ray of Milbridge ME, b. 1 Feb 1826 d. 7 Mar 1862, dau. William and Sophia (Collins) Ray. Sea captain.
468 George Stillman[7], 1845-1893.
469 Gustavus[7], 1848-1923.
Josephine, b. Aug 1851, d. 13 Apr 1852.
Sources: Milbridge ME census 1850. VR Milbridge ME, Harrington ME. M5.

301. **EMERY W.[6] SAWYER** [see 146], b. 20 Nov 1825 Harrington ME, d. 3 Sep 1883 Milbridge ME, m. 24 Oct 1851 Milbridge ME Phebe Turner of Milbridge ME, b. 16 Aug 1833 d. 17 Feb 1911, dau. Solon and Sarah (Pinkham) Turner. Justice of the Peace. Patented a washing machine 1866. W/son Horace 1880.
470 Edgar E.[7], 1853-1892.
471 Horace French[7], 1854-1937.
Eugene, b. 3 Oct 1857 Milbridge ME, d. 3 Sep 1883.
Susan, b. 16 Aug 1859, d. 19 Feb 1891, m. Lewis Todd.
472 Charles Turner[7], 1863-1901.
Sources: Milbridge ME census 1850. ME 1880 census index. VR SA/ME. M5, D51.

302. **FRANKLIN[6] SAWYER** [see 146], b. 29 Aug 1830 Harrington ME, d. 3 Dec 1895 Milbridge ME, m.(I) 29 Jun 1852 Susan C. Wood, b. 20 Apr 1832 d. 16 Jan 1895. Mariner.
473 Frank W.[7], 1853-1921.
Helen C., b. 1856, m. 24 Oct 1880 Augustus H. Wallace.
Sources: Milbridge ME census 1860. VR Milbridge ME, SA/ME. M5.

303 **DAVID[6] SAWYER** [see 146], b. 23 Oct 1833 Harrington ME, d. 26 Jul 1895 Milbridge ME, m. 13 May 1858 Milbridge ME Henrietta Foster of Milbridge ME, b. 27 Feb 1843 d. 13 Sep 1901, dau. Henry and Ann (Sloan) Foster. Sea captain.
Alice E., b. 1862.
Nellie G., b. 1864, m. 8 Dec 1885 James H. Means.
Etta, b. 16 Mar 1867, m. 14 Mar 1888 Lester Strout.
Henry J., b. 17 Aug 1870, d. 27 May 1897.
Mark, b. 1872 Milbridge ME.
Grace A., b. 27 Apr 1874.
Eva J., b. 12 May 1877.
Sources: Milbridge ME census 1870, 1880. ME 1880 census index. VR Milbridge ME, SA/ME. P43.

304. **JOSIAH HANDY[6] SAWYER** [see 147], b. 10 Feb 1825 Cape Elizabeth ME, m.(1) (I) 22 Aug 1847 Elizabeth W. Mitchell, b. ?; m.(2) 26 Mar 1851 Leonice N. Hinkley of Addison ME, b. 15 Jan 1839 d. 20 Feb 1914.
Eva Jane, b. 21 Aug 1860, d. 8 Oct 1933, m. Chester Huntley.

George A., b. 9 Sep 1863 Jonesboro ME, d. 31 May 1913 Jonesport ME, m. 12 Dec 1896 Columbia Falls ME Elvira E. Steele of Addison ME, b. Jan 1865, dau. Alvin and Elvira (Leighton) Steele. He bur. in Jonesport ME. CH: Jessie, b. Feb 1895.

Mary E., b. 1868, m. John H. Connors.

474 James Winslow[7], 1872-1948.

Lydia, b. 1874, d. 6 Mar 1891.

Ida B., b. 24 Sep 1875, m. Arthur C. Reed.

Sources: Jonesboro ME census 1850. VR SA/ME. Doralies Sawyer rec.

305. **EDMUND CHANDLER[6] SAWYER** [see 148], b. 29 Jan 1809 Chebeaque Isle ME, d. 25 Apr 1881, m. Nancy Handley of Harpswell ME, b. 1812 d. 22 Oct 1882. S/land on Chebeaque Isle ME to brother Jacob 1847.

475 Joseph S.[7], b. 1837.

476 Solomon[7], 1839-1896.

Mary Ann, b. 1842, d. 23 Nov 1865.

Freeman, b. 19 Jul 1844, d. 30 Jul 1863.

Stillman, b. 19 Jul 1844 Cumberland ME, m. Hattie D._____, b. 1853. Mariner.

477 George E.[7], b. 1846.

Sarah E., b. ca. 1856.

Sources: Cumberland ME census 1840, 1850. Yarmouth ME census 1870. VR North Yarmouth ME, Cumberland ME, SA/ME. R10a.

306. **JACOB E.[6] SAWYER** [see 148], b. 14 Sep 1825 Chebeaque Island ME, d. 22 Jan 1887, m. 23 Dec 1847 Sarah Hamilton of Chebeaque Island ME, b. 17 Sep 1824 d. 5 Apr 1889. Mariner. B/S/land 1842-1870.

478 Calvin Seavey[7], b. 1850.

Smith Daniel, b. 10 Apr 1853 Cumberland ME, d. 16 Apr 1918 Yarmouth ME, m. Ada F._____, b. ?. Steamboat captain. CH: Florence E., b. 1880.

Serena Ann, b. 26 Apr 1855, d. 6 Oct 1873, m. _____ Graves.

Georgia A., b. 5 May 1860, m. _____ Merrill.

Sources: Cumberland ME census 1850. Yarmouth ME census 1870, 1880. ME 1880 census index. VR SA/ME. R10a.

307. **ABNER J.[6] SAWYER** [see 151], b. 4 Sep 1815 Portland ME, m.(1) (I) 20 Oct 1838 Sophia P. Gilham of Harpswell ME, b. ?; m.(2) 23 Aug 1853 Medford MA Mary Pray of Augusta ME, b. 1810, dau. Edmund Pray. Shipwright.

George, b. 14 Mar 1840 Portland ME. In Medford MA.

Almira, b. 17 Mar 1842.

William, b. 6 Apr 1844 Portland ME. In Medford MA.

Mary A., b. 17 Nov 1846.

Abner A., b. Feb 1849 Portland ME, d. 20 Sep 1851 Medford MA.

Ann M. K., b. 11 Jan 1851.

Sources: Portland ME census 1840.Medford MA census 1850. VR Medford MA, SA/MA.

308. **SEWALL BROWN[6] SAWYER** [see 152], b. 1817 Milbridge ME, m. 19 Sep 1840 Martha J. Stover, b. ?. In Pownal ME, Old Town ME.

479 Charles Henry[7],1840-1911.

Enos, b. 4 Oct 1845 Old Town ME.

480 Horatio M.[7], 1860-1918.

Sources: Old Town ME census 1850. LaGrange ME census 1880. ME 1880 census index. VR Old Town ME, Milbridge ME, SA/ME.

309. **ENOS$^6$ SAWYER** [see 152], b. 28 Aug 1827 Pownal ME, d. 13 Feb 1907 Howland ME, m.(I) 17 Aug 1850 Old Town ME Frances A. Scribner of Jackson ME, b. 23 Aug 1832 d. 24 Mar 1911, dau. James Scribner. In Old Town ME 1850, Stillwater ME 1853, Howland ME 1866. Civil War. He bur. in La Grange ME.

George W., b. 1852 Old Town ME, m. Lottie J. Pearson, b. ?. In Stillwater ME, Howland ME.
Lucy Etta, b. 27 Jun 1853, d. 16 Oct 1918, m. Lewis Spaulding.
Edwin E., b. 1856 Stillwater ME, m. Gertrude Brown, b. ?. In Howland ME.
William (Phileman), b. 1857, m. Angie Brooks, b. ?.
481 Lester Franklin$^7$, b. 1859.
Herbert B., b. 1865, d. 1871.
482 Enos$^7$, 1866-1953.
Elizabeth, b. 1868, d. 1871.
Clara L., b. 22 Feb 1869, m. Elijah Smart.
Lovina Jane, b. 10 Mar 1871, m. Harry D. Smart.
Mary F., b. 24 Aug 1874, d. 1890.
Elisha, b. 2 Jul 1877, m. Blanche M. Holmes, b. ?.

Sources: Old Town Me census 1850. Howland ME census 1880. ME 1880 census index. VR Old Town ME, SA/ME. M7A.

310. **JOSEPH D.$^6$ SAWYER** [see 153], b. 1832 Pownal ME, d. 26 Sep 1894 Bangor ME, m.(I) 20 Jan 1855 Old Town ME Jane David of Old Town ME, b. 1838. In Orono ME 1850, Berlin NH 1860. Civil War.

Frederick L., b. 1856 Orono ME, m. 18 Jan 1879 Old Town ME Mary F. Ayers, b. 1858, dau. B_____ B. Ayers. Millman.
George A., b. 1858 Orono ME. In Berlin NH 1860.
Alvin M., b. 1863.
Myrtle, b. 1865.
Mildred, b. 1869.
Grace, b. 1871.

Sources: Orono ME census 1850. Berlin NH census 1860. Old Town ME census 1880. ME 1880 census index. VR Old Town ME, Bangor ME, SA/ME. M7A.

311. **HORACE C.$^6$ SAWYER** [see 153], b. 19 Nov 1834 Pownal ME, d. 17 Jul 1902 Lancaster NH, m.(1) 3 Nov 1855 Milan ME Julia F. Twitchell of Rhode Island, b. 1837; m.(2) Josephine M. Gilson of Norway (Europe), b. 1839 d. 23 Apr 1921 Portland ME, dau. John and Ingeborg (Oleson) Gilson. In Orono ME, Berlin NH, Columbia NH.

Serena E., b. 1860.
Althea L., b. 1862, m. 14 Mar 1888 Everett Reede.
Minnie G., b. Mar 1877.
Ozman Henry, b. Jun 1880 Berlin NH.

Sources: Berlin NH census 1860, 1880.

312, **ARTHUR G.$^6$ SAWYER** [see 153], b. 20 Oct 1843 Pownal ME, d. 3 Oct 1917 Madison ME, m. 19 Jan 1869 Old Town ME Clara E. Gray, b. 15 Oct 1845 d. 18 Jan 1917, dau. Levi and Margaret (Grant) Gray. Millman.

483 Harry N., b. ca. 1872.

Sources: Berlin NH census 1860. Upper Stillwater ME 1880. ME 1880 census index. VR Old Town ME, SA/ME.

313. **JAMES$^6$ SAWYER** [see 154], b. 3 Dec 1803 Gloucester MA, m. 10 May 1835 Abigail Hotchkiss, b. 1810 d. 26 Jan 1858, dau. Parker and Abigail Hotchkiss. Sailmaker. In Gloucester MA 1850.

Charles W., b. 5 May 1836, d. 14 Jul 1853 Gloucester MA, unm.
Caroline, b. 1838.

Sources: Gloucester MA census 1850. VR Gloucester MA, SA/MA.

314. **WILLIAM MORGAN$^6$ SAWYER** [see 154], b. 14 Oct 1805 Gloucester MA, d. 11 Dec 1845 No. Yarmouth ME, m. 5 Dec 1830 Esther Corliss of No. Yarmouth ME, b. ?, dau. Ebenezer Corliss.

Lydia Ann, b. 18 Oct 1831, d. 9 Apr 1856 Roxbury MA.
Loring Austin, b. Mar 1833 No. Yarmouth ME.
Warren Thaxter, b. Apr 1835, d. 1839.
Charles, b. 2 Sep 1839 No. Yarmouth ME.
Annie M., b. 10 May 1844, m. 9 Feb 1867 Brighton MA Mark Greenleaf.

Sources: VR Gloucester MA, No. Yarmouth ME, SA/MA.

315. **CHARLES$^6$ SAWYER** [see 154], b. 7 Feb 1811 Gloucester MA, m.(1) 30 Dec 1843 Gloucester MA Ellen M. Barrett of Gloucester MA, b. 25 Aug 1824; m.(2) 19 Nov 1871 Gloucester MA Margaret McLew of Nova Scotia, Canada, dau. Daniel and Christiana McLew. Trader, fisherman, saloonkeeper.

Clemina B., b. 25 Jul 1844, m. 4 Oct 1863 Gloucester MA George Fears.
Son, b. 6 Jul 1845.
Helen A., b. 1846, m. 30 Mar 1869 Foxboro MA Julius W. Leonard.
484 Charles Warren$^7$, b. 1854.

Sources: Gloucester MA census 1850. VR Gloucester MA, SA/MA.

316. **ROBERT$^6$ SAWYER** [see 155], b. 11 Mar 1822 Gloucester MA, m. 25 Jun 1844 Gloucester MA Sarah E. Ayers of Gloucester MA, b. 1825. Fisherman.

Emma L., b. 9 Jul 1845, m. 16 Nov 1866 Gloucester MA John H. Ingersoll.
Charles, b. 30 Aug 1846.
John F., b. 27 Apr 1853.

Sources: Gloucester MA census 1850. VR Gloucester MA, SA/MA.

317. **DAVID$^6$ SAWYER** [see 155], b. 10 Mar 1828 Gloucester MA, m. 30 Dec 1858 Gloucester MA Maria Whitman of Nova Scotia, Canada, b. 1836, dau. George and Margaret Whitman. Fisherman, teamster.

Jennie W. b. 12 Sep 1859.
George F. Wonson, b. 26 Jan 1861, m. Agnes Worthysake of Nova Scotia, Canada, b. ?. Butcher. CH: Maria Elizabeth, b. 6 Mar 1892.
Robert S., b. 11 Mar 1862 Gloucester MA, m. 8 Dec 1895 Gloucester MA Grace M. Godet of Nova Scotia, Canada, b. 1876, dau. John and Mary J. (Mallett) Godet.
485 William H.$^7$, b. 1863.
James F. W., b. 20 Apr 1866.
486 Austin B.$^7$, b. ca. 1868.
Alice W., b. 15 Mar 1870.
Daughter, b. 30 Oct 1872.

Sources: Gloucester MA census 1850. VR SA/MA.

318. **AARON I.$^6$ SAWYER** [see 155], b. 29 Aug 1830 Gloucester MA, m. 9 Jan 1855 Gloucester MA Hannah Butler of Chelsea MA, b. 1836, dau. Richard Butler. Mariner.

Richard F., b. 20 Apr 1856.
Meina, b. 13 Sep 1857, m. 24 Feb 1876 Gloucester MA Fitz Hinkley.
George T., b. 12 Dec 1859, d.y.
Ella Florence, b. 25 Dec 1861.
487 Charles H.$^7$, b. ca. 1866.
488 George A.$^7$, b. 1868.
Vestie G., 25 Mar 1877.

Sources: Gloucester MA census 1850. VR Gloucester MA, SA/MA. Frank Sawyer rec.

319. **GEORGE WASHINGTON$^6$ SAWYER** [see 155], b. 29 Aug 1839 Gloucester MA, m. Gloucester MA Josephine Cross of Rockport MA, b. 1847, dau. Joseph and Esther Cross. Mariner. In Rockport MA.

Edward S., b. 6 Jan 1866.
Etta F., b. 19 Jul 1868, m. 20 Apr 1886 Gloucester MA James E. Lovett.
Herbert Everett, b. 16 Mar 1871.
Forest, b. 23 May 1877.
George R., b. 13 Oct 1881.

Sources: VR Gloucester MA, SA/MA.

320. **JOSEPH$^6$ SAWYER** [see 156], b. 22 Oct 1823 Chelsea MA, d. 27 May 1901, m. 10 Jun 1847 Chelsea MA Anna Maria Dillaway, b. 3 Apr 1823. Merchant.

489 Joseph Dillaway$^7$, b. 1849.
490 Arthur Wilkinson$^7$, 1851-1917.
Mary, b. 12 Nov 1853, m. 16 Oct 1879 Boston MA Franklin B. Rogers.
Walter Lawrence, b. 24 Oct 1855 Boston MA, d. 1905, m. 11 May 1887 Boston MA Lizzie E. (Stavell) Farless of Watertown MA, b. 1862, dau. Samuel and Jennie Stavell.
Isabel, b. 1867, d. 1901, m. 9 Nov 1887 Boston MA Lawrence Miller.

Sources: Boston MA census 1850. VR Chelsea MA, SA/MA.

321. **CHARLES$^6$ SAWYER** [see 157], b. 15 Nov 1813 Gloucester MA, d. 1867, m. 1 Jul 1838 Newburyport MA Almira W. Hotchkiss of Newburyport MA, b. 1814 d. 1885. Merchant. He bur. in Oak Grove Cem., Gloucester MA.

Charles A., b. 1839 Gloucester MA, d. 1894 Gloucester MA, m. 27 Feb 1869 Gloucester MA Lillie M. Haskell of Manchester MA, b. 1849, dau. Henry Haskell. He bur. in Gloucester MA. CH: Mabel F., 22 Aug 1869.
Samuel C. Jones, b. Sep 1841, d. Mar 1842.
Samuel Jones, b. 6 Jan 1844 Gloucester MA, d. 1900. He bur. in Gloucester MA.
Frederick H., b. 1846 Gloucester MA, d. 1910 Gloucester MA, m.(1) 6 Aug 1883 Portland ME Winnifred S. Smith of Chelsea MA, b. ?; m.(2) 19 Jan 1892 Gloucester MA (div. 1 Apr 1909) Adelia Etta Smith, b. 1872, dau. Ariel A. and Maria (Roberts) Smith. CH: Agnes Trask, b. 19 Feb 1893. In Rochester NH. Purser. He bur.in Gloucester MA.
Amy C., b. 15 Mar 1848, d. 19 Nov 1853 Gloucester MA.
Lillian M., b. 1849, d. 1932.
Agnes Hunt, b. 13 Dec 1850, m. 1 May 1873 Gloucester MA Abbott Coffin.

Sources: Gloucester MA census 1850. VR Newburyport MA, Gloucester MA, SA/MA. N6.

322. **JOSEPH M.[6] SAWYER** [see 158], b. 1842 New Gloucester ME, m.(1) 5 Jan 1865 No. Yarmouth ME Almira B. Ryder, b. 1847; m.(2) Georgia Plummer, b. ?.

Cora B., b. 17 Mar 1865.
Llewella, b. 15 Apr 1866.
William, b. 1867 New Gloucester ME.
Olive M., b. 8 Aug 1870, m. 26 April 1888 Gorham NH Granville Hawkes.
Josephine Pearl, b. 27 Apr 1883, m. 4 Dec 1897 Gorham NH Myron L. Pickett.

Sources: New Gloucester ME census 1870. VR New Gloucester ME, SA/ME. N6.

## SEVENTH GENERATION

323. **FERNALD J.[7] SAWYER** [see 159], b. 21 Jul 1841 Harrison ME, d. 18 Mar 1912 Norway ME, m. 28 Jun 1871 Lowell MA Mary E. Gilman of Newmarket NH, b. 26 Dec 1841 d. 24 Jan 1921, dau. Lycurgus G. and Rhoda (Wiggins) Gilman. S/land in Otisfield.

Ernest F., b. 30 Jan 1874, d. 12 Aug 1874.
David Fernald, b. 12 Aug 1875 Otisfield ME, d. 27 May 1945, m. Susan A. Hall, b. ?. In Gray ME.
Della M., b. 4 Oct 1878, d. 14 May 1887.

Sources: Otisfield ME census 1880. ME 1880 census index. VR Otisfield ME, SA/ME, SA/MA. S67, R10a.

324. **DAVID E.[7] SAWYER** [see 160], b. 21 Nov 1840 Gorham ME, m. Madeline Hamilton of Missouri, b. 1841. Teacher. In Gorham ME, No. Yarmouth ME.

George H., b. 1867 No. Yarmouth ME.
Martha A., b. 1868.
Charles, b. 1870 No. Yarmouth ME.
Mary F., b. 9 Sep 1875.

Sources: VR No. Yarmouth ME. B74.

325. **GEORGE L.[7] SAWYER** [see 160], b. 13 Jun 1844 Harrison ME, d. 19 Dec 1921 No. Yarmouth ME, m. Harriet M. True of No. Yarmouth ME, b. 1 Sep 1852 d. 19 Dec 1921, dau. Thomas and Rachel (Thomas) True. Farmer. In Westbrook ME, No. Yarmouth ME. He bur. in Pine Grove Cem., No. Yarmouth ME.

Miles, b. 18 May 1872 No. Yarmouth ME, d. 22 Dec 1917.
Fred L., b. 22 Jun 1878, d. 6 Apr 1909.
H. Blanche, b. May 1880, d. 1955.
Harriet B., b. Jan 1882, d. 1921.
Georgia M., b. Jun 1883 North Yarmouth ME.
Frank Luce, b. 26 Mar 1888, d. 12 Dec 1897.

Sources: North Yarmouth ME census 1880. ME 1880 census index. VR SA/ME. R10a, M5, B74.

326. **DANIEL MILLARD[7] SAWYER** [see 160], b. 25 Feb 1856 Gorham ME, m. 22 Dec 1880 Portland ME Jennie M. Cranton of New Brunswick, Canada, b. ?, dau. Dana and Sarah (Tingly) Cranton. In Portland ME, Westbrook ME, Deering ME.

Harry B., b. Oct 1882.
Frederick L., b. 13 Jun 1883.
Edith L., b. Sep 1885.
Wilbur C., b. 16 Jan 1898.

Sources: VR SA/ME. B74.

327. **JOHN RICH$^{7}$ SAWYER** [see 160], b. Jul 1860 Gorham ME, m. 27 Sept 1882 Rosa E. Cameron, b. Nov 1865. Farmer. In Portland ME.

Mildred C., b. 1884.
Philip Brackett, b. 29 Dec 1886.
Estelle F., b. Dec 1890.
Ruth G., b. 21 Jun 1893.

Sources: VR SA/ME. B74.

328. **CUSHMAN JOHN$^{7}$ SAWYER** [see 161], b. 19 Jun 1846 Stoneham ME, d. 14 Nov 1910 Stoneham ME, m. Nellie H. Sterns, b. 28 Jun 1846 d. 9 Sep 1922, dau. William and Betsey (Heald) Stearns.

Elwood B., b. 19 Feb 1870 Stoneham ME, d. 23 Jul 1944 Damariscotta ME, m. Elizabeth Collins, b. ?.
Nellie M., b. ca. 1872, m. _____ McAllister.
Linwood Cushman, b. Nov 1879 Stoneham ME. In Lovell ME.
Carrie S., b. Jul 1889.

Sources: Stoneham ME census 1870, 1880. ME 1880 census index. VR Stoneham ME, Bristol ME, SA/ME.

329. **EDWARD SELDON$^{7}$ SAWYER** [see 164], b. 25 Jan 1847 Lovell ME, m.(1) (I) 2 Oct 1871 Elizabeth O. Hatch of Paris ME, b. 1850; m.(2) Alice _____, b. ?. In Portland ME, Somerville MA.

Edgar, b. ca. 1874 Portland ME.
Nellie, b. 10 Aug 1884 Somerville MA.

Sources: Portland ME census 1880. ME 1880 census index. VR SA/ME, SA/MA. R21.

330. **CHRISTOPHER C. $^{7}$ SAWYER** [see 167], b. Sep 1818 Cornish ME, d. 19 Jun 1898 Porter ME, m. 31 Jul 1853 Buxton ME Betsey C. Webster of Buxton ME, b. 23 Oct 1828, dau. Thomas and Nancy (Cobb) Webster. Farmer, sailor. In Porter ME, Rockport MA. B/S/land in Porter ME 1853-1855.

Amanda P., b. 1854, m.(1) (I) 10 Jul 1882 Alger Parker, m.(2) _____ Stilson.
Mary Ellen, b. 7 Jan 1855, d. 23 Sep 1941, m. Albion Wentworth.
Christopher C., b. 21 Mar 1858 Porter ME, d. 25 Jan 1941 Pownal ME, m. 24 Dec 1881 Hattie A Wilson, b. ?.
491 Rosswell C.$^{8}$, 1861-1916.
William T., b. 1863, m.(1) ?; m.(2) 29 Dec 1823 Rochester NH Annie B. (Hubbard) French of Prince Edward Isle, Canada, b. 1871, dau. George and Eliza (Jery) Hubbard.
492 Sumner Cummings$^{8}$, 1866-1937.
Nancy C., b. 14 Apr 1868, d. 6 Aug 1939, m. 11 Jan 1884 Edwin R. Libby.
Arthur C., b. 17 Mar 1870 Cornish ME, d. 19 Sep 1966 Portland ME, m.(1) 20 Sep 1891 Dover NH Cora Hilton of Biddeford ME, b. 1871, dau. Harry and Abby Hilton; m.(2) 5 Dec 1899 Exeter NH Eva May Hobbs of Haverhill MA, b. 1872, d. 1948. In Haverhill MA, Rockport MA. He bur Linwood Cem., Haverhill MA. No CH.

Sources: Porter ME census 1860, 1870, 1880. ME 1880 census index. VR Porter ME, SA/ME. R10c, M5, Kendal W. Sawyer rec., Karen Sawyer rec.

331. **WILLIAM T.$^{7}$ SAWYER** [see 167], b. 1824 Cornish ME, d. 7 Jul 1904 Porter ME, m.(1) Abigail F. French of Porter ME, b. 5 May 1827 d. 16 Aug 1898; m.(2) Sarah A._____, b. ca. 1828. Cooper. Owned land in Hiram ME. In Porter ME 1850. B/S/land in Porter ME 1851, 1853.

493 Sewall S.$^{8}$, 1846-1892.

494 William Henry[8], 1847-1927.
Ann E., b. 1849, m.(1)_____ French; m.(2) 1880 Charles Tewksbury; m.(3) 1886 Charles Gray.
495 Freeman Wesley[8], 1851-1938.
496 Alphonse[8], 1853-1898.
Sources: Porter ME census 1850, 1860, 1870, 1880. ME 1880 census index. VR Freedom NH, Kezar Falls ME, SA/ME. R10c, Karen Sawyer rec., Kendal W. Sawyer rec.

332. **HENRY H.[7] SAWYER** [see 167], b. 24 Feb 1834 Porter ME, d. 19 May 1909 Porter ME, m. 3 Aug 1857 Johnstown PA, by "Mr. Shanon", Matilda McAteer of Pennsylvania, b. 1840 d. 1923. Farmer. Civil War: Company K, 23d Maine Infantry, 29 Sep 1862-15 Jul 1863. He bur. in Porter ME.
497 Willard Evangeline[8], 1859-1928.
Nemiah T., b. 1861, d. 1864.
Mary R., b. 25 Jan 1868, d. 15 May 1937, m. 16 Apr 1880 John French.
Henry M., b. 2 Nov 1871 Porter ME, d. 22 Mar 1951 Limington ME, m. Alice Blake, b. 20 Jan 1870 d. 4 Nov 1936, dau. Gideon and Cordelia (Staples) Blake. He bur. in No. Limington ME. CH: Vivian E., b. 1891, d. 1941, m. Charles Sawyer.
Clara B., b. 22 Aug 1874 d. 26 Dec 1928, m. 20 Mar 1890 Frank French.
Sources: Porter ME census 1860, 1870, 1880. ME 1880 census index. M5, N6, Obit (Henry H.), Kendal W. Sawyer rec.

333. **EDWARD PAYSON[7] SAWYER** [see 168], b. 24 Mar 1869 Greene ME, d. 2 Feb 1953, m.(1) 27 Jun 1900 Barnet VT Ella Alice Winch of Barnet VT, b. ? d. 1902; m.(2) Marion Littlefield. Salesman.
George Winch, b. 23 Feb 1902, d. 11 Sep 1963, m. 1926 Edith Ford.
Stewart Edward, b. 3 Aug 1910, m. 1937 Ann E. Oldham.
Ashton Parker, b. 2 May 1912, m. Margaret Homans.
Richard Miles, b. 30 Jul 1917, m. Anita Holm.
Sources: D9, Laura E. Sawyer rec.

334. **JOHN MARSHALL[7] SAWYER** [see 168], b. 14 Aug 1874 Greene ME, d. 2 Oct 1946, m. 1 Jul 1905 Greene ME Annie M. Hill of Greene ME, b. 1 Jun 1880. Went to Montana ca. 1912.
Robert Hill, b. 1906, d. 1959, m. Ivy Beckley.
Truth, b. 1907, m. Ward Henderson.
Barbara, b. 1910, m. Clarence Nelson.
June, b. 1913, m. Clifford Wallace.
Sources: M60, D6, D9, Laura E. Sawyer rec.

335. **HENRY STANTON[7] SAWYER** [see 169], b. 9 Jan 1863 Garland ME, d. 1 Jul 1966, m. 21 Nov 1898 Garland ME Florence E. Cole of Corinna ME, b. 25 Dec 1873, d. 19 Jul 1962, dau. Charles A. and Martha (Greeley) Cole.
Thelma I, b. 20 Jun 1900, d. 10 Jul 1977, m. Oliver La France. Went to Massachusetts.
Charles Reuben, b. 22 Dec 1902, d. 14 Dec 1909.
Guy Stanton, b. 23 Apr 1904, d. 8 Jul 1988, m. 14 Jan 1928 Ruth M. Dudley.
Kenneth Sherwood, b. 4 Feb 1908, d. 14 Mar 1959, m. Helen Peavey.
Warren Harding, b. 12 Feb 1922, d. 7 Apr 1969, m. 26 Jun 1943 Anita Gilbert.
Sources: VR SA/ME. C76, Guy S. Sawyer rec.

336. **THOMAS JAMES[7] SAWYER** [see 171], b. 2 Sep 1826 Porter ME, d. 5 Mar 1896 Boston MA hospital, m. 1 Feb 1852 Rutland VT Eliza J. Sawyer, b. 10 Jan 1831, d. 25 Nov 1919, dau. Michael and Margery (Morton) Sawyer. Machinist. Civil War: Captain, Company G, 5th Maine Regiment. In Portland ME, Waterville ME.

Ellen Estella, b. 23 Apr 1852, m. 1 Feb 1872 E. Madison ME Lucius L. Morrison.
Son, b. 23 Apr 1854, d.y.
Abbie F., b. 2 Jan 1856, m. D_____ M. Scribner. Went to Minnesota.
James Morton Gray, b. 3 Sep 1871 Waterville ME, m. 3 Dec 1892 Portland ME Hattie M. Annis of Bangor ME, b.?. Lineman.

Sources: VR Portland ME, SA/ME. M53, Obit.

337. **MELVILLE HENRY[7] SAWYER** [see 172], b. 24 Apr 1843 Limington ME, d. 22 May 1899 Limington ME, m.(I) 18 Jan 1881 Caroline Whitney, b. 21 Jun 1857 d. 19 May 1903. He bur. in No. Limington ME.

498 Guy Emery[8], 1882-1938.
Margery Louise, b. ?, m. Harris P. Ilsley of Limington ME.
Marita, b. ?, unm.
More children.

Sources: VR SA/ME. T6A, N40, L22.

338. **WILLIAM M.[7] SAWYER** [see 173], b. 1837 Phillips ME, d. 1863 Virginia in war, m. 5 Jul 1859 Catherine R. Robinson, b. 1840 d. 1934, dau. Lysander and Jane W. Robinson. Civil War. Millman. Wid. went to Sherman Mills ME.

499 William Asa[8], 1862-1940.

Sources: Buckfield ME census 1860. VR Buckfield ME.

339. **NEWALL H.[7] SAWYER** [see 173], b. 24 Jun 1845 Phillips ME, d. 25 Jul 1912 Madison ME, m. 6 May 1866 Madrid ME Margaret E. Sargent of Madrid ME, b. 30 Apr 1848, dau. Solomon and Alice (Brazier) Sargent. In Madrid ME, Jay Bridge ME.

Flora Augusta, b. 15 Apr 1867.
Andrew N., b. 15 Jun 1869 Madrid ME, m. 9 Jun 1894 Florence Plaisted of Phillips ME, b. ?, dau. Daniel and Mary (Staples) Plaisted. In Madrid ME, Jay Bridge ME.
Adelbert N., b. 8 Mar 1871. In Jay Bridge ME.
Elsie Mary, b. 20 Aug 1875.
Minnie B., b. 20 Jul 1878.
500 Percival B.[8], b. 1883.
Harold C., b. 20 May 1885 Phillips ME, m. 27 Apr 1912 Skowhegan ME Laura (Vigue) Clough of Canada, b. 1878, dau. Ephraim and Lucy (Vigue) Clough. Carpenter.
Ethel A., b. 29 Aug 1888.

Sources: ME 1880 census index. VR Skowhegan ME, SA/ME. S9, G6.

340. **DELBERT N.[7] SAWYER** [see 173], b. Mar 1848 Phillips ME, d. 15 Nov 1875 Standish ME, m. 14 Dec 1872 Standish ME Anna F. Shaw of Standish ME, dau. John Nelson and Almira (Bradley) Shaw. Clothing manufacturer. He. bur. Village Cem., Standish ME.

William A., b. 6 Jun 1874, d. 31 Aug 1922 Augusta ME. Living with Willard E. Thompson in Standish 1880.

Sources: VR SA/ME. F11.

341. **LUTHER S.**[7] **SAWYER** [see 174], b. 11 Jun 1823 Addison ME, d. 29 May 1898 Jonesport ME, m. Lucy A. Drick of Addison ME, b. 1828. Caulker. In Addison Falls ME, Columbia Falls ME.

501 William J.[8], 1850-1917.
502 Walter Preston[8], 1854-1922.

Sources: Addison ME census 1850, 1860. VR SA/ME.

342. **JOSEPH D.**[7] **SAWYER** [see 174], b. 1832 Addison ME, m. Fannie E. Connell of New Brunswick, Canada, b. 1837.

503 Ansel M., 1856-1907.
Arminda, b. 1868.
Judson Heath, b. Dec 1870 Addison ME, m.(1) 22 Mar 1900 Jonesboro ME Elvira C. Smith of Jonesboro ME, b. Sep 1864, dau. Albert and Charlotte (Farnsworth) Smith; m.(2) Isabelle Furgeson of Ireland, b. 12 Feb 1871, d. 13 Jun 1919, dau. John F. and Matilda (Sullivan) Furgeson. Jeweler. In Eden ME.

Sources: Addison ME census 1860, 1880. ME 1880 census index. M8.

343. **GEORGE M.**[7] **SAWYER** [see 174], b. 1835 Addison ME, m. Jane McEachran, b. ?. In Steuben ME.

Joseph, b. 12 Oct 1861 Philadelphia (PA?), m. 7 May 1881 Rebecca Huckins of Milbridge ME, b. 19 Apr 1864, dau. Taft C. and Mary (Evans) Huckins. CH: Ida S., b. 13 Mar 1893, d. 14 Dec 1989, m. Herbert Alexander.

Sources: H18, Obit (Ida).

344. **WILLIAM AUGUSTUS**[7] **SAWYER** [see 174], b. Nov 1838 Addison ME, m. Elva R. Aymar of Addison ME, b. Oct 1848, dau. Francis and Emily (Rushbrook) Aymar. Carpenter.

Frank A., b. 1871 Addison ME.
George Y., b. 1873 Addison ME.
Benjamin Perley, b. 3 Dec 1880 Addison ME.
Sarah Aymar, b. 25 Feb 1883.

Sources: Addison ME census 1880. VR SA/ME. Ken Schoonmaker rec.

345. **LEMUEL B.**[7] **SAWYER** [see 176], b. 1824 Addison ME, m. 1 Jan 1853 Boston MA Amelia A. Whittemore of Bangor ME, dau. Otis Whittemore. Carpenter/engineer. In Boston MA 1853, Charlestown MA.

Edward Everett, b. 6 Apr 1853.
Augustus Wilson, b. 20 Aug 1855.
George Albert, b. 25 Jan 1857.
Minnie Adela, b. 21 Mar 1860, m. 29 Oct 1885 Boston Edgar Timson.
Hollis Huniwell, b. 12 Jun 1863 Charlestown MA, m. 16 Jun 1892 Amesbury MA Florence W. Glover of W. Newton MA, b. 1872, dau. Henry and Mary A. Glover. Bookkeeper. In Malden MA. CH: Doris Elizabeth, b. 15 Nov 1893;
Carrie Wass, b. 16 May 1871.

Sources: VR SA/MA.

346. **ENOS D.**[7] **SAWYER** [see 176], b. 9 Feb 1839 Augusta ME, d. 16 Sep 1907 Cambridge MA, m.(1) Adelaide Duron of Calais ME, b. 1842; m.(2) 31 Dec 1890 Cambridge MA Lucy R. (Smith) Duer of Lexington MA, b. Nov 1850, dau. Billings and Martha Smith. In Cambridge MA.

Edward D., b. 1862 Calais ME, m. 4 Sep 1890 Boston MA Dora Wentworth of Jackson NH, b. 1865, dau. Albert R. and Maria C. Wentworth.

Florence M., b. 1871.

William D., b. Dec 1872 Calais ME, m.(1) ?; m.(2) 15 Apr 1921 Portsmouth NH Marion D. Parker of Salem MA, b. 1891, dau. Joseph and Lilla V. (Hill) Parker. Salesman. In Cambridge MA. Both marriages ended in divorce.

Enos Clifford, b. Nov 1898 Cambridge MA.

Sources: VR SA/MA. H88.

347. **CHARLES ADDISON**[7] **SAWYER** [see 177], b. 11 Feb 1878 Steuben ME, d. 19 May 1968, m. 23 Mar 1907 Josie Dunbar of Steuben ME, b. 1889. Both bur. Sawyer Cem., Steuben ME.

Herman Lemuel, b. 28 Mar 1908, d. 28 Apr 1993, m. Bessie L. Rhodes.

Mary Abigail, b. 8 Dec 1912, m. _____ DeGraff of Alabama.

Charles Lloyd, b. 8 Aug 1920, d. 12 Jun 1990, m. Janet Beardsley.

Sources: Family Bible of Charles L. Sawyer, Obit (Charles L., Herman L.), M5.

348. **BENJAMIN**[7] **SAWYER** [see 179], b. 15 Mar 1813 Baldwin ME, d. 8 Apr 1884 Baldwin ME, m. 6 Jul 1843 Baldwin ME Hannah W. Davis of Baldwin, b. 7 Jul 1820 d. 10 Oct 1893, dau. Lot and Susan (Larrabee) Davis. Selectman for Baldwin ME 1852. B/S/land. He bur. on Emery Farm, Baldwin ME.

Onville, b. 4 May 1844 Baldwin ME, d. 9 Mar 1898 Baldwin ME, m.(1) 14 Jan 1871 Hattie Graffam of Gorham ME, b. ca. 1841 d. 20 Sep 1874; m.(2) (I) 9 Feb 1880 Mary E. (Goodwin) Schermerhorn of Baldwin ME, b. 1850 d. 6 May 1923. CH: Harriet, b. 12 Sep 1880, d. 21 Oct 1952, m.(1) William Archibald, m.(2) Douglass Darrows.

Elwyn F., b. 23 Mar 1847 Baldwin ME, d. 13 Mar 1914 Steep Falls ME, m. 24 Sep 1873 Conway NH Addie L. Mayo of No. Windham ME, b. 24 Sep 1849 d. 27 May 1912, dau. William D. and Eunice (Marean) Mayo. CH: Mabel G., b. 1875 d. 1946.

Henry Wilton, b. 4 Jul 1850, d. 14 Jun 1863.

Wilbur Davis, b. 13 Apr 1852 Baldwin ME, d. 31 Jan 1922 No. Conway NH, m. 5 Nov 1874 Conway NH Abbie C. Larrabee of Standish ME, b. 17 Nov 1857 Standish ME d. 21 Dec 1929, dau. Freeman and Mary (White) Larrabee. Railroad trackman. CH: Mary F., b. 26 Aug 1876, d. 18 Jan 1894; Helen R. b. 10 Sep 1881, m. Willard Russell; Louise, b. 8 Jul 1891.

Frank G., b. 30 Sep 1854, d. 7 May 1898.

Arthur F., b. 9 Aug 1856, d. 14 Jan 1921.

Sources: Standish ME census 1880. VR Baldwin ME, SA/ME, SA/NH. R17, M5, Obit.

349. **CHRISTOPHER DYER**[7] **SAWYER** [see 179], b. 6 Mar 1815 Baldwin ME, d. 25 Sep 1867 Baldwin ME, m. 25 Oct 1838 Limington ME Catherine Marr of Limington ME, b. Feb 1815 d. 13 Mar 1899, dau. William P. and Anna (Sawyer) Marr. Selectman for Baldwin ME 1846. Received land from father 1859.

Susan, b. 11 Apr 1840, d. 5 Jan 1911, m. 30 Dec 1863 Luther S. McCorisin.

504 Charles Franklin[8], 1842-1910.

Joanna Dyer, b. 10 Nov 1845, d. 12 Aug 1847.

John Elmore, b. 31 Nov 1848 Baldwin ME, d. Jun 1869.

Mary C., b. 20 Aug 1850, d. 2 Jul 1851.

Mary A., b. ?, m. 22 May 1870 Baldwin ME John Drost.

Josephine, b. 1856, d. 2 Feb 1865.

Wallace L., b. 1860 Baldwin ME, d. 6 Feb 1892, m. 31 Dec 1884 No. Baldwin ME Susan J. Grace of Baldwin ME, b. ?, dau. Aaron and Lucinda (Sanborn) Grace. Wid. m. 20

Apr 1898 Leander Rounds. CH: Addie J., b. 16 Dec 1886, d. 29 Jan 1974, m. Gilman P. Lewis; Henry W., b. 25 Mar 1889, d. 19 Jun 1892.

Sources: Baldwin ME census 1840, 1850. VR Baldwin ME, SA/ME. R10a, T6A, C62, Robert L. Taylor rec.

350. **THOMAS JEFFERSON⁷ SAWYER** [see 180], b. 3 Oct 1815 Baldwin ME, m. Deborah Elizabeth Hall.

Edwin Forrest, b. 16 May 1849 Cambridge MA, m.(1) 4 Mar 1873 Cambridge MA Susan P. Monroe of Swanzey MA, b. 1855, dau. Albert and Kezia Monroe; m. (2) 1912 Mabel Olmstead, b. ?.

Sources: VR SA/MA.

351. **STEPHEN LITTLE⁷ SAWYER** [see 181], b. 16 Aug 1817 Portland ME, d. 12 May 1860 Boston MA, m.(1) 18 May 1846 Portland ME Annie M. Pritchard, b. 1820 d. 23 Mar 1855, dau. John and Margaret (Hammond) Pritchard; m.(2) 18 Dec 1856 Boston MA Lydia A. Curtin of Boston MA, b. 1839, dau. Daniel Curtin.

Russell, b. 11 Apr 1847 Boston MA, d. 26 Dec 1902 Minneapolis MN, m. 1870 Elizabeth Stewart of Indiana, b. 1854 d. 1931, dau. John H. and Lucinda (Nevitt) Stewart. CH: Ann, b. 1872, m. 1899 Charles J. Geigerdarumer; Lucy P., b. 4 Oct 1873, m. 4 Sep 1894 William A. Thompson.

Lucy Pritchard, b. 1 Feb 1849, d. 14 May 1854.

Frances Walworth, b.4 Oct 1858, m.1 Jan 1896 Clinton G. Stickncy.

Anna Folsom, b. 10 May 1861, d. 25 Nov 1883.

Sources: VR Portland ME, SA/MA. Lucy P. Thompson rec.

352. **NATHAN⁷ SAWYER** [see 181], b. 16 Aug 1819 Portland ME, d. 24 Feb 1889, m. 16 Dec 1841 Emma Henry of Worcester MA, b. 6 Jul 1819 d. 23 Apr 1896. Nathan and son Henry were printers at 70 State Street, Boston MA 1890.

505 Henry Nathan⁸,1842-1912.

Harris Batchelder, b. 27 Oct 1844, d. 3 Sep 1847.

George Edward, b. 6 Nov 1847, d. 21 Apr 1864.

Albert Webster, b. 18 Jan 1853, d. 2 Mar 1885. Went west.

Sources: Boston MA census 1850. VR SA/MA. M5, N5, Lucy P. Thompson rec., Henry Nathan Sawyer rec.

353. **REUBEN S.⁷ SAWYER** [see 181], b. 25 Feb 1822 Portland ME, d. 7 Nov 1863 Detroit ME, m. 1 Jun 1847 Portland ME Anna L. Lincoln, b. 17 Jan 1820 d. 7 May 1865, dau. Royal and Jerusha (Waterman) Lincoln. Civil War: Captain, 3rd Maine Regiment. Bookseller.

Julia P., b. 22 May 1848, m. Daniel H. Towle.

David Tilden Stimson, b. 14 Jul 1851, d. 26 Jul 1859. He bur. in Eastern Cem., Portland ME.

Emma Marie, b. 17 Aug 1853, m. Charles A. Winchester.

Louise H., b. 17 Jan 1854, m.(1) Edward Barrett; m.(2) Charles St. Clair.

Frank Lincoln, b. 28 Nov 1859, d. 13 Sep 1862.

Reuben Frank, b. 29 Jan 1864 Bath ME, unm in 1911. In Portland ME.

Sources: Bath ME census 1850. VR Bath ME. P69, L25, Lucy P. Thompson rec.

354. **HENRY MOSES⁷ SAWYER** [see 182], b. 31 Jul 1825 Bangor ME, m. 4 Mar 1857 Quincy MA Carrie. Emeline Bartlett of Roxbury MA, b. 1835, dau. Abraham and Abigail Bartlett. Salesman. Had a substitute for military service.

George Daws, b. 6 Apr 1863 Quincy MA, m. 17 May 1888 Boston MA Sophia A. Spindler of Roxbury MA, b. ca. 1870, dau. Osmer and Pauline Spindler. CH: Florence May, b. 23 May 1891.

Carrie Ellen, b. 6 Apr 1863, m. 15 Oct 1884 Boston MA Arthur J. Lucas.

Elizabeth Alice, b. 15 Aug 1864, m. 13 Sep 1886 Boston MA Jesse W. Butterfield.

Sources: VR Bangor ME, SA/MA. P19.

355. **JOHN HATHAWAY$^7$ SAWYER** [see 182], b. 15 May 1828 Bangor ME, m. Frances M. Williams, b. ?.

506 Albert E.$^8$, b. ca. 1850.

Sources: VR Bangor ME.

356. **CHARLES HOWARD$^7$ SAWYER** [see 184], b. 8 Aug 1837 Portland ME, d. 8 Aug 1902 Boston MA, m. 9 Sep 1860 Portland ME Louise E. Stevens of Portland ME, b. 20 Nov 1836 d. 6 Apr 1908, dau. Petetiah and Abbie (Adams) Stevens. Lawyer.

507 Fred Howard$^8$, 1861-1898.

508 Walter Sumner$^8$, 1865-1919.

Sources: Portland ME census 1860. VR Portland ME.

357. **NATHAN I.$^7$ SAWYER** [see 185], b. 30 Aug 1843 Cape Elizabeth ME, m. 6 Jan 1881 Boston MA Clara Nute Brooks of Boston MA, b. 22 Oct 1860 d. 16 Dec 1942, dau. Howard W. and Olive Ann (Sawyer) Brooks. Civil War. Farmer.

Nathan H., b. 14 Feb 1886 Cape Elizabeth ME.

Sources: VR Cape Elizabeth ME, SA/MA. C89, M7A, Olive B. Cooper rec.

358. **MELVILLE F.$^7$ SAWYER** [see 186], b. 24 Nov 1840 Cape Elizabeth ME, d. 28 Oct 1907 Portland ME, m. 28 Dec 1870 Portland ME Harriet A. Guilford, b. 1848 d. 1931. Civil War. He bur. in Bayview Cem., So. Portland ME.

Francis Cutter, b. 21 May 1873 Cape Elizabeth ME, d. 1945 Portland ME m. So. Portland ME 26 Jun 1895 Mary A. Richardson of W. Baldwin ME, b. 1872 d. 1951, dau. Edward and Sarah (Chadbourne) Richardson.

Charles E., b. 24 Mar 1875 Cape Elizabeth ME, d. 1939, m. Susan F. Hutchinson, b. 1885 d. 1955. He bur. in Bay View Cem., So. Portland ME.

Melville G., b. 22 Aug 1877 Cape Elizabeth ME.

Minnie A., b. 16 Aug 1880, d. 28 Jan 1881.

Hattie E., b. Feb 1889.

Sources: ME 1880 census index. VR Cape Elizabeth ME, SA/ME. D37, M5, M7A.

359. **FREDERICK T.$^7$ SAWYER** [see 188], b. 1849 Ellsworth ME, m. 30 Oct 1870 New Bedford MA Mary E. Fuller of New Bedford MA, b. 1851, dau. Benjamin and Mary A. Fuller. Teamster.

Frederick C., b. 28 Apr 1871.

Florence E., b. 10 Aug 1873.

Charles S., b. 2 Sep 1875.

Grace A., b. 9 Aug 1880.

Eslah (?) S., b. 28 Sep 1882.

Edith M., b. 7 May 1885.

Annie F., b. 11 Sep 1887.

Helen P., b. 2 Jul 1894.

Sources: VR New Bedford MA, SA/MA.

360. **FREDERICK A.[7] SAWYER** [see 189], b. 12 Jul 1867 Gardiner ME, m.(1) Estelle Jay Moore; m.(2) Lillian _____ of Bangor ME. In Harpswell ME, Bangor ME, Somerville MA 1894.
Margery, b. 12 May 1892.
John A, b. 7 Aug 1893, d.y.
Harold Augustus, b. 21 May 1894.
John A., b. Apr 1897, d. Aug 1897 Harpswell ME.
Sources: VR SA/ME, SA/MA.

361. **THOMAS PENNELL[7] SAWYER** [see 192], b. 21 Jan 1822 Buxton ME, d. 28 Sep 1897, m. 12 Oct 1848 Parsonsfield ME Harriet O. Thompson, b. 1823. Truckman, Carpenter.
509 Frank Leroy[8], 1849-1913.
Lucy E., b. 1858.
Sources: Saco ME census 1850. VR Parsonsfield ME, SA/ME. Joan H. Sawyer rec.

362. **ISAAC DEERING[7] SAWYER** [see 192], b. 11 May 1827 Buxton ME, d. 1864 Gettysburg PA, m. 31 Dec 1859 Buxton ME Mary Jane Sawyer, b. 24 Aug 1822, d. 11 Dec 1899, dau. Ebenezer and Betsey (Knight) Sawyer. Civil War. Note: Mary Jane was declared insane and her father-in-law was appointed her guardian on 6 Sep 1864.
Charles Isaac, b. 1 Nov 1860 Buxton ME, d. 14 Jan 1901. Mentally imcompetent, deaf and dumb.
Sources: Buxton ME census 1850. VR Buxton ME, SA/ME. Y3, P82k, M5.

363. **FREEMAN CHENEY[7] SAWYER** [see 192], b. 12 Mar 1843 Buxton ME, m. 2 Jan 1869 Buxton ME Abbie A. Whitten, b. 1846, dau. Thomas Whitten. Baptised Seth Freeman Cheney.
Herbert F., b. 13 Sep 1870 Buxton ME, m. 1 May 1895 Chelsea MA Clara Augusta Blackmer of New York City, b. 1868, dau. William A. and Letitia (Lamasters) Blackmer. Electrician.
Sources: Saco ME census 1880. ME 1880 census index. VR Buxton ME, SA/ME.

364. **JOHN EMERY[7] SAWYER** [see 193], Dr., b. 24 Dec 1854, d. 9 Jul 1912 Chicago IL, m. 5 Jun 1884 Olive Staples, b. 2 Apr 1860 New Richmond WI d. 17 Apr 1894 St. Paul MN, dau. Silas Staples.
John Emery, b. 7 Mar 1885 Wisconsin, d. 3 May 1961, m. 6 Jul 1915 Louella May Roepken, b. ?.
Marian, b. 20 Jan 1887.
Dorothy, b. 1 Nov 1890, d. 23 Apr 1953, m. 23 Jun 1917 Charles Almer Shay.
Sources: Elliotsville ME census 1860. T11, Delia Libby rec.

365. **NATHAN FREEMAN[7] SAWYER** [see 195], b. 4 Nov 1822 Fryeburg ME, d. 11 Aug 1903 Brooklyn NY, m. Hannah S. Buck of Fryeburg ME, b. 1823. S/land in Bridgton ME 1852.
Albert Frank, b. 24 Mar 1849 Bridgton ME. Went to Pennsylvania.
John Tilson, b. 1856 Bridgton ME. Went to Brooklyn NY.
Sources: Bridgton ME census 1850, 1860. VR Bridgton ME. R10c.

366. **SAMUEL MERRILL[7] SAWYER** [see 195], b. 18 Dec 1825 Fryeburg ME, d. 26 Apr 1881, m.(1) 5 Oct 1846 Ellen F. Freeman, b. 1827 d. 19 Dec 1873; m.(2) Mary J. Hapgood, b. 20 Oct 1825, d. 30 Dec 1915, dau. William and Mary (Harndon) Hapgood. B/S/land in Bridgton ME.
Mary Eliza, b. 7 May 1848, d. 5 Feb 1854.
510 George Austin[8], 1850-1916.

Priscilla Maria, b. 18 Apr 1853, d. 13 Oct 1929, m. John C. Pillsbury.
Frances Ellen, b. 1855, d. 19 Sep 1868.
Mary Susan, b. 1858, m. 5 Mar 1875 Chatham NH Isaac H. Huckins.
Sources: Bridgton ME census 1850, 1860. VR Fryeburg ME, Bridgton ME. R10a.

367. **BENJAMIN FRANKLIN⁷ SAWYER** [see 195], b. 21 Jun 1829 Fryeburg ME, d. 10 Jan 1903 W. Bridgton ME, m.(1) 3 Sep 1854 Rumford ME Abby Bisbee of Bridgton ME, b. 1838 d. 15 Jan 1870; m.(2) 4 Feb 1872 Mary A. Hannon of Island Pond VT, b. Nov 1846. Carriage maker. B/S land Bridgton ME 1855-1862. In Portland ME 1872, Boston MA 1879. He bur. in North Bridgton ME.
Charles D., b. 1857, d. 29 Jul 1859.
Louise, b. ?
Annie L., b. Feb 1872, m. _____ O'Hara.
James David Percival, b. 5 Dec 1874 Portland ME. In Boston MA.
John Hastings, b. 24 Jun 1877 Portland ME. In Boston MA.
511 George Chester⁸, b. 1879.
Sources: Portland ME census 1860. VR Rumford ME, SA/ME, SA/VT. R10a.

368. **STEPHEN EUGENE⁷ SAWYER** [see 196], b. 2 Jul 1853 Sweden ME, d. 14 Mar 1921 Standish ME, m. Delia McLean of Ireland, b. 10 Aug 1868 d. 19 Mar 1921, dau. Thomas McLean. In Standish ME. He bur. in Maplewood Cem., Standish ME.
Mary R., b. Aug 1889.
James Sweat, b. 21 Jul 1892, d. 23 Aug 1949, m. Gertrude F. Morrell, b. 24 Feb 1901. He bur. in Maplewood Cem., Standish ME.
Cynthia A., b. 26 Dec 1894.
Sources: VR SA/ME. M5.

369. **ALBERT G.⁷ SAWYER** [see 197], b. 4 Sep 1842 Buxton ME, d. 28 Mar 1905 Buxton ME, m. 12 Feb 1867 Mary E. Bradbury, of Standish ME, b. Feb 1843 d. 19 Jul 1910. Railroad engineer. He bur. in Tory Hill Cem., Buxton ME.
512 George Mellen⁸,1868-1954.
Carrie M., b. 3 Jun 1879.
Sources: VR SA/ME. M5, E19, Obit.

370. **FRANK DAVIS⁷ SAWYER** [see 198], b. 1852 Sumner ME, m. Fedelia Sawyer of New Portland, b. 11 Jun 1850, dau. William and Emily (Churchill) Sawyer. In Littleton MA 1886.
Nina, b. ca. 1875.
Frank Arthur, b. 4 Dec 1876.
Berkley, b. ca. 1879.
William Victor, b. 23 May 1886.
Eugene Malcolm, b. 19 Feb 1894.
Sources: ME 1880 census index. VR SA/ME, SA/MA.

371. **FRANKLIN⁷ SAWYER** [see 202], b. 23 May 1826 So. Windham ME, d. 16 Apr 1888 Portland ME, m. 2 May 1852 Otisfield ME Mary P. Lombard of Otisfield ME, b. Jan 1827 d. 28 Jul 1887. In Raymond ME, Portland ME. B/S/land in Raymond ME 1843-1860, B/land Casco ME 1860. He bur. in Evergreen Cem., Portland ME.
513 John H.⁸, 1852-1920.
Willis H., b. 10 May 1853 Portland ME, d. 1939 Portland ME, m. Ella Barbour, b. 1869 d. 1944. He bur. in Evergreen Cem, Portland ME.

Clara C., b. 1 Mar 1854.
Gertrude G., b. 5 Jul 1858.
Sources: Raymond ME census 1860. VR Otisfield ME, Raymond ME. R10a, M5.

372. **HAMILTON JOHN⁷ SAWYER** [see 202], b. 9 Feb 1828 South Windham ME, d. 9 Aug 1898 Lowell MA, m. 10 Dec 1858 Nancy R. (Gerald) Stinson of Canaan ME, b. 7 Apr 1827 d. 14 Dec 1891, dau. David and Susannah Gerald. In California Gold Rush 1849.
Edward Everett, b. 28 Nov 1860, m. 5 Oct 1887 Salem MA Harriet Emma Rugg of Canada, b. 4 Aug 1862 d. 10 Feb 1901, dau. Lorenzo and Emeline Rugg. CH: Fanny Rugg, b. 19 Aug 1888. In Lowell MA.
John F., b. Jul 1866, m. 16 Oct 1889 Lowell MA Effie L. Clark of Rutland VT, b. Jun 1866, dau. C. Martin and Martha Clark. In Lowell MA. CH: Beth L., b. May 1892.
Mary G., b. 21 Sep 1869, m. 10 Dec 1895 Lowell MA Charles L Knapp.
Sources: Lowell MA census 1860. VR SA/MA. D6.

373. **CHARLES CARROLL⁷ SAWYER** [see 202], b. 3 Jan 1833 Raymond ME, d. 27 Jun 1904 Boston MA, m. Ellen E. Thomas of Brandon Vt, b. 1835. In Waltham MA, Boston MA, Arlington MA. Merchant.
514 Addison Gage⁸, b. 1861.
515 Carroll Whitman⁸, b. 1864.
Nellie Grace, b. 1867, m. 3 Jul 1894 Waltham MA William C. Ball.
Frederick W., b. 5 May 1870.
Sources: Arlington MA census 1880. VR SA/MA.

374. **DENNIS JENKINS⁷ SAWYER** [see 203], b. 6 Apr 1835 Standish ME, d. 12 Aug 1912 Windham ME, m.(1) 6 Sep 1857 Windham ME Sarah J. Varney of Windham ME, b. 6 Jun 1833, dau. Hiram and Susanna (Green) Varney; m.(2) Charity Anne Smith of Windham ME, b. Feb 1844 d. 23 Jul 1914, dau. Thomas and Susannah (Bodge) Smith. Shoemaker. B/land in Windham ME 1864.
Eugene H., b. 1861 Standish ME, m. 15 Feb 1882 Emma Thurlow of Deering ME, b. ?.
516 George Thomas⁸, 1865-1949.
William Arthur, b. 15 Jul 1873 Windham ME, d. 1952 Windham ME, m. Lulu Nash, b. ?.
Luella A., b. 19 Jun 1884.
Sources: Windham ME census 1880. ME 1880 census index. VR Windham ME, SA/ME. L30, V3, R10a.

375. **ELLERY FOXCROFT⁷ SAWYER** [see 203], b. 13 Mar 1838 Standish ME, d. 19 Mar 1876, m. 10 Jun 1864 Vassalboro ME Ellen Nichols of Windham ME, b. 23 Sep 1840 d. 11 Sep 1894, dau. Charles and Esther (Owen) Nichols. In Lynn MA. Wid. m. David Phinney.
Charles Leonard, b. 5 Apr 1871, d. 13 Apr 1915 Gorham ME, m. 19 Apr 1898 Windham ME Cora Hall, b. 1872, dau. Valentine C. and Mary A. (Libby) Hall. Merchant. In Standish ME, Lynn MA.
Chester, b. 1874 Windham ME. Druggist. In Waltham MA.
Sources: VR SA/ME, SA/MA. L30, D4.

376. **JOHN PURINGTON⁷ SAWYER** [see 203], b. 30 Oct 1839 Standish ME, d. 29 Mar 1917 Westbrook ME, m.(I) 31 Aug 1863 Windham ME Louise (Bodge) Kimball of Windham ME, wid., b. 11 Aug 1838 d. 13 Jun 1910, dau. Thomas and Abigail (Nason) Bodge of Gorham ME. In Windham ME, Westbrook ME.
517 Clarence P.⁸, b. 1865.

Hattie E., b. 3 Mar 1871, d. 16 Jan 1876.
Sources: VR Windham ME, SA/ME. H30.

377. **ALFRED STANFORD[7] SAWYER** [see 203], Dr., b. 13 Aug 1844 Standish ME, m. 23 Mar 1881 Hannah E. Rich of Standish ME, b. 25 Jul 1857, dau. William and Lucy (Freeman) Rich. Dartmouth Medical School 1887. Physician. In Charlestown MA, Plainfield NH, Scarboro ME, So. Portland ME.

Ralph Eldon, b. 1884 Portland ME, m. 18 Jan 1935 Somersworth NH Annie E. Yates, b. 1914 Windham ME, dau. Howard A. and Alice (Burrill) Yates of Standish ME. Harvard College 1908. Civil engineer. In Bath ME.

Sources: L30.

378. **THOMAS C.[7] SAWYER** [see 204], b. 17 Aug 1838 Standish ME, d. 15 Aug 1914 Hollis ME, m. Harriet C. Sawyer of Hollis ME, b. May 1846 d. 1920, dau. John and Lydia (Ridlon) Sawyer.

518 Almon J.[8], 1861-1942.
May Dora, b. Jan 1864, m. J_____ W. Tarbox.
Herbert J., b. 20 Nov 1878, d. 6 Sep 1900.

Sources: Hollis ME census 1870, 1880. ME 1880 census index. VR SA/ME. R17, M8, M5.

379. **WILLIAM PITT[7] SAWYER** [see 204], b. 1 Dec 1840 Standish ME, d. 11 Sep 1916 Standish ME, m. 27 Apr 1867 New Bedford MA Elizabeth Jane Taber of New Bedford MA, b. 16 Jul 1846 d. 5 May 1895, dau. Leonard and Elizabeth (Hervey) Taber. Teamster. He bur. in Maplewood Cem., Standish ME.

Lizzie Sands, b. 14 Feb 1868, d. 23 Aug 1948, m. 20 Apr 1890 George Dole.
Lewis Albert, b. 6 Apr 1871 Standish ME, d. 1945 Standish ME, m. 1 Jan 1894 Gorham ME Nellie Libby, b. 1876. He bur. in Maplewood Cem., Standish ME.
Thomas Elmore, b. 14 Sep 1873 Standish ME, d. 1958 Standish ME, m. 7 Jul 1897 So. Standish ME Eva M. Libby, b. 1876 d. 1960, dau. Lewis B. and Frances J. (Brown) Libby.
Esther E., b. 12 Apr 1875, d. 7 Dec 1943, m. 16 Sep 1893 Orion E. Southwick.
Millard P., b. 25 Nov 1881, d. 21 Apr 1942, m. 13 Jul 1913 Clyde E. Brown. Went to Iowa.
Robert Reed, b. 22 Feb 1884, d. 24 Dec 1961, unm.
Frank Earle, b. 15 Nov 1886 Standish ME, d. 12 Nov 1938 Standish ME, m. 29 Apr 1907 Almeda Dolloff, b. 1885 d. 1965, dau. Charles and Julia (Cousins) Dolloff. Farmer. He bur. in Maplewood Cem., Standish ME.

Sources: Standish ME census 1880. ME 1880 census index. VR Standish ME, SA/ME. R5, M5, M8, C26, Mary E. Jackson rec.

380. **MATTHIAS H.[7] SAWYER** [see 204], b. May 1847 Standish ME, d. 5 Feb 1927, m. 2 Apr 1866 Melinda E. Johnson of Hollis ME, b. Mar 1851 d. 30 Jan 1914. Lumbering. In Hollis ME. Civil War.

519 Charles F.[8], 1867-1932.
520 Algernon A.[8], b. 1871.
Bertha M., b. 1877, d. 1940, m. 16 Nov 1898 John M. Boulter.
George M., b. Jan 1878 Standish ME. In Hollis ME.
Millie, b. Jan 1881.
Louise M., b. 10 Aug 1884, d. 1 Jun 1945, m. Almon T. Barnes.

Sources: Standish ME census 1880. ME 1880 census index. VR Standish ME, Hollis ME, SA/ME. M7A, M8, M5.

381. **ROBERT G.$^{7}$ SAWYER** [see 205], b. May 1828 Hollis ME, m. 1870 Freedom NH Lydia A. Newbegin of Salem MA, b. ca. 1847, dau. John Newbegin.

Fred E., b. 1871.
Warren N., b. Mar 1874.
Myra A., b. Mar 1886.

Sources: Hollis ME census 1850, 1860. Tamworth NH census 1870. Newfields ME census 1880 with John Newbegin. VR Buxton ME. D51.

382. **FRANK$^{7}$ SAWYER** [see 205], b. 29 Sep 1861 Hollis ME, d. 17 Oct 1936 Cornish ME, m. 30 Sep 1883 Buxton ME Sarah Harmon of Buxton ME, b. 17 Jul 1863 d. 20 Jan 1926, dau. Joshua and Deborah (Dunn) Harmon. In Hollis ME.

Elmer F., 1884, d. 23 Jun 1884.
Eugene F., b. May 1887 Hollis ME, d. 1947 Cornish ME, m. Carrie E. ______, b. 1876 d. 20 Aug 1954.
Marion Alma, b. 8 Jun 1890, d. 1976.
Carroll E., b. 15 Jul 1898 Hollis ME, d. 2 May 1963 Cornish ME.
Elmer Francis, b. 13 Sep 1913, d. 19 Nov 1932 Cornish ME.

Sources: VR Buxton ME, SA/ME. F34, M8, M5.

383. **ELBRIDGE L.$^{7}$ SAWYER** [see 206], b. 20 Dec 1846 Buxton ME, d. 1878 Saco ME, m. Serena Shackford of Springvale ME, b. 1843 d. 18 Oct 1905, dau. Christopher and Mehitable (Maddox) Shackford. He bur. in Laurel Grove Cem., Saco ME.

521 Charles Elbridge$^{8}$,1874-1959.
Harry Shackford, b. 1877 Rochester NH, d. 1941, m. 27 Apr 1904 Carrie A. Rice, b. 1878 d. 1949, dau. Alonzo and Lydia (Ward) Rice. He bur. in Laurel Grove Cem., Saco ME. CH: Son, b. 10 May 1905; Son, b. 16 Sep 1906.

Sources: ME 1880 census index. M5.

384. **GEORGE ALMON$^{7}$ SAWYER** [see 206], b. 8 Oct 1851 Buxton ME, m. 5 Nov 1872 Arlington MA Mary A. Rafter of Portland ME, b. 1854, dau. Edward and Mary Rafter. Carpenter. In Boston MA, Arlington MA.

Elbridge Freeman, b. 21 Oct 1873.
522 Frank Almon$^{8}$, b. 1875.
Abbie May, b. 9 Jun 1878.
Blanche Lona, b. 22 Aug 1882.
Edith Emeline, b. 3 Oct 1886.

Sources: VR SA/MA. George P. Sawyer rec.

385. **MARSHALL PIERCE$^{7}$ SAWYER** [see 206], b. 2 Oct 1853 Buxton ME, d. 28 Aug 1895, m. 1 Jan 1878 Abbie F. Tibbetts of Hollis ME, b. 1854, d. Saco ME, dau. Ephraim and _____ (Foster) Tibbetts. Carpenter.

Gertrude L., b. 1879.
Ralph Ernest, b. 15 Jun 1881 Buxton ME, m. 19 Sep 1906 Vergie M. Ellis, b. ca. 1885.
523 John Marshall$^{8}$, 1890-1927.
Edith Louise, b. 12 Jun 1898.

Sources: Hollis ME census 1880. ME 1880 census index. VR SA/ME. Robert L. Taylor rec.

386. **ANSEL G.$^{7}$ SAWYER** [see 207], b. 11 Nov 1856 Buxton ME, d. 10 Feb 1913 Portland ME, m.(1) 18 Nov 1879 Hattie M. Howe, b. 17 Nov 1855 d. 12 Oct 1886 Arlington MA, dau.

Henry M. and Prudence (Lancaster) Howe; m.(2) (I) 19 Nov 1888 Georgia E. Hamblin of Saco ME, b. Dec 1864 d. 1916. Livery stable. In Portland ME.

524 Harry Ansel[8], b. 1882.

Ralph Joseph, b. 23 Aug 1884 Portland ME.

Philip A., b. 27 Feb 1892 Portland ME.

Sources: VR Saco ME, SA/ME. W11.

387. **GEORGE EDWIN[7] SAWYER** [see 208], b. 12 Jun 1850 Buxton ME, d. 1936 Buxton ME, m.(1) 14 Feb 1875 Buxton ME Olive E. Pennell, b. 1854 d. 1879; m.(2) 4 Nov 1891 Gorham ME Leona M. Deering of Gorham ME, b. 31 Jan 1860 d. 1935. He bur. in Tory Hill Cem., Buxton ME.

Harold D., b. 9 Nov 1894 Windham ME.

Ralph E., b. 10 Mar 1896 Buxton ME, d. 1939 Buxton ME. Bur. in Tory Hill Cem., Buxton ME.

Zilpah B., b. 1 Jul 1898.

Luella R., b. 28 Mar 1900, d. 1972, m. Albertine Pierce.

Sources: VR Buxton ME, SA/ME. M5.

388. **GEORGE WESLEY[7] SAWYER** [see 210], b. 22 Apr 1848 Standish ME, d. 21 May 1927 Hebron ME, m. 16 Jan 1875 Hebron ME Rose H. Farris of Hebron ME, b. 2 Apr 1852 d. 16 Oct 1928, dau. James F. and Sarah (Farr) Farris. In Minot ME 1876, Poland ME 1879, Mechanics Falls ME 1893.

Ellen Jane, b. 25 Jun 1876, d. 15 Jul 1945, m. 29 Aug 1893 Joseph A. Hibbs.

Alice Maud, b. 16 Oct 1877, d. 16 Nov 1950, m. 21 Jun 1896 Elmer F. Perkins.

525 Charles Francis[8], 1879-1954.

Grace D., b. 21 Jul 1893, d. 7 Apr 1953, m. 4 Mar 1912 Henry Bacon.

Sources: ME 1880 census index. VR Hebron ME. Father's will, Inez Sawyer rec.

389. **CURTIS B. MERRILL[7] SAWYER** [see 210], b. 29 Sep 1849 Standish ME, d. 7 Feb 1925 Auburn ME, m. 10 Jan 1880 Judith E. Staples of Raymond ME, b. 26 Sep 1853 d. 25 May 1925, dau. Nathaniel and Esther (Mann) Staples. In Minot ME.

John Hermon, b. 4 Aug 1880 d. 3 Mar 1956, m. 29 Nov 1907 Eva Crocker, b. ?. In Minot ME.

Carroll Merton, b. 20 Jul 1886, m. 27 Jul 1907 Evelyn Frost, b. ?. In Minot ME.

Sources: Father's will.

390. **FRANKLIN[7] SAWYER** [see 212], b. ca. 1828 Boston, MA. m. 16 Nov 1859 Boston MA Mary Jones of Ireland, b. 1837, dau. Bernard and Catherine Jones. Upholsterer. In Boston MA, Cambridge MA.

Franklin Edward, b. 11 Jun 1859.

Catherine, b. 4 Apr 1862.

Margaret Adams, b. 9 Jul 1865.

Benjamin, b. 24 May 1869.

Mary Elizabeth, b. 26 May 1871.

Walter Lewis, b. 13 Aug 1873.

Ellen, b. 2 Jan 1876.

Daughter, b. 5 Sep 1877.

George Joseph, b. 14 Mar 1880.

Sources: VR SA/MA.

391. **EDWARD GORHAM⁷ SAWYER** [see 214], b. 31 Dec 1829 Boston MA, d. 17 Feb 1915, m. 29 Dec 1850 Allston MA Mary Farrington of Waterford VT, b. ?. In Boston MA, Chelsea MA, Brighton MA.

Susan Lydia, b. 10 Nov 1851, m. 12 Jun 1873 Brighton MA Horace F. Burr.

Mary Farrington, b. 14 Feb 1854.

Edward Joseph., b. 29 Jan 1860 Chelsea MA, d. 5 Jan 1921 Malden MA, m. 28 Jul 1886 Waterford VT Carrie Amanda Green of Waterford VT, b. ?. CH: Edward, b. 16 Mar 1888, d.y.; Mildred, b. 14 Jul 1890, m. 26 Sep 1916 George C. Stickney of Newburyport MA.

Hattie, b. 14 Sep 1861.

Carrie, b. 14 Sep 1861.

Elisha Brown, b. 27 Dec 1869.

Sources: Chelsea MA census 1860. VR SA/MA.

392. **ABEL HARGROVE⁷ SAWYER** [see 215], b. 1846 Portland ME, d. 22 Jan 1912 Cambridge MA, m. 25 Dec 1873 Boston MA Emily (Evelina?) V. Belcher of Farmington ME, b. ?.

Philip Brett, b. 13 Jul 1875 Farmington ME, m. Helen Preston, b. ?.

Frederica, b. ?, m. Stafford D. Noble.

Lucy B., b. ?.

Sources: VR SA/ME. G18.

393. **HENRY HOLMES⁷ SAWYER** [see 218], b. 24 Jun 1854 Charlestown MA, m. 12 May 1883 Boston MA (div. 7 Apr 1909) Lelia Lucy Slade of Boston MA, b. 1 Jan 1857 d. 13 Jun 1940, dau. Lucius and Lucy C. (Rust) Slade. Superintendent of Mill. In Manchester VT, Hudson NY, Walpole NH 1901.

Robert Stanley, b. 5 Oct 1884 Charlestown MA, m. 19 Apr 1911 Walpole NH Bessie S. Tidd, b. 6 Apr 1873 d. 22 Mar 1962, dau. Frank and Elizabeth A. (Wells) Tidd. Farmer.

526 Franklin Lucius⁸, b. 1886.

Arthur Henry, b. 8 May 1889 Hudson NY, m. Eleanor Morse Sani, b. ?.

Elizabeth, b. 31 Jul 1912.

Sources: VR SA/MA, SA/NH. P25, Edward S. Sawyer rec.

394. **HORACE AUSTIN⁷ SAWYER** [see 222], b. 1845 Boston MA, m. 19 Jun 1867 Lynn MA Hannah Abby Berry of Lynn MA, b. 1847, dau. John and Ann Berry. Civil War.

Walter Mayhew, b. 30 Apr 1868 Lynn MA, m. 17 Sep 1892 Lynn MA May Herbert of New Hampshire, b. 1871, dau. George A. and Annie Herbert.

Sources: VR SA/MA. S15.

395. **WALTER SCOTT⁷ SAWYER** [see 222], b. 10 Feb 1849 Chelsea MA, m. 25 Sep 1872 Lynn MA Hannah Abbie Weston of Lynn MA, b. 1850, dau. Jonas and Adaline Weston. Machinist. In Boston MA, Lynn MA.

George Fred, b. 28 Jan 1873.

Horace Weston, b. 2 Sep 1874.

Sources: VR SA/MA.

396. **GEORGE FREDERICK⁷ SAWYER** [see 222], b. 3 Feb 1852 Chelsea MA, d. 14 Nov 1915 Boston MA, m. 25 Nov 1874 Boston MA Mary E. Carlton of Boston MA, b. 23 Dec 1848 d. 11 May 1908. Bookkeeper. In Boston MA, Chelsea MA.

George Frederick, b. 9 Sep 1875 Boston MA, d. 1941 Boston MA. In Rhode Island.

Ernest Alexander, b. 26 Aug 1876 Boston MA, d. 1960.
Herbert A., b. 23 Feb 1879 Boston MA.
Grace May, b. 12 Nov 1880.
Alfred Chester, b. 19 Dec 1883 Boston MA.
Mabel F., b. 1888.
Sources: D6, M1.

397. **FRANK AUGUSTUS[7] SAWYER** [see 224], b. 2 Jun 1856 Cape Elizabeth ME, m. 1 Jun 1882 Cape Elizabeth ME Josie A. Turner, b. Jul 1861. In New York, Wakefield MA, Keene NH.
Clyde A., b. 12 Jan 1883.
Phebe J., b. May 1895.
Arleigh C., b. Aug 1897.
Sources: VR Cape Elizabeth ME. S15.

398. **DANIEL M.[7] SAWYER** [see 226], b. 23 Jul 1827 Cape Elizabeth ME, d. 1905, m. (I) 20 Nov 1855 Cape Elizabeth ME Mary A. Morton of Winthrop ME, b. 15 Nov 1829 d. 1895, dau. Mordica E. and Christian Morton. He bur. Pleasant Hill Cem., So. Portland ME.
Mary E., b. 5 Nov 1859.
527 Henry Morton[8], 1865-1932.
Sources: Cape Elizabeth ME census 1860, 1870. VR Cape Elizabeth ME.

399. **WILLIAM E.[7] SAWYER** [see 228], b. 1850 Machiasport ME, d. 10 Aug 1881, m. 28 Sep 1872 Margaret Phinney, b. 1849.
Edward W., b. 1874.
Ernest M., b. 1875.
Harry B., b. 1878.
Sources: Machiasport ME census 1880. ME 1880 census index.

400. **JOHN F.[7] SAWYER** [see 229], b. 23 Nov 1859 Jonesboro ME, d. 8 Apr 1923, m. 26 Mar 1884 Alice B. Crowley of Addison ME, b. ?.
Son, b. 25 Jun 1898.
Sources: VR SA/ME.

401. **DANIEL JAMES[7] SAWYER** [see 229], b. Feb 1866 Jonesboro ME, d. 27 Mar 1912 Portsmouth NH, m. Carrie E. Smith, b. ?. Mariner.
Ezra, b. 18 Feb 1896.
Daughter, b. 21 Dec 1897.
Catherine Myrtle, b. 18 Aug 1900, d. 10 Jun 1969, m. Perley Dow.
James F., b. 4 May 1901, d. 10 Aug 1989, m. Frances Goodrich, b. ?.
Wilbur F., b. 27 Mar 1906, d. 18 Jan 1986, m. Marjorie Mackenzie, b. ?.
Ida May, b. 26 May 1907, d. 25 Aug 1907 Rye NH.
More children.
Sources: VR SA/ME, SA/NH. D50, Obit (James).

402. **JOHN VASSAR[7] SAWYER** [see 231], b. Jan 1878 Jonesport ME, d. 1958 Jonesport ME, m. Annie M. Morrison of Lawrence MA, b. 1878 d. 1957.
Frances V., b. ?, m. Homer Worcester.
Daniel James, m. Evelyn B. Wind, CH: John Vassar II, m. Betty M. Wersebe; Judith Ann, m. Andre White.
Dorothy, m.(1) Alfred McMichael, m.(2) Donald Shory.

Sources: John V. Sawyer II rec.

403. **JOHN HENRY$^7$ SAWYER** [see 232], b. 29 Jun 1833 Brooks ME, d. 10 Jan 1914 Blaine ME, m.(1) 29 Jun 1856 Brooks ME Augusta Tasker of Monroe ME, b. 3 Mar 1833 d. 3 Jun 1883; m.(2) 10 Nov 1884 Old Town ME Viola Witham of Lagrange ME, b. Jan 1862 d. 30 Oct 1895; m.(3) 24 Feb 1897 Emeline (Tapley) Perkins, b. 9 May 1849, d. 13 Nov 1921, dau. Sherman and Esther (Kinny) Perkins. Carpenter. In Jackson ME 1860, Old Town ME 1868.

Charles W., b. 1857 Jackson ME.

Fred W., b. 1860 Old Town ME, d. 6 Jun 1892 Lubec ME, m.(1) 28 May 1879 Minnie H. Clark of New Brunswick, Canada, b. ?; m.(2) 16 Jun 1888 Mary Fitzhenry of Machais ME, b. ?. CH: Myrtle A. b. 9 Mar 1880.

Anna A., b. 1868, d. 12 Apr 1942, m. 1 Sep 1887 Eugene W. Bradeen.

Allen J., b. 1874 Old Town ME.

Grace Bruce, b. 7 Nov 1886, d. 16 Feb 1975, m. 20 Oct 1904 Valere J. Morin.

Sources: Jackson ME census 1860. ME 1880 census index. VR Old Town ME, Rockland ME, SA/ME.

404. **ENOCH C.$^7$ SAWYER** [see 232], b. Feb 1837 Monroe ME, d. 2 Nov 1915 Old Town ME, m. Evaline P Pattee of Jackson ME, b. 1837, d. 15 Mar 1911 Old Town ME, dau. James Pattee. Carriagemaker. In Medfield MA 1869.

Julia Augusta, b. Mar 1869.

H. Everett, b. Jul 1875 Monroe ME.

Sources: Monroe ME census 1850. Old Town ME census 1880. ME 1880 census index. VR SA/ME.

405. **CHARLES HENRY$^7$ SAWYER** [see 233], b. 3 Nov 1829 Dixmont ME, d. 20 Jan 1903 in Los Angeles CA, m. 6 Mar 1864 Boston MA Etta H Farnham of Jefferson ME, b. 1839, dau. Daniel and Mary Farnham. Sea captain. US Navy.

Gertrude, b. 1866, m. Frank Hovey. Went to California.

Reginald S., b. 1879, d.y. in Pittsfield ME.

Rex, b. ?. In Calais ME.

Sources: Pittsfield ME census 1880. ME 1880 census index. VR SA/ME. D51, Family Bible.

406. **DANIEL ROSCOE$^7$ SAWYER** [see 233], b. 1 Sep 1840 Dixmont ME, d. 11 Dec 1920 Caribou ME, m. 29 Dec 1861 Bangor ME Susan M. Green of Lisbon ME, b. 1830 d. 19 May 1901, dau. Elbridge and Maria (Holland) Green. Civil War.

528 Charles L.$^8$, b. 1863.

Sources: VR Bangor ME, SA/ME. M7A, Family Bible.

407. **CHARLES LAURISTON$^7$ SAWYER** [see 235], b. 2 May 1849 Limington ME, d. 9 Dec 1930 Portland ME, m. 14 Dec 1872 Ida Freeman of Blaine ME, b. 21 Jan 1850 d. 27 Apr 1910, dau. William and Mary (Phinney) Freeman. He bur. Standish Village Cem.

Carrie, b. 1874, m. George Mountford of Portland ME.

Charles Lauriston, b. 1876 of Westbrook ME.

Lucy F., b. 1879.

Sources: Standish ME census 1880 with father. ME 1880 census index. VR SA/ME.

408. **EDMUND P.$^7$ SAWYER** [see 237], b. 28 Apr 1841 Limington ME, d. 3 Sep 1915 Freedom NH, m. 3 Mar 1861 Zelma Z. Philbrook of Ipswich MA, b. Dec 1844 d. 5 Nov 1918, dau. Oliver Philbrick. Teamster. In Freedom NH 1878.

Charles H., b. 1862 Eaton NH, m. 30 Jul 1887 Boston MA Minnie B. Bartlett of New York City, b. 1862, dau. Daniel A. and Hannah G. Bartlett. In Boston MA. Clerk.
Abner J., b. 24 Jan 1864 Eaton NH.
Jessie, b. 1866.
Sources: Eaton NH census 1860. VR SA/MA, SA/NH. T6.

409. **JOSIAH C.[7] SAWYER** [see 237], b. 1845 Limington ME, m. 31 Mar 1864 Mary Augusta Haley of Biddeford ME, b. 1847. Coachman.
Alonzo Hathorne, b. 19 Jan 1874 Boston MA, m. 15 Jan 1893 Boston MA B. Sadie Doyle of Boston MA, b. ca. 1874, dau. Michael and Rosa Doyle. Bookkeeper. CH: Pearl A., b. 27 Aug 1894.
James William, b. 4 Apr 1877 Boston MA.
Sources: Eaton NH census 1860. VR SA/MA.

410. **EDGAR HOWARD[7] SAWYER** [see 238], b. 4 Feb 1856 Bridgton ME, d. 31 Mar 1922 Holliston MA, m. E. Fryeburg ME Jennie Emerson of Saco ME, b. 1854 d. 1922. Lumberman. In Limington ME, Standish ME, Holliston MA.
Nellie E., b. ca. 1875, m. James Perrin. Went to California.
Perley H., b. ca. 1877.
Charles Henry, b. 1 Sep 1882, m. ?.
529 Justus Wilson[8], 1886-1947.
Fred Emerson, b. 2 Jul 1891 Holliston MA, d. 3 Apr 1978 Porter ME, m. Georgie _____, b. ?.
George, b. ?. Went to Indiana.
Sources: Standish ME census 1880. ME 1880 census index. VR SA/MA. Richard S. Sawyer rec., Arlene Gallot rec.

411. **CHARLES FRANK[7] SAWYER** [see 240], b. 25 Jun 1879 Sebago ME, d. 20 Aug 1954 W. Rye NH, m. 25 Dec 1903 Sebago ME Elsie Maude Johnson, b. ? d. 26 May 1978. Guide, farmer. He bur. in Convene ME.
Marion Elva, b. 19 Jun 1904, m. 1934 John E. Lockwood, Jr.
Harry Wilson, b. 5 Mar 1906 Sebago ME, d. 18 Jun 1984 Presque Isle ME, m. 6 Jun 1934 Frances Louise Roberts. CH: Robert Harry, b. 14 Apr 1935, m. 20 Jun 1959 Barbara J. Conover; Sallyann, b. 20 Mar 1936, m. 28 Sep 1957 Philip Joseph of Massachusetts.
Hazel Louise, b. 25 Mar 1911, m.(1) Chester Wormhood, m.(2) Theodore Ham.
Sources: Family Bible, Frances L. Sawyer rec.

412. **SAMUEL GUY[7] SAWYER** [see 241], b. 1 Dec 1871 Limington ME, d. 3 Mar 1956 Cornish Me, m. 30 Nov 1905 Helen L. Pierce of Newton MA, b. 1 Mar 1883 d. 1981, dau. Alfred and Marcia (Kendrick) Pierce. Physician. In Cornish ME.
Kendrick B., b. 20 May 1907 Cornish ME, d. 1976 Cornish ME, m.(1) ? (div.); m.(2) 20 Feb 1932 Portsmouth NH Elizabeth C. Carter of Fairfield ME, b. 1912, dau. Howard R. and Ethel (Deering) Carter. In Portland ME.
Norman Pierce, b. 25 Jan 1910, d. 1970.
Donald G., b. 22 Apr 1912, d. 21 Mar 1967 Poughkeepsie NY, m. Pauline McKinney.
Samuel Philip, b. 8 Jul 1920.
Sources: VR Cornish ME. T5, N40, F34.

413. **FRED B.[7] SAWYER** [see 242], b. 15 Feb 1868 Maysville ME, d. 23 Aug 1945, m. 5 Jan 1892 Lillian McCubrey of Caribou ME, b. 24 Jun 1871 d. 28 Mar 1920, dau. Robert A. and Sarah (Marks) McCubrey. Farmer. In Ft. Fairfield ME.

Earl, b. 12 Jul 1892 Fort Fairfield ME.
Lewis, b. 14 Oct 1894 Fort Fairfield ME.
Mildred Marguerette, b. 19 Jun 1896.

Sources: VR SA/ME.

414. **JOSEPH WALLACE[7] SAWYER** [see 242], b. 8 Mar 1870 Maysville ME, d. 8 Feb 1944 Easton ME, m. 26 Jul 1902 Easton ME Alice Elizabeth Gould of Easton ME, b. 11 Jul 1881 d. 16 Jul 1942, dau. William and Mary A.(Pratt) Gould.

Daughter, b. 1914, d. at birth.
530 Neil Gould[8], b. 1916.

Sources: Neil G. Sawyer rec.

415. **CHARLES W.[7] SAWYER** [see 244], b. Aug 1826 Portland ME, d. 1 Nov 1904 Milbridge ME, m. 5 Jan 1849 Steuben ME Caroline P. Fickett of Steuben ME, b. Apr 1830 d. 3 Nov 1902, dau. Elias and Beulah (Gray) Fickett. Both bur. Sanborn Cem., Milbridge ME.

Frederick W., b. 1850 Milbridge ME, d. 10 Apr 1881.
Florence, b. 1851.
Hattie B., b. 1856, m. 18 Oct 1875 Lynn MA H. Gardiner Alley.
Bartlett D., b. ca. 1859 Milbridge ME, d. 28 Dec 1877.
Albert G., b. 1867 Milbridge ME.
Augustus F., b. 6 Aug 1868 Milbridge ME, d. 15 Jun 1899 Milbridge ME, m. 20 Dec 1892 Harrington ME Grace Strout of Harrington ME, b. 1876 d. 1918, dau. Charles and Emma Strout. Stonecutter.

Sources: Milbridge ME census 1850. VR SA/ME, SA/MA. M5.

416. **GEORGE F.[7] SAWYER** [see 244], b. 18 Nov 1832 Cape Elizabeth ME, d. 16 Aug 1894 Scarboro ME, m. 7 May 1857 Milbridge ME Theresa C. Preble of Milbridge ME, b. 1835. Carpenter.

531 George Irving[8], 1858-1912.
Lizzie D., b. 3 Jun 1860.
Nellie F., b. 9 Jul 1862.
Charles H., b. ca. 1865 Portland ME.
Alice J., b. Feb 1867, d. 5 Jan 1868.
Susie J., b. ca. 1868.
Hattie, b. 15 Jan 1870, d. 15 Feb 1870.
Emma G., b. 1871.
Carrie L., b. 1875.

Sources: Portland ME census 1860, 1870, 1880. ME 1880 census index. VR Milbridge ME, SA/ME. M5, R10a.

417. **WINTHROP R.[7] SAWYER** [see 247], b. 18 Nov 1834 Danville ME, d. 22 Oct 1918, m. 27 Nov 1856 New Gloucester ME Susan A. Penney of New Gloucester ME, b. 21 Jul 1832 d. 1 Jun 1888, dau. Aaron and Drusilla (Witham) Penney. B/S/land in New Gloucester ME, 1856-1870. In New Gloucester ME, North Yarmouth ME. He bur. in Evergreen Cem., Portland ME.

William W., b. 27 May 1858 New Gloucester ME.
Lillian W., b. 27 May 1858, m. 12 Sep 1888 Wesley S. Sweetsir.
Annie Priscilla, b. ?

532 Herbert Thomas Penney[8], b. 1867.
Sources: New Gloucester ME census 1860. VR New Gloucester ME, SA/ME. P28.

418. **JOSEPH WILLIAM[7] SAWYER** [see 248], b. 28 Nov 1844 Danville ME, d. 7 Mar 1929 New Gloucester ME, m. 20 Jan 1872 New Gloucester ME Ella E. Merrill of New Gloucester ME, b. 11 May 1851 d. 19 Sep 1919. He bur. Gloucester Hill Cem., New Gloucester ME.
Edwin L. b. 20 Sep 1872 New Gloucester ME, m. 21 May 1900 New Gloucester ME Florence E. Goff of Gray ME, b. 1879 Gray ME, dau. Barrillas and Ruby Goff.
Lottie Mae, b. 13 Feb 1878, d. 1 Nov 1930, m. 1896 John W. Humphrey, Jr.
Nathaniel, b. 25 May 1882 New Gloucester ME.
Sources: New Gloucester ME census 1880. ME 1880 census index. VR SA/ME. Gravestone.

419. **HORATIO M.[7] SAWYER** [see 248], b. 27 Jul 1856 Danville ME, d. 9 Jan 1945, m. (I) 28 Oct 1884 New Gloucester ME Addie C. Staples of Roxbury MA, b. Jul 1863 d. 18 Jul 1939. Farmer. Storekeeper in North Gray ME, 1891-1945. He bur. in Gray ME.
533 Perley Clair[8], 1885-1958.
Ralph White, b. 19 Jul 1894 Danville ME, d. 1967, m. 1 Jan 1912 Evelyn Bishop, b. ?. In Gray ME.
Sources: VR Gray ME, SA/ME. Margaret C. Sawyer rec.

420. **JAMES FRANKLIN[7] SAWYER** [see 249], b. Mar 1854 Danville ME, m. Nellie M. Patterson of No. Waterford ME, b. ca. 1859. Farmer. In Norway ME, Minot ME.
Frank True, b. 20 May 1879.
Sources: Norway ME census 1880. ME 1880 census index. VR SA/ME.

421. **GEORGE E.[7] SAWYER** [see 249], b. 1856 Danville ME, d. 18 Oct 1882, m. 18 Feb 1879 Ida M. Libby of Bridgton ME, b. 22 Dec 1857, dau. Samuel Libby. In Oxford ME.
George Lynwood, b. 8 Oct 1879.
Sources: Danville ME census 1860. Oxford ME census 1880 with Samuel Libby. ME 1880 census index. VR SA/ME. L20.

422. **JOHN MILTON[7] SAWYER** [see 252], b. 10 Apr 1863 New Gloucester ME d. 5 Feb 1920, m. 25 Dec 1888 Lenora Sawyer of Gray ME, b. 6 Jan 1870 d. 6 Jan 1945, dau. George Washington Royal and Asenath (Witham) Sawyer. In New Gloucester ME. He bur. in Gray ME.
Maude B., b. Apr 1889, m. James Nally.
Bessie M., b. 4 Sep 1890, m. _____ Brackett.
Fred, b. ca. 1892, m. Gertrude Hanscom, b. ?. CH: Fred Rowland, b. ?.
John M., b. 29 Mar 1897, m. Erla Whitney, b. ?. In New Gloucester ME. CH: Ronald, b. ?; Milton, b. ?.
Lucelia A., b. 28 Dec 1898, m. _____ Day.
Velma, m. John Toohill.
Eva, m. Donald Nichols.
Harry V., b. 1905, d. 1956, m. Adelaide R._____, b. ca. 1901. CH: Richard, b. ?.
Leola, m. Paul Stanford.
Sources: VR SA/ME. M5, Gerald M. Kimball rec, Gertrude Sawyer rec.

423. **FRANCIS M.[7] SAWYER** [see 253], b. 16 Oct 1826 Westbrook ME, d. 1 Sep 1894 Portland ME, m. 18 Nov 1847 Portland ME Phebe H. Horr of Norway ME, b. Nov 1829 d. 28 Oct 1904, dau. William and Hannah (Holt) Horr. Tin worker. Phebe B/S/land in Portland ME.
534 William F.[8],1848-1880.

Rosa B., b. ca. 1850.

Sources: Portland ME census 1850. VR Portland ME, SA/ME. R10a.

424. **ALONZO W.**[7] **SAWYER** [see 253], b. Apr 1833 Portland ME, d. 25 May 1897 Portland ME, m. 24 Oct 1856 Portland ME Sarah Elizabeth Gould, b. May 1840 d. 24 Jul 1912, dau. Abner and Elizabeth Gould. Civil War. S/land Portland ME 1869. He bur. in Evergreen Cem., Portland ME.

Edward Francis, b. 30 May 1857 Portland ME, d. 1928 Portland ME, m. Alice G._____ b. Apr 1865 d. 1914. He bur. in Evergreen Cem., Portland ME. CH: Millie E., b. Aug 1884.

Annie V., b. 26 Mar 1860.

535 Henry Jackson[8], 1862-1939.

Charles Eugene, b. 29 Aug 1866 Portland ME, d. 1954.

Ellen S., b. 1869.

Sources: ME 1880 census index. VR Portland ME, SA/ME. M5, D37, R10a.

425. **WILLIAM KIMBALL**[7] **SAWYER** [see 256], b. 15 Jun 1840 Westbrook ME, m. 20 Jun 1867 Portland ME Lucy A. Buck of Buckfield ME, b. 13 Mar 1839 d. 7 Apr 1910. Mason. Civil War. S/land inherited from father, 1867 and 1869.

Harris Eastman (aka Harry Elmer), b. 3 Apr 1868 Portland ME, d. 5 Jul 1911 Andover NH, m. Copenhagen, Denmark, a member of German Royalty. PHD from Harvard College. In Buckfield ME, Washington DC. CH: Helen M., b. 1890.

Helen A., b. 23 Oct 1874.

536 Clarence Buck[8], 1879-1951.

Sources: Boston MA census 1870. VR SA/ME, SA/MA, SA/NH. R10a, C63.

426. **MICHAEL S.**[7] [see 257], b. ca. 1841 Portland ME, m. Ellen R. _____ of Portland ME, b. 1844. House carpenter. In Boston MA.

Francis H., b. 1859, d.y.

Ferdinand, b. ca. 1863.

537 Francis Howard[8], b. 1866.

Eva Margaret, b. 26 Jul 1871.

George St. John, b. 31 Oct 1874 Boston MA.

Sources: VR SA/MA.

427. **HOWARD DEWOLF**[7] **SAWYER** [see 257], b. 19 Mar 1846 Portland ME, m. 25 May 1872 Boston MA Mary A. Roper of England, b. ca. 1853, dau. James and Hannah Roper. Engineer. In Boston MA.

538 Harrison Hill[8], b. 1873.

Elizabeth Octave, b. 29 Feb 1876, m. 30 Dec 1894 Boston MA John S. Dalzell.

Sources: VR SA/MA. May Sawyer rec.

428. **BENJAMIN LEONARD**[7] **SAWYER** [see 263], b. 19 Apr 1840 Portland ME, d. 1927 Portland ME, m. 14 Jul 1881 Portland ME Susan J. Googins, b. 18 Jul 1859 d. 1926, dau. William and Mary E. (Wardell) Googins. Fire Department driver in Great Portland Fire 1866.

Emily M., b. 6 Oct 1883, m. 1911 G. Wilmot Carle.

Mildred L., b. 19 Nov 1886, m. 1916 Harold N Fisk.

539 Benjamin H.[8], 1888-1968.

William Edward, b. 30 Jan 1890, d. 1962.

Sources: M8, G22, Lewis B. Sawyer rec., Susan Szewczyk rec.

429. **DANIEL C.[7] SAWYER** [see 264], b. 11 Apr 1832 Eaton NH, d. 2 May 1903 Eaton NH, m. 15 Apr 1858 Lydia A. White of Parsonsfield ME, b. 1842.

Asa M., b. Apr 1859, d. 11 Jul 1866.
Susan N., b. 1862, m. 27 Mar 1884 Eaton NH Thaddeus E. Bryant.
Clara E., b. 10 Oct 1868, d. 1 Jan 1871.
Carrie Bell, b. ca. 1870, m. 18 Oct 1888 Orren N. Currier.
Frank D., b. 3 May 1871, d. 24 Dec 1875.
Orra L., b. 21 Sep 1873, d. 11 Aug 1889, m. 7 Oct 1888 Freedom NH Irving W. Young.
Mary L., b. 1878, m. 3 Jun 1894 Conway NH Irving W. Young.
Ida E., b. 22 May 1879, m. 1 Oct 1896 Conway NH Myron S. Allard.
540 Carle D.[8], 1881-1966.

Sources: Eaton NH census 1860, 1870, 1880. VR SA/NH. N6, N14, H17.

430. **LOREN D.[7] SAWYER** [see 264], b. 1835 Eaton NH, m. 29 Jun 1863 Ruth J. Kezar of Parsonsfield ME, b. ?.

George S., b. 1864 Eaton NH, m. 25 Sep 1890 Portland ME Carrie M. Robertson of Conway NH, b. 1866. In E. Hiram ME. CH: Marjorie Ruth b. 14 Nov 1895.

Sources: VR SA/ME.

431. **IRVIN A.[7] SAWYER** [see 264], b. 27 May 1851 Eaton NH, d. 5 May 1932 Conway NH, m. 14 Jun 1880 Portsmouth NH Carrie S. Hayes of Conway NH, b. 1860 d. 1948. Carpenter.

Frederick Hayes, b. 25 May 1881 Conway NH, d. 1966, m. 26 Jun 1929 Conway NH Minerva C. Thomas of Eaton NH, b. 1876 d. 1959, dau. Elijah and Lurana L. (Sanborn) Carlton. Liveryman.

Samuel, b. 16 Jun 1891 Conway NH, d. 1916, m. 5 Aug 1915 Conway NH Hazel Roarty of E. Weymouth MA, b. 1893, dau. James A. and Marcia (Dyer) Roarty. Civil engineer.

Sources: VR Eaton NH, SA/NH. R15.

432. **LEANDER L.[7] SAWYER** [see 266], b. Jun 1843 Westbrook ME, m.(1) 2 Jan 1863 Boston MA Angelina (Ellis) McBride of Marietta OH, b. 1841, dau. Ira and Julia Ellis; m.(2) 22 Jul 1880 Portsmouth NH Lizzie E. Freeman of Vermont, b. 1847, dau. James and Mary E. Freeman; m.(3) 2 Aug 1892 Deering ME Linnie E. Scribner of Unity ME, b. 1857. In Westbrook ME 1870, Deering ME 1894.

541 Harry M.[8], b. 1864.
Frank E., b. 1867 Westbrook ME.
Allen S., b. 1869 Westbrook ME, m. 19 Jul 1895 Brockton MA Mabel E. Perry of Oakland ME, b. 1874, dau. Charles and Melenthia (Pearson) Perry.
Netta Ward, b. 1 Feb 1894.

Sources: Westbrook ME census 1870. VR SA/ME, SA/MA.

433. **EUGENE WILLIS[7] SAWYER** [see 266], b. 16 Mar 1855 Charlestown MA, d. 8 Dec 1926, m.(1) 1 Jun 1880 Deering ME Ida L. Merrill, b. 1857 d. 18 Apr 1902; m.(2) 5Aug 1914 Addie Inez Randall, b. 15 Mar 1880 d. 29 Dec 1944. Silversmith.

Willis Randall, b. 20 May 1915 Deering ME, m. Irma C. Collamore, b. ?.

Theodore Lewis, b. 13 Mar 1919 Deering ME, m. 21 Aug 1940 Ida Alice Libby. In Boxford MA, Scarboro ME. CH: Quenton Theodore, b. 12 Jun 1941; Stephen Lewis, b. 1 Apr 1944.

Sources: VR Deering ME.

434. **FRANK H.[7] SAWYER** [see 267], b. 1854 Westbrook ME, d. 1927, m. 5 Jul 1889 Deering ME Elzina C. Bennett of Deering ME, b. ?.

F. Bennett, b. 1898, d. 24 Jan 1986 Kennebunk ME.

Sources: VR SA/ME. Obit (F. Bennett).

435. **EDWARD HENRY[7] SAWYER** [see 268], b. 18 Dec 1837 Portland ME, d. 5 Apr 1905 Boston MA, m. 5 Jul 1865 Portland ME Mary J. Corey of St. Johns, New Brunswick, Canada, b. Dec 1839. Carpenter.

542 Edward Whitmore[8], 1866-1957.

George Washington, b. 1 Jun 1869 Boston MA, m. 8 Jan 1890 Boston MA Fannie I. Hurd of Roxbury MA, b. 1872, dau. Sylvester and Hannah Hurd. CH: Daughter, b. 30 Sep 1891; Marion Hurd, b. 17 Sep 1892.

Charles F., b. 13 Nov 1870, d. 8 Aug 1871.

Lillie May, b. 14 Nov 1871.

Grace M., b. Nov 1872.

Sources: Boston MA census 1870. VR Portland ME, SA/MA, SA/ME. Bickford Sawyer rec.

436. **PHILIP WEEKS[7] SAWYER** [see 268], b. 27 May 1840 Portland ME, d. 11 Nov 1905 Vinal Haven ME, m. 14 Apr 1861 Bath ME Sarah J. Coombs of Bath ME, b. 2 Sep 1847 d. 3 Aug 1896. In Portland ME 1863, Freeport ME 1864. B/S/land 1866-1869.

Hannah A., b. 13 Dec 1863.

Anne, b. 14 Sep 1864.

Robert Franklin, b. 2 Nov 1872 Freeport ME, m. 10 Aug 1891 Boston MA Mary A. Carron of Newfoundland, Canada, b. 1872. In New Haven CT.

Martha, b. ca. 1875.

John H., b. ca. 1877 Freeport ME, m. 24 Oct 1894 Boston MA Margaret Decosta of Nova Scotia, Canada, b. 1873, dau. Henry and Eliza Decosta. In Vinal Haven ME.

Ansel, b. ca. 1878.

Sources: Vinal Haven census 1880. ME 1880 census index. VR Portland ME, Bath ME, Freeport ME, SA/ME. R10a.

437. **HADWIN[7] SAWYER** [see 268], b. 6 Sep 1850 Portland ME, d. 23 Jun 1923 Lynn MA, m. 4 Aug 1872 Boston MA Ruth Ann Elliott of Portland ME, b. ca. 1852, dau. Moses and Mary J. Elliot. Painter, fireman.

George, b. 14 Jun 1873.

Maud Loring, b. ca. 1874.

Ruth Ann, b. 21 Feb 1880.

Daughter, b. 18 Dec 1881.

543 Hadwin[8], b. 1882.

Son, b. 1884.

Joseph Emery, b. 3 Aug 1886.

Samuel Sargent, b. 13 Aug 1891.

Sources: VR SA/MA. Ruth H. Sawyer rec.

438. **ROBERT[7] SAWYER** [see 269], b. 3 Jun 1809 Dresden ME, m. 27 Oct 1831 Hallowell ME Nancy D. Moores, b. ca. 1817. Tailor. Paymaster, 42d Regiment, 8 Jul 1844. Surveyor of Highways for Lancaster NH 1848, Postmaster 1850-1853.

Edmund M., b. ca. 1833, d. 1856 in New York. Laborer.

Sources: Lancaster NH census 1850, 1860. VR Hallowell ME. S61.

439. **ISAAC$^7$ SAWYER** [see 269], b. 2 Nov 1813 Hallowell ME, d. 23 Oct 1851, m.(I) 13 Aug 1837 Augusta ME Harriet Bickford, b. ca. 1819.

Charles S., b. 1841 Hallowell ME, m. 4 Nov 1866 Boston MA Mary L. Lewis of Kittery ME, b. ?, dau. Joseph and Rebecca Lewis. Blacksmith. CH: Evelyn, b. 26 Jul 1871.
Sarah A., b. 1842.
Georgianna, b. 1843.
Harriet F., b. 1846, m. 29 Apr 1867 So. Hadley MA P____ E. Snow.
Mary L., b. 1847, m. 10 Mar 1869 Newton MA Albert G. Blunt.

Sources: Hallowell ME census 1850. Waterville ME census 1860. VR Augusta ME, SA/MA.

440. **WILLIAM W.$^7$ SAWYER** [see 269], b. 2 Jun 1817 Hallowell ME, m.(1) Hannah A. _____, b. 14 Apr 1822; m.(2) 23 Nov 1882 Georgia Dudley, b. ?. Blacksmith, carriage manufacturer. In Chelsea MA, Malden MA, Charlestown MA 1865.

William, b. 1846.
Eugene, b. ca. 1849.
Emily Adeline, b. 29 Apr 1850.

Sources: Malden MA census 1850. VR Hallowell ME, SA/MA. L30, M2A.

441. **GEORGE ADDISON$^7$ SAWYER** [see 269], b. 16 Jun 1826 Hallowell ME, m. 1 Jul 1851 Boston MA Hannah E. Russell of Bath ME, b. ?. Clerk, merchant.

Mary Jane, b. 18 Aug 1854.
Frederick Russell, b. 17 Jul 1857 Boston MA, m. 6 Nov 1879 Melrose MA Cora F. Austin of Boston MA, b. 1859, dau. John S. and Harriet Austin.
Son, b. 6 May 1867.

Sources: VR SA/MA.

442. **CHARLES H.$^7$ SAWYER** [see 272], b. 1847 Madison ME, d. 23 Aug 1914 Portsmouth NH, m. Abbie M Patterson of No. Anson ME, b. 30 May 1851 d. 24 Mar 1920 Portland ME, dau. Caleb and Caroline (Mantor) Patterson.

George Henry, b. 17 Jan 1874.
Eugenia M., b. 23 Sep 1880.
John Patterson, b. 22 May 1882.

Sources: Madison ME census 1880. ME 1880 census index. VR SA/ME.

443. **ELMER ELLSWORTH$^7$ SAWYER** [see 273], b. Mar 1851 Madison ME, d. 1924 North Anson ME, m. Sarah F. Gahan of North Anson ME, b. Mar 1855.

Emily M., b. 16 Apr 1886.
Everett R., b. Jul 1889.
Elmer W., b. 25 Jan 1892.

Sources: VR Anson ME, SA/ME.

444. **ALONZO WILLARD$^7$ SAWYER** [see 276], b. ca. 1835 Westbrook ME, d. 6 May 1864 in Civil War, m. Martha M. Bennett, b. ca. 1841. S/land in Westbrook ME 1859, 1860.

Lewis B., b. ca. 1860 Westbrook ME.

Sources: Westbrook ME census 1860. R10a, M55, Theodore L. Sawyer rec.

445. **RUFUS M.$^7$ SAWYER** [see 277], b. 1 Sep 1820 Otisfield ME, d. 1872, m. 27 Nov 1851 Otisfield ME Sophia C. Blake, b. 19 Apr 1821, d. 21 Nov 1891, dau. Silas Blake. Minister. In Bangor ME, Somersworth NH, Middleboro MA.

Silas B., b. ca. 1853.

Julia E., b. ca. 1855.
Clara C., b. ca. 1857.
Susan, b. ca. 1858.
Charles L., b. ca. 1859.
Sources: Bangor ME census 1850. Somersworth NH census 1860. VR Otisfield ME.

446. **NATHANIEL K.[7] SAWYER** [see 277], b. 12 Feb 1822 Otisfield ME, d. 15 May 1904 Portland ME, m.(1) 1 Sep 1844 Westbrook ME Sarah A. Morrill, b. 1822 d. 1872; m.(2) (I) 11Mar 1874 Harriet B.Bell of Deering ME, b. ca. 1848. Tanner.
Edward, b. 5 Oct 1845, d. 10 Nov 1847.
Willard G., b. 1846 Westbrook ME.
Frank W., b. 21 Jun 1848, d. 22 Nov 1860.
Willard, b. 26 Oct 1857, d. 20 Oct 1860.
Mary Bell, b. May 1876, d. 1 Oct 1893.
Sources: Westbrook ME census 1850. VR Westbrook ME, SA/ME. R10a.

447. **OLIVER P.[7] SAWYER** [see 279], b. 17 Jun 1817 Harpswell ME, d. 11 Apr 1867 Harpswell ME, m.(1) Mar 1838 Harpswell ME Elizabeth A. Toothaker, b. 24 Dec 1818 d. 3 Jun 1853, dau. John and Sarah (Ridley) Toothaker; m.(2) 24 Oct 1854 Mary White, b. ?. Sailor, ship carpenter, cooper. He bur. in Great Island ME. Tombstone of Elizabeth, Curtis Cem., Richmond ME, says she d. 18 Oct 1852 at 34 yrs, 6 mos.
Mary A., b. 8 Jan 1840, m.(1) 3 Sep 1856 Lyman Doyle, m.(2) Daniel R. Hodgden.
544 William Snow[8], 1841-1873.
545 John Whitmore[8], 1843-1925.
Sarah E., b. ?, d. 10 May 1844.
Eugene, b. 1846, d. Sep 1853.
Oliver E., b. 1 Aug 1848 Richmond ME.
Sarah A., b. 8 Feb 1850, d. 3 Mar 1892, m. 2 Nov 1866 Samuel J. Toothaker.
Charles Edwin, b. Sep 1852, d. 2 Oct 1852.
Elizabeth A., b. 25 Sep 1853, d. 7 Nov 1912, m. 14 Jan 1872 Charles Storer.
Sources: Richmond ME census 1850. VR Harpswell ME, Topsham ME, Richmond ME. M5, David Parker rec.

448. **JOSEPH E.[7] SAWYER** [see 280], b. 4 Nov 1837 Westbrook ME, d. 18 Dec 1916 Portland ME, m. 18 Apr 1872 Portland ME Lucille Daughty of Gray ME, b. ?. Clerk.
Charles, b. ?, d. 1875.
Henry P., b. 1878, d. 22 Mar 1911.
Sources: Deering ME census 1880. ME 1880 census index. VR Deering ME, SA/ME.

449. **CHARLES EDWIN[7] SAWYER** [see 281], b. 23 Aug 1834 Bath ME, m.(1) 1 Jan 1857 Bath ME Lucy B. Sylvester, b. ?; m.(2) 6 Jun 1877 Mary E. Gordon of Bath ME, b. ca. 1840.
546 Edwin S.[8], b. 1858.
Herbert Meade, b. 18 May 1863 Bath ME, m. 12 Sep 1888 Brunswick ME Annie C. Lunt of Brunswick ME, b. ?, dau. Robert and Jane A. (Gross) Lunt. In Worcester MA. Journalist, author.
Sources: VR Augusta ME. N44.

450. **CHARLES WINTHROP[7] SAWYER** [see 282], b. 17 Oct 1868 Dorchester MA, d. 1943, m. 18 Jun 1895 Boston MA Mabel L. Warren of Boston, b. 1871, dau. John C. and Katherine Warren.

Albion T., b. 1901 Dorchester MA, d. 1971, m. 1929 Mary H. Blood. CH: Albion T.; Joanna B.

Constance, b. 11 Aug 1902, d. 13 Sep 1938.

Harriet B., b. ?, m. Carroll Wilson.

Philip Warren, b. ?, d. 1970.

Sources: VR SA/MA. Albion T. Sawyer rec.

451. **CHARLES P.⁷ SAWYER** [see 283], b. 1859 Westbrook ME, d. 1922 Westbrook ME, m.(I) 29 Mar 1884 Almeda C. Lord of Windham ME, b. ?. Stablekeeper.

Sumner Cleveland, b. 27 Oct 1884 Westbrook ME, m. 4 Nov 1937 Manchester NH Lorena M. Cheney of New Brunswick Canada, b. 1906, dau. Owen and Agnes (Franklin) Cheney. Woodworker.

Sarah S. b. ?, m. _____ Leighton.

Addie, b. ?, m. David Loftus.

Daughter, b. ?, m. Everett Wilson.

Sources: VR Windham ME, SA/NH.

452. **LEVI WILLIS⁷ SAWYER** [see 285], b. 13 Feb 1857 Windham ME, d. 10 May 1932, m. 8 Feb 1897 So. Windham ME Ina E. Nealey, b. Jul 1878 d. 16 Sep 1963, dau. Frank W. and Mary A. (Holmes) Nealey. Farmer.

Clyde Milton, b. 30 May 1901 Windham ME, d. 21 Jan 1982, m. Hazel J. Hill.

Sources: VR SA/ME. Clyde M. Sawyer rec.

453. **WALTER H.⁷ SAWYER** [see 285], b. 29 Apr 1863 Windham ME, d. 12 Jul 1929, m. 25 May 1885 Windham ME Carrie Lord of Windham ME, b. 1865 d. 1900, dau. Nathan and Lucy J. (Verrill) Lord.

Irving W., b. 5 Feb 1888 Windham ME, d. Jan 1958 Portland ME, m.(1) Dolly Carter, b. ?; m.(2) Olivette McClellan, b. ?. CH: Ella, b. ?, m. _____ Folland.

Alice F., b. 5 Mar 1893, m. Charles E. Knowles.

Ella, b. 1897, m. Edward Axelson.

Sources: VR SA/ME. R28, Bertha E. Sawyer rec., Clyde M. Sawyer rec.

454. **EUGENE J.⁷ SAWYER** [see 285], b. 27 Dec 1865 Windham ME, d. 22 Apr 1943 Westbrook ME, m. Mary E Davis of Bridgton ME, b. 24 Feb 1869 d. 22 Dec 1919, dau. Samuel and Phebe (Durgin) Davis. Carpenter.

Edith May, b. 28 Nov 1888, d. 23 Oct 1968, m. George Durgin.

Mabel Edna, b. 7 Jul 1891 d. 6 Dec 1984, m.(1) Guy Jack, m.(2) Frank Foster.

Warren Louville, b. 16 Dec 1893, d. 24 Nov 1944, m. 8 Jul 1922 Portland ME Mildred M. McCubrey, b. ?. CH: Jean, b. 6 Mar 1924, m. 14 Sep 1946 Edward Philip Lefebvre.

Bernice Elizabeth, b. 7 Dec 1901, m. Robert Woodman.

Bertha E., b. 7 Dec 1901.

Sources: VR SA/ME. Bertha E. Sawyer rec., Kay Soldiers rec., Thomas W. Lefebvre rec.

455. **GEORGE W.⁷ SAWYER** [see 285], b. 6 Sep 1871 Windham ME, d. 9 Sep 1918 Westbrook ME, m. 26 Oct 1898 Windham ME Alfreda Jaquis of Casco ME, b. Mar 1830, dau. Walter G. and Martha (Smith) Jaquis. Farmer. In Westbrook 1907.

Ralph M., b. 28 Nov 1899.

Phyllis, b. ?.

Sources: VR SA/ME. Bertha E. Sawyer rec.

456. **FRANK SANFORD[7] SAWYER** [see 285], b. 12 May 1875 Windham ME, d. 1951 Windham ME, m. Anne Jorgensen of New Brunswick, Canada, b. 1 Jun 1884, d. 2 Feb 1953. Farmer, veterinary.

Chester Francis, b. ?.
Guy Edward, b. 11 Jul 1911, d. 17 Sep 1958, m. Charlotte Rolfe.
Arthur Leon, stillborn 26 Jan 1916.
Agnes Marie, b. ?, m. Fred Kelley.

Sources: VR SA/ME. Obit, Clyde M. Sawyer rec.

457. **JAMES ALEXANDER[7] SAWYER** [see 290], b. 1852 No. Yarmouth ME, m. 13 Nov 1891 Springfield MA Edith Maud Sawyer of Cumberland ME, b. 14 Nov 1870, dau. Asa and Eliza (Clough) Sawyer.

James Milton, b. 14 Jun 1893 No. Yarmouth ME.
Randall Asa, b. 24 Sep 1894 No. Yarmouth ME.

Sources: VR SA/ME, SA/MA.

458. **WESLEY[7] SAWYER** [see 291], b. Feb 1849 Cumberland ME, d. Aug 1934, m.(1) (I) 3 Mar 1873 Mary Ellen Cash of Cape Elizabeth ME, b. May 1855; m.(2) ?. Physician. In Lowell MA, Pelham NH.

Ardella J., b. ca. 1874, m. 3 Aug 1893 Salem MA Frederick W. Hand.
Olive J., b. ca. 1876.
Elizabeth Mabel, b. ca. 1878.
John Wesley, b. ca. 1879, d. World War I.
Hattie M., b. 26 Feb 1882, d. 16 Apr 1883.
Georgiann, b. Jan 1884.
Lauretta, b. Nov 1885.
Mary E., b. 28 May 1888.
Joseph H., b. 7 Jun 1890 Pelham NH, d.y.
Joseph, b. 1893, d. 30 May 1893.

Sources: Cape Elizabeth ME census 1880. Pelham NH census 1890. ME 1880 census index. VR Cape Elizabeth ME, SA/MA.

459. **CARLETON[7] SAWYER** [see 291], b. 1 Nov 1855 Cumberland ME, d. 1 Oct 1924 Foxboro MA, m.(1) Emma Barbour, b. ?; m.(2) 30 Apr 1889 Cambridge MA E. Louise Richardson of Walpole MA, b. 1863, dau. Horace R. and Hannah Richardson; m.(3) 20 Nov 1895 Bridgton ME Mary Abbie Mead of Bridgton ME, b. 5 Sep 1865 d. 18 Aug 1938, dau. Thomas and Sarah (Bean) Mead. In North Conway NH, Foxboro MA.

Henry Carleton, b. ?, d. of tuberculosis.
Stella Richarson, b. 31 Oct 1890, d. 17 May 1955, m. John Parker.
Olive L., b. 12 Apr 1897, unm. Went to New York.

Sources: North Conway NH census 1890. VR SA/ME, SA/MA. B40.

460. **EDWARD IRVING[7] SAWYER** [see 291], b. 28 Nov 186? Cumberland ME, d. at 75 yrs, m. Jun 1897 Ella Chamberlain, b. ? d. 26 Dec 1955.

Walter Emerson, b. 9 Aug 1898, d. 24 Nov 1957, m. 26 Aug 1934 Rose Bruce, b. 2 Dec 1897. In California. No CH.
547 Stanley Brooks[8], 1899-1957.
Harold Irving, b. 11 Jun 1905, d. 9 Dec 1971, m. 16 Jun 1934 Ida Smith, b. 26 Nov 1904. In Needham MA. No CH.
Edwin, b. ?, d.y.

Sources: VR SA/MA.

461. **FRED LELAND[7] SAWYER** [see 292], b. 16 Feb 1858 Alna ME, m. 24 Nov 1881 Nashua NH Mary E. Condaite of England, b. 1860. Harvard Law School. Lawyer.

Warren Lovering, b. 28 Nov 1886.

Sources: VR SA/MA. H29.

462. **CHARLES WILLIAM[7] SAWYER** [see 295], b. 11 Nov 1848 Brewer ME, d. 22 Dec 1933 Lynn MA, m. Apr 1871 Flora Deering of Brewer ME, b. 27 Mar 1851 d. 18 Feb 1944, dau. Samuel and Mary A. (Downes) Deering.

William G., b. 10 Feb 1874 Brewer ME, m. Harriet Collins, b. ?. In Lynn MA.
Fred, b. ca. 1876.
Elbridge Patten, b. 24 May 1880 Brewer ME.
Lottie J., b. 3 Jul 1886, m. 24 May 1905 Benjamin F. Hudson.

Sources: Brewer ME census 1850. VR SA/ME, SA/MA. Merle Graffam rec.

463. **ASA D.[7] SAWYER** [see 296], b. 14 Apr 1859 Milbridge ME, d. 19 Jul 1901 Bangor ME, m. 29 Sep 1892 Cherryfield ME Lillian V. Hutchins of Franklin ME, b. Jul 1863, dau. John and Sophia (Wentworth) Hutchins. Carpenter. In Ellsworth ME, Bangor ME. He bur. Milbridge ME.

Julia M., b. 9 Nov 1893.
Gladys V., b. 1895, d. 20 Jan 1896.
Sherly (male), b. 5 Jan 1898.
Daughter, b. 5 Sep 1900.

Sources: VR Ellsworth ME, Bangor ME, SA/ME. M5.

464. **WARREN[7] SAWYER** [see 298], b. 15 Apr 1850 Milbridge ME, d. 19 Apr 1914 Milbridge ME, m.(I) 18 Oct 1875 Mary A. Knowles of Addison ME, b. ?. Shipbuilder.

Joseph Warren, b. 29 Sep 1878 Addison ME.

Sources: Milbridge ME census 1880. ME 1880 census index. VR Milbridge ME, SA/ME.

465. **ELMER EBEN[7] SAWYER** [see 298], b. 24 Feb 1862 Milbridge ME, d. 2 Jan 1917 Milbridge ME, m. 11 May 1897 Cherryfield ME Frances G. Archer, b. 7 Mar 1872 d. 27 Jan 1954, dau. Charles and _____(Shaw) Archer. Shipbuilder. Both bur. Evergreen cem., Milbridge ME.

Jeanette, b. 19 Mar 1902, m. _____ Penfield. Went to Connecticut.
E. Philip, b. 31 Dec 1905, d. 19 May 1989, m. Madeline Stanley.
Allana, b. 8 Aug 1911, m. _____ Saywell. Went to Rhode Island.

Sources: VR SA/ME. Obit. M5.

466. **ALONZO[7] SAWYER** [see 298], b. 19 Feb 1864 Milbridge ME, d. 1939 Milbridge ME, m. 7 Sep 1898 Addison ME Eva A. Ingersoll, b. 25 Jan 1877 d. 1956, dau. Frank and Louise B. (McCaslin) Ingersoll. Shipbuilder. Both bur. Evergreen Cem., Milbridge ME.

Donald Frank, b. 24 Dec 1899.
Mortena A., b. 11 Mar 1901.
Roger I., b. 1908, d. 5 Feb 1986, m. Myra Honekley.

Sources: VR SA/ME. A38, M5, Obit (Roger).

467. **GEORGE A.[7] SAWYER** [see 299], b. 3 Feb 1859 Milbridge ME, d. 19 Aug 1936 Milbridge ME m.(1) 17 Apr 1883 Lillian Friend, b. Feb 1864 d. 7 Aug 1891; m.(2) Frances S. _____ of Brooklin ME, b. ?. Physician.

William Roberts, b. 25 Apr 1884, m. ?.

Edgar John, b. 10 Mar 1886, m. Amclia Cronk.
Sources: VR Milbridge ME. M5.

468. **GEORGE STILLMAN[7] SAWYER** [see 300], b. 11 Dec 1845 Milbridge ME, d. 20 May 1893 Milbridge ME, m.(1) 8 May 1869 Milbridge ME Josephine Greely, b. Oct 1848 d. 15 Apr 1873; m.(2) 24 Aug 1876 Margaret Hayland of Cherryfield ME, b. 12 May 1850 d. 1938. Master mariner. Wid. m. ca. 1900 Edwin Wallace.
548 Carroll Ray[8], b. 1877.
Sources: Milbridge ME census 1880. ME 1880 census index. VR Milbridge ME, SA/ME.

469. **GUSTAVUS[7] SAWYER** [see 300], b. 3 Jan 1848 Milbridge ME, d. 21 Mar 1923 Portland ME, m. 14 Nov 1868 Frances I. Fickett of Milbridge ME, b. 21 Sep 1851 d. 29 Dec 1908, dau. Rufus and Thirza Fickett. Merchant. Both bur. Evergreen Cem., Milbridge ME.
549 Ira Stillman[8], 1869-1941.
Effie D., b. 17 May 1873, d. 13 Apr 1964, m. Warren Pray.
Susie May, b. 1878, d. 6 Jan 1933, m. Raymond D. Fickett.
Eugene F., b. 8 Feb 1879 Milbridge ME, m. 4 Aug 1899 Cherryfield ME Gertrude M. Nichols of Cherryfield ME, b. 4 Aug 1880 d. 9 Dec 1918, dau. John and Harriet (Grant) Nichols. In Boothbay ME. Merchant. CH: Marjorie, b. 23 Jan 1900.
Everett W., b. 31 Jul 1882 Milbridge ME, d. 20 Mar 1960, m. Alice L. Colby, b. ?.
Sources: Milbridge ME census 1870, 1880. ME 1880 census index. VR Milbridge ME, SA/ME. M5.

470. **EDGAR E.[7] SAWYER** [see 301], b. 10 Apr 1853 Milbridge ME, d. Feb 1892 at sea, m. 25 May 1874 Milbridge ME Emma F. Dyer of Milbridge ME, b. 12 Oct 1855 d. 1 Apr 1920 Bangor ME, dau. James and Flora (Foster) Dyer. Sea captain. She bur. Evergreen Cem., Milbridge ME.
Josie E., b. 17 Feb 1877.
James, b. May 1882, d. 3 Mar 1903.
Myra H., b. 30 Mar 1889, m. 15 Jun 1920 Fred Avery.
Sources: VR Old Town ME, Skowhegan ME, SA/ME. M5, S44.

471. **HORACE FRENCH[7] SAWYER** [see 301], b. May 1854 Milbridge ME, d. 1937, m. Emily E. Orr of Prince Edward Island, Canada, b. Jun 1858 d. 1927. Canning business.
Gertrude, b. ca. 1879.
Lonnie, b. Jul 1881.
Guy, b. 14 Jan 1884 Milbridge ME.
Margaret W., b. 22 Apr 1888.
Natalie, b. 23 Apr 1895, d. 14 Feb 1896.
Claude, b. 10 Oct 1896, d. 13 Oct 1896.
Sources: ME 1880 census index. VR SA/ME. M5, S44.

472. **CHARLES TURNER[7] SAWYER** [see 301], b. 3 Oct 1863 Milbridge ME, d. 1901 at sea, m. 15 Dec 1886 Steuben ME Ella N. Brown of Milbridge ME, b. 23 Oct 1869, dau. John and Mary Ann Brown. Engineer. In Portland ME 1889. He bur. Evergreen Cem., Milbridge ME.
Edna, b. 22 Sep 1887, m. 2 Jun 1906 Oscar Barstow.
Eugene, b. 29 Nov 1889 Portland ME, m. 14 Sep 1926 Portsmouth NH Ethel M. (Clifford) Colby of Wiscasset ME, b. 1889, dau. Isaac F. and Bertha B. Clifford. Mechanic.
Susie C., b. 1 Jan 1891.
Ralph, b. 2 Feb 1892.
Phebe M., b. 2 Jul 1897.

Sources: VR Milbridge ME, Portland ME, Portsmouth NH, SA/ME. R2. M5.

473. **FRANK W.[7] SAWYER** [see 302], b. 10 Jun 1853 Milbridge ME, d. 14 Dec 1921 Milbridge ME m. 10 Nov 1879 Effie J. Wallace of Milbridge ME, b. Jan 1850. Merchant.

Carl Wallace, b. 7 Jul 1881 Milbridge ME, m. Olive _____, b. ?.

Allen Frank, b. 30 Oct 1889 Milbridge ME.

Sources: VR Milbridge ME, SA/ME. M5.

474. **JAMES WINSLOW[7] SAWYER** [see 304], b. 19 Jan 1872 Rogue Bluff ME, d. 21 Jan 1948 Jonesport ME, m. 29 Aug 1903 Christine Bagley, b. 13 Nov 1885 d. 16 Dec 1958. He bur. in Greenwood Cem., Jonesport ME.

Hollis Vinal, b. 11 Apr 1904, d. 12 Jul 1956, m. 1 Sep 1928 Doralies M. Libby, b. 20 May 1913. CH: Paul Vinal, b. 1 Dec 1928, m. 15 Aug 1958 Carol Wheatly; Richard Eugene, b. 16 Feb 1931, m. 21 May 1955 Betty M. Crowley; Carolyn A. N., b. 26 Dec 1934, m. 23 Jul 1958 Vincent Bonofiglio.

Martha A., b. 17 Apr 1909, d. 13 May 1946, m. 22 Sep 1928 Adrian Fish.

Fred, b. 21 Aug 1911, d. 10 Jul 1987, m. 8 Dec 1931 Edith Hoffens. Went to Connecticut.

Sources: Doralies M. Sawyer rec.

475. **JOSEPH S.[7] SAWYER** [see 305], b. 19 Sep 1837 Portland ME, m. 23 Dec 1858 Cumberland ME Abbie P. Grannell of New Brunswick, Canada, b. Sep 1835 d. 23 Jan 1904. Seaman. At Cape Elizabeth ME, Cumberland ME.

550 Walter L.[8], b. 1863.

Ada, b. 1869.

Sources: Cape Elizabeth ME census 1850. VR Cumberland ME.

476. **SOLOMON[7] SAWYER** [see 305], b. 20 Feb 1839 Chebeaque Isle ME, d. 16 Apr 1896 Yarmouth ME, m. 13 Dec 1861 Cumberland ME Margaret D. Grannell of New Brunswick, Canada, b. 1836. Seaman.

Anna M., b. 1867, d. 13 Aug 1869.

Wilmer Eugene, b. 29 Aug 1869 Yarmouth ME, m. 5 Feb 1896 Yarmouth ME Bertha E. Corliss of Vinalhaven ME, b. Mar 1874, dau. Octavius and Cora (Pierce) Corliss.

Fanny L., b. 1872.

Sources: Yarmouth ME census 1870, 1880. ME 1880 census index. VR Cumberland ME, SA/ME.

477. **GEORGE E.[7] SAWYER** [see 305], b. 8 Sep 1846 Cumberland ME, m. 29 Nov 1866 Attleboro MA Addie E. Bates, b. 1845, dau. William and Martha Bates. Seaman. In Lynn MA 1876.

Angie, b. 1869.

Ernest A., b. Aug 1876 Cumberland ME. In Lynn MA.

Edwin K., b. Aug 1883 Cumberland ME.

Sources: Yarmouth ME census 1880. ME 1880 census index. VR SA/MA.

478. **CALVIN SEAVEY[7] SAWYER** [see 306], b. 10 May 1850 Cumberland ME, m. Elizabeth Cushing Prince of No. Yarmouth ME, b. Dec 1850. Farmer. In Yarmouth ME.

Emery Smith, b. 29 Dec 1876 Yarmouth ME.

Louise Ethel, b. 17 Nov 1879.

Rena B., b. Apr 1884.

Harold Smith, b. 2 Oct 1896 Yarmouth ME.

Sources: Yarmouth ME census 1880. ME 1880 census index. VR Yarmouth ME.

479. **CHARLES HENRY[7] SAWYER** [see 308], b. 14 Nov 1840 Freeport ME, d. 7 Jun 1911 LaGrange ME, m.(I) 28 Jun 1869 Milbridge ME Susie J. Wallace, b. ?. Civil War.

Newell E., b. ca. 1870.

Mattie A., b. ca. 1872.

Sources: Old Town ME census 1850. LaGrange ME census 1880. ME 1880 census index. VR Milbridge ME, Old Town ME, SA/ME. M7A.

480. **HORATIO M.[7] SAWYER** [see 308], b. 26 Feb 1860 Milbridge ME, d. 26 Jun 1918 Laconia NH, m.(1) Cora B. Durgin of Medford MA, b. ?; m.(2) 23 Sep 1904 Old Town ME Mary L. Drew of Wakefield NH (div. 2 Mar 1912), b. ?; m.(3) 30 Mar 1912 Farmington NH Adeline Fontaine of Lawrence MA, widow, b. 1875. Fireman. In LaGrange ME, Farmington NH, Lawrence MA.

Sewall Brown, b. 14 May 1896 Lagrange ME, m. 18 Jul 1917 Laconia NH (div. 26 1921) Elsie G. (Downes) Mitchell of Belmont NH, b. 1882, dau. William H. and Mary E. (Randal) Downes.

Rosco I., b. 1910 Farmington NH, m. 20 Oct 1935 Venna M. Rollins.

Sources: VR SA/ME, SA/NH.

481. **LESTER FRANKLIN[7] SAWYER** [see 309], b. Mar 1859 Stillwater ME, m. Harriet Smart of Maxfield ME. b. ?. In Howland ME, Maxfield ME.

Bernard L., b. Aug 1886 Howland ME.

Raymond L., b. Jun 1888 Howland ME.

Edna E., b. 7 Nov 1890.

Harriet Mary, b. 7 Jan 1893.

Florence J., b. 16 May 1896, m._____ Cummings.

551 Lester Franklin[8], b. 1898.

Sources: Maxfield ME census 1890. VR SA/ME. Obit.

482. **ENOS[7] SAWYER** [see 309], b. 1 Apr 1866 Howland ME, d. 13 Dec 1953 Howland ME, m. 15 Oct 1890 Addie W. Lancaster of Maxfield ME, b. Mar 1876. Lumberman.

Son, b. 17 Jun 1892, d. 27 Jul 1892.

552 Stanley Enos[8], 1895-1982.

Sheldon I., b. 27 Sep 1902, m. 17 Jun 1933 Wilma Roberts, b. ?.

Florence A., b. 8 Jul 1904, m. 1 Jan 1927 Theodore P. Emery.

Irma G., b. 13 Jun 1906, m. 26 Aug 1928 Roland B. Andrews.

Sources: VR SA/ME. Obit (Irma and Sheldon), Theodore P. Emery rec.

483. **HARRY N.[7] SAWYER** [see 312], b. ca. 1877 Upper Stillwater ME, m. 9 Sep 1899 Madison ME Edith E. McKenney of New Sharon, b. 11 Apr 1882 d. 29 Mar 1964, dau. Joseph and Elvira (Withee) McKenney.

Cecil A., b. 1900, m. 5 Oct 1929 Olive O. Calway.

Levi Gray, b. 1903, m.(1) 9 Mar 1925 Berlin NH Caroline Sawyer of Jackman, ME, b. 6 Feb 1902, dau. Orrin and Viola (Colby) Sawyer; m.(2) 2 May 1936 Skowhegan ME Ellen Labon of Fairfield ME, b. 1914, dau. Anthony and Olga H. (Colus) Labon of Russia.

Sources: Upper Stillwater ME census 1880. ME 1880 census index. VR Skowhegan ME, SA/ME.

484. **CHARLES WARREN SAWYER** [see 315], b. 1 Jun 1854 Gloucester MA, m. 2 Jun 1879 Gloucester MA Clara M. McPherson of Gloucester MA, b. ca. 1859, dau. E. Fletcher and Nancy P. (McDonald) McPherson. Fisherman, shoemaker. In Beverly MA 1879.
553 Arthur Fletcher[8], b. 1879.
Sources: VR SA/MA.

485. **WILLIAM H.[7] SAWYER** [see 317], b. 20 Nov 1863 Gloucester MA, m. Bertie A. Doughty of New Brunswick Canada, b. ?. Mariner.
William A., b. 12 Aug 1885.
Sources: VR SA/MA.

486. **AUSTIN B.[7] SAWYER** [see 317], b. ca. 1868 Gloucester MA, m. 24 Nov 1892 Gloucester MA Annie J. McKay of Nova Scotia, Canada, b. ca. 1872, dau. John and Kitty (Casey) McKay. Hostler.
John David, b. 30 Sep 1894.
Everett Austin, b. 31 Dec 1895.
James F., b. ca. 1903, m. 4 Nov 1936 Portsmouth NH Eleanor M. Storment of Boston MA, b. 1913, dau. David and Ella Dwyer.
Sources: VR SA/MA.

487. **CHARLES H.[7] SAWYER** [see 318], b. ca. 1866 Gloucester MA, m.(1) 16 Sep 1891 Angie C. Howe of Gloucester MA, b. ca. 1873, dau. William H. and Louisa (Tarr) Howe; m.(2) 21 Dec 1893 Gloucester MA Annie E. Creamer of Ireland, b. ca. 1871, dau. Daniel J. and Annie (Shea) Creamer.
Charles H., b. 26 Dec 1891.
Sources: VR SA/MA.

488. **GEORGE A.[7] SAWYER** [see 318], b. 11 Mar 1868 Gloucester MA, m. 13 Jan 1893 Salem MA Elizabeth J. Deward of Gloucester MA, b. 1875, dau. Albert and Jennie (Decosta) Deward. Butcher.
Helen Elizabeth, b. 28 Jul 1893.
George Irving, b. 28 Nov 1895.
Sources: VR Gloucester MA, SA/MA.

489. **JOSEPH DILLAWAY[7] SAWYER** [see 320], b. 16 Nov 1849 Boston MA, m.(1) 10 Jun 1872 Boston MA Mary L. Wiggin of Boston MA, b. 21 Sep 1851, dau. Charles E. and Rebecca Wiggin; m.(2) 6 Jan 1881 Cambridge MA Lilla Ann Babcock, b. ?, dau. John M. and Mariam C. Babcock.. Woolen manufacturer. In Newton MA, Stanford CT.
Ethel, b. 30 Jul 1873, m. 25 Sep 1895 Boston MA T. Abbott Williams Jr.
Joseph, b. 18 Jun 1875.
Harold Stewart, b. 1 Jun 1878, d. 31 Mar 1882.
Lilla, b. 9 Jun 1882.
Mildred, b. 7 Dec 1885.
Leslie, b. 23 Oct 1886.
Sources: VR Gloucester MA, SA/MA. E16.

490. **ARTHUR WILKINSON[7] SAWYER** [see 320], b. 1851 Boston MA, d. 1917, m. 7 Oct 1873 Boston MA Carrie A. Lodge of Roxbury MA, b. 1851, dau. John and Elizabeth Lodge. Salesman.
Gordon Lodge, b. 24 May 1875.

Marguerite, b. 31 Mar 1879.
Sources: VR SA/MA.

## EIGHTH GENERATION

491. **ROSSWELL C.[8] SAWYER** [see 330], b. 30 Aug 1861 Porter ME, d. 1 Jan 1916 Parsonsfield ME, m. 7 Apr 1882 Susan F. Day of Cornish ME, b. ?. In Kezar Falls ME 1883. He bur. Riverside Cem., Cornish ME.

Sadie, b. 1883, d.y.
Eugene, b. 1884, d.y.
Gertrude M., b. 16 Aug 1886, d. 27 May 1970, m. Perley Stacy of Kezar Falls ME.
554 Ransom Towle[9], 1890-1974.
Amy E., b. ca. 1892, d. 1969, m. Leon R. Hussey of Kezar Falls ME.
555 Allen[9], 1893-1958.
556 Burton Smith[9], 1894-1972.
Anna Rose, b. 1900, d. 1958.
Wilfred, b. 20 Nov 1907, d. 29 Aug 1922 Parsonsfield ME.
Sources: VR SA/ME. F34, D25, A22, Allen Sawyer rec.

492. **SUMNER CUMMINGS[8] SAWYER** [see 330], b. 12 Mar 1866 Porter ME, d. 22 Oct 1937 Mineola NY, m.(1) 18 Sep 1885 Somersworth NH Lottie Ward of Portland ME, b. 1867, dau. Seth and Esther Ward; m.(2) 12 Oct 1900 Providence RI Almeda J. Morrison, b. ca. 1870, dau. William B. and Emily (Jeffrey) Morrison. In Portsmouth NH, Everett MA.

Daughter, b. 20 Apr 1889.
557 Paul Jeffrey[9], b. 1903.
Howard Gordon, b. 22 Feb 1905 Everett MA, d. 16 Nov 1976, m. 1935 Marion M. Wood, b. ca. 1910.
Esther Phyllis, b. 20 Apr 1914, m. 14 Oct 1930 Arthur Ringwall.
Sources: Paul J. Sawyer rec.

493. **SEWELL S.[8] SAWYER** [see 331], b. 22 Jan 1846 Porter ME, d. 23 Mar 1892 Porter ME, m. Susan Cressie of Pennsylvania, b. 24 Jul 1850 d. 16 Sep 1943. Farmer. Civil War: Company H, 171st Pennsylvania Infantry, 24 Oct 1862-8 Aug 1863, 27 Mar 1865-30 Jun 1865. In Porter ME 1870, 1880.

Elmer H., b. 1868 Porter ME, d. 1947. Carpenter. In Parsonsfield ME.
558 Mark Steven[9], 1873-1963.
Sources: Porter ME census 1870, 1880. VR Porter ME, SA/ME. M7A.

494. **WILLIAM HENRY[8] SAWYER** [see 331], b. 1847 Porter ME, d. 1927, m.(I) 27 Dec 1869 Sarah M. Stacy of Porter ME, b. 1850 d. 1919. Laborer. In Porter ME 1880.

Nehemia E., b. 1871 Porter ME, d. 12 May 1914, m. 24 Aug 1895 Freedom NH Eva M. Bickford of Porter ME, b. 1868, dau. Isaac and Mary J. Bickford. CH: Agnes S., b. May 1897.
Lula F., b. 1877, m. _____ Mason.
559 Charles R.[9], 1885-1972.
Sources: Porter ME census 1880. ME 1880 census index. VR Porter ME. R10c.

495. **FREEMAN WESLEY[3] SAWYER** [see 331], b. 3 Sep 1851 Porter ME, d. 14 Sep 1938 Kezar Falls ME, m. Sarah E. Towle of Porter ME, b. 7 Nov 1850 d. 1 Jan 1921, dau. John and

Ruth (Rice) Towle. Laborer. In Porter ME 1880. Note: Sarah was commonly called "Jo Razor" because of her sharp tongue.

Clarence W., b. 1873, d. 31 Dec 1875.

Cassie M., b. 1875, d. same year.

560 Ellsworth William$^{9}$, 1877-1932.

Sources: Porter ME census 1880. VR Porter ME. Kendal W. Sawyer rec.

496. **ALPHONSE$^{8}$ SAWYER** [see 331], b. 6 Mar 1853 Porter ME, d. 24 Nov 1898 Porter ME, m. 7 Apr 1878 Emma S. Tewksbury of Albany NH, b. 1858 d. 1901. Farmer. In Porter ME 1880. He bur. in Porter ME.

Burley E., b. 13 Jan 1879 Porter ME, m.(1) 4 May 1907 Freedom NH (div. May 1916) Mamie E. Wyman of Effingham NH, b. 1891, dau. Melvin and Idella (Thompson) Wyman; m.(2) 1 Jul 1916 Wolfboro NH (div. 15 Jul 1921) Alice May (Marden) Swett of Ossipee NH, b. 1894, dau. Alex and Ruth (Sharpe) Marden; m.(3) 6 May 1922 Wolfeboro NH Susie (Patee) Gray of Harrison ME, b. 1879, dau. George and Ann M. (Brown) Patee. CH: Son, b. 28 Nov 1908, d. same day Effingham NH; Mildred, b. 21 Oct 1916, d. 10 Dec 1916 Wolfboro NH.

Mabel, b. ?, m. _____ Thomas of Springfield IL.

Ruth Martha, b. 9 Oct 1888, d. 1948, m. Fred Mason.

Laura, b. 20 Nov 1894.

Sources: Porter ME census 1880. VR Porter ME, SA/ME, SA/NH. M5.

497. **WILLARD EVANGELINE$^{8}$ SAWYER** [see 332], b. 29 Jan 1859 Johnstown PA, d. 15 Feb 1928 in State Hospital, Danvers MA, m.(1) (I) 31 May 1885 Angie May Hurd of Portland ME, b. 2 May 1865 Freedom NH d. 5 Mar 1911 Somerville MA, dau. John and Frances (Grant) Hurd; m.(2) Jennie F. Edgerly of Porter ME, b. 29 Dec 1870 d. 8 Dec 1920 Parsonsfield ME, dau. Charles O. and Maria J. (Towle) Edgerly. In Porter ME, Somersworth NH, Charlestown MA, Roxbury MA, Somerville MA, Kezar Falls ME. Salesman. He bur. in Porter ME.

561 Kendal Willard$^{9}$, 1887-1981.

Sources: VR Porter ME, SA/ME. Gravestone (Jennie), Kendal W. Sawyer rec.

498. **GUY EMERY$^{8}$ SAWYER** [see 337], b. 8 May 1882 Limington ME, d. 5 May 1938, m. 17 Jun 1907 Marion Small, b. 15 Aug 1886 d. 18 Aug 1927, dau. Winfield Scott and Kate L. (Mitchell) Small. Marion bur. in North Limington ME.

Ralph Sherwood, b. 1 Oct 1908, m. Althea Haley.

Donald Small., b. 10 Apr 1910.

Eleanor Marguerite, b. 31 Jan 1913, d. 21 Sep 1987, m. Arthur W. Libby.

Justin S., b. 15 Aug 1921, d. 27 Jan 1922.

Marion Virginia, b. 3 Jan 1923, m. Manley Brackett of Limington ME.

Sources: L22, M8, Obit (Eleanor), Nancy Welch rec.

499. **WILLIAM ASA$^{8}$ SAWYER** [see 338], b. 14 Jan 1862 Buckfield ME, d. 10 Jan 1940 Sherman Mills ME, m.(1) Jeanette Bryant of Sherman Mills ME, b. 7 Feb 1870 d. 17 Mar 1910, dau. Albion and Lois (Stubbs) Bryant; m.(2) 1912 Jean Daigle, b. ? d. 29 Dec 1981; m.(3) Frances Constantine, b. ?. Attended Bryant and Stratton Commercial School of Boston MA. Farmer, lumberman. He bur. in Sherman Mills ME.

Mary E., b. 1 May 1890, d. 23 Feb 1920, m. 5 Jun 1911 Sidney Holmes.

Leo Harold, b. 10 Jul 1894 Sherman Mills ME, d. 13 Feb 1966, m.(1) Jesse Rideout, b. ?; m.(2) Lora Sleeper, b. ?.

Thelma D., b. 18 Dec 1899, d. May 1982, m. Royce Sleeper.

Delbert, b. 2 Mar 1901 Sherman Mills ME, m. Hazel Drinkwater, b. ?.
William Eugene, b. 28 Nov 1912 Sherman Mills ME, d. 1940, m. Wilma Dearborn, b. ?.
Evelyn, b. 15 Sep 1914, m. 15 Sep 1939 Glen Smith of Portsmouth NH.
John, b. 5 Apr 1917, m. 1939 Lillian Duffy of Sandwich MA.
Sources: VR SA/ME. N8 (William Asa Sawyer's letter), Evelyn Glenn Smith rec.

500. **PERCIVAL B.[8] SAWYER** [see 339], b. 17 Feb 1883 Phillips ME, m. 16 Mar 1904 Skowhegan ME Clara M. Shortier of Skowhegan ME, b. 25 Jun 1885 d. 20 Dec 1954, dau. Joseph and Louisa (Clukey) Shortier. In Skowhegan ME, Marlboro MA, Madison ME, Anson ME, Gardiner ME.

Raymond Percival, b. 25 Dec 1905 Skowhegan ME, m. 23 Jun 1956 Skowhegan ME Lucille V. Chapman of Skowhegan ME, b. ca. 1910, dau. Walter H. and Lillian (Daggett) Chapman.
Louise, b. 21 Jun 1908.
Armond, b. 30 Oct 1911 Marlboro MA, d. 7 Jul 1963, m. Beryl Flood of Farmington ME. CH: Stephen Clayton, b. ca. 1943, m. 16 Apr 1966 Carolyn A. Hunt; David William, b. ?.
Irene, b. 13 Nov 1913.
Robert, b. 2 Mar 1917. Went to South Carolina.
Kenneth, b. 11 May 1920.
Lucille, b. 10 Oct 1922, d. Dec 1979.
Barbara, b. 8 Jul 1929.
Sources: VR Skowhegan ME. Irene Sawyer rec.

501. **WILLIAM J.[8] SAWYER** [see 341], b. 21 Oct 1850 Addison ME, d. 30 Nov 1917 Columbia Falls ME, m. Almeda L. Ingersoll of Columbia ME, b. Nov 1855 d. 12 Mar 1906, dau. F. Greene and Lucy (Worcester) Ingersoll. In Columbia Falls ME, Jonesport ME.

Lucy b. 1875, d. in teens.
Luther Green, b. 11 May 1887 Columbia Falls ME, d. 1 Apr 1963 Columbia Falls ME, m. Jennie A. Worcester, b. 22 Oct 1890 d. 31 Jan 1987. CH: Marion, b. 29 Mar 1915, d. 25 Jan 1986, m. Reginald Hathaway; Lillian, b. 25 Jul 1917, m. Wilfred E. Rogers of Claremont NH.
Sources: Columbia Falls ME census 1880. ME 1880 census index. VR SA/ME. A38, Lillian Rogers rec.

502. **WALTER PRESTON[8] SAWYER** [see 341], b. 14 May 1854 Addison ME, d. 15 Aug 1922 Machias ME, m. 18 Jun 1879 Annie S. Tupper of Jonesport ME, b. Dec 1857 d. 1940. Blacksmith. In Columbia Falls ME.

Myra D., b. Jan 1880.
562 Percy Arlington[9], 1883-1961.
Madeline D., b. 20 Apr 1900.
Lizzie T., b. ?.
Sources: Columbia Falls ME census 1880. ME 1880 census index. VR SA/ME. Burton A. Sawyer rec.

503. **ANSEL M.[8] SAWYER** [see 342], b. Aug 1856 Addison ME, d. 9 Sep 1907, m.(I) 15 Sep 1885 Winifred B. Wallace of Providence RI, b. May 1862. Watchmaker. In Milbridge ME 1886.

Armida W., b. 24 Sep 1886.
Louis C., b. 1 Mar 1888.
Percival Ansell, b. 10 Jan 1890.

Corrine W., b. 10 Jan 1890.
Sources: VR SA/MA.

504. **CHARLES FRANKLIN[8] SAWYER** [see 349], b. 7 Nov 1842 Baldwin ME, d. 15 Jul 1910 Sanford ME, m. 4 Apr 1872 Baldwin ME Eliza A. Thorne of Sebago ME, b. 15 Jul 1850 d. 15 Nov 1912, dau. Bartholomew and Mary Thorne. Civil War: 17th Maine Regiment. B/S/land 1868-1869. Received pension 1871. Carpenter.

563 John Elmore[9], 1873-1967.
564 Fred Wilson[9], 1874-1952.
Annie J., b. 23 Dec 1877, d. 19 Jul 1900, m. in Sebago ME Sumner Shaw.
Georgia E., b. 16 Aug 1879, d. 16 May 1896 Sebago ME, unm.
Bertie, b. ?, d.y.
Frank, b. 21 Sep 1886, d. 25 Nov 1888.

Sources: Baldwin ME census 1880. ME 1880 census index. VR SA/ME. R10a, Obit (Georgia), Joyce R. Sawyer rec., Robert L. Taylor rec.

505. **HENRY NATHAN[8] SAWYER** [see 352], b. 29 Sep 1842 Boston MA, d. 12 Jul 1912 Canaan NH, m. 7 Nov 1871 Mary A. Neff of Philadelphia PA, b. ?. Printer.

565 Henry Nathan[9], 1872-1935.
Emma Georgie, b. 7 Sep 1874, d. 2 Mar 1875 Philadelphia PA.

Sources: VR SA/MA, SA/NH. Henry Nathan Sawyer rec.

506. **ALBERT E.[8] SAWYER** [see 355], b. ca. 1850, m.(1) 6 Nov 1878 Clinton MA Henrietta Schumacher of Boston MA, b. ca. 1850, dau. Hermon H. and Ellen Schumacher; m.(2) 25 May 1893 Fitchburg MA Julia E. (Harvey) Adams of Monson MA, b. ca. 1850, dau. Edward and Betsey (Tirrell) Harvey. In Lancaster MA 1878, Sterling MA 1893.

Edward R., b. 27 Mar 1880 Lancaster MA.

Sources: VR SA/MA.

507. **FRED HOWARD[8] SAWYER** [see 356], b. 17 Jul 1861 Portland ME, d. 28 Dec 1898 Melrose MA, m.(1) 27 Aug 1883 Chelsea MA Winifred Smith of Chelsea MA, b. 1863, dau. Charles G. and Frances Smith; m.(2) 12 Oct 1892 West Medford MA Elizabeth Alice Hatch of Andover MA, b. 25 Aug 1861 d. 26 Sep 1901, dau. George F. and Matilda E. (Learwell) Hatch. In Melrose MA. Clerk.

Bertram Hatch, b. 5 Jul 1894 Melrose MA, d. 28 Aug 1973, m. 17 Jun 1922 Concord MA Doris Moulton Worthen of Concord MA, b. 1898 Concord MA, dau. John H. and Dell M. (Moulton) Worthen. Dentist. In Salem MA.
Muriel, b. 14 Apr 1896, d. 23 Jan 1902 Salem MA.
Charles Bowker, b. 8 Oct 1898, d. 26 Jan 1902 Salem MA.

Sources: Dr. Bertram Hatch Sawyer rec.

508. **WALTER SUMNER[8] SAWYER** [see 356], b. 15 Sep 1865 Portland ME, d. 15 Dec 1919 Boston MA, m. 17 Dec 1906 Teckla B. Cummins, b. ?.

Walter, b. ?.

Sources: Dr. Bertram Hatch Sawyer rec.

509. **FRANK LEROY[8] SAWYER** [see 361], b. Aug 1849 Saco ME, d. 7 Sep 1913, m. 27 Dec 1873 Abby A. Moulton of Scarboro ME, b. 21 Aug 1849 d. 5 Jun 1888. In Leominster MA.

566 Fred Sturdevant[9], 1875-1961.
Elizabeth M., b. 1877, m. John Burnham.

Sources: Saco ME census 1880. ME 1880 census index. VR Scarboro ME. Wendell F. Sawyer rec., Joan H. Sawyer rec.

510. **GEORGE AUSTIN⁸ SAWYER** [see 366], b. 18 Oct 1850 Bridgton ME, d. 28 Mar 1916 Bridgton ME, m. 11 May 1879 Chatham NH Anna M. Douglas of Bridgton ME, b. 14 Sep 1853 d. 16 Apr 1926, dau. Earl and Eunice (Emerson) Douglas. Farmer. He bur. in W. Bridgton ME.

Lester D., b. 5 Mar 1879, d. 12 Oct 1881.
Chester S., b. 29 Sep 1881. Farmer. In Fryeburg ME.
Earle D., b. 1 Apr 1889. Physician. Went to Washington State.
Leon George, b. Dec 1890.

Sources: Bridgton ME census 1880. ME 1880 census index. VR Bridgton ME, SA/ME.

511. **GEORGE CHESTER⁸ SAWYER** [see 367], b. 7 Oct 1879 Bridgton ME, m. ?.

George F., b. ?, m. Ethel _____, b. ?.

Sources: Ethel Sawyer's rec.

512. **GEORGE MELLEN⁸ SAWYER** [see 369], b. 18 Feb 1868 Buxton ME, d. 1954 Buxton ME, m. 12 Oct 1895 Buxton ME Daisy P. Towle, b. 1876 d. 1958, dau. Arthur E. and Fanny (Ladd) Towle. He bur. Tory Hill Cem., Buxton ME.

Child, b. 13 Jul 1896.
Kenneth E., b. 20 Aug 1897.

Sources: VR SA/ME. M5.

513. **JOHN H.⁸ SAWYER** [see 371], b. 7 Aug 1852 Portland ME, d. 11 Apr 1920 Portland ME, m. 13 Sep 1875 Fannie S. Means, b. ?. In No. Raymond ME.

Alice M., b. 13 Sep 1875.
Lewis, b. 27 Jul 1877 Portland ME.
Lena C., b. 27 Jul 1877.
Robert F., b. 19 Sep 1879 Portland ME.

Sources: VR SA/ME.

514. **ADDISON GAGE⁸ SAWYER** [see 373], b. 17 Aug 1861 Arlington MA, m. 6 Jun 1886 Fitchburg MA Ida Blanche Ganong of New Brunswick, Canada, b. ?, dau. Samuel F. and Isabelle Ganong. Expressman. In Fitchburg MA, Waltham MA.

Charles Addison, b. 7 Dec 1887.
Rachel Ganong, b. 25 Sep 1893.

Sources: VR SA/MA.

515. **CARROLL WHITMAN⁸ SAWYER** [see 373], b. Jan 1864 Waltham MA, m. 11 Apr 1893 Cambridge MA Jennie Mabel Clapp of Allston MA, b. Mar 1866, dau. Moody C. and Flora A. (Goding) Clapp. Salesman. In Somerville MA, Waltham MA.

Whitman, b. 9 Mar 1894.

Sources: VR SA/MA.

516. **GEORGE THOMAS⁸ SAWYER** [see 374], b. 12 Aug 1865 Windham ME, d. 1949 Buxton ME, m. 1 Aug 1885 Windham ME Georgianna Manning Phinney, b. 21 Dec 1861, d. 1959. He bur. Tory Hill Cem., Buxton ME.

Arthur Thomas, b. 6 Jun 1889 Windham ME, d. 1970 Bar Mills ME. World War I.
Harold D., b. 1894 Windham ME.

Sources: VR Windham ME. M5, D4.

517. **CLARENCE P.[8] SAWYER** [see 376], b. 1865 Windham ME, m. 6 Jun 1891 Boston MA Louise Dunn of Deering ME, b. ca. 1870, dau. George C. and Grace Dunn. Painter.

John Philip, b. 31 Dec 1912.

Sources: VR SA/MA. H30.

518. **ALMON J.[8] SAWYER** [see 378], b. 1862 W. Buxton ME, d. 1942, m. 24 Oct 1888 Boston MA Elizabeth Jackson of Prince Edward Island, Canada, b. 1872, dau. Michael and Margaret Jackson. Tinsmith. In Boston MA. He bur. Hollis ME.

Elmer Frederick, b. 6 Dec 1894.

567 Bruce S.[9], 1898-1943.

Sources: VR SA/MA. M5, Nancy Welch rec.

519. **CHARLES F.[8] SAWYER** [see 380], b. 10 May 1867 Standish ME, d. 22 Dec 1932 Manchester NH, m. 10 May 1889 Dover NH Ellen C. Dodge of Wolfeboro NH, b. 11 Feb 1872 d. 29 Feb 1944, dau. Elwell and Emma Dodge. In Hollis ME, Portsmouth NH, Manchester NH. He bur. in Maplewood Cem., Standish ME.

Gary C., b. Mar 1890.

Sources: VR SA/NH. M8, M5.

520. **ALGERNON A.[8] SAWYER** [see 380], b. 1871 Standish ME, m. 28 May 1891 Haverhill MA Carrie Isabel Devereaux of Castine ME, b. Jan 1871, dau. Samuel and Iyrinna Devereaux. Farmer, shoemaker. In Hollis ME, Plaistow NH.

Addie Melinda, b. Sep 1892.
Ethel (Edith?) M., b. 16 Mar 1894.
Bernice I., b. 18 Nov 1896.
Burley Emery, b. 18 Nov 1896 Plaistow NH.
Paul E., b. 24 Jan 1898 Plaistow NH.
Dorothy M., b. 31 Oct 1899.
Harold Walter, b. 22 Apr 1903.

Sources: VR Plaistow NH, SA/MA.

521. **CHARLES ELBRIDGE[8] SAWYER** [see 383], b. 7 Apr 1874 Rochester NH, d. 29 Aug 1959 Haverhill MA, m.(1) 12 Feb 1895 Providence RI Elsie Deering of Nashua NH, b. 1872; m.(2) Katherine Pearl, b. ?. Justice of Court.

Mildred S., b. ?, m. Harold Ryan.
Russell Floyd, b. 14 Jan 1899, d. 17 Jun 1960, m. Dorothy Merrill.

Sources: VR Haverhill MA. H32.

522. **FRANK ALMON[8] SAWYER** [see 384], b. 17 Jul 1875 Arlington MA, m. 10 Oct 1901 Louise Randall of Fort Wayne IN, b. ?.

Frank Almon, b 8 Aug 1902, m. Jun 1925 Elizabeth Clarke.
Randall F., b. 27 Sep 1903, m Jun 1930 Margaret Ward.
James E., b. 30 Nov 1907, m. Mary E. Harvey.
Louise, b. 4 Apr 1910.
George P., b. 6 Aug 1918, m. 31 Aug 1940 Shirley Simmons.

Sources: George P. Sawyer rec.

523. **JOHN MARSHALL[8] SAWYER** [see 385], b. 1890 Buxton ME, d. 1927 Wellsley MA, m. 16 Sep 1914 Mary E Weymouth, b. ?, dau. Frank E. and Elizabeth (Mahoney) Weymouth. In Saco ME, Portland ME.

John Marshall, b. 22 Nov 1915.

Sources: W31, John M. Sawyer, Jr rec.

524. **HARRY ANSEL[8] SAWYER** [see 386], b. 17 Apr 1882 Portland ME, m. 12 Sep 1911 Gertrude M. Burns, b. ?. In Cumberland Mills ME.

John Phillips, b. 20 Sep 1912 Portland ME. In Cumberland Mills ME.

Sources: W11.

525. **CHARLES FRANCIS[8] SAWYER** [see 388], b. 3 Aug 1879 Poland ME, d. 2 Apr 1954, m. 13 Aug 1898 Oxford ME Inez I. McAllister, b. 1881 d. 1969, dau. George and Nettie (Webber) McAllister. Store owner. In Hebron ME. He bur. in W. Minot ME.

Charles Francis, b. 1901, d. 1960, m. (div. 1950) Marion Rollins. CH: Keith Marvin, b. 12 May 1932, m. 20 Dec 1957 Marilyn Newcombe.

Cynthia, b. ?, d. 1981, m. Guy Libby of W. Minot ME.

Nettie, m. _____ Dimock of Norway ME.

Sources: VR SA/ME. Grandfather's will [210], Nettie Dimock rec., Keith M. Sawyer rec.

526. **FRANKLIN LUCIUS[8] SAWYER** [see 393], b. 29 May 1886 Manchester VT, m. Martha Clay Wright, b. 6 Mar 1884. In Walpole NH.

Edward S., b. 18 Nov 1925, m. Margaret G. Hale.

Sources: P25, Edward S. Sawyer rec.

527. **HENRY MORTON[8] SAWYER** [see 398], b. 3 Aug 1865 Cape Elizabeth ME, d. 1932, m. 20 May 1887 Cape Elizabeth ME Elizabeth M. Small of Cape Elizabeth ME, b. 1865, d. 1926.

Margaret F., b. 1890, d. 1911.

Annie Elizabeth, b. 8 Oct 1892.

Daniel, b. 10 Feb 1895.

Sources: VR Cape Elizabeth ME, SA/ME.

528. **CHARLES L.[8] SAWYER** [see 406], b. Mar 1863 Hermon Pond ME, m. 1 Feb 1894 Limestone ME Mary H. Browne, b. ?. Teacher.

Bernice May, b. 13 Jan 1895.

Maria Hortense, b. 9 Sep 1896.

Madelene Beatrice, b. 1 Apr 1898.

Bela, b. ?.

Charles, b. ?.

Sources: VR SA/ME.

529. **JUSTUS WILSON[8] SAWYER** [see 410], b. 8 Jan 1886 Holliston MA, d. 1947, m. Caroline Elizabeth Johnson, b. 31 Oct 1886.

Evelyn Frances, b. 10 Dec 1910, m _____ McDonald. Went to Virginia.

Herbert Wilson, b. 1912, m. ?. Went to Medway MA.

Edgar Perley, b. 8 Jan 1916, m. ?.

Richard Stanley, b. Oct 1920, m. ?. Went to Mendon MA.

Arlene Edith, b. 25 Jul 1924, m. _____ Gallot. Went to Pennsylvania.

Barbara Ann, b. 30 Sep 1929, m. _____ Straight.

Sources: VR SA/MA. Richard S. Sawyer rec.

530. **NEIL GOULD[8] SAWYER** [see 414], b. 20 Sep 1916 Easton ME, m. 30 May 1945 Portland ME Sarah Louise Parsons, b. 19 Jan 1920 Presque Isle ME, dau. Vaughan William and Margaret Louise (Boone) Parsons. In Bangor ME.

Richard Wallace, b. 9 Apr 1946 Riverside CA, m. 12 Jul 1969 Elizabeth Hersey.

Margaret Alice, b. 10 May 1949, m. 30 Jul 1977 Anton Finelli.

Louise, b. 2 Feb 1951, m.(1) (div. 1978) Roger Ballou, m.(2) 11 Sep 1982 Michael Elefante.

Elizabeth, b. 27 Oct 1956, m.(1) 30 Jun 1979 (div. 1983) George Soules, m. (2) 29 Apr 1989 Joshua D. Cutler.

Sources: Neil G. Sawyer rec.

531. **GEORGE IRVING[8] SAWYER** [see 416], b. 5 Jul 1858 Portland ME, d. 31 Aug 1912 So. Portland ME, m. 28 Jul 1887 Ada A. Bryant, b. Feb 1867 d. 4 Sep 1892, dau. Amos S. and Jeanette (Durham) Bryant. Woodworker.

Philip Bryant, b. 18 Dec 1890, d. 4 Mar 1891.

John Irving, b. 22 Aug 1892.

Sources: VR SA/ME. M5.

532. **HERBERT THOMAS PENNEY[8] SAWYER** [see 417], b. 17 Feb 1867 Hebron ME, m. 24 Jun 1893 Conway NH Minnie M. Blake of Gray ME, b. 25 Dec 1875 Gray ME, dau. O. G. and Abbie W. Blake. In No. Yarmouth ME. He bur. in Evergreen Cem., Portland ME.

Susan A., b. 26 Aug 1894.

Hugh, b. 1903 No. Yarmouth ME.

Rodney Lee, b. 9 Mar 1905 No. Yarmouth ME, d. 17 Dec 1973 Vergennes VT, m. 27 Jun 1931 Colebrook NH Alice Cole of Stewartstown VT, b. 1912. In Colebrook NH. CH: Ruth L., b. 9 Jun 1934, m. 27 Jun 1952 Bernard Stewart.

Phillip, b. 1907 No. Yarmouth ME.

Priscilla, b. ?.

Sources: VR SA/ME. P28.

533. **PERLEY CLAIR[8] SAWYER** [see 419], b. 6 Feb 1885 Gray ME, d. 31 Oct 1958 Gray ME, m. Jennie M. Bohnsen of Cumberland Mills ME, b. 27 Jan 1885 d. 23 Jun 1979.

Kenneth Horatio, b. 22 Jan 1908, m. 1931 Evelyn Pierce, b. ?.

Elbert Carsten, b. 5 Jan 1911 Gray ME, d. 6 Mar 1983, m. 18 May 1935 Stratham NH Hazel J. Parkhurst of Gray ME, b. 1909, dau. Arthur D. and Lillian L. (Marsden) Parkhurst. Mechanic.

Margaret Clair, b. 29 Jul 1919.

Sources: Margaret C. Sawyer rec.

534. **WILLIAM F.[8] SAWYER** [see 423], b. 13 Mar 1848 Portland ME, d. 22 Jul 1880 Durham ME, m. 28 Nov 1867 Rosa P. Bennett of Westbrook ME, b. 1 Jan 1849 d. 16 Oct 1937.

Albert F., b. 1868, d. 1937, m. Mary E. Lanigan, b. 1868, d. 1927.

568 Charles Henry[9], 1871-1946.

Sources: Durham ME census 1880. Vaughn Sawyer rec.

535. **HENRY JACKSON[8] SAWYER** [see 424], b. 16 Jun 1862 Portland ME, d. 1939 Portland ME, m. 26 Jul 1885 Cora M. Wiggins of Portland ME, b. May 1862 d. 1948. He bur. in Evergreen Cem., Portland ME.

Bessie M., b. 22 Jul 1886.

Sadie E., b. 17 Oct 1887.
Jennie L., b. 13 Dec 1888.
Alice G., b. 12 Nov 1890, d. 17 Nov 1910.
Cora Estelle, b. 25 Jan 1893.
Alonzo W., b. Feb 1898.
Clifford Henry, b. 26 Feb 1900, d. 18 Apr 1900.

Sources: VR Portland ME, SA/ME. M5.

536. **CLARENCE BUCK[8] SAWYER** [see 425], b. 5 Mar 1879 So. Boston MA, d. 13 Jan 1951 Naval Hospital, Chelsea MA, m. 15 Jun 1904 Bertha May Watson of Boston MA, b. 23 Feb 1879 d. 15 Jul 1916. Mechanical engineer. In Boston MA, Dennisport MA. Note: [C63] says that Clarence was awarded the Congressional Medal of Honor during the Spanish American War, but official records do not support this claim.

Richard Merrill, b. 3 Jul 1907 W. Roxbury MA, d. 29 Sep 1974 Peterborough NH, m. 6 Jul 1935 E. Kingston NH Frances (Sanborn) Knight, b. 16 Jan 1910, d. 8 Oct 1952, dau. Charles F. and Josephine M. Sanborn. U.S.Army officer. In Salem OR, Exeter NH, New York, Peterborough NH. CH: Susan Ann, b. 31 Mar 1937; George Merrill, b. 29 Sep 1938.

Arthur Gilman, b. 22 Aug 1912, W. Roxbury MA, d. 25 Mar 1987 Hamden CT, m. 26 Oct 1939 Exeter NH Muriel R. Smith of Exeter NH, dau. Chester H. and Mabel F. (Babcock) Smith. Traveling saleman. In Exeter NH, Waban MA. CH: John Gilman, b. 21 Aug 1942.

Sources: C63, Obit.

537. **FRANCIS HOWARD[8] SAWYER** [see 426], b. 15 Nov 1866 Boston MA, m. 23 Jun 1889 Lynn MA Annie G. Geary of Rockland MA, b. 1870, dau. Thomas H. and Mary A. Geary. Clerk, In Lynn MA.

Edison, b. 29 Mar 1891 Boston MA.

Sources: SA/ME, SA/MA.

538. **HARRISON HILL[8] SAWYER** [see 427], b. 1 May 1873 Boston MA, m. Mary Louise Goode of E. Boston MA, b. ?. Part of family lived in Boylston; farm is now under waters of Quabban Reservoir.

Harrison J., m. Beatrice _____.
John Francis, m. Florence May _____.

Sources: F. May Sawyer rec.

539. **BENJAMIN H.[8] SAWYER** [see 428], b. 14 Sep 1888 Portland ME, d. 6 Dec 1968 Portland ME, m. Danietta D. Miller, b. 6 Apr 1898 d. 7 Oct 1986. Fireman.

Robert, b. ?, m. Joann _____.
Lewis Benjamin, m. Theresa Jane Powell.
William A., m. Byle Ann Carson.
Benjamin, m. Sandra _____.

Sources: Lewis B. Sawyer rec., Susan Szewczyk rec.

540. **CARLE D.[8] SAWYER** [see 429], b. 26 Jan 1881 Eaton NH, d. 30 May 1966, m.(1) 14 Nov 1901 Madison NH Mabel S. Moses of Freedom NH, b. 2 Jun 1882 d. 24 Apr 1910, dau. William Isaac and Sarah J. (Wilkinson) Moses; m.(2) 29 May 1912 Eaton NH Lillian Osgood of Boston MA, b. 9 Mar 1887 d. 20 Jun 1956, dau. Andrew B. and Harriet (Billings) Osgood. In California. He bur. in Freedom NH.

Everett Daniel, b. 1903, m. 6 Mar 1931 Elmona E. Browne, b. ca. 1905.
Sources: VR SA/NH. M56, M5.

541. **HARRY M.[8] SAWYER** [see 432], b. Apr 1864 Deering ME, m. 21 May 1883 Mary Hanlin of Ireland, b. Jan 1863. In Portland ME.

Frank Ellis, b. 28 Feb 1885 Portland ME.
Mary A., b. 10 Apr 1891.

Sources: VR Portland ME.

542. **EDWARD WHITMORE[8] SAWYER** [see 435], b. 17 Apr 1866 Portland ME, d. 1957, m. 30 Sep 1891 Milan NH Flora B. Bickford of Milan ME, b. 30 Jul 1863 d. Jul 1946, dau. Charles and Amanda (Folsom) Bickford. In Milan NH, Boston MA, Melrose MA. Clerk.

Bickford E., b. 1 Aug 1894, m. 19 Aug 1917 Grace Bell, b. ?. Went to Florida.
Helen, b. 5 May 1899, m. 1 Oct 1923 Herbert Shimmon.

Sources: VR SA/NH, SA/MA. F1.

543. **HADWIN[8] SAWYER** [see 437], b. 1882, m. Pearl Tucker, b. ca. 1885. In Holbrook MA.

Hadwin Emery, b. 4 Mar 1908, m. Ruth H. Gray.

Sources: Ruth H. Sawyer rec.

544. **WILLIAM SNOW[8] SAWYER** [see 447], b. 9 Aug 1841 Richmond ME, d. Feb 1873 Danielsville CT, m. 1 May 1864 Emma E. Jones of Richmond ME, b. 12 Jun 1844 Richmond ME d. 8 Feb 1876 Acton ME. Civil War. Both bur. Curtis Cem., Richmond ME.

Waldron Eugene, b. 7 Feb 1864 Richmond ME, d. 14 Jul 1939 Waltham MA, m. 8 Nov 1888 Ida Florence Mitchell, b. 14 Nov 1864 d. 24 Nov 1948. CH: Ethel Mae, b. 16 Apr 1890, m. 15 Jan 1918 Warren K. Green.
Mary Louise, b. 1867, d. 1904, m.(1) 1 Dec 1891 William H. Curtis, m.(2) Frank Foster.
George Prescott, b. 1869, d. 3 May 1887 Acton ME.

Sources: VR SA/MA. F33, M5.

545. **JOHN WHITMORE[8] SAWYER** [see 447], b. 14 Jul 1843 Richmond ME, d. 31 Mar 1925 at Naval Hospital, Chelsea MA, m.(1) 9 Feb 1867 Louise M. Merrill of Freeport ME, b. 1848 d. 1899, dau. Richard and Elizabeth (Hill) Merrill; m.(2) 11 Dec 1900 Revere MA Phoebe Jane (Merrill) Colson of Bath ME, wid. of Clark, b. ? d. 9 Jan 1914. Civil War: Enl. US Navy 24 Dec 1861 Boston MA, discharged 30 Sep 1863.

Guy C., b. 31 Dec 1869 Bath ME, d. 1910 Revere MA.
Jennie Louise, b. 10 Mar 1872, d. 1872 Woburn MA.

Sources: Bath ME census 1880. VR Bath ME. N1A.

546. **EDWIN S.[8] SAWYER** [see 449], b. 1858 Bath ME, m. 25 Oct 1877 Bath ME Fanny M. Bradford of Bath ME, b. ?. Painter. In Lynn MA.

Charles Edwin, b. 4 May 1887.
Don Linwood, b. 20 Dec 1892.

Sources: VR SA/ME, SA/MA. M5.

547. **STANLEY BROOKS[8] SAWYER** [see 460], b. 29 Dec 1899 Cumberland ME, d. 9 Apr 1957 Jamaica Plain MA, m. 12 Oct 1927 (later div.) Gertrude Woods, b. 25 Jan 1898.

Richard Irving, b. 10 Sep 1930, m. 2 Oct 1954 Cynthia Bailey, b. ?. In Cheshire CT. CH: Debra, b. ?; Donna, b. ?.
Priscilla, b. 25 Jan 1935, m. 23 Apr 1954 Howard W. Hammond.

Sources: VR SA/MA.

548. **CARROLL RAY$^8$ SAWYER** [see 468], b. 15 May 1877 Milbridge ME, m. Bertha Clark of Nova Scotia, b. 1878. Chauffeur. In Jamaica Plain MA.

Margaret Wallace, b. ca. 1899, unm.

Ray Stillman, b. 1909 Jamaica Plain MA, m. 20 Jun 1936 Manchester NH Miriam S. Riford, b. 1914, dau. James C. Simpson of Edinborough, Scotland. CH: Robert C., Barrie J.

Sources: VR SA/MA, SA/NH.

549. **IRA STILLMAN$^8$ SAWYER** [see 469], b. 11 Mar 1869 Milbridge ME, d. 5 Apr 1941 Portland ME, m.(I) 20 Aug 1890 Lillian May White of Columbia Falls ME, b. 20 May 1870 d. 1956, dau. Augustine S. and Mary E. (Allen) White. Insurance agent. In Columbia Falls ME.

569 Merrill Ray$^9$, b. 1892.

Clarence A., b. 18 Aug 1898 Milbridge ME, d. 1943, m. Grace Louise McIntosh, b. ca. 1899.

Lawrence White, b. 7 Feb 1907 Milbridge ME, m. Alice (Bette) Crosby b. 23 Sep 1908. In Kennebunk ME. CH: Lawrence, b. 19 Dec 1932, m. Barbara Turner; Lillian M., b. 19 Sep 1935, m. Cedric Porter.

Sources: VR Milbridge ME. Theodora Hoyt Sawyer rec.

550. **WALTER L.$^8$ SAWYER** [see 475], b. 1863 Cumberland ME, m. 12 Nov 1884 Portland Flora M. Farmer., b. ca. 1870. Editor.

Chapman Ford, b. 20 Jun 1894 Boston MA.

Sources: VR SA/ME, SA/MA.

551. **LESTER FRANKLIN$^8$ SAWYER**. [see 481], b. Feb 1898 Maxfield ME, m.(1) Clara Casey, b. ?, m.(2) June Vilsia, b. ?

Frank Herbert

Clarence Irving, b. 17 Mar 1921, d. 27 Jan 1989, m. _____Merrill.

Donald W.

Lester Franklin

Agatha Hillery, m. _____ Cummings.

Shirley Marie, m. _____ Delong.

Maynard Elliot

Byron Arthur

Marilyn Florence, m. _____ Weatherbee.

David Edwin

Blanche Estes, m.(1) _____ Stevens; m.(2)_____ Armstrong.

Sources: Obit, Agatha Cummings rec.

552. **STANLEY ENOS$^8$ SAWYER** [see 482], b. 10 May 1895 Howland ME, d. 2 Jan 1982, m. 20 Oct 1917 Marjorie Bartlett, b. ?. Trucker. In Milo ME.

Waldron E., b. 1921, m. Winona Cole.

Sources: Winona C. Sawyer rec.

553, **ARTHUR FLETCHER$^8$ SAWYER** [see 484], b. 13 Aug 1879 Beverly MA, m. Nellie S. Page of Salem MA, b. ?. In Winchester ME.

Albert K., b. ca. 1907, m. 18 Sep 1932 Phyllis Jackson.

Sources: VR SA/MA.

## NINTH GENERATION

554. **RANSOM TOWLE⁹ SAWYER** [see 491], b. 9 Sep 1890 Parsonsfield ME, d. 3 Jan 1974 New Port Richey FL, m. 2 Apr 1911 Freedom NH Agnes V. Weeks of Porter ME, b. 2 Oct 1893 d. 1960, dau. Lester and Cora (Stanley) Weeks. Electrician. In Five Islands (Bath) ME. He bur. in Cornish ME.

Theresa, b. 7 Nov 1912, d. 1983, m. Arthur Nelson.
Raymond E., b. 25 Aug 1913, m. 31 May 1937 Celia Meserve. Went to Utah.
Ethelyn (Lillian), b. 6 Dec 1914, m. _____.
Cora M., b. 25 Jun 1916, d. 11 Sep 1916 Parsonsfield ME.
Melia Frances, b. 20 Jun 1918.
Shirley W., b. 15 Apr 1921, m. Richard Bowman.
Ransom Towle, b. 1923, d. 22 Jun 1988, m. Phyllis Stover of Lewiston ME.
Lincoln K., b. 12 Feb 1924, d. 7 May 1924.
Ellen Lorraine, b. 3 Sep 1927, m. Warren Mank.
Jacqueline Ruth, b. 10 Feb 1929, unm.
Donald Marvin, b. Jan 1934, d. 15 Jan 1939.

Sources: F34, H17, D25.

555. **ALLAN⁹ SAWYER** [see 491], b. 6 Aug 1893 Parsonsfield ME, d. 5 Nov 1958 Togus ME, m. 29 Jan 1920 North Wilmington MA Anna Frolio, b. 20 Jun 1900 d. 22 Sep 1958. In Kezar Falls ME.

Maxine, b. 29 Jan 1921, m. 19 Jan 1946 John Lyle.
Allan, b. 23 Jan 1923 No. Wilmington MA, m. 7 Sep 1947 Jeanette Huber. CH: Gary Allan, b. 31 Mar 1950.
Mildred, b. 23 Aug 1932, m. 5 May 1952 Charles Metcalf.

Sources: VR SA/ME. Maxine Lyle rec., Allan Sawyer rec.

556. **BURTON SMITH⁹ SAWYER** [see 491], b. 7 Nov 1894 Parsonsfield ME, d. 11 Sep 1972 Porter ME, m.(1) 11 Oct 1919 Hollis ME Lyle N. Harmon of Amesbury MA, b. 5 Jun 1890 d. 12 Apr 1935, dau. Henry and Minnie (Watson) Harmon; m.(2) 19 Dec 1936 Madison ME Mary Elizabeth Webster of Nova Scotia, Canada, b. 1898, dau. George L. and Mary L. (Ramsdell) Webster. Mechanic, carpenter. World War I. In Madison ME, Bradenton FL. He bur. in Madison NH.

Boyce H., b. ca. 1920.

Sources: VR SA/NH. Will, Obit.

557. **PAUL JEFFREY⁹ SAWYER** [see 492], b. 22 Jun 1903 Everett MA, m. 1 Nov 1928 New York City Dorothy M. Warwick of Revere MA, b. 12 Aug 1909, dau. Louis R. and Rachel (Patterson) Warwick. In Flushing NY.

Paul Jeffrey, b. 3 Sep 1929, m. 12 Jun 1953 Anne Shaffer, b. ca. 1932.
Priscilla D., b. 3 Mar 1932, d. 29 May 1965, m. 1953 Clinton Schmieg.
Robert Warwick, b. 20 Apr 1937, m. 26 Aug 1966 Jo Ann Foulk, b. ?.
Thomas Richard, b. 5 Oct 1945, m. 19 Aug 1967 Vicki Gould, b. ?.

Sources: Paul J. Sawyer rec.

558. **MARK STEVEN⁹ SAWYER** [see 493], b. 27 Jun 1873 Porter ME, d. 7 Apr 1963 Gorham ME, m. 30 Jul 1898 Porter ME Ida Cross of Parsonsfield ME, b. 10 Sep 1875 d. 2 Aug 1948, dau. Moses and Rebecca (Eastman) Cross. Clerk.

Gladys B., b. 18 Mar 1898, d. 22 Jul 1977, m.(1) 24 Nov 1915 Sidney Libby, m.(2) Walter Ward.

Carl C., b. 17 July 1901 Porter ME, d. 9 May 1967 Kezar Falls ME, m. 7 Nov 1936 Portsmouth NH Annie T. West of Freedom NH (her 3rd m.), b. 1889, dau. Alvin A. and Carrie F. (Hayes) Thurston. Weaver. He bur. Riverside Cem., Cornish ME.

Daughter, b. 5 Feb 1903, d.y.

Daughter, b. 20 Mar 1904, d.y.

Minnie A., b. ?, m. Nov 1919 John Mason of Kezar Falls ME.

Ivy H., b. May 1906, d. 23 Mar 1907.

Sewell E., 24 Jul 1909 Kezar Falls ME, d. 31 Aug 1968 Kezar Falls ME, m. 1 Oct 1927 Doris Jewell of W. Baldwin ME. CH: Harold Elwin, Eugene Elmer, Rodney Ellsworth.

Sources: VR SA/ME. A22, Obit.

559. **CHARLES R.$^9$ SAWYER** [see 494], b. 12 Jul 1885 Porter ME, d. 1972 Fryeburg ME, m. Vivian E. Sawyer, b. 1891 d. 13 Dec 1941, dau. Henry M., and Alice (Blake) Sawyer. He bur. in Porter ME.

Fred, b. 14 Feb 1910 Porter ME.

Elwyn G., b. 9 Nov 1915 Porter ME, d. 1980.

Lula F., b. ?, m. 12 Oct 1940 Roland Wentworth of Porter ME.

Sources: Lula F. Wentworth rec.

560. **ELLSWORTH WILLIAM$^9$ SAWYER** [495], b. 5 Aug 1877 Porter ME, d. 14 May 1932 Kezar Falls ME, m. 3 Jan 1898 Porter ME Mabel S. Stanley of Porter ME, b. 19 Nov 1878 d. 30 Jul 1966, dau. Samuel and Judy Stanley. Postmaster, teacher. He bur. in Riverside Cem., Kezar Falls ME.

Clarence Stanley, b. 30 Aug 1898 Kezar Falls ME, d. 16 Mar 1956 Kezar Falls ME, m. 30 Jul 1921 Harriet Bibber of Kezar Falls ME, b. ?.

Frank W., b. 3 Jul 1900, d. 13 Aug 1900.

Child, b. Jun 1901, d. 14 Aug 1901.

Beatrice E., b. 9 Jun 1902, m. 3 Jul 1920 Leroy S. Pierce of Gray ME.

Frances J., b. 12 Jul 1905, d. 31 Mar 1966, m. 22 Jun 1925 Russell Cutting of Porter ME.

Allison M., b. 13 Jul 1908, d. 29 Aug 1959, m. Ervin Curtis of Kezar Falls ME.

Robert Ellsworth, b. 20 Jul 19ll Kezar Falls ME, d. 4 Mar 1976, m. 6 Aug 1932 Grace A. Stacy. CH: Robert Bruce, William Brian, Stanley Hilton, Karen Ruth, Cheryl F.

Evelyn D., b. 11 Sep 1915, d. 4 Jan 1977, m. 25 Sep 1942 Donald Shover.

Samuel S., b. 20 Oct 1917 Kezar Falls ME, m. 25 Jul 1942 Florence Boyd.

Sources: VR SA/ME. A22, Karen Sawyer rec.

561. **KENDAL WILLARD$^9$ SAWYER** [see 497], b. 12 Sep 1887 Charlestown MA, d. 25 Mar 1981 Los Angeles CA, m.(1) 6 Oct 1915 Emma A. Perry of Somerville MA, b. 16 Jul 1890 d. 25 Sep 1918 (in flu epidemic) W. Somerville MA, dau. Warren Andrew and Elizabeth (Andrews) Perry of Somerville MA; m.(2) 5 Apr 1919 Elizabeth Sears Perry (sister of Emma), b. 1 Sep 1892 Hyannis MA d. 30 Sep 1968 Boston MA. Postal letter carrier. In Wilmington MA, Somerville MA, Dorchester MA, Strafford NH, Los Angeles CA. All bur. in Wyoming Cem., Melrose MA.

Richard Warren, b. 9 Jun 1917 Somerville MA, d. 11 May 1991 Los Angeles CA, unm. World War II: B-24 Navigator. In Boston MA, New York City, Los Angeles CA. Ashes scattered in Pacific Ocean.

570 Robert Kendal$^{10}$, b. 1920.

Dorothy Emma, b. 16 Jul 1922 Somerville MA, unm.

571 Allan Willard$^{10}$, b. 1923, d. 1995.

Sources: VR SA/MA. Kendal W. Sawyer rec., Robert Kendal Sawyer rec.

562. **PERCY ARLINGTON[9] SAWYER** [see 502], b. Sep 1883 Jonesport ME, d. 1961, m. 14 Nov 1915 Bangor ME Lillian P. Burton, b. 1892 d. 1978. In Brewer ME.

Burton Arlington,b. 3 Nov 1922, m. 28 Jul 1945 Christine M. Jones.

Walter Preston, b. 1925, d. 1928.

Sources: Burton A. Sawyer rec.

563. **JOHN ELMORE[9] SAWYER** [see 504], b. 7 Jan 1873 Baldwin ME, d. 11 Jan 1967 Sanford ME, m. 23 Dec 1897 Sanford ME Esther Simmons of Kennebunkport ME, b. 1878, dau. George H. and Mary C. (Ghen) Simmons. Mill operator.

Paul Simmons, b. 27 May 1905, d. 11 Mar 1993 Rochester NH, m. 18 Aug 1928 Edna A. Monahan, b. 23 Dec 1900, d. 21 Dec 1992.

Cynthia, m.(1) Leo Flamme, m.(2) Charles Smith.

Sources: VR SA/ME. Joyce C. Sawyer rec., Paul Simmons Sawyer rec.

564. **FRED WILSON[9] SAWYER** [see 504], b. 18 Nov 1874 Baldwin ME, d. 8 Aug 1952 Denmark ME, m. 13 Oct 1900 Emma E. Crawford of Sebago ME, b. 1878 d. 14 Jun 1951.

Charles, b. 10 Jul 1901, d. an infant.

Frank Wilson, b. 8 May 1904, m. Feb 1930 Bessie M. Hale.

Bert Alna, b. 18 Feb 1906, d. 29 Feb 1983, m. Edith Blake, b. ?.

Sources: M5, Bessie M. Sawyer rec., Robert L. Taylor rec.

565. **HENRY NATHAN[9] SAWYER** [see 505], b. 2 Sep 1872 Boston MA, d. 28 Feb 1935 Newton Highlands MA, m.(1) 28 Aug 1890 Edith A. I. Anstey, b. ?, dau. _____ and Louise (Lee) Anstey; m.(2) 7 Dec 1901 Kate M. (Woolfe) Currier, dau. Lorenzo and Kate M. (Quiden) Woolfe. Printer.

572 Herbert Anstey[10], 1891-1964.

Sources: Henry Nathan Sawyer rec.

566. **FRED STURDEVANT[9] SAWYER** [see 509], b. 5 Feb 1875 Saco ME, m. 2 Oct 1900 E. Machias ME Estelle M. Barker of Canada, b. 13 Mar 1875 d. 29 Mar 1958, dau. J. A. and Eliza (Taylor) Barker. In Boston MA, West Newton MA.

Helen T., b. 1900, m. Feb 1933 Willis V. Dougherty.

Wendell Frank, b. 10 Nov 1902, d. 18 Mar 1872, m. 10 Jun l933 Virginia Armstrong.

Allen W., b. 29 Aug 1904 W. Newton MA, m. Charlotte Boss, b. ?. In Concord MA, Boston MA. CH: Anne Wilson, b. 17 Sep 1947; Joan Hathaway, b. 23 Nov 1948.

Sources: Wendell F. Sawyer rec., Agnes Ames rec., Joan H. Sawyer rec.

567. **BRUCE S.[9] SAWYER** [see 518], b. 1898 Brighton MA, d. 11 May 1943 Portland ME m.(1) ?; m.(2) 11 Sep 1924 Gorham ME Frances Smith of W. Buxton ME, b. 1905, dau. Edward H. and Julia (Russell) Smith. In So. Windham ME, Hollis ME. He bur. on Meeting House Hill, Hollis ME.

Stanley Wayne, b. 14 May 1931.

Sources: M5, Nancy Welch rec.

568. **CHARLES HENRY[9] SAWYER** [see 534], b. 18 May 1871 Durham Me, d. 1945, m. Ella A. Allen of Gray ME, b. ?.

Charles Allen, b. 19 Apr 1914, d. 24 Dec 1916.

William A., b. 26 May 1917, m. ?. CH; Vaughn Carl, b. 13 Nov 1940.

Sources: Vaughn Carl Sawyer rec.

569. **MERRILL RAY[9] SAWYER** [see 549], b. 8 Dec 1892 Milbridge ME, d. 4 Nov 1958 Portland ME, m. 3 Mar 1919 Marion Louise Pitcher, b. 3 Nov 1891 d. 25 Mar 1984, dau. Wilbert R. and Lydia C. (Johnson) Pitcher.

Ira Stillman, b. 3 Sep 1924, m. Theodora Helen Hoyt, b. 10 Feb 1922. In Virginia, Freeport ME, St. Augustine FL. CH: Deborah Susan, b. 21 Aug 1951, m. Charles Tolhurst; Lydia Helen, b. 13 Sep 1953, m. Peter Tate.

Sources: Theodora Hoyt Sawyer rec.

## TENTH GENERATION

570. **ROBERT KENDAL[10] SAWYER** [see 561], b. 22 Oct 1920 Melrose MA, m. 12 Apr 1946 Somerville MA Eleanor Grace Rideout of Somerville MA, b. 29 May 1921, dau. William Robert and Alice Mabel (Brooks) Rideout. World War II, Korean War. Colonel US Army. In Strafford NH after retirement in 1974.

Kenneth Robert, adopted, b. 1 Sep 1942 Somerville MA, d. 12 Feb 1969 Xuan Loc, Vietnam. Captain, US Army. Bur. in Arlington National Cem., Washington DC.

Janice Elaine, adopted, b. 9 Jun 1944, m. 28 Jun 1965 Quinton Dennis Gabriel. In Pittsburgh PA.

573 Robert Kendal[11], Jr., b. 1947.
574 William Howard[11], b. 1950.
575 Peter Allan[11], b. 1952.

Sources: Robert Kendal Sawyer rec.

571. **ALLAN WILLARD[10] SAWYER** [see 561], b. 3 Sep 1923 Dudley MA, d. 27 May 1995 Quincy MA, m. 16 Nov 1946 Edith MacDonald, b. 21 May 1922 d. 12 Jun 1966. Boston Elevated Railway employee.

576 Donald Allan[11], b. 1948.

Sources: Allan Willard Sawyer rec.

572. **HERBERT ANSTEY[10] SAWYER** [see 565], b. 2 Aug 1891 Dorchester MA, d. 21 Sep 1964 Malden MA, m. Janet Holmes Stumble, b. ?. Printer.

Henry Nathan, b. 20 Mar 1917.
Herbert Anstey, b. 25 Jun 1918.
Stephen Trenamon, b. 17 Dec 1920.

Sources: Henry Nathan Sawyer rec.

## ELEVENTH GENERATION

573. **ROBERT KENDAL[11] SAWYER, Jr.** [see 570], b. 14 Dec 1947 Boston MA, m. 24 Aug 1969 Westerly RI (div. 1993) Nancy Marie Scola of Worcester MA, b. 26 Oct 1948, dau. William and Marie (Holden) Scola. University of Massachusetts 1969, Suffolk University Law School 1980. Lawyer. In Worcester MA, Medfield MA.

David Andrew, b. 4 May 1972 Worcester MA.
Elizabeth Anne, b. 1 Mar 1978 Worcester MA.

Sources: Robert Kendal Sawyer rec., Robert Kendall Sawyer, Jr rec.

574. **WILLIAM HOWARD[11] SAWYER** [see 570], b. 29 Dec 1950 Boston MA, m. 30 Apr 1978 Alexandria VA (div. 1993) Karen Monroe of Scottsville VA, b. 4 Feb 1953, dau. Charles and

Freda Monroe. University of Massachusetts 1973. VOLVO auto parts manager. In Alexandria VA, Springfield VA, Portland OR 1988-1989, Burtonsville MD, Laurel MD, Columbia MD.

Kimberly Hope, b. 17 Oct 1979 Falls Church VA.

Kelly Joy, b. 19 Oct 1981 Richmond VA.

Sources: Robert Kendal Sawyer rec., William Howard Sawyer rec.

575. **PETER ALLAN[11] SAWYER** [see 570], b. 15 Mar 1952 Boston MA, m. 17 Sep 1977 Alexandria VA Susan Joan Craig of Springfield VA, b. 29 Apr 1953, dau. Donald (Commander, US Navy, Ret) and Jeanne (Hartman) Craig. University of Massachusetts 1974. Artist. In Alexandria VA, Burke VA, Fairfax Station VA. Painted "Archean Age" mural at Smithsonian Museum of Natural History, Washington DC 1985.

Jason Kenneth, b. 8 May 1981 Falls Church VA.

Erin Marie, b. 20 Jul 1984 Falls Church VA.

Sources: Robert Kendal Sawyer rec., Peter Allan Sawyer rec.

576. **DONALD ALLAN[11] SAWYER** [see 571], b. 10 Jul 1948 Boston MA, m. 9 Sep 1977 Quincy MA Helen L. Clements, b. 15 Dec 1949 Boston MA, dau. Robert Francis and Helen Virginia (Anderson) Clements. Telephone Co. employee.

James Stephen, b. 25 Nov 1979 Quincy MA.

Heather Elizabeth, b. 13 Sep 1981 Weymouth MA.

Sources: Donald Allan Sawyer rec.

# PART V

# ꟷ WILLIAM OF READING ꟷ

1. **WILLIAM[1] SAWYER**, b. ca. 1675, m.(1) Abigail Lilly, b. 15 Aug 1672 d. 1698, dau. George and Jane Lilly; m.(2) 30 Apr 1700 Reading MA Dorcas Burnap, b. 22 Aug 1679, dau. Robert and Sarah (Brown) Burnap. In Reading MA.

Nothing whatever is known of William of Reading's birthplace, nor is it known where or when he died. As suggested in fourth paragraph of Part I, a possible clue to his parentage lies in the fact that his oldest boy was named Henry at a time when first sons were often named after their grandfather. Aside from his family however, the only facts we have concerning this William include a purchase of land on both sides of the Ipswich River in 1711, on the road from Salem to Chelmsford (now Park Street). Also, because his will was executed on 24 March 1732, we know that he was alive on that date.

William[1] of Reading was father of the following children:

2 Henry[2], b. 1697.
Dorcas, b. 22 Feb 1701, m. 30 Jun 1726 Nathaniel Sherman of Lynn MA.
Rachel, b. 18 Feb 1703, m. 12 Mar 1723 Thomas Rich.
Lidy, b. 12 Sep 1705, d. 30 Apr 1749, m. 18 Oct 1726 Daniel Townsend of Lynn MA.
3 William[2], b. 1708.
Isaac, b. 10 Jul 1711 Reading MA.
4 Jacob[2], b. ca. 1713.
Susanna, b. 20 Oct 1717.
Bethyah, b. 15 Jul 1720.

Sources: VR Reading MA, Lynn MA. B41, E5, N5, E21, R19.

## SECOND GENERATION

2. **HENRY[2] SAWYER** [see 1], b. 15 Feb 1697 Reading MA, m. 18 Apr 1718 Reading MA Sarah Nurse, b. 27 Jan 1697, dau. Francis Jr. and Sarah (Tarbell) Nurse. S/land in Amherst NH 1758. In Methuen MA, Andover MA.

Abigail, b. 15 Jul 1719, m. 6 May 1738 Ebenezer Flint of Reading MA.
5 Josiah[3], 1721-1813.
6 Reuben[3], b. 1723.
Sarah, b. 31 Mar 1726, m. 1757 Charles Mason.
7 Francis[3], 1728-1827.
Hepsibah, b. 2 Jun 1730.
8 Caleb[3], b. 1732.
Bulah, b. 17 May 1733, m. 19 Mar 1752 Thomas Austin of Andover MA.
Ebenezer, b. 13 Oct 1736 Andover MA. In Methuen MA.
Rebecca, b. 1739, m. 25 Oct 1759 Joseph Griffen of Methuen MA.

Sources: VR Reading MA, Andover MA. A27.

3. **WILLIAM[2] SAWYER** [see 1], b. 28 Jan 1708 Reading MA, d. Reading MA, m. 6 Jan 1730 Reading MA Margaret Wood, b. ?. Will probated 8 Oct 1776.

9 William[3], 1730-1815.
Margaret, b. 1732, m. 1750 Benjamin Flint.
10 Nathaniel[3], 1738-1797.
11 Jonathan[3], 1739-1823.
Amos, b. 1744, d. 21 Sep 1769. Pastor of Church of Christ, Danvers MA.

Sources: VR Reading MA. B41, S97.

4. **JACOB[2] SAWYER** [see 1], b. ca. 1713, m.(1) 28 Jun 1733 Reading MA Elizabeth Damon, b. ?; m.(2) (I) 10 Mar 1758 Danvers MA Mary (Eaton) Pope, wid. of John.
Elizabeth, b. 7 Nov 1734, m. 26 May 1761 Jonathan Dix.
Rachel, b. 25 Oct 1736, m. 19 Jul 1759 Ebenezer Jones of Wilmington MA.
Dorcas, b. 1743, d.y.
Dorcas, b. 1744.
12 Jacob[3], 1748-1843.
13 Daniel[3], 1752-1824.
Sources: VR Reading MA, Danvers MA.

## THIRD GENERATION

5. **JOSIAH[3] SAWYER** [see 2], b. 10 Aug 1721 Reading MA, d. Apr 1813 Sharon NH, m. 11 Dec 1742 Andover MA Hannah Gowing of Lynn MA, b. 23 Apr 1721 d. 1807, dau. Nathaniel and Hannah (Eaton) Gowing. In Monson NH 1746. B/land in Amherst NH 1758, Monson NH 1760. Revolutionary War: Private in Captain S. Peabody's Co., Colonel Nichols' Regiment, 1797. Four sons in Revolutionary War. In Methuen MA, Hancock NH, Amherst NH, Sharon NH.
14 Josiah[4], 1744-1829.
Hannah, b. 26 Aug 1746.
Sarah, b. 12 Jul 1748.
15 Nathaniel[4], 1750-1807.
16 Jonathan[4], 1752-1812.
Nurse, b. 24 Feb 1755, d. Jul 1776 at Crown Point on Lake Champlain NY in Revolutionary War. In Amherst NH, Wilton NH.
17 Benjamin[4], 1757-1846.
Persellar (Priscilla?), b. 9 May 1760, m. 11 Mar 1789 Amherst NH Roger Elliot.
Sources: Sharon NH census 1790, 1800, 1810. VR Andover MA, Lynn MA, SA/MA. F6, R10i.

6. **REUBEN[3] SAWYER** [see 2], b. 9 Aug 1723 Reading MA, m. 15 Nov 1752 Andover MA Sarah Bailey of Bradford MA, b. 8 Dec 1734, dau. Nathan and Mary (Palmer) Bailey. In Methuen MA, Dracut MA.
18 Amos[4], b. 1753.
19 Ebenezer[4], 1755-1842.
Sarah, b. 2 Dec 1757, d.y.
Hannah, b. 21 Sep 1759.
Rebekah, b. 23 Sep 1761, m. 22 Nov 1794 Daniel Hardy.
20 Reuben[4], 1763-184?.
21 Henry[4], 1765-1849.
Sarah, b. 11 Apr 1767, m. 7 Mar 1785 Moses Davis.
22 Nathan[4], b. 1769.
Rachel, b. ?, m. 20 Dec 1795 Josiah Galleron.
Sources: Dracut MA census 1790, 1800. VR Andover MA, Methuen MA. E20, M39.

7. **FRANCIS[3] SAWYER** [see 2], b. 21 Feb 1728 Reading MA, d. 31 Dec 1827 Canterbury NH, m.(1) 22 Mar 1749 Elizabeth Richardson of Middleton MA, b. 20 Aug 1730 d. 1772, dau. Solomon and Elizabeth (Goodale) Richardson; m.(2) 31 Aug 1773 Methuen MA Tamar Barker of Methuen MA, b. 22 Sep 1746 d. 23 Apr 1819, dau. Timothy and Sarah (Davis) Barker. Ferry keeper. Revolutionary War. In Methuen MA 1759, Dracut MA, Canterbury NH.

Elizabeth, b. 8 Oct 1750, d. 17 Mar 1816, m. Oct 1770 Joshua Pillsbury.

Francis, b. 22 Feb 1752 Methuen MA, d. 1777 Saratoga NY in Revolutionary War, m. 11 Jun 1772 Dracut MA Susannah Clough, b. ?.

Molly, b. 9 Oct 1753, m. 1789 Timothy Astin.

Ebenezer, b. 25 Dec 1755 Methuen MA, d. 1840 New York, m. 2 Aug 1786 Salem NH Hannah Whittier, b. 7 Jan 1766. In Dracut MA 1790, Henderson NY 1812. CH: Rhoda, b. 1795, m. 1817 William Wilkinson of NY. Note: Dracut MA census 1790 says five CH.

Abigail, b. 15 Apr 1758, m. 9 Mar 1780 Samuel Clark, Jr.

23 David$^4$, 1760-1832.

24 Amos Richardson$^4$, 1764-1846.

25 Aaron$^4$, 1766-1854.

Hannah, b. 18 Jan 1769, d. 2 Oct 1869, m.(1) 9 Aug 1792 Paul Pettengill, m.(2) _____ Brown.

26 Moses$^4$, b. 1773.

Sarah, b. 7 Aug 1774.

Ruth, b. 25 Aug 1779, d. 15 Apr 1868, m. 21 Jan 1800 Abraham Cross.

27 Francis$^4$, b. 1781.

Olive, b. 8 Aug 1783, d. 17 Jan 1875, m.(1) 12 Jul 1809 James French, m.(2) Morrill Shepard.

Daniel, b. 4 Sep 1785 Dracut MA, killed rolling logs into river in Canterbury NH, m. 29 Dec 1812 Canterbury NH Apphia Clough, b. 3 Mar 1793, dau. Jeremiah and Martha (Foster) Clough. CH: Mary, b. ?, m. Joseph W. Gale of Pembroke NH; Sarah, b. ?, m. Hascall Comb of Lowell MA; Nancy, b. ?, m. Jonathan Kimball; Hannah, b. ?, m. George Fox.

28 Jeremiah P.$^4$, 1787-1851.

Lois, b. 1 Aug 1789, d. 1823, m. 30 Dec 1817 John Batchelder.

Sources: Dracut MA census 1790. Canterbury NH census 1800, 1820. Templeton MA census 1800. VR Methuen MA, Middleton MA, Carmel ME, Dracut MA. C87, R34, A27, N9, P37, N14, P41, V8, E20, F11A.

8. **CALEB$^3$ SAWYER** [see 2], b. 21 Apr 1732 Reading MA, m. 4 Oct 1752 Methuen MA Mary Griffen of Methuen MA, b. Oct 1731, dau. John and Mehitable Griffen. S/land in Amherst NH 1758, Pelham NH 1770. In Pelham NH 1767, Dracut MA 1790, Methuen MA 1800.

Susannah, b. 3 Aug 1754, m. 20 Apr 1784 Amos Morse of Dracut MA.

Molle, b. 2 Oct 1756, m. 20 Sep 1777 Rufus Mors (Morse?), Jr.

Sarah, b. 10 Apr 1762.

Thomas, b. 15 Sep 1764 Pelham NH, d. 13 Jun 1836 Concord NH, m. ?, CH: Son, b. (1810-1820).

29 Caleb$^4$, 1767-1837.

Rebecca, b. 21 Oct 1769.

30 Joshua$^4$, 1772-1864.

Benjamin Griffen, b. 23 Sep 1779 Dracut MA.

Sources: Dracut MA census 1790. Methuen MA census 1800, 1810. VR Methuen MA, Dracut MA.

9. **WILLIAM$^3$ SAWYER** [see 3], b. 18 Nov 1730 Reading MA, d. 26 Feb 1815 Reading MA, m. Priscilla _____, b. 1730 d. 20 Apr 1804. French and Indian War. He left a will.

31 William$^4$, 1758-1816.

32 Thomas$^4$, 1760-1818.

Priscilla, b. 19 May 1762, d. 4 Jun 1849, m. 24 Jan 1883 Daniel Flint.
Ebenezer, b. 16 Apr 1764 Reading MA.
Molly, b. 24 Apr 1770, m. 1 May 1789 Daniel Upton.
33 Porter[4], ca. 1771-1840.
Sources: Reading MA census 1790, 1800. VR Reading MA.

10. **NATHANIEL[3] SAWYER** [see 3], b. 1738 Reading MA, d. 26 Jul 1797 Westminster MA, m. 11 Jun 1761 Reading MA Jerusha Flint, b. 28 Jun 1739 d. 20 Feb 1824, dau. William and Susannah Flint.
Jerusha, b. 25 May 1762, d. 13 Aug 1844, m. 23 Jun 1778 Zachariah Rand of Vermont.
34 Nathaniel[4], 1764-1851.
35 Eli[4], 1765-1841.
Rebecca, b. 7 Dec 1767, d. 24 Nov 1825, m. 11 Mar 1788 Asa Brooks.
Elizabeth, bp. Nov 1769.
36 Amos[4], 1769-1848.
Dorcas, b. 28 Aug 1772, m. 29 May 1790 Joseph Edgell.
37 William[4], 1774-1860.
Taymor, b. 28 Nov 1776, d. same day.
38 Aaron Flint[4], 1779-1847.
Rachel, b. 28 Mar 1783, m. 16 Nov 1805 Daniel McIntire.
Sources: Westminster MA census 1790. VR Reading MA, Westminster MA. P85, H45.

11. **JONATHAN[3] SAWYER** [see 3], b. 1739 Reading MA, d. 5 Mar 1823 Westminster MA, m. 15 Nov 1764 Reading MA Susannah Flint, b. 30 Aug 1741 d. 12 Aug 1819, dau. William and Susannah Flint. In Westminster MA 1765. Revolutionary War: Lieutenant.
Jonathan, b. 8 Feb 1768 Westminster MA, m. Betsey McCormick, b. ?.
Susannah, b. 22 Feb 1770, m. 17 Oct 1792 John Jackson.
39 Jacob[4], 1772-1852.
Peggy, b. 9 Dec 1773, d. 9 Feb 1813, m. 9 Jan 1794 Cyrus Winship.
40 Zadock[4], 1776-1858.
Zibah, b. 5 May 1779, unm. Went west.
Nancy, b. 1 Jul 1781, d. 1801.
Levi, b. 13 Jul 1783 Westminster MA, m. 29 Dec 1833 Westminster MA Fanny Rand, b. 1798, wid. of Crosby. CH: Julia Augusta, b. 19 May 1835, m. 19 Aug 1857 Fitchburg MA Charles L. Harris.
Julah, b. 6 Aug 1785.
Sources: Westminster MA census 1790, 1810, 1830, 1840, 1850. VR Reading MA, Westminster MA. H45.

12. **JACOB[3] SAWYER** [see 4], b. 24 Apr 1748 Reading MA, d. 1843 Farmington ME, m.(1) 24 Nov 1768 Reading MA Sarah Flint, b. 1 Jun 1750; m.(2) Eunice (Eaton) Reed of Strong ME, wid. of William, b. ?; m.(3) 22 Jun 1800 Elizabeth Fry, b. ?. Wheelwright. B/land in Lincoln County ME 1771. Revolutionary War: Penobscot Expedition; Siege of Boston. B/land at mouth of Union River 1792. Land sold for taxes in Sedgewick ME 1800. At Plantation #6 in 1800, Surry ME 1810, Dixmont ME 1840. He bur. in Dixmont ME.
41 Jacob[4], 1768-1863.
Rachel, b. ?, m. Samuel Butterfield.
Lucretia, b. ?, m. Daniel H. Morse.
More unnamed children listed in census.

Sources: Plantation #6 ME census 1800. Surry ME census 1810. Dixmont ME census 1840. VR Reading MA. C25, M5A, M3A, N5. R10b.

13. **DANIEL[3] SAWYER** [see 4], b. 26 Jul 1752 Reading MA, d. 14 Jun 1824 Sandown NH, m.(1) 2 May 1775 Reading MA Hephzibah Hart, b. 20 Oct 1753 d. 5 Jun 1816; m.(2) 12 Mar 1817 Abigail (Colby) Tabor of Candia NH, wid., b. 1765 d. 13 Aug 1862, dau. Beniah and Abigail (Emerson) Colby. Storekeeper. In Westminster MA 1790, Sandown NH 1800.

Hepzibeth, b. 6 Oct 1778, m. 22 Jul 1799 John Wheeler of Hooksett NH.
42 Daniel[4], 1781-1847.
43 Asa[4], b. 1783. Went to Ohio.
Rachel, b. 5 Oct 1785, m. 25 Mar 1808 Thomas Williams of Hooksett NH.
Lydia, b. 19 Sep 1787, d. 1 Jan 1857, m. Henry Dutton of Candia NH.
Dorcas, b. 16 Aug 1789, m. 25 May 1812 Edward Hill of Chester NH.
Nancy, b. 27 Jan 1793, m. 26 Oct 1825 Chester NH Ephraim French.
Jacob, b. 26 Dec 1794 Sandown NH, m. _____ McGowan of Carlisle PA, b. ?. Physician.
44 Ebenezer J.[4], 1798-1844.
45 Benjamin Eaton[4], 1801-1878.

Sources: Westminster MA census 1790. Sandown NH census 1800, 1810, 1820. VR Reading MA, Hampstead NH. C11, H84, N14, N6, P82g.

## FOURTH GENERATION

14. **JOSIAH[4] SAWYER** [see 5], b. 17 Sep 1744 Milford NH, d. 2 Oct 1829 Sharon NH, m. 3 Sep 1767 Andover MA Lydia Barnard of Andover MA, b. 20 Jan 1746 d. 10 Feb 1829, dau. John and Alice (Holt) Barnard. Revolutionary War: In Colonel Reed's Regiment at Battle of Bunker Hill. In Methuen MA, Andover MA, Milford NH, Sharon NH.

Lydia, b. 21 Feb 1768 Andover MA, d. 28 Aug 1850, m. William Nay.
46 Josiah[5], 1770-1800.
Hannah, b. 10 Feb 1772 Methuen MA, d. 27 Sep 1860, m. Phinehas Everett.
47 Moses[5], 1774-1851.
Alice, b. 1781, d. 4 Sep 1849, m. 26 Nov 1801 George Shedd.
Rebecca, b. 14 Apr 1783, d. 24 Dec 1869, m. 22 Nov 1810 William Pettengill.
48 Abial[5], 1784-1870.

Sources: Sharon NH census 1800, 1810, 1820. VR Andover MA. P37, D6, S34, S26, E27, A27, S48, D10, N6.

15. **NATHANIEL[4] SAWYER** [see 5], b. 10 Jun 1750 Methuen MA, d. 15 Oct 1807 Wilton NH, m. 13 Oct 1778 Andover MA Prudence Abbot of Andover MA, b. 3 Oct 1757 d. 15 Dec 1839 Salem NY, dau. David and Prudence (Sheldon) Abbot. In Amherst NH 1779, Wilton NH 1790. Wid. in Wilton NH 1810.

Fanny, b. 6 Jul 1779, m. 13 Mar 1800 Silas Buss.
Hannah, b. 6 Dec 1780, m. 31 May 1804 Leonard Barker.
Sally, b. 25 Nov 1782, d. 10 Jun 1863, m. 7 Jun 1808 Timothy Holt.
Nathaniel, b. 25 Nov 1784 Wilton NH, d. 20 Jun 1875, m. 2 Apr 1818 Jane C. Waterhouse of New Brunswick, Canada, b. 1800. B/land in Cooper ME 1825.
Olive, b. 14 Feb 1787, m. 10 May 1808 Joseph Parker.
Asaph, b. 11 May 1789, d. 6 Feb 1790.
Anna, b. 17 Jan 1791, d. 30 May 1809.
49 Asaph[5], 1793-1875. Went to Maine.
Amos, b. 26 Oct 1795, d. 20 Oct 1799.

Achsah, b. 15 Sep 1800, d. 28 May 1886, m. 12 Nov 1825 John C. Allen.
Sources: Wilton NH census 1790, 1800, 1810. Dennysville ME census 1820. Cooper ME census 1830, 1840, 1850. VR Andover MA, Wilton NH. E20, A2, S26.

16. **JONATHAN[4] SAWYER** [see 5], b. 30 Jun 1752 Monson NH, d. 14 Mar 1812 Hancock NH, m. 24 Sep 1774 Hollis NH Isobel Grimes of Groton MA, b. 1749 d. 14 Jul 1832. Revolutionary War: In Captain Nathan Ballard's Company, Colonel Nichols' Regiment. In Hancock NH 1782. Wid. in Hancock NH 1820.

50 Jonathan[5], b. 1774.
Rhoda, b. 16 Aug 1776, d. 9 Mar 1779.
51 Daniel[5], 1778-1857.
52 Josiah[5], 1780-1858. Went to New York.
53 Nathaniel[5], 1783-ca. 1868.
54 Abel[5], 1785-1860.
Rhoda, b. 30 May 1787, d. 6 Mar 1867, unm.
55 Henry[5], 1789-1861.
Polly, b. 25 Apr 1791, m. Asa Hart.

Sources: Hancock NH census 1790, 1800, 1810, 1820. N14, S26, H37, N9, D10.

17. **BENJAMIN[4] SAWYER** [see 5], b. 19 Jul 1757 Monson NH, d. 18 Mar 1846 Nelson NH, m. 1778 Tabitha Kittredge, b. 24 Jul 1759 d. 26 Nov 1845, dau. Solomon and Tabitha (Ingalls) Kittredge. Revolutionary War: Enl. in Colonel James Reed's Regiment, Amherst NH 1775; fought in Battle of Bennington VT. He bur. on Nelson NH Town Common.

Benjamin, b. 4 Mar 1779 Nelson NH.
Nourse, b. 4 Aug 1780 Nelson NH.
56 Asa[5], 1782-1845.
Sally, b. 30 Sep 1783, m. 2 Jun 1807 Nelson NH Nathaniel Belnap.
57 Jesse A.[5], 1786-1856.
58 Joel[5], 1787-1833.
59 Amos[5], 1789-1841.
Levi, b. 22 Jan 1791 Nelson NH, m. 7 Jun 1818 Aurilla Flint, b. ?.
Tabitha, b. 16 Jul 1792, m. 3 Apr 1810 Daniel Stevens of Stoddard NH.
60 Ingalls Kittredge[5], b. 1794.
Fanny, b. 19 Oct 1795, m. 2 Dec 1816 Daniel K. Stevens of Nelson NH.
Nancy, b. 19 Sep 1797, d. 3 Aug 1800.
Silas, b. 16 Sep 1799, d. 4 Aug 1800.
Nancy, b. 21 Mar 1801, d. 7 Dec 1846, m. 31 Oct 1827 Henry C. Stickney.
Asenath, b. 19 Nov 1802.

Sources: Packersfield (later Nelson) NH census 1790, 1800, 1810. Nelson NH census 1820, 1830. Hebron NH census 1840. VR SA/VT. N5, N4, N14, N6, S89.

18. **AMOS[4] SAWYER** [see 6], b. 28 Oct 1753 Methuen MA, m. 8 Jan 1778 Methuen MA Mary Morrell of Londonderry NH, b. ?. In Dracut MA, Londonderry NH, Lancaster NH 1795, Newport VT 1797 where he was Town Clerk, Selectman, Town Representative, and Justice of the Peace.

Hannah, b. 29 Jul 1778.
61 Jeremiah[5], b. 1779.
Polly, b. 22 Mar 1781.
Rhoda, b. 6 Jun 1782, m. 4 Apr 1805 Oliver Stiles.
Lydia, b. 20 Jun 1784, d. 1 Jul 1867, m. 11 Apr 1802 Joshua Coburn.

Abigail, b. 7 Apr 1786, m. 10 Jul 1808 John McBede.
Amos, b. 23 Feb 1788 Londonderry NH, m. 29 Jul 1813 Newport VT Betsey Adams, b. ?. In Duncansboro (Newport) VT.
Marion, b. 24 Feb 1790, m. 3 Jan 1811 Lindon Chapin.
Betsey, b. Nov 1792, m. 23 Jun 1811 Newport VT Nathaniel Martin, Jr.
Mary, b. 16 Nov 1795, d. 29 Mar 1864.
Sarah, b. 8 Mar 1797.

Sources: Londonderry NH census 1790. VR Dracut MA, Methuen MA, SA/VT. G24, N2, G47.

19. **EBENEZER$^4$ SAWYER** [see 6], b. 30 Dec 1755 Methuen MA, d. 6 Dec 1842 Danville VT, m. 23 Feb 1755 Danvers MA Sarah Russell, b. ?.

62 Benjamin$^5$, 178?-1841.
Ebenezer, b. 1787 Danville VT.
Polly, b. ?, m. 5 Jan 1806 John Russell.
63 Charles$^5$, 1790-1870.

Sources: Danville VT census 1790, 1800, 1810, 1820, 1830. 1840. VR Danville VT, SA/VT. N1A.

20. **REUBEN$^4$ SAWYER** [see 6], b. 21 Apr 1763 Dracut MA, d. 184?, m. 12 May 1785 Pelham NH Trayefney Messor b. ?. Revolutionary War. Surveyor of Highways for Londonderry NH 1794-1810. Went to Manchester NH.

64 Asa M.$^5$, 1786-1860.
Reuben G., b. ? Londonderry NH, m. 6 Feb 1827 Sophia Brown of Chester VT, b. ?. In Manchester NH 1840.
Lucy, B., b. ?, m. _____ Greeley.

Sources: Londonderry NH census 1790, 1800, 1810. Manchester NH census 1820, 1830, 1840. VR Dracut MA, SA/VT.

21. **HENRY$^4$ SAWYER** [see 6], b. 25 May 1765 Dracut MA, d. 14 Feb 1849 Dracut MA, m. 9 Jul 1789 Dracut MA Kezia Coburn, b. 17 Nov 1766 d. 21 Jul 1847, dau. Simon and Kezia (Durant) Coburn.

Henry, b. 21 Oct 1789, d. 2 Nov 1811.
Sarah, b. 20 Nov 1792.
Simon, b. 9 Nov 1794 Dracut MA.
Miriam, b. 3 Nov 1797.
Mary Ann, b. 18 Sep 1799, m. 16 Feb 1824 Caleb Sawyer.
Sybel, b. 16 Jul 1802.
65 Ralpha W.$^5$, b. 1805.
66 James Madison$^5$, b. 1809.

Sources: Dracut MA census 1800, 1810, 1840. Pelham MA census 1830. VR Dracut MA, Lowell MA. G24.

22. **NATHAN$^4$ SAWYER** [see 6], b. 30 Aug 1769 Dracut MA, d. in New York, m.(1) 10 Jun 1799 Dracut MA Sally Flint, b. 7 Mar 1777 d. 3 Mar 1807; m.(2) 19 Oct 1809 Dracut MA Azubah Austin, b. ?.

Sally Flint, b. 23 Aug 1799, m. 22 Feb 1818 New York John H. Jennison.
Nathan, b. 16 Apr 1801 Dracut MA.
Hannah, b. 7 Apr 1803, d. Dec 1879, m. Valentine Putnam of New York.
James Sullivan, b. 13 Jul 1805 Dracut MA, d. 15 Apr 1895, m. 12 Mar 1833 Polly Alma Aylsworth, b. 10 Nov 1815 d. 25 Mar 1890. CH: Sylvia Rosetia, b. 31 Jul 1852, d. 2 Apr 1928, m. 4 Jul 1871 Henry A. Cobb.

Erastus, b. 28 Feb 1807 Dracut MA, d. 29 May 1893, m. Hannah Williams of New York, b. ?.
Benjamin Franklin, b. 27 Jun 1810 Dracut MA, m. 1841 Sophia Hatch of New York, b. ?.
Mary Jane, b. 3 Nov 1811.
Reuben, b. ?.
John Quincy Adams, b. 22 Nov 1822.
Louisa, b. ?.
Charles Carroll, b. 2 Aug 1831 New York, d. 5 Dec 1898.
Sources: Dracut MA census 1800, 1810. VR Dracut MA. D6.

23. **DAVID[4] SAWYER** [see 7], b. 17 Mar 1760 Dracut MA, d. 22 Sep 1832 Westford VT, m. 27 Apr 1787 Methuen MA Judith Harris, b. 14 Jun 1766. Revolutionary War. In Methuen MA 1790, Nottingham NH 1802, Manchester NH 1810, Landgrove VT, Peru VT 1820, Westford VT 1828.
67 David[5], 1787-1866.
Asa, b. 14 May 1789, d. 14 Nov 1790.
Achsah, b. 30 Dec 1790, d. 8 May 1817, m. 8 Jun 1815 John Mulk.
68 Thaddeus Colburn[5], 1792-1863.
Hannah, b. 7 Nov 1794, m. 1 Nov 1818 Joseph Farnum. Went to New York.
Judith, b. 4 Jul 1797, d. 3 Nov 1831, m. 19 Oct 1817 Moody Roby.
Elizabeth, b. 21 Jan 1800, d. 1843.
69 John Harris[5], 1802-1850.
70 Alfred[5], 1804-1880.
Mary B., b. 13 May 1807, m. 15 Jan 1829 John Wood.
Sources: Methuen MA census 1790. Manchester NH census 1810. Peru VT census 1820. VR Dracut MA, Methuen MA. D6, N5.

24. **AMOS RICHARDSON[4] SAWYER** [see 7], b. 25 Jan 1764 Dracut MA, d. 1 Oct 1846 Denmark ME, m. 30 Mar 1790 Middleton MA Elizabeth Bixby of Dracut MA, b. 26 Sep 1767 d. 6 Feb 1843, dau. Nathaniel and Mary (Stowers) Bixby. In Methuen MA 1790. B/S/land in Andover ME 1799-1835. In Andover ME 1800, Denmark ME 1840. He bur. in Denmark ME.
John Calvin, b. 1792, d.y.
Levi Pillsbury, b. 16 Jan 1794 Methuen MA, d. 11 Oct 1864 Denmark ME, m. Hannah A. Kimball, b. 1812. Physician. B/S/land in Bridgton ME 1853-1854.
Eliza, b. 22 May 1800, d. 1843, m. and went to Colebrook NH.
Mary B., b. 29 Jun 1802, m. Luther C. Kinsbury of New Hampshire.
Mehitable, b. 1 Oct 1806, d. 30 Jun 1886, m. 1827 Benjamin K. Hill.
Sources: Methuen MA census 1790. Andover ME census 1800, 1810, 1820, 1830. Denmark ME census 1840, 1850, 1860. VR Methuen MA, Middleton MA. E20, R10a, M5.

25. **AARON[4] SAWYER** [see 7], b. 11 Sep 1766 Dracut MA, d. 28 Aug 1854 Methuen MA, m. 5 Aug 1793 Methuen MA Sally Griffin, b. 24 Jun 1773. In Methuen MA.
Sally, b. 23 Dec 1793, m. 17 Nov 1814 Amos Morse.
Abigail, b. 11 Sep 1795, m. 12 Jan 1817 Ezekiel Clark.
71 Aaron[5], 1801-1870.
72 Samuel[5], b. 1803.
Asa, b. 27 Feb 1806 Methuen MA, d. bef. 1851, m. 5 Jan 1837 New Ipswich NH Lydia Sawyer, b. 5 Apr 1813 New Ipswich NH, dau. Francis and Lydia (Hibbard) Sawyer. Wid. m. 14 May 1851 Henry J. Gray. CH: Lydia A., b. 16 Sep 1840, m. 1 Mar 1866 Andover MA Aaron Cummings.

73 John[5], b. 1808.
Asenath, b. 10 Nov 1810, d. 27 Mar 1905 Boscawen NH, m. 10 Nov 1835 Francis S. French.
Rebecca Griffin, b. 25 May 1813, m. 5 Nov 1847 Eliphalet Mansur.
74 Francis[5], b. 1815.
Sources: Methuen MA census 1800, 1810, 1820, 1830, 1840, 1850. VR Methuen MA, SA/MA. L47, D6, N9, E14.

26. **MOSES[4] SAWYER** [see 7], b. 16 Dec 1773 Dracut MA, m.(1) 26 Dec 1796 Methuen MA Hannah Currier, b. Mar 1773 d. 8 May 1797 Gardner MA; m.(2) 28 Sep 1798 Templeton MA Sarah Byam of Templeton MA, b. 24 Apr 1768; m.(3) Polly Carll of Saco ME, b. 24 Apr 1784 d. 5 Sep 1849. In Templeton MA 1800, Carmel ME 1810, Plymouth ME 1830. Moses and Polly are bur. Unity ME.
Miles, b. 25 May 1800 Carmel ME.
75 Phineas B.[5], b. 1802.
Mary, b. 15 Aug 1804, d. 26 Dec 1804.
Hannah, b. 15 Sep 1805, d. 9 Jan 1806.
Lydia, b. 18 Jan 1807.
76 Moses[5], 1809-1882.
Daughter, b. (1815-1820).
Son, b. (1820-1825).
Daughter, b. (1825-1830).
Sources: Templeton MA census 1800. Carmel ME census 1810. VR Methuen MA, Templeton MA, Gardner MA, Dracut MA. M5.

27. **FRANCIS[4] SAWYER** [see 7], b. 21 Sep 1781 Dracut MA, m. 1 Sep 1809 Methuen MA Lydia Hibbard of Methuen MA, b. ?. In Canterbury NH, Northfield NH 1810, Rindge NH 1812-1826, New Ipswich NH 1830.
Lovina, b. 14 Jun 1811.
Lydia, b. 5 Apr 1813, m.(1) 5 Jan 1837 New Ipswich NH Asa Sawyer of Methuen MA, m.(2) 14 May 1851 Henry J. Gray.
Francis, b. 21 Jul 1815 Rindge NH.
Lois, b. 6 Jan 1818.
Charles, b. 27 Dec 1819 Rindge NH.
Clarissa, b. 27 Dec 1819.
Timothy, b. 20 Aug 1822 Rindge NH.
Martha, b. 25 Oct 1825.
Alfred A., b. ?, m. 8 Nov 1860 Mary Frances Fletcher, b. ?.
Son, b. (1825-1830).
Sources: Northfield NH census 1810. New Ipswich (Hillsboro) NH census 1830. VR Dracut MA, Methuen MA. S82, N6.

28. **JEREMIAH P.[4] SAWYER** [see 7], b. 9 Mar 1787 Dracut MA, d. 16 Feb 1851 Andover NH, m. 27 Dec 1810 Gilmanton NH Hepsibah P. Edwards, b. 23 May 1788 d. 27 Dec 1865, dau. John Edwards. Blacksmith.
John Edward, b. 25 Mar 1812 Dracut MA, m. 1838 Harriet Fields, b. ?. In Exeter NH 1830, Boston MA.
Jeremiah Francis, b. 20 May 1814 Dracut MA. In Exeter NH 1830.
Hepsibah E., b. 30 Jan 1816 Hooksett NH, m. 10 Jan 1840 John Buzzell.
Olive, b. 28 Apr 1820 Hooksett NH, d. 1841, m. 1838 Simeon Brown.

Louisa A., b. 2 Jan 1823 Concord NH, d. 1862, m. 22 Sep 1852 Daniel Swan of Lowell MA.
Emeline L., b. 20 Sep 1826 Hopkinton NH, m. 23 Jun 1852 Lowell MA Charles Geer.
77 Daniel E.$^5$, b. 1828.
Sources: Canterbury NH census 1800. Bow NH census 1820. Boscawen NH census 1830. Exeter NH census 1830. Andover NH census 1850. VR Dracut MA, Gilmanton NH. E2, N14, E9.

29. **CALEB$^4$ SAWYER** [see 8], b. 1 Jun 1767 Pelham NH, d. 13 Aug 1837 Bristol NH, m. 26 Jan 1790 Dracut MA Susannah Hall of Dracut MA, b. 25 May 1773 d. 26 Jan 1843. In Dracut MA 1800, Hopkinton NH 1810, Bristol NH 1816.
Sarah Hall, b. 7 Aug 1790 d. 29 Dec 1838, m. 14 Oct 1823 Robert Smith.
78 Richard Hall$^5$, b. 1792-1877.
Alvah, b. 7 Feb 1795 Pelham NH, d. Bergen NY, m. 13 Feb 1826 Boston MA Elizabeth McMurphy of Bristol NH, b. ?. In Buffalo NY, Bergan NY. Both Alvah and Elizabeth d. in an epidemic. CH: Susan Hall, b. ?, adopted by Uncle Richard Hall; Catherine, b. ?, adopted by Aunt Sarah Smith. Note: VR Boston MA says Alvah m. there 7 Feb 1825.
79 Caleb$^5$,1797-1871.
Putnam, b. 4 May 1799, unm. Went to Canada.
Henry I., b. 13 May 1801, d. 18 Jul 1817 Boscawen NH.
Mary, b. 2 Jul 1803, d. 17 May 1832 Cambridge MA, unm.
Milton, b. 27 Jun 1805 Hopkinton NH, d. 4 Aug 1884 Portland MI, m. 8 Jul 1832 Kesiah Ingalls of Bristol NH, b. 1810 d. 1882. In Nashua NH 1840. No CH.
80 Moody Currier$^5$, 1807-1854.
Emily, b. 2 Feb 1810, m. Peter A. Sleeper.
Charlotte Augusta, b. 5 Apr 1812, d. 2 Oct 1813 Boscawen NH.
Sources: Dracut MA census 1800. Hopkinton NH census 1810. Nashua NH census 1840. Alexandria NH census 1860. VR Dracut MA, Boston MA, Salem MA. N14, M64, N9.

30. **JOSHUA$^4$ SAWYER** [see 8], b. 14 May 1772 Pelham NH, d. 1864 Warner NH, m. 12 Jul 1798 Sally George, b. 21 Apr 1776 d. 26 Feb 1844. He bur. in Lower Village Cem., Warner NH.
Caleb, b. 27 Jan 1799 Warner NH.
81 Alvah$^5$, 1800-1874.
John G., b. 29 Nov 1802, d. 18 Nov 1805.
Fanny, b. 24 Jun 1804, d. 1885, m. 16 Apr 1835 Elijah Eaton.
82 George$^5$, 1806-1883.
Emily, b. 16 Jun 1810, d. 21 Feb 1880, m. John Aiken.
83 Joshua$^5$, 1813-1882.
Laura, b. 20 Dec 1815, d. 9 Mar 1875, m. 1 Jul 1847 Warner NH Aaron Dutton.
Susan, b. 14 Mar 1819, d. 25 Sep 1884, unm.
Sources: Warner NH census 1800, 1810, 1820, 1830, 1840, 1850, 1860. VR Warner NH, SA/VT.

31. **WILLIAM$^4$ SAWYER** [see 9], b. 8 Aug 1758 Reading MA, d. 17 Jan 1816 Bradford NH, m.(1) 15 Jul 1784 Hannah Upton, b. ?; m.(2) 1 Jun 1797 Elizabeth Upton, b. 11 Jun 1771 d. 25 May 1839. Revolutionary War: Captain. In Reading MA 1790, New Boston NH 1800. On tax roll Bradford NH 1805. B/land in Bradford NH 1812. Wid. in Bradford NH 1820, 1830.
84 William$^5$, b. 1785.
85 Jabez$^5$, 1787-1837.
Mary Upton, b. 1790, d. 15 Sep 1817.
Margaret, b. (1790-1794).
Hannah, b. (1790-1794), m. 3 Oct 1811 Cyrus Creasey.

Ebenezer, b. Mar 1798 New Boston NH, d. 25 Sep 1898 Nashua NH. Drover. In Bradford NH 1820-1850, Nashua NH 1860.

86 Oliver[5], 1801-1891.

Lydia, b. (1800-1810).

Porter, b. 1803 (New Boston NH?), d. 18 Mar 1838 Bradford NH, m. 5 Jul 1835 Wealthy Marshall of Bradford NH, b. ?, dau. Walker and Dorcas Marshall. Wid. m. 29 Jul 1859 Allen Creasey. CH: Dorcas H., b. 27 Apr 1836, d. 27 Aug 1841.

Daniel, b. (1800-1810).

Melinda, b. (1800-1810).

Priscilla, b. (1800-1810), m. 13 Nov 1828 Warner NH Gilman Presby.

Sophia, b. ca. 1807.

Betsey, b. (1810-1820).

Benjamin, b. (1810-1820) (Bradford NH?), m. 6 Nov 1838 Goshen NH Phebe N. Cain of Goshen NH, b. ?. In Goshen NH. CH: Sarah E., b. 1839, m. 13 Dec 1865 Lawrence MA John R. Penniman.

Flint, b. (1810-1820).

87 Joseph Warren[5], 1815-1899.

Sources: Reading MA census 1790. New Boston NH census 1800. Bradford NH census 1810, 1820, 1830, 1850. Nashua NH census 1860, 1870. VR Reading MA, Bradford NH. N14, N9, N6, D10, Donald F. Sawyer rec.

32. **THOMAS[4] SAWYER** [see 9], b. 8 Mar 1760 Reading MA, d. 3 Nov 1818 Reading MA, m.(1) 19 Jul 1781 Reading MA Elizabeth Damon, b. 5 Jul 1755 d. 28 Nov 1796; m.(2) 26 Sep 1799 Polly Richardson, b. ? d. 24 Sep 1805; m.(3) 29 Jan 1807 Betsey (Eaton) Stove, b. 24 Feb 1767 d. 24 Nov 1842, dau. Joseph and Sarah (Webster) Eaton. Revolutionary War: Captain. In Massachusetts Muster 1778.

Thomas, b. 21 Dec 1781 Reading MA, d. 14 Mar 1826 Reading MA, m. 24 Apr 1815 Methuen MA Rebecca Hardy, b. ?.

88 Samuel[5], 1783-1827.

Amos, b. 25 Oct 1785 Reading MA, d. 16 Feb 1826 Reading MA, m. 14 Sep 1820 Andover MA Betsey O. Hayward, b. ?. Wid. remarried. CH: Nehemiah, b. 8 Feb 1821, d. 12 Aug 1823; Sarah J., b. 28 Sep 1822, m. 14 Oct 1846 Willard Mason of Andover MA.

Betsey, b. 3 Feb 1789, d. 8 Oct 1824, m. 21 Sep 1813 Bowman Viles of Lynnfield MA.

Anna, b. 2 Aug 1792, m. 6 May 1819 Dennis Gillet of Granby CT.

Sally U., b. 13 Jun 1796, m. 26 Mar 1829 Josiah Blanchard of Andover MA.

Joseph Eaton, b. 22 Jan 1808 Reading MA, m.(1) 2 Nov 1842 Reading MA Elizabeth Goodrich, b. ?; m.(2) 4 Apr 1859 Salem MA Jane McIntire, b. ca. 1830.

Sources: Reading MA census 1790, 1800, 1810. VR Reading MA, Methuen MA, Andover MA, SA/MA. B32, H88, N5.

33. **PORTER[4] SAWYER** [see 9], b. ca. 1771 Reading MA, d. Nov 1840 Ellsworth ME, m.(1) 15 Nov 1796 Nancy Upton, b. ?; m.(2) Abigail (Lord) Ross, b. 1769 d. 31 May 1829, wid. of Donald, dau. Abraham and Phebe (Heard) Lord; m.(3) Susan Osgood, b. Nov 1776 d. 5 Mar 1861. Boarding house owner.

Porter, b. 31 Dec 1797 Reading MA.

Charlotte P., b. ?, m. Daniel Rolfe.

John B., b. 1810, d. 21 Oct 1833.

Sources: New Boston NH census 1800. Ellsworth ME census 1810, 1820, 1830, 1840. VR Reading MA, Ellsworth ME.

34. **NATHANIEL$^4$ SAWYER** [see 10], b. 14 Feb 1764 Reading MA, d. 26 Aug 1851 Rutland MA, m. 1 Jun 1786 Westminster MA Elizabeth Pierce, b. 6 Jan 1763, dau. John and Abigail (Demport) Pierce; m.(2) 7 Oct 1794 Westminster MA Betsey Martin, b. 1770 d. 2 Sep 1851. Farmer. In Westminster MA, Rutland MA.

89 Nathaniel$^5$, 1786-1879.
Betsey, b. (1790-1800), m. Josiah Underwood.
Lucinda, b. 1802, d. 23 Nov 1838.
Roxana, b. 25 Nov 1804, d. 9 Jan 1877, m. 6 Apr 1824 Samuel Boyden.
Clarissa J., b. ?, m. 16 Jun 1831 Silas Davis.
More unnamed children listed in census.

Sources: Rutland MA census 1800, 1810, 1820, 1830, 1840. VR Reading MA, Rutland MA, Westminster MA, SA/MA. B71, B51, P434, H88, L16., Gravestone.

35. **ELI$^4$ SAWYER** [see 10], b. 18 Oct 1765 Reading MA, d. 30 Jun 1841 Westminster MA, m. 1 Jul 1790 Westminster MA Anna Laws of Billerica MA, b. 18 Feb 1768 d. 3 Oct 1856, dau. James and Anna (Danforth) Laws. Farmer. In Westminster MA 1790.

Anna, b. 16 May 1791, d. 29 Aug 1883, m. 27 Apr 1809 Levi Rice of Ashburnham MA.
Polly, b. 24 Nov 1792, m. 7 Apr 1818 Nathan Hartwell of Fitchburg MA.
Joel, b. 13 Dec 1794, d. 11 Aug 1797.
Rebekah, b. 8 Sep 1796, m. 18 Jan 1821 Josiah Hartwell of Fitchburg MA.
Abel, b. 4 Sep 1798 Westminster MA, d. 9 Apr 1883, m.(1) 12 Nov 1822 Ashburnham MA Lucy Holt, b. 20 Jan 1803 d. 28 Dec 1841; m.(2) 27 May 1845 (recorded in Westminster and Ashburnham MA) Rhoda Weston, b. 1799 d. 22 Dec 1855; m.(3) 13 May 1856 Fitchburg MA Ann (Hamilton) Kenney of New York, b. ca. 1814, dau. Elijah Hamilton. Farmer. CH: Lucy Ann, b. 28 Jul 1823, d. 5 May 1870, m. 12 Dec 1843 Soloman E. Jacquith; Child, b. 1826, d. 7 Jul 1828; Abigail D., b. 13 Jun 1828, m. 10 Apr 1845 Ashburnham MA Jerome S. Gibson; Adeline M., b. 15 Aug 1830, d. 14 Aug 1886, m. 11 Nov 1855 Fitchburg MA Ezra M. Merritt; Sarah J., b. 2 Mar 1833, m. 20 Sep 1852 Ashburnham MA Andrew J. Adams; Harriet Augusta, b. 28 Mar 1837; James W., b. 11 Aug 1841, d. 28 Aug 1851 Ashburnham MA. Note: Sarah J.'s m. was recorded in Templeton MA on 18 Sep 1852.
Rhonda, b. 11 Jul 1800, m.(I) 22 Apr 1824 Nathan Hartwell.
Mariah, b. 29 Jan 1802, m. 24 Mar 1818 Joseph Bruges of Ashburnham MA.
Sophia, b. 30 Nov 1803.
Roena, b. 20 Feb 1806, m. 19 May 1831 John M. Sawyer.
James Laws, b. 18 Jan 1810 Westminster MA.

Sources: Westminster MA census 1790, 1800, 1810, 1820, 1830, 1840. VR Reading MA, Westminster MA, Ashburnham MA, SA/MA. H45.

36. **AMOS$^4$ SAWYER** [see 10], b. 13 Dec 1769 Reading MA, d. 31 Jan 1848 Westminster MA, m.(1) 11 Apr 1793 Fitchburg MA Anna Willard, b. 1770 d. 1 May 1795; m.(2) 15 Dec 1796 Westminster MA Abigail B. Willard of Fitchburg MA, b. 30 Aug 1776 d. 6 Jan 1855, dau. Charles Willard.

Jerusha, b. 29 Jul 1793, m. 9 Feb 1815 Amos Polly.
90 Amos$^5$, b. 1797.
Betsey N., b. 23 Mar 1800, m. 5 Jun 1821 Amos Sheldon of Fitchburg MA.
91 John$^5$, 1802-1891. Went to New York.
92 Charles Willard$^5$, 1804-1845.
Child, b. 1809, d. same year.
93 Sanford$^5$, 1810-1889.

Sarah, b. 11 Jun1813, m. 1 May 1838 Joseph Pierce of Fitchburg MA.

Stillman, b. 19 May 1818 Westminster MA, m.(1) 23 Oct 1845 Westminster MA Charlotte Gates of Gardner MA, b. 11 Aug 1818 d. 30 Aug 1852, dau. Daniel and Phebe (Moseman) Gates; m.(2) 4 Oct 1855 Phebe L. (Wilson) Wyman of Cambridge MA, b. ?. Farmer. In Fitchburg MA 1850. CH: Merrich W., b. 15 May 1847, d. 15 Aug 1849; Abbie Jane, b. 18 Oct 1858, m. 7 Jul 1886 Fitchburg MA Samuel Ware.

Sources: Westminster MA census 1810, 1820, 1830. Fitchburg MA census 1850. VR Reading MA, Westminster MA, SA/MA. H45.

37. **WILLIAM⁴ SAWYER** [see 10], b. 26 Oct 1774 Westminster MA, d. 5 Jul 1860 Wakefield NH, m. 5 Jan 1804 Mary Yeaton of Portsmouth NH, b. 1774 d. 8 Nov 1852. Harvard College 1800. Lawyer. In Wakefield NH 1805. B/land in Eastport and Lubec ME 1820. He bur. in Spencer Cem., Wakefield NH.

94 William⁵, 1804-1881.

95 George Yeaton⁵, 1805-1882.

96 Charles Haven⁵, 1814-1850.

Mary, b. ?.

Augusta, b. ?, m. 22 Feb 1838 Joseph Pike.

Sources: Wakefield NH census 1810, 1830, 1840, 1850, 1860. VR Westminster MA. N6, M37, Haven Sawyer rec., Robert L. Taylor rec.

38. **AARON FLINT⁴ SAWYER** [see 10], b. 21 Apr 1779 Westminster MA, d. 4 Jan 1847 Nashua NH, m. 20 Aug 1811 Hannah Locke of Westminster MA, b. 5 Nov 1783, dau. Samuel and Hannah (Cowden) Locke. Dartmouth College 1804. Lawyer. Director of Farmers Bank, Amherst NH. In Mont Vernon NH 1807, Nashua NH 1828.

97 Samuel Locke⁵, 1812-1890. Went to Missouri.

Charlotte L., b. 1 Jul 1816, m. 17 Nov 1845 Aaron P. Hughes.

98 Aaron Worcester⁵, 1818-1882.

Flint Holyoke, b. 2 Nov 1821 Mont Vernon NH, m. Martha J. Colburn of Massachusetts, b. 1820. In Nashua NH 1850. No CH.

Catherine A., b. 25 Apr 1825, m. John Taft of Worcester MA.

Sources: Mont Vernon NH census 1820. Nashua NH census 1840, 1850. VR Westminster MA. L35, S26, M52, S51, P82k.

39. **JACOB⁴ SAWYER** [see 11], b. 15 Jun 1772 Westminster MA, d. 15 Jan 1852 Boston MA, m. 25 Aug 1801 Westminster MA Polly Rice, b. Jun 1778, dau. Rev. Asaph and Elizabeth (Clough) Rice.

Mary Almira, b. 28 Nov 1803, d. 7 Mar 1811.

Nancy Aurelia, b. 28 Aug 1805, unm. In Boston MA.

Benjamin Rice, b. 1 Jan 1807, d. 15 Mar 1807.

Benjamin Rice, b. 4 Feb 1808 Westminster MA.

Elizabeth Clough, b. 14 Mar 1810, unm. In Boston MA.

99 George Washington⁵, b. 1812.

Mary Almira, b. 13 Sep 1814, d. 1898, m. 9 Sep 1835 Rev. William Jackson.

Julia, b. 11 Mar 1816.

Susannah Flint, b. 9 May 1817, d. 8 Jul 1838.

Jacob, b. 4 Jun 1820, d. 2 May 1837.

Catherine, b. 7 Jun 1822.

Sources: Westminster MA census 1810. Boston MA census 1840. VR Westminster MA, Boston MA. J1, E16, N5.

40. **ZADOCK⁴ SAWYER** [see 11], b. 4 Feb 1776 Westminster MA, d. 24 Dec 1858 Townsend VT, m. 12 May 1805 Westminster MA Sally Kendall, b. 12 Aug 1786 d. 12 Dec 1863. Innkeeper, farmer.

100 John Milton[5], 1806-1871.

Julia Ann, b. 10 Mar 1808, m. 31 Aug 1830 Oliver Farr.

Edwin H., b. 6 Oct 1810 Westminster MA, d. 25 Nov 1889 Brattleboro VT, m. 20 Dec 1865 Springfield VT Sarepta Holmes Goodell, b. 15 Dec 1843 d. 19 Aug 1912. Merchant. CH: Sarah Goodell, b. 28 Oct 1866, m.(1) 17 Nov 1888 Frederick Pellerin, m.(2) 2 Oct 1900 Moritz Capen.

101 Francis Dana[5], 1813-1871.

Franklin H., b. 2 Jun 1815 Newfane VT, d. 27 Dec 1871 Brattleboro VT, m. 12 Jul 1841 Newfane VT Nancy Ann Taft, b. 1822 d. 12 Jan 1892 Brattleboro VT, dau. Nathan and Olive (Willard) Taft. Merchant, Bank Director. In Brattleboro VT 1869. CH: Florence, b. 1850, d. 6 Feb 1918, teacher; Son, b. 1850; Mary Evelyn, b. 1853, m. 17 Jun 1875 Dr. Charles E. Severence.

Henry, b. 8 Jun 1817, d. 11 Nov 1817.

Sarah Kendall, b. 3 Sep 1818, d. 14 Mar 1855, m. 27 Oct 1842 George Smith.

Mary Delia, b. 29 Nov 1822.

Augusta, b. 28 Dec 1825, m. 25 Sep 1848 Edward O. Whipple.

Henry, b. 29 Aug 1828, d. 7 Aug 1845.

Sources: Windham VT census 1820, 1830. Townshend VT census 1850. Newfane VT census 1850. VR Westminster MA, Rockingham VT, SA/VT. C14, P39.

41. **JACOB⁴ SAWYER** [see 12], b. 1768 Reading MA, d. 22 Nov 1863 Phelps NY, m. 27 Dec 1791 Nobleboro ME Eunice Keen, b. ?. In Wilton ME 1810, Avon ME 1820. S/B/land in Avon ME 1825, 1826.

102 Jacob[5], b. 1794.

Son, b. 30 Jun 1796, d. 5 Jul 1796.

Lucretia, b. 4 Sep 1797.

Daughter, b. 30 Jul 1799, d. 31 Jul 1799.

Son, b. 7 Jun 1800, d. 9 Jun 1800.

Nancy, b. 18 Jun 1802.

Porter, b. 1 Sep 1804 Wilton ME. Tavern keeper.

Sources: Wilton ME census 1810. Avon ME census 1820, 1830. VR Nobleboro ME, Strong ME, Wilton ME, Bristol ME. H26.

42. **DANIEL⁴ SAWYER** [see 13], b. 4 Sep 1781 Westminster MA, d. 1 Oct 1847 Pembroke NH, m. 22 Sep 1803 Hampstead NH Sarah Ferren of Sandown NH, b. 23 Oct 1783 d. 26 Jun 1864, dau. Alphonse and Margaret (Currier) Ferren. Captain of militia. B/mill in Chester NH 1805. In Sandown NH 1810, Chester NH 1820, Hooksett NH 1830, Pembroke NH 1835.

Sally, b. 23 Jan 1804 Sandown NH, d. 12 Feb 1826, m. 26 Jan 1825 William G. Buell.

Alpheus Ferren, b. 26 Oct 1805 Sandown NH, d. 21 Jun 1833, unm.

Daniel, b. 3 Apr 1808 Sandown NH, d. 30 Apr 1827, unm.

Sylvester Thompson, b. 6 Mar 1810 Sandown NH, d. 5 Dec 1827, unm.

103 Jacob[5], 1812-1892.

Edward Hill, b. 24 Jul 1815 Hooksett NH, d. 7 Sep 1818.

Mary, b. 6 Aug 1817 Hooksett NH, d. 19 Apr 1818.

Asa, b. 18 Jun 1819 Hooksett NH, d. 18 Feb 1821.

Benjamin, b. 27 Jan 1822 Hooksett NH, d. 13 May 1827.

Mary Elizabeth, b. 21 Mar 1824 Hooksett NH, d. 15 Feb 1897, m. 1841 George Noyes. Went to Concord NH.

Sarah, b. 8 Jul 1826 Hooksett NH, d. 14 Sep 1829.

Sources: Sandown NH census 1810. Chester NH census 1820. Hooksett NH census 1830. Pembroke NH census 1840. VR Hampstead NH. N9, C11, N40, F15, C31, N6.

43. **ASA[4] SAWYER** [see 13], b. 11 Aug 1783 Sandown NH, d. in Keysville NY, m. 4 Jul 1809 Brentwood NH Mary Ann Garland of Kingston NH, b. ?. Physician. In Kingston NH 1810, Pembroke NH 1830.

Maria, b. ca. 1810.

Joseph, b. ca. 1812.

Asa, b. ca. 1814.

Elvira Garland, b. ca. 1815.

Hepsibah, b. ca. 1817.

Sarah Jane, b. ca. 1819.

Amos Milton Gale, b. ca. 1820 Pembroke NH.

Daniel, b. ca. 1822 Pembroke NH.

Nathaniel Rogers, b. 13 Feb 1824, d. 28 Jul 1825.

Sylvester, b. ca. 1825 Pembroke NH. 2 Sons, b. (1825-1830).

Sources: Kingston NH census 1810. Pembroke NH census 1830. C11, N9, N14.

44. **EBENEZER J.[4] SAWYER** [see 13], b. 27 Feb 1798 Sandown NH, d. 12 Jan 1844 Sandown NH, m. 25 Sep 1833 Mary Jack of Massachusetts, b. 12 Apr 1810 d. 2 Mar 1868.

Sarah Ann, b. 13 Nov 1834, m. _____ Gale.

Jacob M., b. 8 Aug 1836 Sandown NH, d. 5 Apr 1874 Haverhill MA, m.(1) 28 Nov 1861 Gilford NH Olive J. Davis, b. ?; m.(2) 4 Jul 1867 Haverhill MA Nellie F. Belmont of Haverhill MA, b. 1851, dau. Charles A. and Sarah A. Belmont. Carpenter. CH: Ida M., b. ?, m. 23 Oct 1888 Claremont NH Edgar M. Gordon. He bur. in Sandown NH.

Abigail, b. 29 Nov 1838, m. 26 Nov 1857 Franklin Fitts.

Mary Elizabeth, b. 11 May 1841, m. I Jan 1867 Newton NH John Griffin.

Rachel Jones, b. 2 Apr 1844, d. 28 May 1867, unm.

Sources: Sandown NH census 1830, 1840. VR SA/MA. C11, D10, N6.

45. **BENJAMIN EATON[4] SAWYER** [see 13], b. 28 Nov 1801 Sandown NH, d. 23 Aug 1878 Candia NH, m. 14 Jun 1827 Lucinda Kimball of Manchester NH, b. 6 Nov 1805 d. 10 Jan 1872, dau. Nathan and Eunice (Hoyt) Kimball. Farmer.

Susan Maria, b. 9 Feb 1828 Hooksett NH, d. 24 Jan 1907, m. 14 Feb 1860 Manchester NH Rev. Otis Russell.

Lucinda Jane, b. 13 Jun 1831 Manchester NH, m. 18 May 1856 Manchester NH A_____ H. Elliott.

Rachel Amanda, b. 6 Jun 1833 Manchester, d. 12 Apr 1834 Hampstead NH.

Daniel Sylvester, b. 8 Nov 1834 Candia NH, d. 1 Jun 1913 Candia NH, m. 1 Oct 1873 Dollie Clark of Candia NH, b. 7 Jan 1828 d. 2 Jul 1890.

Son, b. 12 Jul 1836, d. 13 Jul 1836.

Ebenezer Benjamin, b. 26 Dec 1839 Candia NH, d. 23 May 1861 Candia NH.

Ann Celestia, b. 5 May 1846 Candia NH, d. 2 Jun 1866 Candia NH.

George Hart, b. 7 Oct 1847 Candia NH, d. 20 May 1872 Candia NH.

Sources: Candia NH census 1840, 1850, 1860, 1870. VR Candia NH. N6, C11, M54, P82g.

## FIFTH GENERATION

46. **JOSIAH⁵ SAWYER** [see 14], b. 24 Jun 1770 Methuen MA, d. 23 Apr 1800 Peterboro NH, m. Martha Wyman of Woburn MA, b. 12 Jun 1777. In Peterboro NH 1795.

Martha, b. 23 Nov 1795 Peterboro NH, d. 23 Jul 1842, m. 22 Oct 1816 Benjamin Haywood.
Sally, b. 14 Aug 1797, m. Lot Nichols.
104 Josiah[6], 1800-1864.
Sources: A27, H93.

47. **MOSES[5] SAWYER** [see 14], b. 25 Aug 1774 Sharon NH, d. 26 Apr 1851 Sharon NH, m.(1) 22 Nov 1795 Jaffrey NH Hepzibah Hathorn, b. 28 Nov 1771 d. 25 Jun 1816, dau. Collins and Sarah (Dean) Hathorn; m.(2) Sarah Ingalls, b. 13 Aug 1783 d. 16 Nov 1871, dau. Josiah and Sarah (Bowers) Ingalls. In Peterborough NH 1800, Sharon NH 1810.

Sally, b. 11 Oct 1797, d. 19 Aug 1866, m. 19 Nov 1822 Peterborough NH Levi W. Porter.
Moses, b. 30 Oct 1799 Peterborough NH, d. 7 Mar 1829 Sharon NH.
Naomi, b. 20 Aug 1801, d. 14 Apr 1802.
Oliver, b. 18 Feb 1803 Sharon NH, d. 26 May 1834.
Naomi, b. 2 May 1805.
105 Alvin[6], 1808-1865.
Harvey, b. 18 Sep 1810 Sharon NH, d. Sep 1885 Topeka KS, m. 31 May 1838 Jaffrey NH Adeline Haywood of Jaffrey NH, b. 25 Jan 1818 d. 22 Mar 1896, dau. Benjamin and Polly (Sawyer) Haywood. Manufacturer. In Jaffrey NH 1854, Topeka KS 1872. CH: Mary Ann, b. 16 Nov 1841, d. 6 Dec 1932, m.(1) 14 Mar 1865 Addison Farnsworth, m.(2) 16 Nov 1886 Albert H. Horton; Erminia, b. 12 Aug 1844, d. 29 Sep 1874.
Sidney, b. 18 Sep 1812, d. 14 Jul 1814.
Sources: Peterborough NH census 1800. Sharon NH census 1810, 1820, 1830, 1840, Jaffrey NH census 1860, 1870. A27, N9, B98, N6.

48. **ABIAL[5] SAWYER** [see 14], b. 25 Mar 1784 Sharon MA, d. 23 Oct 1870 Peterborough NH, m. 15 Sep 1807 Wilton NH Sybel Buss of Wilton NH, b. 16 Jan 1787 d. 26 Feb 1866. Farmer. Selectman for Peterborough NH.

106 Josiah[6], 1808-1883. Went to Illinois.
107 Silas[6], 1810-1879.
108 Joseph A.[6], b. 1812.
Almira, b. 10 Dec 1814, d. 10 Jan 1836, m. 19 Mar 1833 Wirling Gregg.
Louise, b. 17 Dec 1816, d. 24 Aug 1867.
Albert, b. 16 Aug 1819 Sharon NH, d. 13 Jan 1889 Fitchburg MA, m. 26 Aug 1845 Sophia M. Gowing, b. 28 Dec 1826. In Peterborough NH 1850-1870. CH: Emma S., b. 25 May 1847, m. 13 Feb 1870 Fitchburg MA Joseph Farnsworth.
Susannah, b. 5 Aug 1821, d. 21 Sep 1873, m. 1852 Miflin Bailey.
Anna, b. 25 May 1825, m. 25 Nov 1851 Albert S. Scott.
Andrew J., b. 19 Aug 1827, d. 25 Sep 1829.
Sources: Sharon NH census 1810, 1820, 1830. Peterborough NH census 1840, 1850, 1860, 1870. VR Wilton NH, SA/MA. N6, J14, S48.

49. **ASAPH[5] SAWYER** [see 15], b. 15 Jul 1793 Wilton NH, d. 1 Aug 1875 Cooper ME, m.(1) 23 Feb 1819 Wilton NH Betsey Russell, b. 4 Mar 1797 d. in New York, dau. Daniel and Elizabeth Russell; m.(2) 3 Nov 1845 Cooper ME Alice C. Allen of Cooper ME, b. 1818. Brickmaker. In Castleton VT, Cohoes NY, California, Cooper ME.

Charlotte E., b. 1846.

Alice A., b. 1848.

Nathaniel Gates, b. 1850 Cooper ME, m. 3 Dec 1790 Wesley ME Josephine Rollins of Wesley ME, b. ?, dau. Davis W. and Clorinda G. Rollins.

Sources: Cooper ME census 1850. VR Brockton MA, Bangor ME. A1.

50. **JONATHAN$^5$ SAWYER** [see 16], b. 2 Apr 1774 Hancock NH, d. Peru NY, m. 18 Mar 1800 Hancock NH Abigail Cummings, b. 11 Feb 1774 d. Weston VT, dau. John and Rebecca (Reed) Cummings.

Isobel, b. 1801, d. 20 Jan 1873.

George, b. ca. 1808 Hancock NH. In Weston VT.

Abigail, b. Mar 1810, m. Eli Buxton.

Sources: Hancock NH census 1800. Weston VT census 1810. H37, S31, C90.

51. **DANIEL$^5$ SAWYER** [see 16], b. 15 Sep 1778 Hancock NH, d. 18 May 1857 Andover VT, m. 10 Apr 1800 Hancock NH Jane S. Miller, b. 5 Apr 1775 d. 184?, dau. John Miller. Farmer. Daniel's d. rec. in Ludlow VT.

109 Daniel$^6$, 1800-1877.

110 Leonard$^6$, 1807-1861.

111 Addison$^6$, 1814-1851.

Sources: Hancock NH census 1800. Andover VT census 1810, 1820, 1830, 1840, 1850. VR Hancock NH, SA/VT. H37.

52. **JOSIAH$^5$ SAWYER** [see 16], b. 28 Oct 1780 Hancock NH, d. 15 Apr 1858 Owego NY, m. 20 Nov 1804 Greenfield NH Martha Pollard of Billerica MA, b. ? d. 10 Aug 1862. In Greenfield NH 1827.

Susanna, b. 8 Jan 1805.

William, b. 17 Nov 1806 Peterborough NH, d. 26 Apr 1882 Owego NY, m. 1835 Nancy Bosworth, b. ?.

Lucy, b. 2 Apr 1809, d. 20 Dec 1818 Hancock NH.

Nathan, b. 2 Dec 1810 Hancock NH, m. 1836 Huldah Barker of Owego NY, b. ?. In Greenfield NH, Owego NY.

Clarissa, b. 24 May 1814, m. 1855 George Fuller of Bennington VT.

Martha M., b. 9 Jun 1818, m. Alonzo P. Buck of Owego NY.

Malinda, b. 23 Sep 1820, m. Oren Camp of New York.

Francis Edwin, b. 7 Jun 1824 Greenfield NH, m. Catherine Camp of New York, b. ?.

Roena, b. 31 May 1827, d. 9 Jul 1831.

Sources: Hancock NH census 1810, 1820. H37, N9, 14.

53. **NATHANIEL$^5$ SAWYER** [see 16], b. 6 Jan 1783 Hancock NH, d. ca. 1868 Temple ME, m. Mary Richards of Lunenburg MA, b. 1793, dau. Michael Richards. In Temple ME 1820, w/son Dennis in 1860.

Mary, b. 22 Nov 1815.

Pemela, b. 5 Sep 1817, d. 3 Mar 1898 Farmington ME.

Leonard, b. 31 Jul 1819 Temple ME, b. 21 Nov 1851 Charlestown MA, unm.

Albion K., b. 29 Mar 1822 Temple ME, d. 9 Jan 1877.

Abiel, b. 31 Dec 1824 Temple ME, d. 20 Oct 1848 Charlestown MA.

Sophia A., b. 10 Feb 1827.

Dennis, b. 23 Feb 1829 Temple ME.

112 Edwin$^6$, 1831-1915.

Phirella, b. 23 Aug 1835.

Sources: Temple ME census 1820, 1830, 1840, 1850, 1860. VR SA/ME. H37, M8A.

54. **ABEL$^5$ SAWYER** [see 16], b. 18 Jan 1785 Hancock NH, d. 30 Jul 1860 Hancock NH, m. 15 Nov 1807 Hancock NH Elizabeth Goodhue of Hancock NH, b. 17 Nov 1788 d. 1 Mar 1863, dau. Ebenezer and Sally Goodhue. Farmer.

Lucy, b. 2 Feb 1811, m. 13 May 1834 Samuel Matthews.
113 Charles$^6$, 1812-1872.
114 Leonard$^6$, b. 1814.
Emeline, b. 12 Jan 1817, m. Roland Goodhue.
Elizabeth, b. 17 Jun 1819, d. 26 Jan 1848, m. 19 Dec 1844 Cyrus Estabrook of Hancock NH.
115 Wallace$^6$, 1821-1887.
Arvilla, b. 1 Oct 1823, d. 26 Feb 1833.

Sources: Hancock NH census 1820, 1830, 1840, 1850. N6, H37, N9, E22.

55. **HENRY$^5$ SAWYER** [see 16], b. 6 Mar 1789 Hancock NH, d. 20 Mar 1861 Marlborough NH, m. 1 Apr 1821 Stoddard NH Roxelana Emerson of Richmond NH, b. 28 Feb 1797 d. 24 Sep 1860. In Marlow NH 1830, Marlborough NH 1845. He bur. in East Cem., Marlborough NH.

Mary A., b. 30 Dec 1821, m. 23 May 1853 Marlborough NH James M. Johnson.
Rhoda, b. 14 Mar 1823, d. 2 Feb 1842.
Caroline M., b. 26 Oct 1824, d. 29 Apr 1844.
Adeline E., b. 6 Jul 1826, d. 26 Aug 1856.
Harriet N., b. 3 Mar 1828, d. 29 Oct 1843.
Elizabeth Wood, b. 26 Feb 1830, d. 27 May 1844.
116 Daniel Henry$^6$, 1832-1909.
117 Wyman$^6$, b. 1835.

Sources: Marlow NH census 1830, 1840. Marlborough NH census 1850. N6, B42, H37, N9.

56. **ASA$^5$ SAWYER** [see 17], b. 23 Feb 1782 Nelson NH, d. 1 Feb 1845 Mt. Holly VT, m. 11 Jan 1803 Polly Barnard of Peterborough NH, b. 22 Feb 1780 d. 6 Sep 1858, dau. Benjamin Barnard. In Mt. Holly VT 1810-1840. Wid. in Mt. Holly VT 1850.

118 Asa$^6$, 1806-1885.
Emily, b. 5 Jul 1808, m. 5 Jul 1828 Isaac G. Wheeler.
Louisa, b. 11 Sep 1810, m. 11 Dec 1837 Clark Shattuck of Weston VT.
Alvina, b. 1 Feb 1813.
Polly, b. 2 Jul 1814.
119 Benjamin$^6$, b. 1815.
120 David B.$^6$, b. 1818.
Emily, b. 5 Jul 1819.
121 William$^6$, b. 1820.
122 Winslow Hartwell$^6$, 1821-1890.

Sources: Mt. Holly VT census 1810, 1820, 1830, 1840, 1850. VR SA/VT. S33, D32.

57. **JESSE A.$^5$ SAWYER** [see 17], b. 5 Jan 1786 Nelson NH, d. 23 Dec 1856 Mt. Holly VT, m. 21 Dec 1808 Ashburnham MA Mary Reed, b. 18 May 1790 d. 21 Feb 1865. Justice of the Peace. In Mt. Holly VT 1810.

Daughter, b. (1809-1810).
Son, b. (1810-1820).
123 Jesse$^6$, 1814-1898.
124 Amos$^6$, 1816-1882.

Daughter, b. (1820-1825).
Helen, b. 1838.
Sources: Mt Holly VT census 1810, 1820, 1830, 1840, 1850. VR Bolton MA, Ashburnham MA. L17, D6.

58. **JOEL[5] SAWYER** [see 17], b. 8 Sep 1787 Nelson NH, d. 1833, m. 9 May 1809 Susannah Davis of Stoddard NH, b. 1782 d. 9 Sep 1856. Wid. in New Ipswich NH 1850.
125 Joel[6], 1810-1856.
Lucy, b. 3 Oct 1811, d. 2 Mar 1884, m. Eli Foster.
Asenath, b. 25 Oct 1813, m. 16 Feb 1837 Benjamin Sawyer of Vermont.
Alvinia, b. 24 Oct 1816.
Arvilla, b. 10 Mar 1819, d. 24 Sep 1836.
126 Benjamin[6], 1821-1882.
Josiah, b. 1824, d. 22 Feb 1826.
Mary, b. 20 Aug 1826.
Francis, b. 31 Dec 1830, d. 22 Dec 1850.
Note: One dau. m. George Kittredge of Nelson NH.
Sources: Packersfield (early Nelson) NH census 1810. Nelson NH census 1820, New Ipswich NH 1850. S100, C24, N6.

59. **AMOS[5] SAWYER** [see 17], b. 12 Jun 1789 Nelson NH, d. 1841 Hartland NY, m. Fanny _____, b. ?. In Philadelphia VT 1810. Both bp. in Goshen VT 1815.
Silas, b. (Philadelphia VT?), m. Eliza Jane Leonard, b. ?. In Hartland NY.
Armena, b. 15 Sep 1809.
Elvira, b. 12 Jul 1811.
Fanny, b. 12 Oct 1813.
Rosina, b. 29 May 1815.
Sources: Philadelphia VT census 1810. Goshen VT census 1820. VR SA/VT. H43.

60. **INGALLS KITTREDGE[5] SAWYER** [see 17], b. 22 Mar 1794 Nelson NH, m. 23 Jan 1818 Rachel White of Nelson NH, b. 27 Oct 1796 d. 23 Aug 1858, dau. John White. Rachel bur. in Mt. Holly VT.
Horace, b. 30 Oct 1820 Chester VT.
Eliza A., b. 23 Feb 1823, m. 10 Oct 1843 Nelson C. Earl.
Horatio, b. 2 Dec 1824 Chester VT.
Harvey, b. 7 Sep 1827 Chester VT.
Henry Hubbard, b. 10 Aug 1829 Chester VT, m. 23 Jun 1850 Ida Brown, b. ?.
Lucy, b. 20 Jun 1832, m. 31 Oct 1855 Ludlow VT Calvin Wheeler.
Olive Parker, b. 20 Sep 1834.
Ann Elizabeth, b. 27 Nov 1836.
Arterisia, b. 16 Oct 1841, d. 16 Sep 1843.
Sources: Goshen VT census 1820. Chester VT census 1830, 1840. VT SA/VT. E1, W32.

61. **JEREMIAH[5] SAWYER** [see 18], b. 16 Nov 1779 Dracut MA, m. 2 Mar 1809 Newport VT Nancy Hacket, b. ?. Selectman for Newport VT 1811, 1814. Justice of the Peace.
Reuben, b. 11 Aug 1809 Duncansboro (Newport) VT.
Ira, b. 21 Feb 1811 Newport VT.
Milley, b. 11 Feb 1813.
Sources: VR SA/VT. N2.

62. **BENJAMIN[5] SAWYER** [see 19], b. 178? (Methuen MA?), d. 5 Jul 1841 Danville VT, m. Betsey _____ of Massachusetts, b. 1784. In Danville VT 1820-1840. Wid. in Danville VT 1850.

Sally Pillsbury, b. 9 Mar 1807, m. 30 Apr 1825 Parker Woodward.
Elizabeth Stevens, b. 18 Oct 1810.
Harriet Taylor, b. 2 Apr 1813.
Mary Hawley, b. 30 May 1816.
Pamela, b. 5 Aug 1819, m. 22 Jan 1838 Amasa McDonald.
Uri B., b. 1827, d. 11 May 1851.
Frank, b. 26 Mar 1831 Danville VT, d. 15 May 1901, m. 12 Sep 1882 Eliza Bently.

Sources: Danville VT census 1820, 1830, 1840, 1850. VR SA/VT. J2, S41.

63. **CHARLES[5] SAWYER** [see 19], b. 1790 Danville VT, d. 24 Jun 1870 Henderson NY, m. 29 Dec 1822 Danville VT Sarah B. Shepard, b. ? d. 4 Feb 1899, dau. James and Sarah (Richards) Shepard of Cabot VT. War of 1812.

Harriet, b. 1826.
Frederick, b. 1828 (Danville VT?). In Craftsbury VT 1850.
Asabel, b. 1830.
Catherine, b. 1833.
Charles, b. 1836 Craftsbury VT.

Sources: Craftsbury VT census 1840, 1850. VR SA/VT. F11A.

64. **ASA M.[5] SAWYER** [see 20], b. 7 Jun 1786 Dracut MA, d. 26 May 1860 Waterbury VT, m. Ann _____, b. ?. Farmer. In Thetford VT 1833.

127 John M.[6], b. 1833.

Sources: VR SA/VT. D11.

65. **RALPHA W.[5] SAWYER** [see 21], b. 24 Oct 1805 Dracut MA, m. 30 Apr 1829 Dracut MA Polly Webster, b. ?. Blacksmith. In Dracut MA 1850.

Mary Ann, b. 1830, d. 3 Jul 1833.
Alfred W., b. 27 Mar 1832, d. 23 Jun 1833.
Letitia Blood, b. 27 Jan 1834, d. 12 Jan 1903, m. Lowell MA Robert Park.
128 Francis Albert[6], b. 1835.
Ralpha A., b. ca. 1837 Dracut MA, m. 1 May 1856 Dracut MA Susan F. Coburn of Dracut MA, b. 19 May 1835, dau. Benjamin and Mary Coburn. Farmer. CH: Emily Frances, b. 19 Mar 1857; Helen F., b. 27 Feb 1868 New Bedford MA.
Aurilla, b. 15 May 1839.
Lydia Ann, b. 7 Oct 1843, m. 29 Nov 1863 Lowell MA Jessie Marshall.

Sources: Dracut MA census 1830, 1840, 1850. VR Dracut MA, SA/MA. P7, G24.

66. **JAMES MADISON[5] SAWYER** [see 21], b. 9 Jun 1809 Dracut MA, m. 12 Dec 1836 Lowell MA Dorcas A. Upton of Lowell MA, b. ?.

129 Frank P.[6], b. 1839.

Sources: VR Dracut MA, Lowell MA, SA/MA.

67. **DAVID[5] SAWYER** [see 23], b. 11 Nov 1787 Dracut MA, d. 24 Dec 1866 Landgrove VT, m. 3 Jul 1812 Methuen MA Lydia Clark of Methuen MA, b. 1790 d. 23 Sep 1870, dau. Samuel and Abigail (Sawyer) Clark. In Peru VT 1820, Mt. Tabor VT 1840. He bur. in Old Cemetery Landgrove VT.

Mary, b. 15 Nov 1812, d. 6 Sep 1879, m. 6 Dec 1832 Royal Bryant.
Achsah, b. Jan 1822, d. 9 Sep 1831.

Lydia, b. ?, d. Jan 1879.
Abigail C., b. 5 Nov 1825, m. 2 May 1850 S. Merritt Pease.
Milo C., b. 1828, d. 13 Jun 1852.
Alvira, b. ?, m. George Pease. Went to Langdon VT.
Lucinda, b. 1832, d. 1894, m. Ira French. Went to Nebraska.
Hannah, b. ?, m. 28 Aug 1844 Allen Barber.

Sources: Peru Vt census 1820. Mt. Tabor VT census 1840, 1850. VR Methuen MA, SA/VT.

68. **THADDEUS COLBURN⁵ SAWYER** [see 23], b. 11 Nov 1792 Methuen MA, d. 3 Mar 1863 Essex VT, m.(1) 11 Feb 1816 Corinth VT Polly Wood, b. 1794 d. 14 Jul 1837; m.(2) 19 Feb 1838 Burlington VT Marian (Fleming) Gilmore of Scotland, b. Oct 1796 d. 7 Jan 1867. Farmer. In Corinth VT 1820, Westford VT 1830, Burlington VT 1840, Essex VT 1850.

Seth W., b. 1817, d. 5 Oct 1838.
Hampden A., b. 1827, d. 8 Feb 1858.
Albert H., b. 1836, d. 2 Mar 1836.
Albert F., b. 1838, d. Sep 1863.
Alfred F., b. 1842, d. 30 Aug 1862.
Isabelle Graham, b. 9 Jan 1844, m. 26 Oct 1867 James A. Parsons.
130 Frederick Parker[6], b. 1846. Went to California.

Sources: Corinth VT census 1820. Westford VT census 1830. Burlington VT census 1840. Essex VT census 1850. VR SA/VT. D11, D41, P13.

69. **JOHN HARRIS[5] SAWYER** [see 23], b. 7 Aug 1802 Nottingham NH, d. 26 Oct 1850 Peru VT, m. 9 Feb 1829 Hannah R. Roby, b. 12 Nov 1800 d. 31 May 1871. In Landgrove VT, Peru VT 1850.

Harvey, b. 16 Oct 1829, d. 1 Sep 1850.
131 John[6], 1831-1897. Went to California.
Sorel Allen, b. 1 Jun 1833 Peru VT, d. 1 Dec 1919 Townshend VT, m. 17 Mar 1863 Barnardston MA Susan J. Connable of Barnardston MA, b. 7 Apr 1842 d. 28 Apr 1915. Farmer. CH: Susan Jennie, b. 4 Nov 1866, d. 1906, m. 1 Jun 1887 Irving Watson; Hattie C., b. 27 Jan 1868, d. Jan 1895, m. 5 Nov 1890 Sylvester Blodgett; Mary C., b. 23 Feb 1870, d. 22 Dec 1952, m. 30 Oct 1889 Fred Watson, to Townshend VT; Sorel Horton, b. 5 Nov 1871 d. 3 Aug 1872; Harlan, b. 15 Sep 1875, d. 31 Oct 1883; Seth Samuel, b. 29 Aug 1879, d. 31 Oct 1883.
Ambrose W., b. 15 Jul 1834 Peru VT, d. 31 Mar 1866 Chittenden/Peru VT, m. 12 Sep 1857 Rutland VT Ellen Hill of England, b. ? d. 19 Sep 1900. CH: Helen B., b. 20 Mar 1858, m. 25 Dec 1877 Emmet Crapo; May, b. 15 Mar 1859.
Hannah, b. 23 Apr 1836, d. 13 Jul 1871, m. 26 Nov 1864 Thomas Cross.
Ann, b. 8 Feb 1838, d. 8 May 1875, m. 22 Mar 1855 Charles E. Morrill.
Harlan, b. 9 Nov 1839, d. 21 Oct 1850.
Edward P., b. 25 Oct 1843 Peru VT, d. 8 May 1873 Marlboro NH, m. 6 Sep 1869 Anna (Savage) Dickerman of Stockbridge VT, b. ?. Farmer.
Seth L., b. 12 Nov 1846, d. 19 Sep 1871.

Sources: Peru VT census 1850. VR Peru VT, SA/VT, SA/MA.

70. **ALFRED[5] SAWYER** [see 23], b. 21 Jun 1804 Nottingham NH, d. 24 Oct 1880 Lowell VT, m.(1) Jericho VT Laura _____ of Massachusetts, b. 1812; m.(2) 22 Jan 1862 Ruth Manley of Milton VT, b. Apr 1843 d. 15 May 1873, dau. Howard and Hattie Manley; m.(3) 20 Jul 1875 Lowell VT Delia M. Demerit, b. ?. Farmer, miller. In Landgrove VT, Westford VT.

Abby M., b. 1833, d. 25 Aug 1861, m. 1 Apr 1859 George W. Mardin.

Lewis, b. 1835 Westford VT.
Seth, b. 1841 Westford VT.
Eugene, b. 1843 Westford VT.
Alison, b. 1848.
Lettie M., b. 14 Jan 1863, m. 5 Jun 1880 George M. Demerit.
Lottie A., b. 1865, m. 23 Nov 1887 Milton VT William L. Bean.
Ella A., b. 2 Oct 1866, m. 4 Jul 1883 Eugene A. Coolidge.
Ida May, b. 5 May 1868, m. 29 Oct 1884 Dennis Hines.
Alma M., b. 20 Dec 1871, m. 12 Oct 1891 Milton VT Fred A. Walston.

Sources: Westford VT census 1840, 1850. VR SA/VT. N6, G6, B40.

71. **AARON$^5$ SAWYER** [see 25], b. 14 Jan 1801 Methuen MA, d. 1870, m. 3 May 1821 Methuen MA Mary P. Sinclare, b. 1800 d. 1875. Blacksmith. In Andover MA 1840, Wilbraham MA 1852.

Mary, b. 15 Aug 1821, m.(1) ?, m.(2) Burnham S. White of Stoneham MA.
Aaron, b. 29 Jun 1823, d. 5 May 1826.
132 Joseph Warren$^6$, b. 1825.
Aaron, b. 2 Dec 1827, d. 25 Sep 1829.
Rhoda Flint, b. 25 Dec 1829, d. 1928, m. 4 Sep 1854 William S. Webster.
Susan, b. 16 Jun 1832, m. 25 Oct 1852 Andover MA Francis H. Webster.
Adelia, b. 6 Feb 1835, m. 4 May 1859 Bluehill ME George Stevens.
George Francis, b. 26 Dec 1837, d. 29 May 1842.
Charles Murray, b. 18 Jan 1840 Methuen MA, d. 23 Jun 1928 Wilbraham MA, m. 16 May 1865 Methuen MA Sarah A. Dowding of Methuen MA, b. 1840, dau. Nathaniel and Ann Dowding. Civil War: In Company B, 6th Massachusetts Volunteers, under Captain Bradley, April 1861. Farmer. He bur. in Elmwood Cem., Wilbraham MA. CH: Grace Ella, b. 30 Sep 1867, m. 28 Mar 1889 Lawrence MA Charles W. Mansise.
Emily J., b. 5 Jan 1842, m. _____ Cole.
Walter, b. 20 May 1849 Methuen MA.

Sources: Methuen MA census 1830. Andover MA census 1840, 1850. VR Methuen MA, Wilbraham MA, SA/MA. T1.

72. **SAMUEL$^5$ SAWYER** [see 25], b. 28 Feb 1803 Methuen MA, m. 19 Jul 1835 Methuen MA Sarah Adeline Frye, b. ? d. 7 Aug 1851, dau. Samuel and Mary (Fetcher) Frye. In Lowell MA, Salem NH 1840. Wid. m. brother-in-law Francis$^5$.

Samuel Frye, b. 7 Jul 1836 Lowell MA. In Salem NH 1840.

Sources: Salem NH census 1840. B23.

73. **JOHN$^5$ SAWYER** [see 25], b. 27 Jul 1808 Methuen MA, m. 21 May 1848 Methuen MA Irene Hobbs of New Hampshire, b. 19 Jun 1819, dau. Daniel Hobbs. Farmer, blacksmith.

Daniel H., b. 25 Sep 1849 Methuen MA, m. 8 May 1873 Camden ME Sarah B. Haskell of Deer Isle ME, b. ?. Machinist. CH: Asenath T., b. 25 Jun 1874, m. 21 Nov 1874 Lawrence MA Carleton A. Welton.
Susan I, b. 28 Feb 1852, m. 14 Feb 1887 Lawrence MA Norman Fuller.

Sources: Methuen MA 1850. VR Methuen MA, Dracut MA, Camden ME, SA/MA.

74. **FRANCIS$^5$ SAWYER** [see 25], b. 13 Jul 1815 Methuen MA, m.(1) 7 Nov 1840 Methuen MA Sarah Adeline (Frye) Sawyer, b. ? d. 7 Aug 1851, wid. of Samuel$^5$, [see 72], dau. Samuel and Mary (Fletcher) Frye; m.(2) 17 Jan 1852 Lawrence MA Belinda B. Parker of Dracut MA, b. ca. 1834, dau. Nathan and Fanny Parker. Shoemaker.

133 Aaron Lorain[6], b. 1841.

Asa Francis, b. 11 Jan 1846 Methuen MA, m. 25 Jun 1868 Mary Malery, b. ca. 1846, dau. William Malery. Mason. In Lawrence MA 1874. CH: Blanche, b. ca. 1874, m. 13 Apr 1894 Bradford MA Edwin N. Sawyer.

Walter F., b. 1849 Methuen MA, m.(1) 19 Jul 1871 Lizzie F. Harris of Methuen MA, b. ca. 1853; m.(2) 10 Aug 1889 Alice J. Dyer of Rochester NH, b. 18 Dec 1859 d. 21 Feb 1891; m.(3) 17 Jun 1893 Katie T. Clough of Alton NH, b. 1877. Butcher. In Farmington NH.

134 Granville[6], b. ca. 1852.

Mary A., b. ca. 1853, d. 1 Feb 1928, m. 25 Jun 1871 Michael Kincane.

Daughter, b. 30 Sep 1856.

Thornton W., b. ca. 1857 (Methuen MA?), m. 4 Aug 1880 Annie L. Cook, b. ?. Went to Alabama.

Henry, b. ca. 1858 Methuen MA, m. 16 Mar 1882 Lawrence MA Nellie Simmonds of No. Andover MA, b. ca. 1862. Butcher. CH: Bernice Irving, b. 18 Oct 1881; Kate M., b. 16 Feb 1887.

Fred, b. ca. 1861 Methuen MA, m. 14 Jun 1882 Lawrence MA Kate Cahill of Ireland, b. ca. 1861. Butcher.

Jennie L., b. 23 Oct 1864.

Bertram Sumner, b. 10 May 1867 Methuen MA, m. 9 Nov 1885 Ellen C. McKinstry of Prince Edward Island, Canada, b. ca. 1861. In Concord NH.

Inez F., b. ca. 1869, m. 21 Nov 1887 Lowell MA Edward Smith.

Ina F., b. 25 Apr 1870.

Rupert, b. 7 Oct 1872 Methuen MA.

Nathan Parker, b. 19 Apr 1876 Methuen MA.

Sources: VR Methuen, SA/MA. B23.

75. **PHINEAS B.[5] SAWYER** [see 26], b. 8 Jun 1802 Carmel ME, d. Plymouth ME, m. Sabrina _____, b. 1809. In Plymouth ME 1830-1850. Wid. in Plymouth ME 1880.

David, b. 1827 Plymouth ME.

Daniel, b. 1829 Plymouth ME.

Amos, b. 1833 Plymouth ME.

Sarah L. b. 1838, m. 16 Nov 1869 Boston MA James C. Frost.

Melinda, b. 1840.

Mehitable, b. 1843.

Lucy, b. 1844.

135 Lyman[6], b. 1846.

Edward, b. 1848 Plymouth ME.

Charles, b. 1851 Plymouth ME.

Sources: Plymouth ME census 1830, 1840, 1850, 1880 (wid.). VR Carmel ME, SA/MA. M5.

76. **MOSES[5] SAWYER** [see 26], b. 28 Oct 1809 Carmel ME, d. 4 Jul 1882 Hope ME, m. 4 Jul 1850 Bangor ME Mary Jane Wilton of Bangor ME, b. 1815. Laborer. In Bangor ME 1840, Brooks ME 1860.

Daughter, b. (1825-1830).

Daughter, b. (1830-1835).

Daughter, b. (1835-1840).

Son, b. (1835-1840).

William, C., b. ca. 1842 Bangor ME, m.(1) ?; m.(2) 10 Feb 1899 Boston MA Annie L Morris of England, b. ?.

Sources: Bangor ME census 1840, 1850. Brooks ME census 1860. VR Carmel ME, Bangor ME, SA/MA.

77. **DANIEL E.$^5$ SAWYER** [see 28], b. 4 Sep 1828 Hopkinton NH, m.(1) 1851 Julia Gibbons, b. ? d. 24 Feb 1874; m.(2) 24 Feb 1875 Sarah R. Burpee, b. ?. Superintendent of Yellowstone National Park. In East Andover NH, Concord NH.

Charles L., b. 26 Jun 1852 East Andover NH, m. Nettie Hegler, b. ?.
Caleb Marston, b. 19 Aug 1854, m. 1876 Zella Dickey of Pine Island MN, b. ?.
Daniel J., b. 24 Jun 1857 (East Andover MA?).
Francis E., b. 24 May 1859 (East Andover MA?).
Mary Ellen, b. 15 Nov 1862.
Edward Lynn, b. 3 Jul 1876 (East Andover MA?).

Sources: E2, E9.

78. **RICHARD HALL$^5$ SAWYER** [see 29], b. 1 Nov 1792 Pelham NH, d. 26 Feb 1877 Bristol NH, m. 2 Dec 1819 Bridgewater NH Relief Brown of Landaff NH, b. 11 Aug 1804 d. 17 Dec 1861. Farmer, blacksmith. In Bristol NH 1830. Note: Relief was sister of Sarah, wife of Moody Currier$^5$ [see 80].

Ann Maria, b. 24 Jun 1829, d. 22 Jun 1872, m. 5 May 1850 Dr. Albert A. Moulton.
Edward Payson, b. 15 Jul 1840 Bristol NH, d. 2 May 1925 Bristol NH, m. 2 Feb 1859 Mary Blodgett of Kalamazoo MI, b. 5 Jul 1842 d. 28 Aug 1919, dau. William R. and Deborah (Hedge) Blodgett. CH: Harry Edward, b. 22 Feb 1866, d. 19 Oct 1874.
Susan Hall, b. ?, adopted (dau. of Alvah$^5$), m. Benjamin Flanders.

Sources: Bristol NH census 1830, 1840, 1850, 1860, 1870. N14, A19, R34, C60, T4.

79. **CALEB$^5$ SAWYER** [see 29], b. 12 Feb 1797 Dracut MA, d. 11 Jul 1871 Alexandria NH, m.(1) 16 Feb 1824 Salem MA Mary Ann Sawyer, b. 18 Sep 1799, dau. Henry and Kez1a (Coburn) Sawyer; m.(2) 5 Nov 1843 Hannah (Hastings) Wallace of Bristol NH, b. 24 Jan 1808 d. 5 Sep 1853. In Bristol NH, Alexandria NH 1860, Meredith NH 1870.

William Henry, b. ca. 1825 Bristol NH, m. 26 Jan 1846 Mary Grey, b. ?.
Frances A., b. 1828, d. 30 Jan 1841.
Mary Jane, b. 11 Mar 1830, d. 15 Apr 1880, m. 20 Apr 1847 Danvers MA George Whittier.
Mary Frances, b. 11 Apr 1845, m. 6 Dec 1865 George M. Bean.

Sources: Alexandria NH census 1860. Meredith NH census 1870. VR Dracut MA, Salem MA, SA/MA. W43, M64, B40.

80. **MOODY CURRIER$^5$ SAWYER** [see 29], b. 2 Oct 1807 Hopkinton NH, d. 24 Jul 1854 Bristol NH, m. 1 Jun 1835 Sarah Brown, b. 1 Nov 1809 d. 10 Feb 1853. Physician. In Concord VT, Bristol NH. Sarah was sister of Relief, wife of Richard Hall [see 78].

Moody A., b. 30 Apr 1836 Concord VT, d. 26 May 1895 Boscobel WI, m. 2 Jul 1865 Milwaukee WI Annie Maria Prescott of Claremont NH, b. 19 Aug 1837 d. 3 Feb 1895, dau. Jonathan and Helen (Mansur) Prescott. Civil War: Hospital Steward, Colonel Enoch O. Fellows' 3rd Regiment, 1861. In Milwaukee WI.
Ellen Augusta, b. 20 Oct 1843, d. 20 Oct 1873, m. 18 Oct 1862 Ichabod C. Bartlett.

Sources: Bristol NH census 1840, 1850, 1860. M64, C60, N6.

81. **ALVAH$^5$ SAWYER** [see 30], b. 8 Oct 1800 Warner NH, d. 1 Aug 1874 Topsham VT, m.(1) 17 May 1825 Topsham VT Sally F. George of New Hampshire, b. 1802 d. 11 Oct 1845; m.(2) 13 Apr 1846 Newbury VT Lucia Flanders of Warner VT, b. 1803 d. 19 Oct 1860; m.(3) 30 May 1861 Topsham VT Eliza Ann Hood of Topsham VT, b. 1838 d. 5 Feb 1889. Farmer.

Frances Jane, b. 1825, d. 30 Nov 1838.
Ruth D., b. 1832, d. 19 Jul 1838.
Laura Ann, b. Sep 1839, d. 4 Dec 1839.
Laura Bell, b. 2 Dec 1862, d. 5 Jan 1864.
136 Alvah George$^{6}$, b. 1864.
John R., b. 14 Oct 1868, unm. Went west.
137 Milo B.$^{6}$, b. 1872.
Sources: Topsham VT census 1840, 1850. VR Warner NH, SA/VT.

82. **GEORGE$^{5}$ SAWYER** [see 30], b. 11 Dec 1806 Warner NH, d. 26 Jun 1883 Stewartstown NH, m. 2 Mar 1840 Mary C. Tewksbury, b. 23 Nov 1815 d. 21 Feb 1886, dau. Stephen and Sally (Flanders) Tewksbury of Warner NH. Farmer. In Warner NH 1850, Topsham VT 1857, Stewartstown NH 1870.
Mary A., b. 11 Jun 1841, d. 14 Mar 1853.
George, b. 2 Jan 1843, d. 8 Dec 1862 near Fredericksburg VA.
Sarah, b. 12 May 1844, d. 28 Aug 1867.
138 Alvah$^{6}$, 1846-1930.
139 Charles Nathan$^{6}$, 1847-1931.
Franklin, b. 13 Sep 1849 Warner NH, d. 3 Sep 1897 Concord NH, m. 16 Mar 1872 Roseltha A. Hodgkins, b. 31 Mar 1850 d. 6 May 1944. CH: Edna, b. 30 Jan 1887.
Henry D., b. 29 Nov 1854 Warner NH, d. 23 Apr 1921, m. 21 Jan 1878 Clara Anne Ayer of Quebec, Canada, b. ? d. May 1949. Farmer. In Stewartstown NH 1880. CH: Fannie May, b. 12 Sep 1878, d. Jun 1955, m. James Congdon.
Fannie E., b. 22 Aug 1857, d. 16 Nov 1867.
Sources: Warner NH census 1840, 1850. Stewartstown NH census 1870, 1880. VR SA/VT. H27, Patricia Sawyer rec.

83. **JOSHUA$^{5}$ SAWYER** [see 30], b. 27 Jun 1813 Warner NH, d. 1882 Warner NH, m. 29 Sep 1840 Lavinia Foster of Pembroke NH, b. 17 Jun 1816 d. 19 Jul 1906, dau. Joseph F. and Mary (Jewett) Foster. Note: Joshua and Lavinia are listed separately in the 1850 Warner census.
Frank Orra, b. 8 Sep 1842, d. 2 Mar 1844.
140 William Herbert$^{6}$, 1844-1898.
Susan A., b. 17 Sep 1846, m. 17 Sep 1870 Harlon S. Willis.
Frances Ellen, b. 13 Feb 1848, d. 27 Jun 1863.
Orin, b. 11 Jan 1850, d. 21 Feb 1850.
Orin A., b. 2 Jan 1852 Warner NH, d. 6 Sep 1919 Warner NH, m. 26 Jan 1892 Sadie M. Jones of Warner NH, b. 1873. CH: Mildred May, b. 8 Nov 1892.
Mary E., b. 3 Jan 1854, m. 1 Jan 1889 Warner NH Alphonso Ingalls.
Walter, b. 7 Jul 1857, d. 21 Nov 1889.
Sources: Warner NH census 1850, 1860, 1870. VR SA/NH. H27, N6,

84. **WILLIAM$^{5}$ SAWYER** [see 31], b. 1785 Reading MA, m. 26 Jan 1813 Reading MA Esther Damon, b. ?. Drover. In Bradford NH 1820-1850.
141 William$^{6}$, 1813-1863.
Daughter, b. (1815-1820).
Joshua D., b. 1818 Bradford NH, m. 28 Feb 1849 Palmer MA Catherine E. Gallop of Guilford VT, b. 1818, dau. Amos and Polly Gallop. Soap maker. In Palmer MA 1850. CH: Daughter, b. 14 Dec 1854.
142 Benjamin$^{6}$, b. ca. 1820.
Daughter, b. (1820-1825).

Esther O., b. 19 Nov 1824, m. 30 Dec 1848 Marcus Tyler.

Daughter, b. (1825-1830).

Hannah, b. 1827, m. 8 Apr 1861 Northhampton MA Orsin M. Graves.

Amos, b. ca. 1830 Bradford NH, m. 2 Jul 1857 Cambridge MA Cordelia Tandy of Newport NH, b. ca. 1832, dau. James Tandy. Soap boiler. In Bradford NH 1850, Northhampton MA 1865. CH: Daughter, b. 17 Feb 1859; Mary, b. 14 Aug 1865; Fanny, b. 10 Jul 1867, m. 6 Aug 1891 Cambridge MA John G. Atkinson.

Sources: Bradford NH census 1820, 1830, 1840, 1850. Palmer MA census 1840, VR Reading MA, Bradford NH, SA/MA. B85.

85. **JABEZ$^5$ SAWYER** [see 31], b. 1787, d. 27 Mar 1837, m. 24 Jul 1816 Hannah Emerson of Henniker NH, b. 20 Jun 1794 d. 23 Sep 1884. In New Boston NH, Bradford NH 1830. Wid. in Bradford NH 1840. Wid., sons George W. and Charles P., all bur. in Davis Mill Cem., Warner NH.

Harriet M., b. (1810-1820), m. Jere F. Bailey.

Jerome, b. 1817 Bradford NH, d. 7 Oct 1878 Quereturo, Mexico, m. 2 Apr 1846 Adeline Whitney of Nashua NH, b. 1824 d. 9 Dec 1862. In No. Chelmsford MA. He bur. in American Cem., Mexico City. Wife and one son bur. in Warner NH. CH: George Washington, b. Jun 1847 d. 25 Sep 1848; Geronimo, b. 25 Nov 1858 d. 10 Jun 1859.

143 Frederick Train$^6$, 1819-1898.

Charles Pettee, b. 17 Feb 1821 Bradford NH, d. 16 Nov 1897, unm.

144 Jabez Augustus$^6$, b. 1824.

George W., b. 1830, d. 17 Apr 1847.

Sources: Bradford NH census 1820, 1830, 1840. VR Henniker NH, Bradford NH, Chelmsford MA, SA/MA. N9, M39, C59, Donald F. Sawyer rec.

86. **OLIVER$^5$ SAWYER** [see 31], b. 3 Mar 1801 New Boston NH, d. 29 Mar 1891 Bradford NH, m. 12 May 1828 Sutton NH Lucinda Presby, b. 1801 d. Feb 1870. Farmer. In Bradford NH 1830.

William D., b. 6 Nov 1828 Bradford NH, d. 14 Oct 1900 Bradford NH.

145 George Oscar$^6$, 1832-1884.

Lydia P., b. 1835.

Malinda S., b. 1836, d. 2 Jan 1923.

Pamelia F., b. 1838, m. 7 Dec 1865 Bradford NH B_____ Monroe.

Sources: Bradford NH census 1830, 1840, 1850, 1860, 1870. VR SA/NH. N14, N6.

87. **JOSEPH WARREN$^5$ SAWYER** [see 31], b. 17 Nov 1815 Bradford NH, d. 13 Jan 1899, m. 27 Oct 1841 Martha J. Hoyt of Tunbridge VT, b. 10 May 1822 d. 21 Aug 1894, dau. Enoch and Lydia (Presby) Hoyt of Bradford NH. In Manchester NH, Bradford NH.

Adeline, b. 1842, m. 18 Feb 1862 Nathan Knight.

George Marcell, b. 13 Feb 1844 Bradford NH, d. 13 Jul 1918 Springfield VT, m. 13 May 1868 Nancy J. Plummer of Henniker NH, b. 26 Oct 1848 d. 19 Aug 1870, dau. Ira and Lydia (Folsom) Plummer. Farmer. CH: Addie M., b. 18 May 1869, d. 27 Sep 1895.

Daniel Upton, b. 29 Mar 1846 Bradford NH, d. 2 Apr 1921 Bradford NH, m.(1) 5 Nov 1868 Abbie West of Hillsboro NH, b. Jun 1850 d. 14 Apr 1889, dau. Leonard A. and Mary (Ayers) West; m.(2) 5 Oct 1890 Alice J. Nichols of Bradford NH, b. ca. 1854. Town Clerk 1884. CH: Mary, b. 23 May 1874, d. 8 May 1888.

Warren Flint, b. 27 Aug 1848 Lowell MA, d. 2 Jan 1916 Bradford NH, m. 19 Feb 1879 Clara B. Woodward of Wolcott VT, b. 4 Feb 1851 d. 30 Jan 1911, dau. Samuel P. and Sarah Ann (Leavitt) Woodward. In Bradford NH, Franklin NH.

146 Frederick E.$^6$, 1854-1928.

Sources: Bradford NH census 1850, 1860, 1870, 1880. N6.

88. **SAMUEL$^5$ SAWYER** [see 32], b. 12 Dec 1783 Reading MA, d. 24 Mar 1827 Reading MA, m. 19 Jan 1817 Reading MA Mary J. Campbell, b. ?. Wid. m. John Stevens, went to Illinois.

Edward Tucker, b. 16 Dec 1817 Reading MA, d. 13 Jul 1891 Tishilwa IL, m. 26 Jun 1838 Boscawen NH Louise Stevens, b. 2 Mar 1821 d. 4 Aug 1903.

Sources: Reading MA census 1820. VR Reading MA. N21.

89. **NATHANIEL$^5$ SAWYER** [see 34], b. 26 Mar 1786 Rutland MA, d. 13 Jan 1879, m. 26 Mar 1816 Hubbardston MA Sally Underwood of Hubbardston MA, b. 28 Oct 1793 d. 24 Jan 1878, dau. Isreal and Rhoda (Newton) Underwood. War of 1812. [P46] says Sally was dau. of Isaiah and Abigail (Whitney) Underwood.

Sally, b. 30 Apr 1817, d. 30 Aug 1840 Athol MA, unm.
147 Diodorus$^6$, 1818-1890.
Betsey Pierce, b. 21 Oct 1823, d. 14 Oct 1863, m. 11 Nov 1851 George Sawyer.

Sources: Athol MA census 1820, 1830, 1840. Readsborough VT census 1850. VR Athol MA, Hubbardston MA. P46, J18, L16.

90. **AMOS$^5$ SAWYER** [see 36], b. 17 Aug 1797 Westminster MA, m.(1) 30 Dec 1823 Westminster MA Mary Brooks of Ashburnham MA, b. 1796, dau. Simeon Brooks; m.(2) 26 Nov 1865 Fitchburg MA Susan (Andrews) Phillips of England, b. 1820, dau. Robert and Jemima Andrews. Farmer. In Westminster MA 1830, Fitchburg MA 1840-1850.

148 Augustus$^6$, 1825-1901.
149 William Porter$^6$, 1829-1907.

Sources: Westminster MA census 1830. Fitchburg MA census 1840, 1850. VR Westminster MA, SA/MA. H45, C76.

91. **JOHN$^5$ SAWYER** [see 36], b. 24 Jun 1802 Westminster MA, d. 4 Jun 1891 Mills Corner NY, m. Salome Smith of Vermont, b. 1811 d. 28 May 1894, dau. Benjamin and Lucy (Ellis) Smith.

Andrew Benjamin, b. 8 Nov 1827, d. ca. 1918, m. ca. 1853 Vermont Maria Houseman, b. ?.
Aaron Flint, b. 26 Sep 1831, d. 7 Mar 1862.
Levi Willard, b. 11 Nov 1833, d. 5 Aug 1908, m. 6 Oct 1852 Mary Ann Due, b. ?.
Lucy Delecta, b. 18 Oct 1835, d. 29 Jun 1918, m. Edward P. Hall.
Flavious Josephius, b. 1 Jun 1837, d. 1907, m. Hannah Brown, b. ?.
Mary Jerusha, b. 23 Aug 1839, d. 20 Oct 1910, m. Martin Tymerson.
Henry Theodore, b. 23 May 1841, d. 26 Feb 1927, m. Matilda Gardner, b. ?.
John Tunis, b. 23 Apr 1843, d. 9 Dec 1917, m. 23 Sep 1866 Lois M. Hall, b. ?.
Nancy Marinda, b. 7 May 1845, d. 21 Mar 1925, m. Edward Drake.
Cornelia Ann, b. 20 Jan 1847, d. 30 Mar 1922, m. Arch Pinckney.
George Erastus, b. 17 Mar 1850, d. 1888.
Helen Augusta, b. 26 Sep 1851.

Sources: Gloria Sawyer Brown rec.

92. **CHARLES WILLARD$^5$ SAWYER** [see 36], b. 6 Dec 1804 Westminster MA, d. 9 Oct 1845 Westminster MA, m. 29 Nov 1827 Westminster MA Melezinda T. Cobb, b. ?, dau. Samuel and Lucinda (Shumway) Cobb. Farmer. Wid. m. Reuben Fisher, went to Vermont.

Charles Francis, b. 8 Nov 1828 Westminster MA.
Harriet Elizabeth, b. 2 Jul 1831, d. 30 Apr 1897, m. 2 Aug 1849 John W. Burns.
150 Cyrus Willard$^6$, 1837-1895.

George S., b. 28 Apr 1839, d. 18 Nov 1847.

Mary E., b. 23 Oct 1842 d. 14 Nov 1912, adopted by Aunt Sarah Pierce, m. 20 Nov 1866 Henry A. Coburn of Lowell MA.

John L., b. 21 Apr 1845, d. 1 Oct 1846.

Sources: Westminster MA census 1830, 1840. VR Westminster MA, SA/MA. G24, H45.

93. **SANFORD[5] SAWYER** [see 36], b. 13 May 1810 Westminster MA, d. 28 Jan 1889, m.(1) Samantha A. Ellis of Vermont, b. 1816 d. 10 Jan 1852; m.(2) 11 Jan 1853 Fitchburg MA Martha Cutler of Westminster MA, b. 28 Feb 1814, dau. Jonas and Martha (Marrett) Cutler. Carriage maker, restauranteur.

Sanford A., b. 1832 New York. In Fitchburg MA 1850. Civil War.

Walter E., b. 1839 Fitchburg MA, d. 25 Apr 1856 unm.

Charles, b. 4 Jun 1846 Fitchburg MA, m. 22 Jun 1876 Julia A. Farrington, b. ?. In Somerville MA.

Emily M., b. 23 May 1854, d. 21 Jul 1854 Fitchburg MA.

Andrew Cutler, b. 1 Aug 1855, d.y.

Frank Merrett, b. 31 May 1857 Westminster MA, m. 20 Sep 1879 Westminster MA Marion T. Ames of Westminster MA, b. 1850, dau. Jacob and Frances Ames. Chair manufacturer. CH: Bernice, b. 1880; Kathleen, b. 14 Oct 1886.

Sources: Fitchburg MA census 1840, 1850, 1880. Westminster MA census 1880. VR Westminster MA, SA/MA. C94A, D58, H45, D20.

94. **WILLIAM[5] SAWYER** [see 37], b. 1804 Wakefield NH, d. 13 May 1881 Wakefield NH, m. 27 Jan 1824 Mehitable Richards of Brookfield NH, b. 10 Feb 1805 d. 29 Jan 1887. Student at Wolfeboro/Tuftonboro Academy 1823. Merchant.

151 Charles Augustine[6], 1825-1893.

152 George William[6], 1830-1890.

Mary Ann, b. 26 Nov 1844, d. 9 Jan 1897 Brookfield NH.

Sources: Wakefield NH census 1830, 1840, 1850, 1860, 1870. VR Brookfield NH. P9, N6.

95. **GEORGE YEATON[5] SAWYER** [see 37], b. 5 Dec 1805 Wakefield NH, d. 15 Jun 1882 Nashua NH, m. Oct 1834 Meredith Bridge (Laconia) NH Emeline Tucker of Laconia NH, b. 1810 d. 16 Sep 1891. Judge. Practiced law in Laconia NH until 1834 when he went to Nashua NH to be partners with Aaron Flint Sawyer.

Emeline A., b. ?, d. in infancy.

William Edward, b. ?, d. in infancy.

George Yeaton, b. ca. 1838 Nashua NH, d. 20 Nov 1906 New Bedford MA, m. Amanda Roby of Nashua NH, b. 24 Dec 1835 d. 26 Apr 1907 Nashua NH. Civil War: Enl. 2 May 1861, mustered 7 May 1861, discharged 9 Aug 1861. CH: Anne G., b. ?, m. 12 Dec 1894 Charles Reed.

Charles Albert, b. 1840. Civil War: Army, 1863.

Helen Mary, b. 1843, m. 27 Aug 1873 Nashua NH Elisha Hubbard.

Clara H., b. 16 Oct 1844, d. 30 Apr 1926 Concord NH.

Alice M., b. 1850, d. 21 Nov 1893, m. 5 Nov 1879 Fred W. Estabrook.

Sources: Laconia NH census 1830. Nashua NH census 1840, 1850, 1860, 1870. VR SA/NH. E22, N6, P10, B68, M37.

96. **CHARLES HAVEN[5] SAWYER** [see 37], b. 16 Jul 1814 Wakefield NH, d. 8 Oct 1850 Wakefield NH, m. 17 Nov 1837 Brookfield NH Susan Hanson Pike of Wakefield NH, b. 6 May 1814 d. 11 Feb 1895 Bangor ME. Farmer. Wid. in Wakefield NH 1860.

153 Charles Haven$^{6}$, 1839-1910.
Anna H., b. 1844.
154 Robert William$^{6}$, b. 1850.
Sources: Wakefield NH census 1850, 1860, VR Bangor ME. W68, Haven Sawyer rec.

97. **SAMUEL LOCKE$^{5}$ SAWYER** [see 38], b. Nov 1812 Mont Vernon NH d. 30 Mar 1890 Independence MO, m. Mary Calloway, b. ?.
Mary Greene, b. ?.
Aaron Flint, b. ?.
Thomas Calloway, b. ?.
Fanny Ingalls, b. ?.
Sources: C8, S51.

98. **AARON WORCESTER$^{5}$ SAWYER** [see 38], b. 11 Oct 1818 Mont Vernon NH d. 23 Aug 1882 Nashua NH, m.(1) Mary F. Ingalls of NY City, b. 6 Jul 1827; m.(2) 11 Sep 1856 Fanny Winch of Nashua NH, b. 11 Dec 1833 d. 12 Nov 1917, dau. Francis and Almira (Stetson) Winch. Lawyer, teacher, judge.
Mary G., b. 1859.
Fanny Ingalls, b. 7 Apr 1860, d. 4 Feb 1861.
Fanny Locke, b. 1862, m. 4 Oct 1893 Dr. George A. Bowers.
Aaron Frank, b. 8 Jan 1867, d. 15 Oct 1874.
William Merriam, b. 9 Sep 1873 Nashua NH, d. 8 Jan 1899, m. 23 Jun 1898 Marion Stimpson of Brooklyn NY, b. ?. Harvard Law School 1898. Lawyer.
Sources: Nashua NH census 1850, 1860, 1870, 1880. VR SA/NH. N6, P10, S51, B98, N9.

99. **GEORGE WASHINGTON$^{5}$ SAWYER** [see 39], b. 25 Apr 1812 Westminster MA, m. 14 May 1841 Framingham MA Betsey Sargent of Barton VT, b. 27 Dec 1817. In Lowell MA. Note: Both of their sons took name of Sargent and moved to Springfield MA.
George Washington, b. 12 Feb 1842.
Stephen A., b. 13 Nov 1843.
Sources: VR Westminster MA, Lowell MA. R21.

100. **JOHN MILTON$^{5}$ SAWYER** [see 40], b. 11 Feb 1806 Westminster MA d. 11 May 1871 Winchester NH, m. 19 May 1831 Westminster MA Roena Sawyer, b. 20 Feb 1806, dau. Eli and Anna (Laws) Sawyer. In Richmond NH 1840, Winchester NH 1850.
Joseph, b. 1832 Richmond NH, m. 29 Nov 1860 Winchester NH Emily N. Prince, Swanzey NH, b. ?. Grocer. CH: Grace Emma, b. 31 Jan 1871.
155 Samuel$^{6}$, b. 1836.
156 David$^{6}$, 1841-1908.
157 Henry$^{6}$, b. 1843.
Son, b. 14 Nov 1850.
Sources: Richmond NH census 1840. Winchester NH census 1850, 1860. Boston MA census 1860. VR Winchester NH, Richmond NH, Westminster MA, SA/MA.

101. **FRANCIS DANA$^{5}$ SAWYER** [see 40], b. 7 Apr 1813 Westminster MA, d. 17 Nov 1871 Townshend VT, m. Hannah Dunklee, b. 23 Mar 1811 d. 2 Jan 1897. Merchant. In Townshend VT 1840. Representative to the General Assembly 1851, 1853, 1861.
Mary E., b. 1840, d. 9 Sep 1887, m. 6 Jan 1873 William H. Ingalls.
Sarah E., b. 1842, d. 14 Jan 1928, m. 28 Sep 1862 Charles E. Goodhue.
Edwin E., b. 28 Nov 1849 Townshend VT d. 25 Apr 1935 Townshend VT.

Julia Elizabeth, b. 1853, d. 23 Aug 1863.

Sources: Townshend VT census 1840, 1850. VR Westminster MA, SA/VT. D6, P39, F22, B98.

102. **JACOB[5] SAWYER** [see 41], b. 2 Nov 1794 Strong ME, m. 2 Feb 1813 Sabrina _____, b. 1794 d. 11 Aug 1886. In Avon ME 1820.

Sullivan Kendall, b. 17 Jan 1815 Avon ME.

Armina T., b. 3 Jul 1817.

Martha Goodell, b. 23 Jan 1820.

Sources: Avon ME census 1820.

103. **JACOB[5] SAWYER** [see 42], b. 24 Mar 1812 Sandown NH, d. 25 Apr 1892 Pembroke NH, m.(1) 31 Dec 1840 Sarah Whittemore, b. 24 Nov 1815 d. 9 Sep 1845; m.(2) 2 Dec 1849 Manchester NH Mary Ann Doland of Derry NH, b. 18 Feb 1829 d. 17 Sep 1892, dau. John and Eliza (Burnham) Doland. In Pembroke NH 1842.

Helen Victoria, b. 13 Aug 1841, d. 19 Mar 1878, unm.

Frances Augusta, b. 11 Dec 1842, m. Edward Brown.

Daniel Jacob, b. 19 Aug 1851 Pembroke NH, d. 8 Mar 1920 Pembroke NH, m. 28 Nov 1878 Addie Phelps of Woodstock NH, b. 9 Jul 1858 d. 8 Aug 1886. Note: Death record says he was b. 7 Aug 1851.

John Murray, b. 28 May 1853 Sandown NH, d. 3 Sep 1890 Pembroke NH. In Middletown CT.

Lizzie Marion, b. 24 Mar 1855, m.(1) 30 Dec 1875 Charles L. Dow, m.(2) 16 Feb 1884 George A. Woodward of Rhode Island.

Mary Capitola, b. 16 Feb 1859, d. 23 May 1879.

Susan Abby, b. 10 May 1861.

Belle, b. 2 Aug 1870, m. 7 Jun 1893 James Ahmuty.

Sources: Pembroke NH census 1850, 1860, 1880. C11, N9, N6.

## SIXTH GENERATION

104. **JOSIAH[6] SAWYER** [see 46], b. 7 Jul 1800 Peterborough NH, killed by a runaway horse 14 Sep 1864 Jaffrey NH, m. 30 Dec 1823 Margerite C. French, b. 18 Dec 1794 d. 1 Jan 1882, dau. Thomas French.

158 Cummings[7], 1824-1894.

Emily C., b. 19 Apr 1827, m. 13 Sep 1854 Jaffrey NH Albert Bass.

George W., b. 21 Jun 1829, d. 23 Nov 1830.

159 Alfred[7], 1831-1930.

Lydia Ann, b. 2 Dec 1833, d. 18 Aug 1852.

Adeline H., b. 3 Feb 1836, d. 5 Sep 1852.

Leonard F., b. 8 Aug 1839 Jaffrey NH, d. 23 Nov 1903 Jaffrey NH, m. 17 Jan 1866 Mary B. Adams of Rindge NH, b. 4 Feb 1847 d. 17 Dec 1924, dau. Albert and Mary (Pollard) Adams. Farmer. CH: Etta M., b. 23 Oct 1866, d. 5 Jan 1931 (twin); Ella M., b. 23 Oct 1866 d. 3 Dec 1933 (twin).

Levi B., b. 12 Oct 1841 Jaffrey NH, d. 9 Sep 1852.

Sources: Jaffrey NH census 1840, 1850, 1860, 1870 (wid.). N6, A27, B92, F8.

105. **ALVIN[6] SAWYER** [see 47], b. 28 Feb 1808 Sharon NH, d. 26 Nov 1865 Groton MA, m. 19 Aug 1830 Wilton NH Esther Cram, b. 1810 d. 26 Jun 1898. In Sharon NH 1830, Vermont 1839-1847, Peterborough NH 1850.

Moses W., b. 4 Jan 1836, d. 21 Jul 1852.

Helen H., b. 23 Apr 1839, m.(1) (I) 13 Sep 1856 Charles Dix, m.(2) 1883 Orin Sherman.
Iantha, b. ?.
Almira A., b. 1843, m. 2 Oct 1861 Fitchburg MA Charles H. Sweeney.
160 Alvin C. L.[7], 1847-1881.
161 Charles M.[7], b. ca. 1850.
Sources: Sharon NH census 1830. Peterborough NH census 1850. VR Wilton NH, SA/MA.

106. **JOSIAH[6] SAWYER** [see 48], b. 25 Jun 1808 Sharon NH, d. 3 Oct 1883 Tremont IL, m. 15 Nov 1832 Harriet Bates, b. 17 Jul 1805 d. 18 Oct 1887.
Abial B., b. ? Tremont IL.
Josiah M., b. ? Tremont IL.
Sources: S48.

107. **SILAS[6] SAWYER** [see 48], b. 8 Jun 1810 Sharon NH, d. 2 May 1879 Peterborough NH, m.(1) 1 Jun 1837 Harriet N. Bacon of Sharon NH, b. 31 Jul 1815 d. 19 Aug 1856, dau. Stephen and Mary (Porter) Bacon; m.(2) 26 Jan 1858 Annie Lawrence, b. 31 Dec 1808. Selectman for Sharon NH for four years.
Stephen A., b. 25 Apr 1840 Sharon NH. Went to Kansas.
George A., b. 25 Sep 1850, d. 28 Oct 1850.
Mary L., b. 11 Aug 1856, d. 16 Jun 1869.
Sources: Sharon NH census 1840, 1850, 1860. Peterborough NH census 1870. S48.

108. **JOSEPH A.[6] SAWYER** [see 48], b. 10 Apr 1812 Sharon NH, m.(1) Martha Richmond, b. ?; m.(2) Almeda Wells, b. ?.
Edward F., b. ca. 1840 (Sharon NH?).
Emma E., b. ?.
Albert, b. ca. 1844 (Sharon NH?).
Sarah L., b. ?.
Lucy A., b. ?.
Laura, b. ?.
Ella, b. ?.
Henry, b. ca. 1850.
Sources: S48.

109. **DANIEL[6] SAWYER** [see 51], b. 29 Jul 1800 Hancock NH, d. 1 Jul 1877 Ludlow VT, m. 4 Dec 1827 Andover VT Sarah Batchelder of New Hampshire, b. 28 Aug 1801 d. 11 Oct 1890, dau. David and Sarah (Adams) Batchelder. Farmer. In Andover VT 1830, Ludlow VT 1850.
Harriet, b. 13 Dec 1828, d. 25 Sep 1832.
Cordelia, b. 4 Sep 1831, d. 13 Oct 1840.
Alonzo, b. 22 Aug 1835, d. 16 Apr 1836.
Harriet, b. 4 Feb 1839, d. 27 Nov 1862.
Elizabeth, b. 28 Jan 1843, m. 22 May 1860 Charles M. Giddens.
162 Charles H.[7], 1856-1924.
Sources: Andover VT census 1830. Ludlow VT census 1850. VR SA/VT. H37, P41.

110. **LEONARD[6] SAWYER** [see 51], b. 1807 Andover VT, d. 14 Jul 1861 Ludlow VT, m. 26 Nov 1832 Ludlow VT Lucia Gould of Windsor VT, b. Apr 1813 d. 18 Feb 1905, dau. Asa and Hannah Gould. Farmer. Wid. m. Charles Burpee 1863.
Charles L., b. 1837, d. 2 Oct 1840.
Hannah E., b. 1841, d. 4 Dec 1843.

Charles N., b. Nov 1844, d. 27 Aug 1845.

George M., b. 16 Jul 1847 Ludlow VT, m.(1) 24 Oct 1871 Rutland VT Anna Richardson of Andover MA, b. 1846 d. 18 Oct 1879, dau. Mark D. and Mary (Jenness) Richardson; m.(2) 15 Nov 1882 Putney VT Amelia DeKalb, b. ?. Railroad engineer.

LuciaE., b. 18 Jan 1849, m. 9 Oct 1866 Windsor VT Alphonse Sawyer.

Sources: Andover VT census 1840. Ludlow VT census 1850, 1860. VR SA/VT.

111. **ADDISON$^6$ SAWYER** [see 51], b. 1814 Andover VT, killed by a falling tree 2 May 1851 Ludlow VT, m. 12 Dec 1836 Benson VT Laura Hazelton, b. 16 Jun 1815 d. 14 Dec 1872. Farmer. Note: Marriage recorded in Montpelier VT 1 Dec 1836.

163 Hiland Addison$^7$, 1838-1903.

Oscar Martin, b. 5 Jan 1840 Andover VT, d. 1910 Ludlow VT, m. Mary Warren, b. ca. 1840 d. 15 Apr 1881, dau. Pierce Warren. CH: Jane, b. 7 Nov 1863, d. 4 Jul 1871.

Caroline Minerva, b. 11 Feb 1842, m. 29 Nov 1860 Albert D. Hazelton.

164 Albert Delno$^7$, 1844-1923.

Sources: Andover VT census 1840, 1850. VR SA/VT. H37, William Edward Sawyer rec.

112. **EDWIN$^6$ SAWYER** [see 53], b. 5 Jul 1831 Temple ME, d. 27 May 1915 Farmington ME, m. 27 Mar 1859 Aphia J. Voter, b. 24 Jan 1835, dau. Warren and Lucy (Corbett) Voter.

George E., b. 16 Jan 1860, d. 3 Jun 1865.

Persis E., b. 3 Sep 1861, m. Charles R. Hall.

Hamlin, b. 1864.

Ernest G., b. 17 Feb 1869, d. 18 Jul 1873.

Bernice E., b. 20 May 1879, d. 5 Dec 1965, m. 24 Jun 1896 Charles Goodwin.

Sources: ME 1880 census index. VR SA/ME. M8A.

113. **CHARLES$^6$ SAWYER** [see 54], b. 19 Dec 1812 Hancock NH, d. 8 May 1872 Antrim NH, m. 4 Oct 1838 Olivia B. Priest of Dublin NH, b. 24 Aug 1817 d. 4 May 1900. In Hancock NH 1840, Stoddard NH 1850, Antrim NH 1870. He bur. in North Branch Cem., Antrim NH.

Charles Dennis, b. 26 Jul 1839 Hancock NH, d. 23 Nov 1910 Antrim NH, m. 5 Nov 1863 Keene NH Martha A. Swett of Windsor NH, b. 27 Mar 1841 d. 21 Nov 1920, dau. Daniel and Roxah (Bootwell) Swett. Carpenter. He bur. in North Branch Cem., Antrim NH. CH: Mabel J., b. 1875, m. 9 Jan 1895 Antrim NH Charles M. Prentiss.

Mary A., b. 26 Feb 1841, d. Mar 1928, m. 4 Apr 1867 Asher S. Burbank of Boston MA.

165 Allen Levi$^7$, 1843-1904.

George A., b. 26 Oct 1848, d. 19 Jun 1849.

166 Clarence E.$^7$, 1857-1933.

Sources: Hancock NH census 1840. Stoddard NH census 1850, 1860. Antrim NH census 1870. Clinton NH census 1880. C54, N9.

114. **LEONARD$^6$ SAWYER** [see 54], b. 6 Nov 1814 Hancock NH, m.(1) 24 Nov 1835 Hancock NH Sarah L. Davis, b. 1814 d. 24 May 1863 Shrewsbury VT, dau. Asa and Lydia Davis; m.(2) 15 May 1864 Shrewsbury VT Betsey Hazeltine, wid., b. 1815 d. 7 Aug 1867; m.(3) 30 Nov 1867 Ludlow VT Abigail Gibson, b. 27 Jan 1822 d. 31 Jul 1899, dau. Isaac and Nabby (Pettengill) Gibson. In Shrewsbury VT, Plymouth VT, South Dakota.

167 Walter G.$^7$, b. 1838.

168 Hiram E.$^7$, 1840-1910.

Lydia Adeline, b. 1843, m. 26 Dec 1861 Almon Johnson of Shrewsbury VT.

Caroline Elizabeth, b. 1846, d. 21 Apr 1882, m. 18 Jul 1866 Eli Marble of Springfield VT.

Sources: Hancock NH census 1840, 1850. VR SA/VT. H37, W59.

115. **WALLACE⁶ SAWYER** [see 54], b. 10 Sep 1821 Hancock NH, d. 4 Mar 1887 Hancock NH, m.(1) 4 Feb 1847 Mary Jane Clyde of Bradford NH, b. 24 May 1825 d. 14 Apr 1853; m.(2) 4 Jan 1855 Washington NH Sarah Burney of Hancock NH, b. 9 Jan 1828 d. 12 Oct 1863, dau. Theodoria Burney; m.(3) 12 May 1864 Antrim NH Priscilla (Atwood) Brown of Deering NH, b. 10 Aug 1821 d. 21 Mar 1894, dau. Joshua and Priscilla (Patten) Atwood.

Daughter, b. 14 Apr 1853.
169 Hubbard Dudley[7], b. 1856.
Son, b. 24 Jan 1858, d. 6 Feb 1858.
Mary Emma, b. 24 Sep 1860, m.(1) 10 Oct 1878 Jerome Bailey, m.(2) 27 Jan 1880 Manchester NH Charles Blakey, m.(3) Edward A. May.
Maria Jane, b. 16 Apr 1866, d. 22 Dec 1866.

Sources: Hancock NH census 1860. H37, N9, N6, W10.

116. **DANIEL HENRY⁶ SAWYER** [see 55], b. 6 Jan 1832 Marlow NH, d. 3 Feb 1909 Fitchburg MA, m. 28 Jun 1865 Sarah W. Fairbanks of Troy NH, b. 8 May 1832 d. 26 Oct 1895, dau. Cyrus and Betsey Fairbanks. Carpenter, photographer. In Fitchburg MA 1903.

170 Walter Fairbanks[7], b. 1868.

Sources: Keene NH census 1860, 1870. VR SA/NH. G46, H37, F2, A27.

117. **WYMAN⁶ SAWYER** [see 55], b. 3 Feb 1835 Marlow NH, m. 2 May 1861 Keene NH Carrie M. Knight of Dudley MA, b. 29 Jul 1842 d. 16 Feb 1887 Worcester MA, dau. Josiah and Martha (Mason) Knight. Merchant, Farmer. In Winchendon MA, Marlborough NH 1870.

Edson E., b. 3 Dec 1861 Marlborough NH, m. 15 Jun 1892 Winchendon MA Lona E. Plummer of Winchendon MA, b. ca. 1862, dau. Charles and Frances E. (Nutting) Plummer. Farmer.
Martha F., b. 8 Aug 1874.

Sources: Marlborough NH census 1870. R30, L17, S31, T19.

118. **ASA⁶ SAWYER** [see 56], b. 16 Jul 1806 Mt. Holly VT, d. 15 Mar 1885 Mt. Holly VT, m.(1) Lucy M. Morse of Shrewsbury VT, b. 4 Apr 1805 d. 18 May 1865, dau. Squire and Priscilla Morse; m.(2) 13 Dec 1866 Minerva L. Leavitt, b.?. Farmer.

Elliot Clinton, b. 27 Jul 1831, d. 22 Feb 1859.
Miranda L., b. 24 Nov 1832, d. 15 Jan 1899, m. Joel L. Barrett of Belmont VT.
Marisa E., b. 11 Nov 1835, d. 16 Jan 1845.
Elizabeth H., b. 26 Mar 1837, d. 9 Feb 1858.
Oscar C., b. 1 Mar 1845, d. 11 Dec 1858.
Edwin A., b. 14 Jan 1846, d. 1 Aug 1863.

Sources: VR SA/VT.

119. **BENJAMIN⁶ SAWYER** [see 56], b. 3 Feb 1815 Mt. Holly VT, m. 16 Feb 1837 Asenath Sawyer of Nelson NH, b. 25 Oct 1813, dau Joel and Susannah (Davis) Sawyer. In Hillsboro NH 1850.

Wallace, b. 1838 Mt. Holly VT. In Hillsboro NH 1850.
Tyler, b. 1841, d. 28 Apr 1842 Holly VT.
Mary A., b. 1843.

Sources: Hillsboro NH census 1850. VR SA/VT. N6.

120. **DAVID B.⁶ SAWYER** [see 56], b. 4 Jan 1818 Mt. Holly VT, m. 5 Sep 1843 Plymouth VT Eleanor Goff, b. ?. In Plymouth VT 1850, Bridgewater VT 1860, Colburn VT 1870.

Edwin A., b. 25 Jul 1845 Plymouth VT.
Adeline I., b. 13 Jan 1848.
Sources: Plymouth VT census 1850. Bridgewater VT census 1860. Colburn VT census 1870. VR SA/VT.

121. **WILLIAM[6] SAWYER** [see 56], b. 1 Aug 1820 Mt. Holly VT, m. Sophronia _____, b. 1818. Landlord. In Plymouth VT.
Frances M., b. 1842.
Alphonse, b. 1844 Plymouth VT, m. 9 Oct 1866 Windsor VT Lucia E. Sawyer of Ludlow VT, b. 18 Jan 1849, dau. Leonard and Lucia (Gould) Sawyer. Carriage maker. In Ludlow VT.
Hannah J., b. 1847.
Sources: VR SA/VT.

122. **WINSLOW HARTWELL[6] SAWYER** [see 56], b. 8 Mar 1821 Mt. Holly VT, d. 2 Dec 1890 Plymouth VT, m. 21 Feb 1843 Plymouth VT Martha Lovina Brown of Plymouth VT, b. Oct 1823 d. 6 Nov 1894, dau. Isreal and Sally (Briggs) Brown. Farmer. He bur. in Ludlow VT.
Leroy Winslow, b. 2 Feb 1844, d. 15 Jul 1865.
171 Herbert Brown[7], 1848-1903. Went to Nebraska.
172 Merritt Angelo[7], 1852-1926.
Clarence Everett, b. 25 Apr 1854 Plymouth VT, m. 27 Jan 1885 Fairmont NE Alice Elizabeth Davis of Iowa, b. Jul 1851 d. 23 Mar 1913, dau. _____ and Sophia (Spoon) Davis. CH: Alice Agatha, b. 19 Apr 1887, m. 10 Apr 1912 Floyd B. Reed.
Agatha Martha, b. 10 Feb 1856, m. 14 Jun 1876 Frank C. Moor.
Silas Eldon, b. 9 Sep 1866 Plymouth VT.
Sources: Plymouth VT census 1850, 1860, 1870. VR SA/VT.

123. **JESSE[6] SAWYER** [see 57], b. 1814 Mt. Holly VT, d. 1898, m.(1) Hannah Whitcomb of Alstead NH, b. 5 May 1812 d. 24 Nov 1839; m.(2) Mary (Giles) Wheeler of New York, b. 1803 d. 14 Jun 1877, dau. Joseph and Penelope Giles; m.(3) 29 Mar 1880 Lucia Burpee, b. ?. Farmer, mechanic. Hannah bur. in Cavendish VT.
Helen Miranda, b. 1 Apr 1838.
Mary Amarilla, b. 9 May 1844, m. 31 Jan 1867 Charles T. Griffith.
Royal Tyler, b. 25 Apr 1848 Mt. Holly VT d. 21 Aug 1898 Worcester VT, m. Clara Jane Stowe of Hampton NY, b. 6 Sep 1849 d. 28 Nov 1891 Quincy MA. Tufts College. Universalist minister. In Gardner MA, Newmarket NH, Milford MA. CH: Angie Mary, b. 24 Sep 1879, m. 12 Dec 1900 Milton E. Hutchinson; Susie Marion, b. 26 Mar 1884, d. 30 Jul 1907 Danbury VT, unm, teacher.
Sources: Mt. Holly VT census 1850. VR SA/VT, SA/MA.

124. **AMOS[6] SAWYER** [see 57], b. 10 Sep 1816 Mt. Holly VT, d. 2 Jul 1882 Mt. Holly VT, m.(1) 31 Dec 1838 Benson VT Nancy M. Hooper, b. 13 Nov 1816 d. 10 Nov 1871, dau. Asa and Samantha Hooper; m.(2) 7 Jun 1879 Angie M. Allen, b. ?. Farmer. In Benson VT. He bur. in Belmont VT.
Esther Almina, b. 27 Feb 1840, d. 12 Jun 1908, m. 1858 John E. White.
Viola, b. 1841.
Henry, b. 1841 Mt. Holly VT.
Emily A., b. 1847, m. 19 Jan 1868 Merrill H. Benson.

Adelbert L., b. 1853 Mt Holly VT, d. 10 Jun 1901 Vergennes VT, m.(1) 29 Mar 1872 Emma S. Hamlin, b. Sep 1855 d. 15 Mar 1878; m.(2) 1879 Carrie Allen, b. ?. Farmer. CH: Grace E., b. 15 Mar 1878, m. 18 May 1899 Edgar L. Hier.

Sources: Mt. Holly VT census 1850. VR SA/VT. D6.

125. **JOEL[6] SAWYER** [see 58], b. 5 Feb 1810 Nelson NH, d. 21 Aug 1856 Mason NH, m. Dorcas Foster of Massachusetts, b. Feb 1817 d. 8 Oct 1899. Farmer. He bur. in Greenville NH. Wid. in Mason NH 1860, m. 4 Jul 1861 Aaron Wheeler of Fitchburg MA.

Lucy Ann, b. 26 Dec 1839, m. 29 May 1859 Temple NH Albert F. Stone.

George A., b. 1842 Nelson NH, m. 12 Jan 1864 Wilton NH Betsey A. Herrick of Wilton NH, b. 24 Jun 1846, dau. Amos and Betsey (Larkin) Herrick. In Mason NH 1850, Fitchburg MA 1864.

Caroline E., b. 1844, m. 4 Jul 1867 Fitchburg MA Willard Blanchard.

Henry W., b. 1846 Nelson NH, m.(1) 23 Sep 1866 Acton MA Sarah E. Lawrence of Ashby MA, b. ?, dau. John W. and Emily Lawrence; m.(2) 10 Jul 1844 Hudson MA Almira Gates of Stow MA, b. 1850, dau. David and Elizabeth Stow; m.(3) 1 Jan 1893 Boston MA Emma J. (Nash) Rand of Charlestown MA, b. ca. 1846, dau. William H. and Mary A. Nash. Teamster. In Mason NH 1850. CH: Caroline D., b. 12 Aug 1886.

Charles M., b. 20 Feb 1854, d. 20 Jul 1856.

Sources: Hebron NH census 1840. Mason NH census 1850, 1860. VR SA/MA. D10, B33,N6.

126. **BENJAMIN[6] SAWYER** [see 58], b. 6 Jul 1821 Nelson NH, d. 6 Aug 1882 New Ipswich NH, m. 29 Sep 1852 Martha Morey of Strafford VT, b. 1 Nov 1826 d. 17 Mar 1905, dau. Ellis and Nancy (Robinson) Morey. Laborer. In Fairlee VT, Mason Hills VT, Greenville NH.

Frank E., b. 29 Mar 1853 Mason NH, d. 24 Dec 1895 Greenfield NH, m. 11 Oct 1875 Maria Octavia Farnsworth of Ellsworth ME, b. 4 May 1854. In West Fairlee VT. Wid m. 22 Dec 1898 Charles Kendall.

173 Charles Elwin[7], 1858-1929.

Sources: Mason Hills VT census 1850. VR SA/NH. N9, N6.

127. **JOHN M.[6] SAWYER** [see 64], b. 1833 Thetford VT, m. Aug 1861 Waterbury VT Martha DeLigne of Canada, b. 1837 d. 6 Aug 1896 Berlin VT. Laborer. In Waterbury VT 1861, Northfield VT 1868, Duxbury VT 1870, Georgia VT 1882.

George McClellan, b. Aug 1861 Waterbury VT, d. 6 Nov 1889 Montpelier VT, m. 15 Jan 1883 Georgia VT Julia Rowe, b. 1862, dau. Joseph and Mary Rowe. In Georgia VT, Berlin VT. Wid. m. 1891 Northfield VT Albert H. Johnson. CH: Aurelia, b. 19 Oct 1883; Mary Agnes, b. 15 Jul 1884, m. 9 Sep 1899 David Moyle; Fred R., b. 1887, d. 23 Jun 1905, unm.

Asa, b. 1862 Waterbury VT, m. 30 Aug 1883 Montpelier VT Julia Howe, b. ?. Farmer.

Adah, b. 1865, m. 28 Jan 1882 William Bevins.

Myron G., b. 21 Mar 1868 Northfield VT, m. 9 May 1892 Mattie Goneo, b. ?. CH: Son, b. 31 Aug 1897.

Carrie C., b. 11 Dec 1870, m. 20 Sep 1886 William Cayhue.

Archie R., b. 16 Jul 1873, d. 4 Oct 1893.

William (Wellington) Wilhamton, b. 1 Aug 1875 Waterbury VT, m. 16 Mar 1895 Montpelier VT Aurelia Nellie Sears of Braintree VT, b. ?, dau. Asa and Ellen (Bruce) Sears. Laborer. Wid. m. 1903 John F. Mitchell. CH: Stanley Arthur, b. 9 Jan 1900, d. 10 Jan 1900. Note: William's birth also recorded in Johnston VT.

James Arthur, b. Sep 1884, d. 16 Nov 1886.

Addie, b. 4 Apr 1886.

Sources: Duxbury VT census 1870. VR SA/VT.

128. **FRANCIS ALBERT[6] SAWYER** [see 65], b. 9 Aug 1835 Dracut MA, m. Emily A._____, b. Feb 1835. Butcher. In Lowell MA 1861.

Deforest Albert, b. 19 Sep 1861 Lowell MA, m. 1 Jan 1891 Lowell MA Cassie M. McDougald of Boston MA, b. ca. 1868, dau. Hugh J. and Catherine H. McDougald. Plumber. In Brockton MA 1893. CH: Emily Frances, b. 21 Jul 1891; Catherine Mabel, b. 19 Aug 1893.

Leonard Francis, b. 20 Nov 1863 Dracut MA, m. 2 Jun 1886 Lowell MA Carrie B. Huntoon of Lowell MA, b. ?, dau. Timothy V. and Matilda C. Huntoon. Clerk. In Boston MA.

Sources: VR Dracut MA, SA/MA.

129. **FRANK P.[6] SAWYER** [see 66], b. 14 Feb 1839 Lowell MA, m. 4 May 1865 Worcester MA Susan King Broughton of Conway NH, b. 27 Mar 1846, dau. Mark and Lydia (Wentworth) Broughton. Hotel keeper. In Northfield MA.

Daughter, b. 24 Oct 184?.

James Andrew, b. 3 Nov 1867 Brookfield MA.

Wilson Lane, b. 21 May 1869 Boston MA, m. 20 Oct 1895 Tyngsboro MA Sarah Etta Loveland of Goffstown NH, b. ca. 1874, dau. Hollis and Ida (Vance) Loveland. Caterer.

Mark Henry, b. 17 May 1871 Boston MA.

Sources: VR SA/MA. W26.

130. **FREDERICK PARKER[6] SAWYER** [see 68], b. Aug 1846 Essex VT, m.(1) 31 Dec 1874 Frances A. Bates of Essex VT, b. Sep 1852 d. 13 Jun 1900, dau. Halman and Achsa Bates; m.(2) 5 Oct 1903 Leonora (Wade) Wright of Jericho VT, wid. of Edward, b. 16 May 1849, dau. George R. and Ruth (Smith) Wade. Cabinet maker. In Essex VT 1850. In Pomona CA. Note: Vermont VR says Leonore E. Hopkins.

Wilbur C., b. 8 May 1877.

Elizabeth M., b. 23 Jun 1880.

Sources: Essex VT census 1850. VR SA/VT.

131. **JOHN[6] SAWYER** [see 69], b. 16 Jun 1831 Landgrove VT, d. 15 Aug 1897 California, m. Sarah McClennon, b. ?. In Peru VT 1850, Winchester MA 1857.

Sarah I., b. 1857, m. George Herr.

Warren H., b. Nov 1862, m. Nettie _____, b. ?.

Son, b. 10 Feb 1870.

Son, b. Aug 1871.

Sources: Peru VT census 1850. VR SA/VT.

132. **JOSEPH WARREN[6] SAWYER** [see 71], b. 31 Aug 1825 Methuen MA, m.(1) 18 Nov 1846 Andover MA Miranda Mills of Norway ME, b. 1824, dau. Andrew and Olive Mills; m.(2) 3 Oct 1862 Boston MA Mary A. Ford of Hampton CT, b. 1834, dau. Isaac and Abigail Ford. Civil War. Gunsmith. In Hartford ME, Portland ME 1850. He bur. Norway Lake ME.

Joseph Warren, b. 1848 Andover MA, m.(1) 12 Nov 1867 Athol MA Etta Greenwood of Athol MA, b. ca. 1847, dau. William F. and Hope Greenwood; m.(2) 12 May 1881 Boston MA Joanna J.E. Murray of Cambridge MA, b. ca. 1849, dau. Timothy and Mary Murray. CH: Lillian Maud, b. 25 May 1876.

Henry W., b. 1852 Hartford ME, m.(1) 28 Mar 1874 Chatham MA Laura (Walker) Sylvester of Denmark ME, b. 1856, dau. Daniel and Julia A. Walker; m.(2) 11 Mar

1902 Portsmouth NH Lenora (McCorison) Deering of Knox ME, wid., b. 1859, dau. Alvin and Johanna (Rowe) McCorison. In Norway ME.

Sources: Portland ME census 1850. VR Methuen MA, Haverhill MA, SA/MA. M7A.

133. **AARON LORAIN[6] SAWYER** [see 74], b. 20 Sep 1841 Methuen MA, m. 20 Mar 1866 Methuen MA Sarah Marlin of Athens ME, b. ca. 1846, dau. William and Elizabeth Marlin. Went to Chicago IL.

Edwin N., b. ca. 1873 Methuen MA, m. 13 Apr 1894 Bradford MA Blanche Sawyer, b. ca. 1874, dau. Asa Francis and Mary (Malery) Sawyer.

Sources: VR Methuen MA, SA/MA.

134. **GRANVILLE[6] SAWYER** [see 74], b. ca. 1852 Methuen MA, m. 31 Oct 1875 Methuen MA Fanny E. Pierce of Temple NH, b. ?. Butcher.

Warner Granville, b. 6 May 1878 Haverhill MA.

Henry Franklin, b. 8 Feb 1880 Brighton MA.

Sources: VR SA/MA.

135. **LYMAN[6] SAWYER** [see 75], b. 1846 Plymouth ME.

Lyman, b. 1867.

Lizzie, b. 1871.

Sources: Plymouth ME census 1850.

136. **ALVAH GEORGE[6] SAWYER** [see 81], b. 24 Nov 1864 Topsham VT, m. 22 Nov 1890 Hattie B. Smith of Topsham VT, b. Nov 1871. Farmer.

Clinton Ora, b. 11 Nov 1890 Topsham ME, d. Jul 1965, m. Gladys M._____, b. ?.

Ruth Avis, b. 13 Sep 1893.

Ethel Frances, b. 22 Jan 1898.

Sources: VR SA/VT.

137. **MILO B.[6] SAWYER** [see 81], b. 1872 E. Topsham VT, m. 27 Dec 1896 Alice B. Rodimon of Piermont NH, b. 1879. Farmer. In Piermont NH, Haverhill NH.

Mildred Virginia, b. 16 Oct 1896, m. _____ Howe.

Clyde Bailey, b. 2 Jan 1898 Piermont NH, m. 30 Jun 1920 No. Haverhill NH Lily Ward of Monroe NH, b. 1897, dau. Robert and Mary Ward, both of England. Laborer.

Lucy A., b. 7 Aug 1899, m. _____ Jones.

Wilhemina, m. _____ Hood.

Leona M., b. ca. 1903, d. 6 Jun 1994, m. _____ Wheeler.

Maynard, b. ca. 1912 Piermont NH, m. 26 Oct 1934 Haverhill MA Margaret (Eastman) Smith of Haverhill NH, b. 1914, dau. Edwin and Beatrice Eastman.

Wesley.

Sources: VR SA/VT, SA/MA. Obit (Leona), Gladys M. Sawyer rec.

138. **ALVAH[6] SAWYER** [see 82], b. 25 Mar 1846 Warner NH, d. 29 May 1930 Littleton NH, m. 11 Jan 1873 Canaan VT Betsey Jane Tewksbury, b. 27 Aug 1848 d. 18 Jun 1893. Laborer. In Stewartstown NH 1880, Watertown NY, Littleton NH 1924.

Phebe E., b. 20 Nov 1873, d. 13 Feb 1953, m. 28 Aug 1895 Stewartstown NH Hubbard Placey.

174 George Alvah[7], 1876-1925.

Frank Willis, b. 21 Jun 1881 Stewartstown NH, d. 12 Jul 1911 (suicide by hanging) Northumberland NH, m. 4 Apr 1911 Lancaster NH Estelle. J. Blodgett of Columbia NH, b. ?, dau. Fred A. and Julia E. (Barnett) Blodgett

Sources: Stewartstown NH census 1880. VR SA/NH, SA/VT. N6, Patricia Sawyer rec.

139. **CHARLES NATHAN⁶ SAWYER** [see 82], b. 28 Sep 1847 Warner NH, d. 30 Jan 1931 Huntington Park CA, m. 2 Sep 1877 Estella Ann Giddings of Hooksett NH, b. 2 Apr 1858 Loudon NH d. 29 Nov 1943 Gloversville NY, dau. Isaac B. and Julia Ann (Butterfield) Giddings. In Concord NH 1880.

Harry Herbert, b. 20 Dec 1878 Warner NH, d. 24 Oct 1954 Huntington Park CA, m. Gertrude Stears, b. ?. CH: Lynn, Ross.

Eva, b. 2 Jul 1887, d. Jul 1968, m. 11 Apr 1916 Charles Serfis.

Harley Willis, b. 6 Jan 1885, d. 17 Jun 1974, m. 28 Aug 1905 Ione P. Prinyer, b. 28 Feb 1883 Cleveland OH d. 26 Jan 1938, dau. Archibald J. and Sophia H. (Davis) Prinyer. CH: Harley Edward, Bessie Margeret, Roger W.

Charles Frank, b. 4 May 1892, d. Nov 1987 Tampa FL, m. 1908 Emma Prinyer. CH: Francis, Estella Mae, Fred.

Sources: Concord NH census 1880. Patricia Sawyer rec., Estelle P. Boomsma rec.

140. **WILLIAM HERBERT⁶ SAWYER** [see 83], b. 18 Nov 1844 Warner NH, d. 12 Dec 1898 Warner NH, m.(1) 2 Oct 1873 Minnie L. Bartlett of Salmon Falls NH, b. 24 Oct 1850 d. 10 Aug 1885; m.(2) 17 Dec 1887 (div. 14 Nov 1898) Jennie E. Runnels of Warner NH, b. ?. Butcher. Civil War.

Annie L., b. ca. 1875.

Helen Frances, b. 23 Jun 1876, m. 28 Jan 1896 Warner NH George G. Martin.

Herbert B., b. 20 Jul 1879 Warner NH, d. 1969, m. 11 Dec 1907 Concord NH Alys M. Guernsey of E. Calais VT, b. 1880 d. 1957, dau. Oscar W. and Jennie (Leach) Guernsey. Merchant. In Sunapee NH.

Sources: Warner NH census 1880. VR SA/NH. N6.

141. **WILLIAM⁶ SAWYER** [see 84], b. 22 Nov 1813 Bradford NH, d. 9 Nov 1863 Bradford NH, m. 6 Dec 1838 Elizabeth Hale of Bradford NH, b. 6 Jan 1817 d. 3 Oct 1882, dau. Daniel and Betsey (Campbell) Hale of West Newbury MA. Farmer. In Swanzey NH 1860.

William, b. 1840 Bradford NH.

Ira W., 1843 Bradford NH.

Daniel F., b. Mar 1844, d. 12 Aug 1844.

Daniel F., b. 1849 Bradford NH.

Sources: Bradford NH census 1850. Swanzey NH census 1860. VR Bradford NH.

142. **BENJAMIN⁶ SAWYER** [see 84], b. 1820 Bradford NH, m.(1) Samantha Waterman, b. ? d. 3 Aug 1861 Bradford NH; m.(2) 8 Nov 1867 Barton VT Maria (Sanborn) Dorian, b. ?.

Warner, b. 1851 Wheelock VT, d. 26 Jun 1884 Barton VT.

Sources: VR Bradford NH, SA/NH, SA/VT.

143. **FREDERICK TRAIN⁶ SAWYER** [see 85], b. 13 May 1819 Bradford NH, d. 14 Jul 1898 Milford NH, m. 6 Jan 1859 Sarah S. Lovejoy of Amherst NH, b. 22 Aug 1833 d. Oct 1905, dau. William H. and Hannah (Shedd) Lovejoy. Bank cashier. Town Treasurer for Milford NH. In Nashua NH 1840, Milford NH 1854. In State Legislature 1864-65.

Bertha Caroline, b. 22 Jun 1860, m. 28 Jul 1881 David Blanpied.

175 Frederick Willis⁷, 1862-1946.

Chester Ayer, b. 16 Jul 1869 Milford NH, m. 6 Sep 1904 Nashua NH Anna A. Kendall of Temple NH, b. 25 Apr 1859 d. 18 May 1920, dau. Charles C. and Hannah C. (Jewett) Kendall. Furniture finisher.

Gertrude Wallace, b. 4 Aug 1874, m. 17 Apr 1900 Milford NH George D. White of New York City.

Sources: Nashua NH census 1840, 1880. Milford NH census 1860. VR Milford NH, Nashua NH. N6, R3, V2, B92, Donald F. Sawyer rec.

144. **JABEZ AUGUSTUS$^6$ SAWYER** [see 85], b. 1 Jun 1824 Bradford NH, m. 13 Sep 1855 Hollis MA Sarah Caroline Worcester of Hollis NH, b. 10 Oct 1827 d. 2 Aug 1873. Lawyer. In Townsend MA 1850, Cambridge MA 1861, Pepperell MA, Milford MA. Alderman 1868. M. also recorded in Roxbury MA.

George Augustus, b. 25 May 1857 Roxbury MA, m. 18 Jun 1884 Cambridge MA Florence Emeline Ellis, b. 1858. Harvard College 1877. Lawyer.

Rollin Worcester, b. 12 Jan 1861, d. 6 Oct 1868 Cambridge MA.

176 John Howard$^7$, b. 1862.

Caroline, b. 6 Apr 1864.

177 Walter Dean$^7$, b. 1866.

Lillian Whitney, b. 26 Apr 1869.

Edward Holden, b. 16 Nov 1870, d. 30 Apr 1871 Pepperell MA.

Sources: Townsend MA census 1850. VR SA/MA. W67, J14, W68, P1.

145. **GEORGE OSCAR$^6$ SAWYER** [see 86], b. 21 Jan 1832 Bradford NH, d. 22 Jul 1884 Concord NH, m. 20 Nov 1861 Windsor VT Lucretia S. Haskell of Weare NH, b. 20 Sep 1843 d. 3 Jan 1915 Malden MA. Merchant.

Harry, b. 21 Feb 1866 Bradford NH.

Sources: VR SA/NH, SA/VT. N9.

146. **FREDERICK E.$^6$ SAWYER** [see 87], b. 15 Jan 1854 Bradford NH, d. 20 Dec 1928, m. 21 Nov 1875 Shrewsbury VT Luella J. Lord, b. Mar 1853. Farmer. In Springfield VT 1875.

Edward W., b. 25 Jul 1876 Shrewsbury VT, m. Rachel E. Jackson, b. 1876 d. 1939 Pittsford VT.

Albert E., b. Mar 1897 Shrewsbury VT.

Sources: VR SA/NH, SA/VT.

147. **DIODORUS$^6$ SAWYER** [see 89], b. 10 Nov 1818 Athol MA, d. 13 Nov 1890, m. 16 Sep 1847 Whitingham VT Permelia Waste of Whitingham VT, b. 5 May 1818 d. 17 Mar 1884. Carpenter. In Whitingham VT 1847, Readsboro VT 1850.

George E., b. Sep 1848 Readsboro VT, m. 2 Feb 1871 Charlemont MA Amanda A. Albee of Colrain MA, b. Nov 1848, dau. George L. and Betsey Albee.

Charles L., b. Jan 1851, d. 9 Sep 1872.

Fred W., b. 1854 Readsboro VT.

Sarah R., b. Apr 1856, d. 13 May 1856.

Alice Carrie, b. 19 Jul 1857, m. 21 Apr 1881 Templeton MA Fred Whitney.

Merritt R., b. 29 Apr 1862, d. 26 Oct 1874.

Sources: Readsboro VT census 1850. VR SA/VT, SA/MA. M17, H43.

148. **AUGUSTUS$^6$ SAWYER** [see 90], b. 6 Jun 1825 Westminster MA, d. 18 Sep 1901 Nashua NH, m. 27 Mar 1850 Brattleboro VT Almira Copeland of Lancaster MA, b. 27 Jun 1829 d. 3 Jan

1878, dau. Charles and Mary (Divoll) Copeland. Harness maker. In Fitchburg MA 1850, Worcester MA 1857, Nahsua NH 1863, Gardner MA 1870.

George, b. 3 Sep 1850, d. 6 Jul 1858.

Nellie Frances, b. 27 Sep 1857, d. 13 Feb 1863.

Hattie Louisa, b. 6 Oct 1863, m. 7 Apr 1891 Nashua NH Joseph Hamblett.

Henry Copeland, b. 17 Jan 1866, m.(1) 17 Sep 1890 Chester NH Delia T. O'Brien, b. ?; m.(2) 15 Aug 1912 Nellie R. Hull, b. ?. Carpenter. CH: Marie Copeland, b. 9 Nov 1891.

Sources: Fitchburg MA census 1850. Gardner MA census 1870. VR SA/MA, SA/NH, SA/VT. N6, W39, D20, C76, C31.

149. **WILLIAM PORTER[6] SAWYER** [see 90], b. 30 Apr 1829 Westminster MA, d. 28 Apr 1907 Keene NH, m. 30 Oct 1856 Fitchburg MA H. Maria Litchfield of Littleton MA, b. 12 Jul 1834 d. 10 Mar 1914, dau. Samuel (or Hiram) and Hannah (Sargent) Litchfield. Harness maker. In Fitchburg MA 1840, Springfield VT 1857, Keene NH 1862, Swanzey NH 1880.

Luella Maria, b. 19 Oct 1857, d. 7 May 1927, unm.

Etta Adelaide, b. 2 Mar 1861.

Milton Porter, b. 6 Sep 1873 Keene NH, d. 6 Oct 1904 Concord NH.

Sources: Fitchburg MA census 1840, 1850. Keene NH census 1870. Swanzey NH census 1880. VR SA/MA, SA/NH, SA/VT. G46, F7.

150. **CYRUS WILLARD[6] SAWYER** [see 92], b. 12 Feb 1837 Westminster MA, d. 13 Mar 1895 Keene NH, m. 24 Jan 1866 Brattleboro VT Mary A. Rice, b. ?. Glue manufacturer. In Brattleboro VT, Keene NH 1880.

Milton, b. 17 Jan 1870, d. 19 Jun 1870.

Clinton Willard, b. 7 May 1872 Brattleboro VT, m. 14 Apr 1900 Lillian V. Wood of New York, b. Jul 1870. Watchmaker.

Mabel M., b. 1874.

Sources: Keene NH census 1880. VR Westminster MA, Brattleboro VT, SA/VT.

151. **CHARLES AUGUSTINE[6] SAWYER** [see 94], b. 1 Mar 1825 Wakefield NH, d. 11 Feb 1893 Deering ME, m. 1 May 1853 Amanda M. Horne of Farmington NH, b. 1835. Confectioner. In Wakefield NH 1850, Milton NH 1860, Portland ME.

Ella A., b. 16 Mar 1855, d. 30 Apr 1866. Bur. in Deering ME.

George E., b. Mar 1858 Milton NH, d. 25 Dec 1920 Portland ME, m. 17 Oct 1882 Portland ME Ada F. Hodgkins of Chelsea MA, b. Jul 1858. Confectioner. He bur. in Evergreen Cem., Portland ME. CH: Florence E., b. 7 Nov 1883, d. 1955, m. Herbert M. Haven; Ada A., b. 3 Dec 1892, d. 1951.

Anna M., b. ca. 1868.

John G., b. 19 Aug 1870 Milton NH.

Sources: Wakefield NH census 1850. Milton NH census 1860, 1870. Portland ME census 1880. ME 1880 census index. VR Grimball ME, Portland ME, SA/ME.

152. **GEORGE WILLIAM[6] SAWYER** [see 94], b. 24 Jun 1830 Wakefield NH, d. 19 Jun 1890 Wakefield NH, m.(1) 12 Aug 1850 Hannah C. Young of Milton NH, b.? d. 1873; m.(2) 19 Nov 1882 Lucy A. (Bickford) Richardson of Wakefield NH, b. 18 Oct 1841 d. 24 Nov 1910, dau. Charles and Mary B. (Remick) Bickford. Harnessmaker.

Daughter, b. 31 Jan 1852.

178 William A.[7], 1854-1920.

Carrie M., b. 1858.

179 Frederick Eugene[7], 1861-1941.

Sources: Wakefield NH census 1860. VR SA/NH.

153. **CHARLES HAVEN$^6$ SAWYER** [see 96], b. 18 Dec 1839 Wakefield NH, d. 5 Mar 1910 Mt. Clemens MI, m. 1 Jan 1874 Louise E. Jewett of Bangor ME, b. 26 Feb 1850 d. 11 May 1939, dau. George K. and Maria (Marsh) Jewett of Portsmouth NH. Construction engineer. Civil War. In Wakefield NH 1860, Bangor ME 1880. B/S/land in Portland ME 1862-1867.

Charles Jewett, b. 26 Oct 1874 Bangor ME, d. 15 Jul 1913 Bangor ME, m. 10 Jul 1901 Margaret E. Davis, b.?. Mechanical engineer.
180 Haven$^6$, 1876-1952.
William McCrillis, b. 15 Jan 1879 Bangor ME, m. 9 Sep 1903 Lucy E. Peck, b. ?.
Louise, b. 30 Jul 1881.
Susan M., b. 1 Dec 1887.

Sources: Wakefield NH census 1860. Bangor ME census 1880. ME 1880 census index. VR Bangor ME, SA/ME. J14, R10a, Obit (Charles H).

154. **ROBERT WILLIAM$^6$ SAWYER** [see 96], b. Jan 1850 Wakefield NH, m. 12 Nov 1878 Wakefield NH Martha Copp Paul of Wakefield NH, b. Oct 1850 d. 31 Dec 1922, dau. Hiram and Mary (Copp) Paul. Harvard graduate 1874. In Exeter NH 1870, Bangor ME 1878.

181 Robert William$^7$, b. 1880.
Eugene Mitchell, b. 9 Jan 1882.
Pauline D., b. 16 Apr 1887.

Sources: Exeter NH census 1870. ME 1880 census index. VR Bangor ME, SA/ME. C94, W68.

155. **SAMUEL$^6$ SAWYER** [see 100], b. 1836 Richmond NH, m.(1) 13 Jun 1856 Winchester NH Sarah H. Starkey of Winchendon MA, b. ?; m.(2) 15 Apr 1868 Orange MA Sarah S. Pratt of Shutesbury MA, b. 28 Nov 1838, dau. Ephraim Pratt. Laborer.

Hattie Marie, b. 27 Sep 1859.
Charles L., b. 5 Dec 1869 Montague MA, m. 27 Jun 1895 Chester NH Alice M. Dibble of Chester NH, b. ca. 1874, dau. S_____ E. and Mary A. (Blood) Dibble. Mechanic.

Sources: VR Richmond NH, Winchester NH, SA/MA. C73A.

156. **DAVID$^6$ SAWYER** [see 100], b. 25 Dec 1841 Richmond NH, d. 10 May 1908 Winchester NH, m.(1) 25 Dec 1874 Richmond NH Mattie A. Luther of Westport NY, b. 1855 d. 1887; m.(2) 25 Jun 1906 Winchester NH Cora B. (Smith) Rixford of Winchester NH, b. 9 Jul 1861 d. 8 Jul 1933, dau. Daniel and Lydia (Darling) Smith. In Winchester NH.

Walter David, b. 5 Oct 1875 Winchester NH, m.(1) 7 Jun 1899 Winchester NH Gertrude Stetson of Winchester NH, b. 28 May 1882 d. 5 Nov 1899; m.(2) Clara M. Manning of Winchester NH, b. 29 Nov 1871 d. 14 Dec 1926, dau. Joseph H. and Mary J. (Thompson) Manning; m.(3) 2 May 1936 Winchester NH Helena Stone of Haverhill MA, b. 1876, wid., dau. George A. and Sarah E. (Beckford) Young.
Son, stillborn 10 Jun 1877.

Sources: Winchester NH census 1850, 1860, 1870, 1880. VR Winchester NH, SA/NH.

157. **HENRY$^6$ SAWYER** [see 100], b. 1843 Richmond NH, m.(1) 1867 Andover NH Ella Augusta Brown, b. 12 Feb 1848 d. 10 Nov 1868, dau. True and Lucinda (Blake) Brown; m.(2) 16 Jan 1870 Boston MA Caroline C. Acorn of Wiscassett ME, b. ca. 1846, dau. William and Elizabeth Acorn. Bookkeeper. In Winchester NH, Malden MA 1880.

George H., b. 5 Sep 1880 Malden MA.

Sources: Malden MA census 1880. VR SA/MA. E2, B91.

## SEVENTH GENERATION

158. **CUMMINGS[7] SAWYER** [see 104], b. 26 Nov 1824 Sharon NH, d. 27 Jan 1894 Jaffrey NH, m. 16 Dec 1858 Elizabeth Young of Woburn MA, b. 3 Mar 1839 d. 7 Aug 1908, dau. William E. and Parnell (Beers) Young. Farmer.

Albert Cummings, b. 6 Jan 1860 Sharon NH, d. 21 Jul 1918 Manatee FL, m. 30 Dec 1903 Carrie Elizabeth Bailey, b. 8 Aug 1866 d. 1931, dau. Clarence and Sarah E (Whitcomb) Bailey. CH: Allison E. b. 11 Jun 1905, m. 31 Aug 1930 Durwood M. Hussey of Florida.

Emily Jane, b. 31 Jan 1863, d. 25 May 1934 Boston MA, unm.

182 Fred Lincoln[8], b. 1866.

William Edward, b. 29 Jan 1868, d. 14 Mar 1868.

Sources: Jaffrey NH census 1870. VR SA/MA, SA/NH. A27, C32.

159. **ALFRED[7] SAWYER** [see 104], b. 12 Aug 1831 Sharon NH, d. 17 May 1930 Jaffrey NH, m. 7 Jun 1854 Lucy M. Parker of Nelson NH, b. 9 Jul 1829 d. 19 Jan 1892, dau. Nathaniel Parker. Dairy Farmer. Selectman 11 years, Justice of Peace 25 years.

Mary A., b. 30 Sep 1855, d. 30 Sep 1928, m. 20 Oct 1880 Will J. Mower.

183 Clifton Alfred[8], 1861-1921.

Sources: Jaffrey NH census 1850, 1860, 1870. VR SA/NH. A27, H93.

160. **ALVIN C. L.[7] SAWYER** [see 105], b. 1847 Roxbury VT, d. 5 Dec 1881 Groton MA, m. 17 Nov 1866 Groton MA Alice E. Wright of Pepperell MA, b. 1845 d. 1931, dau. Abel and V. Wright. Furrier, teamster. In Peterborough NH 1850.

Esther V., b. 15 Apr 1871.

Elmer, b. 21 Nov 1877 Pepperell MA, d. 1951. In Groton MA.

Ida Louise, b. 24 Apr 1880.

Sources: Peterborough NH census 1850. VR SA/MA. Roland Sawyer rec.

161. **CHARLES M.[7] SAWYER** [see 105], b. ca. 1850 Sharon NH, m. 29 May 1872 Cambridge MA Carrie G. Knowlton of Manchester NH, b. ?, dau. Benjamin and Grace L. Knowlton. Baker.

Albert Edward, b. 13 May 1875 Cambridge MA.

Grace Nichols, b. 3 Aug 1882.

Sources: VR SA/MA.

162. **CHARLES H.[7] SAWYER** [see 109], b. 21 Mar 1856 Ludlow VT, d. 14 Dec 1924 Westport NH, m. 20 Feb 1879 Swanzey NH Ella M.(Talbot) Knight of Sharon MA, b. 13 Aug 1854 d. 10 Jan 1937, dau. Charles and Ella M. Talbot. In Swanzey NH, Westport NH 1879.

Hattie Ella, b. 22 Aug 1880, m. 8 Oct 1898 Swanzey NH Albert Plummer.

Charles B., b. 26 Jan 1883 Swanzey NH.

Flora M., b. 21 Aug 1886.

Barnum Bailey, b. 23 Dec 1894 Swanzey NH.

Sources: VR SA/NH, SA/VT. R7, N6.

163. **HILAND ADDISON[7] SAWYER** [see 111], b. 14 Jan 1838 Andover VT, d. 13 Apr 1903 Ludlow VT, m. 8 May 1859 Ludlow VT Melissa Snell of Ludlow VT, b. 1840 d. 1903. Carpenter.

Laura Ella, b. 15 Feb 1860, m. 1 Jan 1878 Chester VT Will Sanders.

Ann Amanda, b. 1 Mar 1863, d. 1921, m. 5 Jul 1882 William H. Henderson. CH: Mark A., b. 20 May 1880.

Alma Lenore, b. 22 Mar 1866, m. 25 May 1884 Springfield VT George Peram.

Son, b. ?, d. 30 Apr 1870.

William M., b. 29 Aug 1871 Ludlow VT, m. 16 May 1891 Plymouth MA Kate D. Willis of Winchester NH, b. ca. 1872, dau. Fayette P. and Frances Willis. Stockbroker. In Chicago IL, Winchester NH 1891. CH: Fayette, b. ?, d. at 30 yrs, m. ?, no CH.

Emma Jane, b. 18 Apr 1874, d. 24 May 1892.

Edward, b. 21 May 1876 Ludlow VT, m. Kathleen Parsons, b. ?.

184 John Guy[8], 1881-1957.

Sources: VR SA/VT, SA/MA. William Edward Sawyer rec.

164. **ALBERT DELNO[7] SAWYER** [see 111], b. 20 Jan 1844 Andover VT, d. 2 Dec 1923 Keene NH, m. 14 Mar 1871 Flora T. Pike of Orange VT, b. 6 Apr 1847 d. 18 Jun 1914, dau. William and Felicia Pike. Carpenter. In Marlborough NH 1850-1880, Keene NH 1917.

Jennie Laura, b. 14 Mar 1872, m. 12 Sep 1894 Keene NH Alonzo Tupper.

Carrie M., b. 11 Jan 1874, m. 11 Jan 1898 Fred J. Pratt.

Charles A., b. 8 May 1876 Marlborough NH.

Flora Belle., b. 9 Nov 1880, m. 3 Jul 1908 George Henry Oliver.

Sources: Marlborough NH census 1850, 1870 (alone), 1880. VR SA/NH. B42, N6.

165. **ALLEN LEVI[7] SAWYER** [see 113], b. 6 Oct 1843 Hancock NH, d. 4 Apr 1904 Antrim NH, m.(1) 2 Nov 1865 Keene NH Carrie E. Wilson of Stoddard NH, b. 1846 d. 16 Sep 1880; m.(2) 18 Apr 1883 Antrim NH Mary F. Case of Antrim NH, b. 1856. In Stoddard NH 1865, Clinton NH 1880. He bur. in Antrim NH. Stoddard NH census says Levi Allen.

185 George A.[8], b. 1866.

Mary L., b. 11 Nov 1870, m. 5 Sep 1888 Milford NH Albert H. Brown.

Lora, b. 7 Dec 1874, m. 15 Apr 1896 Antrim NH Charles L. Holt.

Sources: Stoddard NH census 1870. VR SA/NH. C54, N9, N6.

166. **CLARENCE E.[7] SAWYER** [see 113], b. 22 Feb 1857 Stoddard NH, d. Nov 1933 Russell MA, m. 1 Oct 1882 Antrim NH Nellie M. Burnham of Francestown NH, b. 14 Nov 1864 d. 4 May 1906, dau. Clark W. and Ellen (Pratt) Burnham. Paper maker. In Antrim NH 1867-1879, Bennington VT 1880-1890. Nellie bur. in Bennington VT.

Rose A., b. 8 Jun 1883, m. Richard Day.

Edith M., b. 9 Jan 1884, d. 26 Mar 1935 Concord NH.

Norman P., b. 21 Sep 1885 Stoddard NH, m. 31 Mar 1906 Antrim NH Bertha Paquette, b. ?, dau. Alex Paquette of Canada. In Gardner MA, Manchester NH. CH: Carroll, b. 10 Mar 1908, d. 22 Jan 1911; Dau., stillborn 12 Dec 1909 Concord NH.

Earle Anthony, b. 2 Mar 1888, d. 30 Jul 1890.

Clark Ernest, b. 6 May 1890, d. 23 Jul 1890.

Sources: Bennington VT census 1880, 1890. VR SA/NH, SA/VT.

167. **WALTER G.[7] SAWYER** [see 114], b. 1838 Hancock NH, m.(1) Hartford VT Sarah Danver of Shrewsbury VT, b. 1840 d. 2 Oct 1886, dau. Peter and Mary Danver of Ireland; m.(2) 22 Feb 1888 Mary (Colston) Thompson, b. ?. Farmer. Civil War: 14th Regiment, Vermont Volunteer Militia, Oct 1862-28 Jan 1863. In White River Junction VT, Stockbridge VT.

Lee Arthur, b. 29 Dec 1891 Stockbridge VT.

Sources: VR SA/VT. H13.

168. **HIRAM E.[7] SAWYER** [see 114], b. 19 Feb 1840 Hancock NH, d. 9 May 1910 Shrewsbury VT, m. 22 Nov 1860 Shrewsbury VT Clara E. Aldrich of Shrewsbury VT, b. 5 Mar 1843 d. 11 Mar 1904. Tavern keeper, postmaster. In Plymouth VT.

George W., b. ca. 1863 Shrewsbury VT, m. 4 Sep 1881 Northhampton MA Addie R. Wilder of Wilmington VT, b. ca. 1864, dau. John and Lydia Wilder. Railroad engineer. In Springfield MA 1884. CH: Maria C., b. 17 Feb 1882; Grace M., b. 4 Aug 1884.

Charles H., b. 14 Dec 1868 Jamaica VT, d. 23 Oct 1945 Shrewsbury VT, m. 9 Jan 1899 Northhampton MA Clara Angie Mills of Unionville CT, b. 19 Apr 1868 d. 8 Mar 1942, dau. Edward and Angeline (Hill) Mills. CH: Corinne Constance, b. 4 Sep 1895.

Sources: VR SA/VT, SA/MA. B60.

169. **HUBBARD DUDLEY⁷ SAWYER** [see 115], b. 22 Jan 1856 Hancock NH, m.(1) 27 Apr 1880 Martha A. Cutler of Woburn MA, b. 1847 d. 30 Apr 1886, dau. David and Martha (Nutting) Cutler; m.(2) 17 Apr 1892 Minnie Joslyn of New York, b. 1858, dau. Daniel and Rhoda (Blackman) Joslyn. In East Jaffrey NH.

William A., b. 2 Aug 1881 Hancock NH. In East Jaffrey NH.

Daughter, stillborn 23 Apr 1886.

Sources: N25.

170. **WALTER FAIRBANKS⁷ SAWYER** [see 116], b. 5 Feb 1868 Keene NH. Harvard Medical School. Physician, practiced in Fitchburg MA.

Walter Fairbanks, b. 1902, d. 1981.

Sources: Kenne NH census 1870. H29.

171. **HERBERT BROWN⁷ SAWYER** [see 122], b. 29 May 1848 Plymouth VT, d. 27 Apr 1903 Lincoln NE, m. 23 May 1871 Lina Frances Pursell of Michigan, b. 7 May 1853 d. 24 Dec 1922.

Willits H., b. 31 Oct 1873 Lincoln NE, d. 1 Mar 1966, m. 11 May 1908 Frances G. Case, b. ?.

Everett Brown, b. 9 Feb 1877, d. 25 Jun 1967, m. 12 Jun 1901 Nellie E. Conly, b. ?.

Leroy Pursell, b. 26 Dec 1878, d. 9 Mar 1950, m. 7 Jun 1907 Jessimine Pike, b. ?.

Helen A., b. 8 Dec 1890, d. 4 Apr 1981.

Proctor Herbert, b. 11 Dec 1895 d. 23 Oct 1877, m. 15 Oct 1927 Elizabeth Jack, b. ?.

Sources: VR SA/VT. Willits H. Sawyer rec.

172. **MERRITT ANGELO⁷ SAWYER** [see 122], b. 22 Aug 1852 Plymouth VT, d. 9 May 1926 Los Angeles CA, m. 2 Feb 1876 Walpole NH Jennie R. McWain of Dorset VT, b. 1852 d. 21 Feb 1910, dau. Harmon and Amanda (Coolidge) McWain. Farmer. He bur. in Ludlow VT.

186 Merle Merritt⁸, 1876-1959.

Mary Angela, b. 26 Jan 1878, m. 18 Jul 1899 Woodstock VT Fred Brown Handy.

Clifton Winslow, b. 29 Aug 1879 Plymouth VT, d. May 1955, m. 25 Mar 1905 Silver City IA Nellie Colburn of Iowa, b. 20 Apr 1881, dau. J.S. and Estelle (Herrick) Colburn. CH: Kenneth Winslow, b. 6 May 1908; Vadio Burdette, b. 3 May 1911; Max DeVon, b. 27 Aug 1916.

Wayne Harmon, b. 22 Sep 1881, d. 10 Apr 1884.

Charles Field, b. 20 Mar 1886 Plymouth VT, d. 3 Oct 1957 Sierra Madre CA, m. 22 Dec 1908 Rutland VT Zilpah May Lamb of Mendon VT, b. 29 Sep 1886, dau. Willie and Ida Jane (Bennett) Lamb. In Keokuk IA. CH: Charles Field, b. 6 Oct 1910, m. Mary Esther Welshons, b. ?.

Sources: VR SA/VT. C75.

173. **CHARLES ELWIN⁷ SAWYER** [see 126], b. 28 Jul 1858 Mason NH, d. 30 May 1929 Greenville NH, m.(1) 27 Jan 1881 Ayer MA Harriet E. Winship of Townsend MA, b. 14 Nov 1858

d. 26 Mar 1885, dau. Adrian and Harriet Winship; m.(2) 1 May 1890 in Townsend MA (div. 1 Jun 1894) Alice E. Sellars of England, b. 1870, dau. James and Elizabeth (Cooper) Sellars; m.(3) 4 May 1895 Harriet M. White of New Ipswich NH, b. 4 Feb 1868 d. 10 May 1896; m.(4) 10 Sep 1898 Alice E. (Sellars) Sawyer of England, b. 1870. Hotel keeper. In New Ipswich NH, Greenville NH.

Lucy, b. 6 Nov 1881, d. 13 May 1884.

Ashubul C., b. 17 May 1883, d. 3 Apr 1888.

Charles Elwin, b. 1890 New Ipswich NH, m. 27 Jun 1910 Romula M. Doucet of Greenville NH, b. 1893.

Marion Lucy, b. 16 Dec 1899.

Sources: VR Ayer MA, SA/MA.

174. **GEORGE ALVAH[7] SAWYER** [see 138], b. 21 Dec 1876 Stewartstown NH, d. 1 Sep 1925 Littleton NH, m. 20 Dec 1903 Tilton NH Inez B. Goodale of Tilton NH, b. 2 Apr 1882 d. 9 Oct 1928, dau. Augustus M. and Susie P. (Evans) Goodale. In Auburn ME.

Oscar Fay, b. 12 May 1907, d. 17 Jun 1972, m. 3 Feb 1929 Ruth Healy, b. 29 Sep 1900 d. 21 Aug 1965. CH: Richard Lewis, b. 1 Oct 1929; James Winston, b. 6 Feb 1931; Patricia Ruth, b. 14 Apr 1932; Dorothy Marion, b. 17 May 1933; Duane Healy, b. 17 May 1938.

Mabel Evelyn, b. 5 Jun 1909, d. 11 Mar 1966, m. 8 Sep 1934 Benjamin F. Moulton.

Ruth Inez, b. 30 Jun 1912, m. 14 Mar 1931 Ralph Spencer.

Helen Phoebe, b. 11 Aug 1915, m. 12 Oct 1940 Raymond M. Fletcher.

Edna Louise, b. 3 May 1917, d. 16 May 1958, m. 3 Nov 1938 Lawrence Bauman.

Sources: VR SA/NH. Patricia R. Sawyer rec.

175. **FREDERICK WILLIS[7] SAWYER** [see 143], b. 16 Apr 1862 Milford NH, d. 3 Feb 1946 Milford NH, m. 26 Oct 1893 Bertha (Wilkins) Hyde of Amherst NH, b. 17 Dec 1863 d. 9 Jan 1941, dau. Aaron S. and Sarah (Kendall) (Flint) Wilkins. Bank cashier.

Grace Miriam, b. 10 Aug 1894, m. 24 Nov 1923 John E. Miltimore.

Marguerite, b. 19 Feb 1899, unm.

Donald Frederick, b. 13 Feb 1900 Milford NH, m.(1) 11 Jul 1925 Lisbon NH Alice L. Oliver of Lisbon NH, b. 1899 d. 23 Jun 1983, dau. William W. and Alice M.(Boynton) Oliver; m.(2) 14 Sep 1984 Josephine K. Lorimer, b. ?. Banker. In Brooklyn NY. CH: Mary Louise, b. 25 Jul 1926; Betsey Boynton, b. 22 Oct 1928; Sarah Wilkins, b. 5 Oct 1932.

Sources: R3, H50, Donald F. Sawyer rec.

176. **JOHN HOWARD[7] SAWYER** [see 144], b. 10 Dec 1862 Cambridge MA, m. 12 Sep 1906 Theresa May Hardy, b. 26 Nov 1880. In Arlington MA.

John Howard, b. 10 Aug 1907, m. Caroline Aiken, b. ?.

Sources: W68.

177. **WALTER DEAN[7] SAWYER** [see 144], b. 5 Jul 1866 Cambridge MA, m.(1) 10 Mar 1896 Anna B. Coursen, b. 25 Mar 1866 d. 22 Apr 1897; m.(2) 20 Oct 1906 Lucie Adelia Learned, b. 13 Jan 1871. In Arlington MA.

Belle Coursen, b. ?, d. in infancy.

Geoffrey Augustus, b. 29 Jul 1909.

Sources: W68.

178. **WILLIAM A.[7] SAWYER** [see 152], b. 5 Jan 1854 Milton NH, d. 28 May 1920 Wakefield NH, m.(1) 2 Nov 1872 (div. 16 Oct 1894) Stella Augusta Day of Bradford NH, b. Oct 1854 d. 31 Aug 1898, dau. Alfred and Louisa (Kimball) Day; m.(2) 1 Dec 1894 Conway NH Mary E. (Pierce) Brown of South Berwick ME, b. 1860 d. 1940, dau. Charles and Laura (Rand) Pierce. Railroad conductor. In Wakefield NH 1860 and 1906, Conway NH, Topsfield MA 1875.

Nellie E., b. 13 May 1874, d. 14 Apr 1893.

Alfred Leo, b. 3 Sep 1875 Wakefield NH, d. 9 Nov 1924 Conway NH, m. 22 Feb 1907 Nashua NH (later div.) Ella (Templeness) Winterbone of Webster MA, b.?, dau. John and Ella (Rogers) Templeness. Granite cutter. In Barre VT.

Daughter, b. 2 Oct 1878, d. 20 Nov 1880.

Son, b. 22 Mar 1882, d. same day.

Daughter, b. 12 Oct 1885.

Sources: Wakefield NH census 1860, 1880. VR Conway NH, SA/ME.

179. **FREDERICK EUGENE[7] SAWYER** [see 152], b. 30 Sep 1861 Wakefield NH, d. 26 Jan 1941 Skowhegan ME, m.(1) 13 Oct 1880 Rosie Edith Waite of Portland ME, b. ? d. 1907; m.(2) 21 Jun 1910 Sanbornville NH Mary L. Dyer of Burnham ME, b. 22 Dec 1874 d. 26 Feb 1959, dau. Benjamin and Fidelia (Stearns) Dyer. Candy maker. In Waterville ME, Portland ME, Falmouth ME. He bur. Burnham ME.

Alice G., b. 20 Oct 1881.

Frank L., b. 12 Jan 1883 Portland ME.

Robert Henry, b. 22 Jul 1885 Portland ME, d. 3 Jul 1905, m. 6 Jun 1904 Effingham NH Nellie O. Hobbs of Parsonsfield ME, b. 1886, dau. Victory and Augusta M.(Brown) Hobbs.

Paul L., b. 1888, d. 9 May 1905.

Beatrice I., b. 26 Mar 1895.

George W., b. 1896, d. 6 Jan 1898.

Leslie Austin, b. 19 Mar 1897, d. 20 Oct 1897.

Sources: VR Skowhegan ME, SA/NH, SA/ME. M5.

180. **HAVEN[7] SAWYER** [see 153], b. 27 Jul 1876 Bangor ME, d. 9 Mar 1952 Bangor ME, m. 26 Mar 1918 Lorena Fellows, b. ?.

Haven, b. 26 Jan 1919. In New Harbor ME.

Adelle, b. 22 Oct 1920, d. 29 Jul 1988, m. 1944 Dr. George Wood of Bangor ME.

Kimball J., b. ?.

Virginia, b. ?, m. _____ Wilder. Went to California.

Sources: Obit, Haven Sawyer rec.

181. **ROBERT WILLIAM II[7] SAWYER** [see 154], b. 12 May 1880 Bangor ME, m. 2 Aug 1905 Louise C. Dunn, b. 7 Jul 1878, dau. George and Lucinda (Cushing) Dunn. Harvard College 1902. Lawyer, judge. In Oregon 1912. He bur. in Ashland ME.

Robert William III, b. 1905 Bangor ME, d. 1965, m. Anita Jacobson, b. 1911 d. 1951. CH: Robert William IV; Gerry Dunn; John Bancroft, b. 1941, d. 1949; Charles Russell, b. 1946, d. 1966. He bur. in Ashland ME.

George Cushing, b. 1909 Bangor ME, m.(1) Elizabeth Markel, m.(2) Irene Rand. In Houlton ME, Ashland ME. CH: George Cushing; Laura; m. George Pike; Elizabeth, m. _____ Buehring; Peter Dunn; Nancy C., m. Elvin Goggins; Donald Rand; Janice Rand; Peter Rand; Barbara Rand; Teddy Rand; Susan Rand.

Alfred Worcester, b. 1911 Bangor ME, d. 1965. CH: John Cushing; Valerie Kay.

Sources: C94, W68, M5, Robert W. Sawyer VI rec.

## EIGHTH GENERATION

182. **FRED LINCOLN$^8$ SAWYER** [see 158], b. 25 Feb 1866 Jaffrey NH, m.(1) 6 Jul 1891 Boston MA Genevieve Archibald of New York City, b. 1870 d. 26 Apr 1892, dau. John and Sarah Archibald; m.(2) 4 Jun 1896 Mary Houston, b. ? d. Sep 1919. Lumber dealer. In Boston MA, Waltham MA.

Fred Archibald, b. 8 Apr 1892, d. 27 Oct 1917.

Cecil, b. ca. 1897, m. 14 Jul 1917 Eva M Thomas. CH: Virginia E., b. 8 Mar 1921; Belle, b. 19 Jan 1924.

Sources: VR SA/MA.

183. **CLIFTON ALFRED$^8$ SAWYER** [see 159], b. 11 Sep 1861 Jaffrey NH, d. 30 Oct 1921 Jaffrey NH, m. 28 Dec 1887 Jennie M. Hale of Rindge NH, b. 10 May 1865, dau. Julius A. and Eliza (Perry) Hale. Farmer.

Bernice L., b. 28 Apr 1889.

187 Roscoe Alfred$^9$, b. 1892.

188 Jason Clifton$^9$, 1898-1973.

Sources: VR SA/NH.

184. **JOHN GUY$^8$ SAWYER** [see 163], b. 17 May 1881 Ludlow VT, d. 1957, m. 20 Mar 1912 Hillsboro NH Edith M. Morgan of Hillsboro NH, b. 7 Aug 1889 d. 1961, dau. Charles H. and Nellie (Gay) Morgan. Weaver. Note: M. also recorded in Ludlow VT.

William Edwin, b. 6 Feb 1913, m. 19 Jun 1937 Sarah A. Garland. Went to Texas.

Charles Henry, b. 24 Jun 1915, m. 23 Aug 1941 Ruth E. Schaeffer. Went to California.

Sources: B92, M63, William Edwin Sawyer rec.

185. **GEORGE A.$^8$ SAWYER** [see 165], b. 6 Sep 1866 Stoddard NH, m. 6 Aug 1906 Antrim NH Ines E. Hildreth of Antrim NH, b. 1880, dau. William A. and Helen J. (Smith) Hildreth. In Antrim NH, Clinton NH.

Winslow A., b. 1912 Antrim NH, m. 26 Jun 1937 Antrim NH Frances E. Wheeler of Stoddard NH, b. 1912, dau. Frank E. and Amy B. (Gammon) Wheeler. Draftsman.

Sources: C54, N9.

186. **MERLE MERRITT$^8$ SAWYER** [see 172], b. 17 Aug 1876 Plymouth VT, d. 28 Sep 1959 White River Junction VT, m. Maude F. Kneeland of Boston MA, b. ?. Plumber. In Woodstock VT. He bur. in Worcester MA.

Merle L., b. 17 Oct 1902.

Sources: VR SA/VT.

## NINTH GENERATION

187. **ROSCOE ALFRED$^9$ SAWYER** [see 183], b. 22 Sep 1892 Jaffrey NH, m. 21 Aug 1914 Rita C. Parsons, b. ?, dau. John Parsons of Newburyport MA.

Marie Parsons, b. 13 dec 1915.

Nancy Hale, b. 6 Jan 1917.

Phyllis Cushing, b. 11 Nov 1918.

Alfred Perry, b. 25 Nov 1919.

David Russell, b. 20 May 1925.

Sources: A27.

188. **JASON CLIFTON⁹ SAWYER** [see 183], b. 14 Nov 1898 Jaffrey NH, d. 1973, m. 12 Oct 1928 Elizabeth Scott Doty of Smithfield PA, b. 22 Nov 1905 d. 31 Dec 1988, dau. James S. and Emma (Scott) Doty. Farmer.

Clifton Doty, b. 18 Oct 1929.
Donald Harvey, b. 9 Dec 1931. Went to Boonville NY.
Jeremy Jason, b. 12 Nov 1933.
Sheldon Scott, b. 25 May 1935, m. 5 May 1962 Carol Jean Holms.
R. Peter, b. ?.
Perry H., b. ?, m. Linda Kendall.

Sources: A27.

# PART VI

# ∞ UNCONNECTED LINES ∞

This section lists family lines based on Sawyer males who suddenly appeared in the census or other records with no clue as to their parentage or where their lines originated. Although I have been able to trace forward the lines of some of these individuals, I have not been able to identify the Sawyers who preceded them. In each case, therefore, I have assigned the primary individual sequence number (1), with his descendants following in the manner used elsewhere in this work. For convenience, the lines are listed chronologically, based on the birth date of the earliest family head in each case.

## LINE 1

1. **JOHN[1] SAWYER**, b. ca. 1640, m.(1) Nov 1666 Mercy Little, b. ? d. 10 Feb 1693, dau. Thomas and Ann (Warren) Little of Marshfield MA; m.(2) 23 Nov 1694 Rebekah (Barker) Snow of Duxbury MA, wid. of Josiah, b. ? d. 28 Apr 1711, dau. Robert and Lucy (Williams) Barker. Constable for Marshfield MA 1672.

___ke, son, b. 19 Aug 1667.
Mercy, b. 1 Feb 1668, d. 1702, m. 2 Dec 1686 Anthony Eames.
Susanne, b. 27 May 1671, d. 15 Dec 1682.
Thomas, b. 11 Feb 1672 Marshfield MA. B/land in Middleboro MA 1688.
2 Josias[2], 1675-1733. Went to Rhodc Island.
__ry, dau., b. 12 Oct 1677.

Sources: VR Marshfield MA.

2. **JOSIAS[2] SAWYER** [see 1], b. 7 Jan 1675 Marshfield MA, d. Aug 1733 Little Compton RI, m.(1) 20 Dec 1705 Duxbury MA Martha Seabury of Duxbury MA, b. 23 Dec 1679 d. 1712, dau. Samuel and Martha (Peabody) Seabury; m.(2) Martha Fobes, b. 1681, dau. William and Elizabeth (Southworth) Fobes. In Tiverton RI. Mentioned in will of William Fobes, Littleton RI 1712. Witnessed will of John Woodman 1710 and William Ladd 1720 or 1729, Little Compton RI. Own will filed in Taunton MA 15 Sep 1733.

John, b. 20 Feb 1707 Tiverton RI.
Hannah, b. 27 Nov 1710, d. 1780, m. 27 Aug 1730 John Williston.
Mercy, b. 28 Jan 1712, d. 1 Oct 1790, m. 6 Feb 1741 Samuel Reed. Went to Freetown MA.
Mary, b. 28 Aug 1714, d. 4 Mar 1775, m. G____ B____.
Abigail, b. 4 Oct 1716, d. 1777, m. 1 Nov 1743 Newport RI Joseph Taber.
Priscilla, b. Feb 1719.
3 Josiah[3], 1725-1792.

Sources: VR SA/RI.

3. **JOSIAH[3] SAWYER** [see 2], b. 15 May 1725, d. 1792 Little Compton RI, m.(1) 1746 Sarah Pearce of Little Compton RI, b. 12 Jan 1729 d. 28 Aug 1780, dau. George and Deborah (Searles) Pearce; m.(2) 27 Jan 1791 Anstress Wilcox, b. ?. In Tiverton RI.

4 Lemuel[4], 1748-1804.
Thomas, b. ca. 1749 Little Compton RI.
Antrace, b. 30 Oct 1751, d. 12 Oct 1835, m. 1771 Wright Pearce.
Priscilla, b. 20 Mar 1754.
Josiah, b. 26 Jun 1756 Little Compton RI, d. Jan 1800, m. 14 Jul 1782 Betsey Pierce, b. 17 Oct 1756 d. 15 Jul 1849, dau. Jepthiar and Elizabeth (Roose) Pierce. CH: 2 sons, b. ?.
Martha, b. ca. 1757.

5 John$^4$, 1759-1794.
Sarah, b. 17 Sep 1761, d. 6 May 1832, m. Samuel Sherman.
Isaac, b. 29 Oct 1763.
Child, b. 1765.
Jeremiah, b. 1768 Little Compton RI.
George, b. 1768 Little Compton RI.
Child, b. 1770.
Isaac, b. 1772 Little Compton RI, d. Jan 1804.
6 William$^4$, ca. 1774-1837.
Sources: Little Compton RI census 1790. VR Little Compton RI, New Bedford MA.

4. **LEMUEL$^4$ SAWYER** [see 3], b. 13 Nov 1748 Little Compton RI, d. 4 Mar 1804 Little Compton RI, m. 2 Nov 1777 Betsey Woodman, b. 23 Mar 1755, dau. William and Mary Woodman.
Thomas, b. 31 Oct 1779, d.y.
Sarah, b. 17 Jun 1781.
Cynthia, b. 22 Jun 1783, m. 23 Jun 1812 Thomas Manchester.
7 Stephen$^5$, b. 1785.
Ruth, b. 27 Feb 1787.
Thomas, b. 6 Feb 1788 Little Compton RI, d. 26 Dec 1850, m. Ruth Boardman, b. ?.
Sources: Little Compton RI census 1790. VR Little Compton RI.

5. **JOHN$^4$ SAWYER** [see 3], b. 19 Sep 1759 Little Compton RI, d. 17 Apr 1794 Little Compton RI, m. 3 May 1787 Ruth Stoddard, b. ?, dau. Benjamin and Phebe (Brownell) Stoddard. Wid. m. 9 Apr 1799 Captain Gideon Simmons.
Phebe Brownell, b. 5 Oct 1788.
John, b. 22 Jul 1790 Little Compton RI, d. 17 Sep 1847.
Sources: VR SA/RI.

6. **WILLIAM$^4$ SAWYER** [see 3], b. ca. 1774 Tiverton RI, d. 1837 Tiverton RI, m.(1) 11 Feb 1796 Judeth Tabor, b. 1773 d. 1818, dau. Gideon and Judith Tabor; m.(2) 16 Sep 1819 Rebecca Pearce, b. ?. Wid. in Tiverton RI 1840.
Priscilla, b. 30 May 1799, m. 20 Oct 1825 Edward Cannon.
Andrew, b. 8 Jul 1801 Tiverton RI, m. 1 Jul 1828 New Bedford MA Priscilla Divol, b. ?. Cooper, mason. CH: Pardon, b. 19 Apr 1829, d. 2 Jul 1840; Judith T., b. 19 Aug 1832, d. 1 Sep 1833; William, b. ?, d. 12 Feb 1834; Rachel D., b. ca. 1836, m. 1 Jun 1864 New Bedford MA Charles Fails; Cornelia M., b. 5 Mar 1844, m. 29 Apr 1859 New Bedford MA Edward Howland.
8 Gideon Tabor$^5$, 1803-1896.
Hannah Record, b. 5 Nov 1806, m. 21 Sep 1830 Captain Russell Maxfield.
Mary Ann, b. 9 Jan 1809.
William, b. 9 Nov 1811 Tiverton RI.
Thomas, b. 30 May 1816 Tiverton RI.
Sources: Tiverton RI census 1800, 1810, 1820, 1830, 1840. New Bedford MA census 1830, 1840, 1850. VR New Bedford MA, SA/MA.

7. **STEPHEN$^5$ SAWYER** [see 4], b. 14 Feb 1785 Little Compton RI, m. 21 Mar 1813 Westport MA Nancy Earle, b. 30 Aug 1794, dau. Benjamin and Mary (Soule) Earle. Marriage record says he was a colonel.
9 Henry S.$^6$, b. 1822.
Sources: VR Little Compton RI, Westport MA.

8. **GIDEON TABOR[5] SAWYER** [see 6], b. 13 Sep 1803 Tiverton RI, d. 31 Mar 1896, m. 17 Sep 1828 New Bedford MA Olive H. Potter, b. 1808. Mason. In New Bedford MA 1830.
10 Stephen Potter[6], 1828-1912.
Drusilla, b. 3 Jan 1831, d. 23 Feb 1895, m. 23 Feb 1852 New Bedford MA William C. Knight.
Mary B., b. 1840, d. 1891, m. 13 Aug 1862 New Bedford MA Daniel M. Sampson.
Olive P., b. 22 Jun 1845, m. 11 Nov 1869 New Bedford MA George O. Buckley.
Sources: New Bedford MA census 1830, 1840, 1850. VR New Bedford MA, SA/MA.

9. **HENRY S.[6] SAWYER** [see 7], b. ca. 1822 Westport MA, d. 15 Nov 1858 Taunton MA, m. 28 Oct 1851 Fall River MA Sophia M. Allen of Westport MA, b. 1829, dau. George and Phebe Allen. Carpenter. In Fall River MA, Providence RI.
11 Charles E.[7], b. ca. 1851.
George Henry, b. 1 Aug 1852.
Phebe Alice, b. 22 Jan 1858, m. 1 Jun 1895 New Bedford MA William W. Cranston.
Sources: VR SA/MA.

10. **STEPHEN POTTER[6] SAWYER** [see 8], b. 12 Sep 1828 New Bedford MA, d. 19 Mar 1912, m.(1) 26 Nov 1851 Fairhaven MA Helen W. Collins of New Bedford MA, b. 17 Mar 1832 d. 27 Jul 1868, dau. David and Jane Collins; m.(2) 12 Jan 1876 Fairhaven MA Elizabeth Bryden of Canada, b. 5 Feb 1847 d. 10 Feb 1947, dau. Ebenezer and Nancy B. Bryden. Tinplate worker.
Clara, b. Nov 1852, m. 26 Jan 1876 New Bedford MA William G. Lamb.
Gideon, b. 8 Apr 1856 New Bedford MA.
Helen L., b. 28 Apr 1858, m. 12 Nov 1879 New Bedford MA Oliver Harvey Gardner.
12 Albert C.[7], b. 1860.
William Knight, b. Mar 1879, d. 1971, m. three times, no CH.
13 Charles Prescott[7], 1884-1948.
Sources: New Bedford MA census 1860. VR New Bedford MA, SA/MA.

11. **CHARLES E.[7] SAWYER** [see 9], b. ca. 1842 Fall River MA, m. 27 Nov 1877 Fall River MA Lizzie A. Houghton of Fall River MA, b. 1858, dau. James and Alice Houghton.
George F., b. 2 Aug 1883 Fall River MA.
Sources: VR SA/MA.

12. **ALBERT C.[7] SAWYER** [see 10], b. 29 Apr 1860 New Bedford MA, m. 28 Nov 1883 Boston MA Laura Belle Williams of New Brunswick, Canada, b. ca. 1858. Machinist. In Boston MA.
Gideon Thomas, b. 9 Oct 1887 Boston MA. Machinist.
Mildred, b. 13 Aug 1893.
Sources: VR SA\MA.

13. **CHARLES PRESCOTT[7] SAWYER** [see 10], b. 20 Mar 1884 New Bedford MA, d. Oct 1948, m. 6 Dec 1906 Mabelle Winch, b. 12 Apr 1884 d. Feb 1972.
14 Charles Prescott[8], b. 1909.
Sources: VR SA/MA. Charles Prescott Sawyer, Jr rec.

14. **CHARLES PRESCOTT[8] SAWYER** [see 13], b. 10 Oct 1909 New Bedford MA, m. 14 Jul 1938 Helen Reddy, b. 27 Jan 1913.
15 Peter Bryden[9], b. 1944.
16 Richard Prescott[9], b. 1947.

Sources: Charles Prescott Sawyer, Jr rec.

15. **PETER BRYDEN$^9$ SAWYER** [see 14], b. 25 Dec 1944, m. 1 Nov 1980 Merle Finn, b. 20 Jan 1953

Stephen Bryden, b. 4 Feb 1984.

Sources: Charles Prescott Sawyer, Jr rec.

16. **RICHARD PRESCOTT$^9$ SAWYER** [see 14], b. 7 Dec 1947, m. 20 Dec 1971 Naomi Leonard, b. 21 Jan 1948.

Ian Prescott, b. 27 Jan 1972.

Shannon Elizabeth, b. 8 Sep 1981.

Sources: Charles Prescott Sawyer, Jr rec.

---

## LINE 2

1. **THOMAS$^1$ SAWYER**, b. ca. 1646, d. 9 Dec 1732 Cohasset MA, m.(1) 26 Nov 1673 Hingham MA Sarah Prince of Hingham MA, b. 22 Feb 1652, dau. John and Margery Prince; m.(2) 13 Oct 1685 Hingham MA Mary Chamberlin, b. ca. 1664 d. Weymouth MA, dau. Henry and Sarah (Jones) Chamberlin; m.(3) 21 May 1713 Mary (Whiton) Jordan, b. 1645 d. 3 Dec 1732, wid. of Baruch, dau. James and Mary (Beal) Whiton. Farmer, constable. In Marshfield MA, Hingham MA. B/land in Middleboro Township MA 1663, Hingham MA 1674.

2 Thomas$^2$, b. 1685.

Sarah, b. 27 Oct 1689, d.y.

Sarah, b. 17 Aug 1690, d. 12 Oct 1773, m. 24 Jun 1708 Benjamin Dyer of Weymouth MA.

Sources: VR Cohasset MA, Weymouth MA.

2. **THOMAS$^2$ SAWYER** [see 1], b. 12 Apr 1685 Hingham MA, m. 11 Sep 1711 Jerusha Eames, b. ?, dau. Anthony and Mercy (Sawyer) Eames of Marshfield MA. Constable.

Sarah, b. 15 Aug 1712, m. 15 Jan 1730 Isreal Nichols, Jr.

Submit, b. 22 Apr 1714.

John, b. 7 Sep 1717 Hingham MA.

Jerusha, b. 22 May 1721.

Mercy, b. 14 Nov 1725.

Sources: H56.

---

## LINE 3

1. **MOSES$^1$ SAWYER**, b. ca. 1720 Yorkshire, England, d. Noank CT, m. Phebe Havens, b. ?. Father was a British admiral, secured a grant of land on Long Island Sound for his son. Moses came to America in 1740, settled on Long Island, then Mystic CT, Noank CT. He bur. in Old Noank Burial Ground CT.

Mary, b. ?, m. Zebulon Weeks. Went to New York.

Martha, b. ?, m. Wakeman Foster. Went to New York.

Sarah, b. ?, d. 13 Jan 1822, m. 24 Dec 1778 William Wilbur.

Phebe, b. ?, m. William Brown. Went to Long Island NY.

John, b. ?, d. at 18 yrs on American privateer *Eagle* during engagement with British man-of-war.

2 James$^2$, 1765-1813.

3 William$^2$, 1767-1852.

Sources: N18, A20.

2. **JAMES² SAWYER** [see 1], b. Apr 1865 in Connecticut, d. 24 Apr 1813 Mason's Island CT, m.(1) Betsey Rathbun, b. ?; m.(2) Mercy Burrows, b. (1760-1770). Wid. w/son Benjamin in 1830.

Nancy, b. (1784-1790).
John, b. ?, d.y.
Frederick, b. (1784-1790). In Stonington CT.
Betsey, b. (1794-1800).
James, b. (1794-1800).
Winthrop, b. (1794-1800).
John Havens, b. (1800-1810) Stonington CT.
Benjamin, b. (1800-1810) Stonington CT.
Phebe, b. ?.

Sources: Groton CT census 1800, 1830, 1840. Stonington CT census 1810, 1840. N18.

3. **WILLIAM² SAWYER** [see 1], b. 19 Apr 1767 in Connecticut, d. 15 Sep 1852, m. Prudence Ashbey, b. 29 Jun 1771 d. 19 Apr 1851. Sea captain.

Marsha, b. 1 Sep 1791.
4 James Ashbey³, 1793-1839.
Maty, b. 29 Oct 1794.
Moses Havens, b. 28 Aug 1796 Stonington CT, m. Iantha Wilcox, b. 3 Nov 1799.
5 William Riley³, b. 1797.
Joshua, b. 15 Aug 1799.
Prudence, b. 15 May 1802.
6 Jeremiah Niles³, 1805-1841.
7 Thomas Jefferson³, b. 1807.
Priscilla, b. 15 Oct 1808.
Asa, b. 12 Jan 1812 Stonington CT, m. 1840 Phebe _____, b. ?.
Sarah Ann, b. 12 Jan 1814, m. George Washington Ashbey.

Sources: Stonington CT census 1800, 1810, 1830, 1840, 1850. N18, S55.

4. **JAMES ASHBEY³ SAWYER** [see 3], b. 5 Jul 1793 Stonington CT, d. 1839, m. Betsey _____, b. ?.

John, b. (1815-1820).
Emanual, b. (1815-1820).

Sources: Stonington CT census 1830, 1840. N18.

5. **WILLIAM RILEY³ SAWYER** [see 3], b. 20 Oct 1797 Stonington CT, m. Lucretia Minor Baker, b. ?.

Jeremiah, b. ca. 1823 Stonington CT. Sailor.
Ann E., b. ca. 1831, d. 12 May 1876, m. Captain Charles C. Sisson.
Frances Jane, b. ca. 1833, m.(1) 1852 Captain Thomas E. Wolfe, m.(2) Captain Charles Sisson.
8 William Albert⁴, b. 1841.

Sources: Stonington CT census 1830. Groton CT census 1840. N18, William D. Sawyer rec.

6. **JEREMIAH NILES³ SAWYER** [see 3], b. 15 May 1805 Stonington CT, d. 8 May 1841 on ship *Hero,* m. 7 Jul 1826 Emerline O. Kelly, b. ?. Sea captain.

Moses Havens, b. 6 Jun 1827 Stonington CT, d. 1909.

Jeremiah Niles, b. 28 Jun 1829 Stonington CT, m. Mystic CT Mary E. Sawyer, b. ?. Lawyer, sea captain, CH: Emerline O., b. 30 Mar 1861, m. 4 Jun 1879 Hampton Young. Went to Texas.
Emerline, b. 22 Apr 1831, d. 8 Oct 1831.
Lodawick Latham, b. 27 Oct 1832.
Lucy Latham, b. 5 Feb 1835.
Franklin Kelly, b. 1 Jun 1839, d. 24 Feb 1847.
Sources: N18.

7. **THOMAS JEFFERSON[3] SAWYER** [see 3], b. 12 Apr 1807 Mason's Island CT, m. Mary Palmer, b. ?. Fisherman.
Mary Ann, b. ?, m. Asa Ashbey.
Prudence A., b. 1835, m. John A. Carrington.
Thomas Jefferson, b. ca. 1837 Groton CT, m. Louisa Williams, b. ?.
Rosswell Palmer, b. 5 Feb 1843 Groton CT, m. 19 Nov 1863 Adelaide Fitch, b. ?.
Charles, b. ?, d.y.
Georgianna, b. ?, d.y.
Sources: Groton CT census 1840, 1850. N18.

8. **WILLIAM ALBERT[4] SAWYER** [see 5], b. 1841 Mystic CT, m. 9 Oct 1873 Katherine D. Brand of Mystic CT, b. 1850 d. 1940. Sea captain.
Mary, b. 1881, d. 1975, m. Leo Doyle.
George, b. 1883, d. 1940.
9 William Albert[5], 1887-1916.
Sources: William D. Sawyer rec.

9. **WILLIAM ALBERT[5] SAWYER** [see 8], b. ca. 1887, d. 1916, m. Eugenia Walkley, b. 1887 d. 1918. Draftsman. In West Hartford CT.
David Walkley, b. 13 May 1912, d. 10 Dec 1968, m. 1933 Sylvia Francis.
William, b. 1913, d. 1915.
Albert, b. 1916, m. Dorothy Herlihy. Adopted by Aunt Mary Doyle.
Sources: William D. Sawyer rec.

---

## LINE 4

1. **BENJAMIN[1] SAWYER**, b. ca. 1742 Cape Elizabeth ME, d. 12 Apr 1830 Cumberland ME, m.(I) 7 Aug 1761 Falmouth ME Rebecca Blackstone of Falmouth ME, b. ?, dau. Benjamin Blackstone. Blacksmith. B/S/land in Cumberland County 1763, 1764. In Falmouth ME 1764. On Falmouth ME tax list 1766. In North Yarmouth ME 1790.
2 John[2], 1762-1828.
3 Benjamin[2], 1764-1852.
4 Jeremiah[2], 1766-1815.
5 Asa[2], 1767-ca. 1830.
6 William[2], 1769-1856.
7 Samuel[2], ca. 1773-1844.
Rebecca, b. ?, m.(1) ?, m.(2) 4 Jul 1825 William Thompson. Rebecca had illegitimate son, Edward, b. ca. 1814 [see 23].
Polly, b. ?, d. at 20 yrs.
Sources: North Yarmouth ME census 1790, 1800. VR Falmouth ME, North Yarmouth ME. G37.

2. **JOHN² SAWYER** [see 1], b. Jul 1762 Falmouth ME, d. 4 Mar 1828 Durham ME, m. 30 Sep 1790 North Yarmouth ME Mary Hannaford, b. ca. 1776 d. 27 Mar 1834, dau. Thomas and Mary (Parker) Hannaford. Revolutionary War. B/S/land in Cumberland County 1788-1800. In North Yarmouth ME 1790, Pownal ME 1795, Monmouth ME 1800, Durham ME 1820. Wid. in Durham ME 1830. He bur. in Cedar Grove Cem., Durham ME.

8 John³, 1791-1870.
9 Asa G.³, 1794-1864.
Sarah D., b. 24 Dec 1795.
Daughter, b. (1800-1810).
10 Reuben Allen³, 1809-1880.
Jerusha, b. ?.

Sources: North Yarmouth ME census 1790. Monmouth ME census 1800, 1810. Durham ME census 1820, 1830. VR North Yarmouth ME, Pownal ME, SA/ME. R10a, H26, C46, G37, Charles F. Sawyer rec.

3. **BENJAMIN² SAWYER** [see 1], b. 4 Mar 1764 Falmouth ME, d. 17 Mar 1852 Pownal ME, m.(1)(I) 29 Oct 1785 North Yarmouth ME Huldah Pomeroy, b. ?; m.(2) 26 May 1791 Cumberland or No. Yarmouth ME Miriam True, b. 1772 d. 20 Jun 1856, dau. Abner True. Yoeman. B/S/land in Cumberland County 1799-1841. On Pownal ME tax list 1808. He bur. Lake Cemetery, North Pownal ME.

Edward M., b. 14 Aug 1792 Freeport ME, d. 28 May 1827 Durham ME, m. 7 Jun 1818 Sarah Dame of Pownal ME, b. 21 Dec 1791 d. 6 Apr 1827, dau. John and Mary (Webb) Dame. He bur. in Lake Cem, Pownal ME. CH: Esther Ann, b. 18 Jul 1819, d. 3 Jul 1893, m. 11 Feb 1841 William Johnson; Rachel, b. 1823 m. 1880 George Hunnewell. Daughters B/S/land in Pownal ME.
Rebecca, b. 26 Jan 1796, m. Joshua Marston.
11 Samuel³, b. 1798.
12 Paul³, 1800-1896.
Salome, b. 1 May 1803, d. 7 Nov 1816.
Rachel, b. 7 Sep 1805, d. 13 Nov 1806.
Hannah, b. 8 Aug 1808, d. 7 Feb 1809.
Hugh Nevens, b. 2 Oct 1815 Pownal ME, drowned 20 May 1856 Pownal ME, m. 1 Jan 1850 Mary J. Wilbur, b. 1817. Mariner. In Durham ME 1850. He bur. in Lake Cem., Pownal ME. CH: Annie L., b. 1851, m. 17 Jun 1870 Ashburnham MA J. Frank Haywood.
13 Andrew Nelson³, 1818-1882.
Daughter, b. ca. 1820.

Sources: Freeport ME census 1800. Pownal ME census 1810, 1820, 1830, 1840, 1850. VR Cumberland ME, Freeport ME, Pownal ME, SA/ME, SA/MA. R10a, L10, M5.

4. **JEREMIAH² SAWYER** [see 1] , b. (1765-1774), drowned 6 Jul 1815 in Casco Bay ME, m.(I) 12 Sep 1795 Elizabeth Dodd of Falmouth ME, b. 1770 d. 21 Jan 1839, dau. _____ and Abigail (Blackstone) Dodd. Wid. B/land in New Gloucester ME 1824.

Eunice, b. 1796, m. 23 Sep 1815 Benjamin Woodbury of New Gloucester ME.
14 Rufus³, ca. 1800-1873.
Almira, b. ?.
Abigail, b. ?.

Sources: North Yarmouth ME census 1800, 1810. Freeport ME census 1820. New Gloucester ME census 1830. VR North Yarmouth ME. G37, M5, R10a, H40.

5. **ASA² SAWYER** [see 1], b. (1765-1774) Falmouth ME, d. bef. 1830, m. Jerusha Thrasher, b. 18 May 1773 d. 10 May 1856, dau. Joseph and Susanna (York) Thrasher. S/land 1815. He bur. in Pine Grove Cem., Falmouth ME. Wid. in Pownal ME 1830, w/son in Raymond ME 1850.

2 sons, b. (1794-1800).
2 daughters, b. (1794-1800).
2 sons, b. (1800-1810).
1 daughter, b. (1800-1810).
15 Joseph Thrasher³, 1804-1853.
16 George³, b. ca. 1812.

Sources: Falmouth ME census 1800, 1810. Pownal ME census 1830. Raymond ME census 1850.

6. **WILLIAM² SAWYER** [see 1], b. 9 Feb 1769 Falmouth ME, d. 8 Feb 1856 Pownal ME, m. 1 Aug 1795 North Yarmouth ME Susannah Blake of Falmouth ME, b. ? d. bef. 1830, dau. William Blake of Westbrook ME. In Falmouth ME 1795, Freeport ME 1797, Pownal ME 1810. S/land in Pownal ME 1825-1828.

3 daughters, b. (1794-1800).
17 Benjamin³, 1795-1882.
18 William Blake³, 1797-1885.
19 Jeremiah³, 1799-1864.
Susannah, b. 28 Mar 1802, d. 18 Jan 1888, m. 24 Jan 1839 William Larabee.
Abigail, b. 6 Jun 1807, d. 19 Jan 18??, m. 1 Feb 1827 Ezra W. Field.
20 John Blake³, 1810-1855.
21 Charles S.³, 1812-1897.
Charlotte Blake, b. 29 Sep 1815, d. 15 Nov 1881, m. William Dunlop.
Rebecca Knight, b. 10 May 1818, d. 28 Oct 1885, m. Owen Wilbur.

Sources: Pownal ME census 1810, 1820, 1830, 1840, 1850. VR North Yarmouth ME, Pownal ME, SA/ME. S44.

7. **SAMUEL² SAWYER** [see 1], b. ca. 1773 North Yarmouth ME, d. 12 Dec 1844 Durham ME, m.(1) 11 Oct 1798 North Yarmouth ME Elizabeth Jacobs, b. ?; m.(2) 2 Sep 1824 Durham ME Joanna (Roberts) Turner, b. 1772 d. 27 Mar 1858. In North Yarmouth 1800, Durham ME 1810. S/land in Durham ME 1815. He bur. in Harmony Grove Cem., West Durham ME. Wid. in Durham ME 1850.

22 Samuel S.³, 1799-1840.
Daughter, b. ca. 1800.

Sources: North Yarmouth ME census 1800. Durham ME census 1810, 1820, 1830, 1840, 1850. R10a, M5, G37.

23 Edward³ ca. 1814 [see Rebecca² under Benjamin¹].

8. **JOHN³ SAWYER** [see 2], b. 13 Feb 1791, d. 5 May 1870 Monmouth ME, m.(1) Philena (Mary) Allen, b. 1792 d. 8 Jul 1826, dau. Joseph and Olive (Thompson) Allen; m.(2) 11 Mar 1827 Comfort W. Towle of New Hampshire, b. 12 Nov 1795, dau. Benjamin and Abigail (Edgerly) Towle. Farmer.

Mary, b. 13 Sep 1817, d. 12 Aug 1818.
Allen B., b. 21 May 1819, d. 19 Jan 1842.
24 Harlow Harrison⁴, 1821-1869.
Joseph Augustus, b. 12 Mar 1823, murdered 19 May 1894 Monmouth ME, unm. In Monmouth ME 1850, 1860.
John, b. 29 Jun 1826, d. 15 Oct 1826.

Sources: Monmouth ME census 1820, 1830, 1840, 1850, 1860. VR SA/ME. E7.

9. **ASA G.[3] SAWYER** [see 2], b. 1 Jan 1795 Pownal ME, d. 4 Apr 1864 Litchfield ME, m. 13 Jun 1822 Lisbon ME Dorothy Jordan of Lisbon ME, b. 1803 d. 1875, dau. William Jordan, Jr.

Emily, b. 27 May 1823, m. 27 Jul 1856 B. Frank Rowe.
25 George W.[4], 1825-1895.
Mary J., b. 6 Apr 1827, m. 9 Nov 1854 Boston MA John T. Manson.
Celia A., b. 18 Oct 1831, m. 22 Nov 1854 Boston MA Elbridge Moulton.
Elizabeth D., b. 7 Feb 1834, d. 4 Oct 1857.
Frances E., b. 4 Oct 1837, m. 4 Jul 1854 Daniel Powers.
Almira G., b. 7 Jan 1841, d. 14 Aug 1871 Litchfield ME.

Sources: Lisbon ME census 1830. Webster ME census 1840, 1850. VR SA/ME. C46, M57.

10. **REUBEN ALLEN[3] SAWYER** [see 2], b. Jun 1809 Durham ME, d. 3 Jul 1880 Lisbon ME, m. 22 Mar 1838 Durham ME Hannah Libby of Pownal ME, b. 30 May 1812 d. 28 Nov 1885, dau. Alexander and Elizabeth Libby. Farmer.

26 John Fairfield[4], b. 1839.
27 Greenfield Thompson[4], b. 1841.
28 Joseph Warren[4], 1843-1902.
Frances M. E., b. 7 Jan 1845, d. 1865, m. 4 Nov 1863 Boston MA James Tryon.
Irving Washington, b. 7 Sep 1846, d. 21 Jan 1850.
29 Allen Irving[4], 1849-1921.
30 Alfred Dow[4], 1855-1921.

Sources: Pownal ME census 1840, 1850. Durham ME census 1860. VR Pownal ME, SA/ME, SA/MA. M4, R10a, H26, L20, David Young rec.

11. **SAMUEL[3] SAWYER** [see 3], b. 13 Feb 1798 Freeport ME, m. 23 Sep 1827 Hannah Brown, b. ca. 1791 d. 23 Nov 1868. Had business in Pownal ME 1820-1830. Wid. bur. in Lake Cem., Pownal ME.

Charles W., b. ca. 1834 Pownal ME, m. 17 May 1856 Mary E. Fletcher of Milford MA, b. ?, dau. Martin and Mary Fletcher. Bootmaker.

Sources: M5, L10.

12. **PAUL[3] SAWYER** [see 3], b. 25 Aug 1800 Freeport ME, d. 28 May 1896 Durham ME, m. 18 Oct 1826 Durham ME Lydia Jones of Pownal ME, b. 25 Jul 1806 d. 30 Apr 1877, dau. William Jones. Farmer. In Pownal ME 1830, Durham ME 1865, w/son William 1880.

31 Edward Herman[4], 1827-1882.
32 John Lufkin[4], b. 1830.
Seward Nelson, b. 3 Mar 1832 Durham ME.
Mary Blake, b. 12 Mar 1836.
33 William Jones[4], 1838-1916.
Henry Harrison, b. 1 Apr 1840, d. 18 Oct 1841.
Rachel True, b. 30 Jul 1842, d. 1936, m. Orin Loring.
34 Lyman Fobes[4], 1844-1904.

Sources: Pownal ME census 1830, 1840, 1850, 1860. Durham ME census 1880. ME 1880 census index. VR Durham ME, Pownal ME. M5, R10a, G37.

13. **ANDREW NELSON[3] SAWYER** [see 3], b. 18 Aug 1818 Pownal ME, d. 25 Nov 1882 Durham ME, m. 16 Dec 1841 Durham ME Martha A. Littlefield, b. ca. 1824 d. 6 Sep 1883. Farmer. B/S/land in Cumberland County, 1841-1867.

Alonzo, b. 1844 Durham ME. Farmer.
Harriet D., b. 1851, m. _____ Partridge.

Hannah E., b. 1854.

Sources: Durham ME census 1850, 1860, ME 1880 census index. VR Durham ME. M5, R10a.

14. **RUFUS³ SAWYER** [see 4], b. 1800 North Yarmouth ME, d. 26 Feb 1873 Bangor ME, m.(I) 21 Sep 1839 New Gloucester ME Jerusha Cobb of Poland ME, b. ? d. 11 Dec 1876, dau. Joseph and Elizabeth (Loring) Cobb. B/S/land in Cumberland County, 1818-1856.

George, b. 8 Feb 1841 New Gloucester ME, d. 1922 Bangor ME, m. 5 May 1868 Bangor ME Angeline Prince of New Gloucester ME, b. 29 May 1843 d. 1927, dau. Rufus and Sophia (Brewster) Prince. Civil War: Company B, 22nd Maine Regiment. In Old Town ME 1860, Bangor ME 1880. CH: Bertha Lewella, b. 13 Apr 1877.

Joseph C., b. 6 Aug 1845, d. 7 Aug 1848.

Sources: New Gloucester ME census 1820, 1830, 1840, 1850. Old Town ME census 1860. Bangor ME census 1880. ME 1880 census index. VR Bangor ME, SA/ME. R10a, J20.

15. **JOSEPH THRASHER³ SAWYER** [see 5], b. 1804 Falmouth ME, d. 19 Jan 1853 Raymond ME, m. 29 Nov 1827 Pownal ME Elizabeth Sweetser of Portland ME, b. 1808. Farmer. In Pownal ME 1830, Portland ME 1840, Raymond ME 1850. Wid. S/land in Raymond ME 1855. All CH S/land in Raymond ME 1861.

John Henry, b. 21 Jul 1828 Raymond ME, m.(1) 9 Nov 1853 Almira Leach of Raymond ME, b. ?; m.(2) 23 Nov 1859 by Franklin Sawyer, JP, Amelia Brown of Raymond ME, b. 4 Jun 1840 d. 25 Feb 1918, dau. Samuel and Mary Ann (Whitten) Brown. Seaman, trader. In Hanover ME 1860.

Albion K. P., b. 1830 Pownal ME, m. 2 Feb 1855 Clara D. Leach of Raymond ME, b. 1833. Carpenter. In Raymond ME. Bethel ME, Bath ME, Portland ME 1864. CH: Alice, b. 14 Dec 1856; Joseph, b. Jul 1859, d. 16 Sep 1860; Charles C., b. May 1862, d. 13 Apr 1863; Nellie G., b. 9 Apr 1864.

35 Bethuel S.⁴, b. 1832.

Mary E., b. 21 Jul 1836, m. 11 Aug 1887 Portsmouth NH Ephraim Brown.

36 Joseph C.⁴, 1839-1863.

George Oscar, b. 8 Aug 1842 Raymond ME, m. 1 Feb 1865 Portland ME Ione Amelia Pingree of Oxford ME, b. 25 Jan 1842, dau. Luther and Elizabeth (Dexter) Pingree. In Hartford ME. CH: Edith Pingree, b. 26 Dec 1871, m. 17 Oct 1900 Charles L. Pettee; Judson Albro, b. 29 Jan 1874, d. 2 Oct 1877; Dudley Pingree, b. 24 May 1878, d. 19 Nov 1882.

Helen L., b. 13 Dec 1844.

Sources: Pownal ME census 1830. Portland ME census 1840. Raymond ME census 1850. Hanover ME census 1860. VR Raymond ME, SA/ME. N6, R10a, D36, K10, P27, L7.

16. **GEORGE³ SAWYER** [see 5], b. ca. 1812 (Falmouth ME?), m. 6 Jun 1837 Mary McArthur of Limington ME, b. 1818. Grocer. In Portland ME 1850.

Charles Stewart, b. 21 Feb 1838 Portland ME, m. 17 Oct 1872 Fall River MA Mary A. Keyes of Fall River MA, b. 1849, dau. Henry and Rebecca Keyes. Painter.

James M., b. 16 Dec 1839 Portland ME.

Laura, b. 9 Mar 1842, m. 20 Nov 1861 Roxbury MA Joseph H. Hammond.

Sources: Portland ME census 1840, 1850. VR SA/MA.

17. **BENJAMIN³ SAWYER** [see 6], b. 11 Aug 1795 Falmouth ME, d. 15 Oct 1882 Durham ME, m.(1) 27 Jan 1825 Durham ME Lydia Field, b. 1800 d. 17 Sep 1848, dau. Zacheriah Field; m.(2) 11 Aug 1849 New Gloucester ME Esther Maxfield of Cumberland ME, b. 1801 d. 29 Aug 1882. B/S/land in Cumberland County 1840. In Freeport ME, Pownal ME, New Gloucester ME 1840. He bur. in Davis Randall Cem., Freeport ME.

Lydia Ann, b. 26 Jun 1825, m. Simon Fickett.
37 Elijah Field[4], 1828-1906.
Lewis Field, b. 19 Jun 1829 Freeport ME, m. 7 Feb 1856 Laura Plummer, b. ?. S/land in Cumberland County 1853. In Alna ME.
Harriet B., b. 2 Nov 1832, m. Joshua Witham of Gray ME.
Melissa E., b. 12 Nov 1843, m. Edward Bowie of Durham ME.

Sources: New Gloucester ME census 1840, 1850. VR New Gloucester ME, Freeport ME. R10a, G37, S69, Bowie family Bible.

18. **WILLIAM BLAKE[3] SAWYER** [see 6], b. 25 Feb 1797 Freeport ME, d. 5 Aug 1885 New Gloucester ME, m. 11 Jan 1823 Freeport ME Eunice E. Fields of Windham ME, b. 1797 d. 1878. War of 1812. B/S/land in Cumberland County 1826-1854. He bur. in Lake Cem., Pownal ME.
Rosanna, b. 2 Oct 1823, d. 11 Mar 1912 New Gloucester ME.
Mary D., b. 15 Feb 1825, m. _____ Hunnewell.
John B., b. 7 Mar 1826 Pownal ME, d. 10 Apr 1914 New Gloucester ME. B/S/land in New Gloucester ME 1852-1860.
38 Moses F.[4], 1828-1903.
William S., b. 25 May 1829 New Gloucester ME, d. 24 Sep 1903 Portland ME, m. Amanda _____, b. ?. CH: Jennie, b. 25 Feb 1859.
Dexter W., b. 18 Feb 1831 New Gloucester ME, d. 26 Mar 1858 New Gloucester ME.
Susan A., b. 12 Jan 1833.
Joseph L., b. 26 Jul 1834 New Gloucester ME, m. 1 Jan 1859 Frances A. Coffin of Freeport ME, b. ?. In Portland ME 1859. CH: Julia V., b. 17 Oct 1859.
Sarah S., b. 10 Aug 1836.
Andrew H., b. 27 Mar 1838 New Gloucester ME, d. 18 Aug 1863 Washington DC of Civil War wounds. In Pownal ME 1860.
Eunice E., b. 17 Sep 1839.
Charlotte, b. 6 Feb 1841.

Sources: New Gloucester ME census 1830, 1840, 1850, 1860. Pownal ME census 1860. VR Freeport ME, SA/ME. M5, G37, L10, R10a.

19 **JEREMIAH[3] SAWYER** [see 6], b. 12 May 1799 Freeport ME, d. 19 Feb 1864 New Gloucester ME, m.(1) 18 Apr 1827 Durham ME Elizabeth M. Merrill of Westbrook ME, b. 1802 d. 26 Dec 1849; m.(2) 30 Mar 1851 Laura Tirney, b. ?. B/S/land in Cumberland County 1838-1864. In Pownal ME, New Gloucester ME 1840. Wid. m. _____ Small.
Charles W., b. 8 Nov 1826 New Gloucester ME, d. 13 Dec 1874 Auburn ME, m. 12 Dec 1852 Durham ME Jane H. Goss of Danville ME, b. 5 Dec 1834 d. 22 Mar 1867, dau. Benjamin and Cyrene F. (Dyer) Goss. Farmer. In New Gloucester ME 1850, Danville ME 1860. B/S/land in Cumberland County 1861-1864. CH: Eliza J., b. 27 Feb 1854, d. 14 Dec 1876, m. _____ Wright; Mary E., b. 10 Jun 1858; Emma F., b. 28 Mar 1860; Annie, b. 6 May 1865,d. 7 May 1879.
Catherine, b. 19 Nov 1832, m. 1860 Chandler Knight.
39 Royal Greenleaf[4], 1839-1908.
Mary Jane, b. ?.

Sources: New Gloucester ME census 1840, 1850. Danville ME census 1860. VR New Gloucester ME, Durham ME, Westbrook ME. R10a, Robert L. Taylor rec., David Young rec.

20. **JOHN BLAKE[3] SAWYER** [see 6], b. 5 Jul 1810 Pownal ME, d. 30 Apr 1855 Durham ME, m. 17 Jul 1831 Hannah Getchell of Durham ME, b. ca. 1813. Farmer. In Durham ME 1850. He bur. in Lake Cem., Pownal ME. Wid. in Danville ME 1860.
Mary G., b. 1832.

Almira, b. 1833.
Antress, b. 1835.
40 Henry H.[4], 1836-1919.
George W., b. 1840 Durham ME, m.(1) Lois Noyes, b. ?; m.(2) 25 Jul 1883 Watertown MA Mary A. Chase of Salem MA, b. 1856, dau. Benjamin E. and Mary S. Chase. Carpenter.
Greenleaf, b. 1842 Durham ME. In Danville ME 1860.
Emerline, b. 1846.

Sources: Durham ME census 1850. Danville ME census 1860. VR Durham ME, SA/ME, SA/MA. M5, G37.

21. **CHARLES S.[3] SAWYER** [see 6], b. 14 May 1812 Pownal ME, d. 13 Feb 1897 Pownal ME, m. 30 Apr 1840 Durham ME Abigail Wilbur of Durham ME, b. 1814 d. 1859. Farmer. B/S/land in Pownal ME 1835, 1844. In Pownal ME 1850, Poland ME 1870.

Elizabeth J., b. 15 May 1841, m. James Tuttle of New Gloucester ME.
Sophia W., b. 15 Jan 1845.
41 Albert Lewellyn[4], 1847-1916.
Martha A., b. 1851, d. 18 Feb 1939, m. _____ Fields.
Joseph R., b. Dec 1854 Pownal ME, d. 27 Nov 1912 Pownal ME, m. 14 Feb 1907 Abbie M. Arey of Durham ME, b. Aug 1860 d. 11 Nov 1921, dau. Lenos and Jeanette (Cushing) Arey. Farmer.
Hiram David, b. 3 Sep 1856 Pownal ME, m. 3 Mar 1894 Auburn ME Laura M. Gore of Gray ME, b. Jul 1855, dau. Jessie and Harriet Gore. Farmer.
Henrietta T., b. 1859.

Sources: Pownal ME census 1850, 1860. Poland ME census 1870. VR Pownal ME, Durham ME, SA/ME. M5, G37.

22. **SAMUEL S.[3] SAWYER** [see 7], b. Sep 1799 North Yarmouth ME, d. 17 Dec 1840 Durham ME, m. 13 Sep 1827 Rhoda A. Nutting of Pownal ME, b. ca. 1804. Wid. m. Samuel Jackson.

Irene, b. 1829.
Joseph David, b. ca. 1832 Durham ME. In New Gloucester ME.
42 Emery W.[4], b. 1834-1862.
Martha Ann, b. 4 Nov 1839.

Sources: Durham ME census 1830, 1840. New Gloucester ME census 1850. Lisbon ME census 1850. VR SA/ME. R10a, David Young rec.

23. **EDWARD[3] SAWYER** [see 1], b. ca. 1814 Portland ME, m. 27 May 1832 Cumberland ME Maria Stanwood of New Hampshire, b. 1805 d. 6 Jun 1878. Truckman. In Portland ME.

43 William F.[4], b. 1832.
Albert H., b. ca. 1836 Portland ME, d. 6 Sep 1899 Portland ME, m. 5 May 1873 Portsmouth NH Lizzie F. Bibber of Yarmouth ME, b. 1853 d. 20 May 1906. Blacksmith. In Portland ME. CH: William F., b. 1875.
Charles M., b. 1842 Portland ME, drowned 22 Aug 1879 Portland ME, m. 3 Sep 1861 Eliza J. Russell, b. ca. 1842. Boat fitter. In Portland ME. CH: Charles A., b. 13 Sep 1861; Clara M., b. 25 Oct 1865; Frank H., 29 Mar 1870, d. 18 Jun 1870; Sarah H., b. 29 Mar 1870, d.y.; Walter E., b. 1 Sep 1871; Cora M., b. ca. 1874; Arthur C., b. 26 Jul 1877; Elmer M., b. ca. 1879.
Henry W., b. Apr 1848, d. 31 Aug 1848.

Sources: Portland ME census 1840, 1850, 1860. ME 1880 census index. VR SA/ME. P69, M5, R10a.

24. **HARLOW HARRISON[4] SAWYER** [see 8], b. 26 Aug 1821 Monmouth ME, d. 15 Jun 1869, m. Margarette A. Atwood of Readville ME, b. 1828 d. 5 Dec 1914 Gardiner ME, dau. Jonathan and Mary (Brede) Atwood.

Alton, b. 23 Sep 1848 Wayne ME, d. 1 Mar 1922 Gardiner ME, m.(I) 12 Sep 1882 Gardiner ME Lizzie Leavitt, b. ?. Physician. In Monmouth ME.
Augusta, b. 20 Dec 1850, m. 1 Jun 1876 Frank Rideout.
44 Albert Arthur[5], 1853-1914.
Mary A., b. 21 Jun 1856, m. 21 Oct 1879 John Hinkley.
Ida M., b. 21 Jul 1859, d. 9 Aug 1867.
Ruth A. W., b. 4 Nov 1861, d. Jul 1894, m. 23 Nov 1892 Emerson Smith.
John W., b. 7 Jul 1865 Monmouth ME, d. 22 Jan 1919 Dexter ME. Physician.

Sources: VR Gardiner ME, SA/ME. C53A.

25. **GEORGE W.[4] SAWYER** [see 9], b. 16 Apr 1825 Webster ME, d. 1 Jan 1895 Lewiston ME, m. 29 Aug 1852 Harriet A. Rollins, b. 2 Jan 1828 d. 6 Sep 1908. In Litchfield ME 1860, 1870.

George M., b. 18 Jul 1853 Litchfield ME.
Elizabeth L., b. 29 Oct 1856.

Sources: Litchfield ME census 1860, 1870. VR Litchfield ME, SA/ME. C46, David Young rec.

26. **JOHN FAIRFIELD[4] SAWYER** [see 10], b. 25 Nov 1839 Pownal ME, m. Chelsea MA Fannie A. Burrill of Bangor ME, b. ?. Agent. In West Roxbury MA 1868, Chelsea MA 1873.

Emma F., b. 1863, m. 23 Nov 1883 Winthrop MA John B. Tewksbury.
Mary J., b. 3 Aug 1868, m. 25 Apr 1888 Winthrop MA Ora French.
Helen A., b. 1872, m. 22 Jan 1891 Winthrop MA Alonzo F. Coggins.
John F., b. 27 May 1873 Chelsea MA, m. Delia Sullivan, b. ?. CH: Gertrude E., b. 2 Oct 1895.
William Henry, b. 15 Aug 1874 Chelsea MA.

Sources: Chelsea MA census 1880. VR SA/MA. L20, Charles F. Sawyer rec.

27. **GREENFIELD THOMPSON[4] SAWYER** [see 10], b. 27 May 1841 Pownal ME, m. 17 Sep 1865 Boston MA Melinda B. Rice of Durham ME, b. 1843, dau. George and Dorcas Rice. Fruit dealer. In Chelsea MA 1880.

Helen, b. 23 Jul 1867.
Gertrude W., b. 1868, m. 7 Sep 1887 Chelsea MA George H. Kimball.
Grace E., b. 8 Feb 1876.
45 Greenfield Thompson[5], ca. 1886-1980.
Guy, b. ?.
Frank, b. ?.
Stephen, b. ?.

Sources: Chelsea MA census 1880. VR SA/MA. L20, Charles F. Sawyer rec., Richard B. Sawyer rec.

28. **JOSEPH WARREN[4] SAWYER** [see 10] b. 30 Mar 1843 Pownal ME, d. 22 Apr 1902 Wales ME, m. 15 Jun 1869 Biddeford ME Frances E. Bangs of Sabattus ME, b. 1844 d. 1927, dau. Stephen Bangs of Limington ME. In Biddeford ME, Wales ME 1880, Durham ME. He bur. in Pleasant Hill Cem., Sabattus ME.

46 Fred Everett[5], 1870-1945.
Mary L., b. 1872, m. _____ Dickson.
Guy W., b. 1875 Biddeford ME.
Eva L., b. 1878, m. _____ Doane.
Stephen R., b. 1882 Biddeford ME.

Greenfield, b. 1886 Biddeford ME.
Frank E., b. 1887 Biddeford ME.
Sources: Wales ME census 1880. ME 1880 census index. L20, D57, Obit, Charles F. Sawyer rec.

29. **ALLEN IRVING[4] SAWYER** [see 10], b. 17 Nov 1849 Pownal ME, d. 1 Apr 1921 Webster ME, m. 24 Aug 1871 Chelsea MA Almeda Mitchell of Webster ME, b. Jul 1850 d. 1934, dau. Charles and Ann Mitchell. Salesman. In Lisbon ME 1871, Boston MA 1883.
Willie, b. 1872, d. 1880.
Irving, b. 1880, d. same year.
47 Charles Llewellyn[5], 1883-1914.
Sources: VR SA/ME, SA/MA. L20, Charles F. Sawyer rec., Daniel Young rec.

30. **ALFRED DOW[4] SAWYER** [see 10], b. 8 Jan 1855 Pownal ME, d. 20 Jun 1921 Fort Fairfield ME, m. 1880 Mabel Carrie Spears of Lisbon ME, b. 25 Feb 1856. Graduate of NY University 1880, went to medical school in Maine. Physician, Superintendent of Schools. In Lisbon Falls ME 1881, Fort Fairfield ME 1885.
Alfred Loomis, b. 23 Dec 1881 Lisbon Falls ME, d. 14 Aug 1939, m. Eva Mills, b. ?. Went to California.
Warren, b. 5 Sep 1883 Lisbon Falls ME, d. in California. Farmer.
Herbert G., b. Apr 1886 Ft. Fairfield ME, d. Ft. Fairfield ME. Druggist. In Boston MA.
Sources: VR SA/ME, SA/MA. L20, G20A, Eva M. Sawyer rec.

31. **EDWARD HERMAN[4] SAWYER** [see 12], b. 6 Jul 1827 Durham ME, d. 18 Apr 1882 Durham ME, m. Harriet C._____, b. 1830 d. 29 Aug 1905. Wheelwright. B/land in Durham ME 1854.
48 Clarence H.[5], 1857-1889.
Sources: Durham ME census 1850, 1860. R10a.

32. **JOHN LUFKIN[4] SAWYER** [see 12], b. 18 Sep 1830 Durham ME, m. Sarah E. _____ of Richmond ME, b. ?. Housewright. In Winthrop MA.
49 Millard T.[5] (aka Sylvester), b. 1856.
Lizzie L., b. 1863, m. 1 Jun 1884 Winthrop MA Wilber H. Smith.
Albert C., b. 13 Sep 1865 Winthrop MA.
Sources: VR SA/ME, SA/MA.

33. **WILLIAM JONES[4] SAWYER** [see 12], b. 18 Feb 1838 Pownal ME, d. 3 Mar 1916 Durham ME, m. 18 May 1870 Ada A. Smith of Biddeford ME, b. 5 Sep 1853 d. 6 Jul 1922, dau. Shipley and Florilla (Bean) Smith. In Durham ME 1880. He bur. Harmony Grove Cem., Durham ME.
Son, b. 5 Dec 1870, d. 7 Dec 1870.
Mabel A., b. 4 Oct 1874, d. 20 Mar 1954 Lewiston ME.
Shepley P., b. 24 Dec 1882 Durham ME.
Ralph M., b. 14 May 1883 Durham ME, d. 10 Mar 1962 Lewiston ME, m. Carrie M. Parker, b. ?.
Cybelle M., b. 8 Oct 1884, d. 18 May 1959 Portland ME.
Charles D., b. 16 Nov 1887 Durham ME.
Perlie Winfield, b. 21 Mar 1889 Durham ME, d. 2 Oct 1918 Lisbon Falls ME, m. Meta E. Buliot of Germany, b. ?. Paper maker. CH: Ida Marie, b. Aug 1911, d. 26 Dec 1911.
Harold L., b. 14 Feb 1892 Durham ME, d. 7 Sep 1919 Freeport ME.
Lizzie J., b. 1 Aug 1900, d. 4 Jun 1939 New Gloucester ME.
Sources: Durham ME census 1880. ME 1880 census index. VR SA/ME.

34. **LYMAN FOBES[4] SAWYER** [see 12], b. 5 Nov 1844 Pownal ME, d. 28 Oct 1904 Pownal ME, m.(1) 26 Mar 1864 Durham ME Esther W. Parker, b. Jan 1845 d. 30 Jul 1875; m.(2) 30 Jun 1877 Brunswick ME Marcia E. Pollard of Brunswick ME, b. 23 Nov 1850 d. 11 Oct 1915 Lisbon Falls ME, dau. George (or Charles) and Anna (Parker) Pollard. General store owner.

Mary E., b. 21 Dec 1865.
Dora B., b. 1868, m. 9 Aug 1888 Fred T. Merrill.
Charles W., b. 1870, d.y.
50 Seward Nelson[5], 1872-1951.
Lillie J., b. 1874.
Rachel A., b. 1879, m. 22 Aug 1896 Elbridge Wallace.
Seth W., b. Jan 1883 Pownal ME. Store owner.
Harry G., b. 27 Sep 1886 Pownal ME. World War I.
Clarence A., b. 11 Apr 1889, d. 18 Apr 1892.
Carroll, b. ca. 1891 Pownal ME.

Sources: Pownal ME census 1880. ME 1880 census index. VR Pownal ME, Durham ME, Brunswick ME, SA/ME. M5, L10.

35. **BETHUEL S.[4] SAWYER** [see 15], b. 12 Aug 1832 Raymond ME, m. Sarah P.____, b. ca. 1835. B/S/land in Raymond ME 1854-1861. In Newry ME 1860, Bethel ME 1870.

Fred, b. 1854 Newry ME. In Bethel ME.
Cate L., b. 1856.
Frank H., b. 1858 Newry ME. In Bethel ME.
George O., b. 1866 Newry ME. In Bethel ME.

Sources: Newry ME census 1860. Bethel ME census 1870. R10c.

36. **JOSEPH C.[4] SAWYER** [see 15], b. 3 May 1839 Portland ME, d. 3 May 1863 Chancellorsville VA, m. 22 Jun 1861 Windham ME by Rev. Luther Wiswall Abba M. Gerry of Raymond ME, b. ?. S/father's homestead in Raymond ME 1861. Civil War. Wid. m. in Raymond ME Robert T. Smith.

51 Joseph C.[5], b. 1863.

Sources: Raymond ME census 1850. VR Windham ME, Raymond ME. C89.

37. **ELIJAH FIELD[4] SAWYER** [see 17], b. 24 Sep 1828 Freeport ME, d. 1 Sep 1906 Bath ME, m. 28 Dec 1851 Durham ME Sarah Noyes Marston of Durham ME, b. 27 Jun 1830 d. 28 May 1904, dau. Joshua and Rebecca (Sawyer) Marston. Shipbuilder. In Cumberland ME, New Gloucester ME, Bath ME 1847.

Emma, b. ?, d.y.
Ada R., b. 25 May 1856, m. 27 Dec 1876 Howard Spear.
George, b. ? d.y.
Harry Banks, b. 27 Dec 1863 Bath ME, m. 22 Aug 1889 Gertrude H. Frank of Bath ME, b. 2 Dec 1863. School teacher. In Bath ME, Washington DC, St. Paul MN. CH: Jennie May, b. 28 Jun 1894.
Jennie May, b. 27 Sep 1867, d. 20 Dec 1880.

Sources: VR Durham ME. S69, L30.

38. **MOSES F.[4] SAWYER** [see 18], b. Jan 1828 New Gloucester ME, d. 1903, m. 3 Oct 1852 Louisa Larrabee of Durham ME, b. Mar 1828 d. 17 May 1910, dau. Josiah and Elizabeth (Libby) Larrabee. In Durham ME 1860, 1880. He bur. in Maplewood Cem., Pownal ME.

Mary E., b. 1853.
Eunice E., b. 1856.

52 William L.[5], 1859-1932.
Rozener O., b. 1861.
53 Andrew Franklin[5], 1863-1956.
Alfred M., b. May 1867 Durham ME, m. 28 May 1893 Durham ME Mabel M. Currier of Durham ME, b. 1878. Farmer. He bur. Mapelwood Cemetery, Pownal ME. CH: Etta L., b. 22 Sep 1894; Winnie M., b. 31 Jul 1896, d. 30 Apr 1916 Durham ME; Millie M., b. 21 Feb 1899.
Sources: Durham ME census 1860, 1880. ME 1880 census index. VR SA/ME.

39. **ROYAL GREENLEAF[4] SAWYER** [see 19], b. 4 Jan 1839 New Gloucester ME, d. 7 Oct 1908 Derry NH, m.(1) 19 Jan 1861 Elizabeth J. Proctor of Corinna ME, b. 1840; m.(2) Lucina Anne Lunston of Londonderry NH, b. 27 Dec 1852 d. 13 May 1917, dau. John E. and Mary E. (Bancroft) Lunston. Mill worker. B/land in New Gloucester ME 1864. In Lewiston ME, Lowell MA 1874, Londonderry NH. He bur. in Forest Hill Cem., East Derry NH.
Levi Clough, b. 2 Sep 1862 New Gloucester ME, m. Etta F. Morgan of Augusta ME, b. ?. CH: Charles K., b. 3 Jun 1888, d. 5 Jun 1899.
Elizabeth D., b. 25 Jan 1863.
Charles Henry, b. 7 Mar 1874 Lowell MA, d. 31 Oct 1958 Derry NH, m. 29 Mar 1902 West Derry NH Mary Emma Quinn of Texas, b. ?, dau. James A. and Sarah J. (Hennigan) Quinn. Carpenter. In West Derry NH 1880. CH: Laurel, b. ?, m. Russell Scribner.
Annie Bell, b. 25 Jan 1877, m. 28 Sep 1893 Frank A. Ford.
Royal Greenleaf, b. 18 Jun 1882 Derry NH, d. 17 May 1903 Derry NH, unm.
54 Wilmot[5], 1886-1977.
Lillian M., b. 17 Jan 1891, d. 1981, unm.
Winfield Scott, b. 3 Dec 1895 Derry NH, d. 7 Apr 1926 Derry NH, unm.
Sources: West Derry NH census 1880. VR SA/ME, SA/MA. R10a, N6.

40. **HENRY H.[4] SAWYER** [see 20], b. 8 Apr 1836 Pownal ME, d. 17 Oct 1919 New Gloucester ME, m. 6 Jul 1859 Mary A. Libby of Auburn ME, b. 17 Apr 1836 d. 29 Mar 1916, dau. Isaac and Abigail (Hanscomb) Libby. In Danville ME, New Gloucester ME 1860. Civil War.
Victoria A., b. 1860.
Henrietta, b. 24 Feb 1861.
James Edward, b. 28 Mar 1862 New Gloucester ME, m. 20 Jan 1887 Maria Wilson of Poland ME, b. ?.
Albert Henry, b. 1 Jun 1865 New Gloucester ME, d. 27 Apr 1896 New Gloucester ME.
55 Mellen Walter[5], 1868-1943.
Sanford, b. 28 Jan 1870, d. same day.
Abby L., b. Apr 1871.
Harry, b. Aug 1872, d. 18 Mar 1873.
Almira, b. 1 Jul 1874.
Sources: New Gloucester ME census 1860, 1880. ME 1880 census index. VR SA/ME. M7A.

41. **ALBERT LEWELLYN[4] SAWYER** [see 21], b. 19 Oct 1847 Pownal ME, d. 8 Jul 1916 Pownal ME, m. 23 May 1869 Mary Abigail Campbell of Belfast ME, b. 26 Aug 1846 d. 30 Apr 1898, dau. Robert M. and Abigail (Banks) Campbell. He bur. in Lake Cem., Pownal ME.
Jessie M., b. 1871, m. 21 Sep 1898 Weare NH John L. Dow.
56 Harry Emerson[5], b. ca. 1881.
Sources: VR Pownal ME, SA/ME. N6, M5.

42. **EMERY W.⁴ SAWYER** [see 22], b. 25 Jul 1834 New Gloucester ME, d. 24 Nov 1862, m.(1) Anna B. _____, b. ca. 1831 d. 4 Feb 1856; m.(2) Elvina Bickford of Lewiston ME, b. ?. W/mother in Lisbon ME 1850.

Warren Davis, b. 8 Dec 1860 Lisbon ME, d. 8 Jan 1912 Lewiston ME, m. 10 Oct 1881 Boston MA Isabell Jones Coombs of Bath ME, b. 20 Nov 1851 d. 23 Dec 1922, dau. Isaiah and Mindwell (Curtis) Coombs. CH: Mabel Isabel, b. 11 Feb 1885.

Sources: Lisbon ME census 1850. VR SA/ME, SA/MA.

43. **WILLIAM F.⁴ SAWYER** [see 23], b. 1832 Cumberland ME, m. 7 Aug 1853 Asenath H. Libby of Windham ME, b. Mar 1828, dau. Isaac and Sally (Humphrey) Libby. Farmer. In Windham ME. S/L in Windham ME 1868.

Sarah M., b. 1854.

Mary S., b. 1860, m. 15 Jan 1881 Conway NH Andrew Johnson.

Charles W., b. ca. 1862 Windham ME, m. 9 Feb 1889 Windham ME Bertha R. Sylvester, b. ?. Farmer. In Westbrook ME. CH: Asenath, b. ca. 1891, d. 10 May 1989, m. Howard Dyer; George Sylvester, b. 2 Mar 1893; Daughter, b. 10 Nov 1894.

Howard L. b. Feb 1864 Windham ME, d. 27 May 1919 Scarborough ME, m. 4 May 1900 Conway Center NH Lizzie M.(Lion) Jordan of Nova Scotia, Canada, b. 1862, dau. John and Martha (Brown) Lion.

Nathan N., b. 1868 Windham ME.

Sources: Windham ME census 1850, 1860. VR Windham ME, SA/ME. N6, L20, R10a, Obit (Asenath).

44. **ALBERT ARTHUR⁵ SAWYER** [see 24], b. 21 Feb 1853 Monmouth ME, d. 8 Jul 1914 Monmouth ME, m.(1) 3 May 1879 Ada Trask, b. ?; m.(2) 8 Jul 1893 Monmouth ME Addie O. Brown of Hopkinton MA, b. Jun 1864. Farmer.

Harry Augustus, b. 11 Nov 1884 Monmouth ME.

Leveta, b. 7 Apr 1896, d. 8 Apr 1896.

Carl A., b. 2 Aug 1900 Monmouth ME.

Sources: VR SA/ME, SA/MA.

45. **GREENFIELD THOMPSON⁵ SAWYER** [see 27], b. ca. 1887 Monmouth ME, d. 1980 New London NH, m. Gladys Brown of Winthrop MA, b. ca. 1895 d. 11 Mar 1980. In Winthrop MA, New London NH 1942. Note: Wid. obit. says he d. 1977.

Richard B., b. ?. In Tuftonboro NH.

John C., b. ?. Went to Colorado.

Sources: Obit, Richard B. Sawyer rec.

46. **FRED EVERETT⁵ SAWYER** [see 28], b. Apr 1870 Biddeford ME, d. 1945 Sabattus ME, m. 26 Dec 1894 Auburn ME Laura Spofford, b. 1863 d. 1953. In Webster ME. He bur. in Pleasant Hill Cem., Sabattus ME.

Ray Frank, b. 23 Jun 1896.

Emma Augusta, b. 30 Dec 1897.

Sources: VR SA/ME.

47. **CHARLES LLEWELLYN⁵ SAWYER** [see 29], b. 4 Mar 1883 Boston MA, d. 14 Sep 1914 Webster ME, m. 14 Apr 1906 Margaret Wood, b. ?.

Allen Irving, b. 4 Nov 1907, m.(1) ?; m.(2) Edith _____, b. ?.

John William, b. 13 Jul 1910, d. 1982, m.(1) ?; m.(2) Dorothy M. Mooers, b. ?, dau. Walter Franklin and Edith M.(Leighton) Mooers.

Sources: VR SA/ME. Charles F. Sawyer rec.

48. **CLARENCE H.[5] SAWYER** [see 31], b. 1857 Durham ME, d. 25 Sep 1889 Durham ME, m. Boston MA Susan E. Rice of Whiting ME, b. 14 Dec 1860 d. 17 Sep 1913 Portland ME. Clerk. In Medford MA 1880.

George B., b. 10 Aug 1880 Durham ME, m. 14 Jun 1930 Portsmouth NH Mary V. D'Antuono of Boston MA, b. 1906, dau. Anthony B. (b. Italy) and Julia (Healy, b. Ireland) D'Antuoso. In Binghamton NY.

Sources: Medford MA census 1880. VR SA/ME, SA/MA.

49. **MILLARD SYLVESTER[5] SAWYER** [see 32], 14 Dec 1856 Richmond ME, m. 2 Aug 1884 Winthrop MA Elizabeth F. Howard of Plymouth MA, b. 1860, dau. Chauncey M. and Lucy J. Howard. Clerk. In Winthrop MA, Melrose MA 1885, Medfield MA 1893.

57 Howard Winthrop[6], 1885-1950.

John Stanley, b. 11 Dec 1893 Medfield MA, d. 1983, m. Margaret _____, b. ?.

Kenneth, b. ?, d. 1917, unm.

Sources: VR SA/MA. Margaret Sawyer rec.

50. **SEWARD NELSON[5] SAWYER** [see 34], b. 5 Apr 1872 Pownal ME, d. 30 Mar 1951 Saugus MA, m. Boston MA Jessie Ann Squires, b. ?. Meat cutter.

George Henry, b. ?, d.y.

Winifred Marion, b. ?, d. at 20 yrs.

Clarence A., b. ca. 1902.

Carl Augustus, b. 11 Jun 1908 Saugus MA, d. 1953, m. Edith Sproul, b. ?. CH: Carl Augustus, b. ?; Nancy Ann, b. ?, m. _____ Bertram; Thomas Seward, b. ?.

Sources: VR SA/MA. Clarence Sawyer rec., Edith Sawyer rec.

51. **JOSEPH C.[5] SAWYER** [see 36], b. 11 Nov 1863 Raymond ME, m. Louise Harmon of Harrison ME, b. 1868. Salesman. In Portland ME.

Clifford H., b. 21 Apr 1896 Portland ME, m. 3 May 1919 Portsmouth NH Elsie Smith of Portland ME, b. ?, dau. Anna Smith of England. Yoeman, US Navy. CH: Son, stillborn 30 Oct 1919.

58 Earle L.[6], b. 1898.

Sources: VR Portsmouth NH.

52. **WILLIAM L.[5] SAWYER** [see 38], b. 1859 Durham ME, d. 1932, m. 27 Nov 1895 Pownal ME Elizabeth M. Trott of Nova Scotia, Canada, b. 1868 d. 1949, dau. Henry and Sarah (Fisher) Trott. He bur. in Pownal ME.

Elsie M., b. 1 May 1897, d. 1923.

Norman L., b. 24 Oct 1898 Pownal ME, d. 1959, m.(1) 14 Apr 1930 Raymond ME Elsie E. Edwards, wid., b. 1915 d. 1935 Nova Scotia; m.(2) 15 Dec 1937 Portsmouth NH Lillian D. (McKenny) Blake of North Portland ME, b. 1900, dau. Fred W. and Nellie M.(Greenleaf) McKenny. He bur. in Pownal ME.

Sources: VR SA/ME, SA/NH.

53. **ANDREW FRANKLIN[5] SAWYER** [see 38], b. 6 Nov 1863 Durham ME, d. 21 Jun 1956 No. Yarmouth ME, m. 2 Nov 1892 Gray ME Abbie Susan Hall of Gray ME, b. 16 Feb 1869 d. 8 Nov 1949. He bur. in Walnut Hill Cem., North Yarmouth ME.

59 Elmer Hartley[6], 1893-1969.

Clifford Stanley, b. 21 Apr 1895 in Maine, d. 25 Jan 1969, m. 27 Aug 1925 Ruby H. Dodge, b. ?. CH: Jean Barbara, b. 26 May 1926, d. 6 Jun 1926.

Sources: VR SA/ME. M5, Ruby Sawyer rec.

54. **WILMOT[5] SAWYER** [see 39], b. 26 Apr 1886 Derry NH, d. 14 Oct 1977, m. Laura Lupien, b. ?.

Charlotte, b. 20 Aug 1916, m. 30 Jul 1937 Frederick Dalton of Laconia NH.

William Cleve, b. 16 Mar 1930 Manchester NH, m. Eleanor Gothberg, b. ?. In East Newport ME. Six CH.

Sources: William C. Sawyer rec.

55. **MELLEN WALTER[5] SAWYER** [see 40], b. 15 Apr 1868 New Gloucester ME, d. 1943, m. 20 May 1892 Emily E. Edwards of New Gloucester ME, b. 1874 d. 1955. In North Raymond ME. He bur. in New Gloucester ME.

Inez, b. 25 Apr 1893, d. 17 Aug 1893.

Herman P., b. 3 Jul 1895, d. 30 Jun 1914.

Lottie Ella, b. 28 May 1897.

Sources: VR SA/ME. M5, E9.

56. **HARRY EMERSON[5] SAWYER** [see 41], b. ca. 1881 Pownal ME, m. 15 Feb 1901 Portsmouth NH Mercy L. Chadsey of Pownal ME, b. ca. 1885, dau. William H. and Mary J. (Loring) Chadsey.

Hazel Eveline, b. 2 Oct 1902, m. _____.

Louise, b. ca. 1906, m. _____ Milton.

Edward Chadsey, b. 15 May 1908 Portland ME, d. 8 Feb 1979 East Hartford CT, m. Jun 1930 Dorothy Frances Bell of Brewer ME, b. 6 Mar 1906 d. 8 Jan 1973. In Berlin NH, Lewiston ME, Augusta ME, New York, New Jersey.

Elizabeth, b. ?, m. Lionel Etcher.

Sources: Raymond B. Sawyer rec.

57. **HOWARD WINTHROP[6] SAWYER** [see 49], b. 1885 Winthrop MA, d. 1950.

Priscilla, b. 1914, m. Sherwood Avery.

Winthrop, b. 1916. Went to Florida.

Marion, b. 1919, d. 1987, m. George Gunrud.

Kenneth, b. 1921. Went to Texas.

Janet F., b. 1923, m. Herbert Bartlett.

Sources: Margaret Sawyer rec.

58. **EARLE L.[6] SAWYER** [see 51], b. 17 Oct 1898 Raymond ME. In Portland ME.

Heywood A., b. ca. 1925. In Portland ME.

Linwood B., b. ca. 1926.

Sources: Heywood A. Sawyer rec.

59. **ELMER HARTLEY[6] SAWYER** [see 53], b. 21 Aug 1893, d. 23 May 1969, m. Helen M. Pike, b. 31 Oct 1895. He bur. in Walnut Hill Cem., North Yarmouth ME.

Bernard L., b. ?.

Eleanor B., b. ?.

Sources: M5, Ruby Sawyer rec.

---

## LINE 5

1. **BARNABAS[1] SAWYER**, b. ca. 1750 Cape Elizabeth ME, d. 1779 at sea on Brig *Civil Usage*, m. 26 Nov 1775 at Cape Elizabeth ME Thankful Parker, b. 1751 d. 21 Aug 1834. Mariner.

Revolutionary War: Enl. 1778. In Durham ME 1778. S/L between North Yarmouth and Durham ME 1778. Wid. m. Bradstreet Boatman.

2 Reuben[2], 1778-1862.

Barnabas, b. 31 Mar 1779 Cape Elizabeth ME, m. 24 Aug 1800 Cape Elizabeth ME Hannah Pearson of Cape Elizabeth ME, b. ?. Mariner. B/S/land in Cumberland County 1801-1824. CH: Elizabeth, b. 19 May 1801, m. 31 Aug 1830 Joseph Simonton; James L., b. 20 Mar 1803, d. 1824 in Havana, Cuba; John, b. 24 May 1805, d. 3 Jun 1805; William, b. 15 Oct 1806, d. 10 Nov 1806.

Sources: Cape Elizabeth ME census 1810, 1820, 1830, 1840. VR Cape Elizabeth ME. F21, R10a, Obit.

2. **REUBEN[2] SAWYER** [see 1], b. 8 Mar 1778 Cape Elizabeth ME, d. 4 Jul 1862 Gray ME, m. Aug 1799 Gray ME Anna Fowler of Gray ME, b. Aug 1779 d. 3 Feb 1858, dau. John and Mary (Webster) Fowler. B/S/land in Gray ME, 1801-1803. S/land on Cape Elizabeth ME. He bur. in Gray ME.

3 Reuben[3], 1801-1867.

Charlotte, b. 7 Jun 1804, d. 28 Apr 1877, m. 4 May 1828 Reuben Morse.

4 John Fowler[3], 1807-1897.

Caroline F., b. 4 Nov 1811, d. 12 Jul 1852, m. 7 Nov 1837 James Merrill.

5 Joseph Parker[3], 1814-1898.

Mary E., b. 1818, d. 22 Aug 1835.

Rebecca, b. ?

Julia A., b. 3 Jul 1825, d. 18 Feb 1897, m. 18 Oct 1847 John W. Stubbs.

Sources: Gray ME census 1810, 1830, 1840, 1850, 1860. New Gloucester ME census 1820. VR Gray ME, SA/ME. R10a, H26, M36, H40, P33, Gerald Kimball rec.

3. **REUBEN[3] SAWYER** [see 2], b. Jan 1801 Gray ME, d. 17 Apr 1867 Gray ME, m. 20 Feb 1823 Hebron ME Mary Chadbourne of Oxford ME, b. 30 Jun 1801 d. 31 Jul 1850. In New Gloucester ME, Gray ME. He bur. in Gray ME.

Adelaid, b. 18 Jan 1824, d. 23 Jan 1845.

Lucy, b. 16 Apr 1825, d. 5 Feb 1908, m.(I) 1 Jun 1855 James Hall.

Daughter, b. 1827, d. 14 Jun 1827.

Samuel B., b. 18 Feb 1828 Poland ME, d. 3 Dec 1910 Gorham ME, m. 29 Aug 1849 in Gray ME Elizabeth B. Strout of Raymond ME, b. 25 Oct 1827 d. 2 Jan 1899, dau. Joshua and Martha (Tyler) Strout. Minister, butcher. S/land in Gray ME 1851, Gorham ME 1858. He bur. in North Street Cem., Gorham ME. CH: Son, b. Apr 1850, d. 23 May 1850; Mary Ella, b. 25 Jun 1851, d. 14 Mar 1836, m.(1) Herbert Johnson, m.(2) Mayne Johnson; Annie E., b. 25 Sep 1853, m. 3 Jan 1873 Howard D. Cloudman; SarahH., b. ?, m. 30 Oct 1876 Norris Wescott; Eliza C., b. 29 Jan 1861, d. 27 Mar 1908, m. Van W. Carll; Fannie E., b. 22 Apr 1874, d. 30 Apr 1895 Gorham ME.

Sarah M., b. Sep 1831, d. 26 Jan 1854 Boston MA, m. Bella Prince.

6 John Durgin[4], 1838-1917.

Sources: Gray ME census 1830, 1840, 1850. Gorham ME census 1860, 1870, 1880. ME 1880 census index. VR Gray ME, SA/ME. K10, R10a, Obit, Clifton Sargent rec., Gerald Kimball rec.

4. **JOHN FOWLER[3] SAWYER** [see 2], b. 12 Oct 1807 New Gloucester ME, d. 11 May 1897 Gray ME, m. 21 Nov 1833 in Gray ME Melinda Perley of Gray ME, b. 12 Oct 1812 d. 16 Nov 1903, dau. Isaac and Eunice (Hancock) Perley. Farmer. Selectman for Gray ME 1841. B/S/land in Gray ME 1833-1848. Will dated 31 Jul 1892. Bur. in Gray ME.

7 Albert Newell[4], 1834-1879.

Lucinda Perley, b. 13 Jul 1837, d. 29 Oct 1878, m. 30 Jun 1861 Frank Lawrence.

Janette B., b. 23 Jan 1843, d. 21 Mar 1920, unm.

Willard P., b. 17 Aug 1848 Gray ME, d. 4 Dec 1928 Gray ME, m. 3 May 1873 Mary L. Perley, b. 19 Jan 1847, dau. John H. and Mary S. (Starbird) Perley. He bur. in Gray ME. No CH.

8 Cephas Franklin[4], 1852-1937.

Sources: Gray ME census 1840, 1850. VR SA/ME. P82a, R10a, P33, Clifton Sargent rec., Gerald Kimball rec.

5. **JOSEPH PARKER[3] SAWYER** [see 2], b. 6 Jun 1814 Gray ME, d. 10 Jan 1898 Gray ME, m. 18 Jan 1838 Gray ME Jane Tyler Strout of Raymond ME, b. 15 Aug 1818 d. 17 Sep 1889 Raymond ME, dau. Joshua and Martha (Tyler) Strout. B/land in Gray ME 1837. S/L in Gray ME 1839. S/land 1842. He bur. in Gray ME.

9 Greenleaf[4], 1839-1918.

Parker W., b. 25 Feb 1840 Westbrook ME, d. 19 May 1900 Dry Mills (Gray) ME, m. 28 Aug 1866 Gray ME Annie M. Morse of Gray ME, b. 26 Feb 1850 d. 2 Jul 1919, dau. Marshall and Maria (Foster) Morse. Town Treasurer for Gray ME 1884-1888. In North Yarmouth ME, Gray ME. No CH.

10 Alonzo[4], 1842-1916.

Lewis M., b. 24 Jun 1847 North Yarmouth ME, d. 9 Mar 1917 Gray ME, m.(1) 9 Jan 1877 Portland ME Helen M. Wilbur, b. ?; m.(2) Emma _____, b. Apr 1866. Salesman. In No. Yarmouth ME 1850, Winthrop MA.

Clara J., b. 1850, m. 1 Sep 1884 Thomas King.

Annie, b. ?.

Ada, b. ?.

Sources: Gray ME census 1840. North Yarmouth ME census 1850. VR SA/ME. R10a, Obit (Parker), Gerald Kimball rec.

6. **JOHN DURGIN[4] SAWYER** [see 3], b. 31 Jun 1838 Gray ME, d. 19 Dec 1917 Gray ME, m. 15 Apr 1867 Clara A. Thayer, b. 29 Jun 1845 d. 7 May 1925, dau. Warren and Mary (Goff) Thayer. Civil War. Bur. in Gray ME.

Mary H., b. 30 Oct 1867, d. 14 Feb 1923, m. 14 Jun 1891 Fred Barton of Gray ME.

Horace A., b. Nov 1869 Gray ME, d. 1914 in California.

Cora Adelaide, b. 13 Sep 1871, d. 1945, m. 6 Jun 1901 Elmer Perley.

Samuel, b. 21 Aug 1874 Gray ME, d. 30 Oct 1949 Gray ME, unm. Blind.

Reuben, b. 11 Jan 1878 Gray ME, d. 3 Sep 1957 Fryeburg ME, m. Mary Rackley, b. ?. He bur. in Sebego ME. No CH.

Susie, b. Nov 1880, d. 22 Jun 1957, m. Esruff Townsend.

John Durgin, b. 1882, d. 1948, unm.

Winfield, b. 15 Nov 1884 Gray ME, d. 2 Mar 1961.

Sources: Gray ME census 1880. ME 1880 census index. VR SA/ME. M7A, C89, P33, Gerald Kimball rec.

7. **ALBERT NEWELL[4] SAWYER** [see 4], b. 6 Sep 1834 Gray ME, d. 21 Jan 1879 Gray ME, m. 15 Oct 1863 in Portland ME Clarice O. Small of Gray ME, b. Nov 1836 d. 4 Sep 1912, dau. James and Susan (Huston) Small. Teacher. School Supervisor 1861, Town Treasurer for Gray ME 1867, State Representative 1870. He bur. in Gray ME.

Abbie H., b. 21 May 1865, d. 7 Mar 1922, unm. Teacher in Portland ME.

Wilbert Perley, b. 13 Dec 1867 Gray ME, d. 1918 Chicago IL, m. Gertrude A. Davis of Lewiston ME, b. 20 May 1868 d. 7 Nov 1948, dau. Amos and Mary E. (Judkins) Davis. He bur. in Clough Cem., Lewiston ME. CH: Agnes G., b. 18 Oct 1894, m. 2 Aug 1916 Kingsbury E. Parker.

Sources: VR Gray ME, Portland ME, SA/ME. P33, Clifton Sargent rec., Gerald Kimball rec.

8. **CEPHAS FRANKLIN⁴ SAWYER** [see 4], b. 4 Sep 1852 Gray ME, d. 2 Jan 1937 Gray ME, m. 3 Aug 1876 Gray ME Florence Marion Low of Amesbury MA, b. Aug 1855 d. 10 Jun 1920, dau. Robert and Joanna (Skillins) Low. He bur. in Gray ME.

Cephas Henry, b. ca. 1880 Gray ME, d. Gray ME, unm. Bur. in Gray ME.

Percy W., b. 18 Sep 1882 Gray ME, d. 2 Mar 1939 Augusta ME. Bur. in Gray ME.

Eva, b. 1883, d. 23 Dec 1933, m. Roland Whitney.

Henry William, b. 7 Mar 1893 Gray ME.

Sources: VR SA/ME. P33, Gerald Kimball rec.

9. **GREENLEAF[4] SAWYER** [see 5], b. 2 Feb 1839 North Yarmouth ME, d. 27 Nov 1918 Gray ME, m. 5 May 1858 in Gray ME Phebe E. Prince, b. Mar 1838. Carpenter. In North Yarmouth ME 1850, Gray ME 1860. He bur. in Gray ME.

11 George Freeman[5], 1858-1940.

12 Herbert James[5], 1866-1956.

Lizzie A., b. 1868, d. 22 Jun 1924, m. 7 Jan 1888 Boston MA Eben Harmon.

Charles Greenleaf, b. 13 Jun 1871 Gray ME, d. 17 Apr 1945 Gray ME, m.(1) 25 Nov 1896 Gray ME Edith W. Mayberry of Lawrence MA, b. ca. 1879; m.(2) Gray ME Josephine Sawyer, b. 1882 d. 5 May 1952, dau. Fred and Ada (Carlton) Sawyer. He bur. in Gray ME. CH: Mary (adopted), b. ?, m.(1) Forrest Gay, m.(2) Louis Vellieux, m.(3) Elwood Hersey; Vera, b. ?, m.(1) ?, m.(2) _____ White, m.(3) _____ Ring.

Clarence J., b. 24 Feb 1874 Gray ME, d. 15 May 1950 New Gloucester ME, m. Ethel Estes, b. ?, dau. Alverdo and Mary (Strout) Estes. He bur. in Upper Gloucester ME.

13 Ira Prince[5], 1878-1945.

Joseph Parker, b. 4 Oct 1880 Gray ME, d. 31 Dec 1949 Gray ME, m. Emma Tweedie of New Brunswick, Canada, b. 1880 d. 1948. Carpenter, farmer. Bur. in Gray ME. CH: Isabelle K., b. 20 Sep 1908, m.(1) Ormond Hayes, m.(2) Harold Manson.

Sources: North Yarmouth ME census 1850. Gray ME census 1860, 1870, 1880, 1900. ME 1880 census index. VR SA/ME. Gerald Kimball rec.

10. **ALONZO[4] SAWYER** [see 5], b. 5 Nov 1842 Gray ME, d. 4 Feb 1916 North Yarmouth ME, m. 27 Feb 1868 in Gray ME Emma (Eunice?) Hall, b. 12 Dec 1848 d. 15 Oct 1924, dau. Joshua and Eliza (Lufkin) Hall. Fish dealer. He bur. in Gray ME.

Cora B., b. 1869, m. _____ Chapman of New Hampshire.

Irwin J., b. 29 Mar 1888 North Yarmouth ME, d. 8 Apr 1972 Portland ME, m. Florence P. Libby of Portland ME, b. ?, dau. Willis and Kate (Walker) Libby. He bur. in Pine Grove Cem., Falmouth ME. CH: Constance, b. ?, m. Joseph J. Dugan of Watertown MA.

Sources: North Yarmouth ME census 1850, 1860, 1870, 1880, 1900. Gerald Kimball rec.

11. **GEORGE FREEMAN[5] SAWYER** [see 9], b. 23 Jul 1858 North Yarmouth ME, d. 20 May 1940 Phillips ME, m.(1) 22 Aug 1880 in Gray or Windham ME by Rev. Luther Wiswell Mary A. Mayberry of Windham ME, b. 14 Aug 1850 d. 30 Jan 1886; m.(2) 6 Aug 1888 in Gray ME Nellie H. (Wood) Chase of Lewiston ME, b. 19 Sep 1861 d. 6 Jan 1907, dau. Samuel M. and Sarah P. Wood; m.(3) 3 Apr 1909 in Bridgton ME (later div.) Elizabeth Roes of Bridgton ME, b. ?. Farmer. He bur. in Gray ME.

Elizabeth A., b. 23 Apr 1881, d. 13 Jan 1949, m.(1) Daniel Donovan, m.(2) Fred S. Calden.

14 Hannabal William[6], 1882-1961.

Bertha C., b. 21 Sep 1884, d. Aug 1950, m. George Burleigh.

15 Walter[6], 1889-1963.

16 Orrin Higgins[6], 1891-1941.

17 Greenleaf Freeman[6], 1893-1952.
Sadie E., b. 25 Nov 1895, d. Jun 1954, m. Rufus Spiller.
Sources: VR Windham ME. Gerald Kimball rec.

12. **HERBERT JAMES[5] SAWYER** [see 9] b. 2 Apr 1866 Gray ME, d. 24 Apr 1956 Windham ME, m.(I) 7 Jul 1891 Dixmont ME Alice E. Daman of Bangor ME, b. May 1875 d. 1949. In Bridgton ME. He bur. in Gray ME.
Harriet H., b. 11 Feb 1893, d. 24 Sep 1955, m.(1) Roy Webb, m.(2) Azel Faunce.
Harold John, b. 31 May 1902, d. 25 Dec 1960, m. Alice C. Delano
Sources: VR Gray ME, SA/ME. Robert L. Taylor rec., Gerald Kimball rec.

13. **IRA PRINCE[5] SAWYER** [see 9], b. 14 Mar 1878 Gray ME, d. 17 Jun 1945 Gray ME, m.(1) 24 Nov 1900 Mildred E. Foster, b. 2 Jun 1881 d. 20 Feb 1918, dau. Levi S. and Mary (Higgins) Foster; m.(2) Alice Vannah of Jefferson ME, b. 8 Sep 1876 d. 14 Dec 1945, dau. Ambrose and Mary (Mosher) Vannah. Millwright. He bur. in Gray ME.
Bernard, m. Grace Anderson.
Leroy P., b. 1914, d. 1984, m. Ada Grover Hunt. Went to California.
Sources: VR SA/ME. Gerald Kimball rec.

14. **HANNABAL WILLIAM[6] SAWYER** [see 11], b. 23 Sep 1882 Gray ME, d. Oct 1961 Yarmouth ME, m. Lucy Ann Whitney, b. ?, dau. Peter and Mary (Foster) Whitney. In Gray ME, Dover-Foxcroft ME. He bur. in Gray ME.
Victoria, b. 24 May 1909, d. 1969, m. Stanley M. Skillings.
Philip J., b. 11 Apr 1911, m. Kathleen _____, b. ?. Went to Fryeburg ME.
Gwendolyn, b. 4 Jan 1913, d. Sep 1970, m. Elmer A. Skillings.
Frank Wilbur, b. 29 Mar 1914, d. 1963, m. Bertha Burleigh, b. ?.
Mary, b. 4 Mar 1916, d. 23 Jul 1990, m. James S. King.
Thurza, b. 15 Oct 1922, m. Howard Hines.
Sources: Obit (Mary), Gerald Kimball rec.

15. **WALTER[6] SAWYER** [see 11], b. 18 Aug 1889, d. 21 Jan 1963 Harrison ME, m. Marcia Guilford, b. ?. He bur. in Bridgton ME.
Isabelle, m. Harvey Chapman. Irma, m. Alvah Nason.
Clifford, m. Anna Scappaticci.
Everett, m. Althea Lord.
Sources: Gerald Kimball rec.

16. **ORRIN HIGGINS[6] SAWYER** [see 11], b. 18 Jun 1891 Gray ME, d. 24 Jul 1941 (Dunston ME?), m. Nina (Guilford) Ayer of Hiram ME, b. 30 Jun 1885 d. 1 Nov 1918, dau. Herbert and Hattie (Stores? Stoves?) Guilford. In Bridgton ME.
Marguerite, b. 3 Sep 1908, m. 24 Oct 1935 Phineas Meserve.
Hiram, b. 21 Sep 1910, d. 22 Sep 1910.
Raymond, b. 19 Oct 1911, m. Geraldine Church, b. ?.
Harriet L., b. 13 Jun 1913, m. Laurel Haynes.
Earl Herbert, b. 24 Feb 1918, m. Helen Church, b. ?.
Sources: VR SA/ME. Gerald Kimball rec.

17. **GREENLEAF FREEMAN[6] SAWYER** [see 11], b. 21 Sep 1893 Gray ME, d. 20 Sep 1952 Wilton ME, m. 30 Jan 1916 Lottie A. Smith, b. 24 Feb 1893 d. 16 Sep 1959. In Bridgton ME. He bur. in Wilton ME.

Leland, adopted, b. 5 Dec 1913 Pittsfield ME, d. 17 Jan 1977, m. Ruth Crockett. In Wilton ME, Farmington ME, Pittsfield ME, New York. He bur. Wilton ME. CH: Sylvia, Meredith, Leland Dwight, Faith, Darien, Candyce, Darleen.

Earl, b. ?, d. 1917.

William, b. 3 Nov 1918 Wilton ME, m. Louise Ranger. CH: David E., b. 2 Mar 1947, m. Judith Martin; Anita, b. 22 Mar 1948, m.(div.) Garnit Wilson; Robert W., b. 4 Apr 1949, d. 23 Aug 1968 in Vietnam; Irene, b. 26 Jun 1950, m. James Sullivan.

Sources: Gerald Kimball rec.

---

## LINE 6

1. **ABRAM[1] SAWYER**, b. ca. 1750 in Maine, d. bef. Oct 1821 Kittery ME, m.(I) 27 Mar 1773 Wells ME Eunice Cutts, b. 15 Nov 1752, dau. Robert and Hannah (Bartlett) Cutts.

Sarah L. b. ?, m. William Shillabar.

2 Richard Cutts[2], ca. 1777-1844.

Sources: Kittery ME census 1800. VR Wells ME. P82k, S70, P69.

2. **RICHARD CUTTS[2] SAWYER** [see 1], b. ca. 1777 in Maine, d. 24 Nov 1844 Portland ME, m.(I) 2 Oct 1803 Portland ME Lydia Woodbury of Portland ME, b. 1787 d. 7 Dec 1846. Blacksmith. He bur. in Eastern Cem., Portland ME.

3 Enoch[3], 1806-1878.

Woodbury, b. 9 Aug 1808, d. 16 Sep 1810.

Lydia, b. 16 Apr 1811, d. 10 Jan 1813.

Thomas C., b. 10 Jan 1813, d. 29 Feb 1832 Portland ME.

Harriet C., b. 10 Jan 1813.

Sources: Portland ME census 1820, 1830, 1840. H78, M5, P69.

3. **ENOCH[3] SAWYER** [see 2], b. 20 Apr 1806 Portland ME, d. 24 Sep 1878 Portland ME, m. 14 Jul 1829 Priscilla H. Bartlett, b. Nov 1809 d. 1 May 1888. Blacksmith. B/S/land in Portland ME 1831.

Woodbury Dean, b. 29 Apr 1830 Portland ME, d. Jun 1892, m. Oct 1878 E____ Somerville, b. ?. Printer. CH: Harriet W., b. 6 Feb 1881.

4 Melville[4], 1833-1901.

Enoch, b. 2 Nov 1837, d. 24 Feb 1854.

Mary A., b. 18 Aug 1839, d. 23 May 1869, m. 7 Apr 1869 Robert Bryant.

John Hanson, b. 2 May 1844 Portland ME, m. Mary Quinn, b. ?.

Sources: Portland ME census 1830, 1840, 1850, 1860. VR SA/ME. R10a, H78, P69.

4. **MELVILLE[4] SAWYER** [see 3], b. 28 May 1833 Portland ME, d. 24 Nov 1901 Nashua NH, m. 16 Aug 1859 Lewiston ME Harriet A. Hayes of Lewiston ME, b. 24 Oct 1837, dau. William and Hannah (Boynton) Hayes. Blacksmith. Went to St Louis MO.

Harriet P., b. 11 Nov 1861.

Melville Woodbury, b. 4 Nov 1863 Portland ME. Colonel in Missouri militia.

Sources: VR SA/NH. H78, R15.

---

## LINE 7

1. **EPHRAIM[1] SAWYER**, b. 5 Aug 1751, d. 12 May 1823 E. Granby CT, m. 20 Nov 1774 Lyme CT Jemima Hill, b. ?. Revolutionary War: Served one year with Captain Jewett. In Lyme CT, New London CT, Saybrook CT, E. Haddam CT.

Betsey, b. 1 Nov 1775, m. 3 Apr 1797 Elijah Hill of Granby CT.
Polly, b. 22 Nov 1777.
2 David[2], 1780-1851.
Temperance, b. 30 Dec 1784.
Ephraim, b. 1786, d. 6 Nov 1789.
3 John[2], b. 1789.
Ephraim, b. 10 Feb 1792 E. Haddam CT.
Jemima, b. 10 Feb 1792.
Clarinda, b. ?, m. 22 Sep 1799 Harris Watrous.

Sources: New London CT census 1790. Saybrook CT census 1800. E. Haddam CT census 1810. VR Lyme CT.

2. **DAVID[2] SAWYER** [see 1], b. 6 Feb 1780 Lyme CT, d. 23 May 1851 Chester CT, m. 14 Mar 1804 Chester CT Lydia Baldwin, b. 20 Sep 1776, dau. James and Ruth (Shipman) Baldwin. Ship carpenter. In Killingworth CT, Saybrook CT, Chester CT. Lydia received inheritance from her grandfather James Baldwin 1819.

Martha Baldwin, b. 1805, d. 28 Feb 1885, m. 27 Sep 1828 Amos Dickinson.
4 David L.[3], b. 1809.
Lucia, b. 14 Jan 1811, m. 5 Sep 1852 Jonathan Morgan of Lyme CT.
Son, b. 14 Jan 1811, d. 3 Feb 1811.
Lydia A., b. ?, m. Edwin Ackley.
John M., b. ca. 1814 Killingworth CT (?), m. Maria Snow, b. ?.
Ephraim G., b. ca. 1815, m.(1) Wealthy Ann _____, b. 1816 d. 2 Jan 1842; m.(2) 9 Oct 1842 Julia Wooding of Massachusetts, b. 1818. Locksmith. In New Haven CT. CH: Son, b. Aug 1841, d. 15 Nov 1842; Ellen, b. 1844; Son, b. 1846, d. 8 Jan 1849; Laura, b. 1848; Child, stillborn, b. 13 Nov 1849.
5 Daniel M.[3], b. ca. 1817.
Lucy A., b. 1819, m. Enoch Barnes.

Sources: Killingworth CT census 1810. Saybrook CT census 1830. Chester CT census 1840, 1850. VR Saybrook CT. B11, H65, S52.

3. **JOHN[2] SAWYER** [see 1], b. 14 Sep 1789 East Haddam CT, m. Lucy _____, b. 1794. In East Haddam CT.

L. Melissa, b. 1831.
John A., b. ca. 1833 East Haddam CT.

Sources: East Haddam CT census 1810, 1850.

4. **DAVID L.[3] SAWYER** [see 2], b. 1 Jan 1809 (Killingworth CT ?), m.(1) 27 Nov 1834 H. Almira Watrous Willard of Chester CT, b. 31 Aug 1812 d. 11 May 1841, dau. Daniel and Sarah (Stillman) Willard; m.(2) 12 Mar 1843 Eunice J. Wilcox of Killingworth CT. In Saybrook CT, Chester CT, Deep River CT.

Son, b. (1835-1840).
Caroline, b. ca. 1837.
Edwin A., b. ca. 1844 Chester CT.
Frederick, b. ca. 1846 Chester CT.
Almira, b. ca. 1848.

Juniata M., b. ca. 1850.
Sources: Chester CT census 1840, 1850. B11, P63.

5. **DANIEL M.$^3$ SAWYER** [see 2], ca. 1817, m. 22 May 1841 Maryann Woodstock of Clinton CT, b. ?. Mechanic. In Chester CT.
Daughter, b. 11 Sep 1843, d. 2 Oct 1843.
Enoch A., b. 21 Dec 1848 Chester CT.
Daughter, b. 3 Nov 1856.
Sources: Chester CT census 1850. B11.

---

## LINE 8

1. **JOHN$^1$ SAWYER**, b. 1752 Falmouth ME, d. 6 Apr 1810 Freedom ME, m. 27 Oct 1771 Falmouth ME Lettice Whitney, b. 1752 d. 23 Nov 1841. Revolutionary War. Both joined 1st Church of Falmouth 25 Oct 1772. B/S/land in Standish ME 1782-1804. Note: John may have been the son of Thomas$^3$ (Isaac$^2$, James$^1$), 1711-1765 and Mehitable Sawyer of Falmouth ME. One of John's CH was named Thomas, both he and Thomas$^3$ had a son named Jonathan, and each had a daughter named Jerusha. Moreover, the timing of John's birth was right. As these links are tenuous, however, John and his descendants are carried here as an unconnected line.
Jerusha, b. 14 Sep 1772, d 18 Apr 1851, m. 11 Jun 1791 Seth Hamblin of Brownfield ME.
Susannah, b. 7 Aug 1774.
2 Thomas$^2$, ca. 1775.
3 John$^2$, 1777-1846
Jonathan Lowell, b. 28 Feb 1779 Standish ME.
Selina, b. 1781, d. 27 Jan 1826, m. 17 Jul 1800 William Chick.
Polly, b. Oct 1783, m. Stephen G. Wiggin.
Barbara, bp. 23 Sep 1787, m. Charles Wiggin.
Lettice, bp. 9 Oct 1791, m. 17 Mar 1809 Thomas McLaughlin.
Anna, b. ?, m. Henry Beal.
Dorcas, b. 22 Jul 1796, d. 31 Jan 1885, m. John Wiggin.
Sources: Standish ME census 1790, 1800, VR Brownfield ME, SA/ME. W44, K10A, H26, R10a, M5, Will.

2. **THOMAS$^2$ SAWYER** [see 1], b. ca. 1775 Standish ME, lost at sea bef. 1806, m. 13 Sep 1798 Standish ME Hannah Simpson of Standish ME, b. ?, dau. Jonathan and Alice (Peach) Simpson. Mariner. B/land in Hampden ME 1791, Falmouth ME 1797, 1804, Standish ME 1801. Wid. remarried 1806.
4 William$^3$, b. 1799.
Sources: Hampden ME census 1800. R10d, P30.

3. **JOHN$^2$ SAWYER** [see 1], b. 31 Jan 1777 Standish ME, d. 5 Feb 1846 Knox ME, m.(1) 22 Jan 1797 Gorham ME Susannah Hamblen of Gorham ME, b. 7 Aug 1774 d. 1 Jan 1824 Knox ME, dau. Ebenezer and Deborah (Lovell) Hamblen; m.(2) 21 Oct 1825 Mary Todd, b. ?. B/S/land in Knox ME 1810. Will dated 6 Sep 1842.
Fanny, b. 21 Jun 1797, m. John Colby.
5 John$^3$, 1799-1870.
Ebenezer, b. 6 Apr 1801 Knox ME, m. 11 Sep 1823 Abigail Thompson, b. ?. In Montville ME. CH: Mary Ann, b. ca. 1826, m. 26 Apr 1874 Chicopee MA Orlando Rich.
6 Isaac$^3$, 1804-1862.
7 Thomas$^3$, 1806-1884.

Lettis, b. 22 Aug 1808.
Susannah, b. 11 Jun 1811.
8 William C.[3], 1814-1850.
Eliza H., b. 31 Jul 1817, m. _____ Tucker.
Sources: Standish ME census 1800. Knox ME census 1810, 1820, 1830, 1840. VR SA/MA. M8A, D51, P82j, R10e, Obit.

4. **WILLIAM[3] SAWYER** [see 2], b. 13 Nov 1799 Gorham or Hermon ME, m.(1) 1819 Eliza Hewes of Hermon ME, b. ? d. 1829; m.(2) 8 Mar 1832 Hampden ME Jane Miller of Hampden ME, b. 1800. Farmer. B/land in Hampden ME 1826, 1828, 1831. Note: Son William's death record says his father was b. in Freedom NH.
9 Sylvester H.[4], 1828-1884.
William, b. 25 Jan 1830 Hermon ME, d. 28 Aug 1894 Newburgh ME, m. Hannah _____, b. ?. Butcher. In Newburgh ME 1850.
Eliza J., b. 1833, m.(I) 3 Sep 1856 Ray Cooper of Hampden ME.
Elizabeth A., b. 1835, m. Job Collett of Bangor ME.
Ruth M., b. 1837, m. Lyman Miller of Newburgh ME.
Henrietta, b. 1839.
John, b. 16 May 1841 (twin) Hermon ME, d. 12 Jun 1902, m. 19 Nov 1874 Chelsea MA Elizabeth Fernald of Shapleigh ME, b. 1838, dau. Frederick B. and Betsey Fernald. Farmer. Civil War: Company K, 2nd Maine Infantry for two years; Sergeant; wounded three times.
Lucetta, b. Mar 1841 (twin), d. 5 Sep 1922, m. 5 Oct 1862 Peter Works.
10 Charles T.[4], b. 1843.
Sources: Hermon ME census 1830, 1840. Newburgh ME census 1850. VR Bangor ME, SA/ME, SA/MA. P30, D51, R10d, M7A.

5. **JOHN[3] SAWYER** [see 3], b. 12 Feb 1799 Knox ME, d. 14 Apr 1870 Knox ME, m. 3 Sep 1820 Knox ME Lavina Blodgett of Freedom ME, b. 13 Dec 1801 d. 5 Sep 1879, dau. Luther and Sally (Hilyard) Blodgett of Camden ME. B/land in Montville ME 1827, 1832, 1844. S/land in Knox ME 1848. In Bradley ME. Both bur. East Knox ME Cem.
Alfred Marshall, b. 1820, d. 1 Apr 1840 Belfast ME.
Ann B., b. 18 May 1823, d. 18 Jan 1862, m. _____ Brown.
Lucy W., b. 3 Nov 1831, m. Lemuel Wentworth.
Thomas Albert, b. 14 Oct 1833 Montville ME, d. 16 May 1896 Belfast ME, m. 12 Aug 1852 Appleton ME Phebe Farnham of Knox ME, b. 27 Apr 1828 d. 28 Oct 1910, dau. Joseph and Hannah (Clough) Farnham. In Knox ME. Appointed executor of father's will. He bur. East Knox ME cem. CH: John Herbert, b. 1 Feb 1854, d. 16 Dec 1863; Flora M., b. 1855, d. 1916, m. Joel E. Dodge; Lucinda E., b. 29 Oct 1857, d. 10 May 1902, m.(I) 9 Jun 1874 Elisha Sherman.
Lucinda Esther, b. 24 Jan 1836, d. 15 Sep 1856 Bradley ME.
11 John Gilbert[4], 1837-ca. 1867.
Alfred Marshall, b. 4 Jul 1841, d. 4 Feb 1862 in Civil War, unm.
Emma J., b. 1844.
Sources: Montville ME census 1820, 1840. VR Appleton ME, SA/ME. P82j, R10e, T12, W26, M5.

6. **ISAAC[3] SAWYER** [see 3], b. 7 Mar 1804 Knox ME, d. 16 May 1862 Knox ME, m. 3 Oct 1824 Susan Gowin, b. 8 Nov 1803 d. 6 Sep 1865. Farmer. B/land in Unity ME 1828, 1831, 1832. In Montville ME 1840, Thorndike ME 1850. He bur. Knox Station cem.
12 Nathan[4], 1825-1908.

Lettis, b. 1830.
Betsey A., b. 1832.
Fanny, b. 1835.
Augustus, b. 1838 (Montville ME?), d. 1872 Knox ME, m.(I) 16 Nov 1861 Thorndike ME Lydia P. Batchelder, b. 1831.
Rachel, b. 1840.
13 James Loring[4], 1843-1888.
Riley, b. 1845 (Thorndike ME?).
14 Asa[4], 1848-1920.
Sources: Montville ME census 1840, 1870. Thorndike ME census 1850. VR Thorndike ME, Belfast ME, Rockland ME, SA/ME. P82j, R10e, M8A, M5.

7. **THOMAS[3] SAWYER** [see 3], b, 12 Apr 1806 Knox ME, d. 28 Mar 1884 Knox ME, m. 4 Nov 1832 Montville ME Betsey A. Murray of Belfast ME, b. 27 Mar 1810 d. 30 Mar 1893, dau. Jonathan and Ann (Grant) Murray. S/land in Knox ME 1842. Will dtd 30 Jun 1881. Both bur. Knox Ridge ME cem.
Mary E., b. 17 Oct 1833, d. 16 Oct 1861 m. A. V. Sawtelle.
Orland, b. 1835 Knox ME.
Almeda, b. 9 Jul 1839, d. 28 Nov 1858.
Laura M., b. 1844, m. _____ Evans.
Weston, b. 26 Oct 1847, d. 13 Feb 1848.
Flora A., b. 18 Dec 1850, d. 29 Mar 1873.
Sources: Knox ME census 1840, 1850, 1860, 1870. VR SA/ME. M8A, P82j, R10e, M5.

8. **WILLIAM C.[3] SAWYER** [see 3], b. 18 Apr 1814 Knox ME, d. 29 Oct 1850 Bradley ME, m. 3 Dec 1837 Waldo County ME Hannah Hutchings, b. 21 Jun 1815 d. 7 Oct 1879, dau. John and Roxy (Hatch) Hutchings. Cooper.
Eliza E., b. 1838.
Caroline D., b. 1840.
15 Avander Charles[4], 1842-1904.
16 Ferdinand E.[4], 1844-1897.
Sarah E., b. 1847.
Frederick, b. 1850 Bradley ME.
Sources: Knox ME census 1840. Bradley ME census 1850. VR SA/ME, SA/MA.

9. **SYLVESTER H.[4] SAWYER** [see 4], b. 12 Jul 1828 Newburgh ME, d. 26 Jul 1884 Rockland ME, m. 23 Jan 1855 Rockland ME Abbie S. Bean of China ME, b. ?. Joiner.
Frederick W., b. 8 Sep 1851 Rockland ME, d. 20 Jul 1893, unm.
17 Arthur L.[5], b. 1868.
Sources: VR Rockland ME, SA/ME, SA/MA. E3.

10. **CHARLES[4] SAWYER** [see 4], b. ca. 1843 Newburgh ME, d. Apr 1882, m. 10 May 1856 Hampden ME Eliza G. Lennan of Hampden ME, b. ?. In Bangor ME.
John, b. ?.
Eliza G., b. ?. Executrix of father's will.
Sources: VR Rockland ME.

11. **JOHN GILBERT[4] SAWYER** [see 5], b. 1837 Montville ME, d. bef. 1867, m. Rachel D._____, b. 1841. Farmer. Guardian appointed for his minor CH 22 Mar 1867. Left will.
Edgar W., b. 1861 Montville ME.
Ardell, b. 1863.

Delbert R., b. 1865 Montville ME.
Sources: Montville ME census 1860. P82j, R10e.

12. **NATHAN⁴ SAWYER** [see 6], b. 7 Jul 1825 (Thorndike ME?), d. 1 Jun 1908 Montville ME, m. 20 Mar 1861 Belfast ME Susan Rosillia Hassel of Belfast ME, b. 31 Jan 1828 d. 28 Jun 1905. Farmer. In Belfast ME. Both bur. White's Corner cem., Montville ME.
Caro N., b. 1864.
Eliza, b. 1868.
Sources: Montville ME census 1870. VR Belfast ME, Rockland ME. M5.

13. **JAMES LORING⁴ SAWYER** [see 6], b. 1843 Montville ME, d. 1888 m. 21 Feb 1867 Montville ME Cora C. Reeves of Montville ME, b. 24 Aug 1850 d. 3 Sep 1921, dau James Reeves. In Thorndike ME, Unity ME, Burnham ME 1880. Both bur. Pond cem., Unity ME.
George, b. Jun 1870, d. 3 Dec 1880.
Sources: Burnham ME census 1880. ME 1880 census index. VR SA/ME. M5.

14. **ASA⁴ SAWYER** [see 6], b. 1848 Thorndike ME, d. 1920, m.(I) 30 Sep 1870 Burnham ME Nancy Jones of Freedom ME, b. Apr 1852 d. 5 Aug 1884. In Burnham ME 1880. Both bur. Pond cem., Unity ME.
Frederick, b. 1872 Burnham ME, m. 5 Dec 1896 Burnham ME Hattie D. Fernald of Troy ME, b. ?, dau. Laban A. and Martha (Lakeman) Fernald. Laborer.
Addie, b. 1875.
Abbie, b. 1875.
Irving Loring, b. ca. 1878 Burnham ME, m. Augusta L. Crawford of Waterville ME, b. 1877. Painter. In Lowell MA, Marlow NH. CH: Stanley Asa, b. 1907, m. 8 Oct 1932 Alice Barey.
Asa Willis, b. 18 Mar 1880 Burnham ME, d. 16 Dec 1923 Concord NH. Death certificate says Willis Asa.
Sources: Thorndike ME census 1850. Burnham ME census 1880. ME 1880 census index. VR Burnham ME, SA/ME, SA/NH. M5.

15. **AVANDER CHARLES⁴ SAWYER** [see 8], b. 29 Jul 1842 Knox ME, d. 26 Nov 1904 Old Town ME, m. 21 Jan 1864 Lowell MA Almeda Boulter of Knox ME, b. Sep 1837 d. 27 Nov 1911, dau. Simeon and Huldah (Hutchings) Boulter. In Bradley ME 1850, Old Town ME 1880.
Charles Avander, b. 18 Jun 1865, d. 21 Apr 1900.
Tadie F., b. 27 Apr 1866, d.y.
Nellie May, b. 6 Jan 1867, d. May 1906, m. 9 Sep 1885 Ansel E. Carroll.
18 Avander Henry⁵, 1874-1945.
19 William Herbert⁵, 1879-1942.
Sources: Bradley ME census 1850. Old Town ME census 1880. ME 1880 census index. VR SA/ME, SA/MA. Mary Anne Sawyer rec.

16. **FERDINAND E.⁴ SAWYER** [see 8], b. 18 Jul 1844 Knox ME, d. 26 Oct 1897 Knox ME, m. 19 Feb 1865 Knox ME Sabrina J. Patterson of Knox ME, b. 1847 d. 1928, dau. David and Ellsa Patterson. Civil War. In Knox ME 1870. Both bur. East Knox ME cem.
Sadie F., b. 1866.
Arthur William, b. 12 Jan 1869, d. 4 Apr 1893.
Eugene L., b. 1871 Knox ME.
Sources: Bradley ME census 1850. Knox ME census 1870, 1880. ME 1880 census index. VR SA/ME. M7A, M5.

17. **ARTHUR L.$^5$ SAWYER** [see 9], b. 1868 Rockland ME, m.(1) ?; m.(2) 21 Nov 1891 Ella (Sanger) Fairbanks of Hopkinton ME, b. ca. 1857, dau. J. W. and Susan L. Sanger. In Westboro MA.

Sylvester P., b. 26 Jun 1885.

Sources: VR Rockland ME, SA/ME.

18. **AVANDER HENRY$^5$ SAWYER** [see 15], b. 26 Oct 1874 Old Town ME, d. 2 Jan 1945, m. 15 Oct 1919 Bar Harbor ME Elizabeth E. Mooney of Bucksport ME, b. ?. Bank cashier. In Eden ME 1910.

Charlotte S., b. 12 Mar 1903, d. 1 Jun 1994, m. Ralph C. Hilyard.

Sherman A., b. 1904, m. 19 Nov 1926 Bangor ME Eloise M. Carlisle of Ellsworth ME, b. 1910.

Sources: Eden ME census 1910. VR Ellsworth ME. Obit (Charlotte).

19. **WILLIAM HERBERT$^5$ SAWYER** [see 15], b. 10 Jul 1879 Old Town ME, d. 21 Jan 1942 Old Town ME, m. 12 Sep 1909 Andover, New Brunswick, Canada, Lucretia A. Roberts, b. 16 Jul 1881 d. 1964, dau. George B. and Hannah (Weeks) Roberts.

Ralph Herbert, b. 22 Mar 1911, d. 1 Mar 1964, m. 5 Sep 1957 Etta Grange.

Charles Avander, b. 14 Jun 1914, m. 25 Feb 1941 Rita Cormier.

Hannah Almeda, b. 19 Mar 1916, m. 30 Dec 1939 Baxter O. Willey.

George Roberts, b. 22 Apr 1917, m. 12 Oct 1941 Jean Grange.

Sources: Mary Anne Sawyer rec.

---

## LINE 9

1. **JAMES$^1$ SAWYER**, b. Oct 1755 Falmouth ME, d. 23 Nov 1834 Sullivan NH, m. 13 Nov 1777 Mary Ellis of Gilsum NH, b. 1758 d. 5 Feb 1843. Revolutionary War: Enl. in Captain Jeremiah Hill's Company, Falmouth ME. In Gilsum NH, Keene NH before 1783. B/land in Sullivan NH 1798. In Sullivan NH 1820. Farm was on Keene NH town line.

Prudence, b. 11 Jan 1778.

Sarah, b. 2 Apr 1780.

Joseph, b. 9 Mar 1782 Keene NH, d. 11 Dec 1848 Mannsville NY, m. Mary Harper, b. ?. Had 10 CH.

Lydia, b. 25 Oct 1783.

Sidney (female), b. 10 Mar 1788.

James, b. 5 Aug 1790 Keene NH, d. Watertown NY.

Mary, b. ca. 1792.

Melissa, b. ca. 1793.

2 Elisha Ellis$^2$, b. 1794.

Releaf, b. ca. 1799, unm.

Rachel, b. ca. 1803, d. 11 Dec 1825, m. 1 Apr 1823 Abijah Ellis of Roxbury VT.

Sources: Keene NH census 1790, 1800. Sullivan NH census 1820, 1830. G46, H36, A27, N12.

2. **ELISHA ELLIS$^2$ SAWYER** [see 1], b. 1794 Keene NH, d. Winchendon MA, m. 26 Dec 1822 Sally Palmer, b. ?. War of 1812. In Sullivan NH, Sarasota NY.

3 Loren M.$^3$, b. ca. 1836.

Silas, b. ?.

Sources: Sullivan NH census 1820.

3. **LOREN M.[3] SAWYER** [see 2], b. ca. 1836 Sarasota NY, m.(1) 5 Nov 1866 Orange MA Clarissa A. Flagg of Wendell MA, b. ?, dau. Jonathan and Clarissa Flagg; m.(2) 4 Jul 1870 Lucretia Bridge of Harvard MA, b. 31 Jul 1843, dau. John A. and Lucretia (Nichols) Bridge. Mechanic. In Orange MA, Winchendon MA.

John, b. 26 Apr 1869 Winchendon MA.

Lulu Bell, b. 26 Aug 1872, m. 28 Nov 1895 Herbert O. Collins.

Hattie Lillian, b. 1 Jan 1875.

Charles Holman, b. 5 May 1877.

Sources: VR SA/MA. R30, W39.

---

## LINE 10

1. **BENJAMIN[1] SAWYER**, b. ca. 1761, d. 7 Feb 1834 Warner NH, m. 30 May 1792 Methuen MA Rebecca (Hardy) Sawyer of Bradford MA, b. ca. 1761 d. 12 Apr 1836. Revolutionary War. In Methuen MA 1800, Warner NH 1804.

2 Theodore[2], 1793-1881.

Hepsibeth H., b. 24 Nov 1799, d. 10 Nov 1886, m. 13 Dec 1825 Damon Annis.

Fanny, b. ca. 1802, d. 4 Mar 1805.

Cynthia, b. ca. 1808, d. 20 Apr 1832.

Note: According to the census records, the fol. CH were b. in the periods shown: 1 son, 1 dau. (1784-94); 1 dau. (1794-1800); 3 dau. (1800-1810); 1 dau. (1810-1820). Also, it is interesting to note that many descendants of William of Reading (Part V) lived in Warner NH.

Sources: Methuen MA census 1800. Warner NH 1810, 1820, 1830. A29, B40, N9, Dorothy C. Sawyer rec.

2. **THEODORE[2] SAWYER** [see 1], b. 30 Jun 1793 Methuen MA, d. 27 Nov 1881 Warner NH, m. 3 Jun 1832 Bradford NH Mary C. Bean of Canada, b. Feb 1801 d. 22 Jul 1884, dau. Nathaniel and Elizabeth (Barnard) Bean.

Nathaniel Bean, b. 22 Jul 1833 Warner NH, d. 1 Nov 1917, m.(1) Emma C. Stone of Peterboro NH, b. ca. 1838; m.(2) 14 Oct 1869 Mary J. Robertson, b. 10 Sep 1845 d. 21 Feb 1929. In Warner NH, Cherrydale KA.

3 James Bean[3], 1836-1923.

Sources: Warner NH census 1840, 1850. Sutton NH census 1860, 1870, 1880. B40, W69, N14, N9, Dorothy C. Sawyer rec.

3. **JAMES BEAN[3] SAWYER** [see 2], b. 19 Jan 1836 Warner NH, d. 27 Jan 1923 Sutton NH, m. 29 Nov 1860 Lucy Ann Richards of Sunapee NH, b. 6 Feb 1845 d. 18 Feb 1922, dau. Sylvanus and Clarissa (Hurd) Richards. In Sutton NH 1860.

Elmer E., b. 17 Apr 1862 Sutton NH, d. 27 Mar 1934 Hopkinton NH, m. 28 Aug 1889 Hopkinton NH Lillian C. Mudgett of Contoocook NH, b. 5 May 1867, dau. John F. Mudgett. Teacher. In Pepperell MA 1894, Topsham ME.

4 Charles E.[4], b. 1864.

5 Fred A.[4], 1872-1929.

Mary Ella, b. 11 Mar 1874.

Sources: Sutton NH census 1860, 1870, 1880. VR SA/NH. W69, N9, Dorothy C. Sawyer rec.

4. **CHARLES E.[4] SAWYER** [see 3], b. 13 Oct 1864 Sutton NH, m. 23 Jan 1890 Grace E. Flanders of Warner NH, b. ?. In Warner NH.

Lucy A., b. 23 Feb 1891, d. 21 Sep 1964 Haverhill MA.

Benjamin Flanders, b. 18 May 1893 Warner NH, m. 19 Apr 1913 Warner NH Hilery L. Perkins of Allston MA, b. ca. 1892, dau. John L. and Emma Perkins of Boston MA.
Raymond E., b. ?. Went to California.

Sources: H32, Dorothy C. Sawyer rec.

5. **FRED A.[4] SAWYER** [see 3], b. 27 Aug 1872 Sutton NH, d. 27 Aug 1929 Sutton NH, m. 30 Jun 1897 Maude B. Eaton of Newbury MA, b. ca. 1874 d. 1956. Farmer.

Bernice M., b. 20 Feb 1898, m. Ernest MacWilliams.
Lula, b. 10 Dec 1899, m. Edwin Porter.
Clifford A., b. 1903 Sutton NH, d. 1984, m. 19 Jun 1924 Sunapee NH Dorothy C. Gove of Sunapee NH, b. ca. 1905, dau. Archie O. and Harriet M. (Hoitt) Gove. Farmer. In Warner NH. CH: Charlotte; Barbara; Phyllis; Judith; Patricia.
Howard, m. Bertha LaMontiane.

Sources: VR SA/NH. Dorothy C. Sawyer rec.

---

## LINE 11

1. **ISAAC[1] SAWYER**, b. ca. 1762 Falmouth ME, d. 11 May 1847 Gardiner ME, m. Lavinia Atkins of Bowdoin ME, b. 1765 d. 20 Dec 1840 Gardiner ME. In Bowdoin ME, Gardiner ME. Both bur. Cannard Cem., So. Gardiner ME.

2 Ezekiel[2], ca. 1798-1877.
Daughter, b. (1810-1815).

Sources: Bowdoin ME census 1800, 1810. Gardiner ME census 1820, 1830, 1840. VR Gardiner ME. M5.

2. **EZEKIEL[2] SAWYER** [see 1], b. ca. 1798 Gardiner ME, b. 21 Sep 1877 Gardiner ME, m. 20 Jan 1825 Gardiner ME Sally Atkins, b. 1800 d. 21 Dec 1873. Both bur. Mt. Hope Cem., So. Gardiner ME.

Mary A., b. 15 Jan 1827, m. 3 Aug 1854 Lewis Moore.
Charles N., b. 9 Aug 1829 Gardiner ME, d. 10 Feb 1888, m. 14 Jun 1853 Gardiner ME Eliza S. McLellan, b. ?.
3 Henry R.[3], b. 1833-1907.
Ezekiel W., b. 3 Dec 1836, d. 25 Feb 1847.
Augusta, b. 15 Aug 1840, d. 24 Oct 1856.

Sources: Gardiner ME census 1830, 1840, 1850. VR Gardiner ME. M5.

3. **HENRY R.[3] SAWYER** [see 2], b. 13 Apr 1833 Gardiner ME, d. 1907 Gardiner ME, m. 1 May 1861 Gardiner ME Philena W. S. Hathorn, b. 1845 d. 1925. Real estate broker. In Gardiner ME. Both bur. Mt. Hope Cem., So. Gardiner ME.

Ida L., b. 20 Sep 1864, m. 17 Nov 1886 Thomas E. Gorton.
Hattie Charlene, b. 21 Oct 1867, m. Dr. _____ Packard.
4 Ezekiel Joseph[4], 1871-1938.
Henry Hathorn, b. 10 May 1876 Gardiner ME, d. 28 Dec 1915 So. Gardiner ME, m. Hattie _____, b. ?. In New York City.
Jefferson Southard, b. 21 Jul 1883, unm.

Sources: Gardiner ME census 1880. ME 1880 census index. VR Gardiner ME, SA/ME, SA/MA. G28.

4. **EZEKIEL JOSEPH[4] SAWYER** [see 3], b. 20 May 1871 Gardiner ME, d. 1938, m.(1) 4 Oct 1891 Abigail L. Durant of Boothbay ME, b. 16 May 1870 d. 9 Feb 1910, dau. John and Sarah (Neal) Durant; m.(2) Lucy _____, b. ?. Farmer. Abigail bur. Mt. Hope Cem., So. Gardiner ME.

Vivian F., b. 7 May 1892, m. Frank A. Morris.
Ruth, b. 30 Dec 1894, d. 1949, m. Carleton Adams.
Richard, b. 13 Mar 1896.
Lewis M., b. 17 Jun 1897, d. 1 Sep 1897.
Maxwell Durant, b. 29 Sep 1898 So. Gardiner ME, d. 14 Mar 1967 Brunswick ME, m. Mary E. Hill, b. 28 Dec 1910. World War I. CH: Nadine M., b. 11 Aug 1920, m. Frank L. Allen.

Sources: VR SA/ME. M5, Nadine Allen rec.

---

## LINE 12

1. **NEHEMIAH[1] SAWYER**, b. ca. 1762, m. Rebecca Sawyer of Jonesport ME, b. ca. 1771, dau. John and Mary (Jordan) Sawyer. See Part IV, [39].

Hannah, b. 26 May 1788, d. 8 Aug 1846, m. 24 Jul 1810 Jeremiah Norton.
Mary, b. 1 Jan 1790, d. 15 Jan 1794.
John, b. 7 Nov 1792, d. 20 Dec 1792.
Rebecca, b. 2 Aug 1794, d. 15 Dec 1853, m. 26 Dec 1811 Nathaniel Church.
Mary J., b. 9 Jul 1797, d. 28 Sep 1853, m. Thomas Beal.
Elizabeth B., b. 14 Mar 1800, d. 10 Jan 1876, m. 16 Nov 1826 Stephen Watts.
Ebenezer, b. 23 Aug 1803, d. 15 Jul 1806.
2 Ebenezer[2], 1806-1878.
3 Oliver[2], 1809-1881.
Susan E., b. 1812, m. Ezekiel N. Smith.
Ann W., b. 29 Apr 1816, d. 1 Jan 1893, m. 5 May 1835 John Johnson.
(Emma, b. ?, m. Jewett Bryant.) ?

Sources: Jonesport ME census 1790, 1800, 1810, 1820, 1830. VR Jonesport ME. R10f, Agnes Ames rec., Leonard F. Tibbetts rec.

2. **EBENEZER[2] SAWYER** [see 1], b. 2 Jul 1806 Jonesport ME, d. 30 Apr 1878, m.(I) 4 Oct 1827 Eliza Drisco of Addison ME, b. 1804, dau. Joseph and Eunice (Parker) Drisco. Boat builder. Wid. w/son Ebenezer J. 1880.

4 Stephen E.[3], 1828-1910.
Eunice D., b. 8 Feb 1830, d. 22 Dec 1910, m. 1844 Henry Kelley.
5 Joseph W.[3], 1831-1876.
M____ Emily, b. 15 Mar 1833, d. 7 Mar 1923, m. 23 Apr 1854 Benjamin Bryant.
Eliza A., b. 10 May 1835, d. 4 Jun 1912, m. John Sawyer.
Lois M., b. 1837, b. 11 Aug 1877, m. 12 Dec 1866 Samuel Jenkins.
Harriet N., b. 1839, m. 1859 Reuben Beal.
6 Ebenezer J.[3], 1842-1917.
7 George Washington[3], 1844-1878.
Clara E., b. 1845, d. 7 Oct 1931, m. 3 Aug 1867 John R. J. Bryant.
William H., b. 1847 Jonesport ME, m. Catherine _____, b. ?. CH: Mary A., b. ?.
Andrew J., b. ca. 1852.
Sabrina A., b. ca. 1858.

Sources: Jonesport ME census 1830, 1840, 1850, 1880. VR SA/ME. Agnes Ames rec., Leonard F. Tibbetts rec.

3. **OLIVER² SAWYER** [see 1], b. 16 Dec 1809 Jonesport ME, d. 25 Sep 1881, m.(1) Eunice Drisco, b. 1813 d. Mar 1850, dau. Joseph and Eunice (Parker) Drisco; m.(2) 1851 Mary Norton, b. 1832 d. 18 Apr 1870. Sea captain, carpenter.

Elizabeth D., b. Oct 1832, d. 28 Dec 1910, m. Barnabas C. Beal.
Rebecca, b. 18 Jan 1834, d. 30 Nov 1900, m. Jefferson J. Dobbins.
8 Frederick A.³, 1836-1885.
Mary A., b. Dec 1851, d. 25 Dec 1911, m. 24 Feb 1874 Orrin Cummings.
Oliver W., b. 1853, d. 1854.
Wellington Oliver, b. ca. 1855 Jonesport ME, m.(1) 30 Jul 1877 Laura Anna Watts of Rogues Bluff ME, b. May 1854, dau. Henry and Olive (Simpson) Watts; m.(2) 25 Jan 1894 Boston MA Carrie C. Messervy of Appleton ME, b. ca. 1865, dau. Thomas G. and Lucinda G. Messervy. Sea captain. In Jonesport ME. CH: Ernestine, b. 1878; Mary O., b. 1880, d. 25 Feb 1899.
9 Ellery Augustin³, 1857-1907. Went to Mississippi.
Orlando Chester, 1860-1861.
10 Orlando Chester³, 1862-1929.
William Arthur, b. 11 May 1864 Jonesport ME, d. 11 Aug 1911 Portland ME, m. 1897 Katie C._____ of New Brunswick, Canada, b. Nov 1876. Sea captain.
Lillian B., b. 25 Oct 1866, d. 1 Feb 1911, m. 27 Apr 1889 Rufus Doyle.
Daughter, b. 1870, d. 1870.

Sources: Jonesport ME census 1840, 1850, 1860, 1870, 1880. ME 1880 census index. VR Bristol ME, SA/ME, SA/MA. Leonard F. Tibbetts rec.

4. **STEPHEN E.³ SAWYER** [see 2], b. 12 Oct 1828 Jonesport ME, d. 20 Feb 1910 Jonesport ME, m. Dorcas E. Kelley, b. ca. 1841. Painter.

Lowell A., b. 1858, d.y.
Ella M., b. ca. 1859, d.y.
11 George William⁴, b. 1863.
Minnie, b. ?, m. 10 Mar 1888 Wellington R. Pendleton.
Anna M., b. ca. 1868, d.y.
Ebenezer J., b. ca. 1870, d.y.
Eliza L., b. ca. 1872, m. 22 Sep 1891 Boston MA William Dupee.
Frank B., b. Jul 1873 Jonesport ME, d. 5 Apr 1906 Jonesport ME, m. 11 Nov 1893 Venetta Vaulkengham of Jonesport ME, b. Mar 1878. CH: Annie B., b. 16 Mar 1894; Lizzie May, b. 13 Oct 1897.
Nellie R., b. ca. 1875, d.y.
Lowell, b. ca. 1879, d.y.

Sources: Jonesport ME census 1860, 1880. ME 1880 census index. VR SA/ME, SA/MA. P26, Agnes Ames rec.

5. **JOSEPH W.³ SAWYER** [see 2], b. 5 Dec 1831 Jonesport ME, lost at sea 9 Dec 1876, m. 4 Feb 1855 Rebecca E. Watts, b. 15 Aug 1834 d. 13 Apr 1905. Sea captain. Wid. in Jonesport ME 1880.

Lester, b. 21 Oct 1858, d. 9 Dec 1876.
Eugene M., b. 17 Apr 1862, d. 5 Jun 1900.
Cora L., b. 1870.

Sources: Jonesport ME census 1860, 1880. VR Jonesport ME. Leonard F. Tibbetts rec.

6. **EBENEZER J.³ SAWYER** [see 2], b. 7 Jul 1842 Jonesport ME, d. 3 Jul 1917, m. 1871 Philina A. Kelley, b. Jul 1852 d. 1933. Ship carpenter.

Stephen, b. Feb 1872 Jonesport ME, m. Laura Lakeman, b. ?.

Julia C., b. Jun 1875, m. Alton V. Rogers.
Eliza, b. ?, d. at 2 yrs.
Sources: Jonesport ME census 1880, 1900. VR SA/ME. Leonard F. Tibbetts rec.

7. **GEORGE WASHINGTON[3] SAWYER** [see 2], b. 1844 Jonesport ME, lost at sea 1878, m. Mary E. Kelley of Milbridge ME, b. Jan 1841 d. 2 Mar 1925. Sea captain. In Milbridge ME.
12 William A.[4], 1867-1902.
Edith May, b. 16 Jun 1878.
Sources: Leonard F. Tibbetts rec.

8. **FREDERICK A.[3] SAWYER** [see 3], b. 1836 Jonesport ME, d. 20 Apr 1885 Augusta ME, m. 15 Jun 1863 Machias ME Melinda J. Foss of Machias ME, b. 31 Jul 1843 d. 9 Dec 1921, dau. Benjamin and Adeline (Davis) Foss. Sea captain. In Jonesport ME, Harrington ME, Augusta ME.
Laura F., b. ca. 1863.
Charles M., b. ca. 1865 (Jonesport ME?). In Augusta ME.
13 Ivory P.[4], b. 1869.
William A., b. ca. 1870 Jonesport ME, m. 27 Dec 1899 Augusta ME Ellen S. Donahue of Augusta ME, b. 1869, dau. William and Catherine (Murphy) Donahue. Plumber. In Augusta ME.
Frederick A., b. ca. 1873 Jonesport ME. In Jonesport ME 1880.
14 Carroll R.[4], 1877-1949.
Son, b. ca. 1879.
Milton, b. ?.
15 Ernest S.[4], b. ?.
Sources: Jonesport ME census 1880. ME 1880 census index. VR SA/ME. Leonard F. Tibbetts rec., Melinda Regnell rec.

9. **ELLERY AUGUSTIN[3] SAWYER** [see 3], b. 8 Mar 1857 Jonesport ME, d. 28 Jan 1907 Scranton MS, m. 30 Jan 1784 Carrie E. Watts of Rogues Bluff ME, b. Dec 1863 d. 1922, dau. Henry L. and Olive L. (Simpson) Watts. Sea captain.
Lillian B., b. Feb 1887, d. ca. 1971.
16 Wellington Oliver[4], 1890-ca. 1959.
Daughter, b. 8 Oct 1894.
Sources: VR Bristol ME, Jonesboro ME, SA/ME. Hazel Sawyer rec., Leonard F. Tibbetts rec.

10. **ORLANDO CHESTER[3] SAWYER** [see 3], b. 4 Jan 1862 Jonesport ME, d. 4 Jan 1929, m.(1) 25 Feb 1886 Malden MA Mary E. Fossett of Bristol ME, b. Jul 1861 d. 5 Apr 1895, dau. Thomas M. and Jane E. Fossett; m.(2) 14 Sep 1899 Newcastle ME Rachel Loud of Bristol ME, b. ca. 1872, dau. Samuel and Amanda (Bassett) Loud. Sea captain. In Bristol ME.
17 Arthur Ellery[4], 1888-1960.
Ethel A., b. 1890, m. Winfred March.
Daughter, b. 17 Sep 1900.
Sources: VR Bristol ME, SA/ME. Stanley A. Sawyer rec., Leonard F. Tibbetts rec.

11. **GEORGE WILLIAM[4] SAWYER** [see 4], b. Mar 1863 Jonesport ME, m. Mary Lorena Flaherty of Columbia ME, b. ?. In Harrington ME, Jonesport ME.
Rhoda W., b. 13 Apr 1892.
Roscoe, b. 6 Jun 1893 Jonesport ME.
Son, b. 3 May 1895.
Gerald, b. Apr 1896 Jonesport ME.
Sources: Jonesport ME census 1890. VR SA/ME.

12. **WILLIAM A.[4] SAWYER** [see 7], b. 11 Jan 1867 Jonesport ME, d. 2 Feb 1902 at sea, m.(I) 19 Aug 1890 Gertrude A. Strout of Milbridge ME, b. 1871 d. 1 May 1906, dau. Albert A. and Abby (Leighton) Strout. In Milbridge ME.

George Harold, b. 26 Nov 1891 Milbridge ME.
Son, b. 29 Jun 1893, d. 2 Oct 1893.
Lester W., b. 24 Apr 1895 Milbridge ME.
Lillian A., b. 13 Oct 1898.

Sources: VR SA/ME. M5.

13. **IVORY P.[4] SAWYER** [see 8], b. Feb 1869 Jonesport ME, m. Lettie R. Kelley of Jonesport ME, b. May 1868. Seaman.

Burt, b. 7 Feb 1894 Jonesport ME.
Laura Frances, b. 2 Nov 1896.
Elva Etta, b. 18 Mar 1899.

Sources: VR SA/ME.

14. **CARROLL R.[4] SAWYER** [see 8], b. Nov 1877 Jonesport ME, d. 1949, m. 8 May 1897 Belgrade ME Annie L. Yeaton of Belgrade ME, b. 1880 d. 1940, dau. Howard B. and Susie (Cummings) Yeaton. In Belgrade ME.

Son, b. 11 Mar 1898.
Son, b. 21 Feb 1900, d. 8 Mar 1900.
Chester M., b. 1911, d. 1977, m. Bertha S. Bickford.

Sources: VR SA/ME.

15 **ERNEST S.[4] SAWYER** [see 8], b. ?, m. Margaret Murray, b. ?.

Richard F., b. 1915, d. 27 Dec 1985, m. Faith Groves.
Ernest, b. ?, m. _____, no CH.
Edward P., b. ?.
Robert P., b. ?. Went to Idaho.

Sources: Obit, Melinda Regnell rec.

16. **WELLINGTON OLIVER[4] SAWYER** [see 9], b. 29 Nov 1890, d. ca. 1959, m. 1914 Bridgeport CT Edith A. Kelley, b. ?, dau. Henry A. and Alice (Ackley) Kelley.

Sherman, b. ?, m. Hazel _____, b. ?.

Sources: Hazel Sawyer rec.

17. **ARTHUR ELLERY[4] SAWYER** [see 10], b. 30 Nov 1888 Bristol ME, d. 1960 Damariscotta ME, m. Verna M. Yates, b. 1892.

Muriel.
Ellery Chester.
Kenneth Yates.
Stanley Arthur.

Sources: VR Bristol ME. M5, Stanley A. Sawyer rec.

---

## LINE 13

1. **ELIAS[1] SAWYER**, b. ca. 1763, d. 10 Feb 1851 Grantham NH, m. Polly Dutton of Vershire VT, b. ca. 1763 d. 1861. Farmer. In No. Grantham NH, Grantham NH.

Betsey, b. ca. 1790.

2 Oliver[2], b. ca. 1791.
Charlotte, b. ca. 1794, d. 1881, m. _____ Abbott.
Roxane, b. ca. 1795, d. 1 May 1824, m. John Haggett.
Elisha, b. ca. 1798 North Grantham NH.
Rebecca, b. ca. 1802, d. 1882, m. 10 Feb 1825 John Haggett.
Azubah, b. Aug 1805, d. 5 Apr 1893, unm.
3 David[2], ca. 1806-1880.
Sources: North Grantham NH census 1790, 1800, 1810. Grantham NH census 1820, 1830, 1840, 1850. W6, Elizabeth Larkin rec.

2. **OLIVER[2] SAWYER** [see 1], b. ca. 1791 Windsor VT, m. 24 Sep 1815 Cornish NH Betsey Russell of Plymouth MA, b. ca. 1791. Farmer. In Grantham NH.
Laura, b. 22 Oct 1816, m. 21 Mar 1842 William West.
Mary Ann, b. 18 Feb 1819.
Susan, b. 18 Feb 1823.
Lyman, b. ca. 1827 Grantham NH, d. 27 Sep 1898 Concord NH, m.(1) 5 Jul 1853 Esther C. Glines, b.?; m.(2) 22 Sep 1859 Northfield NH Susan G. Hanaford of Northfield NH, b. 4 Aug 1830 d. 11 Jun 1904, dau. Amos and Hannah (Lyford) Hanaford. Farmer. In Croyden NH, Concord NH 1860. Official in Ward 3, Concord NH, 1874-75. CH: Gertrude, b. 1867.
4 Elias[3], 1832-1896.
Sources: Grantham NH census 1820, 1830, 1840, 1850, 1860. Croyden NH census 1850. Concord NH census 1860, 1870.

3. **DAVID[2] SAWYER** [see 1]. ca. 1806 North Grantham NH, d. 1880, m. 10 Apr 1839 Sophia Muzzey of Grantham NH, b. ca. 1813. Milwright. In Cornish NH 1850.
Caroline, b. ca. 1840.
Thomas, b. ca. 1843 Cornish NH.
Ethan, b. ca. 1845 Cornish NH.
Edgar A., b. ca. 1848 Cornish NH.
Sources: Cornish NH census 1850.

4. **ELIAS[3] SAWYER** [see 2], b. 29 Mar 1832 Grantham NH, d. 19 Jul 1896 Concord NH, m. 1853 Augusta C. Heath of Croyden NH, b. ?. Joiner. In Croyden NH, Newport NH 1852. He bur. in Concord NH.
Son, b. 25 Feb 1854.
Charles F., b. 1855, d. 10 Feb 1859.
Ada F., b. ca. 1856, d. 13 Feb 1859.
Herbert W., b. 8 Sep 1861 Newport NH, m. 10 Nov 1886 Lillian K. Gove of Alexandria NH, b. 1867. In Concord NH.
Sources: Croyden NH census 1850, 1870. Newport NH census 1860, W33.

---

## LINE 14

1. **WILLIAM[1] SAWYER**, b. ca. 1763 Wells ME, d. 11 Jan 1851 Greene ME, m.(1)(I) 4 Sep 1784 Rhoda Hatch, b. ? d. 13 Mar 1813; m.(2) Nov 1815 Mary Graffam, b. ?. Revolutionary War. W/son Thaddeus 1850. Pension record says he was b. 1761.
2 Thaddeus[2], 1785-1863.
Sally, b. 31 Jan 1787, d. 14 Jan 1836.

Sources: Wells ME census 1790. Greene ME census 1800, 1810, 1820, 1830, 1840, 1850. VR Saco ME. M60, N11.

2. **THADDEUS² SAWYER** [see 1], b. 18 Nov 1785 Wells ME, d. 1863 Greene ME, m. Sep 1811 Margaret Larrabee of Greene ME, b. 26 Aug 1787, dau. Deacon John Larrabee. Served in militia. In Greene ME.

John Emerson, b. 4 Aug 1812 Greene ME, d. 19 Jan 1894 Greene ME, m. 4 Aug 1838 Bristol/Nobleboro ME Electa A. Mower of Greene ME, b. 22 Jan 1821 d. 23 Jan 1877, dau. Leonard and Lydia (Robbins) Mower. Farmer, selectman, tax collector, school board member. CH: Ann A., b. 15 Feb 1840, d. Oct 1914 Lewiston ME.

Nathaniel Larrabee, b. 8 Apr 1814, d. 13 Oct 1845.

Jane, b. 16 Mar 1816, d. 1898, m. Aug 1840 Samuel R. Lamont.

William Ellery, b. 5 Aug 1818, d. 11 Sep 1819.

3 William Ellery³, 1820-1882.

Josephine B., b. ?, m. 29 Aug 1846 Gardiner ME Daniel Hamilton.

Rhoda, b. 1 Aug 1823, d.y.

Sources: Greene ME census 1820, 1830, 1840, 1850, 1860. Bristol/Nobleboro ME. VR SA/ME. M60, R17.

3. **WILLIAM ELLERY³ SAWYER** [see 2], b. 23 Oct 1820 Greene ME, d. 1 Oct 1882, m. 19 Dec 1850 Mary P. Cummings of Greene ME, b. 29 Nov 1826 d. 15 Apr 1915 Auburn ME, dau. Deacon Lemuel and Polly (Pitt? Waterman?) Cummings.

4 William Pitt⁴, 1856-1917.

Mary, b. ?, m. Lawrence Pettengill.

Sources: Greene ME census 1850, 1860. VR SA/ME. M60.

4. **WILLIAM PITT⁴ SAWYER** [see 3], b. 24 Sep 1856 Greene ME, d. 4 Sep 1917 Auburn ME, m. May 1878 Rosetta Austin, b. ?.

Alson A., b. 1883 Greene ME, m.(1) ?; m.(2) 12 Jun 1933 Berlin NH Ida M.(Reynolds) Card, b. 1874, dau. James and Mary E. Reynolds. In Auburn ME.

Sources: M60.

---

## LINE 15

1. **TOPPAN (Topham)¹ SAWYER**, b. (1770-1774), m. 12 Apr 1801 Gorham ME Rachel Hamblen, b. ?. S/land in Standish ME 1801. In Gorham ME 1810, Hollis ME 1820, Landaff NH 1830. B/land in Lincoln NH 1832. In Franconia NH 1840. Note: Marriage rec. says he was "of Standish."

Sophia, b. 27 Nov 1801, m.(I) 6 Feb 1825 Jonathan Bean of Hollis ME.

Eliza, b. 7 Mar 1804, m. Abel Bean of Hollis ME.

John Russell, b. 6 Apr 1806 Gorham ME, m. and had one son b. (1825-1830). In Landaff NH 1830.

2 James Sullivan², b. 1808.

Thomas Jefferson, b. 28 Feb 1808 Gorham ME.

3 Daniel R.², 1812-1871.

Mary, b. 18 Jan 1818, m.(I) 11 Sep 1837 Hollis ME Abel Bean.

Toppan Robie, b. 7 Jul 1820 Hollis ME.

Judith, b. 21 Apr 1823.

Sources: Gorham ME census 1810. Hollis ME census 1820. Landaff NH census 1830. Franconia NH census 1840. VR Gorham ME. R10d.

2. **JAMES SULLIVAN[2] SAWYER** [see 1], b. 28 Feb 1808 Gorham ME, d. at Ft. Ann NY, m. 25 Feb 1830 Gorham ME Hannah Sturgis of Gorham ME, b. 13 Jul 1811 d. 3 Feb 1857, dau. Joseph and Hannah (Blake) Sturgis. In Gorham ME 1830, Bethlehem NH 1840.

Eliza Jane, b. ca. 1830 Landaff NH, m. 13 Sep 1849 Lowell MA James Webb.
4 Thomas Jefferson[3], 1831-1908.
Almira P., b. 29 Jan 1832, d. 25 Sep 1902, m. 1849 Joseph F. Hale.
5 James Samuel[3], 1834-1905.
Daughter, b. (1835-1840).
6 Adenirian Judson[3], 1841-1917.

Sources: Gorham ME census 1830. Bethlehem NH census 1840. VR Gorham ME, Lowell MA, Hopkinton NH, Dunbarton NH, SA/MA. D6.

3. **DANIEL R.[2] SAWYER** [see 1], b. 1812 in Maine, d. 14 Jul 1871 Lisbon NH, m.(1) Abigail Morse of Lisbon NH, b. 14 Jan 1815; m.(2) 28 May 1859 Bethelhem NH Phebe Kenney of Bethlehem NH, b. 1825. In Lisbon NH 1840, Franconia NH 1860, Bethlehem NH 1870.

James Harrison, b. 2 Nov 1838 Lisbon NH, d. 4 Mar 1895 Bethlehem NH, m. Lydia F. Watson of Franconia NH, b. 28 Mar 1841 d. 19 Mar 1912. CH: Gertrude E., b. ?, m. 4 Jul 1896 Landaff NH Frank R. Eastman.
Marcella M., b. 11 Nov 1840, d. 6 Jan 1858.
Myron A., b. 6 May 1842, d. 25 May 1864.
Henry A., b. ca. 1843 Lisbon NH.
Elzora S., b. 1854, m. 7 Dec 1878 Lisbon NH Henry Whipple.

Sources: Lisbon NH census 1840, 1850. Franconia NH census 1860. Bethlehem NH census 1870. N6.

4. **THOMAS JEFFERSON[3] SAWYER** [see 2], b. Aug 1831 Gorham ME, d. 10 Feb 1908 Derry NH, m.(1) 27 Oct 1855 Lawrence MA Ellen West Whittier of Boscawen NH, b. 1 Nov 1835 d. 13 May 1869, dau. Joseph and Victoria (Elkins) Whittier; m.(2) Carrie McLaughlin of Prince Edward Island, Canada, b. 25 Jan 1835 d. 3 Mar 1911, dau. Daniel and Jennie (Henderson) McLaughlin, both of Scotland. Blacksmith, shoemaker. Civil War: 7th Maine Regiment. In Concord NH 1850, 1860, Londonderry NH 1880.

7 William Whittier[4], 1855-1948.
Gilbert J., b. 23 Sep 1857, d. 28 Oct 1880, unm.
Martha M., b. 1870, m. 11 Dec 1890 Edmund G. Anderson.
Walter A., b. 11 Mar 1873 Londonderry NH.
Ella Mabel, b. 26 Jan 1878, d. 29 Jul 1889.

Sources: Concord NH census 1850, 1860. VR Londonderry NH, SA/MA, SA/NH. N6, W43.

5. **JAMES SAMUEL[3] SAWYER** [see 2], b. 1834 Bethlehem NH, d. 1905 Dunbarton NH, m. Ellen M. Lufkin of Dunbarton NH, b. 1829 d. 28 Apr 1882. Farmer. In Dunbarton NH 1860.

George Henry, b. 17 Oct 1859 Dunbarton NH, d. 8 May 1920 Concord NH, m. 23 Nov 1887 Sarah Jane Nelson of Pembroke NH, b. 1850, dau. John and Lydia (Moses) Nelson. No CH.
8 James William[4], 1864-1927.
9 Fred[4], 1866-1905.
Ellen M., b. 28 Mar 1867, m. 15 Oct 1886 Melrose MA George W. Hale.

Sources: Dunbarton NH census 1860, 1870. Concord NH census 1880. VR SA/NH, SA/MA.

6. **ADENIRIAN JUDSON[3] SAWYER** [see 2], b. 16 Feb 1841 Hopkinton NH, d. 26 Jun 1917 Newton NH, m.(1) 4 Oct 1865 Lawrence MA Susie M. Currier of Durham NH, b. 1843, dau.

Joseph and Sarah Currier; m.(2) 25 Oct 1884 Adelaide L. (Hoyt) Boswell of Merrimac MA, b. 5 Mar 1844 d. 31 Jan 1924, dau. William and Elvira (Morse) Hoyt. Shoemaker. In East Kingston NH.

Son, b. 2 Aug 1866.

Fred Earl, b. 2 Sep 1867 East Kingston NH, d. 21 Jan 1933 Concord NH, m. 4 Aug 1888 Newton NH Etta E. Batchelder of East Kingston NH, b. 3 Nov 1865 d. 31 May 1933, dau. Nathaniel and Abbie (Marsh) Batchelder.

Eva P., b. 24 Dec 1868, d. 19 Mar 1869.

Sources: East Kingston NH census 1870. VR SA/MA, SA/NH. P41.

7. **WILLIAM WHITTIER**[4] **SAWYER** [see 4], b. 3 Aug 1855 Boscawen NH, d. 18 Dec 1948 Exeter NH, m. Malden MA Clara M. Burnham of Gloucester MA, b. 1865, dau. Robert W. and Medora C. Burnham. In Malden MA. He bur. in Woodlawn Cem., Boscawen NH.

10 Robert Whittier[5], 1897-1981.

Sources: VR SA/MA.

8. **JAMES WILLIAM**[4] **SAWYER** [see 5], b. 6 Aug 1864 Dunbarton NH, d. 25 Oct 1927 Boscawen NH, m. 19 Sep 1891 Dunbarton NH (div. 6 Oct 1909) Ellen(Webber) Knowles of Bow NH, b. 14 Jul 1853 d. 3 Oct 1924, dau. John B. and Rhoda (Simpson) Webber. Carpenter. In Concord NH, Epsom NH, Boscawen NH 1925.

Frank William, b. 18 Jan 1892 Concord NH, m.(1) 24 Dec 1913 Epsom NH Lena A. Marden of Epsom NH, b. 6 Jul 1887 d. 31 Dec 1933, dau. Cyrus and Angie M. Marden; m.(2) 2 Apr 1936 Chichester NH Elizabeth (Marin) Hilliard of Troy NH, b. 1906, dau. George J. and Rebecca (Rogers) Marin. Mechanic.

Walter Alfred, b. 26 Oct 1893 Concord NH, m. 25 Nov 1924 Chichester NH Eliza Wheeler of Epsom NH, b. 1905, dau. Frank A. and Lillian C. Wheeler. Mechanic.

Sources: VR SA/NH.

9. **FRED**[4] **SAWYER** [see 5], b. 5 Jan 1866 Dunbarton NH, d. 29 Apr 1905 Concord NH, m. 11 Jun 1891 Marlborough MA Ada MacLean of Nova Scotia, Canada, b. 1872 d. 1 Aug 1948, dau. Ries and Annie (Northrop) MacLean. Blacksmith. In Concord NH 1890.

Son, stillborn 2 Jun 1892.

Marion M., b. 26 Jul 1896, d. 16 Aug 1896.

Daughter, stillborn 24 May 1897.

11 Earl Maclean[5], 1900-1977.

12 Russell DeWight[5], 1904-1993

Sources: Concord NH census 1890. VR SA/NH, SA/MA. Richard D. Sawyer rec.

10. **ROBERT WHITTIER**[5] **SAWYER** [see 7], b. 13 Jan 1897 Malden MA, d. 27 Jan 1981 Hancock NH, m. 14 Nov 1917 Elizabeth Florence Lane, b. ?. He bur. in Exeter NH.

William Lane, b. 18 Nov 1920, m. 10 Jan 1943 Gene Belle Cram.

Sources: M50.

11. **EARL MacLEAN**[5] **SAWYER** [see 9], b. 13 Apr 1900 Concord NH, d. 21 Jan 1972 Concord NH, m.(1) 12 Jun 1922 Concord NH Mary E. Morin of Camden ME, b. 1897, dau. Leonide and Nora (Twohig) Morin; m.(2) Aug 1961 Concord NH Frances E. West, b. 25 Oct 1913 d. 10 Apr 1989 in Florida, dau. George and Elizabeth (Bean) West. Auto mechanic.

Robert Earle, b. 1922, d. 29 Dec 1982, m. Betty Baker.

Daughter, stillborn 6 Feb 1931.

Jane, b. 1933, m. Robert Pokigo of Goffstown NH.

Sources: VR SA/NH. B40, Richard Dewight Sawyer rec.

12. **RUSSELL DeWIGHT[5] SAWYER** [see 9], b. 19 Oct 1904 Concord NH, d. 25 Jun 1993, m. 12 Jun 1926 Concord NH Ida C. Carlson of Concord NH, b. 31 May 1902, dau. Richard A. and Ida O. (Rybery) Carlson, both of Sweden. Commander, USNR (Ret).

Richard DeWight, b. 6 Jun 1930, m. Mary Louise Gilman. Teacher.

Sources: Richard DeWight Sawyer rec.

---

## LINE 16

1. **JOSIAH[1] SAWYER**, b. ca. 1772 (Andover MA?), d. 4 May 1845 Greenfield NH, m. 29 Oct 1801 Wilmington MA Sally Gowing of Wilmington MA, b. 18 Jan 1781 d. 29 Jun 1843.

Sally, b. ca. 1803.
Mary, b. (1800-1810).
Daughter, b. (1800-1810).
2 Daniel[2], 1807-1884.
Daughter, b. (1810-1820).
Joseph, b. ca. 1815 (Greenfield NH?), m. Sarah Belton Patterson, b. 1817 d. 7 Apr 1897. In Amherst NH, Manchester NH, Syracuse NY, Titusville PA. B/quarry in Brunswick ME 1855; S/part 1864. CH: Joseph Henry, b. 9 Sep 1843 Francestown NH; Frank W., b. ?.
3 James Henry[2], 1817-1881 (1891?).
Daughter, b. (1825-1830).

Sources: Greenfield NH census 1810. 1820, 1830, 1840. VR Wilmington MA. N9, R10a.

2. **DANIEL[2] SAWYER** [see 1], b. Sep 1807 Greenfield NH, d. 19 Mar 1884 Greenfield NH, m.(1) Mary Day of Wilmington MA, b. Jan 1819 d. 24 May 1872, dau. Sarah (Frost) Day; m.(2) 7 May 1874 Martha L. Weston of Peterboro NH, b. 1823.

John, b. 1845 Greenfield NH, d. 23 Jul 1877 Greenfield NH, m. 14 Oct 1866 Mary Caroline Day of Woburn MA, b. 1846, d. 25 Jul 1868. CH: Daniel G., b. 1867, d. 15 Aug 1868. Note: Greenfield NH census 1850 says John was b. in Massachusetts.

Sources: Greenfield NH census 1840, 1850, 1860, 1870. N9.

3. **JAMES HENRY[2] SAWYER** [see 1], b. 29 Dec 1817 Greenfield NH, d. 23 Dec 1881 (or 1891) Greenfield NH, m. Sarah Dodge, b. Aug 1815 d. 6 Dec 1890, dau. Levi and Keziah (Stanley) Dodge. Farmer. In Amherst NH 1868. B/land in Brunswick ME 1868.

Emily, b. 1838.
Daughter, b. ca. 1840.
Henrietta, b. ca. 1842, m. 30 Jun 1869 Lowell MA James E. Stearns.
Julia, b. ca. 1845.
Mary E., b. ca. 1849.
4 Newall James[3], 1852-1887.

Sources: Greenfield NH census 1840, 1850, 1870. VR SA/MA. N9.

4. **NEWALL JAMES[3] SAWYER** [see 3], b. Dec 1852 Greenfield NH, d. 25 Jan 1887 Greenfield NH, m.(1) 1878 Viola M. Holt of Greenfield NH, b. ca. 1856 d. 13 Jan 1882, dau. Levi S. and Caroline B. (Marsh) Holt; m.(2) 11 Sep 1884 Peterborough NH MaryE. Wheeler of Bangor ME, b. ca. 1849 d. 29 Dec 1932.

Newall Wheeler, b. 14 Jan 1886 Greenfield NH.

Sources: N9, W32.

---

## LINE 17

1. **PHILIP[1] SAWYER**, b. ca. 1771, d. 10 Feb 1837 Foxboro MA, m.(1) 16 Sep 1800 Keziah Billings, b. 1778 d. 18 May 1808; m.(2) 18 Sep 1810 Mansfield MA Abigail Simmonds, b. ?. In Foxboro MA, Providence RI, Cumberland RI.

2 Otis[2], 1801-1855.
  Hannah H., b. 16 Jul 1803, d. 29 Sep 1804.
  William, b. 12 Sep 1805.
  Susan, b. 4 Apr 1808, m. 1830 Benjamin Wiswell of Newton MA.

Sources: Providence RI census 1820. Cumberland RI census 1830. VR Foxboro MA, Mansfield MA. R11A, C82.

2. **OTIS[2] SAWYER** [see 1], b. 25 Aug 1801 Foxboro MA, d. 9 Jul 1855 Needham MA, m. 26 Sep 1830 Newton MA Charlotte M. Boynton, b. ca. 1806. Farmer. In Needham MA.

  William O., b. ca. 1831.
  Charlotte M., b. ca. 1833, m. 24 Oct 1872 Needham MA Luther A. Kingsbury.
  Harriet E., b. ca. 1836, m. Ezra C. Dudley.
  Susan A., b. ca. 1841, m. 12 Nov 1864 Eleazer H. Stanwood.
  Decatur M., b. 1 Feb 1849, m. 22 May 1879 Boston MA Annie E. Shapleigh of Lowell MA, b. 1853, dau. Samuel C. and Amy Shapleigh. Merchant. Went to New York City.

Sources: Needham MA census 1850. VR Newton MA, SA/MA. C44, C82, B73.

---

## LINE 18

1. **MOSES[1] SAWYER**, b. ca. 1772 in New Hampshire, d. 24 Aug 1853 Ossipee NH, m. Sally Ham, b. 1777 d. 11 Oct 1853, dau. David Ham. Carpenter. He bur. in Sawyer Farm Cem., Ossipee NH.

2 Joseph H.[2], b. ca. 1800.
3 George, [2], 1803-1880.
  Daughter, b. (1800-1810).
4 David H.[2], b. ca. 1810.
  Daughter, b. (1810-1815).

Sources: Ossipee NH census 1810, 1820, 1830, 1840, 1850. L41, C3.

2. **JOSEPH H.[2] SAWYER** [see 1], b. ca. 1800 Ossipee NH, m.(I) Feb 1823 Tuftonboro NH Abigail B. Hall of Tuftonboro NH. In Tuftonboro NH.

  Adeline A., b. ca. 1829, m. 16 Sep 1849 Boston MA William G. Grant.
  John H., b. 4 Feb 1830 Boston MA, d. 1 Jan 1901, m. 4 Nov 1856 Jennie C. Newcomb, b. 6 May 1832 d. Jan 1907, dau. Samuel E. and Eva Ann (Johnson) Newcomb.

Sources: Tuftonboro NH census 1830. VR SA/MA. C3, H5, N21.

3. **GEORGE[2] SAWYER** [see 1], b. 13 Apr 1803 Ossipee NH, d. 14 Apr 1880 Masardis ME, m. Feb 1828 Tuftonboro NH Eliza Kennison of Tuftonboro NH, b. 22 Mar 1806 d. 26 Jun 1871. Farmer. In Tuftonboro NH, Old Town ME, Fish Township 1840, Masardis ME.

  Lydia Frances, b. 29 Apr 1829, d. 13 Jul 1908, m. Andrew Sutherland. Went to Montana.
5 Hosea B.[2], 1832-1914.

Sources: Tuftonboro NH census 1830. Fish Township ME census 1840. Masardis ME census 1860, 1870. SA/ME. D51, H5.

4. **DAVID H.$^{2}$ SAWYER** [see 1], b. ca. 1810 Ossipee NH, d. Ossipee NH, m. Mary J. Willard of Tuftonboro NH, b. ca. 1813 d. 9 Oct 1861, dau. John and Polly Willard. Farmer. He bur. in Sawyer Farm Cem., Ossipee NH.

Susan D., b. ca. 1834.
Maria J., b. ca. 1836, d. 5 Aug 1860, m. 28 Feb 1857 Wolfeboro NH George I. Jordan.
David M., b. Sep 1842, d. 24 Jan 1873.
Mary A., b. Apr 1845, d. 5 Jul 1846.
Sydna A., b. Feb 1847, d. 19 May 1848.
Daughter, b. 18 Apr 1850.
6 Frank$^{3}$ b. ca. 1852.
San Francisco (*sic.*), b. ca. 1853.

Sources: Ossipee NH census 1840, 1850, 1860. L41.

5. **HOSEA B.$^{3}$ SAWYER** [see 3], b. 19 Mar 1832 Tuftonboro NH, d. 7 Feb 1914 Island Falls ME, m.(1) Mary Ann Thompson, b. ca. 1832; m.(2) 4 Jun 1895 Ashland ME Caroline Rowe of Alna ME, b. 16 Jul 1838 d. 16 Apr 1909 Masardis ME, dau. John and Mary (Dole) Messinger. In Masardis ME 1870, 1880.

William N., b. ca. 1864 Masardis ME.
Andrew J., b. ca. 1866 Masardis ME.
7 George W.$^{3}$, 1868-1941.
8 Hosea B.$^{3}$, b. 1870.
Mary Ann, b. 1872, m. Charles Gadding.

Sources: Masardis ME census 1870, 1880. ME 1880 census index. VR Old Town ME, SA/ME. M7A.

6. **FRANK$^{3}$ SAWYER** [see 4], b. ca. 1852 Ossipee NH, m. 19 Nov 1887 Ossipee NH (div. Apr 1901) Adaline (Hall) Chapman of Sunapee NH, b. ca. 1867. In Goshen NH, Milford NH, West Concord NH.

9 Charles Edwin$^{4}$, 1890-1937.

Sources: VR SA/NH. S31.

7. **GEORGE W.$^{4}$ SAWYER** [see 5], b. 23 Mar 1868 Masardis ME, d. 26 Dec 1941, m.(1) Etta M. Greenlough of Presque Isle ME, b. Apr 1869 d. Jan 1892, dau. George W. and Martha (Sprague) Greenlough; m.(2) 20 Oct 1896 Masardis ME Lillian H. Leavitt of Ludlow ME, b. 4 Oct 1867 d. 30 Jun 1961, dau. William T. and Anna (Smith) Leavitt.

10 George Greenlough$^{4}$, 1892-1974.
11 Frank Dewey$^{4}$, 1898-1968.
Annie, b. ?, m. Brayley Webb.
Arolyn, b. ?, m. Roy Wheeler.

Sources: Masardis ME census 1880. VR SA/ME. Obit, Nina Sawyer rec.

8. **HOSEA B.$^{4}$ SAWYER** [see 5], b. 1870 Oxbow ME, m. 19 Aug 1892 Annie P. Condon of Atkinson ME, b. ca. 1875. Farmer.

Earle L., b. 11 Jun 1893 Masardis ME.
Laura M., b. 27 Apr 1895.
Jennie, b. 11 Jul 1897.

Sources: Masardis ME census 1880. VR SA/ME. Obit, Nina Sawyer rec.

9. **CHARLES EDWIN$^{4}$ SAWYER** [see 6], b. 1890 Milford NH, d. 1937, m. 2 Oct 1911 Claremont NH Ruth E. Angier of Brattleboro VT, b. ca. 1842, dau. Will and Verna (Fowler) Angier.

Charles Edwin, b. 1921.
Sources: Charles E. Sawyer rec.

10. **GEORGE GREENLOUGH[5] SAWYER** [see 7], b. 7 Jan 1892 Masardis ME, d. 25 Dec 1974, m. Abbie Tank, b. ?
Evelyn Etta, b. ?. m. Irving A. Cope.
George W., b. 1923, d. 1964.
Sources: Evelyn Cope rec.

11. **FRANK DEWEY[5] SAWYER** [see 7], b. 22 Jul 1898 Masardis ME, d. 31 Dec 1968 Island Falls ME, m.(1) (later div.) Eva Cyr, b. ? d. 1976; m.(2) Nina G. Caldwell, b. ?
Hosea Frank, Colonel, b. 25 Jul 1922, d. 14 Nov 1984, m. Emma L. Talmadge.
Sources: Obit, Nina Sawyer rec.

---

## LINE 19

1. **SAMUEL[1] SAWYER**, b. ca. 1774, m. Mary _____, b. 1776 d. Nov 1817. In Dresden ME 1800, Wiscasset ME. Mother was Hepzebah.
Jane Stevens, b. 29 Aug 1798, d. 16 Jan 1831.
Hepzebah, b. 11 Feb 1800, m. 10 Jul 1825 James Pinkham of Wiscasset ME.
2 Samuel E.[2], 1802-1890.
John Jones, b. 1 Aug 1803 Wiscasset ME, d. 1875. Shoemaker. In Charlestown MA 1865.
Mary, b. 1 Aug 1803, m. 10 Jan 1846 in Massachusetts Joseph Mace.
Sources: Dresden ME census 1800. VR SA/MA. D51.

2. **SAMUEL E.[2] SAWYER** [see 1], b. 23 Aug 1802 Wiscasset ME, d. 1890 Woburn MA, m. Matilda Ann _____, b. 1808 d. 21 Sep 1849. Baker. In Charlestown MA 1833, Woburn MA 1850.
3 Samuel Edwin[3], b. 1833.
Matilda J., b. 1836, d. 1876.
4 Willard F.[3], b. 1846.
Sources: Woburn MA census 1850. Charlestown MA census 1865. VR Woburn MA, SA/MA.

3. **SAMUEL EDWIN[3] SAWYER** [see 2], b. 1833 Charlestown MA, m. 27 Apr 1855 Burlington MA Sarah F. McIntire of Reading MA, b. 1835, dau. Aaron and Jerusha McIntire. Shoemaker.
Edwin Russell, b. 12 Jun 1857, d. 21 Dec 1863.
Frederick Loring, b. 5 Oct 1861, d. 5 Dec 1863.
James Willard, b. 17 Jul 1865, d. 29 Aug 1868.
Charles H., b. 10 Dec 1875 Woburn MA.
Sources: VR Woburn MA, SA/MA.

4. **WILLARD F.[3] SAWYER** [see 2], b. 17 Jun 1846 Woburn MA, m. 10 Jun 1869 Charlestown MA Nettie A. Hayward of Charlestown MA, b. 1848, dau. Martin and Mary Hayward. Glue manufacturer. In Woburn MA 1850.
Harry H., b. 6 Aug 1870 Woburn MA.
Willie Reed, b. 10 Mar 1872 Woburn MA.
Son, b. 25 Oct 1874.
Hattie Augusta, b. 25 May 1876.
Sources: VR SA/MA.

---

## LINE 20

1. **LARKIN[1] SAWYER**, b. 1779 in Vermont, m. Jennie _____ of Rhode Island, b. 1779. Farmer.

Lucretia, b. 1800.
2 Edwin A.[2], b. 1803.
Isaiah, b. 1815 in Vermont. Farmer. In Sharon VT 1850.

Sources: Sharon VT census 1850.

2. **EDWIN A.[2] SAWYER** [see 1], b. 1803 in Vermont, m. Matilda Harrington of Sharon VT, b. 27 Jul 1805 d. 9 May 1873. In Sharon VT 1850.

Mary, b. 1840.
3 Charles Henry[3], 1842-1907.
Isaiah, b. 1845.

Sources: Sharon VT census 1850. VR SA/VT.

3. **CHARLES HENRY[3] SAWYER** [see 2], b. Nov 1842 Sharon VT, d. 22 Nov 1907 Pomfret VT, m. 16 Nov 1867 Sharon VT Sarah A. Barrows, b. ?. Farmer.

4 George H.[4], b. 1870.

Sources: Sharon VT census 1850. Stafford VT census 1870. VR SA/VT. Florence Sawyer rec.

4. **GEORGE H.[4] SAWYER** [see 3], b. Nov 1870 Pomfret VT, m. 4 Mar 1893 Pomfret VT Alice B. Chapman of Manchester NH, b. ?. Farmer.

5 Harland Chapman[5], 1893-1928.
Daughter, b. 15 Aug 1897.

Sources: VR SA/VT.

5. **HARLAND CHAPMAN[5] SAWYER** [see 4], b. 3 Oct 1893 in Vermont, d. 25 Oct 1928, m. Florence St. John, b. ? d. 29 Aug 1988.

Harland Chapman, b. ?, d. 21 Apt 1988, m. Christine Olmstead. CH: Arland Harland, m. Jane I. ______
George, m. Carmen ______.
Robert
John

Sources: VR Pomfret VT, SA/NH.

---

## LINE 21

1. **PHINEAS[1] SAWYER**, b. in Ireland, d. Feb 1821, m. 6 Aug 1809 Boston MA Susanna Fowler of Kittery ME, b. 1783 d. 25 Dec 1861. War of 1812: Enl. in Salem MA. In Boston MA.

2 Joseph J.[2], 1820-1897.

Sources: VR Boston MA, SA/ME. H26, M5.

2. **JOSEPH J.[2] SAWYER** [see 1], b. 10 Sep 1820 Boston MA, d. 4 Sep 1897 Kittery ME, m. Sarah Peters of Kittery Point ME, b. 1819. Fisherman, shoemaker. In Kittery ME 1860. He bur. Kittery ME.

Hugh A., b. 1853, d. 18 Sep 1854 in Kittery ME.
Hugh A., b. 23 Oct 1854 Kittery ME, d. 30 Mar 1892 South Berwick ME, m. 10 Dec 1884 Portsmouth NH Frances Philpot of Iowa, b. 1862. Sea captain. In South Berwick ME. CH: Alta F., b. 13 Mar 1889.

3 Charles C.$^3$, 1856-1932.
4 Leonidas H.$^3$, 1860-1938.
Sources: Kittery ME census 1860. VR SA/ME. M5.

3. **CHARLES C.$^3$ SAWYER** [see 2], b. Jan 1856 Kittery ME, d. 14 Apr 1932 Kittery ME, m. 26 Mar 1882 Portsmouth NH Abbie F. Randall of Kittery ME, b. 11 Dec 1862 d. 31 Oct 1931, dau. Reuben Randall. Sea captain. In Kittery ME 1880. Both bur. Kittery ME.
Victor C., b. May 1883 Kittery ME, d. 3 Jul 1937 Kittery ME, m. Sarah E. _____, b. 1883 d. 1965.
Burton W., b. Dec 1888 Kittery ME.
Mildred Abbie, b. 2 Oct 1894.
Sources: Kittery ME census 1860, 1900. VR SA/ME. M5.

4. **LEONIDAS H.$^3$ SAWYER** [see 2], b. 9 Aug 1860 Kittery ME, d. 27 Feb 1938 Kittery ME, m. 2 Sep 1883 Portsmouth NH Malvina M. Bridges of Kittery ME, b. 8 Jul 1864 d. 26 Jun 1937, dau. Samuel and Jane Bridges. Both bur. Kittery ME.
5 Justin A.$^4$, 1885-1972.
Bessie, b. Jul 1887.
Sources: Kittery ME census 1990. M5.

5. **JUSTIN A.$^4$ SAWYER** [see 4], b. 5 Jan 1885 Kittery Point ME, d. 5 May 1972, m. 16 Sep 1902 Portsmouth NH Annie M. Mitchell of Kittery Point ME, b. 8 Jul 1885 d. 3 Oct 1941, dau. Daniel and Jane (Kimball) Mitchell. Both bur. Kittery ME.
Clayton Leonides, b. 6 Dec 1902 Kittery Point ME, d. 1984 Kittery Point ME, m.(1) 26 Apr 1921 Hazel E. Twombly of Portsmouth NH, b. 9 Dec 1902 d. 2 Dec 1951; m.(2) Josephine B. _____. CH: Elaine, b. Mar 1922, d. 28 Jun 1922; Daughter, stillborn 13 Jun 1931.
Sources: VR SA/NH. M5.

---

## LINE 22

1. **DAVID$^1$ SAWYER**, b. ca. 1784, d. 1835 Castine ME, m. 17 Oct 1808 Hepsebeth Foster, b. 1793. Wid. in Castine ME in 1840, 1850. Note: The only possible clue to David's origin is a deed (Ellsworth, Hancock County ME 6\21) in which a David Sawyer of Boston MΛ B/land in Hancock County 1798. This buyer could have been David's father.
Phebe Brooks, b. 29 Dec 1808.
Eliza, b. 4 May 1812, d. 15 Aug 1812.
Angelina D., b. 6 Dec 1815, m.(I) 18 Sep 1836 Joseph Bithee.
Ingerson Procter, b. 11 Aug 1816 Castine ME.
William, b. 18 Mar 1817, d. 4 Jan 1890.
Susan A., b. 21 Dec 1818, m. 1 Jun 1839 John Q. Adams of Boston MA.
Jane Augusta, b. 1 Oct 1820, d. Apr 1879.
David Charles, b. 25 Nov 1825, d. 13 Dec 1827.
John Clifton, b. 25 Dec 1826 Castine ME, m.(1) 6 Apr 1856 Olive Thomas, b. 1841 d. 3 Oct 1856; m.(2) 31 Oct 1863 Harriet Cox, b. ?. Mariner. CH: John, b. ?, d. 1856; Jennie F., b. Aug 1870, d. 6 Oct 1884 Castine ME.
Abigail, b. 1 Apr 1829.
2 David H.$^2$, 1832-1914.
Sources: Castine ME census 1810, 1820, 1830, 1840, 1850. VR Castine ME. P82b, R10b, N39.

2. **DAVID H.² SAWYER** [see 1], b. 3 Apr 1832 Castine ME, d. 12 Mar 1914 Castine ME, m.(1) 15 Nov 1859 Susan J. Coombs, b. 18 Mar 1836 d. 12 Dec 1874, dau. Jessie and Desire Coombs; m.(2) 27 May 1889 Janette P. Mills, b. 1860 d. 9 Mar 1901. David received a pension for his father April 1869. Second wife left a will.

Ella, b. 8 Mar 1857, d. 25 Jun 1857.
Ingerson, b. 6 Feb 1861.
Frederick I., b. 1862 Castine ME.
3 Charles Lincoln³, 1863-1942.
Laura S., b. 19 Jan 1892.
Harry E., b. 20 Apr 1893 Castine ME.

Sources: Castine ME census 1860. VR Castine ME, SA/ME. P82b, M5A.

3. **CHARLES LINCOLN³ SAWYER** [see 2], b. 1863 Castine ME, d. 1942, m.(1) 28 Apr 1882 Castine ME Ella J. Hackett, b. ? d. 10 Nov 1892, dau. Joseph and Mercy Hackett; m.(2) 29 Aug 1894 Castine ME Mary G. Fay of Boston MA, b. 1874 d. 1929, dau. George and Mary (Conley) Fay. Sailor, mason. Note: Ella's will mentions seven CH. He bur. in Castine ME.

4 Fred Harrison⁴, 1884-1972.
Hattie B., b. 21 Sep 1888.
5 Charles Arthur⁴, b. 1890.
Osgood C., b. 8 Nov 1892.
Joseph, b. ?.
John, b. ?.
Ebenezer, b. ?
Margaret V., b. 26 Jan 1896.
Bernard David, b. 23 Oct 1898 Castine ME, m. Alice Gray, b. ?. CH: Roger W., b. 1927, d. 1928 Castine ME.
Leonard, b. ca. 1900 Castine ME, d. Dec 1985 Castine ME.
6 James Goodwin⁴, 1918-1973.
Charlotte, b. ?, m. John Butler.

Sources: VR Castine ME, SA/ME. Will, Charles M. Sawyer rec., Lloyd V. Sawyer rec.

4. **FRED HARRISON⁴ SAWYER** [see 3], b. 22 Sep 1884 Castine ME, d. 17 Sep 1972, m.(1) Ada M. Jordan of Waltham (MA?), b. ?; m.(2) Leola _____, b. ?. Had total of nine sons, four daughters?

Lloyd V., m. Dolores _____.
Lowell J., b. 1918, d. 28 Oct 1920 Brewer ME.
Charles Lawrence, b. 14 Sep 1931.
Ada Mertice, b. 27 Nov 193?.

Sources: VR SA/ME. Lloyd V. Sawyer rec.

5. **CHARLES ARTHUR⁴ SAWYER** [see 3], b. 24 Jun 1890 Castine ME, m. Emma B. Lawrence, b. ?. In Brewer ME.

Arthur A.
Marion, m.(1) _____ Ellis, m.(2) _____ Grover.

Sources: P82d.

6. **JAMES GOODWIN⁴ SAWYER** [see 3], b. 17 Feb 1918 Castine ME, d. 25 Feb 1973, m. Winifred Laura Perkins, b. 12 Nov 1925. Wid. m. _____ Leach.

Donna Lee.
Sally Ann, m. _____ Grant.
James Edward.

Charles M., m. Debora C. Gilley. CH: Charles Leonard, Jessica Marie.
Sources: Charles M. Sawyer rec.

---

## LINE 23

1. **LEWIS[1] SAWYER**, b. ca. 1785, m. Margaret Brown, b. ?. In Westport NY 1820, Mendon VT.

Raney, b. 30 Dec 1805, d. 17 Oct 1889, m. Ziba Plumley.
Deborah, b. 5 Aug 1810, d. 24 Dec 1824.
Louisa Ann, b. 16 Jan 1813, m. _____ Wilkins.
Albina, b. 19 Jan 1815.
Julia Ann, b. 25 Feb 1818.
2 George W.[2], 1820-1880.
John B., b. 11 May 1822 Rutland VT, d. 23 Sep 1890 Mendon VT, m. Arosina E. Sargent, b. 1826 d. 5 Jun 1893. In Mendon VT 1860.
Margaret, b. 27 Jan 1825, m. 3 Oct 1856 Mendon VT Daniel Eames.
Sources: Mendon VT census 1860. VR SA/VT. Sawyer family Bible, Ann Page rec.

2. **GEORGE W.[2] SAWYER** [see 1], b. 12 Apr 1820 Westport NY, d. 20 or 21 May 1880 Rutland VT, m. Lucretia C. Rowe of Rutland VT, b. 1827 d. 10 Nov 1920, dau. Joel and Eliza Rowe. Farmer. In Sherburne VT 1850, Mendon VT 1860. Representative, 1861-62. Wid. m. 23 Sep 1890 Warren Green.

Julia A., b. 1849, d. 7 Mar 1885, m. 4 Mar 1868 Forest C. Fisk.
3 Charles D.[3], b. 1850.
Frances E., b. 23 Aug 1852, d. 25 Aug 1870.
John B., b. 1854 Mendon VT, m. 23 Sep 1876 EllaJ. Ranger of Mendon VT, b. ?. Farmer. In Pittsfield VT. CH: Julia C., b.2 Jun 1877, m. 30 Aug 1893 Charles Shanghausse; Anna, b. ca. 1878, m. 25 Dec 1897 Albert Lary.
Lucinda, b. 1 Nov 1856, d. 18 Jul 1874 Mendon VT.
Daughter, b. 17 Nov 1859.
George W., b. 9 May 1863 Mendon VT, m. 3 Jul 1890 Pittsfield VT Blanche L. Ranger, b. Dec 1873. Laborer. CH: Ella May, b. 1892; Beryl Frances, b. 2 Jun 1899, m. Earl T. Kilburn; Dorothy Isabelle, b. 23 Mar 1907.
Sources: Sherburne VT census 1850. Mendon VT census 1860. VR Mendon VT, SA/VT.

3. **CHARLES D.[3] SAWYER** [see 2], b. 1850 Sherburne VT, m. 3 Nov 1870 Pittsfield VT Lucia McGee, b. 1854. Farmer. In Mendon VT, Pittsfield VT, Woodford VT.

Frances Belle, b. 11 Jul 1871.
George J., b. 1873, d. 13 Apr 1874.
John B., b. 1874, d. 4 Jul 1874.
John, b. 18 Nov 1875, d. 3 Jun 1876.
Durrell P., b. 6 Nov 1889 Woodford VT.
Sources: VR Woodford VT, SA/VT.

---

## LINE 24

1. **JOHN[1] SAWYER**, b. 10 Feb 1787 in Massachusetts, d. 18 Dec 1875 Sheldon VT, m.(1) 31 Oct 1813 Highgate VT Mrs. Hannah Stimmets, b. 25 Dec 1790 d. 14 Jan 1851; m.(2) 10 Mar

1859 Sheldon VT Ellen Irwin. In Highgate VT, Franklin VT. He bur. Old Cemetery of Franklin Center VT.

John, b. Jul 1826, d. 5 Jul 1901.

2 Charles$^2$, 1829-1902.

More unnamed children listed in census.

Sources: Franklin VT census 1830, 1840. VR SA/VT.

2. **CHARLES$^2$ SAWYER** [see 1], b. Mar 1829 Franklin VT, d. 6 Jun 1902, m. Huldah Wait of Swanton VT. Farmer. In Lowell VT.

Henry A., b. 20 Dec 1863 Lowell VT, m. 31 Dec 1884 Lowell VT Mary A LaRoch, b. ?. CH: Son, b. 19 Jun 1886, d. 21 Jun 1886; Roy Eldon, b. 23 Sep 1887, d. 28 Dec 1887.

Mary J., b. 4 Dec 1866, m. 10 Oct 1885 William J. Morton.

Sources: VR SA/VT.

---

## LINE 25

1. **LEWIS$^1$ SAWYER**, b. ca. 1792, m. Angeline _____, b. ?. In Pownal VT, New Bedford MA.

2. John, b. 1817.

Augustus, b. 1824 Pownal VT, d. 1 Aug 1872 Pownal VT.

Sources: VR New Bedford MA, Pownal VT

2. **JOHN$^2$ SAWYER**, b. ca. 1817 Stanford VT, m. 23 Nov 1845 Dartmouth MA Silvia P. Hathaway of Dartmouth MA, b. ?, dau. Isreal J. and Hannah Hathaway. Cordwainer. In New Bedford MA, Dartmouth MA.

Augustus H., b. 10 Mar 1846 New Bedford MA.

Daughter, b. 15 Feb 1848.

Orrin P., b. 5 Mar 1851 New Bedford MA, m.(1) 17 May 1875 New Bedford MA Louisa R. Wilbur of New Bedford MA, b. 1849, dau. James Wilbur; m.(2) 2 Jun 1884 Dartmouth MA Annie H. Pinkham of New Bedford MA, b. 1867, dau. Charles H. and Louisa Pinkham. Shoemaker. CH: Daughter, b. 24 Dec 1875.

Son, b. Aug 1860.

Sources: VR New Bedford MA, SA/MA.

---

## LINE 26

1. **ISAAC$^1$ SAWYER**, b. ca. 1796 Pittston ME, d. 24 May 1860, m.(I) 19 Oct 1829 Abigail Douglas of Litchfield ME, b. 1810 d. 20 Feb 1850. In Pittston ME 1830. Abigail bur. Riverside Cem., Pittston ME.

2 Elijah L.$^2$, 1831-1894.

Sources: Pittston ME census 1830, 1840, 1850. VR SA/ME. M5.

2. **ELIJAH L.$^2$ SAWYER** [see 1], b. 1831 Pittston ME, d. 7 Oct 1894 Hallowell ME, m.(1) 5 Jun 1852 Pittston ME Ann Dorcas Baker of Nova Scotia, Canada, b. 1830 d. 4 Mar 1871; m.(2) 9 Mar 1872 Hallowell ME Lucretia R. Clarke of Hallowell ME, b. 1827 d. 3 Aug 1899, dau. Peter and Susan (Kimball) Clarke. In Hallowell ME 1860.

3 Frank Lorenso$^3$, 1853-1915.

Abigail A., b. 16 Nov 1854, m. 30 Nov 1874 Scott. W. Haynes.

Carrie P., b. 25 May 1857.

Warren W. H., b. 17 Sep 1860 Hallowell ME, m. 23 Nov 1882 Georgia A. Dudley of Augusta ME, b. 1862. Farmer. CH: Barbara D., b. 5 Sep 1890.
Delia A., b. 29 Jun 1869.
Alice D., b. 21 Feb 1871.
Sources: Hallowell ME census 1860. VR Pittston/Hallowell ME, Gardiner ME, SA/ME.

3. **FRANK LORENSO[3] SAWYER** [see 2], b. 7 Apr 1853 Pittston ME, d. 15 Oct 1915 Augusta ME, m.(I) 14 Oct 1872 Nellie R. Steward of Farmingdale ME, b. 11 Jul 1853 d. 20 Apr 1901, dau. Daniel and Philena (Gould) Steward. In Chelsea MA 1880.
Harry E., b. ca. 1877.
Alice, b. ca. 1885.
Sources: Chelsea MA census 1880. ME 1880 census index. VR Farmingdale ME, SA/ME.

---

## LINE 27

1. **JOHN B.[1] SAWYER**, b. ca. 1800 in Vermont, m.(1) Mar 1820 SallyHaywood, b. 1799 d. 20 Jul 1827; m.(2) 8 Aug 1832 Southboro MA Louisa Newton, b. ca. 1810. Bootmaker. In New York City, Upton MA 1850, Hopkinton MA.
Child, b. ?, d. 20 Jul 1833.
2 Ephraim H.[2], b. ca. 1823.
3 Henry James[2], b. 1825.
4 Angelo L.[2], b. ca. 1835.
5 William L.[2], b. ca. 1837.
Louisa S., b. ca. 1840, m. 8 May 1870 Bolton MA George E. Wales.
6 Charles L.[2], b. ca. 1849.
Sources: VR Upton MA, Hopkinton MA, SA/MA. B18, H28, B19.

2. **EPHRAIM H.[2] SAWYER** [see 1], b. ca. 1823 New York City, m. 15 Nov 1844 Milford MA Lydia A. Pond of Milford MA, b. 16 Sep 1826, dau. Jonas and Hopestill (Corbett) Pond. Bootmaker. In Upton MA, Hopkinton MA.
Arthur J., b. 19 Dec 1846, d. 7 Jan 1847.
Henry Lloyd, b. 1 Sep 1849, d. 7 Sep 1850.
7 Henry Lloyd[3], b. ca. 1850.
Cora Arabella, b. 29 Sep 1851.
Helen Frances, b. 10 Jan 1855.
Sources: VR Milford MA, Hopkinton MA, SA/MA. H28.

3. **HENRY JAMES[2] SAWYER** [see 1], b. 22 Jan 1825 New York City, m.(1) 27 Jun 1850 Chloe S. Comey of Hopkinton MA, b. ? d. 4 Apr 1857, adopted dau. Lovett H. and Alma Bowker; m.(2) 27 Jan 1869 Milford MA Sarah A. Cook, b. ?, dau. Arthur and Adeline (Purington) Cook. Shoe manufacturer. In Milford MA, Chicago IL 1870.
Alma Marie, b. 6 Apr 1853, m. 12 Jun 1877 Hopkinton MA Clarence A. Claflin.
Mary B., b. 27 Mar 1855, m. 18 Oct 1877 Hopkinton MA Clarence Thompson.
Henry James, b. 9 Jan 1870 Chicago IL.
Gordon Hayward, b. 2 Nov 1871 Chicago IL.
Mabel Aurilla, b. 25 Mar 1873 Chicago IL.
Gertrude Lovice, b. Feb 1876 Chicago IL.
Sources: VR SA/MA. B18.

4. **ANGELO L.[2] SAWYER** [see 1], b. ca. 1835 Upton MA, m. 22 Jun 1862 Sutton MA Mary E. (Gould) Sawyer of Douglas MA, b. ?, dau. Willard and Joanna Gould. Shoemaker, gunsmith. In Sutton MA, Millbury MA 1863.

Son, b. 8 Dec 1860.
Emily Louisa, b. 23 Jun 1863.

Sources: VR SA/MA.

5. **WILLIAM L.[2] SAWYER** [see 1], b. ca. 1837 New York City, m. Chloe C. Jennings of Hopkinton MA, b. ?. Shoemaker. In Sutton MA, Hopkinton MA.

Emma Frances, b. 9 Aug 1860.
Winslow L., b. 18 May 1862 Hopkinton MA.

Sources: VR SA/MA.

6. **CHARLES L.[2] SAWYER** [see 1], b. ca. 1849 Upton MA, m. 8 Oct 1870 Bolton MA Harriet G. Perkins of Acton MA, b. ?, dau. Stephen and Harriet Perkins. Bootmaker.In New York City, Milford MA 1872.

Ralph Leroy, b. 3 Oct 1872 Milford MA.

Sources: VR SA/MA.

7. **HENRY LLOYD[3] SAWYER** [see 2], b. ca. 1850 Hopkinton MA, m. 21 Dec 1877 Boston MA Martha A. Pope of Watertown MA, b. ca. 1855, dau. Frederick and Mary A. Pope. Teacher. In Boston MA 1881.

Ethel Louise, b. 5 Mar 1879.
Frederick Haywood, b. 21 Feb 1881 Boston MA.

Sources: VR SA/MA.

---

## LINE 28

1. **JOSEPH[1] SAWYER**, b. ca. 1800, m. Susan _____, b. ca. 1800. Trader. In Center Harbor NH.

2 Joseph C[2], 1824-1864.

Sources: Center Harbor NH census 1850.

2. **JOSEPH C.[2] SAWYER** [see 1], b. 1824, d. 6 Jan 1864 Londonderry NH, m.(1) Apphia T. Plumer of Gilmanton NH, b. 17 Sep 1826, m.(2) Leonora W. Cummings of Ireland, b. 1825 d. 11 Jan 1875. In Newton NH, Salem NH, Derry NH. Wid. m. 19 Apr 1873 Derry NH William H Redfield.

Clark, b. 21 Sep 1852.
Matthew A., b. 9 Oct 1855 Newton NH, m. 3 Feb 1900 Angeline I. (Rollins) Clark of Pelham NH, b. 15 Dec 1873 d. 13 Jul 1907, dau. Samuel and Lydia (Hansell) Rollins. In Nashua NH.

3 Cleon Josiah[3], b. 1859.

Sources: Derry NH census 1860. VR SA/NH. W53, N6.

3. **CLEON JOSIAH[3] SAWYER** [see 2], b. 26 May 1859 Salem NH, m. 18 Apr 1881 Dummerston VT Jennie M. Roberts of Williamstown MA, b. ?. Clerk. In Williamstown MA, Washington DC.

Maria, b. 3 May 1884.
Harold Cleon, b. 8 Dec 1885.

Sources: VR SA/MA. W53.

---

## LINE 29

1. **EPHRAIM W.[1] SAWYER**, b. ca. 1805 Erving MA, m. 14 Oct 1835 Phillipston MA Rosanna K. Wesson of Fairfield VT, b. ca. 1807. Shoemaker. In Phillipston MA, Canada, Vermont.

Laura M., b. 2 Sep 1836.

2 Elmer Warren, b. 1838.

Charles Wood, b. 25 Sep 1839 Phillipston MA, m. 26 Sep 1863 Wilbraham MA LucyM. Kendall of Stafford CT, b. 1841, dau. John and Eucina Kendall. Machinist. In Athol MA, Springfield MA. CH: Grace, b. 11 Nov 1866.

Eunice Elanna, b. ca. 1841, m. 18 Sep 1862 Phillipston MA George G. Smith.

3 Oscar L., b. ca. 1844.

Mary A., b. ca. 1846.

Flora, b. ca. 1849.

Ellen Frances, b. 23 Dec 1851.

Sources: Phillipston ME census 1840, 1850. VR Phillipston MA, SA/MA.

2. **ELMER WARREN[2] SAWYER** [see 1], b. 3 May 1838 Phillipston MA, m. Sarah Ann Hager of Petersham MA, b. Apr 1846, dau. George Hager. Chair manufacturer. In Phillipston MA. Civil War: 20 Jul 1863 to 29 Jun 1865.

Willis L., b. ca. 1867 Phillipston MA, m. 9 Feb 1890 Phillipston MA Nellie A. Sears of Greenwich CT, b. 1866, dau. Henry T. and Mary P. Sears. Farmer. CH: Son, stillborn 6 May 1891.

Eveline A., b. 19 Jul 1870, m. 30 May 1891 Phillipston MA Albert Sampson.

Sources: Phillipston MA census 1880. VR SA/MA. T13.

3. **OSCAR L.[3] SAWYER** [see 1], b. ca. 1844 Troy VT, m. 8 Aug 1865 Phillipston MA Adeline E. Stratton of Brighton MA, b. 1843, dau. Nathan and Harriet Stratton. Butcher, expressman. In Phillipston MA, Ware MA.

William H., b. 18 Jul 1866 Phillipston MA.

Mary Ellen, b. 15 Jul 1868.

Harriet A., b. 15 Jul 1868, m. 1 May 1889 Templeton MA Fred A. Hunting.

Sources: Phillipston MA census 1850. VR SA/MA.

---

## LINE 30

1. **ZEBULON K.[1] SAWYER**, b. ca. 1805 Westbrook ME, d. bef. 1834, m. 18 Nov 1828 Portland ME Rebecca S. Langford, b. 15 Oct 1807 d. 12 Mar 1891, dau. Smith and Grace (Atkins) Langford. In Westbrook 1830. Wid. S/L 1834. Wid. m. 1834 Edward B. Randall.

2 Smith Langford[2], 1829-1905.

Sources: VR SA/ME. R10a.

2. **SMITH LANGFORD[2] SAWYER** [see 1], b. 2 Sep 1829 Portland ME, d. 28 Jul 1905 New Gloucester ME, m.(1)(I) 25 Apr 1856 ElizabethM. Strout of Limington ME, b. 23 Nov 1836 d. 28 Apr 1865; m.(2) Almeda E. Dearborn of Limington ME, b. 29 Aug 1835 d. 13 Sep 1915, dau. Jacob and Nancy (Braden) Dearborn. Farmer. In Limington ME 1850, New Gloucester ME. Selectman for Limington ME 1869.

Grace A., b. 24 Nov 1857, d. 15 Nov 1910, m. 24 Jan 1900 George H. Dutton.

Charles F., b. 1860, d. 29 Mar 1889.
3 Willard Smith[3], 1864-1937.
Elizabeth E., b. 1 Dec 1872, d. 9 Apr 1940, m. 31 Dec 1891 Herbert Blake.
Sources: Limington ME census 1850, 1860, 1880. ME 1880 census index. VR SA/ME. N39, Robert L. Taylor rec.

3. **WILLARD SMITH[3] SAWYER** [see 2], b. 9 Apr 1864 Limington ME, d. 7 Feb 1937 Haverhill MA, m. 1 Jan 1887 Edith B. DeShon of Limington ME, b. 24 May 1865 d. Feb 1943. Motorman. In Portland ME, Haverhill MA. He bur. New Gloucester Hill ME.
Grace E., b. 4 May 1888, d. 12 Apr 1890.
Emma G., b. 7 Jun 1890, d. 22 Jan 1929.
4 Charles Franklin[4], b. 1891.
Ralph Deshon, b. 17 Jan 1894, d. 2 May 1966.
Ruth Elizabeth, b. 29 Jan 1906, d. 10 Mar 1913.
Sources: VR SA/MA. Robert L. Taylor rec.

4. **CHARLES FRANKLIN[4] SAWYER** [see 3], b. 17 Oct 1891 Portland ME, m. 20 Jun 1923 Virginia E. Gindorff of Boston MA, b. 24 May 1899 d. 19 Apr 1961. In Haverhill MA.
Willard Joseph, b. 18 Mar 1926.
Mary Lucille, b. 4 Jun 1928.
Virginia Ruth, b. 7 Nov 1930.
Sources: Robert L. Taylor rec.

---

## LINE 31

1. **JAMES P.[1] SAWYER**, b. 1805, d. 29 Sep 1879 Bradley ME, m.(1) Maria Sturdivant, b. 1815 d. 5 Jun 1850, m.(2) 13 Jun 1852 SarahH. Patterson, b. Mar 1815 d. 25 Aug 1881. In Hudson ME, Bradley ME.
Hannah A., b. 1836, m.(I) 11 Jul 1853 Charles C. Smith.
Harriet, b. 1837.
Helen M., b. 1839.
Harrison, b. 1842 Hudson ME.
2 Horatio Beal[2], 1843-1918.
Horace A., 1845, d. 2 Jul 1870. Civil War.
Henrietta A., b. 1848.
James P., b. 2 Jul 1853 Bradley ME, d. 15 Aug 1876, m. 7 Apr 1875 Bradley ME Clara A. Brown.
Ada M., b. 13 Feb 1857, d. 18 Oct 1879.
Sources: Kirkland (Hudson) ME census 1850. VR Bradley ME, SA/ME. P82f, M5.

2. **HORATIO BEAL[2] SAWYER** [see 1], b. 7 May 1843 Hudson ME, d. 24 Mar 1918 Auburn ME, m. 27 Mar 1870 Bradley ME Malvina Mason of Bradley ME, b. 1852, dau. T. W. and Zaben (Sawyer) Mason. Box manufacturer. In Auburn ME. Horatio received military pension 1878. Appointed administrator to stepmother's will.
Lois Anderson, b. 1 Sep 1878, m. _____ Arnold of Worcester MA.
Bernice E., b. 13 Nov 1890.
Sources: ME 1880 census index. VR SA/ME. D82f, N1A, M7A.

---

## LINE 32

1. **CHARLES S.[1] SAWYER**, b. 25 Aug 1805 Portland ME, d. 28 Oct 1877 Portland ME, m. 27 Nov 1823 Cumberland ME Sarah Ross of Gray ME, b. ?. Shipbuilder, sea captain. S/land on Chebeaque Island ME 1834. B/land in Portland ME 1863.

Charles W., b. 15 Oct 1824, d. 10 Sep 1825.
2 Greenleaf T.[2], 1828-1888.
3. James David[2], 1830-1892.
Emily, b. 24 Nov 1833, d. Jul 1834.
Lucinda, b. 28 Apr 1835, d. Mar 1836.
Martha A., b. 15 Nov 1842, d. 21 May 1895, m. _____ White.
John W., b. 4 Sep 1845, d. 5 Dec 1848.
Minnie, b. ca. 1846.

Sources: Portland ME census 1850, 1860. VR SA/ME. P69, M5.

2. **GREENLEAF T.[2] SAWYER** [see 1], b. 10 Jan 1828 Portland ME, d. 2 Apr 1888 Portland ME, m.(1) 12 Nov 1850 Portland ME Mary J. Rackliff of Portland ME, b. ?; m.(2) 7 Oct 1865 Margaret J. Hickey of Eastport ME, b. ?. Confectioner. Mary S/land in Portland ME 1863.

John W., b. Apr 1852, d. 30 Oct 1854.
Albion, b. 16 Nov 1853 Portland ME.
Ida M., b. 1 May 1855, m. 13 Mar 1883 Boston MA Edward A. Robie.
Minnie H., b. 1856, d. 20 May 1875.
Hattie E., b. 20 Jan 1857.
Green L., b. Feb 1858, d. 16 Aug 1858.
Mary E., b. 6 Jan 1860.
Edward E., b. Aug 1867, d. 11 Sep 1868.
Nellie, b. 4 Dec 1868.

Sources: Portland ME census 1860. VR SA/ME. M5, R10a.

3. **JAMES DAVID[2] SAWYER** [see 1], b. 5 Oct 1830 Portland ME, d. 9 Jul 1892, m.(1) 25 Mar 1853 Calais ME Lydia E. McCardy b. ?; m.(2) 13 Aug 1856 Portland ME Eliza A. Sawyer, b. 1830 d. 26 Sep 1868; m.(3) Mary A. Swett of Hampden ME, b. 25 Jan 1837 d. 21 Feb 1917, dau Benjamin and Hannah (Morse) Swett. Fruit dealer. B/S/land in Portland ME 1867-1870.

Lizzie M., b. 22 Apr 1859, d. 18 May 1863.
Howard Harry, b. 20 Feb 1871 Portland ME, m. 11 Jul 1894 Blanche L. Grant, b. ?.
Mary A., b. 1873.

Sources: Portland ME census 1850, 1860, 1880. ME 1880 census index. VR SA/ME. R10a.

---

## LINE 33

1. **SAMUEL[1] SAWYER**, b. ca. 1808 Westbrook ME, d. Feb 1900 Millbury MA, m. 2 May 1832 Lucinda B. Bacon of Palmer MA, b. ca. 1811 d. 1 May 1891. Blacksmith. Civil War. Arrived in Millbury MA 1833. His father lost an arm in War of 1812.

Harriet Maria, b. 17 Dec 1833, m. 24 Jul 1858 Sutton MA Ezra W. Marble. She had illegitimate son named Walter Frederick.
Mary Jane, b. 22 Jul 1835, m. 16 Apr 1864 Millbury MA Gardner Lewis.
Sarah Ann, b. 20 Mar 1838, m. 6 Sep 1864 Millbury MA Alonzo Sabin.
Emma Augusta, b. 21 Jun 1842, m. 16 Nov 1869 Charles Morrill.
2 Franklin B.[2], b. 1844.
3 Charles Herbert[2], b. 1846.

4 George O.[2], b. 1849.
Ellen Louise, b. 9 Jan 1856, m. 25 Jan 1881 Springfield MA Rev. Willis H. Stone.
Alphonse P., b. ?
Sources: Millbury MA census 1840, 1850. VR SA/MA. M42, B32.

2. **FRANKLIN B.[2] SAWYER** [see 1], b. 9 Oct 1844 Millbury MA, m. 23 Mar 1871 Ada A. Gardner of Leominster MA, b. ca. 1851. Occupation shown as "Billiards." In Worcester MA.
Harry Norman, b. 10 Aug 1871 Millbury MA, m. Helen J. French, b. ?. Clerk. In Worcester MA. CH: Cornelia, b. 17 Mar 1895.
Edith Louise, b. 25 Sep 1873.
Inez G., b. 5 Jun 1880.
Son, b. 27 Jun 1882.
Frank K., b. 21 Jul 1884 Worcester MA.
Ralph Victor, b. 7 Jan 1887 Worcester MA.
Charles Alan, b. 26 Dec 1891 Worcester MA.
Sources: VR SA/MA. M42.

3. **CHARLES HERBERT[2] SAWYER** [see 1], b. 30 Oct 1846 Millbury MA, m. 25 Dec 1878 in Worcester MA Clara E. (Gay) Wells of Plymouth MA, b. 1855, dau. Timothy and Harriet Gay. Bookkeeper. In Melrose MA 1879, Boston MA 1882.
Edward Asa, b. 13 Feb 1879 Melrose MA.
Mabel Eveline, b. 17 Apr 1882.
Sources: VR SA/MA. M42.

4. **GEORGE O.[2] SAWYER** [see 1], b. 30 Oct 1849 Millbury MA, m. 14 Mar 1872 Grafton MA Margaret A. Ferguson of Bristol RI, b. 1847, dau. John and Charlotte Ferguson. Blacksmith.
Henry Herbert, b. 18 Jun 1873 Millbury MA.
Sources: VR SA/MA. M42.

---

## LINE 34

1. **ARTHUR M.[1] SAWYER**, b. ca. 1811 Portland ME, m. 12 Sep 1841 Portland ME Eunice P. Nash of Portland ME, b. Dec 1821 d. 28 Dec 1907, dau. John and Eunice (Poland) Nash. Mariner, painter. In Portland ME 1844, Bath ME 1850.
Arthur M., b. 7 Jan 1842 Portland ME, d. 12 Mar 1909 Portland ME, m. Mary E. Gatecomb, b. ?. Janitor.
Edward H., b. 1 Nov 1843, d. 2 Dec 1847 Bath ME.
Eunice Sarah, b. 1846, d. 20 Jun 1910, unm.
2 Edward H.[2], b. 1850.
Ellen A., b. 1852.
George L., b. ca. 1856 Bath ME.
Frederick S., b. ca. 1858, m. Isabella Risteen, b. ?.
Sources: Bath ME census 1850. VR SA/ME. P69.

2. **EDWARD H.[2] SAWYER** [see 1], b. 1850 Bath ME, m. 26 Jun 1873 Bath ME Mary E. Mason, b. ?.
Edward H., b. ca. 1874 Bath ME, m. 16 Jan 1892 Hoosick Falls NY Minnie M. Webb, B. ca. 1874, dau. Henry and Elizabeth (Adams) Webb. Machinist. In Fitchburg MA. CH: Ruth Mae, b. 15 Jul 1892.
Sources: Bath ME census 1880. ME 1880 census index. VR SA/ME, SA/MA.

## LINE 35

1. **JAMES[1] SAWYER**, b. ca. 1813, d. bef. 1863, m. 11 Mar 1839 Rochester MA Ann Brown Leonard, b. ca. 1823, dau. Ichabod and Hope Leonard. In Freetown MA, Dartmouth MA. Wid. m. 20 Feb 1863 Lakeville MA George Robbins.

Mary B., b. ca. 1839, m. 5 Jul 1856 Noah Parker, Jr.
2 Lorenzo L.[2], b. ca. 1845.
Susan B., b. ca. 1846, m. 1 Jul 1864 Lakeville MA William J. Parris.
Jane M., b. ca. 1848, m. 3 Aug 1865 Freetown MA Franklin Keith.

Sources: VR Freetown MA, Franklin MA.

2. **LORENZO L.[2] SAWYER** [see 1], b. ca. 1845 Dartmouth MA, m.(1) 17 Jun 1867 Taunton MA Lydia M. Davis of Fall River MA, b. ca. 1846, dau. Lephaniah and Sarah Davis, m.(2) 31 Jul 1884 Dartmouth MA Lizzie M.(Burbank) Coon of Taunton MA, b. 1846, dau. Leonard and Betsey Burbank. Farmer, mariner. In Lakeville MA.

Elmer E., b. ca. 1869, m. 4 Jun 1889 Lakeville MA Nellie E. Tripp of Rochester MA, b. 1869, dau. James H. and Lydia C. Tripp. CH: Lucy Ellsworth, b. 3 May 1891; Lily Claftin, b. 2 Apr 1892. In Rochester MA.
Jenny B., b. ca. 1871, m. 23 Oct 1893 Brockton MA John F. Thompson.
James, b. 7 Oct 1877.
Amelia, b. 29 Mar 1881.
Daughter, b. 4 Jun 1882.

Sources: VR Taunton MA, SA/MA.

## LINE 36

1. **WILLIAM[1] SAWYER**, b. ca. 1816 Charlestown MA, m. 27 Oct 1841 Athol MA Betsey P. Chase of Athol MA, b. 16 Nov 1812, dau. Ebenezer and Barsylvia (Peck) Chase. Shoemaker. In Stoneham MA, Athol MA.

Iner, b. May 1843, d. 17 Oct 1848 Royalston MA.
William O., b. ca. 1846.
Ellen Sylvia, b. 11 Jun 1848, m. 17 Dec 1866 Orange MA William Spaulding.
Elizabeth, b. 11 Aug 1850.
2 Solon James[2], b. 1852.

Sources: VR Athol MA, Stoneham MA, SA/MA. C30.

2. **SOLON JAMES[2] SAWYER** [see 1], b. 26 Sep 1852 Athol MA, m. 13 Jan 1874 Orange MA Stella Bosworth, b. 1856, dau. Harmon and Miranda Bosworth. Railroad worker. In Royalston MA.

Leslie Solon, b. 23 Dec 1874.
Luna Aurora, b. 17 Jan 1879.
Sadie Isabella, b. 25 Mar 1882.
Lillian, b. 30 May 1885.
Charles E., b. 28 Mar 1892 Royalston MA.

Sources: VR SA/MA.

## LINE 37

1. **JAMES H.[1] SAWYER**, b. ca. 1820, m. Frances Lee of Addison ME, b. 12 Aug 1824 d. 5 Jan 1910, dau. John Lee. Ship carpenter. In Addison ME.

Marcella, b. 1846, m.(1) ?, m.(2) 8 Jul 1884 Boston MA Benjamin F. Gleason.
Henry I., b. ca. 1852.
2 Winslow Marshall[2], 1855-1893.
Alice B., b. 1858.

Sources: Addison ME census 1850, 1860, 1870. VR SA/ME, SA/NH.

2. **WINSLOW MARSHALL[2] SAWYER**, b. 5 Jan 1855 Addison ME, d. 25 Nov 1893 Milbridge ME, m. 25 Jul 1885 Alice Farnsworth of Harrington ME, b. 21 Nov 1864 d. 21 Sep 1939. Merchant. In Milbridge ME.

Vera Lee, b. 17 Jan 1887, d. 24 Jan 1958.
Gladys F., b. 16 Aug 1891.

Sources: VR SA/ME.

---

## LINE 38

1. **CHARLES HENRY E.[1] SAWYER**, b. ca. 1822 Portland ME, d. Mar 1906, m. Rebecca .J. Parker of Webster MA, b. 1831. Teamster, trader. In Mansfield MA 1850, Lewiston ME 1860, w/son Charles W. in 1880.

2 Charles William[2], 1848-1931.
Benjamin Franklin, b. 3 May 1850 Mansfield MA.
Lena S., b. 12 Mar 1853.
Eva E., b. 1859.

Sources: Mansfield MA census 1850. Lewiston ME census 1860. Poland ME census 1880. VR SA/MA.

2. **CHARLES WILLIAM[2] SAWYER** [see 1], b. 11 Sep 1848 Webster MA, d. Feb 1931 Newry ME, m. Annie M. Dunham of Boston MA, b. ?. In North Berwick ME, Poland ME.

Annie Mabel, b. 17 Jan 1876, d. 1944, m. _____ Ingraham.
3 Fred Everett[3], 1877-1935.
Bertha M., b. 1879, d. 1966, m. _____ Erlach.
Nellie G., b. 1882, d. 1966, m. _____ Hanscom.

Sources: Poland ME census 1880. ME 1880 census index.

3. **FRED EVERETT[3] SAWYER** [see 2], b. 1877 No. Berwick ME, d. 1935, m. Florence Irvine of Solon ME, b. 1885. Car salesman. In Portland ME, Auburn ME.

4 Mellen Clement[4], 1899-1981.
Frank Clifford, b. 1901, d. 1981.
Wellington Irvine, b. 1911, d. 1965, m. 19 Oct 1935 Margaret E. Hay.

Sources: Poland ME census 1880. ME 1880 census index.

4. **MELLEN CLEMENT[4] SAWYER** [see 3], b. 1899, d. 1981, m. _____, b. ?. In Portland ME.

Mellen C., b. 1918.
Fred William, b. 1920.
Walter, b. 1922.
Clifford Frank.

Ida Anne.
George Orin.
Sources:

---

## LINE 39

1. **GRANVILLE DENNEN[1] SAWYER**, b. 30 Dec 1827 New Gloucester ME, d. 4 Sep 1867 Auburn ME, m. 16 Oct 1853 Danville ME Cordelia Goding of Livermore ME, b. 6 Jul 1827 d. 17 Mar 1900, dau. Asa and Rhoda (Goding) Goding. Farmer. In Boston MA 1850, Danville ME 1860, Auburn ME. He bur. in Hotel Road Cem., Auburn ME. Note: His mother was ElizaSarah, b. 1771, m. William Stanley. Both with Granville in 1860 census.

2 Norman Alberto[2], 1854-1920.
Sarah Eliza, b. 2 Apr 1857, d. 10 Oct 1932, m. 15 Nov 1881 Auburn ME Clarence L. Goding.
Lewis Cyrus, b. 4 Mar 1859 Auburn ME, d. 29 Nov 1880, m. Mary _____, b. ?.
3 William Stanley[2], 1865-1941.
Granville Leighton, b. 8 Nov 1867 Auburn ME, d. 6 Mar 1937 Lynn MA, m. 28 Nov 1912 Lynn MA Carrie J. Blackadar of Nova Scotia, Canada, b. 6 Jan 1869, dau. Charles and Marguerite (Bell) Blackadar.

Sources: Boston MA census 1850. Danville ME 1860. VR Danville ME, Auburn ME. M5, Robert L. Taylor rec., Carleton Labdon rec.

2. **NORMAN ALBERTO[2] SAWYER** [see 1], b. 17 Jul 1854 Auburn ME, d. 28 May 1920 Wells ME, m. 8 Oct 1883 Lynn MA Margaret J. MacConley of Prince Edward Island, Canada, b. 27 Sep 1858 d. 27 Jan 1913, dau. Michael and Mary Jane (MacIsaac) MacConley. Stone cutter. In Lynn MA 1883.

Frank Warren, b. 25 Oct 1884 Lynn Ma.
Elmer Everett, b. 21 Jan 1886 Lynn Ma, m. Evie Maria Haynes, b. ?. CH: AliceMiriam, b. 4 Apr 1914, m. 3 Aug 1936 Elmer W. Widell; Hermione Margaret, b. 3 Dec 1915, m. 18 Aug 1940 Carleton W. Labdon.
Frederick Granville, b. 4 Mar 1888 Lynn Ma, m. 22 Oct 1913 Eva Greeley, b.?.
4 Clarence Ralph[3], b. 1891.

Sources: VR SA/ME, SA/MA. Carleton Labdon rec.

3. **WILLIAM STANLEY[2] SAWYER** [see 1], b. 4 Oct 1865 Danville ME, d. 29 Jun 1941 Auburn ME, m. 30 Jan 1897 Poland ME Gertrude Larrabee of New Gloucester ME, b. 14 Feb 1878 d. 27 Jan 1958, dau. Richard M. and Mary Lizzie (Sawyer) Larrabee. In Auburn ME. He bur. in Hotel Road Cem., Auburn ME. Note: Three different VR give his birthplace variously as Auburn ME, Danville ME, and New Gloucester ME.

Eva Cordelia, b. 17 Sep 1898, d. 15 Sep 1901 Auburn ME.
Marguerita Rose, b. 28 Nov 1899, m. Frank Beal. Went to Maryland.
Norman Asa, b. 23 Dec 1901, m. Marie _____. Went to Michigan.
Gladys, b. 28 Jul 1904, m. Arthur Peach.
Herman Goding, b. 22 Jan 1907, d. 19 Jul 1964, m. 6 Oct 1928 Ruth Briggs. Went to New York.
Stanley Monroe, b. 12 May 1909, m. Mildred E. _____.
Lewis Granville, b. 3 Dec 1916, d. 6 Feb 1918.
Daughter, d. in infancy.

Sources: VR SA/ME. M5, Mildred Sawyer rec., Carleton Labdon rec.

4. **CLARENCE RALPH[3] SAWYER** [see 2], b. 18 Mar 1891 Lynn MA, m. Marjorie Frances Fifield, b. ?. In Medford MA.

Clarence Haskell, b. 29 Mar 1916, m. 4 Dec 1936 Beulah Louise Cragie.

Sources: VR SA/MA. M5, Mildred Sawyer rec., Carleton Labdon rec.

---

## LINE 40

1. **OBEDIAH SAWYER**, ca. 1840, m. Elizabeth _____, b. ?. In Biddeford ME. Civil War: Served 1863 to 1865.

Franklin P., b. 17 Mar 1866 Biddeford ME.

2. Fred A., b. ca. 1869.

Eunice M., b. ?, m. 31 Aug 1891 Nashua NH James H. Paige.

Sources: VR SA/ME. N6.

2. **FRED A. SAWYER** [see 1], b. ca. 1869 Biddeford ME, m. 2 Aug 1893 Manchester NH Lizzie A. Breen of Nova Scotia, Canada, b. 1873. Mason. In Braintree MA, Quincy MA.

Daughter, b. 22 Oct 1893.

Rodman J., b. 24 Oct 1895 Quincy MA.

Sources: VR Braintree MA, Manchester NH, SA/MA.

---

## LINE 41

1. **CONRAD[1] SAWYER**, b. ca. 1846 in Germany, m. 10 Jul 1876 Boston MA Margaret. C. Pepper of Ireland, b. ca. 1852, dau. Thomas C. and Margaret Pepper, b. ?. Grocer. His parents were Charles and Elizabeth, b. ?

2 Carl Francis[2], b. 1877.

Sources: VR SA/MA. Mrs. James R. Sawyer rec.

2. **CARL FRANCIS[2] SAWYER** [see 1], b. 1 Nov 1877 Malden MA, m. 3 Jun 1903 Warrentine F. Lincoln, b. ?.

Warren, b. ?, d. 1977.

Carl, b. ?, d. Mar 1984.

Pearl Margaret, b. ?, d. Dec 1984.

Harold, b. ?, d. 1950, m. Margaret M. Ramsey, b. ?.

Sources: VR SA/MA. Mrs. James R. Sawyer rec.

---

## LINE 42

1. **FREDERICK J. SAWYER**, b. ca. 1848 Germany, son of John and Sophia Sawyer, m. 12 May 1869 Boston MA Mary Stuart of Boston MA, b. ca. 1850, dau. John and Margaret Stuart. Painter. In Boston MA.

Eliza Ann, b. 14 Mar 1870.

2. John J., b. 1872.

Frederick Joseph, b. 14 Nov 1873 Boston MA.

Mary, b. 5 Jul 1877.

Sources: VR SA/MA.

2. **JOHN J. SAWYER** [see 1], b. 18 Feb 1872 Boston MA, m. 14 Apr 1890 Boston MA Ann F. McElkinney of Boston MA, b. ca. 1872, dau. Michael and Bridget McElkinney. Butcher. In Boston MA.

John Joseph, b. 9 Feb 1891 Boston MA.
Leo F., b. 14 Nov 1895 Boston MA.

Sources: VR SA/MA.

---

## LINE 43

1. **FRANK A.[1] SAWYER**, b. ca. 1855 Searsport ME, m. 16 Dec 1873 Concord NH Almira J. Ash of Concord NH, b. 26 Dec 1857 d. 26 Aug 1881. Freight brakeman. In Enfield NH 1870, Concord NH 1880.

Mabel A., b. 1 Dec 1875, d. 21 Jul 1891.
2 Willis James[2], 1878-1955.
Frank A., b. 2 Mar 1881 Concord NH, d. 1 Aug 1881.

Sources: Enfield NH census 1870. Concord NH census 1880. VR Concord NH. Richard H. Sawyer rec.

2. **WILLIS JAMES[2] SAWYER** [see 1], b. 13 Sep 1878 Concord NH, d. 28 Mar 1955, m. 20 Dec 1899 Nettie J. Woodbury of Milton VT, b. 1882. Machinist.

Marion, b. 6 Jun 1901, d. 8 Jun 1901.
Willis James, b. 1902 Concord NH, m. 17 May 1924 Concord NH Ruth E. Tyler of Greenfield MA, b. 1905, dau. William E. and Blanch (Carbee) Tyler. CH: Kenneth; Sallie, m. Malcolm Edmonds.
Earl Woodbury, b. 1904, d. 1965, m. 27 Apr 1929 Edna M. Dunn.
Infant, b. 30 Dec 1905, d. 3 Jan 1906.
Richard Hall, b. 9 Jan 1920, m. 3 Aug 1944 Mary L. DuVal. In Hampden VA. CH: Susan DuVal, m. Charles Edmonson; Richard James; Mary Hall; Ann Modena m. Casey Stratton.

Sources: VR Concord NH. B68, Richard H. Sawyer rec.

---

## LINE 44

1. **CHESTER A.[1] SAWYER**, b. ?, d. 1892, m. Delia Kingsley, b. ?. Innkeeper. In Port Kent NY.

George Luther, b. ?, m.(1) Mildred Snow, b. ?; m.(2) Jean Marsham of Sciota NY, b. ?.
Delia, b. 1884, m. William Sawyer.
2 Allen Chester[2], 1886-1931.

Sources: George T. Sawyer rec., Dorothy Antoloci rec.

2. **ALLEN CHESTER[2] SAWYER** [see 1], b. 5 Mar 1886, d. 1931, m. 13 Feb 1915 South Hadley MA Eva May Thayer, b. ?.

Bessie Thelma, b. 6 Mar 1918, m. 1941 Marciene Ramsdell Whitcomb.
Dorothy Evelyn, b. 17 Feb 1921, m.(1) Roger Bouebonnais, m.(2) Charles Antoloci.
Allen Chester, b. 17 May 1925, d. 1975, m. Phyllis June Strong.
3 George Thayer[3], b. 1927.

Sources: George T. Sawyer rec., Dorothy Antoloci rec.

3. **GEORGE THAYER$^3$ SAWYER** [see 2], b. 2 Dec 1927 South Hadley Falls MA, m. Annette A. Authier, b. ?.

George Phillip, m. Margaret Lazarz. Stephen Paul.
Gail, m.(1) Paul Memard, m.(2) David Bergeron.
Judith, m. Michael Roy.
Liza, m. Edward Scott.
Dawn.
Amy.
Eva.

Sources: George Thayer Sawyer rec.

---

## CANADIAN LINES

1. **ESAU$^1$ SAWYER**, b. 24 Nov 1784 Canada, d. 9 Mar 1870 Morristown VT, m. Victoria Rum of France, b. Feb 1794 d. 18 Apr 1882 Wolcott VT. Laborer. In Morristown VT 1840, Elmore VT 1850.

2 Zara B.$^2$, 1831-1910.
3 Peter$^2$, 1832-1907.
Adelia, b. ca. 1835, m. 12 Jun 1851 Joseph LaFleur.
Moses, b. ca. 1838.
Thomas, b. ca. 1840.
William, b. ca. 1842.
Solomon, b. ca. 1844.

Sources: Morristown VT census 1840. Elmore VT census 1850. VT SA/VT.

2. **ZARA B.$^2$ SAWYER** [see 1], b. 22 Oct 1831 Canada, d. 1 May 1910 Manchester NH, m.(1) 27 Nov 1856 Evaline Tillotson of Orange VT, b. 30 Jun 1835 d. 1 Mar 1878, dau. Lester and Sophia (Lord) Tillotson; m.(2) 5 Feb 1881 Ellen L. McLaren of Nashua NH, b. 26 Oct 1849 d. 28 Nov 1929. In Morrisville VT 1850, Manchester NH 1880.

Fred A., b. 25 Nov 1857, m. Marie L. Huard of North Brookfield MA, b. ?. Laborer. In Manchester NH, North Brookfield MA, New Bedford MA 1893. CH: Louise L., b. 29 Jul 1892.

Elmer E., b. 27 Nov 1861 Manchester NH, m. Cora A. Hawes, b. 1866. Farmer. CH: Catherine Rosannah, b. 29 Jun 1900.

John F., b. ca. 1862 Manchester NH, m.(1) 5 Jan 1887 Matilda J. Dowd of Manchester NH, b. 1863 d. 16 Dec 1887, dau. John and Mary B. Dowd; m.(2) 28 Nov 1894 Lowell MA L. Bridget Gilbride of Ireland, b. ca. 1866, dau. Patrick and Alice Gilbride. In Lowell MA. CH: John F., b. 26 Oct 1887, d. 19 Apr 1888; Francis J., b. 28 Dec 1895.

Harry Wesley, b. 5 Jan 1874 Manchester NH, d. 21 Apr 1932 Manchester NH, m. 28 Dec 1910 Manchester NH Betsey M.(Stevens) Burbank of Manchester NH, b. 1887, dau. Charles D. and Fannie E. Stevens. Civil engineer.

Carrie, b. 24 Sep 1875.
Bertie A., b. 5 Jan 1882, d. 26 May 1890.
Walter L., b. 31 May 1883 Manchester NH.
Alfred G., b. 22 Sep 1885 Manchester NH.
Son, b. 26 Oct 1888.

Sources: Morrisville VT census 1850. Manchester NH census 1880. VR Manchester NH, SA/VT, SA/NH, SA/MA. L39.

3. **PETER[2] SAWYER** [see 1], b. 26 Oct 1832 Canada, d. 10 Jul 1907 Sutton NH, m. 1 Jan 1861 Wolcott VT Lucinda Bingham of Pomfret VT, b. 12 Jun 1844 d. 3 Sep 1927, dau. Asa and Sarah (Hart) Bingham. Farmer. In Wolcott VT, Sutton NH.

Daughter, b. 12 Nov 1861.

Wallace G., b. 28 Apr 1863 Sutton NH, d. 14 Jan 1924 Henniker NH, m. 12 Dec 1886 Ella M. Connor of Henniker NH, b. 18 Jan 1864 d. 1 Sep 1934, dau. Ichabod and Eliza (Gordon) Connor. In Warner NH. CH: Nellie May, b. 27 May 1889; Addie Inez, b. 16 Sep 1893; Flossie Lucinda, b. 8 Nov 1895, d. 12 Sep 1896.

Maurice A., b. ca. 1866.

Ida A., b. 1 Dec 1870, m. 2 Jun 1897 Webster NH Edgar J. Jones.

Daughter, stillborn 19 Aug 1873.

Sadie Inez, b. 24 Sep 1878.

Archie Lucine, b. 7 Dec 1883 Sutton NH, m. 26 Jul 1919 Sutton NH Lottie M. Jackman of Cambridge MA, b. ca. 1900, dau. George A. and Lillian G. (Elliot) Jackman. CH: Son, b. 3 Jun 1928, d. 30 Jun 1928; Daughter, b. ?, d. 31 Jul 1929.

Sources: Sutton NH census 1880. VR SA/VT, SA/NH. N6.

---

1. **JAMES N.[1] SAWYER** (James, Daniel), b. 1808 Fredrickton, New Brunswick, Canada, d. 16 Apr 1898 Pembroke ME, m. Mary Frost of Pembroke ME, b. 1818 d. 28 Jun 1892. Mill worker. In Lubec ME 1850, Pembroke ME. He bur. Pembroke ME.

Phylinda, b. 18 May 1840, d. 14 Jun 1911, m. Ezra McLaughlin.

Lorinda, b. 1842, d. 1917, m. Edward Phinney.

Elira A., b. 17 May 1845, m. George Bridges.

2 James Monroe[2], 1853-1900.

Sources: Lubec ME census 1850. H18, Alton L.Sawyer rec., Clayton L. Sawyer rec., George Sawyer rec.

2. **JAMES MONROE[2] SAWYER** [see 1], b. 1853 Lubec ME, d. 29 Jan 1900 Pembroke ME, m.(1) Laura E. Antone of Pembroke ME, b. 1859 d. 25 May 1877; m.(2) Mary E. Vance of Cooper ME, b. 18 Aug 1860 d. 13 Jan 1941. Mill worker. He bur. Pembroke ME.

James A., b. 25 May 1877, d. 16 Sep 1877.

Maude, b. 1881, d. 4 Jul 1914, m. Edward A. Crowell.

3 Lewis Edward[3], 1882-1957.

Willie Cleveland, b. 9 Nov 1884 Pembroke ME, d. Oct 1864 Medfield MA, m. Bessie Maude Hilton of Pembroke ME, b. 10 May 1887 d. 28 Apr 1976. CH: Doris Evelyn, b. 30 Apr 1911, m. Herbert Frink of Millis MA; Hazel Gladys, b. 1 Oct 1921, m. Henry Allen Kingsbury of Medfield MA.

Jennie Eveline, b. 25 Aug 1886, d. 31 Mar 1970, m.(1) William B. Carter, m.(2) Leon B. Taylor.

George Maynard, b. 24 May 1889 Princeton ME, d. 1 Oct 1975 Eastport ME, m. Lillian Maude Harris, b. 11 May 1876 d. 21 Jan 1962. In Medfield MA. CH: Jennie Marie, b. 3 Mar 1915, m. Charles Elihu Bridges of Pembroke ME; George Maynard, b. 10 Jan 1917, m. Alicia C. Sawyer of Pembroke ME, b. 11 Apr 1918.

Hattie Gertrude, b. 9 Dec 1892, d. 1987, m. Joseph Wall.

Nellie, b. 30 Apr 1895, d. 3 Jul 1979 m. George Robinson.

Vera Myrtle, b. 30 Apr 1895, d. 1895.

Sources: VR SA/ME. Thursa Sawyer rec., George M. Sawyer, Jr. rec.

3. **LEWIS EDWARD[3] SAWYER** [see 2], b. 3 Oct 1882 in Maine, d. 19 Feb 1957 Calais ME, m. Lara Bell Brown of Pembroke ME, b. 2 May 1890 d. 16 Dec 1976. Millworker, railroad worker. He bur. Pembroke ME.

Lara Mae, d. at three days in Pembroke ME.
Essie Brown, b. 22 Aug 1909, d. 16 Jul 1933, m. Carl Edgar Carter.
Ellis E., b. 14 Mar 1911, d. 16 Feb 1983, m. Evelyn Mae (Brown) Roy.
Myrtle, b. 7 Apr 1913, m. Wellington C. James.
Cecil, b. 4 Feb 1915, d. 4 Aug 1937.
S. Kenneth, b. 13 May 1916, m. Ruth E. Brown.
Alton Lewis, b. 9 May 1919, m. Barbara J. Cook.
Clayton Lee, b. 17 Nov 1920, m. Thursa Elizabeth Consins.
James Franklin, b. 6 Sep 1922, m. Mary C._____.
Eleanor Louise, b. 15 May 1924, m. William George Baker.
Florence Evelyn, b. 22 Jan 1926, m. Donald Frederick Hatton.
Roy Calvin, b. 5 Jan 1928, d. 4 May 1980, m. Rae June Lashi.

Sources: Thursa Sawyer rec.

---

1. **LEWIS[1] SAWYER**, b. ca. 1810 Canada, m. Emelia St. John of Canada, b. ?. In Coopersville NY.

2 Solomon[2], 1839-1925.
Henry, b. ca. 1845 Coopersville NY, d. 18 May 1926 Goffstown NH, m.(1) ?; m.(2) ?; m.(3) 10 Jan 1891 Zoe Desmarais of St. Simon, Canada, b. 29 May 1848 d. 5 Jun 1927, dau. Alex and Zoe (Girard) Desmarais. CH: Anna M., b. ?, m. 30 Aug 1894 Alphonse Holbrook; Daughter, stillborn 2 Feb 1893; Elizabeth, b. 20 Apr 1895, d. 25 Apr 1895. More children.

Sources: VR SA/NH. N6.

2. **SOLOMON[2] SAWYER** [see 1], b. 6 May 1839 Coopersville NY, d. 31 Mar 1925 Nashua NH, m. Josephine Woods of Coopersville NY, b. ca. 1846.

Oscar, b. ca. 1872 Coopersville NY, m. 9 Nov 1891 Valeria Evon of Canada, b. ?. In Nashua NH.
Charles J., b. ca. 1877 Cooperville NY, m. 10 Feb 1898 Elizabeth Adams of Bedford NH, b. ca. 1881. In Nashua NH.
Lillian, b. ?, m. 30 Oct 1897 Nashua NH Eugene Foster.
Chandler, b. 6 Apr 1878 Manchester NY, d. 31 Jul 1932 Goffstown NH, m.(1) 10 Feb 1896 (div. 28 Oct 1902) Emma Adams of Manchester NH, b. ca. 1881; m.(2) 8 Jun 1904 Nashua NH (div. 1 Feb 1916) Rosa Cheriault of Nashua NH, b. 1887, dau. Henry and Mary (Belanger) Cheriault. CH: Son, stillborn 13 Apr 1896. Painter. In Nashua NH.

Sources: VR SA/NH, N6.

---

1. **CHARLES[1] SAWYER**, b. ca. 1810 Canada, m. Allix (Adeline) Martin of Canada, b. ?. Laborer. In South Hero VT 1859, Grand Isle VT 1860, Brandon VT 1862.

Eliza, b. ca. 1840.
2 Charles[2], b. ca. 1842.
Moses J., b. ca. 1846 Canada, m. Lucy Merno of Canada, b. ?. In Chicopee MA, Worcester MA 1882. CH: Charles J., b. 27 Apr 1882.
Agnes, b. ca. 1849.
Emma, b. ca. 1851.

Levi C. or E., b. ca. 1856 Grande Isle VT, m. 24 Nov 1881 Worcester MA Delia Noe, b. 1850, dau. Paul and Taulois Noe. Laborer. In Worcester MA. CH: Arthur E., b. 13 Nov 1883; Fanny D., b. 9 Jan 1886.
James, b. 5 Jan 1857 South Hero VT, m. 16 Oct 1882 Lowell MA Ozile Duchance of Canada, b. 1864. In Brandon VT, Lowell MA. CH: John, b. 23 Jun 1885.
Mary, b. 19 Jun 1862, m. 4 May 1878 Rutland VT Peter Marshall.
Sources: VR SA/VT, SA/MA. Edward C. Sawyer rec.

2. **CHARLES[2] SAWYER** [see 1], b. ca. 1842 Canada, m. Philinda _____ of Canada, b.?. Road builder. In Brandon VT, Sudbury VT 1863, Mt. Holly 1870, Chicopee MA 1880.
3 Charles A.[2], 1863-1926.
Nancy, b. 4 Apr 1865.
Frank, b. ca. 1867. Went to California.
Rose, b. ca. 1869, m. 18 Oct 1886 John Hicks.
Eli M., b. Jul 1877, d. 24 Nov 1878.
Phebe, b. 22 Jun 1873.
Mary, b. ?.
Sources: VR SA/VT, SA/MA. Edward C. Sawyer rec.

3. **CHARLES A.[3] SAWYER** [see 2], b. 18 Jul 1863 Sudbury VT, d. 1926, m. CelinaGoyette of Canada, b. 1865 d. 1932. Mill operator. In Chicopee MA 1887.
4 John Arthur[4], 1887-1983.
Carl Lionel, b. ca. 1892 Taunton MA, m. Helen N. Boyd, b. 1900. CH: Carl Lionel, m. Agnes T. Field.
5 Edward Herbert[4], 1894-1951.
Alfred, b. 1900 Chicopee MA, d. 1958, m. Euphrasia, b. 1902 d. 1952. CH: Donald A.
Sources: VR SA/MA. Edward C. Sawyer rec., Lois Ricci rec.

4. **JOHN ARTHUR[4] SAWYER** [see 3], b. 26 Jun 1887 Chicopee MA, d. 1983, m. Mabel House, b. ?. In Chicopee MA.
Ralph Vincent, b. 26 Jul 1913, d. 27 Nov 1979, m. 17 Oct 1936 Phyllis Tomkins.
Edith, d. 18 Dec 1980, m. ______Goddu.
Sources: VT SA/MA.

5. **EDWARD HERBERT[4] SAWYER** [see 3], b. 8 Apr 1894 Chicopee MA, d. 28 Jul 1951, m. Mary Agnes Moynahan, b. 15 Aug 1897 d. Oct 1955, dau. Michael F. and Mary (Fitzgerald) Moynahan.
Margaret M., b. 10 Nov 1917, d. Jan 1985, m. Glen Bach.
Doris I, b. 1 Aug 1919, m. Francis O'Hare.
Ethel M., b. 15 Sep 1920, d. Oct 1964, m. John Healy.
Edward Charles, b. 19 Aug 1923, m. Roberta Bodi.
Robert F., b. 12 May 1926, m. Lucille Wirfel.
Sources: VR SA/MA. Edward C. Sawyer rec.

---

1. **ISAAC[1] SAWYER**, b. ca. 1812 New Brunswick, Canada, d. 1847. m. Eunice Bither of Linneus ME, b. ?. In Linneus ME.
2 Orville L.[2], b. ca. 1841.
3 David T.[2], b. ca. 1843.
Julia A., b. ca. 1844.

4 Isaac², 1847-1920.
Sources: VR SA/ME.

2. **ORVILLE L.[2] SAWYER** [see 1], b. ca. 1841 Linneus ME, m.(1) 31 Aug 1864 Linneus ME Augusta L. Warner, b. ?; m.(2) Nancy J. Starrett of Linneus ME, b. 6 Jan 1845 d. 17 Nov 1920, dau. James and Lillian (Wilson) Starrett. In Linneus ME. Civil War.
Isaac S., b. May 1869 Linneus ME, m. 17 Jun 1894 Ellen D. Kervin, b. ?.
Eunice A., b. ca. 1871.
Nora W., b. ca. 1875.
Edwin B., b. ca. 1876 Linneus ME.
Freda B., b. ca. 1879.
Sources: Linneus ME census 1880, ME 1880 census index. VR SA/ME. M7A.

3. **DAVID T.[2] SAWYER** [see 1], b. ca. 1843 Linneus ME, m. Mary C. Risteen of New Brunswick, Canada, b. 22 Mar 1849 d. 30 Aug 1919, dau. John B. and Maria (Greene) Risteen. In Linneus ME. Civil War.
Harry, b. ca. 1876 Linneus ME, m. 13 Mar 1897 Minnie Ruth ______ of Linneus ME, b. ?. CH: Daughter, b. 28 Apr 1897.
Georgie M., b. ca. 1877.
Son, b. 1880.
Sources: Linneus ME census 1880. ME 1880 census index. VR SA/ME. M7A.

4. **ISAAC[2] SAWYER** [see 1], b. 7 Jul 1847 Linneus ME, d. 13 Jul 1920 Houlton ME, m. Rebecca S.______, b. 1847. In Linneus ME.
Arthur O., b. ca. 1873 Linneus ME.
Orville D., b. ca. 1875 Linneus ME, m. 16 Oct 1898 New Limerick ME Mabel Lucia Thompson of Linneus ME, b. ca. 1879, dau. John and Martha (Bragg) Thompson. Farmer. In Linneus ME. CH: Alta, b. 15 Mar 1899; Norman A., b. 23 Sep 1902, d. 12 Jun 1918.
Edna R., b. ca. 1878.
Sources: Linneus ME census 1880. ME 1880 census index. VR SA/ME.

---

1. **FRANK[1] SAWYER**, b. ca. 1820 in Canada, m. Zoe Marlow of Canada, b. Oct 1822 d. 6 Sep 1890 Berkshire VT. In Franklin VT.
Eli, b. ca. 1851 in Canada, d. 19 Oct 1897 Burlington VT, m. 31 Jan 1875 Williston VT (later div.) Cornelia Sisters, b. ?. Harness maker. In Montgomery VT. CH: Lettie E., b. 24 Nov 1875, m. 28 Aug 1894 Richmond VT Albert Crandall.
Cliff A., b. ca. 1853 in Canada, m. 17 Mar 1894 Franklin VT Frances (Pease) Brown, b. ?.
Sources: VR SA/VT.

---

1. **WILLIAM T.[1] SAWYER**, b. ca. 1823 New Brunswick, Canada, m. Susan Page of Portland ME, b. ca. 1825 d. 1896 Chelsea MA. Printer. In Boston MA 1850.
William, b. Nov 1847, d. 8 Sep 1852.
2 Calvin W.², b. 1850.
Son, b. 5 Nov 1852 Boston MA.
Joseph, b. Jul 1854, d. 15 Aug 1854.
Frank, b. 1856 Boston MA, m. 14 Sep 1880 Chelsea MA Maria L. Davis of Chelsea MA, b. ca. 1862, dau. John and Maria H. Davis. Currier.

3 William Morris[2], 1859-1927.
Sources: Boston MA census 1850. VR SA/MA.

2. **CALVIN W.[2] SAWYER** [see 1], b. 7 Oct 1850 Boston MA, m. 2 Nov 1873 Chelsea MA Eliza J. Long, b. 1852 of Chelsea MA, dau. George M. and Eliza J. Long. Clerk. In Chelsea MA, Melrose MA 1900.
4 Roswell Whitney[3], 1876-1961.
Susan L., b. 20 Jan 1878 Chelsea MA.
Lotta L., b. 19 Jul 1881 Chelsea MA.
Winnifred Warren, b. 16 Feb 1884 Chelsea MA, m. Robert Metcalf of Rhode Island.
Sources: Melrose MA census 1900. VR SA/MA. Douglas W. Sawyer rec.

3. **WILLIAM MORRIS[2] SAWYER** [see 1], b. 18 Nov 1859 Boston MA, d. 14 Feb 1927 Somerville MA, m. 25 Dec 1880 Boston MA Cora Pike of Barrington, Nova Scotia, Canada, b. ca. 1856 d. 1915 Somerville MA, dau. Josiah Pike. Railroad shifter. In Chelsea MA, Everett MA.
Frank Mansfield, b. 11 May 1882 Chelsea MA.
Son, b. 2 Nov 1883 Chelsea MA.
Catherine, b. 29 Mar 1885 Chelsea MA.
Beatrice, b. 10 Aug 1886.
Gertrude M., b. 23 Oct 1891 Everett MA.
William R., b. 23 Feb 1893 Everett MA.
Harold Edgar, b. 26 Apr 1894 Everett MA.
Sources: VR SA/MA.

4. **ROSWELL WHITNEY[3] SAWYER** [see 2], b. 21 Jun 1876 Chelsea MA, d. 1961, m. Ethel Turner, b. 1889 d. 1974. In Melrose Highlands MA.
Donald Whitney, b. 11 Dec 1924 Melrose Highlands MA, m. Nancy _____. In Reading MA. CH: Ronald, Pamela, Lisa, Deborah.
Calvin Delancy, b. 14 Jan 1926 Melrose Highlands MA, m. Winifred Nona Young. In Reading MA. CH: Steven Wayne, Douglas Calvin, David Leonard.
Sources: VR SA/MA. Douglas W. Sawyer rec.

---

1. **FREDERICK[1] SAWYER**, b. ca. 1840 Canada, m. Selina Saunville, b. ? of Canada. Shoemaker. In Marlborough MA.
Selina, b. 3 Feb 1866.
Frederick, b. 16 Apr 1867 Marlborough MA.
Oliver, b. 16 Oct 1868 Marlborough MA.
Philemon, female, b. ?.
Lewis, b. 1870 Marlborough MA.
Sources: VR SA/MA.

---

1. **JOSEPH[1] SAWYER**, b. ca. 1841 in Canada, son of Eli and Margaret Sawyer, m.(1) ?; m.(2) 14 Jul 1872 Milford MA Agnes Plant of Canada, b. ca. 1844, dau. Edward and Agnes Plant. In Milford MA, Southboro MA.
Walter O., b. 11 May 1873 Milford MA.
William, b. 16 May 1875 Southboro MA.
Willard, b. 6 Dec 1881 Southboro MA.
Sources: VR SA/MA.

---

1. **FELIX[1] SAWYER**, b. in Canada, m.(1) Ella ______ of Canada; m.(2) Minnie Fountain of Manchester NH. Shoe maker. In Milford MA, Southboro MA.

Joseph F., b. ca. 1871 Milford MA, m. 11 Mar 1892 Natick MA Cora C. Sullant of Warren RI, b. ca. 1871, dau. Lewis and Clara (Bissoner) Sullant. Shoemaker. In Wayland MA. CH: Chester Henry, b. 25 Nov 1894.

Williford, b. 2 Jun 1874.

Henry, b. 1 Jul 1877 Southboro MA.

Nettie Lelia, b. 24 Aug 1880.

Sources: VR SA/MA.

---

1. **ANDREW[1] SAWYER**, b. in Canada, m. Esther Boombower of Bedford, Quebec, Canada, b. ?. In Swanton VT.

Philip Gilbert, b. ca. 1873 Bedford, Quebec, Canada, m.(1) LillianM. Winters, b. ca. 1881 d. 14 Jun 1899, dau. William and Rachel (Stinehour) Winters; m.(2) 18 May 1901 Franklin VT Ellen Derosin, b. ?. In Swanton VT. CH: Son, b. 1 Aug 1899; Daughter, b. 5 Jan 1902; Daughter, b. 22 Aug 1903.

Carrie, b. ca. 1875, m. 20 May 1896 Swanton VT George Adams.

Moses, b. ca. 1880 Stanbridge, Canada, m. 23 Mar 1901 Franklin VT Minnie Savage of Swanton VT, b. ?. CH: Eddie, b. 24 Oct 1901, d. 13 Aug 1903; Son, b. 4 Aug 1903 Swanton VT; Daughter, b. 17 May 1905; Son, b. 17 Aug 1907 Swanton VT.

William, b. ca. 1882 East Dunham, Quebec, Canada, m. 25 Sep 1906 Franklin VT Kate Wing, b. ?. Mason. In Franklin VT

Sources: VR Swanton VT, SA/VT.

---

1. **WILLIAM H.[1] SAWYER**, b. 10 Jan 1842 New Brunswick, Canada, m. Eliza_____, b. 20 Feb 1850. In North Lubec ME 1874, Eastport ME 1880.

Eliza Jane, b. 18 Sep 1868.

Mary Ann, b. 24 Mar 1870.

James Henry, b. 15 Apr 1874 North Lubec ME, m. 30 Sep 1894 Eastport ME Georgie I. Wilson of North Lubec ME, b. 1875, dau. David and Linda Wilson.

Frank, b. 27 Feb 1881 Lubec ME.

Child, b. 18 Jun 1886.

Sources: Eastport ME census 1880. ME 1880 census index. VR SA/ME.

---

1. **DANIEL[1] SAWYER**, b. 28 Dec 1845 New Brunswick, Canada, d. 14 Aug 1918 Gardiner ME, m. Elizabeth DeGoff of New Brunswick, Canada, b. 24 May 1849 d. 16 Dec 1914, dau. Felix and Elizabeth DeGoff.

Alfred E., b. Mar 1885, d. 9 Jul 1885.

Alexander, b. 27 Oct 1886, d. 21 Jul 1908 in Pennsylvania.

Catherine H., b. 13 Feb 1888, d. 26 Aug 1888.

Cecilia L., b. 28 Feb 1892, d. 9 Mar 1893.

Edmund A., b. ca. 1893 Gardiner ME, m.(1) Harriet Smith of New York, b. ?; m.(2) 9 Feb 1935 Portsmouth NH Mildred (Dyer) Purrington of Owls Head ME, b. ca. 1895, dau. Alden and Rose (Hudson) Dyer. Shoemaker. In Gardiner ME, Berlin NH. CH: William Daniel, b. 1910, d. 2 Aug 1911.

Sources: VR Gardiner ME, SA/ME.

---

1. **JOHN B.[1] SAWYER**, b. 1869 Montreal, Canada, m. 7 Aug 1894 Harriet Taylor of Middlebury VT. Stone cutter. In Alburg VT.

Raymond, b. 8 Feb 1894 Arlburg VT.
John Henry, b. 19 Aug 1895 Alburg VT, d. 28 Aug 1978 Rutland VT, m. ?. CH: Merritt of Manchester Ct; Henry of Florida; Robert of Jackson TN; Marvin of Derry NH; Richard of Poultney VT; Madeline Beach of Virginia; Edith Pratt of Hubbardton VT.
Margaret, b. ?.
Lillian Mary, b. 18 Feb 1898, m. ______ Peer of Rutland VT.
Charles Lawrence, b. 29 May 1899.
Louis, b. 22 Nov 1900.
Ethylen, (male), b. 9 Feb 1904.
Ethel, b. 3 Apr 1905.
Harriet Elizabeth, b. 10 Nov 1906, m. ______ Mordue of Illinois.
Daughter, b. 10 Oct 1908.

Sources: VR SA/VT. Obit, Richard Sawyer rec.

---

## CHANGED NAME TO SAWYER

1. **JOHN[1] SAWYER**, b. 1795 Canada East, d. 28 Jul 1862 Westfield VT, m. Mary Shortsleeves, b. 1794 d. 24 Jun 1882 Lowell VT.

Ezra, b. ca. 1823 Canada East, m. 4 Apr 1858 Troy VT Elmira Ramsdell, b. ?.
2. Francis (Frank)[2], ca. 1828-1906.
3. Lewis (Louis)[2], b. ca. 1830.
Abby, b. ca. 1836.
Ezekiel, b. ca. 1838, m. 1850 Emerline _____, b. ?.
Lyman, b. ca. 1839 Canada East.

Sources: Westfield VT census 1850. VR Troy VT, Lowell VT.

2. **FRANCIS (FRANK)[2] SAWYER** [see 1], b. ca. 1828 Canada East, d. 20 Apr 1906 Lowell VT, m. 3 Jul 1857 Westfield VT Esther Martin of Fairfax VT, b. ?. Farmer. In Westfield VT, Lowell VT.

Ferdinand, b. 27 Mar 1858 Westfield VT, m. 1 Jan 1883 Lowell VT Rosa Murphy of Lowell VT, b. ?. CH: Harlan Henry, b. 10 Oct 1886 Lowell VT.
Abel Joseph, b. 5 May 1859 Westfield VT, m. 29 Sep 1877 Lowell VT Rogene Sarah Gelo of Georgia VT, b. ?. Farmer. In Westfield VT, Lowell VT. CH: Ida Abbie, b. 29 Jan 1878; Wallace Frank, b. 19 Jul 1880, d. 30 Jan 1881; Gladys Bell, b. 3 Jul 1891.
4 Elbridge J.[3], b. 1861.
Edward, b. 17 May 1863, d. 28 Jun 1867 Westfield VT.
Alberta May, b. 6 Nov 1864, m. 9 Aug 1884 Millbury MA Frederick Greenwood.

Sources: VR Lowell VT, SA/VT, SA/MA.

3. **LEWIS (LOUIS)[2] SAWYER** [see 1], b. ca. 1830 Canada East, m. Lucinda B. Hoyt of Bolton, Canada. Farmer. In Westfield VT, Lowell VT.

5 Chauncy L.[3], 1850-1875.
Florence Elizabeth, b. 19 Jul 1860, m. 1 May 1881 Henry A. Woods.
Frank Wallace, b. 12 Jun 1864 Westfield VT.
Sanford, b. 12 Apr 1868 Lowell VT.

Almon, b. ?, m. Belle Willis, b. ?.
Sources: Westfield VT census 1850. VR Lowell VT, SA/VT.

4. **ELBRIDGE J.[3] SAWYER** [see 2], b. 16 Jul 1861 Westfield VT, m. 5 Feb 1881 Grafton MA Mary Guthrie of Canada, b. 1864, dau. Henry and Victoria Guthrie.

Wallace Elbridge, b. 31 Oct 1884 Lowell VT, m. 24 Jun 1903 Barton VT Ethel M. Perley of Barton Landing VT, b. 13 Apr 1881. Printer. In Millbury MA, Orleans VT, Newport VT. CH: Richard Elbridge, b. 1914 Orleans VT, m. 5 Mar 1937 Conway NH Ruth (Church) Clark of Long Island ME, dau. Ralph and Thelma (Johnson) Church. Soldier. At Ft. Williams ME.

Maud Effie, b. 10 Jul 1886.

Sources: VT Lowell VT, SA/VT, SA/MA, SA/NH. P33.

5. **CHAUNCY L.[3] SAWYER** [see 3], b. 10 May 1850 Westfield VT, d. 4 Dec 1875 Lowell VT, m. 4 Feb 1873 Lowell VT Hannah Maria Martin of Fairfax VT.

Isadore Agnew, b. 5 Apr 1874 Lowell VT.

Orrin Chauncy, b. 22 Jun 1875 Lowell VT.

Sources: VR Lowell VT.

---

1. **JOHN BAPTIST[1] SAWYER**, b. 13 Oct 1829 Hyacintha, Quebec, Canada, d. 23 Nov 1899 Granville VT, m.(1) 1 Jan 1850 Salisbury VT Mary Bushee, b. ?; m.(2) 25 Sep 1852 Middlebury VT Mary Effie Baker of Plattsburg NY, b. 15 Sep 1839 d. 28 Oct 1920. Farmer. In Salisbury VT, Middlebury VT, Granville VT. His parents were Celestin and Maria (Moreau) Decelles.

Ellen, b. 4 Nov 1853, d. 9 Feb 1858 Middlebury VT.

Louise Luella, b. 19 Apr 1855, d. 19 Apr 1927, m. 23 Jun 1869 James Riley.

2 Frank E.[2], 1856-1938.

Moses Aaron, b. 28 Jul 1857 Middlebury VT, d. 14 Oct 1918, m. 26 Feb 1885 Granville VT Nell Pennington of Salsbury VT, b. ?. Farmer. In Granville VT, Salisbury VT. CH: Edith M., b. 2 Nov 1885; Ethel, b. 25 Dec 1887, m. 11 Oct 1905 Herbert L. Morgan; Eva, b. 13 Jan 1889, m. 5 Jun 1907 Cassius C. Seeley.

Mary Ann, b. 27 Jan 1859, d. 22 Jan 1913, m. 4 Nov 1874 Gilman A. Spooner.

Isaac Isreal, b. 14 Dec 1860 Salisbury VT, d. 7 Mar 1941.

Abraham Lincoln, b. 3 Jan 1863, d. 21 Aug 1865 Granville VT.

Minnie Ann, b. 22 Feb 1868, d. 17 Nov 1949, m. 23 Nov 1887 Sharon VT Alpha C. Gidson.

Harriet May, b. 6 Feb 1877, d. 10 May 1927, m. 8 Mar 1900 Granville VT Robert J. Marsh.

Emogene Della, b. 29 Oct 1878, d. 3 Oct 1953, m. 16 Apr 1901 Granville VT Bernie J. Swinyer.

Flora Alice, b. 1 Dec 1881, m. 15 Dec 1904 Granville VT Verlon E. Wood.

Sources: Salisbury VT census 1850. VR SA/VT.

2. **FRANK E.[2] SAWYER** [see 1], b. 10 Mar 1856 Salisbury VT, d. 26 Dec 1938, m. 16 Oct 1878 Granville VT Mary Jennie Kendall of Hancock VT, b. Mar 1861. Laborer. In Granville VT, St. Albans VT, Randolph VT.

Charles W., b. Oct 1879 Granville VT.

Ernest F., b. 18 Jun 1883 St. Albans VT, m. 7 Dec 1903 Randolph VT Grace Mabel White of Randolph VT. Laborer. In Randolph VT. CH: Elsie Genevive, b. 7 Jul 1904; Clifford Earl, b. 17 Sep 1907; John Francis, b. 28 Nov 1908.

Wesley E., b. 5 Oct 1888 Granville VT.

Ralph John, b. 28 Apr 1896 Randolph VT.

Stella, b. 8 Apr 1903.
Sources: VR SA/VT.

---

1. **ANDREW FREEMAN[1] SAWYER**, b. 11 Mar 1835 Amherst NH, m.(1) 26 Sep 1858 Harriet E. Bartlett of Nashua NH, b. 13 Jun 1830 d. 11 Oct 1909; m.(2) 11 Jan 1912 Levinia Vallely of Ireland, b. 1872. In Amherst NH. His parents were William and Fanny (Burnham) Peacock.

Anna Eveline, m. 1 Jan 1885 Charles H. Mickey.
Sources: Amherst NH census 1860. VR SA/NH.

---

1. **EDWARD[1] SAWYER**, b. ca. 1847 Canada, m. 30 Jul 1868 Milford MA Josephine Dufremme of Manchester NH, b. ca. 1853, dau. Charles and Clara (Pelter) Dufremme. Bootmaker. Milford MA, Worcester MA. His parents were Eli and Mary Seynoir.

William, b. 15 Apr 1870 Milford MA.
Son, b. 22 Feb 1871.
Exilda Agnes, b. 20 Mar 1872 Milford MA.
Lydia Mabel, b. 2 Nov 1878 Worcester MA.
Rose Ann, b. 11 Nov 1880 Worcester MA.
Sources: VR SA/MA.

# SOURCES

A.


1. Abbot, Abiel, *History of the Town of Wilton, New Hampshire*, Livermore and Sewall Putnam, Lowell MA, 1888. NHHS.
2. Abbot, Abiel and Ephraim, *Genealogical Register of the Descendants of George Abbot of Andover, Massachusetts*, Boston MA, 1847.
3. Abbott, Major Lemuel A., *Descendants of George Abbot of Rowley, Massachusetts*, 2 vol., Boston MA, 1906.
4. Adams, Andrew Napoleon, *A Genealogical History of Henry Adams of Braintree, Massachusetts, and his Descendants*, Rutland VT, 1898.
5. Adams, Andrew Napoleon, *Genealogical History of Robert Adams of Massachusetts, and his Descendants*, Rutland VT, 1900.
6. Adams, Charles Collard, *Middleton, Conn., Upper Houses*, Phoenix Publ. Co., Canaan NH, 1983. Reprint of 1908 Edn. NHHS.
7. Adams, Frank David, *Ancestors and Descendants of Elias Adams, The Pioneer*, Kaysville UT, n. d.
8. Alden, Ebenezer, Dr., "Historical Sketches of the Town of Randolph Before 1800 With Genealogical Notices of Early Families, by Dr. Ebenzer Alden in the Randolph Transcript, 1857-1858," under title *History of Randolph, Mass.*, bound ms, n. d. NHHS.
9. Aldrich, Louis Cass, Ed., *History of Franklin and Grand Isle Counties, Vermont*, D. Mason and Co., Syracuse NY, 1891. NHHS.
10. Alexander, DeSilva S., *The Alexanders of Maine,*, Buffalo NY, 1898.
11. "Congregational Church Records, Alfred, Maine," Vol. I and II, 1782 1866, copied by Benapeag Chapter, DAR, Sanford ME, 1949. MHS.
12. Alfred ME, "Transcript of Marriage Intentions Entered in Original Town Record Book," Vol. 1, 1794-1834.
13. Allen, Charles Edwin, *History of Dresden, Maine*, 1931. NHHS.
14. Allen, Francis Olcott, *The History of Enfield, Connecticut*, 3 vol., The Wickersham Printing Co., Lancaster PA, 1900. NHHS.
15. Allen, Orrin Peer, *Descendants of Nicholas Cady*, Palmer MA, 1910.
16. Allen, Orrin Peer, *The Allen Memorial: Descendants of Edward Allen of Nantucket, Massachusetts, 1690-1905*, C. B. Fiske and Co., Palmer MA, 1905.
17. Allen, William, *The History of Norridgewock*, E. J. Peet, Norridgewock ME, 1949. MHS.
18. Alvord, Samuel M., *A Genealogy of the Descendants of Alexander Alvord*, Webster MA, 1908.
19. Ambrose, John Lee, "Ambrose Genealogy," ms., n. d. NHHS.
20. *The National Cyclopedia of American Biographies*, James T. White and Co., New York NY, 1906, w/index and conspectus. NHHS.
21. Amesbury MA, Records of the Town Clerk.
22. Ancient Landmarks Society of Parsonsfield (ALSOP), Maine.
23. Anderson, Joseph, *The Town and City of Waterbury, Ct.*, 3 vol., The Price and Lee Co., New Haven CT, 1896. NHHS.
24. Anderson, Martha, and Norton Bagley, "Some Descendants of Orlando Bagley of Amesbury, Massachusetts," 1973. 3 vol., mimeographed.
25. Anderson, Mary A. Smith, *Ancestry of Joseph Smith and Emma Hale*, Herald Publishing Co., Independence MO, 1924. NHHS.
26. Andrews, Henry Franklin, *The Hamlin Family of Giles Hamlin*, Exira IA, 1900. NHHS.
27. Annett, Albert, and Alice E. Lehtinen, *History of Jaffrey, New Hampshire*, Vol. II, PBT, 1934. NHHS.
28. Annis, Daniel G. and George W. Browne, *Londonderry, N. H., Vital Records*, Granite State Publishing Co., Manchester NH, 1914.
29. Annis, Verle L., *The Annis Genealogy*, Laguna Beach CA, 1978. NHHS.
30. Appleton ME, Vital Records, 21 Nov 1835 to 11 Sep 1858. Based on original records in possession of town clerk, 1938.
31. Appleton, William Sumner, *Some Descendants of William Sawyer*, Boston MA, 1891. NHHS.
32. Arnold, James N., *Vital Records of Rhode Island, 1636-1850*, 7 vols., Providence RI, 1895. NHHS.
33. Atkinson NH, Town Records, Book I.
34. Atwater, Francis, *History of Kent, Connecticut*, The Journal Publishing Co., Meridan CT, 1897. NHHS.
35. Atwater, Francis, *History of the Town of Plymouth, Connecticut*, The Journal Publishing Co., Meriden CT, 1891. NHHS.
36. Avery, Clara, *Averill-Averell-Avery Family: A Record of the Descendants of William and Abigail Averell of Ipswich, Massachusetts*, 2 vol., n. d.
37. Avery, Elroy M. and Catherine, *The Groton Avery Clan*, Cleveland OH, 1912.
38. Avery, Lelian Drake, *Genealogy of the Ingersoll Family in America*, Fred H. Hitchcock, New York NY, 1926.

B.

1. Babson, John J., *History of the Town of Gloucester, Cape Ann*, Procter Bros., Gloucester MA, 1860. NHHS.
2. Babson, John J., *Notes and Additions to the History of Gloucester*, Second Series, Salem Press, Salem MA, 1891. NHHS.
3. Bailey, Frederic W., Ed., *Early Connecticut Marriages as Found in Ancient Church Records Prior to 1800*, 7 vol., Bureau of American Ancestry, New Haven CT, 1896. MSL.
4. Bailey, F. W., *Massachusetts: Early Marriages Prior to 1800*, 3 vol., n. d. MHS. LOC.
5. Bailey, Hollis R., *James, John, and Thomas Bailey and Their Descendants*, Somerville MA, 1899.
6. Bailey, Marietta Pierce, *Solomon Peirce Family Genealogy*, Press of George M. Ellis Company, Boston MA, 1912. NHHS.
7. Bailey, Richard, *Genealogy of the Descendants of Richard Bailey*, Vol. I, No. 2, Jan 1858. NHHS.
8. Bailey, Sarah Loring, *Historical Sketches of Andover*, Cambridge MA, 1800.
9. Baker, Eleanor Johnson, *Genealogy of the Descendants of William Johnson of Charlestown, Massachusetts*, Newburyport MA Press, 1969.
10. Baker, Mary Eva, *Folklore of Springfield, Vermont*, Springfield VT, 1922. NHHS.
11. Baldwin, Charles C., *Baldwin Genealogy (1500 to 1881)*, Cleveland OH, 1881.
12. Baldwin, John D. and William Clift, *A Record of the Descendants of George Denison*, Tyler and Seagram, Worcester MA, 1881. NHHS.
13. Baldwin ME, town records
14. Baldwin ME, Town Register 1905. MHS.
15. Baldwin, Thomas W., *Cambridge, Mass., Vital Records to the Year 1850*, Wright and Potter Printing Co., Boston MA, 1914. NHHS.
16. Baldwin, Thomas W., *Michael Bacon of Dedham, 1640, and his Descendants*, Cambridge MA, 1915.
17. Baldwin, Thomas William, *Patten Genealogy*, PBA, Boston MA, 1908. NHHS.
18. Ballou, Adin, *History of the Town of Milford to 1881*,PBT, 1882.
19. Ballou, Adin, *Elaborate History and Genealogy of the Ballous of America*, Providence RI 1888, and addendum, WPA, Boston MA 1937. NHHS.
20. Banks, Charles Edward, MD, *Topographical Dictionary of English Emigrants to New England, 1620-1650*, Genealogical Publishing Co., Baltimore MD, 1963. NHHS.
21. Banks, Charles Edward, MD, *The History of Martha's Vineyard*, Vol. II, George E. Dean, Boston MA, 1911.
22. Barber, Eunice Miena, *The Wright-Chamberlin Genealogy*, The Vail Ballou Company, Binghamton NY, 1914. NHHS.
23. Barker, Ellen Frye, *Frye Genealogy*, Tobias A. Wright, Printer, New York NY, 1920. NHHS.
24. *History of Barnard, Vermont, 1761-1927*, 2 vol., Vermont Hist. Soc., 1928. NHHS.
25. Barney, Elvira Stevens, *Stevens Genealogy*, Skelton Publishing Co., Salt Lake City UT, 1907. NHHS.
26. Barney, Keith Richard, *The History of Springfield, Vermont, 1885-1961*, Springfield VT, 1972. NHHS.
27. Barnum, Louise Noyes, *Atkinson Then and Now*, Atkinson NH Hist. Soc., 1976. NHHS.
28. Barrington NH, Records of the Town Clerk.
29. Bartholomew, George W., *Record of the Bartholomew Family*, Austin TX, 1885.
30. Bartlett, Genevieve Wilson, *Forefathers and Descendants of Willard and Genevieve Wilson Bartlett and of Allied Families*, St. Louis MO, 1952. NHHS.
31. Bartlett, Hubert Carlton, *Reflections on Royalston, Worcester County, Massachusetts, USA*, Published by *The Reflector*, Fitchburg MA, 1927. NHHS.
32. Bartlett, J. Gardner, *Gregory Stone Genealogy*, Murray Printing Co., Cambridge MA, 1918. NHHS.
33. Bartlett, J. Gardner, *Simon Stone Genealogy*, Pinkham Press, Boston MA, 1926. NHHS.
34. Bartlett, Levi, *Genealogy and Biographical Sketches of the Bartlett Family, in England and America*, Lawrence MA, 1876.
35. Bassett, Buel B., *One Bassett Family in America*, New Britain CT, 1926.
36. Bates, Albert C., *Vital Records of Granby, Connecticut*, 1947.
37. Bates, Edward Craig, *The History of Westborough, Massachussets*, Part III, PBT, Westborough MA, 1891. NHHS.
38. Baylor, Richard M., *History of Windham County, Connecticut*, W. W. Preston and Company, New York NY, 1889. NHHS.
39. Beach, Moses S. and William Ely, *The Ely Ancestry*, The Calumet Press, New York NY, 1902. NHHS.
40. Bean, Bernie, *The Life and Family of John Bean of Exeter, New Hampshire and his Cousins*, Seattle WN Genealogical Society, 1970.
41. Belknap, Henry W., *The Burnap-Burnett Genealogy*, The Essex Institute, Salem MA, 1925.
42. Bemis, Charles A., *History of the Town of Marlborough, New Hampshire*, Marlborough NH, 1974. Facs. of 1881 edn. NHHS.
43. Benedict, Henry M., *Genealogy of the Benedicts in America*, Albany NY, 1870.
44. Best, Frank E., *The Amidon Family Descendants of Roger Amadowne of Rehoboth, Massachusetts*, Chicago IL, 1904.

45. Bicknell, Zachery, *History and Genealogy of the Bicknell Family*, Providence RI, 1913. NHHS.
46. "Biddeford Town Records, Book Three," cy. in Dyer Library, Saco ME.
47. Bigelow, Ella A., *Historical Reminiscences of the Early Times in Marlborough, Massachusetts*, Times Publishing Co., Marlborough MA, 1910.
48. Binney, Charles J. F., *The History and Genealogy of the Prentice or Prentiss Family, 1631-1883*, PBA, Boston MA, 1883. NHHS.
49. Blake, Carlton E., *Descendants of Jasper Blake,*, Gateway Press, Inc., Baltimore MD, 1980.
50. Blake, Frances E., *Increase Blake of Boston: His Ancestors and Descendants*, Boston MA, 1898.
51. Blake, Francis E., *History of the Town of Princeton, Massachusetts*, Vol. I and II, PBT, Princeton MA, 1915. NHHS.
52. Bliss, John H., *Genealogy of the Bliss Family of America,* PBA, Boston MA, 1881. NHHS.
53. Blodgett, George B., *Early Settlers of Rowley, Masachusetts*, Salem MA, 1933. NHHS.
54. Boardman, Anna C., *Robert Calef of Boston and Some of His Descendants*, Reprinted from Essex Institute Historical Collections, Salem MA, 1940.
55. Boardman, William F. J., *Ancestry of Jane Maria Greenleaf*, PP, Hartford CT, 1906. NHHS.
56. Bodge, George Madison, *Soldiers of the King Philip's War*, PBA, Leominster MA, 1896. NHHS.
57. Bolton, Ethel Stanwood, *Stanwood Family*, Rockwell and Churchill Press, Boston MA, 1899. NHHS.
58. Bolton CT: *Vital Records of Bolton to 1854 and Vernon to 1852*, Hartford CT Hist. Soc., 1909.
59. Bolton, Thaddeus L., *Genealogy of the Dart Family in America*, Cooper Printing Co., Philadelphia PA, 1927. NHHS.
60. Booker, Warren E., DDS, *Historical Notes, Jamaica, Vermont*, E. L. Hildreth and Co., Inc., Brattleboro VT, 1940. NHHS.
61. *One Hundred and Fiftieth Anniversary of the Settlement of Boscawen and Webster, New Hampshire*, Concord NH, 1884. NHHS
62. Boston MA: *9th Report of the Record Commissioners, Containing Births, Baptisms, Marriages, Deaths, 1630-1699*, Rockwell and Churchill, Boston MA, 1883. Dover NH Public Library.
63. Boston MA: *24th Report of the Record Commissioners, Containing Births From A. D. 1700 to A. D. 1800*, Rockwell and Churchill, Boston MA, 1894. Dover NH Public Library.
64. Boston MA: *28th Report of the Record Commissioners, Containing Marriages, 1700-1751*, Municipal Printing Office, Boston MA, 1898. Dover NH Public Library.
65. Boston MA: *30th Report of the Record Commissioners, Containing Marriages, 1752-1809*, Municipal Printing Office, Boston MA, 1903. Dover NH Public Library.
66. Boston MA: *A Report of the Record Commissioners, Containing the Records From 1729-1742*, Rockwell and Churchill, Boston MA, 1885. Dover NH Public Library.
67. Bourne, Edward E., *The History of Wells and Kennebunkport*, B. Thurston and Co., Portland ME, 1875. NHHS.
68. Bouton, Nathaniel, *History of Concord, New Hampshire*, 2 vol., Benning W. Sanborn, Concord NH, 1856. NHHS.
69. Bowen, Clarence Winthrop, *The History of Woodstock, Connecticut*, 8 vol., PP, The Plimpton Press, Norwood MA, 1926. NHHS.
70. Bowen, Edward A., *Lineage of the Bowens of Woodstock, Connecticut*, Riverside Press, Cambridge MA, 1897.
71. Boyden, Wallace Clarke, *Thomas Boyden and his Descendants*, Boston MA, 1901.
72. Boyle, Frederick R., *Early Families of Sanford-Springvale, Maine*, Peter E. Randall, Portsmouth NH, 1988. ALSOP files.
73. Boynton, John F. and Caroline, *Boynton Family, Descendants of William and John*, 1897.
74. Brackett, Herbert I., *Brackett Genealogy*, PBA, Washington DC, 1907. NHHS.
75. Brainard, Homer W., *Survey of the Ishams of England and America*, Tuttle Publishing Co., Rutland VT, 1938.
76. Brainard, Lawrence, *Gary Genealogy: The Descendants of Arthur Gary*, T. R. Marvin and Sons, Boston MA, 1918. NHHS.
77. Brainard, Lucy Abigail, *Genealogy of the Brainard-Brenard Family in America, 1644-1908*, Vol. 3, Hartford Press, 1908.
78. *A History of the Town of Brandon, Vermont, 1761-1961*, PBT, 1961. NHHS.
79. Bridge, Rev. William D., *Genealogy of the John Bridge Family in America*, Murray Printing Co., Cambridge MD, 1924.
80. *Bridgton, Maine, 1768-1968*, Bridgton ME Historical Society, 1968. NHHS.
81. Briggs, L. Vernon, *Briggs History and Genealogy*, Charles Goodspeed and Co., Boston MA, 1938.
82. Brigham, Emma E. (Neal), *Neal Family*, Springfield MA, 1938. NHHS.
83. Brigham, Theda Page, *Descendants of John Page (1614-1687) of Hingham and Haverhill*, Haverhill NH Historical Society, 1972. NHHS.
84. Brigham, W. Tyler, *History of the Brigham Family*, Grafton Press, New York NY, 1907. MHS.
85. Brigham, Willard Tyler, *Tyler Genealogy*, Cornelius and Rollin Tyler, Plainfield NJ, 1912. NHHS.
86. Brookfield NH, Records of the Town Clerk.
87. Brooklin ME, Vital Records, compiled by Grace Lineburger, March 1941.
88. Brooks, Charles, *History of the Town of Medford, 1630-1855*, Rand, Avery and Co., Boston MA, 1886.

89. Brown, Cyrus Henry, *Brown Genealogy*, Vol. II, Pt. III, Everett Press, Boston MA, 1915. NHHS.
90. Brown, Katherine, *Stockman-Gallison Ancestry*, PP, 1984. NHHS.
91. Brown, Mary W., *Genealogy of John Brown of Hampton, New Hampshire*, Amesbury MA, 1977.
92. Browne, George W., *History of Hillsborough, New Hampshire*, 2 vol., Manchester NH, 1921.
93. Buckminster, Lydia N. (Hastings), *Hastings Memorial, 1634-1864*, Samuel G. Drake, Boston MA, 1866. NHHS.
94. Bull, Sidney A., *History of the Town of Carlisle, Massachusetts, 1754-1920*, The Murray Printing Co., Cambridge MA, 1920.
95. Burgess, E., *Burgess Genealogy Memorial of the Family of Thomas and Dorothy Burgess*, T. R. Marvin and Son, Boston MA, 1865. NHHS.
96. Burke, Arthur M., *The Prominent Families of the United States of America*, Vol. 1, Genealogical Publishing Co., Baltimore MD, 1991. Reprint of 1908 Edn. NHHS.
97. Burleigh, Charles, *The Genealogy and History of the Guild, Guile, and Gile Family*, Brown Thurston and Co., Portland ME, 1887. NHHS.
98. Burleigh, Charles, *Genealogy and History of the Ingalls Family in America*, George E. Dunbar, Malden MA, 1903.
99. Burnham, E. P., "Saco Families," ms., n. d., Dyer Library, Saco ME.
100. Butler, George H., *Thomas Butler and his Descendents*, Trow Printing and Publishing Co., New York NY, 1886.
101. "Records of Births and Deaths in the Town of Buxton," copied for Maine Gen. Soc. by Charles A. Meserve, MD, Portland ME, 1891.

C.

1. Cabot, Mary Rogers, *Annals of Brattleboro, 1681-1895*, 2 vol., Brattleboro VT, 1921. NHHS.
2. "Campton N. H. Congregational Church Records (1811-1857)," ms., no author, n. d. NHHS.
3. Canney, Robert S., *Early Marriages of Strafford County, New Hampshire*, Heritage Books, Inc., Bowie MD, 1991. NHHS.
3A Cape Elizabeth ME, "Intentions of Marriages and Marriages, 1765 1895," ms. MHS.
4. Carleton, Hiram, *Genealogical and Family History of the State of Vermont*, 2 vol., New York NY, 1903. NHHS.
5. Carpenter, Amos B., *Genealogical History of the Carpenter Family in America*, Carpenter and Morehouse, Amherst MA, 1898. NHHS.
6. Carr, Edison I., *The Carr Family Record*, Herald Printing Co., Rockton IL, 1894.
7. Carr, Jonathan R., *Photographs and Memories of Cornish*, Vol. 2, Dec 1984.
8. Carter, Amory, *Sawyers in America: A History of the Immigrant Sawyers*, Edward R. Fiske, Worcester MA, 1883. NHHS.
9. Carter, Clara A. and Sarah A., *Descendants of Samuel and Thomas, Sons of Rev. Samuel Carter, 1640-1886*, Printed by W. J. Coulter, Clinton MA, 1887. NHHS.
10. Carter, HowardWilliston, *Genealogy of the Descendants of Thomas Carter*, PBA, Norfolk CT, 1909.
11. Carter, N. F., Rev., and Hon. T. L. Fowler, *History of Pembroke, New Hampshire, 1730-1895*, 2 vol., Allenstown and Pembroke Bicentennial Committee, 1976. NHHS.
12. Cary, Seth C., *John Cary, The Plymouth Pilgrim*, PBA, Boston MA, 1911. NHHS.
13. Case, Lafayette W., *The Goodrich Family in America*, Chicago IL, 1889. NHHS.
14. Case, Lafayette W., *Hollister Family of America*, Fergus Printing Co., Chicago IL, 1886.
15. Case, Leland D. and Edith E. H. Grannis, *Memoirs of Samuel H. Grannis, 1839-1939*, Tucson AZ, 1962. NHHS.
16. Case, Lynn M. and Page Sanderson, *The Family of John Page of Haverhill, Massachusetts*, The Gateway Press, Baltimore MD, 1978. NHHS.
17. Caswell, Lilly B., *Athol, Massachusetts, Past and Present*, 1899.
18. Caswell, Lilly B., *The History of the Town of Royalston, Massachusetts*, PBT, Royalston MA, 1917. NHHS.
19. Caverly, Robert Boodey, *Annals of the Boodeys in New England*, Lowell MA, 1880.
20. Chaffin, William L., *History of the Town of Easton, Massachusetts*, University Press, Cambridge MA, 1886. NHHS.
21. Chaffin, William L., *A Biographical History of Robert Randall and his Descendants, 1608-1909*, Grafton Press, New York NY, MCMIX. NHHS.
22. Chamberlain, George W., *Descendants of Charles Glidden*, Boston MA, 1925. NHS
23. Chamberlain, George Walter, *The Webber Genealogy, 1639-1934*, Webber Foundation, Wellesley MA, 1935. NHHS.
24. Chandler, Charles H. and Sarah F. Lee, *The History of New Ipswich, New Hampshire, 1735-1914*, Fitchburg MA, 1914.
25. Chandler, George, *The Chandler Family, Descendants of William and Annis Chandler*, Press of Charles Hamilton, Worcester MA, 1883.
26. Chapman, F. W., Rev., *The Chapman Family or the Descendants of Robert Chapman*, Case, Tiffany and Co., Hartford Ct, MDCCCLIV. NHHS.
27. Chapman, Jacob and James H. Fitts, *Lane Genealogy*, Vol. 1, Exeter NH NewsLetter Press, 1891.
28. Chase, Benjamin, *History of Old Chester From 1719 to 1839*, PBA, Auburn NH, 1869. NHHS.

29. Chase, George Wingate, *The History of Haverhill, Massachusetts From its First Settlement in 1640 to the Year 1860*, Haverhill MA, 1861.
30. Chase, John C. and George W. Chamberlain, *Seven Generations of the Descendants of Aquila and Thomas Chase*, Derry NH, 1928. NHHS.
31. Chase, John Carroll, *History of Chester, New Hampshire*, Derry NH, 1926. NHHS.
32. *Cheshire County Gazeteer*, Comp. and Publ. by Hamilton Childs, Syracuse NY, 1885. NHHS.
33. Cheshire County NH, Index to Probate Records, 1769-1800, copied from card index in Office of Probate Clerk, Keene NH. NHHS.
34. "Chickering Family," ms., no author, 1939. Revised by Lucy D. Pratt. NHHS.
35. Child, Hamilton, *Gazetteer of Grafton County, New Hampshire*, Syracuse NY, 1886. NHHS.
36. Child, Hamilton, *Gazetteer of Orange County, Vermont, 1762-1888*, Syracuse NY, 1888. NHHS.
37. Child, Hamilton, *Gazetteer of Washington County, Vermont, 1783-1889*, (Berlin VT), The Syracuse Journal Co., Syracuse NY, 1889.
38. Child, William H., *History of the Town of Cornish, New Hampshire, 1763-1910*, Vol. I, The Rumford Press, Concord NH, n. d. NHHS.
39. Childs, Ethel B., *History of Stow*, Tercentenary Edition, 1863-1893, Stow MA Hist. Soc. Publishing Company, 1983. NHHS.
40. Childs, Francis L., "Henniker, New Hampshire, Inscriptions," ms., 1925. NHHS.
41. Chipman, Bert L., *The Chipman Family, 1631-1920*, Winston Salem NC, 1920.
42. Churchill, Gardner A. and Nathaniel W., *Churchill Family in America*, published by the family of the author, n. d.
43. Clarke, George Kuhn, *Genealogy of Descendants of Nathaniel Clarke of Newbury, Massachusetts*, Boston MA, 1883.
44. Clarke, George Kuhn, *History of Needham, Massachusetts, 1711-1911*, University Press, Cambridge MA, 1912.
45. Clarke, Louise B., *The Greenes of Rhode Island*, New York NY, 1903. NHHS.
46. Clason, Oliver B., *History of Litchfield*, Heritage Books, Bowie MD, 1992. MHS.
47. Claypool, Edward A. and Azalea Clizbee, *Genealogy of the Descendants of William Kelsey*, 2 vol., Tuttle, Morehouse, Taylor Co., New Haven CT, 1929.
48. Cleaveland, Edmund J. and Horace G., *Genealogy of the Cleveland and Cleaveland Families*, Hartford CT, 1899. NHHS.
49. Clemens, William M., *Early Connecticut Marriage Records Before 1699*, The Biblo Company, Pompton Lakes NJ, 1926.
50. Clement, Percival W., *Ancestors and Descendants of Robert Clement*, 2 vol., Press of Patterson and White, Philadelphia PA, 1927. NHHS.
51. Clemens, William M., Ed., *American Marriages Before 1699*, The Biblo Company, Pompton Lakes NJ, 1926.
52. Clemons, Hubert W., *Cemetery Records of Brownfield, Maine*, Hiram ME, n. d. ALSOP files.
53. Clemons, Hubert W., "Cemeteries and Burial Grounds in Hiram, Maine," ms. ALSOP files.
53A. Cochrane, Harry H., *History of Monmouth and Wales, Maine*, Banner Co., East Winthrop ME, 1894. NHHS.
54. Cochrane, Rev. W. R.,*History of the Town of Antrim, New Hampshire*, Manchester NH, 1880.
55. Cochrane, Rev. W. R., and George K. Wood, *History of Francestown, N. H.*, PBT, Nashua NH, 1895. NHHS.
56. Coffin, Joshua, *A Sketch of the History of Newbury, Newburyport, and West Newbury*, Peter E. Randall, Hampton NH, 1972 reprint of 1845 edn. NHHS. Cy. in ALSOP files.
57. Coggeshall, Charles P. and J. Russell, *The Coggeshalls in America*, G. E. Goodspeeds, Boston MA, 1930.
58. Cogswell, Elliott C., *History of Nottingham, Deerfield, and Northwood*, NH Publishing Co., Somersworth NH, 1972. NHHS.
59. Cogswell, Leander W., *History of the Town of Henniker, New Hampshire*, New Hampshire Publishing Co, Somersworth NH, 1973. NHHS.
60. Colby, Harrison, "History of Bow, N. H. ", Vol. 2, ms., 1930. NHHS.
61. Coldham, Peter W., *The Complete Book of Emigrants, 1607-1660*, Genealogical Publishing Co., Baltimore MD, 1988. NHHS.
62. Cole, Rev. Albert, "Baptismal, Marriage and Funeral Records (1818 1881) of Cornish, Maine," reproduced by ALSOP, 1983.
63. Cole, Alfred and Whitman, Charles Foster, *A History of Buckfield*, Buckfield ME, 1915. MHS. NHHS.
64. Cole, Kenneth E. and Dudy, *Cemetery Inscriptions of Pine Grove, Falmouth Foreside (Old Part)*, Saco ME, 1979. MHS.
65. Colesworthy, Daniel C., *Casco Bay, Maine*, Sanborn and Carter, Portland ME, 1850. MHS.
66. Colton, Margaret Kelly Ashe, "Evergreen Cemetery Inscriptions at Milbridge, Maine," n. d. MHS.
67. Colton, Margaret Kelly Ashe, "Intentions and Marriages Recorded in the Town of Milbridge, Maine, From its Incorporation in 1848 to 1892. " Copied from original records, 1937. MHS.
68. Colton, Margaret Kelly Ashe, Harrington ME Vital Records, copied from original records in 1936. MHS.
69. Colton, Margaret Kelly Ashe, "Sanborn-Sawyer Cemetery Inscriptions, Fickett's Point, in Field Back of Sanborn Farmhouse, East of Road, Milbridge, Maine," n. d. MHS.
69A. Conant, Frederick Odell, *Conant Family of England and American*, PP, Portland ME, 1887. NHHS.

70. Concord NH: South Congregational Church Records, 1956. NHHS.
71. Cone, William W., *Cone Family in America*, Topeka KS, 1903.
72. "Conway N. H. Village Cemetery," ms., n. d. ALSOP files.
73. Cook, H. Ruth, *Times and Generations of the Driver Family*, New York, NY, 1889. NHHS.
73A Cooley, Mortimer E., *Cooley Genealogy*, The Tuttle Publishing Co., Rutland VT, n. d. NHHS.
74. Coolidge, Mabel Cook, *The History of Petersham, Massachusetts, Incorporated April 20, 1754*, The Petersham MA Hist. Soc., Inc., 1948. NHHS.
75. Coolidge, Emma D., *Descendants of John and Mary Coolidge of Watertown, Massachusetts*, Wright and Potter Printing Co., Boston MA, 1930.
76. Copeland, Warren T., *The Copeland Family*, The Tuttle Publishing Co.,Rutland VT, 1937. NHHS.
77. Corey, Deloraine Pendre, *The History of Malden, Massachusetts, 1633-1785*, PBA, Malden MA, 1899.
78. Corliss, Augustus W., *Old Times of North Yarmouth, Maine*, Vol. 6, No. 3, July 1882. MHS.
79. Corser, Samuel G. B., *Genealogy of the Corser Family in America*, Ira C. Evans Co., Concord NH, 1902. NHHS.
80. Cowley, Charles, *History of Lowell*, Lee and Shepard, Boston MA, 1868.
81. Cox, Louis S., "A Pease Family", ms., Mimeograph Shop, Haverhill MA, 1947. NHHS.
82. Crafts, James M. and William F., *The Crafts Family*, Gazette Printing Co., Northampton MA, 1893.
83. Crafts, James Monroe, *History of the Town of Whately, Mass., 1661 1899*, PBT, 1899. NHHS.
84. Craig, Frank H., *Sketches of the Town of Topsham, Orange County, Vermont*, The Green Mt. Press, Bradford VT, 1929. NHHS.
85. Crandall, Adelaide B., *Blanchards of Rhode Island*, Ann Arbor MI, 1942.
86. Crocker, Henry G., *Nathaniel Crocker, His Descendants and Ancestors*, Rumford Press, Concord NH, 1923. NHHS.
87. Cross, Lucy R. H., *History of Northfield, New Hampshire*, Rumford Press,Concord NH, 1905.
88. Cross, Rev. R. T., *My Children's Ancestors*, Twinsberg OH, 1913. NHHS.
89. Cumberland County ME, Civil War Roster, 1880.
90. Cummins, Albert O., *Cummins Genealogy*, Montpelier VT, 1904. NHHS.
91. Currier, Harvey L. and John McNab, *Richard Currier of Salisbury and Amesbury, Mass., 1616-1686/7*, Newport VT, 1910. NHHS.
91A. Currier, John J., *History of Newbury, Massachusetts, 1635-1902*, Damrell and Upham, Boston MA, 1902.
92. Currier, John J., *"Ould Newbury"; Historical and Biographical Sketches*, Boston MA, 1896. NHHS.
93. Currier, John M., *Genealogy of Richard Currier and his Descendants*, Newport VT, 1910. NHHS.
94. Cushing, James S., *Genealogy of the Cushing Family*, The Perrault Printing Co., Montreal, Canada, 1905. NHHS.
94A. Cutler. Nahum S., *A Cutler Memorial*, Press of E. A. Hall and Co., Greenfield MA, 1889. MHS.
95. Cutter, Benjamin and William, *History of the Town of Arlington*, Boston MA, 1880.
96. Cutter, Daniel B., *History of the Town of Jaffrey, 1749-1880*, Republican Press Assn., Concord NH, 1881. NHHS.
97. Cutter, William R., *Genealogies of Boston and Eastern Massachusetts*, Lewis Historical Publishing Co., New York NY, 1908. MHS.
98. Cutter, William R., *Middlesex, Massachusetts*, 4 vol., Lewis Historical Publ. Co., New York NY, 1908. NHHS.
99. Cutter, William Richard, The New England Families, 1914. Zeroxed.
100. Cutter, William Richard, *Genealogical and Personal Memoires Massachusetts*, Vol. 1, Lewis History Publ. Co., NY 1910.

D.

1. Daggett, Samuel B., *A History of the Doggett-Daggett Family*, Press of Rockwell and Churchill, Boston MA, 1894. NHHS.
2. Damon, Samuel C., *The History of Holden, Massachusetts, 1667-1841*, Holden MA, 1841. NHHS.
3. Dana, Elizabeth E., *The Dana Family in America*, Cambridge MA, 1956. NHHS.
4. Daniel, Elizabeth S. and Jeanne E. Sawtelle, *Thomas Rogers, Pilgrim, and Some of his Descendants*, The Gateway Press, Baltimore MD, 1980. NHHS.
5. Daniels, George F., *History of the Town of Oxford, Massachusetts*, PBA, Oxford MA, 1892.
6. DAR Grandfathers File, DAR Library, Washington DC.
7. DAR: *Index of the Rolls of Honor in the Lineage Books of the National Society of the Daughters of the American Revolution*, 4 vol., Pittsburgh PA, 1916. NHHS.
8. *DAR Lineage Books*, Vol. 1-166, Washington DC. NHHS.
9. DAR, Misc. Records of Maine.
10. DAR, Misc. Records of New Hampshire.
11. DAR, Misc. Records of Vermont.
12. DAR, Misc. Records of Massachusetts.
13. DAR, Misc. Records of Connecticut.
14. DAR, Misc. Records of Rhode Island.
15. Davis, Albert H., *History of Ellsworth, Maine*, Lewiston Journal Printshop, Lewiston ME, 1927. NHHS.

16. Davis, Charles H. S., *History of Wallingford, Conn.*, PBA, Meriden CT, 1870. NHHS.
17. Davis, George W., *John Grow of Ipswich*, PBA, Washington DC, 1913. NHHS.
18. Davis, Gilbert A., *History of Reading*, Bellows Falls VT, 1874. NHHS.
19. Davis, Mitchell T., *Sebago, Maine, Town Register*, H. E. Mitchell Co., Brunswick ME, 1910. MHS.
20. Davis, Walter A., City Clerk, *The Old Records of the Town of Fitchburg, Massachusetts, 1764-1789*, Vol. I-VII, 1898. NHHS.
21. Davis, Walter G., *Ancestors of Bethia Harris*, Southworth Press, Portland ME, 1934.
22. Davis, Walter Goodwin, *The Ancestry of James Patten, 1747?-1817*, Southworth-Anthoeson Press, Portland ME, 1941. NHHS.
23. Davis, Walter Goodwin, *The Ancestry of Phoebe Tilton, 1775-1847* (facs. of 1947 edn. ), Parker River Researchers, Newburyport MA, 1987. NHHS.
24. Davis, W. T., *New England States*, Vol. 3 and 4, 1897.
25. Day, Ina Harris, *William Day and Dorothy Littlefield and Many of Their Ancestors, Descendants, and Cousins*, DACOMM Family Orgn., Murray UT, 1989. ALSOP files.
26. Dean, John Gilmore and Edgar Crosby Smith, "History of Portland," *Sprague's Journal of Maine History*, Vol. 6, No. 1, May-Jul 1918. MHS.
27. Dearborn, J. W., *et. al.*, *A History of the First Century of the Town of Parsonsfield, Maine, Incorporated August 29, 1785....*, Brown Thurston and Co., Portland ME, 1888. ALSOP files. NHHS.
28. Dearborn, John J., *The History of Salisbury, New Hampshire,*, William E. Moore, Manchester NH, 1890. NHHS.
29. DeForest, Louis Effingham, *Our Colonial and Continental Ancestors:The Ancestry of Mr. and Mrs. Louis William Dommerich*, Deforest Publishing Co., New York NY, 1930. AAS.
29A. Delorey, Janet Ireland, *A Line of Descent from James Sawyer of Gloucester, Massachusetts to Obediah Sawyer of Falmouth, Maine*, Shrewsbury MA, 1987. MHS.
30. Deming, Judson K., *Genealogy of the Descendants of John Deming*, Mathis-Mets Company, Dubuque IA, 1904. NHHS.
31. Denio, Francis B. and Herbert W., *A Genealogy of Aaron Denio of Deerfield, Massachusetts, 1704-1925*, Capital City Press, Montpelier VT, 1926. NHHS.
32. Denison, E. Glenn, *et. al.*, *Denison Genealogy*, The Pequot Press, Stonington CT, 1963. NHHS.
33. "Cemetery Records, Denmark, Maine," ms., n. d. ALSOP files.
34. Dewey, Louis Marinus, *Life of George Dewey, Rear Admiral, USN, and Dewey Family History*, Dewey Publishing Co., Westfield MA, 1898. NHHS.
35. Dewing, Benjamin F., *Descendants of Andrew Dewing of Dedham, Mass.*, PP, Boston MA, 1904. NHHS.
36. Dexter, Orrando P., *History of the Descendants of Richard Dexter of Malden, Massachusetts, 1642-1904*, J. J. Little, New York NY, 1904. NHHS.
37. Dilts, Bryan Lee, *1890 Maine Census Index of Civil War Veterans or Their Widows*, Index Publishing Co., Salt Lake City UT, 1984. NHHS.
38. Dimock, Susan Whitney, *Births, Marriages, Baptisms and Deaths From the Records of the Town and Churches in Coventry, Connecticut, 1711-1844*, The Baker and Taylor Co., New York NY, 1897. NHHS.
39. Dimock, Susan W., *Births, Baptisms, Marriages and Deaths, From the Records of the Town and Churches in Mansfield, Connecticut, 1703 1850*, The Baker and Taylor Co., New York NY, 1898. NHHS.
40. Dodge, Joseph T., *Genealogy of the Dodge Family of Essex County,, Mass., 1629-1894*, 2 vol., Madison WI, 1894. NHHS.
41. Dodge, Nancy, *Settlement and Cemeteries in Vermont Northeast Kingdom*, Higginson Books, Salem MA, 1988. NHHS.
42. Dodge, Prentiss C., *Encyclopedia of Vermont Biography*, Burlington VT, 1912. NHHS.
43. Doe, Elmer E., *The Descendants of Nicholas Doe*, Orleans VT, 1918. NHHS.
44. Dole, Samuel T., "Inscription From Headstones in Gorham, Maine," 1902, ms., Gorham ME Library.
45. *Dorchester NH 1772-1972*, The Dorchester NH Bicentennial Committee, n. d. NHHS.
46. Doty, Ethan A., *The Doty-Doten Family in America*, PBA, Brooklyn NY, 1897. NHHS.
47. Dover NH, *A Bill of Mortality for The Society of Friends in Dover, 1708-1791*, Scales and Quimby, Dover NH, 1894. Dover NH Public Library.
48. Dover NH, *Vital Statistics, Births, Marriages, and Deaths Registered in Dover, 1887-1899*, Dover NH Public Library.
49. Dow, George Francis, *History of Topsfield, Massachusetts*, Topsfield MA Hist. Soc., 1940. NHHS.
50. Dow, John J., *All in a Family-Dow Genealogy*, PP, Exeter NH, 1980. NHHS.
51. "Down East Ancestry," PO Box 398, Machias ME, 04654:
    a. Vol. 4, No. 2, Nov 1979.
    b. Vol. 4, No. 4, Dec 1980.
    c. Vol. 4, No. 5, Feb 1981.
    d. Vol. 5, No. 2, Aug 1981.
    e. Vol. 5, No. 4, Dec 1981.
    f. Vol. 6, No. 4, 1982.

g. Vol. 6, No. 5, Feb 1983.
h. Vol. 6, No. 6, Apr 1983.
i. Vol. 7, No. 1, Jun 1983.
j. Vol. 7, No. 2, Aug 1983.
k. Vol. 7, No. 3, Oct 1983.
l. Vol. 7, No. 4, Dec 1983.
m. Vol. 8, No. 1, Jun 1984
n. Vol. 8, No. 2, Aug 1984.
o. Vol. 8, No. 3, Oct 1984.
p. Vol. 8, No. 5, Feb 1985.
q. Vol. 9, No. 3, Oct 1985.
r. Vol. 9, No. 4, Dec 1985.
s. Vol. 9, No. 5, Feb 1986.

52. Downer, David R., *The Downers of America, With Genealogical Record*, Newark NJ, 1900. NHHS.
53. Dows, Azro M., *The Dows or Dowse Family in America, 1642-1890*, Lowell MA, 1890. NHHS.
54. Drake, Samuel G., *Founders of New England*, John Wilson and Son Press of Boston MA, 1865.
55. Draper, Thomas, *Bemis History and Genealogy*, San Francisco CA, 1900. NHHS.
56. Dudley, Dean, *History of the Dudley Family*, 2 vol., PP, Wakefield MA, 1886. NHHS.
57. Dudley, Dean, *History and Genealogy of the Bangs Family in America*, PBA, Montrose MA, 1896. NHHS.
58. Dunster, Samuel, *Henry Dunster and his Descendants*, E. L. Freeman and Co., Central Falls RI, 1876. NHHS.
59. Durand, Celia C., *Genealogical Register of the Durand Family*, Oberlin OH, 1925. NHHS.
60. Dwight, Benjamin W., *The History of John Dwight of Dedham, Mass.*, 2 vol., John F. Trow and Son., New York NY, 1874. NHHS.
61. Dwight, Benjamin W., *History of the Descendants of Elder John Strong*, Joel Musell, Albany NY, 1871. NHHS.

E.

1. Earle, Pliney, *The Earle Family: Ralph Earle and his Descendants*, Press of Charles Hamilton, Worcester MA, 1888. NHHS.
2. Eastman, John R., *History of the Town of Andover, New Hampshire, 1751-1906*, Concord NH, 1910. NHHS.
3. Eaton, Cyrus, *History of Thomaston, Rockland, and South-Thomaston, Maine*, 2 vol., Masters Smith and Co., Hallowell ME, 1865. 2 vol. MHS.
4. Eaton, Francis L., *Berlin, Massachusetts Vital Records to 1899*, Marlborough MA, 1935. NHHS.
5. Eaton, Lilley, *Genealogical History of the Town of Reading, Mass., Including the Present Towns of Wakefield, Reading, and North Reading, 1639-1874*, Alfred Mudge and Son, Boston MA, 1874. NHHS.
6. Eddy, Ruth, S. D., *The Eddy Family in America*, T. O. Metcalf Co., Boston MA, 1930. NHHS.
7. Edgerly, Edwin L., *Edgerly and Allied Families*, PP, 1959. NHHS.
8. Edson, Carroll A., Ed., *Family History and Genealogical Descendants of Samuel Edson*, 2 vol., Edward Brothers, Ann Arbor MI, n. d. NHHS.
9. Edwards, Llewellyn N., *Genealogical Record of the Descendants of John Edwards, 168 to 1915*, Bangor, ME, 1916. NHHS.
10. Ela, David H., *Vital Records of Anson, Maine*, Part I, 1975.
11. Eldridge, Jane J., *The Leavitts of America*, Leavitt Family Association, Salt Lake City UT, 1924.
12. Ellis, Leonard Bolles, *History of New Bedford and its Vicinity, 1602-1892*, Syracuse NY, 1892. NHHS.
13. Ellis, Leola C. and Kera C. Millard, *More About Early Cornish*, 1975. NHHS.
14. Ellis, Mary R., *The House of Mansur*, The Hugh Stevens Press, Jefferson City MO, 1926. NHHS.
15. Ellis, Milton and Leola Chaplin, *John Chaplin of Rowley, Massachusetts, and Bridgton, Maine*, Westbrook ME, 1949.
16. Ellis, Roy Lowther, Ed., *A Genealogical Register of Edmund Rice Descendants*, The Charles Tuttle Company, Rutland VT, 1970. NHHS.
17. Elwell, John Lewis, *The Story of Byfield*, George E. Littlefield, Boston MA, 1904.
18. Emery, Edwin, *The History of Sanford, Maine, 1661-1900*, PBA, Fall River MA, 1901. NHHS.
19. Emery, Rufus, *Genealogical Records of Descendants of John and Anthony Emery*, Emery Cleaves, Salem MA, 1890. NHHS.
20. *The Essex Antiquarian*, published quarterly, Vol. I-XIII, 1897-1909, Salem MA.
21. *Essex Institute Historical Collections*, Vol. 56-58, Salem MA, 1921.
22. Estabrook, William B., *Genealogy of the Estabrook Family*, Andrus and Church, Ithaca NY, 1891. NHHS.
23. Estes, Charles, *Estes Genealogies*, Eden Putnam, Publishers, Salem MA, 1894. NHHS.
24. Estes, David Foster, *The History of Holden, Massachusetts, 1684 1894*, Worcester MA, 1894. NHHS.
25. Evans, Harry W., *Evans Families*, PP, 1949. NHHS.
26. Evans, Helen F., Ed., "Abstracts of the Probate Records of Strafford County, New Hampshire, 1771-1799," *The Bibliographer*, Bedford NH, 1983. NHHS.

27. Everett, Edward F., *Descendants of Richard Everett of Dedham of Dedham, Mass.*, Boston MA, 1902. NHHS.

F.

1. Fahnestock, Catherine B., *Three Hundred and Fifty Years of Bickfords in New Hampshire*, Cottonport LA, 1971. NHHS.
2. Fairbanks, Lorenzo S., *Genealogy of the Fairbanks Family in America, 1633-1897*, Boston MA, 1897. NHHS.
3. Family Records of Ancient Landmarks Society of Parsonsfield ME, Vol. S. ALSOP files.
4. Family records on microfilm, NHHS.
5. Farlow, Charles F., *Ballard Genealogy*, Boston MA, 1911. NHHS.
6. Farmer, John, *Historical Sketch of Amherst in the County of Hillsborough in New Hampshire, From its First Settlement to the Year MDCCCXXXVII*, Concord NH, 1837. NHHS.
7. Farnham, Charles H. *History of the Descendants of John Whitman of Weymouth Massachusetts*, Tuttle, Morehouse and Taylor, New Haven CT, 1889. NHHS.
8. Farnsworth, Moses F., *Farnsworth Memorial*, L. A. Lauber, Manti UT, 1897. NHHS.
9. Farrin, Frank M., *Captain Jonathan Farrin of Amesbury, Massachusetts, and Some of his Descendants*, Murray Printing Co., Cambridge MA, 1941. NHHS.
10. *Farrington Memorial*, Press of Southworth Bros., Portland ME, 1899. NHHS.
11. Farwell, Harriette F., *Shaw Records*, E. C. Bowler, Bethel ME, 1904.
11A. Faulkner, Gerald, *Shepard Family of New England*, Vol. 1, New Haven Colony Historical Society, New Haven CT, 1971. NHHS.
12. Felt, Joseph B., *Annals of Salem*, 2 vol., W. and S. B. Ives, Salem MA, 1845. NHHS.
13. Felt, Joseph B., *History of Ipswich, Essex, and Hamilton*, Cambridge MA, 1834. NHHS.
14. Felton, William R., *Genealogical History of the Felton Family*, Tuttle Publishing Co., Rutland VT, 1935. NHHS.
15. Ferrin-Hollinger, Lavisa, *A Genealogical Record of the Ancestors and Descendants of Joseph Ferrin and Elizabeth Preston*, Cherokee IA, 1915. NHHS.
16. Ferris, Mary Walton, *Dawes-Gates Ancestral Lines*, Vol. 1, Chicago IL, 1943. NHHS.
17. Fisher, Albert V., *A Brief History of Alton Corners, 1765-1810*, Alton NH, 1973.
18. Fisher, Philip A., *The Fisher Genealogy*, Massachusetts Publishing Co., Everett MA, 1898. NHHS.
19. Fitts, James H., *Fitts or Fitz Family in America*, Port Orange Press, Albany NY, 1897. NHHS.
20. Fitts, James H., *History of Newfields, New Hampshire*, Concord NH, 1912.
21. Flagg, Charles Alcott, "An Alphabetical Index of Revolutionary Pensioners Living in Maine", reprinted from *Sprague's Journal of Maine History*, publ. quarterly, Dover ME 1920.
22. Fletcher, Edward H., *The Descendants of Robert Fletcher of Concord, Mass*, Rand, Avery and Co., Boston MA, 1881. NHHS.
23. Folsom, Elizabeth Knowles, *Genealogy of the Folsom Family, A Revised and Extended Edition, Including English Records, 1638-1938*, 2 vol., Rutland VT, 1938. NHHS.
24. Foote, Abram W., *Foote Family*, Vol. 1, The Tuttle Co., Rutland Vt., 1907. NHHS.
25. Ford, Andrew E., *History of the Origin of the Town of Clinton, Massachusetts, 1635-1865*, Press of W. J. Coulter, Clinton MA, 1896. NHHS.
26. Foster, Rev. Amos, *The History of the Town of Putney*, Ludlow VT, 1884. NHHS.
27. Foster, Helen M. and William W. Streeter, *Only One Cummington*, Cummington MA Historical Commission, 1974. NHHS.
28. Fox, N. M., *History of That Part of the Fox Family Descended From Thomas Fox*, Union Printing Co., St. Joseph MO, 1899. NHHS.
29. Freedom NH Cemetery. ALSOP files.
30. French, Edward A., *History of the Church Family*, Narragansett Publishing Co., Providence RI, 1887.
31. Frizzell, Martha McDanolds, *A History of Walpole, New Hampshire*, Vol. 1, Walpole NH Hist. Soc., 1963. NHHS.
32. Frost, John E., *The Nicholas Frost Family*, The Cabinet Press, Milford NH, 1943. NHHS.
33. Frost, John E., "The Acton (Maine) Record Book," 1964. MHS.
34. Frost, John E., "The Cornish (Maine) Record Book," 1965. MHS.
35. Frost, John E., "The Alfred (Maine) Record Book," 1968. MHS.
36. Frost, John E., "The Biddeford (Maine) Record Book, 1968. ALSOP.
37. Frost, John E., "The Buxton (Maine) Record Book," 1968. MHS.
38. Frost, John E., "York County (Maine) Record Book," addenda to record books of towns, 1975. MHS.
39. Frost, Josephine C., *Ancestors of Frank Davol and his Wife Phebe Downing Willets*, Fred H. Hitchcock Genealogical Publications, New York NY, 1925. NHHS.
40. Frost, Josephine C., *Ancestors of Alden Smith Swan and his Wife Mary Althea Farwell*, The Hills Press, New York NY, 1923. NHHS.
41. Frost, Josephine C., *Strong Genealogy*, Bowles Printer, Brooklyn NY, 1915. NHHS.
42. Frost, Josephine C., *Underhill Genealogy*, Myron C. Taylor, 1912.
43. Fuess, Claude M., *Andover: Symbol of New England*, The Andover Hist. Soc., Andover MA, 1959.

44. Fuller, William H., *Genealogy of Some Descendants of Edward Fuller*, 4 vol., C. B. Fiske and Co., Palmer MA, 1908. NHHS.

## G.

1. Gannett, Michael R., *Gannett Descendants of Matthew and Hannah Gannett of Scituate*, Chevy Chase MD, 1976. NHHS.
2. Gard, Nellie A., *Ancestors and Descendants of Phineas and Polly Dunsmoor*, Richardson Printing Corp., Marietta OH, 1971. NHHS.
3. Garrett, Margery Z., *From AB to Z*, A Bryant Family Genealogy, PP, Burlington KS, 1974.
4. Gates, Charles O., *Stephen Gates*, Willis McDonald and Co., New York NY, 1898. NHHS.
5. George, Georgia Cook, *The Melendy Family in America, 1701-1981*, Gateway Press, Baltimore MD, 1982. NHHS.
6. Getchell, Sylvia Fitts, *Marden Family Genealogy*, PP, 1974. NHHS.
7. Gilbert, Edgar, *History of Salem, New Hampshire*, Rumford Printing Co., Concord NH, 1907. NHHS.
8. Gilbert, George G. and Geoffrey, *Gilberts in New England*, Ward and Phillips, Ltd., Victoria B. C., Canada, 1959. NHHS.
9. "Gilmanton, New Hampshire, Church Records, 1773-1865," ms., no author, n. d. NHHS.
10. Gilmore, George C., *New Hampshire Soldiers at Bennington*, John B. Clarke, Manchester NH, 1891. NHHS.
11. Gloucester MA: Gravestones, Oak Grove Cemetery, copied by Helen M. Rideout.
12. Gloucester MA: (a) Microfilm/fiche records, 1634-1979; (b) 4th Parish records, 1742-1839; (c) Town papers, 1645-1826; (d) Town records, 1642-1874. Sawyer Free Library, Gloucester MA.
13. Glover, Anna, *An Account of John Glover of Dorchester*, David Clapp and Son, Boston MA, 1867. NHHS.
14. Goddard, M. E. and Henry V. Partridge, *A History of Norwich, Vermont*, The Dartmouth Press, Hanover NH, 1905. NHHS.
15. Goding, Frederick W., *Genealogy of the Goding Family*, PBA, Richmond IN, 1906. NHHS.
16. Goldthwaite, Charlotte, *Boardman Genealogy, 1525-1895*, Hartford CT, 1895.
17. Goldthwaite, Charlotte, *Descendants of Thomas Goldthwaite*, Hartford CT Press, 1899.
18. Goodenow, L. B., *The Brett Genealogy*, Cambridge MA, 1915. NHHS.
19. Goodhue, Rev. Josiah F., *History of the Town of Shoreham, Vermont*, A. H. Copeland, Middlebury VT, 1861. NHHS.
20. Goodwin, "History of Sterling MA," Worcester Magazine. AAS.
20A. Goodwin, Walter, *Ancestry of Annis Spear, 1775-1858*, facsimile of original edn., Anthoensen Press, Portland ME, 1945.
21. Goodwin, William F., *Records of the Proprietors of Narraganset Township No. 1, Now the Town of Buxton*, Book 1, PP, Concord NH, 1871. NHHS.
22. Googins, Charlotte Hannah, *The Googins Family in American*, LeFavorTower Co., Portland ME, 1914. NHHS.
23. Goold, William, *Portland in the Past*, B. Thurston and Co., Portland ME, 1886. NHHS.
24. Gordon, George A. and Silas R. Coburn, *Genealogy of the Descendants of Edward Colburn or Coburn*, published by Walter Coburn, Lowell MA, 1913.
25. Gorham ME, Births and Marriages, 1753-1799. MSA.
26. Gorham ME Proprietor Records, microfilm reel 199, MSA.
27. *Gorham Maine, Records of*, Maine Genealogical Society Special Pub. No. 7, 2d edn., Picton Press, Camden ME, 1991. ALSOP files.
28. Gorton, Adelos, *The Life and Times of Samuel Gorton*, Philadelphia PA, 1907. NHHS.
29. Goss, Elbridge Henry, *The History of Melrose (Mass. )*, PBT, 1902.
30. Gove, William Henry, *The Gove Book*, Salem MA, 1922. NHHS.
31. *Grafton County, New Hampshire, Book of Biographies*, Biographical Publishing Co., Buffalo NY, 1897. No author listed. NHHS.
32. Grafton County NH, "Index to Probate Records, 1769-1800," copied from card index in Office of Probate Clerk, Woodsville NH. NHHS.
33. *The Granite Monthly*, John N. MacClintock and Co., Concord NH, 1889. NHHS.
34. Graves, John C., *Genealogy of the Graves Family in America*, Vol. 1, Buffalo NY, 1896. NHHS.
35. Gray, George A., *George Holmes*, David Clapp and Sons, Boston MA, 1908.
35A. Gray, Ruth, *Maine Families in 1790*, Vol. 2, Picton Press, Camden ME, 1990. MHS.
36. Greeley, George Hiram, *Genealogy of the Greely-Greeley Family*, Boston MA, 1905. NHHS.
37. Greeley, Rev. Seth, "Families of North Yarmouth," ms., written in the 1850s. Androscoggin Hist. Soc., Auburn ME.
38. Green, Samuel A., MD, *Groton During the Indian Wars*, Groton MA, 1883.
39. Green, Samuel A., MD, *The Boundary Lines of Old Groton*, Groton MA, 1885.
40. Green, Samuel A., MD, *Groton Historical Series*, Vol. I-IV, Groton MA, 1899. NHHS.
41. Greene, Richard Walden, Jr., *History of Boothbay*, Ivers Washburn Inc., New York NY, ca. 1949.
42. Greenleaf, James Edward, *Genealogy of the Greenleaf Family, 1574-1896*, Frank Wood, Printer, Boston MA, 1896. NHHS.

43. Greenwood, Frederick, *Greenwood Genealogies, 1154-1914*, The Lyons Genealogical Company, New York NY, 1914. NHHS.
44. Gregory, John, *History of the Town of Northfield*, Montpelier VT, 1878. NHHS.
45. Griffin, Barton McLain, *History of Alton, NH*, New Hampshire Publishing Co., Somersworth NH, 1965.
46. Griffin, S. G., *A History of the Town of Keene, 1732-1874*, Sentinal Publishing Company, Keene NH, 1904. NHHS.
47. Griffin, Sarah Swan, *Quaint Bits of Lowell History*, Butterfield Printing Co., Lowell MA, 1948.
48. "Highland Cemetery, Groveville," ms., rec. of Nancy Welch. ALSOP.
49. Guild, Mary Stiles (Paul), *Strobridge, Morrison or Morison Strawbridge*, S. W. Huse and Co., Lowell MA, 1891. NHHS.
50. *Official History of the Town of Guilford, Vermont*, PBT, 1961. NHHS.
51. Gupples, Joseph G., *Record of the Commemoration on 2 and 3 July 1890 on the 250th Anniversary of the Settlement of Haverhill, Massachusetts*, 1891.

H.

1. Hadley, George P., *History of the Town of Goffstown, 1733-1920*, PBT, 1922. NHHS.
2. Hager, Lucie Caroline, *Boxborough: A New England Town and Its People*, J. W. Lewis Co., Philadelphia PA, 1891.
3. Haines, Andrew M. and Thomas V., *Deacon Samuel Haines and his Descendants in America, 1635-1901*, North Hampton NH, 1902.
4. Hale, Robert, *Descendants of Thomas Hale*, Weed, Parsons and Co., Albany NY, 1889.
5. Haley, John W., DD, *History of Tuftonboro, New Hampshire*, Tuftonboro NH, 1923. NHHS.
6. Hall, Ruth Gardin, *Descendants of Governor William Bradford*, Bradford Family Compact, 1951.
7. Ham, John R., "Dover, N. H., Marriages, 1623-1828," ms. NHHS.
8. Hammatt, Abraham, *Early Inhabitants of Ipswich, Massachusetts*, Augustine Caldwell, 1880. NHHS.
9. Hammond, Otis G., *Notices From New Hampshire Gazette, 1765-1800*, Lambertville NJ, w/index by Thomas Wilson, 1970. NHHS.
10. Hammond, Priscilla, "Vital Records of Hampstead, N. H., 1731-1870," ms., Concord NH, 1938. NHHS.
11. Hammond, Priscilla, "Vital Records of Plaistow, N. H., 1726-1871," Concord NH, 1937. NHHS.
12. Hanaford, Mary E. (Neal), *Family Records of Hanaford and Allied Families*, Rockford IL, 1915.
13. Hance, Dawn D., *Shrewsbury, Vermont, Our Town As It Was*, Rutland Academy Books, Rutland VT, 1980. NHHS.
14. Hanson, J. W., *History of the Town of Danvers*, PBA, Danvers MA, 1848. NHHS.
15. Hanson, J. W., *History of the Old Towns Comprising Norridgewock, Canaan, Skowhegan and Bloomfield*, PBA, Boston MA, 1849. NHHS.
16. Hapgood, Warren, *The Hapgood Family, Descendants of Shadrack, 1656-1898*, Boston MA, 1898. NHHS.
17. Hardon, Henry W., "Huckins Collaterals," ms., Vol. 3, New York NY, n. d. NHHS.
18. Hardon, Henry W., *Huckins Family*, PP, Boston MA, 1916. NHHS.
19. Hardon, Henry W., "Huntress Collaterals," ms., New York NY, n. d. NHHS.
20. Hardon, Henry W., *Huntress Family*, ms., 2 vol., n. d. NHHS.
21. Hardon, Henry W., "Lord Family," ms., New York NY, n. d. NHHS.
22. Hardon, Henry W., "Roberts Family," bound ms., Vol. 2,4, New York NY, ca. 1920. NHHS.
23. Hardon, Henry W., "Seward Family," ms., New York NY. NHHS.
24. Hardy, H. Claude and Edwin U., *Hardy and Hardie, Past and Present*, Greewich CT, 1935.
25. Harmon, Artemas C., *The Harmon Genealogy*, Gibson Bros., Washington DC, 1920. NHHS.
26. Harmon, Zebulon K. of Portland ME, pension records. MHS.
27. Harriman, Walter, *The History of Warner, New Hampshire*, fasc. of 1879 edn., Warner NH, 1975. NHHS.
28. Harris, Edward Doubleday, Ed., *A Genealogical Record of Daniel Pond and his Descendants*, William Parsons Lunt, Boston MA, 1873. NHHS.
29. Harvard Law School, Catalogue from the Beginning to 1858. NHHS.
30. Harvey, George, *Bodge Family of Massachusetts, New Hampshire, and Maine*, Sacramento CA, 1982.
31. Haskell, T. H., *The New Gloucester Centennial, September 7, 1874*, Hoyt, Fogg and Denham, Portland ME, 1875. MHS.
32. Haverhill MA, Biography of Residents. Haverhill MA Public Library.
33. Haverhill MA, Records of the City Clerk.
34. Hayden, Charles A., *Descendants of Bernard Capen of Dorchester*, Augsburg Publishing House, Minneapolis MN, 1929. NHHS.
35. Hayes, Lyman Simpson, *History of the Town of Rockingham, Vermont, 1753-1907*, PBT, Bellows Falls VT, 1907. NHHS.
36. Hayward, Silvanus, *History of the Town of Gilsum, New Hampshire, 1752-1879*, PBA, Manchester NH, 1881. NHHS.
37. Hayward, William W., *The History of Hancock, New Hampshire, 1764-1889*, 2 vol., Lowell MA, 1889. NHHS.
37A. Haywood, L. S., *The Sawyer Family*, Pomfret CT Centenial 1899.

38. Hazelett, Charles A., *History of Rockingham County, New Hampshire*, Richmond-Arnold Publishing Co., Chicago IL, 1915. NHHS.
39. Hazen, Tracy E., *The Hazen Family in America*, Thomaston CT, 1947. NHHS.
40. Heaney, Marjory Anne Stubbs, *Descendants of Richard Stubbs, 1619-1677, of Hull, Massachusetts*, E. O. Painter Printing Co., Deleon Springs FL, 1984. NHHS.
41. Heitman, Francis B., *Historical Register of Officers of the Continental Army, 1775-83*, Washington DC, 1893. MHS.
42. Heitman, Francis B., *Historical Register and Dictionary of the U. S. Army, 1789-1903*, Vol. 1and2, GPO, Washington DC, 1903. MHS.
43. Hemenway, Abbey Maria, *The Vermont Historical Gazetteer*, Vol. 1-4, Burlington VT, 1868. NHHS.
44. Herrick, William D., Rev., *History of the Town of Gardner, Worcester County, Massachusetts*, Gardner MA, 1878. NHHS.
45. Heywood, William Sweetzer, *History of Westminster, Massachusetts, 1728-1893*, Vox Populi Press, Lowell MA, 1893. NHHS.
46. Hibner, Aldis E., *Genealogy of the Descendants of Joseph Bartlett of Newton, Massachusetts*, Rutland VT, 1934.
47. Higgins, Katherine C., *Richard Higgins and his Descendants*, Worcester MA, 1918.
48. Hill, Mary Pelham, *Phippsburg, Maine, Vital Statistics to the Year 1892*, Press of Merrill and Webber Co., Auburn ME, 1935. MHS.
49. Hill, Mary Pelham, *Topsham, Maine, Vital Records to the Year 1892*, Rumford Press, Concord NH, 1929. Vol. I, II. MHS.
50. Hill, William Carroll, *The Family of Bray Wilkins*, The Cabinet Press, Milford NH, 1943. NHHS.
51. Hill, William G., *Family Records of Deacons James W. and Elisha S. Converse*, Boston MA, 1887.
52. Hillsboro County NH, Index to Probate Records, 1769-1884, copied from card index in Office of Probate Clerk, Nashua NH. NHHS.
53. *The State of New Hampshire, Hillsborough County Register of Probate Index, 1771-1884*, published 1973. NHHS.
54. Hilton, Fannie Mulloy, *The Family-Molloy*, The Chronicle Print Shop, South Berwick ME, 1869. ALSOP files.
55. Hinds, Albert H., *History and Genealogy of the Hinds Family*, Thurston Print, Portland ME, 1899.
56. *History of the Town of Hingham, Massachusetts*, 3 vol., PBT, 1893. NHHS.
57. Hodge, Orlando J., *Hodge Genealogy*, Rockwell and Churchill Press, Boston MA, 1900. NHHS.
58. Hodges, Almon D. Jr., *Hodges Family of New England*, Boston MA, 1896.
58A. Hodgson, Alice Doan, *Thanks to the Past-The Story of Orford, New Hampshire*, Historical Publications, Orford NH, 1965. NHHS.
59. Holbrook, Jay Mack, *New Hampshire 1776 Census*, Holbrook Research Institute, Oxford MA, 1976. NHHS.
60. Holbrook, Jay Mack, *Vermont's First Settlers*, Holbrook Research Institute, Oxford MA, 1976. NHHS.
61. Hollis ME, Vital Records, rec. of Nancy Welch, ALSOP.
62. Hollis ME, "Riverside Cemetery," records of Nancy Welch, ALSOP.
63. Holman, Mary Lovering, *Ancestry of Charles Stinson Pillsbury and John Sargent Pillsbury*, 2 vol., Rumford Press, Concord NH, 1938. NHHS.
64. Holman, Mary Lovering, *Descendants of William Sherman*, Rumford Press, Concord NH, 1936. NHHS.
65. Holman, Mary Lovering, *Ancestors of Colonel John Harrington Stevens and Frances Helen Miller*, Vol. 1, Rumford Press, Concord NH 1948. NHHS.
66. Holman, Winifred Lovering, *Remick Genealogy*, Rumford Press, Concord NH, 1933. NHHS.
67. Hooker, Edward, *Rev. Thomas Hooker*, Rochester NY, 1909.
68. Hopkins, Hannah B., *Records of the Bailey Family: Descendants of William Bailey of Newport, Rhode Island*, Providence RI, 1895.
69. Hopkins, Timothy, *John Hopkins and Some of his Descendants*, Stanford University Press, CA, 1932. NHHS.
70. Hopkins, Timothy, *The Kelloggs in the Old World and the New*, 2 vol., Sunset Press, San Francisco CA, 1903.
71. Horn, Mrs. Ray Huntly, *John Huntley and his Descendants*, 1953.
72. Hosford, Henry H., *Horsford-Hosford Family in America*, Tower Press, Cleveland OH, 1936.
73. Hosmer, George L., *An Historical Sketch of the Town of Deer Isle, Maine*, The Fort Hill Press, Boston MA, 1905. NHHS.
74. Hotten, John Camden, *The Original Lists of Persons of Quality, 1600-1700*, Genealogical Publishing Co., Inc., Baltimore MD, 1968. First published in London, England, 1874.
75. Houghton, John Wesley, MD, *Houghton Genealogy: The Descendants of Ralph and John Houghton of Lancaster, Massachusetts*, New York NY, 1912.
76. Houghton, William A., Rev., *History of the Town of Berlin*, Worcester MA, 1895.
77. *The Hovey Book*, Hovey Press, Haverhill MA, 1913.
78. Howard, Cecil H. Cutts, *Cutts Family in America*, Joel Munsell's Sons, Albany NY, 1892. NHHS.
79. Howard, Herman, *Howard Genealogy*, Standard Print Co., Brockton MA, 1903.
80. Howe, Daniel W., *Howe Genealogy*, NEHGS, Boston MA, 1929.
81. Howe, Gilman Bigelow, *Genealogy of the Bigelow Family of America, From the Marriage in 1642 of John Bigelow and Mary Warren to the Year 1890*, Worcester MA, 1890. NHHS.

82. Howland, Franklyn, *Genealogical History-Howland*, New Bedford MA, 1895.
83. Hoyt, David W., *Hoyt Family*, C. Benjamin Richardson, Boston MA, 1857.
84. Hoyt, David W., *Old Families of Salisbury and Amesbury, Massachusetts, 1817-1919*, Vol. II, Providence RI, 1902. NHHS.
85. Hubbard, B. F., *History of Stanistead County, Province of Quebec. Canada*, Lovell Printing and Publishing Co., Montreal, Canada 1874. NHHS.
86. Hudson, Alfred Sereno, *The History of Sudbury, Wayland, and Maynard, Massachusetts, 1638-1889*, PBT, 1889. NHHS.
87. Hudson, Charles, *History of the Town of Marlborough, 1657-1861*, Boston MA, 1862.
88. Hudson, Charles, *History of the Town of Lexington, Massachusetts*, 2 vol., Houghton Miflin Co., Boston and NY, 1913.
89. Hufbauer, Virginia Knowles, *Descendants of John Knowles*, Edward Brothers, Inc., Ann Arbor MI,
90. Hunnewell, James F., *A Century of Town Life: A History of Charlestown, Massachusetts, 1775-1887*, Little Brown and Co., Boston MA, 1888.
91. Hunt, W. L. G., *Genealogy of the Hunt Family*, John Wilson and Son, Boston MA, 1862-3.
92. *Huntington Family*, Published by the Huntington Family Assn., Hartford CT, 1915.
93. Hurd, D. Hamilton, *History of Hillsboro County, New Hampshire*, J. W. Lewis Co., Philadelphia PA, 1885. NHHS.
94. Hurd, D. Hamilton, *History of Merrimac and Belknap Counties, New Hampshire*, J. W. Lewis Co., Philadelphia PA, 1885. NHHS.
95. Hurd, D. Hamilton, *History of Rockingham and Strafford Counties, New Hampshire*, J. W. Lewis Co., Philadelphia PA, 1882. NHHS.
96. Huse, Harry P., *The Descendants of Abel Huse of Newbury, 1602-1690*, Washington DC, 1935. NHHS.
97. Hutchinson, Eleanor Jones, *Town of Wheelock*, Emerson Publishing Co., Rochester VT, 1961. NHHS.
98. *Hyde Park Vermont*, PBT, 1976. NHHS.

I.

1. Inscriptions From Cemeteries in Auburn, Minot, Poland, Poland Corner, Minot, West Minot, South Poland, Maine, indexed by Mina E. Hayden. MHS.

J.

1. Jackson, Blake S., *Nicholas Jackson of Rowley and his Descendants, 1635-1976*, Belchertown MA, 1977. NHHS.
2. Jackson, James R., *History of Littleton, New Hampshire*, 3 vol., University Press, Cambridge MA, 1905.
3. Jacobus, Donald L., *American Genealogist*, Vol. 1, 45, 48, Clarence D. Smith, Rome NY, 1923. NHHS.
4. Jacobus, Donald L., *Families of Ancient New Haven, Ct.*, Rome (NY?), 1923-32. NHHS.
5. Jacobus, Donald L., *The Bulkeley Genealogy: Rev. Peter Bulkeley*, Tuttle, Morehouse and Taylor Co., New Haven CT, 1933. NHHS.
6. Jacobus, Donald L., *Descendants of Robert Waterman*, Edgar F. Waterman, New Haven CT, 1939. NHHS.
7. Jacobus, Donald L. and Edgar F. Waterman, *Hale, House, and Related Families*, Genealogical Publishing Co., Baltimore MD, 1978. NHHS.
8. Jameson, E. O., *The History of Medway, Massachusetts, 1713-1885*, PBT, 1886.
9. Jameson, E. O., *The Jamesons in America*, Rumford Press, Concord NH, 1901.
10. Jameson, E. O., *The Military History of Medway, Massachusetts, 1745-1885*, Providence RI, 1886.
11. Jenkins, Robert E., *Jenkins Family Book*, Chicago IL, 1904. NHHS.
12. Jewell, Thomas, *Jewell Register*, Press of Case, Lockwood and Co., Hartford CT, 1860. NHHS.
13. Jewett, Amos E. and Emily M. A., *Rowley, Massachusetts, "Mr Ezechi Rogers Plantation," 1639-1850*, Rowley MA, 1946. NHHS.
14. Jewett, Frederick Clarke, MD, *History and Genealogy of the Jewetts of America*, Vol. 1, Rowley MA, 1908. NHHS.
15. Jillsen, David, *Genealogy of Gillson and Jillsen Families*, E. L. Freeman and Co., Central Falls RI, 1876. NHHS.
16. Johnson, Carol C., *A Genealogical History of the Clark and Worth Families*, PP, 1970. NHHS.
17. Johnson, Henrietta D., "Dolloff Family," ms., 1936. NHHS.
18. Johnson, Herbert T., "Vermont Roster of Soldiers in the War of 1812," ms., xeroxed, AG 1933. NHHS.
19. *History of the Town of Johnson, Vermont, 1784-1907*, published by the OREAD Literary Club, 1907. NHHS.
20. Jones, Emma C. Brewster, *Brewster Genealogy, 1866-1907*, 2 vol., New York, 1908.
21. Jones, Hazel Parker, *Nathaniel Parker and his Descendants, 1651-1737*, Vogue Press, Columbia SC, 1966. NHHS.
22. Jones, Matt Bushnell, *History of the Town of Waitsfield, Vermont, 1782-1908*, Boston MA, 1909. NHHS.
23. Jordan, Tristram Frost, *The Jordan Memorial*, New England History Press, Somersworth NH, 1982.
24. Joy, James Richard, *Thomas Joy and his Descendants*, New York NY, MDCCCC. NHHS.
25. Judkins, Elizabeth Littlefield, "Job Judkins of Boston and his Descendants," ms., 1962. NHHS.

K.


1. Kellogg, Allyn S., *Memorials to Elder John White*, Hartford CT, 1860. NHHS.
1A. Kaster, Katherine Prescott, *History of Cousins and Little John Islands, 1645-1893*, no publ., no date. MHS.
2. Kelly, Giles M., *A Genealogical Account of the Descendants of John Kelly of Newbury, Mass.*, 1986. NHHS.
3. Kendall, Oliver, *Memorial of Josiah Kendall*, PBA, Providence RI, MDCCCLXXXIV. NHHS.
4. Kendrick, Fannie Shaw, *The History of Buckland, 1779-1935*, Buckland MA, 1937.
5. Ketcham, Mary E., Ed., *Ketcham Genealogy*, Rutland VT, n. d. NHHS.
6. Keyser, Leon, "The Keyser Family of Maine," ms., Portland ME, 1912.
7. Kimball, E. A., *The Peaslees and Others of Haverhill and Vicinity*, Press of Charles Bros., Haverhill MA, 1899. NHHS.
8. Kimball, Henry A., *John Eliot Family of Boscawen, New Hampshire*, Rumford Press, Concord NH, 1918. NHHS.
9. King, Harvey B., *King Genealogy and its Branches*, Hartford CT, 1897.
10. King, Marquis F., *Annals of Oxford, Maine, 1829-1850*, Portland ME, 1903. MHS.
10A. King, Marquis F., *First Parish Church of Falmouth, Maine*. LOC.
11. King, Marquis F., *Name Changes in Maine*, 1901. MHS.
12. Kingman, Bradford, *History of North Bridgewater*, PBA, Boston MA, 1866. NHHS.
13. Kingman, Bradford, *History of Brockton*, D. Mason and Co., Syracuse NY, 1895.
14. Kingsbury, Arthur Murray, *Kingsbury Genealogy*, Burgen, Beckwith, Inc., Minneapolis MN, 1962. NHHS.
15. Kingsbury, Frank B.,*History of the Town of Surry, New Hampshire*, PBT, 1925. NHHS.
16. Kirkpatrick, Doris, *The City and the River*, Vol. 1, Fitchburg MA Hist. Soc., 1971. NHHS.
17. Kittredge, Mabel T., *The Kittredge Family in America*, The Tuttle Publishing Co., Rutland VT, 1936.
18. Knapp, Alfred A., MD, *Nicholas Knapp Generalogy*, Winter Park FL, 1953.
19. Knight, Ernest H., "Families of Early Raymond Settlers and Residents," Jan 1981. Mimeographed copy of data in Town Office, Raymond ME, presumeably compiled by Orrin B. Lane, Town Clerk, 1864-1910. Sources of his data thought to be original town records, which were destroyed by fire in the early 1930's.


L.


1. Ladd, Warren, *Ladd Family*, Edmund Anthony and Sons, New Bedford MA, 1890.
2. Lamson, D. F., Rev., *History of the Town of Manchester, Massachusettts, 1645-1895*, PBT, 1895.
3. Lamson, William J., *Descendants of William Lamson of Ipswich, Mass., 1634-1917*, Tobias A. Wright, New York NY, 1917. NHHS.
4. Lancaster, Daniel, *The History of Gilmanton NH*, Printed by Alfred Prescott, Gilmanton NH, 1845. NHHS.
5. Landon, James O., *Landon Genealogy*, Clark Boardman Co., South Hero VT, 1928.
6. Lapham, Wm. B. and Silas P. Maxim, *History of Paris, Maine*, PBA, Paris ME, 1884. MHS.
7. Lapham, William Berry, *Centennial History of Norway, Oxford County, Maine, 1786-1886*, Brown Thurston and Co., Portland ME, 1886. ALSOP files.
8. Lapham, William Berry, *Bradbury Memorial*, Portland ME, 1890.
9. Lapointe, Gladys E., "Leighton Family and Allied Lines," n. p., 1972. MHS.
10. Latham, Ettie J., *History of the Town of Pownal*, Lewiston Journal Co., Lewiston ME, 1908. NHHS.
11. Lawrence, Cora B., "Moses Fellows, 1755-1846, With Genealogical Notes," ms., 48 pp. NHHS.
12. Lazell, Theodore S., *John Lazell of Hingham and Some of His Descendants*, Record Publishing Co., Haverhill MA, 1936.
13. Lee, Helen B. Joy, *The Joy Genealogy*, Pequot Press, Essex CT, 1968. NHHS.
14. Lee, William, *John Leigh of Ipswich and His Descendants*, Albany NY, 1888.
15. Leland, Sherman, "Genealogical Records of Henry Leland," *Leland Magazine*, Wier and White, Boston MA, 1850.
16. Leonard, Ermina Newton, *Newton Genealogy*, De Pere WI, 1915. NHHS.
17. Leonard, Levi W. and Josiah L. Seward, *The History of Dublin, N. H.*, Dublin NH, 1920. NHHS.
18. Lewis, George H., *Edmund Lewis of Lynn, Massachusetts*, Essex Institute, Salem MA, 1908.
19. Lewis, Theodore Graham, *History of Waterbury, Vermont, 1763-1915*, Harry C. Whitehill, Waterbury VT, 1915. NHHS.
20. Libby, Charles T., *Libby Family in America*, B. Thurston Co., Portland ME, 1882.
21. Limeburner, Grace M., *A Record of the Very Early Settlers of Sedgwick, Maine*, 1918. MHS.
22. Limington, Maine, Old Record Book. ALSOP files.
23. Limington Town Records (Marriages). ALSOP files.
24. *The Probate Records of Lincoln County, Maine, 1760-1800*, Maine Genealogical Society Publication No. 6, Picton Press, Camden ME, 1991.
25. Lincoln, Waldo, *History of the Lincoln Family, Samuel of Hingham*, Commonwealth Press, Worcester MA, 1923.
26. Lincoln, William, *History of Worcester to 1836*, Charles Hersey, Worcester MA, 1862.
27. Linzee, John William, *The History of Peter Parker and Sarah Ruggles of Roxbury, Mass.*, PP, Boston MA, 1913. NHHS.

28. *History of Litchfield and an Account of its Centennial Collection, 1895*, Kennebec Journal Print, Augusta ME, 1897. Xerox cy. NHHS.
29. Little, George T. *Descendants of George Little*, Augurn ME, 1882.
30. Little, Thomas, Rev., Ed., *Genealogical and Family History of the State of Maine*, Vol. III, Lewis Historical Publishing Co., NY, 1909. MHS.
31. Little, William, *The History of Weare, New Hampshire, 1735-1888*, PBT, Lowell MA, 1888. NHHS.
32. Little, William D., "Portland Vital Records, 1765-1893," typed cy. MHS.
33. *Proceedings of the Littleton Historical Society*, No. 1, 1894-1895, Littleton MA, 1896.
34. Locke, Arthur H., *A History and Genealogy of Captain John Locke, [1627-1696]*, Reprinted by Locke Family Assn., Rye NH, 1979. NHHS.
35. Locke, John Goodwin, *Genealogy and Historical Record of William Locke of Woburn*, James Runroe and Co., Boston MA, 1853. NHHS.
36. Long, E. Waldo, Ed., *The Story of Duxbury, 1637-1937*, The Duxbury Tercentenary Committee, 1937. NHHS.
37. Lord, Charles Edward, *Ancestors and Descendants of Lt. Tobias Lord*, PP, 1913. NHHS.
38. Lord, John King, *A History of the Town of Hanover, N. H.*, The Dartmouth Press, Hanover NH, 1928. NHHS.
39. Lord, Kenneth, *Genealogy of the Descendants of Thomas Lord*, Tuttle, Morehouse and Taylor, New Haven CT, 1946. NHHS.
40. Lord, Myra, *A History of the Town of New London (1779-1899)*, The Rumford Press, Concord NH, 1899.
41. Loud, Eva Blake and Mable E. Blake, *Early Cemetery Records of Ossipee, New Hampshire*, Bicentennial Committee of Ossippee, 1976. NHHS.
42. Lovejoy, Evelyn M. Wood, *History of Royalton, Vermont, With Family Genealogies, 1769-1911*, PBT and the Royalton Woman's Club, Burlington VT, 1911. NHHS.
43. Lovejoy, Mrs. Rupert, Baldwin Maine Cemetery Records, 1953.
44. Lowell, Daniel Ozro, *A Munsey-Hopkins Genealogy*, PP, Boston MA, 1920. NHHS.
45. Lowell, Delmar R., *Historic Genealogy of the Lowells of America, 1639-1899*, Tuttle Company, Rutland VT, 1899. NHHS.
46. Lunt, Thomas S., *A History of the Lunt Family in America*, Salem Press Co., Salem MA, 1913. NHHS.
47. Lyford, James Otis, *The History of Canterbury, New Hampshire, 1727-1912*, Canterbury NH Hist. Soc., 1973. Facs. of 1912 Edn. NHHS.
48. *Vital Records of Lyme, Connecticut, 1665-1850*, Publ. by The American Revolution Bicentennial Commission of Lyme, CT, 1976. NHHS.

## M.

1. MacDougal, Catherine Finney, *The Babson Genealogy: Descendants of Isabel Babson, Who Arrived in Salem, 1637*, Watertown MA, 1978.
2. Maine census records, on microfilm, MSA.
2A. *Maine Genealogical Society, Journal of The*, Vol. 16, Penmor Lithographers, Lewiston ME, 1994. MHS.
3. *Maine Historical and Genealogical Recorder*, 9 vol., S. M. Watson, Portland ME, 1884. NHHS.
3A. *Maine Historical Magazine, 1885-1894*, Vol. 8, Picton Press, Camden ME, 1993. MHS.
4. Maine Historical Society Collection, 1890, Vols. 1-9.
4A. Maine Deeds, *Pejepscot Claim*, ms., COL S-5431, Box 122/16. MHS.
5. Maine Old Cemetery Association (MOCA), Series I-II, III, Augusta ME, 1982/1987. Inscriptions listed in vol. by county, town, and cemetery.
6. *Maine Pension Roll-Revolutionary War*, Excerpt From US War Department Report From the Secretary of War, 1835. MHS.
7. Maine Revolutionary War Bounty Records. MSA.
7A. Maine Veterans in 1890. MHS.
8. Maine town registers/directories. MHS.
8A. Maine town records, on microfilm. MSA.
9. Maine vital records, on microfilm. MSA.
10. Manning, William H., *The Manning Family of New England*, The Salem Press, Salem MA, 1902. NHHS.
11. Manwaring, Charles William, *Early Connecticut Probate Records*, Hartford CT, 1904.
12. "Maplewood Cemetery, Standish ME," ms., rec. of Nancy Welch, ALSOP.
13. Marsh, Dwight W., *Marsh Genealogy*, Carpenter and Morehouse Press, Amherst MA, 1895. NHHS.
14. Marsh, Col. Lucius R., *The Genealogy of John Marsh of Salem and his Descendants, 1633-1898*, Amherst MA, 1888. NHHS.
15. Marshall, J. M., *A Report of the Proceedings at the Celebration of the First Centennial Anniversary of the Incorporation of the Town of Buxton, Maine*, Portland ME, 1874. MHS. NHHS.
16. Marston, Nathan W., *The Marston Genealogy*, So. Lubec ME, 1888. NHHS.
17. Martyn, Charles, *William Ward Genealogy*, Artemus Ward, Publ., New York NY, 1925. NHHS.
18. Marvin, Abijah P., *History of the Town of Winchendon*, PBA, Winchendon MA, 1868. NHHS.

19. Marvin, Abijah P., *History of the Town of Lancaster, Massachusetts:From the First Settlement to the Present Time, 1643-1879*, PBT, 1879. Cy. in files of Town Clerk, Lancaster MA.
20. Marvin, George Franklin, *Descendants of Reinold and Matthew Marvin*, T. R. Marvin and Son, Boston MA, 1904.
21. "The Sampson Mason Family," ms., no author, n. d. NHHS.
22. Massachusetts bible records, DAR Library, Washington DC.
23. Massachusetts: *Journal of the Constitutional Convention, 1779-80.* Containing a List of Delegates by County, Boston MA, 1832. NHHS.
24. Massachusetts vital records, 1790-1850, in separate volumes by town, NHHS.
25. May, John J., *Danforth Genealogy: Nicholas Danforth*, Charles H. Pope, Boston MA, 1902. NHHS.
26. McDaniel, Charles, *History of Springfield, New Hampshire*, The Coventry Press, New London NH, 1872. NHHS.
27. McDuffee, Franklin F., *History of the Town of Rochester, New Hampshire, 1722-1890*, 2 vol., The John C. Clarke Co., Manchester NH, 1892. Reprint by Rochester NH Hist. Soc., 1988. NHHS.
28. McGregor, Alma G. Watson, and Daniel Clark Watson, Jr., *Lorenzo Dow Watson*, J. Grant Stevenson, Provo UT, 1970. NHHS.
29. McIntyre, Robert Harry, *Descendants of William McIntyre*, Book Crafters, Chelsea MI, 1984. NHHS.
30. McKeen, Rev. Silas, *A History of Bradford, Vermont*, J. D. Clark and Sons, Montpelier VT, 1875. NHHS.
31. McQuiston, Leona B., *McQuiston Family*, Standard Press, Louisville KY, 1937. NHHS.
32. Mead, Spencer P., *History and Genealogy of the Mead Family*, Knickerbocker Press, New York NY, 1901.
33. Mears, Neal F., *History of the Heverly Family*, Bates Publishing Co., Chicago IL, 1945.
34. "Meeting House Hill Cemetery," ms., rec. of Nancy Welch, ALSOP.
35. Merle, Elinor I., Ed., *The History of Jericho, Vermont*, Vol. Two, PBT, 1963. NHHS.
36. Merrick, George B., *Merrick Genealogy*, Tracy, Gibbs and Co., Madison WI, 1902.
37. Merrill, Georgia Drew, *History of Carroll County, New Hampshire*, New Hampshire Publ. Co., Somersworth NH, 1971. Facs. of 1889 Edn. NHHS.
38. Merrill, J. L., Rev., *History of the Town of Acworth NH*, The Proceedings of the Centennial Anniversary, Genealogical Records and Register of Farms, Town History, 1869. (2d Printing, Charlestown NH 1978. ) NHHS.
38A. Merrill, Samuel, *A Merrill Memorial*, Cambridge MA, 1917-1928. NHHS.
39. *Historical and Genealogical Researches and Records of Passing Events of Merrimack Valley*, Vol. 1, Nos. 1 (Apr 1857) and 2 (Jan 1858). NHHS.
40. Merrow, Oscar E., *Henry Merrow of Reading, Massachusetts*, Winchester MA, 1954. NHHS.
41. Metcalf, John G., MD, *Annals of the Town of Mendon, From 1659 to 1880*, Providence RI, 1880.
42. *Centennial History of the Town of Millbury, Massachusetts, Including Vital Statistics, 1850-1899*, Millbury MA, 1915.
43. Milliken, J. A., *The Narraguagus Valley*, Portland ME, 1910. MHS.
44. *History of Monkton, Vermont, 1734-1961*, PBT, n. d.
45. Mitchell, Harry E., *Town Register of Otisfield, Harrison, Naples, Sebago*, 1906. MHS.
46. Moore, Esther Gilman, *History of Gardner, Massachusetts, 1785-1967*, Hatton Printing, Gardner MA, 1967. NHHS.
47. Moore, Howard P., *Maine Lang Families*, The Tuttle Publishing Co., Rutland VT, 1935.
48. Moore, Howard Parker, *The Patten Families*, Edwards Brothers, Inc., Ann Arbor MI, 1939. NHHS.
49. Moran, Edward C., Jr., *Bunker Genealogy*, Rockland ME, 1942.
50. Morison, George A. and Etta M. Smith, *History of Peterborough, New Hampshire*, 2 vol., Rindge NH, 1954. NHHS.
51. Morris, Tyler Semour, *Ephraim and Pamela (Converse) Morris, Their Ancestors and Descendants*, Chicago IL, 1894. NHHS.
52. Morrison, L. A., *History of Windham in New Hampshire, 1719-1883*, Phoenix Publishing, Caanan NH, 1975. NHHS.
53. Morrison, Leonard, *History of the Morison, Morrison Family*, A. Williams and Company, Boston MA, 1880.
54. Morrison, Leonard A. and Stephen P. Sharples, *History of the Kimball Family of America*, Dambrell and Upham, Boston MA, 1897.
55. Morrison, Leonard Allison, *Lineage and Biographies of the Norris Family in America*, Damrell and Upham, Boston MA, 1892. NHHS.
56. Moses, Zebina, *Moses Family*, Vol. II, Hartford CT, 1907. NHHS.
57. Moulton, Henry W., *Moulton Annals*, Edward A. Claypool, Chicago IL, 1906. NHHS.
58. Moulton, J., *Porter, a Portion of Maine*, Portland ME, 1879. MHS.
59. Mower, Anna L., *History of Morristown, Vermont*, Morrisville Woman's Club, 1935. NHHS.
60. Mower, Walter L., *History of Greene, 1775-1900*, Press of Merrill and Webber Co., Auburn ME, 1938. MHS.
61. Mudge, Alfred, *Mudge Memorials*, Boston MA, 1868. NHHS.
62. Mudgett, Mildred D. and Bruce D.,*Thomas Mudgett of Salisbury, Massachusetts, and his Descendants*, Bennington VT, 1961.
63. Munroe, Richard S., *History and Genealogy of the Lexington, Massachusetts, Munroes*, Florence MA, 1966. NHHS.

64. Musgrave, Richard W., *History of Bristol, New Hampshire*, 2 vol., 1904.

## N.

1. Nason, Rev. Elias, *A History of the Town of Dunstable*, Alfred Mudge and Son, Boston MA, 1877. NHHS.
1A. National Archives Military Records and Pensions, Washington DC.
2. Nelson, Emily M., *Frontier Crossroads*, Published for the Newport History Committee, Canaan NH, 1977. NHHS.
3. Nelson, Walter R., *History of Goshen, New Hampshire*, Concord NH, 1957. NHHS.
4. New England Historic Genealogical Society, *Memorial Biographies, 1880-1908*, Boston MA, NHHS.
5. *New England Historical and Genealogical Register*, Vol. 1-52. NHHS.
6. New Hampshire Brides List, on microfilm, NHSA.
7. New Hampshire church records, ms., in separate vol. by town. NHHS.
8. New Hampshire family Records, microfilm FS 40. NHHS.
9. New Hampshire graves and cemetery records, in vol. by towns. NHHS.
10. New Hampshire Gravestones of Early Date. NHHS.
11. New Hampshire Revolutionary Pension Records, Vol. 44. NHHS.
12. *New Hampshire State Papers, 1775-1777*, Vol. 1-14, publ. by the State. See index, part 2. NHHS.
13. New Hampshire Town Registers: Ashland, Plymouth, Sandwich, Campton, Holderness, Center Harbor, Moultonboro, NH, Mitchell-Cony Co., Inc., 1900.
14. New Hampshire town records w/index, on microfilm. NHSL.
15. New Hampshire vital records. NHSA
16. New Hampshire wills and deeds, on microfilm. NHHS.
17. *New Haven Vital Records, 1649-1850*, Pts. I and II, The Connecticut Society of the Order of the Founders and Patriots of America, 1924. NHHS.
18. New London County, Connecticut, Genealogy and Biographic Records.
19. Newbury MA, Tax Assessor's list, Aug 1688.
20. *The History of Newbury, Vermont, 1900-1977*, PBT, Bradford VT, 1978. NHHS.
21. Newcomb, Bethuel Merritt, *Andrew Newcomb and his Descendants*, rev., Tuttle, Moorehouse and Taylor Co., New Haven CT, 1923. NHHS.
22. Newfield ME Cemetery Records, ALSOP files.
23. Newton, Rev. EphraimHolland,*The History of Marlborough, Vermont*, Vermont Hist. Soc., Montpelier VT, MDCCCCXXX. NHHS.
24. Nicely, Charlotte A., *Hanson Relatives*, Gateway Press, Baltimore MD, 1977.
25. Nichol, Nathan Round, Ed., *Round-Rounds Genealogy*, n. p., n. d. NHHS.
26. Nicholson, Nettie Gove, *A Tenth Generation Yankee From Maine*, AandR Printing and Stationers, Inc., West Palm Beach FL, n. d. ALSOP files.
27. Norris, D. W. and H. A. Feldmann, *The Wells Family*, Cramer-Krasselt Co., Milwaukee WI, 1942. NHHS.
28. Norris, Henry McCoy, *Ancestors and Descendants of Lt. Jonathan and Tamesin (Barker) Norris of Maine*, Grafton Press, New York NY, 1906.
29. North, James W., *The History of Augusta, Maine*, Augusta ME, 1870. MHS. NHHS.
30. North Anson ME: "Sunset Cemetery, North Anson, Maine," inscriptions copied by Ruth Heald Cragin Chapter. DAR.
31. "North Yarmouth Baptisms, 1731-1776." First Congregational Church, Yarmouth ME. MHS.
32. North Yarmouth ME, *Vital Records to 1850*, Society of Mayflower Descendants of Rhode Island, 1980. NHHS.
33. Norwich: *Vital Records of Norwich, 1659-1848*, Pts. I, II, Hartford Society of Colonial Wars in the State of Connecticut, 1913. NHHS.
34. Nourse, Henry S., *Military Annals of Lancaster, Massachusetts, 1740-1865*, Lancaster MA, 1889.
35. Nourse, Henry S., *Birth, Marriage, and Death Register, Church Records and Epitaphs of Lancaster Massachusetts*, W. J. Coulter Printer, Clinton MA, 1890. NHHS.
36. Nourse, Henry S., *History of the Town of Harvard, Massachusetts, 1732-1893*, Harvard MA, 1894.
37. Noyes, Edward D. Jr., Deering Noyes Collection, 1764-1971, six boxes, 62 vol. MHS.
38. Noyes, Henrietta E., *Memorial History of Hampstead, New Hampshire*, Vol. 2, Boston MA, 1903. NHHS.
39. Noyes, Vital Records of Maine, 2 vol. LOC.
40. Noyes, Col. Henry E. and Henrietta E., *Genealogical Record of Some of the Noyes Descendants of James, Nicholas, and Peter Noyes*, 2 vol., Boston MA, 1904. NHHS.
41. Noyes, Mabel F. and Minna B., *West Methuen of Long Ago*, Bedford MA, 1929. NHHS.
42. Noyes, Sybil, *et. al.*, *Genealogical Dictionary of Maine and New Hampshire*, The Southworth-Athoensen Press, Portland ME, 1928 1939. NHHS.
43. Nutt, Charles, *Descendants of George Puffer, of Braintree, Massachusetts, 1639-1915*, Worcester MA, 1915. NHHS.
44. Nutt, Charles, *History of Worcester and Its People*, Vol. III, IV, Lewis Historical Publishing Co., New York NY, 1919. NHHS.

45. Nye, George Hyett and Frank Eugene Best, *A Genealogy of the Nye Family*, Published by the Nye Family of America Assn., 1907. NHHS.
46. Nye, Mary Greene, *Early History of Berlin, Vermont, 1763-1820*, Town and Dodge, Montpelier VT, 1951. NHHS.

## O.

1. O'Connor, Florence E., *The Ancestors and Descendants of Asa F. Ellingwood*, Western Maine Graphics, Oxford ME, 1979. NHHS.
2. Odiorne, Joseph Milton, *A Rundlett-Randlett Genealogy*, The Knowlton and McLeary Co., Farmington ME, 1976. NHHS.
3. Olmstead, Henry King, *The Olmstead Family in America*, De La Mare Printing and Publishing Co., New York NY, 1912. NHHS.
4. Orcutt, Samuel, *History of New Milford and Bridgewater, Conn.*, Case, Lockwood, and Brainard Co., Hartford CT, 1882. NHHS.
5. Osgood, Frank S., "Gilmore Genealogy," ms., Newburyport MA, 1926. NHHS.
6. Osgood, Ira, *Genealogy of the Descendants of John, Christopher, and William Osgood*, Salem Press, Salem MA, 1894. NHHS.
7. Oxford County ME, Cemetery Inscriptions, Series I and II. MOCA.

## P.

1. Paige, Lucius R., *History of Cambridge, Massachusetts, 1630-1877*, H. O. Houghton and Co., Boston MA, 1877.
2. Paine, Albert Ware, *Paine Genealogy, Ipswich Branch*, O. F. Knowles and Co., Bangor ME, 1887. NHHS.
3. Paine, Nathaniel Emmons,*Thomas Payne of Salem and his Descendents*, Record Publishing Co., Haverhill MA, 1928. NHHS.
4. Palmer, Horace Wilber, *Palmer Family of America*, Vol. III, New Hampshire Publishing Co., Somersworth NH, 1973. NHHS.
5. Parish, Roswell, *New England Parish Families*, The Tuttle Publishing Co., Rutland VT, 1938. NHHS.
6. Park, Lawrence, *Major Thomas Savage of Boston*, David Clapp and Sons Press, 1914.
7. Parke, Frank Sylvester, *Genealogy of the Parke Family of Massachusetts*, PP, Washington DC, 1909. NHHS.
8. Parker, Benjamin Franklin, *History of the Town of Wolfborough, New Hampshire*, Wolfeboro NH Hist. Soc., 1974. NHHS.
9. Parker, Benjamin Franklin, *History of the Town of Westborough, New Hampshire*, Wolfeboro NH Historical Society, 1988. ALSOP files.
10. Parker, Edward E., *History of the City of Nashua, N. H.*, Nashua NH, 1897. NHHS.
11. Parker, Francis J., Colonel, *Genealogy of the Ainsworth Family in America*, Boston MA, 1894.
12. Parker, Theodore, *Genealogical and Biographical Notes of John Parker of Lexington*, Charles Hamilton Press, Worcester MA, 1893. NHHS.
13. Parlin, Frank Edson, *The Parlin Genealogy-The Descendants of Nicholas Parlin of Cambridge, Mass.*, T. R. Marvin and Son, Cambridge MA, 1913. NHHS.
14. Parmenter, C. O., *History of Pelham, Mass. From 1738 to 1898*, Press of Carpenter and Morehouse, Amherst MA, 1898. NHHS.
15. Parsons, Henry, *Parsons Family*, 2 vol., Frank Allaben Genealogical Company, New York NY, 1912. NHHS.
16. Parsons, Langdon B., *History of the Town of Rye, New Hampshire*, Rumford Printing Co., Concord NH, 1905. NHHS.
17. Parsons, Nancy S., *Stockton Spring Vital Records, 1857-1891*, Orrington ME, 1978.
18. Pastors of the First Church of Portland, *Journals of Rev. Thomas Smith and Rev. Samuel Deane*, publ. by J. S. Bailey, Portland ME. 1849. MHS.
19. Pattee, William S., MD, *A History of Old Braintree and Quincy*, Green and Prescott, Quincy MA, 1878.
20. Patten, A. S., *Historical Sketch of the Hampden, Maine, Sawyer Family*, read at annual reunion at Hermon Pond, 25 Aug 1909. MHS.
21. Payne, Charles T., *Litchfield and Morris, Connecticut, Inscriptions*, Dwight Kilbourne, Litchfield CT, 1905. NHHS.
22. Peabody, Selim Hobart, *A Peabody (Paybody, Pabody, Pabodie) Genealogy*, Charles H. Pope, Boston MA, 1909. NHHS.
23. Peck, Thomas B., *The Bellows Genealogy, or John Bellows, the Boy Emigrant of 1635 and his Descendants*, Keene NH, 1898. NHHS.
24. Peck, Thomas B., *Vital Records, Rockingham, Vermont*, George E. Littlefield, Boston MA, 1908. NHHS.
25. Peck, Thomas B., *William Slade of Windsor, Connecticut, and His Descendants*, Sentinal Printing Co., Keene NH, 1910. NHHS.
26. Pendleton, Everett Hall, *Brian Pendleton and his Descendants, 1599-1910*, PP, 1911. NHHS.
27. Pengry, William M., *Genealogical Record of the Descendants of Moses Pengry of Ipswich, Mass.*, Warner and Hyde, Ludlow VT, 1881. NHHS.

28. Penney, John W., *A Genealogical Record of the Descendants of Thomas Penney of New Gloucester, Maine*, The Thurston Press, Portland ME, 1897. NHHS.
29. Penniman, Rev. George Wallace, *The Penniman Family, 1631-1900*, The Gateway Press Inc., Baltimore MD, 1981. NHHS.
30. Penobscot County: *History of Penobscot County*, 2 vol., Cleveland, Williams, Chase and Co., Bangor ME, 1882. MHS.
31. "Penobscot Marriages and Intentions," 2 vol., n. d., copied from town records by Mrs. Grace G. Limeburner. MHS
32. Perkins, Thomas Allen, *Jacob Perkins of Wells, Maine, and his Descendants, 1583-1936*, Record Publishing Co., Haverhill MA, 1947. NHHS
33. Perley, Martin Van Buren, *History and Genealogy of the Perley Family*, PBA, Salem MA, 1906. NHHS.
34. Perley, Sidney, *The History of Boxford*, PBA, Boxford MA, 1880. NHHS.
35. Perley, Sidney, *The Plumer Genealogy*, The Essex Institute, Salem MA, 1917 (reprinted 1983). NHHS.
36. Perley, Sidney, *The History of Salem, Massachusetts (1626-1637)*, 3 vol., Salem MA, 1924. NHHS.
37. Pettingill, John Mason, *A Pettingill Genealogy*, Ft. Hill Press, Boston MA, 1906. NHHS.
38. Phalen, Harold R., *History of the Town of Acton*, Cambridge MA, 1954. NHHS.
39. Phelps, James H., *Collections Relating to the History and Inhabitants of the Town of Townshend*, Part II, Brattleboro VT, 1884. NHHS.
40. Phelps, Judge Oliver S., *The Phelps Family of America*, Vol. 2, Eagle Publishing Company, Pittsfield MA, 1899. NHHS.
41. Pierce, Fred C., *Batchelder, Batcheller, Bachiler Genealogy: Descendants of Rev. Stephen Bachiler of England*, Chicago IL, 1898. NHHS.
42. Pierce, Frederic Beech, *Pierce Genealogy of Thomas of Charlestown*, Press of Charles Hamilton, Worcester MA, 1882. NHHS.
43. Pierce, Fred C., *Foster Genealogy: Reginald Foster*, Press of W. B. Conkey Co., Chicago IL, 1899. NHHS.
44. Pierce, Frederick Clifton, *Pierce Genealogy of John Pers*, Press of Charles Hamilton, Worcester MA, 1880. NHHS.
45. Pierce, Frederick Clifton, *Pierce Genealogy*, Rockford IL, 1888.
46. Pierce, Frederick Clifton, *The Descendants of John Whitney, Who Came From London, England, to Watertown, Massachusetts, in 1634*, PBA, Chicago IL, 1895. NHHS.
47. Pierce, Frederick Clifton, *History of Grafton*, Press of Charles Hamilton, Worcester MA, 1879. NHHS.
48. Pierce, Frederick Clifton, *Pierce Genealogy*, PP, Albany NY, 1889. NHHS.
49. Pierce, Frederick Clifton, *Forbes and Forbush Genealogy*, Chicago IL, 1892. NHHS.
50. Pierce, Frederick Clifton, *Field Genealogy*, 2 vol., Hammond Press, Chicago IL, 1901. NHHS.
51. Pierce, Joshua, *A History of the the Town of Gorham, Maine*, Portland ME, 1862. NHHS.
51A. *Piermont New Hampshire, 1764-1947*, prepared by a committee, pub. by The Green Mountain Press, Bradford VT, 1947. NHHS.
52. Pitcher, Grace Whipple, *A Genealogy of the Pitcher Family of Milton, Massachusetts*, Capital Offset Co., Concord NH, n. d. NHHS.
53. Pitkin, Ozias C. and Fred E., "History of Marshfield, VT.," ms., 1941. NHHS.
54. Pixley, Edward Evans and Franklin Hanford, *William Pixley of Hadley, Northampton, and Westfield, Mass., and Some of his Descendants*, Peter Paul and Co., Buffalo NY, 1900. NHHS.
55. Plaistow NH, records of the Town Clerk.
56. Plimpton, Elizabeth B., *Vital Records of Saybrook Colony, 1635-1860*, 1985. NHHS.
57. Plummer, George F., *History of the Town of Wentworth, New Hampshire*, The Rumford Press, Concord NH, 1930. NHHS.
58. Pomfret CT family records, microfilm #F540. NHHS.
59. Poore, Alfred, *A Memoir and Genealogy of John Poore, 1615-1880*, PBA, Salem MA, 1881. NHHS.
60. Pope, Charles H., *The Cheney Family*, PBA, Boston MA, 1897. NHHS.
61. Pope, Charles Henry, *Loring Genealogy*, Murray and Emery Co., Cambridge MA, 1917. NHHS.
62. Charles Henry Pope, *Pioneers of Massachusetts*, n.p., 1900. MHS.
63. Pope, Charles Henry, *Willard Genealogy*, Willard Family Association, Boston MA, 1915. NHHS.
64. Pope, Charles H. and Thomas Hooper, *Hooper Genealogy*, Boston MA, 1908.
65. Porter, Juliet, *A Porter Pedigree*, Worcester MA, 1907. NHHS.
66. "Porter, Maine, Cemetery Records and Tombstone Inscriptions," copied by Ina M. Emery, 1944-45. MHS.
67. Porter ME, "Record of Deaths as Kept by Warren Libby From 1854, as Taken From His Diary. " Photostats. MHS.
68. "Porter/South Hiram Cemetery," ms., no author, n.d. ALSOP files.
69. Portland, Maine, *City-Directory, 1844*. MHS.
70. Portland, Maine, 1st Parish Church (Unitarian) Baptism and Admission Records, compiled by Marquis F. King, Maine Hist. Soc., Portland ME, 1898. MHS.
71. "Portland, Maine, Vital Statistics, 1786-1814," Second Book of Records, 1951. Typed cy. MHS.
72. Powers, Amos H., *The Powers Family*, Fergus Printing Co., Chicago IL, 1884. NHHS.
73. Powers, Franklin E., "A Genealogical Record of the Powers Family," ms., 1974. NHHS.
74. Pownal Scenic and Historical Society, *Pownal A Rural Maine History*, Grace Press, Falmouth ME, 1977. NHHS.

75. Pratt, Walter Merriam, *Seven Generation-A Story of Prattville and Chelsea*, PP, 1930. NHHS.
76. Prescott, William, *The Prescott Memorial of John Prescott of 1640*, Henry W. Dutton and Son, Boston MA, 1870. NHHS.
77. Prescott, Worrall Dumont, *A Genealogical Record Concerning Captain Samuel Reed and Mary Winship Reed and all of Their Descendants*, Webber Print, Inc., New York NY, 1953. NHHS.
78. Pressy, Edward Pearson, *History of Montague, A Typical Puritan Town*, The New Clairvaux Press, Montague MA, 1910.
79. Preston, Belle, *Bassett Preston Ancestors*, New Haven CT, 1930.
80. Preston, Charles Henry, *Descendants of Roger Preston of Ipswich and Salem Village*, Essex Institute, Salem MA, 1931. NHHS.
81. Pringle, James R., *History of the Town and City of Gloucester, Cape Ann, Massachusetts, 1623-1892*, PBA, Gloucester MA, 1892. NHHS.
82. Probate Records:
    a. Cumberland County Court House, Portland ME.
    b. Essex County Court House, Salem MA.
    c. Grafton County Court House, No. Haverhill NH.
    d. Hancock County Court House, Ellsworth ME.
    e. Oxford County Court House, So. Paris ME.
    f. Penobscot County Court House, Bangor ME.
    g. Rockingham County Court House, Exeter NH.
    h. Somerset County Court House, Skowhegan ME.
    i. Strafford County Court House, Dover NH.
    j. Waldo County Court House, Belfast ME.
    k. York County Court House, Alfred ME.
83. Proctor, William and Mrs., *A Genealogy of Robert Proctor*, Republican and Journal, Printers, Ogdensburg NY, 1898. NHHS.
84. Purdy, Jessie W. P., *The Whitmore Genealogy*, 1907.
85. Putnam, Eben, *Holden Genealogy*, 2 vol., Boston MA, 1923.
86. Putnam, Eben, *Marriage Notices, 1785-1794, for the Whole United States*, Salem MA, 1900. Copied from the *Massachusetts Centinal* and the *Columbian Sentinal* by Charles Knowles Bolton, Baltimore MD, 1980.

## Q.

1. Quaker Burial Ground in West Newbury MA. Copied by Nathalie Potts.
2. Quint, Alonzo Hall, *Concerning Persons and Places in Old Dover N. H. Published in The Dover Enquirer From 1850 to 1888, by John Scales,* Vol. 1, Dover NH, 1900. Dover NH Public Library.

## R.

1. Radasch, Arthur H., "Barstow-Bester Genealogy: Descendants of John Barstow and George Barstow," 1964. Mimeographed ms. MHS.
2. Radasch, Arthur H., "The Barstow Family: Genealogy of the Descendants of William Barstow, 1635-1965," 1966. Mimeographed ms. MHS.
3. Ramsdell, George A., and William P. Colburn,*The History of Milford*, The Rumford Press, Concord NH, 1901.
4. Rand, Florence Osgood, *A Genealogy of the Rand Family of the United States*, The Republic Press, New York NY, 1898. NHHS.
5. Randall, George L., *Taber Genealogy*, Viking Press, New Bedford MA, 1924. NHHS.
6. Raymond, John Marshall, *Teel and Thomas Genealogy*, Runnymeade Press, Palo Alto CA, 1964. NHHS.
7. Read, Benjamin, *The History of Swanzey, New Hampshire From 1734 to 1898*, Salem MA, 1892. NHHS.
8. Read, George H., *Some of the Descendants of John Read, Senior,, 1646-1924*, PP, n.d. NHHS.
9. Reed, John L., *The Reed Genealogy-Descendants of William Reade of Weymouth, Massachusetts, 1635-1902*, Lord Baltimore Press, Baltimore MD, 1901. NHHS.
10. Registry of Deeds:
    a. Cumberland County Court House, Portland ME.
    b. Hancock County Court House, Ellsworth ME.
    c. Oxford County, So. Paris ME and Fryeburg ME.
    d. Penobscot County, District Court House, Bangor ME.
    e. Waldo County, Belfast ME.
    f. Washington County, Machias ME.
    g. York County, Alfred ME.
    h. Worcester County, Worcester MA.
11. Rhode Island Vital Records, 1636-1850, vol. 2.

12. Rice, Edward P., *The Worcester of Eighteen Hundred and Ninety Eight*, F. S. Blanchard and Co., Worcester MA, 1899. NHHS.
13. Rice, Franklin P., *Worcester, Mass: Births, Marriages, and Deaths, 1714-1848*, The Worcester Society of Antiquity, Worcester MA, 1894. NHHS.
14. Richards, Lysander Salmon, *History of Marshfield*, Vol. I and II, The Memorial Press, Plymouth MA, 1901.
15. Richmond, Katherine F., *John Hayes of Dover, New Hampshire*, 2 vol., Tyngsboro MA, 1936.
16. Ridlon, Gideon T., Rev., *History of the Ancient Ryedales, 360-1884*, Lowell MA, 1884. NHHS.
17. Ridlon, Gideon T., Rev., *Saco Valley Settlements and Families*, 2 vol., PBA, Portland ME, 1895. MHS.
18. Ridlon, Gideon T., Rev., *Sole, Soule, Sowle History*, Vol. 2, Journal Press, Lewiston ME, 1926. NHHS.
19. Rifford, Elizabeth M. Leach, *300 Colonial Ancestors and War Service*, Tuttle Co., Rutland VT, 1934.
20. Ring, Lena C., "Marriage records of Winter Street Congregational Church, Bath ME," 1947. MHS.
21. Rix, Guy Scobie, *History and Genealogy of the Eastman Family of America*, 2 vol., Ira C. Evans Press, Concord NH, 1901. NHHS.
22. Robinson, H. L.,*History of Pittsfield, New Hampshire, in the Great Rebellion*, American Press Association, Concord NH, 1893. NHHS.
23. Rockey, J. L., Ed., *History of New Haven County, Connecticut*, Vol. 2, W. W. Preston and Co., New York NY, 1892. NHHS.
24. Rogers, James Swift, *James Rogers of New London, Connecticut, and his Descendants*, PBA, Boston MA, 1902. NHHS.
25. Rollins, John R., *Records and Families of the Name Rawlins or Rollins in the United States*, George S. Merrill and Crocker Printers, Lawrence MA, 1874 (reprinted 1985). NHHS.
26. Roper, Ella E., *The Roper Book of Sterling and Rutland*, Fred H. Calvin, East Orange NJ, 1904. NHHS.
27. Ross, Emma Howell, *Descendants of Edward Howell*, University Press, Winchester MA, 1968.
28. Round, Harold F., *Varreel-Verrill*, PP, 1968. NHHS.
29. Rowley Town Committee, *The Early Records of the Town of Rowley, Massachuseetts, 1639-1672*, Vol. One, Rowley MA, 1894. NHHS.
30. Rugg, Ellen R., *The Descendants of John Rugg*, Frederick H. Hitchcock, New York NY, 1911. NHHS.
31. Ruggles, Harry Stoddard, *Ruggles Family of England and America*, PP, Boston MA, 1893. NHHS.
32. Rumery, Samuel D., "Marriages in Town of Anson, Maine, 1801-1802," ms., 1928. MHS.
33. Runnels, Moses T., *A Genealogy of Runnells-Reynolds Family*, Alfred Mudge and Sons, Printers, Boston MA, 1873.
34. Runnels, Moses T., *History of Sanbornton, New Hampshire*, 2 vol., Alfred Mudge and Sons, Boston MA, 1882. NHHS.
35. Rust, Albert D., *Record of the Rust Family*, PBA, Waco TX, 1891. NHHS.

## S.

1. Saco ME: *First Book of Records, First Church of Pepperellboro (Saco), 1763-1797*, York Institute, Saco ME, 1914. MHS.
2. Saco ME, Vital Records, rec. of Nancy Welch, ALSOP.
3. *Saco Register*, 1906. McArthur Library, Biddeford ME.
4. Safford, Marion Fuller, *The Story of Colonial Lancaster*, The Tuttle Publishing Co., Rutland VT, 1937.
5. Saint Francis District of Canada, marriage records. Copied by Wilfred Sawyer.
6. Salisbury Association, Inc., *Historical Collections Relating to the Town of Salisbury, Litchfield County, Connecticut*, Vol. I, and II, 1913. NHHS.
7. Samuels, Edward A., and Henry H. Kimbal, Ed., *Somerville, Past and Present*, PBA, Boston MA, 1897. NHHS.
8. Sanborn, V. C., *Samborne or Sanborne in England and America*, PP, 1899 (reprinted 1969). NHHS.
9. Sargent, Aaron, *Sargent Genealogy*, Somerville MA, 1895. NHHS.
10. Sargent, Edwin Everett, *Sargent Record*, Caledonian Company, St. Johnsbury VT, 1899. NHHS.
11. Sargent, John S. and Aaron, *Sargent Genealogy*, Boston MA, 1895. NHHS.
11A. Sargent, William M., *The Skillings Family*, Portland ME, 1885. MSL.
12. Savage, James A., *Genealogical Dictionary of the First Settlers of New England*, 4 vol., Little Brown and Co., Boston MA, 1862. NHSL.
13. Sawtelle, Ithmar B., *History of the Town of Townsend, 1676-1878*, PBA, Fitchburg MA, 1878. NHHS.
14. Sawyer, Arthur H., "Sawyer Family, Limington and Limerick," ms., zeroxed copy. MHS.
15. Sawyer, Ernest A., "Sawyer Family of Maine," ms., Somerville MA, 1932. AAS.
16. Sawyer, Nathaniel, and J. S. Walker, *Sawyer Family*, Manchester NH, 1889. MHS.
17. Sawyer, Roland D., Rev., *The History of Kensington, New Hampshire, 1663 to 1945*, Farmington ME, 1946.
18. Sawyer, Roland D., Rev., *Sawyer Family of Hill, New Hampshire: Betfield and Thomas Sawyer, Their Ancestry and Posterity*, n.p., n.d. NHHS.
19. Sawyer, Timothy T., *Old Charlestown*, James H. West Co., Boston MA, 1902. NHHS.
20. Sawyers of Rhode Island, IGI, LDS Library, Concord NH.

21. Scales, John, *Colonial Era History of Dover, N. H.,* Vol. I, Heritage Books, Inc., Bowie MD, 1977. Facs. of 1923 edn. NHHS.
22. Scales, John, *History of Strafford County, New Hampshire*, Richmond Arnold Publishing Co., Chicago IL, 1914. NHHS.
22A. Scarborough ME: "First Parish Church of Scarborough ME," ms., 1926. MHS.
23. Scarborough ME: "Records of the First Congregational Church in Scarborough," ms., copied by Augustus F. Moulton, 1895. MHS.
24. Schofield, George A., *The Ancient Records of the Town of Ipswich*, Vol. I (1634-1650), Ipswich MA, 1899, pp. not numbered.
25. Sears, Albert J., "Early Families of Standish," ms., n.d. ALSOP files. Based on his original papers at MHS.
26. Secomb, Daniel F., *History of Amherst, New Hampshire*, June 1728 to March 1882, Concord NH, 1883.
27. "*The Second Boat*," a genealogical booklet published quarterly by the *News-Journal*, Machias ME, 04654, Vol. 4, No. 2; Vol. 6, Nos. 1-3; Vol. 7, No. 1.
28. Sedgley, George B., *Genealogy of the Burbank Family*, The Knowlton and McLeary Co., Farmington ME, 1928.
29. Selleck, Lillian L., *Miner Family*, Donald L. Jacobus, New Haven CT, 1928.
30. Sewall, Samuel, *The History of Woburn, Massachusetts, 1640-1860*, Wiggen and Lunt, Boston MA, 1868. NHHS.
31. Seward, JosiahL.,*History of the Town of Sullivan, New Hampshire, 1777-1917*, 2 vol., J. L. Seward Estate, Keene NH, 1921. NHHS.
32. Sharon CT, *Vital Statistics, Record of Births, Marriages, and Deaths, 1721-1879*, Lawrence Van Alstyne, Sharon CT, 1897. NHHS.
33. Shattuck, Lemuel, *Memorials of the Desendants of William Shattuck*, Dutton and Wentworth, Boston MA, 1855. NHHS.
34. Shedd, Frank Edson, *Daniel Shed Genealogy*, PP. Boston MA, 1921.
35. Sherman, Jeanette Johnson, *Johnson-Mitchell Ancestry With Allied Families*, Edward Bros., Ann Arbor MI, 1967. NHHS.
36. Sherman, Robert M., *Vital Records of Marshfield to the Year 1850*, Published by the Society of Mayflower Descendants in the State of Rhode Island. NHHS.
37. Sherman, Roy V., *Some of the Descendants of Philip Sherman*, PP, 1968. NHHS.
38. Sherman, Roy V., *The New England Shermans*, PP, 1974. NHHS.
39. Sherwood, George, *American Colonists*, 1st Series, London, England, 1930.
40. Shurtleff, Benjamin, *The History of the Town of Revere*, Beckler Press, Boston MA, 1938. NHHS.
41. Shurtluff, Benjamin, *Descendants of William Shurtluff*, 2 vol., rev. edn., PP, 1976.
42. Sias, Azaariah Boody, *The Sias Family in America*, Florida Press Inc., Orlando FL, 1952.
43. Sinnett, Rev. Charles N., "The Farr Genealogy," ms., Carthage SD, n.d. NHHS.
44. Sinnett, Rev. Charles Nelson, *Richard Pinkham of Old Dover and His Descendants*, Rumford Printing Company, Concord NH, 1908. NHHS.
45. Skowhegan ME, Vital Records, town clerk's files.
46. Slafter, Edmund F., Rev., *The Slafter Memorial*, Henry W. Dutton and Son Press, Boston MA, 1869. NHHS.
47. Small, Mrs. Addie B., Cornish ME, records.
48. Smith, Albert, MD, *History of the Town of Peterborough, New Hampshire*, Press of George H. Ellis, Boston MA, 1876. NHHS.
49. Smith, Alven Martyn, *Three Blackmore Genealogies*, PBA, South Pasadena CA, 1932. AAS.
50. Smith, Annie M., *Morrill Kindred in America*, Vol. 2, The Grafton Press, New York, 1926. NHHS.
51. Smith, Charles James, *The History of the Town of Mont Vernon, New Hampshire*, Boston MA, 1907.
52. Smith, Dr. Elinor V., *Descendants of Nathaniel Dickinson*, The Dickenson Family Assn., 1978. NHHS.
53. Smith, Ethel F., *Adam Hawkes of Saugus, Massachusetts, 1605-1672*, Gateway Press, Baltimore MD, 1980.
54. Smith, Frank, *Dover Farms*, Historical and Natural History Society of Dover MA, 1914. NHHS.
55. Smith, Henry Allen, *Genealogical History of Rev., Nehemiah Smith*, Munsell's Sons, Albany NY, 1889. NHHS.
56. Smith, John Montague, *History of the Town of Sunderland, Massachusetts*, E. A. Hall and Co., Greenfield MA, 1899.
57. Smith, Joseph E. A., *The History of Pittsfield, Massachusetts, 1800-1876*, C. W. Bryan and Co., Springfield MA, 1876. NHHS.
58. Smith, Samuel F., *History of Newton, Massachusetts, 1630-1880*, The American Logotype Co., Boston MA, 1880. NHHS.
59. Snow, Edwin H., *The William Snow Family*, Snow and Farnham Company, Printers. Providence RI, 1908. NHHS.
60. Snow, Nora, *Snow-Estes Ancestry*, Hillburn NY, 1939. NHHS.
61. Somers, Amos Newton, *History of Lancaster, New Hampshire*, The Rumford Press, Concord NH, 1899.
62. "South Hampton Church Records," ms., no author, n.d. NHHS.
63. Spaulding, Charles W., *Spaulding Memorial of Edward Spaulding*, Chicago IL, 1897. NHHS.
64. Spear, Eva Clough, Ed., *The Genealogy and Descendants of John Clough*, The John Clough Gen. Soc., Bethel ME, 1968.

65. Spofford, Jeremiah, *Genealogical Record of John Spofford and Elizabeth Scott*, Alfred Mudge and Son, Boston MA, 1888. NHHS.
66. Spooner, Thomas, *Memorial of William Spooner*, Robert Clarke and Co., Cincinnati OH, 1871. NHHS.
67. Spurr, William S., *A History of Otisfield, From the Original Grant to the Close of the Year 1944*, n.p., 1944. MHS.
68. Stackpole, Everett S. *et. al., History of the Town of Durham, New Hampshire*, NH Publishing Co., Somersworth NH, 1973. NHHS.
69. Stackpole, Everett S., *History of Durham, Maine*, Lewiston ME, 1899. NHHS.
70. Stackpole, Everett S., *Kittery, Maine*, Press of Lewiston Journal Co., Lewiston ME, 1903. MHS.
71. Stackpole, Everett S., *History and Genealogy of the Stackpole Family*, Journal Bindery, Lewiston ME, 1920. MHS.
72. Stackpole, Everett S., *Swett Genealogy*, Journal Printshop, Lewiston ME, 1913. MSL.
73. Stackpole, Everett S., *History of Winthrop, Maine*, PBT, Auburn ME, 1925. MHS.
74. Stafford, Morgan Hewett, *The Kidder Family, Descendants of Ensign James Kidder*, The Tuttle Publishing Co., Rutland VT, 1941.
75. Stark, Caleb, *History of the Town of Dunbarton, New Hampshire, 1751-1860*, G. Parker Lyon, Concord NH, 1860. NHHS.
76. Stark, Charles R., *Groton, Conn., 1705-1905*, The Palmer Press, Stonington CT, 1922. NHHS.
77. Stark, Charles R., *Aaron Stark Family*, Wright and Potter, Boston MA, 1927. NHHS.
78. Starr, Edward C., *A History of Cornwall, Connecticut*, New Haven CT, 1926. NHHS.
79. Stearns, Ezra S., *History of Ashburnham, Massachusetts*, 1887.
80. Stearns, Ezra S., Ed., *Genealogical and Family History of the State of New Hampshire*, 4 vol., The Lewis Publishing Co., New York NY, 1908. NHHS.
81. Stearns, Ezra S., *History of Plymouth, New Hampshire*, 2 vol., PBT, Cambridge MA, 1906. NHHS.
82. Stearns, Ezra S., *History of the Town of Rindge, New Hampshire, 1736-1874*, Press of George H. Ellis, Boston MA, 1875. NHHS.
83. "Steep Falls Cemetery," rec. of Nancy Welch, ALSOP.
84. Stein, S. G., III, *The Steins of Muscatine*, PP. Muscatine IA, 1962. MHS.
85. Sterling MA, *Vital Records*, The Sterling Historical Commission, 1976. Xeroxed. NHHS.
86. "Steuben, Maine, Births, Intentions and Marriages (A-M)," copied from original VR by Margaret Kelley Ashe Colton, 1937. MHS.
87. "Steuben, Maine, Births, Intentions and Marriages (N-Z)," copied from original VR by Margaret Kelley Ashe Colton, 1937. Also includes Beddington ME and Cherryfield ME.
88. Early Records of Intentions and Marriages in Steuben, Washington County, Maine, copied by Dorothy Parker Phelan, 1961. MHS.
89. Stickney, Matthew A., *Stickney Family: Descendants of William and Elizabeth Stickney*, Essex Institute Press, Salem MA, 1869. NHHS.
90. Stickney, Matthew A., *The Fowler Family: A Genealogical Memoir of the Descendants of Philip and Mary Fowler*, Salem Press, Salem MA, 1883. NHHS.
91. Stiles, Henry R., *The History of Ancient Wethersfield, Connecticut*, 2 vol., The Grafton Press, New York NY, MCMIIII. NHHS.
92. Stockin, Edwin, and Harold Hill Blossom, "Blossom Genealogy," ms., 280 pp., a family record of the children of Benjamin Blossom and Margaret R. Blackwell, 1870. NHHS.
93. Stocking, H. W., Rev.,*History and Genealogy of the Knowltons of New England*, Knickerbocker Press, New York NY, 1897.
94. Stockwell, Mary LeBaron, *Descendants of Francis LeBaron of Plymouth, Massachusetts*, T. R. Marvin and Sons, Boston MA, 1904.
95. Stoeckel, Carl and Ellen Battelle, "Baptisms, Marriages, Burials, and List of Members Taken From the Church Records of the Reverend Amni Ruhamah Robbins, First Minister of Norfolk, Connecticut, 1761-1831," n.p., 1910. NHHS.
96. Stowe, John M., Rev., *History of the Town of Hubbardston*, Hubbardston MA, 1881.
97. Stowell, William Henry H., *The Stowell Genealogy*, Tuttle Co., Rutland VT, 1922. NHHS.
98. Strafford NH, rec. of the Town Clerk.
99. Stratton, Harriet Russell, *A Book of Strattons*, Grafton Press, New York NY, 1908. NHHS.
100. Struthers, Parke Hardy, Ed., *A History of Nelson, New Hampshire, 1767-1967*, Keene NH, 1968.
101. Stubbs, Albert R., "Rolls of the Maine Militia in the War of 1812-1814. " Scrapbook. MHS.
102. Sumner, Edith B., *Ancestry of Edward Wales Blake and Clarissa Matilda Glidden With Ninety Allied Families*, Los Angeles CA, 1948. NHHS.
103. Surry ME, Record Book (1829 and later). Town Clerk's Office.

## T.

1. Tapley, Harriet Silvester, *The Tapley Family*, Endicott Press, Danvers MA, 1900. NHHS.

2. Tapley, Harriet Silvester, *Chronicles of Danvers (Old Salem Village), Massachusetts, 1632-1923*, Danvers MA Hist. Soc., 1923. NHHS.
3. Taylor, Charles J., *History of Great Barrington, Massachusetts*, Clark W. Bryan Co., Great Barrington MA, 1882. NHHS.
4. Taylor, Ellery Kirke, *Descendants of Stephen Flanders of Salisbury, Mass., 1646*, PP, Rutland VT, 1932. NHHS.
5. Taylor, Robert L., *Early Families of Cornish, Maine*, Danville ME, 1985. MHS.
6. Taylor, Robert L., *Early Families of Limington, Maine*, n.d. MHS.
6A. Taylor, Robert L., *History of Limington, Maine, 1668-1900*, Oxford Hills Press, Norway ME, 1975. NHHS.
7. Teg, William, *History of Porter*, The Parsonsfield-Porter Hist. Soc., Kezar Falls ME, 1957. NHHS. ALSOP.
8. Temple, Joseph H., *A History of the Town of Northfield, Massachusetts, for 150 Years*, Joel Munsell, Albany NY, 1875. NHHS.
9. Temple, Josiah H., Rev., *History of North Brookfield, Masssachusetts*, PBT, 1887. NHHS.
10. Tenney, Martha Jane, *The Tenney Family, 1638-1904*, Revised, The Rumford Press, Concord NH, 1904. NHHS.
11. Thompson, Alice Smith, *The Drake Family of New Hampshire*, NH Hist. Soc., Concord NH, 1962. NHHS.
12. Thompson, Bradley and Franklin, "Blodget-Blodgett Descendents of Thomas of Cambridge," 6 vol., typescript, Concord NH, 1955.
13. Thompson, Francis M., *History of Greenfield*, Vol. I and II, Greenfield MA, 1904. NHHS.
14. Thompson, Joseph P., "Births, Marriages, and Deaths from First Book of Town Records, Wells, Maine, 1619-1809." MHS.
14A. Thompson, Rev. Leander, *Memorial of James Thompson*, L. Barta Co., Boston MA, 1887. MHS.
15. Thurston, Florence G. and Harmon S. Cross, *Three Centuries of Freeport, Maine*, Freeport ME, 1940. NHHS.
16. Tibbals, Rev. Ralph Howard, *Genealogical Record, Antrim NH Families*, PBT, Concord NH, 1967. NHHS.
17. Tibbets, Charles S., *Cemeteries of Falmouth, Maine, and Vicinity*, 1933. MHS.
18. Tibbets, Charles S., *Falmouth Marriages and Deaths, 1737-1849*, n.p., n.d. MHS.
19. Tibbets, Charles S., "The Knight Family," ms., 1941. NHHS.
20. Tibbets, Charles W., *New Hampshire Genealogical Record*, Vol. 1-7, PBA, Dover NH, 1904. NHHS.
21. Tilden, William S., *History of the Town of Medfield, Massachusetts, 1650-1886*, Boston MA, 1887.
21A. Titcomb, Gilbert M., *Descendants of William Titcomb of Newbury Massachusetts, 1635*, Aroostook State College of the University of Maine, 1969. NHHS.
22. Toppan, David Langdon, *Ancestors and Descendants of Abraham Toppan*, PP, 1915.
23. Topsfield MA Hist. Soc., *Amesbury MA Vital Records to the Year 1849*, 1913. NHHS.
24. Topsfield MA Hist. Soc., *Vital Records of Haverhill, Massachusetts, to the End of the Year 1849*, Vol. 1. 1910.
25. Topsfield MA Hist. Soc., *Vital Records of Topsfield, Massachusetts, to the End of the Year 1849*, 2 vol. 1903.
26. Topsham ME: Original family rec. on file at Selectman's Office, copied by Mary Pelham Hill, March 1942.
27. Torrey, Clarence Almon, *New England Marriages Prior to 1700*, Genealogical Publishing Co., Inc., Baltimore MD, 1985. NHHS.
28. Totten, John R., *Thatcher Genealogy*, NY Genealogical and Biographical Society., 1910. NHHS.
29. Trowbridge, Francis B., *A History of the Descendants of Robert Ashley of Springfield, Massachusetts*, New Haven CT, 1896.

## U.

1. Underhill, Lora Altine (Woodbury), *Descendants of Edward Small and Allied Families*, 3 vol., Revised Edn., The Riverside Press, Cam bridge MA, 1934. NHHS.

## V.

1. Valentine, Thomas W., *The Valentines in America*, Clarke and Maynard, New York NY, 1874. MSL.
2. Van Wagenen, Avis Stearns, *Genealogy and Memoirs of Isaac Stearns*, Courier Publishing Co., Syracuse NY, 1901. NHHS.
3. Varney, Herbert Clarkson, *Genealogy of William Varney of Ipswich, Massachusetts*, 1949. NHHS.
4. Varnum, John Marshall, *Varnums of Dracut*, David Clapp and Son, Boston MA, 1907. NHHS.
5. *Vermont Marriages*, Vol. 1, Genealogical Publishing Co., Baltimore MD, 1967. NHHS.
6. Vermont vital records, VSA.
7. Vinton, John Adams, *Giles Genealogical Memoirs*, Dutton and Son, Boston MA, 1864. NHHS.
8. Vinton, John Adams, *The Richardson Memorial*, Brown Thurston and Co., Portland ME, 1876. NHHS.
9. Virkus, Frederick A., Ed., *The Compendium of American Genealogy*, Vol. 1,3,4,6, The Institute of American Genealogy, Chicago IL, 1937. NHHS.

## W.

1. Wade, Hugh Mason, *A Brief History of Cornish, 1763-1974*, PBT, 1976. NHHS.

2. Waite, Otis F. R., *History of the Town of Claremont, New Hampshire*, PBT, Manchester NH, 1895. NHHS.
3. Wakefield NH Spenser Cemetery, inscriptions copied by Eleanor G. Sawyer.
4. Wakefield, Homer, MD, *Wakefield Memorial*, PP, Bloomington IL, 1897. NHHS.
5. Wakefield NH, rec. of the Town Clerk.
5A. Walker, Ernest G., *Embden Town of Yore*, Independent Reporter Co., Skowhegan ME, 1929. MHS.
6. Wallace, William Allen, *The History of Caanan, New Hampshire*, The Rumford Press, Concord NH, 1910. NHHS.
7. Walsh, Ruth T., "Benjamin Franklin Chase," mimeographed ms., n.d.
8. Walworth, Reuben W., *Hyde Genealogy*, J. C. Munsee, Albany NY, 1864.
9. Ward, Andrew H., *History of the Town of Shrewsbury, Massachusetts, 1717-1829*, Samuel G. Drake, Boston MA, 1847. NHHS.
10. Ware, Emma Forbes, *Ware Genealogy: Robert Ware*, Charles H. Pope, Boston MA, 1901. NHHS.
11. Ware, Josephine S., *Lancaster Genealogy*, The Tuttle Publishing Co., Rutland VT, n.d. NHHS.
12. Warren, Orin, *Genealogy of Descendants of James Warren*, Chase Press, Haverhill ME, 1902. MSL.
13. Waters, Thomas Franklin, *Ipswich in the Massachusetts Bay Colony*, Vol. I (1633-1700), The Ipswich MA Hist. Soc., 1905. NHHS.
14. Waters, Thomas Franklin, *Ipswich in the Massachusetts Bay Colony*, Vol. II (1700-1917), The Ipswich MA Hist. Soc., 1917. NHHS.
15. Waters, Rev. Wilson, *History of Chelmsford, Massachusetts*, Courier Citizen Co., Lowell MA, 1917.
16. *Watertown's Military History*, Published Under the Direction of the Committee Representing the Sons of the American Revolution and Isaac B. Patten Post, GAR, 1907. NHHS.
17. *Watertown Records, Sixth Book of Town Proceedings, 1769 to 1792*, prepared under the direction of the Town Clerk, 1928. NHHS.
18. *Webster's History of Hudson, New Hampshire, 1673/1913*, Hudson NH Historical Society, 1977. Reprint of 1913 Edn. NHHS.
19. Weeks, John M., *History of Salisbury, Vermont*, A. H. Copeland, Middlebury VT, 1860. NHHS.
20. Weeks, Robert D., *Genealogy of George Weeks*, L. J. Hardman Press, Newark NJ, 1885. NHHS.
21. Weis, Frederick Lewis, "Early Families of Lancaster, Massachusetts," ms., presented to the AAS, Worcester MA, on 22 August 1942, pp. not numbered.
22. Welch, Nancy, Notebook #2. ALSOP files.
23. Welch, William Lewis, *Francis Lyford of Boston and Exeter and Some of his Descendants*, Essex Institute, Salem MA, 1902. NHHS.
24. Wells, Frederick Palmer, *History of Newbury, Vermont*, The Caledonian Co., St. Johnsbury VT, 1902. NHHS.
25. Wellman, Rev. Jushua W., *Descendants of Thomas Wellman*, Arthur H. Wellman, Boston MA, 1918. NHHS.
26. Wentworth, John, *Wentworth Genealogy*, 3 vol., Little Brown and Co., Boston MA, 1878. NHHS.
27. Westbrook ME Vital Records (Marriages). Microfilm file. MHS.
28. Weston, Thomas, *History of the Town of Middleboro, Massachusetts*, The Riverside Press, Cambridge MA, 1906.
29. Weston: *Town of Weston Tax Lists, 1757-1827*, PBT, Alfred Mudge and Sons, Boston MA, 1897. NHHS.
30. Wetherbee, Winthrop, "Wetherbee Family in New England,," ms., n.d. NHHS.
31. Weymouth, Ruth Ella, *Weymouth Family History*, J. Grant Stevenson, Provo UT, 1978. NHHS.
32. Wheeler, Albert Gallatin Jr., *Wheeler Family in America*, 2 vol., American College of Genealogy, Boston MA, 1914. NHHS.
33. Wheeler, Edmund, *The History of Newport, New Hampshire From 1766 to 1878*, Republican Press Assn., Concord NH, 1879. NHHS.
34. Wheeler, George Augustus, MD, *History of Brunswick, Topsham, and Harpswell, Maine*, Pejepscot ME Hist. Soc., Boston MA, 1974. Facs. of 1878 edn. NHHS.
35. Wheeler, Richard Anson, *History of the Town of Stonington, Ct.*, Day Publishing Co., New London CT, 1900. NHHS.
36. Whitcher, William F., *History of the Town of Haverhill, New Hampshire*, The Rumford Press, Concord NH, 1919. MHS.
37. Whitcher, William F., *Some Things About Coventry-Benton, New Hampshire*, New Print, Woodsville NH, 1905. NHHS.
37A. Whitcomb, Charlotte, *Whitcomb Family in America*, Minneapolis MN, 1904. NHHS.
38. White, Almira L., Ed., *Nicholas Hodson-Hodgdon*, Published by Andrew J. Hodgdon, Haverhill MA, 1904.
39. White, Almira L., *Genealogy of the Descendants of John White*, Vol. III, IV, 1905. NHHS.
40. White, Almira L., Ed., *Ancestry of John Barber White*, Vol. I-IV, C. H. Webster, Haverhill MA, 1913. NHHS.
40A. Whitney, Peter, *Worcester County Massachusetts History*, Worcester MA, 1793. NHHS.
41. Whiton, John M., Rev., *History of the Town of Antrim, New Hampshire (1744-1844)*, Concord NH, 1852.
42. Whitten, Phyllis O., *Samuel Fogg, 1628-1672: His Ancestors and Descendants*, 2 vol., Columbia Planograph Co., Washington DC, n.d.
43. Whittier, Charles Collier, *The Descendants of Thomas Whittier and Ruth Green*, The Tuttle Publishing Co., Rutland VT, 1937. NHHS.
44. Wiggin, Arthur C. *et. al.*, "Wiggin Genealogy," Vol. 1, n.d., a compilation of manuscripts in NHHS Library.

45. Wight, Charles H., *Genealogy of the Chaflin Family*, Press of William Green, New York NY, 1903. MHS.
46. Wight, William Ward, *The Wights*, Swain and Tate, Milwaukee WI, 1890. NHHS.
47. Wilbor, John Reid and Benjamin Franklin, *The Wildbores in America*, 2d. Edn., George W. King Printing Co., Baltimore MD, 1933. NHHS.
47A. Wilbur, Asa, "Genealogical Record of The Wilbur Family," Boston MA, 1871. Bound photocopy. MHS.
48. *Wildbore Index Register*, NHHS file 929. 2/W669wl. No other ID.
49. Wilder, Moses H., Rev., *Book of the Wilders*, PBA, New York NY, 1878. MHS.
50. Wildey, Anna C., *Genealogy of the Descendants of William Chesebrough*, T. A. Wright, New York NY, 1903.
51. Willard, Joseph, *Willard Memoir*, Phillips, Sanford and Co., Boston MA, 1858. NHHS.
52. Willard Woodman Collection. MHS.
53. Willey, George F., *Willey's Book of Nutfield*, PBA, Derry Depot NH, 1895. NHHS.
54. Williams, Charles C., MD, "Ancestry and Posterity of Richard Williams and Frances Dighton, his Wife, of Taunton, Massachusetts," ms., Los Angeles CA, 1924. NHHS.
55. Williamson, Lois F., *Morrill Lineage*, 2 vol., n.p., 1980.
56. Willis, J. L. M., Ed., *Old Eliot*, a Quarterly Magazine of the History and Biographies of the Upper Parish of Kittery, Now Eliot, Maine, Vol. 1-9, Jan. 1897 to Dec 1909. MHS.
57. Willis, William, *The History of Portland, Maine, From 1632-1864*, Bailey and Noyes, Portland ME, 1865. MHS.
58. Wilson, Lillian, *Barber Genealogy: Thomas Barber, Connecticut. . . John Barber, Massachusetts*, Haverhill MA, 1909. NHHS.
59. Wilson, Mehitable C. C., *John Gibson of Cambridge, Massachusetts, and his Descendants*, Press of McGill and Wallace, Washington DC, 1900. NHHS.
60. Windham CT: *Records of the Congregational Church in Windham, Conn., 1700-1851*, Conn. Hist. Soc., Hartford CT, 1943. NHHS.
61. Winship, J. P. C., *Historical Brighton*, George A. Warren, Boston MA, 1899.
62. Wood, William Smith, *Descendants of the Brothers Jeremiah and John Wood*, Press of Charles Hamilton, Worcester MA, 1885. NHHS.
63. Woodard, Florence May, *Town Proprietors of Vermont*, New York NY 1968. Reprint of Columbia University Studies, No. 418, 1936. NHSL.
64. Wooden, Emily Beaman, *Beaman and Clark Genealogy: A History of the Descendants of Gamaliel Beaman and Sarah Clark of Dorchester and Lancaster, Massachusetts*, 1909.
65. Woodman, Cyrus, *The Woodmans of Buxton, Maine*, PP, Boston MA, 1874. NHHS.
66. Woodstock CT: *Vital Records of Woodstock, 1686-1854*, Case, Lockwood and Brainard Co., Hartford CT, 1914. NHHS.
67. Worcester, Samuel T., *History of the Town of Hollis*, Nashua NH, 1879.
68. Worcester, Sarah Alice, *The Descendants of Rev. William Worcester*, E. F. Worcester, Boston MA, 1914. NHHS.
69. Worthen, Augusta H., *The History of Sutton, New Hampshire*, facs. of 1890 edn., PBT, Sutton NH, 1975. NHHS.
70. Wright, Gertrude B., *Hinman Family*, Hanover NH, 1966.
71. Wright, Henry B. and E. D. Harvey, *The Settlement and Story of Oakham, Massachusetts*, Vol. 2, Ernest L. Hayward, New Haven CT, 1947.
72. Wyman, Thomas B., *The Genealogies and Estates of Charlestown, 1629-1818*, 2 vol., David Clapp and Son., Boston MA 1879. Dover NH Public Library.

## Y.

1. Yates, Edgar A. P., *First Book of Records, First Church of Pepperellboro, Maine*, 1914. MHS.
2. *York County Genealogical Society Journal*, Ogunquit ME 03907, Vol 1, No. 1 (Jan), No. 2 (Apr), No. 3 (Jul) 1986.
3. *York County Maine, History of*, Everts and Peck, Philadelphia PA 1880. NHHS.
4. Young, David C. and Robert L. Taylor, *Death Notices From Free Will Baptist Publications, 1811-1851*, Heritage Books, Inc., Bowie MD. 1985. MHS.
5. Young, David C. *Maine Newspaper Listings Up to 1821*, Heritage Books, Inc., Bowie MD.

# — SAWYER INDEX —

**E**

**H**

I

**J**

**M**

**N**

**S**

U



V



W

# — OTHER NAMES INDEX —

C

I



J



K



L

**Q**



**R**

## Y